More information about this series at https://link.springer.com/bookseries/558

Manuel V. Hermenegildo ·
José F. Morales
Editors

Static Analysis

30th International Symposium, SAS 2023
Cascais, Portugal, October 22–24, 2023
Proceedings

Springer

Editors
Manuel V. Hermenegildo
U. Politécnica de Madrid (UPM)
and IMDEA Software Institute
Pozuelo de Alarcón, Madrid, Spain

José F. Morales
U. Politécnica de Madrid (UPM)
and IMDEA Software Institute
Pozuelo de Alarcon, Spain

ISSN 0302-9743 ISSN 1611-3349 (electronic)
Lecture Notes in Computer Science
ISBN 978-3-031-44244-5 ISBN 978-3-031-44245-2 (eBook)
https://doi.org/10.1007/978-3-031-44245-2

This Springer imprint is published by the registered company Springer Nature Switzerland AG
The registered company address is: Gewerbestrasse 11, 6330 Cham, Switzerland

Preface

This volume contains the proceedings of the 30th edition of the International Static Analysis Symposium, SAS 2023, held on October 22–24, 2023, in Cascais, Portugal. The conference was a co-located event of SPLASH, the ACM SIGPLAN conference on Systems, Programming, Languages, and Applications: Software for Humanity.

Static analysis is widely recognized as a fundamental tool for program verification, bug detection, compiler optimization, program understanding, and software maintenance. The series of Static Analysis Symposia serves as the primary venue for the presentation of theoretical, practical, and applied advances in the area. Previous symposia were held in Auckland, Chicago, Porto, Freiburg, New York, Edinburgh, Saint-Malo, Munich, Seattle, Deauville, Venice, Perpignan, Los Angeles, Valencia, Kongens Lyngby, Seoul, London, Verona, San Diego, Madrid, Paris, Santa Barbara, Venice, Pisa, Paris, Aachen, Glasgow, and Namur.

SAS 2023 called for papers on topics including, but not limited to, abstract interpretation, automated deduction, data flow analysis, debugging techniques, deductive methods, emerging applications, model checking, data science, program optimizations and transformations, program synthesis, program verification, machine learning and verification, security analysis, tool environments and architectures, theoretical frameworks, type checking, and distributed or networked systems. Besides the regular papers, authors were encouraged to submit short submissions in the NEAT category to discuss experiences with static analysis tools, industrial reports, and case studies, along with tool papers, brief announcements of work in progress, well-motivated discussions of new questions or new areas, etc. Authors were encouraged to submit artifacts accompanying their papers to strengthen evaluations and the reproducibility of results.

The conference employed a double-blind reviewing process with an author response period, supported on EasyChair. This year, SAS had 40 full submitted papers (38 regular and two NEAT).The Program Committee used a two-round review process, where each remaining submission received at least three first-round reviews, and most four reviews, which the authors could then respond to. In addition to the PC members, 23 external reviewers were also involved in the process. The author response period was followed by a Program Committee discussion where consensus was reached on the papers to be accepted, after a thorough assessment of the relevance and the quality of the work. Overall, 20 papers were accepted for publication (19 regular and one NEAT) and appear in this volume. The submitted papers were authored by researchers around the world: China, USA, France, Germany, Italy, Sweden, India, Macedonia, Taiwan, UK, Israel, Cuba, Denmark, Switzerland, the Netherlands, Czechia, Japan, Mexico, and Canada.

We view the artifacts as being equally important for the success and development of static analysis as the written papers. It is important for researchers to be able to independently reproduce experiments, which is greatly facilitated by having the original artifacts available. Marc Chevalier, the artifact committee chair, set up the artifact committee. In line with SAS 2022, the authors could submit either Docker or Virtual Machine images as artifacts. A public archival repository for the artifacts is available on Zenodo, hosted at https://zenodo.org/communities/sas-2023. The artifacts have badges awarded at three levels: Validated (correct functionality), Extensible (with source code), and Available (on the Zenodo repository). The artwork for the badges is by Arpita Biswas (Harvard University) and Suvam Mukherjee (Microsoft). SAS 2023 had 12 valid artifact submissions. The review process for the artifacts was similar to that for the papers. Each artifact was evaluated by three members of the artifact evaluation committee, and 11 out of 12 valid artifacts were accepted, at different levels.

In addition to the contributed papers, SAS 2023 also featured four invited talks by distinguished researchers: Gagandeep Singh (University of Illinois at Urbana-Champaign, VMware Research, USA), Bor-Yuh Evan Chang (U. of Colorado at Boulder, USA), Loris D'Antoni (U. of Wiscounsin at Madison, USA), and Daniel Kästner (AbsInt Gmbh, Germany). The Program Committee also selected the recipient of the Radhia Cousot Young Researcher Best Paper Award, given to a paper with a significant contribution from a student. This award was instituted in memory of Radhia Cousot, for her fundamental contributions to static analysis and having been one of the main promoters and organizers of the SAS series of conferences.

The SAS program would not have been possible without the efforts of many people. We thank them all. The members of the Program Committee, the artifact evaluation committee, and the external reviewers worked tirelessly to select a strong program, offering constructive and helpful feedback to the authors in their reviews. We would also like to thank the organizing committee of SPLASH 2023, chaired by Vasco T. Vasconcelos (LASIGE, University of Lisbon, Portugal) for all their efforts to make the conference a success, and the 2022 chairs Caterina Urban and Gagandeep Singh and the whole SAS Steering Committee for their help in passing the torch. We also thank our sponsors, Google, ENS Foundation, Meta, AbsInt, Springer, and the IMDEA Software Institute for their generous support of the conference. Finally, we thank Springer for publishing these proceedings.

August 2023

Manuel V. Hermenegildo
José F. Morales

Organization

Program Committee Chairs

Manuel Hermenegildo (Co-chair)	Universidad Politécnica de Madrid and IMDEA Software Institute, Spain
Jose F. Morales (Co-chair)	Universidad Politécnica de Madrid and IMDEA Software Institute, Spain

Steering Committee

Gagandeep Singh	VMware Research and UIUC, USA
Caterina Urban	Inria and ENS|PSL, France
Bor-Yuh Evan Chang	University of Colorado Boulder, USA
Patrick Cousot	New York University, USA
Cezara Dragoi	Inria and ENS|PSL and Informal Systems, France
Kedar Namjoshi	Nokia Bell Labs, USA
David Pichardie	Meta, France
Andreas Podelski	University of Freiburg, Germany

Program Committee

Gogul Balakrishnan	Google, USA
Liqian Chen	National University of Defense Technology, China
Yu-Fang Chen	Academia Sinica, Taiwan
Patrick Cousot	New York University, USA
Michael Emmi	Amazon Web Services, USA
Pietro Ferrara	Ca' Foscari University of Venice, Italy
Roberto Giacobazzi	University of Airzona, USA
Roberta Gori	Università di Pisa, Italy
Francesco Logozzo	Facebook, USA
Isabella Mastroeni	Università di Verona, Italy
Antoine Miné	LIP6, UPMC - Sorbonne Université, France
Kedar Namjoshi	Nokia Bell Labs, USA
Jorge A. Navas	Certora Inc., USA
Martin Rinard	Massachusetts Institute of Technology, USA
Daniel Schoepe	Amazon, UK
Helmut Seidl	Technical University of Munich, Germany
Mihaela Sighireanu	ENS Paris-Saclay, France
Gagandeep Singh	University of Illinois Urbana-Champaign (UIUC) and VMware Research, USA

Fu Song	ShanghaiTech University, China
Yulei Sui	University of New South Wales, Australia
Laura Titolo	National Institute of Aerospace, NASA LaRC, USA
Jingling Xue	University of New South Wales, Australia
Xin Zhang	Peking University, China

Artifact Evaluation Committee Chair

Marc Chevalier (Chair)	Snyk, Switzerland

Artifact Evaluation Committee

Vincenzo Arceri	University of Parma, Italy
Dorra Ben Khalifa	Université de Perpignan Via Domitia, France
Jérôme Boillot	École Normale Supérieure and INRIA, France
Marco Campion	Inria & École Normale Supérieure, Université PSL, France
Yifan Chen	Peking University, China
Xiao Cheng	University of Technology Sydney, Australia
Kai Jia	Massachusetts Institute of Technology, USA
Daniel Jurjo	IMDEA Software Institute and U. Politécnica de Madrid, Spain
Jonathan Laurent	Carnegie Mellon University, USA
Denis Mazzucato	Inria and École Normale Supérieure, France
Facundo Molina	IMDEA Software Institute, Spain
Luca Negrini	Corvallis SRL, Ca' Foscari University of Venice, Italy
Vivek Notani	University of Verona, Italy
Luca Olivieri	Ca' Foscari University of Venice, Italy
Francesco Parolini	Sorbonne Université, France
Louis Rustenholz	IMDEA Software Institute and U. Politécnica de Madrid, Spain
Ryan Vrecenar	Sandia National Laboratories, USA

Publicity Chair

Louis Rustenholz	IMDEA Software Institute and U. Politécnica de Madrid, Spain

Additional Reviewers

Arceri, Vincenzo
Ascari, Flavio
Assolini, Nicola
Bruni, Roberto
Cheng, Xiao
Dalla Preda, Mila
Demangeon, Romain
Dolcetti, Greta
Feliu Gabaldon, Marco Antonio
Izycheva, Anastasiia

Kan, Shuangxiang
Lei, Yuxiang
Liu, Jiaxiang
Lo, Fang-Yi
Petter, Michael
Ren, Jiawei
Stucki, Sandro
Tsai, Wei-Lun
Wang, Jiawei
Xu, Feng
Yan, Zhenyu
Zaffanella, Enea
Zhang, Min

Goal-Directed Abstract Interpretation and Event-Driven Frameworks (Abstract of Invited Talk)

Bor-Yuh Evan Chang[1,2]

[1] University of Colorado Boulder, USA
evan.chang@colorado.edu
[2] Amazon, USA

Abstract. Static analysis is typically about computing a global over-approximation of a program's behavior from its source code. But what if most of the program code is missing or unknown to the analyzer? What if even where the program starts is unknown? This fundamentally thorny situation arises when attempting to analyze interactive applications (apps) developed against modern, event-driven software frameworks.

Rich event-driven software frameworks enable software engineers to create complex applications on sophisticated computing platforms (e.g., smartphones with a broad range of sensors and rich interactivity) with relatively little code by simply implementing callbacks to respond to events. But developing apps against them is also notoriously difficult. To create apps that behave as expected, developers must follow the complex and opaque asynchronous programming protocols imposed by the framework. So what makes static analysis of apps hard is essentially what makes programming them hard: the specification of the programming protocol is unclear and the possible control flow between callbacks is largely unknown.

While the typical workaround to perform static analysis with an unknown framework implementation is to either assume it to be arbitrary or attempt to eagerly specify all possible callback control flow, this solution can be too pessimistic to prove properties of interest or too burdensome and tricky to get right. In this talk, I argue for a rethinking of how to analyze app code in the context of an unknown framework implementation. In particular, I present some benefits from taking a goal-directed or backward-from-error formulation to prove just the assertions of interest and from designing semantics, program logics, specification logics, and abstract domains to reason about the app-framework boundary in a first-class manner. What follows are hopefully lines of

I would like to especially thank the following for making significant contributions to the research described in this talk: Ph.D. students Shawn Meier, Benno Stein, and Sam Blackshear; postdoc Sergio Mover; and collaborators Manu Sridharan and Gowtham Kaki.The University of Colorado Programming Languages and Verification (CUPLV) Group has offered the essential community with insightful discussions to conduct this work. This research was supported in part by NSF awards CCF-1055066, CCF-1619282, CCF-2008369 and DARPA award FA8750-14-2-0263.

Bor-Yuh Evan Chang holds concurrent appointments at the University of Colorado Boulder and as an Amazon Scholar. This talk describes work performed at the University of Colorado Boulder and is not associated with Amazon.

work that make analyzing modern interactive applications more targeted, more compositional, and ultimately more trustworthy.

Keywords: Goal-directed verification · Backwards abstract interpretation · Event-driven framework modeling

Contents

Invited Talks

Verifying Infinitely Many Programs at Once 3
Loris D'Antoni

Abstract Interpretation in Industry – Experience and Lessons Learned 10
Daniel Kästner, Reinhard Wilhelm, and Christian Ferdinand

Building Trust and Safety in Artificial Intelligence with Abstract Interpretation 28
Gagandeep Singh

Regular Papers

Modular Optimization-Based Roundoff Error Analysis of Floating-Point Programs 41
Rosa Abbasi and Eva Darulova

Unconstrained Variable Oracles for Faster Numeric Static Analyses 65
Vincenzo Arceri, Greta Dolcetti, and Enea Zaffanella

Symbolic Transformation of Expressions in Modular Arithmetic 84
Jérôme Boillot and Jérôme Feret

A Formal Framework to Measure the Incompleteness of Abstract Interpretations 114
Marco Campion, Caterina Urban, Mila Dalla Preda, and Roberto Giacobazzi

BREWasm: A General Static Binary Rewriting Framework for WebAssembly 139
Shangtong Cao, Ningyu He, Yao Guo, and Haoyu Wang

Quantum Constant Propagation 164
Yanbin Chen and Yannick Stade

Error Invariants for Fault Localization via Abstract Interpretation 190
Aleksandar S. Dimovski

Generalized Program Sketching by Abstract Interpretation and Logical Abduction 212
Aleksandar S. Dimovski

Mutual Refinements of Context-Free Language Reachability 231
Shuo Ding and Qirun Zhang

ADCL: Acceleration Driven Clause Learning for Constrained Horn Clauses 259
Florian Frohn and Jürgen Giesl

How Fitting is Your Abstract Domain? 286
Roberto Giacobazzi, Isabella Mastroeni, and Elia Perantoni

A Product of Shape and Sequence Abstractions 310
Josselin Giet, Félix Ridoux, and Xavier Rival

Error Localization for Sequential Effect Systems 343
Colin S. Gordon and Chaewon Yun

Scaling up Roundoff Analysis of Functional Data Structure Programs 371
Anastasia Isychev and Eva Darulova

Reverse Template Processing Using Abstract Interpretation 403
Matthieu Lemerre

Domain Precision in Galois Connection-Less Abstract Interpretation 434
Isabella Mastroeni and Michele Pasqua

Lifting On-Demand Analysis to Higher-Order Languages 460
Daniel Schoepe, David Seekatz, Ilina Stoilkovska, Sandro Stucki, Daniel Tattersall, Pauline Bolignano, Franco Raimondi, and Bor-Yuh Evan Chang

Octagons Revisited: Elegant Proofs and Simplified Algorithms 485
Michael Schwarz and Helmut Seidl

Polynomial Analysis of Modular Arithmetic 508
Thomas Seed, Chris Coppins, Andy King, and Neil Evans

Boosting Multi-neuron Convex Relaxation for Neural Network Verification 540
Xuezhou Tang, Ye Zheng, and Jiaxiang Liu

Correction to: Octagons Revisited: Elegant Proofs and Simplified Algorithms C1
Michael Schwarz and Helmut Seidl

Author Index 565

Invited Talks

Verifying Infinitely Many Programs at Once

Loris D'Antoni(✉)

University of Wisconsin, Madison, WI 53706-1685, USA
loris@cs.wisc.edu

Abstract. In traditional program verification, the goal is to automatically prove whether a program meets a given property. However, in some cases one might need to prove that a (potentially infinite) *set* of programs meets a given property. For example, to establish that no program in a set of possible programs (i.e., a search space) is a valid solution to a synthesis problem specification, e.g., a property φ, one needs to verify that all programs in the search space are incorrect, e.g., satisfy the property $\neg\varphi$. The need to verify multiple programs at once also arises in other domains such as reasoning about partially specified code (e.g., in the presence of library functions) and self-modifying code. This paper discusses our recent work in designing systems for verifying properties of infinitely many programs at once.

1 Introduction

In traditional program verification, the goal is to automatically prove whether **a program** meets a given property. However, in some cases we might need to prove that **a potentially infinite set of programs** meets a given property.

For example, consider the problem of establishing that a program-synthesis problem is *unrealizable* (i.e., has no solution in a given search space of programs) [4,5,9]. To establish unrealizability, i.e., that no program in a set of possible programs (i.e., a search space) is a valid solution to a synthesis problem specification, e.g., a property φ, one needs to verify that all programs in the search space are incorrect, e.g., satisfy the property $\neg\varphi$.

Example 1 (Proving Unrealizability). Consider the synthesis problem sy_{first} where the goal is to synthesize a function f that takes as input a state (x, y), and returns a state where $y = 10$. Assume, however, that the search space of possible programs in sy_{first} is defined using the following grammar G_{first}:

$$Start \rightarrow y := E \quad E \rightarrow x \mid E + 1$$

Work done in collaboration with Qinheping Hu, Jinwoo Kim, and Thomas W. Reps. Supported by NSF under grants CCF-{1750965, 1918211, 2023222}; by a Facebook Research Faculty Fellowship, by a Microsoft Research Faculty Fellowship. Any opinions, findings, and conclusions or recommendations expressed in this publication are those of the authors, and do not necessarily reflect the views of the sponsoring entities.

M. V. Hermenegildo and J. F. Morales (Eds.): SAS 2023, LNCS 14284, pp. 3–9, 2023.
https://doi.org/10.1007/978-3-031-44245-2_1

Clearly $y := 10 \notin L(Start)$; moreover, all programs in $L(Start)$ are incorrect on at least one input. For example, on the input $x = 15$ every program in the grammar sets y to a value greater than 15. Consequently, sy_{first} is unrealizable.

While it is trivial for a human to establish that sy_{first} is indeed unrealizable, it is definitely not trivial to *automatically verify* that all the infinitely many programs accepted by the grammar G_{first} are incorrect on at least one input.

Another setting where one may want to prove a property about multiple programs is when verifying partial programs—i.e., programs where some components are unknown [10].

Example 2 (Symbolically Executing Partial Programs). Consider the following program `foo` that outputs the difference between the number of elements of an array for which applying a function `f` results in a positive number and the number of elements for which the result of applying `f` is a negative number.

```
1 def foo(f, array):
2     count = 0
3     for i in range(len(array)):
4         if f(array[i]) > 0:
5             count += 1
6         else:
7             count -= 1
8     return count
```

Now assume that we know this program will always receive a function `f` drawn from the following grammar:

$$
\begin{aligned}
&F \rightarrow \lambda \mathtt{x}.G \\
&G \rightarrow \mathtt{abs}(H) \mid \mathtt{-abs}(H) \\
&H \rightarrow \mathtt{x} \mid H\mathtt{+}H \mid H\mathtt{*}H \mid H\mathtt{-}H \mid \mathtt{abs}(H)
\end{aligned}
$$

We might be interested in symbolically executing the program `foo` to identify feasible paths and understand if the program can be pruned or whether perhaps it is equivalent to a simpler program. One can do so using an uninterpreted function to model the behavior of `f`, but this approach would be imprecise because the grammar under consideration is such that all the infinitely many programs in $L(F)$ either always return a positive number (i.e., `f` is of the form $\lambda \mathtt{x}.\mathtt{abs}(H)$) or always return a negative number (i.e., `f` is of the form $\lambda \mathtt{x}.\mathtt{-abs}(H)$). Using an uninterpreted function one would detect that the path that follows the line numbers $[1, 2, 3, 4, 5, 3, 6, 7]$—i.e., the path that reaches line 5 in the first iteration of the loop and line 7 in the second iteration—is feasible, which is a false positive since the witness for `f` for this path is a function that does not have a counterpart in $L(F)$. We would like to devise a verification technique that can symbolically execute `foo` and avoid this source of imprecision.

The examples we showed illustrate how verification sometimes requires one to reason about more than one program at once. In fact, our examples require one to reason about *infinitely many programs* at once! Our work introduced automated techniques to prove properties of infinite sets of programs. First, we designed sound but incomplete automated verification techniques specialized in proving unrealizability of synthesis problems [4,5,9] (Sect. 2). Second, we designed unrealizability logic [8] a sound and relatively complete Hoare-style logical framework for expressing proofs that infinitely many programs satisfy a pre-post condition pair (Sect. 3). We conclude this extended abstract with some reflections of the current limitations and directions of our work.

2 Proving Unrealizability of Synthesis Problems

Program synthesis refers to the task of discovering a program, within a given search space, that satisfies a behavioral specification (e.g., a logical formula, or a set of input-output examples) [1,2,11].

While tools are becoming better at synthesizing programs, one property that remains difficult to reason about is the *unrealizability* of a synthesis problem, i.e., the non-existence of a solution that satisfies the behavioral specification within the search space of possible programs. Unrealizability has many applications; for example, one can show that a certain synthesized solution is optimal with respect to some metric by proving that a better solution to the synthesis problem does not exist—i.e., by proving that the synthesis problem where the search space contains only programs of lower cost is unrealizable [6].

In our work, we built tools that can establish unrealizability for several types of synthesis problems. Our tools Nay [5] and Nope [4] can prove unrealizability for syntax-guided synthesis (SyGuS) problems where the input grammar only contains expressions, whereas our tool MESSY [9] can prove unrealizability for semantics-guided synthesis (SemGuS) problems.

Nay The key insight behind Nay is that one can, given a synthesis problem, build a nondeterministic recursive program that always satisfies an assertion if and only if the given problem is unrealizable. For example, for the problem in Example 1, one would build a program like the following to check that no program in the search space of the synthesis problem, when given an input that sets x to 15, can produce an output where y is set to 10.

```
def genE(x, y):
    if nondet(): # nondeterministic guard
        return x  # simulates E -> x
    return genE(x, y) + 1  # simulates E -> E+1
def genStart(x, y):
    return (x, genE(x, y)) # simulates Start -> y:=E
def main():
    genStart(15, nondet()) # if we set x to 15
    assert y != 10 # y is never 10
```

NOPE The key observation of NOPE is that for problems involving only expressions, unrealizability can be checked by determining what set of values $\eta(i)$ a certain set of programs can produce for a given input i, and making sure that the output value we would like our program to produce for input i does not lie in that set $\eta(i)$. For example, for the problem in Example 1, one can define the following equation that computes the possible values $\eta_{Start}(15)$ of x and y, when the input value of x is 15.

$$\begin{aligned} \eta_{Start}(15) &= \{(v_x, v_y) \mid v_y \in \eta_E(15)\} \\ \eta_S(15) &= \{v \mid v = 15 \vee (v' \in \eta_E(15) \wedge v = v' + 1)\} \end{aligned}$$

NOPE can solve this type of equations for a limited set of SyGuS problems using fixed-point algorithms and can then check if $\eta_{Start}(15)$ contains a pair where the second element is 10 (in this case it does not). NOPE can automatically prove unrealizability for many problems involving linear integer (LIA) arithmetic and is in fact sound and complete for conditional linear integer arithmetic (CLIA) when the specification is given as a set of examples—i.e., NOPE provides a decision procedure for this fragment of SyGuS (Theorem 6.2 in [4]). Some of the techniques presented in NOPE have been extended to design specialized unrealizability-checking algorithms for problems involving bit-vector arithmetic [7].

MESSY SemGuS is a general framework for specifying synthesis problems, which also allows one to define synthesis problems involving, for example, imperative constructs. In SemGuS, one can specify a synthesis problem by providing a grammar of programs and constrained Horn clauses (CHCs) that describe the semantics of programs in the grammar. For the problem in Example 1, the following CHC can capture the semantics of the assignment $y := e$ using two relations: (i) The relation $Sem_{Start}(p, (x, y), (x', y'))$ holds when evaluating the program p on state (x, y) results in the state (x', y'), and (ii) The relation $Sem_E(e, (x, y), v)$ holds when evaluating expression p on state (x, y) results in the value v.

$$\frac{Sem_E(e, (x, y), v) \quad x' = x \quad y' = v}{Sem_{Start}(y := e, (x, y), (x', y'))}\; y := E \tag{1}$$

Once a problem is modeled with CHCs (i.e., we have semantic rules for all the possible constructs in the language), proving unrealizability can be phrased as a proof search problem. In particular, if we add the following CHC to the set of CHCs defining the semantics, the relation $Solution(p)$ captures all programs that on input $x = 15$ set the value of y to 10.

$$\frac{Sem_{Start}(p, (x, y), (x', y') \quad x = 15 \quad y' = 10}{Solution(p)}\; y := E \tag{2}$$

MESSY then uses a CHC solver to find whether there exists a program p such that $Solution(p)$ is provable using the given set of CHCs. If the answer is no, the problem is unrealizable. MESSY is currently the only automated tool that can (sometimes) prove unrealizability for problems involving imperative programs and could, for example, prove that no imperative program that only uses bitwise *and* and bitwise *or* can implement a bitwise *xor*.

3 Unrealizability Logic

The works we discussed in Sect. 3 provide automatic techniques to establish that a problem is unrealizable; however, these techniques are all *closed-box*, meaning that they conceal the reasoning behind *why* a synthesis problem is unrealizable. In particular, these techniques typically do not produce a proof artifact that can be independently checked.

Our most recent work presents *unrealizability logic* [8], a Hoare-style proof system for reasoning about the unrealizability of synthesis problems (In this section, we include some excerpts from [8].). In addition to the main goal of reasoning about unrealizability, unrealizability logic is designed with the following goals in mind:

- to be a *general* logic, capable of dealing with various synthesis problems;
- to be amenable to *machine reasoning*, as to enable both automatic proof checking and to open future opportunities for automation;
- to *provide insight* into why certain synthesis problems are unrealizable through the process of completing a proof tree.

Via unrealizability logic, one is able to (*i*) reason about unrealizability in a principled, explicit fashion, and (*ii*) produce concrete proofs about unrealizability.

To prove whether the problem in Example 1 is unrealizble, one would use unrealizability logic to derive the following triple, which states that if one starts in a state where $x = 15$, executing any program in the set $L(Start)$ will result in a state where y is different than 10:

$$\{\!|x = 15|\!\}\ L(Start)\ \{\!|y \neq 10|\!\}$$

Unrealizability logic shares much of the intuition behind Hoare logic and its extension toward recursive programs. However, these concepts appearing in Hoare logic alone are insufficient to model unrealizability, which motivated us to develop the new ideas that form the basis of unrealizability logic.

Hoare logic is based on triples that overapproximate the set of states that can be reached by a program s; i.e., the Hoare triple

$$\{P\}\,\mathsf{s}\,\{Q\}$$

asserts that Q is an *overapproximation* of all states that may be reached by executing s, starting from a state in P. The intuition in Hoare logic is that one will often attempt to prove a triple like $\{P\}\,\mathsf{s}\,\{\neg X\}$ for a set of bad states X, which ensures that execution of s cannot reach X.

Unrealizability logic operates on the same overapproximation principle, but differs in two main ways from standard Hoare logic. The differences are motivated by how synthesis problems are typically defined, using two components: (*i*) a search space S (i.e., a set of programs), and (*ii*) a (possibly infinite) set of related input-output pairs $\{(i_1, o_1), (i_2, o_2), \cdots\}$.

To reason about *sets* of programs, in unrealizability logic, the central element (i.e., the program s) is changed to a *set* of programs S. The unrealizability-logic triple

$$\{\!|P|\!\}\ S\ \{\!|Q|\!\}$$

thus asserts that Q is an overapproximation of all states that are reachable by executing *any possible combination* of a pre-state $p \in P$ *and* a program $\mathsf{s} \in S$.

The second difference concerns *input-output pairs*: in unrealizability logic, we wish to place the input states in the precondition, and overapproximate the set of states reachable from the input states (through a set of programs) as the postcondition. Unfortunately, the input-output pairs of a synthesis problem cannot be tracked using standard pre- and postconditions; nor can they be tracked using auxiliary variables, because of a complication arising from the fact that unrealizability logic must reason about a *set* of programs—i.e., we want our possible output states to be the results of executing the *same* program on the given input (for all possible programs) and prevent output states where different inputs are processed by different programs in the search space.

To keep the input-output relations in check, the predicates of unrealizability logic talk instead about (potentially infinite) *vector-states*, which are sets of states in which each individual state is associated with a unique index—e.g., variable x of the state with index i is referred to as x_i. We defer the reader to the original unrealizability logic paper for these details [8].

The proof system for unrealizability logic has sound underpinnings, and provides a way to build proofs of unrealizability similar to the way Hoare logic [3] provides a way to build proofs that a given program cannot reach a set of bad states. Furtheremore the systems is relatively complete in the same sense as Hoare logic is.

4 Conclusions

This paper outlines recent advances in reasoning about infinite sets of programs at once. We presented techniques for proving unrealizability of synthesis problems that draw inspiration from traditional program verification. However, such techniques did not provide ways to produce proof artifact and to address this limitation, we discussed *unrealizability logic*, the first proof system for overapproximating the execution of an infinite set of programs. This logic is also the first approach that allows one to prove unrealizability for synthesis problems that require infinitely many inputs to be proved unrealizable.

The name "unrealizability logic" is perhaps misleading as the logic allows one to reason about many properties beyond unrealizability. The fact that unrealizability logic is both sound and relatively complete means that this proof system can prove (given powerful enough assertion languages) any property of a given set of programs expressed as a grammar. For example, the problem given in Example 2 of identifying whether a symbolic execution path is infeasible can be phrased as proving whether an unrealizability triple holds.

It is thus natural to conclude with two open questions: (*i*) What applications besides unrealizability can benefit from unrealizability logic as a proof system? (*ii*) Can unrealizability logic be automated in the same successful way Hoare logic has been automated for traditional program verification?

References

1. Feser, J.K., Chaudhuri, S., Dillig, I.: Synthesizing data structure transformations from input-output examples. ACM SIGPLAN Not. **50**(6), 229–239 (2015)
2. Gulwani, S.: Automating string processing in spreadsheets using input-output examples. ACM SIGPLAN Not. **46**(1), 317–330 (2011)
3. Hoare, C.A.R.: An axiomatic basis for computer programming. Commun. ACM **12**(10), 576–580 (1969)
4. Hu, Q., Breck, J., Cyphert, J., D'Antoni, L., Reps, T.: Proving unrealizability for syntax-guided synthesis. In: Dillig, I., Tasiran, S. (eds.) CAV 2019. LNCS, vol. 11561, pp. 335–352. Springer, Cham (2019). https://doi.org/10.1007/978-3-030-25540-4_18
5. Hu, Q., Cyphert, J., D'Antoni, L., Reps, T.: Exact and approximate methods for proving unrealizability of syntax-guided synthesis problems. In: Proceedings of the 41st ACM SIGPLAN Conference on Programming Language Design and Implementation, pp. 1128–1142 (2020)
6. Hu, Q., D'Antoni, L.: Syntax-guided synthesis with quantitative syntactic objectives. In: Chockler, H., Weissenbacher, G. (eds.) CAV 2018. LNCS, vol. 10981, pp. 386–403. Springer, Cham (2018). https://doi.org/10.1007/978-3-319-96145-3_21
7. Kamp, M., Philippsen, M.: Approximate bit dependency analysis to identify program synthesis problems as infeasible. In: Henglein, F., Shoham, S., Vizel, Y. (eds.) VMCAI 2021. LNCS, vol. 12597, pp. 353–375. Springer, Cham (2021). https://doi.org/10.1007/978-3-030-67067-2_16
8. Kim, J., D'Antoni, L., Reps, T.: Unrealizability logic. Proc. ACM Program. Lang. **7**(POPL), 659–688 (2023). https://doi.org/10.1145/3571216
9. Kim, J., Hu, Q., D'Antoni, L., Reps, T.: Semantics-guided synthesis. Proc. ACM Programm. Lang. **5**(POPL), 1–32 (2021)
10. Mechtaev, S., Griggio, A., Cimatti, A., Roychoudhury, A.: Symbolic execution with existential second-order constraints. In: Proceedings of the 2018 26th ACM Joint Meeting on European Software Engineering Conference and Symposium on the Foundations of Software Engineering, pp. 389–399 (2018)
11. Phothilimthana, P.M., et al.: Swizzle inventor: data movement synthesis for GPU kernels. In: Proceedings of the Twenty-Fourth International Conference on Architectural Support for Programming Languages and Operating Systems, pp. 65–78 (2019)

Abstract Interpretation in Industry – Experience and Lessons Learned

Daniel Kästner[1(✉)], Reinhard Wilhelm[2], and Christian Ferdinand[1]

[1] AbsInt GmbH, Science Park 1, 66123 Saarbrücken, Germany
kaestner@absint.com

[2] Saarland University, Stuhlsatzenhausweg 69, 66123 Saarbrücken, Germany

Abstract. In this article we will give an overview of the development and commercialization of two industry-strength Abstract Interpretation-based static analyzers, aiT WCET Analyzer and Astrée. We focus on development steps, adaptations to meet industry requirements and discuss criteria for a successful transfer of formal verification methods to industrial usage.

Keywords: abstract interpretation · WCET analysis · runtime error analysis · functional safety · cybersecurity

1 Introduction

Abstract interpretation is a formal method for sound semantics-based static program analysis [8]. It supports formal correctness proofs: it can be proved that an analysis will terminate and that it is sound in the sense that it computes an over-approximation of the concrete program semantics. Abstract interpretation-based static analyzers provide full control and data coverage and allow conclusions to be drawn that are valid for all program runs with all inputs.

As of today, abstract interpretation-based static analyzers are most widely used to determine non-functional software quality properties [22,23]. On the one hand that includes source code properties, such as compliance to coding guidelines, compliance to software architectural requirements, as well as absence of runtime errors and data races [34]. On the other hand also low-level code properties are covered, such as absence of stack overflows and violation of timing constraints [24,25].

Violations of non-functional software quality requirements often either directly represent safety hazards and cybersecurity vulnerabilities in safety- or security-relevant code, or they can indirectly trigger them. Corresponding verification obligations can be found in all current safety and security norms, such as DO-178C [48], IEC-61508 [15], ISO-26262 [17], and EN-50128 [6].

Many formal verification tools, including abstract interpretation-based static analyzers, originate from academic research projects. However, the transition from academia into industry is far from straightforward. In this article we will

M. V. Hermenegildo and J. F. Morales (Eds.): SAS 2023, LNCS 14284, pp. 10–27, 2023.
https://doi.org/10.1007/978-3-031-44245-2_2

give an overview of our experience in development and commercialization of two industry-strength sound analyzers, aiT WCET analyzer and Astrée. We will discuss the lessons learned, and present recommendations to improve dissemination and acceptance in industrial practice.

2 Sound Worst-Case Execution Time Analysis

Time-critical embedded systems have deadlines derived from the physical environment. They need assurance that their execution time does not exceed these deadlines. Essential input to a response-time analysis are the safe upper bounds of all execution times of tasks to be executed on the same execution platform. These are commonly called *Worst-case Execution times, WCET*. The WCET-analysis problem had a solution for architectures with constant execution times for instructions, so-called *Timing Schemata* [54]. These described how WCETs could be computed by structural induction over programs. However, in the 1990s industry started using microprocessors employing performance-enhancing architectural components and features such as caches, pipelines, and speculation. These made methods based on timing schemata obsolete. The execution-time of an instruction now depended on the execution state in which the instruction were executed. The variability of execution times grew with several architectural parameters, e.g. the cache-miss penalty and the costs for pipeline stalls and for control-flow mis-predictions.

2.1 Our View of and Our Solution to the WCET-Analysis Problem

We developed the following view of the WCET-analysis problem for architectures with state-dependent execution times: Any architectural effect that lets an instruction execute longer than its fastest execution time is a *Timing Accident*. Some of such timing accidents are cache misses, pipeline stalls, bus-access conflicts, and branch mis-predictions. Each such timing accident has to be paid for, in terms of execution-time cycles, by an associated *Timing Penalty*. The size of a timing penalty can be constant, but may also depend on the execution state. We consider the property that an instruction in the program will not cause a particular timing accident as a safety property. The occurrence of a timing accident thus violates a corresponding safety property.

The essence of our WCET-analysis method then consists in the attempt to verify for each instruction in the program as many safety properties as possible, namely that some of the potential timing accidents will never happen. The proof of such safety properties reduces the worst-case execution-time bound for the instruction by the penalties for the excluded timing accidents. This so-called *Microarchitectural Analysis*, embedded within a complex tool architecture, is the central innovation that made our WCET analysis work and scale. We use Abstract Interpretation to compute certain invariants at each program point, namely an upper approximation of the set of execution states that are possible when execution reaches this program point and then derive safety properties, that certain timing accidents will not happen, from these invariants.

2.2 The Development of Our WCET-Analysis Technique

We started with a *classifying cache analysis* [1,12], an analysis that attempts to classify memory accesses in programs as either always hitting or always missing the caches, i.e. instruction and data caches. Our *Must* analysis, used to identify cache hits, computes an under-approximation of the set of cache states that may occur when execution reaches a program point. Our *May* analysis determines an over-approximation of this set of cache states. Both can be represented by compact, efficiently updatable *abstract cache states*. At the start of the development, the caches we, and everybody else, considered used LRU replacement. This made our life easy, but application to real-life processors difficult since the hardware logic for implementing LRU replacement is expensive, and therefore LRU replacement is rarely used in real-life processors.

Involved in the European project Daedalus with Airbus we were confronted with two processors using very different cache-replacement strategies. The first processor, flying the Airbus A340 plane, was a Motorola Coldfire processor which used a cheap emulation of a random-replacement cache. The second projected to fly the A380 plane was a Motorola PowerPC 755. It used a Pseudo-LRU replacement strategy. We noticed that our cache analysis for the Coldfire processor could only track the last loads into the cache, and that our cache analysis for the PowerPC 755 could only track 4 out of the 8 ways in each cache set. This inspired us to very fruitful research about *Timing Predictability* [60] and in particular to the first formal notion of timing predictability, namely that for caches [50].

Next Stephan Thesing developed our pipeline analysis [39]. Unfortunately, pipelines in real-life processors do not admit compact abstract pipeline states. Therefore, expensive powerset domains are used. The pipeline analysis turned out to be the most expensive part of the WCET analysis. A basic block could easily generate a million pipeline states and correspondingly many transitions for analysis. There was a tempting idea to follow only local worst-case transitions and ignore all others. However, real-life processors exhibit *Timing Anomalies* [51]. These entail that a local non-worst-case may contribute to a global worst case.

In the Daedalus project, Airbus also asked for a modeling of their system controller. So far, all WCET research had concentrated on processors. However, a system controller contributes heavily to overall system timing and therefore needs an accurate model and precise analysis [59].

The Micro-architectural analysis was applied to basic blocks, i.e. maximally long straight-line code sequences that can only be entered at the beginning and only be left at the end. The control flow, which had been extracted from the binary executable [57], was translated into an Integer Linear Program (ILP) [58]. The solution of this ILP presented a longest path through the program and the associated execution time. This approach, termed *Implicit Path Enumeration Technique (IPET)*, had been adopted from [40].

At EMSOFT 2001 we presented our breakthrough paper [11]. In summary, a generic tool architecture has emerged which consists of the following stages:

Decoding: The instruction decoder identifies the machine instructions and reconstructs the call and control-flow graph.

Value analysis: Value analysis aims at statically determining enclosing intervals for the contents of the registers and memory cells at each program point and for each execution context. The results of the value analysis are used to predict the addresses of data accesses, the targets of computed calls and branches, and to find infeasible paths.

Micro-architectural analysis: The execution of a program is statically simulated by feeding instruction sequences from the control-flow graph to a micro-architectural timing model which is centered around the cache and pipeline architecture. It computes the system state changes induced by the instruction sequence at cycle granularity and keeps track of the elapsing clock cycles.

Path analysis: Based on the results of the combined cache/pipeline analysis the worst-case path of the analyzed code is computed with respect to the execution timing. The execution time of the computed worst-case path is the worst-case execution time for the task.

We had shown that our sound WCET-analysis method not only solved the single-core WCET-analysis problem, but was even more accurate than the unsound, measurement-based method Airbus had previously used. This meant that their worst-case execution times they had presented in certification had been reliable. Consequently we collaborated with Airbus to satisfy their needs for a sound, industrially viable WCET analysis.

2.3 Improvements

Although the results of our our analysis were already quite accurate, over-estimating the ever observed worst-case execution times by roughly 25%, Airbus wanted more accurate results. Also the integration into industrial development processes needed consideration and some effort.

Increasing Precision. Programs are known to spend most of their time in (recursive) procedures and in loops. The IPET approach using worst-case execution times of basic blocks as input was theoretically pleasing, but lost too much accuracy at the border between basic block and between loop iterations. Controlled loop unrolling increased the accuracy by the necessary extent. However, until today we confuse the competition by using the IPET approach in our explanations.

Often, the software developers knew what they were doing, i.e., they knew properties of their software that influenced execution time, but which were not explicit in the software. Our tool offered to be instructed by adding annotations to the software. Some annotations were even absolutely necessary, like loop and recursion bounds if those could not be automatically derived by our *Value Analysis*, essentially an interval analysis [9], modified to work on binary programs. We will later see that annotations could be automatically inserted if the WCET-analysis tool had been integrated with a model-based design tool.

Integration with Model-Based Design and Schedulability Tools. Much of the safety-critical embedded software is developed using *Model-based Design (MBD)* tools. These automatically generate code from models specified by the software developer. When our WCET tool aiT is integrated with such a MBD tool, model information can be automatically inserted as annotations. Also approximate timing information can be provided on the model level to the developer by back annotation during the development process.

The determined WCETs are typically input into a schedulability analysis. Consequently, aiT has been integrated with several such tools.

2.4 Tool Qualification

Whenever the output of a tool is either part of a safety-critical system to be certified or the tool output is used to eliminate or reduce any development or verification effort for such a system, that tool needs to qualified [22]. Safety norms like DO-178C and ISO 26262 impose binding regulations for tool qualification; they mandate to demonstrate that the tool works correctly in the operational context of its users and/or that the tool is developed in accordance to a safety standard. To address this, a Qualification Support Kit has been developed, which consists of several parts.

The Tool Operational Requirements (TOR) document lists the tool functions and technical features which are stated as low-level requirements to the tool behavior under normal operating conditions. Additionally, the TOR describes the tool operational context and conditions in which the tool computes valid results. A second document (Tool Operational Verification and Validation Cases and Procedures, TOVVCP) defines a set of test cases demonstrating the correct functioning of all specified requirements from the TOR. Test case definitions include the overall test setup as well as a detailed structural and functional description of each test case. The test part contains an extensible set of test cases with a scripting system to automatically execute them and generate reports about the results. These tests also include model validation tests, in fact, a significant part of the development effort for aiT is to validate the abstract hardware model; [25] gives an overview.

In addition, the QSK provides a set of documents that give details about the AbsInt tool development and verification processes and demonstrate their suitability for safety-critical software.

2.5 Impact in Industry and Academia

A painful insight was that hardly any two WCET customers of AbsInt used the same hardware configuration in his systems. The costs for an instantiation of our WCET-analysis technology for a new processor can take quite an effort, making the resulting tool by necessity quite expensive. Still, aiT has been successfully employed in industry and is available for a variety of microprocessors ranging from simple processors like ARM7 to complex superscalar processors with timing anomalies and domino effects like Freescale MPC755, or MPC7448, and multi-core processors like Infineon AURIX TC27x. Our development of a sound method that actually solved a real problem of real industry was considered a major success story for the often disputed formal-methods domain. AbsInt became the favorite partner for the industrialization of academic prototypes. First, Patrick Cousot and his team offered their prototype of Astrée, which in cooperation with some of the developers has been largely extended by AbsInt – more about this in Sect. 3. Then, we entered a cooperation with Xavier Leroy on the result of his much acclaimed research project, CompCert, the first formally verified optimizing C compiler [29,30]. The CompCert front-end and back-end compilation passes, and their compositions, are all formally proved to be free of miscompilation errors. The property that is formally verified, using machine-assisted mathematical proofs, is *semantic preservation* between the input code and output code of every pass. Hence, the executable code CompCert produces is proved to behave exactly as specified by the formal semantics of the source C program. Both Astrée and CompCert are now available as AbsInt products.

2.6 Application to Non-Timing-Predictable Architectures

Multi-core processors with shared resources pose a severe problem for sound and precise WCET analysis. To interconnect the several cores, buses, meshes, crossbars, and also dynamically routed communication structures are used. In that case, the interference delays due to conflicting, simultaneous accesses to shared resources (e.g. main memory) can cause significant imprecision. Multi-core processors which can be configured in a timing-predictable way to avoid or bound inter-core interferences are amenable to static WCET analysis [27,63,64]. Examples are the Infineon AURIX TC275 [16], or the Freescale MPC 5777.

The Freescale P4080 [13] is one example of a multi-core platform where the interference delays have a huge impact on the memory access latencies and cannot be satisfactorily predicted by purely static techniques. In addition, no public documentation of the interconnect is available. Nowotsch et al. [46] measured maximal write latencies of 39 cycles when only one core was active, and maximal write latencies of 1007 cycles when all eight cores were running. This is more than 25 times longer than the observed single-core worst case. Like measuring task execution on one core with interference generators running on all other cores, statically computed WCET bounds will significantly overestimate the timing delays of the system in the intended final configuration.

In some cases, robust partitioning [64] can be achieved with approaches approaches like [53] or [46]. For systems which do not implement such rigorous software architectures or where the information needed to develop a static timing model is not available, hybrid WCET approaches are the only solution.

For hybrid WCET analysis, the same generic tool architecture as described in Sect. 2.2 can be used, as done in the tool TimeWeaver [37]. It performs Abstract Interpretation-based context-sensitive path and value analysis analysis, but replaces the Microarchitectural Analysis stage by non-intrusive real-time instruction-level tracing to provide worst-case execution time estimates. The trace information covers interference effects, e.g., by accesses to shared resources from different cores, without being distorted by probe effects since no instrumentation code is needed. The computed estimates are upper bounds with respect to the given input traces, i.e., TimeWeaver derives an overall upper timing bound from the execution time observed in the given traces. This approach is compliant to the recommendations of CAST-32a and AMC 20–193 [7,10].

2.7 Spin-Off: Worst-Case Stack Usage Analysis

In embedded systems, the run-time stack (often just called "the stack") typically is the only dynamically allocated memory area. It is used during program execution to keep track of the currently active procedures and facilitate the evaluation of expressions. Each active procedure is represented by an activation record, also called stack frame or procedure frame, which holds all the state information needed for execution.

Precisely determining the maximum stack usage before deploying the system is important for economical reasons and for system safety. Overestimating the maximum stack usage means wasting memory resources. Underestimation leads to stack overflows: memory cells from the stacks of different tasks or other memory areas are overwritten. This can cause crashes due to memory protection violations and can trigger arbitrary erroneous program behavior, if return addresses or other parts of the execution state are modified. In consequence stack overflows are typically hard to diagnose and hard to reproduce, but they are a potential cause of catastrophic failure. The accidents caused by the unintended acceleration of the 2005 Toyota Camry illustrate the potential consequences of stack overflows: the expert witness' report commissioned by the Oklahoma court in 2013 identifies a stack overflow as probable failure cause [3,61].

The generic tool architecture of Sect. 2.2 can be easily adapted to perform an analysis of the worst-case stack usage, by exchanging the Microarchitectural analysis step with a dedicated value analysis for the stack pointer register(s) [24]. In 2001, the resulting tool, called StackAnalyzer, was released, which was the first commercial tool to safely prove the absence of stack overflows in safety-critical systems, and since then has been widely adopted in industry.

3 Sound Runtime Error Analysis

The purpose of the Astrée analyzer is to detect source-level runtime errors due to undefined or unspecified behaviors of C programs. Examples are faulty pointer manipulations, numerical errors such as arithmetic overflows and division by zero, data races, and synchronization errors in concurrent software. Such errors can cause software crashes, invalidate separation mechanisms in mixed-criticality software, and are a frequent cause of errors in concurrent and multi-core applications. At the same time, these defects also constitute security vulnerabilities, and have been at the root of a multitude of cybersecurity attacks, in particular buffer overflows, dangling pointers, or race conditions [31].

3.1 The Origins

Astrée stands for Analyseur statique de logiciels temps-réel embarqués (real-time embedded software static analyzer). The development of Astrée started from scratch in Nov. 2001 at the Laboratoire d'Informatique of the École Normale Supérieure (LIENS), initially supported by the ASTRÉE project, the Centre National de la Recherche Scientifique, the École Normale Supérieure and, since September 2007, by INRIA (Paris-Rocquencourt).

First industrial applications of Astrée appeared two years after starting the project. Astrée has achieved the following unprecedented results on the static analysis of synchronous, time-triggered, real-time, safety critical, embedded software written or automatically generated in the C programming language:

- In Nov. 2003, Astrée was able to prove completely automatically the absence of any RTE in the primary flight control software of the Airbus A340 fly-by-wire system.
- From Jan. 2004 on, Astrée was extended to analyze the electric flight control codes then in development and test for the A380 series.
- In April 2008, Astrée was able to prove completely automatically the absence of any RTE in a C version of the automatic docking software of the Jules Vernes Automated Transfer Vehicle (ATV) enabling ESA to transport payloads to the International Space Station [4].

In Dec. 2009, AbsInt started the commercialization of Astrée in cooperation with LIENS, in particular Patrick Cousot, Jérôme Feret, Laurent Mauborgne, Antoine Miné, and Xavier Rival.

3.2 Further Development

From a technical perspective, the ensuing development activities can be grouped into several categories:

Usability. The original version of Astrée was a command-line tool, however, to facilitate commercial use, a graphical user interface was developed. The purpose is not merely to make the tool more intuitive to use, but – even more importantly – to help users understand the results. Astrée targets corner cases of the C semantics which requires a good understanding of the language, and it shows defects due to behavior unexpected by the programmer. To facilitate understanding the unexpected behavior, we have developed a large set of graphical and interactive exploration views. To give some examples, all parents in the call stack, relevant loop iterations or conditional statements that lead to the alarm can be accessed by mouse click, tool tips show the values of values, the call graph can be interactively explored, etc. [28]. In all of this, there is one crucial requirement: all views and graphs have to be efficiently computable and suitable for large-scale software consisting of millions of lines of code [20].

Further usability enhancements were the integration of a preprocessor into Astrée (the original version read preprocessed C code), automated preprocessor configuration based on JSON compilation files, Windows support, and the ability to classify and comment findings from the GUI.

Apart from easy usability, an important requirement of contemporary development processes is the ability to integrate a tool in a CD/CI (continuous development/continuous integration) platform. To support this, Astrée can be started from the command line with full functionality, the configuration is given as an XML file which can be automatically created, results can be exported in machine-readable formats (xml, csv, html) that support post-processing. Furthermore, there is a large number of plugins and tool couplings which have been developed, e.g., to model-based development tools like Matlab/Simulink/TargetLink [26,38], as well as CI tools and IDEs such as Jenkins, Eclipse, and Keil μVision.

Formal Requirements. The primary use-case of Astrée is to find defects in safety-critical or security-relevant software, hence the same tool qualification requirements apply as described in Sect. 2.3. So, the development of a Qualification Support Kit for Astrée was a mandatory; its structure is similar to the aiT QSK as described above.

Another constraint is that in certain safety processes, no code modifications are allowed which cannot be traced to functional software requirements. Also, in the case of model-based software development, where the code is automatically generated, it is infeasible to modify the source code to interact with a static analyzer.

Astrée provides numerous analysis directives that allow users to interact with the tool, e.g., to pass certain preconditions such as constraints on input value ranges or volatile variable ranges to the analyzer. Alarms can be classified (e.g., as true defect or false alarms) via source code comments or analysis directives. Finally Astrée's domains have been specifically developed to support fine-grained precision tuning to eliminate false alarms. One example is the trace partitioning domain, a generic framework that allows the partitioning of traces based on the history of the control flow [52]. By inserting analysis directives into the code, users can influence the partitioning strategy of the analyzer for limited parts of the code.

To also support use cases where code modifications are infeasible, a formal language AAL has been developed [36] which provides a robust way to locate analyzer directives in the abstract syntax tree without modifying the source code. It is also possible to automatically generate such annotations from the build environment or an interface specification.

New Capabilities

Interleaving Semantics and Integration Analysis. While the first versions of Astrée targeted sequential code, most of today's industry applications are multi-threaded. In such software systems, it is highly desirable to be able to do runtime error analysis at the integration verification stage, i.e., to analyze the entire software stack in order to capture the interactions between all components of the system, determine their effect on data and control flow and detect runtime errors triggered by them.

To support this, Antoine Miné has developed a low-level concurrent semantics [42] which provides a scalable sound abstraction covering all possible thread interleavings. The interleaving semantics enables Astrée, in addition to the classes of runtime errors found in sequential programs, to report data races and lock/unlock problems, i.e., inconsistent synchronization. The set of shared variables does not need to be specified by the user: Astrée assumes that every global variable can be shared, and discovers which ones are effectively shared, and on which ones there is a data race. To implement its interleaving semantics, Astrée provides primitives which expose OS functionality to the analyzer, such as mutex un-/locks, interrupt dis-/enabling, thread creation, etc. Since Astrée is aware of all locks held for every program point in each concurrent thread, Astrée can also report all potential deadlocks. Astrée also supports several stages of concurrent execution so that initialization tasks can be separated from periodic/acyclic tasks. Each thread can be associated to one or several concurrent execution stages.

Using the Astrée concurrency primitives, abstract OS libraries have been developed, which currently support the OSEK/AUTOSAR and ARINC 653 norms [2,43]. A particularity of OSEK/AUTOSAR is that system resources, including tasks, mutexes and spin-locks, are not created dynamically at program startup; instead they are hardcoded in the system: a specific tool reads a configuration file in OIL (OSEK Implementation Language) or ARXML (AutosaR XML) format describing these resources and generates a specialized version of the system to be linked against the application. A dedicated ARXML converter has been developed for Astrée which automatically generates the appropriate data structures and access functions for the Astrée analysis, and enables a fully automatic integration analysis of AUTOSAR projects [20].

Code Guideline Checking. Coding guidelines aim at improving code quality and can be considered a prerequisite for developing safety- or security-relevant software. In particular, obeying coding guidelines is strongly recommended by all current safety standards. Their purpose is to reduce the risk of programming errors by enforcing low complexity, enforcing usage of a language subset, using well-trusted design principles, etc. According to ISO 26262, the language subset to be enforced should exclude, e.g., ambiguously defined language constructs, language constructs that could result in unhandled runtime errors, and language constructs known to be error-prone. Since the Astrée architecture is well suited for sound and precise code guideline checking, over the years, the analyzer has been extended to support all major coding guidelines, such as MISRA C/C++ [41,44,45], SEI CERT C/C++ [55], CWE [56], etc.

Cybersecurity Vulnerability Scanning. Many security attacks can be traced back to behaviors undefined or unspecified according to the C semantics. By applying sound static runtime error analyzers, a high degree of security can be achieved for safety-critical software since the absence of such defects can be proven. In addition, security hyperproperties require additional analyses to be performed which, by nature, have a high complexity. To support this, Astrée has been extended by a generic abstract domain for taint analysis that can be freely instantiated by the users [33]. It augments Astrée's process-interleaving interprocedural code analysis by carrying and computing taint information at the byte level. Any number of taint hues can be tracked by Astrée, and their combinations will be soundly abstracted. Tainted input is specified through directives attached to program locations. Such directives can precisely describe which variables, and which part of those variables is to be tainted, with the given taint hues, each time this program location is reached. Any assignment is interpreted as propagating the join of all taint hues from its right-hand side to the targets of its left-hand side. In addition, specific directives may be introduced to explicitly modify the taint hues of some variable parts. This is particularly useful to model cleansing function effects or to emulate changes of security levels in the code. The result of the analysis with tainting can be explored in the Astrée GUI, or explicitly dumped using dedicated directives. Finally, the taint sink directives may be used to declare that some parts of some variables must be considered as taint sinks for a given set of taint hues. When a tainted value is assigned to a taint sink, then Astrée will emit a dedicated alarm, and remove the sinked hues, so that only the first occurrence has to be examined to fix potential issues with the security data flow.

The main intended use of taint analysis in Astrée is to expose potential vulnerabilities with respect to security policies or resilience mechanisms. Thanks to the intrinsic soundness of the approach, no tainting can be forgotten, and that without any bound on the number of iterations of loops, size of data or length of the call stack. Based on its taint analysis, Astrée provides an automatic detection of Spectre-PHT vulnerabilities [32].

Data and Control Flow. All current safety norms require determining the data and control flow in the source code and making sure that it is compliant to the intended control and data flow as defined in the software architecture. To meet this requirement, Astrée has been extended by a data and control flow analysis module, which tracks accesses to global, static, and local variables. The soundness of the analysis ensures that all potential targets of data and function pointers are discovered. Data and control flow reports show the number of read and write accesses for every global, static, and out-of-frame local variable, lists the location of each access and shows the function from which the access is made. All variables are classified as being thread-local, effectively shared between different threads, or subject to a data race.

To further support integration verification, a recent extension of Astrée provides a generic concept for specifying software components, enabling the analyzer to lift the data and control flow analysis to report data and control flow interactions between software components. This is complemented by an automatic taint analysis that efficiently tracks the flow of values between components, and automatically reports undesired data flow and undesired control dependencies.

The combination of augmented data and control analysis and the taint analysis for software components provides a sound interference analysis [35].

C++. To respond to the increasing interest in C++ even in the domain of safety-critical software, since 2020 Astrée also provides a dedicated analysis mode for C++ and mixed C/C++. It uses the same analysis technology as Astrée's semantic C code analysis and has similar capabilities. At the same time it is also subject to the same restrictions. The analyzer is designed to meet the characteristics of safety-critical embedded software. Typical properties of such software include a static execution model that uses a fixed number of threads, no or limited usage of dynamic memory allocation and dynamic data structures. Astrée provides an abstract standard template library, that models the behavior of STL containers in an abstract way suitable for analysis with Astrée. Astrée does not attempt to analyze the control flow of exceptions; it only reports if an exception could be raised.

Precision and Efficiency. Constant development effort is required to work at precision and scalability of the analyzer. Over the years, various additional abstract domains have been developed to avoid false alarms on common embedded software elements. Examples are domains for finite integer sets, gauges [21,62], domains for precise analysis of interpolation functions, finite state machines, etc. Astrée's state machine domain heuristically detects state variables and disambiguates them by state partitioning in the relevant program scope [14]. In consequence the analyzer becomes aware of the exact transitions of the state machine and the false alarms due to control flow over-approximation can be avoided. Over the past years, the size of embedded software has grown significantly; typical automotive AUTOSAR projects span 5–50 million lines of (preprocessed) code. One prerequisite to enable an efficient analysis of such large-scale projects is an efficient strategy to heuristically control the context-sensitivity of the analyzer and distinguish critical call chains where full flow- and context-sensitivity is needed from less critical ones where building a summary context is enough [20].

4 The User Perspective

Whereas from an academic perspective, software verification can be fun and is a topic of great merit, this is not necessarily a view shared by every software developer working in the field. In fact, the ISO 26262 norm puts en emphasis on the need to embrace functional safety in the company organization and establish a safety culture [18]. Verification activities should not be – as they often are – perceived as a burden that drains on development cost, delays delivery and does not provide an added value to the end product. Introducing new verification steps should not be perceived as admitting a mistake. The capability of defect prevention, the efficiency in defect detection, and the degree of automation is crucial for user acceptance.

Advanced program analysis requires significant technical insights, including knowledge about the programming language semantics, microprocessor design, and system configuration. Without the necessary understanding, program analysis tools are hard to use. On the other hand, it is necessary for tools to expose the information users need to understand the results as intuitively as possible.

Finally, users expect tools to solve real problems, e.g., the worst-case execution time on a particular microcontroller in the configuration given, or the occurrence of runtime errors in the tasks as they are deployed in the real system. When providing partial solutions to a problem, it is necessary to explain how to use them to help dealing with the full problem.

5 The Role of Safety Norms

Functional safety and security are aspects of dependability, in addition to reliability and availability. *Functional safety* is usually defined as the absence of unreasonable risk to life and property caused by malfunctioning behavior of the system. Correspondingly, cybersecurity can be defined as absence of unreasonable risk caused by malicious misusage of the system. Functional safety norms aim at formalizing the minimal obligations for developers of safety-critical systems to make sure that unreasonable safety risks are avoided. In addition, advances in system development and verification since the publication date of a given norm have to be taken into account. In other words, safety norms define the minimal requirements to develop safety-relevant software with due diligence. Safety standards typically are domain-specific; examples DO-178B/DO-178C [47,48] (aerospace), ISO 26262 [17] (automotive), CENELEC EN 50128/EN 50657 [5,6] (railway), IEC 61508 [15] (general electrical and/or electronic systems), IEC 62304 (medical products), etc.

The DO-178C [48] has been published with supplements focusing on technical advances since release of the predecessor norm DO-178B, in particular the DO-333 (Formal Methods Supplement to DO-178C and DO-278A) [49], that addresses the use of formal methods to complement or replace dynamic testing. It distinguishes three categories of formal analyses: deductive methods such as theorem proving, model checking, and abstract interpretation. The computation of worst-case execution time bounds and the maximal stack usage are listed as reference applications of abstract interpretation. However, the standard does not mandate the use of formal methods.

Table 7 and Table 10 of ISO 26262 Part 6 [19] give a list of recommended methods for verification of software unit design and implementation, and integration verification, respectively. They contain separate entries for formal verification, control flow analysis, data flow analysis, static code analysis, and static analysis by abstract interpretation. Static analysis in general is *highly recommended* for all criticality levels (ASILs), Abstract Interpretation is *recommended* for all ASILs. The current versions of EN 50128 and IEC 62304 lack an explicit reference to Abstract Interpretation.

Since for industrial system development, functional safety norms are defining what is considered to be (minimal) state of the art, the availability of mature development and verification techniques should be reflected in them. To create the necessary awareness, an exchange between software and safety communities is essential.

6 Conclusion

The focus of this article is to describe the application of Abstract Interpretation to two different real-life problems: to compute sound worst-case execution time bounds, and to perform sound runtime error analysis for C/C++ programs. We have summarized the development history of aiT WCET Analyzer and Astrée, discussed design choices, and illustrated the exigencies imposed by commercial users and industrial processes. We also addressed derived research and applications to other topics, in particular hybrid WCET analysis and worst-case stack usage analysis. In summary, the tools discussed in this article provide a formal methods-based ecosystem for verifying resource usage in embedded software projects. The three main causes of software-induced memory corruption in safety-critical systems are runtime errors, stack overflows, and miscompilation. The absence of runtime errors and stack overflows can be proven by abstract interpretation-based static analyzers. With the formally proven compiler CompCert, miscompilation can be ruled out, hence all main sources of software-induced memory corruption are addressed. Industrial application of mathematically rigorous verification methods strongly depends on their representation in industrial safety norms; the corresponding methods and tools have to become better known to the safety community and their advantages compared to legacy methods better explained.

Acknowledgment. Many people contributed to aiT and Astrée and their success. We want to thank them all.

References

1. Alt, M., Ferdinand, C., Martin, F., Wilhelm, R.: Cache behavior prediction by abstract interpretation. In: Cousot, R., Schmidt, D.A. (eds.) SAS 1996. LNCS, vol. 1145, pp. 52–66. Springer, Heidelberg (1996). https://doi.org/10.1007/3-540-61739-6_33
2. AUTOSAR: AUTOSAR (AUTomotive Open System ARchitecture). http://www.autosar.org
3. Barr, M.: Bookout v. Toyota, 2005 Camry software Analysis by Michael Barr (2013). http://www.safetyresearch.net/Library/BarrSlides_FINAL_SCRUBBED.pdf
4. Bouissou, O., et al.: Space software validation using abstract interpretation. In: Proceedings of the 13thData Systems in Aerospace (DASIA 2009) (2009)
5. BS EN 50657: Railway applications - Rolling stock applications - Software on Board Rolling Stock (2017)
6. CENELEC EN 50128: Railway Applications - Communication, Signalling and Processing Systems - Software for Railway Control and Protection Systems (2011)

7. Certification Authorities Software Team (CAST): Position Paper CAST-32A Multi-core Processors (2016)
8. Cousot, P., Cousot, R.: Abstract interpretation: a unified lattice model for static analysis of programs by construction or approximation of fixpoints. In: Proceedings of the POPL'77, pp. 238–252. ACM Press (1977). http://www.di.ens.fr/~cousot/COUSOTpapers/POPL77.shtml. Accessed Sep 2017
9. Cousot, P., Cousot, R.: Static determination of dynamic properties of generalized type unions. In: Wortman, D.B. (ed.) Proceedings of an ACM Conference on Language Design for Reliable Software (LDRS), Raleigh, North Carolina, USA, 28-30 March 1977, pp. 77–94. ACM (1977). https://doi.org/10.1145/800022.808314
10. EASA: AMC-20 - amendment 23 - AMC 20–193 use of multi-core processors (2022)
11. Ferdinand, C., et al.: Reliable and precise WCET determination for a real-life processor. In: Henzinger, T.A., Kirsch, C.M. (eds.) EMSOFT 2001. LNCS, vol. 2211, pp. 469–485. Springer, Heidelberg (2001). https://doi.org/10.1007/3-540-45449-7_32
12. Ferdinand, C., Wilhelm, R.: Efficient and precise cache behavior prediction for real-time systems. Real-Time Syst. **17**(2–3), 131–181 (1999)
13. Freescale Inc.: QorIQ^{TM} P4080 Communications Processor Product Brief (2008). rev. 1
14. Giet, J., Mauborgne, L., Kästner, D., Ferdinand, C.: Towards zero alarms in sound static analysis of finite state machines. In: Romanovsky, A., Troubitsyna, E., Bitsch, F. (eds.) SAFECOMP 2019. LNCS, vol. 11698, pp. 3–18. Springer, Cham (2019). https://doi.org/10.1007/978-3-030-26601-1_1
15. IEC 61508: Functional safety of electrical/electronic/programmable electronic safety-related systems (2010)
16. Infineon Technologies AG: AURIX^{TM} TC27x D-Step User's Manual (2014)
17. ISO 26262: Road vehicles - Functional safety (2018)
18. ISO 26262: Road vehicles - Functional safety - Part 2: Management of functional safety (2018)
19. ISO 26262: Road vehicles - Functional safety - Part 6: Product development at the software level (2018)
20. Kaestner, D., Wilhelm, S., Mallon, C., Schank, S., Ferdinand, C., Mauborgne, L.: Automatic sound static analysis for integration verification of AUTOSAR software. In: WCX SAE World Congress Experience. SAE International (2023). https://doi.org/10.4271/2023-01-0591
21. Karos, T.: The Gauge Domain in Astrée. Master's thesis, Saarland University (2015)
22. Kästner, D.: Applying abstract interpretation to demonstrate functional safety. In: Boulanger, J.L. (ed.) Formal Methods Applied to Industrial Complex Systems. ISTE/Wiley, London, UK (2014)
23. Kästner, D., Ferdinand, C.: Efficient verification of non-functional safety properties by abstract interpretation: timing, stack consumption, and absence of runtime errors. In: Proceedings of the 29th International System Safety Conference ISSC2011. Las Vegas (2011)
24. Kästner, D., Ferdinand, C.: Proving the absence of stack overflows. In: Bondavalli, A., Di Giandomenico, F. (eds.) SAFECOMP 2014. LNCS, vol. 8666, pp. 202–213. Springer, Cham (2014). https://doi.org/10.1007/978-3-319-10506-2_14
25. Kästner, D., Pister, M., Gebhard, G., Schlickling, M., Ferdinand, C.: Confidence in timing. In: SAFECOMP 2013 Workshop: Next Generation of System Assurance Approaches for Safety-Critical Systems (SASSUR) (2013)

26. Kästner, D., et al.: Model-driven code generation and analysis. In: SAE World Congress 2014. SAE International (2014). https://doi.org/10.4271/2014-01-0217
27. Kästner, D., et al.: Meeting real-time requirements with multi-core processors. SAFECOMP 2012 Workshop: Next Generation of System Assurance Approaches for Safety-Critical Systems (SASSUR) (2012)
28. Kästner, D., et al.: Astrée: proving the absence of runtime errors. In: Embedded Real Time Software and Systems Congress ERTS ^{2} (2010)
29. Kästner, D., et al.: CompCert: practical experience on integrating and qualifying a formally verified optimizing compiler. In: ERTS2 2018 - Embedded Real Time Software and Systems. 3AF, SEE, SIE, Toulouse, France (2018). https://hal.inria.fr/hal-01643290, archived in the HAL-INRIA open archive, https://hal.inria.fr/hal-01643290/file/ERTS_2018_paper_59.pdf
30. Kästner, D., Leroy, X., Blazy, S., Schommer, B., Schmidt, M., Ferdinand, C.: Closing the gap - the formally verified optimizing compiler CompCert. In: SSS 2017: Developments in System Safety Engineering: Proceedings of the Twenty-fifth Safety-critical Systems Symposium, pp. 163–180. CreateSpace (2017)
31. Kästner, D., Mauborgne, L., Ferdinand, C.: Detecting safety- and security-relevant programming defects by sound static analysis. In: Falk, R., Chan, J.C.B.S. (eds.) The Second International Conference on Cyber-Technologies and Cyber-Systems (CYBER 2017). IARIA Conferences, vol. 2, pp. 26–31. IARIA XPS Press (2017)
32. Kästner, D., Mauborgne, L., Ferdinand, C.: Detecting spectre vulnerabilities by sound static analysis. In: Anne Coull, R.F., Chan, S. (ed.) The Fourth International Conference on Cyber-Technologies and Cyber-Systems (CYBER 2019). IARIA Conferences, vol. 4, pp. 29–37. IARIA XPS Press (2019). http://www.thinkmind.org/download.php?articleid=cyber_2019_3_10_80050
33. Kästner, D., Mauborgne, L., Grafe, N., Ferdinand, C.: Advanced sound static analysis to detect safety- and security-relevant programming defects. In: Falk, R., Steve Chan, J.C.B. (eds.) 8th International Journal on Advances in Security. vol. 1 & 2, pp. 149–159. IARIA (2018), https://www.iariajournals.org/security/
34. Kästner, D., Mauborgne, L., Wilhelm, S., Ferdinand, C.: high-precision sound analysis to find safety and cybersecurity defects. In: 10th European Congress on Embedded Real Time Software and Systems (ERTS 2020). Toulouse, France (2020). https://hal.archives-ouvertes.fr/hal-02479217
35. Kästner, D., Mauborgne, L., Wilhelm, S., Mallon, C., Ferdinand, C.: Static data and control coupling analysis. In: 11th Embedded Real Time Systems European Congress (ERTS2022). Toulouse, France (2022). https://hal.archives-ouvertes.fr/hal-03694546
36. Kästner, D., Pohland, J.: Program analysis on evolving software. In: Roy, M. (ed.) CARS 2015 - Critical Automotive applications: Robustness & Safety. Paris, France (2015). https://hal.archives-ouvertes.fr/hal-01192985
37. Kästner, D., Hümbert, C., Gebhard, G., Pister, M., Wegener, S., Ferdinand, C.: Taming Timing - Combining Static Analysis With Non-intrusive Tracing to Compute WCET Bounds on Multicore Processors. Embedded World Congress (2021)
38. Kästner, D., Salvi, S., Bienmüller, T., Ferdinand, C.: Exploiting synergies between static analysis and model-based testing (2015). https://doi.org/10.1109/EDCC.2015.20
39. Langenbach, M., Thesing, S., Heckmann, R.: Pipeline modeling for timing analysis. In: Hermenegildo, M.V., Puebla, G. (eds.) SAS 2002. LNCS, vol. 2477, pp. 294–309. Springer, Heidelberg (2002). https://doi.org/10.1007/3-540-45789-5_22

40. Li, Y.T.S., Malik, S.: Performance analysis of embedded software using implicit path enumeration. In: Proceedings of the 32nd ACM/IEEE Design Automation Conference, pp. 456–461 (1995)
41. Limited, M.: MISRA C++:2008 Guidelines for the use of the C++ language in critical systems (2008)
42. Miné, A.: Static analysis of run-time errors in embedded real-time parallel C programs. Logic. Meth. Comput. Sci. (LMCS) **8**(26), 63 (2012)
43. Miné, A., Delmas, D.: Towards an industrial use of sound static analysis for the verification of concurrent embedded avionics software. In: Proceedings of the 15th International Conference on Embedded Software (EMSOFT 2015), pp. 65–74. IEEE CS Press (2015)
44. MISRA (Motor Industry Software Reliability Association) Working Group: MISRA-C:2012 Guidelines for the use of the C Language in Critical Systems. MISRA Limited (2013)
45. MISRA (Motor Industry Software Reliability Association) Working Group: MISRA-C:2023 Guidelines for the use of the C Language in Critical Systems. MISRA Limited (2023)
46. Nowotsch, J., Paulitsch, M., Bühler, D., Theiling, H., Wegener, S., Schmidt, M.: Multi-core interference-sensitive wcet analysis leveraging runtime resource capacity enforcement. In: ECRTS 2014: Proceedings of the 26th Euromicro Conference on Real-Time Systems (2014)
47. Radio Technical Commission for Aeronautics: RTCA DO-178B. Software Considerations in Airborne Systems and Equipment Certification (1992)
48. Radio Technical Commission for Aeronautics: RTCA DO-178C. Software Considerations in Airborne Systems and Equipment Certification (2011)
49. Radio Technical Commission for Aeronautics: RTCA DO-333. Formal Methods Supplement to DO-178C and DO-278A (2011)
50. Reineke, J., Grund, D., Berg, C., Wilhelm, R.: Timing predictability of cache replacement policies. Real-Time Syst. **37**(2), 99–122 (2007)
51. Reineke, J., et al.: A definition and classification of timing anomalies. In: Mueller, F. (ed.) International Workshop on Worst-Case Execution Time Analysis (WCET) (2006)
52. Rival, X., Mauborgne, L.: The trace partitioning abstract domain. ACM Trans. Program. Lang. Syst. **29**(5), 26 (2007). https://doi.org/10.1145/1275497.1275501
53. Schranzhofer, A., Chen, J.J., Thiele, L.: Timing predictability on multi-processor systems with shared resources. In: Workshop on Reconciling Performance with Predictability (RePP), 2010 (2009)
54. Shaw, A.C.: Reasoning about time in higher-level language software. IEEE Trans. Softw. Eng. **15**(7), 875–889 (1989). https://doi.org/10.1109/32.29487
55. Software Engineering Institute SEI - CERT Division: SEI CERT C Coding Standard - Rules for Developing Safe, Reliable, and Secure Systems. Carnegie Mellon University (2016)
56. The MITRE Corporation: CWE – Common Weakness Enumeration. https://cwe.mitre.org. Accessed Sep 2017
57. Theiling, H.: Extracting safe and precise control flow from binaries. In: Proceedings of the 7th Conference on Real-Time Computing Systems and Applications. Cheju Island, South Korea (2000)
58. Theiling, H.: ILP-based interprocedural path analysis. In: Sangiovanni-Vincentelli, A., Sifakis, J. (eds.) EMSOFT 2002. LNCS, vol. 2491, pp. 349–363. Springer, Heidelberg (2002). https://doi.org/10.1007/3-540-45828-X_26

59. Thesing, S.: Modeling a system controller for timing analysis. In: Min, S.L., Yi, W. (eds.) Proceedings of the 6th ACM & IEEE International conference on Embedded software, EMSOFT 2006, 22-25 October 2006, Seoul, Korea, pp. 292–300. ACM (2006). https://doi.org/10.1145/1176887.1176929
60. Thiele, L., Wilhelm, R.: Design for timing predictability. Real-Time Syst. **28**(2–3), 157–177 (2004). https://doi.org/10.1023/B:TIME.0000045316.66276.6e
61. Transcript of Morning Trial Proceedings had on the 14th day of October, 2013 Before the Honorable Patricia G. Parrish, District Judge, Case No. CJ-2008-7969 (2013). http://www.safetyresearch.net/Library/Bookout_v_Toyota_Barr_REDACTED.pdf
62. Venet, A.: The gauge domain: scalable analysis of linear inequality invariants (2012). https://doi.org/10.1007/978-3-642-31424-7_15
63. Wegener, S.: Towards multicore WCET analysis. In: Reineke, J. (ed.) 17th International Workshop on Worst-Case Execution Time Analysis (WCET 2017). OpenAccess Series in Informatics (OASIcs), vol. 57, pp. 1–12. Schloss Dagstuhl–Leibniz-Zentrum fuer Informatik, Dagstuhl, Germany (2017). https://doi.org/10.4230/OASIcs.WCET.2017.7, http://drops.dagstuhl.de/opus/volltexte/2017/7311
64. Wilhelm, R., Reineke, J., Wegener, S.: Keeping up with real time. In: Durak, U., Becker, J., Hartmann, S., Voros, N.S. (eds.) Advances in Aeronautical Informatics, pp. 121–133. Springer, Cham (2018). https://doi.org/10.1007/978-3-319-75058-3_9

Building Trust and Safety in Artificial Intelligence with Abstract Interpretation

Gagandeep Singh[1,2](✉)

[1] University of Illinois at Urbana-Champaign (UIUC), Champaign, USA
ggnds@illinois.edu
[2] VMware Research, Palo Alto, USA

1 Introduction

Deep neural networks (DNNs) are currently the dominant technology in artificial intelligence (AI) and have shown impressive performance in diverse applications including autonomous driving [9], medical diagnosis [2], and text generation [10]. However, their black-box construction [46] and vulnerability against environmental and adversarial noise [30,57] have raised concerns about their safety, when deployed in the real world. Standard training [28] optimizes the model's accuracy but does not take into account desirable safety properties such as robustness [48], fairness [18], and monotonicity [49]. The standard practice of testing and interpreting DNN behavior on a finite set of unseen test inputs cannot guarantee safe and trustworthy DNN behavior on new inputs seen during deployment [59,66]. This is because the DNN can misbehave if the inputs observed during deployment deviate even slightly from those in the test set [20,23,36].

To address these limitations, there is growing work on checking the safety of DNN models [3,5,11,17,25,27,31,42–45,50–53,58,61,62,65,68,70] and interpreting their behavior [7], on an infinite set of unseen inputs using formal certification. Testing and interpreting with formal methods provide a more reliable metric for measuring a model's safety than standard methods [12]. Formal methods can also be used during training [6,22,38,40,69,72,74] to guide the model to satisfy desirable safety and trustworthy properties.

DNN Certification Problem. The certification problem consists of two main components: (i) a trained DNN f, (ii) a property specification in the form of a tuple (ϕ, ψ) containing symbolic formulas ϕ and ψ. Here the formula ϕ is a precondition specifying the set of inputs on which, the DNN should not misbehave. The formula ψ is a postcondition that determines constraints that the DNN outputs $f(\phi)$ [26] or its gradients $f'(\phi)$ [33,34] corresponding to the inputs in ϕ should satisfy, for its behaviors to be considered safe and trustworthy. A DNN certifier tries to check whether $f(\phi) \subseteq \psi$ (or $f'(\phi) \subseteq \psi$) holds. Both ϕ, ψ are typically specified as disjunctions of convex polyhedra. The property specifications are domain dependent and usually designed by DNN developers.

Local vs Global Properties. The precondition ϕ for local properties defines a local neighborhood around a sample input from the test set. For example,

M. V. Hermenegildo and J. F. Morales (Eds.): SAS 2023, LNCS 14284, pp. 28–38, 2023.
https://doi.org/10.1007/978-3-031-44245-2_3

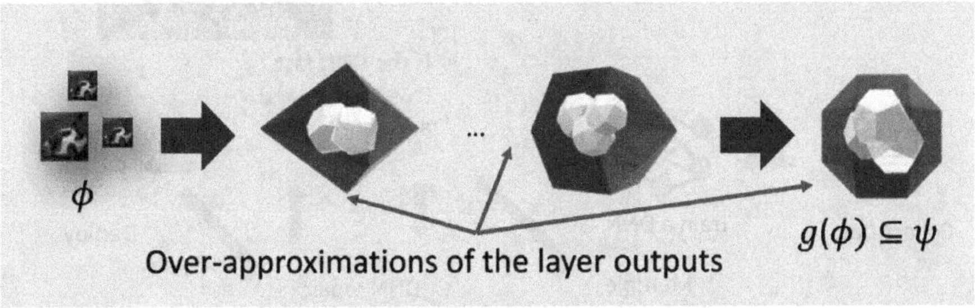

Fig. 1. Neural network certification with abstract interpretation involves computing an abstract element (in blue) containing the true network output $f(\phi)$ (in white) at each layer using the corresponding abstract transformer. (Color figure online)

given a test image correctly classified as a car by a DNN, the popular local robustness property specifies that all images generated by rotating the original image within ± 5 degrees are also classified as a car [5]. In contrast, ϕ for global properties does not depend upon a test input. For domains where the input features have semantic meaning, e.g., air traffic collision avoidance systems [26] or security classifiers [13], global properties can be specified by defining a valid range for the input features expected in a real-world deployment. Certifying global properties yields stronger safety guarantees, however, they are difficult to formulate for popular domains, such as vision and NLP, where the individual features processed by the DNN have no semantic meaning. While certifying local properties is not ideal, the local certification results enable testing the safety of the model on an infinite set of unseen inputs, not possible with standard methods.

2 Certification for Testing Model Safety

DNN certification can be seen as an instance of program verification (DNNs can be written as programs) making it undecidable. State-of-the-art certifiers are therefore incomplete in general. These certifiers can be formulated using the elegant framework of abstract interpretation [15]. While abstract interpretation-based certifiers can certify both local and global properties, for the remainder of this paper, we focus on the certification of local properties as they are more common in real-world applications. Figure 1 shows the high-level idea behind DNN certification with abstract interpretation. Here, the certifier is parameterized by the choice of an abstract domain. The certifier first computes an abstract element $\alpha(\phi) \supseteq \phi$ that includes the input region ϕ. Next, the analyzer symbolically propagates $\alpha(\phi)$ through the different layers of the network. At each layer, the analyzer computes an abstract element (in blue) overapproximating the exact layer output (in white) corresponding to ϕ. The element is computed by applying an abstract transformer that approximates the effect of the operations (e.g., ReLU, affine) applied at the layer. Propagation through all the layers yields an abstract element $g(\alpha(\phi)) \supseteq f(\phi)$ at the output layer. Next, the certifier checks

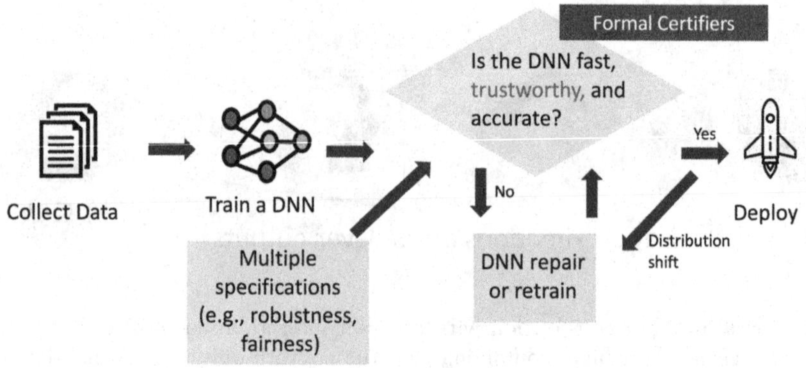

Fig. 2. Development pipeline for building fast, accurate, and trustworthy DNNs. Certification is used for testing model trustworthiness (green diamond). (Color figure online)

if $g(\alpha(\phi)) \subseteq \psi$ holds for the bigger region $g(\alpha(\phi))$. If the answer is yes, then $f(\phi) \subseteq \psi$ also holds for the smaller region $f(\phi)$. Because of the overapproximation, it can be the case that $g(\alpha(\phi)) \subseteq \psi$ does not hold while $f(\phi) \subseteq \psi$ holds. To reduce the amount of overapproximation, refinements [41,47,53,62,63,68,71] can be applied.

To obtain an effective certifier, it is essential to design an abstract domain and corresponding abstract transformers such that $g(\alpha(\phi))$ is as close as possible to the true output $f(\phi)$ while g can also be computed in a reasonable amount of time for practical networks. The classical domains, such as Polyhedra [16,55] and Octagons [37,54], used for analyzing programs are not well suited for DNN certification. This is because the DNNs have a different structure compared to traditional programs. For example, DNNs have a large number of non-linear assignments but typically do not have infinite loops. For efficient certification, new abstract domains and transformers tailored for DNN certification have been developed. Examples include DeepPoly [52], DeepZ [51], Star sets [58], and DeepJ [33]. These custom solutions can scale to realistic DNNs with upto a million neurons [39], or more than 100 layers [68], certifying diverse safety properties in different real-world applications including autonomous driving [72], job-scheduling [68], data center management [12], and financial modeling [32].

Incremental Certification. By leveraging formal certification to check DNN safety and trust, the development pipeline shown in Fig. 2 can be employed [61] to obtain fast, accurate, and trustworthy DNNs. First, a DNN is trained to maximize its test accuracy. Next, a domain expert designs a set of safety specifications (e.g., robustness, fairness) defining the expected network behavior in different real-world scenarios. If the model satisfies the desired specifications, then the DNN is considered fit for deployment. Otherwise, it is iteratively repaired (e.g., by fine-tuning [1] or LP-solving [56]) till we obtain a fast, accurate, and trustworthy DNN. We note that repair is preferred over retraining as it is cheaper.

However, if a repair is not possible, then the DNN is retrained from scratch. After deployment, the DNN is monitored to check for distribution shifts, generating inputs not covered by the specifications. If a distribution shift is detected, then new specifications are designed, and the model is repaired or retrained.

Domain experts usually design a large number of local properties (around 10-100K). Therefore, the certifier needs to be run several thousand times on the same DNN. Further, as shown in Fig. 2, the model repair is applied, before or after deployment, in case the DNN does not satisfy the desired specifications. The certifier is needed again to check the safety of the repaired model. Existing certifiers do not *scale* in such a deployment setting: they can precisely certify individual specifications in a few seconds or minutes, however, the certification of a large and diverse set of specifications on a single DNN can take multiple days to years or the certifier can run out of memory. Given multiple DNNs are generated due to repair or retraining, it makes using existing certifiers for safe and trustworthy development infeasible. The inefficiency is because the certifier needs to be run from scratch for every new pair of specifications and DNNs. A straightforward approach to overcome this limitation is to run the certifier on several machines. However, such an approach is not sustainable due to its huge environmental cost [8,67]. Further, in many cases, large computational resources are not available. For example, to preserve privacy, reduce latency, and increase battery lifetime, DNNs are increasingly employed on edge devices with limited computational power [14,64]. Therefore, for sustainable, democratic, and trustworthy DNN development, it is essential to develop new general approaches for incremental certification to improve the certifier scalability, when certifying multiple specifications and networks.

The main challenge in developing incremental certifiers is determining information that (i) can be reused across multiple specifications and DNNs to improve scalability, and (ii) is efficient to compute and store. Recent works [19,61] have developed general mechanisms to enable incremental certification by reusing proofs across multiple specifications and DNNs. These methods can be plugged into state-of-the-art certifiers based on abstract interpretation [51,52] to improve their scalability inside the development pipeline of Fig. 2. [19] introduced the concept of *proof sharing* across multiple specifications on the same DNN. Proof sharing is based on the key insight that it is possible to construct a small number of abstract elements as proof templates at an intermediate DNN layer, that capture the intermediate proofs of a large number of specifications. To certify a new specification, we run the certifier partially till the layer at which the templates are available. If the intermediate proof is subsumed by an existing template, then the specification is proved without running the certifier till the end, saving time and memory. The work of [61] introduced the concept of *proof transfer* across similar networks obtained after incremental changes to an original network (e.g., after fine-tuning [1]). The key insight behind this concept is that it is possible to efficiently transfer the proof templates generated on the original network to multiple similar networks, such that the transformed templates capture the proofs of a large number of specifications on similar networks. The transferred templates

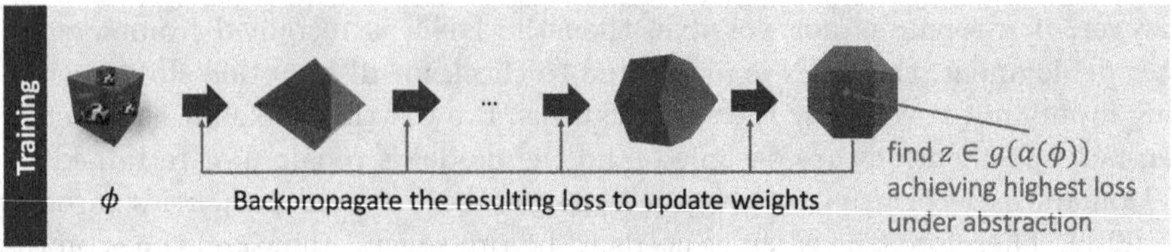

Fig. 3. Certified training involves computing the point $z \in g(\alpha(\phi))$ where the robust loss if maximum. The resulting loss is backpropagated through the certifier code to update the model parameters.

can improve certifier precision and scalability when certifying multiple specifications on similar networks. [60] considers incremental certification for certifiers combining abstract interpretation with branch and bound (BaB) [11] and uses the trace of BaB as proof templates to improve certification speed across multiple similar DNNs.

3 Certification for Training Safe DNNs

DNNs trained to only maximize accuracy with standard training [28] are often unsafe [36]. Next, we describe how certifiers can be leveraged during training to obtain safe DNNs. While the description here applies to different safety properties, we focus on robustness as it is the most common property for safe training considered in the literature. Robust training involves defining a robust loss function $\mathcal{L}_R$ for each point $x \in \phi$ with the property that $\mathcal{L}_R$ at x is ≤ 0 iff in the DNN output $z = f(x)$, the score z_c for the correct class c is higher than all other classes z_i, i.e., $z_c > z_i$. The DNN is robust iff $\mathcal{L}_R \leq 0$ for all $x \in \phi$. The DNN parameters can be updated during training to minimize the maximum value of $\mathcal{L}_R$. This min-max formulation makes robust training a harder optimization problem than standard training. Computing the worst-case robust loss exactly requires computing $f(\phi)$ which is infeasible. Therefore an approximation of $\mathcal{L}_R$ is computed in practice. Adversarial training methods [36] compute a lower bound on the worst-case robust loss by heuristically computing a point $x \in \phi$ at which the robust loss is high. x is then added to the training dataset. On the other hand, certified training [6,21,38,69,72,74] methods compute an upper bound on the worst-case robust loss using abstract interpretation-based DNN certifiers. Figure 3 shows the high-level idea behind certified training which leverages the output $g(\alpha(\phi))$ computed by the DNN certifier. Here one computes $z \in g(\alpha(\phi))$ where the robust loss is maximum and then updates the model with respect to the resulting loss value. State-of-the-art certified training methods employ differentiable certifiers [38,51], which makes the computation of the worst-case robust loss differentiable. As a result, the parameter updates are performed by differentiating through the certifier code directly.

Since certified training computes an upper bound on the worst-case robust loss when this loss is ≤ 0, the actual loss is also ≤ 0. This is not the case with the lower bound computed by adversarial training. As a result, DNNs trained with certified training achieve higher robustness guarantees than those trained with adversarial training [38]. They are also easier to certify than those trained with adversarial and standard training. Even imprecise abstract domains such as intervals give precise certification results for DNNs trained with certified training. The work of [4] theoretically shows the existence of two DNNs f, f' such that (i) they have the same accuracy, and (ii) interval analysis achieves the same certification results on f' as a more precise certifier on f.

Training with only the robust loss deteriorates model accuracy, therefore in practice, robust loss is combined with standard accuracy loss during training using custom mechanisms [21]. While one would expect that training with precise certifiers yields more accurate and robust DNNs than imprecise ones, as they reduce the approximation error in computing the robust loss, in practice, the highly imprecise interval domain performs the best for certified training. This is because the optimization problem for training becomes harder with more complex abstract domains [24]. Most certified training methods target robustness with respect to norm-based changes to pixel intensities in images. Even with all the progress in this direction, DNNs trained with state-of-the-art certified training methods [6,40,74] suffer significant loss of accuracy on popular datasets such as CIFAR10 [29]. There have been conflicting hypotheses in the literature about whether accuracy conflicts with norm-based robustness [59] or not [73]. The work of [72] is the first to build a certified training method for challenging geometric robustness by developing a fast geometric certifier that can be efficiently parallelized on GPUs. Interestingly, the work shows that it is possible to achieve both high accuracy and robustness on the autonomous driving dataset [9]. Therefore, in certain practical scenarios, both high accuracy and safety may be achievable.

4 Certification for Interpreting DNNs

Abstract interpretation-based DNN certifiers [51,52,70] generate high-dimensional abstract elements at different layers capturing complex relationships between neurons and DNN inputs to prove DNN safety. However, the individual neurons and inputs in the DNN do not have any semantic meaning, unlike the variables in programs, therefore it is not clear whether the safety proofs are based on any meaningful features learned by the DNN. If the DNN is proven to be safe but the proof is based on meaningless features not aligned with human intuition, then the DNN behavior cannot be considered trustworthy. While there has been a lot of work on interpreting black-box DNNs, standard methods [46,66] can only explain the DNN behavior on individual inputs and cannot interpret the complex invariants encoded by the abstract elements capturing DNN behavior on an infinite set of inputs. The main challenge in interpreting DNN proofs is in mapping the complex abstract elements to human understandable interpretations.

The work of [7] is the first to develop a method for interpreting robustness proofs computed by DNN certifiers. The method can interpret proofs computed by different certifiers. It builds upon the novel concept of *proof features* that are computed by projecting the high-dimensional abstract elements onto individual neurons. The proof features can be analyzed independently by generating the corresponding interpretations. Since certain proof features can be more important for the proof than others, a priority function over the proof features that signify the importance of each individual proof feature in the complete proof is defined. The method extracts a set of proof features by retaining only the more important parts of the proof that preserve the property.

A comparison of proof interpretations for DNNs trained with standard and robust training methods [6,36,74] on the popular MNIST [35] and CIFAR10 datasets [29] shows that the proof features corresponding to the standard networks rely on meaningless input features while the proofs of adversarially trained DNNs [36] filter out some of these spurious features. In contrast, the networks trained with certifiable training [74] produce proofs that do not rely on any spurious features but they also miss out on some meaningful features. Proofs for training methods that combine both empirical and certified robustness [6] not only preserve meaningful features but also selectively filter out spurious ones. These observations are empirically shown to be not contingent on any specific DNN certifier. These insights suggest that DNNs can satisfy safety properties but their behavior can still be untrustworthy.

References

1. Agrawal, P., Girshick, R., Malik, J.: Analyzing the performance of multilayer neural networks for object recognition. In: Fleet, D., Pajdla, T., Schiele, B., Tuytelaars, T. (eds.) ECCV 2014. LNCS, vol. 8695, pp. 329–344. Springer, Cham (2014). https://doi.org/10.1007/978-3-319-10584-0_22
2. Amato, F., López, A., Peña-Méndez, E.M., Vaňhara, P., Hampl, A., Havel, J.: Artificial neural networks in medical diagnosis. J. Appl. Biomed. **11**(2) (2013)
3. Anderson, G., Pailoor, S., Dillig, I., Chaudhuri, S.: Optimization and abstraction: a synergistic approach for analyzing neural network robustness. In: Proceedings of the Programming Language Design and Implementation (PLDI), pp. 731–744 (2019)
4. Baader, M., Mirman, M., Vechev, M.: Universal approximation with certified networks. In: International Conference on Learning Representations (2020)
5. Balunovic, M., Baader, M., Singh, G., Gehr, T., Vechev, M.: Certifying geometric robustness of neural networks. In: Advances in Neural Information Processing Systems, vol. 32. Curran Associates, Inc. (2019)
6. Balunovic, M., Vechev, M.T.: Adversarial training and provable defenses: bridging the gap. In: 8th International Conference on Learning Representations, ICLR 2020, Addis Ababa, Ethiopia, 26–30 April 2020. OpenReview.net (2020)
7. Banerjee, D., Singh, A., Singh, G.: Interpreting robustness proofs of deep neural networks (2023)
8. Bender, E.M., Gebru, T., McMillan-Major, A., Shmitchell, S.: On the dangers of stochastic parrots: can language models be too big? In: Elish, M.C., Isaac, W., Zemel, R.S. (eds.) FAccT '21: 2021 ACM Conference on Fairness, Accountability, and Transparency, Virtual Event/Toronto, Canada, 3–10 March 2021, pp. 610–623. ACM (2021)

9. Bojarski, M., et al.: End to end learning for self-driving cars. arXiv preprint arXiv:1604.07316 (2016)
10. Brown, T.B., et al.: Language models are few-shot learners. In: Proceedings of the Advances in Neural Information Processing Systems (NeurIPS) (2020)
11. Bunel, R., Lu, J., Turkaslan, I., Kohli, P., Torr, P., Mudigonda, P.: Branch and bound for piecewise linear neural network verification. J. Mach. Learn. Res. **21**(2020) (2020)
12. Chakravarthy, A., Narodytska, N., Rathis, A., Vilcu, M., Sharif, M., Singh, G.: Property-driven evaluation of rl-controllers in self-driving datacenters. In: Workshop on Challenges in Deploying and Monitoring Machine Learning Systems (DMML) (2022)
13. Chen, Y., Wang, S., Qin, Y., Liao, X., Jana, S., Wagner, D.A.: Learning security classifiers with verified global robustness properties. In: Proceedings of the Conference on Computer and Communications Security (CCS), pp. 477–494. ACM (2021)
14. Chugh, U., et al.: An automated approach to accelerate DNNs on edge devices. In: ISCAS, pp. 1–5. IEEE (2021)
15. Cousot, P., Cousot, R.: Abstract interpretation: a unified lattice model for static analysis of programs by construction or approximation of fixpoints. In: Conference Record of the Fourth ACM Symposium on Principles of Programming Languages, Los Angeles, California, USA, January 1977, pp. 238–252. ACM (1977)
16. Cousot, P., Halbwachs, N.: Automatic discovery of linear restraints among variables of a program. In: Conference Record of the Fifth Annual ACM Symposium on Principles of Programming Languages, Tucson, Arizona, USA, January 1978, pp. 84–96. ACM Press (1978)
17. Dathathri, S., et al.: Enabling certification of verification-agnostic networks via memory-efficient semidefinite programming. In: Advances in Neural Information Processing Systems, vol. 33: Annual Conference on Neural Information Processing Systems 2020, NeurIPS 2020, 6–12 December 2020, virtual (2020)
18. Dwork, C., Hardt, M., Pitassi, T., Reingold, O., Zemel, R.S.: Fairness through awareness. In: Innovations in Theoretical Computer Science 2012, Cambridge, MA, USA, 8–10 January 2012, pp. 214–226. ACM (2012)
19. Fischer, M., Sprecher, C., Dimitrov, D.I., Singh, G., Vechev, M.T.: Shared certificates for neural network verification. In: Shoham, S., Vizel, Y. (eds.) Computer Aided Verification. CAV 2022. LNCS, vol. 13371, pp. 127–148. Springer, Cham (2022). https://doi.org/10.1007/978-3-031-13185-1_7
20. Goodfellow, I.J., Shlens, J., Szegedy, C.: Explaining and harnessing adversarial examples. arXiv preprint arXiv:1412.6572 (2014)
21. Gowal, S., et al.: On the effectiveness of interval bound propagation for training verifiably robust models. CoRR abs/1810.12715 (2018)
22. Gowal, S., et al.: Scalable verified training for provably robust image classification. In: Proceedings of the IEEE/CVF International Conference on Computer Vision (ICCV), pp. 4842–4851 (2019)
23. Heo, J., Joo, S., Moon, T.: Fooling neural network interpretations via adversarial model manipulation. In: Advances in Neural Information Processing Systems (NeurIPS), pp. 2921–2932 (2019)
24. Jovanovic, N., Balunovic, M., Baader, M., Vechev, M.T.: On the paradox of certified training. Trans. Mach. Learn. Res. **2022** (2022)
25. Kabaha, A., Drachsler-Cohen, D.: Boosting robustness verification of semantic feature neighborhoods. In: Singh, G., Urban, C. (eds.) Static Analysis. SAS 2022.

LNCS, vol. 13790, pp. 299–324. Springer, Cham (2022). https://doi.org/10.1007/978-3-031-22308-2_14
26. Katz, G., Barrett, C., Dill, D., Julian, K., Kochenderfer, M.: Reluplex: an efficient SMT solver for verifying deep neural networks. In: Proceedings of the 29th International Conference on Computer Aided Verification (CAV), pp. 97–117 (2017)
27. Katz, G., et al.: The Marabou framework for verification and analysis of deep neural networks, pp. 443–452, July 2019
28. Kingma, D.P., Ba, J.: Adam: a method for stochastic optimization. In: 3rd International Conference on Learning Representations, ICLR 2015, San Diego, CA, USA, 7–9 May 2015, Conference Track Proceedings (2015)
29. Krizhevsky, A.: Learning multiple layers of features from tiny images (2009)
30. Kurakin, A., Goodfellow, I.J., Bengio, S.: Adversarial examples in the physical world. In: ICLR (Workshop). OpenReview.net (2017)
31. Lan, J., Zheng, Y., Lomuscio, A.: Tight neural network verification via semidefinite relaxations and linear reformulations. In: Thirty-Sixth AAAI Conference on Artificial Intelligence, AAAI 2022, pp. 7272–7280. AAAI Press (2022)
32. Laurel, J., Qian, S.B., Singh, G., Misailovic, S.: Synthesizing precise static analyzers for automatic differentiation. Proc. ACM Program. Lang. (OOPSLA2) (2023)
33. Laurel, J., Yang, R., Singh, G., Misailovic, S.: A dual number abstraction for static analysis of Clarke Jacobians. Proc. ACM Program. Lang. **6**(POPL), 1–30 (2022)
34. Laurel, J., Yang, R., Ugare, S., Nagel, R., Singh, G., Misailovic, S.: A general construction for abstract interpretation of higher-order automatic differentiation. Proc. ACM Program. Lang. **6**(OOPSLA2), 1007–1035 (2022)
35. LeCun, Y., et al.: Handwritten digit recognition with a back-propagation network. In: NIPS, pp. 396–404 (1989)
36. Madry, A., Makelov, A., Schmidt, L., Tsipras, D., Vladu, A.: Towards deep learning models resistant to adversarial attacks. arXiv preprint arXiv:1706.06083 (2017)
37. Miné, A.: The octagon abstract domain. High. Order Symb. Comput. **19**(1), 31–100 (2006)
38. Mirman, M., Gehr, T., Vechev, M.: Differentiable abstract interpretation for provably robust neural networks. In: Proceedings of the International Conference on Machine Learning (ICML), pp. 3578–3586 (2018)
39. Müller, C., Serre, F., Singh, G., Püschel, M., Vechev, M.T.: Scaling polyhedral neural network verification on GPUs. In: Proceedings of Machine Learning and Systems 2021, MLSys 2021, virtual, 5–9 April 2021. mlsys.org (2021)
40. Müller, M.N., Eckert, F., Fischer, M., Vechev, M.T.: Certified training: small boxes are all you need. In: The Eleventh International Conference on Learning Representations, ICLR 2023, Kigali, Rwanda, 1–5 May 2023. OpenReview.net (2023)
41. Müller, M.N., Makarchuk, G., Singh, G., Püschel, M., Vechev, M.: Precise multi-neuron abstractions for neural network certification. arXiv preprint arXiv:2103.03638 (2021)
42. Munakata, S., Urban, C., Yokoyama, H., Yamamoto, K., Munakata, K.: Verifying attention robustness of deep neural networks against semantic perturbations. In: Rozier, K.Y., Chaudhuri, S. (eds.) NASA Formal Methods. NFM 2023. LNCS, vol. 13903, pp. 37–61. Springer, Cham (2023). https://doi.org/10.1007/978-3-031-33170-1_3
43. Palma, A.D., Behl, H.S., Bunel, R., Torr, P.H.S., Kumar, M.P.: Scaling the convex barrier with active sets. In: 9th International Conference on Learning Representations, ICLR 2021, Virtual Event, Austria, 3–7 May 2021. OpenReview.net (2021)

44. Paulsen, B., Wang, J., Wang, C.: Reludiff: differential verification of deep neural networks. In: Proceedings of the ACM/IEEE 42nd International Conference on Software Engineering, pp. 714–726. ICSE '20 (2020)
45. Ranzato, F., Urban, C., Zanella, M.: Fairness-aware training of decision trees by abstract interpretation. In: CIKM '21: The 30th ACM International Conference on Information and Knowledge Management, Virtual Event, Queensland, Australia, 1–5 November 2021, pp. 1508–1517. ACM (2021)
46. Ribeiro, M.T., Singh, S., Guestrin, C.: Why should I trust you?: explaining the predictions of any classifier. In: Proceedings of the ACM SIGKDD International Conference on Knowledge Discovery and Data Mining, pp. 1135–1144. ACM (2016)
47. Ryou, W., Chen, J., Balunovic, M., Singh, G., Dan, A., Vechev, M.: Scalable polyhedral verification of recurrent neural networks. In: Silva, A., Leino, K.R.M. (eds.) CAV 2021. LNCS, vol. 12759, pp. 225–248. Springer, Cham (2021). https://doi.org/10.1007/978-3-030-81685-8_10
48. Shafique, M., et al.: Robust machine learning systems: challenges, current trends, perspectives, and the road ahead. IEEE Des. Test **37**(2), 30–57 (2020)
49. Sill, J.: Monotonic networks. In: Advances in Neural Information Processing Systems, vol. 10, [NIPS Conference, Denver, Colorado, USA, 1997], pp. 661–667. The MIT Press (1997)
50. Singh, G., Ganvir, R., Püschel, M., Vechev, M.: Beyond the single neuron convex barrier for neural network certification. Adv. Neural Inf. Process. Syst. (2019)
51. Singh, G., Gehr, T., Mirman, M., Püschel, M., Vechev, M.: Fast and effective robustness certification. Adv. Neural Inf. Process. Syst. **31** (2018)
52. Singh, G., Gehr, T., Püschel, M., Vechev, M.: An abstract domain for certifying neural networks. Proc. ACM Program. Lang. **3**(POPL) (2019)
53. Singh, G., Gehr, T., Püschel, M., Vechev, M.: Robustness certification with refinement. In: International Conference on Learning Representations (2019)
54. Singh, G., Püschel, M., Vechev, M.T.: Making numerical program analysis fast. In: Proceedings of the 36th ACM SIGPLAN Conference on Programming Language Design and Implementation, Portland, OR, USA, 15–17 June 2015, pp. 303–313. ACM (2015)
55. Singh, G., Püschel, M., Vechev, M.T.: Fast polyhedra abstract domain. In: Proceedings of the 44th ACM SIGPLAN Symposium on Principles of Programming Languages, POPL 2017, Paris, France, 18–20 January 2017, pp. 46–59. ACM (2017)
56. Sotoudeh, M., Thakur, A.V.: Provable repair of deep neural networks. In: PLDI '21: 42nd ACM SIGPLAN International Conference on Programming Language Design and Implementation, Virtual Event, Canada, 20–25 June 2021, pp. 588–603. ACM (2021)
57. Szegedy, C., et al.: Intriguing properties of neural networks. In: ICLR (Poster) (2014)
58. Tran, H.-D., et al.: Star-based reachability analysis of deep neural networks. In: ter Beek, M.H., McIver, A., Oliveira, J.N. (eds.) FM 2019. LNCS, vol. 11800, pp. 670–686. Springer, Cham (2019). https://doi.org/10.1007/978-3-030-30942-8_39
59. Tsipras, D., Santurkar, S., Engstrom, L., Turner, A., Madry, A.: Robustness may be at odds with accuracy. In: Proceedings of the International Conference on Learning Representations, ICLR. OpenReview.net (2019)
60. Ugare, S., Banerjee, D., Misailovic, S., Singh, G.: Incremental verification of neural networks. Proc. ACM Program. Lang. **7**(PLDI) (2023)
61. Ugare, S., Singh, G., Misailovic, S.: Proof transfer for fast certification of multiple approximate neural networks. Proc. ACM Program. Lang. **6**(OOPSLA1), 1–29 (2022)

62. Wang, S., Pei, K., Whitehouse, J., Yang, J., Jana, S.: Efficient formal safety analysis of neural networks. Adv. Neural Inf. Process. Syst. (2018)
63. Wang, S., et al.: Beta-crown: efficient bound propagation with per-neuron split constraints for complete and incomplete neural network verification. arXiv preprint arXiv:2103.06624 (2021)
64. Wang, X., Hersche, M., Tömekce, B., Kaya, B., Magno, M., Benini, L.: An accurate EEGNet-based motor-imagery brain-computer interface for low-power edge computing. In: IEEE International Symposium on Medical Measurements and Applications, (MeMeA), pp. 1–6. IEEE (2020)
65. Wong, E., Kolter, J.Z.: Provable defenses against adversarial examples via the convex outer adversarial polytope. In: Proceedings of the International Conference on Machine Learning, ICML. Proceedings of Machine Learning Research, vol. 80, pp. 5283–5292. PMLR (2018)
66. Wong, E., Santurkar, S., Madry, A.: Leveraging sparse linear layers for debuggable deep networks. In: Proceedings of the 38th International Conference on Machine Learning, ICML. Proceedings of Machine Learning Research, vol. 139, pp. 11205–11216. PMLR (2021)
67. Wu, C., et al.: Sustainable AI: environmental implications, challenges and opportunities. In: MLSys. mlsys.org (2022)
68. Wu, H., Barrett, C., Sharif, M., Narodytska, N., Singh, G.: Scalable verification of GNN-based job schedulers. Proc. ACM Program. Lang. **6**(OOPSLA2) (2022)
69. Xu, K., et al.: Automatic perturbation analysis for scalable certified robustness and beyond. In: Proceedings of the Neural Information Processing Systems (NeurIPS), pp. 1129–1141 (2020)
70. Xu, K., et al.: Fast and complete: Enabling complete neural network verification with rapid and massively parallel incomplete verifiers. In: International Conference on Learning Representations (2021)
71. Yang, P., et al.: Improving neural network verification through spurious region guided refinement. In: Groote, J.F., Larsen, K.G. (eds.) Tools and Algorithms for the Construction and Analysis of Systems. TACAS 2021. LNCS, vol. 12651, pp. 389–408. Springer, Cham (2021). https://doi.org/10.1007/978-3-030-72016-2_21
72. Yang, R., Laurel, J., Misailovic, S., Singh, G.: Provable defense against geometric transformations. In: The Eleventh International Conference on Learning Representations, ICLR 2023, Kigali, Rwanda, 1–5 May 2023. OpenReview.net (2023)
73. Yang, Y., Rashtchian, C., Zhang, H., Salakhutdinov, R., Chaudhuri, K.: A closer look at accuracy vs. robustness. In: Advances in Neural Information Processing Systems, vol. 33: Annual Conference on Neural Information Processing Systems (NeurIPS) (2020)
74. Zhang, H., et al.: Towards stable and efficient training of verifiably robust neural networks. In: Proceedings of the International Conference on Learning Representations (ICLR) (2020)

Regular Papers

Modular Optimization-Based Roundoff Error Analysis of Floating-Point Programs

Rosa Abbasi[1] and Eva Darulova[2(✉)]

[1] MPI-SWS, Kaiserslautern and Saarbrücken, Germany
rosaabbasi@mpi-sws.org
[2] Uppsala University, Uppsala, Sweden
eva.darulova@it.uu.se

Abstract. Modular static program analyses improve over global whole-program analyses in terms of scalability at a tradeoff with analysis accuracy. This tradeoff has to-date not been explored in the context of sound floating-point roundoff error analyses; available analyses computing guaranteed absolute error bounds effectively consider only monolithic straight-line code. This paper extends the roundoff error analysis based on symbolic Taylor error expressions to non-recursive procedural floating-point programs. Our analysis achieves modularity and at the same time reasonable accuracy by automatically computing abstract procedure summaries that are a function of the input parameters. We show how to effectively use first-order Taylor approximations to compute precise procedure summaries, and how to integrate these to obtain end-to-end roundoff error bounds. Our evaluation shows that compared to an inlining of procedure calls, our modular analysis is significantly faster, while nonetheless mostly computing relatively tight error bounds.

Keywords: modular verification · floating-point arithmetic · roundoff error · Taylor approximation

1 Introduction

One of the main challenges of automated static program analysis is to strike a suitable trade-off between analysis accuracy and performance [6]. This trade-off is inevitable, as a certain amount of abstraction and thus over-approximation is necessary to make an analysis feasible for unbounded (or very large) input domains. There are typically different ways to introduce abstractions; for instance by considering abstract domains that are more or less accurate [6,17,22],

M. V. Hermenegildo and J. F. Morales (Eds.): SAS 2023, LNCS 14284, pp. 41–64, 2023.
https://doi.org/10.1007/978-3-031-44245-2_4

or in the context of procedural code, by abstracting procedure calls by summaries or specifications to obtain a *modular* analysis [8].

A modular analysis allows each procedure to be analyzed independently once, regardless of how often it is being called in an application, rather than being re-analyzed in possibly only slightly different contexts at every call site. This saves analysis time and thus increases the scalability of the analysis at the expense of some loss of accuracy: the procedure summaries need to abstract over different calling contexts.

This paper presents a modular roundoff error analysis for non-recursive procedural floating-point programs without conditional branches. Our approach extends the roundoff error analysis first introduced in the FPTaylor tool [27] that is based on symbolic Taylor expressions and global optimization and that has been shown to produce tight error bounds for straight-line arithmetic expressions. Our analysis first computes, for each procedure separately, error specifications that provide an abstraction of the function's behavior as a function of the input parameters. In a second step, our analysis instantiates the error specifications at the call sites to compute an overall roundoff error bound for each procedure.

The main challenge is to achieve a practically useful tradeoff between analysis accuracy and performance. A naive, albeit simple, approach would simply compute the worst-case roundoff error for each procedure as a constant, and would use this constant as the error at each call site. This approach is, however, particularly suboptimal for a roundoff error analysis, because roundoff errors depend on the magnitude of arguments. For reasonable analysis accuracy, it is thus crucial that the error specifications are *parametric* in the procedure's input parameters. At the same time, the error specifications need to introduce some *abstraction* as we otherwise end up re-analyzing each procedure at each call site.

We achieve this balance by computing error specifications that soundly over-approximate roundoff errors using *first-order* Taylor approximations separately for propagation of input and roundoff errors. By keeping first-order terms of both approximations unevaluated, we obtain parametric procedure summaries, and by eagerly evaluating higher-order terms we achieve abstraction that has a relatively small impact on accuracy.

Available sound floating-point roundoff error analyses have largely focused on abstractions for the (global) analysis of straight-line code and require function calls to be inlined manually [10,18,24,27] and are thus non-modular. The tool PRECiSA [26,28] analyzes function calls compositionally, however, does not apply abstraction when doing so. The analysis can thus be considered modular (in principle), but the computed symbolic function summaries can be very large and negatively affect the efficiency of the analysis. Goubault et al. [19] present a modular roundoff error analysis based on the zonotopic abstract domain that does apply abstraction at function calls. However, the implementation is not available and the roundoff error analyses based on zonotopes have been shown to be less accurate than the alternative approach based on symbolic Taylor expressions.

Like most existing roundoff error analyses, our analysis computes absolute roundoff errors for programs without loops or recursive procedure calls and without conditional branches; these remain an open, but orthogonal, challenge for floating-point roundoff error analysis [11,28]. The optimization-based approach that we extend in this paper has been used for the computation of relative error bounds [21] as well, however, relative errors are fundamentally undefined for input domains that include zeros and are thus less widely applicable.

We implement our analysis in a tool called HUGO and evaluate it on two case studies that are inspired by existing floating-point benchmarks [2]. Our evaluation shows that compared to an approach based on procedure inlining and an analysis by state of the art roundoff analysis tools, our modular analysis provides an interesting tradeoff: it is significantly faster, while computing comparable error bounds that are often within the same order of magnitude and thus, in our opinion, practically useful.

Contributions. To summarize, this paper presents the following contributions:

- a sound modular roundoff error analysis for non-recursive procedural code without conditionals that combines modularity and abstraction when analyzing function calls;
- a prototype implementation of our analysis is available open-source at https://doi.org/10.5281/zenodo.8175459;
- an empirical evaluation of the accuracy-performance tradeoff of our analysis.

2 Background

In this section, we provide necessary background on floating-point arithmetic and roundoff error analysis, focusing on the symbolic Taylor expression-based roundoff error analysis that has been implemented in several tools. We extend this analysis in Sect. 3 to support procedure calls. Throughout, we use bold symbols to represent vectors.

Floating-Point Arithmetic. The IEEE754 standard [1] formalizes floating-point numbers and the operations over them. A floating-point number is defined as a triple (sng, sig, exp) indicating its sign, significant, and exponent, with the numerical value being $(-1)^{sng} \times sig \times 2^{exp}$. The standard introduces four general binary formats (16, 32, 64 and 128 bits) varying on the sizes of sig and exp. We assume 64 bit double precision throughout this paper, but our approach generalizes to other formats as well.

The standard introduces several rounding operators that return the floating-point number that is closest to the input real number where the closeness is defined by the specific rounding operator. The most common rounding operator is rounding to nearest (ties to even), which we assume in this paper.

The distance between the real value and the floating-point representation is called the *roundoff error*. Computing this difference exactly is practically infeasible for all but very short computations. Instead, we and most other roundoff error analysis tools assume the following rounding model that holds for the rounding to nearest mode:

$$rnd(op) = op(1 + e) + d \quad \text{where } |e| \leq \epsilon, |d| \leq \delta \tag{1}$$

where *op* is an arithmetic operation (or an input value or constant), ϵ bounds the relative error and δ bounds the absolute error. For the standard arithmetic operations $+, -, *, /$, the IEEE754 standard specifies for double precision $\epsilon = 2^{-53}$ and $\delta = 2^{-1075}$, where the latter captures the roundoff error of subnormal floating-point numbers, i.e. numbers very close to zero. For library function calls to common mathematical functions, e.g. *sin*, *exp*, etc., the library specification typically specifies the corresponding error(s); in this paper we assume $2 * \epsilon$ (most libraries provide this bound or better, but our analysis is parametric).

Sound Roundoff Error Analysis. The goal of a roundoff error analysis is to compute the worst-case absolute error:

$$\max_{\mathbf{x},\tilde{\mathbf{x}} \in I} |f(\mathbf{x}) - \tilde{f}(\tilde{\mathbf{x}})| \tag{2}$$

where $f(\mathbf{x})$ denotes an idealized (purely) numerical program, where $\mathbf{x}$ is a possibly multivariate input, and $\tilde{f}(\tilde{\mathbf{x}})$ represents the function corresponding to the floating-point implementation, which has the same syntax tree but with operations interpreted in floating-point arithmetic. Note that the input to $\tilde{f}$, $\tilde{\mathbf{x}}$, is a rounded version of the real-valued input since that may not be exactly representable in finite precision and may need to be rounded.

We want to maximize the above equation for a set of meaningful inputs I that depends on a particular application. Bounding roundoff errors for unbounded input ranges is not practically useful as the error bounds are then in general unbounded.

In this paper, we consider programs that consist of several procedures and the goal is to compute an error bound for each of them. The procedure bodies consists of arithmetic expressions, mathematical library function calls, (immutable) variable declarations and (possibly) calls to procedures defined within the program.

To estimate the rounding error for such programs with existing roundoff error analyses, the procedure calls need to be effectively inlined—either manually by a user before an analysis tool is run, or automatically by the tool [26]. For larger programs, especially with more procedure calls, this can result in very large (symbolic) expressions and thus long analysis times. This approach is also fundamentally not suitable for integration into modular verification frameworks, such as KeY [3] or Frama-C [23].

For our modular analysis, the procedure calls do not need to be inlined. Instead, for each procedure of the program, our analysis first computes an error specification that is a function of the input parameters and that abstracts some of the error computation. Our analysis instantiates these error specifications at the call sites to compute an overall roundoff error bound (it also checks that the preconditions of the called procedures are respected).

Symbolic Taylor Expression-Based Roundoff Analysis. The approach to roundoff error analysis (for straight-line code) that we extend in Sect. 3 was first proposed in the tool FPTaylor [27]. This approach abstracts the floating-point function $\tilde{f}(\tilde{\mathbf{x}})$ using the rounding model from Eq. 1 into a real-valued function $\hat{f}(\mathbf{x}, \mathbf{e}, \mathbf{d})$ to compute a bound on the roundoff error:

$$\max_{\mathbf{x} \in I} |f(\mathbf{x}) - \hat{f}(\mathbf{x}, \mathbf{e}, \mathbf{d}))|$$

However, while now entirely real-valued, this expression is in general too complex for (continuous, real-valued) optimization tools to handle. To reduce complexity, FPTaylor applies a Taylor expansion:

$$f(\mathbf{x}) = f(\mathbf{a}) + \sum_{i=1}^{k} \frac{\partial f}{\partial x_i}(\mathbf{a})(x_i - a_i) + 1/2 \sum_{i,j=1}^{k} \frac{\partial^2 f}{\partial x_i \partial x_j}(\mathbf{p})(x_i - a_i)(x_j - a_j) \quad (3)$$

that allows to approximate an arbitrary sufficiently smooth function by a polynomial expression around some point $\mathbf{a}$. $\mathbf{p}$ is a point which depends on $\mathbf{x}$ and $\mathbf{a}$ and k is the number of input parameters of f. Taylor series define infinite expansions, however, in practice these are terminated after some finite number of terms, and a remainder term soundly bounds (over-estimates) the skipped higher-order terms. In Eq. 3 the last term is the remainder.

Applying a first-order Taylor approximation to the abstracted floating-point function $\hat{f}(\mathbf{x}, \mathbf{e}, \mathbf{d})$ around the point $(\mathbf{x}, \mathbf{0}, \mathbf{0})$ we get:

$$\hat{f}(\mathbf{x}, \mathbf{e}, \mathbf{d}) = \hat{f}(\mathbf{x}, 0, 0) + \sum_{i=1}^{k} \frac{\partial \hat{f}}{\partial e_i}(\mathbf{x}, 0, 0)(e_i - 0) + \sum_{i=1}^{k} \frac{\partial \hat{f}}{\partial d_i}(\mathbf{x}, 0, 0)(d_i - 0) + R_2(\mathbf{x}, \mathbf{e}, \mathbf{d})$$

$$R_2(\mathbf{x}, \mathbf{e}, \mathbf{d}) = 1/2 \sum_{i,j=1}^{2k} \frac{\partial^2 \hat{f}}{\partial y_i \partial y_j}(\mathbf{x}, \mathbf{p}) y_i y_j \quad (4)$$

where $y_1, \ldots y_{2k}$ range over $e_1, \ldots, e_k, d_1, \ldots, d_k$ respectively. Since $\hat{f}(\mathbf{x}, 0, 0) = f(\mathbf{x})$, one can approximate $|\hat{f}(\mathbf{x}, \mathbf{e}, \mathbf{d}) - f(\mathbf{x})|$ by:

$$|\hat{f}(\mathbf{x}, \mathbf{e}, \mathbf{d}) - f(\mathbf{x})| = |\sum_{i=1}^{k} \frac{\partial \hat{f}}{\partial e_i}(\mathbf{x}, 0, 0) e_i + \sum_{i=1}^{k} \frac{\partial \hat{f}}{\partial d_i}(\mathbf{x}, 0, 0) d_i + R_2(\mathbf{x}, \mathbf{e}, \mathbf{d})| \quad \text{(FPTaylor Error)}$$

To compute a concrete roundoff error bound, the above expression is maximized over a given input domain I using rigorous global optimization techniques such as interval arithmetic [25] or branch-and-bound [27].

The above model can be straight-forwardly extended to capture input errors on (particular) variables by increasing the bound on the corresponding error variables e_i and/or d_i. Similarly, library functions for mathematical functions such as *sin*, *cos*, *exp*, ..., are supported by setting the bound on their corresponding error variables according to the specification. Note that since the derivatives of the standard mathematical library functions are well-defined, the partial derivatives in the equations can be immediately computed.

3 Modular Roundoff Error Analysis

In principle, one can apply FPTaylor's approach (Equation FPTaylor Error) directly to programs with procedure calls by inlining them to obtain a single arithmetic expression. This approach, however, results in potentially many re-evaluations of the same or very similar expressions. In this section, we extend FPTaylor's approach to a modular analysis by considering procedure calls explicitly.

At a high-level, our modular error computation is composed of two stages:

1. The *abstraction* stage computes an error specification for each procedure of the input program (Sect. 3.1 and Sect. 3.2);
2. The *instantiation* stage instantiates the pre-computed error specifications for each procedure at their call-sites with their appropriate contexts.

Note that each procedure is processed only once in each of these stages, regardless of how often it is called in other procedures.

The main challenge is to compute the error specifications such that they, on one hand, abstract enough over the individual arithmetic operations to provide a benefit for the analysis in terms of performance, and on the other hand do not lose too much accuracy during this abstraction to still provide meaningful results.

A naive way to achieve modularity is to compute, for each procedure, a roundoff error bound as a constant value, and use that in the analysis of the procedure calls. This simple approach is, however, not enough, since in order to analyze a calling procedure, we do not only need to know which new error it contributes, but we also need to bound its effect on already existing errors, i.e. how it propagates them. The situation is even further complicated in the presence of nested procedure calls.

Alternatively, one can attempt to pre-compute only the derivatives from Equation FPTaylor Error and leave all evaluation to the call sites. This approach then effectively amounts to caching of the derivative computations, and does not affect the analysis accuracy, but its performance benefit will be modest as much of the computation effort will still be repeated.

Our approach rests on two observations from the above discussion. We first split the error of a procedure into the propagation of input errors and roundoff errors due to arithmetic operations, following [11]:

$$|f(\mathbf{x}) - \tilde{f}(\tilde{\mathbf{x}})| = |f(\mathbf{x}) - f(\tilde{\mathbf{x}}) + f(\tilde{\mathbf{x}}) - \tilde{f}(\tilde{\mathbf{x}})| \leq \underbrace{|f(\mathbf{x}) - f(\tilde{\mathbf{x}})|}_{\text{propagation error}} + \underbrace{|f(\tilde{\mathbf{x}}) - \tilde{f}(\tilde{\mathbf{x}})|}_{\text{round-off error}}$$

and compute error specifications for each of these errors separately. This allows us to handle the propagation issue from which the naive approach suffers. We employ suitable, though different, Taylor approximations for each of these parts.

Secondly, we pre-evaluate, at the abstraction stage already, part of the resulting Taylor approximations, assuming the context, resp. input specification of each procedure. This results in some accuracy loss when the procedure is called in a context that only requires a narrower range, but saves analysis time.

Naturally, our pre-computed error specifications are only sound if they are called from contexts that satisfy the assumed input specifications. Our implementation checks that this is indeed the case.

Running Example. We use the following simple example for explaining and illustrating our technique:

$$g(x) = x^2 \quad \text{where} \quad x \in [0.0, 100.0]$$
$$f(y, z) = g(y) + g(z) \quad \text{where} \quad y \in [10.0, 20.0], z \in [20.0, 80.0] \tag{Running Example}$$

Here, g is being called twice with arguments with different input specifications, but which are both within the allowed range of g of $[0, 100]$. We will consider nested procedure calls in Sect. 3.4.

Notation. We use f, g and h to denote procedures, $\mathbf{x}$, $\mathbf{y}$, $\mathbf{z}$, $\mathbf{w}$ and $\mathbf{t}$ for input parameters and also as input arguments if a procedure contains procedure calls, and $\mathbf{a}$, $\mathbf{b}$ and $\mathbf{c}$ for input arguments. Bold symbols are used to represent vectors. Each error specification of a procedure f consists of a roundoff error function denoted by β_f and the propagation error function, denoted by γ_f. We use $\beta_f(\mathbf{a})$ and $\gamma_f(\mathbf{a})$ to denote the evaluation of roundoff and propagation error specifications for a procedure f with $\mathbf{a}$ as the vector of input arguments. We denote the initial errors of input parameters by $\mathbf{u}$, the relative error of a rounding operator by $\mathbf{e}$, and the absolute error by $\mathbf{d}$. The maximum values for the relative and absolute errors are represented by ϵ and δ respectively. We assume ϵ to denote the maximum error for our default precision, i.e. double precision. We will use the notation $\left.\frac{\partial \hat{g}}{\partial e_i}\right|_{x,0,0}$ to denote $\frac{\partial \hat{g}}{\partial e_i}(x, 0, 0)$ for readability reasons.

3.1 Roundoff Error Abstraction

In this section, we extend FPTaylor's approach with a *rounding model for procedure calls* and show how it can be used to compute roundoff error specifications. Since input errors are handled by the propagation error specification (Sect. 3.2), we assume here that procedure inputs have no errors.

One of the main challenges of such an extension is that contrary to how the library function calls are handled (see Sect. 2), there is no given derivative and fixed upper-bound on the rounding error for arbitrary procedure calls.

If g is a procedure with input arguments $\mathbf{a}$ at the call site, and β_g the corresponding roundoff error specification of g, then we extend the IEEE754 rounding model to procedure calls by:

$$\tilde{g}(\mathbf{a}) = g(\mathbf{a}) + \beta_g(\mathbf{a})$$

That is, we abstract the rounding error by an absolute error, whose magnitude is determined by the error specification of f that is a function of the input arguments.

With this, we can proceed to extend the (FPTaylor Error) with procedure calls. Suppose we have a procedure $f(\mathbf{x})$ that contains the procedure calls $g_1(\boldsymbol{a_1}), \dots g_l(\boldsymbol{a_l})$ to procedures $g_1, \dots g_l$, where $\boldsymbol{a_1}, \dots, \boldsymbol{a_l}$ are the input arguments, and $\boldsymbol{\beta_g}(\boldsymbol{a}) = (\beta_{g_1}(\boldsymbol{a_1}), \dots, \beta_{g_l}(\boldsymbol{a_l}))$ is the vector of corresponding roundoff error specifications. Then the roundoff error specification β_f for the procedure $f(\mathbf{x})$ is given by:

$$\begin{aligned}\beta_f &= \hat{f}(\mathbf{x}, \mathbf{e}, \mathbf{d}, \boldsymbol{\beta}_g(\boldsymbol{a})) - f(\mathbf{x}) \\ &= \sum_{i=1}^{k} \left.\frac{\partial \hat{f}}{\partial e_i}\right|_{\mathbf{x},0} e_i + \sum_{i=1}^{k} \left.\frac{\partial \hat{f}}{\partial d_i}\right|_{\mathbf{x},0} d_i + \sum_{i=1}^{l} \left.\frac{\partial \hat{f}}{\partial \beta_{g_i}(\boldsymbol{a_i})}\right|_{\mathbf{x},0} \beta_{g_i}(\boldsymbol{a_i}) + R_2(\mathbf{x}, \mathbf{e}, \mathbf{d}, \boldsymbol{\beta_g}(\mathbf{a})),\end{aligned}$$

where

$$R_2(\mathbf{x}, \mathbf{e}, \mathbf{d}, \boldsymbol{\beta_g}(\mathbf{a})) = 1/2 \sum_{i,j=1}^{2k+l} \left.\frac{\partial^2 \hat{f}}{\partial y_i \partial y_j}\right|_{\mathbf{x},\mathbf{p}} y_i y_j$$

(Roundoff Specification)

where $y_1, \dots y_{2k}$ define $e_1, \dots, e_k, d_1, \dots, d_k$ as before, and $y_{2k+1}, \dots, y_{2k+l}$ correspond to $\beta_{g_1}(\boldsymbol{a_1}), \dots, \beta_{g_l}(\boldsymbol{a_l})$ respectively.

Note that to derive the roundoff error specification for f, the concrete roundoff specifications for g_i are not required, i.e. we treat β_g as a symbolic variable in the same way as e_i and d_i. They are only instantiated at the evaluation phase, at which point all β_gs are available.

Correctness. Note that if we were to inline all β_g roundoff specifications in β_f above (potentially recursively), we would reach the same roundoff error formula as given by (FPTaylor Error) for a program where all procedure calls are inlined. Depending on the nesting, one needs higher-order terms of the Taylor expansion to achieve such equivalence.

Running Example. To see this, lets consider our (Running Example). In order to compute the roundoff specifications for procedures g and f, we first compute the real-valued abstractions of the floating-point procedures of g and f, (i.e., $\hat{g}(x, e_1, d_1)$ and $\hat{f}(y, z, e_2, \beta_g(y), \beta_g(z))$ respectively) by applying the floating-point rounding model and the rounding model for procedure calls, on the floating-point functions $\tilde{g}$ and $\tilde{f}$:

$$\begin{aligned}&\hat{g}(x, e_1, d_1) = x^2(1 + e_1) + d_1 \\ &\hat{f}(y, z, e_2, \beta_g(y), \beta_g(z)) = (g(y) + \beta_g(y) + g(z) + \beta_g(z))(1 + e_2)\end{aligned}$$

The next step is to compute the roundoff error specifications β_g and β_f. Since g does not contain any procedure calls, then β_g follows the (FPTaylor Error) formula directly:

$$\beta_g = \left.\frac{\partial \hat{g}}{\partial e_1}\right|_{x,0,0} e_1 + \left.\frac{\partial \hat{g}}{\partial d_1}\right|_{x,0,0} d_1$$

Next, we compute the roundoff specification for f:

$$\beta_f = \left.\frac{\partial \hat{f}}{\partial e_2}\right|_{y,z,0} e_2 + \left.\frac{\partial \hat{f}}{\partial \beta_g(y)}\right|_{y,z,0} \beta_g(y) + \left.\frac{\partial \hat{f}}{\partial \beta_g(z)}\right|_{y,z,0} \beta_g(z) + R_2(y,z,e_2,\beta_g(y),\beta_g(z)), \tag{5}$$

where,

$$\begin{aligned} R_2(y,z,e_2,\beta_g(y),\beta_g(z)) = 1/2(& \left.\frac{\partial^2 \hat{f}}{\partial \beta_g(y)\partial e_2}\right|_{y,z,e_2,\beta_g(y),\beta_g(z)} \beta_g(y)e_2 + \\ & \left.\frac{\partial^2 \hat{f}}{\partial \beta_g(z)\partial e_2}\right|_{y,z,e_2,\beta_g(y),\beta_g(z)} \beta_g(z)e_2 + \\ & \left.\frac{\partial^2 \hat{f}}{\partial e_2\partial \beta_g(y)}\right|_{y,z,e_2,\beta_g(y),\beta_g(z)} e_2\beta_g(y) + \\ & \left.\frac{\partial^2 \hat{f}}{\partial e_2\partial \beta_g(z)}\right|_{y,z,e_2,\beta_g(y),\beta_g(z)} e_2\beta_g(z)). \end{aligned}$$

If we replace the β_g functions in Eq. 5 by their respective Taylor expansions we reach the following:

$$\begin{aligned} \beta_f = R_2(y,z,e_2,\beta_g(y),\beta_g(z)) \; & + \left.\frac{\partial \hat{f}}{\partial e_2}\right|_{y,z,0} e_2 \\ & + \left.\frac{\partial \hat{f}}{\partial \beta_g(y)}\right|_{y,z,0} \underbrace{\left(\left.\frac{\partial \hat{g}(y)}{\partial e_1}\right|_{y,0,0} e_1 + \left.\frac{\partial \hat{g}(y)}{\partial d_1}\right|_{y,0,0} d_1 \right)}_{\beta_g(y)} \\ & + \left.\frac{\partial \hat{f}}{\partial \beta_g(z)}\right|_{y,z,0} \underbrace{\left(\left.\frac{\partial \hat{g}(z)}{\partial e_1}\right|_{z,0,0} e_1 + \left.\frac{\partial \hat{g}(z)}{\partial d_1}\right|_{z,0,0} d_1 \right)}_{\beta_g(z)} \end{aligned} \tag{6}$$

Based on the rounding model for procedure calls, we can deduce that $\frac{\partial \hat{f}}{\partial \beta_g(\mathbf{a})} = \frac{\partial \hat{f}}{\partial \hat{g}(\mathbf{a})}$. If we replace $\frac{\partial \hat{f}}{\partial \beta_g(\mathbf{y})}$ and $\frac{\partial \hat{f}}{\partial \beta_g(\mathbf{z})}$ in Eq. 6 and also apply the chain rule (e.g., $\frac{\partial \hat{f}}{\partial \hat{g}(y)} \times \frac{\partial \hat{g}(y)}{\partial e_1} = \frac{\partial \hat{f}}{\partial e_1}$), we reach a formula that is equal to applying the (FPTaylor Error) on

$$\hat{f}_{in} = (y^2(1+e_1) + d1 + z^2(1+e_2) + d_2)(1+e_3),$$

which is the abstraction of the floating-point inlined version of f, i.e. $\tilde{f}_{in}(y,z) = y^2 + z^2$. For simplicity, here we did not expand on the remainder. However, the reasoning is similar.

Partial Evaluation. Besides abstraction that happens in the presence of nested function calls due to considering only first-order Taylor expansions and no higher-order terms, we abstract further by evaluating those error terms in (Roundoff Specification) that tend to be small already at the abstraction phase.

Specifically, we evaluate:

- the first-order derivatives w.r.t. absolute errors for subnormals, i.e. d_is,
- the remainder terms that do not contain any β terms themselves.

For this evaluation, we use the input specification of the procedure call. By doing so, we skip the re-instantiation of these small term at the call sites and over-approximate the (small) error of these terms. Since these terms are mostly of higher-order (especially the remainder terms) over-approximating them improves the analysis performance while having small impact on the analysis accuracy.

3.2 Propagation Error Abstraction

The goal is to compute the propagation error specification γ_f for a procedure f as a function of the input parameters, while achieving a reasonably tight error bound. We over-approximate the propagation error, i.e., $\max|f(\mathbf{x}) - f(\tilde{\mathbf{x}})|$ by following the approach proposed in [11] while extending it to also support procedure calls. We first explain how the propagation error specification is computed, when there are no procedure calls (or they are inlined) and then we explain our extension to support procedure calls.

Suppose $u_i, \ldots u_k$ are the initial errors of the input variables $x_1, \ldots, x_k$, i.e. $\tilde{\mathbf{x}} = \mathbf{x} + \mathbf{u}$. Similarly to the roundoff specification, we apply the Taylor expansion to $f(\tilde{\mathbf{x}})$, but this time we take the derivatives w.r.t. the input variables:

$$f(\tilde{\mathbf{x}}) - f(\mathbf{x}) = \sum_{i=1}^{k} \frac{\partial f}{\partial x_i} u_i + 1/2 \sum_{i,j=1}^{k} \frac{\partial^2 f}{\partial x_i \partial x_j} u_i u_j \tag{7}$$

Now consider the case where $f(\mathbf{x})$ contains procedure calls of $g_1(\boldsymbol{a_1}), \ldots g_l(\boldsymbol{a_l})$, where $\boldsymbol{a_1}, \ldots, \boldsymbol{a_l}$ are the input arguments and $\boldsymbol{\gamma}(\mathbf{a}) = (\gamma_{g_1}(\boldsymbol{a_1}), \ldots, \gamma_{g_l}(\boldsymbol{a_l}))$ is the vector of corresponding propagation error specifications. We compute the propagation error specification for a procedure f as follows:

$$\gamma_f = \sum_{i=1}^{k} \frac{\partial f}{\partial x_i} u_i + \sum_{i=1}^{l} \frac{\partial f}{\partial g_i(\boldsymbol{a_i})} \gamma_{g_i}(\boldsymbol{a_i}) + R_2(\mathbf{x}, \mathbf{u}, \boldsymbol{\gamma}(\mathbf{a}))$$

(Propagation Specification)

where,

$$R_2(\mathbf{x}, \mathbf{u}, \boldsymbol{\gamma}(\mathbf{a})) = 1/2(\sum_{i,j=1}^{k} \frac{\partial^2 f(\mathbf{x})}{\partial x_i \partial x_j} u_i u_j + \sum_{i,j=1}^{k,l} \frac{\partial^2 f(\mathbf{x})}{\partial x_i \partial g_j} u_i \gamma_{g_j}(\boldsymbol{a_j}) +$$
$$\sum_{i,j=1}^{l} \frac{\partial^2 f(\mathbf{x})}{\partial g_i \partial g_j} \gamma_{g_i}(\boldsymbol{a_i}) \gamma_{g_j}(\boldsymbol{a_j}) + \sum_{i,j=1}^{l,k} \frac{\partial^2 f(\mathbf{x})}{\partial g_i \partial x_j} \gamma_{g_i}(\boldsymbol{a_i}) u_j)$$

That is, we compute and add the propagation error of the called procedures by computing the derivatives of the calling procedure w.r.t the called procedures and multiplying such terms by their respective γ function, which is the propagation error of the called procedure. The remainder terms w.r.t called procedures are computed similarly.

Correctness. Just as with the roundoff specifications, if we were to replace the γ_{g_i}s by their corresponding formulas in γ_f, we would reach the same propagation error specification as if we had computed it with Eq. 7 for a program with all procedures inlined. Again, higher-order Taylor expansion terms may be needed for an equivalence.

Running Example. To see this, lets consider our (Running Example). Suppose u_x, u_y, and u_z are the initial errors for procedures g and f respectively. The propagation specifications for g and f are computed as follows:

$$\gamma_g = \frac{\partial g}{\partial x} u_x + 1/2(\frac{\partial^2 g}{\partial x} u_x^2) = 2x u_x + u_x^2$$
$$\gamma_f = \frac{\partial f}{\partial g(y)} \gamma_g(y) + \frac{\partial f}{\partial g(z)} \gamma_g(z) = \gamma_g(y) + \gamma_g(z) = 2x u_y + 2y u_z + u_y^2 + u_z^2$$

Note that replacing the γ_g functions with their equivalent Taylor expansion in γ_f and applying the chain rule (e.g., $\frac{\partial f}{\partial g(y)} \times \frac{\partial g(y)}{\partial y} = \frac{\partial f}{\partial y}$), would result in the Taylor expansion of the inlined version of $f(\tilde{\mathbf{x}})$.

Partial Evaluation. While computing the propagation specification γ, we evaluate the small error terms of the error specification and add them as constant error terms to the error specification. These small terms are the remainder terms that do not contain any γ terms themselves. Doing so, we skip the re-evaluation of these small terms at the call sites and therefore, speed-up the analysis.

3.3 Instantiation of Error

In the second step of our analysis, we instantiate the propagation and roundoff error specifications of each procedure of the program using its input intervals. In other words, for each procedure, we compute upper bounds for the β and γ error specifications. For the instantiation of the error specifications, one can use different approaches to maximize the error expressions. In HUGO, one can chose between interval arithmetic and a branch-and-bound optimization.

The instantiation of an error specification for a procedure is conducted in a recursive fashion. In order to compute an upper bound on the error for a procedure, we instantiate the error terms of the corresponding error specification using interval analysis. While instantiating the error, we may come across β or γ functions corresponding to the called procedures. In such cases, we fetch the error specification of these called procedures and instantiate them using the input intervals of the calling procedure.

Note that in the first stage of the analysis and while computing the error specifications, we over-approximated the error by pre-evaluating the smaller terms there and adding them as constants to the error specifications. As a result, in this stage and before instantiating an error specification of a called procedure, we check that the input intervals of input parameters of the called procedure—for which the error specification function is computed—enclose the intervals of input arguments at the call site. This precondition check can also be applied post analysis.

For the (Running Example), instantiating the roundoff error specification of g results in the following evaluated β functions.

$$\begin{aligned}\beta_g &= \epsilon \max|x^2| + \delta,\\ \beta_f &= \epsilon \max|g(y) + g(z)| + (1 + 2\epsilon) \max|\beta_g(y) + \beta_g(z)|\end{aligned}$$

3.4 Handling Nested Procedures

We now explain how our analysis extends beyond the simple case discussed so far, and in particular how it supports the case when a procedure argument is an arithmetic expression or another procedure call.

In such a case, one needs to take into account the roundoff and propagation error of such input arguments. We treat both cases uniformly by observing that arithmetic expression arguments can be refactored into separate procedures, so that we only need to consider nested procedure calls.

We compute the roundoff and propagation error specification of the nested procedure call in a similar fashion as before. Though, while computing the β and γ specifications with nested procedure calls we incorporate their respective β and γ functions in the solution. That is, we take the β function of a nested procedure into account while we create a rounding abstraction for a procedure call. For example, for the procedure call $f(g(\mathbf{a}))$, the rounding model is:

$$\tilde{f}(g(\mathbf{a})) = f(g(\mathbf{a}) + \beta_g(\mathbf{a})) + \beta_f(g(\mathbf{a}) + \beta_g(\mathbf{a}))$$

On the other hand, while computing the propagation error specification of a procedure call such as $f(g(\mathbf{a}))$, instead of multiplying the computed derivatives by their respected initial error, they get multiplied by the respective propagation error specification, i.e. $\gamma_g(\mathbf{a})$.

Example. We illustrate how we handle nested procedure calls with a slightly more involved example:

$$\begin{aligned}&g(x) = x^2, \quad \text{where} \quad x \in [0.0, 500.0]\\ &h(y, z) = y + z, \quad \text{where} \quad y \in [10.0, 20.0], z \in [10.0, 20.0]\\ &f(w, t) = g(h(w, t)) \quad \text{where} \quad w \in [12.0, 15.0], t \in [12.0, 15.0]\end{aligned} \tag{8}$$

The roundoff error specification for g is computed as before for our (Running Example) and since h does not contain any procedure calls, β_h is computed straight-forwardly as before.

The abstraction of the floating-point procedure of f is as follows:

$$f(w,t,\beta_g,\beta_h) = g(\chi(w,t)) + \beta_g(\chi(w,t))$$

where,

$$\chi(w,t) = h(w,t) + \beta_h(w,t)$$

Next we compute β_f:

$$\begin{aligned}\beta_f =& \frac{\partial \hat{f}}{\partial \beta_h(w,t)}\beta_h(w,t) + \frac{\partial \hat{f}}{\partial \beta_g(\chi(w,t))}\beta_g(\chi(w,t)) + 1/2\frac{\partial^2 \hat{f}}{\partial \beta_h(w,t)}\beta_h^2(w,t) = \\ & \frac{\partial g(\chi(w,t))}{\partial(h(w,t)\beta_h(w,t) + \beta_h(w,t))}\beta_h(w,t) + \beta_g(\chi(w,t)) + \beta_h^2(w,t)\end{aligned}$$

If β_f is instantiated then we obtain:

$$\beta_f = \max|3\epsilon(w+t)^2 + 3\epsilon^2(w+t)^2 + \epsilon^3(w+t)^2|$$

If we compute the roundoff specification for the inlined version of f i.e., $(w+t)^2$, using the Taylor expansion, however up to the third-order derivative terms, we reach the same error specification as in β_f above.

To compute the propagation error, consider u_x as the initial error for g, u_y and u_z as initial errors for h and u_w and u_t as initial errors in f. The propagation error specification for g is as computed before for (Running Example) and is equal to $2xu_x + u_x^2$. The propagation error specifications of h and f are as follows:

$$\begin{aligned}\gamma_h &= \frac{\partial h}{\partial y}u_y + \frac{\partial h}{\partial z}u_z = u_y + u_z \\ \gamma_f &= \frac{\partial f}{\partial g(h(w,t))}\gamma_g(h(w,t)) = \gamma_g(h(w,t)) = 2h(w,t)\gamma_h(w,t) + \gamma_h^2(w,t)\end{aligned}$$

Therefore,

$$\gamma_f = 2(w+t)(u_w + u_t) + (u_w + u_t)^2$$

The inlined version of f has the same propagation error specification.

4 Implementation

We have implemented our proposed modular error analysis technique in a prototype tool that we call Hugo in the Scala programming language. We did not find it feasible to extend an existing implementation of the symbolic Taylor expression-based approach in FPTaylor [27] (or another tool) to support procedure calls. We thus opted to re-implement the straight-line code analysis inside the Daisy analysis framework [10] which supports function calls at least in the frontend. We implement our modular approach on top of it and call it Hugo in our evaluation.

Our implementation does not include all of the performance or accuracy optimizations that FPTaylor includes. Specifically, it is *not* our goal to beat existing optimized tools in terms of result accuracy. Rather, our aim is to evaluate the feasibility of a modular roundoff error analysis. We expect that most, if not all, of FPTaylor's optimizations (e.g. detecting constants that can be exactly represented in binary and thus do not incur any roundoff error) to be equally beneficial to Hugo. Nevertheless, our evaluation suggests that our re-implementation is reasonable.

Hugo takes as input a (single) input file that includes all of the procedures. Integrating Hugo into a larger verification framework such as KeY [3] or Frama-C [23] is out of scope of this paper.

In Hugo, we use intervals with arbitrary-precision outer bounds (with outwards rounding) using the GNU MPFR library [15] to represent all computed values, ensuring a sound as well as an efficient implementation. Hugo supports three different procedures to bound the first-order error terms in equations Roundoff Specification and Propagation Specification: standard interval arithmetic, our own implementation of the branch-and-bound algorithm or Gelpia [4], the branch-and-bound solver that FPTaylor uses. However, we have had difficulties to obtain reliable (timely) results from Gelpia. Higher-order terms are evaluated using interval arithmetic.

5 Evaluation

We evaluate our modular roundoff error analysis focusing on the following research questions:

RQ1: What is the trade-off between performance and accuracy of our modular approach?
RQ2: How does the modular approach compare to the state-of-the-art?

5.1 Experimental Setup

We evaluate Hugo on two case studies, `complex` and `matrix`, that reflect a setting where we expect a modular analysis to be beneficial. Each case study consists of a number of procedures; some of these would appear as library functions that are (repeatedly) called by the other procedures. Each procedure consists of arithmetic computations and potentially procedure calls, and has a precondition describing bounds on the permitted input arguments.

Our two case studies are inspired by existing floating-point benchmarks used for verifying the absence of floating-point runtime errors in the KeY verification

Table 1. Case study statistics

benchmark	# top level procedures	# procedure calls	# arith. ops.	# arith. ops. inlined
matrix	5	15	26	371
matrixXL	6	33	44	911
matrixXS	4	6	17	101
complex	15	152	98	699
complexXL	16	181	127	1107
complexXS	13	136	72	464

framework [2]. We adapted the originally object-oriented floating-point Java programs to be purely procedural. We also added additional procedures and procedure calls to reflect a more realistic setting with more code reuse where a modular analysis would be expected to be beneficial. Note that the standard floating-point benchmark set FPBench [9] is not suitable for our evaluation as it consists of only individual procedures.

matrix. The `matrix` case study contains library procedures on 3×3 matrices, namely for computing the matrix' determinant and for using this determinant to solve a system of three linear equations with three variables, using Cramer's Rule. Finally, we define a procedure (`solveEquationsVector`) that solves three systems of equations and computes the average of the returned values, representative of application code that uses the results of the systems of equations. See Listing 1.2 in the Appendix for the (partial) `matrix` code.

complex. The `complex` case study contains library procedures on complex numbers such as division, reciprocal and radius, as well as procedures that use complex numbers for computing properties of RL circuits. For example, the `radius` procedure uses Pythagoras' theorem to compute the distance to the origin of a point represented by a complex number in the complex plane. The `computeRadiusVector` demonstrates how the `radius` library procedure may be called to compute the radius of a vector of complex numbers. The `approxEnergy` procedure approximates the energy consumption of an RL circuit in 5 time steps.

Listing 1.1 shows partial code of our `complex` case study. The procedure `_add` is a helper procedure that implements an arithmetic expression (and not just a single variable) that is used as argument of a called procedure; see Sect. 3.4 for how our method modularly incorporates the roundoff and propagation errors resulting from such an expression. For now this refactoring is done manually, but this process can be straight-forwardly automated.

Table 1 gives an overview of the complexity of our case studies in terms of the number of procedures and procedure calls, as well as the number of arithmetic operations in both the inlined and the procedural (original) versions of

Listing 1.1. complex case study

```
object complex {
 def _add(rm1: Real): Real = {...}
 def divideRe(re1: Real, im1: Real, re2: Real, im2: Real): Real = {...}
 def divideIm(re1: Real, im1: Real, re2: Real, im2: Real): Real = {...}
 def reciprocalRe(re1: Real, im1: Real): Real = {...}
 def reciprocalIm(re1: Real, im1: Real): Real = { ... }
 def impedanceIm(frequency5: Real, inductance: Real): Real = {...}
 def instantVoltage(maxVoltage: Real, frequency4: Real, time: Real): Real = {...}
 def computeCurrentRe(maxVoltage: Real, frequency3: Real, inductance: Real,
  resistance: Real): Real = {...}
 def computeCurrentIm(maxVoltage: Real, frequency2: Real, inductance: Real,
  resistance: Real): Real = {...}
 def radius(re: Real, im: Real): Real = {...}
 def computeInstantCurrent(frequency1: Real, time: Real, maxVoltage: Real,
  inductance: Real, resistance: Real): Real = {...}

 def approxEnergy(frequency: Real, maxVoltage: Real, inductance: Real,
  resistance: Real): Real = {
  require(((frequency >= 1.0) && (frequency <= 100.0) && (maxVoltage >= 1.0) &&
  (maxVoltage <= 12.0) && (inductance >= 0.001) && (inductance <= 0.004) &&
  (resistance >= 1.0) && (resistance <= 50.0)))

  val t1: Real = 1.0
  val instCurrent1: Real = computeInstantCurrent(frequency, t1, maxVoltage,
       inductance, resistance)
  val instVoltage1: Real = instantVoltage(maxVoltage, frequency, t1)
  val instantPower1: Real = instCurrent1 * instVoltage1
  val t2: Real = _add(t1)
  val instCurrent2: Real = computeInstantCurrent(frequency, t2, maxVoltage,
       inductance, resistance)
  val instVoltage2: Real = instantVoltage(maxVoltage, frequency, t2)
  val instantPower2: Real = instCurrent2 * instVoltage2
  ...
  (0.5 * instantPower1) + (0.5 * instantPower2) + (0.5 * instantPower3) +
   (0.5 * instantPower4) + (0.5 * instantPower5)
 }
 def computeRadiusVector(re: Real, im: Real): Real = {
  require(((re >= 1) && (re <= 2.0) && (im >= 1) && (im <= 2.0)))

  val v1 = radius(re, im)
  val re2 = _add(re)
  val im2 = _add(im)
  val v2 = radius(re2, im2)
  ...
  v1 + v2 + v3 + v4 + v5 + v6 + v7 + v8 + v9 + v10
 }
...
}
```

the code. We inline all procedure calls for comparison with state-of-the-art tools FPTaylor [27] and Daisy [10], since they do not handle them.

We additionally create extended and shortened versions of our two case studies, denoted with the suffixes `XL` and `XS`, respectively. The `XL` versions contain one additional procedure that is an extended version of an existing procedure with twice as many procedure calls. In `matrix`, we extend `solveEquationsVector`, and for `complex` we extend `approxEnergy`. In the `XS` version of `matrix`, we remove `solveEquationsVector` and for `complex` we remove the two procedures that were particularly problematic for FPTaylor (it times out), i.e. `computeInstantCurrent` and `approxEnergy`.

We run our experiments on a server with 1.5 TB memory and 4×12 CPU cores at 3 GHz. However, HUGO runs single-threadedly and does not use more than 8GB of memory. We consider a timeout of one hour for analyzing each case study. We assume uniform 64 bit double precision for all floating-point operations.

5.2 RQ1: Accuracy-Performance Trade-Off

We first evaluate the effectiveness of our modular approach in terms of the trade-off between the performance of the analysis and the accuracy of the computed error bounds. To do so, we compare HUGO's computed error bounds and performance on our case studies in an ablation study with and without inlining procedures, and by varying the specified input ranges of procedure's parameters.

The accuracy of our modular analysis is influenced by the input range specifications of procedures. Wider input ranges will typically lead to looser error bounds, but will enable procedures to be used in more contexts. We thus define two versions of our case studies: one with tighter input parameter bounds and one with wider ones. We widen the input specifications of the procedures such that for each input interval $[a, b]$ we generate the interval $[a-(b-a), b+(b-a)]$, resulting in a new interval three times as wide as the original interval. We do this widening only for the library procedures (i.e. procedures without procedure calls that are called in other procedures) and only when it is feasible; occasionally it results in division by zero and illegal argument to library procedures errors, and in those cases we only do a more limited widening.

The most accurate error bounds will be computed by inlining all procedure calls at their call site, since by doing so no over-approximation is committed due to procedure summaries. This effectively corresponds to always having the tightest input range bounds at each call site. This comes at the expense of having to potentially repeatedly re-analyze the same procedure many times and thus increase the analysis time.

The results of this experiment are shown in Table 2. The running time (in seconds) is the time for analyzing an entire case study with all procedures and including the check that preconditions are satisfied. We ran each experiment three times and recorded the average runtime in Table 2. We only show the error bounds for procedures containing procedure calls, since those are the ones with over-approximated errors with a modular analysis.

Table 2. HUGO runtimes (with precondition check) for original procedures and procedures with widened and tightened input intervals

case	procedure	original		inlined proced.		3× interval	
		err	time(s)	error	time(s)	err	time(s)
matrix	solveEquationX	4.14e−15	3.9	1.50e−15	519.0	3.59e−14	3.9
	solveEquationY	4.68e−15		2.12e−15		4.04e−14	
	solveEquationZ	5.16e−15		2.57e−15		4.46e−14	
	solveEquationsVector	4.73e−15		2.88e−16		4.04e−14	
complex	computeCurrentRe	6.12e−10	239.7	–	TO	8.00e−10	239.2
	computeCurrentIm	6.71e−10		–		2.55e−09	
	computeInstantCurrent	3.34e−03		–		3.77e−03	
	approxEnergy	1.00e−01		–		1.13e−01	
	computeRadiusVector	1.47e−11		–		5.84e−11	
	computeDivideVector	2.39e−10		–		2.39e−10	
	computeReciprocalRadiusV.	3.12e−14		–		3.12e−14	

As expected, inlining the procedures for the `matrix` case study results in smaller errors compared to the original procedures. However, the runtime increases more than 130 times. For the inlined version of the `complex` case study the runtime exceeds the timeout and hence no errors are reported.

Widening the input intervals for library procedures in both case studies results—also as expected—in equal or less accurate error bounds, however, the difference is mostly quite small. We thus conclude that our modular analysis is clearly more efficient than the baseline analysis with inlined procedures, and effectively supports procedures with wider input ranges, while producing reasonable error bounds.

5.3 RQ2: Comparison with the State of the Art

We next compare HUGO in terms of performance and accuracy with the state of the art tools FPTaylor [27] and Daisy [10]. We choose FPTaylor as it implements the baseline symbolic Taylor expression approach to roundoff error analysis and has been shown to generally outperform other tools. Additionally, we include Daisy which is also open-source and implements a different, dataflow-based, roundoff error analysis that has been shown to be generally less accurate, but often faster than FPTaylor—it thus represents a different point in the accuracy/performance tradeoff space.

We use Daisy's default settings that implement a dataflow-based roundoff error analysis using interval arithmetic to track ranges and affine arithmetic to track errors. For FPTaylor, we used for the most part the default configuration setting with the following exceptions:pg

Table 3. Comparison of HUGO's, Daisy's and FPTaylor's runtimes and computed errors

case study	procedure	HUGO		Daisy		FPTaylor	
		err	time(s)	error	time(s)	err	time(s)
matrix	solveEquationX	4.14e–15	**3.9**	1.07e–15	10.5	**3.83e–16**	539.7
	solveEquationY	4.68e–15		1.55e–15		**6.11e–16**	
	solveEquationZ	5.16e–15		1.90e–15		**4.96e–16**	
	solveEquationsVector	4.73e–15		2.09e–16		**1.83e–16**	
matrixXL	solveEquationsVectorXL	4.78e–15	**5.9**	2.53e–16	24.2	**2.27e–16**	1342.0
matrixXS			**3.5**		4.0		158.9
complex	computeCurrentRe	6.12e–10	**239.7**	4.90e–10	439.1	**9.65e–14**	TO
	computeCurrentIm	6.71e–10		2.46e–11		**2.42e–13**	
	computeInstantCurrent	**3.34e–03**		5.57e+01		-	
	approxEnergy	**1.00e–01**		1.67e+03		-	
	computeRadiusVector	1.47e–11		**6.20e–14**		7.26e–14	
	computeDivideVector	2.39e–10		8.26e–14		**3.85e–14**	
	computeReciprocalRadiusV.	3.12e–14		3.89e–14		**4.67e–15**	
complexXL	approxEnergyXL	**2.00e–01**	**969.3**	3.34e+03	1315.1	-	TO
complexXS			181.7		**13.4**		140.7

1. We set the option for the improved rounding model to false to reduce running time; we haven't observed a noticeable effect on accuracy for our case studies.
2. We set FPTaylor to compute the maximum possible initial rounding error for all input variables to match HUGO's behavior.
3. We turned the debugging option off to decrease running time.

Since neither Daisy nor FPTaylor support procedure calls, we inline all procedure calls and call the tools on the fully inlined code. Just like for HUGO, we report running times for computing roundoff error bounds for all procedures in a case study. For Daisy, we prepare one file with all procedures, for FPTaylor we sum up the running times for analyzing each procedure separately, since FPTaylor supports only a single expression per input file (we report the running times for individual procedures in the appending in Table 4). We ran each experiment three times and report the average runtimes.

The results of this experiment are shown in Table 3. As before, we only show the error bounds for procedures containing procedure calls. For the `XL` versions we only report the error of the additional procedure, and for the `XS` version we do not report errors, since this version has a procedure removed.

HUGO is faster than Daisy and FPTaylor on all but the `complexXS` case study, and often significantly so. For `matrix`, HUGO is 2.6× and 138× faster than Daisy and FPTaylor, respectively. For `matrixXL`, the improvements are 4.1× and 227×. These improvements come with error bounds that are within an order of magnitude of those of Daisy and FPTaylor.

FPTaylor is not able to compute errors for two of the longest procedures of `complex`, reporting infinite errors using the default settings. We changed FPTaylor's configuration for these two procedures to be more precise (evaluating second-order terms with a more accurate procedure), however, with this setting FPTaylor timed out, i.e. it took more than one hour for *each* procedure.

For the `complexXS` case study, which does not include the two longest procedures, HUGO is slower than both Daisy and FPTaylor. This is not unexpected, as HUGO's modular analysis has a certain (implementation) overhead and is thus most effective if there are many procedure calls with a lot of code reuse.

For the full `complex` and `complexXL` case studies, HUGO is faster than Daisy by 1.8× and 1.3×, respectively. We suspect that the improvements for the `XL` version are smaller than for the original one due to inefficiencies in our implementation (e.g. due to missed caching opportunities). That said, HUGO can even produce *tighter error bounds* than Daisy for 4 procedures. This is due to HUGO using a different, generally more accurate, type of analysis. FPTaylor also uses this more accurate analysis, but as our experiments show, the non-modular version does not scale well for larger programs.

HUGO can potentially produce tighter error bounds by applying the branch and bound algorithm instead of the interval analysis for range evaluation. However, for the current set of procedures Hugo was only able to produce (slightly) tighter bounds for four procedures, while taking significantly longer.

In conclusion, compared to FPTaylor and Daisy, HUGO's modular analysis is significantly faster for code with many procedure calls. While HUGO generally does not match the accuracy of existing tools exactly (it fundamentally cannot), our evaluation shows that it nonetheless produces error bounds that are reasonably close to be useful for many (though obviously not all) applications. For the largest procedures, our modular analysis even enables to compute significantly tighter error bounds, resp. any error bounds at all.

6 Related Work

Automated sound static analyses for floating-point arithmetic programs have recently seen much interest. Dataflow-based techniques track floating-point ranges and errors using abstract domains, typically using interval or affine arithmetic, in a forward analysis through a program [10,13,18]. The advantage of these techniques is that they are relatively efficient [10,27]. Alternative approaches construct symbolic constraints that are then solved using global optimization techniques [24,26,27]. These have been shown to produce, in general, tighter error bounds [26,27]. We extend the approach implemented in the tool FPTaylor [27] that applies Taylor approximations to make the optimization problem computationally feasible. The tool PRECiSA generates different constraints (though for addition, subtraction and multiplication they coincide) but also solves them with branch-and-bound techniques. PRECiSA supports function calls in its input programs; it computes the error constraints compositionally but inlines them before evaluation of concrete error bounds and does not perform additional abstractions.

The tool Satire [12] also implements the symbolic Taylor expression-based approach, with additional optimizations for efficiency. Some of these, such as dropping higher-order terms, make the analysis unsound, i.e. the computed error bounds are not guaranteed to be an over-approximation. Our analysis is sound.

The only work that we are aware of that proposes a floating-point roundoff error analysis combining modularity with function summary abstraction [19] extends the less accurate data-flow-based analysis approach with the zonotope abstract domain. It uses the zonotopes to compute summaries of procedure bodies, which is effectively a first-order—though different—approximation of the roundoff errors that we apply in our approach. Unfortunately, the implementation is not available for comparison. The paper describes an approach to recompute summaries when the preconditions of the called procedures are not valid at particular call sites. Our implementation currently assumes that preconditions provided by users are sufficiently weak, but a more automated procedure, similar to the above, could be integrated with our approach as well.

Floating-point programs have also been analyzed by deductive verification techniques that are fundamentally modular [2,14]. These tools generate verification conditions that are typically discharged by external SMT solvers or theorem provers, and do not automatically compute (over-approximations of) floating-point roundoff errors. As a consequence, automated roundoff verification is limited to relatively simple computations [2], or requires substantial user interaction in form of annotations [16].

The tools FPTaylor [27], PRECiSa [26], Daisy [5] and real2Float [24] can generate proof certificates that can be independently checked by an interactive theorem prover to ensure the soundness of the computed error bounds. Interactive theorem provers have also been used to prove complex functional properties about floating-point programs, including roundoff errors [7,20]. While they provide an additional level of assurance by their proofs being verified in Coq or HOL, such proofs are manual and require substantial expertise in both theorem proving as well as floating-point arithmetic.

7 Conclusion

We showed how to extend the optimization-based roundoff error analysis for floating-point arithmetic to effectively support (nested) procedure calls. Our evaluation shows that our analysis provides an interesting tradeoff between analysis accuracy and performance, offering substantially smaller analysis times for programs with many procedure calls. Our prototype implementation allows to analyze purely procedural programs; but we expect our approach to be useful in the future as a building block in (existing) modular verification tools.

A Appendix

The code for the `matrix` case study is shown (partially) in Listing 1.2. The runtimes of FPTaylor for individual procedures are shown in Table 4.

Listing 1.2. `matrix` case study

```
object matrix {
 def determinant(a: Real, b: Real, c: Real, d: Real, e: Real, f: Real, g: Real,
  h: Real, i: Real): Real = {
  require((0.8 <= a) && (a <= 20.4) && (0.8 <= b) && (b <= 75.9) && (0.8 <= c) &&
   (c <= 50.4) && (0.8 <= d) && (d <= 57.3) && (-60.0 <= e) && (e <= 10.2) &&
   (-92.0 <= f) && (f <= 10.2) && (0.8 <= g) && (g <= 93.6) && (-3.6 <= h) &&
   (h <= 10.2) && (-15.3 <= i) && (i <= -2.4))

  a * ((e * i) - (f * h)) - b * ((d * i) - (f * g )) + c * ((d * h) - (e * g))
 }
 // solves a system of equations using the Cramer's rule (variable x)
 def solveEquationX(a1: Real, b1: Real, c1: Real, d1: Real, a2: Real, b2: Real,
  c2: Real, d2: Real, a3: Real, b3: Real, c3: Real, d3: Real): Real = {
  require((19.3 <= a1) && (a1 <= 20.3) && (74.8 <= b1) && (b1 <= 75.8) &&
   (49.3 <= c1) && (c1 <= 50.3) && (0.9 <= d1) && (d1 <= 10.1) && ...))

  val d: Real = determinant(a1, b1, c1, a2, b2, c2, a3, b3, c3)
  val d_x: Real = determinant(d1, b1, c1, d2, b2, c2, d3, b3, c3)
  val x: Real = d_x / d
  x
 }
 // solves a system of equations using the Cramer's rule (variable y)
 def solveEquationY(a1: Real, b1: Real, c1: Real, d1: Real, a2: Real, b2: Real,
  c2: Real, d2: Real, a3: Real, b3: Real, c3: Real, d3: Real): Real = {...}
 // solves a system of equations using the Cramer's rule (variable z)
 def solveEquationZ(a1: Real, b1: Real, c1: Real, d1: Real, a2: Real, b2: Real,
  c2: Real, d2: Real, a3: Real, b3: Real, c3: Real, d3: Real): Real = {...}
// solves three sytems of equations
 def solveEquationsVector(a1: Real, b1: Real, c1: Real, a2: Real, b2: Real, c2: Real,
  a3: Real, b3: Real, c3: Real, aa1: Real, bb1: Real, cc1: Real, aa2: Real,
  bb2: Real, cc2: Real, aa3: Real, bb3: Real, cc3: Real, ...): Real = {
  require((19.49 <= a1) && (a1 <= 19.69) && ...)

  val x: Real = solveEquation_x(a1, b1, c1, d1, a2, b2, c2, d2, a3, b3, c3, d3)
  val y: Real = solveEquation_y(a1, b1, c1, d1, a2, b2, c2, d2, a3, b3, c3, d3)
  val z: Real = solveEquation_z(a1, b1, c1, d1, a2, b2, c2, d2, a3, b3, c3, d3)
  val x2: Real = solveEquation_x(aa1, bb1, cc1, d1, aa2, bb2, cc2, d2, aa3, bb3,
   cc3, d3)
  ...
  (x + y + z + x2 + y2 + z2 + x3 + y3 + z3) / 9.0
 }
}
```

Table 4. Runtimes of FPTaylor for individual procedures

case study	procedure	time (s)
matrix	solveEquationX	56.3
	solveEquationY	51.2
	solveEquationZ	50.8
	solveEquationsVector	380.9
complex	computeCurrentRe	18.8
	computeCurrentIm	22.1
	computeRadiusVector	1.5
	computeDivideVector	53.1
	computeReciprocalRadiusV	31.4

References

1. IEEE Standard for Floating-Point Arithmetic: IEEE Std 754-2019 (Revision of IEEE 754-2008) (2019). https://doi.org/10.1109/IEEESTD.2019.8766229
2. Abbasi, R., Schiffl, J., Darulova, E., Ulbrich, M., Ahrendt, W.: Deductive verification of floating-point Java programs in KeY. In: Groote, J.F., Larsen, K.G. (eds.) TACAS 2021. LNCS, vol. 12652, pp. 242–261. Springer, Cham (2021). https://doi.org/10.1007/978-3-030-72013-1_13
3. Ahrendt, W., Beckert, B., Bubel, R., Hähnle, R., Schmitt, P.H., Ulbrich, M. (eds.): Deductive Software Verification - The KeY Book - From Theory to Practice. LNCS, vol. 10001. Springer, Cham (2016). https://doi.org/10.1007/978-3-319-49812-6
4. Baranowski, M.S., Briggs, I.: Global extrema locator parallelization for interval arithmetic (2023). https://github.com/soarlab/gelpia. Accessed 20 Apr 2023
5. Becker, H., Zyuzin, N., Monat, R., Darulova, E., Myreen, M.O., Fox, A.C.J.: A verified certificate checker for finite-precision error bounds in Coq and HOL4. In: Formal Methods in Computer Aided Design (FMCAD) (2018). https://doi.org/10.23919/FMCAD.2018.8603019
6. Blanchet, B., et al.: A static analyzer for large safety-critical software. In: Programming Language Design and Implementation (PLDI) (2003). https://doi.org/10.1145/781131.781153
7. Boldo, S., Clément, F., Filliâtre, J.C., Mayero, M., Melquiond, G., Weis, P.: Wave equation numerical resolution: a comprehensive mechanized proof of a C program. J. Autom. Reasoning **50**(4), 423–456 (2013). https://doi.org/10.1007/s10817-012-9255-4
8. Cousot, P., Cousot, R.: Modular static program analysis. In: Horspool, R.N. (ed.) CC 2002. LNCS, vol. 2304, pp. 159–179. Springer, Heidelberg (2002). https://doi.org/10.1007/3-540-45937-5_13
9. Damouche, N., Martel, M., Panchekha, P., Qiu, C., Sanchez-Stern, A., Tatlock, Z.: Toward a standard benchmark format and suite for floating-point analysis. In: Bogomolov, S., Martel, M., Prabhakar, P. (eds.) NSV 2016. LNCS, vol. 10152, pp. 63–77. Springer, Cham (2017). https://doi.org/10.1007/978-3-319-54292-8_6
10. Darulova, E., Izycheva, A., Nasir, F., Ritter, F., Becker, H., Bastian, R.: Daisy - framework for analysis and optimization of numerical programs (tool paper). In: Beyer, D., Huisman, M. (eds.) TACAS 2018. LNCS, vol. 10805, pp. 270–287. Springer, Cham (2018). https://doi.org/10.1007/978-3-319-89960-2_15
11. Darulova, E., Kuncak, V.: Towards a compiler for reals. ACM Trans. Program. Lang. Syst. (TOPLAS) **39**(2), 1–28 (2017). https://doi.org/10.1145/3014426
12. Das, A., Briggs, I., Gopalakrishnan, G., Krishnamoorthy, S., Panchekha, P.: Scalable yet rigorous floating-point error analysis. In: International Conference for High Performance Computing, Networking, Storage and Analysis (SC) (2020). https://doi.org/10.1109/SC41405.2020.00055
13. De Dinechin, F., Lauter, C.Q., Melquiond, G.: Assisted verification of elementary functions using Gappa. In: ACM Symposium on Applied Computing (2006). https://doi.org/10.1145/1141277.1141584
14. Filliâtre, J.-C., Paskevich, A.: Why3—where programs meet provers. In: Felleisen, M., Gardner, P. (eds.) ESOP 2013. LNCS, vol. 7792, pp. 125–128. Springer, Heidelberg (2013). https://doi.org/10.1007/978-3-642-37036-6_8
15. Fousse, L., Hanrot, G., Lefèvre, V., Pélissier, P., Zimmermann, P.: MPFR: a multiple-precision binary floating-point library with correct rounding. ACM Trans. Math. Softw. **33**(2), 13 (2007). https://doi.org/10.1145/1236463.1236468

16. Fumex, C., Marché, C., Moy, Y.: Automating the verification of floating-point programs. In: Paskevich, A., Wies, T. (eds.) VSTTE 2017. LNCS, vol. 10712, pp. 102–119. Springer, Cham (2017). https://doi.org/10.1007/978-3-319-72308-2_7
17. Gehr, T., Mirman, M., Drachsler-Cohen, D., Tsankov, P., Chaudhuri, S., Vechev, M.T.: AI2: safety and robustness certification of neural networks with abstract interpretation. In: Symposium on Security and Privacy (SP) (2018). https://doi.org/10.1109/SP.2018.00058
18. Goubault, E., Putot, S.: Static analysis of finite precision computations. In: Jhala, R., Schmidt, D. (eds.) VMCAI 2011. LNCS, vol. 6538, pp. 232–247. Springer, Heidelberg (2011). https://doi.org/10.1007/978-3-642-18275-4_17
19. Goubault, E., Putot, S., Védrine, F.: Modular static analysis with zonotopes. In: Miné, A., Schmidt, D. (eds.) SAS 2012. LNCS, vol. 7460, pp. 24–40. Springer, Heidelberg (2012). https://doi.org/10.1007/978-3-642-33125-1_5
20. Harrison, J.: Floating point verification in HOL light: the exponential function. Formal Methods Syst. Des. **16**(3), 271–305 (2000). https://doi.org/10.1023/A:1008712907154
21. Izycheva, A., Darulova, E.: On sound relative error bounds for floating-point arithmetic. In: Formal Methods in Computer Aided Design (FMCAD) (2017). https://doi.org/10.23919/FMCAD.2017.8102236
22. Jeannet, B., Miné, A.: APRON: a library of numerical abstract domains for static analysis. In: Bouajjani, A., Maler, O. (eds.) CAV 2009. LNCS, vol. 5643, pp. 661–667. Springer, Heidelberg (2009). https://doi.org/10.1007/978-3-642-02658-4_52
23. Kirchner, F., Kosmatov, N., Prevosto, V., Signoles, J., Yakobowski, B.: Frama-C: a software analysis perspective. Formal Aspects Comput. **27**(3), 573–609 (2015). https://doi.org/10.1007/s00165-014-0326-7
24. Magron, V., Constantinides, G., Donaldson, A.: Certified roundoff error bounds using semidefinite programming. ACM Trans. Math. Softw. (TOMS) **43**(4), 1–31 (2017). https://doi.org/10.1145/3015465
25. Moore, R.E., Kearfott, R.B., Cloud, M.J.: Introduction to Interval Analysis. Society for Industrial and Applied Mathematics (2009). https://doi.org/10.1137/1.9780898717716
26. Moscato, M., Titolo, L., Dutle, A., Muñoz, C.A.: Automatic estimation of verified floating-point round-off errors via static analysis. In: Tonetta, S., Schoitsch, E., Bitsch, F. (eds.) SAFECOMP 2017. LNCS, vol. 10488, pp. 213–229. Springer, Cham (2017). https://doi.org/10.1007/978-3-319-66266-4_14
27. Solovyev, A., Baranowski, M.S., Briggs, I., Jacobsen, C., Rakamaric, Z., Gopalakrishnan, G.: Rigorous estimation of floating-point round-off errors with symbolic Taylor expansions. ACM Trans. Program. Lang. Syst. **41**(1), 2:1–2:39 (2019). https://doi.org/10.1145/3230733
28. Titolo, L., Feliú, M.A., Moscato, M., Muñoz, C.A.: An abstract interpretation framework for the round-off error analysis of floating-point programs. In: VMCAI 2018. LNCS, vol. 10747, pp. 516–537. Springer, Cham (2018). https://doi.org/10.1007/978-3-319-73721-8_24

Unconstrained Variable Oracles for Faster Numeric Static Analyses

Vincenzo Arceri(✉), Greta Dolcetti, and Enea Zaffanella

Department of Mathematical, Physical and Computer Sciences, University of Parma, 43124 Parma, Italy
{vincenzo.arceri,enea.zaffanella}@unipr.it,
greta.dolcetti@studenti.unipr.it

Abstract. In the context of static analysis based on Abstract Interpretation, we propose a lightweight pre-analysis step which is meant to suggest, at each program point, which program variables are likely to be unconstrained for a specific class of numeric abstract properties. Using the outcome of this pre-analysis as an oracle, we simplify the statements of the program being analyzed by propagating this lack of information, aiming at fine-tuning the precision/efficiency trade-off of the analysis. A preliminary experimental evaluation shows that the idea underlying the approach is promising, as it improves the efficiency of the more costly analysis while having a limited effect on its precision.

Keywords: Abstract Interpretation · Static Analysis · Unconstrained Variables · Abstract Compilation

1 Introduction

Static analyses based on Abstract Interpretation [12] correctly approximate the collecting semantics of a program by executing it on an abstract domain modeling the properties of interest. In the classical approach, which follows a pure program interpretation scheme, the concrete statements of the original program are abstractly executed step by step, updating the abstract property describing the current program state: while being correct, this process may easily incur avoidable inefficiencies and/or precision losses. To mitigate this issue, static analyzers sometimes apply simple, safe program transformations that are meant to better tune the trade-off between efficiency and precision. For instance, when trying to improve efficiency, the evaluation of a complex nonlinear numeric expression (used either in a conditional statement guard or as the right hand side expression in an assignment statement) may be abstracted into a purely nondeterministic choice of a value of the corresponding datatype; in this way, the overhead incurred to evaluate it in the considered abstract domain is avoided, possibly with no precision loss, since its result was likely imprecise anyway. On the other hand, when trying to preserve precision, a limited form of constant propagation may be enough to transform a nonlinear expression into a linear one, thereby allowing

M. V. Hermenegildo and J. F. Morales (Eds.): SAS 2023, LNCS 14284, pp. 65–83, 2023.
https://doi.org/10.1007/978-3-031-44245-2_5

for a reasonably efficient and precise computation on commonly used abstract domains tracking relational information. As another example, some tools apply a limited form of loop unrolling (e.g., unrolling the first iteration of the loop [8]) to help the abstract domain in clearly separating those control flows that cannot enter the loop body from those that might enter it; this transformation may trigger significant precision improvements when the widening operator is applied to the results of the loop iterations.

Sometimes, the program transformations hinted above are only performed at the semantic level, without actually modifying the program being analyzed; hence, the corresponding static analysis tools can still be classified as pure program interpreters. However, in principle the approach can be directly applied at the syntactic level, so as to actually translate the original program into a different one, thereby moving from a pure program interpretation setting to a hybrid form of (abstract) compilation and interpretation. Note that the term *Abstract Compilation*, introduced in [21,31], sometimes has been understood under rather constrained meanings: for instance, [17] and [1] assume that the compiled abstract program is expressed in an existing, concrete programming language; [9] and [32] focus on those inefficiencies that are directly caused by the interpretation step, without considering more general program transformations. Here we adopt the slightly broader meaning whereby portions of the approximate computations done by the static analysis tool are eagerly performed in the compilation (i.e., program translation) step and hence reflected in the abstract program representation itself. Clam/Crab [18] and IKOS [10] are examples of tools adopting this hybrid approach for the analysis of LLVM bitcode, leveraging on specific intermediate representations designed to accomodate several kinds of abstract statements. A similar approach is adopted in LiSA [16,27], to obtain a uniform program intermediate representation when analyzing programs composed by modules written using different programming languages.

Paper Contribution. Adopting the Abstract Compilation approach, we propose a program transformation that is able to tune the trade-off between precision and efficiency. The transformation relies on an *oracle* whose goal is to suggest, for each program point, which program variables are *likely unconstrained* for a target numeric analysis of interest. By systematically propagating the guessed lack of information, the oracle will guide the program transformation so as to simplify those statements of the abstract program for which the target analysis is *likely* unable to track useful information.

We model our oracles as pre-analyses on the abstract program, considering two Boolean parameterizations and thus obtaining four possible oracle variants: we will have *non-relational* or *relational* numeric analysis oracles and each of them can be *existential* or *universal*. The proposed program transformation can be guided by any one of these variants, allowing different degrees of program simplification, thereby obtaining different trade-offs between the precision and the efficiency of the target analysis. It is important to highlight that the oracles we are proposing have no intrinsic correctness requirement; as we will discuss in Sect. 2, whatever oracle is adopted to guess the set of unconstrained variables, its use will always result in a correct program transformation. The (im-)precision of the oracle guesses can only affect the precision and efficiency of the target numeric analysis: *aggressive* oracles, which predict more variables to be unconstrained, will result in faster but potentially less precise analyses; *conservative* oracles, by predicting fewer unconstrained variables, will result in slower analyses, potentially preserving more precision.

Our proposal will be experimentally evaluated on two benchmark suites: the first one, distributed with PAGAI [20], is a classical set of benchmarks for WCET (worst-case execution time) analysis; the second one contains 10 Linux drivers taken from the SV-COMP repository. We will test the four oracle variants on these benchmarks, considering as target analyses the classical numeric analyses using the abstract domains of intervals and convex polyhedra. This experimental evaluation allows us to measure the trade-off between efficiency and precision of the proposed variants, showing that it is possible to fine-tune the efficacy of the oracle and, in turn, of the program transformation.

Paper Structure. In Sect. 2, after introducing the notion of likely unconstrained variable for a target numeric analysis, we define four different oracles as variants of a dataflow analysis tracking variable unconstrainedness; we also formalize the program transformation that, guided by these oracles, simplifies the abstract program being analyzed. The design and implementation of our experimental evaluation are described in Sect. 3, where we also comment the results obtained on the considered benchmarks. Related work is briefly discussed in Sect. 4, while Sect. 5 concludes, also describing future work.

2 Detecting Likely Unconstrained Variables

In the concrete (resp., abstract) semantics of programming languages, the evaluation of an expression is formalized by a suitable set of semantic equations, which specify the result of the expression by using concrete (resp., abstract) operators to combine the current values of program variables, as recorded in the concrete (resp., abstract) environment. The efficiency of the evaluation process can be improved by propagating *known* information (e.g., constant values). In the abstract evaluation case, efficiency improvements may also be obtained by propagating *unknown* information. As an example, when evaluating the numeric expression $x + expr$ using the abstract domain of intervals [12], if no information is known about program variable x, then it is likely that no information at all will be known about the whole expression. Even when considering the more precise abstract domain of convex polyhedra [14], if x is unconstrained and $expr$ is a rather involved, non-linear expression, then it is likely that little information will be known about the whole expression. Hence, in both cases, there is little incentive in providing an accurate (and maybe expensive) over-approximation for the subexpression $expr$.

In this section we propose a heuristic approach to efficiently detect and propagate this lack of abstract information. We focus on the concept of *likely unconstrained* (LU) variables: we say that $x \in \mathbb{Var}$ is an LU variable (at program point

p) if the considered static analysis is likely unable to provide useful information on x. Thus, whenever x is LU, the static analysis can just forget it, since it brings little knowledge. It is worth stressing that the one we are proposing is an informal and heuristics-based definition, with no intrinsic correctness requirement: as we will see, whatever technique is adopted to compute the set of LU variables, its use will always result in a correct static analysis; the only risk, when forgetting too many variables, is to suffer a greater precision loss.

2.1 A Dataflow Analysis for LU Variables

We now informally sketch several variants of a forward dataflow analysis for the computation of LU variables, to be used on a CFG representation of the source program; if needed, the approach can be easily adapted to work with alternative program representations.

The Transfer Function for Non-relational Analyses. Let $\mathbb{Stmt}$ be the set of statements occurring in the CFG basic blocks, which for simplicity we assume to resemble 3-address code. Then, given the set $lu \subseteq \mathbb{Var}$ of variables that are LU before (abstractly) executing $s \in \mathbb{Stmt}$, the transfer function

$$[\![\cdot]\!]\colon \mathbb{Stmt} \times \wp(\mathbb{Var}) \to \wp(\mathbb{Var})$$

computes the set $[\![s]\!](lu)$ of variables that are LU after the execution of s. Clearly, the definition of $[\![\cdot]\!]$ depends on the target analysis: a more precise abstract domain will probably expose fewer LU variables. We first consider, as the reference target analysis, the *non-relational* abstract domain of intervals [12]. Intuitively, in this case a variable is LU if the corresponding interval is (likely) unbounded, i.e., $[-\infty, +\infty]$. Note that, in our definitions, we explicitly disregard those constraints that can be implicitly derived from the variable datatype; for instance, for a nondeterministic assignment $(x \leftarrow ?) \in \mathbb{Stmt}$, even when knowing that x is a signed integer stored in an 8-bit word, we will ignore the implicit constraints $-128 \leq x \leq 127$ and flag the variable x as LU. Hence, the transfer function for nondeterministic assignments is

$$[\![x \leftarrow ?]\!](lu) = lu \cup \{x\}.$$

The transfer function for the assignment statement $(x \leftarrow y \; op \; z) \in \mathbb{Stmt}$, where $op \in \{+, -, *, /, \%\}$ is an arithmetic operator and $x, y, z \in \mathbb{Var}$, is

$$[\![x \leftarrow y \; op \; z]\!](lu) = \begin{cases} lu \setminus \{x\}, & \text{if } y \notin lu \text{ and } z \notin lu, \\ & \text{or if } op = \% \text{ and } z \notin lu, \\ & \text{or if } op = - \text{ and } y = z; \\ lu \cup \{x\}, & \text{otherwise.} \end{cases}$$

Namely, x is going to be constrained (and hence removed from set lu) when both y and z are constrained, or when z is constrained and op is the modulus operator, or when hitting the corner case $x \leftarrow y - y$. For the special case when the third variable z is replaced by a constant argument $k \in \mathbb{Z}$, we can define

$$[\![x \leftarrow y \; op \; k]\!](lu) = \begin{cases} lu \setminus \{x\}, & \text{if } y \notin lu, \text{ or if } op = \%, \\ & \text{or if } op = * \text{ and } k = 0; \\ lu \cup \{x\}, & \text{otherwise.} \end{cases}$$

When evaluating Boolean guards, the abstract semantics works in a similar way: letting $(x \bowtie y) \in \mathbb{Stmt}$, where $x, y \in \mathbb{Var}$ and $\bowtie \in \{<, \leq, =, \geq, >\}$, we can define

$$[\![(x \bowtie y)]\!](lu) = \begin{cases} lu \setminus \{x\}, & \text{if } y \notin lu; \\ lu \setminus \{y\}, & \text{if } x \notin lu; \\ lu, & \text{otherwise.} \end{cases}$$

Similar definitions can be easily provided for all the other statements of the language.

As already said above, the transfer function we are proposing is just a way to heuristically *suggest* LU variables and hence it is subject to *both* false positives and false negatives. A false positive is obtained, for example, when processing the assignments $y \leftarrow 0$ and $x \leftarrow y * z$: since z is LU, the transfer function will also flag x as LU, even though the interval analysis would compute $x \in [0, 0]$. A false negative is obtained by processing the Boolean guards $(y \geq 0)$, $(z \leq 0)$ and the assignment $x \leftarrow y + z$: the transfer function will predict variable x to be constrained, even though the interval analysis computes $x \in [-\infty, +\infty]$.

The Case of Relational Analyses. If the target static analysis is based on an abstract domain tracking relational information, such as the domain of convex polyhedra [14], then the notion of LU variable no longer corresponds to the notion of unboundedness (as an example, consider the constraint $x = y$). Hence, the definition of the transfer function can be refined accordingly. As an example, when assuming that the domain is able to track linear constraints, a relational version $[\![\cdot]\!]^{\mathrm{rel}} \colon \mathbb{Stmt} \times \wp(\mathbb{Var}) \to \wp(\mathbb{Var})$ of the transfer function for the arithmetic assignment statements can be defined as follows:

$$[\![x \leftarrow y \; op \; z]\!]^{\mathrm{rel}}(lu) = \begin{cases} lu \setminus \{x, y, z\}, & \text{if } op \in \{+, -\}; \\ [\![x \leftarrow y \; op \; z]\!](lu) & \text{otherwise;} \end{cases}$$

$$[\![x \leftarrow y \; op \; k]\!]^{\mathrm{rel}}(lu) = \begin{cases} lu \setminus \{x\}, & \text{if } op = \%; \\ lu \setminus \{x, y\}, & \text{otherwise.} \end{cases}$$

Similarly, the relational version for the evaluation of Boolean guards can be defined as follows:

$$[\![(x \bowtie y)]\!]^{\mathrm{rel}}(lu) = lu \setminus \{x, y\}.$$

Once again, the definition of $[\![\cdot]\!]^{\mathrm{rel}}$ for the other kinds of statements poses no problem.

The Propagation of LU Information. Starting from the set lu_{pre} of variables that are LU at the start of a basic block, by applying function $[\![\cdot]\!]$ (resp., $[\![\cdot]\!]^{\text{rel}}$) to each statement in the basic block we can easily compute the set lu_{post} of LU variables at the end of the basic block. In order to complete the definition of our dataflow analysis we need to specify how this information is propagated through the CFG edges. As a first option we can say that a variable x is LU at the start of a basic block if there *exists* an edge entering the block along which x is LU; this corresponds to an analysis defined on the usual powerset lattice

$$\mathsf{LU}^{\exists} \triangleq \langle \wp(\mathbb{Var}), \subseteq, \varnothing, \mathbb{Var}, \cap, \cup \rangle,$$

having set inclusion as partial order and set union as join operator. This *existential* approach may be adequate when our goal is to obtain an *aggressive* LU oracle, which eagerly flags variables as LU, in particular when adopting the non-relational transfer function.

As an alternative, we can say that a variable x is LU at the start of a basic block only if x is LU along *all* the edges entering the block; this corresponds to an analysis defined on the dual lattice

$$\mathsf{LU}^{\forall} \triangleq \langle \wp(\mathbb{Var}), \supseteq, \mathbb{Var}, \varnothing, \cup, \cap \rangle,$$

having set intersection as join operator. When using this *universal* alternative, we will obtain a more *conservative* LU oracle, in particular when adopting the relational transfer function.

In all cases, the dataflow fixpoint computation is going to converge after a finite number of iterations, since the two transfer functions are monotone and the two lattices are finite. In summary, we have obtained four simple LU oracles ($\mathsf{LU}^{\exists}$, $\mathsf{LU}^{\forall}$, $\mathsf{LU}^{\exists}_{\text{rel}}$, $\mathsf{LU}^{\forall}_{\text{rel}}$) that, to some extent, should be able to guess which variables can be forgotten with a limited effect on the precision of the analysis; each of these can be used to guide a program transformation step that simplifies the target analysis, with the goal of improving its efficiency.

2.2 The Program Transformation Step

Algorithm 1 describes how the information about LU variables computed by any one of the oracles described before can be exploited to transform the input CFG. Intuitively, the program transformation should instruct the target static analysis to forget those variables that are not worth tracking. Hence, for each basic block $bb \in N$, we retrieve the corresponding set $lu = \text{LU}_{\text{post}}(bb)$ of program variables that, according to the chosen oracle, are LU at the exit of the basic block; then, each assignment statement $x \leftarrow expr$ in bb having as target a variable $x \in lu$ is replaced with the nondeterministic assignment $x \leftarrow ?$. Note that, for simplicity and ease of exposition, we are assuming that each program variable is assigned at most once in each basic block; this is not a significant restriction, since in most cases the input CFG satisfies much stronger assumptions, such as SSA form.

We now provide an example simulating the LU variable analysis and transformation steps on a simple portion of code, focusing on the $\mathsf{LU}^{\exists}$ and $\mathsf{LU}^{\forall}$ oracles, i.e., the non-relational case.

Algorithm 1: Program transformation

Input: $\langle N, E\rangle$ (input CFG), $\mathsf{LU}_{\text{post}} \colon N \to \wp(\mathbb{V}\mathrm{ar})$ (LU variables map)

foreach $bb \in N$ **do**
  let $lu = \mathsf{LU}_{\text{post}}(bb)$
  foreach $s = (x \leftarrow expr) \in bb$ **do**
    if $x \in lu$ **then**
      replace s with $s' = (x \leftarrow ?)$ in bb
    end
  end
end

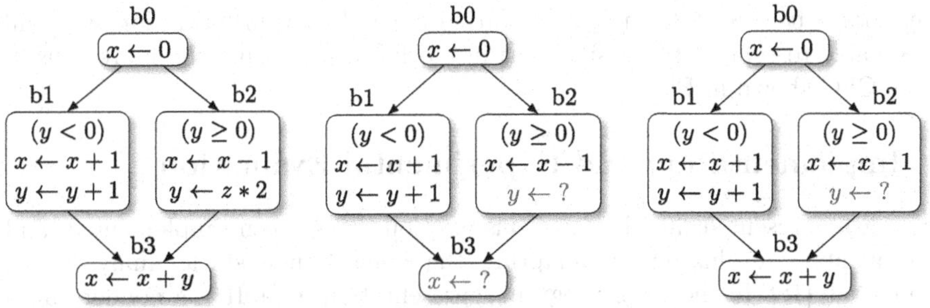

(a) Original CFG. (b) $\mathsf{LU}^{\exists}$ CFG. (c) $\mathsf{LU}^{\forall}$ CFG.

Fig. 1. The effect of LU variable propagation on a simple CFG.

Example 1. Consider the simple CFG in Fig. 1a, defined on the set of program variables $\mathbb{V}\mathrm{ar} = \{x, y, z\}$. Note that the CFG has no loops at all: this is a deliberate choice for exposition purposes, since our goal here is to show the basic steps of the LU analysis, rather than any detail related to the fixpoint computation (whose convergence poses no problems at all, as explained before). When considering the $\mathsf{LU}^{\exists}$ variant of the analysis, the set of LU variables at the start of the initial block b0 is initialized as $\mathrm{LU}_{\text{pre}}(\mathrm{b0}) = \mathbb{V}\mathrm{ar}$, i.e., all variables are assumed to be initially unconstrained. After processing the assignment in b0, we have that variable x is constrained, so that $\mathrm{LU}_{\text{post}}(\mathrm{b0}) = \{y, z\}$; this set is propagated to the start of basic blocks b1 and b2. The abstract execution of the Boolean guard statement at the start of b1 causes variable y to become constrained too; the following two assignments keep both x and y constrained, so that we obtain $\mathrm{LU}_{\text{post}}(\mathrm{b1}) = \{z\}$. Similarly, the Boolean guard statement at the start of b2 causes variable y to become constrained; however, the last assignment in b2 reinserts y in the LU set, because variable z is unconstrained; hence we obtain $\mathrm{LU}_{\text{post}}(\mathrm{b2}) = \{y, z\}$. The LU set at the start of block b3 is computed as

$$\mathrm{LU}_{\text{pre}}(\mathrm{b3}) = \mathrm{LU}_{\text{post}}(\mathrm{b1}) \cup \mathrm{LU}_{\text{post}}(\mathrm{b2}) = \{z\} \cup \{y, z\} = \{y, z\}.$$

Hence, after processing the assignment in b3, we obtain

$$\mathrm{LU}_{\text{post}}(\mathrm{b3}) = [\![x \leftarrow x + y]\!](\{y, z\}) = \{x, y, z\}.$$

At the end of the $\mathsf{LU}^{\exists}$ analysis, the CFG transformation of Algorithm 1 is applied, producing the CFG shown in Fig. 1b: here, two of the assignment statements have been replaced by nondeterministic assignments (highlighted in red).

When considering the $\mathsf{LU}^{\forall}$ heuristic variant, the analysis goes on exactly as before up to the computation of the LU set at the start of block b3: since in the universal variant the join operator is implemented as set intersection, we have

$$\mathrm{LU_{pre}}(\mathrm{b3}) = \mathrm{LU_{post}}(\mathrm{b1}) \cap \mathrm{LU_{post}}(\mathrm{b2}) = \{z\} \cap \{y, z\} = \{z\}$$

so that, when processing the assignment in b3, we obtain

$$\mathrm{LU_{post}}(\mathrm{b3}) = [\![x \leftarrow x + y]\!](\{z\}) = \{z\}.$$

Therefore, when using the universal variant, the CFG transformation step will not be able to replace the assignment in block b3, producing the more conservative CFG shown in Fig. 1c.

3 Implementation and Experimental Evaluation

The ideas presented in the previous section have been implemented and experimentally evaluated by adapting the open source static analysis tool Clam/Crab [18]. In the Crab program representation (CrabIR), a nondeterministic assignment to a program variable `var` is encoded by the abstract statement `havoc(var)`: the variable is said to be *havocked* by the execution of this statement. By adopting the Crab terminology, we will call *havoc analyses* the heuristic pre-analyses detecting LU variables, described in Sect. 2.1; similarly, we will call *havoc transformation* the program transformation described in Sect. 2.2; and we will call *havoc processing* the combination of these two computational steps. In contrast, we will call *target analysis* the static analysis phase collecting the invariants that are of interest for the end-user.

We now describe the steps of the overall analysis process, which are summarized in Fig. 2.

Step A. The input program under analysis is parsed by Clang/LLVM, producing the corresponding LLVM bitcode representation which is then fed as input to `clam-pp`, the Clam preprocessor component. By default, `clam-pp` applies a few program transformations, such as the lowering of switch statements into chains of conditional branches; more importantly, in our experiments we systematically enabled the inlining of known function calls, so as to improve the call context sensitivity of the analysis when performing an intra-procedural analysis. Note that Clam/Crab also supports inter-procedural analyses: these are typically faster than full inlining, but quite often produce less precise results.

Step B. The Clam component translates the LLVM bitcode representation into CrabIR, which is an intermediate representation specifically designed for static analysis; in this translation phase a few program constructs that the analysis is unable to model correctly and precisely, e.g., calls to unknown external functions, are replaced by (sequences of) `havoc` statements.

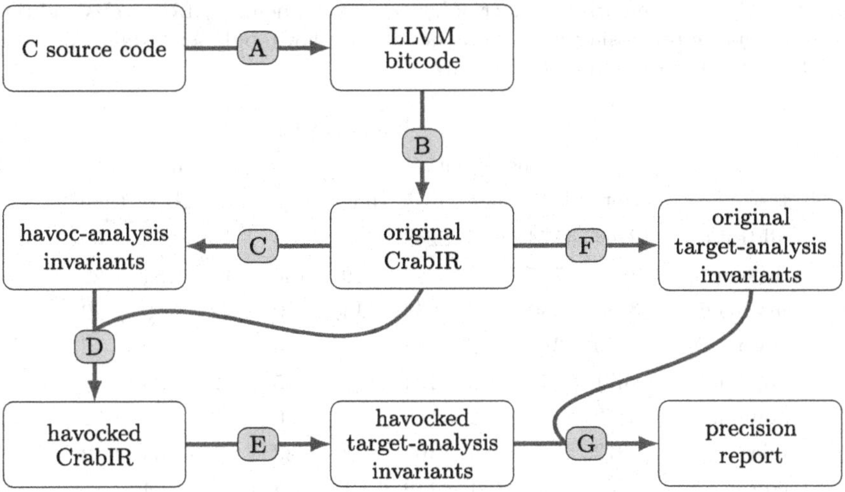

Fig. 2. Processing steps of the Clam/Crab toolchain, also including the precision comparison. Legenda: A = Clang/LLVM+clam-pp; B = Clam; C = havoc-analysis; D = havoc-propagation; E/F = target-analysis; G = clam-diff.

Step C. The *havoc analysis* computes the set of program variables that are likely unconstrained at the exit of each basic block of the CrabIR representation. As discussed in Sect. 2, this step is not subject to a strict safety requirement and hence, in principle, its implementation could be based on any reasonable heuristics; in our prototype we decided to model it as a classical static analysis and we implemented it by using the Crab component itself.

Step D. This step performs the *havoc transformation*, using the results of the analysis of Step C to rewrite the CrabIR representation produced by Step B; this is implemented as a simple visitor of the CrabIR CFG, corresponding to Algorithm 1, replacing assignment statements with `havoc` statements.

Step E. The final processing step is the target static analysis, which reuses the Crab component to compute an over-approximation of the semantics of the *havocked* CrabIR representation produced by Step D, using the target abstract domain chosen at configuration time. In our experimental evaluation, we considered the classical abstract domains of intervals and convex polyhedra. The invariants computed are stored and made available to the post-analysis processing phases (assertion checks, program annotations, etc.).

Step F. In contrast, when the havoc analysis is disabled (i.e., when the analysis toolchain is used without modification), the target static analysis is computed as described in Step E above, but starting from the *original* CrabIR representation produced by Step B.

Step G. The loop invariants produced in Steps E and F are systematically compared for precision using the `clam-diff` tool.

Table 1. WCET benchmarks: number of havocked statements by LU oracles and time spent in the havoc processing (ms). Note: details are shown only for tests having more than 200 abstract statements after inlining.

		stmts havocked							
		non-relational				relational			
test	stmts	$\mathsf{LU}^{\exists}$	time	$\mathsf{LU}^{\forall}$	time	$\mathsf{LU}^{\exists}_{\mathrm{rel}}$	time	$\mathsf{LU}^{\forall}_{\mathrm{rel}}$	time
all tests	12294	4578	35	2248	51	264	42	263	65
decompress	4332	2757	13	472	19	185	17	184	22
nsichneu	3582	630	10	630	14	0	12	0	20
cover	779	386	3	386	4	0	3	0	5
adpcm	671	194	2	194	3	25	2	25	4
statemate	562	5	2	5	2	0	2	0	2
ndes	372	103	1	102	2	33	1	33	2
edn	263	122	1	119	1	4	1	4	1
compress	214	30	1	29	1	2	1	2	1

3.1 The Impact of the Havoc Transformation

In our preliminary experimental evaluation, we first considered the C source files distributed with PAGAI [20], which are variants of benchmarks taken from the SNU real-time benchmark suite for WCET (worst-case execution time) analysis. When evaluating the precision of the target analyses we will focus on the invariants computed at widening points; for this reason, we discarded those few tests having no widening point at all, leaving us with 34 benchmarks. Table 1 summarizes the effects, on the CrabIR representation, of the 4 havoc transformation variants: the number of abstract statements in the original CrabIR is shown in the 2nd column; in the following 4 pairs of columns, for each variant of the havoc analysis, we show the number of assignment statements that are havocked when adopting this variant, as well as the time spent in the havoc processing steps (steps C and D of Fig. 2).

According to Table 1, the overall effect of the havoc transformation varies significantly depending on the considered test; also, the choice between non-relational and relational variants of the havoc analysis seems to have a much greater impact than the choice between existential and universal variants. Some of the tests are completely unaffected by the transformation (i.e., no statement at all is havocked): this happens only 8 times for the non-relational variants (only for the smallest benchmarks), but as many as 25 times for the relational variants (also including some of the biggest benchmarks). The percentage of havocked statements on all tests is 37.2% for the most aggressive variant $\mathsf{LU}^{\exists}$, while being 2.1% for the most conservative one $\mathsf{LU}^{\forall}_{\mathrm{rel}}$. Focusing on the 8 tests reported in the table, which are those having more than 200 statements after inlining, when using $\mathsf{LU}^{\exists}$ the percentage of havocked statements ranges from 0.9% to 63.6%

(median value 28.3%); in contrast, when using $\mathsf{LU}^{\forall}_{\mathrm{rel}}$ the percentage ranges from 0% to 8.9% (median value 1.2%).

Table 2. SV-COMP benchmarks: number of havocked statements by LU oracles and time spent in the havocking process (ms).

		stmts havocked							
		non-relational				relational			
test	stmts	$\mathsf{LU}^{\exists}$	time	$\mathsf{LU}^{\forall}$	time	$\mathsf{LU}^{\exists}_{\mathrm{rel}}$	time	$\mathsf{LU}^{\forall}_{\mathrm{rel}}$	time
all tests	353544	119509	7014	104509	12653	14591	6771	14411	12533
wl12xx	109101	89543	332	75667	578	942	453	915	726
rtlwifi	53456	5873	1481	5873	3391	5813	1418	5813	3049
w83781d	52909	5452	2933	5450	4366	2605	2645	2605	4706
brocade	37587	4703	308	4495	666	2098	309	2039	614
libfc	31272	3108	1285	2811	2472	66	1263	65	2227
vmxnet3	19598	3983	175	3849	311	496	184	495	327
mdc	17104	2333	154	2168	314	1017	149	981	322
firewire	13196	1902	185	1701	284	800	185	747	282
solos	12465	2302	122	2301	199	732	131	730	210
abituguru	6856	310	39	194	72	22	34	21	70

Since many of considered benchmarks are synthetic ones, we extended our experimental evaluation by also considering 10 Linux drivers from the SV-COMP repository.[1] The results for these bigger benchmarks, shown in Table 2, confirm most of the observations done above, except that now the havoc transformation affects all the tests. Considering first the most aggressive variant $\mathsf{LU}^{\exists}$, the percentage of havocked statements on all tests is 33.8%, ranging from 4.5% to 82.1% (median value 13.1%); in contrast, when considering the most conservative variant $\mathsf{LU}^{\forall}_{\mathrm{rel}}$, the percentage of havocked statements on all tests is 4.1%, ranging from 0.2% to 10.9% (median value 5.2%).

In summary, on the considered benchmarks, the transformations based on the relational variants seem really conservative, whereas the non-relational ones look rather aggressive, probably leading to significant effects on the precision and efficiency of the target analysis. Regarding efficiency, it should be stressed that the current implementation of the havoc analysis and transformation steps is just a prototype, hence subject to optimizations; this holds in particular for step C (havoc analysis), as only a small percentage of the havoc processing time is spent in step D (havoc transformation).

[1] https://github.com/sosy-lab/sv-benchmarks/c/ldv-linux-4.2-rc1.

3.2 Precision and Efficiency of the Target Analyses

The next step in our experiments is the evaluation of the effect of the considered program transformation on the precision and efficiency of the target analyses. To this end, we consider the classical numerical analyses based on the abstract domains of intervals [12] and convex polyhedra [14]. For the first domain we adopted the implementation that is built-in in Crab, whereas for the latter we opted for the domain of convex polyhedra provided by the PPLite library [5–7], which is accessible in Crab via the generic Apron interface [23]. Note that we are considering the Cartesian factored variant [19,29] of the domain of convex polyhedra, which greatly improves the efficiency of the classical polyhedral analysis by dynamically computing *optimal* variable packs, thereby incurring no precision loss; a recent experimental evaluation [2] has shown that the PPLite's implementation of this domain is competitive with the one provided by ELINA [29], which is considered state-of-the-art. We stress that the goal of our oracle-based program transformation is to obtain further, significant efficiency improvements and, to this end, a limited precision loss is an acceptable trade-off.

Intervals. When considering a non-relational target analysis, it is natural to also consider a non-relational variant for the havoc analysis step. For the WCET benchmarks, even when using the most aggressive havoc analysis $\mathsf{LU}^{\exists}$, we obtain the same precision of the original interval analysis for all the 34 C programs of the benchmark suite; that is, we compute the same invariants on all the 288 widening points. The differences in precision for the Linux drivers are summarized in Table 3. The first (resp., second) row shows the results of the overall comparison in terms of number (resp., percentage) of widening points on which the invariant computed on the havocked CrabIR is equivalent (EQ), stronger (LT), weaker (GT) and uncomparable (UN) with respect to the invariant computed on the original CrabIR. In this case, we record precision losses for 2 tests for the $\mathsf{LU}^{\exists}$ havoc analysis and 1 test for the $\mathsf{LU}^{\forall}$ havoc analysis, whose details are shown in the next two rows of the table; the same precision is obtained on the other 8 tests, whose details are omitted. For the $\mathsf{LU}^{\exists}$ analysis, the precision loss affects 121 invariants (~4% of all invariants computed); this number decreases to 97 invariants (~3%) when using $\mathsf{LU}^{\forall}$. Note that, quite often, these precision losses are due to just one or two interval constraints missing from the weaker invariants: as a matter of fact, when counting the number of constraints occurring in the invariants, it can be seen that the havocked analyses are able to compute ~ 99% of the constraints computed by the original interval analysis. This is an impressive result, when considering that it has been obtained by using rather aggressive program transformations; for instance, we obtain no precision loss on driver `wl12xx` even when havocking more than 80% of its 109K statements (see the first line in Table 2).

Regarding the impact on the efficiency of the target analysis, our experiments on the domain of intervals have shown that the havocked analysis pipeline seems unable to trigger significant efficiency improvements: no matter if considering the WCET or the SV-COMP benchmarks, the original analysis is as efficient

Table 3. SV-COMP benchmarks: invariant comparison for the interval domain. Boldface text highlights the differences between $\mathsf{LU}^{\exists}$ and $\mathsf{LU}^{\forall}$.

		$\mathsf{LU}^{\exists}$ *vs* original				$\mathsf{LU}^{\forall}$ *vs* original			
		EQ	LT	GT	UN	EQ	LT	GT	UN
# INVS	3102	2981	0	121	0	3005	0	97	0
% INVS	100.00	96.10	0	3.90	0	96.87	0	3.13	0
vmxnet3	513	416	0	97	0	416	0	97	0
mdc	112	**88**	0	**24**	0	**112**	0	**0**	0

as (sometimes even more efficient than) the havocked ones. This was somehow expected, since in our prototype we are only replacing deterministic assignment statements with nondeterministic ones and, in both cases, the abstract execution on the interval domain is very efficient; hence, any small efficiency improvement obtained is likely masked by the overheads of the modified analysis toolchain. Roughly speaking, in order to obtain a measurable effect on the precision/efficiency trade-off, we have to consider abstract domains that are computationally more expensive.

Table 4. WCET benchmarks: invariant comparison for the polyhedra domain. Boldface text highlights the differences between $\mathsf{LU}^{\exists}$ and $\mathsf{LU}^{\forall}$ analyses.

		$\mathsf{LU}^{\exists}$ *vs* original				$\mathsf{LU}^{\forall}$ *vs* original			
		EQ	LT	GT	UN	EQ	LT	GT	UN
# INVS	288	244	0	44	0	249	0	39	0
% INVS	100.00	84.72	0	15.28	0	86.46	0	13.54	0
decompress	79	67	0	12	0	67	0	12	0
adpcm	27	12	0	15	0	12	0	15	0
edn	12	9	0	3	0	9	0	3	0
lms	12	10	0	2	0	10	0	2	0
ndes	12	9	0	3	0	9	0	3	0
qsort-exam	6	**1**	0	**5**	0	**6**	0	**0**	0
cover	3	0	0	3	0	0	0	3	0
insertsort	2	1	0	1	0	1	0	1	0

Convex Polyhedra. When considering a relational target analysis, it would seem natural to consider the relational variants, $\mathsf{LU}^{\exists}_{\text{rel}}$ and $\mathsf{LU}^{\forall}_{\text{rel}}$, of the havoc analysis. Our first experiments, however, have shown that these variants are too conservative and hence probably unable to obtain the efficiency improvements we are looking for. Since our end goal is to obtain a practical way to effectively tune the efficiency/precision trade-off of the target analysis, we keep focusing on the non-relational variants $\mathsf{LU}^\exists$ and $\mathsf{LU}^\forall$, trading the corresponding precision losses for efficiency.

In Table 4, having the same structure of Table 3, we report the precision comparison for the WCET benchmarks. In this case, we obtain the same results, no matter if using $\mathsf{LU}^\exists$ or $\mathsf{LU}^\forall$, for 26 of the 34 tests; hence the table shows the details of the precision regressions for the remaining 8 tests. When comparing the precision of $\mathsf{LU}^\exists$ and $\mathsf{LU}^\forall$ with respect to the classification of the invariants into the EQ, LT, GT and UN categories, we observe a single difference on the `qsort-exam` test, where $\mathsf{LU}^\forall$ is able to maintain the same precision of the original analysis on all the 6 widening points. Note that $\mathsf{LU}^\forall$ obtains other precision improvements with respect to $\mathsf{LU}^\exists$ on test `decompress`, in terms of the number of constraints computed, but these are not sufficient to influence the invariant classification (i.e., $\mathsf{LU}^\forall$ obtains smaller precision losses).

Table 5. SV-COMP benchmarks: invariant comparison for the polyhedra domain; Boldface text highlights the precision differences between $\mathsf{LU}^\exists$ and $\mathsf{LU}^\forall$ analyses. The last 3 columns report the efficiency comparison for $\mathsf{LU}^\forall$.

		$\mathsf{LU}^\exists$ *vs* original				$\mathsf{LU}^\forall$ *vs* original						
		EQ	LT	GT	UN	EQ	LT	GT	UN			
# INVS	3102	1389	0	1713	0	1485	0	1617	0	time (secs)		speed-up
% INVS	100.00	44.78	0	55.22	0	47.83	0	53.17	0	original	$\mathsf{LU}^\forall$	
vmxnet3	513	190	0	323	0	190	0	323	0	134.21	36.39	3.69
brocade	511	154	0	357	0	154	0	357	0	141.10	105.92	1.33
firewire	499	319	0	180	0	319	0	180	0	65.39	20.92	3.13
w83781d	356	95	0	261	0	95	0	261	0	110.76	110.47	1.00
solos	303	104	0	199	0	104	0	199	0	79.56	9.67	8.23
libfc	295	295	0	0	0	295	0	0	0	167.17	104.68	1.60
rtlwifi	208	5	0	203	0	5	0	203	0	79.86	68.64	1.16
abituguru	169	**91**	0	**78**	0	**168**	0	**1**	0	94.16	54.22	1.74
wl12xx	136	92	0	44	0	92	0	44	0	182.22	22.29	8.17
mdc	112	**44**	0	**68**	0	**63**	0	**49**	0	107.30	24.31	4.41

The precision comparison for the Linux driver benchmarks is reported in Table 5: on these bigger tests the havocked target analysis reports precision losses on all tests with the exception of `libfc`. The universal variant $\mathsf{LU}^\forall$ is able to significantly improve precision with respect to $\mathsf{LU}^\exists$, increasing the number of EQ invariants for tests `abituguru` and `mdc`; precision improvements are also obtained by $\mathsf{LU}^\forall$ on another three drivers (`vmxnet3`, `brocade`, `wl12xx`), but again these do not affect the invariant classification.

A more detailed analysis of the experimental results shows that, when comparing the overall number of constraints that compose the computed invariants, the havocked target analyses are able to produce approximately 90% of all the constraints that are obtained when using the original target analysis, with the $\mathsf{LU}^{\forall}$ variant scoring ~ 1% better than the $\mathsf{LU}^{\exists}$ variant.

Our efficiency comparison for the domain of convex polyhedra focuses on the havoc transformation based on the $\mathsf{LU}^{\forall}$ oracle, which as discussed above is able to obtain slightly better results with respect to the $\mathsf{LU}^{\exists}$ oracle. The results for the SV-COMP benchmarks are reported in the last three columns of Table 5: the first of these columns shows the baseline for the comparison, i.e., the time spent when the convex polyhedra analysis works on the original CrabIR; the second column shows the time spent when the target analysis works on the havocked CrabIR obtained when using the $\mathsf{LU}^{\forall}$ oracle; in the third column we report the speed-up obtained. We observe a speed-up for all the tests with the exception of `w83781d`; the positive speed-ups range from 1.16 (`rtlwifi`) to 8.23 (`solos`); the geometric mean of the speed-ups, computed on all the 10 tests, is 2.61.

We are omitting the details of a corresponding efficiency comparison for the WCET benchmark, mainly due to the synthetic nature of the tests: in practice, most of them complete the analysis immediately, making a reliable comparison almost impossible; the others are characterized by (relatively) much higher analysis times, so that they could be interpreted as outliers when compared to the first group. When restricting attention to the few WCET tests whose target analysis takes more than a second, the speed-up obtained ranges between 1.11 and 2.49 (geometric mean 1.59).

It is worth stressing that the time shown are those spent in the *overall* analysis pipeline, only excluding the post-analysis steps that are meant to store and later compare the loop invariants. Namely, with reference to Fig. 2, the time spent in steps A, B and F by the original analysis is compared to the time spent in steps A, B, C, D and E by the modified pipeline. The reader interested in factoring out the time spent during the havoc processing phases (C and D) is referred to Tables 1 and 2 discussed previously.

4 Related Work

The four variants of LU variable analysis described in Sect. 2.1 and the abstract program transformation outlined in Sect. 2.2, as a whole, can be seen as an instance of the Abstract Compilation approach [21,31] to Abstract Interpretation [12]. A few examples [1,9,17,32] of application of Abstract Compilation have already been briefly recalled in Sect. 1; other examples have been recently discussed in [15]. A notable distinction between the current proposal and most of the approaches in the literature is that we do not require the program transformation to *fully* preserve the abstract semantics of the program: since our goal is to tune the efficiency/precision trade-off, we explicitly allow for (hopefully limited) precision losses in the transformation step. In our opinion, this is one of the most relevant differences between abstract and concrete (i.e., traditional) compilation.

It would be tempting to cast our pre-analyses as instances of the A^2I framework [13] and, in particular, as examples of offline meta-abstract interpretations.

This would not be fully appropriate: as we already noted, our oracles have no formal correctness requirement (e.g., they can incur both false positives and false negatives, without affecting the correctness of the target analysis) and hence they cannot be seen as *proper* abstract interpretations. This is also the main difference between our current proposal and similar approaches that, in contrast, are firmly based on the theory of Abstract Interpretation. As notable examples we mention the research work on abstract program slicing (e.g., [22,25]) and more generally dependency analysis [11]. For instance, abstract program slicing aims at removing from the program those instructions that are definitely not affecting the end result of the analysis (possibly modulo a specific slicing criterion); hence, precision losses are explicitly forbidden, while they are legitimate when using our havoc transformation.

The idea to use heuristic approaches to tune the precision/efficiency trade-off of a static analysis is clearly not new to this paper. For the case of numeric properties, the most known example is probably the variable packing technique adopted by Astrée [8, Section 7.2.1]: here, a pre-analysis phase based on a syntactic heuristics, with no formal correctness requirement as in our case, computes for each portion of the program some relatively small variable packs, which are later used during the proper analysis phase to enable the precision of a relational analysis (in that case, the abstract domain of octagons) while keeping under control its computational cost. Similarly, [28] proposes a pre-analysis phase to estimate the impact on precision of context-sensitivity for an inter-procedural program analysis, so as to enable it (and the corresponding computational costs) only when a precision improvement is likely obtained. The overall approach has been extended to non-numeric properties: for instance, [30] and [24] propose two lightweight pre-analyses that can improve the precision of pointer analyses by driving them to dynamically switch between different levels of (context, object, type) sensitivity.

5 Conclusion

In this paper we have proposed a program transformation that improves the efficiency of a classical numeric static analysis by trading some of its precision: this works by selectively havocking some of the abstract assignments in the program, so as to forget all information on the assigned variable. The havocking process is guided by an oracle, whose goal is to predict whether or not the assigned variable would likely be unconstrained anyway, thereby limiting the precision loss. A main contribution of this paper is the design and experimental evaluation of four variants of a lightweight dataflow analysis that implement reasonably precise oracles. The precision and efficiency of the target static analysis using the program transformation as a preprocessing step have been evaluated on two benchmark suites, identifying the universal non-relational oracle as the most promising one. When the havoc transformation is guided by this oracle, the static analysis based on the domain of convex polyhedra is able to achieve significant efficiency improvements, while facing limited precision losses.

Other aspects of the proposed technique will be investigated in future work. In the first place, the current oracle can be refined by applying other heuristics or machine learning techniques, so as to further mitigate the precision losses in the target analysis while maintaining an aggressive transformation leading to efficiency gains. Secondly, the program transformation itself can be enhanced, by considering the propagation of unknown information to other kinds of abstract statements and the interaction of the havocking process with other program transformations, such as abstract dead code elimination and CFG simplifications. Also, the analysis and program transformation can be extended to be integrated in source-level program analysis tools, such as MOPSA [26], so as to investigate its effectiveness when going beyond 3-address code syntax and considering more general arithmetic expressions. Finally, it would be interesting to evaluate the applicability of the approach to non-numerical analyses, such as string analyses [3,4].

Acknowledgements. The authors would like to thank the anonymous reviewers for their useful comments and suggestions. This work was partially supported by Bando di Ateneo per la ricerca 2022, founded by University of Parma, project number: MUR_DM737_2022_FIL_PROGETTI_B_ARCERI_COFIN.

References

1. Amato, G., Spoto, F.: Abstract compilation for sharing analysis. In: Kuchen, H., Ueda, K. (eds.) FLOPS 2001. LNCS, vol. 2024, pp. 311–325. Springer, Heidelberg (2001). https://doi.org/10.1007/3-540-44716-4_20
2. Arceri, V., Dolcetti, G., Zaffanella, E.: Speeding up static analysis with the split operator. In: Ferrara, P., Hadarean, L. (eds.) Proceedings of the 12th ACM SIGPLAN International Workshop on the State of the Art in Program Analysis, SOAP 2023, Orlando, FL, USA, 17 June 2023, pp. 14–19. ACM (2023). https://doi.org/10.1145/3589250.3596141
3. Arceri, V., Mastroeni, I.: Analyzing dynamic code: a sound abstract interpreter for *Evil* eval. ACM Trans. Priv. Secur. **24**(2), 10:1–10:38 (2021). https://doi.org/10.1145/3426470
4. Arceri, V., Olliaro, M., Cortesi, A., Ferrara, P.: Relational string abstract domains. In: Finkbeiner, B., Wies, T. (eds.) VMCAI 2022. LNCS, vol. 13182, pp. 20–42. Springer, Cham (2022). https://doi.org/10.1007/978-3-030-94583-1_2
5. Becchi, A., Zaffanella, E.: A direct encoding for NNC polyhedra. In: Chockler, H., Weissenbacher, G. (eds.) CAV 2018. LNCS, vol. 10981, pp. 230–248. Springer, Cham (2018). https://doi.org/10.1007/978-3-319-96145-3_13
6. Becchi, A., Zaffanella, E.: An efficient abstract domain for not necessarily closed polyhedra. In: Podelski, A. (ed.) SAS 2018. LNCS, vol. 11002, pp. 146–165. Springer, Cham (2018). https://doi.org/10.1007/978-3-319-99725-4_11
7. Becchi, A., Zaffanella, E.: PPLite: zero-overhead encoding of NNC polyhedra. Inf. Comput. **275**, 104620 (2020). https://doi.org/10.1016/j.ic.2020.104620
8. Blanchet, B., et al.: A static analyzer for large safety-critical software. In: Cytron, R., Gupta, R. (eds.) Proceedings of the ACM SIGPLAN 2003 Conference on Programming Language Design and Implementation 2003, San Diego, California, USA, 9–11 June 2003, pp. 196–207. ACM (2003). https://doi.org/10.1145/781131.781153

9. Boucher, D., Feeley, M.: Abstract compilation: a new implementation paradigm for static analysis. In: Gyimóthy, T. (ed.) CC 1996. LNCS, vol. 1060, pp. 192–207. Springer, Heidelberg (1996). https://doi.org/10.1007/3-540-61053-7_62
10. Brat, G., Navas, J.A., Shi, N., Venet, A.: IKOS: a framework for static analysis based on abstract interpretation. In: Giannakopoulou, D., Salaün, G. (eds.) SEFM 2014. LNCS, vol. 8702, pp. 271–277. Springer, Cham (2014). https://doi.org/10.1007/978-3-319-10431-7_20
11. Cousot, P.: Abstract semantic dependency. In: Chang, B.-Y.E. (ed.) SAS 2019. LNCS, vol. 11822, pp. 389–410. Springer, Cham (2019). https://doi.org/10.1007/978-3-030-32304-2_19
12. Cousot, P., Cousot, R.: Abstract interpretation: a unified lattice model for static analysis of programs by construction or approximation of fixpoints. In: Graham, R.M., Harrison, M.A., Sethi, R. (eds.) Conference Record of the Fourth ACM Symposium on Principles of Programming Languages, Los Angeles, California, USA, January 1977, pp. 238–252. ACM (1977). https://doi.org/10.1145/512950.512973
13. Cousot, P., Giacobazzi, R., Ranzato, F.: A^2I: abstract^2 interpretation. Proc. ACM Program. Lang. **3**(POPL), 42:1–42:31 (2019). https://doi.org/10.1145/3290355
14. Cousot, P., Halbwachs, N.: Automatic discovery of linear restraints among variables of a program. In: Aho, A.V., Zilles, S.N., Szymanski, T.G. (eds.) Conference Record of the Fifth Annual ACM Symposium on Principles of Programming Languages, Tucson, Arizona, USA, January 1978, pp. 84–96. ACM Press (1978). https://doi.org/10.1145/512760.512770
15. De Angelis, E., Fioravanti, F., Gallagher, J.P., Hermenegildo, M.V., Pettorossi, A., Proietti, M.: Analysis and transformation of constrained horn clauses for program verification. Theory Pract. Log. Program. **22**(6), 974–1042 (2022). https://doi.org/10.1017/S1471068421000211
16. Ferrara, P., Negrini, L., Arceri, V., Cortesi, A.: Static analysis for dummies: experiencing LiSA. In: Do, L.N.Q., Urban, C. (eds.) SOAP@PLDI 2021: Proceedings of the 10th ACM SIGPLAN International Workshop on the State of the Art in Program Analysis, Virtual Event, Canada, 22 June 2021, pp. 1–6. ACM (2021). https://doi.org/10.1145/3460946.3464316
17. Giacobazzi, R., Debray, S.K., Levi, G.: Generalized semantics and abstract interpretation for constraint logic programs. J. Log. Program. **25**(3), 191–247 (1995). https://doi.org/10.1016/0743-1066(95)00038-0
18. Gurfinkel, A., Navas, J.A.: Abstract interpretation of LLVM with a region-based memory model. In: Bloem, R., Dimitrova, R., Fan, C., Sharygina, N. (eds.) NSV VSTTE 2021. LNPSE, vol. 13124, pp. 122–144. Springer, Cham (2021). https://doi.org/10.1007/978-3-030-95561-8_8
19. Halbwachs, N., Merchat, D., Gonnord, L.: Some ways to reduce the space dimension in polyhedra computations. Formal Methods Syst. Des. **29**(1), 79–95 (2006). https://doi.org/10.1007/s10703-006-0013-2
20. Henry, J., Monniaux, D., Moy, M.: PAGAI: a path sensitive static analyser. In: Jeannet, B. (ed.) Third Workshop on Tools for Automatic Program Analysis, TAPAS 2012. Electronic Notes in Theoretical Computer Science, Deauville, France, 14 September 2012, vol. 289, pp. 15–25. Elsevier (2012). https://doi.org/10.1016/j.entcs.2012.11.003
21. Hermenegildo, M.V., Warren, R.A., Debray, S.K.: Global flow analysis as a practical compilation tool. J. Log. Program. **13**(4), 349–366 (1992). https://doi.org/10.1016/0743-1066(92)90053-6

22. Hong, H.S., Lee, I., Sokolsky, O.: Abstract slicing: a new approach to program slicing based on abstract interpretation and model checking. In: 5th IEEE International Workshop on Source Code Analysis and Manipulation (SCAM 2005), Budapest, Hungary, 30 September–1 October 2005, pp. 25–34. IEEE Computer Society (2005). https://doi.org/10.1109/SCAM.2005.2
23. Jeannet, B., Miné, A.: APRON: a library of numerical abstract domains for static analysis. In: Bouajjani, A., Maler, O. (eds.) CAV 2009. LNCS, vol. 5643, pp. 661–667. Springer, Heidelberg (2009). https://doi.org/10.1007/978-3-642-02658-4_52
24. Li, Y., Tan, T., Møller, A., Smaragdakis, Y.: A principled approach to selective context sensitivity for pointer analysis. ACM Trans. Program. Lang. Syst. **42**(2), 10:1–10:40 (2020). https://doi.org/10.1145/3381915
25. Mastroeni, I., Zanardini, D.: Abstract program slicing: an abstract interpretation-based approach to program slicing. ACM Trans. Comput. Log. **18**(1), 7:1–7:58 (2017). https://doi.org/10.1145/3029052
26. Monat, R., Ouadjaout, A., Miné, A.: A multilanguage static analysis of Python programs with native C extensions. In: Drăgoi, C., Mukherjee, S., Namjoshi, K. (eds.) SAS 2021. LNCS, vol. 12913, pp. 323–345. Springer, Cham (2021). https://doi.org/10.1007/978-3-030-88806-0_16
27. Negrini, L., Ferrara, P., Arceri, V., Cortesi, A.: LiSA: a generic framework for multilanguage static analysis. In: Arceri, V., Cortesi, A., Ferrara, P., Olliaro, M. (eds.) Challenges of Software Verification. ISRL, vol. 238, pp. 19–42. Springer, Singapore (2023). https://doi.org/10.1007/978-981-19-9601-6_2
28. Oh, H., Lee, W., Heo, K., Yang, H., Yi, K.: Selective X-sensitive analysis guided by impact pre-analysis. ACM Trans. Program. Lang. Syst. **38**(2), 6:1–6:45 (2016). https://doi.org/10.1145/2821504
29. Singh, G., Püschel, M., Vechev, M.T.: Fast polyhedra abstract domain. In: Castagna, G., Gordon, A.D. (eds.) Proceedings of the 44th ACM SIGPLAN Symposium on Principles of Programming Languages, POPL 2017, Paris, France, 18–20 January 2017, pp. 46–59. ACM (2017). https://doi.org/10.1145/3009837.3009885
30. Tan, T., Li, Y., Xue, J.: Efficient and precise points-to analysis: modeling the heap by merging equivalent automata. In: Cohen, A., Vechev, M.T. (eds.) Proceedings of the 38th ACM SIGPLAN Conference on Programming Language Design and Implementation, PLDI 2017, Barcelona, Spain, 18–23 June 2017, pp. 278–291. ACM (2017). https://doi.org/10.1145/3062341.3062360
31. Warren, R.A., Hermenegildo, M.V., Debray, S.K.: On the practicality of global flow analysis of logic programs. In: Kowalski, R.A., Bowen, K.A. (eds.) Logic Programming, Proceedings of the Fifth International Conference and Symposium, Seattle, Washington, USA, 15–19 August 1988, vol. 2, pp. 684–699. MIT Press (1988)
32. Wei, G., Chen, Y., Rompf, T.: Staged abstract interpreters: fast and modular whole-program analysis via meta-programming. Proc. ACM Program. Lang. **3**(OOPSLA), 126:1–126:32 (2019). https://doi.org/10.1145/3360552

Symbolic Transformation of Expressions in Modular Arithmetic

Jérôme Boillot[1] (✉) and Jérôme Feret[1,2]

[1] École Normale Supérieure, Université PSL, Paris, France
{jerome.boillot,jerome.feret}@ens.fr
[2] INRIA, Paris, France

Abstract. We present symbolic methods to improve the precision of static analyses of modular integer expressions based on Abstract Interpretation. Like similar symbolic methods, the idea is to simplify on-the-fly arithmetic expressions before they are given to abstract transfer functions of underlying abstract domains. When manipulating fixed-length integer data types, casts and overflows generally act like modulo computations which hinder the use of symbolic techniques. The goal of this article is to formalize how modulo operations can be safely eliminated by abstracting arbitrary arithmetic expressions into sum, product, or division of linear forms with integer coefficients, while simplifying them. We provide some rules to simplify arithmetic expressions that are involved in the computation of linear interpolations, while ensuring the soundness of the transformation.
All these methods have been incorporated within the ASTRÉE static analyzer that checks for the absence of run-time errors in embedded critical software, but also in an available toy abstract interpreter. The effects of our new abstract domain are then evaluated on several code excerpts from industrial code.

Keywords: Modular Arithmetic · Program Transformation · Symbolic Propagation · Abstract Intepretation · Interpolation

1 Introduction

An important Computer Science challenge is to prove that given programs cannot crash. It is particularly needed in critical embedded applications such as planes, where potential errors can be fatal. Because of RICE's theorem, we know that it is impossible to create an analyzer that is both *automatic* (it does not require user interaction to finish, and can do so in finite time), *sound* (any proved

M. V. Hermenegildo and J. F. Morales (Eds.): SAS 2023, LNCS 14284, pp. 84–113, 2023.
https://doi.org/10.1007/978-3-031-44245-2_6

```c
int x, y;
if (x >= y) {
  unsigned int r = (unsigned int) x - y;
  assert(r == (int64_t) x - y);
}
```

(a). C language

$X \leftarrow [-2^{31}, 2^{31}[;$
$Y \leftarrow [-2^{31}, 2^{31}[;$
if $X + -Y \geq 0$ **then**
  $R \leftarrow ((X \textbf{ mod } [0, 2^{32}[) + -(Y \textbf{ mod } [0, 2^{32}[))$
    $\hookrightarrow \textbf{ mod } [0, 2^{32}[;$
  $//\ R = X - Y$
endif

(b). Article's language

Fig. 1. Distance computation example.

property of the program actually holds), and *complete* (it is able to prove any property that holds). Because in general the most precise invariants are not computable, we decide to drop the completeness constraint. This means such analyzer can raise alarms that are false-positives. We are particularly interested in the Abstract Interpretation framework [5,6] and properties of integer expressions. Thus, the static analyzer we will present is parameterized by an auxiliary numerical abstract domain we will use to compute and represent numerical properties of program instructions.

There exist different numerical abstract domains that vary in precision, but also in time and memory costs. For example, we could name the interval domain [4] that computes sound variable bounds, and the polyhedra domain [8] that discovers linear inequalities. In order to prove the correctness of a program, it is sometimes necessary to retain information about the relationships between variables (*e.g.*, equalities between variables, or linear inequalities like in the polyhedron domain). Such abstract domains are called relational, and their usage can be very costly. That is why symbolic methods have been developed: to keep relations between variables by reasoning directly over the arithmetic expressions, and to apply sound program transformations on-the-fly to ease the analysis. This is what [21] describes with its abstraction of any arithmetic expressions into linear forms with interval coefficients. This abstraction allows algebraic simplifications.

When programming in languages, like C, that allow usage of fixed-length integers, it is important to consider how overflows and casts between different integer data types are handled. In C, this semantics is detailed in the C Standard [14]; we take into account that, in addition to explicit casts, some implicit casts are performed in arithmetic operations (*e.g.*, via the integer promotion). Unsigned integers do not overflow, the result is reduced modulo the largest value of the resulting type plus one. Casts also correspond to the use of a modulo. Thus, if we want to use symbolic methods, it appears necessary to deal with those modulo computations in the abstract representation.

In this paper, we present symbolic enhancement techniques similar to the ones described in [21], but that allow safe modulo elimination when it is possible. Consider, for instance, the program of Fig. 1 that computes the distance between X and Y when $X \geq Y$. As for every further introducing examples, we provide the C code in Fig. 1a and the representation in our internal language in Fig. 1b. Please note that in all the following examples the `int` data type is

```c
int x, p0, p1;
unsigned int a = (unsigned int) x - p0;
unsigned int b = (unsigned int) p1 - x;
if (p1 >= p0) {
  unsigned int r = a + b;
  assert(r == (int64_t) p1 - p0);
}
```

(a). C language

$X \leftarrow [-2^{31}, 2^{31}[$;
$P_0 \leftarrow [-2^{31}, 2^{31}[$;
$P_1 \leftarrow [-2^{31}, 2^{31}[$;
$A \leftarrow ((X \textbf{ mod } [0, 2^{32}[) + -(P_0 \textbf{ mod } [0, 2^{32}[))$
↪ $\textbf{mod } [0, 2^{32}[$;
$B \leftarrow ((P_1 \textbf{ mod } [0, 2^{32}[) + -(X \textbf{ mod } [0, 2^{32}[))$
↪ $\textbf{mod } [0, 2^{32}[$;
if $P_1 + -P_0 \geq 0$ **then**
  $R \leftarrow (A + B) \textbf{ mod } [0, 2^{32}[$;
  // $R = P_1 - P_0$
endif

(b). Article's language

Fig. 2. Variable elimination example.

```c
unsigned int x, x0, x1, y0, y1;
if (x0 <= x && x <= x1) {
  if (x0 != x1 && y0 <= y1) {
    unsigned int r = y0 + ((uint64_t)
    ↪ (x-x0) * (y1-y0) / (x1-x0));
    assert(y0 <= r && r <= y1);
  }
}
```

(a). C language

if $X + -X_0 \geq 0$ **then**
  if $X + -X_1 \leq 0$ **then**
    if $X_0 + -X_1 \neq 0$ **then**
      if $Y_0 + -Y_1 \leq 0$ **then**
        $R \leftarrow Y_0 + ((X + -X_0) \times (Y_1 + -Y_0)) /$
        ↪ $(X_1 + -X_0)$;
        // $Y_0 \leq R \leq Y_1$
      endif;
    endif;
  endif;
endif

(b). Article's language (simplified)

Fig. 3. First example of linear interpolation computation.

consistently represented using a 32-bit format. Nevertheless, this representation remains a parameter of the analysis. We expect the analyzer to infer that, when $X \geq Y$ is verified, $R = X - Y$. Note that $X \textbf{ mod } [0, 2^{32}[\neq X$ and the same holds with Y. So, traditional abstract domains like integers or polyhedron, or even linearization, could not infer this invariant. But our *modulo elimination* technique allows us to compute it. In our second example in Fig. 2 we would like to replace the expression $A+B$ by $P_1 - P_0$ by making the occurrences of the variable X in the expressions A and B cancel each other. This is made possible by the *symbolic constant propagation* domain. In addition, in our latest example in Fig. 3 (modulos are omitted for readability), if all conditions are met R is the linear interpolation of some function f in X such that $f(X_0) = Y_0$ and $f(X_1) = Y_1$. Then, R should be between Y_0 and Y_1. The abstract domain we present is able to compute such invariants thanks to the *interpolation detection step* in the reduction heuristic.

Related Work. The problem of analyzing programs with modular computations has already been addressed in the literature. Accurate results are especially important when inferring properties about pointer alignments and arrays lookup parallelization algorithms. The domains of congruences [11], linear congruences [12,22], trapezoidal congruences [18] have been used in that context. They offer several trade-offs for describing modular properties on intervals, linear inequalities, and rational linear inequalities. Modular arithmetic usually involves non-convex properties. A generic domain functor has been introduced in [23] to adapt abstract domains, so they can deal with modular properties.

The granularity of expression assignments is also important. For instance, while the single step assignment [9] method helps static analysis by decomposing the evaluation of expressions and by distinguishing multiple usages of each variable, it may also make more difficult symbolic simplifications of expressions. In contrast, symbolic constant propagation [21] allows composite assignments to be recombined to form composite expressions that can be simplified more easily. In the static analyzer MOPSA [16], abstract domains can rewrite expressions by resolving some aspects (such as pointers, floating point arithmetic), and simplify them symbolically. Lastly, some work has been done on fixed point arithmetic in the context of deductive methods [10].

Adapting symbolic simplification approaches in the context of modular arithmetic is different from detecting modular numerical properties. This is the issue we address in the present paper. Note that, while we focus on the simplification of expressions, the analysis of interpolation algorithms also requires precise handling of array lookup procedures. Analyzing array lookup loops and expressions involved in interpolation algorithms are orthogonal issues. The literature already describes some methods to address the former one [13,24].

In this work, we use an intermediate language inspired by the one used in [21]. We focus on integer arithmetic rather than floating-point computations, and we have introduced modulo computations and bound check operators. Moreover, we have adapted our rewriting relation from the one that is given in [21] by adding an explicit treatment of error alarms.

Outline. The paper is organized as follows. In Sect. 2, we present some preliminary results on modular integer arithmetic, which suggest it should be possible to effectively simplify expressions evaluated over modular rings. In Sect. 3, we introduce a toy arithmetic language that allows modulo computations and bound checks. The semantics of this language describes two kinds of error alarms: divisions by zero and failed bound checks. In Sect. 4 we explain how the integration of the expression rewriting technique can be done soundly. Then, in Sect. 5 we introduce an abstract representation of expressions that can be tuned by the parameters of a generic numerical abstract domain described in Sect. 6. Such a generic abstract domain is then instantiated in Sect. 7, by making explicit the heuristics used to symbolically simplify expressions. Finally, Sect. 8 describes some aspects of our implementations and an evaluation of the introduced abstract domain over several code excerpts from industrial code.

2 Preliminary Results on Modular Integer Arithmetic

In this section, we give basic properties to reason on Euclidean division and modular arithmetic. First, we introduce the set of modulo specifications $\mathbb{M}$ that is defined as follows:

$$\mathbb{M} \stackrel{\text{def}}{=} \{[l,u[\mid l,u \in \mathbb{Z},\ l < u\} \cup \{\mathbb{Z}\}.$$

The set $\mathbb{M}$ contains two kinds of elements. Intervals of the form $[l,u[$ denote operations modulo $u-l$ with result in the interval $[l,u[$, whereas the element $\mathbb{Z}$ denotes arithmetic operations without modulo. This is formalized in the following definition:

Definition 1. *We define the modulo of* $k \in \mathbb{Z}$ *by an element of* $\mathbb{M}$ *as*

$$\begin{aligned} k \bmod [l,u[&\stackrel{\text{def}}{=} l + \operatorname{irem}(k-l, u-l) \\ k \bmod \mathbb{Z} &\stackrel{\text{def}}{=} k \end{aligned}$$

where $\operatorname{irem}(m,n)$ *denotes the remainder of the Euclidean division of the integer* m *by the strictly positive integer* n, *that is to say the unique integer* r *such that* $0 \le r < n$ *and* n *divides* $m-r$.

In particular, when the integer k belongs to the interval $[l,u[$ we have $k \bmod [l,u[= k$.

Definition 2. *An element* $m \in \mathbb{M}$ *is said to be* k*-splittable, with* k *a strictly positive integer, if* m *can be split in* k *sets of same cardinality. We define* $\mathbb{S} : \mathbb{N}^* \to \wp(\mathbb{M})$ *such that* $\mathbb{S}(k)$ *is the set of elements of* $\mathbb{M}$ *that are* k*-splittable. More formally,*

$$\forall k > 0,\ \mathbb{S}(k) \stackrel{\text{def}}{=} \{[l,u[\in \mathbb{M} \mid (k \mid (u-l))\} \cup \{\mathbb{Z}\}.$$

Example 1. The intervals $[0, 2^{16}[$ and $[-2^{15}, 2^{15}[$ both are 2^{16}-splittable and 2^8-splittable.

We use the notion of k-splittability to reason about the application of consecutive modulo computations. In particular, when two modulo operations follow each other, the inner one can be ignored under some specific conditions. This is formalized in the following property.

Property 1. Let $n \in \mathbb{Z}$ be an integer. Let $[l,u[$ and m be two elements of $\mathbb{M}$. If m is $(u-l)$-splittable (*i.e.*, if $m \in \mathbb{S}(u-l)$), then $(n \bmod m) \bmod [l,u[= n \bmod [l,u[$.

We now give two other properties to simplify consecutive modulo computations under some conditions.

Property 2. Let $n \in \mathbb{Z}$ be an integer. Let $[l_1,u_1[$ and $[l_2,u_2[$ be two elements of $\mathbb{M}$ such that $[l_1,u_1[\subseteq [l_2,u_2[$. Then, $(n \bmod [l_1,u_1[) \bmod [l_2,u_2[= n \bmod [l_1,u_1[$.

Property 3. Let $n \in \mathbb{Z}$ be an integer. Let $[l_1,u_1[$ and $[l_2,u_2[$ be two elements of $\mathbb{M}$. We consider $\alpha \stackrel{\text{def}}{=} l_1 \bmod [l_2,u_2[$. If $\alpha + u_1 - l_1 \le u_2$ and $(u_1 - l_1) \mid (\alpha - l_1)$, then we have $(n \bmod [l_1,u_1[) \bmod [l_2,u_2[= n \bmod [\alpha, \alpha+u_1-l_1[$. This is pictured in Fig. 4.

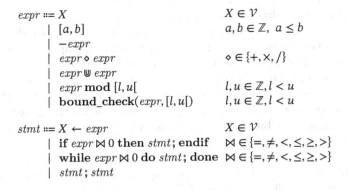

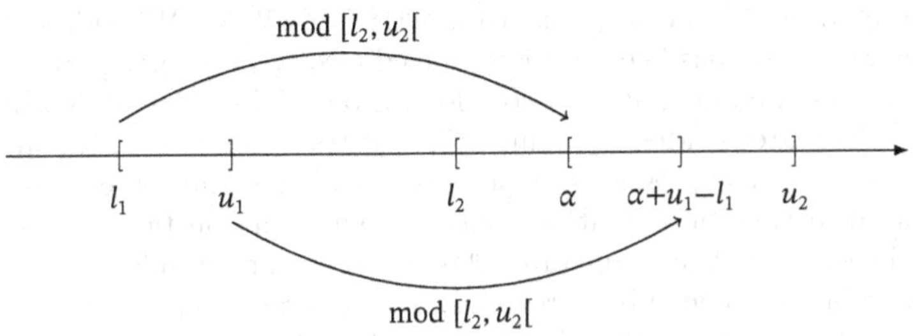

Fig. 4. Translation when applying consecutive modulos.

$expr ::= X$	$X \in \mathcal{V}$
$\mid\ [a, b]$	$a, b \in \mathbb{Z},\ a \leq b$
$\mid\ -expr$	
$\mid\ expr \diamond expr$	$\diamond \in \{+, \times, /\}$
$\mid\ expr \uplus expr$	
$\mid\ expr$ **mod** $[l, u[$	$l, u \in \mathbb{Z}, l < u$
$\mid$ **bound_check**($expr, [l, u[$)	$l, u \in \mathbb{Z}, l < u$
$stmt ::= X \leftarrow expr$	$X \in \mathcal{V}$
$\mid$ **if** $expr \bowtie 0$ **then** $stmt$; **endif**	$\bowtie \in \{=, \neq, <, \leq, \geq, >\}$
$\mid$ **while** $expr \bowtie 0$ **do** $stmt$; **done**	$\bowtie \in \{=, \neq, <, \leq, \geq, >\}$
$\mid\ stmt\,; stmt$	

Fig. 5. Syntax of our extended language.

Note that Prop. 2 is a particular case of Prop. 3. Indeed, with the notations of Prop. 3, if $[l_1, u_1[\subseteq [l_2, u_2[$ we have $\alpha = l_1$. Then, $\alpha + u_1 - l_1 = u_1$ and $\alpha - l_1 = 0$. So, $\alpha + u_1 - l_1 \leq u_2$ and $(u_1 - l_1) \mid (\alpha - l_1)$. We can conclude, thanks to Prop. 3, that $(n \text{ mod } [l_1, u_1[) \text{ mod } [l_2, u_2[= n \text{ mod } [l_1, u_1[$.

We finish this preliminary results section, with few examples about modulo computations.

Example 2. Let n be an integer in $\mathbb{Z}$. Then,
- by Prop. 1, $(n \text{ mod } [-2^{15}, 2^{15}[) \text{ mod } [0, 2^8[= n \text{ mod } [0, 2^8[$,
- because $23 \in [0, 2^8[$, $23 \text{ mod } [0, 2^8[= 23$,
- by Prop. 2, $(n \text{ mod } [0, 2^8[) \text{ mod } [0, 2^{16}[= n \text{ mod } [0, 2^8[$,
- by Prop. 3, $(n \text{ mod } [2, 4[) \text{ mod } [10, 20[= n \text{ mod } [12, 14[$ (with $\alpha = 12$).

3 Syntax and Semantics of the Language

3.1 Syntax of the Language

The syntax of our language is introduced in Fig. 5. The analysis that is described in this paper only refines the result of integer computations. Thus, the description of pointers and floating point arithmetic is omitted. We indeed suppose that lvalue resolution has been partially solved (see [2, Sect. 6.1.3]) and that the abstraction presented here assigns no information to the value of floating point variables (which are handled by some other abstract domains of the analyzer). We focus on integer expressions, which are made of variables, constant intervals, classical arithmetic operations, modulo within a constant modular ring, and bound checks. A specific operator $\uplus$ is added to our extended syntax to represent the value of some sub-expressions. This operator represents the convex join of two integer expressions, that is any value between its operands. This is especially helpful to deal with expressions involved in interpolation procedures. For example, in Fig. 3, if it is defined, the value of R is between the values of Y_0 and Y_1, regardless of their order. We then denote $R \leftarrow Y_0 \uplus Y_1$. Assuming we can establish that $Y_0 \leq Y_1$, it follows that $Y_0 \leq R \leq Y_1$.

The variables involved in the program belong to a finite set, denoted $\mathcal{V}$. We use interval constants to represent constants or to model non-determinism that may be due to some unknown inputs or potentially imprecise abstraction. Implicit and explicit casts have been decomposed by means of two operators: as it will be seen in the description of the semantics, the bound check operator **bound_check** checks whether the value of an expression does not overflow, and the modulo operator **mod** extracts the remainder of the Euclidean division. Lastly, we assume that bit shifting has been replaced with equivalent arithmetic operations.

Statements include assignments, sequential composition, conditional branching (we only consider positive branches, negative ones can be encoded consequently), and loops. The conditions of branching and loops compare expressions with the value 0. This toy language is enough to encode the semantics of the integer arithmetic restriction of real-life programming languages like C.

For the rest of the paper, every constant expression of the form $[\alpha, \alpha]$ with $\alpha \in \mathbb{Z}$ is denoted α_{cst}.

3.2 Concrete Semantics of the Language

We now describe the *concrete semantics* of our language, that is a mathematical expression of its behaviors. It is worth noting that, due to the use of intervals and convex join operators, the evaluation of an expression may induce non-determinism. Additionally, our semantics tracks *erroneous computations*.

We introduce a set of possible errors that we note Ω. We assume that Ω contains in particular two distinct elements ω_d and ω_o: the error ω_d stands for a division by zero, whereas the error ω_o denotes a bound check failure. The other elements of Ω can be raised by the other domains of the analyzer, especially during the resolution of the lvalues.

A *memory state* is a function that maps each variable from the set $\mathcal{V}$ to an integer in $\mathbb{Z}$. The set of all memory states is denoted $\mathcal{E}$. The concrete semantics $[\![\mathit{expr}]\!] \in \mathcal{E} \rightarrow (\wp(\mathbb{Z}) \times \wp(\Omega))$ of an expression maps a memory state to sets of values and errors. To simplify the formulas, given an expression $e \in \mathit{expr}$ and a memory state $\rho \in \mathcal{E}$, the first component of $[\![e]\!]\rho$ is often written $[\![e]\!]^V \rho \in \wp(\mathbb{Z})$,

$$\llbracket X \rrbracket \rho \stackrel{\text{def}}{=} \langle \{ \rho(X) \},\ \varnothing \rangle$$
$$\llbracket [a,b] \rrbracket \rho \stackrel{\text{def}}{=} \langle \{ x \in \mathbb{Z} \mid a \leq x \leq b \},\ \varnothing \rangle$$
$$\llbracket -e \rrbracket \rho \stackrel{\text{def}}{=} \langle \{ -x \mid x \in \llbracket e \rrbracket^V \rho \},\ \llbracket e \rrbracket^\Omega \rho \rangle$$
$$\llbracket e_1 + e_2 \rrbracket \rho \stackrel{\text{def}}{=} \langle \{ x + y \mid x \in \llbracket e_1 \rrbracket^V \rho, y \in \llbracket e_2 \rrbracket^V \rho \},\ \llbracket e_1 \rrbracket^\Omega \rho \cup \llbracket e_2 \rrbracket^\Omega \rho \rangle$$
$$\llbracket e_1 \times e_2 \rrbracket \rho \stackrel{\text{def}}{=} \langle \{ x \times y \mid x \in \llbracket e_1 \rrbracket^V \rho, y \in \llbracket e_2 \rrbracket^V \rho \},\ \llbracket e_1 \rrbracket^\Omega \rho \cup \llbracket e_2 \rrbracket^\Omega \rho \rangle$$
$$\llbracket e_1 / e_2 \rrbracket \rho \stackrel{\text{def}}{=} \langle \{ \text{truncate}(x / y) \mid x \in \llbracket e_1 \rrbracket^V \rho, y \in \llbracket e_2 \rrbracket^V \rho, y \neq 0 \},\ \llbracket e_1 \rrbracket^\Omega \rho \cup \llbracket e_2 \rrbracket^\Omega \rho \cup \Omega_1 \rangle$$
$$\text{with } \Omega_1 \stackrel{\text{def}}{=} \begin{cases} \{ \omega_d \} & \text{if } 0 \in \llbracket e_2 \rrbracket^V \rho \\ \varnothing & \text{otherwise} \end{cases}$$
$$\llbracket e_1 \Cup e_2 \rrbracket \rho \stackrel{\text{def}}{=} \left\langle \left\{ z \in \mathbb{Z} \;\middle|\; \begin{array}{l} x \in \llbracket e_1 \rrbracket^V \rho,\ y \in \llbracket e_2 \rrbracket^V \rho \\ x \leq z \leq y \ \vee\ y \leq z \leq x \end{array} \right\},\ \llbracket e_1 \rrbracket^\Omega \rho \cup \llbracket e_2 \rrbracket^\Omega \rho \right\rangle$$
$$\llbracket e \textbf{ mod } [l,u[\rrbracket \rho \stackrel{\text{def}}{=} \langle \{ x \bmod [l,u[\mid x \in \llbracket e \rrbracket^V \rho \},\ \llbracket e \rrbracket^\Omega \rho \rangle$$
$$\llbracket \textbf{bound\_check}(e, [l,u[) \rrbracket \rho \stackrel{\text{def}}{=} \langle \llbracket e \rrbracket^V \rho,\ \llbracket e \rrbracket^\Omega \rho \cup \Omega_1 \rangle \text{ with } \Omega_1 \stackrel{\text{def}}{=} \begin{cases} \{ \omega_o \} & \text{if } \llbracket e \rrbracket^V \rho \not\subseteq [l,u[\\ \varnothing & \text{otherwise} \end{cases}$$

Fig. 6. Concrete semantics of expressions.

while the second one is written $\llbracket e \rrbracket^\Omega \rho \in \wp(\Omega)$. These notations are used in the inductive definition given in Fig. 6 and also until the rest of the paper.

The evaluation of a variable raises no error, it only gives the value that is fetched from the memory state. The evaluation of an interval constant raises no error either. It provides an arbitrary value in the corresponding interval. Classical arithmetic operators and modulo consist in applying the corresponding operations element-wise while propagating the errors potentially raised when evaluating their sub-expressions. Additionally, the result of every division between two integers is *truncated*, that is rounded towards zero, while raising the error ω_d when the denominator can take the value 0. The convex join operator $\Cup$ outputs any value between the potential values of its operands and propagates the errors, but does not raise new ones. Finally, bound-checking propagates values while raising the error ω_o when they do not fit in the interval given as an argument.

It is worth to note that division by 0 and overflows are handled differently: executions that perform divisions by 0 are halted (they produce no memory states), whereas those that cause overflows are continued without modifying the current value. It corresponds to user-defined semantics assumptions [1], which are more specific than C standard which assumes the result is non-deterministic.

We now define the concrete semantics of statements. The semantics domain $\mathcal{D}$ collects both sets of memory states and errors. Thus, it is defined as follows:

$$\mathcal{D} \stackrel{\text{def}}{=} \wp(\mathcal{E}) \times \wp(\Omega).$$

It is equipped with the component-wise join $\sqcup$ and order $\sqsubseteq$.

The concrete semantics of a statement, $\{\!| \mathit{stmt} |\!\} : \mathcal{D} \to \mathcal{D}$, maps each element of the semantics domain $\rho \in \mathcal{D}$ to another one. For a given statement, it applies

$$\llbracket X \leftarrow e \rrbracket \langle R_0, \Omega_0 \rangle \stackrel{\text{def}}{=} \langle \emptyset, \Omega_0 \rangle \sqcup \bigsqcup_{\rho \in R_0} \left\{ \langle \{ \rho[X \mapsto v] \}, \llbracket e \rrbracket^{\Omega} \rho \rangle \;\middle|\; v \in \llbracket e \rrbracket^{V} \rho \right\}$$

$$\llbracket e \bowtie 0? \rrbracket \langle R_0, \Omega_0 \rangle \stackrel{\text{def}}{=} \langle \emptyset, \Omega_0 \rangle \sqcup \bigsqcup_{\rho \in R_0} \left\{ \langle \{ \rho \}, \llbracket e \rrbracket^{\Omega} \rho \rangle \;\middle|\; \exists v \in \llbracket e \rrbracket^{V} \rho,\ v \bowtie 0 \right\}$$

$$\llbracket s_1 \,;\, s_2 \rrbracket \stackrel{\text{def}}{=} \llbracket s_2 \rrbracket \circ \llbracket s_1 \rrbracket$$

$$\llbracket \textbf{if } e \bowtie 0 \textbf{ then } s;\ \textbf{endif} \rrbracket \langle R_0, \Omega_0 \rangle \stackrel{\text{def}}{=} (\llbracket s \rrbracket \circ \llbracket e \bowtie 0? \rrbracket) \langle R_0, \Omega_0 \rangle \sqcup \llbracket e \not\bowtie 0? \rrbracket \langle R_0, \Omega_0 \rangle$$

$$\llbracket \textbf{while } e \bowtie 0 \textbf{ do } s;\ \textbf{done} \rrbracket \langle R_0, \Omega_0 \rangle \stackrel{\text{def}}{=} \llbracket e \not\bowtie 0? \rrbracket \Big(\bigsqcup_{n \in \mathbb{N}} (\llbracket s \rrbracket \circ \llbracket e \bowtie 0? \rrbracket)^n \langle R_0, \Omega_0 \rangle \Big)$$

Fig. 7. Concrete semantics of statements.

the transformation over the possible memory states and accumulates the potential errors. It is defined by induction over the syntax in Fig. 7. The operator $\bigsqcup$ refers to the iteration of the binary associative and commutative operator $\sqcup$ over the elements of the set given as an argument.

Roughly speaking, the set of potential memory states, after assigning an expression $e \in expr$ to a variable $X \in \mathcal{V}$, is obtained by considering each potential memory state before the execution of the assignment and each potential value for the expression in that memory state ; for each combination, the memory state is updated by taking into account the potential value of the expression. $\rho[X \leftarrow x]$ denotes the function equal to ρ on $\mathcal{V} \backslash \{X\}$ and that maps X to x. The evaluation of the expression can also yield errors, which are also collected. The semantics of the sequential composition of two statements is the composition of their semantics. Lastly, the semantics of conditional branching and loops rely on the handling of guarding conditions: the execution of the guard restricts the set of memory states to those that satisfy the corresponding condition. The potential errors raised when evaluating the expression are also collected. The semantics of conditional branching apply the semantics of the true branch on the result of the application of the guard, and join it to the result of the application of the negation of the guard. Lastly, the semantics of loops is obtained by unfolding the loop according to its number of iterations.

4 Soundness Requirements of Expression Rewriting

We now introduce a rewriting order over expressions, noted $\preccurlyeq$, and parameterized by a set of error alarms. Rewriting an expression may rely on some conditions about the current state of the system. Additionally, it can simplify some parts of the initial expression, which could potentially raise some error alarms. The set of these error alarms are reported as side-conditions.

Definition 3. *The relation $\preccurlyeq_{\Omega_1}$, with $\Omega_1 \in \wp(\Omega)$ a set of potential error alarms, is defined as follows:*

$$\langle R_0, \Omega_0 \rangle \models e_1 \preccurlyeq_{\Omega_1} e_2 \stackrel{\text{def}}{=} \forall \rho \in R_0,\ \llbracket e_1 \rrbracket^{V} \rho \subseteq \llbracket e_2 \rrbracket^{V} \rho \ \wedge\ \llbracket e_1 \rrbracket^{\Omega} \rho \subseteq \llbracket e_2 \rrbracket^{\Omega} \rho \cup \Omega_1$$

with $\langle R_0, \Omega_0 \rangle \in \mathcal{D}$ *a semantics element and* $e_1, e_2 \in expr$ *two expressions.*

The definition of the rewriting relation $\preccurlyeq_{\Omega_1}$ is based on the semantics of expressions. Given a semantics element $\langle R_0, \Omega_0 \rangle \in \mathcal{D}$, an expression e_1 can be rewritten in the expression e_2 if and only if, in every memory state $\rho \in R_0$, the potential values of the expression e_1 are all potential values of the expression e_2. Yet, simplifications of the expression e_1 may hide error alarms, which are reported in the set Ω_1.

Example 3. We wonder whether the expression $0_{cst} \times \textbf{bound\_check}(X, [0, 2^8[)$ can be simplified into the expression 0_{cst}. It depends on the potential range of the variable X. Let R_0 be a set of memory states. If, for every memory state $\rho \in R_0$, we have $\rho(X) \in [0, 2^8[$, then $\langle R_0, \emptyset \rangle \models 0_{cst} \times \textbf{bound\_check}(X, [0, 2^8[) \preccurlyeq_{\emptyset} 0_{cst}$. Otherwise, we can prove that $\langle R_0, \emptyset \rangle \models 0_{cst} \times \textbf{bound\_check}(X, [0, 2^8[) \preccurlyeq_{\{\omega_o\}} 0_{cst}$. We can check that the rewriting order warns about the potential failure of the bound check, despite the fact that the expression that contains this bound check has been removed by simplifications.

Example 4. The expression $((X \textbf{ mod } [0, 2^8[) + -(Y \textbf{ mod } [0, 2^8[)) \textbf{ mod } [0, 2^8[$ can be rewritten as $X - Y$ under some specific assumptions. Let R_0 be a set of memory states. If for every memory state $\rho \in R_0$, we have $\rho(X), \rho(Y) \in [-2^7, 2^7[$ and $\rho(X) - \rho(Y) \in [0, 2^8[$, it follows that $\langle R_0, \emptyset \rangle \models ((X \textbf{ mod } [0, 2^8[) + -(Y \textbf{ mod } [0, 2^8[)) \textbf{ mod } [0, 2^8[\preccurlyeq_{\emptyset} X + -Y$. Indeed, either no cast wraps-around, or exactly two among the three that appear in the expression. In the later case, they compensate each other.

The following property states the transitivity of the rewriting relation.

Property 4. For every semantics element $\langle R_0, \Omega_0 \rangle \in \mathcal{D}$, expressions $e_1, e_2, e_3 \in expr$, and sets of error alarms $\Omega_1, \Omega_1' \in \wp(\Omega)$, if $\langle R_0, \Omega_0 \rangle \models e_1 \preccurlyeq_{\Omega_1} e_2$ and $\langle R_0, \Omega_0 \rangle \models e_2 \preccurlyeq_{\Omega_1'} e_3$, then $\langle R_0, \Omega_0 \rangle \models e_1 \preccurlyeq_{\Omega_1 \cup \Omega_1'} e_3$.

Transitivity is obtained by evaluating the expression with the same memory states and by collecting all the error alarms that may be hidden by the expression rewritings.

In statements, expressions can be rewritten. The following theorem states the soundness of the replacement of an expression by another one in assignments or guards. It would also be true for every statement of the language, yet we omit this result since it is not necessary to prove the soundness of our analysis.

Theorem 1. *For every semantics element* $\langle R_0, \Omega_0 \rangle \in \mathcal{D}$*, expressions* $e, e' \in expr$*, set of error alarms* $\Omega_1 \in \wp(\Omega)$*, and variable* $X \in \mathcal{V}$ *such that* $\langle R_0, \Omega_0 \rangle \models e \preccurlyeq_{\Omega_1} e'$*, we have:*
- $\{\!| V \leftarrow e |\!\}(\langle R_0, \Omega_0 \rangle) \sqsubseteq \langle \emptyset, \Omega_1 \rangle \sqcup (\{\!| V \leftarrow e' |\!\}(\langle R_0, \Omega_0 \rangle))$,
- $\{\!| e \bowtie 0? |\!\}(\langle R_0, \Omega_0 \rangle) \sqsubseteq \langle \emptyset, \Omega_1 \rangle \sqcup (\{\!| e' \bowtie 0? |\!\}(\langle R_0, \Omega_0 \rangle))$.

This way, when an expression is replaced by another one in an assignment or a guard, while following the rewriting order, all the possible memory states and error alarms are kept in the result. Note that the approximation may lead to the introduction of additional memory states or false-negative error alarms.

$$
\begin{aligned}
expr^\sharp ::= &\ \boxed{\mathcal{L}}(a_0 + \textstyle\sum_{X_i \in \mathcal{V}} a_i X_i) \ \ \forall i, a_i \in \mathbb{Z} \\
|\ & expr^\sharp \boxplus expr^\sharp \\
|\ & expr^\sharp \boxtimes expr^\sharp \\
|\ & expr^\sharp \boxslash expr^\sharp \\
|\ & expr^\sharp \boxed{\cup} expr^\sharp
\end{aligned}
$$

Fig. 8. Syntax of abstract expressions.

5 Abstract Representation of Expressions

As far as it is possible to totally order their variables, *linear expressions* have a canonical representation. It is obtained by factorizing occurrences of each variable and ordering their terms increasingly, with respect to the order on the variables. We introduce in this section an abstract syntax for expressions, in which some linear expressions are described canonically. The main goal is to highlight the patterns that can be simplified symbolically.

5.1 Abstract Syntax of Expression

The abstract syntax of expressions is given in Fig. 8. Apart from linear combinations, abstract expressions are defined using the same operators as in the language syntax. For the sake of rigor, and to distinguish them from their concrete counterparts, all the abstract operators are enclosed within a box.

Linear combinations are written as $\boxed{\mathcal{L}}(a_0 + \sum_{X_i \in \mathcal{V}} a_i X_i)$ with $a_0 \in \mathbb{Z}$ and $\forall i, a_i \in \mathbb{Z}$. In particular, we use the convention that every variable in the set $\mathcal{V}$ has to occur in the expression, would it be with a zero coefficient. This eases the definition of operations over linear forms. Constants are specific linear combinations, where all coefficients, except potentially the first one, are equal to 0. We write $\boxed{\mathcal{L}}(\alpha)$ the constant whose first coefficient is equal to $\alpha \in \mathbb{Z}$. The set of all such abstract expressions is denoted $Const^\sharp$. A variable is a linear combination of which all the coefficients are fixed at 0, except that of the variable, which is equal to 1. It is denoted $\boxed{\mathcal{L}}(X)$. Lastly, variable differences are linear combinations of which all the coefficients are fixed to 0, except for two variables. One of them has the coefficient 1 and the other -1. The variable difference between X and Y, two variables of $\mathcal{V}$, is written $\boxed{\mathcal{L}}(X - Y)$.

Intervals are introduced by the means of the convex join operator $\boxed{\cup}$. Lastly, bound checks and modulo computations are not described. Indeed, bound checks are assumed to have been eliminated while reporting the potential error alarms. About modulo computations, abstract expressions are given with an evaluation context. This context takes the form of a modular ring specified by an element of $\mathbb{M}$. Inner modulo computations are assumed to have been resolved, either by proving that they leave the value of the expression unchanged, or by replacing them conservatively by an interval.

The meaning of an abstract expression is defined thanks to a function toExpr which translates abstract expressions in the set $expr^\sharp$ back to expressions in the set *expr*.

Definition 4. *The function* toExpr : $expr^\sharp \to expr$ *is defined inductively as follows:*

$$\begin{aligned}
\text{toExpr}\left(\boxed{\text{C}}\left(a_0 + \textstyle\sum_{X_i \in \mathcal{V}} a_i X_i\right)\right) &\stackrel{\text{def}}{=} a_{0\,cst} + (a_{1\,cst} X_1 + (\cdots + (a_{n\,cst} X_n))) \\
\text{toExpr}(e_1^\sharp \boxplus e_2^\sharp) &\stackrel{\text{def}}{=} \text{toExpr}(e_1^\sharp) + \text{toExpr}(e_2^\sharp) \\
\text{toExpr}(e_1^\sharp \boxtimes e_2^\sharp) &\stackrel{\text{def}}{=} \text{toExpr}(e_1^\sharp) \times \text{toExpr}(e_2^\sharp) \\
\text{toExpr}(e_1^\sharp \boxslash e_2^\sharp) &\stackrel{\text{def}}{=} \text{toExpr}(e_1^\sharp) \; / \; \text{toExpr}(e_2^\sharp) \\
\text{toExpr}(e_1^\sharp \; \boxed{\Cup} \; e_2^\sharp) &\stackrel{\text{def}}{=} \text{toExpr}(e_1^\sharp) \Cup \text{toExpr}(e_2^\sharp)
\end{aligned}$$

6 Generic Abstraction

The translation of classical expressions into abstract ones is parametric, with respect to the choice of an abstract domain, to reason about semantics states. The abstract domain describes a set of properties about semantics states $\mathcal{D}^\sharp$, which are mapped to the least upper bound of the semantics states which satisfy them by a concretization function γ. It also contains a sound abstract counterpart to the join operator $\sqcup$ noted $\sqcup^\sharp$, a primitive $\mathbf{lfp}^\sharp$ to approximate the increasing iteration of concrete operators, and two abstract transformers ASSIGN$^\sharp$ and GUARD$^\sharp$ to lift the execution of assignments and guards on properties. It also contains the primitives ι and **reduce**. The primitive ι extracts the range of abstract expressions and **reduce** performs sound expression rewriting for all the memory states contained in the semantics state given as an argument.

Definition 5. *An abstract domain consists of a tuple comprising eight elements* $\langle \mathcal{D}^\sharp, \gamma, \sqcup^\sharp, \mathbf{lfp}^\sharp, \textit{ASSIGN}^\sharp, \textit{GUARD}^\sharp, \iota, \mathbf{reduce} \rangle$, *such that:*

5.1 $\mathcal{D}^\sharp$ *is a set of properties,*

5.2 $\gamma : \mathcal{D}^\sharp \to \mathcal{D}$ *is a concretization function that, given an abstract element* $R^\sharp$, *outputs all the memory states and error alarms that verify the property* $R^\sharp$,

5.3 for every two abstract elements $R^\sharp, S^\sharp \in \mathcal{D}^\sharp$, $\gamma(R^\sharp) \sqcup \gamma(S^\sharp) \sqsubseteq \gamma(R^\sharp \sqcup^\sharp S^\sharp)$,

5.4 for every abstract element $R^\sharp \in \mathcal{D}^\sharp$ *and every abstract transformer* $\mathbb{F}^\sharp : \mathcal{D}^\sharp \to \mathcal{D}^\sharp$, $lfp^\sharp_{R^\sharp}(\mathbb{F}^\sharp)$ *is an abstract element that satisfies* $\bigsqcup_{n \in \mathbb{N}} \mathbb{F}^n(\langle R_0, \Omega_0 \rangle) \sqsubseteq \gamma(lfp^\sharp_{R^\sharp}(\mathbb{F}^\sharp))$ *for every semantics element* $\langle R_0, \Omega_0 \rangle \in \mathcal{D}$ *and every* $\sqcup$*-complete morphism*[1] $\mathbb{F} : \mathcal{D} \to \mathcal{D}$ *such that:*
  (i) $\langle R_0, \Omega_0 \rangle \sqsubseteq \mathbb{F}(\langle R_0, \Omega_0 \rangle)$,
  (ii) $\langle R_0, \Omega_0 \rangle \sqsubseteq \gamma(R^\sharp)$,

[1] That is to say $\mathbb{F}(\bigsqcup P) = \bigsqcup\{\mathbb{F}(\langle R_0, \Omega_0 \rangle) \mid \langle R_0, \Omega_0 \rangle \in P\}$ for every set $P \subseteq \mathcal{D}$.

$$\{\!| X \leftarrow e |\!\}^{\sharp} \stackrel{\text{def}}{=} \text{ASSIGN}^{\sharp}(X, E)$$
$$\{\!| s_1 \,;\, s_2 |\!\}^{\sharp} \stackrel{\text{def}}{=} \{\!| s_2 |\!\}^{\sharp} \circ \{\!| s_1 |\!\}^{\sharp}$$
$$\{\!| \textbf{if } e \bowtie 0 \textbf{ then } s; \textbf{endif} |\!\}^{\sharp} R^{\sharp} \stackrel{\text{def}}{=} ((\{\!| s |\!\}^{\sharp} \circ \text{GUARD}^{\sharp}(e, \bowtie)) R^{\sharp}) \sqcup \text{GUARD}^{\sharp}(e, \not\bowtie) R^{\sharp}$$
$$\{\!| \textbf{while } e \bowtie 0 \textbf{ do } s; \textbf{done} |\!\}^{\sharp} R^{\sharp} \stackrel{\text{def}}{=} \text{GUARD}^{\sharp}(e, \not\bowtie)(\text{lfp}^{\sharp}\, [X^{\sharp} \mapsto R^{\sharp} \sqcup^{\sharp} (\{\!| s |\!\}^{\sharp} \circ \text{GUARD}^{\sharp}(e, \bowtie)) X^{\sharp}])$$

Fig. 9. Abstract semantics.

(iii) for every abstract element $S^{\sharp} \in \mathcal{D}^{\sharp}$, $(\mathbb{F} \circ \gamma)(S^{\sharp}) \sqsubseteq (\gamma \circ \mathbb{F}^{\sharp})(S^{\sharp})$,

5.5 *for every variable* $X \in \mathcal{V}$, *and every expression* $e \in expr$, $\text{ASSIGN}^{\sharp}(X, e) : D^{\sharp} \rightarrow D^{\sharp}$ *is a function that satisfies* $(\{\!| X \leftarrow e |\!\} \circ \gamma) R^{\sharp} \sqsubseteq (\gamma \circ \text{ASSIGN}^{\sharp}(X, e)) R^{\sharp}$ *for every abstract element* $R^{\sharp} \in \mathcal{D}^{\sharp}$,

5.6 *for every comparison relation* $\bowtie \in \{=, \neq, <, \leq, \geq, >\}$, *and every expression* $e \in expr$, $\text{GUARD}^{\sharp}(e, \bowtie) : D^{\sharp} \rightarrow D^{\sharp}$ *is a function that satisfies* $(\{\!| e \bowtie 0? |\!\} \circ \gamma) R^{\sharp} \sqsubseteq (\gamma \circ \text{GUARD}^{\sharp}(e, \bowtie)) R^{\sharp}$ *for every abstract element* $R^{\sharp} \in \mathcal{D}^{\sharp}$,

5.7 *for every expression* $e \in expr$, $\iota(e) : \mathcal{D}^{\sharp} \rightarrow \mathbb{I}$ *is a function that satisfies* $[\![e]\!]^{V} \rho \subseteq \iota(e) R^{\sharp}$ *for every abstract element* $R^{\sharp} \in \mathcal{D}^{\sharp}$ *and for every memory state* $\rho \in R_0$ *with* $\langle R_0, \Omega_0 \rangle = \gamma(R^{\sharp})$ *and* $\mathbb{I} \stackrel{\text{def}}{=} \{\emptyset\} \cup \{[a, b] \mid a \in \{-\infty\} \cup \mathbb{Z}, b \in \mathbb{Z} \cup \{+\infty\}, a \leq b\}$, *the set of intervals over* $\mathbb{Z} \cup \{-\infty, +\infty\}$,

5.8 *for every abstract expression* $e^{\sharp}$, $\textbf{reduce}(e^{\sharp}) : \mathcal{D}^{\sharp} \rightarrow expr^{\sharp}$ *is an abstract expression transformer such that the rewriting relation* $\gamma(R^{\sharp}) \models \text{toExpr}(e^{\sharp}) \preccurlyeq_{\emptyset} \text{toExpr}(\textbf{reduce}(e^{\sharp}) R^{\sharp})$ *holds for every abstract element* $R^{\sharp}$.

The $\text{lfp}^{\sharp}$ operator is usually described as an increasing iteration, followed by a decreasing iteration. These are defined by the means of a base abstract element, a widening operator, and a narrowing operator [?]. We now assume that such an abstract domain has been chosen.

The abstract semantics of a statement $\{\!| stmt |\!\}^{\sharp} : \mathcal{D}^{\sharp} \rightarrow \mathcal{D}^{\sharp}$ maps a property about semantics states, before applying the statement *stmt*, to the property that is satisfied after applying this statement. It is obtained by lifting the concrete semantics (*e.g.* see Fig. 7) in the abstract domain. Its definition is given in Fig. 9. Each concrete operation is replaced with its abstract counterpart. The abstraction of loops requires more explanations. In order to apply the abstract operator $\text{lfp}^{\sharp}$, we must ensure that the first argument is a sound approximation of a monotonic function, and that the second argument is an abstraction of a pre-fixpoint of this function. Hence, we replace the function $(\{\!| s |\!\} \circ \{\!| e \bowtie 0? |\!\})$ from the iteration, in the concrete semantics, by the function $\langle R_0, \Omega_0 \rangle \mapsto \langle R_0, \Omega_0 \rangle \sqcup (\{\!| s |\!\} \circ \{\!| e \bowtie 0? |\!\}) \langle R_0, \Omega_0 \rangle$, where $\langle R_0, \Omega_0 \rangle$ is the semantics state just before interpreting the loop. This does not change the result of the concrete iterations.

We can now state the soundness of the abstract semantics.

Theorem 2. *Let* $\langle R_0, \Omega_0 \rangle \in \mathcal{D}$ *be a semantics state. Let* $R^\sharp \in \mathcal{D}^\sharp$ *be an abstract state. Let* $s \in stmt$ *be a statement. Then* $\langle R_0, \Omega_0 \rangle \sqsubseteq \gamma(R^\sharp) \implies \{\!|\, s \,|\!\}\langle R_0, \Omega_0 \rangle \sqsubseteq \gamma(\{\!|\, s \,|\!\}^\sharp R^\sharp)$.

Thm. 2 states that the abstract semantics ignores no concrete behavior. Nevertheless, it may introduce fictitious ones due to the abstraction.

6.1 Primitives over Abstract Expressions

We now introduce two primitives that operate over abstract expressions.

The opposite function pushes unary minus to the leafs of abstract expressions (that are linear forms).

Definition 6. *The function* opposite : $expr^\sharp \to expr^\sharp$ *is defined inductively as follows:*

$$\begin{aligned}
&\text{opposite}\left(\boxed{\mathcal{L}}\left(a_0 + \textstyle\sum_{X_i \in \mathcal{V}} a_i X_i\right)\right) \stackrel{\text{def}}{=} \boxed{\mathcal{L}}\left(-a_0 + \textstyle\sum_{X_i \in \mathcal{V}} (-a_i) X_i\right)\\
&\text{opposite}(e_1^\sharp \boxplus e_2^\sharp) \stackrel{\text{def}}{=} \text{opposite}(e_1^\sharp) \boxplus \text{opposite}(e_2^\sharp)\\
&\text{opposite}(e_1^\sharp \boxtimes e_2^\sharp) \stackrel{\text{def}}{=} \text{opposite}(e_1^\sharp) \boxtimes e_2^\sharp\\
&\text{opposite}(e_1^\sharp \boxslash e_2^\sharp) \stackrel{\text{def}}{=} \text{opposite}(e_1^\sharp) \boxslash e_2^\sharp\\
&\text{opposite}(e_1^\sharp \boxed{\uplus} e_2^\sharp) \stackrel{\text{def}}{=} \text{opposite}(e_1^\sharp) \boxed{\uplus} \text{opposite}(e_2^\sharp)
\end{aligned}$$

This way, the opposite of a linear form is obtained by taking the opposite of each coefficient. The function **opposite** propagates over the sub-expressions of the $\boxplus$ and the $\boxed{\uplus}$ operators. Lastly, the opposite of a product or a quotient between two sub-expressions is obtained by propagating it to only one of them (the first one has been chosen arbitrarily).

We now introduce an operator to propagate a modulo computation over an abstract expression. Given an abstract expression and a modulo specification, it applies the modulo on the expression.

Definition 7. *For any abstract expression* $e^\sharp \in expr^\sharp$ *and any modulo specification* $m \in \mathbb{M}$, *the function* $\text{rmMod}(e, m) : \mathcal{D}^\sharp \to expr^\sharp$ *is defined as follows:*

$$\text{rmMod}(e^\sharp, m)R^\sharp \stackrel{\text{def}}{=} \begin{cases}
e^\sharp & \textit{if } m = \mathbb{Z},\\
\boxed{\mathcal{L}}(\alpha \bmod m) & \textit{else if } e^\sharp = \boxed{\mathcal{L}}(\alpha) \textit{ with } \alpha \in \mathbb{Z},\\
e^\sharp & \textit{else if } \iota(\text{toExpr}(e^\sharp))R^\sharp \subseteq m,\\
\textit{reduce}(\boxed{\mathcal{L}}(l)\ \boxed{\uplus}\ \boxed{\mathcal{L}}(u-1))R^\sharp & \textit{otherwise, with } m = [l, u[.
\end{cases}$$

In the previous definition, if the modulo specification is equal to the set $\mathbb{Z}$, nothing has to be done. When the abstract expression is a constant, the modulo computation can be directly applied on the constant. Lastly, if the value of the abstract expression ranges within the interval of the modulo, then the modulo computation can be safely discarded. In all other cases, no information can be kept about the expression. It is then replaced with the interval of the modular ring (or more precisely its reduction).

The following theorem states that any abstract expression that is evaluated over a modular ring can be rewritten in the expression in which the modulo computation has been forced, that is to say the output of the function **rmMod**. Moreover, this rewrite does not hide any potential error alarms.

Theorem 3. *For all abstract value $R^\sharp \in \mathcal{D}^\sharp$, abstract expression $e^\sharp \in expr^\sharp$, and potential modular ring $m \in \mathbb{M}$, the following property holds,*

$$\gamma(R^\sharp) \models \text{toExpr}(e^\sharp)\ \boldsymbol{mod}\ m \preccurlyeq_\emptyset \text{toExpr}(\text{rmMod}(e^\sharp, m)).$$

Example 5. We give two examples of elimination of modulo computations. We compute the result of the abstract expression $\boxed{\mathcal{C}}(0)\ \boxed{\uplus}\ \boxed{\mathcal{C}}(25)$, that intuitively denotes the interval $[0, 25]$, respectively modulo $[0, 2^8[$ and $[10, 26[$. We assume that the primitive ι provides the exact range of this expression, that is to say that $\iota(\text{toExpr}(\boxed{\mathcal{C}}(0)\ \boxed{\uplus}\ \boxed{\mathcal{C}}(25)))R^\sharp = \iota(0_{cst} \uplus 25_{cst}) = [0, 25]$. Since the interval $[0, 25]$ is included in the interval $[0, 2^8[$, the corresponding modulo computation can be eliminated without modifying the abstract expression. We obtain $\text{rmMod}(\boxed{\mathcal{C}}(0)\ \boxed{\uplus}\ \boxed{\mathcal{C}}(25), [0, 2^8[)R^\sharp = \boxed{\mathcal{C}}(0)\ \boxed{\uplus}\ \boxed{\mathcal{C}}(25)$. In the second case, the result of the modulo computation cannot be described precisely as an abstract expression. It is then soundly replaced by the abstract expression $\textbf{reduce}(\boxed{\mathcal{C}}(10)\ \boxed{\uplus}\ \boxed{\mathcal{C}}(25))R^\sharp$. We keep the primitive **reduce** uninterpreted, since it is a parameter of our abstraction.

6.2 Translation from Classical to Abstract Expressions

We now have all the material needed to define the translation of classical expressions into abstract ones. Given an expression $e \in expr$, its translation $(\!(\, e \,)\!) : \mathcal{D}^\sharp \to expr^\sharp \times \mathbb{M} \times \wp(\Omega)$ is a function that maps an abstract element $R^\sharp$ to a triple $(e^\sharp, m, \Omega_e)$. Remember that abstract expressions do not have modulo operators. However, the element $m \in \mathbb{M}$ stands for a modulo computation to be applied on the potential values of the abstract expression. This way, the outermost modulo computation can be kept precisely, whereas inner modulo computations must be translated conservatively. This can be done thanks to the **rmMod** operator, yet it may yield a loss of information. Bound checks also cannot be described in abstract expressions, so potential bound check failures are reported in the set Ω_e. The translation is only valid for the semantics states satisfying the property $R^\sharp$ (*i.e.*, for the states in $\gamma(R^\sharp)$). Thus, the abstract element $R^\sharp$ should be used to drive the translation process to get a more accurate result.

The translation $(\!(\, e \,)\!)R^\sharp$ of an expression e, in the context of an abstract element $R^\sharp$, is defined inductively and by cases by the means of a set of inference rules.

Variable. A variable is replaced by a linear combination where all the coefficients are set to 0, except the one corresponding to the variable which is set to 1.

Such a replacement hides no error alarms, and the abstract expression obtained this way can be interpreted in $\mathbb{Z}$. This is formalized in the following inference rule.

$$\textsc{Variable}\ \frac{X \in \mathcal{V}}{(\!|\, X \,|\!)R^\sharp \stackrel{\text{def}}{=} (\boxed{\square}(X), \mathbb{Z}, \emptyset)}$$

Interval. An interval is encoded by the means of the convex join operator $\boxed{\Cup}$. The bounds of the interval are given as operands (their order has been chosen arbitrarily). Then, the **reduce** operator is applied to potentially simplify the resulting abstract expression. This translation yields no potential errors and its result can be interpreted in $\mathbb{Z}$. This is formalized in the following inference rule.

$$\textsc{Interval}\ \frac{a, b \in \mathbb{Z} \qquad a \leq b}{(\!|\, [a, b] \,|\!)R^\sharp \stackrel{\text{def}}{=} (\textbf{reduce}(\boxed{\square}(a)\ \boxed{\Cup}\ \boxed{\square}(b))R^\sharp, \mathbb{Z}, \emptyset)}$$

Unary Minus. The translation of an expression starting with a unary minus is defined inductively. First, the argument is translated, which provides an abstract expression, a modulo specification, and a set of potential errors. The primitive opposite is then applied to the abstract expression, which yields no additional error alarms. Furthermore, when the abstract expression is evaluated over a modular ring, the ring is kept the same, but the elements of the potential modular interval are also negated.

This is formalized in the two following inference rules, which distinguish two cases according to whether the translation of the argument can be interpreted in $\mathbb{Z}$, or in a modular ring.

$$\textsc{OppositeNoMod}\ \frac{(e^\sharp, \mathbb{Z}, \Omega_e) \stackrel{\text{def}}{=} (\!|\, e \,|\!)R^\sharp}{(\!|\, -e \,|\!)R^\sharp \stackrel{\text{def}}{=} (\textbf{reduce}(\text{opposite}(e^\sharp))R^\sharp, \mathbb{Z}, \Omega_e)}$$

$$\textsc{OppositeMod}\ \frac{(e^\sharp, [l, u[, \Omega_e) \stackrel{\text{def}}{=} (\!|\, e \,|\!)R^\sharp}{(\!|\, -e \,|\!)R^\sharp \stackrel{\text{def}}{=} (\textbf{reduce}(\text{opposite}(e^\sharp))R^\sharp, [-u+1, -l+1[, \Omega_e)}$$

Convex Join. An expression of the form $e_1 \Cup e_2$ is translated thanks to its abstract counterpart $\boxed{\Cup}$. First, the sub-expressions are translated, which provides abstract expressions, modulo specifications, and sets of potential errors. The outermost modulo computations are conservatively suppressed using the rmMod primitive before the results are passed to the $\boxed{\Cup}$ abstract operator. The final result may be simplified by the means of the **reduce** operator before being interpreted in $\mathbb{Z}$. No additional potential errors are collected. This is formalized in the following inference rule.

$$\textsc{ConvexJoin}\ \frac{\begin{array}{cc} (e_1^\sharp, m_1, \Omega_1) \stackrel{\text{def}}{=} (\!|\, e_1 \,|\!)R^\sharp & (e_2^\sharp, m_2, \Omega_2) \stackrel{\text{def}}{=} (\!|\, e_2 \,|\!)R^\sharp \\ e_1'^\sharp \stackrel{\text{def}}{=} \text{rmMod}(e_1^\sharp, m_1)R^\sharp & e_2'^\sharp \stackrel{\text{def}}{=} \text{rmMod}(e_2^\sharp, m_2)R^\sharp \end{array}}{(\!|\, e_1 \Cup e_2 \,|\!)R^\sharp \stackrel{\text{def}}{=} (\textbf{reduce}(e_1'^\sharp\ \boxed{\Cup}\ e_2'^\sharp)R^\sharp, \mathbb{Z}, \Omega_1 \cup \Omega_2)}$$

Addition. According to the result of the translation of its arguments, more or less precise inference rules can be used to translate a sum of two expressions.

Whenever both operands are translated into constants, whether they need to be respectively interpreted in modular rings or not, the potential application of the modulo operations can be directly applied on the constant values. The result can be interpreted in $\mathbb{Z}$. Whenever exactly one operand is translated into a constant, and the other one must be interpreted in modular arithmetic, the potential modulo operator of the constant expression can be directly applied. Then, the result is added to the other abstract expression and to the bounds of its modular ring. The resulting abstract expression may be simplified by the means of the **reduce** operator. In the context of real programming languages, branching is generally not limited to comparisons to 0. Then, we would like to take advantage of the algebraic simplifications of our abstract domain and rewrite `e1 == e2` into `e1 - e2 == 0`. We then need a rule that simplifies addition of abstract expressions interpreted in the same modular ring that sum to $\boxed{\mathbb{Z}}(0)$. In such a case, the result is $\boxed{\mathbb{Z}}(0)$ and can be interpreted in $\mathbb{Z}$. Otherwise, the operator **rmMod** is used to remove modulo operators in both translations of the arguments. It yields abstract expressions which can be interpreted in $\mathbb{Z}$, but may result in loss of information. The resulting abstract expression can be potentially simplified by the means of the **reduce** parametric operator.

In all cases, the computation yields no additional error alarms. This is formalized in the following four inference rules (we recall that by convention $\alpha \bmod \mathbb{Z}$ is equal to α for every integer $\alpha \in \mathbb{Z}$).

$$\textsc{Plus2Const}\ \frac{\begin{array}{c}\alpha_1 \in \mathbb{Z} : (\boxed{\mathbb{Z}}(\alpha_1), m_1, \Omega_1) \stackrel{\text{def}}{=} (\!| e_1 |\!) R^\sharp \\ \alpha_2 \in \mathbb{Z} : (\boxed{\mathbb{Z}}(\alpha_2), m_2, \Omega_2) \stackrel{\text{def}}{=} (\!| e_2 |\!) R^\sharp\end{array}}{(\!| e_1 + e_2 |\!) R^\sharp \stackrel{\text{def}}{=} (\boxed{\mathbb{Z}}(\alpha_1 \bmod m_1 + \alpha_2 \bmod m_2), \mathbb{Z}, \Omega_i \cup \Omega_j)}$$

$$\textsc{PlusConst}\ \frac{\begin{array}{c}i, j \in \{1,2\} : i \neq j \qquad \alpha \in \mathbb{Z} : (\boxed{\mathbb{Z}}(\alpha), m_i, \Omega_i) \stackrel{\text{def}}{=} (\!| e_i |\!) R^\sharp \\ (e_j^\sharp, [l_j, u_j[, \Omega_j) \stackrel{\text{def}}{=} (\!| e_j |\!) R^\sharp \qquad \alpha' \stackrel{\text{def}}{=} \alpha \bmod m_i \qquad e_j^\sharp \notin Const^\sharp\end{array}}{(\!| e_1 + e_2 |\!) R^\sharp \stackrel{\text{def}}{=} (\mathbf{reduce}(\boxed{\mathbb{Z}}(\alpha') \boxplus e_j^\sharp) R^\sharp, [l_j + \alpha', u_j + \alpha'[, \Omega_i \cup \Omega_j)}$$

$$\textsc{PlusEqZero}\ \frac{\begin{array}{c}(e_1^\sharp, [l_1, u_1[, \Omega_1) \stackrel{\text{def}}{=} (\!| e_1 |\!) R^\sharp \\ (e_2^\sharp, [l_2, u_2[, \Omega_2) \stackrel{\text{def}}{=} (\!| e_2 |\!) R^\sharp \qquad \mathbf{reduce}(e_1^\sharp \boxplus e_2^\sharp) R^\sharp = \boxed{\mathbb{Z}}(0) \\ l_2 = -u_1 + 1 \qquad u_2 = -l_1 + 1 \qquad e_1^\sharp \notin Const^\sharp \qquad e_2^\sharp \notin Const^\sharp\end{array}}{(\!| e_1 + e_2 |\!) R^\sharp \stackrel{\text{def}}{=} (\boxed{\mathbb{Z}}(0), \mathbb{Z}, \Omega_1 \cup \Omega_2)}$$

$$\textsc{PlusNoMod}\ \frac{\begin{array}{c}(e_1^\sharp, m_1, \Omega_1) \stackrel{\text{def}}{=} (\!| e_1 |\!) R^\sharp \qquad (e_2^\sharp, m_2, \Omega_2) \stackrel{\text{def}}{=} (\!| e_2 |\!) R^\sharp \\ e_1'^\sharp \stackrel{\text{def}}{=} \mathrm{rmMod}(e_1^\sharp, m_1) R^\sharp \qquad e_2'^\sharp \stackrel{\text{def}}{=} \mathrm{rmMod}(e_2^\sharp, m_2) R^\sharp \\ \text{neither the rule } \textsc{Plus2Const} \text{ nor } \textsc{PlusConst} \text{ nor } \textsc{PlusEqZero} \text{ can be applied}\end{array}}{(\!| e_1 + e_2 |\!) R^\sharp \stackrel{\text{def}}{=} (\mathbf{reduce}(e_1'^\sharp \boxplus e_2'^\sharp) R^\sharp, \mathbb{Z}, \Omega_1 \cup \Omega_2)}$$

Note that in case one argument is translated into a constant and the other one into an abstract expression interpreted in $\mathbb{Z}$, then applying the **rmMod** operator produces no loss of information. Thus, the rule PlusNoMod is enough.

Multiplication. The translation of a multiplication between two expressions works similarly.

In the case both operands are translated into constants, the potential application of the modulo operation can be directly applied on the constant values. The result can then be interpreted in $\mathbb{Z}$. Whenever exactly one operand is translated into a constant and the other abstract expression must be interpreted in modular arithmetic, the potential modulo operator of the constant expression can be directly applied on the constant value. The resulting abstract expression is multiplied by the constant and then potentially simplified by the **reduce** operator. The update of the modular interval depends on the sign of the constant, which splits the inference rule into three ones, depending on whether the constant is positive, zero, or negative. In all other cases, the **rmMod** operator is used to suppress the modulo computations in both arguments translations. Once again, the resulting abstract expression can be potentially simplified by the means of the **reduce** parametric operator.

In all cases, the computation yields no additional error alarms. This is formalized in the following five inference rules.

$$\textsc{Mult2Const}\ \frac{\alpha_1 \in \mathbb{Z} : (\boxed{\mathbb{Z}}(\alpha_1), m_1, \Omega_1) \stackrel{\text{def}}{=} (\!|\, e_1 \,|\!)R^\sharp \qquad \alpha_2 \in \mathbb{Z} : (\boxed{\mathbb{Z}}(\alpha_2), m_2, \Omega_2) \stackrel{\text{def}}{=} (\!|\, e_2 \,|\!)R^\sharp}{(\!|\, e_1 \times e_2 \,|\!)R^\sharp \stackrel{\text{def}}{=} (\boxed{\mathbb{Z}}((\alpha_1 \bmod m_1) \times (\alpha_2 \bmod m_2)), \mathbb{Z}, \Omega_i \cup \Omega_j)}$$

$$\textsc{MultPosConst}\ \frac{\begin{array}{c} i, j \in \{1,2\} : i \neq j \\ \alpha \in \mathbb{Z} : (\boxed{\mathbb{Z}}(\alpha), m_i, \Omega_i) \stackrel{\text{def}}{=} (\!|\, e_i \,|\!)R^\sharp \qquad (e_j^\sharp, [l_j, u_j[, \Omega_j) \stackrel{\text{def}}{=} (\!|\, e_j \,|\!)R^\sharp \\ \alpha' \stackrel{\text{def}}{=} \alpha \bmod m_i \qquad \alpha' > 0 \qquad e_j^\sharp \notin \mathit{Const}^\sharp \end{array}}{(\!|\, e_1 \times e_2 \,|\!)R^\sharp \stackrel{\text{def}}{=} (\mathbf{reduce}(e_j^\sharp \boxtimes \boxed{\mathbb{Z}}(\alpha'))R^\sharp, [l_j{\times}\alpha', u_j{\times}\alpha'[, \Omega_i \cup \Omega_j)}$$

$$\textsc{MultZeroConst}\ \frac{\begin{array}{c} i, j \in \{1,2\} : i \neq j \\ \alpha \in \mathbb{Z} : (\boxed{\mathbb{Z}}(\alpha), m_i, \Omega_i) \stackrel{\text{def}}{=} (\!|\, e_i \,|\!)R^\sharp \qquad (e_j^\sharp, m_j, \Omega_j) \stackrel{\text{def}}{=} (\!|\, e_j \,|\!)R^\sharp \\ \alpha' \stackrel{\text{def}}{=} \alpha \bmod m_i \qquad \alpha' = 0 \qquad e_j^\sharp \notin \mathit{Const}^\sharp \end{array}}{(\!|\, e_1 \times e_2 \,|\!)R^\sharp \stackrel{\text{def}}{=} (\boxed{\mathbb{Z}}(0), \mathbb{Z}, \Omega_i \cup \Omega_j)}$$

$$\textsc{MultNegConst}\ \frac{\begin{array}{c} i, j \in \{1,2\} : i \neq j \\ \alpha \in \mathbb{Z} : (\boxed{\mathbb{Z}}(\alpha), m_i, \Omega_i) \stackrel{\text{def}}{=} (\!|\, e_i \,|\!)R^\sharp \qquad (e_j^\sharp, [l_j, u_j[, \Omega_j) \stackrel{\text{def}}{=} (\!|\, e_j \,|\!)R^\sharp \\ \alpha' \stackrel{\text{def}}{=} \alpha \bmod m_i \qquad \alpha' < 0 \qquad e_j^\sharp \notin \mathit{Const}^\sharp \end{array}}{(\!|\, e_1 \times e_2 \,|\!)R^\sharp \stackrel{\text{def}}{=} (\mathbf{reduce}(e_j^\sharp \boxtimes \boxed{\mathbb{Z}}(\alpha'))R^\sharp, [u_j\alpha'{+}1, l_j\alpha'{+}1[, \Omega_i \cup \Omega_j)}$$

$$\textsc{MultNoMod}\ \frac{\begin{array}{c} (e_1^\sharp, m_1, \Omega_1) \stackrel{\text{def}}{=} (\!|\, e_1 \,|\!)R^\sharp \qquad (e_2^\sharp, m_2, \Omega_2) \stackrel{\text{def}}{=} (\!|\, e_2 \,|\!)R^\sharp \\ e_1'^\sharp \stackrel{\text{def}}{=} \text{rmMod}(e_1^\sharp, m_1)R^\sharp \qquad e_2'^\sharp \stackrel{\text{def}}{=} \text{rmMod}(e_2^\sharp, m_2)R^\sharp \\ \text{neither the rule } \textsc{Mult2Const} \text{ nor } \textsc{MultPosConst} \\ \text{nor } \textsc{MultZeroConst} \text{ nor } \textsc{MultNegConst} \text{ can be applied} \end{array}}{(\!|\, e_1 \times e_2 \,|\!)R^\sharp \stackrel{\text{def}}{=} (\mathbf{reduce}(e_1'^\sharp \boxtimes e_2'^\sharp)R^\sharp, \mathbb{Z}, \Omega_1 \cup \Omega_2)}$$

Division. Propagating modular computations across divisions is quite tricky. Indeed, it can be done precisely only when the following conditions are met. First, the numerator has to be positive. We then consider the modulo interval of the numerator. The denominator has to be a nonzero constant that divides both bounds of this interval (or the bounds of the interval that contains the opposite values when the constant is negative). In addition, this interval must not include both negative (*i.e.*, < 0) and positive (*i.e.*, > 0) values. That is why two inference rules are provided, depending on the sign of both the denominator and the elements of the modulo interval. In such a case, the abstract expression is obtained by reducing the result of the application of the $\boxslash$ operator to the translation of its operands, thanks to the **reduce** primitive. This expression can be evaluated in modular arithmetic: the resulting modular ring is obtained by dividing by the constant both bounds of the modular ring of the numerator (or its opposite when the constant is negative). Because the constant is not 0, the computation does not yield additional error alarms. In all other cases, the **rmMod** operator is used to suppress the modulo computations in both translations of its arguments, and its result can be directly interpreted in $\mathbb{Z}$, at the cost of a possible loss of information. The resulting abstract expression can be potentially simplified by the means of the **reduce** parametric operator. Such computation also has to collect the potential error alarm ω_d when the primitive ι is unable to prove that the value of the denominator cannot be 0.

This is formalized in the following three inference rules.

$$\textsc{DivPosConst}\ \frac{\begin{array}{c}\alpha' \in \mathbb{Z} : (e_1^\sharp, [\alpha' l_1, \alpha' u_1[, \Omega_1) \stackrel{\text{def}}{=} \llparenthesis\, e_1 \,\rrparenthesis R^\sharp \\ \alpha \in \mathbb{Z} : (\boxed{\mathbb{Z}}(\alpha), m_2, \Omega_2) \stackrel{\text{def}}{=} \llparenthesis\, e_2 \,\rrparenthesis R^\sharp \qquad \alpha' \stackrel{\text{def}}{=} \alpha \bmod m_2 \\ \alpha' > 0 \qquad \iota(\text{toExpr}(e_1^\sharp))R^\sharp \subseteq [0, +\infty[\qquad l_1 \geq 0\end{array}}{\llparenthesis\, e_1 \mathbin{/} e_2 \,\rrparenthesis R^\sharp \stackrel{\text{def}}{=} (\textbf{reduce}(e_1^\sharp \boxslash \boxed{\mathbb{Z}}(\alpha'))R^\sharp, [l_1, u_1[, \Omega_1 \cup \Omega_2)}$$

$$\textsc{DivNegConst}\ \frac{\begin{array}{c}\alpha' \in \mathbb{Z} : (e_1^\sharp, [\alpha'(u_1-1), \alpha'(l_1-1)[, \Omega_1) \stackrel{\text{def}}{=} \llparenthesis\, e_1 \,\rrparenthesis R^\sharp \\ \alpha \in \mathbb{Z} : (\boxed{\mathbb{Z}}(\alpha), m_2, \Omega_2) \stackrel{\text{def}}{=} \llparenthesis\, e_2 \,\rrparenthesis R^\sharp \qquad \alpha' \stackrel{\text{def}}{=} \alpha \bmod m_2 \\ \alpha' < 0 \qquad \iota(\text{toExpr}(e_1^\sharp))R^\sharp \subseteq [0, +\infty[\qquad u_1 \leq 1\end{array}}{\llparenthesis\, e_1 \mathbin{/} e_2 \,\rrparenthesis R^\sharp \stackrel{\text{def}}{=} (\textbf{reduce}(e_1^\sharp \boxslash \boxed{\mathbb{Z}}(\alpha'))R^\sharp, [l_1, u_1[, \Omega_1 \cup \Omega_2)}$$

$$\textsc{DivNoMod}\ \frac{\begin{array}{c}(e_1^\sharp, m_1, \Omega_1) \stackrel{\text{def}}{=} \llparenthesis\, e_1 \,\rrparenthesis R^\sharp \\ (e_2^\sharp, m_2, \Omega_2) \stackrel{\text{def}}{=} \llparenthesis\, e_2 \,\rrparenthesis R^\sharp \qquad e_1'^\sharp \stackrel{\text{def}}{=} \text{rmMod}(e_1', m_1)R^\sharp \\ e_2'^\sharp \stackrel{\text{def}}{=} \text{rmMod}(e_2', m_2)R^\sharp \qquad \Omega_3 \stackrel{\text{def}}{=} \begin{cases}\{\omega_d\} & \text{if } 0 \in \iota(\text{toExpr}(e_2'^\sharp))R^\sharp \\ \emptyset & \text{otherwise}\end{cases} \\ \text{neither the rule } \textsc{DivPosConst} \text{ nor } \textsc{DivNegConst} \text{ can be applied}\end{array}}{\llparenthesis\, e_1 \mathbin{/} e_2 \,\rrparenthesis R^\sharp \stackrel{\text{def}}{=} (\textbf{reduce}(e_1'^\sharp \boxslash e_2'^\sharp)R^\sharp, \mathbb{Z}, \Omega_1 \cup \Omega_2 \cup \Omega_3)}$$

Bound check. Bound check expressions may warn about potential overflows and underflows. First, the expression in the argument of the bound check is translated. Then, if its potential values can be proven to be necessarily within the bounds checked, no additional alarm has to be collected. Otherwise, a potential error ω_o is collected.

Different methods can be used to compute the range of possible values of the translated expression. Whenever the interval of the outermost modulo of the inner expression is included in the interval of the bound check, there is no additional alarm to record. Otherwise, the primitive **rmMod** is used to eliminate the outermost modulo applied to the abstract expression. Then, the ι primitive is used to collect the range of the result. This range is checked against the bounds of the bound check.

This is formalized in the following two inference rules.

$$\text{BoundCheckMod}\ \frac{(e^\sharp, m, \Omega_e) \stackrel{\text{def}}{=} (\!| e |\!) R^\sharp \qquad m \subseteq [l, u[}{(\!| \textbf{bound\_check}(e, [l, u[) |\!) R^\sharp \stackrel{\text{def}}{=} (e^\sharp, m, \Omega_e)}$$

$$\text{BoundCheckNoMod}\ \frac{\begin{array}{c}(e^\sharp, m, \Omega_e) \stackrel{\text{def}}{=} (\!| e |\!) R^\sharp \qquad m \not\subseteq [l, u[\\ \Omega_1 \stackrel{\text{def}}{=} \begin{cases} \{\omega_o\} & \text{if } \iota(\text{toExpr}(\text{rmMod}(e^\sharp, m) R^\sharp)) R^\sharp \not\subseteq [l, u[\\ \varnothing & \text{otherwise} \end{cases}\end{array}}{(\!| \textbf{bound\_check}(e, [l, u[) |\!) R^\sharp \stackrel{\text{def}}{=} (e^\sharp, m, \Omega_e \cup \Omega_1)}$$

Modulo. The latest inference rules aim to propagate the outermost modulo computation in expressions of the form e **mod** $[l, u[$ into the sub-expression e. The premises of these conditions are not mutually exclusive. They are displayed according to their levels of priority. That is, only the first inference rule that can be applied is applied. In all following rules, any alarms encountered during the translation of sub-expressions are propagated, but no extra alarms are forwarded.

We begin with the case of a sum of two expressions such that the modulo specifications of the two abstract translations of the operands are compatible with the outermost modulo computation of the main expression. This compatibility is checked thanks to the notion of k-splittability. If they are compatible, the modulo specifications of the translations of both sub-expressions are discarded. Then, the abstract counterpart of the sum is used. Lastly, the resulting abstract expression is simplified by the means of the **reduce** parametric operator. This is formalized in the following inference rule.

$$\text{ModPlusExpr}\ \frac{\begin{array}{c}(e_1^\sharp, m_1, \Omega_1) \stackrel{\text{def}}{=} (\!| e_1 |\!) R^\sharp \\ (e_2^\sharp, m_2, \Omega_2) \stackrel{\text{def}}{=} (\!| e_2 |\!) R^\sharp \qquad m_1 \in \mathbb{S}(u_3 - l_3) \qquad m_2 \in \mathbb{S}(u_3 - l_3)\end{array}}{(\!| (e_1 + e_2) \textbf{ mod } [l_3, u_3[|\!) R^\sharp \stackrel{\text{def}}{=} (\textbf{reduce}(e_1^\sharp \boxplus e_2^\sharp) R^\sharp, [l_3, u_3[, \Omega_1 \cup \Omega_2)}$$

The case of a product between two sub-expressions works exactly the same way. This is formalized in the following inference rule.

$$\text{ModMultExpr}\ \frac{\begin{array}{c}(e_1^\sharp, m_1, \Omega_1) \stackrel{\text{def}}{=} (\!| e_1 |\!) R^\sharp \\ (e_2^\sharp, m_2, \Omega_2) \stackrel{\text{def}}{=} (\!| e_2 |\!) R^\sharp \qquad m_1 \in \mathbb{S}(u_3 - l_3) \qquad m_2 \in \mathbb{S}(u_3 - l_3)\end{array}}{(\!| (e_1 \times e_2) \textbf{ mod } [l_3, u_3[|\!) R^\sharp \stackrel{\text{def}}{=} (\textbf{reduce}(e_1^\sharp \boxtimes e_2^\sharp) R^\sharp, [l_3, u_3[, \Omega_1 \cup \Omega_2)}$$

For any other expression, or when the modulo computations are not compatible, the sub-expression e of the modulo computation is translated, which provides the specifications of a potential inner modulo computation m. Then, the application of the modulo m is followed by the application of the initial modulo $[l, u[$. We now introduce three cases, according to specific properties of m and $[l, u[$ to simplify these modulo computations.

As seen in Prop. 1, when one modulo computation follows another, the inner one can be discarded provided that the outer one is compatible with it. The compatibility between those modulo computations is checked thanks to the notion of k-splittability. This is formalized in the following inference rule.

$$\textsc{ModIdentity}\ \frac{(e^\sharp, m, \Omega_e) \stackrel{\text{def}}{=} (\!| e |\!)R^\sharp \qquad m \in \mathbb{S}(u-l)}{(\!| e \textbf{ mod } [l, u[\ |\!)R^\sharp \stackrel{\text{def}}{=} (e^\sharp, [l, u[, \Omega_e)}$$

As seen in Prop. 3, in some cases, the outermost modulo interval is large enough and compatible with the modular ring of the translated sub-expression. This happens when elements of the second interval are only translated when applying the modulo on the first interval. In such a case, we return the sub-expression without forgetting to translate the bounds of its modular ring. We can then discard the outermost modulo of the main expression. This is formalized in the following inference rule.

$$\textsc{ModTranslation}\ \frac{\begin{array}{c}(e^\sharp, [l', u'[, \Omega_e) \stackrel{\text{def}}{=} (\!| e |\!)R^\sharp \\ \alpha \stackrel{\text{def}}{=} l' \bmod [l, u[\qquad \alpha + u' - l' \leq u \qquad (u' - l') \mid (\alpha - l')\end{array}}{(\!| e \textbf{ mod } [l, u[\ |\!)R^\sharp \stackrel{\text{def}}{=} (e^\sharp, [\alpha, \alpha + u' - l'[, \Omega_e)}$$

When no other rules can be applied the primitive rmMod is used to eliminate the modulo specifications from the translated sub-expression, and the result is returned along the outermost modulo from the main expression as modular specifications. This is formalized in the following inference rule.

$$\textsc{ModIdentityNoMod}\ \frac{(e^\sharp, m, \Omega_e) \stackrel{\text{def}}{=} (\!| e |\!)R^\sharp}{(\!| e \textbf{ mod } [l, u[\ |\!)R^\sharp \stackrel{\text{def}}{=} (\text{rmMod}(e^\sharp, m)R^\sharp, [l, u[, \Omega_e)}$$

The following theorem states that the evaluation of a translated expression keeps all the possible values of the evaluation of the original expression. Moreover, the set of potential error alarms returned by the translation contains at least all the potential error alarms of the evaluation of the original expression. This is a stronger statement than the one needed to rewrite expressions, that corresponds to the corollary below, because the error alarms that may be yield by the evaluation of the abstract expression are discarded.

Theorem 4. *For all abstract element $R^\sharp$ and every expression $e \in expr$, with $\langle R_0, \Omega_0 \rangle \stackrel{\text{def}}{=} \gamma(R^\sharp)$ and $(e^\sharp, m, \Omega_e) \stackrel{\text{def}}{=} (\!| e |\!)R^\sharp$, then*

$$\forall \rho \in R_0,\ [\![e]\!]^\Omega \rho \subseteq \Omega_e \ \wedge\ [\![e]\!]^V \rho \subseteq \begin{cases} [\![\text{toExpr}(e^\sharp)]\!]^V \rho & \textit{if } m = \mathbb{Z}, \\ [\![\text{toExpr}(e^\sharp)\ \textit{mod}\ [l, u[\ ]\!]^V \rho & \textit{if } m = [l, u[. \end{cases}$$

By abuse of notation, we allow the syntactic sugar e **mod** $\mathbb{Z}$ *that represents* e.

Corollary 1 (of theorem 4). *For all abstract element $R^\sharp$ and expression $e \in expr$, with $\langle R_0, \Omega_0 \rangle \stackrel{\text{def}}{=} \gamma(R^\sharp)$, and $(e^\sharp, m, \Omega_e) \stackrel{\text{def}}{=} (\!| e |\!) R^\sharp$, the following rewriting property holds:*

$$\langle R_0, \Omega_0 \rangle \models e \preccurlyeq_{\Omega_e} \text{toExpr}(e^\sharp)\ mod\ m.$$

6.3 Integration with a Numerical Abstract Domain

We introduce a new numerical abstract domain with expression abstraction, noted $\mathcal{D}^\sharp_{\mathcal{L}}$, that is identical to $\mathcal{D}^\sharp$ except for the assignment and guard statements.

For any expression $e \in expr$ and any abstract element $R^\sharp \in \mathcal{D}^\sharp$, let us denote $(e^\sharp, m, \Omega_e) \stackrel{\text{def}}{=} (\!| e |\!) R^\sharp$. Then,

$$\text{ASSIGN}^\sharp{}_{\mathcal{L}}(X, e)R^\sharp \stackrel{\text{def}}{=} \langle \varnothing, \Omega_e \rangle \sqcup \text{ASSIGN}^\sharp(X, \text{toExpr}(\text{rmMod}(e^\sharp, m)R^\sharp))R^\sharp$$
$$\text{GUARD}^\sharp{}_{\mathcal{L}}(e, \bowtie)R^\sharp \stackrel{\text{def}}{=} \langle \varnothing, \Omega_e \rangle \sqcup \text{GUARD}^\sharp(\text{toExpr}(\text{rmMod}(e^\sharp, m)R^\sharp), \bowtie)R^\sharp$$

The soundness of these rewritings comes from Theorems. 1 and 3, as well as Corollary. 1.

7 Instantiation of the Generic Framework

In this section, we provide more explicit definitions for the ι and **reduce** primitives of our parametric abstraction. The other components are supposed to be defined in an underlying domain.

7.1 Intervalization

During the expression abstraction, the ι primitive is used multiple times, either to verify that modulo computations and bound checks can be safely suppressed, or to check that simplifications can be performed, as in the DIVPOSCONST inference rule. Thus, it appears that the more this primitive is precise, the more translations of expression will be precise.

A first possibility would be to represent the possible values of every expression by intervals over $\mathbb{Z}$ as presented in [4]. However, this method lacks the ability to represent relations between variables, which can be necessary to simplify modulo computations. For instance, in the program example introduced at the beginning of the paper Fig. 1, in order to suppress the modulo computations it is necessary to check that $X \geq Y$ holds. Thus, a domain able to represent the range of variables and the inequalities between pairs of variable, as the pentagon domain [17], is enough for our current study cases. However, it would be possible to use more precise abstract domains such as the difference bound matrices domain [?] that detects upper-bounds of the difference between pairs of variables, the octagon abstract domain [20] that handles inequalities of the form $\pm X \pm Y \leq c$ with X, Y variables and c a constant, or the polyhedron abstract domain [8] that keeps trace of linear inequality properties. Although using relational domains might be costly, it is possible to limit it by restraining the number of variables involved in the numerical constraints by a method named packing [2].

7.2 Simplification of Abstract Expressions

We now introduce a **reduce** implementation, denoted as $\mathbf{reduce}_0$, that is a heuristic which attempts to simplify abstract expressions without concealing potential error alarms. The purpose of this function is to achieve maximum expression canonization by using linear forms whenever possible.

The reduction $\mathbf{reduce}_0(e^\sharp)R^\sharp$ of an abstract expression $e^\sharp$, in the context of an abstract element $R^\sharp$, is defined inductively and by cases, by the means of a set of inference rules. Their premises are mutually exclusive, except for the NoReduce rule that is used only when no other rule can be applied.

Addition. When $\boxed{\mathcal{L}}(0)$ (that is the translation of 0_{cst}) is summed with another abstract expression, the latter abstract expression is returned. This is because 0_{cst} is a neutral element of $(expr, +)$. Also, when linear forms are summed, we return the canonical linear form of their sum. Lastly, when a linear form is added to a convex join expression, the addition is distributed over the operands of the convex join. In such case, it is possible to reduce both the new additions and the resulting abstract expression in order to simplify them. Those behaviors are formalized in the three following inference rules. If neither of the three can be applied, no reduction is performed.

$$\text{PlusZero}\ \frac{i, j \in \{1,2\} : i \neq j \qquad e_i^\sharp = \boxed{\mathcal{L}}(0)}{\mathbf{reduce}_0(e_1^\sharp \boxplus e_2^\sharp)R^\sharp \stackrel{\text{def}}{=} e_j^\sharp}$$

$$\text{PlusLinearForms}\ \frac{\begin{array}{ll} e_1^\sharp = \boxed{\mathcal{L}}\left(a_0 + \sum_{X_i \in \mathcal{V}} a_i X_i\right) & e_1^\sharp \neq \boxed{\mathcal{L}}(0) \\ e_2^\sharp = \boxed{\mathcal{L}}\left(b_0 + \sum_{X_i \in \mathcal{V}} b_i X_i\right) & e_2^\sharp \neq \boxed{\mathcal{L}}(0) \end{array}}{\mathbf{reduce}_0(e_1^\sharp \boxplus e_2^\sharp)R^\sharp \stackrel{\text{def}}{=} \boxed{\mathcal{L}}\left((a_0 + b_0) + \sum_{X_i \in \mathcal{V}} (a_i + b_i) X_i\right)}$$

$$\text{PlusConvexJoin}\ \frac{\begin{array}{c} i, j \in \{1,2\} : i \neq j \\ e_i^\sharp = e_{i,1}^\sharp \boxed{\cup} e_{i,2}^\sharp \qquad e_j^\sharp = \boxed{\mathcal{L}}\left(\alpha_0 + \sum_{X_i \in \mathcal{V}} a_i X_i\right) \qquad e_j^\sharp \neq \boxed{\mathcal{L}}(0) \\ e_1'^\sharp \stackrel{\text{def}}{=} \mathbf{reduce}_0(e_{i,1}^\sharp \boxplus e_j^\sharp)R^\sharp \qquad e_2'^\sharp \stackrel{\text{def}}{=} \mathbf{reduce}_0(e_{i,2}^\sharp \boxplus e_j^\sharp)R^\sharp \end{array}}{\mathbf{reduce}_0(e_1^\sharp \boxplus e_2^\sharp)R^\sharp \stackrel{\text{def}}{=} \mathbf{reduce}_0(e_1'^\sharp \boxed{\cup} e_2'^\sharp)R^\sharp}$$

Multiplication. Multiplying a linear form by a constant is the same thing as multiplying the linear form component-wise to its coefficients. One could think this reduction could hide potential errors when the multiplication is performed with 0. However, this is not possible because evaluation of linear forms does not trigger errors. Also, when a linear form is multiplied by a convex join expression, the multiplication is distributed over the operands of the convex join. In such case, it is possible to reduce both the new products and the resulting abstract expression in order to simplify them. Those reductions are formalized in the two following inference rules. If neither of the two can be applied, no reduction is performed.

$$\textsc{MultConst}\ \frac{i, j \in \{1, 2\} : i \neq j \qquad e_i^\sharp = \boxed{\mathcal{L}}\left(a_0 + \sum_{X_i \in \mathcal{V}} a_i X_i\right) \qquad e_j^\sharp = \boxed{\mathcal{L}}(b_0)}{\mathbf{reduce}_0(e_1^\sharp \boxtimes e_2^\sharp)R^\sharp \stackrel{\text{def}}{=} \boxed{\mathcal{L}}\left((a_0 \times b_0) + \sum_{X_i \in \mathcal{V}} (a_i \times b_0) X_i\right)}$$

$$\textsc{MultConvexJoin}\ \frac{\begin{array}{c} i, j \in \{1, 2\} : i \neq j \\ e_i^\sharp = e_{i,1}^\sharp \boxed{\cup}\, e_{i,2}^\sharp \qquad e_j^\sharp = \boxed{\mathcal{L}}\left(\alpha_0 + \sum_{X_i \in \mathcal{V}} a_i X_i\right) \\ e_1'^\sharp \stackrel{\text{def}}{=} \mathbf{reduce}_0(e_{i,1}^\sharp \boxtimes e_j^\sharp)R^\sharp \qquad e_2'^\sharp \stackrel{\text{def}}{=} \mathbf{reduce}_0(e_{i,2}^\sharp \boxtimes e_j^\sharp)R^\sharp \end{array}}{\mathbf{reduce}_0(e_1^\sharp \boxtimes e_2^\sharp)R^\sharp \stackrel{\text{def}}{=} \mathbf{reduce}_0(e_1'^\sharp \boxed{\cup}\, e_2'^\sharp)R^\sharp}$$

Division. The only rule introduced for specific reduction of abstract division expressions is the division of a linear form by a nonzero constant that divides all the coefficients of the linear form. In such a case, the resulting linear form is the original one divided component-wise by the coefficient. Like for the reduction rules of multiplication expressions, no errors can be hidden during this process because evaluation of linear forms does not trigger errors. If it cannot be applied, no reduction is performed.

$$\textsc{DivConst}\ \frac{e_2^\sharp = \boxed{\mathcal{L}}(b_0) \qquad b \neq 0 \qquad e_1^\sharp = \boxed{\mathcal{L}}\left((a_0 \times b_0) + \sum_{X_i \in \mathcal{V}} (a_i \times b_0) X_i\right)}{\mathbf{reduce}_0(e_1^\sharp \boxslash e_2^\sharp)R^\sharp \stackrel{\text{def}}{=} \boxed{\mathcal{L}}\left(a_0 + \sum_{X_i \in \mathcal{V}} a_i X_i\right)}$$

Convex Join. The convex join operator abstracts an idempotent, associative, and commutative operator. This can be exploited in the three following rules. If none of the three can be applied, no reduction is performed.

$$\textsc{ConvexJoinIdem1}\ \frac{e_1^\sharp = e_2^\sharp}{\mathbf{reduce}_0(e_1^\sharp \boxed{\cup}\, e_2^\sharp)R^\sharp \stackrel{\text{def}}{=} e_1^\sharp}$$

$$\textsc{ConvexJoinIdem2}\ \frac{i, j \in \{1, 2\} : i \neq j \qquad e_i^\sharp = e_{i,1}^\sharp \boxed{\cup}\, e_{i,2}^\sharp \qquad e_j^\sharp = e_{i,1}^\sharp \vee e_j^\sharp = e_{i,2}^\sharp}{\mathbf{reduce}_0(e_1^\sharp \boxed{\cup}\, e_2^\sharp)R^\sharp \stackrel{\text{def}}{=} e_i^\sharp}$$

$$\textsc{ConvexJoinIdem3}\ \frac{\begin{array}{c} e_1^\sharp \neq e_2^\sharp \qquad e_1^\sharp = e_{1,1}^\sharp \boxed{\cup}\, e_{1,2}^\sharp \qquad e_2^\sharp = e_{2,1}^\sharp \boxed{\cup}\, e_{2,2}^\sharp \\ i, j \in \{1, 2\} : i \neq j \qquad e_{1,i}^\sharp = e_{2,1}^\sharp \vee e_{1,i}^\sharp = e_{2,2}^\sharp \end{array}}{\mathbf{reduce}_0(e_1^\sharp \boxed{\cup}\, e_2^\sharp)R^\sharp \stackrel{\text{def}}{=} \mathbf{reduce}_0(e_{1,j}^\sharp \boxed{\cup}\, e_2^\sharp)R^\sharp}$$

```c
unsigned int x, a;
int16_t b;
if (a <= x && x-a <= 256 && b >= 0) {
  int16_t r = ((x - a) * b) >> 8;
  assert(0 <= r && r <= b);
}
```

(a). C language

```
if X + −A ≥ 0 then
  if X + −A ≤ 2^8 then
    if B ≥ 0 then
      R ← ((X + −A) × B) / 2^8;
      // 0 ≤ R ≤ B
    endif
  endif
endif
```

(b). Article's language (simplified)

Fig. 10. Second example of linear interpolation computation.

Default Rule. As described earlier, if no other reduction rule can be applied, the abstract expression is returned unmodified. This is formalized in the following inference rule that has no premises.

$$\textsc{NoReduce}\ \frac{}{\mathbf{reduce}_0(e^\sharp)R^\sharp \stackrel{\text{def}}{=} e^\sharp}$$

The soundness of the reduction rules of $\mathbf{reduce}_0$ is stated in the following theorem.

Theorem 5. *The* $\mathbf{reduce}_0$ *operator we introduced is a* **reduce** *operator as described in Def. 5.8.*

7.3 Linear Interpolation

One advantage of handling abstract expressions in the **reduce** function is that they are potentially simpler than the original expressions (*e.g.*, without modulo computations). Moreover, this function is applied during several stages of the reduction. Thus, it is possible to introduce new reduction rules that try to match patterns in order to simplify the matched abstract expressions.

We illustrate this method with the *interpolation detection step* that aims at finding and simplifying linear interpolation patterns. This step consists in the introduction of two new inference rules in $\mathbf{reduce}_0$. The first one matches a product of a linear form $\boxed{\mathcal{L}}(X - A)$ and an abstract expression $e_z^\sharp$, quotient by a linear form $\boxed{\mathcal{L}}(B - A)$ with $A, B, X \in \mathcal{V}$. It claims the quotient can be reduced to $\boxed{\mathcal{L}}(0) \boxed{\uplus} e_z^\sharp$ (or more precisely its reduction) when the denominator is nonzero and X is between A and B. This is the rule that can be used in the program example given at the beginning of the paper in Fig. 3. The second inductive rule introduced is quite similar, but the denominator is a strictly positive constant. Under the condition that $X - A$ is between 0 and kd, with k the maximum nonzero integer that verifies the property (that exists because $\mathbb{N}^*$ is well-founded), the reduction rule returns $\boxed{\mathcal{L}}(0) \boxed{\uplus} (e_z^\sharp \boxtimes \boxed{\mathcal{L}}(k))$ (modulo two reductions). This rule can, for example, be used to prove that, in Fig. 10, $0 \leq R \leq B$ holds if R is assigned. If these induction rules cannot be applied, the usual default rule NoReduce is used.

$$\text{INTERP1}\ \frac{\begin{array}{c} y,z \in \{1,2\} : y \neq z \\ X,A,B \in \mathcal{V} \qquad e^{\sharp}_{y} \stackrel{\text{def}}{=} \boxdot(X-A) \qquad \iota(B-A)R^{\sharp} \subseteq [1,+\infty[\\ \iota(X-A)R^{\sharp} \subseteq [0,+\infty[\qquad \iota(B-X)R^{\sharp} \subseteq [0,+\infty[\end{array}}{\mathbf{reduce}_0((e^{\sharp}_1 \boxtimes e^{\sharp}_2) \boxslash \boxdot(B-A))R^{\sharp} \stackrel{\text{def}}{=} \mathbf{reduce}_0(\boxdot(0) \boxed{\uplus}\, e^{\sharp}_z)R^{\sharp}}$$

$$\text{INTERP2}\ \frac{\begin{array}{c} y,z \in \{1,2\} : y \neq z \qquad d \in \mathbb{N}^* \qquad X,A \in \mathcal{V} \\ e^{\sharp}_{y} = \boxdot(X-A) \qquad k \stackrel{\text{def}}{=} \min\{\, k \in \mathbb{N}^* \mid \iota(X-A)R^{\sharp} \subseteq [0,kd]\,\} \\ e'^{\sharp}_{z} \stackrel{\text{def}}{=} \mathbf{reduce}_0(e^{\sharp}_z \boxtimes \boxdot(k))R^{\sharp} \end{array}}{\mathbf{reduce}_0((e^{\sharp}_1 \boxtimes e^{\sharp}_2) \boxslash \boxdot(d))R^{\sharp} \stackrel{\text{def}}{=} \mathbf{reduce}_0(\boxdot(0) \boxed{\uplus}\, e'^{\sharp}_z)R^{\sharp}}$$

In this section, we have introduced a reduction heuristic over abstract expressions. We have then presented that we can take advantage of the simplified form of the abstract expressions to recognize patterns, such as linear interpolations. Even if they allow some flexibility (*e.g.*, commutation of the operands in multiplications), the capability to recognize all linear interpolations can cause the number of rules to explode. It can then be interesting to memoize the result of pattern recognition so that further iterations would explore fewer cases.

8 Implementation Presentation

All the methods we have described have been implemented in the ASTRÉE [1,2] static analyzer but also in an extra toy abstract interpreter of C code [3] we submitted along this article to emphasize our work. Some implementation details and results of our artifact are detailed in this section.

The approach we have presented in this paper is sensitive to program transformations, and particularly to the usage of temporary variables, as in Fig. 2 In the implementations we also use adopted the *Symbolic Constant Propagation* methods [21] to eliminate them by propagating and simplifying the expressions assigned to them. A strategy has to be provided to the symbolic constant propagation domain to decide which variable substitute by its expression. The one we currently use consists in propagating the expressions as soon as they still contain variables.

The artifact has been evaluated on several code excerpts from industrial code. The improvement of both the analysis time and the number of false-alarms returned by the analyzer when adding the rewriting abstract domain that we presented is summarized in Fig. 11. The comparison has been made using three different underlying abstract domains implemented in the library APRON [15]: intervals (boxes), octagons, and polyhedra. If the analysis times out (after 5 seconds), the corresponding bars are hatched and the bar height is set to the height of the graph, so other bars are not flattened.

The C code excerpts that have been tested are the following ones:

- `fig1.c`, `fig2.c`, `fig3.c` and `fig10.c` respectively correspond to Figs. 1, 2, 3, and 10,
- `fig1_promo.c` and `fig2_promo.c` respectively correspond to Figs. 1 and 2 with the extra usage of integer promotion instead of `unsigned` data type,

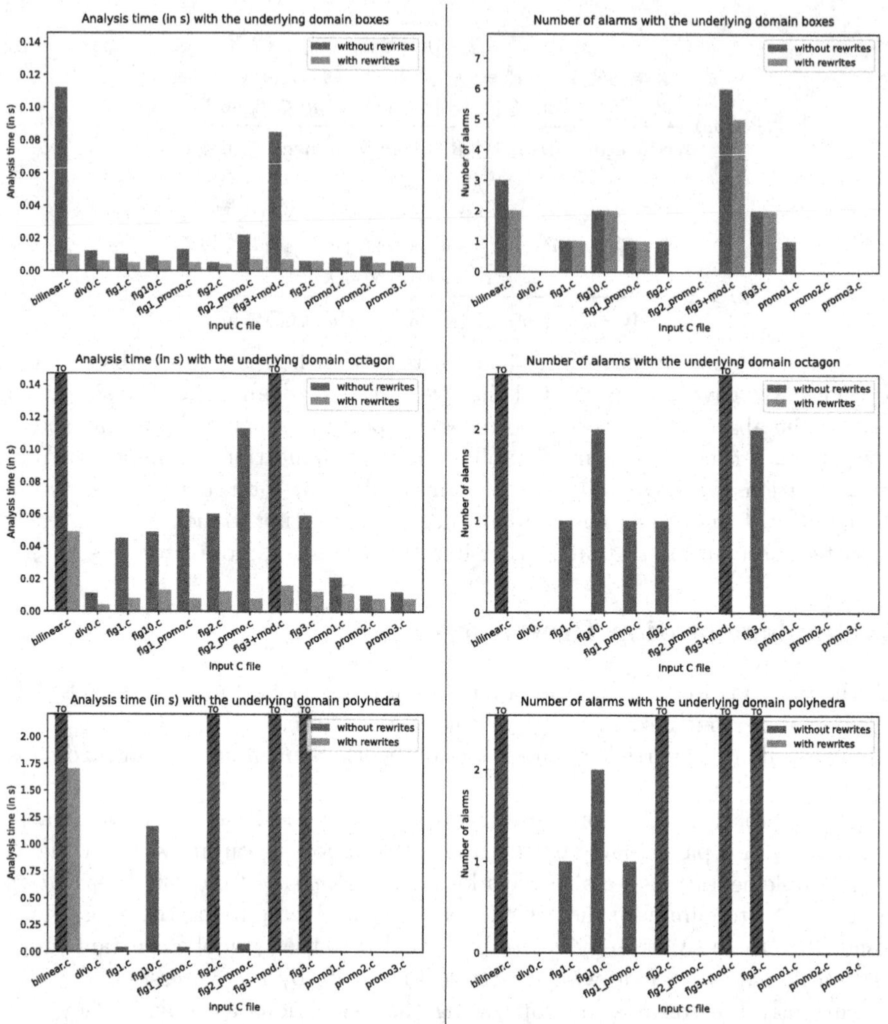

(a). Analysis time comparison. **(b).** Number of false alarms comparison.

Fig. 11. Comparison of the analysis of C files with and without the usage of the rewriting abstract domain, respectively with the interval, octagon, and polyhedron abstract domain as the underlying one.

- `fig3+mod.c` corresponds to Fig. 3 with the extra usage of variable differences as introduced in Fig. 1,
- `promo{1,2,3}.c` present different counter-intuitive effects of integer promotion in C code,
- `div0.c` is a demonstration that rewritings do not hide potential errors, in particular divisions by zero that are discarded during the rewriting,

- `bilinear.c` computes a bilinear interpolation that consists in 8 nested linear interpolations. Its exact range then has to be proven.

The results of our artifact 11 show that, as soon as the underlying abstract domain is able to prove obligation inequalities, the symbolic domain is able to eliminate inner modulo computations and discover more precise numerical properties. In general, the overhead cost is compensated by the fact that, due to the increase of accuracy, the time spent in the other domains is reduced.

9 Conclusion

We have proposed in this article a method to safely rewrite arithmetic expressions into simpler ones. In particular, modulo computations, that are frequent in the semantics of real-world programming languages, are safely discarded ; either by proving that they can be precisely described, or by replacing them conservatively. Then, a reduction operator has been introduced to achieve maximum expression canonization by using linear forms to the fullest extent possible. Those reductions allow us to match and simplify expression patterns, such as linear interpolations, for a low cost. Nevertheless, this technique remains general and could be used with other patterns. This method has been implemented within the ASTRÉE static analyzer, and a toy abstract interpreter that is available. An evaluation of the accuracy and the overhead cost induced by the new abstract domain has been presented and supports its effectiveness in the presence of modulo computations. The cost is generally compensated by the fact that, due to the increase of accuracy, the time spent in the other domains is reduced.

The reduction operator can be easily tuned to adapt to a wider class of interpolation scheme or other application domains. We would like to investigate further the accuracy of our analysis in a wider context and develop further refinement of the reduction operator.

Acknowledgements We thank the anonymous referees for their constructive comments and suggestions. Furthermore, we extend our gratitude to Josselin Giet, Marc Chevalier and Antoine Miné for granting us permission to publish a toy abstract interpreter they created, which served as the foundation for our artifact.

References

1. Blanchet, B., et al.: Design and implementation of a special-purpose static program analyzer for safety-critical real-time embedded software. In: Mogensen, T.Æ., Schmidt, D.A., Sudborough, I.H. (eds.) The Essence of Computation. LNCS, vol. 2566, pp. 85–108. Springer, Heidelberg (2002). https://doi.org/https://doi.org/10.1007/3-540-36377-7_5

2. Blanchet, B., et al.: A static analyzer for large safety-critical software. In: Programming Language Design and Implementation. ACM (2003). https://doi.org/https://doi.org/10.1145/781131.781153
3. Boillot, J., Feret, J.: Artifact for "symbolic transformation of expressions in modular arithmetic" (2023). https://doi.org/https://doi.org/10.5281/zenodo.8186873
4. Cousot, P., Cousot, R.: Static determination of dynamic properties of programs. In: International Symposium on Programming. Dunod (1976). https://doi.org/https://doi.org/10.1145/390019.808314
5. Cousot, P., Cousot, R.: Abstract interpretation: a unified lattice model for static analysis of programs by construction or approximation of fixpoints. In: Principles of Programming Languages. ACM (1977). https://doi.org/https://doi.org/10.1145/512950.512973
6. Cousot, P., Cousot, R.: Abstract interpretation and application to logic programs. J. Log. Program. (1992). https://doi.org/https://doi.org/10.1016/0743-1066(92)90030-7
7. Cousot, P., Cousot, R.: Comparing the Galois connection and widening/narrowing approaches to abstract interpretation. In: Bruynooghe, M., Wirsing, M. (eds.) PLILP 1992. LNCS, vol. 631, pp. 269–295. Springer, Heidelberg (1992). https://doi.org/https://doi.org/10.1007/3-540-55844-6_142
8. Cousot, P., Halbwachs, N.: Automatic discovery of linear restraints among variables of a program. In: Principles of Programming Languages. ACM (1978). https://doi.org/https://doi.org/10.1145/512760.512770
9. Cytron, R., Ferrante, J., Rosen, B.K., Wegman, M.N., Zadeck, F.K.: Efficiently computing static single assignment form and the control dependence graph. Trans. Program. Lang. Syst. **13**, 451–490 (1991). https://doi.org/https://doi.org/10.1145/115372.115320
10. Gallois-Wong, D.: Formalisation en Coq des algorithmes de filtre numérique calculés en précision finie. (Coq formalization of digital filter algorithms computed using finite precision arithmetic). Ph.D. thesis, University of Paris-Saclay, France (2021). https://tel.archives-ouvertes.fr/tel-03202580
11. Granger, P.: Static analysis of arithmetical congruences. Int. J. Comput. Math. **30**, 165–190 (1989). https://doi.org/https://doi.org/10.1080/00207168908803778
12. Granger, P.: Static analysis of linear congruence equalities among variables of a program. In: Abramsky, S., Maibaum, T.S.E. (eds.) CAAP 1991. LNCS, vol. 493, pp. 169–192. Springer, Heidelberg (1991). https://doi.org/https://doi.org/10.1007/3-540-53982-4_10
13. Halbwachs, N., Péron, M.: Discovering properties about arrays in simple programs. In: Programming Language Design and Implementation. ACM (2008). https://doi.org/https://doi.org/10.1145/1375581.1375623
14. ISO: International Standard ISO/IEC 9899:1999. International Organization for Standardization (2007). http://www.open-std.org/jtc1/sc22/wg14/www/docs/n1256.pdf
15. Jeannet, B., Miné, A.: APRON: a library of numerical abstract domains for static analysis. In: Bouajjani, A., Maler, O. (eds.) CAV 2009. LNCS, vol. 5643, pp. 661–667. Springer, Heidelberg (2009). https://doi.org/https://doi.org/10.1007/978-3-642-02658-4_52
16. Journault, M., Miné, A., Monat, R., Ouadjaout, A.: Combinations of reusable abstract domains for a multilingual static analyzer. In: Chakraborty, S., Navas, J.A. (eds.) VSTTE 2019. LNCS, vol. 12031, pp. 1–18. Springer, Cham (2020). https://doi.org/https://doi.org/10.1007/978-3-030-41600-3_1

17. Logozzo, F., Fähndrich, M.: Pentagons: a weakly relational abstract domain for the efficient validation of array accesses. In: Symposium on Applied Computing. ACM (2008). https://doi.org/https://doi.org/10.1016/j.scico.2009.04.004
18. Masdupuy, F.: Array abstractions using semantic analysis of trapezoid congruences. In: International Conference on Supercomputing. ACM (1992). https://doi.org/https://doi.org/10.1145/143369.143414
19. Miné, A.: A new numerical abstract domain based on difference-bound matrices. In: Danvy, O., Filinski, A. (eds.) PADO 2001. LNCS, vol. 2053, pp. 155–172. Springer, Heidelberg (2001). https://doi.org/https://doi.org/10.1007/3-540-44978-7_10
20. Mine, A.: The octagon abstract domain. In: Proceedings Eighth Working Conference on Reverse Engineering. IEEE Computer Society (2001). https://doi.org/https://doi.org/10.1109/WCRE.2001.957836
21. Miné, A.: Symbolic methods to enhance the precision of numerical abstract domains. In: Emerson, E.A., Namjoshi, K.S. (eds.) VMCAI 2006. LNCS, vol. 3855, pp. 348–363. Springer, Heidelberg (2005). https://doi.org/https://doi.org/10.1007/11609773_23
22. Müller-Olm, M., Seidl, H.: Analysis of modular arithmetic. In: Sagiv, M. (ed.) ESOP 2005. LNCS, vol. 3444, pp. 46–60. Springer, Heidelberg (2005). https://doi.org/https://doi.org/10.1007/978-3-540-31987-0_5
23. Simon, A., King, A.: Taming the wrapping of integer arithmetic. In: Nielson, H.R., Filé, G. (eds.) SAS 2007. LNCS, vol. 4634, pp. 121–136. Springer, Heidelberg (2007). https://doi.org/https://doi.org/10.1007/978-3-540-74061-2_8
24. Venet, A.J.: The gauge domain: scalable analysis of linear inequality invariants. In: Madhusudan, P., Seshia, S.A. (eds.) CAV 2012. LNCS, vol. 7358, pp. 139–154. Springer, Heidelberg (2012). https://doi.org/https://doi.org/10.1007/978-3-642-31424-7_15

A Formal Framework to Measure the Incompleteness of Abstract Interpretations

Marco Campion[1(✉)], Caterina Urban[1], Mila Dalla Preda[2], and Roberto Giacobazzi[3]

[1] INRIA & École Normale Supérieure, Université PSL, Paris, France
{marco.campion,caterina.urban}@inria.fr

[2] Department of Computer Science, University of Verona, Verona, Italy
mila.dallapreda@univr.it

[3] Department of Computer Science, University of Arizona, Tucson, AZ, USA
giacobazzi@arizona.edu

Abstract. In program analysis by abstract interpretation, backward-completeness represents no loss of precision between the result of the analysis and the abstraction of the concrete execution, while forward-completeness stands for no imprecision between the concretization of the analysis result and the concrete execution. Program analyzers satisfying one of the two properties (or both) are considered precise. Regrettably, as for all approximation methods, the presence of false-alarms is most of the time unavoidable and therefore we need to deal somehow with incompleteness of both. To this end, a new property called partial completeness has recently been formalized as a relaxation of backward-completeness allowing a limited amount of imprecision measured by quasi-metrics. However, the use of quasi-metrics enforces distance functions to adhere precisely the abstract domain ordering, thus not suitable to be used to weaken the forward-completeness property which considers also abstract domains that are not necessarily based on Galois Connections. In this paper, we formalize a weaker form of quasi-metric, called pre-metric, which can be defined on all domains equipped with a pre-order relation. We show how this newly defined notion of pre-metric allows us to derive other pre-metrics on other domains by exploiting the concretization and, when available, the abstraction maps, according to the information and the corresponding level of approximation that we want to measure. Finally, by exploiting pre-metrics as our imprecision meter, we introduce the partial forward/backward-completeness properties.

Keywords: Abstract Interpretation · Partial Completeness · Completeness · Program Analysis · Distances

1 Introduction

The theory of Abstract Interpretation introduced by Cousot and Cousot [20–22], is a general theory for the approximation of formal program semantics based on

M. V. Hermenegildo and J. F. Morales (Eds.): SAS 2023, LNCS 14284, pp. 114–138, 2023.
https://doi.org/10.1007/978-3-031-44245-2_7

a simple but striking idea that extracting properties of programs' execution means over-approximating their semantics. It is an invaluable framework that helps programmers design sound-by-construction program analysis tools as it makes possible to express mathematically the link between the output of a practical, approximated analysis, also called abstract semantics, and the original, uncomputable program semantics, also called concrete semantics.

The abstract interpretation of a program P consists of an abstract domain of properties of interest $\mathcal{A}$ ordered by a partial-order $\leq_{\mathcal{A}}$, a concretization map γ and an abstract interpreter $[\![\cdot]\!]_{\mathcal{A}}$, designed for the language used to specify P and on the abstract domain $\mathcal{A}$. Let $[\![P]\!]S$ be the result of the concrete (collecting) program semantics on a set of concrete inputs S. *Soundness* means that for all possible abstract inputs $S^\sharp \in \mathcal{A}$ it holds $[\![P]\!]\gamma(S^\sharp) \subseteq \gamma([\![P]\!]_{\mathcal{A}}S^\sharp)$. Furthermore, when $[\![P]\!]_{\mathcal{A}}$ also satisfies $[\![P]\!]\gamma(S^\sharp) = \gamma([\![P]\!]_{\mathcal{A}}S^\sharp)$ then $[\![P]\!]_{\mathcal{A}}$ is said to be *forward-complete* [32], while if the equation holds for a given input $S^\sharp \in \mathcal{A}$, then it is *locally* forward-complete at $S^\sharp$. In abstract interpretation forward-completeness intuitively encodes the greatest achievable precision for an abstract interpreter $[\![\cdot]\!]_{\mathcal{A}}$ applied on a program P, meaning that $[\![P]\!]_{\mathcal{A}}S^\sharp$ exactly matches the concrete result of the concrete counterpart $[\![P]\!]\gamma(S^\sharp)$. When the abstraction $\mathcal{A}$ also admits a Galois Connection (GC) with the concrete domain through an abstraction map α, then $[\![P]\!]_{\mathcal{A}}$ is said to be *backward-complete* when $\alpha([\![P]\!]S) = [\![P]\!]_{\mathcal{A}}\alpha(S)$ holds for all possible concrete set of inputs S, while *locally* backward-complete [5,7] at S if it holds for the input S. The backward-completeness property encodes an optimal behavior of the abstract interpreter $[\![\cdot]\!]_{\mathcal{A}}$ with respect to the abstraction in $\mathcal{A}$ of the concrete behavior $[\![P]\!]S$. Forward- and backward-completeness and their local versions are both highly desirable properties in program analysis for verifying safety properties of programs (also called correctness properties) [21,29,33,39]. Unfortunately, it is well known that whenever a non-trivial abstract domain is used, the analysis will be necessarily (locally) forward/backward-incomplete, meaning that false alarms or spurious counterexamples will arise also for correct programs [11,29]. In fact, forward/backward-completeness and their local definitions in program analysis are extremely hard, if not even impossible, to achieve [11,33]. For this reason, instead of trying to reach forward/backward-completeness, we need to deal with incompleteness of both and therefore with imprecision [27].

In this direction, the notion of *partial completeness* has been introduced in [11] in order to weaken the equality requirement of the local backward-completeness property. Partial completeness allows a limited amount of incompleteness and this amount is measured by quasi-metrics $\delta_{\mathcal{A}} : \mathcal{A} \times \mathcal{A} \to \mathbb{R}^{\infty}_{\geq 0} \cup \{\bot\}$ (where the symbol $\bot$ means undefined) compatible with the underlying abstract domain partial-ordering. More specifically, for a distance function $\delta_{\mathcal{A}}$ being a quasi-metric $\mathcal{A}$-compatible means satisfying for all $a_1, a_2, a_3 \in \mathcal{A}$: ($i$) the partial-ordering $\leq_{\mathcal{A}}$: $a_1 \leq_{\mathcal{A}} a_2 \;\Leftrightarrow\; \delta_{\mathcal{A}}(a_1, a_2) \neq \bot$; ($ii$) identity of indiscernibles: $a_1 = a_2 \;\Leftrightarrow\; \delta(a_1, a_2) = 0$; and ($iii$) the weak triangle inequality, namely, the triangle inequality only along chains $a_1 \leq_{\mathcal{A}} a_2 \leq_{\mathcal{A}} a_3$. So for instance, consider the intervals abstract domain [19] $\mathsf{Int} \overset{def}{=} \{[a, b] \mid a, b \in \mathbb{Z}^*,\ a \leq b\} \cup \{\bot_{\mathsf{Int}}\}$, where $\mathbb{Z}^* \stackrel{def}{=} \mathbb{Z} \cup \{-\infty, +\infty\}$, endowed with the standard ordering $\leq_{\mathsf{Int}}$ induced by the interval containment. We can consider as quasi-metric Int-compatible the distance $\delta^{\mathrm{m}}_{\mathsf{Int}}$ that counts how many more integer values has one interval with respect to another comparable interval. For instance, $\delta^{\mathrm{m}}_{\mathsf{Int}}([0,0],[0,5]) = 5$, $\delta^{\mathrm{m}}_{\mathsf{Int}}([0,+\infty],[-2,+\infty]) = 2$, while $\delta^{\mathrm{m}}_{\mathsf{Int}}([0,5],[0,0]) = \bot$ as $[0,5] \not\leq_{\mathsf{Int}} [0,0]$. The analysis $[\![P]\!]_{\mathcal{A}}\alpha(S)$ on a program P with input S is said to be ε-partial complete at input S for an amount $\varepsilon \in \mathbb{R}^{\infty}_{\geq 0}$ whenever $\delta_{\mathcal{A}}(\alpha([\![P]\!]S), [\![P]\!]_{\mathcal{A}}\alpha(S)) \leq \varepsilon$ holds, namely, the distance between the abstraction of the concrete execution and the result of the abstract interpreter is at maximum ε. In this setting, requiring 0-partial completeness at S corresponds to require local backward-completeness at S.

Main Contribution. In this paper we generalize the partial completeness property in order to be able to weaken both the local backward-completeness property in presence of a GC, *and* the local forward-completeness property in case only the concretization function γ is available. In this last scenario, as we may need to define distances on concrete domains, a weakening of the definition of quasi-metrics $\mathcal{A}$-compatible is necessary. This is because, in the original formalization [11], the definition of quasi-metric $\mathcal{A}$-compatible is specifically tailored for the structure of abstract domains and their relative partial-ordering: the axiom (i) forces the quasi-metric to return a value different from $\bot$ only if the two elements are comparable according to $\leq_{\mathcal{A}}$, namely $\delta_{\mathcal{A}}$ induces the partial-order $\leq_{\mathcal{A}}$. This is in fact not necessary: as our aim is to measure the incompleteness of an abstract interpreter with respect to the concrete execution, these two results are guaranteed to be comparable by soundness, therefore the distance may even return values on non-comparable elements as long as it is defined on all comparable ones. Moreover, the identity of indiscernibles axiom (ii) requires the quasi-metric to be precise enough to recognize equal elements since it constraints the distance to return zero whenever the two elements are equal. This is a too strong requirement especially in the scenario where only γ is available and we have to define a distance on the concrete domain where elements contain more information than what we are interested in for measuring the incompleteness. For instance, by considering the concrete domain $\wp(\mathbb{Z}^n)$ where n is the number of variables used in a program and elements in $S \in \wp(\mathbb{Z}^n)$ are program states, we might need a distance function $\delta_{\wp(\mathbb{Z}^n)}$ that measures the imprecision of certain variables only, say x and y. A possible estimate of this imprecision could be done by calculating the volume of their abstraction into the intervals abstract domain, namely, the area of the rectangle abstracting the values of x and y.

To this end, in Sect. 3 we reason on the *weakest* axioms that a distance function should meet so that it can be used to measure the local forward/backward-incompleteness. We just require a relaxed version of the identity of indiscernibles axiom (only the $\Leftarrow$ implication) and a condition on chains. As domains may not be complete lattices or partial-orders, such as the convex polyhedra abstract domain [24], we only require one of the weakest form of ordering relation known as a pre-order. The resulting distance function will be called *pre-metric* $\preceq_D$-

compatible where D is a pre-ordered set according to the pre-order $\preceq_D$. We will provide several useful examples of pre-metrics compatible to generic pre-ordered sets, as well as well-known numerical abstract domains, that can be used in practice. In Sect. 4 we show how this newly defined notion of pre-metric $\preceq_D$-compatible allows us to derive other pre-metrics from one domain to another by exploiting the concretization γ or, when available, the abstraction map α. Finally, in Sect. 5 we define the new properties *partial backward-completeness* and *partial forward-completeness* using pre-metrics compatible with the underlying domain ordering. We show that, when a certain condition on the precision of the pre-metric is met, then we can characterize the local forward/backward-completeness as the 0-partial forward/backward-completeness. The proposed framework is general enough to be instantiated by most known metrics for abstract interpretation [11,13,25,36,42]. Since imprecision, i.e., incompleteness, is unavoidable in program analysis, our ambition is to help abstract interpretation designers in defining distances able to measure the imprecision they *want to track* regardless of the domain on which they want to define the distance, hence providing the appropriate tools to fully control the imprecision propagation.

2 Background

Orderings. Given two sets S and T, $\wp(S)$ denotes the powerset of S, $\varnothing$ is the empty set, $S \subseteq T$ denotes sets inclusion, $|S|$ denotes the cardinality where S is finite if $|S| < \omega$, countably infinite if $|S| = \omega$, countable if $|S| \leq \omega$. A binary relation $\sim$ over a set S is a subset of the Cartesian product $\sim \subseteq S \times S$. We will emphasize the set S on which a binary relation $\sim$ is defined by the subscript $\sim_S$ except for the straightforward equivalence relation $=$ unless it has a different definition. We denote with $\mathbb{Z}$ and $\mathbb{R}$ the sets of all, respectively, integer and real numbers. We will use subscripts in order to limit their range, while the superscript symbol ∞ denotes the inclusion of the infinite symbol. For example, $\mathbb{R}^{\infty}_{\geq 0}$ denotes the set of all non-negative real numbers together with the symbol ∞ such that, for all $\varepsilon \in \mathbb{R}_{\geq 0}$, $\varepsilon < \infty$.

A binary relation $\preceq_L \in \wp(L \times L)$ is a *pre-order* iff it is reflexive ($\forall l \in L.\ l \preceq_L l$) and transitive ($\forall l_1, l_2, l_3 \in L.\ l_1 \preceq_L l_2 \wedge l_2 \preceq_L l_3 \Rightarrow l_1 \preceq_L l_3$). A set L endowed with a pre-order relation $\preceq_L$ is called a *pre-ordered set*, and it is denoted by $(L, \preceq_L)$. Furthermore, if $\preceq_L$ is anti-symmetric ($\forall l_1, l_2 \in L.\ l_1 \preceq_L l_2 \wedge l_2 \preceq_L l_1 \Rightarrow l_1 = l_2$) then it is a *partial-order* and the pair $(L, \preceq_L)$ is called a *partially-ordered set.* Clearly, every partially-ordered set is also a pre-ordered set. A subset $Y \subseteq L$ of a pre-ordered set $(L, \preceq_L)$ is a *chain* iff for all $y_1, y_2 \in Y$, $y_1 \preceq_L y_2$ or $y_2 \preceq_L y_1$.

Measures and Distances. A σ-algebra on a set X is a collection of subsets of X that includes X itself, it is closed under complement and it is closed under countable unions. The definition implies that it also includes the empty set $\varnothing$ and that it is closed under countable intersections. Consider a σ-algebra A over X. The tuple (X, A) is called a *measurable space.*

Definition 1 (Measure). *A function $\mu : A \to \mathbb{R}^{\infty}_{\geq 0}$ is called a measure iff it satisfies the following properties:*

(1) non-negativity: $\forall S \in A.\ \mu(S) \geq 0$;
(2) null empty set: $\mu(\varnothing) = 0$;
(3) countable additivity: if $S_i \in A$ is a countable sequence of disjoint sets, then $\mu(\bigcup_i S_i) = \sum_i \mu(S_i)$.

The triple (X, A, μ) is called a measure space. ■

A *metric* is a function that defines a distance between pairs of elements of a set S. Formally:

Definition 2 (Metric). *A metric on a non-empty set S is a map $\delta_S : S \times S \to \mathbb{R}_{\geq 0}$ that $\forall x, y, z \in S$ satisfies:*

(1) identity of indiscernibles: $x = y \Leftrightarrow \delta_S(x, y) = 0$;
(2) symmetry: $\delta_S(x, y) = \delta_S(y, x)$;
(3) triangle inequality: $\delta_S(x, z) \leq \delta_S(x, y) + \delta_S(y, z)$.

A set provided with a metric is called a metric space. ■

A function $\delta_S : S \times S \to \mathbb{R}_{\geq 0}$ satisfying all axioms of Definition 2 except for symmetry, is called a *quasi-metric*, while if δ_S does not satisfy the $\Leftarrow$ direction of the identity of indiscernibles axiom then it is called a *pseudo-metric*. A pseudoquasi-metric relaxes both the indiscernibility axiom and the symmetry axiom of a metric. δ_S is said to be a *pre-metric* if it satisfies only the $\Rightarrow$ implication of the identity of indiscernibility axiom (symmetry and triangle inequality may not hold).

Abstract Interpretation. We consider here the abstract interpretation framework as defined in [22] and based on the correspondence between a domain of concrete or exact properties $\mathcal{C}$ and a domain of abstract or approximate properties $\mathcal{A}$. Concrete and abstract domains are assumed to be at least pre-ordered sets, respectively $(\mathcal{C}, \preceq_{\mathcal{C}})$ and $(\mathcal{A}, \preceq_{\mathcal{A}})$, and be related by a monotone *concretization* function $\gamma : \mathcal{A} \to \mathcal{C}$. Furthermore, when they enjoy a *Galois Connection* (GC) through a monotone *abstraction* function $\alpha : \mathcal{C} \to \mathcal{A}$, denoted by the symbols $(\mathcal{C}, \preceq_{\mathcal{C}}) \underset{\alpha}{\overset{\gamma}{\leftrightarrows}} (\mathcal{A}, \preceq_{\mathcal{A}})$, then for all $a \in \mathcal{A}$ and $c \in \mathcal{C}$: $\alpha(c) \preceq_{\mathcal{A}} a \Leftrightarrow c \preceq_{\mathcal{C}} \gamma(a)$. A GC is a *Galois Insertion* (GI), denoted by $(\mathcal{C}, \preceq_{\mathcal{C}}) \underset{\alpha}{\overset{\gamma}{\leftrightarrows}} (\mathcal{A}, \preceq_{\mathcal{A}})$, when it holds $\alpha \circ \gamma = id$, where $\circ$ denotes functions composition and id is the identity function. A concrete element $c \in \mathcal{C}$ is said to be *exactly representable* in the abstract domain $\mathcal{A}$ when $\gamma(\alpha(c)) = c$.

Soundness and Completeness. Let $f_{\mathcal{C}} : \mathcal{C} \to \mathcal{C}$ be a concrete monotone operator (to keep notation simple we consider unary functions) and let $f_{\mathcal{A}} : \mathcal{A} \to \mathcal{A}$ be a corresponding monotone abstract operator defined on some abstraction $\mathcal{A}$. Then, $f_{\mathcal{A}}$ is a *sound* (or *correct*) approximation of $f_{\mathcal{C}}$ on $\mathcal{A}$ when for all $a \in \mathcal{A}$, $f_{\mathcal{C}}(\gamma(a)) \preceq_{\mathcal{C}} \gamma(f_{\mathcal{A}}(a))$ holds. When dealing with GCs, between all abstract functions that approximate a concrete one we can define the most precise one called *best correct approximation* (*bca* for short): $f^{\alpha}_{\mathcal{A}} \stackrel{def}{=} \alpha \circ f_{\mathcal{C}} \circ \gamma$. It turns out that any abstract function $f_{\mathcal{A}}$ is a correct approximation of $f_{\mathcal{C}}$ if and only if it holds $f^{\alpha}_{\mathcal{A}} \preceq_{\mathcal{A}} f_{\mathcal{A}}$ [20].

Given an abstract input $a \in \mathcal{A}$, when the concretization of $f_{\mathcal{A}}(a)$ matches the concrete counterpart $f_{\mathcal{C}}(\gamma(a))$ then $f_{\mathcal{A}}$ is said to be *locally forward-complete*[1] at the input $a \in \mathcal{A}$.

Definition 3 (Local forward-completeness). *Let $f_{\mathcal{A}} : \mathcal{A} \to \mathcal{A}$ be a sound approximation of $f_{\mathcal{C}} : \mathcal{C} \to \mathcal{C}$. Given an input $a \in \mathcal{A}$, $f_{\mathcal{A}}$ is said to be locally forward-complete at the input a, when $f_{\mathcal{C}}(\gamma(a)) = \gamma(f_{\mathcal{A}}(a))$ holds.* ■

When $\mathcal{C}$ and $\mathcal{A}$ admit a GC, then we can also define the property of *local backward-completeness* [5,7].

Definition 4 (Local backward-completeness). *Let $(\mathcal{C}, \preceq_{\mathcal{C}}) \underset{\alpha}{\overset{\gamma}{\leftrightarrows}} (\mathcal{A}, \preceq_{\mathcal{A}})$ and $f_{\mathcal{A}}$ be a sound approximation of $f_{\mathcal{C}}$. Given an input $c \in \mathcal{C}$, $f_{\mathcal{A}}$ is said to be locally backward-complete at the input c, when $\alpha(f_{\mathcal{C}}(c)) = f_{\mathcal{A}}(\alpha(c))$.* ■

The local forward- and backward-completeness properties are a weakening of the standard notions of forward- [32] and backward-completeness[2] [20,21,33], respectively, which require Definition 3 and 4 to hold over all possible, respectively, abstract and concrete inputs. Intuitively, when $f_{\mathcal{A}}$ is an abstract transfer function on $\mathcal{A}$ used in some static program analysis algorithm, local backward-completeness at input $c \in \mathcal{C}$ encodes an optimal precision for $f_{\mathcal{A}}$ at input $\alpha(c)$, meaning that the abstract behavior of $f_{\mathcal{A}}(\alpha(c))$ on $\mathcal{A}$ exactly matches the abstraction in $\mathcal{A}$ of the concrete behavior of $f_{\mathcal{C}}(c)$. On the other hand, if $f_{\mathcal{A}}$ is locally forward-complete at the abstract input $a \in \mathcal{A}$ means that $f_{\mathcal{A}}$ acts on the abstract input a precisely as $f_{\mathcal{C}}$ does on its concretization. As a remark, when $f_{\mathcal{A}}$ is locally forward-complete on an input $a \in \mathcal{A}$ and $(\mathcal{C}, \preceq_{\mathcal{C}}) \underset{\alpha}{\overset{\gamma}{\leftrightarrows}} (\mathcal{A}, \preceq_{\mathcal{A}})$, then $f_{\mathcal{A}}$ is locally backward-complete at $\gamma(a)$, namely, $f_{\mathcal{A}}(a)$ corresponds to the bca $f^{\alpha}_{\mathcal{A}}(a)$.

A relaxation of Definition 4 has been introduced in [11], called *partial completeness*, where quasi-metrics compatible with the underlying abstract domain are considered to measure the imprecision of $f_{\mathcal{A}}(\alpha(c))$ compared to $\alpha(f_{\mathcal{C}}(c))$.

Definition 5 (ε-Partial (backward-)completeness). *Consider the Galois Connection $(\mathcal{C}, \preceq_{\mathcal{C}}) \underset{\alpha}{\overset{\gamma}{\leftrightarrows}} (\mathcal{A}, \preceq_{\mathcal{A}})$, a sound approximation $f_{\mathcal{A}}$ of $f_{\mathcal{C}}$, a quasi-metric $\delta_{\mathcal{A}}$ $\mathcal{A}$-compatible, and $\varepsilon \in \mathbb{R}^{\infty}_{\geq 0}$. The abstract operator $f_{\mathcal{A}}$ is said to be an ε-partial (backward-)complete approximation of $f_{\mathcal{C}}$ on input $c \in \mathcal{C}$ when the following inequality holds: $\delta_{\mathcal{A}}(\alpha(f_{\mathcal{C}}(c)), f_{\mathcal{A}}(\alpha_{\mathcal{A}}(c))) \leq \varepsilon$.* ■

[1] The term "forward-completeness" was introduced in [32] in order to distinguish it from the well known backward-completeness property requiring an abstraction function.

[2] In the standard abstract interpretation framework [20,21] dealing with GCs, the backward-completeness property is simply called completeness or exactness.

Establishing ε-partial (backward-)completeness at input $c \in \mathcal{C}$ of an abstract operator $f_{\mathcal{A}}$, means that when computing $f_{\mathcal{A}}(\alpha(c))$, the output result is allowed to have an imprecision limited to ε compared to the abstraction of the concrete execution at c, namely, $\alpha(f_{\mathcal{C}}(c))$. The meaning of the value ε depends on the quasi-metric $\mathcal{A}$-compatible chosen. Note that the ε-partial (backward-)completeness property is always considered with respect to a specified input.

3 Distances on Orderings

The goal of this section is to set the minimum requirements that a distance function must meet so that it can be used to measure the local forward/backward-incompleteness generated by a sound abstract function $f_{\mathcal{A}} : \mathcal{A} \rightarrow \mathcal{A}$, operating on a set of approximated properties $\mathcal{A}$, with respect to the concrete function $f_{\mathcal{C}} : \mathcal{C} \rightarrow \mathcal{C}$, operating on a set of properties $\mathcal{C}$ some of which may be undecidable. The target distance function could be defined either on the concrete domain $\mathcal{C}$ in order to calculate the distance between $f_{\mathcal{C}}(\gamma(a))$ and $\gamma(f_{\mathcal{A}}(a))$ for an input $a \in \mathcal{A}$, that is the local forward-(in)completeness, or, e.g. when they enjoy a GC, directly on the abstract domain $\mathcal{A}$ for measuring the distance between $\alpha(f_{\mathcal{C}}(c))$ and $f_{\mathcal{A}}(\alpha(c))$ for $c \in \mathcal{C}$, that is the local backward-(in)completeness (as, e.g., formalized in [11] through the use of quasi-metrics).

In abstract interpretation both $\mathcal{C}$ and $\mathcal{A}$ are often based on a qualitative notion of precision in order to know when an element is more precise respect to another. More generally, given an unordered set D, a basic relation able to accomplish this task is a pre-order relation $\preceq_D \in \wp(D \times D)$ where $x \preceq_D y$ for $x, y \in D$ intuitively means that y *approximates* x [22]. Therefore, we need to define a general notion of distance able to exploit *any* pre-ordered structure. Let us informally analyze each property that we may expect on a distance measuring the local incompleteness, either backward or forward, of abstract interpretations.

When comparing two elements $x, y \in D$ in a pre-ordered set $(D, \preceq_D)$, the distance function $\delta_D(x, y)$ must return a non-negative real value for all $x, y \in D$. We also give δ_D the possibility to return the symbol ∞ meaning an infinite distance between two elements. Thus, the type of a distance function δ_D will be:

$$\delta_D : D \times D \rightarrow \mathbb{R}^{\infty}_{\geq 0} \tag{1}$$

If we are calculating the distance between two identical elements, then we expect δ_D to output zero:

$$x = y \Rightarrow \delta_D(x, y) = 0 \tag{2}$$

However, we do not require the converse implication: we allow $x \neq y$ even if $\delta_D(x, y) = 0$. This gives us the freedom to say that, e.g., the distance between two distinct elements is zero because the distance itself is considering the information represented by x and y *up to some abstraction of interest*. That is, the distance itself can be considered as *another* layer of approximation between the elements of D and, thus, it may output zero even if they are represented differently in D. For example, consider the poset $(\wp(\mathbb{Z}), \subseteq)$ corresponding to the powerset of integers together with the subset inclusion relation (i.e., a partial-order). Given two sets $X, Y \in \wp(\mathbb{Z})$ such that $X \subseteq Y$ (e.g., $X = \{2, 9, 19\}$ and $Y = \{2, 9, 15, 19\}$), we might be interested in a function $\delta_{\wp(\mathbb{Z})}$ that calculates the distance of an approximated representation of both X and Y, for instance, by taking their interval abstraction. In this case, it might happen that X and Y are mapped to the same interval (i.e., the interval $[2, 19]$ for the chosen X and Y) and therefore $\delta_{\wp(\mathbb{Z})}(X, Y) = 0$ even though $X \neq Y$. As another example, when considering the convex polyhedra domain $(\mathsf{Poly}, \preceq_{\mathsf{Poly}})$ [24] over $\mathbb{R}^n$ we might want that the distance between two polyhedra $p_1, p_2 \in \mathsf{Poly}$ is zero when they represent the same set of vectors in $\mathbb{R}^n$. That is, if $\gamma(p_1) = \gamma(p_2)$ then $\delta_{\mathsf{Poly}}(p_1, p_2) = 0$ even if p_1 and p_2 are represented by different inequalities in Poly, i.e., $p_1 \neq p_2$.

The requirements (1)–(2) define δ_D to be a generalization of a metric: by relaxing the identity of indiscernibles axiom and dropping the symmetry and triangle inequality axioms of metrics, we get a *pre-metric*[3]. Similarly to the relation between pre-orders and other stronger orderings (e.g., partial-orders and equivalence relations), pre-metrics are more general than pseudoquasi-metrics, quasi-metrics and metrics (see Sect. 2): a pre-metric satisfying the triangle inequality axiom is a pseudoquasi-metric, furthermore if it also satisfies the identity of indiscernibles then it is a quasi-metric, while a symmetric quasi-metric is a metric. Pre-metrics can be considered as one of the weakest forms of distance functions from which we can build on top of pre-ordered sets.

Until now the definition of pre-metric does not consider the pre-order relation between elements of D. Recall that we are interested in computing a distance between the result of a concrete operator $f_{\mathcal{C}}$ working on $(\mathcal{C}, \preceq_{\mathcal{C}})$ and a *sound* abstract operator $f_{\mathcal{A}}$ working on $(\mathcal{A}, \preceq_{\mathcal{A}})$. Therefore, we already know that for any $a \in \mathcal{A}$ the two results $f_{\mathcal{C}}(\gamma(a))$ and $\gamma(f_{\mathcal{A}}(a))$ are comparable according to $\preceq_{\mathcal{C}}$, namely $f_{\mathcal{C}}(\gamma(a)) \preceq_{\mathcal{C}} \gamma(f_{\mathcal{A}}(a))$ thanks to the soundness assumption of $f_{\mathcal{A}}$. This means that our definition of distance should have a meaning when used to calculate distances between elements being part of the same chain, i.e., comparable according to $\preceq_D$, while we do not care about the result of $\delta_D(x, y)$ when $x \not\preceq_D y$. That said, suppose $x, y, z \in D$ are related by $x \preceq_D y \preceq_D z$, i.e., z is an approximation of y and y approximates x. If we ascend the chain from x to y, then we would expect that the remaining distance from y to z to be less than or equal the entire distance from x to z. Similarly, if we descend the chain from z to y then we would expect the remaining distance from x and y to be less than or equal the whole distance from x to z. Formally:

$$x \preceq_D y \preceq_D z \Rightarrow \delta_D(x, y) \leq \delta_D(x, z) \wedge \delta_D(y, z) \leq \delta_D(x, z) \tag{3}$$

This axiom gives us the possibility to reason on distance results between elements on the same chain. For example, suppose that the concrete and abstract domains are related by a GC $(\mathcal{C}, \preceq_{\mathcal{C}}) \underset{\alpha}{\overset{\gamma}{\leftrightarrows}} (\mathcal{A}, \preceq_{\mathcal{A}})$ and that we have defined a distance $\delta_{\mathcal{A}}$

[3] This is not a standard term in the literature: sometimes it is used to refer to other generalizations of metrics such as pseudosemi-metrics [8] or pseudo-metrics [34]; it sometimes appears as pra-metric [3]. This definition is taken from Wikipedia [1].

on the elements of $\mathcal{A}$. Given an input $c \in \mathcal{C}$, we already know that the result of the bca of $f_\mathcal{C}$ on $\mathcal{A}$ is in the middle between the abstraction of $f_\mathcal{C}(c)$ and the result of the abstract sound operator $f_\mathcal{A}(\alpha(c))$, namely, it holds $\alpha(f_\mathcal{C}(c)) \preceq_\mathcal{A} f^\alpha_\mathcal{A}(\alpha(c)) \preceq_\mathcal{A} f_\mathcal{A}(\alpha(c))$. In this case, we would expect that the distance between $\alpha(f_\mathcal{C}(c))$ and the best possible approximation of $f_\mathcal{C}$, i.e., $\delta_\mathcal{A}(\alpha(f_\mathcal{C}(c)), f^\alpha_\mathcal{A}(\alpha(c)))$ to be less than or equal to the distance between the concrete and the chosen abstract operator $f_\mathcal{A}$, namely, $\delta_\mathcal{A}(\alpha(f_\mathcal{C}(c)), f_\mathcal{A}(\alpha(c)))$, and the same for $\delta_\mathcal{A}(f^\alpha_\mathcal{A}(\alpha(c)), f_\mathcal{A}(\alpha(c)))$. Note that the triangle inequality axiom required by metrics and some of their weakening, like pseudo-metrics and quasi-metrics, does not imply axiom (3), and (3) does not imply the triangle inequality. For example, if $D = \{x, y, z\}$ with $x \preceq_D y \preceq_D z$ and $\delta_D(x, y) = 2$, $\delta_D(y, z) = 1$, $\delta_D(x, z) = 1$, then $\delta_D(x, z) = 1 < 3 = \delta_D(x, y) + \delta_D(y, z)$ but $\delta_D(x, y) = 2 > \delta_D(x, z) = 1$. Instead, if $\delta_D(x, y) = 1$, $\delta_D(y, z) = 1$, $\delta_D(x, z) = 3$ then (3) holds while $\delta_D(x, z) = 3 > 2 = \delta_D(x, y) + \delta_D(y, z)$. In fact, we do not require the triangle inequality axiom (neither its weaker form on chains as formalized, e.g., in [11,25,36]): as we are focusing on incompleteness results and, therefore, elements on chains according to the ordering $\preceq_D$, the distance $\delta_D(x, z)$ could be greater or lower than the sum between $\delta_D(x, y)$ and $\delta_D(y, z)$ as long as it respects (3).

We now have all the ingredients needed to formalize the distance that matches our purposes: it must be a pre-metric (axioms (1)–(2)) compatible with the underlying pre-order (axiom (3)). Functions that meet these requirements over a pre-ordered set $(D, \preceq_D)$ are called *pre-metrics $\preceq_D$-compatible.*

Definition 6 (Pre-metric $\preceq_D$-compatible) *Let $(D, \preceq_D)$ be a pre-ordered set. The function δ_D is a pre-metric $\preceq_D$-compatible if and only if the following axioms are satisfied for all $x, y, z \in D$:*

(1) $\delta_D \in D \times D \to \mathbb{R}^\infty_{\geq 0}$;
(2) $x = y \Rightarrow \delta_D(x, y) = 0$;
(3) $x \preceq_D y \preceq_D z \Rightarrow \delta_D(x, y) \leq \delta_D(x, z), \wedge, \delta_D(y, z) \leq \delta_D(x, z)$. ■

Pre-ordered sets equipped with a compatible pre-metric are called *pre-metric $\preceq_D$-compatible spaces.*

Definition 7 (Pre-metric $\preceq_D$-compatible space). *Given a pre-ordered set $(D, \preceq_D)$ and a pre-metric $\preceq_D$-compatible δ_D, the triple $(D, \preceq_D, \delta_D)$ is a pre-metric $\preceq_D$-compatible space. We use $Pre((D, \preceq_D))$ to refer to the the set of all pre-metric $\preceq_D$-compatible spaces: $(D, \preceq_D, \delta_D) \in Pre((D, \preceq_D))$.* ■

The following is a list of pre-metrics compatible with a generic pre-ordered set $(D, \preceq_D)$ or tailored for specific domains.

Example 1 (Zero-distance). One of the most trivial pre-metric $\preceq_D$-compatible definable on any pre-ordered set is the distance that always returns the value zero for all $x, y \in D$:

$$\delta^0_D(x, y) \stackrel{def}{=} 0$$

Although it satisfies all axioms from Definition 6, it does not provide any information about the distance between elements in D since it treats them as they are close to each other. ♦

Example 2 (Ordering-distance). The following distance

$$\delta_D^{\preceq_D}(x,y) \stackrel{def}{=} \begin{cases} 0 & \text{if } x = y, \\ 1 & \text{if } x \neq y \wedge x \preceq_D y, \\ \infty & \text{otherwise} \end{cases}$$

is clearly a pre-metric $\preceq_D$-compatible. In fact, it extends the pre-order relation $\preceq_D$ with the function $\delta_D^{\preceq_D}$ having three output values: 0 for equal elements, 1 for not equal but comparable elements and ∞ for non-comparable elements. ♦

Example 3 (Measure-distance). Let (Z, D, μ) be a measure space, i.e., D be a domain that forms a σ-algebra over a set Z and $\mu : D \to \mathbb{R}^{\infty}_{\geq 0}$ be a measure function. We define the function δ_D^{μ} for every $X, Y \in D$ as follows:

$$\delta_D^{\mu}(X,Y) \stackrel{def}{=} Av(\mu(Y) - \mu(X))$$

where Av is the absolute value function. Note that, because D is composed by measurable properties, δ_D^{μ} can exploit the measure function μ in order to quantify the distance between elements of D. However, depending on how $\preceq_D$ is defined, it still may not be a pre-metric $\preceq_D$-compatible as axiom (3) may be violated. Let us show two examples where δ_D^{μ} is compatible with $\preceq_D$.

Consider the measure space $(D, \wp(D), \mu^c)$, where $(\wp(D), \subseteq)$ and μ^c is the *counting measure*, namely, for all $X \in \wp(D)$, $\mu^c(X) \stackrel{def}{=} |X|$ if $|X|$ is finite, ∞ otherwise. Intuitively, $\delta_{\wp(D)}^{\mu^c}(X,Y)$ counts the elements in X and Y and returns the absolute value of their difference. Note that: axioms (1)–(2) are satisfied since $\delta_{\wp(D)}^{\mu^c}(X,Y)$ is either non-negative or ∞, and if $X = Y$ then they have the same number of elements which implies[4] $\delta_{\wp(D)}^{\mu^c}(X,Y) = 0$. Furthermore, axiom (3) holds as $X \subseteq Y \subseteq Z$ implies that Z has more elements than Y and Y has more elements than X, thus ascending (resp. descending) a chain implies that the distance will increase (resp. decrease). The function $\delta_{\wp(D)}^{\mu^c}$ fulfills all axioms (1)–(3) and, therefore, it is a pre-metric $\subseteq$-compatible. Dually, the same reasoning holds with $\wp(D)$ being partially-ordered by $\supseteq$. This is one of the most common distance used for evaluating the outcome of a program analysis: you simply count the elements generated by the abstract analysis and the elements generated by the concrete execution and then the absolute value of the difference tells you the quality of the analysis result. The bigger this difference is, the worse the result will be. ♦

Example 4 (Volume-distance). Let us consider the pre-ordered domain of convex polyhedra $(\mathsf{Poly}, \preceq_{\mathsf{Poly}})$. We define the pre-metric

$$\delta_{\mathsf{Poly}}^{Vol}(p_1,p_2) \stackrel{def}{=} Av(Vol(p_1) - Vol(p_2))$$

[4] We assume the following results when the ∞ symbol is involved: $Av(k - \infty) = Av(\infty - k) = \infty$ with $k \in \mathbb{R}$, while $\infty - \infty = 0$.

calculating the absolute value of the difference between the volume of two convex polyhedra $p_1, p_2 \in \mathsf{Poly}$. The volume function $Vol : \mathsf{Poly} \to \mathbb{R}^{\infty}_{\geq 0}$ could be a monotone (namely, if $\gamma(p_1) \subseteq \gamma(p_2)$ then $Vol(p_1) \leq Vol(p_2)$) overapproximation of the exact volume computation (see, e.g., [15,35]). This means that Vol may not be a measure according to Definition 1 as the countable-additivity axiom may be violated. However, $\delta^{Vol}_{\mathsf{Poly}}$ satisfies the two axioms of Definition 6 and therefore it is $\preceq_{\mathsf{Poly}}$-compatible. ♦

Example 5 (Trace-Length distance). Let Σ be a set of program states and let $\Sigma^{+\infty} \stackrel{def}{=} \Sigma^{+} \cup \Sigma^{\infty}$ be the set of all non-empty finite (Σ^{+}) and infinite (Σ^{∞}) sequences of program states. We consider the domain of sets of program traces ordered by set inclusion, i.e., $(\wp(\Sigma^{+\infty}), \subseteq)$, and define the following function Len: $\wp(\Sigma^{+\infty}) \to \mathbb{R}^{\infty}_{\geq 0}$:

$$Len(T) \stackrel{def}{=} \begin{cases} 0 & \text{if } T = \varnothing, \\ \max\{|\sigma| \mid \sigma \in T\} & \text{if } T \cap \Sigma^{\infty} = \varnothing, \\ \infty & \text{otherwise} \end{cases}$$

where $|\sigma|$ applied on a trace denotes its length. Len computes the length of the longest program trace in a set of traces T. The following pre-metric

$$\delta^{Len}_{\wp(\Sigma^{+\infty})}(T_1, T_2) \stackrel{def}{=} Av(Len(T_1) - Len(T_2))$$

looking at the absolute value of the difference between the lengths of the longest traces in two sets $T_1, T_2 \in \wp(\Sigma^{+\infty})$ is a pre-metric $\subseteq$-compatible. Note that $Len(T)$ does not form a measure as the countable-additivity axiom does not hold. ♦

Example 6 (Weighted path-length distance). We consider the weighted path-length distance $\delta^{\mathfrak{w}}_{D}$ defined in [11] for posets. We propose a slightly modified version able to work with any pre-ordered structures $(D, \preceq_D)$. Intuitively, $\delta^{\mathfrak{w}}_{D}$ considers a pre-ordered set as a directed weighted graph where the set of edges $E_D \subseteq D \times D$ is defined as $E_D \stackrel{def}{=} \{(x, y) \mid x \prec\!\!\cdot_D\, y\}$, and $\mathfrak{w} : E_D \to \mathbb{R}_{\geq 0}$ is the weight function which assigns a non-negative real value to each edge. The relation $x \prec\!\!\cdot_D\, y$ is true whenever $x \prec_D y$ and there is no element $z \in D$ such that $x \prec_D z \prec_D y$. Clearly, if $\preceq_D$ is a partial-order then the graph is acyclic. Given $x, y \in D$ such that $x \neq y$, let $\mathfrak{C}^{y}_{x}$ denotes the set of all possible chains $\mathbf{c} \subseteq E_D$ between x and y such that if $(z, u) \in \mathbf{c}$ then $x \preceq_D z \prec\!\!\cdot_D\, u \preceq_D y$. It is clear that if $x \not\preceq_D y$ then $\mathfrak{C}^{y}_{x} = \varnothing$. The weighted path-length distance $\delta^{\mathfrak{w}}_{D} : D \times D \to \mathbb{R}^{\mathfrak{w}}_{\geq 0}$ is defined as follows:

$$\delta^{\mathfrak{w}}_{D}(x, y) \stackrel{def}{=} \begin{cases} 0 & \text{if } x = y, \\ \infty & \text{if } \forall \mathbf{c} \in \mathfrak{C}^{y}_{x}.\ |\mathbf{c}| = \omega, \\ \min\left\{ \sum_{e \in \mathbf{c}} \mathfrak{w}(e) \,\middle|\, \begin{array}{l} \mathbf{c} \in \mathfrak{C}^{y}_{x} \\ |\mathbf{c}| < \omega \end{array} \right\} & \text{if } \exists \mathbf{c} \in \mathfrak{C}^{y}_{x}.\ |\mathbf{c}| < \omega. \end{cases}$$

Intuitively, when $\delta^{\mathfrak{w}}_{D}$ is used to calculate the distance between x and y such that $x \prec_D y$ then it outputs the minimum weighted path w.r.t. $\mathfrak{w}$ between x and y, while if $x \not\preceq_D y$ then it outputs ∞. Note that $\delta_D^{\mathfrak{w}}$ is a pre-metric that does not satisfy symmetry, while it satisfies the triangle inequality axiom only on chains. However, it may not be compatible with the underlying ordering $\preceq_D$ as axiom (3) may turn false. For instance, consider the $\mathsf{Sign} \overset{def}{=} \{\mathbb{Z}, -, 0, +, \varnothing\}$ domain for sign analysis of integer variables [19]. Sign is ordered by the following partial-order: $\varnothing \preceq_{\mathsf{Sign}} 0 \preceq_{\mathsf{Sign}} - \preceq_{\mathsf{Sign}} \mathbb{Z}$ and $\varnothing \preceq_{\mathsf{Sign}} 0 \preceq_{\mathsf{Sign}} + \preceq_{\mathsf{Sign}} \mathbb{Z}$. Suppose the weight function $\mathfrak{w}$ assigns $\mathfrak{w}((0,-)) = 5$ while for the others couple $(a,b) \in E_{\mathsf{Sign}}$, $\mathfrak{w}((a,b)) = 1$. Then, the weighted path-length $\delta_{\mathsf{Sign}}^{\mathfrak{w}}$ is not a pre-metric $\preceq_{\mathsf{Sign}}$-compatible as $\delta_{\mathsf{Sign}}^{\mathfrak{w}}(0,-) = 5 > 2 = \delta_{\mathsf{Sign}}^{\mathfrak{w}}(0,\mathbb{Z})$ thus violating (3). On the other hand, if we set $\forall (a,b) \in E_{\mathsf{Sign}}, \mathfrak{w}((a,b)) = 1$ then we get a pre-metric $\preceq_{\mathsf{Sign}}$-compatible.

As a final case of application of $\delta_D^{\mathfrak{w}}$, consider the domain of integer intervals Int also known as the box domain. Given any two intervals $i_1, i_2 \in \mathsf{Int}$ such that $(i_1, i_2) \in E_{\mathsf{Int}}$, if we define $\mathfrak{w}((i_1,i_2)) = 1$, then $\delta_{\mathsf{Int}}^{\mathfrak{w}}$ is a pre-metric $\preceq_{\mathsf{Int}}$-compatible. Intuitively, $\delta_{\mathsf{Int}}^{\mathfrak{w}}(i_1,i_2)$ for $i_1 \preceq_{\mathsf{Int}} i_2$ counts how many more elements one interval has compared to the other: if $\delta_{\mathsf{Int}}^{\mathfrak{w}}(i_1,i_2) = k$ for some $k \in \mathbb{N}$, then the interval i_2 contains exactly k more elements than i_1. For instance, $\delta_{\mathsf{Int}}^{\mathfrak{w}}([0,0],[-1,2]) = 3$ as the interval $[-1,2]$ has 3 more elements than the singleton $[0,0]$, namely: $-1, 1, 2$; $\delta_{\mathsf{Int}}^{\mathfrak{w}}([0,10],[0,+\infty]) = \infty$ as $[0,+\infty]$ has an infinite number of more elements than $[0,10]$, while $\delta_{\mathsf{Int}}^{\mathfrak{w}}([0,+\infty],[-5,+\infty]) = 5$. ♦

When a pre-metric $\preceq_D$-compatible is precise enough to assign zero only when two comparable elements are identical, namely, when it satisfies the identity of indiscernibles axiom on chains, it will be called *strong.*

Definition 8 (Strong pre-metric $\preceq_D$-compatible). *Consider the pre-ordered space $(D, \preceq_D, \delta_D)$. The pre-metric $\preceq_D$-compatible δ_D is said to be strong if and only if the following implication holds for every $x, y \in D$:*

$$x \preceq_D y \;\Rightarrow\; (\delta_D(x,y) = 0 \;\Rightarrow\; x = y) \qquad \blacksquare$$

For instance, the ordering-distance $\delta_D^{\preceq_D}$ of Example 2, the weighted path-length $\delta_{\mathsf{Int}}^{\mathfrak{w}}$ defined on intervals in Example 6, $\delta_{\mathsf{Poly}}^{Vol}$ of Example 4 with Vol calculating the exact volume, and the counting measure-distance on integer sets $\delta_{\wp(\mathbb{Z})}^{\mu^c}$, are strong. Conversely, the zero-distance δ_D^0 of Examples 1, the volume-distance $\delta_{\mathsf{Poly}}^{Vol}$ with Vol overapproximating the real volume, and the trace-length distance $\delta_{\wp(\Sigma^{+\infty})}^{Len}$ defined in Example 5, are not. We will see in Sect. 5 that strong pre-metrics $\preceq_D$-compatible play an important rule when measuring the local forward/backward-incompleteness of abstract interpretations.

As a last note, it is worth noting that Definition 6 is general enough to be instantiated with other definitions of metrics specifically tailored in the context of abstract interpretation. For instance, if a pre-metric $\preceq_D$-compatible δ_D is also symmetric and it satisfies the weak triangle inequality then it is a pseudo-metric $\preceq_D$-compatible according to [36], whereas if δ_D both induces the underlying order relation, it is strong and it satisfies the weak triangle inequality then it is a quasi-metric $\preceq_D$-compatible [11,25].

4 Deriving Pre-metrics from Domains

Concrete $\mathcal{C}$ and abstract $\mathcal{A}$ domains of properties in abstract interpretation are often related by a monotonic concretization function $\gamma : \mathcal{A} \to \mathcal{C}$ and sometimes additionally by a monotonic abstraction function $\alpha : \mathcal{C} \to \mathcal{A}$ that maps a concrete element to the best (i.e., the smallest according to $\preceq_{\mathcal{A}}$) abstract element approximating it, such that $(\mathcal{C}, \preceq_{\mathcal{C}}) \underset{\alpha}{\overset{\gamma}{\leftrightarrows}} (\mathcal{A}, \preceq_{\mathcal{A}})$ forms a GC. By exploiting these structures we can *derive* pre-metrics from one domain to another.

Given a pre-metric compatible with the concrete domain $(\mathcal{C}, \preceq_{\mathcal{C}})$, we can exploit the concretization function γ to derive a pre-metric compatible with the underlying abstract domain ordering $(\mathcal{A}, \preceq_{\mathcal{A}})$. Here a GC between $\mathcal{C}$ and $\mathcal{A}$ is not necessary.

Definition 9 (Induced distance from the concrete domain). *Consider* $(\mathcal{C}, \preceq_{\mathcal{C}}, \delta_{\mathcal{C}}) \in Pre((\mathcal{C}, \preceq_{\mathcal{C}}))$. *For all* $a_1, a_2 \in \mathcal{A}$, *we define:*

$$\overrightarrow{\delta}_{\mathcal{A}}(a_1, a_2) \overset{def}{=} \delta_{\mathcal{C}}(\gamma(a_1), \gamma(a_2))$$

as the pre-metric induced on $\mathcal{A}$ *from* $(\mathcal{C}, \preceq_{\mathcal{C}}, \delta_{\mathcal{C}})$. ■

Proposition 1. *The following statements hold:*

(i) $(\mathcal{A}, \preceq_{\mathcal{A}}, \overrightarrow{\delta}_{\mathcal{A}})$ *is a pre-metric* $\preceq_{\mathcal{A}}$*-compatible space;*
(ii) if $\delta_{\mathcal{C}}$ *is strong and* γ *is injective then* $\overrightarrow{\delta}_{\mathcal{A}}$ *is strong.* □

Furthermore, given $(\mathcal{A}, \preceq_{\mathcal{A}}, \delta_{\mathcal{A}}) \in Pre((\mathcal{A}, \preceq_{\mathcal{A}}))$, when the concrete and abstract domains admit a GC through an abstraction function $\alpha : \mathcal{C} \to \mathcal{A}$, we can derive the pre-metric $\preceq_{\mathcal{C}}$-compatible on the concrete properties $(\mathcal{C}, \preceq_{\mathcal{C}})$. This distance will be called the induced distance from the abstract pre-metric $\preceq_{\mathcal{A}}$-compatible space.

Definition 10 (Induced distance from the abstract domain). *Let the concrete and abstract domains be correlated by a GC* $(\mathcal{C}, \preceq_{\mathcal{C}}) \underset{\alpha}{\overset{\gamma}{\leftrightarrows}} (\mathcal{A}, \preceq_{\mathcal{A}})$. *Moreover, let* $(\mathcal{A}, \preceq_{\mathcal{A}}, \delta_{\mathcal{A}}) \in Pre((\mathcal{A}, \preceq_{\mathcal{A}}))$ *be a pre-metric* $\preceq_{\mathcal{A}}$*-compatible space. For all* $c_1, c_2 \in \mathcal{C}$, *we define:*

$$\overleftarrow{\delta}_{\mathcal{C}}(c_1, c_2) \overset{def}{=} \delta_{\mathcal{A}}(\alpha(c_1), \alpha(c_2))$$

as the pre-metric induced on $\mathcal{C}$ *from* $(\mathcal{A}, \preceq_{\mathcal{A}}, \delta_{\mathcal{A}})$. ■

Proposition 2. $(\mathcal{C}, \preceq_{\mathcal{C}}, \overleftarrow{\delta}_{\mathcal{C}})$ *is a pre-metric* $\preceq_{\mathcal{C}}$*-compatible space.* □

The derived pre-metric on the concrete properties is compatible with $\preceq_{\mathcal{C}}$ as it measures the distance between two concrete elements by throwing away non-relevant information according to the abstraction α.

Note how Definition 9 and Definition 10 define a way to build pre-metrics on domains correlated by a concretization function and/or an abstraction function.

This means that the distance itself δ_D defined on a pre-ordered domain D, can view properties of D on different levels of precision: δ_D can exploit a more approximated pre-metric $\delta_{\mathcal{A}}$ defined on an abstraction of properties $\mathcal{A}$ of D, e.g. we can use $\overleftarrow{\delta_D}$ when $(D, \preceq_D) \underset{\alpha}{\overset{\gamma}{\leftrightarrows}} (\mathcal{A}, \preceq_{\mathcal{A}})$. Alternatively, δ_D can exploit a more precise distance $\delta_{\mathcal{C}}$, for instance when $\delta_{\mathcal{C}}$ is defined on a more precise domain $\mathcal{C}$ related with D through the concretization $\gamma : D \to \mathcal{C}$, then we can use $\overrightarrow{\delta_D}$. We can also combine distances in a way similar to combining abstractions.

Example 7. Let Zone be the zone domain [37], and Oct be the octagon domain [38]. Both are relational domains, with Oct more precise than Zone, able to infer affine relationships (inequalities) between variables, although in a more restricted form respect to Poly. Consider the volume-distance $\delta^{Vol}_{\mathsf{Poly}}$ defined on convex polyhedra in Example 4. We can systematically derive other volume-distances on domains which can be represented by Poly, e.g., Int, Zone and Oct. For instance, given $\gamma_{\mathsf{Oct}} : \mathsf{Oct} \to \mathsf{Poly}$, $\gamma_{\mathsf{Zone}} : \mathsf{Zone} \to \mathsf{Poly}$, $\gamma_{\mathsf{Int}} : \mathsf{Int} \to \mathsf{Poly}$, for all $o_1, o_2 \in \mathsf{Oct}$, $z_1, z_2 \in \mathsf{Zone}$, $i_1, i_2 \in \mathsf{Int}$ we get

$$\overrightarrow{\delta^{Vol}_{\mathsf{Oct}}}(o_1, o_2) = \delta^{Vol}_{\mathsf{Poly}}(\gamma_{\mathsf{Oct}}(o_1), \gamma_{\mathsf{Oct}}(o_2))$$

$$\overrightarrow{\delta^{Vol}_{\mathsf{Zone}}}(z_1, z_2) = \delta^{Vol}_{\mathsf{Poly}}(\gamma_{\mathsf{Zone}}(z_1), \gamma_{\mathsf{Zone}}(z_2))$$

$$\overrightarrow{\delta^{Vol}_{\mathsf{Int}}}(i_1, i_2) = \delta^{Vol}_{\mathsf{Poly}}(\gamma_{\mathsf{Int}}(i_1), \gamma_{\mathsf{Int}}(i_2))$$

♦

Depending on a number of factors such as the imprecision we want to track, the quantity of information represented by a domain, and/or the computational complexity needed to implement δ_D, we may switch from one domain to another. This procedure is also common in program analysis by abstract interpretation where it can be useful to convert between one abstract domain and another, for instance to switch abstract domains dynamically during the analysis or benefit from abstract operators available in other more abstract domains (see, e.g., [18, 39]).

Example 8. Let us consider as concrete domain $(\wp(\mathbb{Z}^n), \subseteq)$ and the abstract pre-metric $\preceq_{\mathsf{Int}}$-compatible space $(\mathsf{Int}, \preceq_{\mathsf{Int}}, \delta^{\mathfrak{w}}_{\mathsf{Int}})$ of intervals together with the weighted path-length defined in Example 6. We can derive the pre-metric

$$\overleftarrow{\delta_{\wp(\mathbb{Z}^n)}}(S_1, S_2) = \delta^{\mathfrak{w}}_{\mathsf{Int}}(\alpha_i(S_1), \alpha_i(S_2))$$

where for all $S_1, S_2 \in \wp(\mathbb{Z}^n)$, $\alpha_i : \wp(\mathbb{Z}^n) \to \mathsf{Int}$ calculates the interval of the i-th component only, with $1 \leq i \leq n$, of set of vectors S_1 and S_2. For instance, if $n = 3$ and $S_1 = \{\langle 1, 9, 9\rangle, \langle 1, 0, 10\rangle\}$, $S_2 = \{\langle 1, 5, 0\rangle, \langle -1, 0, 10\rangle, \langle 5, 0, 0\rangle\}$ then $\alpha_1(S_1) = [1, 1]$, $\alpha_1(S_2) = [-1, 5]$, and their distance is $\overleftarrow{\delta_{\wp(\mathbb{Z}^n)}}(S_1, S_2) = \delta^{\mathfrak{w}}_{\mathsf{Int}}([1, 1], [-1, 5]) = 6$. This can be useful, e.g., when $\sigma \in S$ represents a program state and the i-th component of σ corresponds to the value of a program variable, thus, $\overleftarrow{\delta_{\wp(\mathbb{Z}^n)}}(S_1, S_2)$ is interested in calculating the imprecision of that variable only. ♦

5 Partial Forward/Backward-Completeness Properties

As already mentioned in Sect. 2, Campion et al. in [11] proposed a relaxation of the local backward-completeness through the use of quasi-metrics, leading to Definition 5. More specifically, they require $\mathcal{C}$ and $\mathcal{A}$ to be related by a GC. In their formalization, the use of quasi-metrics enforces distance functions to adhere precisely to the underlying partial-ordering (namely, returning a distance for comparable elements only), and to output zero only when both elements are equal (corresponding to (2) but with both implications). These conditions imply that, if we want to define a quasi-metric on the concrete properties $\mathcal{C}$, the distance function must be precise enough to distinguish when two concrete elements are equal, thus limiting the possibility to choose, e.g., computationally less expensive distances at the cost of losing precision. For instance, the volume-distance defined in Example 4 on Poly would not be possible as a quasi-metric Poly-compatible unless Vol exactly calculates the volume of a convex polytope, which has exponential complexity. Similarly, defining a distance that partially considers the information encoded in the concrete elements, e.g. the imprecision of a specific program variable (Example 8), is not allowed.

In this section we exploit the newly introduced notion of pre-metrics $\preceq_{\mathcal{D}}$-compatible to weaken both definitions of local forward-completeness (Definition 3) and local backward-completeness (Definition 4). Thanks to the weaker requirements of pre-metrics, we ask $\mathcal{C}$ and $\mathcal{A}$ to have fewer structures compared to [11]: they must be, at least, pre-ordered sets and be correlated by a monotone concretization function $\gamma : \mathcal{A} \to \mathcal{C}$ but not necessary forming a GC with an abstraction function α. Weakening the local forward-completeness property involves defining a pre-metric $\preceq_{\mathcal{C}}$-compatible on the concrete domain $(\mathcal{C}, \preceq_{\mathcal{C}})$: this can be achieved by either defining a pre-metric specifically tailored for $(\mathcal{C}, \preceq_{\mathcal{C}})$ or, as showed in Sect. 4, by deriving a distance from another domain which may approximate the computation. The new notion of ε-partial forward-completeness is defined as follows.

Definition 11 (ε-Partial forward-completeness). *Let us consider a pre-metric $\preceq_{\mathcal{C}}$-compatible space $(\mathcal{C}, \preceq_{\mathcal{C}}, \delta_{\mathcal{C}}) \in Pre((\mathcal{C}, \preceq_{\mathcal{C}}))$ and let $f_{\mathcal{A}} : \mathcal{A} \to \mathcal{A}$ be a sound approximation of $f_{\mathcal{C}} : \mathcal{C} \to \mathcal{C}$. Given $\varepsilon \in \mathbb{R}^{\infty}_{\geq 0}$, we say that $f_{\mathcal{A}}$ is an ε-partial forward-complete approximation of $f_{\mathcal{C}}$ on input $a \in \mathcal{A}$ if and only if the following predicate holds:*

$$\delta_{\mathcal{C}}(f_{\mathcal{C}}(\gamma(a)), \gamma(f_{\mathcal{A}}(a))) \leq \varepsilon \qquad \blacksquare$$

The value of the distance $\delta_{\mathcal{C}}$ between the result of the concrete operator $f_{\mathcal{C}}(\gamma(a))$ and the concretization of the abstract operator $\gamma(f_{\mathcal{A}}(a)))$ can be interpreted as the measure of the approximation introduced by $f_{\mathcal{A}}$ with respect to $f_{\mathcal{C}}$ at input a. Therefore, this distance encodes a quantitative level of imprecision introduced by $f_{\mathcal{A}}$, more precisely, *the imprecision that we want to measure* according to how we have defined the pre-metric $\preceq_{\mathcal{C}}$-compatible $\delta_{\mathcal{C}}$.

```
var x : int, y : int;
begin
  x = 0; y = 0;
  while (x <= 9) and (y >= 0) do
    if x <= 4 then
      x = x + 1; y = y + 1;
    else
      x = x + 1; y = y - 1;
    endif;
  done;
end
```

Fig. 1. The Program P

```
var x : int;
begin
  while x > 0 do
    x = x - 1;
  done;
end
```

Fig. 2. The Program Q

Example 9 (Static analysis of numeric invariants). We want to analyze the partial forward-completeness of the Interproc[5] [2] static analyzer when used to infer the numerical invariant of the while-loop of program P defined in Fig. 1 using the abstract domains $\mathcal{A} \in \{\mathsf{Oct}, \mathsf{Poly}\}$. The imprecision generated by the abstract execution $[\![P]\!]_{\mathcal{A}}$ with respect to the concrete (collecting) execution $[\![P]\!]$, is measured by using the following pre-metric $\subseteq$-compatible on $(\wp(\mathbb{Z}^n), \subseteq)$:

$$\%Vol(S_1, S_2) \stackrel{def}{=} \frac{(Vol(\alpha_{\mathsf{Int}^n}(S_2)) - Vol(\alpha_{\mathsf{Int}^n}(S_1))) \cdot 100}{Vol(\alpha_{\mathsf{Int}^n}(S_1))}$$

Intuitively, the value returned by $\%Vol(S_1, S_2)$ is to be interpreted as the percentage of more volume that the abstraction (α_{Int^n}) of S_2 into Int^n has compared to the volume of the abstraction of S_1 into Int^n, namely, $Vol(\alpha_{\mathsf{Int}^n}(S_1))$ and $Vol(\alpha_{\mathsf{Int}^n}(S_2))$ are the volumes of the two smallest hyperrectangles containing, respectively, S_1 and S_2. Calculating the exact volume of hyperrectangles is generally much less computationally expensive than computing volumes of octagons and polyhedra, so this choice can be a good trade-off. In our case example, $n = 2$ since P has two variables so that Int^2 represents rectangles and $Vol(\alpha_{\mathsf{Int}^2}(S))$ is the area of the rectangle $\alpha_{\mathsf{Int}^2}(S)$. Note that, since the concrete $[\![P]\!]$ and the two abstract executions $[\![P]\!]_{\mathsf{Poly}}$, $[\![P]\!]_{\mathsf{Oct}}$ respect $[\![P]\!] \subseteq \gamma_{\wp(\mathbb{Z}^2)}([\![P]\!]_{\mathsf{Poly}}) \subseteq \gamma_{\wp(\mathbb{Z}^2)}([\![P]\!]_{\mathsf{Oct}})$ where $\gamma_{\wp(\mathbb{Z}^2)}$ is the concretization of Oct and Poly into $\wp(\mathbb{Z}^2)$, then, thanks to axiom 3, we are sure that

$$\%Vol([\![P]\!], \gamma_{\wp(\mathbb{Z}^2)}([\![P]\!]_{\mathsf{Poly}})) \leq \%Vol([\![P]\!], \gamma_{\wp(\mathbb{Z}^2)}([\![P]\!]_{\mathsf{Oct}}))$$

$$\%Vol(\gamma_{\wp(\mathbb{Z}^2)}([\![P]\!]_{\mathsf{Poly}}), \gamma_{\wp(\mathbb{Z}^2)}([\![P]\!]_{\mathsf{Oct}})) \leq \%Vol([\![P]\!], \gamma_{\wp(\mathbb{Z}^2)}([\![P]\!]_{\mathsf{Oct}}))$$

hold for program P. This means that $\%Vol$ *estimates how more inaccurate* is $[\![P]\!]_{\mathsf{Oct}}$ compared to $[\![P]\!]_{\mathsf{Poly}}$, $[\![P]\!]_{\mathsf{Poly}}$ compared to $[\![P]\!]$, and $[\![P]\!]_{\mathsf{Oct}}$ compared to $[\![P]\!]$.

[5] Interproc is freely available at http://pop-art.inrialpes.fr/interproc/interprocweb.cgi.

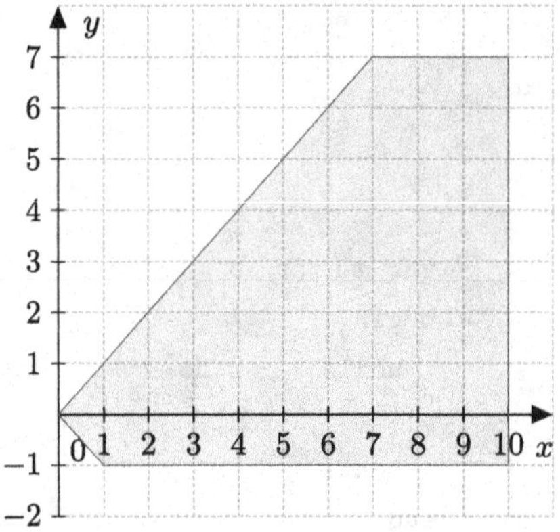

Fig. 3. Loop invariant generated by $[\![P]\!]_{\mathsf{Oct}}$

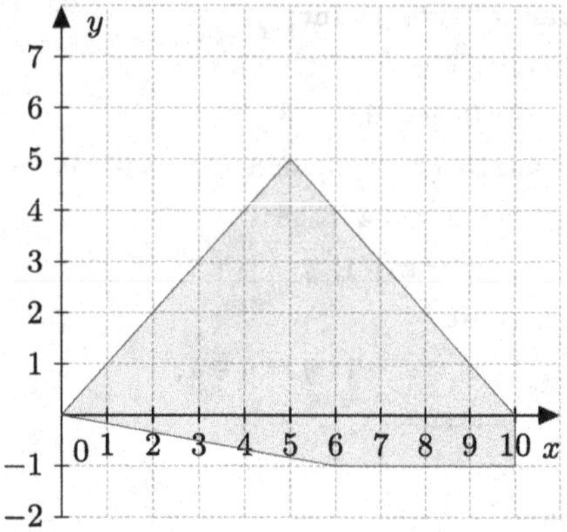

Fig. 4. Loop invariant generated by $[\![P]\!]_{\mathsf{Poly}}$

Suppose our imprecision tolerance measured by $\%Vol$ is 20%. We want to verify when $\%Vol([\![P]\!], \gamma_{\wp(\mathbb{Z}^2)}([\![P]\!]_{\mathcal{A}})) \leq 20$ holds, i.e., whether $[\![P]\!]_{\mathsf{Oct}}$ and $[\![P]\!]_{\mathsf{Poly}}$ are 20-partial forward-complete. By running Interproc using Oct and Poly[6] we get the following inequalities representing the inferred while-loop invariants:

$$\begin{aligned}[\![P]\!]_{\mathsf{Oct}} &= \{x >= 0; -x + 10 >= 0; -x + y + 11 >= 0; x + y >= 0;\\ &\quad y + 1 >= 0; -x - y + 17 >= 0; x - y >= 0; -y + 7 >= 0\}\\ [\![P]\!]_{\mathsf{Poly}} &= \{-x - y + 10 >= 0; -x + 10 >= 0; y + 1 >= 0;\\ &\quad x - y >= 0; x + 6y >= 0\}\end{aligned}$$

Fig. 3 and Fig. 4 depict, respectively, $[\![P]\!]_{\mathsf{Oct}}$ and $[\![P]\!]_{\mathsf{Poly}}$. The pre-metric $\%Vol$ outputs:

$$\begin{aligned}\%Vol(\gamma_{\wp(\mathbb{Z}^2)}([\![P]\!]_{\mathsf{Poly}}), \gamma_{\wp(\mathbb{Z}^2)}([\![P]\!]_{\mathsf{Oct}})) &= 33.33\\ \%Vol([\![P]\!], \gamma_{\wp(\mathbb{Z}^2)}([\![P]\!]_{\mathsf{Poly}})) &= 20\\ \%Vol([\![P]\!], \gamma_{\wp(\mathbb{Z}^2)}([\![P]\!]_{\mathsf{Oct}})) &= 60\end{aligned}$$

These numbers validate the better accuracy of $[\![P]\!]_{\mathsf{Poly}}$ compared to $[\![P]\!]_{\mathsf{Oct}}$ by providing us a quantitative estimation: the rectangle representing $[\![P]\!]_{\mathsf{Oct}}$ has 33.33% more volume than $[\![P]\!]_{\mathsf{Poly}}$, the one representing $[\![P]\!]_{\mathsf{Poly}}$ has 20% more volume than the concrete execution $[\![P]\!]$, while $[\![P]\!]_{\mathsf{Oct}}$ has 60% more volume than $[\![P]\!]$. We can conclude that $[\![P]\!]_{\mathsf{Poly}}$ is 20-partial forward-complete whereas $[\![P]\!]_{\mathsf{Oct}}$ is not.

It is worth noting that, the same results can be drawn by defining a similar (computationally more efficient) pre-metric compatible with the Oct domain $\%Vol(o_1, o_2)$ with $o_1, o_2 \in \mathsf{Oct}$ which abstracts octagons into boxes, thus calculating for instance $\%Vol(\alpha_{\mathsf{Oct}}([\![P]\!]), [\![P]\!]_{\mathsf{Oct}})$ without passing through the concrete domain $\wp(\mathbb{Z}^2)$. ♦

[6] For the convex polyhedra analysis, we activated the option of 2 descending steps.

When $\mathcal{C}$ and $\mathcal{A}$ enjoy a GC and a pre-metric $\preceq_{\mathcal{A}}$-compatible is defined over the abstract elements of $\mathcal{A}$, then we can weaken the notion of local backward-completeness to obtain the ε-partial backward-completeness property.

Definition 12 (ε-Partial backward-completeness). *Let the concrete and abstract domains be correlated by a GC* $(\mathcal{C}, \preceq_{\mathcal{C}}) \underset{\alpha}{\overset{\gamma}{\leftrightarrows}} (\mathcal{A}, \preceq_{\mathcal{A}})$. *Furthermore, assume* $(\mathcal{A}, \preceq_{\mathcal{A}}, \delta_{\mathcal{A}}) \in Pre((\mathcal{A}, \preceq_{\mathcal{A}}))$ *and let* $f_{\mathcal{A}} : \mathcal{A} \to \mathcal{A}$ *be a sound approximation of* $f_{\mathcal{C}} : \mathcal{C} \to \mathcal{C}$. *Given* $\varepsilon \in \mathbb{R}^{\infty}_{\geq 0}$, *we say that* $f_{\mathcal{A}}$ *is an ε-partial backward-complete approximation of* $f_{\mathcal{C}}$ *on input* $c \in \mathcal{C}$ *if and only if the following predicate holds:*

$$\delta_{\mathcal{A}}(\alpha(f_{\mathcal{C}}(c)), f_{\mathcal{A}}(\alpha(c))) \leq \varepsilon \qquad \blacksquare$$

The ε-partial backward-completeness property of an abstract sound operator $f_{\mathcal{A}}$ encodes a limited amount of imprecision measured by $\delta_{\mathcal{A}}$, namely at maximum ε, between the abstraction of the concrete execution $\alpha(f_{\mathcal{C}}(c))$ and the abstract execution $f_{\mathcal{A}}(\alpha(c))$ over the concrete input c. Note the difference between the above definition and Definition 5 presented in [11]: here $\mathcal{C}$ and $\mathcal{A}$ are required to be at least pre-orders, and pre-metrics $\preceq_{\mathcal{A}}$-compatible are employed as distance functions, instead of quasi-metrics $\mathcal{A}$-compatible.

We conclude this section by showing some common characteristics between partial forward- and partial backward-completeness properties.

Proposition 3. *Let* $(\mathcal{C}, \preceq_{\mathcal{C}}, \delta_{\mathcal{C}}) \in Pre((\mathcal{C}, \preceq_{\mathcal{C}}))$ *and* $f_{\mathcal{A}} : \mathcal{A} \to \mathcal{A}$ *be a correct approximation of* $f_{\mathcal{C}} : \mathcal{C} \to \mathcal{C}$. *The following hold for every* $a \in \mathcal{A}$:

(i) $f_{\mathcal{A}}$ *ε-partial forward-complete at* $a \;\Rightarrow\; \forall \xi \geq \varepsilon : f_{\mathcal{A}}$ *ξ-partial forward-complete at* a;
(ii) $f_{\mathcal{A}}$ *∞-partial forward-complete at* a. $\square$

Proposition 4. *Let* $(\mathcal{C}, \preceq_{\mathcal{C}}) \underset{\alpha}{\overset{\gamma}{\leftrightarrows}} (\mathcal{A}, \preceq_{\mathcal{A}})$ *and* $(\mathcal{A}, \preceq_{\mathcal{A}}, \delta_{\mathcal{A}}) \in Pre((\mathcal{A}, \preceq_{\mathcal{A}}))$. *The following hold for every* $c \in \mathcal{C}$:

(i) $f_{\mathcal{A}}$ *ε-partial backward-complete at* $c \;\Rightarrow\; \forall \xi \geq \varepsilon : f_{\mathcal{A}}$ *ξ-partial backward-complete at* c;
(ii) $f_{\mathcal{A}}$ *∞-partial backward-complete at* c. $\square$

If $f_{\mathcal{A}}$ is ε-partial forward-complete at a (resp. ε-partial backward-complete at c) then admitting a larger imprecision ξ according to $\delta_{\mathcal{C}}$ (resp. $\delta_{\mathcal{A}}$) results in the property of ξ-partial forward-completeness (resp. ξ-partial backward-completeness) which is always satisfied by $f_{\mathcal{A}}$. This implies that, if we define the class of all ε-partial forward-complete (sound) abstract operators with respect to $f_{\mathcal{C}}$ and input $a \in \mathcal{A}$, and the class of all ε-partial backward-complete (sound) abstract operators with respect to $f_{\mathcal{C}}$ and input $c \in \mathcal{C}$, namely

$$\mathbb{F}^{\varepsilon}_{f_{\mathcal{C}},a} \stackrel{def}{=} \{f_{\mathcal{A}} \mid \delta_{\mathcal{C}}(f_{\mathcal{C}}(\gamma(a)), \gamma(f_{\mathcal{A}}(a))) \leq \varepsilon\}$$
$$\mathbb{B}^{\varepsilon}_{f_{\mathcal{C}},c} \stackrel{def}{=} \{f_{\mathcal{A}} \mid \delta_{\mathcal{A}}(\alpha(f_{\mathcal{C}}(c)), f_{\mathcal{A}}(\alpha(c))) \leq \varepsilon\}$$

then for all $\xi \geq \varepsilon$: $\mathbb{F}^{\varepsilon}_{f_C,a} \subseteq \mathbb{F}^{\xi}_{f_C,a}$ and $\mathbb{B}^{\varepsilon}_{f_C,c} \subseteq \mathbb{B}^{\xi}_{f_C,c}$. The second point of Proposition 3 and Proposition 4 simply states that any sound approximation $f_{\mathcal{A}}$ of f_C is partial forward/backward-complete when we admit an infinite level of imprecision.

6 Characterizing Local Forward/Backward-Completeness

In the original definition of partial (backward-)completeness given in [11] using quasi-metrics, asking for 0-partial (backward-)completeness at an input $c \in \mathcal{C}$ is equivalent to require local backward-completeness at c [11].

In our more relaxed framework where pre-metrics are involved and the identity of indiscernibles axiom is not satisfied, requiring 0-partial backward-completeness at c may not be the same as demanding local backward-completeness at c and, similarly, requiring 0-partial forward-completeness at input $a \in \mathcal{A}$ may not coincide with local forward-completeness at a. This is a consequence of the possible approximation introduced by the pre-metric when valuating the distance.

Example 10. Given $(\wp(\mathbb{Z}^2), \subseteq)$, consider the pre-metric $\subseteq$-compatible $\%Vol$ defined in Example 9, and the two sets $S_1 = \{\langle 0,2\rangle, \langle 3,5\rangle\}$, $S_2 = \{\langle 0,2\rangle, \langle 1,1\rangle, \langle 3,5\rangle\}$ such that $S_1 \subseteq S_2$. The $\%Vol$ between S_1 and S_2 is $\%Vol(S_1, S_2) = 0$ even if $S_1 \neq S_2$. This is because of the approximation made by $\%Vol$ which considers an approximated representation of S_1 and S_2, namely, rectangles so that $\alpha_{\mathsf{Int}^2}(S_1) = \langle [0,3], [1,5]\rangle = \alpha_{\mathsf{Int}^2}(S_2)$. Therefore, if S_1 and S_2 are the results of, respectively, a concrete operator $f_{\wp(\mathbb{Z}^2)}$ and and abstract operator f_{Int^2}, then f_{Int^2} is 0-partial forward-complete but not local forward-complete. ♦

However, it turns out that the 0-partial forward-completeness property coincides with the local forward-completeness property when the pre-metric $\preceq_C$-compatible is strong.

Theorem 1. *If δ_C is strong then the following equivalence holds for all $a \in \mathcal{A}$:*

$$f_{\mathcal{A}} \text{ 0-partial forward-complete at } a \Leftrightarrow f_{\mathcal{A}} \text{ locally forward-complete at } a \quad \square$$

Example 11. If we define the weighted path-length directly on $(\wp(\mathbb{Z}), \subseteq)$, namely, $\delta^{\mathfrak{w}}_{\wp(\mathbb{Z})}$ where $\mathfrak{w}(S_1, S_2) = 1$ for all $(S_1, S_2) \in E_{\wp(\mathbb{Z})}$, then $\delta^{\mathfrak{w}}_{\wp(\mathbb{Z})}$ is strong. Consider the program Q defined in Fig. 2. We analyze the value of variable x at the end of the program having input the interval $[10, 10]$ using Interproc on the interval abstract domain Int with no widening at the first 10 loop iterations. The result of the analysis is $\gamma([\![Q]\!]_{\mathsf{Int}}[10,10]) = \{0\} = [\![Q]\!]\gamma([10,10])$, and the weighted path-length outputs

$$\delta^{\mathfrak{w}}_{\wp(\mathbb{Z})}([\![Q]\!]\gamma([10,10]), \gamma([\![Q]\!]_{\mathsf{Int}}[10,10])) = 0$$

i.e., $[\![Q]\!]_{\mathsf{Int}}$ is 0-partial forward-complete on input $[10, 10]$ using $\delta^{\mathfrak{w}}_{\wp(\mathbb{Z})}$. Since $\delta^{\mathfrak{w}}_{\wp(\mathbb{Z})}$ is strong, then we are sure that $[\![Q]\!]\gamma([10,10]) = \gamma([\![Q]\!]_{\mathsf{Int}}[10,10])$, i.e., $[\![Q]\!]_{\mathsf{Int}}$ is locally forward-complete. ♦

A similar reasoning also applies to the 0-partial backward-completeness property when strong pre-metrics $\preceq_{\mathcal{A}}$-compatible are employed.

Theorem 2. *If $\delta_{\mathcal{A}}$ is strong then the following equivalence holds for all $c \in \mathcal{C}$:*

$$f_{\mathcal{A}} \text{ 0-partial backward-complete at } c \Leftrightarrow f_{\mathcal{A}} \text{ locally backward-complete at } c \quad \square$$

As a final observation, in cases where the concrete and abstract domains enjoy a GI through an abstraction function $\alpha : \mathcal{C} \rightarrow \mathcal{A}$ and $\mathcal{A}$ is equipped with a strong pre-metric $\preceq_{\mathcal{A}}$-compatible $\delta_{\mathcal{A}}$, we can characterize the local backward-completeness property over exactly representable elements of $\mathcal{C}$ as an instance of the 0-partial forward-completeness property by exploiting the induced pre-metric $\overleftarrow{\delta_{\mathcal{C}}}$ from the abstract pre-metric $\preceq_{\mathcal{A}}$-compatible space.

Theorem 3. *Let $(\mathcal{C}, \preceq_{\mathcal{C}}) \underset{\alpha}{\overset{\gamma}{\leftrightarrows}} (\mathcal{A}, \preceq_{\mathcal{A}})$, $(\mathcal{A}, \preceq_{\mathcal{A}}, \delta_{\mathcal{A}}) \in Pre((\mathcal{A}, \preceq_{\mathcal{A}}))$ and $(\mathcal{C}, \preceq_{\mathcal{C}}, \overleftarrow{\delta_{\mathcal{C}}}) \in Pre((\mathcal{C}, \preceq_{\mathcal{C}}))$. If $\delta_{\mathcal{A}}$ is strong then the following equivalence holds for every $a \in \mathcal{A}$:*

$$f_{\mathcal{A}} 0 \text{ -partial forward-complete at } a \Leftrightarrow f_{\mathcal{A}} \text{ locally backward-complete at } \gamma(a) \square$$

Example 12. Consider again Example 11 analyzing program Q defined in Fig. 2. Let us use this time the weighted path-length $\delta_{\mathsf{Int}}^{\mathrm{rp}}$ on intervals for reasoning on the partial backward-completeness at input $\gamma([10, 10]) = \{10\}$ of variable x at the end of program Q. Recall that $\delta_{\mathsf{Int}}^{\mathrm{rp}}$ is a strong pre-metric $\preceq_{\mathsf{Int}}$-compatible. We get the following equalities:

$$\overleftarrow{\delta}_{\wp(\mathbb{Z})}(\llbracket Q \rrbracket \gamma([10, 10]), \gamma(\llbracket Q \rrbracket_{\mathsf{Int}}[10, 10])) = \delta_{\mathsf{Int}}^{\mathrm{rp}}(\alpha(\llbracket Q \rrbracket \gamma([10, 10])), \llbracket Q \rrbracket_{\mathsf{Int}}[10, 10]) = 0$$

namely, $\llbracket Q \rrbracket_{\mathsf{Int}}$ is 0-partial forward-complete on input $[10, 10]$ using $\overleftarrow{\delta}_{\wp(\mathbb{Z})}$. Since $\delta_{\mathsf{Int}}^{\mathrm{rp}}$ is strong, this implies that $\alpha(\llbracket Q \rrbracket \gamma([10, 10])) = \llbracket Q \rrbracket_{\mathsf{Int}}[10, 10]$, i.e., $\llbracket Q \rrbracket_{\mathsf{Int}}$ is locally backward-complete at $\{10\}$. ♦

7 Related Work

Forward and backward completeness are well known notions in abstract interpretation, especially in static program analysis for verifying safety program properties [20, 29, 33]. The first attempt to weaken the notion of backward-completeness in abstract interpretation has been defined in [5]. Here the authors introduced the notion of local completeness which corresponds to our definition of local backward-completeness (Definition 3). Partial completeness has been recently introduced as a further weakening of the local completeness property by admitting a limited amount of imprecision measured by a quasi-metric compatible with the underlying abstract domain [10, 11].

Besides the partial completeness property, the problem of measuring the imprecision of abstract interpretations is not new. Sotin [42] defines a metric to quantify the result of numerical invariants by calculating the size of the concretization into $\mathbb{R}^n$. This metric can be considered as an instance of pre-metric $\subseteq$-compatible, thus it can be used as distance function for formalizing the partial forward/backward-completeness property of interest.

Crazzolara [25] proposes to substitute partial-orders with quasi-metrics, i.e., the concrete and abstract partially-ordered set turn into quasi-metric spaces. Our approach, instead, preserves the standard abstract interpretation framework and considers the distances as external tools for measuring the incompleteness of abstract operators. A similar idea is proposed by Di Pierro and Wiklicky [41] where partially-ordered domains are replaced by vector spaces lifting abstract interpretation to a probabilistic version where it is possible to apply some well-known distances in linear spaces.

Logozzo et al. [36] adapt the notion of pseudo-metric to be compatible with partially-ordered sets in order to measure the distance between two elements. Their definition of pseudo-metric requires the weak triangle inequality axiom and symmetry, while our definition of pre-metric relaxes those axioms. Moreover, axiom 3 may not be satisfied by pseudo-metrics, therefore their distances may not fit well in our framework.

Casso et al. [13] proposes a list of observations about distance functions when used to measure distances between elements of abstract domains in the context of logic programming. They show that it is possible to induce other distances from one domain to another through the concretization and abstraction functions in a similar way we did in Sect. 4. However, their notion of distance requires more compatibility with the underlying lattice than our approach as they focus on abstract domains commonly used for analyzing logic programs. For instance, they assume abstract domains to be complete lattices related by a GI with the concrete domains, they require another type of triangle inequality called diamond inequality, and consider distances between comparable elements only. As our notion of pre-metric is weaker than what they require for distances, our framework can be easily instantiated with their distances.

8 Conclusion

We weakened both the local backward-completeness, in presence of a GC, and the local forward-completeness properties in case only a concretization function is available (e.g., the case of convex polyhedra or the domain of formal languages [9]) in order to allow a limited amount of imprecision. This imprecision is measured according to a distance function formalized as a pre-metric compatible with the underlying pre-order relation. The definition of pre-metrics is general enough to be instantiated by distance functions having different "levels of view". For instance, a distance may be precise enough to satisfies the identity of indiscernibles axiom on the concrete domain, so that it can be used to reason on the local forward-completeness. Different levels of approximation can be obtain by inducing pre-metrics from one domain to another by the use of the concretization or the abstraction maps. Our framework could assist program analysis designers in controlling the propagation of incompleteness, e.g., by choosing the preferred pre-metric according to the imprecision they want to measure and at which level of details, and then by using it for checking how an invariant generated by the analysis grows with respect to the concrete execution or another comparable analysis. This checking process could also be combined with other repairing techniques that aim to enrich the expressiveness of abstract domains [6,33].

Similarly to the other completeness properties [4,10,11,29] both partial forward and backward-completeness properties are undecidable. As a future work we plan to extend the proof system proposed in [11] in order to be able to overestimate, according to δ_D, a bound of incompleteness (either forward or backward) generated by the abstract interpreter without actually executing the program. This, in fact, can be considered as another abstract interpretation analyzing the abstract interpreter [23].

Understanding the propagation of incompleteness through pre-metrics is closely linked to code obfuscation [16], which finds application in software protection [28,30,31] and malware analysis [12,26,40,44]. Being able to quantify the amount of incompleteness induced in the abstract interpretation by a code-obfuscating program transformation could enable us to measure the potency of these transformations. This remains one of the primary open challenges in software protection [14,17,43].

Acknowledgements. We wish to thank the anonymous reviewers of SAS 2023 for their detailed comments. This work has been partially supported by the grant PRIN2017 (code: 201784YSZ5) "AnalysiS of PRogram Analyses (ASPRA)".

References

1. https://en.wikipedia.org/wiki/Metric_space#Premetrics
2. http://pop-art.inrialpes.fr/people/bjeannet/bjeannet-forge/interproc/index.html
3. Arkhangel'Skii, A., Fedorchuk, V.: General Topology I: Basic Concepts and Constructions Dimension Theory, vol. 17. Springer, Berlin, Heidelberg (2012). https://doi.org/10.1007/978-3-642-61265-7
4. Bruni, R., Giacobazzi, R., Gori, R., Garcia-Contreras, I., Pavlovic, D.: Abstract extensionality: on the properties of incomplete abstract interpretations. Proc. ACM Program. Lang. **4**(POPL), 28:1–28:28 (2020). https://doi.org/10.1145/3371096
5. Bruni, R., Giacobazzi, R., Gori, R., Ranzato, F.: A logic for locally complete abstract interpretations. In: 36th Annual ACM/IEEE Symposium on Logic in Computer Science, LICS 2021, Rome, Italy, June 29–2 July 2021, pp. 1–13. IEEE (2021). https://doi.org/10.1109/LICS52264.2021.9470608
6. Bruni, R., Giacobazzi, R., Gori, R., Ranzato, F.: Abstract interpretation repair. In: Jhala, R., Dillig, I. (eds.) PLDI '22: 43rd ACM SIGPLAN International Conference on Programming Language Design and Implementation, San Diego, CA, USA, 13–17 June 2022, pp. 426–441. ACM (2022). https://doi.org/10.1145/3519939.3523453
7. Bruni, R., Giacobazzi, R., Gori, R., Ranzato, F.: A correctness and incorrectness program logic. J. ACM **70**(2), 15:1–15:45 (2023). https://doi.org/10.1145/3582267
8. Buldygin, V.V., Kozachenko, I.V.: Metric Characterization of Random Variables and Random Processes, vol. 188. American Mathematical Society, Providence (2000). https://doi.org/10.1090/mmono/188

9. Campion, M., Dalla Preda, M., Giacobazzi, R.: Abstract interpretation of indexed grammars. In: Chang, B.-Y.E. (ed.) SAS 2019. LNCS, vol. 11822, pp. 121–139. Springer, Cham (2019). https://doi.org/10.1007/978-3-030-32304-2_7
10. Campion, M., Dalla Preda, M., Giacobazzi, R.: On the properties of partial completeness in abstract interpretation. In: Lago, U.D., Gorla, D. (eds.) Proceedings of the 23rd Italian Conference on Theoretical Computer Science, ICTCS 2022, Rome, Italy, 7-9 September 2022. CEUR Workshop Proceedings, vol. 3284, pp. 79–85. CEUR-WS.org (2022). http://ceur-ws.org/Vol-3284/8665.pdf
11. Campion, M., Dalla Preda, M., Giacobazzi, R.: Partial (in)completeness in abstract interpretation: limiting the imprecision in program analysis. Proc. ACM Program. Lang. **6**(POPL), 1–31 (2022). https://doi.org/10.1145/3498721
12. Campion, M., Dalla Preda, M., Giacobazzi, R.: Learning metamorphic malware signatures from samples. J. Comput. Virol. Hacking Tech. **17**(3), 167–183 (2021). https://doi.org/10.1007/s11416-021-00377-z
13. Casso, I., Morales, J.F., López-García, P., Giacobazzi, R., Hermenegildo, M.V.: Computing abstract distances in logic programs. In: Gabbrielli, M. (ed.) LOPSTR 2019. LNCS, vol. 12042, pp. 57–72. Springer, Cham (2020). https://doi.org/10.1007/978-3-030-45260-5_4
14. Ceccato, M., et al.: Understanding the behaviour of hackers while performing attack tasks in a professional setting and in a public challenge. Empir. Softw. Eng. **24**(1), 240–286 (2018). https://doi.org/10.1007/s10664-018-9625-6
15. Cohen, J., Hickey, T.J.: Two algorithms for determining volumes of convex polyhedra. J. ACM **26**(3), 401–414 (1979). https://doi.org/10.1145/322139.322141
16. Collberg, C., Nagra, J.: Surreptitious Software: Obfuscation, Watermarking, and Tamperproofing for Software Protection. Addison-Wesley Professional, Boston (2009)
17. Collberg, C.S., Davidson, J.W., Giacobazzi, R., Gu, Y.X., Herzberg, A., Wang, F.: Toward digital asset protection. IEEE Intell. Syst. **26**(6), 8–13 (2011). https://doi.org/10.1109/MIS.2011.106
18. Cousot, P.: Principles of Abstract Interpretation. The MIT Press, Cambridge, Mass (2021)
19. Cousot, P., Cousot, R.: Static determination of dynamic properties of programs. In: Proceedings of the 2nd International Symposium on Programming, pp. 106–130. Dunod, Paris (1976). https://doi.org/10.1145/390019.808314
20. Cousot, P., Cousot, R.: Abstract interpretation: a unified lattice model for static analysis of programs by construction or approximation of fixpoints. In: Graham, R.M., Harrison, M.A., Sethi, R. (eds.) Proceedings of the 4th ACM Symposium on Principles of Programming Languages, Los Angeles, California, USA, January 1977, pp. 238–252. ACM (1977). https://doi.org/10.1145/512950.512973
21. Cousot, P., Cousot, R.: Systematic design of program analysis frameworks. In: Aho, A.V., Zilles, S.N., Rosen, B.K. (eds.) Proceedings of the 6th ACM Symposium on Principles of Programming Languages, San Antonio, Texas, USA, January 1979, pp. 269–282. ACM Press (1979). https://doi.org/10.1145/567752.567778
22. Cousot, P., Cousot, R.: Abstract interpretation frameworks. J. Log. Comput. **2**(4), 511–547 (1992). https://doi.org/10.1093/logcom/2.4.511
23. Cousot, P., Giacobazzi, R., Ranzato, F.: A^2i: abstract^2 interpretation. Proc. ACM Program. Lang. **3**(POPL), 1–31 (2019). https://doi.org/10.1145/3290355
24. Cousot, P., Halbwachs, N.: Automatic discovery of linear restraints among variables of a program. In: Aho, A.V., Zilles, S.N., Szymanski, T.G. (eds.) Conference Record of the Fifth Annual ACM Symposium on Principles of Programming Languages,

Tucson, Arizona, USA, January 1978, pp. 84–96. ACM Press (1978). https://doi.org/10.1145/512760.512770
25. Crazzolara, F.: Quasi-metric spaces as domains for abstract interpretation. In: Falaschi, M., Navarro, M., Policriti, A. (eds.) 1997 Joint Conference on Declarative Programming, APPIA-GULP-PRODE'97, Grado, Italy, 16–19 June 1997, pp. 45–56 (1997)
26. Dalla Preda, M., Giacobazzi, R., Debray, S.K.: Unveiling metamorphism by abstract interpretation of code properties. Theor. Comput. Sci. **577**, 74–97 (2015). https://doi.org/10.1016/j.tcs.2015.02.024
27. Distefano, D., Fähndrich, M., Logozzo, F., O'Hearn, P.W.: Scaling static analyses at facebook. Commun. ACM **62**(8), 62–70 (2019). https://doi.org/10.1145/3338112
28. Giacobazzi, R.: Hiding information in completeness holes: new perspectives in code obfuscation and watermarking. In: Cerone, A., Gruner, S. (eds.) Sixth IEEE International Conference on Software Engineering and Formal Methods, SEFM 2008, Cape Town, South Africa, 10–14 November 2008, pp. 7–18. IEEE Computer Society (2008). https://doi.org/10.1109/SEFM.2008.41
29. Giacobazzi, R., Logozzo, F., Ranzato, F.: Analyzing program analyses. In: Rajamani, S.K., Walker, D. (eds.) Proceedings of the 42nd Annual ACM SIGPLAN-SIGACT Symposium on Principles of Programming Languages, POPL 2015, Mumbai, India, 15–17 January 2015, pp. 261–273. ACM (2015). https://doi.org/10.1145/2676726.2676987
30. Giacobazzi, R., Mastroeni, I.: Making abstract interpretation incomplete: modeling the potency of obfuscation. In: Miné, A., Schmidt, D. (eds.) SAS 2012. LNCS, vol. 7460, pp. 129–145. Springer, Heidelberg (2012). https://doi.org/10.1007/978-3-642-33125-1_11
31. Giacobazzi, R., Mastroeni, I., Dalla Preda, M.: Maximal incompleteness as obfuscation potency. Form. Aspects Comput. **29**(1), 3–31 (2016). https://doi.org/10.1007/s00165-016-0374-2
32. Giacobazzi, R., Quintarelli, E.: Incompleteness, counterexamples, and refinements in abstract model-checking. In: Cousot, P. (ed.) SAS 2001. LNCS, vol. 2126, pp. 356–373. Springer, Heidelberg (2001). https://doi.org/10.1007/3-540-47764-0_20
33. Giacobazzi, R., Ranzato, F., Scozzari, F.: Making abstract interpretations complete. J. ACM **47**(2), 361–416 (2000). https://doi.org/10.1145/333979.333989
34. Helemskii, A.Y.: Lectures and Exercises on Functional Analysis, vol. 233. American Mathematical Society, Providence (2006). https://doi.org/10.1090/mmono/233
35. Lawrence, J.: Polytope volume computation. Math. Comput. **57**(195), 259–271 (1991). https://doi.org/10.1090/S0025-5718-1991-1079024-2
36. Logozzo, F.: Towards a quantitative estimation of abstract interpretations. In: Workshop on Quantitative Analysis of Software. Microsoft, June 2009. https://www.microsoft.com/en-us/research/publication/towards-a-quantitative-estimation-of-abstract-interpretations/
37. Miné, A.: A new numerical abstract domain based on difference-bound matrices. In: Danvy, O., Filinski, A. (eds.) PADO 2001. LNCS, vol. 2053, pp. 155–172. Springer, Heidelberg (2001). https://doi.org/10.1007/3-540-44978-7_10
38. Miné, A.: The octagon abstract domain. In: Burd, E., Aiken, P., Koschke, R. (eds.) Proceedings of the Eighth Working Conference on Reverse Engineering, WCRE'01, Stuttgart, Germany, 2–5 October 2001, p. 310. IEEE Computer Society (2001). https://doi.org/10.1109/WCRE.2001.957836

39. Miné, A.: Tutorial on static inference of numeric invariants by abstract interpretation. Found. Trends Program. Lang. **4**(3–4), 120–372 (2017). https://doi.org/10.1561/2500000034
40. Moser, A., Kruegel, C., Kirda, E.: Limits of static analysis for malware detection. In: 23rd Annual Computer Security Applications Conference (ACSAC 2007), 10–14 December 2007, Miami Beach, Florida, USA, pp. 421–430. IEEE Computer Society (2007). https://doi.org/10.1109/ACSAC.2007.21
41. Di Pierro, A., Wiklicky, H.: Measuring the precision of abstract interpretations. In: LOPSTR 2000. LNCS, vol. 2042, pp. 147–164. Springer, Heidelberg (2001). https://doi.org/10.1007/3-540-45142-0_9
42. Sotin, P.: Quantifying the precision of numerical abstract domains. Technical report. HAL Id: inria-00457324, INRIA (2010). https://hal.inria.fr/inria-00457324
43. Sutter, B.D., Collberg, C.S., Dalla Preda, M., Wyseur, B.: Software protection decision support and evaluation methodologies (dagstuhl seminar 19331). Dagstuhl Rep. **9**(8), 1–25 (2019). https://doi.org/10.4230/DagRep.9.8.1
44. You, I., Yim, K.: Malware obfuscation techniques: a brief survey. In: Proceedings of the Fifth International Conference on Broadband and Wireless Computing, Communication and Applications, BWCCA 2010, 4–6 November 2010, Fukuoka Institute of Technology, Fukuoka, Japan (In conjunction with the 3PGCIC-2010 International Conference), pp. 297–300. IEEE Computer Society (2010). https://doi.org/10.1109/BWCCA.2010.85

BREWasm: A General Static Binary Rewriting Framework for WebAssembly

Shangtong Cao[1], Ningyu He[2], Yao Guo[2], and Haoyu Wang[3(✉)]

[1] Beijing University of Posts and Telecommunications, Beijing, China
[2] Key Lab on HCST (MOE), Peking University, Beijing, China
[3] Huazhong University of Science and Technology, Wuhan, China
haoyuwang@hust.edu.cn

Abstract. Binary rewriting is a widely adopted technique in software analysis. WebAssembly (Wasm), as an emerging bytecode format, has attracted great attention from our community. Unfortunately, there is no general-purpose binary rewriting framework for Wasm, and existing effort on Wasm binary modification is error-prone and tedious. In this paper, we present BREWasm, the first general purpose static binary rewriting framework for Wasm, which has addressed inherent challenges of Wasm rewriting including high complicated binary structure, strict static syntax verification, and coupling among sections. We perform extensive evaluation on diverse Wasm applications to show the efficiency, correctness and effectiveness of BREWasm. We further show the promising direction of implementing a diverse set of binary rewriting tasks based on BREWasm in an effortless and user-friendly manner.

Keywords: WebAssembly · Binary Rewriting

1 Introduction

WebAssembly (Wasm) [58], endorsed by Internet giants like Google and Mozilla, is an assembly-like stack-based low-level language, aiming to execute at native speed. Portability of Wasm is achieved by the ability of being a compiling target for mainstream high-level programming languages, e.g., C/C++ [61], Go [48], and Rust [31]. Lots of resource-consumed and -sensitive software have been compiled to Wasm binaries and embedded in browsers [2], like 3D graphic engines and scientific operations Beyond the browser, Wasm is moving towards a much wider spectrum of domains, e.g., IoT [29], serverless computing [18], edge computing [36], and blockchain and Web 3.0 [15].

The rising of Wasm has attracted massive attention from our research community. As an emerging instruction format, our fellow researchers have invested huge effort into Wasm binary analysis, e.g., static analysis for vulnerability detection [7], dynamic analysis based on program instrumentation [25], Wasm

S. Cao and N. He—The first two authors contribute equally.

M. V. Hermenegildo and J. F. Morales (Eds.): SAS 2023, LNCS 14284, pp. 139–163, 2023.
https://doi.org/10.1007/978-3-031-44245-2_8

binary transformation [10], and binary optimization [9]. More or less, most existing studies rely on Wasm binary rewriting to achieve their goals. For example, Wasabi [25] is a dynamic analysis framework against Wasm, which obtain the runtime information of target binaries via instrumenting. However, due to the case-specific demands of existing work, researchers need to implement a specific set of rewriting rules from scratch, or even manually modify Wasm binaries, which are error-prone. We, therefore, argue that a general purpose rewriting framework is necessary to facilitate the research on Wasm binaries.

Binary rewriting is a general technique to modify existing executable programs, which is a well-studied direction for native binaries [13,16,30,33,59]. Unfortunately, there currently is no general-purpose binary rewriting framework for Wasm. Implementing such a rewriting framework is challenging. First, Wasm is unreadable and complicated in syntax. The low-level nature of such an assembly-like language makes it extremely hard to reason about its original intention. Though Wasm formally explains the functionalities of its 11 valid sections, the syntax of them is highly structured and varies. As a user-friendly general rewriting framework, it should handle both the unreadability and the syntactic complexity in a concise way, which is a natural contradiction. Second, modifying a functionality in Wasm may require updating several sections accordingly. For example, if a user intends to insert a new function, he has to update several sections simultaneously. Manually updating all sections is fallible. Third, Wasm enforces a strict verification before executing, while any violations against the Wasm syntax during rewriting Wasm binaries will invalidate them. An invalid Wasm binary cannot be loaded and executed at all. Therefore, the binary rewriting on syntactic level cannot be conducted in an arbitrary way.

This Work. In this paper, we implement BREWasm, a general-purpose binary rewriting framework for Wasm, consisting of: *Wasm parser*, *section rewriter*, *semantics rewriter*, and *Wasm encoder*. Specifically, the Wasm parser and encoder are implemented based on our abstraction of Wasm binaries. Based on these abstracted objects, the section rewriter is able to conduct fine-grained rewriting, e.g., inserting/deleting a new object. The semantics rewriter further combines them and offers another set of high-level APIs, where each of them possesses rich semantics, like inserting a function. Thus, Wasm binaries can be arbitrarily modified without considering the underlying complexity of syntax.

Based on benchmarks consisting of representative Wasm binaries, the evaluation results show the efficiency, correctness, effectiveness, and real-world usability of BREWasm. Specially, it is practical to achieve various kinds of complicated Wasm binary rewriting tasks by combining the APIs provided by BREWasm, including binary instrumentation, binary hardening, and mutation-based fuzzing. Comparing with the cumbersome implementation of these specific tasks, the work built on BREWasm is effortless and user-friendly.

Our contribution can be summarized as follows:

- To the best of our knowledge, we have implemented the first general purpose Wasm binary rewriting framework, named BREWasm, which offers more than 31 semantic APIs that are summarized from real-world usage scenarios. It offers new insights for the design of binary rewriting tools.

```c
extern int sqrt(int x);
extern void print(int x);

void start(int param){
    int var = param;
    while(1){
        var = sqrt(var);
        if(var == 0){
            return;
        }
        print(var);
    }
}
```

```wat
1 (module
2   (type $type1 (func (param i32))) ;; declare types
3   (type $type2 (func (param i32) (result i32)))
4   (import "env" "sqrt"                ;; import sqrt
5     (func $sqrt (type $type2)))       ;; signature is type2
6   (import "env" "print"               ;; import print
7     (func $print (type $type1))       ;; signature is type1
8   (func $start          ;; entry function
9     (type $type1)       ;; signature is type1
10    (local $var i32)    ;; declare another local variable
11    local.get 0
12    local.set $var      ;; assign $var with the param
13    loop                ;; a new code block (#1)
14      block             ;; a new code block (#2)
15        local.get $var  ;; push $var on the stack
16        call $sqrt      ;; call the imported sqrt
17        local.set $var  ;; pop the return value to $var
18      end
19      local.get $var    ;; push $var on the stack
20      i32.const 0       ;; push a 0 on the stack
21      i32.eq            ;; if $var is equal to 0
22      br_if 1           ;; jump out of this function
23      local.get $var
24      i32.const 1       ;; push the offset of the callee
25      call_indirect (type $type2) ;; the callee is with type2
26      br 0              ;; jump to line 13, and restart the loop
27    end)
28  (table 5 5 funcref)
29  (elem (i32.const 1) func $print)) ;; The offset 1 corresponds to $print
```

Fig. 1. A code snippet of WebAssembly in WAT text format with its source code.

- We perform extensive evaluation on diverse Wasm applications to show the efficiency, correctness and effectiveness of BREWASM.
- We show that it is useful, effortless, scalable, and user-friendly to implement a diverse set of binary rewriting tasks based on BREWASM.

To boost further research on Wasm binary rewriting, we release the implementation of BREWASM as well as the corresponding documentation at link.

2 Background

2.1 WebAssembly Binary

WebAssembly (Wasm) is an emerging cross-platform low-level language that can be compiled from various programming languages, e.g., C/C++ [61], Rust [31], and Go [48]. Wasm is designed to be effective and compact. It can achieve nearly native code speed in performance with a sufficiently small size (100KB to 1MB for an ordinary Wasm binary [32]). In addition, some official auxiliary tools are proposed to facilitate the development of Wasm. For example, *wasm2wat* can translate a Wasm binary into WebAssembly Text Format (WAT for short), and *wasm-validate* [51] can validate the syntax of a Wasm binary.

Each Wasm binary is composed of sections with different functionalities. Specifically, in a Wasm binary, functions are implemented in the ***code section***, and their signatures are declared in the ***type section***. The ***function section*** maintains a mapping from the index of each function to the index of its corresponding type. Functions can also be imported from environment through the ***import section***, and be exported via the ***export function***. Except for their independent contexts, data stored in the ***global section***, ***data section***, and

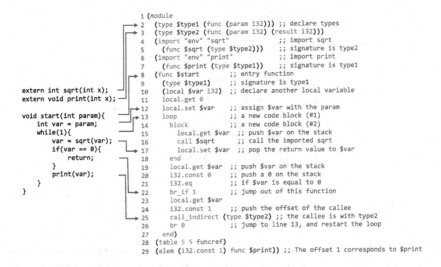

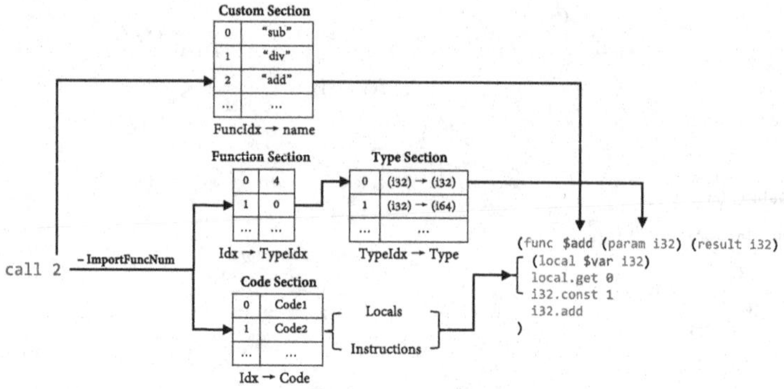

Fig. 2. Function indexing is achieved by coupling several sections.

memory section can be accessed arbitrarily. To implement function pointers, Wasm designs an *indirect call mechanism*, where all possible callees have to be declared in the ***table section*** and ***element section*** (also denoted as elem section). Additionally, debugging information or third-party extensions will be stored in the ***custom section***, which has no effect on execution.

Sections can be further divided into *vectors*, the smallest unit that declares a functionality. For example, Fig. 1 shows a code snippet of Wasm binary (shown in WAT text format) as well as its source code in C. As we can see, L2[1] is a vector belonging to type section, which declares a function signature. A vector may have many attributes, e.g., the vector at L3 consists of its index (`$type2`), parameters type (`i32`), and the return value type (`i32`). In Wasm, however, *a single semantics is often achieved by coupling several sections.* Taking indexing a function as an example, which is shown in Fig. 2. Once an internal function, indexed by 2 in this example, is invoked by a `call` instruction, its readable name can be indexed via the custom section. To obtain its signature, we need a two-layer translation through the function section and the type section. Its implementation can be accessed only via the code section. Note that, all imported functions are located in front of normal functions, thus we need to subtract the number of imported functions, which is 1 in this example, to obtain its real index when indexing in the function section and the code section.

2.2 Binary Rewriting

Binary rewriting[2] refers to the process of taking a binary as an input, rewriting various parts of it, and generating another binary that is properly formatted. The semantics of the rewritten program depends on the rewriting purpose and strategy. This technique has been widely adopted in the software analysis direction, e.g., program instrumentation [8,22,28,41], binary enhancement [23,37,60], and program transformation [5,10,47].

[1] The second line, denoted by L2. We adopt such notations in the following.

[2] In this work, the *binary rewriting* specifically refers to the static binary rewriting.

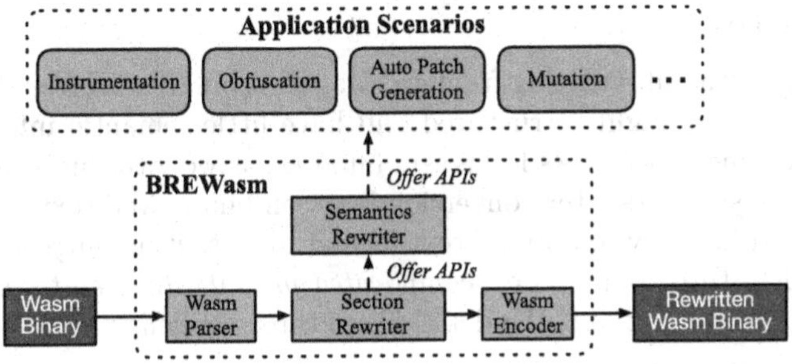

Fig. 3. The architecture and workflow of BREWASM.

Currently, some work specifically conducts rewriting against Wasm binaries. For example, Wasabi [25] is a dynamic analysis framework of Wasm. It can dynamically obtain the runtime information of the target binary via instrumenting Wasm instructions. Fuzzm [27] statically inserts stack canaries into the linear memory to identify memory bugs by conducting fuzzing. SEISMIC [52] also conducts instrumentation against Wasm binaries to determine whether the target is a malicious mining program. At last, Wasm-mutate [4] is a binary mutation tool. It integrates many different strategies for performing mutation on Wasm binaries, e.g., deliberately inserting functions or a piece of memory. All of these tools rely on binary rewriting to implement the core functionalities. However, due to their case-specific demands, developers need to implement a specific set of rewriting rules from scratch, or even manually modify Wasm binaries.

3 BREWasm

3.1 Overview

To the best of our knowledge, we have implemented the first general rewriting framework against Wasm binaries, dubbed as BREWASM, whose architecture and workflow are shown in Fig. 3. As we can see, BREWASM is composed of four components: *Wasm parser*, *section rewriter*, *semantics rewriter*, and *Wasm encoder*. Specifically, the Wasm parser takes a Wasm binary as an input, and parses it as a list of objects. Based on these objects, the section rewriter is able to conduct rewriting, e.g., inserting/deleting a new object or modifying attributes of existing objects. It packs these fine-grained rewriting functions into four basic APIs. The semantics rewriter combines these fine-grained APIs and offers another set of high-level APIs, where each of them possesses rich semantics, like inserting a function, and appending a piece of linear memory. Through these exposed APIs, users can rewrite Wasm binaries for different goals, e.g., obfuscation, instrumentation, or patch generation on vulnerabilities. Finally, these updated objects will be encoded into a valid Wasm binary through the Wasm encoder. The implementation of BREWASM is detailed in Sect. 4, and some usage scenarios will be depicted in Sect. 5.5.

3.2 Challenges

Implementing a general rewriting framework against binaries is often challenging. Because binaries are highly structured and have little semantic information to guide the rewriting process. As for Wasm binaries, as we introduced in Sect. 2.1, although Wasm supports inter-conversion between binary and text formats, it is still infeasible to directly modify its text format for rewriting purposes. This can be attributed to three points, i.e., *complicated format*, *strict static verification*, and *coupling among sections*. We detail these three challenges in the following.

C1: Format Complexity. Conducting efficient and effective static binary rewriting is strongly correlated to the complexity of the rewritten binary. From Fig. 1, we can observe that Wasm is a syntactic complicated format. Specifically, as we introduced in Sect. 2.1, there are 11 valid sections defined under the current specification [56]. Each section is composed of vectors, each of which is further composed of several attributes. As an assembly-like language, each attribute is indispensable and corresponds to a specific and unique meaning. Moreover, these sections are highly structured. For example, for a vector in type section (see L3 in Fig. 1), the attributes `param` and `result` are wrapped by a `func`, which is further wrapped by the corresponding `type`. The same situation also plays for other sections. Therefore, the syntactic complexity of Wasm makes it exceptionally challenging to implement a general rewriting framework.

Our Solution: In order to enhance readability and facilitate the following rewriting process, we implement a parser to translate the given Wasm binary into an array of *objects*, each of which is composed of several *attributes*. During the parsing process, we also omit some auxiliary strings, like the `type` and the `func` at L3 of Fig. 1. Therefore, each highly structured and nested vector will be translated into an object with several side-by-side attributes according to its semantics. Binary rewriting can be easily performed by modifying objects. Meanwhile, we also implement an encoder to conduct the opposite process, i.e., translating objects into a Wasm binary. Please see Sect. 4.1 for more details.

C2: Static Verification. Each Wasm binary will be thoroughly and strictly verified statically before executing [17,57]. Such a static verification performs on several aspects. For example, sections are composed of vectors, each of which is indexed by an index. Thus, if a user inserts/deletes a vector, he has to update vectors of the whole section to ensure the continuity of indices of vectors. Moreover, as we mentioned in **C1**, the encoder has to reassemble objects and complete the auxiliary strings that are discarded in the parsing process. Any negligence will invalidate the rewritten Wasm binary.

Our Solution: To solve this problem, we implement a fixer that will be automatically invoked after each time of invoking the APIs exposed by the section rewriter. Specifically, the fixer is mainly responsible for repairing the incontinuity for indices of the rewritten section. It can also fix some context-aware errors, like increasing the limitation field (if necessary) to hold a newly inserted memory. After the encoding process, the official syntactic checker, wasm-validate, is invoked to examine the validity. Please refer to Sect. 4.2.

C3: Sections Coupling. As we mentioned in Sect. 2.1, some functionalities should be achieved by combining multiple sections. For example, if we add an extra function in a Wasm binary, except for inserting its implementation in the code section, we have to modify the function section and the type section to declare its signature. Moreover, if the added function can be taken as the callee of a function pointer, the table section and the elem section should also be updated accordingly. Manually updating them is tedious and error-prone. Such a section coupling raises another challenge for the user to achieve his intended goal.

Our Solution: To address the sections coupling problem, we abstract the coupling between sections into a set of Wasm program semantics, i.e., *global variable*, *import and export*, *linear memory*, *function* and *custom content*. Based on these five semantics, we expose a set of APIs, e.g., `insertInternalFunc`, which takes a function's body and signature as inputs. Inside the API, we determine if the signature already exists, and insert a new one if necessary. Then, we will insert its declaration and implementation in the function section and the code section, respectively. It is worth noting that if any reference relation goes wrong due to indices mismatch, like the index of callee of a `call` is incremented by 1 due to inserting a function, these reference relations will be repaired automatically after each time of invoking APIs of the semantics rewriter. Please refer to Sect. 4.3.

4 Approach

In this section, we will introduce the technical details of components of BREWASM, and how we address the aforementioned challenges.

4.1 Wasm Parser and Wasm Encoder

Wasm has a highly structured and complicated format. Specifically, a Wasm binary is composed of *sections*, which is a vector of *elements*. Further, an element consists of several *fields* according to the section where it locates. As we mentioned in **C1**, to facilitate the following rewriting process, we hide unnecessary and verbose details and translate Wasm binaries in a semantically equivalent format. Referring to the official Wasm specification, we formally define the relationships among sections, elements, and fields as shown in Fig. 4.

As we can see, each section is composed of a list of elements with the same name, where elements are composed of several fields. Specifically, each *custom* element is composed of a set of *index-name* pairs. These pairs can be parsed as debugging information for different purposes, like keeping readable names of functions, global variables, and a piece of data. Moreover, each *type* element consists of three fields, indicating the function signature $type_{param}{}^* \rightarrow type_{result}{}^*$ is declared by the idx_{type}-th type element. The definitions of *import* elements and *export* elements are similar. An *import* element indicates the idx_{func}-th function with the type declared by idx_{type} is imported from *modulename* and named as *name*, while an *export* element refers to the idx_{func}-th function is

Section, Element & Field

$$
\begin{aligned}
\textit{Section } S &::= \textit{element}^{+} \\
\textit{element} &::= \textit{custom} \mid \textit{type} \mid \textit{import} \mid \textit{function} \mid \textit{table} \mid \textit{memory} \\
&\quad \mid \textit{global} \mid \textit{export} \mid \textit{start} \mid \textit{elem} \mid \textit{code} \mid \textit{data} \\
\textit{custom} &::= (idx_{func|global|data}\ name)^{*} \\
\textit{type} &::= idx_{type}\ type_{param}{}^{*}\ type_{result}{}^{*} \\
\textit{import} &::= idx_{func}\ module\ name\ idx_{type} \\
\textit{function} &::= idx_{func}\ idx_{type} \\
\textit{table} &::= min \mid min\ max \\
\textit{memory} &::= min \mid min\ max \\
\textit{global} &::= idx_{global}\ type_{val}\ mut\ val \\
\textit{export} &::= idx_{export}\ name\ idx_{func} \\
\textit{start} &::= idx_{func} \\
\textit{elem} &::= idx_{elem}\ offset\ idx_{func}{}^{*} \\
\textit{code} &::= idx_{func}\ local^{*}\ instruction^{*} \\
\textit{data} &::= idx_{data}\ offset\ initData \\
\textit{local} &::= idx_{local}\ type_{val} \\
\textit{instruction} &::= op\ operand^{*}
\end{aligned}
$$

Types & Literals

$$
\begin{aligned}
type_{*} &::= \texttt{i32|i64|f32|f64} \\
mut &::= \texttt{0x00|0x01} \\
module|name|initData &::= \texttt{byte}^{*} \\
op|operand &::= \texttt{byte} \\
idx_{*}|val|min|max|offset &::= \texttt{u32}
\end{aligned}
$$

Fig. 4. Formal definition of sections, elements, and fields in Wasm.

exported as *name*, which can be invoked by the environment. Note that, an *function* element only declares a function's index and its signature, where the implementations are defined in the corresponding *code* element. The *min* and *max* defined in *memory* elements jointly limit the available size of the linear memory, and each *data* element declares that the initial value (*initData*) of the idx_{data}-th linear memory starts from the designated *offset*. Similarly, *table* elements and *elem* elements share the pattern, but $idx_{func}{}^{*}$ refers to callee indices for `call_indirect` instructions. Finally, a *global* element declares its value as *val* with type of $type_{val}$, where *mut* indicates whether its value can be updated by instructions. Two extra terms *local* and *instruction* are defined that are nestedly adopted in *code* elements.

For each section, we have defined a class with its fields as attributes. Each element is an object of the corresponding class. To this end, the Wasm parser is able to translate a Wasm binary into a list of objects. For example, Listing 1.1 illustrates the parsed objects of the Wasm binary in Fig. 1.

As we can see from Listing 1.1, the Wasm parser translates each element and packs them into their corresponding objects. The field names are hidden, but we can obtain the corresponding value according to the definition in Fig. 4. For example, L8 is a *code* element, its first parameter 2 indicates that it corresponds to the implementation of the second function. According to L6, its type can be indexed by 0, i.e., returns nothing but takes an `i32` (declared at L2). The second field of the code element is a list of *local* objects, each of which declares the type and the value of local variables. Similarly, the third field declares all its instructions, which are wrapped by `Instruction` objects. The first instruction has an *op* valued as `0x20` and an *operand* as `0`, corresponding to the `local.get 0` at L11 in Fig. 1. Through the opposite direction, the Wasm encoder can translate and reassemble these objects into a Wasm binary in a lossless way.

```
1  parsedWasm = [
2      Type(0, ["i32"], []),
3      Type(1, ["i32"], ["i32"]),
4      Import(0, "env", "sqrt", 0),
5      Import(1, "env", "print", 0),
6      Function(2, 0),
7      # omit following instructions
8      Code(2, [Local(0, "i32")], [Instruction("0x20", [0]),
           ...]),
9      Table(5, 5),
10     Elem(0, 1, [1])
11 ]
```

Listing 1.1. Parsed objects of the Wasm binary of Fig. 1.

4.2 Section Rewriter

The section rewriter plays a vital role for BREWASM. It provides four basic APIs that allow users to manipulate sections on fine-grained level, i.e., *select*, *insert*, *delete*, and *update*. Through combining these four operations, users are able to manipulate any elements or fields we mentioned in Sect. 4.1. The syntax for these operations is formally expressed as follows:

$$select : element_{template} \rightarrow element^*$$
$$insert : element^* \times element_{new} \rightarrow \texttt{true|false}$$
$$delete : element^* \rightarrow \texttt{true|false}$$
$$update : field \times field_{new} \rightarrow \texttt{true|false}$$

Specifically, within the context after parsing the given Wasm binary, the *select* takes an element template ($element_{template}$) to filter out all elements conforming to the $element_{template}$. Note that the wild card, an understrike character, is allowed when designating a field. For example, `select(Type(_, _, ['i32']))` returns all *type* elements that return a single `i32` without considering their arguments. To this end, the object at L3 in Listing 1.1 instead of the one at L2 will be returned. Based on the selected results, the *insert* and *delete* can be conducted to insert a new element ($element_{new}$) after the designated one(s) and delete the given elements, respectively. Take a concrete situation as an instance. Against

Listing 1.1, if a user wants to delete the first type element and insert a new one, with arguments as i64 and returns as i32, he can write:

```
delete(select(Type(0, ['i32'], [])))
insert(select(Type(_, _, _))[-1], Type(_, ['i64'], ['i32'])),
```

where the first statement deletes the object at L2 by an exact match, and the second statement inserts a new type element after the last one. Moreover, the *update* can be used to modify a field by a new value ($field_{new}$). Field values can be retrieved by a dot operator, like getting values of an attribute in an object. For example, the user intends to modify the returns as i64 on the just inserted type element. He can invoke the following statement:

```
update(select(Type(_, ['i64'],['i32'])).resultType,['i64']),
```

where the field $type_{result}$ is accessed by a dot operator with an identical name.

Though we can ensure the flexibility of them, the challenge **C2** still occurs and has to be addressed. For example, the *max* in *memory* elements declares the maximum available space for the corresponding linear memory. It is possible to update the *initData* in a *data* element resulting in exceeding the limitation. Another example is that inserting a new or deleting an existing element from any sections may lead to the incontinuity of indices. Both of these situations invalidate the Wasm binary. Therefore, we implement a fixer that is automatically invoked after each rewriting requests. The fixer can determine which section should be fixed, identify the bugs resulting from rewriting requests, and fix them. Therefore, **C2** can be addressed after a flexible rewriting process.

```
# suppose params, results, locals, and instrs are given
    by the user
# insert the type element
funcType = select(Type(_, params, results))
if funcType:
    typeIdx = funcType[0].typeIdx
else:
    insert(select(Type(_, _, _))[-1], Type(_, params,
        results))
    typeIdx = select(Type(_, _, _))[-1].typeIdx
# insert the function element
insert(select(Function(_, _))[-1], Function(_, typeIdx))
# insert the code element
insert(select(Code(_, _, _))[-1], Code(_, local, instrs))
```

Listing 1.2. Append a function through APIs offered by the section rewriter.

4.3 Semantics Rewriter

Though the section rewriter allows users to rewrite elements and even their fields on a fine-grained level without considering the indices continuity, users still have

Table 1. APIs exposed by the semantics rewriter.

<table>
<tr><th>Semantic</th><th>Sections</th><th>Representative API(s)</th><th>Explanations</th></tr>
<tr><td>Global Variables</td><td>Global</td><td>insertGlobalVariable
idx : u32
valType : i32|i64|f32|f64
mut : 0x00|0x01
initValue : u32</td><td><pre>
globalItem = Global(idx, valType, mut, initValue)
insert(select(Global(idx, _, _)), globalItem)
</pre></td></tr>
<tr><td rowspan="2">Import & Export</td><td rowspan="2">Type
Import
Export</td><td>insertImportFunction
idx : u32
moduleName : byte*
funcName : byte*
paramsType : (i32|i64|f32|f64)
resultsType : (i32|i64|f32|f64)'</td><td><pre>
# insert the type element
functype = select(Type(_, paramsType, resultsType))
if functype:
    typeidx = functype.typeIdx
else:
    insert(select(Type(_, _, _))[-1], functype)
    typeidx = len(Type(_, _, _))[-1].typeIdx
# insert the import element
importFunc = Import(_, moduleName, funcName, typeidx)
if select(importFunc):
    pass
else:
    insert(select(Import(idx, _, _, _)), importFunc)
</pre></td></tr>
<tr><td>insertExportFunction
idx : u32
funcName : byte*
funcidx : u32</td><td><pre>
# insert the global element
exportFunc = Export(_, funcName, funcidx)
if select(exportFunc):
    pass
else:
    insert(select(Export(idx, _, _)), exportFunc)
</pre></td></tr>
<tr><td rowspan="2">Linear Memory</td><td rowspan="2">Memory
Data</td><td>appendLinearMemory
pageNum : u32</td><td><pre>
memory = select(Memory(_, _))
if memory.max != 0:
    memory.max += pageNum
</pre></td></tr>
<tr><td>modifyLinearMemory
offset : u32
bytes : byte*</td><td><pre>
modify the initData of data
for data in select(Data(_, _, _))
    dataEnd = data.offset + len(data.initData)
    if data.offset <= offset and offset < dataEnd:
        pre = data.initData[:offset - data.offset]
        post = data.initData[offset - data.offset + len(bytes):]
        data.initData = pre + bytes + post
        return
# otherwise, insert the data element
data = Data(_, offset, bytes)
insert(select(Data(_, _, _))[-1], data)
</pre></td></tr>
<tr><td rowspan="4">Function</td><td rowspan="4">Type
Function
Code
Start
Table
Element</td><td>insertInternalFunction
funcidx : u32
paramsType : (i32|i64|f32|f64)
resultsType : (i32|i64|f32|f64)'
locals : local*
funcBody : instruction*</td><td><pre>
# insert the import element
functype = Type(_, paramsType, resultsType)
if select(functype):
    typeidx = functype.typeIdx
else:
    insert(select(Type(_, _, _))[-1], functype)
    typeidx = len(Type(_, _, _))[-1].typeIdx
# insert the function element
insert(select(Function(funcidx, _)), Function(funcidx, typeidx))
# insert the code element
code = Code(funcidx, locals, funcBody)
insert(select(Code(funcidx, _, _)), code)
</pre></td></tr>
<tr><td>insertHookFunction
funcidx : u32
hookedFuncIdx : u32
funcBody : instruction*
paramsType : (i32|i64|f32|f64)
resultsType : (i32|i64|f32|f64)'
locals : local*</td><td><pre>
# insert the hook function
hookFuncidx = insertInternalFunction(funcidx,
                paramsType, resultsType, localVec, funcBody)
# Modify call instruction
callInstr = Instruction(Call, hookedFuncidx)
newCallInstr = Instruction(Call, hookFuncidx)
importFuncNum = len(select(Import(_, _, _, _)))
for funcidx in range(importFuncNum, len(select(Code(_, _, _)))):
    if funcidx != hookFuncidx:
        funcInstrs = select(Code(funcidx, _, _)).instrs
        for instr in funcInstrs:
            if instr == Instruction('call', hookedFuncidx)
                instr.operands = hookFuncidx
code = select(Code(funcidx, _, _))
code.insert(code.select(Instruction(_, _)[offset]), instrs)
</pre></td></tr>
<tr><td>modifyFunctionInstr
funcIdx : u32
offset : u32
instrs : instruction*</td><td><pre>
code = select(Code(funcidx, _, _))
# Delete old instructions and insert new ones
code.delete(code.select(Instruction(offset, _, _)))
code.insert(code.select(Instruction(offset, _, _)), instr)
</pre></td></tr>
<tr><td>appendFunctionLocal
funcidx : u32
valType : i32|i64|f32|f64</td><td><pre>
code = select(Code(funcidx, _, _))
code.insert(code.select(Local(_, _))[-1], Local(_, valType))
</pre></td></tr>
<tr><td>Custom Content</td><td>Custom</td><td>modifyFunctionName
funcidx : u32
name : byte*</td><td><pre>
funcName = select(Custom(funcidx=idx, _))
update(funcName, Custom(funcidx=idx, name))
</pre></td></tr>
</table>

to make effort to deal with the *section coupling problem* (see **C3**). For example, the indices mismatch occurs when indices for type elements are changed but still referred by elements in other sections. Fixing them manually is fallible.

Moreover, to achieve a little complex functionality, it may be inconvenient for users to solely adopt such fine-grained APIs offered by the section rewriter. Take appending a function as an example, which is shown in Listing 1.2.

As we can see, L3 firstly checks if the given signature has been declared. If it is, its index is kept (L5), or a new index is calculated by inserting it into the type section (L7 to L8). Then, the user has to manually link the type index to a function index by inserting a function element (L10). Finally, the implementation of the function is appended (L12). We can see that all newly inserted elements have no concrete *idx*, which is because the fixer we mentioned in Sect. 4.2 can automatically calculate these indices.

From the instance, we can conclude that rewriting or updating a functionality of a Wasm binary always needs a series of combinations of APIs exposed by the section rewriter. To ease the burden on users and improve the usability, BREWASM provides another rewriter, named *semantics rewriter*. We have conducted a comprehensive survey in real-world scenarios on applications that require binary rewriting as the prerequisite. The survey has covered lots of representative papers [10,25,27,52] and popular repos on GitHub [4,54]. Consequently, as shown in Table 1, we have abstracted 5 semantics, which cover all 11 sections and offer 31 APIs in total that can be used by these applications. Specifically, the *global semantics* allows users to arbitrarily update values that can be accessed under the global scope. Through the *import & export semantics*, users can import or export designated functions. The *memory semantics* can be used to insert another piece of linear memory with a piece of initiated data, while the *function semantics* mainly focuses on updating functions to achieve some goals. Finally, through the *custom semantics*, users can update the debug information to perform obfuscation by changing names of functions. For example, the 12-LOC Listing 1.2 can be abstracted to:

```
appendInternalFunction(params, results, locals, instrs)
```

Though it is practical to enhance the usability of implementing some functionalities through calling these 31 APIs, **C3** requires another fixer that investigates and maintains reference relations between elements across sections. Therefore, after APIs have been invoked, another fixer will be automatically waked to iterate sections and fix reference relations. Take the `appendInternalFunction` as an instance, it will examine if any element in other sections has to be fixed.

We argue that the semantics rewriter is not limited by the scalability issue. These APIs are concluded from real-world scenarios, which can satisfy most needs. Moreover, it is intuitive and practical to implement case-specific semantics APIs by users themselves through combining four APIs in the section rewriter. The three challenges can be properly handled without their intervention. On the one hand, as for **C1**, the Wasm parser can translate the given Wasm binary with complicated syntax into a list of objects (see Sect. 4.1). On the other hand, the fix against **C2** and **C3** is automatically conducted.

5 Implementation and Evaluation

5.1 Implementation

We have implemented BREWASM with over 4.3K LOC of Python3 code from scratch. To avoid reinventing the wheel, some relied modules are based on open-source GitHub projects. For example, integer literals in Wasm are encoded by LEB128 algorithm [1]. To accelerate the encoding and decoding process, we utilize the highly efficient cyleb128 library [39] implemented by Cython. We have packaged BREWASM into a standard Python library, which can be easily accessed and used by developers.

5.2 Research Questions and Experimental Setup

Our evaluation is driven by the following three research questions:

- **RQ1** Is it efficient to conduct Wasm binaries rewriting through APIs exposed by BREWASM?
- **RQ2** Whether the APIs provided by BREWASM are implemented correctly and effectively?
- **RQ3** Can BREWASM be easily applied to real-world scenarios?

To answer these questions, we first selected 10 Wasm binaries from Wasm-Bench [21], a well-known micro benchmark that collects tens of thousands of Wasm binaries. The basic information for them is shown in Table 2. We believe that these 10 binaries are representative. Specifically, they are compiled from various mainstream programming languages, and cover two typical domains of applying Wasm binaries, i.e., web scripts and standalone applications. Moreover, they range in size from 3 KB to 4 MB, which can effectively reflect the ability of BREWASM to handle Wasm binaries with different sizes. Though we can add more Wasm binaries as candidates for the following evaluations, some APIs (e.g., `insertHookFunction`) require our manual effort to determine concrete parameters. Thus, considering such a trade-off, we argue that these 10 Wasm binaries are representative for the whole ecosystem.

All experiments were performed on a server running Ubuntu 22.04 with a 64-core AMD EPYC 7713 CPU and 256 GB RAM.

5.3 RQ1: Efficiency

As we mentioned in Sect. 4.3, to make it easier for users to conduct rewriting Wasm binaries, the semantics rewriter exposes a total of 31 APIs, which cover all the legal sections of Wasm. Therefore, a thorough evaluation on their efficiency is essential to evaluate BREWASM's usability. Based on each Wasm binary in Table 2, we invoke each of 31 APIs with proper arguments 1,000 times. For example, we call `insertGlobalVariable` to deliberately insert a global value at the beginning of the global section. Then, we record how long it will take to finish the designated behavior, including all necessary stages, i.e., parsing, processing,

Table 2. Representative Wasm binaries.

Name	Language	Type	Size (KB)
zigdom (B_1) [6]	C	web	3
stat (B_2) [55]	C	standalone	45
kindling (B_3) [40]	zig	web	3,373
rustexp (B_4) [38]	Rust	web	935
wasmnes (B_5) [46]	Rust	web	82
base64-cli (B_6) [53]	Rust	standalone	2,415
basic-triangle (B_7) [45]	Go	web	1,394
clock (B_8) [49]	Go	web	1,445
go-app (B_9) [11]	Go	web	4,302
audio (B_{10}) [50]	Go	web	8

fix-up, and encoding. The timing results are listed in Table 3. It is worth noting that in this experiment each API call requires a parsing process and an encoding process. However, under real scenarios, they are one-shot overhead to complete a given task through calling a series of APIs. Therefore, we list the parsing and encoding times in the second and the third row, respectively.

On average, it takes around 1.3 s and 0.5 s to parse and encode a Wasm binary, respectively. Although we can see that it takes 6.6 s to parse B_9. However, this is because the Wasm binary consists of more than one million instructions, which will take up more than 100MB of space when converted to WAT format. Therefore, under normal scenarios, we can conclude that the parsing and encoding time will not exceed 2 to 3 s in total, which is acceptable as a one-shot overhead. Moreover, we can easily observe that each API takes only milliseconds or even less than a millisecond. Interestingly, among all these APIs, the operations related to *insertion* consume more time than other types of operations. This is because inserting an entry into a section requires fixing indices of subsequent entries to ensure continuity between indices. Also, the fixer under the semantics rewriter will have to enumerate all sections to identify if there are mismatched reference relations. Fortunately, these two fixing processes require no manual intervention.

Such a high efficiency is due to our engineering implementation as well as the time complexity. Specifically, four basic operations are defined in the section rewriter. As the `select` requires iterating on the given section, its time complexity is $O(n)$, where n refers to the length of the corresponding section. For the other three operations, their complexity are $O(1)$ because we adopt the hash table to store elements in sections. As for the semantics rewriter, the time complexity of APIs varies and depends on the implementation. Take the most extreme one, `insertHookFunction`, as an example. As we can see from Table 1, the nested loop causes its time complexity to be $O(n \cdot m)$, where n and m are proportional to the number of functions and their instructions. The time complexity of other APIs are typically $O(n)$.

Table 3. Consumed time (*ms*) of invoking APIs provided by the semantics rewriter, as well as the parsing and the encoding time on each Wasm binary.

	B_1	B_2	B_3	B_4	B_5	B_6	B_7	B_8	B_9	B_{10}
parsing	6.46	55.66	173.71	1,023.41	119.09	725.94	2,174.82	1,794.90	6,651.99	2.94
encoding	2.58	21.28	79.29	408.89	42.32	332.95	617.66	586.59	3,294.77	2.00
Global Variable										
appendGlobalVariable	0.01	0.03	0.38	0.02	0.01	0.02	0.02	0.02	0.02	0.01
modifyGlobalVariable	0.06	1.08	1.34	24.14	1.83	48.43	37.07	37.57	123.13	0.04
deleteGlobalVariable	0.06	1.18	0.99	23.64	1.83	42.78	22.98	43.85	121.51	0.04
insertGlobalVariable	0.39	6.84	7.72	176.34	12.26	149.25	71.87	158.33	470.11	0.20
Import & Export										
insertImportFunction	0.31	4.61	4.99	76.62	9.67	101.00	48.13	102.51	300.64	0.16
appendImportFunction	0.08	1.30	1.59	29.48	2.11	38.29	15.62	38.51	118.36	0.05
modifyImportFunction	0.07	1.35	1.10	23.30	1.79	36.41	16.58	37.37	124.53	0.05
deleteImportFunction	0.07	2.52	1.58	36.25	1.77	36.98	16.21	36.67	120.52	0.04
insertExportFunction	0.07	1.64	1.12	23.31	1.85	37.22	16.51	36.84	119.84	0.04
appendExportFunction	0.07	1.89	2.20	23.93	1.91	34.72	16.56	42.74	113.94	0.04
modifyExportFunction	0.07	1.16	0.91	22.11	1.79	34.43	15.88	36.44	132.07	0.04
deleteExportFunction	0.07	1.29	1.85	26.81	2.13	35.22	14.97	33.75	120.78	0.04
Linear Memory										
appendLinearMemory	0.01	0.01	0.01	0.01	0.01	0.01	0.01	0.02	0.02	0.01
modifyLinearMemory	0.01	0.02	0.01	0.03	0.02	0.02	0.03	0.02	0.02	0.01
Function										
insertInternalFunction	0.33	4.48	4.49	65.43	8.16	100.77	47.59	99.82	318.12	0.17
insertIndirectFunction	0.38	4.64	5.87	89.97	10.11	131.80	63.39	132.27	429.44	0.21
insertHookFunction	0.74	9.88	10.87	176.79	20.58	260.23	119.99	261.16	833.86	0.40
deleteFuncInstr	0.09	0.92	2.30	23.25	1.94	32.90	17.11	33.74	121.37	0.05
appendFuncInstrs	0.07	0.86	1.32	23.55	1.81	35.42	17.90	35.13	122.17	0.04
insertFuncInstrs	0.08	0.94	1.95	24.39	1.99	33.39	16.26	33.91	126.50	0.06
modifyFuncInstr	0.08	0.88	2.04	22.69	2.23	34.58	16.80	34.50	121.72	0.05
appendFuncLocal	0.08	0.91	1.23	23.50	2.87	33.95	23.15	33.66	118.26	0.06
Custom Content										
modifyFuncName	0.01	0.02	0.02	0.12	0.04	0.12	0.12	0.12	0.40	0.01
deleteFuncName	0.08	0.91	1.55	23.21	1.96	34.81	15.64	33.60	121.61	0.06
insertFuncName	0.07	0.84	1.77	23.66	1.98	33.73	15.75	34.73	115.16	0.05
modifyGlobalName	0.08	0.91	1.54	22.97	2.07	34.50	15.63	34.56	120.61	0.06
deleteGlobalName	0.07	0.84	1.14	25.27	1.84	34.71	16.14	33.63	114.15	0.05
insertGlobalName	0.08	0.94	1.05	23.53	2.81	36.37	16.06	33.16	120.71	0.06
insertDataName	0.07	0.92	1.20	26.87	1.98	70.41	14.94	35.27	119.47	0.05
modifyDataName	0.08	0.89	1.39	23.40	2.45	35.04	16.10	33.45	119.95	0.05
deleteDataName	0.07	0.86	3.44	23.03	2.21	35.92	15.63	34.45	126.69	0.05

RQ-1 Answer: BREWASM exposes 31 semantics APIs that can efficiently achieve the corresponding goals. Though the parsing and the encoding processes on a Wasm binary take around 1.8 s, it is acceptable as a one-shot overhead compared to the negligible time it takes to execute semantics APIs.

5.4 RQ2: Correctness and Effectiveness

Correctly and effectively achieving the corresponding goals through APIs plays a vital role for BREWASM. However, it is insufficient to require only the correctness of the implementation of APIs in the section rewriter, which is due to the section coupling problem (see **C3** in Sect. 3.2). To evaluate the effectiveness of APIs of the semantics rewriter, we pass each Wasm binary after invoking an API shown in the first column of Table 3 to *wasm-validate*, an official syntax validator. Then, we manually double checked all 310 (31 APIs * 10 Binaries) cases to make sure the results are inline with the original intents.

According to the results, on the one hand, all rewritten Wasm binaries pass the validation of wasm-validate, indicating valid syntax; on the other hand, all 31 APIs perform correctly in their corresponding functionalities. Moreover, all 31 APIs resolve the **C2** and **C3** correctly. For example, when the API `insertImportFunction` is invoked, BREWASM not only rewrites the type section (if necessary) and the import section according to the import function, but also identifies if any instructions are affected, e.g., indices of the callee of `call` instructions and the indirect function table in the element section. BREWASM will automatically fix them to keep original semantics intact. Of course, all these evaluated APIs are passed with valid arguments. If invalid arguments are passed, e.g., inserting a function with a nonexistent index, the underlying `select` will return an empty list, leading to returning `false` by the following `insert` operation (see the formal definitions of `select` and `insert` in Sect. 4.2).

RQ-2 Answer: Based on the results of the automated verification tool and manual checks, we can conclude that these semantic APIs perform correctly in both syntax and functionalities.

5.5 RQ3: Practicability

We next demonstrate the practicability of BREWASM by illustrating some real scenarios that require rewriting Wasm binaries to achieve designated goals.

Case I: Binary Instrumentation. Binary instrumentation can be used to collect various runtime information of a program. D. Lehmann et al. [25] have implemented a dynamic analysis framework, named Wasabi, whose core is a Wasm binary instrumentation module. It specifies instrumentation rules for instructions to obtain runtime information during execution. For example, against a `call`, Wasabi inserts two functions (imported through the import section) before and after it, respectively, to record necessary information. Through APIs provided by BREWASM, the equivalent functionality can be implemented easily, as shown in Listing 1.3.

As we can see, L1 defines an instruction, `i32.const 5`, and L2 and L3 retrieve the type of the callee, i.e., the function indexed by 5. Then, L5 and L6 construct two function signatures according to the callee's type. L8 invokes an API, named `appendImportFunction`, to introduce a function, whose name is `call_pre` belonging to a module named **hooks**, into import section. The same operation is done in L10. Then, at L13, we construct a series of instructions, where the original **call** is wrapped by the newly declared **call_pre** and **call_post**. At L16, through another API, the original instruction will be replaced. Consequently, BREWasm achieves equivalent binary instrumentation like what Wasabi does.

Due to the fixed pattern of instrumentation used in Wasabi, modifying the underlying code is unavoidable to achieve other specific binary instrumentation functionalities. In contrast, BREWasm provides a large number of instruction-related general rewriting APIs, making it more flexible and convenient to implement the required instrumentation functionalities. In addition, in Sect. 4.2, our abstraction reduces the complexity of Wasm binaries, lowering the bars and the learning costs of using BREWasm.

```
1  instrs = [Instruction("i32.const", 5)]
2  calleeTypeidx = select(Function(5, _)).typeIdx
3  calleeType = select(Type(calleeTypeidx, _, _))
4  # construct call_pre and call_post
5  callPreFunctype = Type(_, ["i32"] + calleeType.typeArg,
       calleeType.typeRet)
6  callPostFunctype = Type(_, calleeType.typeArg, calleeType.
       typeRet)
7  # insert declaration to import section
8  appendImportFunction("hooks", "call_pre", callPreFunctype)
9  callPreFuncidx = select(Import(_, _, _, _))[-1].funcIdx
10 appendImportFunction("hooks", "call_post", callPostFunctype)
11 callPostFuncidx = select(Import(_, _, _, _))[-1].funcIdx
12 # replace the original call instruction
13 instrs.extend([Instruction("call", callPreFuncidx),
14                Instruction("call", 5),
15                Instruction("call", callPostFuncidx)])
16 modifyFuncInstr(Instruction("call", 5), instrs)
```

Listing 1.3. Achieve binary instrumentation through APIs provided by BREWasm.

Case II: Software Hardening. Software hardening is to enhance the security and stability of a program by updating it or implementing additional security measures [44]. In Wasm, unmanaged data, like strings, is stored in the linear memory, organized as a stack, and managed by a global variable representing the stack pointer. Because little protection measures are designed and adopted, traditional attacks, e.g., stack overflow, can exploit Wasm binaries leading to out-of-bound read and write [43]. However, through BREWasm, developers can easily conduct software hardening. For example, **callee** is originally potential for buffer overflow. After the hardening, it is wrapped by **hook**, which inserts a stack canary and validates its integrity around the invocation to **callee**. Listing 1.4 illustrates how to implement this goal via BREWasm.

As we can see, at L4, we randomly generate a canary number. Instructions from L5 to L11, responsible for validating the integrity of canary, are proposed by Fuzzm [27]. Similarly, the **funcbody**, the body of the function **hook**, defined from L12 to L30 is also proposed by Fuzzm. To be specific, L12 to L18 deploys the generated canary into the linear memory. From L19 to L22, it dynamically generates the correct number of `local.get` according to the signature of the callee, which is retrieved by the API `getFuncFunctype`. After the instruction `call $callee` (L24), we insert the already defined canary validation piece as the operand of a `block` instruction (L25). If the value of canary is unchanged, indicating no buffer overflow, the instructions from L26 to L30 will restore the stack and give the control back to `caller`.

```
1  # suppose calleeFuncIdx is given by the user
2  # the first global is a stack pointer
3  stackPointerIdx = 0
4  canary = random.randint(1, 10000)
5  canaryValidateInstrs = [
6              Instruction("global.get", stackPointerIdx),
7              Instruction("i64.load"),
8              Instruction("i64.const", canary),
9              Instruction("i64.eq"),
10             Instruction("br_if", 0),
11             Instruction("unreachable")]
12 funcbody = [Instruction("global.get", stackPointerIdx),
13             Instruction("i32.const", 16),
14             Instruction("i32.sub"),
15             Instruction("global.set", stackPointerIdx),
16             Instruction("global.get", stackPointerIdx),
17             Instruction("i64.const", canary),
18             Instruction("i64.store", canary)]
19 calleeTypeidx = select(Function(calleeFuncIdx, _)).typeIdx
20 calleeType = select(Type(calleeTypeidx, _, _))
21 for idx, _ in enumerate(calleeType.paramsType):
22     funcbody.append(Instruction("local.get", idx))
23 funcbody.extend([
24             Instruction("call", calleeFuncIdx),
25             Instruction("block", canaryValidateInstrs),
26             Instruction("global.get", stackPointerIdx),
27             Instruction("i32.const", 16),
28             Instruction("i32.add"),
29             Instruction("global.set", stackPointerIdx),
30             Instruction("return")])
31 insertHookFunction(calleeFuncIdx, calleeType.paramsType,
       calleeType.resultsType, funcbody, locals = [])
```

Listing 1.4. Achieve software hardening through APIs provided by BREWASM.

In Fuzzm, the stack canary protection is implemented in a similar way. However, since a function may have multiple exit points, Fuzzm modifies the control flow of the function to have only one exit point. This might disrupt the original semantics of the function. In contrast, BREWASM's `insertHookFunction` provides a better solution for this issue, as it minimizes the modifications made to the original function's instructions in the Wasm binary.

Case III: Fuzzing. Fuzzing is an automated software testing technique that can discover security and stability issues by using random files as input [34].

One of the widely adopted approaches to generate random files is *mutation-based*, i.e., generating new files by mutating existing files. Wasm-mutate can mutate the given Wasm binary while keeping semantic equivalence. One of its mutation strategies is *module structure mutation*, e.g., introducing an isolated function. This can also be easily done by BREWasm, as shown in Listing 1.5.

```
1  typeSecLen = len(select(Type(_, _, _)))
2  functype = select(Type(random.randint(0, typeSecLen), _, _))
3  # construct a function according to a random signature
4  funcbody = []
5  for retType in functype.resultsType:
6      if retType == "i32":
7          funcbody.append(Instruction("i32.const", 0))
8      elif retType == "i64":
9          funcbody.append(Instruction("i64.const", 0))
10     elif retType == "f32":
11         funcbody.append(Instruction("f32.const", 0.0))
12     elif retType == "f64":
13         funcbody.append(Instruction("f64.const", 0.0))
14 # randomly insert the function
15 importFuncNum = len(select(Import(_, _, _, _)))
16 internalFuncNum = len(select(Function(_, _)))
17 funcNum = importFuncNum + internalFuncNum
18 insertInternalFunction(random.randint(importFuncNum, funcNum),
       functype.paramType, functype.resultType, funcbody, locals =
       [])
```

Listing 1.5. Achieve add function mutation through APIs provided by BREWasm.

As we can see, L1 and L2 randomly select a type serving as a function signature. According to the designated signature, L4 to L13 construct the body of the function by inserting meaningless instructions to ensure stack balance. Finally, at L18, the generated function will be randomly inserted into the Wasm binary, and the original semantic keeps intact.

There is no rewriting component in Wasm-mutate, thus achieving this goal needs to decode and encode the relevant sections. In contrast, BREWasm parses the entire Wasm binary into an object, which simplifies many extra operations. Additionally, since BREWasm implements the semantics rewriter, inserting a function only requires invoking a single API, without the need to rewrite the relevant sections in turn as in Wasm-mutate.

Other Application Scenarios of BREWasm. Except for the three concrete applications we mentioned above, BREWasm can also be applied in other scenarios, as summarized in Table 4.

Code Obfuscation. Some traditional code obfuscation methods can be implemented. For instance, users can insert global variables or internal functions as opaque predicates [12] into a Wasm binary. Moreover, users can change the debug information in the custom section, like obfuscating readable names of functions, to make the Wasm binary unreadable for attackers.

Table 4. Other application scenarios of BREWasm.

Scenario	Applications	Related Semantics APIs

Code Obfuscation	Opaque predicates obfuscation;
	Memory encryption;
	Debug info obfuscation
		`insertGlobalVariable`
		`insertInternalFunction`
		`modifyLinearMemory`
		`modifyFuncName`

Software Testing	Runtime testing; WASI function testing	`modifyFuncInstr` `appendImportFunction`
Program Repair	Bug fixing	`modifyFuncInstr` `appendFuncLocal`
Software optimization	Instruction optimization	`modifyFuncInstr` `appendFuncLocal`

Software Testing. The exposed APIs can also be used in software testing. For example, Y. Zhang et al. [62] have proposed a method to mutate an instruction's operands constantly to examine if the instruction follows the specification. Through `modifyFuncInstr`, users can easily achieve operands rewriting. Users can even call `appendExportFunc` to export the result of the instruction to alleviate the workload of results comparing. The same approach can be applied in testing imported functions as well.

Program Repairing. BREWasm can be used to fix bugs in Wasm binaries without source code. For example, BREWasm can insert a wrapper function around addition instructions. Within the wrapper, as integer overflow can be detected easily, users can choose to either correct results or raise an exception.

Software Optimization. Instructions optimization can be easily achieved. For example, a piece of Wasm bytecode can be optimized with a higher-level optimization during the compilation, which, however, requires accessing the source code. In contrast, through the APIs offered by BREWasm, users can easily match a piece of code with a pre-defined pattern. Then, through `modifyFuncInstr` and `appendFuncLocal`, the code snippet can be updated to an optimized one.

RQ-3 Answer: Our exploration suggests that it is practical to achieve various kinds of complicated Wasm binary rewriting tasks by combing the APIs provided by BREWasm. Comparing with the cumbersome implementation of the specific tasks, the work built on BREWasm is effortless and user-friendly.

6 Related Work

Wasm Binary Analysis. As an emerging stack-based language, WebAssembly can be applied inside or outside the browser [2]. Lots of work focused on Wasm binary analysis [19–21,24,26,35,42]. For example, Lehmann and Pradel [21,24] pay attention to the memory issues in Wasm, e.g., exploitable buffer overflow.

They found that some memory issues in the source code will still be exploitable in compiled Wasm binaries. In addition, Quentin Stiévenart et al. [42] overcame the challenges of dependency analysis at the binary level and presented an approach to statically slice Wasm programs for the following analysis.

Static Binary Rewriting. Researchers have proposed lots of static rewriting tools against native programs [13,16,30,33,59]. Some of them, e.g., Alto [33], SASI [16] and Diablo [13], can only rewrite programs with the assistance of debug information or the ones compiled by a specific compiler. Recently, E9Patch [14] proposes a control-flow-agnostic rewriting method that inserts jumps to trampolines without the need to move other instructions, which significantly improves the scalability and robustness. The Bytecode Alliance provides two tools, wasm-parser [51] and wasm-encoder [51], for parsing and encoding Wasm binaries, while using them would face the same challenge of Wasm binary complexity. As a comparison, our proposed abstraction model in Sect. 4.1 could reduce the complexity of Wasm binaries when implementing the section rewriting. To the best of our knowledge, there is no static binary rewriting framework for Wasm yet.

7 Limitations and Discussion

Structured Control Flow Rewriting. Wasm adopts a special and complicated control flow structure, named *structured control flow* [3]. Specifically, a Wasm function is composed of a set of sequential or nested code blocks, each of which has to be led by a `block` or `loop` instruction. Moreover, some instructions can guide the control flow to the destination code blocks, like `end` and `br`. In other words, by rewriting such instructions, BREWASM can handle the control flow of Wasm binaries to some extent. However, to guarantee the semantic consistency, users cannot simply change a `block` into a `loop` (which turns a normal code block into a loop structure), but have to implement their own APIs with four operations in the section rewriter we proposed, which is tedious, error-prone, and case-specific. No existing work is able to rewrite the structured control flow in a flexible and general way, which will be one of our future work.

Concerns about Reinventing Wheels. Some existing tools have similar design purpose or functionalities with BREWASM, thus there may have concerns about reinventing wheels. We underline that all components in BREWASM are irreplaceable. Specifically, wasm-parser and wasm-encoder are implemented by the Bytecode Alliance official, however, directly adopting them will overwhelm users. Though they can parse and encode the given Wasm binary and fully support all sections defined in the specification, parsing and encoding require approximately 1,300 and 800 lines of code, respectively. It is tedious and infeasible to compose a script with more than 2K LOC to conduct binary rewriting. In addition, though Wasabi has implemented a wasabi_wasm module, which is able to conduct static instrumentation, it is insufficient in binary rewriting. On the one hand, it is designed specifically for binary instrumentation, indicating that it cannot implement removing or updating vectors in sections, which will significantly hinder its ability in terms of binary rewriting. On the other hand, it does not consider the section coupling challenge as we mentioned in **C3**. Moreover, some sections are not supported by its module, like the elem section. The lack of ability on rewriting some sections will dramatically impact the flexibility of rewriting. Consequently, implementing BREWASM instead of combining existing modules or tools does not indicate reinventing wheels.

8 Conclusion

We present BREWASM, a general binary rewriting framework for WebAssembly. BREWASM can properly handle inherent challenges of Wasm binary rewriting, including the highly complicated binary structure, strict static syntax verification, and coupling among sections. Based on representative Wasm binaries, BREWASM illustrates its efficiency and effectiveness in rewriting process. Through three cases inspired by existing work and real-world scenarios, BREWASM also proves its practicality and usability.

Acknowledgement. We have great thanks to all anonymous reviewers and our shepherd, Prof. Jingling Xue. This work was supported in part by National Key R&D Program of China (2021YFB2701000), the National Natural Science Foundation of China (grants No.62072046 and 62141208), and Xiaomi Young Talents Program.

References

1. Leb128 algorithm (2023). https://en.wikipedia.org/wiki/LEB128
2. Official webpage (2023). https://webassembly.org/docs/use-cases/
3. Structured control flow (2023). https://tinygo.org/docs/guides/webassembly/
4. Alliance, B.: GitHub wasm-tools repository (2023). https://github.com/bytecodealliance/wasm-tools/tree/main/crates/wasm-mutate
5. Becker, M., Baldin, D., Kuznik, C., Joy, M.M., Xie, T., Mueller, W.: XEMU: an efficient QEMU based binary mutation testing framework for embedded software. In: Proceedings of the Tenth ACM International Conference on Embedded Software, pp. 33–42 (2012)
6. Bhattarai, S.: Github zig-wasm-dom repository (2023). https://shritesh.github.io/zig-wasm-dom/
7. Brito, T., Lopes, P., Santos, N., Santos, J.F.: Wasmati: an efficient static vulnerability scanner for WebAssembly. Comput. Secur. **118**, 102745 (2022)
8. Bruening, D., Amarasinghe, S.: Efficient, transparent, and comprehensive runtime code manipulation. Ph.D. thesis, Massachusetts Institute of Technology, Department of Electrical Engineering ... (2004)
9. Cabrera Arteaga, J., et al.: Superoptimization of WebAssembly bytecode. In: Companion Proceedings of the 4th International Conference on Art, Science, and Engineering of Programming, pp. 36–40 (2020)
10. Cabrera-Arteaga, J., Monperrus, M., Toady, T., Baudry, B.: WebAssembly diversification for malware evasion. arXiv preprint arXiv:2212.08427 (2022)

11. Charriere, M.: LOFIMUSIC website (2023). https://lofimusic.app/collegemusic-lonely
12. Collberg, C., Thomborson, C., Low, D.: Manufacturing cheap, resilient, and stealthy opaque constructs. In: Proceedings of the 25th ACM SIGPLAN-SIGACT Symposium on Principles of Programming Languages, pp. 184–196 (1998)
13. De Sutter, B., De Bus, B., De Bosschere, K.: Link-time binary rewriting techniques for program compaction. ACM Trans. Programm. Lang. Syst. (TOPLAS) **27**(5), 882–945 (2005)
14. Duck, G.J., Gao, X., Roychoudhury, A.: Binary rewriting without control flow recovery. In: Proceedings of the 41st ACM SIGPLAN Conference on Programming Language Design and Implementation, pp. 151–163 (2020)
15. EOSIO: EOSIO official website (2023). https://eos.io/
16. Erlingsson, U., Schneider, F.B.: SASI enforcement of security policies: a retrospective. In: Proceedings of the 1999 Workshop on New Security Paradigms, pp. 87–95 (1999)
17. Haas, A., et al.: Bringing the web up to speed with webassembly. In: Proceedings of the 38th ACM SIGPLAN Conference on Programming Language Design and Implementation, pp. 185–200 (2017)
18. Hall, A., Ramachandran, U.: An execution model for serverless functions at the edge. In: Proceedings of the International Conference on Internet of Things Design and Implementation, pp. 225–236 (2019)
19. He, N., et al.: EOSAFE: Security analysis of EOSIO smart contracts. In: USENIX Security Symposium, pp. 1271–1288 (2021)
20. He, N., et al.: Eunomia: enabling user-specified fine-grained search in symbolically executing WebAssembly binaries. arXiv preprint arXiv:2304.07204 (2023)
21. Hilbig, A., Lehmann, D., Pradel, M.: An empirical study of real-world WebAssembly binaries: security, languages, use cases. In: Proceedings of the Web Conference 2021, pp. 2696–2708 (2021)
22. Hundt, R.: HP caliper: a framework for performance analysis tools. IEEE Concurr. **8**(4), 64–71 (2000)
23. Kim, T., et al.: RevARM: a platform-agnostic arm binary rewriter for security applications. In: Proceedings of the 33rd Annual Computer Security Applications Conference, pp. 412–424 (2017)
24. Lehmann, D., Kinder, J., Pradel, M.: Everything old is new again: binary security of WebAssembly. In: Proceedings of the 29th USENIX Conference on Security Symposium, pp. 217–234 (2020)
25. Lehmann, D., Pradel, M.: Wasabi: a framework for dynamically analyzing WebAssembly. In: Proceedings of the Twenty-Fourth International Conference on Architectural Support for Programming Languages and Operating Systems, pp. 1045–1058 (2019)
26. Lehmann, D., Pradel, M.: Finding the dwarf: recovering precise types from WebAssembly binaries. In: Proceedings of the 43rd ACM SIGPLAN International Conference on Programming Language Design and Implementation, pp. 410–425 (2022)
27. Lehmann, D., Torp, M.T., Pradel, M.: Fuzzm: finding memory bugs through binary-only instrumentation and fuzzing of WebAssembly (2021). https://arxiv.org/pdf/2110.15433.pdf
28. Luk, C.K., et al.: Pin: building customized program analysis tools with dynamic instrumentation. ACM SIGPLAN Not. **40**(6), 190–200 (2005)

29. Mäkitalo, N., et al.: WebAssembly modules as lightweight containers for liquid IoT applications. In: Brambilla, M., Chbeir, R., Frasincar, F., Manolescu, I. (eds.) ICWE 2021. LNCS, vol. 12706, pp. 328–336. Springer, Cham (2021). https://doi.org/10.1007/978-3-030-74296-6_25
30. McSema: GitHub McSema repository (2023). https://github.com/lifting-bits/mcsema
31. MDN: MDN web docs website (2023). https://developer.mozilla.org/en-US/docs/WebAssembly/Rust_to_wasm
32. Musch, M., Wressnegger, C., Johns, M., Rieck, K.: New kid on the web: a study on the prevalence of WebAssembly in the wild. In: Perdisci, R., Maurice, C., Giacinto, G., Almgren, M. (eds.) DIMVA 2019. LNCS, vol. 11543, pp. 23–42. Springer, Cham (2019). https://doi.org/10.1007/978-3-030-22038-9_2
33. Muth, R., Debray, S.K., Watterson, S., De Bosschere, K.: Alto: a link-time optimizer for the Compaq alpha. Softw. Pract. Exp. **31**(1), 67–101 (2001)
34. Nagy, S., Nguyen-Tuong, A., Hiser, J.D., Davidson, J.W., Hicks, M.: Breaking through binaries: compiler-quality instrumentation for better binary-only fuzzing. In: 30th USENIX Security Symposium (2021)
35. Naseem, F.N., Aris, A., Babun, L., Tekiner, E., Uluagac, A.S.: MINOS: a lightweight real-time cryptojacking detection system. In: NDSS (2021)
36. Nieke, M., Almstedt, L., Kapitza, R.: EdgeDancer: secure mobile WebAssembly services on the edge. In: Proceedings of the 4th International Workshop on Edge Systems, Analytics and Networking, pp. 13–18 (2021)
37. Payer, M., Barresi, A., Gross, T.R.: Fine-grained control-flow integrity through binary hardening. In: Almgren, M., Gulisano, V., Maggi, F. (eds.) DIMVA 2015. LNCS, vol. 9148, pp. 144–164. Springer, Cham (2015). https://doi.org/10.1007/978-3-319-20550-2_8
38. Pilfold, L.: Rustexp website (2023). https://rustexp.lpil.uk/
39. PyPI: PyPI cyleb128 library (2023). https://pypi.org/project/cyleb128/
40. Shenton, C.: GitHub kingling repository (2023). https://github.com/cshenton/kindling
41. Srivastava, A., Eustace, A.: ATOM: a system for building customized program analysis tools. In: Proceedings of the ACM SIGPLAN 1994 Conference on Programming Language design and Implementation, pp. 196–205 (1994)
42. Stiévenart, Q., Binkley, D.W., De Roover, C.: Static stack-preserving intra-procedural slicing of WebAssembly binaries. In: Proceedings of the 44th International Conference on Software Engineering, pp. 2031–2042 (2022)
43. Stiévenart, Q., De Roover, C., Ghafari, M.: Security risks of porting c programs to WebAssembly. In: Proceedings of the 37th ACM/SIGAPP Symposium on Applied Computing, pp. 1713–1722 (2022)
44. Strackx, R., Piessens, F.: Fides: selectively hardening software application components against kernel-level or process-level malware. In: Proceedings of the 2012 ACM Conference on Computer and Communications Security, pp. 2–13 (2012)
45. Suedmeier, E.: wasm-basic-triangle website (2023). https://shritesh.github.io/zig-wasm-dom/
46. Takahiro: NES-rust-ecsy website (2023). https://takahirox.github.io/nes-rust-ecsy/index.html
47. Tian, L., Shi, Y., Chen, L., Yang, Y., Shi, G.: Gadgets splicing: dynamic binary transformation for precise rewriting. In: 2022 IEEE/ACM International Symposium on Code Generation and Optimization (CGO), pp. 155–167. IEEE (2022)
48. TinyGo: TinyGo official docs webpage (2023). https://tinygo.org/docs/guides/webassembly/

49. Ts, J.: GitHub clockexample-go-webassembly repository (2023). https://github.com/Yaoir/ClockExample-Go-WebAssembly
50. Turner, A.: GitHub wasm-by-example repository (2023). https://github.com/torch2424/wasm-by-example/tree/master/examples/reading-and-writing-audio/demo/go
51. WABT: WABT tool website (2023). https://github.com/WebAssembly/wabt
52. Wang, W., Ferrell, B., Xu, X., Hamlen, K.W., Hao, S.: SEISMIC: SEcure in-lined script monitors for interrupting cryptojacks. In: Lopez, J., Zhou, J., Soriano, M. (eds.) ESORICS 2018, Part II. LNCS, vol. 11099, pp. 122–142. Springer, Cham (2018). https://doi.org/10.1007/978-3-319-98989-1_7
53. WAPM: base64-cli app in WAPM (2023). https://takahirox.github.io/nes-rust-ecsy/index.html
54. wasabi: GitHub wasabi repository (2023). https://github.com/danleh/wasabi
55. WAVM: GitHub WAVM repository (2023). https://github.com/WAVM/WAVM/tree/master/Test/wasi
56. WebAssembly: WebAssembly specification webpage (2023). https://webassembly.github.io/spec/core/binary/index.html
57. WebAssembly: WebAssembly static validation algorithm (2023). https://webassembly.github.io/spec/core/appendix/algorithm.html
58. WebAssembly: WebAssembly website (2023). https://webassembly.org/
59. Williams-King, D., et al.: Egalito: layout-agnostic binary recompilation. In: Proceedings of the Twenty-Fifth International Conference on Architectural Support for Programming Languages and Operating Systems, pp. 133–147 (2020)
60. Xu, Y., Xu, Z., Chen, B., Song, F., Liu, Y., Liu, T.: Patch based vulnerability matching for binary programs. In: Proceedings of the 29th ACM SIGSOFT International Symposium on Software Testing and Analysis, pp. 376–387 (2020)
61. Zakai, A.: Emscripten: an LLVM-to-Javascript compiler. In: Proceedings of the ACM International Conference Companion on Object Oriented Programming Systems Languages and Applications Companion, pp. 301–312 (2011)
62. Zhang, Y., et al.: Characterizing and detecting webassembly runtime bugs. arXiv preprint arXiv:2301.12102 (2023)

Quantum Constant Propagation

Yanbin Chen and Yannick Stade(✉)

TUM School of Computation, Information and Technology, Technical University of Munich, Boltzmannstr. 3, 85748 Garching, Germany
{chya,stya}@cit.tum.de

Abstract. A quantum circuit is often executed on the initial state where each qubit is in the zero state. Therefore, we propose to perform a symbolic execution of the circuit. Our approach simulates groups of entangled qubits exactly up to a given complexity. Here, the complexity corresponds to the number of basis states expressing the quantum state of one entanglement group. By doing that, the groups need neither be determined upfront nor be bound by the number of involved qubits. Still, we ensure that the simulation runs in polynomial time - opposed to exponential time as required for the simulation of the entire circuit. The information made available at gates is exploited to remove superfluous controls and gates. We implemented our approach in the tool quantum constant propagation (QCP) and evaluated it on the circuits in the benchmark suite MQTBench. By applying our tool, only the work that cannot be carried out efficiently on a classical computer is left for the quantum computer, hence exploiting the strengths of both worlds.

Keywords: quantum computation · constant propagation · simulation · optimization · static analysis

1 Introduction

Current Status in Quantum Computing. Quantum computers have seen rapid improvements in recent years, especially the capability of the physical realizations of quantum computers has increased significantly [5]. There are applications where quantum computers promise an advantage over classical machines [8,10, 19,23]. Currently, the provided number of qubits does not reach the order of

Y. Chen and Y. Stade—Both authors contributed equally to this research and are ordered alphabetically.

M. V. Hermenegildo and J. F. Morales (Eds.): SAS 2023, LNCS 14284, pp. 164–189, 2023.
https://doi.org/10.1007/978-3-031-44245-2_9

magnitude required for putting the majority of quantum algorithms into practical use. Moreover, current hardware faces significant problems with noise that perturbs the computed results and makes them harder to use as the circuits grow deep [15]. Consequently, the number of gates in the quantum circuit should be reduced as much as possible beforehand. For this purpose, several tools have been developed, e. g., T|ket⟩ [24], pyzx [14], Qiskit [20], staq [2], QGo [27]. More details about existing optimization techniques can be found in Sect. 7.

Considering Initial Configuration. A quantum program is usually executed starting from a state where all qubits are $|0\rangle$. Surprisingly, tools listed above take this information only slightly into account and they heavily rely on gate cancellation rules and pattern matching to simplify circuits. When it comes to the initial state, quantum circuits designers provide ad-hoc arguments why particular controls or gates can be omitted based on the initial configuration, e. g., in the context of Shor's algorithm [17,26]. Jang et al. [13] propose to use the knowledge of the initial state to automatically remove superfluous controls of controlled gates. For their optimization, they need to execute the quantum circuit on a quantum machine many times. In our view, executing a circuit on a quantum computer several thousand times to achieve an optimized version of the same circuit seems to be laborious. More in the spirit of our approach is Liu et al. [16], who propose a Relaxed Peephole Optimization (RPO) approach that leverages the information on single-qubit states which could be efficiently determined at compile time. However, their idea of treating qubits as independent systems has the drawback that information on single qubits is lost when a multi-qubit gate is applied, with few exceptions. Our approach avoids this issue by tracing entangled qubits' states up to a given complexity.

Restricted Polynomial-Time Simulation. Since the full simulation of a quantum circuit takes exponential time in the number of qubits [9] in general, simulating the entire quantum circuit is not a viable solution for efficient optimization. For this reason, we propose a restricted simulation of a quantum circuit in Sect. 3, which simulates the circuit only up to a given complexity. The complexity of an entanglement group (the group of qubits that are entangled) corresponds to the number of basis quantum states. For example, the complexity of the three-qubit state, $\frac{1}{2}(|000\rangle + |001\rangle + |010\rangle + |111\rangle)$, is 4, since there are 4 basis states in the entanglement group, namely $|000\rangle$, $|001\rangle$, $|010\rangle$, and $|111\rangle$. The complexity up to which circuits are simulated is chosen beforehand and thus not depending on the number of qubits. This restriction on complexity ensures that our approach runs in polynomial time, which we will prove in Sect. 5. Using the idea of restricted simulation, we propose to perform a quantum equivalent to constant propagation [22], called *quantum constant propagation* (QCP). We have implemented our idea into a publicly available tool[1].

Objective of QCP. With QCP we aim to reduce the number of controls and eliminate superfluous controlled gates, following the same objective as Jang et al..

[1] The implementation of QCP is accessible under https://github.com/i2-tum/qcp.

Overall QCP reduces quantum circuits in their costs to be executed on target platforms. Nevertheless, the circuit processed by QCP still produces the same desired outcome, as what we prove in Sect. 4.

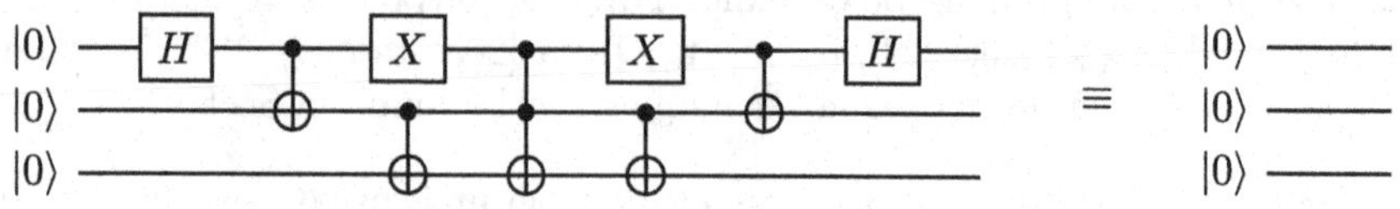

Fig. 1. Our proposed *quantum constant propagation* identifies the doubly controlled not-gate in the middle as superfluous and hence the circuit reduces to the empty circuit on the right.

Effects of QCP. Our proposed optimization technique is capable of identifying the doubly controlled not-gate in the middle of the circuit shown in Fig. 1 as superfluous and, hence, the circuit reduces to the empty circuit. Our evaluation in Sect. 6 MQT Bench [21] demonstrates the impact of our novel optimization technique. Applying our optimization followed by Qiskit using the highest optimization level, we can remove up to 26k more gates compared to just using Qiskit [20], which corresponds to 0.5% of all gates evaluated. When we compare our approach with a similar existing optimization called Relaxed Peephole Optimization (RPO) [16] by running ours after RPO, we can remove 17.2% more gates on the evaluated circuits than just using RPO alone. It shows that this existing optimization even benefits our optimization. We believe that, especially in the future, QCP will become more important when larger circuits are built based on building blocks controlled by one or multiple controls. We comment on this in more detail in Sect. 8. In the next section, Sect. 2, we give a brief introduction to quantum computing on aspects important to this article.

2 Preliminaries

In the following, we give a brief introduction to quantum computing in order to make this article as self-contained as possible; for a more in-depth explanation, the interested reader is referred to the textbooks [12,18].

Quantum Bits. Instead of bits, quantum computers operate on *qubits* (quantum bits). Those cannot just assume the two basis states $|0\rangle$ and $|1\rangle$ but also every state that can be expressed as their linear combination, $|\Psi\rangle = \alpha\,|0\rangle + \beta\,|1\rangle$, where $\alpha, \beta \in \mathbb{C}$—often called *amplitudes*—satisfy $|\alpha|^2 + |\beta|^2 = 1$. Hence, a qubit can be in a so-called *superposition* of both basis states. Upon measured, it collapses into either $|0\rangle$ or $|1\rangle$ with probability $|\alpha|^2$ or $|\beta|^2$, respectively.

Multiple Quantum Bits. The state of a multi-qubit quantum system is denoted by a vector in $\mathbb{C}^2 \otimes \cdots \otimes \mathbb{C}^2 = \mathbb{C}^{2^n}$. The basis vectors are written as $|b_1\rangle \otimes \cdots \otimes |b_n\rangle$ or $|b_1 \ldots b_n\rangle$ for short, with $b_i \in \{0,1\}$. Sometimes the abbreviated notation $|n\rangle$ is used where $n = \sum_{i=0}^{n} b_i \cdot 2^i$.

Gates. Operations on qubits are expressed as *gates*, each of which is denoted by a unitary matrix. A quantum computer only offers a discrete set of basis (parameterized) gates that can be applied to the qubits. Similar to conditioned branches in classical programs, gates can be controlled on the state of one or multiple other qubits. Then the controlled gate is applied to the target qubit if and only if all controlling qubits are in the $|1\rangle$ state.

Entanglement. Entanglement refers to the situation in which the measurement result of one qubit depends on the rest of the quantum system. For example, the circuit in Fig. 2 creates an entanglement among three qubits: The *Hadamard-gate* brings the first qubit into maximal superposition $(|0\rangle + |1\rangle)/\sqrt{2}$; then, two controlled not-gates are applied in sequence; when measuring the resulting quantum state $(|000\rangle + |111\rangle)/\sqrt{2}$, there are only two possible outcomes—"000" and "111"—and no other combination of results, e.g., "010" and "110", can be obtained even if the three qubits are not measured simultaneously.

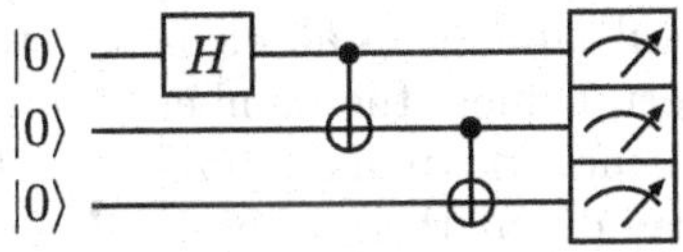

Fig. 2. This circuit creates a GHZ state of three qubits.

Curse of Dimensionality. Entanglement is the root cause of why it is so hard to simulate a quantum computer on a classical machine. As long as all the qubits are separable, i.e., not entangled, one needs to store two complex numbers for each qubit. As soon as some k qubits are entangled with each other, one needs to store potentially $\mathcal{O}(2^k)$ complex numbers, which would immediately lead to exponential running time [1,11].

Concrete Semantics. A quantum program consists of a sequence of quantum gates that are applied on an initial configuration of a quantum system, where usually all qubits are in the $|0\rangle$ state. The application of a gate transforms the concrete quantum state, represented as a state vector, according to the unitary matrix associated with the gate via matrix multiplication.

Interface of an Optimization. In our setting, a quantum circuit is represented as a list of gates. The optimization is expected to accept a list of gates and output an optimized version. For this purpose, an optimization provides a function `transform : gate list -> gate list`. In the next section, we explain how we implement QCP utilizing a restricted simulation.

3 Methodology

As mentioned in Sect. 1, up to now, many quantum circuit designers have argued in complex manners about the superfluousness of specific controls and gates. Our approach aims to automate those reasonings and apply them automatically as an optimization pass to a quantum circuit. For that, we simulate the circuit and identify controls and gates that can be dropped without changing the semantics of the circuit. To make our optimization efficient in terms of a polynomial time complexity, we propose a restricted simulation that simulates the circuit only partially but satisfies the required time-bound, with the help of our specially tailored data structures that efficiently represent quantum states.

3.1 Union-Table

Efficient Union-Find Customization. One central idea of our approach to allow polynomial running time is to keep groups of qubits that are not entangled with each other separated as long as possible. For that, we need a data structure that stores a collection of sequences, i. e., qubits, supports the operation `union`, and can retrieve the position of an element in its sequences. Additionally, it needs to maintain extra information associated with each sequence. The required functionality suggests augmenting a union-find data structure. However, we have the advantage that the total number of all elements stored in our structure is constant and known a priori, namely the number of qubits. For this reason, we use a table-like approach, hence, the name *union-table.* To store n elements in a union-table, we use an array of length n, where each field denotes one element. Each field contains a pointer to a value of type `entry` storing all indices `idxs` also pointing to this entry, their number `card`, and the value `elem` associated with this entry. This leads to the following type definitions for the union-table as an OCaml module where `t` is the type of the union-table itself.

```
module UnionTable : sig
  type 'a entry = { card: int; idxs: int list; elem: 'a }
  type 'a t =
    { size: int; perm: int array; content: 'a entry array }
  ...
```

Use of Permutation. Note that we use an extra attribute `perm` that stores a permutation serving as a view onto the underlying data structure. If one calls a function that accesses an entry at index `i`, then `i` is first looked up in `perm` that returns a potentially different index `j`; the index `j` is then used for actual access to the union-table structure. More information about the functions to operate on a union-table, especially their running times, can be taken from Table 1.

3.2 Representation of a Quantum State

Bitwise Representation. The union-table is polymorphic in the type used to store the extra information for each set. For that, we introduce another module

Table 1. The table lists all functions provided by the module union-table to access and modify the stored data. The type definition of each function is given in script size below it. All functions in the lower block are implemented to run in $\mathcal{O}(1)$ time. The functions `make` and `pos_in_group` take $\mathcal{O}(n)$ time and `union` needs $\mathcal{O}(n + f(n))$ where n is the size of the union-table and f the running time of `combine`.

Function	Description
`make n x` `int -> 'a -> 'a t`	creates a union-table with an initial value `x` in all `n` entries; each entry corresponds to its own set, no entries are united yet into a common set, see also the corresponding paragraph in the text.
`pos_in_group i ut` `int -> 'a t -> int`	returns the position of the qubit referred to by `i` within its entanglement group; this is important to identify its state stored in the quantum state for this group.
`union i j combine ut` `int -> int -> ('a -> 'a -> bool Seq.t -> 'a)-> 'a t -> 'a t`	unites the two entries pointed to by `i` and `j`. To retrieve the new element in the new entry, the `combine` function is used. The boolean sequence passed to `combine` denotes the choices made during the merging of the two sets.
`get i ut` `int -> 'a t -> 'a`	returns the element in the entry pointed to by `i`.
`set i x ut` `int -> 'a -> 'a t -> 'a t`	updates the element in the entry pointed to by `i`.
`swap i j ut` `int -> int -> 'a t -> 'a t`	swaps two elements with each other. It alters the permutation that serves as a view of the content.
`card i ut` `int -> 'a t -> int`	returns the number of elements in the entry pointed to by `i`.
`same i j ut` `int -> int -> 'a t -> bool`	returns `true` if and only if `i` and `j` point to the same entry in the union-table.

`QuantumState` that is a hash table with bit combinations as keys and complex numbers as values inspired by the data structure used in [7]. The bit combinations correspond to basis states, e. g., if there are stored three qubits in a group in the union-table, the binary number 11_{bin} corresponds to the quantum state $|011\rangle$ where the first of the three qubits is in the state $|0\rangle$ and the other two in $|1\rangle$. The values denote the amplitudes for each state. For this to work correctly, the length of keys must not be limited by the number of bits used for an integer, e. g., 32 or 64 bits; instead, we use arbitrary large integers as keys for the hash table. The indices of qubits in each group in the union-table are ordered; this way, one gets a mapping from the global index of a qubit to its position within the state. Figure 3 shows the representation of the state $(|10000\rangle - |10101\rangle + |11000\rangle - |11101\rangle)/2 \otimes (1+i)/\sqrt{2}\,|0\rangle$ using a union-table and bitwise representation of the quantum states.

Merging Entanglement Groups. The correct ordering of indices becomes, in particular, tricky when two entanglement groups are merged and, consequently, also their quantum states must be merged. For this purpose, the `union` func-

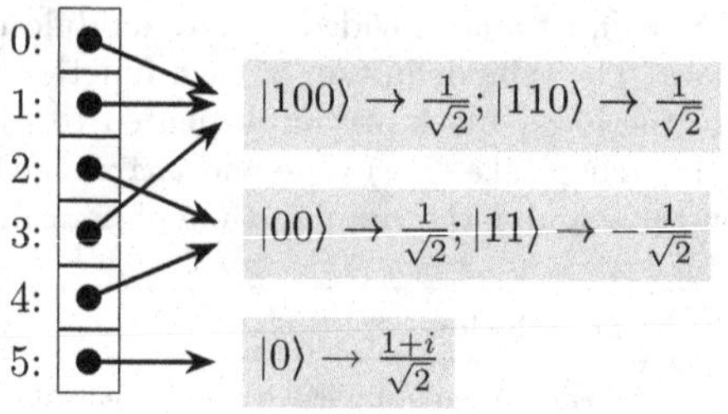

Fig. 3. The representation of a quantum system with six qubits using the union-table data structure (left), where the quantum state of each entanglement group is a hash table with the basis states as keys and their complex amplitudes as values (right). The qubits in each state are indexed from left to right. The represented quantum state is $(|10000\rangle - |10101\rangle + |11000\rangle - |11101\rangle)/2 \otimes (1+i)/\sqrt{2}\,|0\rangle$. Using the usual tensor-product notation, it is not obvious that qubits $\{0,1,3\}$ and $\{2,4\}$ are separable.

tion requires a `combine` function to combine the two entries, i. e., in our case the two quantum states. The union-table merges the sequences of two groups in one merge step known from the merge-sort algorithm. The combine function receives the order in which the elements from the two former groups were merged, in order to apply the same merging behavior to the quantum states. When the quantum state for n qubits contains k many basis states, the `combine` function requires $\mathcal{O}(k \cdot n)$ steps.

Application of Gates. Here, we only describe the application of a single-qubit gate to a state; the approach generalizes to gates operating on multiple qubits. Let U be the matrix representation of some gate that is to be applied on qubit i in a given quantum state where $U = (u_{ij})_{i,j\in\{0,1\}}$. We iterate over the keys in the quantum state: For keys with the i-th bit equal to 0, we map the old key-value pair $(|\Psi\rangle, \alpha)$ to the two new pairs $(|\Psi\rangle, \alpha \cdot u_{11})$ and $(|\Psi'\rangle, \alpha \cdot u_{21})$, where $|\Psi'\rangle$ emerges from $|\Psi\rangle$ by flipping the i-th bit; for keys with the i-th bit equal to 1, we map the old key-value $(|\Phi\rangle, \beta)$ pair to the two new pairs $(|\Phi'\rangle, \beta \cdot u_{12})$ and $(|\Phi\rangle, \beta \cdot u_{22})$, where, again, $|\Phi'\rangle$ emerges from $|\Phi\rangle$ by flipping the i-th bit. Generated pairs with the same key (basis state) are merged by adding their values (amplitudes). For a matrix of dimension 2^d and k states in the quantum state of n qubits, this procedure takes $\mathcal{O}(2^d \cdot k \cdot n)$ steps where d is the number of affected qubits.

3.3 Restricted Simulation

Restrict Complexity. The state in Fig. 2 contains only two basis states as opposed to $2^3 = 8$ possible ones for which a complex number needs to be stored each. Exploiting this fact, the key features of the restricted simulation are

(i) to keep track of the quantum state as separable entanglement groups of qubits, where qubits are included in the same entanglement group if and only if they are entangled, and

(ii) to limit the number of basis states representing the quantum state of an entanglement group by a chosen constant.

Note that the number of basis states allowed in the quantum state of one entanglement group corresponds to the number of amplitudes required to be stored; all other amplitudes are assumed to be zero.

Reaching Maximum Complexity. The careful reader may ask how to proceed when the maximum number of allowed basis states is reached. We set the state of the entanglement group of which the limit is exceeded to $\top$, meaning that we no longer track any information about this group of qubits. By doing so, we can continue simulating the remaining entanglement groups until they may also end up in the $\top$. For this, we utilize a flat lattice that consists of either an element representing a concrete quantum state of an entanglement group, $\top$, or $\bot$ (not used) satisfying the partial order in Fig. 4. The following definitions establish the relation between the concrete quantum states and their abstract description.

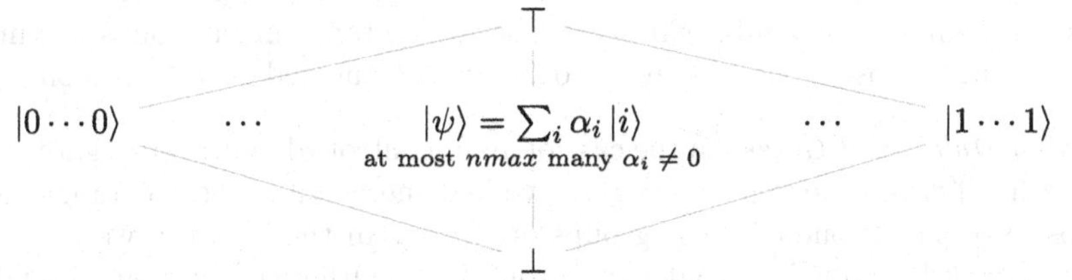

Fig. 4. Lattice for the abstract description of quantum states.

Definition 1 (Abstract state). *The abstract state s is an abstract description of a concrete quantum state if and only if $s = \top$ or $s = |\psi\rangle$ where $|\psi\rangle$ is a concrete quantum state consisting of at most $nmax$ many non-zero amplitudes.*

Definition 2 (Abstract description relation). *Let Δ denote the description relation between quantum states and their abstract description. Furthermore, let $|\psi\rangle$ be a quantum state and s be an abstract description. The quantum state $|\psi\rangle$ is described by s, formally $|\psi\rangle \ \Delta \ s$, if and only if $s = \top$ or $s = |\psi\rangle$.*

Consequently, the entry in the union-table is not the quantum state itself but an element of the flat lattice, an abstract description of the quantum state. Definition 3 defines a concretization operator for abstract states.

Definition 3 (Concretization operator). *Let γ be the concretization operator, and s be an abstract description. Then $\gamma \ s = \{|\psi\rangle \mid |\psi\rangle \ \Delta \ s\}$.*

Next, we define the abstract effect for gates acting on quantum states.

Definition 4 (Abstract gate). *Let $[\![U]\!]^\sharp$ denote the abstract effect of the quantum gate U. For an abstract description s, the abstract effect of U is:*

$$[\![U]\!]^\sharp s = \begin{cases} U\,|\psi\rangle & \text{if} \quad s = |\psi\rangle \\ \top & \phantom{\text{if}} \quad s = \top \end{cases}$$

Theorem 1 justifies the above-defined abstract denotation of quantum states. It follows directly from Definition 1, Definition 2, and Definition 4.

Theorem 1 (Correctness of abstract denotation). *For any quantum state $|\psi\rangle$ and abstract description s satisfying $|\psi\rangle \;\Delta\; s$, $U\,|\psi\rangle \;\Delta\; [\![U]\!]^\sharp s$ holds.*

Operating with Separated States. In the beginning, every qubit constitutes its own entanglement group. Single-qubit gates can be applied without further ado by modifying the corresponding amplitudes accordingly; the procedure behind is matrix multiplication which can be implemented in constant time given the constant size of matrices. The case where multi-qubit gates are applied is split into two subcases. When the multi-qubit gate is applied only to qubits within one entanglement group, the same argument for applying single-qubit gates still holds. Applying a multi-qubit gate across several entanglement groups will most likely entangle those; hence, we need to merge the affected groups into one.

Applying Multi-qubit Gates. In the case of an uncontrolled multi-qubit gate, such as an echoed cross-resonance (ecr) gate, we first merge all affected entanglement groups into one. If one of those groups is already in the $\top$ state, we must set the entire newly formed entanglement group to $\top$. Otherwise, we can apply the merging strategy of the involved quantum states as described in Sect. 3.2. Afterward, matrix multiplication is performed to reflect the expected transformation of the state. A special case is the swap gate: we leave the entanglement groups as is and keep track of the effect of the swap gate in the permutation embedded in the quantum state structure. Before we apply a controlled gate, we perform *control reduction*—the central part of the optimization—which we outline in the next section, to remove superfluous controls.

3.4 Control Reduction

Classically Determined Qubits. The central task of quantum constant propagation is to remove superfluous controls from controlled gates. First, we identify and remove all classically determined qubits, i. e. those that are either in $|0\rangle$ or $|1\rangle$. If we find a qubit always in $|0\rangle$, the controlled gate can be removed. If we find qubits always in $|1\rangle$, those controls can be removed since they are always satisfied.

Satisfiable Combination. By filtering out classically determined qubits as described above, a set of qubits may remain in some superposition. Even then, for the target operation to be applied, there must be a basis-state where each of the controls is satisfied, i. e., each is in $|1\rangle$. If no such combination exists, the gate can be removed entirely.

Implied Qubits. When a combination with all controls in the $|1\rangle$ state was found, there can still be some superfluous controls among the remaining qubits. Consider the situation in Fig. 5. Here, the upper two qubits are both in $|1\rangle$ state when the third qubit is as well; hence, the third qubit implies the first and second one. The semantics of the controlled gate remains unchanged when we remove the two upper controls. To generalize this idea, we consider every group of entangled qubits separately since there can not be any implications among different entanglement groups. Within each entanglement group, we look for implications, i. e., whether one qubit being in $|1\rangle$ state implies that other qubits are also in the $|1\rangle$ state. Those implied qubits can be removed from the list of controls.

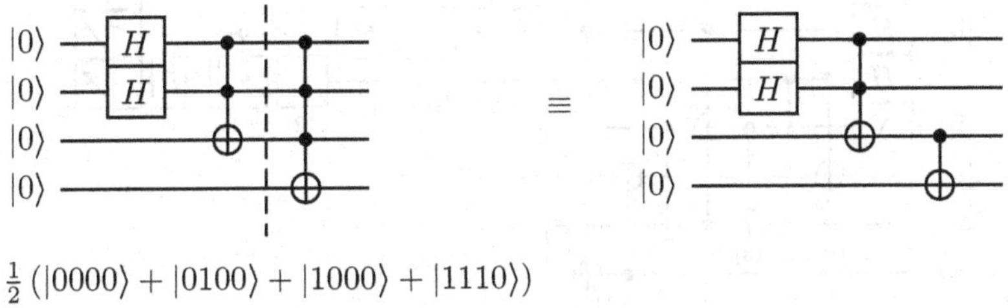

Fig. 5. For the rightmost gate, the third qubit implies the first and second qubit, hence the first and second control qubits can be removed from it.

Further Optimization Potential. In some cases, there might be an equivalence relation between two qubits; here, either one or the other qubit can be removed. This choice is made arbitrarily right now; by considering the circuit to the left or right of the gate, more optimization potential could be exploited. Moreover, the information of more than one qubit might be needed to imply another qubit. Here, we limit ourselves to the described approach because of two reasons: First, in currently common circuits [21] multi-controlled gates with more than two controls rarely occur, and for two controls, our approach finds all possible implications; second, to find the minimal set of controlling qubits is a computationally expensive task that is to the best of our knowledge exponential in the number of controls.

Handle the Abstract State $\top$. If some of the entanglement groups covered by the controls are in $\top$, the optimization techniques can be applied nevertheless. Within groups that are in $\top$ no classically determined qubits or implications between qubits can be identified; however, this is still possible in all other groups. To check whether a satisfiable combination exists across all entanglement groups, we assume one within each group that is $\top$. This is a safe choice: It does not lead to any unsound optimizations since there could be a satisfiable combination in such groups.

Application of Controlled Gates. Before applying a controlled gate, we assume that all superfluous controls are already removed according to the approach described in Sect. 3.4. Like the application of an uncontrolled multi-qubit gate explained in Sect. 3.2, all involved entanglement groups must be merged. Then, all states that satisfy all remaining controls after the control reduction are filtered. To those, the gate is applied to the target qubits via matrix multiplication, whereas the amplitudes of all other states remain unchanged. However, if one of the controls belongs to an entanglement group in $\top$, the resulting state cannot be determined, and we set the merged entanglement group to $\top$.

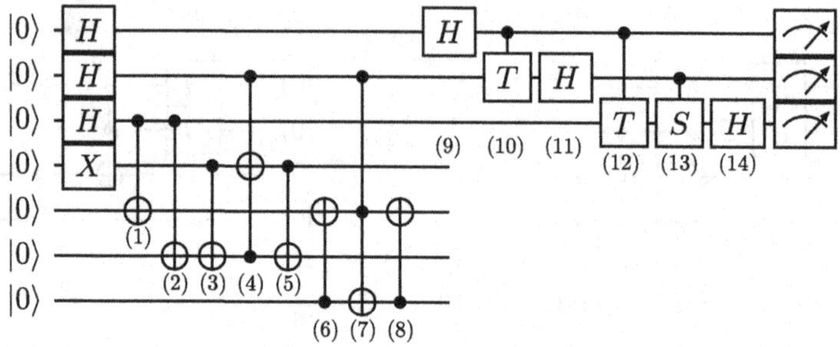

Fig. 6. Quantum constant propagation removes the control from the gate (3) and the gates (6), (10), and (12) entirely. For an explanation, see Example 1

Example 1. We will demonstrate the effect of our optimization on an example taken from [26]. Vandersypen et al. perform Shor's algorithm on 7 qubits to factor the number 15. In this process, they design the circuit from Fig. 6. From the gate labeled with (3), the optimization will remove the control because the state of the controlling qubit is known to be $|1\rangle$ at this point. Gate (6) will be removed entirely because the controlling qubit is known to be in the $|0\rangle$ state. Also, gates (10) and (12) are removed since their controlling qubit will be in the $|0\rangle$ state. These optimizations seem to be trivial. However, the difficult part when automating this process is to scale it to larger and larger circuits without sacrificing efficient running time. Here, we provide the right tool for that with our proposed restricted simulation.[2] ※

4 Correctness of Control Reduction

In this section, we complement the intuitive justification for the correctness of the optimization with a rigorous proof. We first establish the required definitions to characterize the concrete semantics of controlled operations. Similar reasoning

[2] Note that our optimization will not remove redundant gates such as the two Hadamard gates on top; we leave this step for other optimization tools since we already have enough to perform this task sufficiently well.

about the correctness is contained in [13]; we see our style as more comprehensible since it argues only over the superfluousness of one qubit at a time but is still sufficient to show the correctness of the optimization.

Definition 5 (Controlled gate). *Let $U \in \mathbb{C}^{2^n \times 2^n}$ for $n \in \mathbb{N}$ be a unitary matrix of a gate. Let $C^m(U)$ denote the matrix representing the m-controlled version of this gate (the application of gate U is controlled on m qubits).*

Example 2. Consider the X-gate. The corresponding matrix is given by

$$X = \left(\begin{smallmatrix} 0 & 1 \\ 1 & 0 \end{smallmatrix}\right).$$

The doubly-controlled version $C^2(X)$ (the Toffoli-gate), amounts to

$$\begin{pmatrix} 1 &&&&&&& \\ & 1 &&&&&& \\ && 1 &&&&& \\ &&& 1 &&&& \\ &&&& 1 &&& \\ &&&&& 1 && \\ &&&&&& 0 & 1 \\ &&&&&& 1 & 0 \end{pmatrix} \in \mathbb{C}^{8\times 8}.$$

※

Definition 6 (Superfluousness of controls). *Given a state $|\Psi\rangle \in \mathbb{C}^{2^{m+n}}$ and a unitary $U \in \mathbb{C}^{2^n \times 2^n}$. Let $\mathbb{I} \in \mathbb{C}^{2\times 2}$ denote the identity matrix. The first one of m controls is superfluous with respect to $|\Psi\rangle$ if*

$$C^m(U)\,|\Psi\rangle = \mathbb{I} \otimes C^{m-1}(U)\,|\Psi\rangle\,. \tag{1}$$

For the following, we assume without loss of generality that the first m qubits are the controlling ones for a gate applied to the following n qubits.

Theorem 2 (Superfluousness of controls). *With the notation from Definition 6 and $|\Psi\rangle = \sum_{i=0}^{2^m-1}\sum_{j=0}^{2^n-1}\lambda_{i,j}\,|i\rangle \otimes |j\rangle$, the condition from Definition 6 is equivalent to*

$$\left.\begin{pmatrix} \lambda_{i,0} \\ \vdots \\ \lambda_{i,2^n-1} \end{pmatrix}\right|_{i=2^{m-1}-1}$$

being an eigenvector of U for the eigenvalue 1 or the 0 vector.[3]

Proof. When we write out the left-hand side of Eq. (1) in Definition 6 using the definition of $|\Psi\rangle$, we get the following equation:[4]

$$C^m(U)\,|\Psi\rangle = \left.\sum_{j=0}^{2^n-1}\left(\sum_{k=0}^{2^n-1} u_{j,k}\lambda_{i,k}\,|i\rangle\,|j\rangle\right)\right|_{i=2^m-1} + \sum_{i=0}^{2^m-2}\sum_{j=0}^{2^n-1}\lambda_{i,j}\,|i\rangle\,|j\rangle \tag{2}$$

[3] We index elements in matrices starting with 0 as opposed to the mathematical convention with 1 such that the λ corresponding to the basis state $|0\rangle$ has index 0.

[4] For simplicity we omitted the $\otimes$ sign to multiply the states.

We do the same with the right-hand side of Eq. (1), which results in:

$$C^m(U)\left|\Psi\right\rangle = \sum_{i\in\{2^{m-1}-1,2^m-1\}} \sum_{j=0}^{2^n-1} \left(\sum_{k=0}^{2^n-1} u_{j,k}\lambda_{i,k} \left|i\right\rangle \left|j\right\rangle \right) \Bigg|_{i=2^m-1} + \sum_{\substack{i=0 \\ i\notin\{2^{m-1}-1,2^m-1\}}}^{2^m-1} \sum_{j=0}^{2^n-1} \lambda_{i,j} \left|i\right\rangle \left|j\right\rangle \tag{3}$$

Such that Eq. (1) in Definition 6 is satisfied, both, Eq. (2) and (3) must be equal, which gives us:

$$\sum_{j=0}^{2^n-1} \left(\sum_{k=0}^{2^n-1} u_{j,k}\lambda_{i,k} \right) \left|i\right\rangle \left|j\right\rangle \stackrel{!}{=} \sum_{j=0}^{2^n-1} \lambda_{i,j} \left|i\right\rangle \left|j\right\rangle \Bigg|_{i=2^{m-1}-1}$$

By performing a summand-wise comparison, this reduces to:

$$\sum_{k=0}^{2^n-1} u_{j,k}\lambda_{i,k} = \lambda i, j \Bigg|_{i=2^{m-1}-1} \qquad \forall j \in \{0, \dots, 2^n - 1\}$$

This is equivalent to $(\lambda_{i,0}, \dots, \lambda_{i,2^n-1})^\top$ with $i = 2^{m-1} - 1$ being an eigenvector to the eigenvalue 1 or being the zero-vector, concluding the proof. □

From Theorem 2 we can derive a corollary that brings this result in a closer relationship with our optimization using the following definition.

Definition 7 (Implied control). *Using the notation from Definition 5, we say the first control is* implied *by the other controls if* $\lambda_{i,j} = 0$ *for* $i = 2^{m-1} - 1$ *and all* $j \in \{0, \dots, 2^n - 1\}$.

If one interprets the basis states as equal-length bitstrings representing variable assignments of $m + n$ truth variables, then this condition intuitively states that the implication $x_1 \wedge \dots \wedge x_{m-1} \implies x_0$ holds.

Corollary 1 (Sufficient condition for a control to be superfluous). *If the first control is implied by the other controls, it is superfluous.*

The following main theorem shows that each of the three possible modifications, as described in Sect. 3.4, does not change the semantics of the circuit.

Theorem 3. *Quantum constant propagation does not change the semantics relative to the initial configuration with all qubits in the* $\left|0\right\rangle$ *state.*

Proof. Without loss of generality, we can assume that the optimization pass detects the first one of m controlling qubits as superfluous. Depending on the state of the first qubit, the optimization continues in three different ways.

(i) *The first qubit is in* $|0\rangle$: Here, different from the other two cases, not just the controlling qubit is removed from the controlled gate, rather than the entire gate is removed. Thus, we need to show

$$C^m(U)\,|\Psi\rangle = |\Psi\rangle\,.$$

Since all $\lambda_{i,j} = 0$ where $i = 2^m - 1$ the sum on the right of Eq. (2) reduces to 0 and the claim follows.

(ii) *The first qubit is in* $|1\rangle$: Then the amplitude of all basis state with the first qubit in $|0\rangle$ are equal to 0, i.e., $\lambda_{i,j} = 0$ where $i = 2^{m-1} - 1$ and for all $j \in \{1, \ldots, 2^n - 1\}$. Consequently, the condition in Theorem 2 is satisfied, and the first control qubit can safely be removed.

(iii) *Otherwise*: This case can only occur if the optimization found another qubit j among the controlling ones such that the first qubit is only in $|1\rangle$ if the j-th qubit is also in $|1\rangle$. Hence, the sufficient condition from Corollary 1 is satisfied and here the first control qubit can be safely removed.

Altogether, this proves the correctness of the QCP optimization pass. □

We continue with an analysis to show that QCP runs in polynomial time.

5 Running Time Analysis

Variable Definition. For the rest of this section, let m be the number of gates in the input circuit and n the number of qubits. Furthermore, let k be the maximum number of controls attached to any gate in the circuit. Each entanglement group is limited in the number of basis states by the custom constant n_{max}. The achieved asymptotic running time of our QCP is then established by the following lemmas and the main theorem of this section.

Lemma 1. *Control reduction runs in* $\mathcal{O}(k^2 \cdot n)$ *time.*

Proof. As described in Sect. 3.4, the control reduction procedure consists of three steps. First, scanning for classically determined qubits takes $O(n \cdot k)$ time since the state of all controlling qubits needs to be determined and the entanglement group contains at most n_{max} basis states, which is constant. The factor of n comes from retrieving the position and later the state of a specific qubit within the entanglement group which comprises $\mathcal{O}(n)$ qubits, see also Table 1.

Second, the check for a combination where every controlling qubit is in $|1\rangle$, requires splitting the controlling qubits into groups according to their entanglement groups and then checking within each such group whether a combination of all controlling qubits in $|1\rangle$ exists. There can be $\mathcal{O}(k)$ groups containing each $\mathcal{O}(k)$ qubits in the worst case. For each such group, a basis state among the at most n_{max} basis states where all contained controlling qubits are in $|1\rangle$, needs to be found. This requires retrieving the position and then the state of the individual controlling qubits, which takes $\mathcal{O}(n)$ for each of those. Together, this step runs in $\mathcal{O}(k^2 \cdot n)$.

For the third step of finding implications between qubits, we need to consider every pair of qubits in each group already calculated for the previous step. For each pair, we need to retrieve the position and state of the corresponding qubits again, which takes $\mathcal{O}(n)$ times. Since there are $\mathcal{O}(k^2)$ pairs to consider, this gives us a running time of $\mathcal{O}(k^2 \cdot n)$ for this step.

Combined, the running time of the entire control reduction is $\mathcal{O}(k^2 \cdot n)$. □

To perform the control reduction, the current quantum state needs to be tracked. The running time required for that is given by the next lemma.

Lemma 2. *The application of one gate requires $\mathcal{O}(n)$ time.*

Proof. For multi-qubit (un- and controlled) gates, first the affected entanglement groups need to be merged. With the results mentioned in Sect. 3, this requires $\mathcal{O}(n)$ time considering that n_{max} is constant.

For uncontrolled gates, there are only single-qubit and two-qubit gates available in current quantum programming tools, hence, we consider the size of the unitary that defines the transformation of those as constant. We first check whether the number of basis states would exceed n_{max} after the application of the gate; this can be done in $\mathcal{O}(n)$ by iterating over the basis states in the entanglement group and counting the states relevant for the matrix multiplication.

For the application of the associated unitary, one must iterate over the states in the entanglement group and add for each the corresponding states with their modified amplitudes as described in Sect. 3.2. Since the number of states in an entanglement group is bound by n_{max} and the unitary is constant in size, this requires $\mathcal{O}(n)$ time. Checking the state of a specific qubit in a basis state within the entanglement group comprising $\mathcal{O}(n)$ qubits requires $\mathcal{O}(n)$ time.

For the controlled case, the procedure is slightly more complicated, since the unitary transformation shall only be applied to basis states where all controlling qubits are satisfied. This can be done by filtering out the right states and then applying the same procedure as above. Hence, since there are at most n_{max} states, this does not change the overall running time. Consequently, the whole application of one gate can be performed in $\mathcal{O}(n)$ time. □

Theorem 4. *QCP runs in $\mathcal{O}(m \cdot k^2 \cdot n)$.*

Proof. Lemma 1 and Lemma 2 show together, that processing one gate takes $\mathcal{O}(k^2 \cdot n + n) = \mathcal{O}(k^2 \cdot n)$ time. With m the number of gates present in the input circuit, this gives us the claimed result. □

In particular, this shows that the entire QCP runs in polynomial time which we consider important for an efficient optimization. This is due to the restriction of the number of states in each entanglement group since this number could otherwise grow exponentially in the number of qubits, i. e., would be in $\mathcal{O}(2^n)$.

6 Evaluation

The QCP, we propose, only applies control reduction and gate cancellation because of unsatisfiable controls. This may facilitate the elimination of duplicate gates or rotation folding afterward— optimizations which we leave for existing tools capable of this task. In more detail, with the evaluation presented here, we pursue three objectives:

(i) Measure the effectiveness of QCP in terms of its ability to facilitate widely used quantum circuit optimizers.
(ii) Show that QCP extends existing optimizations that also use the idea of constant propagation, namely the Relaxed Peephole Optimization (RPO) [16].
(iii) Demonstrate the efficiency (polynomial running time) of QCP even when processing circuits of large scale.

In the following, we describe the experiments performed to validate our objectives, and afterward, we show and interpret their results. The corresponding artifact [4] provides the means to reproduce the results reported here.

6.1 Experiments

The Benchmark Suite. To provide realistic performance numbers for our optimization, we evaluate it on the comprehensible benchmark suite MQTBench [21]. This benchmark contains circuit representations of 28 algorithms at different abstraction levels; most are scalable in the number of qubits ranging from 2 to 129 qubits. We use the set of circuits at the target-independent level compiled with Qiskit using optimization level 1. This results in a total number of 1761 circuits of varying sizes.

Representation of Numeric Parameters. Due to considerations of practicability and to avoid dealing with symbolic representations of numeric parameters of gates, we convert the parameters to floats and introduce a threshold[5] of $\varepsilon = 10^{-8}$; numbers that differ by less than this threshold are treated as equal, especially numbers less than ε are treated equal to zero. Consequently, some gates in the input circuits reduce to the identity gate; we remove those from the benchmark circuit in a preprocessing step.

Test Settings. For purpose (i), we evaluate the influence of QCP with different values for n_{max} on optimization passes provided by three well-established and widely accepted circuit optimizers—PyZX [14], Qiskit [20], and T$|$ket$\rangle$ [24]. For that, we let those passes run on all benchmark circuits without QCP to create results for a baseline; these numbers are compared with those resulting from first processing the circuits with QCP for different n_{max} values and then applying

[5] Based on personal discussion with Johannes Zeiher from the Max Planck Institute for Quantum Optics, gate parameters can be realized with a precision of $\pi \cdot 10^{-3}$.

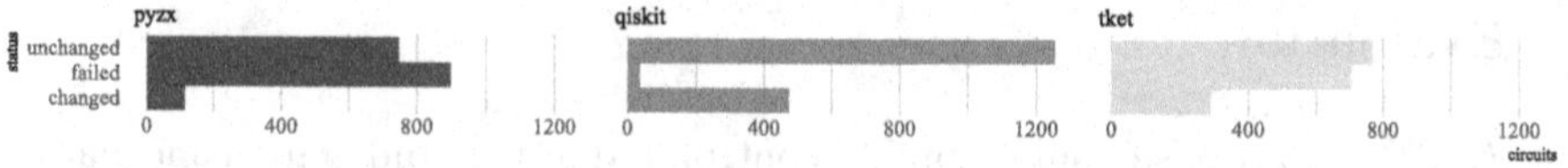

Fig. 7. This shows how many circuits remained unchanged, changed, or failed due to timeout (of one minute) or another error when first applying QCP with $n_{max} = 1024$ and then the corresponding optimization tool.

those passes. For purpose (ii), we compare the results of the optimization composed by RPO and Qiskit with those when placing QCP before or after RPO into this pipeline. The above comparisons are both conducted for two metrics, namely gate count and control count. For purpose (iii), we record the running times of QCP alone on each input circuit. All experiments are executed on a server running Ubuntu 18.04.6 LTS with two Intel® Xeon® Platinum 8260 CPU @ 2.40 GHz processors offering in total 48 physical cores.

Pre-processing to Fit Circuit Optimizer. Each circuit optimizer supports only a specific gate set. Therefore, certain pre-processing is required to adapt the circuits to the circuit optimizer. This pre-processing includes parameter formatting, gate substitution, and gate decomposition. The latter modification leads to a larger gate count than the input circuit. However, this larger gate count will already be included in our baseline for each circuit optimizer and hence, will not lead to a deterioration of the gate count through the optimization.

6.2 Results

Statistics of the Benchmark Suite. As mentioned in the previous section, we evaluate the QCP on 1761 circuits using between 2 and 129 qubits. The smallest circuits comprise only two gates, whereas the largest circuit contains almost 4.9 million gates. However, except for 16 circuits, the majority contain less than 50 thousand gates. The entire benchmark comprises 23.3 million gates and 22.5 million controls, of which approximately 17 thousand belong to a doubly controlled X-gate and the rest to single-controlled gates. The preprocessing of the circuits to make them suitable for the different circuit optimizers must be considered a best-effort approach. Consequently, some circuits still could not be parsed by the corresponding circuit optimizer. Figure 7 shows exemplarily how many of the 1761 circuits failed either due to a timeout of one minute or another error, remained unchanged regarding their gate count, or changed when first applying QCP for $n_{max} = 1024$ and then the corresponding optimizer.

Improvement of Standard Optimizers. Figure 8 shows a summary of the first experiment; the plots show how many more gates and controls, respectively, could be removed in total over the entire benchmark utilizing QCP than just using the corresponding optimizer alone. The plots for Qiskit and T|ket⟩ show

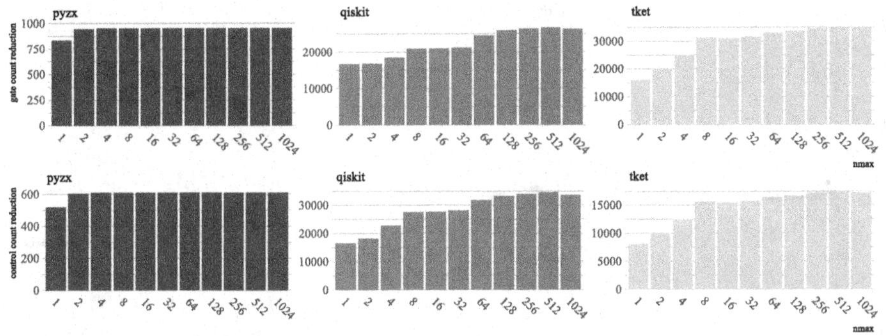

Fig. 8. This plot depicts the aggregated number of gate count (top) and control count (bottom) reduction relative to the baseline, respectively, when applying QCP with different values for n_{max} (x-axis) and then the corresponding optimizer. Note that a y-value greater than 0 corresponds to an improvement over the baseline of only performing the corresponding optimization alone (i. e., PyZX, Qiskit, or T|ket⟩).

that the reduction of gates and controls increases gradually with the value of n_{max}. Note that the absolute numbers for PyZX are smaller since PyZX fails on a lot more circuits compared to the other two optimization tools. In any case, it is evident from the plot that QCP improves the result of each optimizer.

Distribution of Relative Improvement. To show the impact of QCP in more detail, we calculate the relative gate reduction for each circuit by dividing the absolute gate reduction by the total gate count before optimization; analogously, we calculate the relative control reduction for every gate. Only for those circuits that fall into the category changed in Fig. 7, we plot the respective distribution of the relative gate and control count reduction. Figure 9 shows the histograms when applying QCP with $n_{max} = 1024$ before each circuit optimizer. In those plots, the width of each bin amounts to 0.02. We only plot these plots for $n_{max} =$ 1024 because they look almost identical for other values of n_{max}. These plots show that the impact of QCP is small on the majority of circuits. However, some circuits benefit considerably, especially when applying the optimizer T|ket⟩ afterward, which looks for patterns to replace with fewer gates; apparently, QCP modifies the circuit such that more of those patterns occur in the circuit.

Interaction with RPO. RPO [16] propagates the initial state through the circuit as long as the single qubits are in a pure state, see also Sect. 7. To achieve this type of state propagation in our framework, a value for n_{max} of two suffices. Still, QCP with $n_{max} = 2$ can track more information as RPO since also two basis states can suffice to express multiple qubits that are in a superposition of two basis states. Figure 10 and Fig. 11 depict the mutual influence of RPO and QCP. For values 1 and 2 for the parameter n_{max}, QCP does deteriorate the results of RPO when applied before RPO. This is because RPO also implements some circuit pattern matching together with circuit synthesis; when QCP destroys

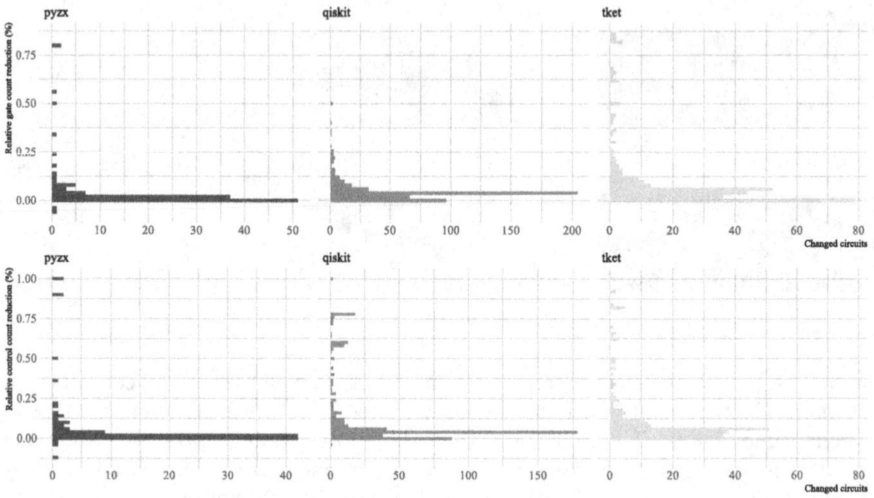

Fig. 9. The relative reduction of gates (top) and controls (bottom) of the circuits that appear in the category changed in the plot from Fig. 7.

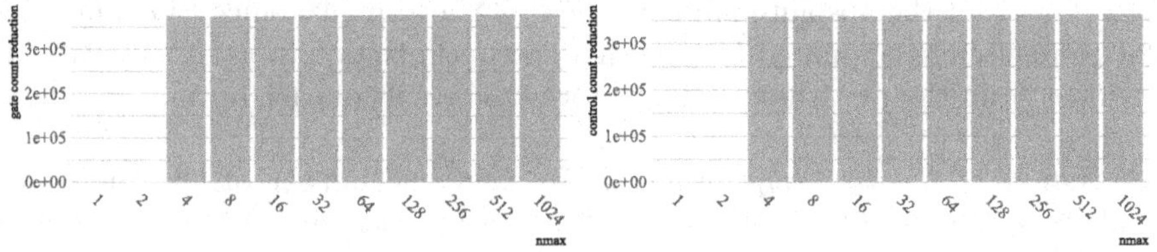

Fig. 10. Those two plots show the reduction of gates and controls, respectively, when applying QCP with different values for n_{max} (x-axis) after RPO and finally Qiskit.

such a pattern, this optimization can not be applied at this position anymore. However, for larger values for n_{max}, those plots show that QCP finds additional optimization potential and is therefore not subsumed by RPO. When looking at Fig. 10, one can see that RPO even benefits QCP: In this setting, approximately 10 times more gates can be removed compared to only using QCP with Qiskit afterward. These remarkable results are mainly due to two circuit families, namely `qpeexact` and `qpeinexact`, where RPO removes some controlled gates with their technique in the first place and facilitates that QCP can remove even more controlled gates.

Analysis of QCP Alone. QCP only fails on six circuits, of which one is a timeout, and five produce an error because of an unsupported gate. QCP needs the most time on the `grover` and `qwalk` circuits; on all other circuits, it finishes processing after at most 3.6 s. In general, the running time of QCP is high if it must track high entanglement for many gates. Accordingly, Fig. 12 shows the running time of QCP on the circuits that belong to the family of Quantum Fourier Transform.

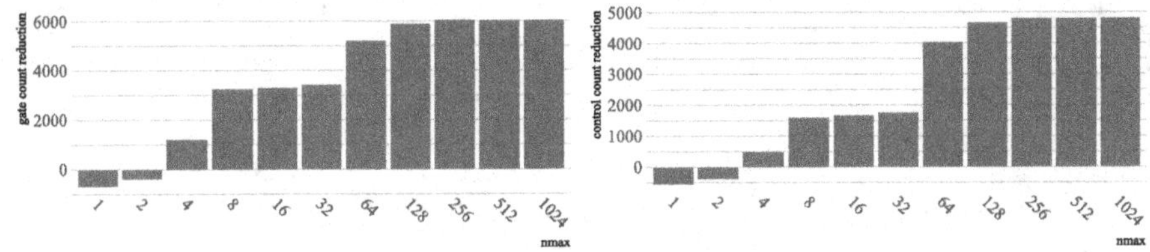

Fig. 11. Those two plots show the reduction of gates and controls, respectively, when applying RPO after QCP with different values for n_{max} (x-axis) and finally Qiskit.

Those produce maximum entanglement among the qubits where all possible basis states are represented at the end of the circuit. The plot displays the running time against the number of qubits. Note that the number of gates, and therefore the size of the circuit, grows quadratically with the number of qubits. A full simulation of those circuits would result in exponential running time. The plots indicate that QCP circumvents the exponential running time by limiting the number of basis states to express the state of an entanglement group by n_{max}.

Explanation of Outliers. The plot in Fig. 12 shows outliers, especially for larger values for n_{max}. Those outliers indicate an exponential running time cut-off at a specific qubit count depending on the value of n_{max}. Considering the circuits reveals that due to the generation pattern of those circuits, the chunk of gates executed on the maximal possible entanglement gradually increases in size until the qubit count where the running time drops again. For example, the maximum outlier in the plot for $n_{max} = 4096$ is reached for 112 qubits. In this circuit, 271 gates are executed on the maximum entanglement comprising 4096 basis states without increasing the entanglement before the gate that increases the entanglement above the limit is processed. In the circuit for one more qubit, i. e., 113 qubits, just 13 gates are executed on the largest possible entanglement. This is due to the order in which the gates in the input file are arranged. In summary, those practical running time measurements underpin our theoretical statements from Sect. 5 since the exponential growth would continue unrestrained otherwise. The results provided indicate differences from existing optimizations. In the next section, we compare our proposed optimization with those and other optimization techniques on a broader basis.

7 Related Work

Other (Peephole) Optimizations. Existing optimization tools [2,20,24] mostly look for known patterns consisting of several gates that can be reduced to a smaller number of gates with the same effect. A special case of those optimizations is *gate cancellation* that removes redundant gates: Many of the common gates are hermitian, i. e., they are self-inverse; when they appear twice directly after each other, both can be dropped without influencing the semantics of the program. When we applied the optimization tools mentioned at the beginning

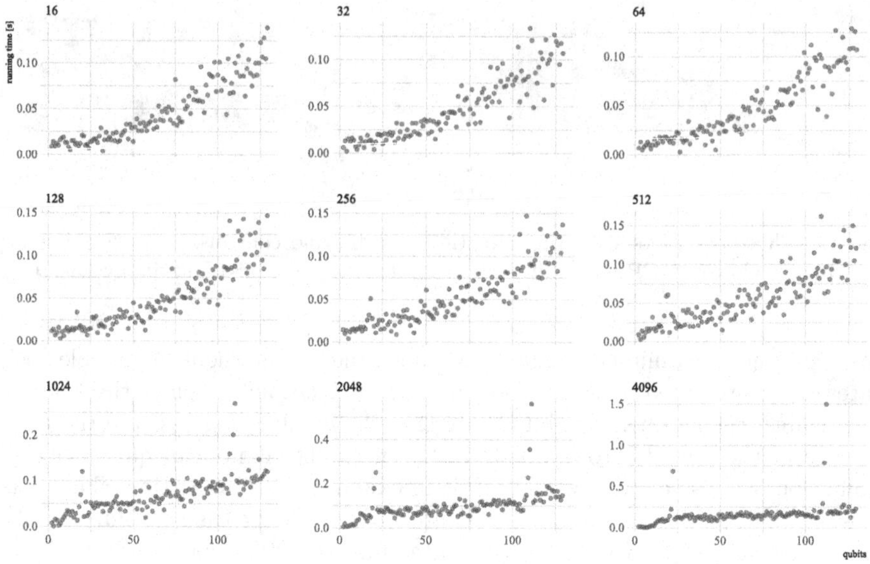

Fig. 12. This plot shows the running time of QCP for different values of n_{max} against the number of qubits (x-axis). The outliers occur due to the structure in which the circuits are generated; more details can be found in the text.

of this paragraph on the circuit shown in Fig. 1, none of those could reduce the circuit to the equivalent empty circuit.

Bitwise Simulation. As already mentioned in Sect. 3.2, the idea to use a hash table to store the quantum state goes back to a simulator developed by Da Rosa et al. [7]. They use a hash table in the same way as we described in Sect. 3.2 with the basis states as keys and their associated amplitudes as values. However, our approach improves upon theirs by keeping qubits separated as long as they are not entangled following the idea in [3] and, hence, be able to store some quantum states even more efficiently. In contrast, Da Rosa et al. use one single hash table for the entire quantum state. Since they want to simulate the circuit and not optimize it as we aim for, they do not change to $\top$ if the computed quantum state becomes too complex. Consequently, their simulation runs still in exponential time even though it is not exponential in the number of qubits but rather in the degree of entanglement [7].

Initial-State Optimizations. Circuit optimization tools developed by Liu et al. [16] and Jang et al. [13] both take advantage of the initial state. Liu et al. leverage the information on the single-qubit state which could be efficiently determined at compile time [16]. They implement state automata to keep track of the single-qubit information on each pure state for circuit simplifications. Single-qubit information is lost though when a multi-qubit gate is applied except for a few special cases since a pure state could then turn into a mixed state. To tackle this issue, users are allowed to insert annotations from which some single-qubit information can be recovered. Our approach, however, avoids treating qubits as independent of each other and tries to trace the global state of the quantum system, enabling us not to lose all the information on qubits even after applying a multi-qubit gate on them. The circuit optimizer proposed by Jang et al. aims to remove redundant control signals from controlled gates based on the state information [13]. Instead of classical simulation, they repeatedly perform quantum measurements at truncation points to determine state information. Besides, in order to consider the noise of quantum computers, they set thresholds depending on gate errors and the number of gates and drop observations that are below the thresholds. Although their approach is lower in computational cost compared to classical simulation, the fact that quantum measurements are needed disallows their tool to run at the compile time only, since shipping circuits to the quantum runtime is necessary for performing measurements. Additionally, in their scheme, it is assumed that the controlled gate in the circuit is either a Toffoli gate or a singly-controlled unitary operation denoted to avoid computations growing exponentially, therefore gate decompositions are needed to guarantee that the assumption holds. In contrast, our approach runs statically at compile time and no prior assumption or pre-processing is required for the success of the analysis. In addition, Markov et al. [17] and Vandersypen et al. [26] optimize their circuits manually using arguments based on initial-state information.

Quantum Abstract Interpretation. Another point of view within the static analysis of quantum programs was established by Yu and Palsberg [28]. They introduce a way of abstract interpretation for quantum programs to verify assumptions on the final state reached after the execution of the program, hence their focus is not on the optimization of the circuit but rather to verify its correctness. Interestingly, their approach to focus on a particular set of qubits mimics our separation of entanglement groups, or to put it the other way around, our separation can be seen as one instantiation of their abstract domain just that we allow to alter the groups during simulation of the circuit instead of keeping them fixed over the entire computation as they do. Consequently, our approach dynamically adapts to the current circuit whereas Yu and Palsberg need to fix the set of qubits to focus on statically for their quantum abstract interpretation.

Classical Constant Propagation. When designing our optimization we were inspired by constant propagation known from classical compiler optimizations for interprocedural programs such as C/C++ programs [22]. However, our QCP differs fundamentally from classical constant propagation: In our case, we just need to pass the information along a linear list of instructions (the gates); the problem here is the sheer mass of information that needs to be tracked. In the classical case, the challenge is to deal with structural program elements such as loops and conditional branches that prevent linearly passing information about values. Here, a constraint system consisting of equations over an abstract domain is derived from the program which then needs to be solved.

8 Conclusions

Summary. In our work, we take the idea of utilizing the most common execution condition of quantum circuits where the initial states of all qubits are in $|0\rangle$ and propose our optimization, QCP, which simulates circuits in a restricted but computationally efficient way and has demonstrated its power in one of the circuit optimization tasks, namely control reduction. In addition, QCP works in harmony with quantum computers: QCP runs in polynomial time and hence can be executed efficiently on classical computers, the output of QCP, optimized circuits, which cannot be efficiently simulated on classical computers, are submitted to quantum computers for execution. That is, we let the classical computer do all where it is good at and leave only the rest for the quantum computer. The success of QCP not only proves the value that resides within initial state information but also contributes to the research on quantum circuit optimization based on methods of static analysis running on classical computers. It is already clear that quantum circuits are expected to grow larger and larger, where building blocks containing multi-controlled gates will be heavily used. For example, OpenQASM 3.0, a highly accepted Quantum assembly language for circuit description, allows users to write arbitrarily many controls for gates [6]. Therefore, it is likely that our QCP will play to its strengths even more in the future.

Future Work. It is worthwhile to consider other abstract domains, e. g., the one used by Yu and Palsberg [28] that keep partial information about the state and still maintain the efficiency we desire. Additionally, it could be useful for QCP to consider an abstract state of meta-superposition which stores possible states after the measurement in a probability distribution. The use of meta-superposition would allow QCP to simulate circuits with intermediate measurements, i. e., measurements that happen not at the end of the circuit. We also plan to incorporate and evaluate the idea of the threshold from [13], so that QCP will be able to discard basis states that are not significant to the simulation and will be indistinguishable from noise on a real quantum computer. Besides, currently QCP is not able to detect when qubits become separable again after they were entangled. Implementing such detection facilitates keeping more state information and thus performs better optimizations. Another direction is to increase the capability of the control reduction itself: For this, we want to generalize the ideas proposed in [16] that use only pure state information of single qubits, to our setting. This includes replacing fully simulated parts of the circuit by means of circuit synthesis methods, such as KAK decomposition [25]. It is possible that performing QCP causes a loss of opportunities for other optimizations. So, one might also be interested to study how to determine the optimal order to perform different optimization passes.

Acknowledgements. We thank our reviewers for their tremendous efforts and their helpful suggestions. This has greatly improved the quality of this article. We are grateful to our supervisor Helmut Seidl for many fruitful discussions and his support at all times.

Johannes Zeiher from Max Planck Institute of Quantum Optics has also provided us with precious advice. This work has been supported in part by the Bavarian state government through the project Munich Quantum Valley with funds from the Hightech Agenda Bayern Plus.

References

1. Aaronson, S., Chen, L.: Complexity-Theoretic Foundations of Quantum Supremacy Experiments (2016). https://doi.org/10.48550/ARXIV.1612.05903
2. Amy, M., Gheorghiu, V.: Staq - a full-stack quantum processing toolkit. Quantum Sci. Technol. **5**(3), 034016 (2020). https://doi.org/10.1088/2058-9565/ab9359
3. Bauer-Marquart, F., Leue, S., Schilling, C.: symQV: automated symbolic verification of quantum programs. In: Chechik, M., Katoen, J.P., Leucker, M. (eds.) FM 2023. LNCS, vol. 14000, pp. 181–198. Springer, Cham (2023). https://doi.org/10.1007/978-3-031-27481-7_12
4. Chen, Y., Stade, Y.: Artifact for Quantum Constant Propagation (2023). https://doi.org/10.5281/zenodo.8033829
5. Chow, J., Dial, O., Gambetta, J.: IBM Quantum breaks the 100-qubit processor barrier (2021). https://research.ibm.com/blog/127-qubit-quantum-processor-eagle
6. Cross, A.W., et al.: OpenQASM 3: a broader and deeper quantum assembly language. ACM Trans. Quantum Comput. **3**(3), 1–50 (2022). https://doi.org/10.1145/3505636
7. Da Rosa, E.C.R., De Santiago, R.: Ket quantum programming. J. Emerg. Technol. Comput. Syst. **18**(1), 1–25 (2022). https://doi.org/10.1145/3474224
8. Farhi, E., Goldstone, J., Gutmann, S., Zhou, L.: The quantum approximate optimization algorithm and the Sherrington-Kirkpatrick model at infinite size. Quantum **6**, 759 (2022). https://doi.org/10.22331/q-2022-07-07-759
9. Feynman, R.P.: Simulating physics with computers. Int. J. Theor. Phys. **21**(6), 467–488 (1982). https://doi.org/10.1007/BF02650179
10. Grover, L.K.: A fast quantum mechanical algorithm for database search. In: Proceedings Twenty-Eighth Annual ACM Symposium Theory Computing, STOC 1996, Philadelphia, Pennsylvania, USA, pp. 212–219. ACM Press (1996). https://doi.org/10.1145/237814.237866
11. Haferkamp, J., Hangleiter, D., Bouland, A., Fefferman, B., Eisert, J., Bermejo-Vega, J.: Closing gaps of a quantum advantage with short-time Hamiltonian dynamics. Phys. Rev. Lett. **125**(25), 250501 (2020). https://doi.org/10.1103/PhysRevLett.125.250501
12. Hidary, J.D.: Quantum Computing: An Applied Approach. Springer, Cham (2021). https://doi.org/10.1007/978-3-030-83274-2
13. Jang, W., et al.: Initial-state dependent optimization of controlled gate operations with quantum computer. Quantum **6**, 798 (2022). https://doi.org/10.22331/q-2022-09-08-798
14. Kissinger, A., van de Wetering, J.: PyZX: large scale automated diagrammatic reasoning. Electron. Proc. Theor. Comput. Sci. **318**, 229–241 (2020). https://doi.org/10.4204/EPTCS.318.14
15. Knill, E.: Quantum computing with very noisy devices. Nature **434**(7029), 39–44 (2005). https://doi.org/10.1038/nature03350

16. Liu, J., Bello, L., Zhou, H.: Relaxed peephole optimization: a novel compiler optimization for quantum circuits. In: 2021 IEEE/ACM International Symposium on Code Generation and Optimization, CGO, Seoul, Korea (South), pp. 301–314. IEEE (2021). https://doi.org/10.1109/CGO51591.2021.9370310
17. Markov, I.L., Saeedi, M.: Constant-Optimized Quantum Circuits for Modular Multiplication and Exponentiation (2015)
18. Nielsen, M.A., Chuang, I.L.: Quantum Computation and Quantum Information: 10th Anniversary Edition, 1st edn. Cambridge University Press (2012). https://doi.org/10.1017/CBO9780511976667
19. Peruzzo, A., et al.: A variational eigenvalue solver on a photonic quantum processor. Nat. Commun. **5**(1), 4213 (2014). https://doi.org/10.1038/ncomms5213
20. Qiskit contributors: Qiskit: an open-source framework for quantum computing (2023). https://doi.org/10.5281/zenodo.2573505
21. Quetschlich, N., Burgholzer, L., Wille, R.: MQT Bench: Benchmarking Software and Design Automation Tools for Quantum Computing (2022). https://doi.org/10.48550/arXiv.2204.13719
22. Seidl, H., Wilhelm, R., Hack, S.: Compiler Design: Analysis and Transformation. Springer, Heidelberg (2012). https://doi.org/10.1007/978-3-642-17548-0
23. Shor, P.: Algorithms for quantum computation: discrete logarithms and factoring. In: Proceedings 35th Annual Symposium on Foundations of Computer Science, Santa Fe, NM, USA, pp. 124–134. IEEE Computer Society Press (1994). https://doi.org/10.1109/SFCS.1994.365700
24. Sivarajah, S., Dilkes, S., Cowtan, A., Simmons, W., Edgington, A., Duncan, R.: T$|$ket$\rangle$: a retargetable compiler for NISQ devices. Quantum Sci. Technol. **6**(1), 014003 (2021). https://doi.org/10.1088/2058-9565/ab8e92
25. Tucci, R.R.: An Introduction to Cartan's KAK Decomposition for QC Programmers (2005)
26. Vandersypen, L.M.K., Steffen, M., Breyta, G., Yannoni, C.S., Sherwood, M.H., Chuang, I.L.: Experimental realization of Shor's quantum factoring algorithm using nuclear magnetic resonance. Nature **414**(6866), 883–887 (2001). https://doi.org/10.1038/414883a
27. Wu, X.C., Davis, M.G., Chong, F.T., Iancu, C.: QGo: Scalable Quantum Circuit Optimization Using Automated Synthesis (2020). https://doi.org/10.48550/ARXIV.2012.09835
28. Yu, N., Palsberg, J.: Quantum abstract interpretation. In: Proceedings of the 42nd ACM SIGPLAN International Conference on Programming Language Design and Implementation, pp. 542–558. ACM, Virtual Canada (2021). https://doi.org/10.1145/3453483.3454061

Error Invariants for Fault Localization via Abstract Interpretation

Aleksandar S. Dimovski(✉)

Mother Teresa University, st. Mirche Acev nr. 4, 1000 Skopje, North Macedonia
aleksandar.dimovski@unt.edu.mk
https://aleksdimovski.github.io/

Abstract. *Fault localization* aims to automatically identify the cause of an error in a program by localizing the error to a relatively small part of the program. In this paper, we present a novel technique for automated fault localization via *error invariants* inferred by abstract interpretation. An error invariant for a location in an error program over-approximates the reachable states at the given location that may produce the error, if the execution of the program is continued from that location. Error invariants can be used for *statement-wise semantic slicing* of error programs and for obtaining concise error explanations. We use an iterative refinement sequence of backward-forward static analyses by abstract interpretation to compute error invariants, which are designed to explain why an error program violates a particular assertion. We demonstrate the effectiveness of our approach to localize errors in realistic C programs.

Keywords: Fault localization · Error invariants · Abstract interpretation · Statement-wise semantic slicing

1 Introduction

Static program analyzers [6,8,22,27,36] are today often applied to find errors in real-world programs. They usually return an error report, which shows how an assertion can be violated. However, the programmers still need to process the error report, in order to isolate the cause of an error to a manageable number of statements and variables that are relevant for the error. Using this information, they can subsequently repair the given program either manually or automatically by running specialized program repair tools [31,33].

In this paper, we present a novel technique for *automated fault localization*, which automatically generates concise error explanations in the form of

M. V. Hermenegildo and J. F. Morales (Eds.): SAS 2023, LNCS 14284, pp. 190–211, 2023.
https://doi.org/10.1007/978-3-031-44245-2_10

statements relevant for a given error that describe the essence of why the error occurred. In particular, we describe a fault localization technique based on so-called *error invariants* inferred via abstract interpretation. An error invariant for a given location in a program captures states that may produce the error, that is, there may be executions of the program continued from that location violating a given assertion. We observe that the same error invariants that hold for consecutive locations characterize statements in the program that are irrelevant for the error. A statement that is enclosed by the same error invariant does not change the nature of the error. Hence, error invariants can be used to find only relevant statements and information about reachable states that helps to explain the cause of an error. They also identify the relevant variables whose values should be tracked when executing the program. The obtained relevant statements constitute the so-called *statement-wise semantic slicing* of the error program, which can be changed (repaired) to make the entire program correct.

Abstract interpretation [7,29] is a general theory for approximating the semantics of programs. It has been successfully applied to deriving computable and approximated static analysis that infer dynamic properties of programs, due to its soundness guarantee (all confirmative answers are indeed correct) and scalability (with a good trade-off between precision and cost). In this paper, we focus on applying abstract interpretation to automate fault localization via inferring error invariants. More specifically, we use a combination of backward and forward refining analyses based on abstract interpretation to infer error invariants from an error program. Each next iteration of backward-forward analyses produces more refined error invariants than the previous iteration. Finally, the error invariants found in the last iteration are used to compute a slice of the error program that contains only relevant statements for the error.

The backward (over-approximating) numerical analysis is used for computing the necessary preconditions of violating the target assertion, thus reducing the input space that needs further exploration. Error invariants are constructed by going backwards step-by-step starting at the property violation, i.e. by propagating the negated assertion backwards. The negated assertion represents an error state space. When there is a precision loss caused by merging the branches of an `if` statement, we collect in a set of predicates the branching condition of that conditional. Subsequently, the forward (over-approximating) numerical analysis of a program with reduced abstract sub-input is employed to refine error invariants in all locations, thus also refining (reducing) the error state space. Based on the inferred error invariants, we can find the relevant statements and relevant variables for the assertion violation. Initially, in the first iteration, both analyses are performed on a base abstract domain (e.g., intervals, octagons, polyhedra). In the subsequent iterations, we use the set of predicates generated by the previous backward analysis to design a binary decision diagram (BDD) abstract domain functor, which can express disjunctive properties with respect to the given set of predicates. A decision node in a BDD abstract element stores a predicate, and each leaf node stores an abstract value from a base abstract domain under specific evaluation results of predicates. When the obtained set of predicates as well as the (abstract) error state sub-space stay the same over two iterations, the iterative process stops and reports the inferred error invariants. Otherwise, the refinement process continues by performing backward-forward analyses on a BDD abstract domain based on the refined set of predicates as well as on a reduced error state sub-space. The BDD abstract domain and the reduced error state sub-space enable our analyses in the subsequent iterations to focus on smaller state sub-spaces, i.e. partitionings of the total state space, in each of which the program may involve fewer disjunctive or non-linear behaviours and thus the analyses may produce more precise results.

We have implemented our abstract interpretation-based approach for fault localization of C programs in a prototype tool. It takes as input a C program with an assertion, and returns a set of statements whose replacement can eliminate the error. The tool uses the numerical abstract domains (e.g., intervals, octagons, polyhedra) from the APRON library [25], and the BDD abstract domains from the BDDAPRON library [24]. BDDAPRON uses any abstract domain from the APRON library for the leaf nodes. The tool also calls the Z3 SMT solver [30] to compute the error invariants from the information inferred via abstract interpretation-based analyses. We discuss a set of C programs from the literature, SV-COMP and TCAS suites that demonstrate the usefulness of our tool.

In summary, this work makes the following contributions:

(1) We define error invariants as abstract representations of the reason why the program may go wrong if it is continued from that location;
(2) We propose an iterative abstract interpretation-based analyses to compute error invariants of a program. They are used to identify statements and program variables that are relevant for the fault in the program;
(3) We implemented the approach in a prototype tool, which uses domains from APRON and BDDAPRON libraries as well as Z3 SMT solver;
(4) We evaluate our approach for fault localization on a set of C benchmarks.

2 Motivating Examples

We demonstrate our technique for fault localization using the illustrative examples in Figs. 1, 2, and 3. The first example, `program1`, in Fig. 1 shows a program code that violates the assertion $(x > y)$ for all values of the parameter x, since $y = x+1$ holds at the end of the program. A static analysis of this program will establish the assertion violation. However, the static analysis returns a full list of invariants in all locations of the program, including details that are irrelevant for the specific error. Similarly, other verification tools will also report many irrelevant details for the error (e.g. full execution paths).

Our technique works as follows. We begin with the first iteration of the backward-forward analyses. The backward analysis defined over the Polyhedra domain starts with the negated assertion $(x \leq y)$ at loc. ④. By propagating it backwards, it infers the preconditions: $(x \leq y)$ at loc. ③, $(x \leq z)$ at loc. ②, and $\top$ at loc. ①. The subsequent forward analysis starts with invariant $\top$ at loc. ①, and then infers invariants: $(z = x+1)$ at loc. ②, $(z = x+1 \wedge y = x+1)$ at loc. ③, and

```
void main(int x){
[ ⊤ ]
① int z := x + 1;
[ z = x + 1 ]
② int y := z;
[ y = x + 1 ]
③ z := z+1;
[ y = x + 1 ]
④ assert (x > y);
```

Fig. 1. program1.

```
void main(int input){
[ input ≤ 41 ]
① int x := 1;
[ input ≤ 41 ]
② int y := input − 42;
[ B ∧ input ≤ 41 ∧ y = input − 42 ]
③ if (y<0) then
[ B ∧ input ≤ 41 ∧ y = input − 42 ]
④      x := 0;
[ B ∧ input ≤ 41 ∧ y = input − 42 ∧ x = 0 ]
⑤ else
[ ⊥ ]
⑥ endif
[ B ∧ input ≤ 41 ∧ y = input − 42 ∧ x = 0 ]
⑦ assert (x>0);
```

Fig. 2. program2 ($B \equiv (y<0)$).

```
void main(int n){
[ n ≥ 11 ]
① int x := 6;
[ n ≥ 11 ∧ x = 6 ]
② int y := n;
[ n ≥ 11 ∧ x = 6 ]
③ while (x < n) do
[ n ≥ 11 ∧ n ≥ x + 1 ]
④      x := x + 1;
[ n ≥ 11 ∧ n ≥ x ]
⑤      y := y + 1;
[ n ≥ 11 ∧ n ≥ x ]
⑥ od;
[ n ≥ 11 ∧ n = x ]
⑦ assert (x ≤ 10);
```

Fig. 3. program3.

$(z = x+2 \wedge y = x+1)$ at loc. ④. Note that we use boxed code, such as $\boxed{z = x + 1}$, to highlight the inferred error invariants by our technique. The computed error invariants after one iteration of backward-forward analysis, shown in Fig. 1, are: $\boxed{\top}$, $\boxed{z = x + 1}$, $\boxed{y = x + 1}$, $\boxed{y = x + 1}$ in locs. ① to ④, respectively. Note how the results of backward analysis are refined using the forward analysis to compute more precise error invariants. For example, the error invariant at loc. ③, $\boxed{y = x + 1}$, is obtained by refining the backward precondition $(x \leq y)$ using the forward invariant $(z = x+1 \wedge y = x+1)$ at loc. ③. By analyzing the inferred error invariants, we get a set of relevant statements that are potential indicators of the error. Since the error invariants at locs. ③ and ④ are the same, the statement at loc. ③, $z := z + 1$, is dropped from the resulting program slice. That is, the program will remain erroneous even if $z := z + 1$ is removed from the program. Hence, this statement is irrelevant for the error. In effect, the computed program slice of relevant statements for the error consists of statements at locs. ① and ②. A fix of the error program would be to change some of those statements. Error invariants also provide information about which variables are responsible for the error. After executing the statement at loc. ②, $y := z$, we can see from the error invariant $\boxed{y = x + 1}$ that z is no longer relevant and only x and y has to be considered to the end of the program. For the purpose of comparison with the state-of-the-art, we also ran the `BugAssist` tool [26] on this example. `BugAssist` returns only the statement at loc. ① as potential bug.

Consider `program2` in Fig. 2 taken from [4]. The assertion is violated if `main` is called with a value less than 42 for the parameter *input*. In this case, the assignment at loc. ④ is executed and the assigned value 0 to x makes the assertion fail. The backward analysis in the first iteration of our procedure starts with the negated assertion $(x \leq 0)$, and it infers that the precondition of `then` branch is $\top$ and the precondition of `else` branch is $(x \leq 0)$. Their join $\top$ is the precondition before the `if` statement at loc. ③, which is then propagated back to loc. ①. Hence, there is a precision loss in analyzing the `if` statement, so we record the `if` condition $(y < 0)$, denoted as B, in the set of predicates $\mathbb{P}$. As a result of this precision loss, the error invariants inferred after first iteration are: $\boxed{\top}$ for locs. ① - ④, $\boxed{(x = 1)}$ for locs. ⑤, ⑦, and $\boxed{\bot}$ for loc. ⑥. In effect, we would drop the statement at loc. ②, `y :=` $input - 42$, as irrelevant for the error. However, the second iteration is performed on the refined BDD abstract domain defined over the Polyhedra leaf domain and the set $\mathbb{P} = \{B \equiv (y < 0)\}$ of predicates for decision nodes. Thus, we can analyze the `if` statement more precisely and obtain more precise analysis results. From the obtained error invariants, shown in Fig. 2, we can see that statement at loc. ② is now relevant for the error, while statement at loc. ①, $x := 1$, is encompassed with the same invariants, so it can be dropped from the resulting program slice as irrelevant for the error. Consider a variant of `program2`, denoted `program2-a`, where the assertion in loc. ⑦ is changed to $(x \leq 0)$. The single backward analysis infers very imprecise results by reporting that all statements are relevant for the error. However, our approach finds more precise results inferring that the whole `if` statement (locs. ③ - ⑥) is irrelevant for the error since it cannot set x to a positive value that contradicts the assertion. `BugAssist` also gives less precise results. It reports locs. ② and ③ as potential bugs for both `program2` and `program2-a`.

Finally, consider `program3` in Fig. 3. The error due to the violation of the assertion occurs when `main` is called with a value greater than 10 for the parameter n. In this case, at the end of the `while` loop, the value of x becomes equal to n, thus conflicting the given assertion. Our technique for fault localization works as follows. In the first iteration, the backward analysis starts with the invariant $(x \geq 11)$ at the assertion location ⑦. After computing the error invariants at the end of the first backward-forward iteration, we infer the more precise invariant $(n \geq 11 \wedge x = n)$ at loc. ⑦. We also obtain the error invariant $\top$ for locs. ④, ⑤, and ⑥, which would make the body of `while` irrelevant for the error. Since the error state space at loc. ⑦ is refined from $(x \geq 11)$ to $(n \geq 11 \wedge x = n)$ after the first iteration, we continue with the second iteration on the reduced error sub-space. Therefore, the second iteration starts with the invariant $(n \geq 11 \wedge x = n)$ at loc. ⑦. It infers the error invariants shown in Fig. 3. We can see that statements at locs. ② and ⑤ are redundant and can be eliminated as irrelevant. Moreover, the error invariants imply that variables n and x are relevant, while y is completely irrelevant for the assertion violation. On the other hand, `BugAssist` fails to report any potential bug locations for `program3` by default. In particular, `BugAssist` builds on the `CBMC` bounded model checker [6] for construction of the logic formula, which is then analyzed using a `MAX-SAT` solver. Hence, it reasons about loops by unrolling them, making it very sensitive to the degree of unrolling. If the loop is unrolled 15 times, `BugAssist` reports some potential bug locations. Still, it wrongly returns loc. ⑤ as potential bug, and misses to return loc. ① as potential bug.

3 The Language and Its Semantics

Syntax. We consider a simple C-like sequential non-deterministic programming language. The program variables *Var* are statically allocated and the only data type is the set $\mathbb{Z}$ of mathematical integers. The control locations before and after each statement are associated to unique syntactic labels $l \in \mathbb{L}$.

$$s\,(s \in \mathit{Stm}) ::= \texttt{skip} \mid \texttt{x=}ae \mid s;s \mid \texttt{if}\,(be)\,\texttt{then}\,s\,\texttt{else}\,s \mid \texttt{while}\,(be)\,\texttt{do}\,s \mid \texttt{assert}(be)$$
$$ae\,(ae \in \mathit{AExp}) ::= n \mid [n,n'] \mid \texttt{x} \in \mathit{Var} \mid ae \oplus ae,$$
$$be\,(be \in \mathit{BExp}) ::= ae \bowtie ae \mid \neg be \mid be \wedge be \mid be \vee be$$

where n ranges over integers $\mathbb{Z}$, $[n,n']$ over integer intervals, $\texttt{x}$ over program variables *Var*, and $\oplus \in \{+,-,*,/\}$, $\bowtie \in \{<,\leq,=,\neq\}$. Without loss of generality, we assume that a program is a sequence of statements followed by a single assertion. That is, a program $p \in \mathit{Prog}$ is of the form: ${}^{l_{in}:}s;{}^{l_{ass}:}\,\texttt{assert}(be^{ass})$.

Concrete Semantics. A *store* $\sigma : \Sigma = \mathit{Var} \to \mathbb{Z}$ is a mapping from program variables to values. The semantics of arithmetic expressions $[\![ae]\!] : \Sigma \to \mathcal{P}(\mathbb{Z})$ (resp., boolean expressions $[\![be]\!] : \Sigma \to \mathcal{P}(\{\text{true}, \text{false}\})$) is the set of possible integer (resp., boolean) values for expression ae (resp., be) in a store σ. E.g.,

$$[\![n]\!]\sigma = \{n\},\ [\![[n,n']]\!]\sigma = \{n,\ldots,n'\},\ [\![\texttt{x}]\!]\sigma = \{\sigma(\texttt{x})\},$$
$$[\![ae_0 \bowtie ae_1]\!]\sigma = \{n_0 \bowtie n_1 \mid n_0 \in [\![ae_0]\!]\sigma, n_1 \in [\![ae_1]\!]\sigma\}$$
$$[\![\neg be]\!]\sigma = \{\neg t \mid t \in [\![be]\!]\}$$

We define a *necessary precondition* (backward) semantics and an *invariance* (forward) semantics on the complete lattice $\langle \mathbb{L} \mapsto \mathcal{P}(\Sigma), \dot{\subseteq}, \dot{\cup}, \dot{\cap}, \lambda l.\emptyset, \lambda l.\Sigma \rangle$ by induction on the syntax of programs. The dotted operators $\dot{\subseteq}, \dot{\cup}, \dot{\cap}$ defined on $\mathbb{L} \mapsto \mathcal{P}(\Sigma)$ are obtained by point-wise lifting of the corresponding operators $\subseteq, \cup, \cap$ defined on $\mathcal{P}(\Sigma)$. The above semantics work on functions from labels to sets of stores. The necessary precondition semantics backtracks from an user-supplied property to its origin [1], so it associates to each label $l \in \mathbb{L}$ a necessary precondition in the form of a set of possible stores $S \in \mathcal{P}(\Sigma)$ that may lead to the execution of the user-supplied property. The stores resulting from the necessary precondition semantics $\overleftarrow{[\![s]\!]} : \mathcal{P}(\Sigma) \to \mathcal{P}(\Sigma)$ are built backwards: each function $\overleftarrow{[\![s]\!]}$ takes as input a set of stores S at the final label of s and outputs a set of possible stores before s from which stores from S may be reached after executing s. The invariance semantics [7] associates to each label $l \in \mathbb{L}$ an invariant in the form of a set of possible stores $S \in \mathcal{P}(\Sigma)$ that may arise each time the execution reaches the label l from some initial store. The stores resulting from the invariance semantics $\overrightarrow{[\![s]\!]} : \mathcal{P}(\Sigma) \to \mathcal{P}(\Sigma)$ are built forward: each function $\overrightarrow{[\![s]\!]}$ takes as input a set of stores S at the initial label of s and outputs a set of possible stores reached after executing s from S. The complete definitions of functions $\overleftarrow{[\![s]\!]}$ and $\overrightarrow{[\![s]\!]}$ are given in Fig. 4.

In this way, we can collect the set of possible stores denoting necessary preconditions, written $\texttt{Cond}_{\mathcal{F}}$, and invariants, written $\texttt{Inv}_{\mathcal{I}}$, at each label $l \in \mathbb{L}$ of

$\overleftarrow{[\![\texttt{skip}]\!]}S = S$
$\overleftarrow{[\![\texttt{x := } ae]\!]}S = \{\sigma \in \Sigma \mid \exists n \in [\![ae]\!]\sigma, \sigma[\texttt{x} \mapsto n] \in S\}$
$\overleftarrow{[\![s_1 \texttt{ ; } s_2]\!]}S = \overleftarrow{[\![s_1]\!]}(\overleftarrow{[\![s_2]\!]}S)$
$\overleftarrow{[\![\texttt{if } be \texttt{ then } s_1 \texttt{ else } s_2]\!]}S = \{\sigma \in \overleftarrow{[\![s_1]\!]}S \mid \text{true} \in [\![be]\!]\sigma\} \cup \{\sigma \in \overleftarrow{[\![s_2]\!]}S \mid \text{false} \in [\![be]\!]\sigma\}$
$\overleftarrow{[\![\texttt{while } be \texttt{ do } s]\!]}S = \texttt{lfp}\ \overleftarrow{\phi}$
$\overleftarrow{\phi}(X) = \{\sigma \in S \mid \text{false} \in [\![be]\!]\sigma\} \cup \{\sigma \in \overleftarrow{[\![s]\!]}X \mid \text{true} \in [\![be]\!]\sigma\}$

$\overrightarrow{[\![\texttt{skip}]\!]}S = S$
$\overrightarrow{[\![\texttt{x := } ae]\!]}S = \{\sigma[\texttt{x} \mapsto n] \mid \sigma \in S, n \in [\![ae]\!]\sigma\}$
$\overrightarrow{[\![s_1 \texttt{ ; } s_2]\!]}S = \overrightarrow{[\![s_2]\!]}(\overrightarrow{[\![s_1]\!]}S)$
$\overrightarrow{[\![\texttt{if } be \texttt{ then } s_1 \texttt{ else } s_2]\!]}S = \overrightarrow{[\![s_1]\!]}\{\sigma \in S \mid \text{true} \in [\![be]\!]\sigma\} \cup \overrightarrow{[\![s_2]\!]}\{\sigma \in S \mid \text{false} \in [\![be]\!]\sigma\}$
$\overrightarrow{[\![\texttt{while } be \texttt{ do } s]\!]}S = \{\sigma \in \texttt{lfp}\ \overrightarrow{\phi} \mid \text{false} \in [\![be]\!]\sigma\}$
$\overrightarrow{\phi}(X) = S \cup \overrightarrow{[\![s]\!]}\{\sigma \in X \mid \text{true} \in [\![be]\!]\sigma\}$

Fig. 4. Necessary precondition (above) and invariance (below) semantics.

a program $^{l_{in}:}s;^{l_{ass}:}\texttt{assert}(be^{ass})$. We assume that at the assertion label l_{ass} the possible stores are $\mathcal{F} \in \mathcal{P}(\Sigma)$, whereas at the initial label l_{in} are $\mathcal{I} \in \mathcal{P}(\Sigma)$. That is, $\texttt{Cond}_{\mathcal{F}}(l_{ass}) = \mathcal{F}$ and $\texttt{Inv}_{\mathcal{I}}(l_{in}) = \mathcal{I}$. For each statement $^{l:}s^{l'}$, the set $\texttt{Cond}_{\mathcal{F}}(l) \in \mathcal{P}(\Sigma)$ (resp., $\texttt{Inv}_{\mathcal{I}}(l') \in \mathcal{P}(\Sigma)$) of possible necessary preconditions (resp., invariants) at the initial label l (resp., final label l'), are:

$$\texttt{Cond}_{\mathcal{F}}(l) = \overleftarrow{[\![s]\!]}\ \texttt{Cond}_{\mathcal{F}}(l'), \qquad \texttt{Inv}_{\mathcal{I}}(l') = \overrightarrow{[\![s]\!]}\ \texttt{Inv}_{\mathcal{I}}(l)$$

We now define the error invariant map $\texttt{ErrInv}_{\mathcal{F}} : \mathbb{L} \to \mathcal{P}(\Sigma)$ as follows. Let $\mathcal{F} = \{\sigma \in \Sigma \mid [\![be^{ass}]\!]\sigma = \text{false}\}$ be a set of stores in which $\texttt{assert}(be^{ass})$ is not valid. Given a set of stores $S \in \mathcal{P}(\Sigma)$, we define the set of *unconstrained variables* in S as $UVar_S = \{x \in Var \mid \forall y \in Var\backslash\{x\}, (\exists n \in \mathbb{Z}.\exists\sigma[y \mapsto n] \in S \implies \forall n' \in \mathbb{Z}.\exists\sigma'[x \mapsto n'][y \mapsto n] \in S)\}$. The set of *constrained variables* of S is $CVar_S = Var\backslash UVar_S$. Given a store $\sigma \in \Sigma$, let $\sigma\,|_{Var'}$ denote the restriction of σ to the sub-domain $Var' \subseteq Var$, such that $\sigma\,|_{Var'}(x) = \sigma(x)$ for all $x \in Var'$. Given a set of stores $S \in \mathcal{P}(\Sigma)$, define $S\,|_{Var'} = \{\sigma\,|_{Var'} \mid \sigma \in S\}$. Then, we define:

$$\texttt{ErrInv}_{\mathcal{F}}(l) = \{\sigma \in \texttt{Cond}_{\mathcal{F}}(l) \mid \sigma\,|_{CVar_{\texttt{Cond}_{\mathcal{F}}(l)}} \in \texttt{Inv}_{\texttt{Cond}_{\mathcal{F}}(l_{in})}(l)\,|_{CVar_{\texttt{Cond}_{\mathcal{F}}(l)}}\} \quad (1)$$

That is, the error invariants at label l is the set of necessary preconditions $\texttt{Cond}_{\mathcal{F}}(l)$ restricted with respect to the constrained variables from $CVar_{\texttt{Cond}_{\mathcal{F}}(l)}$ with the values they obtain in the set $\texttt{Inv}_{\texttt{Cond}_{\mathcal{F}}(l_{in})}(l)$ of invariants at l obtained by taking as the initial set of stores $\texttt{Cond}_{\mathcal{F}}(l_{in})$. For example, let $Var = \{x, y, z\}$, $\texttt{Cond}_{\mathcal{F}}(l) = \{\sigma \in \Sigma \mid \sigma(x) = \sigma(y)\}$, and $\texttt{Inv}_{\texttt{Cond}_{\mathcal{F}}(l_{in})}(l) = \{[x \mapsto 2, y \mapsto 2, z \mapsto 3]\}$. Then, we have $CVar_{\texttt{Cond}_{\mathcal{F}}(l)} = \{x, y\}$, $UVar_{\texttt{Cond}_{\mathcal{F}}(l)} = \{z\}$, and $\texttt{ErrInv}_{\mathcal{F}}(l) = \{[x \mapsto 2, y \mapsto 2, z \mapsto n] \mid n \in \mathbb{Z}\}$.

We now show that the error invariants enable us to locate irrelevant statements for the error as ones that do not change the occurrence of the error if they are replaced by `skip`.

Proposition 1. *Let $p[^{l_1:}-^{l_2}]$ be a program with a missing hole that represents a statement between labels l_1 and l_2, and let $\mathcal{F}$ be a set of final error states. Let $\mathtt{ErrInv}_{\mathcal{F}}$ and $\mathtt{ErrInv}'_{\mathcal{F}}$ be the error invariants for the programs $p[^{l_1:}s^{l_2}]$*[1] *and $p[^{l_1:}\mathtt{skip}^{l_2}]$, respectively. If $\mathtt{ErrInv}_{\mathcal{F}}(l_1) = \mathtt{ErrInv}_{\mathcal{F}}(l_2)$, then $\mathtt{ErrInv}_{\mathcal{F}}(l) = \mathtt{ErrInv}'_{\mathcal{F}}(l)$ for all $l \in \mathbb{L}$.*

Proof. The proof is by structural induction on statements s that can be inserted in the hole $-$ in $p[-]$. We consider the case of assignment $\mathtt{x}\texttt{=}ae$. Let $\mathtt{ErrInv}_{\mathcal{F}}$ be the error invariants inferred for $p[^{l_1:}s^{l_2}]$. Since $\mathtt{ErrInv}_{\mathcal{F}}(l_1) = \mathtt{ErrInv}_{\mathcal{F}}(l_2)$, the variable $\mathtt{x}$ must be unconstrained in $\mathtt{Cond}_{\mathcal{F}}(l_1)$ and $\mathtt{Cond}_{\mathcal{F}}(l_2)$ due to the definition of $\mathtt{ErrInv}_{\mathcal{F}}(l)$ (see Eq. 1). Therefore, the assignment $\mathtt{x}\texttt{=}ae$ has no effect on $\mathtt{Cond}_{\mathcal{F}}$ and $\mathtt{ErrInv}_{\mathcal{F}}$ due to the definition of $\overleftarrow{[\![\mathtt{x}\ \texttt{:=}\ ae]\!]}$ (see Fig. 4). Note that $\overleftarrow{[\![\mathtt{x}\ \texttt{:=}\ ae]\!]}S = S$ when $\mathtt{x}$ is unconstrained in S. That is, $\mathtt{Cond}_{\mathcal{F}}(l_1) = \mathtt{Cond}_{\mathcal{F}}(l_2)$. Hence, we will obtain the same $\mathtt{Cond}_{\mathcal{F}}$ and $\mathtt{ErrInv}_{\mathcal{F}}$ for $p[^{l_1:}\mathtt{x}\texttt{=}ae^{l_2}]$ and $p[^{l_1:}\mathtt{skip}^{l_2}]$. Similarly, we handle the other cases. □

However, the necessary precondition semantics $\overleftarrow{[\![s]\!]}$ and $\mathtt{Cond}_{\mathcal{F}}$, the invariance semantics $\overrightarrow{[\![s]\!]}$ and $\mathtt{Inv}_{\mathcal{I}}$, as well as the error invariants $\mathtt{ErrInv}_{\mathcal{F}}$ are not computable since our language is Turing complete.

Abstract Semantics. We now present computable abstract analyses that over-approximate the concrete semantics. We consider an abstract domain $(\mathbb{D}, \sqsubseteq_{\mathbb{D}})$, such that there exist a concretization-based abstraction $\langle \mathcal{P}(\Sigma), \subseteq \rangle \xleftarrow{\gamma_{\mathbb{D}}} \langle \mathbb{D}, \sqsubseteq_{\mathbb{D}} \rangle$.[2] We assume that the abstract domain $\mathbb{D}$ is equipped with sound operators for ordering $\sqsubseteq_{\mathbb{D}}$, least upper bound (join) $\sqcup_{\mathbb{D}}$, greatest lower bound (meet) $\sqcap_{\mathbb{D}}$, bottom $\bot_{\mathbb{D}}$, top $\top_{\mathbb{D}}$, widening $\triangledown_{\mathbb{D}}$, and narrowing $\triangle_{\mathbb{D}}$, as well as sound transfer functions for assignments $\mathtt{ASSIGN}_{\mathbb{D}} : \mathit{Stm} \times \mathbb{D} \to \mathbb{D}$, tests $\mathtt{FILTER}_{\mathbb{D}} : \mathit{BExp} \times \mathbb{D} \to \mathbb{D}$, and backward assignments $\mathtt{B\text{-}ASSIGN}_{\mathbb{D}} : \mathit{Stm} \times \mathbb{D} \to \mathbb{D}$. We let $\mathtt{lfp}^{\#}$ denote an abstract fix-point operator, derived using widening $\triangledown_{\mathbb{D}}$ and narrowing $\triangle_{\mathbb{D}}$, that over-approximates the concrete $\mathtt{lfp}$. Finally, the concrete domain $(\mathbb{L} \to \mathcal{P}(\Sigma), \dot{\subseteq})$ is abstracted using $\langle \mathbb{L} \to \mathcal{P}(\Sigma), \dot{\subseteq} \rangle \xleftarrow{\dot{\gamma}_{\mathbb{D}}} \langle \mathbb{L} \to \mathbb{D}, \dot{\sqsubseteq} \rangle$.

For each statement s, its abstract necessary precondition semantics $\overleftarrow{[\![s]\!]}^{\sharp}$ and its abstract invariance semantics $\overrightarrow{[\![s]\!]}^{\sharp}$ are defined as mappings $\mathbb{D} \mapsto \mathbb{D}$. The complete definitions of functions $\overleftarrow{[\![s]\!]}^{\sharp}$ and $\overrightarrow{[\![s]\!]}^{\sharp}$ are given in Fig. 5. Suppose that at the assertion label l_{ass} the abstract element is $d_{\mathcal{F}} \in \mathbb{D}$, whereas at the initial label l_{in} is $d_{\mathcal{I}} \in \mathbb{D}$. Thus, $\mathtt{Cond}^{\sharp}_{d_{\mathcal{F}}}(l_{ass}) = d_{\mathcal{F}}$ and $\mathtt{Inv}^{\sharp}_{d_{\mathcal{I}}}(l_{in}) = d_{\mathcal{I}}$. For a statement $^{l:}s^{l'}$, abstract element $\mathtt{Cond}^{\sharp}_{d_{\mathcal{F}}}(l)$ (resp., $\mathtt{Inv}^{\sharp}_{d_{\mathcal{I}}}(l')$) of necessary preconditions (resp., invariants) at initial label l (resp., final label l'), are:

$$\mathtt{Cond}^{\sharp}_{d_{\mathcal{F}}}(l) = \overleftarrow{[\![s]\!]}^{\sharp}\ \mathtt{Cond}^{\sharp}_{d_{\mathcal{F}}}(l'), \qquad \mathtt{Inv}^{\sharp}_{d_{\mathcal{I}}}(l') = \overrightarrow{[\![s]\!]}^{\sharp}\ \mathtt{Inv}^{\sharp}_{d_{\mathcal{I}}}(l)$$

The soundness of abstract semantics follows from the soundness of $\mathbb{D}$ [7,29].

---

1 $p[^{l_1:}s^{l_2}]$ is a complete program in which statement s is inserted at the place of hole.

2 Concretization-based abstraction is a relaxation of the known Galois connection abstraction, which is more used in practice (e.g., Polyhedra domain).

$$\overleftarrow{[\![\texttt{skip}]\!]}^\sharp d = d$$
$$\overleftarrow{[\![\texttt{x := } ae]\!]}^\sharp d = \texttt{B-ASSIGN}_{\mathbb{D}}(\texttt{x := } ae, d)$$
$$\overleftarrow{[\![s_1 \texttt{ ; } s_2]\!]}^\sharp d = \overleftarrow{[\![s_1]\!]}^\sharp(\overleftarrow{[\![s_2]\!]}^\sharp d)$$
$$\overleftarrow{[\![\texttt{if } be \texttt{ then } s_1 \texttt{ else } s_2]\!]}^\sharp d = \texttt{FILTER}_{\mathbb{D}}(be, \overleftarrow{[\![s_1]\!]}^\sharp d) \sqcup_{\mathbb{D}} \texttt{FILTER}_{\mathbb{D}}(\neg be, \overleftarrow{[\![s_2]\!]}^\sharp d)$$
$$\overleftarrow{[\![\texttt{while } be \texttt{ do } s]\!]}^\sharp d = \texttt{lfp}^\sharp\, \overleftarrow{\phi^\sharp}$$
$$\overleftarrow{\phi^\sharp}(x) = \texttt{FILTER}_{\mathbb{D}}(\neg be, d) \sqcup_{\mathbb{D}} \texttt{FILTER}_{\mathbb{D}}(be, \overleftarrow{[\![s]\!]}^\sharp x)$$

$$\overrightarrow{[\![\texttt{skip}]\!]}^\sharp d = d$$
$$\overrightarrow{[\![\texttt{x := } ae]\!]}^\sharp d = \texttt{ASSIGN}_{\mathbb{D}}(\texttt{x := } ae, d)$$
$$\overrightarrow{[\![s_1 \texttt{ ; } s_2]\!]}^\sharp d = \overrightarrow{[\![s_2]\!]}^\sharp(\overrightarrow{[\![s_1]\!]}^\sharp d)$$
$$\overrightarrow{[\![\texttt{if } be \texttt{ then } s_1 \texttt{ else } s_2]\!]}^\sharp d = \overrightarrow{[\![s_1]\!]}^\sharp(\texttt{FILTER}_{\mathbb{D}}(be, d)) \sqcup_{\mathbb{D}} \overrightarrow{[\![s_2]\!]}^\sharp(\texttt{FILTER}_{\mathbb{D}}(\neg be, d))$$
$$\overrightarrow{[\![\texttt{while } be \texttt{ do } s]\!]}^\sharp d = \texttt{FILTER}_{\mathbb{D}}(\neg be, \texttt{lfp}^\sharp\, \overrightarrow{\phi^\sharp})$$
$$\overrightarrow{\phi^\sharp}(x) = d \sqcup_{\mathbb{D}} \overrightarrow{[\![s]\!]}^\sharp(\texttt{FILTER}_{\mathbb{D}}(be, x))$$

Fig. 5. Abstract necessary precondition (above) and invariance (below) semantics.

Algorithm 1: AbsAnalysis$(p, d_{err}, \mathbb{D})$

Input: Program p, error state d_{err}, abstract domain $\mathbb{D}$
Output: Error invariants $\texttt{ErrInv}^\sharp_{d_{err}}$, refined error state d'_{err}, predicates set $\mathbb{P}$

$\texttt{Cond}^\sharp_{d_{err}}, \mathbb{P} := \overleftarrow{[\![p]\!]}^\sharp\, d_{err}$;
$d_{in} := \texttt{Cond}^\sharp_{d_{err}}(l_{in})$;
if $(d_{in} = \bot_{\mathbb{D}})$ **then** $\{\texttt{ErrInv}^\sharp_{d_{err}} := \texttt{Cond}^\sharp_{d_{err}};\ d'_{err} := \bot_{\mathbb{D}};\ \mathbb{P} := \emptyset\ \}$;
if $(d_{in} \neq \bot_{\mathbb{D}})$ **then**
    $\texttt{Inv}^\sharp_{d_{in}} := \overrightarrow{[\![p]\!]}^\sharp\, d_{in}$;
    $\texttt{ErrInv}^\sharp_{d_{err}} := \textsc{MinSupport}(\texttt{Inv}^\sharp_{d_{in}} \sqcap_{\mathbb{D}} \texttt{Cond}^\sharp_{d_{err}}, \texttt{Cond}^\sharp_{d_{err}})$;
    $d'_{err} := \texttt{ErrInv}^\sharp_{d_{err}}(l_{ass})$
return $\texttt{ErrInv}^\sharp_{d_{err}}, d'_{err}, \mathbb{P}$;

Proposition 2. *Let* $\mathcal{F} = \gamma_{\mathbb{D}}(d_{\mathcal{F}})$ *and* $\mathcal{I} = \gamma_{\mathbb{D}}(d_{\mathcal{I}})$. *For any* $l \in \mathbb{L}$, *we have:* $\mathit{Cond}_{\mathcal{F}}(l) \subseteq \gamma_{\mathbb{D}}(\mathit{Cond}^\sharp_{d_{\mathcal{F}}}(l))$ *and* $\mathit{Inv}_{\mathcal{I}}(l) \subseteq \gamma_{\mathbb{D}}(\mathit{Inv}^\sharp_{d_{\mathcal{I}}}(l))$.

4 Inferring Abstract Error Invariants

In this section, we first present one iteration of the backward-forward analysis for generating abstract error invariants. Then, we introduce our procedure for iterative abstract analysis and the BDD abstract domain functor we use.

4.1 Abstract Analysis

Sound abstract error invariants can be computed automatically by backward abstract interpretation, $\texttt{Cond}^\sharp_d$, and forward abstract interpretation, $\texttt{Inv}^\sharp_d$. Both analyses are parameterized by an abstract domain $\mathbb{D}$. In this work, we combine backward and forward abstract analyses to generate for each label the constraints, called *(abstract) error invariants*, that describe states which are reachable from the input and may cause the target assertion fail.

The $\texttt{AbsAnalysis}(p, d_{err}, \mathbb{D})$ procedure is given in Algorithm 1. It takes as input a program p, a target abstract error state d_{err}, and a chosen abstract domain $\mathbb{D}$. First, we call a backward abstract analysis $\overleftarrow{[\![p]\!]}^\sharp d_{err}$ (Line 1), which computes the necessary preconditions $\texttt{Cond}^\sharp_{d_{err}}$ of program p. Additionally, the backward analysis computes a set of predicates $\mathbb{P}$ by selecting branch conditions of $\texttt{if}$ statements, where precision loss is observed. Given a conditional ${}^{l}\texttt{:if}\,(be)\,\texttt{then}\,{}^{l_{tt}}\texttt{:}s_{tt}\,\texttt{else}\,{}^{l_{ff}}\texttt{:}s_{ff}$, the precondition in l is obtained by joining the preconditions found in the $\texttt{then}$ l_{tt} and $\texttt{else}$ branches l_{ff}. If those preconditions are not equal, that is $\texttt{Cond}^\sharp_{d_{err}}(l_{tt}) \neq \texttt{Cond}^\sharp_{d_{err}}(l_{ff})$, then we collect the corresponding branch condition be in $\mathbb{P}$ since some precision loss occurs. Subsequently, we check the precondition found at the initial label $d_{in} = \texttt{Cond}^\sharp_{d_{err}}(l_{in})$ (Lines 2, 3, 4). If $d_{in} = \bot_{\mathbb{D}}$ (which means there is no concrete input state that violates the assertion), the assertion must be valid and the procedure terminates with no further computations (Line 3). Otherwise, a forward analysis $\overrightarrow{[\![p]\!]}^\sharp d_{in}$ is started to refine the inferred $\texttt{Cond}^\sharp_{d_{err}}(l)$ and the abstract error state d_{err} (Line 5). It takes as input the program p and the input abstract state d_{in}, and computes invariants $\texttt{Inv}^\sharp_{d_{in}}$ in all labels. The (abstract) error invariants map $\texttt{ErrInv}^\sharp_{d_{err}}$ is then generated using $\texttt{Cond}^\sharp_{d_{err}}$ and $\texttt{Inv}^\sharp_{d_{in}}$ as follows (Line 6):

$$\texttt{ErrInv}^\sharp_{d_{err}}(l) = \textsc{MinSupport}(\texttt{Inv}^\sharp_{d_{in}}(l) \sqcap_{\mathbb{D}} \texttt{Cond}^\sharp_{d_{err}}(l), \texttt{Cond}^\sharp_{d_{err}}(l)), \text{ for } l \in \mathbb{L}$$

where MinSupport is minimal support set. Finally, the procedure returns as outputs $\texttt{ErrInv}^\sharp_{d_{err}}$, refined abstract error state $\texttt{ErrInv}^\sharp_{d_{err}}(l_{ass})$, and set $\mathbb{P}$.

We now show how the *minimal support set* MinSupport is computed [23].

Definition 1. *Let $P = \{p_1, \ldots, p_n\}$ and $p'_1 \wedge \ldots \wedge p'_k$ be linear constraint formulas over program variables, such that $p_1 \wedge \ldots \wedge p_n \models p'_1 \wedge \ldots \wedge p'_k$. A subset $P' \subseteq P$* supports *the inference $\bigwedge_{p_i \in P} p_i \models p'_1 \wedge \ldots \wedge p'_k$ iff $\bigwedge_{p_j \in P'} p_j \models p'_1 \wedge \ldots \wedge p'_k$. A support set P' is minimal iff no proper subset of P' can support the inference.*

For $P \models p'_1 \wedge \ldots \wedge p'_k$, let the MinSupport$(P, p'_1 \wedge \ldots \wedge p'_k)$ denote the set of minimal supporting conjuncts in P that imply $p'_1 \wedge \ldots \wedge p'_k$. An implementation of MinSupport through unsatisfiability cores is available in existing SMT solvers (e.g., Z3 [30]) for many theories such as linear arithmetic. That is, we ask the SMT solver to find the unsatisfiability core of $\bigwedge_{p_i \in P} p_i \wedge \neg(p'_1 \wedge \ldots \wedge p'_k)$ (which is negation of $\bigwedge_{p_i \in P} p_i \implies (p'_1 \wedge \ldots \wedge p'_k)$). The conjuncts in P that are part of this unsatisfiability core represent a minimal support set for $(p'_1 \wedge \ldots \wedge p'_k)$.

Example 1. Suppose that at a given program location the precondition $(x \geq 0)$ is inferred by the backward analysis, while the invariant $(x = 1 \wedge z = y + 1)$ is inferred using the refined forward analysis. The formulas $p_1 : x = 1, p_2 : z = y+1$ together imply the formula $p' : x \geq 0$. By checking the unsatisfiability core of

Algorithm 2: $\texttt{IterativeAbsAnalysis}(p, be^{ass}, \mathbb{D})$

Input: Program p, assertion be^{ass}, abstract domain $\mathbb{D}$
Output: Program slice p'

$\mathbb{P} := \emptyset$; $\mathbb{P}' := \emptyset$; $d_{err} := \bot_{\mathbb{D}}$; $d'_{err} :=$ **FILTER**$_{\mathbb{D}}(\neg be^{ass}, \top_{\mathbb{D}})$; $\mathbb{A} := \mathbb{D}$;
while $(\mathbb{P} \neq \mathbb{P}')$ *or* $(d_{err} \neq d'_{err})$ **do**
  $\mathbb{P} := \mathbb{P}'$; $d_{err} := d'_{err}$;
  $\texttt{ErrInv}^{\sharp}_{d_{err}}, d'_{err}, \mathbb{P}' := \texttt{AbsAnalysis}(p, d_{err}, \mathbb{D})$;
  if $(d'_{err} = \bot_{\mathbb{D}})$ **then return skip** ;
  if $(d'_{err} \neq \bot_{\mathbb{D}})$ **then** $\mathbb{D} := \mathbb{BD}(\mathbb{P}', \mathbb{A})$;
  if (*Timeout*) **then break** ;
return $Slice(p, \texttt{ErrInv}^{\sharp}_{d_{err}})$;

the formula $p_1 \wedge p_2 \wedge \neg p'$, we can find that the subset $\{p_1\}$ suffices to establish p', and thus $\{p_1 : x = 1\}$ represents a minimal support set. □

We assume that the elements of the abstract domain are finite conjunctions of linear constraints over program variables. The application of MINSUPPORT removes the redundant conjuncts from the invariants in $\texttt{Inv}^{\sharp}_{d_{in}}(l) \sqcap_{\mathbb{D}} \texttt{Cond}^{\sharp}_{d_{err}}(l)$. By using Proposition 2 and definition of $\texttt{ErrInv}^{\sharp}_{d_{err}}$, we can show the following.

Proposition 3. *Let* $\mathcal{F} = \gamma_{\mathbb{D}}(d_{\mathcal{F}})$. *For any* $l \in \mathbb{L}$, $\textit{ErrInv}_{\mathcal{F}}(l) \subseteq \gamma_{\mathbb{D}}(\textit{ErrInv}^{\sharp}_{d_{\mathcal{F}}}(l))$.

4.2 Iterative Abstract Analysis

The $\texttt{AbsAnalysis}(p, d_{err}, \mathbb{D})$ procedure may produce very imprecise (abstract) error invariants due to the over-approximation. One of the major sources of imprecision is that the most commonly used base abstract domains $\mathbb{D}$ (intervals, octagons, polyhedra) have limitations in expressing disjunctive and non-linear properties, which are common in programs. To address these issues, we propose an iterative abstract analysis, wherein the refinement process makes use of the predicates $\mathbb{P}$ inferred at the joins of `if` statements as well as the reduced abstract error sub-space d_{err}. In particular, we use a BDD abstract domain functor, denoted as $\mathbb{BD}(\mathbb{P}, \mathbb{A})$, which can characterize disjunctions of elements from domain $\mathbb{A}$. A decision node in the BDD abstract domain stores a predicate from $\mathbb{P}$, and a leaf node stores an abstract element from the base abstract domain $\mathbb{A}$ under specific evaluation results of predicates found in decision nodes up to the given leaf. We refer to Sect. 4.3 for detailed description of the BDD domain.

The overall $\texttt{IterativeAbsAnalysis}(p, be^{ass}, \mathbb{D})$ procedure is shown in Algorithm 2. The procedure is called with the following parameters: a program p, an assertion be^{ass} to be checked, and a base abstract domain $\mathbb{D}$. Initially, we call $\texttt{AbsAnalysis}(p, \texttt{FILTER}_{\mathbb{D}}(\neg be^{ass}, \top_{\mathbb{D}}), \mathbb{D})$, given in Algorithm 1, with the negated assertion $\neg be^{ass}$ as error state space d_{err} in order to infer error invariants $\texttt{ErrInv}^{\sharp}_{d_{err}}$, a refined abstract error sub-space d'_{err}, and predicate set $\mathbb{P}'$

$$\texttt{Slice}(\texttt{skip}, \texttt{ErrInv}^\sharp_{d_{err}}) = \texttt{skip}$$
$$\texttt{Slice}(\texttt{x := } ae, \texttt{ErrInv}^\sharp_{d_{err}}) = \begin{cases} \texttt{skip}, & \text{if } \texttt{ErrInv}^\sharp_{d_{err}}(l) = \texttt{ErrInv}^\sharp_{d_{err}}(l') \\ \texttt{x := } ae, & \text{otherwise} \end{cases}$$
$$\texttt{Slice}(s_1 \texttt{ ; } s_2, \texttt{ErrInv}^\sharp_{d_{err}}) = \begin{cases} \texttt{skip}, & \text{if } \texttt{ErrInv}^\sharp_{d_{err}}(l) = \texttt{ErrInv}^\sharp_{d_{err}}(l') \\ \texttt{Slice}(s_1, \texttt{ErrInv}^\sharp_{d_{err}}); \texttt{Slice}(s_2, \texttt{ErrInv}^\sharp_{d_{err}}), & \text{otherwise} \end{cases}$$
$$\texttt{Slice}(\texttt{if } be \texttt{ then } s_1 \texttt{ else } s_2, \texttt{ErrInv}^\sharp_{d_{err}}) =$$
$$\begin{cases} \texttt{skip}, & \text{if } \texttt{ErrInv}^\sharp_{d_{err}}(l) = \texttt{ErrInv}^\sharp_{d_{err}}(l') \\ \texttt{if } be \texttt{ then Slice}(s_1, \texttt{ErrInv}^\sharp_{d_{err}}) \texttt{ else Slice}(s_2, \texttt{ErrInv}^\sharp_{d_{err}}), & \text{otherwise} \end{cases}$$
$$\texttt{Slice}(\texttt{while } (be) \texttt{ do } s, \texttt{ErrInv}^\sharp_{d_{err}}) = \begin{cases} \texttt{skip}, & \text{if } \texttt{ErrInv}^\sharp_{d_{err}}(l) = \texttt{ErrInv}^\sharp_{d_{err}}(l') \\ \texttt{while } (be) \texttt{ do Slice}(s, \texttt{ErrInv}^\sharp_{d_{err}}), & \text{otherwise} \end{cases}$$

Fig. 6. Definition of $\texttt{Slice}(s, \texttt{ErrInv}^\sharp_{d_{err}})$, where "$l : s; l'$" is a statement in program whose error invariants map is $\texttt{ErrInv}^\sharp_{d_{err}}$.

(Line 4). If the refinement process is enabled, that is, the newly obtained $\mathbb{P}'$ and d'_{err} are not the same as $\mathbb{P}$ and d_{err} from the previous iteration (Line 2), the call to `AbsAnalysis` is repeated again with refined parameters d'_{err} and $\mathbb{BD}(\mathbb{P}', \mathbb{A})$ (Line 6), where $\mathbb{A}$ is the input base domain $\mathbb{D}$. Note that, if $\mathbb{P}' = \emptyset$ then $\mathbb{BD}(\mathbb{P}', \mathbb{A})$ is simply $\mathbb{A}$. The procedure terminates when either the refinement is no longer enabled (Line 2), or the assertion is proved true when $d'_{err} = \bot_{\mathbb{D}}$ (which means there is no concrete error state, so we return the program slice "`skip`" since no statement is relevant for the error) (Line 5), or a time limit is reached (Line 7). The procedure $\texttt{Slice}(p, \texttt{ErrInv}^\sharp_{d_{err}})$ (Line 8) returns a slice of program p containing only the statements *relevant* for the assertion failure. Given a statement ${}^{l:}s^{l'}$, `Slice` replaces statement s with `skip` if $\texttt{ErrInv}^\sharp_{d_{err}}(l) = \texttt{ErrInv}^\sharp_{d_{err}}(l')$. In this case, we say s is *irrelevant* for the error. That is, the statements for which we can find an encompassing error invariant are not needed to reproduce the error and can be dropped. Otherwise, `Slice` recursively pre-process all sub-statements of compound statements or returns basic statements. The complete definition of $\texttt{Slice}(s, \texttt{ErrInv}^\sharp_{d_{err}})$ is given in Fig. 6.

4.3 BDD Abstract Domain Functor

The binary decision diagram (BDD) abstract domain functor, denoted $\mathbb{BD}(\mathbb{P}, \mathbb{A})$, plays an important role in the iterative abstract analysis procedure. The abstract elements of the domain $\mathbb{BD}(\mathbb{P}, \mathbb{A})$ are disjunctions of leaf nodes that belong to an existing base abstract domain $\mathbb{A}$, which are separated by the values of Boolean predicates from the set $\mathbb{P}$ organized in decision nodes. Therefore, the state space $\mathcal{P}(\Sigma)$ is partitioned with respect to the set of predicates $\mathbb{P}$, such that each top-down path of a BDD abstract element represents one or several partitionings of $\mathcal{P}(\Sigma)$, and we store in the leaf node the property inferred for those partitionings.

We first consider a simpler form of binary decision diagrams called *binary decision trees* (BDTs). A *binary decision tree* (BDT) $t \in \mathbb{BT}(\mathbb{P}, \mathbb{A})$ over the set $\mathbb{P}$

of predicates and the leaf abstract domain $\mathbb{A}$ is either a leaf node $\ll a \gg$ with $a \in \mathbb{A}$ and $\mathbb{P} = \emptyset$, or $[\![P : tl, tr]\!]$, where P is *the smallest element* of $\mathbb{P}$ with respect to its ordering, tl is the left subtree of t representing its true branch, and tr is the right subtree of t representing its false branch, such that $tl, tr \in \mathbb{BT}(\mathbb{P}\backslash\{P\}, \mathbb{A})$. Note that, $\mathbb{P} = \{P_1, \ldots, P_n\}$ is a totally ordered set with ordering: $P_1 < \ldots < P_n$.

However, BDTs contain some redundancy. There are three optimizations we can apply to BDTs in order to reduce their representation [2]: (1) Removal of duplicate leaves; (2) Removal of redundant tests; (3) Removal of duplicate non-leaves. If we apply reductions (**1**)–(**3**) to a BDT $t \in \mathbb{BT}(\mathbb{P}, \mathbb{A})$ until no further reductions are possible, and moreover if the ordering on the Boolean predicates from $\mathbb{P}$ occurring on any path is fixed to the ordered list $[P_1, \ldots, P_n]$, then we obtain a *reduced ordered binary decision diagram* (or only BDD for short) $b \in \mathbb{BD}(\mathbb{P}, \mathbb{A})$. Notice that BDDs have a canonical form, so any disjunctive property from the BDT domain can be represented in an unique way by a BDD.

Given a set of predicates $\mathbb{P}$, an evaluation for $\mathbb{P}$ is a function $\mu : \mathbb{P} \to \{\text{true}, \text{false}\}$. $\texttt{Eval}(\mathbb{P})$ denotes the set of all evaluations for $\mathbb{P}$. Each evaluation $\mu \in \texttt{Eval}(\mathbb{P})$ can be represented as a formula $\bigwedge_{P \in \mathbb{P}} \nu(P)$, where $\nu(P) = P$ if $\mu(P) = \text{true}$ and $\nu(P) = \neg P$ if $\mu(P) = \text{false}$. Given a BDD $b \in \mathbb{BD}(\mathbb{P}, \mathbb{A})$, the concretization function $\gamma_{\mathbb{BD}}$ returns $\gamma_{\mathbb{A}}(a)$ for $\mu \in \texttt{Eval}(\mathbb{P})$, where μ satisfies the constraints reached along the top-down path to the leaf node $a \in \mathbb{A}$.

The abstract operations, transfer functions, and soundness of the domain $\mathbb{BD}(\mathbb{P}, \mathbb{A})$ are obtained by lifting the corresponding operations, transfer functions, and soundness of the leaf domain $\mathbb{A}$. We refer to [3,11,35] for more details. However, the assignment transfer function needs more care, since its application on a leaf node in one partitioning (i.e., one evaluation of $\mathbb{P}$) may cause its result to enter other partitionings. In such a case, the result in each partitioning is updated to be the join of all elements which belong to that partitioning after applying the transfer function to all leaf nodes of the current BDD. This procedure is known as *reconstruction on leaves* [3].

Example 2. Suppose we have a BDD $b = [\![(\mathtt{x} \leq 0) : \ll \mathtt{x} = 0 \gg, \ll 1 \leq \mathtt{x} \leq 10 \gg]\!]$ and an assignment `x := x-1`. Note that the left leaf $\ll \mathtt{x} = 0 \gg$ satisfies the decision node $(\mathtt{x} \leq 0)$, while the right leaf $\ll 1 \leq \mathtt{x} \leq 10 \gg$ satisfies its negation. After performing the (forward) assignment transfer function without reconstruction on leaves, we obtain: $[\![(\mathtt{x} \leq 0) : \ll \mathtt{x} = -1 \gg, \ll 0 \leq \mathtt{x} \leq 9 \gg]\!]$. Hence, the right leaf node $(0 \leq \mathtt{x} \leq 9)$ does not satisfy the predicate leading to it: $\neg(\mathtt{x} \leq 0)$. However, after the reconstruction on leaves, we obtain: $[\![(\mathtt{x} \leq 0) : \ll -1 \leq \mathtt{x} \leq 0 \gg, \ll 1 \leq \mathtt{x} \leq 9 \gg]\!]$.

5 Evaluation

We have implemented a prototype tool based on our approach for fault localization via inferring error invariants. We now evaluate our tool.

Implementation and Experimental Setup. Our tool is based on the APRON library [25], which includes the abstract domains of intervals, octagons, and polyhedra, and the BDDAPRON library [24]. It also calls the Z3 SMT solver [30] to compute minimal support sets. The tool is written in OCAML and consists of around 7K LOC. It supports a subset of the C language. The current tool provides a limited support for arrays, pointers, `struct` and `union` types.

For the aim of evaluation, we ran: (1) our tool, denoted `Full_AI`; (2) a single backward analysis, denoted `Single_AI`; and (3) the logic formula-based fault localization tool `BugAssist` [26].[3] Given an error program, `BugAssist` uses the `CBMC` bounded model checker [6] to generate an error trace as well as to construct the corresponding trace formula, which is then analyzed by a `MAX-SAT` solver. We use a set of numerical benchmarks taken from the literature [4], different folders of SV-COMP (https://sv-comp.sosy-lab.org/) and TCAS [21].

Experiments are executed on 64-bit Intel®Core^{TM} i7-1165G7 CPU@2.80 GHz, VM LUbuntu 20.10, with 8 GB memory, and we use a timeout value of 300 s. All times are reported as average over five independent executions. We report total times, measured via `real` values of the `time` command, needed for the actual tasks to be performed. For all three approaches, this includes times to parse the program, to check the assertion violation of the given program, and to identify potential error locations. The implementation is available from [14]: https://doi.org/10.5281/zenodo.8167960.

SV-COMP Examples. Consider the program in Fig. 7. It represents a suitably adjusted `easy2-1` example from SV-COMP, where the `if` statement is nested inside the `while`. In the first iteration of `Full_AI`, the `if` condition $(x < 3)$ is added to the set of predicates $\mathbb{P}$, due to the analysis imprecision of the `if` statement. Hence, in the following iterations we use the BDD domain based on the predicate set $\mathbb{P} = \{B \equiv (x < 3)\}$. The inferred error invariants by `Full_AI` are shown in Fig. 7. After calling the slicing procedure `Slice`, we see that statements at locs. ③ and ⑥ are redundant, and so can be dropped. E.g., the statement at loc. ⑥ is enclosed by the error invariant $\boxed{\neg B \wedge y \geq 0}$. The computed error invariants further highlight the information about the state that is essential for the error at each location, thus indicating that variable z is completely irrelevant.

If we analyze this program using single backward analysis `Single_AI`, we do not consider separately the `then` and `else` branches of the `if` statement as in `Full_AI`. Thus, we obtain very imprecise analysis results: $\top$ for all locations inside `while` and loc. ①, as well as $(x \geq 1)$ for all other locations. In fact, we would consider as relevant only statement at loc. ① and `while` condition at loc. ④, whereas all other locations would be irrelevant. This way, we would drop statements at loc. ②, ⑤, ⑦, due to the over-approximation of abstraction, although they are relevant for the error. We thus obtain 53% precision for `Single_AI` (see Table 1, column `Prec%`).

Consider the program `Mysore-1` from SV-COMP given in Fig. 8. The inferred error invariants by `Full_AI` are shown in Fig. 8. We can see that the

[3] The other known logic formula-based tool [4,20] is not available online.

```
void main(int n) {
[⊤]
① int x := 7;
[¬B ∧ x = 7]
② int y := 0;
[¬B ∧ x = 7 ∧ y = 0]
③ int z := y;
[¬B ∧ x = 7 ∧ y = 0]
④ while (x>0) do
[(¬B ∧ x ≥ 3 ∧ y ≥ 0) ∨ (B ∧ 1 ≤ x ≤ 2 ∧ x + y ≥ 2)]
⑤    if (x<3) then y := y+1;
⑥    else z := z-1;
⑦    x := x − 1;
[(¬B ∧ x ≥ 3 ∧ y ≥ 0) ∨ (B ∧ 0 ≤ x ≤ 2 ∧ x + y ≥ 2)]
⑧ od;
[(B ∧ x = 0 ∧ y ≥ 2)]
⑨ assert (y ≤ 0);
```

Fig. 7. `easy2-1` example.

```
void main(int x) {
[(x ≤ −1)]
① int c := 0;
[(x ≤ −1 ∧ c = 0)]
② while (x + c ≥ 0) do
[⊥]
⑤    x := x−c;
[⊥]
⑥    c := c+1;
[⊥]
⑧ od;
[(c = 0)]
⑨ assert (c > 0);
```

Fig. 8. `Mysore-1` example.

statements in the body of `while` are redundant and so can be eliminated from the generated program slice. On the other hand, if we use a single backward analysis `Single_AI`, then the loop invariant is $(c \leq 0 \wedge x + c \leq -1)$, and thus no statement is eliminated as irrelevant. As a result, `Single_AI` gives 66% precision (see Table 1).

`BugAssist` again reports less precise results by wrongly identifying as irrelevant statements at locs. ①, ② for `easy2-1` and at loc. ① for `Mysore-1`, as well as statement at loc. ⑥ for `easy2-1` as potential bug. Recall that `BugAssist` reasons about loops by unrolling them. Thus, it needs 10 unrollings of the loop for `easy2-1`. The precision of `BugAssist` is 66% for `easy2-1` and 83% for `Mysore-1`.

TCAS Example. The final example is an error implementation of the Traffic Alert and Collision Avoidance System (TCAS) [21], which represents an aircraft collision detection system used by all US commercial aircrafts. An extract from the error implementation is shown in Fig. 9. The error in this TCAS implementation is caused by a wrong comparison in the function `Non_Crossing_Biased_Climb()`. On some inputs, this error causes the variable `need_upward_RA` to become 1. The effect is that the assertion will get violated. Note that the strict inequality '>' in ¬(`Down_Separation` > `Positive_RA_Alt_Tresh`) from function `Non_Crossing_Biased_Climb()` is problematic, which causes the error. It should be replaced with '≥' for the implementation to be correct.

Our tool first inlines all functions into the `main()` function, which is then analyzed statically. Thus, the complete program has 308 locations in total, and the `main()` function after inlinement contains 118 locations. `Full_AI` needs two iterations to terminate by using the BDD domain with four predicates:

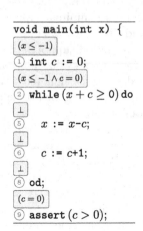

```
int Non_Crossing_Biased_Climb() {
  ⋮
  if (own_below_threat=0)∨((own_below_threat=1)∧¬(Down_Separation>Positive_RA_Alt_Tresh))
  then result := 1;
  else result := 0;
  ⋮
  return result;
}

int alt_sep_test() {
  if (High_Confidence=1)∧(Own_Tracked_Alt_Rate ≤ OLEV)∧(Cur_Vertical_Sep>MAXALTDIFF)
  then enabled := 1;
  else enabled := 0;
  ⋮
  if (enabled=1)∧(((tcas_equipped=1)∧(intent_not_known=1))∨(tcas_equipped=0))
  then {
    if (Non_Crossing_Biased_Climb() = 1)∧(Own_Below_Threat() = 1)
      then need_upward_RA := 1;
      else need_upward_RA := 0;
      ⋮
  }
  assert (need_upward_RA=0)∨(Down_Separation ≥ Positive_RA_Alt_Tresh);
}

void main() {
  ⋮
  int High_Confidence := [0,1];
  int Other_Tracked_Alt := ?;
  ⋮
  int Down_Separation := ?;
  int Other_RAC := [0,1];
  int Other_Capability := [0,1];
  int Climb_Inhibit := [0,1];
  int Positive_RA_Alt_Tresh := 740;
  ⋮
  int res := alt_sep_test() ;
}
```

Fig. 9. An excerpt from an error TCAS implementation.

$B1 \equiv$ (need_upward_RA=1) $\wedge$ (need_downward_RA=1)
$B2 \equiv$ (Own_Tracked_Alt $<$ Other_Tracked_Alt)
$B3 \equiv$ (own_above_threat=0) $\wedge$ (Curr_Vertical_Sep $\geq$ MINSP)$\wedge$
(Up_Separation $\geq$ Positive_RA_Alt_Tresh)
$B4 \equiv$ (own_below_threat=0)$\vee$
(own_below_threat=1 $\wedge \neg$(Down_Separation $>$ Positive_RA_Alt_Tresh))

The slice computed by Full_AI approach contains 44 locations relevant for the error. Some of these statements are shown underlined in Fig. 9. Note that not underlined else branches are classified as irrelevant. The reported relevant statements are sufficient to understand the origins of the error. The generated slice depends only on 15 variables instead of 37 variables in the original program. The number of input variables is also reduced from 12 to 6. Thus, we conclude that the obtained slice significantly reduces the search space for error statements.

The single backward analysis Single_AI reports a slice containing only 28 locations. However, the slice does not contain any statement from the buggy Non_Crossing_Biased_Climb(), thus missing the real reasons for the error. On the other hand, the BugAssist tool reports as potential bugs only 2 locations, the condition 'if (enabled=1)...' and the assertion, both from alt_sep_test() function. Similarly as in the case of Single_AI, none of these locations is from the buggy Non_Crossing_Biased_Climb().

Performances. Table 1 shows the result of running our tool Full_AI, the single backward analysis Single_AI, and the BugAssist tool on the benchmarks considered so far. The column "LOC#" is the total number of locations in the program, "Time" shows the run-time in seconds, "Slice#" is the number of potential (relevant) fault locations, and "Perc%" is the percentage precision of the given approach to locate the relevant statements for the error. This is the ratio of the sum of *correctly* classified erroneous and non-erroneous locations by an approach to the total number of locations in the program. A classification of a location as erroneous given by the concrete semantics is considered correct.

We conclude that our technique, Full_AI, gives more precise information about potential error statements than simply performing a backward analysis and BugAssist. In fact, Full_AI pin-pointed the correct error locations for all examples. On average, the number of locations to check for potential error (Slice#) is reduced to 47.6% of the total code (LOC#). On the other hand, the precision of Single_AI is 70% and the precision of BugAssist is 64%, on average. Although our technique Full_AI is the most precise, it is slower than Single_AI due to the several iterations it needs to produce the fully refined error invariants. Full_AI and BugAssist have often comparable running times, except for the loop benchmarks when BugAssist is slower due to the need to unwind the loops. Moreover, Full_AI reports more fine-grained information by identifying relevant variables for the error, whereas BugAssist reports only potential bug locations. Finally, we should note that the run-time of our technique Full_AI in all examples is still significantly smaller than our human effort required to isolate the fault.

Table 1. Performance results of `Full_AI` vs. `Single_AI` vs. `BugAssist`. `Full_AI` and `Single_AI` use Polyhedra domain. All times in sec.

Bench.	LOC#	Full_AI			Single_AI			BugAssist		
		Time	Slice#	Perc%	Time	Slice#	Prec%	Time	Slice#	Perc%
program1	6	0.056	2	100%	0.013	2	100%	0.031	1	66%
program2	9	0.187	5	100%	0.013	4	83%	0.031	2	50%
program2-a	9	0.088	2	100%	0.015	6	33%	0.030	2	66%
program3	10	0.453	3	100%	0.016	3	100%	2.954	5	71%
easy2-1	15	2.401	10	100%	0.011	3	41%	8.441	9	66%
Mysore-1	9	0.050	4	100%	0.014	6	66%	0.210	3	83%
TCASv.1	118	57.78	44	100%	0.225	28	86%	0.095	1	62%

6 Related Work

Fault localization has been an active area of research in recent years [4,5,20, 26,33]. The most successful approaches for fault localization are based on logic formulae [4,5,20,26,33]. They represent an error trace using an SMT formula and analyze it to find suspicious locations. Hence, they assume the existence of error traces on input. The error traces are usually obtained either from failing test cases or from counterexamples produced by external verification tools. In contrast, our approach is directly applied on (error) programs, thus it needs no specific error traces from other tools making it more self-contained. This way, the two phases of error-detection and error-localization are integrated by our approach.

The closest to our approach for inferring error invariants applied to fault localization is the work proposed by Ermis et al. [4,20]. They use Craig interpolants and SMT queries to calculate error invariants in an error trace. Another similar approach that uses error traces and SAT queries is `BugAssist` [26]. It uses MAX-SAT based algorithm to identify a maximal subset of statements from an error trace that are not needed to prove the unsatisfiability of the logical formula representing the error trace. One limitation of `BugAssist` is that control-dependent variables and statements are not considered relevant. Moreover, `BugAssist` do not report error invariants, which can be especially useful for dense errors where the error program cannot be sliced significantly. Hence, `BugAssist` cannot identify relevancy of variables. Other logic formula-based approaches include using weakest preconditions [5], and syntactic information in the form of graphs for static and dynamic dependency relations [33] to localize the errors.

Rival [32] uses abstract interpretation static analyzer ASTREE [9] to investigate the found alarms and to classify them as true errors or false errors. It uses an refining sequence of forward-backward analyses to obtain an approximation of a subset of traces that may lead to an error. Hence, the above work aims to find a set of traces resulting in an error, thus defining so-called trace-wise semantic slicing. In contrast, our approach aims to find statements that are reasons for the error, thus defining the statement-wise semantic slicing. The under-approximated backward analysis proposed by Mine [28] infers sufficient preconditions ensuring that the target property holds for all non-deterministic choices. It would produce the under-approximations of concrete error invariants if applied to our approach. We could then combine the results of under- and over-approximating error invariants, so that if both are the same for some locations we can be certain that the corresponding statements are either error-relevant or error-irrelevant. The work [19] also uses forward-backward analyses to estimate the probability that a target assertion os satisfied/violated.

Decision-tree domains have been used in abstract interpretation community recently [3,10,35]. Segmented decision tree abstract domains have enabled path dependent static analysis [3,10]. Their elements contain decision nodes that are determined either by values of program variables [10] or by the `if` conditions [3], whereas the leaf nodes are numerical properties. Urban and Miné [35] use decision tree abstract domains to prove program termination. Decision nodes are labelled with linear constraints that split the memory space and leaf nodes contain affine ranking functions for proving termination. Recently, specialized decision tree lifted domains have been proposed to analyze program families (or any other configurable software system) [11,12,16,18]. Decision nodes partition the configuration space of possible feature values (or statically configurable options), while leaf nodes provide analysis information of program variants (family members) corresponding to each partition. The work [11] uses lifted BDD domains to analyze program families with Boolean features. Subsequently, the lifted decision tree domain has been proposed to handle program families with both Boolean and numerical features [18], as well as dynamic program families with features changing during run-time [16].

Once a set of statements relevant for the error has been found, we need to replace those statements in order to fix the error. Recently, abstract interpretation has been successfully applied to program sketching [13,15,17]. The above works leverage a lifted (family-based) static analysis to synthesize program sketches, which represent partial programs with some missing integer holes in them [34]. We can combine our approach for fault localization with the techniques for program sketches to develop an automatic procedure for program repair.

7 Conclusion

In this work, we have proposed error invariants for reasoning about the relevancy of portions of an error program. They provide a semantic argument why certain statements are irrelevant for the cause of an error. We have presented an algorithm that infers error invariants via abstract interpretation and uses them to obtain compact slices of error programs relevant for the error. Our evaluation demonstrates that our algorithm provides useful error explanations.

References

1. Bourdoncle, F.: Abstract debugging of higher-order imperative languages. In: Proceedings of the ACM SIGPLAN 1993 Conference on Programming Language Design and Implementation (PLDI), pp. 46–55. ACM (1993). https://doi.org/10.1145/155090.155095
2. Bryant, R.E.: Graph-based algorithms for Boolean function manipulation. IEEE Trans. Comput. **35**(8), 677–691 (1986). https://doi.org/10.1109/TC.1986.1676819
3. Chen, J., Cousot, P.: A binary decision tree abstract domain functor. In: Blazy, S., Jensen, T. (eds.) SAS 2015. LNCS, vol. 9291, pp. 36–53. Springer, Heidelberg (2015). https://doi.org/10.1007/978-3-662-48288-9_3
4. Christ, J., Ermis, E., Schäf, M., Wies, T.: Flow-sensitive fault localization. In: Giacobazzi, R., Berdine, J., Mastroeni, I. (eds.) VMCAI 2013. LNCS, vol. 7737, pp. 189–208. Springer, Heidelberg (2013). https://doi.org/10.1007/978-3-642-35873-9_13
5. Christakis, M., Heizmann, M., Mansur, M.N., Schilling, C., Wüstholz, V.: Semantic fault localization and suspiciousness ranking. In: Vojnar, T., Zhang, L. (eds.) TACAS 2019, Part I. LNCS, vol. 11427, pp. 226–243. Springer, Cham (2019). https://doi.org/10.1007/978-3-030-17462-0_13
6. Clarke, E., Kroening, D., Lerda, F.: A tool for checking ANSI-C programs. In: Jensen, K., Podelski, A. (eds.) TACAS 2004. LNCS, vol. 2988, pp. 168–176. Springer, Heidelberg (2004). https://doi.org/10.1007/978-3-540-24730-2_15
7. Cousot, P., Cousot, R.: Abstract interpretation: a unified lattice model for static analysis of programs by construction or approximation of fixpoints. In: Conference Record of the Fourth ACM Symposium on POPL, pp. 238–252. ACM (1977). https://doi.org/10.1145/512950.512973, http://doi.acm.org/10.1145/512950.512973
8. Cousot, P., et al.: The ASTREÉ analyzer. In: Sagiv, M. (ed.) ESOP 2005. LNCS, vol. 3444, pp. 21–30. Springer, Heidelberg (2005). https://doi.org/10.1007/978-3-540-31987-0_3
9. Cousot, P., Cousot, R., Feret, J., Mauborgne, L., Miné, A., Rival, X.: Why does ASTRÉE scale up? Formal Methods Syst. Design **35**(3), 229–264 (2009). https://doi.org/10.1007/s10703-009-0089-6
10. Cousot, P., Cousot, R., Mauborgne, L.: A scalable segmented decision tree abstract domain. In: Manna, Z., Peled, D.A. (eds.) Time for Verification. LNCS, vol. 6200, pp. 72–95. Springer, Heidelberg (2010). https://doi.org/10.1007/978-3-642-13754-9_5
11. Dimovski, A.S.: A binary decision diagram lifted domain for analyzing program families. J. Comput. Lang. **63**, 101032 (2021). https://doi.org/10.1016/j.cola.2021.101032
12. Dimovski, A.S.: Lifted termination analysis by abstract interpretation and its applications. In: GPCE 2021: Concepts and Experiences, Chicago, IL, USA, October 2021, pp. 96–109. ACM (2021). https://doi.org/10.1145/3486609.3487202
13. Dimovski, A.S.: Quantitative program sketching using lifted static analysis. In: FASE 2022. LNCS, vol. 13241, pp. 102–122. Springer, Cham (2022). https://doi.org/10.1007/978-3-030-99429-7_6
14. Dimovski, A.S.: Artifact for the paper "error invariants for fault localization via abstract interpretation". Zenodo (2023). https://doi.org/10.5281/zenodo.8167960
15. Dimovski, A.S.: Quantitative program sketching using decision tree-based lifted analysis. J. Comput. Lang. **75**, 101206 (2023). https://doi.org/10.1016/j.cola.2023.101206

16. Dimovski, A.S., Apel, S.: Lifted static analysis of dynamic program families by abstract interpretation. In: 35th European Conference on Object-Oriented Programming, ECOOP 2021. LIPIcs, vol. 194, pp. 14:1–14:28. Schloss Dagstuhl - Leibniz-Zentrum für Informatik (2021). https://doi.org/10.4230/LIPIcs.ECOOP.2021.14
17. Dimovski, A.S., Apel, S., Legay, A.: Program sketching using lifted analysis for numerical program families. In: Dutle, A., Moscato, M.M., Titolo, L., Muñoz, C.A., Perez, I. (eds.) NFM 2021. LNCS, vol. 12673, pp. 95–112. Springer, Cham (2021). https://doi.org/10.1007/978-3-030-76384-8_7
18. Dimovski, A.S., Apel, S., Legay, A.: Several lifted abstract domains for static analysis of numerical program families. Sci. Comput. Program. **213**, 102725 (2022). https://doi.org/10.1016/j.scico.2021.102725
19. Dimovski, A.S., Legay, A.: Computing program reliability using forward-backward precondition analysis and model counting. In: FASE 2020. LNCS, vol. 12076, pp. 182–202. Springer, Cham (2020). https://doi.org/10.1007/978-3-030-45234-6_9
20. Ermis, E., Schäf, M., Wies, T.: Error invariants. In: Giannakopoulou, D., Méry, D. (eds.) FM 2012. LNCS, vol. 7436, pp. 187–201. Springer, Heidelberg (2012). https://doi.org/10.1007/978-3-642-32759-9_17
21. Graves, T.L., Harrold, M.J., Kim, J., Porter, A.A., Rothermel, G.: An empirical study of regression test selection techiques. ACM Trans. Softw. Eng. Methodol. **10**(2), 184–208 (2001). https://doi.org/10.1145/367008.367020
22. Greitschus, M., Dietsch, D., Heizmann, M., Nutz, A., Schätzle, C., Schilling, C., Schüssele, F., Podelski, A.: Ultimate taipan: trace abstraction and abstract interpretation. In: Legay, A., Margaria, T. (eds.) TACAS 2017, Part II. LNCS, vol. 10206, pp. 399–403. Springer, Heidelberg (2017). https://doi.org/10.1007/978-3-662-54580-5_31
23. Harris, W.R., Sankaranarayanan, S., Ivancic, F., Gupta, A.: Program analysis via satisfiability modulo path programs. In: Proceedings of the 37th ACM SIGPLAN-SIGACT Symposium on Principles of Programming Languages, POPL 2010, Madrid, Spain, 17–23 January 2010, pp. 71–82. ACM (2010). https://doi.org/10.1145/1706299.1706309
24. Jeannet, B.: Relational interprocedural verification of concurrent programs. In: Seventh IEEE International Conference on Software Engineering and Formal Methods, SEFM 2009, pp. 83–92. IEEE Computer Society (2009). https://doi.org/10.1109/SEFM.2009.29
25. Jeannet, B., Miné, A.: APRON: a library of numerical abstract domains for static analysis. In: Bouajjani, A., Maler, O. (eds.) CAV 2009. LNCS, vol. 5643, pp. 661–667. Springer, Heidelberg (2009). https://doi.org/10.1007/978-3-642-02658-4_52
26. Jose, M., Majumdar, R.: Cause clue clauses: error localization using maximum satisfiability. In: Proceedings of the 32nd ACM SIGPLAN Conference on Programming Language Design and Implementation, PLDI 2011, pp. 437–446. ACM (2011). https://doi.org/10.1145/1993498.1993550
27. King, J.C.: Symbolic execution and program testing. Commun. ACM **19**(7), 385–394 (1976). https://doi.org/10.1145/360248.360252
28. Miné, A.: Backward under-approximations in numeric abstract domains to automatically infer sufficient program conditions. Sci. Comput. Program. **93**, 154–182 (2014). https://doi.org/10.1016/j.scico.2013.09.014
29. Miné, A.: Tutorial on static inference of numeric invariants by abstract interpretation. Found. Trends Program. Lang. **4**(3–4), 120–372 (2017). https://doi.org/10.1561/2500000034

30. de Moura, L., Bjørner, N.: Z3: an efficient SMT solver. In: Ramakrishnan, C.R., Rehof, J. (eds.) TACAS 2008. LNCS, vol. 4963, pp. 337–340. Springer, Heidelberg (2008). https://doi.org/10.1007/978-3-540-78800-3_24
31. Nguyen, H.D.T., Qi, D., Roychoudhury, A., Chandra, S.: SemFix: program repair via semantic analysis. In: 35th International Conference on Software Engineering, ICSE 2013, pp. 772–781. IEEE Computer Society (2013). https://doi.org/10.1109/ICSE.2013.6606623
32. Rival, X.: Understanding the origin of alarms in ASTRÉE. In: Hankin, C., Siveroni, I. (eds.) SAS 2005. LNCS, vol. 3672, pp. 303–319. Springer, Heidelberg (2005). https://doi.org/10.1007/11547662_21
33. Rothenberg, B.-C., Grumberg, O.: Must fault localization for program repair. In: Lahiri, S.K., Wang, C. (eds.) CAV 2020, Part II. LNCS, vol. 12225, pp. 658–680. Springer, Cham (2020). https://doi.org/10.1007/978-3-030-53291-8_33
34. Solar-Lezama, A.: Program sketching. STTT **15**(5–6), 475–495 (2013). https://doi.org/10.1007/s10009-012-0249-7
35. Urban, C., Miné, A.: A decision tree abstract domain for proving conditional termination. In: Müller-Olm, M., Seidl, H. (eds.) SAS 2014. LNCS, vol. 8723, pp. 302–318. Springer, Cham (2014). https://doi.org/10.1007/978-3-319-10936-7_19
36. Yin, B., Chen, L., Liu, J., Wang, J., Cousot, P.: Verifying numerical programs via iterative abstract testing. In: Chang, B.-Y.E. (ed.) SAS 2019. LNCS, vol. 11822, pp. 247–267. Springer, Cham (2019). https://doi.org/10.1007/978-3-030-32304-2_13

Generalized Program Sketching by Abstract Interpretation and Logical Abduction

Aleksandar S. Dimovski(✉)

Mother Teresa University, st. Mirche Acev nr. 4, 1000 Skopje, North Macedonia
aleksandar.dimovski@unt.edu.mk
https://aleksdimovski.github.io/

Abstract. This paper presents a new approach for synthesizing missing parts from imperative programs by using abstract interpretation and logical abduction. Given a partial program with missing arbitrary expressions, our approach synthesizes concrete expressions that are strong enough to prove the assertions in the given program. Furthermore, the synthesized elements by our approach are the simplest and the weakest among all possible that guarantee the validity of assertions. In particular, we use a combination of forward and backward numerical analyses based on abstract interpretation to generate constraints that are solved by using the logical abduction technique.

We have implemented our approach in a prototype synthesis tool for C programs, and we show that the proposed approach is able to successfully synthesize arithmetic and boolean expressions for various C programs.

Keywords: Program Synthesis · Abstract interpretation · Logical Abduction

1 Introduction

Program synthesis [2] is a task of inferring a program that satisfies a given specification. A sketch [32,33] is a partial program with missing arithmetic and boolean expressions called *holes*, which need to be discovered by the synthesizer. Previous approaches for program sketching [19,32,33] automatically synthesize only integer "constants" for the holes so that the resulting complete program satisfies given assertions for all possible inputs. However, it is more challenging to define a synthesis algorithm that infers arbitrary arithmetic and boolean expressions in program sketches. We refer to this as *generalized sketching problem.*

In this paper, we propose a new approach for solving the generalized sketching problem by using abstract interpretation [5,29,34] and logical abduction

M. V. Hermenegildo and J. F. Morales (Eds.): SAS 2023, LNCS 14284, pp. 212–230, 2023.
https://doi.org/10.1007/978-3-031-44245-2_11

[1,8,12]. Assume that we have a program sketch with an unknown expression indicated by ??. Our synthesis algorithm computes an expression E over program variables such that, when ?? is replaced by E, all assertions within the resulting complete program become valid. Our synthesis algorithm proceeds in two phases, consisting of constraint generation and constraint solving. The constraint generation phase is based on abstract interpretation, whereas the constraint solving phase is based on logical abduction. In particular, we use forward and backward static analyses based on abstract interpretation to simultaneously compute the invariant postcondition before and sufficient precondition that ensures assertion validity after the unknown hole. The forward analysis computes an invariant P representing the facts known at the program location before the hole, whereas the backward analysis provides a sufficient precondition C that guarantees that the code after the hole satisfies all assertions. Then, we use abduction to find missing hypothesis in a logical inference task. In more detail, assume we have a premise P and a desired conclusion C for an inference, where P and C are constraints generated using forward and backward analyses, respectively. The abduction infers the simplest and most general explanation E such that $P \wedge E \models C$ and $P \wedge E \not\models$ false. The first condition states that the abduction solution E together with premise P should imply conclusion C, while the second condition states that the abduction solution E should not contradict premise P. Finally, we use explanation E to synthesize a concrete expression for hole ??.

We have implemented our approach in a prototype program synthesizer. Our tool uses the numerical abstract domains (e.g., intervals, octagons, polyhedra) from the APRON library [25] for static analysis, as well as the EXPLAIN tool [8] for logical abduction in the combination SMT theory of linear arithmetic and propositional logic, and the MISTRAL tool [9] for SMT solving. We illustrate this approach for automatic completion of various numerical C sketches from the SKETCH project [32,33], SV-COMP (https://sv-comp.sosy-lab.org/), and the literature [28]. We compare performances of our approach against the most popular sketching tool SKETCH [32,33] and the FAMILYSKETCHER [15,19] that are used for synthesizing program sketches with missing integer constants.

This work makes several contributions:

(1) We explore the idea of automatically synthesizing arbitrary expressions in program sketches;
(2) We show how this generalized program sketching problem can be solved using abstract interpretation and logical abduction;
(3) We build a synthesizer using tools for static analysis by abstract interpretation and logical abduction, and present the synthesis results for the domain of numerical (linear arithmetic) programs.

2 Motivating Examples

We now present an overview of our approach using motivating examples. Consider the code `intro.c` shown in Fig. 1, where the unknown hole `??` is an arith-

```
void main(int x){
① int z = x+1;
② int y = z;
③ y = ??;
④ z = z+[2,3];
⑤ assert (z>y); }
```

Fig. 1. intro.c.

```
void main(int n){
① int abs = n;
② if (??) ⓣ abs = -n;
③ else ⓔ skip;
④ assert (abs ≥ 0); }
```

Fig. 2. abs.c.

```
void main() {
① int x = 10, y = 0;
② while ⓗ (??) {
③     x = x-1;
④     y = y+1; }
⑤ assert (y==10); }
```

Fig. 3. while.c.

metic expression in an assignment. The goal is to complete the unknown hole in loc. ③ so that the assertion is always valid.

Our approach starts by performing forward and backward static analyses that compute numerical invariants and sufficient conditions. They are abstract interpretation-based static analyses implemented using the Polyhedra abstract domain [7] from the APRON library [25]. The (over-approximating) forward analysis infers the invariant (z=x+1 $\wedge$ y=x+1) at loc. ③ before the hole. The subsequent (under-approximating) backward analysis starts with the assertion fact (z>y) at loc. ⑤, and by propagating it backwards it infers the precondition (z+2>y) at loc. ④ after the hole.[1] We use these inferred facts to construct the following abduction query:

$$(\texttt{z=x+1} \wedge \texttt{y'=x+1}) \wedge R(\texttt{y,y',x,z}) \implies (\texttt{z+2>y})$$

which is solved by calling the EXPLAIN tool [8]. The left-hand side of the implication encodes the generated constraints up to the hole ??, where y' denotes the value of variable y before loc. ③ and the unknown predicate R(y,y',x,z) encodes the constraint over all program variables in scope at loc. ③. The right-hand side of this implication encodes the postcondition ensuring that the assertion must be valid. Hence, this abduction query is looking for a constraint over program variables that guarantees the validity of this implication. Among the class of all solutions, we prefer abductive solutions containing the variable y over others. For this reason, we specify in the abduction query the lowest cost to variable y, while y', x and z have higher costs. The logically weakest and simplest[2] solution containing y is: R(y,y',x,z) $\equiv$ (y $\leq$ y'+1). This represents a weakest specification for the hole, so we can use it to synthesize the unknown expression. That is, we can fill the hole in loc. ③ with: y = y+1 (other solutions are also possible, e.g. y = y-1).

Consider abs.c shown in Fig. 2, where the unknown hole ?? is a boolean expression in the if-guard. The forward analysis infers the invariant (abs=n) at loc. ②. The backward analysis starts with the assertion satisfaction, i.e. by

[1] This condition guarantees that the assertion is valid for any non-deterministic choice [2, 3]. If we have used an over-approximating backward analysis, it would infer the necessary condition (z+3>y) that may lead to the assertion satisfaction for some non-deterministic choices of [2, 3] (e.g., the execution where the non-deterministic choice [2, 3] returns 3).

[2] A solution is simplest if it contains the fewest number of variables.

propagating the assertion fact (abs $\geq$ 0) backwards. After the if-guard, it infers that the precondition of then branch is (n $\leq$ 0) and the precondition of else branch is (abs $\geq$ 0). Thus, we construct two abduction queries: (1) (abs=n) $\wedge$ R_{true}(n,abs) $\implies$ (n $\leq$ 0), and (2) (abs=n) $\wedge$ R_{false}(n,abs) $\implies$ (abs $\geq$ 0), which are solved by EXPLAIN tool [8]. The reported weakest solutions are: R_{true}(n,abs) $\equiv$ (n $\leq$ 0) and R_{false}(n,abs) $\equiv$ (n $\geq$ 0). Subsequently, we check whether $\neg R_{true}$(n,abs) $\implies$ R_{false}(n,abs) using the MISTRAL SMT solver [9]. Since $\neg$(n$\leq$0) $\implies$ (n$\geq$0) is valid, we fill the hole at loc. ② with the boolean guard (n$\leq$0) as a sufficient condition for the assertion to hold.

Consider the code while.c given in Fig. 3, where the unknown hole ?? is a boolean expression in the while-guard. The forward analysis infers the invariant (x $\leq$ 10) $\wedge$ (x+y=10) at loc. ⓗ. We construct the abduction query (x $\leq$ 10) $\wedge$ (x+y=10) $\wedge$ R_{false}(x,y) $\implies$ (y=10). The reported solution by EXPLAIN is R_{false}(x,y) $\equiv$ (x=0). We compute R_{true}(x,y) $\equiv \neg R_{false}$(x,y) $\equiv$ (x<0) $\vee$ (x>0). Hence, we perform two backward analysis of while.c in which the while-guard is (x<0 $\wedge$??$_1$) and (x>0 $\wedge$??$_2$), respectively. They start with the fact (x=0 $\wedge$ y=10) at loc. ⑤. The first backward analysis for (x<0 $\wedge$??$_1$) infers the bottom ($\perp$) condition after the guard at loc. ③, whereas the second backward analysis for (x>0 $\wedge$??$_2$) infers (1 $\leq$ x $\leq$ 11) $\wedge$ (x+y=10) after the guard at loc. ③. We construct two abduction queries: (1) (x $\leq$ 10 $\wedge$ x+y=10) $\wedge$ R^1_{true}(x,y) $\implies$ false, and (2) (x $\leq$ 10 $\wedge$ x+y=10) $\wedge$ R^2_{true}(x,y) $\implies$ (1 $\leq$ x $\leq$ 11) $\wedge$ (x+y=10). The obtained solutions are R^1_{true}(x,y) $\equiv$ false and R^2_{true}(x,y) $\equiv$ true. Hence, we fill the hole with (x>0).

Assume that the assertion at loc. ⑤ of while.c is assert (y $\leq$ 10). In this case, the solution of the first abduction query is R_{false}(x,y) $\equiv$ (x $\geq$ 0). We find one interpretation (x=n), where n $\geq$ 0, of the formula (x $\geq$ 0) using MISTRAL SMT solver. So, we obtain R_{true}(x,y) $\equiv \neg R_{false}$(x,y) $\equiv$ (x<n) $\vee$ (x>n). Then, we proceed analogously to above (basically replacing (x=0) by (x=n)).

3 Language and Semantics

This section introduces the target language of our approach as well as its concrete and abstract semantics. They will be employed for designing the invariance (reachability) and sufficient condition static analyses using the abstract interpretation theory [5,29,34]. Moreover, we formally define the logical abduction problem.

3.1 Syntax

We use a simple C-like imperative language for writing general-purpose programs. The program variables *Var* are statically allocated and the only data type is the set $\mathbb{Z}$ of mathematical integers. To encode unknown holes, we use the construct ??. The hole constructs ??$_i$ are placeholders that the synthesizer must replace with suitable (arithmetic and boolean) expressions, such that the resulting program will avoid any assertion failures. The syntax is given below.

$$\overrightarrow{[\![\texttt{skip}]\!]}S = S$$
$$\overrightarrow{[\![\texttt{x = }ae]\!]}S = \{\sigma[\texttt{x} \mapsto n] \mid \sigma \in S, n \in [\![ae]\!]\sigma\}$$
$$\overrightarrow{[\![s_1 \texttt{ ; } s_2]\!]}S = \overrightarrow{[\![s_2]\!]}(\overrightarrow{[\![s_1]\!]}S)$$
$$\overrightarrow{[\![\texttt{if } be \ s_1 \texttt{ else } s_2]\!]}S = \overrightarrow{[\![s_1]\!]}\{\sigma \in S \mid \text{true} \in [\![be]\!]\sigma\} \cup \overrightarrow{[\![s_2]\!]}\{\sigma \in S \mid \text{false} \in [\![be]\!]\sigma\}$$
$$\overrightarrow{[\![\texttt{while } be \texttt{ do } s]\!]}S = \{\sigma \in \texttt{lfp} \ \overrightarrow{\phi} \mid \text{false} \in [\![be]\!]\sigma\}$$
$$\overrightarrow{\phi}(X) = S \cup \overrightarrow{[\![s]\!]}\{\sigma \in X \mid \text{true} \in [\![be]\!]\sigma\}$$

Fig. 4. Definitions of $\overrightarrow{[\![s]\!]} : \mathcal{P}(\Sigma) \to \mathcal{P}(\Sigma)$.

$$s\,(s \in Stm) ::= \texttt{skip} \mid \texttt{x=}ae \mid s; s \mid \texttt{if}\,(be)\,s\,\texttt{else}\,s \mid \texttt{while}\,(be)\,\texttt{do}\,s \mid \texttt{assert}(be),$$
$$ae\,(ae \in AExp) ::= \texttt{??}_i \mid ae', \quad ae' ::= n \mid [n, n'] \mid \texttt{x} \in Var \mid ae' \oplus ae',$$
$$be\,(be \in BExp) ::= \texttt{??}_i \mid be', \quad be' ::= ae \bowtie ae \mid \neg be' \mid be' \wedge be' \mid be' \vee be'$$

where n ranges over integers $\mathbb{Z}$, $[n, n']$ over integer intervals, x over program variables *Var*, and $\oplus \in \{+, -, *, /\}$, $\bowtie \in \{<, \leq, =, \neq\}$. Integer intervals $[n, n']$ denote a random choice of an integer in the interval. We assume that statements and holes are tagged with unique syntactic labels ⓛ $\in \mathbb{L}$. Without loss of generality, we assume that a program p is a sequence of statements followed by a single assertion "ⓘ s; ⓕ `assert` (be^f)".

The unknown holes $\texttt{??}_i$ occur either as tests (boolean expressions) in `if` and `while` statements or as right-hand sides (arithmetic expressions) in assignments. Let H be a set of uniquely labelled holes $\texttt{??}_i$ in program p. A *control function* ϕ is a mapping from the set of holes H to concrete (arithmetic and boolean) expressions. We say that ϕ is *complete* if $dom(\phi) = H$, i.e. ϕ is defined for each hole in the program. Otherwise, if $dom(\phi) \subset H$, i.e. ϕ is $\perp$ (undefined) for some holes, we say that ϕ is a *partial* control function. We write $p[\phi]$ to denote the program obtained by substituting each $\texttt{??}_i$ with $\phi(\texttt{??}_i)$, if $\phi(\texttt{??}_i)$ is defined.

Definition 1. *A complete control function ϕ is a* solution *to the generalized sketching problem defined by program p if $p[\phi]$ is a complete program that satisfies all its assertions under all possible inputs.*

3.2 Concrete Semantics and Analyses

We now define the concrete semantics of our language, and use it to construct *invariance* (forward) and *sufficient condition* (backward) *concrete analyses.* Such analyses are obviously *uncomputable*, since our language is Turing complete. In the next subsection, we present their sound decidable abstractions, which can statically determine dynamic properties of programs.

A memory *store*, denoted $\sigma \in \Sigma$, is a function mapping each variable to a value: $\Sigma = Var \to \mathbb{Z}$. The concrete domain is the powerset complete lattice $\langle \mathcal{P}(\Sigma), \subseteq, \cup, \cap, \emptyset, \Sigma \rangle$. The semantics of arithmetic expressions $[\![ae]\!] : \Sigma \to \mathcal{P}(\mathbb{Z})$ and boolean expressions $[\![be]\!] : \Sigma \to \mathcal{P}(\{\text{true}, \text{false}\})$ are the sets of possible (numerical and boolean) values for expressions ae and be in a given store σ. For example, $[\![\texttt{??}_i]\!]\sigma = \mathbb{Z}$ and $[\![[n, n']]\!]\sigma = \{n, \ldots, n'\}$ for arithmetic expressions

$$\overleftarrow{[\![\texttt{skip}]\!]}S = S$$
$$\overleftarrow{[\![\texttt{x = } ae]\!]}S = \{\sigma \mid \forall n \in [\![ae]\!]\sigma, \sigma[\texttt{x} \mapsto n] \in S\}$$
$$\overleftarrow{[\![s_1\texttt{ ; }s_2]\!]}S = \overleftarrow{[\![s_1]\!]}(\overleftarrow{[\![s_2]\!]}S)$$
$$\overleftarrow{[\![\texttt{if } be\ s_1 \texttt{ else } s_2]\!]}S = \Big(\overleftarrow{[\![s_1]\!]}S \cup \{\sigma \mid [\![be]\!]\sigma = \{\text{false}\}\}\Big) \cap \Big(\overleftarrow{[\![s_2]\!]}S \cup \{\sigma \mid [\![\neg be]\!]\sigma = \{\text{false}\}\}\Big)$$
$$\overleftarrow{[\![\texttt{while } be \texttt{ do } s]\!]}S = \texttt{gfp}\ \overleftarrow{\phi}$$
$$\overleftarrow{\phi}(X) = \Big(S \cup \{\sigma \mid [\![\neg be]\!]\sigma = \{\text{false}\}\}\Big) \cap \Big(\overleftarrow{[\![s]\!]}X \cup \{\sigma \mid [\![be]\!]\sigma = \{\text{false}\}\Big\}$$

Fig. 5. Definitions of $\overleftarrow{[\![s]\!]} : \mathcal{P}(\Sigma) \to \mathcal{P}(\Sigma)$.

$??_i$ and $[n, n']$. We consider two semantics of statements (programs): an *invariance* (forward) semantics $\overrightarrow{[\![s]\!]} : \mathcal{P}(\Sigma) \to \mathcal{P}(\Sigma)$ that infers a set of reachable stores (invariants) from a given set of initial stores; and a *sufficient condition* (backward) semantics $\overleftarrow{[\![s]\!]} : \mathcal{P}(\Sigma) \to \mathcal{P}(\Sigma)$ that infers a set of stores (sufficient condition) from which only stores satisfying a given postcondition are reached. The definitions of $\overrightarrow{[\![s]\!]}$ and $\overleftarrow{[\![s]\!]}$ are given in Fig. 4 and Fig. 5, respectively. The invariance semantics [5] is built forward, so each function $\overrightarrow{[\![s]\!]}$ takes as input a set of stores S before statement s and returns a set of possible stores reached after executing s from S. The sufficient condition semantics [29] is built backward, so each function $\overleftarrow{[\![s]\!]}$ takes as input a set of stores S after statement s and returns a set of possible stores before s from which only stores from S are reached after executing s. The semantics of a `while` statement is given in a standard fixed-point formulation [5, 29] using the least and greatest fix-point operators `lfp` and `gfp`, where the fixed-point functionals $\overrightarrow{\phi}, \overleftarrow{\phi} : \mathcal{P}(\Sigma) \to \mathcal{P}(\Sigma)$ accumulate possible stores after another `while` iteration from a set of stores X going in a forward and backward direction, respectively.

Assume that a program "ⓘ s; ⓕ `assert` (be^f)" is given. We can use the invariance semantics $\overrightarrow{[\![s]\!]}$ to collect the possible stores in all program locations reachable from a set of initial stores $\mathcal{I} \subseteq \mathcal{P}(\Sigma)$, denoted $\texttt{Inv}_{\mathcal{I}}$. We can also use the sufficient condition semantics $\overleftarrow{[\![s]\!]}$ to infer sufficient conditions in the form of a set of possible stores in all program locations that guarantee the stores after executing the program belong to some user-supplied property $\mathcal{F} \subseteq \mathcal{P}(\Sigma)$, denoted $\texttt{Cond}_{\mathcal{F}}$. We assume that at the initial label ⓘ the set of possible stores is $\mathcal{I} = \mathcal{P}(\Sigma)$, whereas at the final (assertion) label ⓕ the possible stores are $\mathcal{F} = \{\sigma \in \texttt{Inv}_{\mathcal{I}}(ⓕ) \mid [\![be^f]\!]\sigma = \{\text{true}\}\}$. That is, $\texttt{Inv}_{\mathcal{I}}(ⓘ) = \mathcal{I}$ and $\texttt{Cond}_{\mathcal{F}}(ⓕ) = \mathcal{F}$. For each statement "ⓛ s ⓛ'", we define:

$$\texttt{Inv}_{\mathcal{I}}(ⓛ') = \overrightarrow{[\![s]\!]}\ \texttt{Inv}_{\mathcal{I}}(ⓛ), \qquad \texttt{Cond}_{\mathcal{F}}(ⓛ) = \overleftarrow{[\![s]\!]}\ \texttt{Cond}_{\mathcal{F}}(ⓛ')$$

3.3 Abstract Semantics and Analyses

We now define computable abstract analyses that are approximations of the concrete semantics and analyses. We replace the computation in the concrete domain

$\mathcal{P}(\Sigma)$ with a computation in some numerical abstract domain $\mathbb{D}$ that reasons on the numerical properties of variables, such that there exists a concretization-based abstraction $\langle \mathcal{P}(\Sigma), \subseteq \rangle \xleftarrow{\gamma_{\mathbb{D}}} \langle \mathbb{D}, \sqsubseteq_{\mathbb{D}} \rangle$.[3] The abstract domain $\mathbb{D}$ is a set of computer-representable properties, called *abstract elements*, together with effective algorithms to implement sound abstract operators for forward and backward analyses. In particular, they have abstract operators for ordering $\sqsubseteq_{\mathbb{D}}$, least upper bound (join) $\sqcup_{\mathbb{D}}$, greatest lower bound (meet) $\sqcap_{\mathbb{D}}$, bottom $\bot_{\mathbb{D}}$, top $\top_{\mathbb{D}}$, widening $\nabla_{\mathbb{D}}$, and narrowing $\triangle_{\mathbb{D}}$. There are forward transfer functions for assignments $\texttt{ASSIGN}_{\mathbb{D}} : \mathit{Stm} \times \mathbb{D} \to \mathbb{D}$ and tests $\texttt{FILTER}_{\mathbb{D}} : \mathit{BExp} \times \mathbb{D} \to \mathbb{D}$, which are sound over-approximations of the corresponding concrete functions. We let $\texttt{lfp}^{\#}$ denote an abstract fix-point operator, derived using widening $\nabla_{\mathbb{D}}$ and narrowing $\triangle_{\mathbb{D}}$, that over-approximates the concrete $\texttt{lfp}$. There are also backward transfer functions for assignments $\texttt{B-ASSIGN}^{u}_{\mathbb{D}} : \mathit{Stm} \times \mathbb{D} \to \mathbb{D}$, tests $\texttt{B-FILTER}^{u}_{\mathbb{D}} : \mathit{BExp} \times \mathbb{D} \to \mathbb{D}$, and a lower widening $\underline{\nabla}_{\mathbb{D}}$ [29], which are sound under-approximations of the corresponding concrete functions. We let $\texttt{gfp}^{\#}$ denote an abstract fixpoint operator, derived using lower widening $\underline{\nabla}_{\mathbb{D}}$, that under-approximates the concrete $\texttt{gfp}$.

The operators of the abstract domain $\mathbb{D}$ can be used to define abstract invariance (resp., sufficient condition) analysis that is over- (resp., under-) approximation of the corresponding concrete analysis. For each statement s, we define its abstract invariance semantics $\overrightarrow{[\![s]\!]}^{\sharp}$ in Fig. 6 and its abstract sufficient condition semantics $\overleftarrow{[\![s]\!]}^{\sharp}$ in Fig. 7. For a $\texttt{while}$ loop, $\texttt{lfp}^{\sharp}\, \overrightarrow{\phi}^{\sharp}$ and $\texttt{gfp}^{\sharp}\, \overleftarrow{\phi}^{\sharp}$ are the limits of the following increasing and decreasing chains: $y_0 = d$, $y_{n+1} = y_n \nabla_{\mathbb{D}} \overrightarrow{\phi}^{\sharp}(y_n)$ for forward analysis; and $y_0 = \texttt{B-FILTER}^{u}_{\mathbb{D}}(\neg be, d)$, $y_{n+1} = y_n \underline{\nabla}_{\mathbb{D}} \overleftarrow{\phi}^{\sharp}(y_n)$ for backward analysis. Since $\texttt{FILTER}_{\mathbb{D}}(be, d) \sqsubseteq_{\mathbb{D}} d$ and $\texttt{B-FILTER}^{u}_{\mathbb{D}}(be, d) \sqsupseteq_{\mathbb{D}} d$, we use $\texttt{FILTER}_{\mathbb{D}}(??_i, d) = d$ and $\texttt{B-FILTER}^{u}_{\mathbb{D}}(??_i, d) = d$ to handle holes $??_i$ as boolean expressions. We also use $\texttt{ASSIGN}_{\mathbb{D}}(\texttt{x = } ??_i, d) = \texttt{ASSIGN}_{\mathbb{D}}(\texttt{x = } [-\infty, +\infty], d)$ and $\texttt{B-ASSIGN}^{u}_{\mathbb{D}}(\texttt{x = } ??_i, d) = \texttt{B-ASSIGN}^{u}_{\mathbb{D}}(\texttt{x = } [-\infty, +\infty], d)$ to handle holes $??_i$ as arithmetic expressions.

Given a program "ⓘ s; ⓕ $\texttt{assert}$ (be^f)", we assume that at the initial label ⓘ the set of possible stores is described by abstract element $d_{\mathcal{I}}$, whereas at the final label ⓕ the user-supplied property is described by abstract element $d_{\mathcal{F}}$. That is, $\texttt{Inv}^{\sharp}_{d_{\mathcal{I}}}(ⓘ) = d_{\mathcal{I}}$ and $\texttt{Cond}^{\sharp}_{d_{\mathcal{F}}}(ⓕ) = d_{\mathcal{F}}$. Note that $d_{\mathcal{I}} = \top_{\mathbb{D}}$ and $d_{\mathcal{F}} = \texttt{FILTER}_{\mathbb{D}}(be^f, \texttt{Inv}^{\sharp}_{d_{\mathcal{I}}}(ⓕ))$. For each statement "ⓛ$s$ ⓛ'", we define:

$$\texttt{Inv}^{\sharp}_{d_{\mathcal{I}}}(l') = \overrightarrow{[\![s]\!]}^{\sharp}\, \texttt{Inv}^{\sharp}_{d_{\mathcal{I}}}(l), \qquad \texttt{Cond}^{\sharp}_{d_{\mathcal{F}}}(l) = \overleftarrow{[\![s]\!]}^{\sharp}\, \texttt{Cond}^{\sharp}_{d_{\mathcal{F}}}(l')$$

By using the soundness of the operators of abstract domain $\mathbb{D}$ [5,29], we prove the soundness of abstract semantics with respect to concrete semantics. That is, $\texttt{Inv}^{\sharp}_{d_{\mathcal{I}}}$ is an over-approximation and contains some spurious stores that are not reachable in the concrete $\texttt{Inv}_{\mathcal{I}}$, whereas $\texttt{Cond}^{\sharp}_{d_{\mathcal{F}}}$ is an under-approximation and does not contain some stores that are present in the concrete $\texttt{Cond}_{\mathcal{F}}$.

[3] Concretization-based abstraction is a relaxation of the known Galois connection, which uses only a concretization function $\gamma_{\mathbb{D}}$ (e.g. Polyhedra domain).

$$\overrightarrow{[\![\texttt{skip}]\!]}^\sharp d = d$$
$$\overrightarrow{[\![\texttt{x = } ae]\!]}^\sharp d = \texttt{ASSIGN}_{\mathbb{D}}(\texttt{x = } ae, d)$$
$$\overrightarrow{[\![s_1 \texttt{ ; } s_2]\!]}^\sharp d = \overrightarrow{[\![s_2]\!]}^\sharp(\overrightarrow{[\![s_1]\!]}^\sharp d)$$
$$\overrightarrow{[\![\texttt{if } be \ s_1 \texttt{ else } s_2]\!]}^\sharp d = \overrightarrow{[\![s_1]\!]}^\sharp(\texttt{FILTER}_{\mathbb{D}}(be, d)) \sqcup_{\mathbb{D}} \overrightarrow{[\![s_2]\!]}^\sharp(\texttt{FILTER}_{\mathbb{D}}(\neg be, d))$$
$$\overrightarrow{[\![\texttt{while } be \texttt{ do } s]\!]}^\sharp d = \texttt{FILTER}_{\mathbb{D}}(\neg be, \texttt{lfp}^\sharp \overrightarrow{\phi^\sharp})$$
$$\overrightarrow{\phi^\sharp}(x) = d \sqcup_{\mathbb{D}} \overrightarrow{[\![s]\!]}^\sharp(\texttt{FILTER}_{\mathbb{D}}(be, x))$$

Fig. 6. Definitions of $\overrightarrow{[\![s]\!]}^\sharp : \mathbb{D} \rightarrow \mathbb{D}$.

$$\overleftarrow{[\![\texttt{skip}]\!]}^\sharp d = d$$
$$\overleftarrow{[\![\texttt{x = } ae]\!]}^\sharp d = \texttt{B-ASSIGN}^u_{\mathbb{D}}(\texttt{x = } ae, d)$$
$$\overleftarrow{[\![s_1 \texttt{ ; } s_2]\!]}^\sharp d = \overleftarrow{[\![s_1]\!]}^\sharp(\overleftarrow{[\![s_2]\!]}^\sharp d)$$
$$\overleftarrow{[\![\texttt{if } be \ s_1 \texttt{ else } s_2]\!]}^\sharp d = \texttt{B-FILTER}^u_{\mathbb{D}}(be, \overleftarrow{[\![s_1]\!]}^\sharp d) \sqcap_{\mathbb{D}} \texttt{B-FILTER}^u_{\mathbb{D}}(\neg be, \overleftarrow{[\![s_2]\!]}^\sharp d)$$
$$\overleftarrow{[\![\texttt{while } be \texttt{ do } s]\!]}^\sharp d = \texttt{gfp}^\sharp \overleftarrow{\phi^\sharp}$$
$$\overleftarrow{\phi^\sharp}(x) = \texttt{B-FILTER}^u_{\mathbb{D}}(\neg be, d) \sqcap_{\mathbb{D}} \texttt{B-FILTER}^u_{\mathbb{D}}(be, \overleftarrow{[\![s]\!]}^\sharp x)$$

Fig. 7. Definitions of $\overleftarrow{[\![s]\!]}^\sharp : \mathbb{D} \rightarrow \mathbb{D}$.

Proposition 1 ([5,29]). *Let $\mathcal{F} = \gamma_{\mathbb{D}}(d_{\mathcal{F}})$ and $\mathcal{I} = \gamma_{\mathbb{D}}(d_{\mathcal{I}})$. For all $l \in \mathbb{L}$, we have: $\mathit{Inv}_{\mathcal{I}}(l) \subseteq \mathit{Inv}^\sharp_{d_{\mathcal{I}}}(l)$, $\mathit{Cond}_{\mathcal{F}}(l) \supseteq \mathit{Cond}^\sharp_{d_{\mathcal{F}}}(l)$.*

3.4 Abduction

The standard abduction allows the inference of a single unknown predicate $R(\mathbf{x})$ defined over a vector of variables $\mathbf{x}$, known as *abducible*, from a formula $R(\mathbf{x}) \wedge \chi \implies C$. That is, the standard abduction finds a formula ϕ over variables $\mathbf{x}$, such that (1) $\phi \wedge \chi \not\models \text{false}$; and (2) $\phi \wedge \chi \models C$. A solution ϕ to the standard abduction problem is an interpretation of $R(\mathbf{x})$ that strengthens the left-hand side of the implication in order to make the implication logically valid. Every solvable abduction problem has an unique logically weakest solution. The procedure $\texttt{Abduce}(\chi, C, \mathbf{x})$ that solves the problem $R(\mathbf{x}) \wedge \chi \implies C$ is implemented in the `EXPLAIN` tool [8]. It computes the logically weakest solution containing the fewest number of variables. That is, it finds the most general and simple solution.

Proposition 2 ([8]). *If the abduction problem is solvable, $\texttt{Abduce}(\chi, C, \boldsymbol{x})$ terminates with an unique weakest solution containing a fewest number of variables.*

4 Synthesis Algorithm

In this section, we present our synthesis algorithm for solving the generalized sketching problem. In particular, we employ the abstract interpretation-based

Algorithm 1: $\texttt{GenSketching}(p, H)$

Input: Program sketch p, and a set of holes H
Output: Complete control function ϕ or an empty set

1 $\phi := \emptyset$;
2 **for** $(??_i \in H)$ **do**
3 $\quad ⓛ s_i ⓛ' := \texttt{Extract}(p, ??_i)$;
4 $\quad e_i := \texttt{Solve}(p, ⓛ s_i ⓛ')$;
5 $\quad$ **if** $(e_i = \emptyset)$ **then return** $\emptyset$;
6 $\quad \phi := \phi \uplus [??_i \mapsto e_i]$
7 **for** $(??_i \in H)$ **do**
8 $\quad ⓛ s_i ⓛ' := \texttt{Extract}(p, ??_i)$;
9 $\quad \phi_i := \phi[??_i \mapsto \bot]$;
10 $\quad e_i' := \texttt{Solve}(p[\phi_i], ⓛ s_i ⓛ')$;
11 $\quad$ **if** $(e_i = \emptyset)$ **then return** $\emptyset$;
12 $\quad \phi := \phi \uplus [??_i \mapsto e_i']$
13 **return** ϕ

analyses, $\texttt{Inv}^\sharp_{d_\mathcal{I}}$ and $\texttt{Cond}^\sharp_{d_\mathcal{F}}$, as well as the logical abduction procedure, $\texttt{Abduce}$, to automatically find expressions for the holes in a program sketch, so that the resulting complete program satisfies its assertions.

High-Level Description. The $\texttt{GenSketching}(p, H)$ synthesis procedure is shown in Algorithm 1. The procedure takes as input two parameters: a program sketch p, and a set of holes H in p. For each hole $??_i$ in H, we first find an initial solution, an expression e_i, where all other holes are treated as non-deterministic choices over integers or booleans (lines 2–6). This is achieved by identifying the statement "$ⓛ s_i ⓛ'$" in which $??_i$ occurs using $\texttt{Extract}(p, ??_i)$, and by calling the function $\texttt{Solve}(p, ⓛ s_i ⓛ')$ to find the expression e_i corresponding to hole $??_i$. This way, we construct an *initial* complete control function $\phi : [??_i \mapsto e_i]$ by using the above initial solutions for all holes in H. Then, we weaken the solution ϕ by iteratively weakening initial solutions for all holes (lines 7–12). To weaken the solution for each $??_i$, we fix the solutions e_j for all other $??_j$ in a partial control function ϕ_i, such that $\phi_i(??_i) = \bot$ and $\phi_i(??_j) = \phi(??_j)$ for all other $??_j \in H$. Next, we construct a program sketch $p[\phi_i]$ with only one hole $??_i$. Finally, we call $\texttt{Solve}(p[\phi_i], ⓛ s_i ⓛ')$ to find the weaken expression e_i' for $??_i$. That is, we use the existing solution given by the current control function for all other holes and infer the weakest expression for $??_i$ that implies the assertion validity.

Solving One-Hole Sketches. The function $\texttt{Solve}(p, ⓛ s ⓛ')$, shown in Algorithm refAlgorithm2, takes two parameters: a program sketch p and a statement "$ⓛ s ⓛ'$" in which the hole $??$ we want to handle occurs. Note that all other holes in p are treated (analyzed) as non-deterministic choices: $[-\infty, \infty]$ for arithmetic and $\{\text{true}, \text{false}\}$ for boolean expressions. We first call a forward abstract analysis $\overrightarrow{[\![p]\!]}^\sharp d_\mathcal{I}$, where $d_\mathcal{I} = \top_\mathbb{D}$, to compute the invariants $\texttt{Inv}^\sharp_{d_\mathcal{I}}$ (line 1). Then we

Algorithm 2: $\mathtt{Solve}(p, \textcircled{l}s\textcircled{l'})$

Input: Program sketch p, and a statement $\textcircled{l}s\textcircled{l'}$ in which a hole occurs
Output: Expression e or an empty set

1 $\mathtt{Inv}^{\sharp}_{d_{\mathcal{I}}} := \overrightarrow{[\![p]\!]}^{\sharp}\, d_{\mathcal{I}}$;
2 **switch** *(s)* **do**
3   **case** $(x := ??)$ **do**
4     $\mathtt{Cond}^{\sharp}_{d_{\mathcal{F}}} := \overleftarrow{[\![p]\!]}^{\sharp}\, d_{\mathcal{F}}$;
5     $R(\mathbf{x}) := \mathtt{Abduce}(\mathtt{Inv}^{\sharp}_{d_{\mathcal{I}}}(\textcircled{l})[x'/x], \mathtt{Cond}^{\sharp}_{d_{\mathcal{F}}}(\textcircled{l'}), \mathbf{x})$;
6   **if** *(unsat(R(x)))* **then return** $\emptyset$;
7   **return** $\mathtt{SolveAsg}(R(\mathbf{x}), x)$
8   **case** $(\mathit{if}(??)\,\textcircled{t}s_1\ \mathit{else}\,\textcircled{e}s_2)$ **do**
9     $\mathtt{Cond}^{\sharp}_{d_{\mathcal{F}}} := \overleftarrow{[\![p]\!]}^{\sharp}\, d_{\mathcal{F}}$;
10     $R_{true}(\mathbf{x}) := \mathtt{Abduce}(\mathtt{Inv}^{\sharp}_{d_{\mathcal{I}}}(\textcircled{l}), \mathtt{Cond}^{\sharp}_{d_{\mathcal{F}}}(\textcircled{t}), \mathbf{x})$;
11     $R_{false}(\mathbf{x}) := \mathtt{Abduce}(\mathtt{Inv}^{\sharp}_{d_{\mathcal{I}}}(\textcircled{l}), \mathtt{Cond}^{\sharp}_{d_{\mathcal{F}}}(\textcircled{e}), \mathbf{x})$;
12   **if** $(\mathit{unsat}(R_{true}(\boldsymbol{x})) \vee \mathit{unsat}(R_{false}(\boldsymbol{x})))$ **then return** $\emptyset$;
13   **return** $\mathtt{SolveCond}(R_{true}(\mathbf{x}), R_{false}(\mathbf{x}))$
14   **case** $(\mathit{while}\,\textcircled{h}(??_i)\ \mathit{do}\ \textcircled{b}s_1)$ **do**
15     $R_{false}(\mathbf{x}) := \mathtt{Abduce}(\mathtt{Inv}^{\sharp}_{d_{\mathcal{I}}}(\textcircled{h}), d_{\mathcal{F}}, \mathbf{x})$;
16     $(\mathbf{x}{=}\mathbf{n}) = \mathtt{Model}(R_{false}(\mathbf{x}))$;
17     $\mathtt{Cond}^{\sharp,1}_{d_{\mathcal{F}}} = \overleftarrow{[\![p[??_i \mapsto (\mathbf{x} > \mathbf{n}) \wedge ??_i]]\!]}^{\sharp}(d_{\mathcal{F}})$;
18     $\mathtt{Cond}^{\sharp,2}_{d_{\mathcal{F}}} = \overleftarrow{[\![p[??_i \mapsto (\mathbf{x} < \mathbf{n}) \wedge ??_i]]\!]}^{\sharp}(d_{\mathcal{F}})$;
19     $R^1_{true}(\mathbf{x}) := \mathtt{Abduce}(\mathtt{Inv}^{\sharp}_{d_{\mathcal{I}}}(\textcircled{h}), \mathtt{Cond}^{\sharp,1}_{d_{\mathcal{F}}}(\textcircled{b}), \mathbf{x})$;
20     $R^2_{true}(\mathbf{x}) := \mathtt{Abduce}(\mathtt{Inv}^{\sharp}_{d_{\mathcal{I}}}(\textcircled{h}), \mathtt{Cond}^{\sharp,2}_{d_{\mathcal{F}}}(\textcircled{b}), \mathbf{x})$;
21   **if** $(\mathit{unsat}(R_1(\boldsymbol{x})) \vee \mathit{unsat}(R_2(\boldsymbol{x})))$ **then return** $\emptyset$;
22   **return** $(\mathbf{x} > \mathbf{n} \wedge R^1_{true}(\mathbf{x})) \vee (\mathbf{x} < \mathbf{n} \wedge R^2_{true}(\mathbf{x}))$

reason by the structure of the statement "$\textcircled{l}s\textcircled{l'}$". For assignments and `if`-s, we call a backward abstract analysis $\overleftarrow{[\![p]\!]}^{\sharp} d_{\mathcal{F}}$, where $d_{\mathcal{F}} = \mathtt{FILTER}_{\mathbb{D}}(be^f, \mathtt{Inv}^{\sharp}_{d_{\mathcal{I}}}(\textcircled{f}))$, to compute the sufficient conditions $\mathtt{Cond}^{\sharp}_{d_{\mathcal{F}}}$ of program p. When s is an assignment "x = ??" (lines 2–7), we construct an abduction query where the premise is $\mathtt{Inv}^{\sharp}_{d_{\mathcal{I}}}(\textcircled{l})[x'/x]$, the desired conclusion is $\mathtt{Cond}^{\sharp}_{d_{\mathcal{F}}}(\textcircled{l'})$, and the unknown predicate (abducible) $R(\mathbf{x})$ is defined over all variables $\mathbf{x}$ that are in scope of s_i including x and x'. We denote by $[x'/x]$ the renaming of x as x'. Moreover, we configure the call to `Abduce` so that the variable x has the highest priority to occur in the solution $R(\mathbf{x})$ of the given abduction query. Then we call $\mathtt{SolveAsg}(R(\mathbf{x}))$ to find one expression e_i such that $x = e_i$ satisfies the predicate $R(\mathbf{x})$. This is realized by asking an SMT solver for one interpretation (model) of the formula $R(\mathbf{x})$. Finally, we return the expression $e_i[x/x']$ as solution of this case. We recall the example `intro.c` in Sect. 2 to see how this case works in practice.

When s is a conditional statement "`if (??) then` $\textcircled{t}s_1$ `else` $\textcircled{e}s_2$" (lines 8–13), we construct two abduction queries in which the premise is $\mathtt{Inv}^{\sharp}_{d_{\mathcal{I}}}(\textcircled{l})$ and the unknown predicate is defined over all variables $\mathbf{x}$ that are in scope of s. The conclusions are $\mathtt{Cond}^\sharp_{d_\mathcal{F}}(ⓣ)$ and $\mathtt{Cond}^\sharp_{d_\mathcal{F}}(ⓔ)$ in the first and second abduction query, respectively. We then call $\mathtt{SolveCond}(R_{true}(\mathbf{x}), R_{false}(\mathbf{x}))$ to check if $\neg R_{true}(\mathbf{x}) \implies R_{false}(\mathbf{x})$ by an SMT solver, where $R_{true}(\mathbf{x})$ and $R_{false}(\mathbf{x})$ are solutions of the first and second abduction query. If this is true, then $R_{true}(\mathbf{x})$ is returned as solution for this case. Otherwise, $R_{true}(\mathbf{x})$ is strengthen until $\neg R_{true}(\mathbf{x}) \implies R_{false}(\mathbf{x})$ holds, in which case the found $R_{true}(\mathbf{x})$ is returned as solution. For example, see how `abs.c` in Sect. 2 is resolved.

Similarly, we handle the case when s is an iteration "`while` ⓗ`(??) do` ⓑs_1" (lines 14–22). First, we construct an abduction query where the premise is $\mathtt{Inv}^\sharp_{d_\mathcal{I}}(ⓗ)$, the desired conclusion is $d_\mathcal{F}$, and the unknown predicate (abducible) is $R_{false}(\mathbf{x})$. Then, we find one interpretation ($\mathbf{x}$=$\mathbf{n}$) of the formula $R_{false}(\mathbf{x})$, which is obtained by finding a model M of $R_{false}(\mathbf{x})$ by an SMT solver and setting $\mathbf{x} = M(\mathbf{x})$. Next, we perform two backward analyses defined as follows: $\mathtt{Cond}^{\sharp,1}_{d_\mathcal{F}} = \overleftarrow{[\![p[??_i \mapsto (\mathbf{x} > \mathbf{n}) \wedge ??_i]]\!]^\sharp}(d_\mathcal{F})$ and $\mathtt{Cond}^{\sharp,2}_{d_\mathcal{F}} = \overleftarrow{[\![p[??_i \mapsto (\mathbf{x} < \mathbf{n}) \wedge ??_i]]\!]^\sharp}(d_\mathcal{F})$. We create two abduction queries using: (1) $\mathtt{Inv}^\sharp_{d_\mathcal{I}}(ⓗ)$, $\mathtt{Cond}^{\sharp,1}_{d_\mathcal{F}}(ⓑ)$, $R^1_{true}(\mathbf{x})$; and (2) $\mathtt{Inv}^\sharp_{d_\mathcal{I}}(ⓗ)$, $\mathtt{Cond}^{\sharp,2}_{d_\mathcal{F}}(ⓑ)$, and $R^2_{true}(\mathbf{x})$. Finally, the solution is $(\mathbf{x} > \mathbf{n} \wedge R^1_{true}(\mathbf{x})) \vee (\mathbf{x} < \mathbf{n} \wedge R^2_{true}(\mathbf{x}))$. For example, see how `while.c` in Sect. 2 works.

Correctness. The following theorem states correctness of the `GenSketching` algorithm.

Theorem 1. *`GenSketching`(p, H) is correct and terminates.*

Proof. The procedure `GenSketching`(p, H) terminates since all steps in it are terminating. The correctness of `GenSketching`(p, H) follows from the soundness of $\mathtt{Inv}^\sharp_{d_\mathcal{I}}$ and $\mathtt{Cond}^\sharp_{d_\mathcal{F}}$ (see Proposition 1) and the correctness of `Abduce` (see Proposition 2).

The correctness proof is by structural induction on statements s in programs p of the form "ⓘ s; ⓕ `assert` (be^f)". We consider the case of assignment `x=??`. Since there is one hole in p, we call `Solve`$(p,$ ⓘ`x=??` ⓕ$)$. We infer $\mathtt{Inv}^\sharp_{d_\mathcal{I}}(ⓘ) = \top_\mathbb{D}$ and $\mathtt{Cond}^\sharp_{d_\mathcal{F}}(ⓕ) = be^f$, so we obtain the abduction query `Abduce`$(\text{true}, be^f, \mathbf{x})$. The solution is $R(\mathbf{x}) \equiv be^f$, thus we call `SolveAsg`$(be^f, \mathbf{x})$ to find one expression ae such that `x=`ae satisfies be^f. By construction of ae, it follows that the program "ⓘ `x=ae`; ⓕ `assert` (be^f)" is valid. Similarly, we handle the other cases. □

5 Evaluation

We now evaluate our approach for generalized program sketching. The evaluation aims to show that we can use our approach to efficiently resolve various C program sketches with numerical data types.

```
void main(int n1; int n2, int n3){
① int max = n1;
② if (n2>max) max = n2;
③ if (n3>max) max = ??;
// if (??) max = n3;
④ assert (max ≥ n1);
⑤ assert (max ≥ n2);
⑥ assert (max ≥ n3); }
```

Fig. 8. `max.c`.

```
void main(int n){
① int x = n;
② if (??) x = x+2n;
③ else x = x-2n;
④ assert (x ≤ 3); }
```

Fig. 9. `cond.c`.

```
void main() {
① unsigned int j;
② int i = 0;
③ j = [0,9]; //j = ??;
④ while (??) {
   //while (i<100) {
⑤   i = i+1;
⑥   j = j+[0,1];}
⑦ assert (j ≤ 105); }
```

Fig. 10. `mine.c`.

Implementation. We have implemented our synthesis algorithm in a prototype tool. The abstract operations and transfer functions of the numerical abstract domains (e.g. Polyhedra [7]) are provided by the APRON library [25], while the abduction and SMT queries are solved by the EXPLAIN [8] and the MISTRAL [9] tools. Our tool is written in OCAML and consists of around 7K lines of code. Currently, it provides only a limited support for arrays, pointers, `struct` and `union` types.

Experiment Setup and Benchmarks. All experiments are executed on a 64-bit Intel®Core^{TM} i5 CPU, Lubuntu VM, with 8 GB memory, and we use a timeout value of 300 sec. All times are reported as average over five independent executions. We report times needed for the actual synthesis task to be performed. The implementation, benchmarks, and all obtained results are available from [16]: https://zenodo.org/record/8165119. We compare our approach `GenSketching` based on the Polyhedra domain with program sketching tool SKETCH version 1.7.6 that uses SAT-based inductive synthesis [32,33], as well as with the FAMILYSKETCHER that uses lifted (family-based) static analysis by abstract interpretation (the Polyhedra domain) [19]. Note that SKETCH and FAMILYSKETCHER can only solve the standard sketching problem, where the unknown holes represent some integer constants. Therefore, they cannot resolve our benchmarks. We need to do some simplifications, so that the unknown holes refer to integer constants. Moreover, their synthesis times depend on the sizes of hole domains (and inputs for SKETCH). Hence, for SKETCH and FAMILYSKETCHER we report synthesis times to resolve simplified sketches with `5-bits` and `10-bits` sizes of unknown holes. On the other hand, `GenSketching` can synthesize arbitrary expressions and its synthesis time does not depend on the sizes of holes. For `GenSketching`, we report TIME which is the total time to resolve a given sketch, and ABDTIME which is the time to solve the abduction queries in the given synthesis task.

The evaluation is performed on several C numerical sketches collected from the SKETCH project [32,33], SV-COMP (https://sv-comp.sosy-lab.org/), and the literature [28]. In particular, we use the following benchmarks: `intro.c` (Fig. 1), `abs.c` (Fig. 2), `while.c` (Fig. 3), `max.c` (Fig. 8), `cond.c` (Fig. 9), and `mine.c` (Fig. 10).

Table 1. Performance results of `GenSketching` vs. SKETCH vs. FAMILYSKETCHER. All times in sec.

Bench.	`GenSketching`		SKETCH		FAMILYSKETCHER	
	TIME	ABDTIME	`5-bits`	`10-bits`	`5-bits`	`10-bits`
`intro.c`	0.0022	0.0011	0.208	0.239	0.0013	0.0016
`abs.c`	0.0021	0.0013	0.204	0.236	0.0020	0.0021
`while.c`	0.0055	0.0013	0.213	0.224	0.0047	0.0053
`max.c`	0.0042	0.0011	0.229	24.25	0.0025	0.0026
`max2.c`	0.0040	0.0015	0.227	31.88	0.0022	0.0033
`cond`	0.0019	0.0011	1.216	2.362	0.0021	0.0023
`mine.c`	0.0757	0.0012	0.236	1.221	0.0035	0.0042
`mine2.c`	0.0059	0.0013	0.215	1.217	0.0024	0.0031

Performance Results. Table 1 shows the performance results of synthesizing our benchmarks. To handle `intro.c` using SKETCH and FAMILYSKETCHER, we need to simplify it so that the hole represents an integer constant. This is done by replacing `y = ??` by `y = y-??` or `y = y+??`. Moreover, they cannot handle non-deterministic choices, so we use constants instead. SKETCH and FAMILYSKETCHER resolve the simplified `intro.c` in 0.208 sec and 0.0013 sec for 5-bit sizes of holes, while `GenSketching` resolves the `intro.c` in 0.0022 sec.

To resolve `abs.c` using SKETCH and FAMILYSKETCHER, we use the `if`-guard ($\texttt{n} \leq \texttt{??}$). In this case SKETCH and FAMILYSKETCHER terminate in 0.204 sec and 0.0022 sec for 5-bit sizes of holes, while `GenSketching` terminates in 0.0021 sec. Still, FAMILYSKETCHER reports "I don't know" answer due to the precision loss. In particular, it infers the invariant ($\texttt{2*??-n+abs} \geq 0 \land 0 \leq \texttt{??} \leq 31 \land \texttt{n+abs} \geq 0$) at loc. ④, thus it is unable to conclude for which values of `??` the assertion ($\texttt{abs} \geq 0$) will hold. For similar reasons, FAMILYSKETCHER cannot successfully resolve the other simplified sketches that contain holes in `if`-guards (see `max2.c` and `cond.c` below).

We simplify the `while`-guard of `while.c` to (`x>??`). SKETCH still cannot resolve this example, since it uses only 8 unrollments of the loop by default. If the loop is unrolled 10 times, SKETCH terminates in 0.213 sec for 5-bit sizes of holes. FAMILYSKETCHER terminates in 0.0047 sec for 5-bits, while `GenSketching` terminates in 0.0055 sec.

Consider the program sketch `max.c` in Fig. 8 that finds a maximum of three integers. It contains one hole in the assignment at loc. ③. The forward analysis of `GenSketching` generates the invariant ($\texttt{max}' \geq \texttt{n1} \land \texttt{max}' \geq \texttt{n2} \land \texttt{n3} \geq \texttt{max}'$) before the hole (where $\texttt{max}'$ denotes the value of `max` before the hole), while the backward analysis infers the sufficient condition ($\texttt{max} \geq \texttt{n1} \land \texttt{max} \geq \texttt{n2} \land \texttt{max} \geq \texttt{n3}$) after the hole. The result of the corresponding abduction query is ($\texttt{max} = \texttt{n3}$), so we fill the hole with the assignment `max = n3`. For SKETCH and FAMILYSKETCHER, we simplify the hole to `max = n3-??`. Since there are three inputs and one hole, SKETCH takes 24.25 sec to resolve this simplified sketch for 10-bit sizes and timeouts for bigger sizes.

Consider a variant of `max.c`, denoted `max2.c`, where the commented statement in Fig. 8 is placed at loc. ③, so the hole is `if`-guard. The forward analysis of `GenSketching` infers the invariant ($\texttt{max} \geq \texttt{n1} \wedge \texttt{max} \geq \texttt{n2}$) before the hole, while the backward analysis infers the sufficient conditions ($\texttt{n3} \geq \texttt{n1} \wedge \texttt{n3} \geq \texttt{n2}$) at the `then` branch after the hole and ($\texttt{max} \geq \texttt{n1} \wedge \texttt{max} \geq \texttt{n2} \wedge \texttt{max} \geq \texttt{n3}$) at the `else` branch after the hole. We construct two abduction queries, and the results are ($\texttt{max} \leq \texttt{n3}$) and ($\texttt{max} \geq \texttt{n3}$), respectively. Hence, we fill the hole with the boolean expression ($\texttt{max} \leq \texttt{n3}$). For SKETCH and FAMILYSKETCHER, we use the simplified sketch where the `if`-guard is (`max<??`). SKETCH timeouts for bigger than 10-bit sizes of holes and inputs, while FAMILYSKETCHER returns "I don't know" answer.

The sketch `cond.c` contains an `if`-guard hole. The inferred invariant of `GenSketching` is (`x=n`) before the hole, while sufficient conditions are ($\texttt{x+2n} \leq 3$) at the `then` branch and ($\texttt{x-2n} \leq 3$) at the `else` branch after the hole. The results of the two abductions queries are $R_{true}(\texttt{x,n}) \equiv (\texttt{n} \leq 1)$ and $R_{false}(\texttt{x,n}) \equiv$ (`n>-4`). Since ($\neg\texttt{n} \leq 1$) $\Longrightarrow$ (`n>-4`) is valid, the hole is filled with ($\texttt{n} \leq 1$).

Consider the `mine.c` sketch, taken from [28], containing a `while`-guard and the `GenSketching` approach. The forward analysis infers the `while`-invariant ($\texttt{j} \geq 0 \wedge \texttt{i} \geq 0 \wedge \texttt{i} \geq \texttt{j-9}$). Hence, the answer to the first abduction query ($\texttt{j} \geq 0 \wedge \texttt{i} \geq 0 \wedge \texttt{i} \geq \texttt{j-9}) \wedge R_{false}(i,j) \Longrightarrow (\texttt{j} \leq 105)$ is ($\texttt{i} \leq 96$). One solution is ($\texttt{i} = 96$), so we perform two backward analyses with `while`-guards ($\texttt{i} < 96 \wedge \texttt{??}$) and ($\texttt{i} > 96 \wedge \texttt{??}$). We construct two abduction queries and obtain $R^1_{true}(i,j) \equiv$ (true) and $R^2_{true}(i,j) \equiv$ (false). Thus, we fill the hole with ($\texttt{i} < 96$).

Consider a variant of `mine.c`, denoted `mine2.c`, where the commented statements (see Fig. 10) are placed at locs. ③ and ④, so the hole is in the assignment `j = ??`. The invariant at loc. ③ is (`i=0`), while the sufficient condition obtained at loc. ④ is ($\texttt{j} \geq 0 \wedge \texttt{i} \geq 0 \wedge \texttt{i} \geq \texttt{j-5} \wedge \texttt{j} \leq 105$). Note that the backward sufficient condition analysis infers conditions at all locations so that all executions branching from those locations will satisfy the assertion. By solving the corresponding abduction query, we obtain the answer ($0 \leq \texttt{j} \leq 5$), so we fill the hole at loc. ③ with `j =` $[0, 5]$. Even if the non-deterministic choice $[0, 1]$ always evaluates to 1 in the `while`-body, the assertion ($\texttt{j} \leq 105$) will hold in the resulting complete program where the initial value of `j` is in $[0, 5]$. For SKETCH and FAMILYSKETCHER to successfully handle the simplified versions of `mine.c` and `mine2.c` we need to use constants instead of non-deterministic choices.

Discussion. In summary, we can conclude that `GenSketching` can successfully synthesize the holes in all sketches, and it does not depend on the sizes of holes thus outperforming the other tools. The abduction time is proportional to the number of abduction queries that need to be solved in a given synthesis task. FAMILYSKETCHER achieves comparable synthesis times to `GenSketching`. FAMILYSKETCHER performs one forward (lifted) analysis using decision tree abstract elements, in which decision nodes are linear constraints defined over unknown holes and the leaves provide analysis information (in the form of polyhedral constraints) corresponding to each partition of the tree. Furthermore, FamilySketcher has similar synthesis times for 5-bit and 10-bit sizes of holes, since all integer holes in the given simplified examples can be handled symbolically. However, if a hole occurs in more complex expressions, e.g. `??*x+y`, then the performance of FamilySketcher will decline since the hole should be handled explicitly [19].

The current tool supports an interesting subset of C, so we can handle many interesting benchmarks. The selected benchmarks represent the proof-of-concept that our approach can be successfully applied in practice. They are chosen to show some distinctive features of our approach compared to the other state-of-the-art tools. To handle bigger programs, we can use some computationally cheaper abstract domains, such as octagons and intervals, but this will result in additional precision loss that will influence the precision of our approach. For example, if we use intervals domain we cannot handle `abs.c` example from Sect. 2.

6 Related Work

Abstract Interpretation in Program Analysis and Verification. Forward invariance and backward sufficient condition analyses by abstract interpretation have been used in practice for a long time [3,5,7,28,29]. The three most popular forward invariance analyses are based on the Interval [5], the Octagon [27], and the Polyhedra [7] domains that infer variable bounds, unit affine inequalities and arbitrary affine inequalities on variables, respectively. Sufficient condition analysis has been first introduced by Bourdoncle [3] in his work on abstract debugging of deterministic programs. Miné [28] has presented a technique for automatically inferring sufficient conditions of non-deterministic programs by using a polyhedral backward analysis. The under-approximating sound abstract operators are implemented as part of the APRON library in the Banal tool.

Several works use a combination of forward-backward analyses to extract interesting dynamic properties of programs [3,21,30,34]. In particular, the combination of forward-backward analyses are used by Rival [30] to obtain a set of traces that may lead to error; by Bourdoncle [3] to find preconditions for invariant and intermittent assertions to always hold; by Dimovski and Legay [21] to calculate the probability that a target assertion is satisfied/violated; and by Urban and Miné [34] to infer ranking functions for proving termination.

Many recent approaches and tools for program verification use static analysis by abstract interpretation. ASTREE [6] is an industrial-scale static analyzer for verifying avionics software. SeaHorn [23] combines Horn-clause solving techniques with abstract interpretation, Pagai [24] combines SMT-solving with abstract interpretation, whereas Ulitimate Taipan [22] is a CEGAR-based software model checker that uses abstract interpretation to derive invariants for the path program corresponding to a given spurious counterexample. VATer [35] uses input space partitioning to iteratively refine static analyses by abstract interpretation, and moreover it uses bounded exhaustive testing to complement static analyses.

Program Sketching. The goal of the so-called standard sketching problem is to synthesize program sketches in which some missing holes are integer constants. One of the earliest and widely-known approach to solve the standard sketching problem is the SKETCH tool [32,33], which uses SAT-based counterexample-guided inductive synthesis. It iteratively generates a finite set of inputs and performs SAT queries to identify values for the holes so that the resulting program satisfies all assertions for the given inputs. Further SAT queries are then used to check if the resulting program is correct on all possible inputs. Hence, SKETCH may need several iterations to converge reporting only one solution. Moreover, SKETCH reasons about loops by unrolling them, so is very sensitive to the degree of unrolling. Our approach does not have this constraint, and is able to handle unbounded loops in a sound way. Still, our approach can be applied to numerical programs, while SKETCH is more general and especially suited for bit-manipulating programs. Another works for solving this standard sketching problem are proposed in [15,17,19], which use a lifted (family-based) static analysis by abstract interpretation [13,14,18,20]. The key idea is that the set of all possible sketch realizations represent a program family with numerical features. Thus, the effort of conducting an effective search of all possible hole realizations is delegated to an efficient lifted static analyzer for program families, which uses a specifically designed decision tree abstract domain. However, the above works address the standard sketching problem, where each unknown hole can be replaced by one value from a finite set of integers. In this work, we pursue this line of work by considering the generalized sketching problem, where each hole can be replaced by an arbitrary expression. This way, we broaden the space of program sketches that can be resolved.

Recently, abstract interpretation has been successfully applied to program synthesis [31,36]. The work [31] efficiently synthesizes imperative programs from input-output examples. It combines the enumerative search with static analysis, which is used to identify and ignore partial programs that fail to be a solution. The work [36] uses specifications given as input-output examples and a bitvector abstract domain to synthesize bitvector-manipulating programs without loops. We could replace the Polyhedra domain with the bitvector domain from [36] in our approach in order to scale to bigger programs. However, the abduction solver EXPLAIN currently supports only the linear arithmetic SMT theory (not other theories, such as bitvector). If an abduction solver that supports bitvecotrs becomes available in the future, we can extend our approach to handle bitvector-manipulating programs as well.

Abduction in Program Analysis. Logical abduction has found a number of applications in program analysis. In the context of separation logic for shape analysis, abduction (or bi-abduction) are used for performing modular heap reasoning [4]. An abduction algorithm for first-order SMT theories is described in [8] for computing a maximally simple and general solution. This form of SMT-based abduction has also been applied for loop invariant generation [11], for error explanation and diagnosis of error reports generated by verification tools [10], and for construction of circular compositional program proofs [26].

Abduction in Program Synthesis. The abduction has been used before in program synthesis to infer missing guards from low-level C code such that all buffer accesses are memory safe [12]. However, this is the constraint-based approach that uses Hoare logic-style verification condition (VC) generation with a logical abduction algorithm to solve the generated constraints. To generate verification conditions, the approach computes the strongest postcondition before the missing guard, as well as the weakest precondition that guarantees memory safety after the missing guard. Since this approach uses loop invariants provided by an external tool in the VC generation phase, the quality of the solutions is relative to the used loop invariants. Unlike the prior constraint-based approach to synthesis [12], our method uses exclusively abstract interpretation-based techniques to infer invariant postconditions before the hole and sufficient preconditions after the hole. Hence, no assist from external tools is used. Moreover, our approach can synthesize arbitrary expressions in general C programs, whereas the prior approach [12] can only synthesize boolean guards in `if`-s that ensure memory safety in buffer accessing C programs.

7 Conclusion

In this paper, we present an approach for program synthesis by interaction between abstract interpretation and logical abduction. We introduce a synthesis algorithm that infers arbitrary expressions for unknown holes in program sketches, so that the resulting complete programs satisfy all assertions. We experimentally demonstrate the effectiveness of our approach for generating correct solutions of a variety of C benchmarks.

In the future, we would like to extend our approach for program synthesis by considering program sketches in which apart from expressions, unknown holes can be arbitrary statements as well. We hope further fruitful interplay between abstract interpretation and logical abduction will be possible.

References

1. Albarghouthi, A., Dillig, I., Gurfinkel, A.: Maximal specification synthesis. In: Proceedings of the 43rd Annual ACM SIGPLAN-SIGACT Symposium on Principles of Programming Languages, POPL 2016, pp. 789–801. ACM (2016). https://doi.org/10.1145/2837614.2837628
2. Alur, R., Bodík, R., et al.: Syntax-guided synthesis. In: Formal Methods in Computer-Aided Design, FMCAD 2013, pp. 1–8. IEEE (2013). https://ieeexplore.ieee.org/document/6679385/
3. Bourdoncle, F.: Abstract debugging of higher-order imperative languages. In: Proceedings of the ACM SIGPLAN 1993 Conference on Programming Language Design and Implementation (PLDI), pp. 46–55. ACM (1993). https://doi.org/10.1145/155090.155095
4. Calcagno, C., Distefano, D., O'Hearn, P.W., Yang, H.: Compositional shape analysis by means of bi-abduction. In: Proceedings of the 36th ACM SIGPLAN-SIGACT Symposium on Principles of Programming Languages, POPL 2009, pp. 289–300. ACM (2009). https://doi.org/10.1145/1480881.1480917

5. Cousot, P., Cousot, R.: Abstract interpretation: a unified lattice model for static analysis of programs by construction or approximation of fixpoints. In: Conference Record of the Fourth ACM Symposium on POPL, pp. 238–252. ACM (1977). https://doi.org/10.1145/512950.512973. https://doi.acm.org/10.1145/512950.512973
6. Cousot, P., et al.: The ASTREÉ analyzer. In: Sagiv, M. (ed.) ESOP 2005. LNCS, vol. 3444, pp. 21–30. Springer, Heidelberg (2005). https://doi.org/10.1007/978-3-540-31987-0_3
7. Cousot, P., Halbwachs, N.: Automatic discovery of linear restraints among variables of a program. In: Conference Record of the Fifth Annual ACM Symposium on POPL 1978, pp. 84–96. ACM Press (1978). https://doi.org/10.1145/512760.512770
8. Dillig, I., Dillig, T.: Explain: a tool for performing abductive inference. In: Sharygina, N., Veith, H. (eds.) CAV 2013. LNCS, vol. 8044, pp. 684–689. Springer, Heidelberg (2013). https://doi.org/10.1007/978-3-642-39799-8_46
9. Dillig, I., Dillig, T., Aiken, A.: Cuts from proofs: a complete and practical technique for solving linear inequalities over integers. In: Bouajjani, A., Maler, O. (eds.) CAV 2009. LNCS, vol. 5643, pp. 233–247. Springer, Heidelberg (2009). https://doi.org/10.1007/978-3-642-02658-4_20
10. Dillig, I., Dillig, T., Aiken, A.: Automated error diagnosis using abductive inference. In: ACM SIGPLAN Conference on Programming Language Design and Implementation, PLDI 2012, pp. 181–192. ACM (2012). https://doi.org/10.1145/2254064.2254087
11. Dillig, I., Dillig, T., Li, B., McMillan, K.L.: Inductive invariant generation via abductive inference. In: Proceedings of the 2013 ACM SIGPLAN International Conference on Object Oriented Programming Systems Languages & Applications, OOPSLA 2013, pp. 443–456. ACM (2013). https://doi.org/10.1145/2509136.2509511
12. Dillig, T., Dillig, I., Chaudhuri, S.: Optimal guard synthesis for memory safety. In: Biere, A., Bloem, R. (eds.) CAV 2014. LNCS, vol. 8559, pp. 491–507. Springer, Cham (2014). https://doi.org/10.1007/978-3-319-08867-9_32
13. Dimovski, A.S.: A binary decision diagram lifted domain for analyzing program families. J. Comput. Lang. **63**, 101032 (2021)
14. Dimovski, A.S.: Lifted termination analysis by abstract interpretation and its applications. In: GPCE 2021: Concepts and Experiences, pp. 96–109. ACM (2021). https://doi.org/10.1145/3486609.3487202
15. Dimovski, A.S.: Quantitative program sketching using lifted static analysis. In: FASE 2022. LNCS, vol. 13241, pp. 102–122. Springer, Cham (2022). https://doi.org/10.1007/978-3-030-99429-7_6
16. Dimovski, A.S.: Artifact for the paper "generalized program sketching by abstract interpretation and logical abduction". Zenodo (2023)
17. Dimovski, A.S.: Quantitative program sketching using decision tree-based lifted analysis. J. Comput. Lang. **75**, 101206 (2023)
18. Dimovski, A.S., Apel, S.: Lifted static analysis of dynamic program families by abstract interpretation. In: 35th European Conference on Object-Oriented Programming, ECOOP 2021. LIPIcs, vol. 194, pp. 14:1–14:28. Schloss Dagstuhl - Leibniz-Zentrum für Informatik (2021). https://doi.org/10.4230/LIPIcs.ECOOP.2021.14
19. Dimovski, A.S., Apel, S., Legay, A.: Program sketching using lifted analysis for numerical program families. In: Dutle, A., Moscato, M.M., Titolo, L., Muñoz, C.A., Perez, I. (eds.) NFM 2021. LNCS, vol. 12673, pp. 95–112. Springer, Cham (2021). https://doi.org/10.1007/978-3-030-76384-8_7

20. Dimovski, A.S., Apel, S., Legay, A.: Several lifted abstract domains for static analysis of numerical program families. Sci. Comput. Program. **213**, 102725 (2022)
21. Dimovski, A.S., Legay, A.: Computing program reliability using forward-backward precondition analysis and model counting. In: FASE 2020. LNCS, vol. 12076, pp. 182–202. Springer, Cham (2020). https://doi.org/10.1007/978-3-030-45234-6_9
22. Greitschus, M., et al.: Ultimate taipan: trace abstraction and abstract interpretation. In: Legay, A., Margaria, T. (eds.) TACAS 2017. LNCS, vol. 10206, pp. 399–403. Springer, Heidelberg (2017). https://doi.org/10.1007/978-3-662-54580-5_31
23. Gurfinkel, A., Kahsai, T., Komuravelli, A., Navas, J.A.: The SeaHorn verification framework. In: Kroening, D., Păsăreanu, C.S. (eds.) CAV 2015. LNCS, vol. 9206, pp. 343–361. Springer, Cham (2015). https://doi.org/10.1007/978-3-319-21690-4_20
24. Henry, J., Monniaux, D., Moy, M.: PAGAI: a path sensitive static analyser. Electron. Notes Theor. Comput. Sci. **289**, 15–25 (2012)
25. Jeannet, B., Miné, A.: APRON: a library of numerical abstract domains for static analysis. In: Bouajjani, A., Maler, O. (eds.) CAV 2009. LNCS, vol. 5643, pp. 661–667. Springer, Heidelberg (2009). https://doi.org/10.1007/978-3-642-02658-4_52
26. Li, B., Dillig, I., Dillig, T., McMillan, K., Sagiv, M.: Synthesis of circular compositional program proofs via abduction. In: Piterman, N., Smolka, S.A. (eds.) TACAS 2013. LNCS, vol. 7795, pp. 370–384. Springer, Heidelberg (2013). https://doi.org/10.1007/978-3-642-36742-7_26
27. Miné, A.: The octagon abstract domain. High.-Order Symb. Comput. **19**(1), 31–100 (2006)
28. Miné, A.: Backward under-approximations in numeric abstract domains to automatically infer sufficient program conditions. Sci. Comput. Program. **93**, 154–182 (2014)
29. Miné, A.: Tutorial on static inference of numeric invariants by abstract interpretation. Found. Trends Program. Lang. **4**(3–4), 120–372 (2017)
30. Rival, X.: Understanding the origin of alarms in Astrée. In: Hankin, C., Siveroni, I. (eds.) SAS 2005. LNCS, vol. 3672, pp. 303–319. Springer, Heidelberg (2005). https://doi.org/10.1007/11547662_21
31. So, S., Oh, H.: Synthesizing imperative programs from examples guided by static analysis. In: Ranzato, F. (ed.) SAS 2017. LNCS, vol. 10422, pp. 364–381. Springer, Cham (2017). https://doi.org/10.1007/978-3-319-66706-5_18
32. Solar-Lezama, A.: Program sketching. STTT **15**(5–6), 475–495 (2013)
33. Solar-Lezama, A., Rabbah, R.M., Bodík, R., Ebcioglu, K.: Programming by sketching for bit-streaming programs. In: Proceedings of the ACM SIGPLAN 2005 Conference on Programming Language Design and Implementation, pp. 281–294. ACM (2005). https://doi.org/10.1145/1065010.1065045
34. Urban, C., Miné, A.: A decision tree abstract domain for proving conditional termination. In: Müller-Olm, M., Seidl, H. (eds.) SAS 2014. LNCS, vol. 8723, pp. 302–318. Springer, Cham (2014). https://doi.org/10.1007/978-3-319-10936-7_19
35. Yin, B., Chen, L., Liu, J., Wang, J., Cousot, P.: Verifying numerical programs via iterative abstract testing. In: Chang, B.-Y.E. (ed.) SAS 2019. LNCS, vol. 11822, pp. 247–267. Springer, Cham (2019). https://doi.org/10.1007/978-3-030-32304-2_13
36. Yoon, Y., Lee, W., Yi, K.: Inductive program synthesis via iterative forward-backward abstract interpretation. In: PLDI 2023: 44th ACM SIGPLAN International Conference on Programming Language Design and Implementation, pp. 1657–1681. ACM (2023). https://doi.org/10.1145/3591288

Mutual Refinements of Context-Free Language Reachability

Shuo Ding(✉) and Qirun Zhang

Georgia Institute of Technology, Atlanta, GA 30332, USA
{sding,qrzhang}@gatech.edu

Abstract. Context-free language reachability is an important program analysis framework, but the exact analysis problems can be intractable or undecidable, where CFL-reachability approximates such problems. For the same problem, there could be many over-approximations based on different CFLs $C_1, \ldots, C_n$. Suppose the reachability result of each C_i produces a set P_i of reachable vertex pairs. Is it possible to achieve better precision than the straightforward intersection $\bigcap_{i=1}^{n} P_i$?

This paper gives an affirmative answer: although CFLs are not closed under intersections, in CFL-reachability we can "intersect" graphs. Specifically, we propose *mutual refinement* to combine different CFL-reachability-based over-approximations. Our key insight is that the standard CFL-reachability algorithm can be slightly modified to trace the edges that contribute to the reachability results of C_1, and C_2-reachability only need to consider contributing edges of C_1, which can, in turn, trace the edges that contribute to C_2-reachability, etc. We prove that there exists a unique optimal refinement result (fix-point). Experimental results show that mutual refinement can achieve better precision than the straightforward intersection with reasonable extra cost.

1 Introduction

Context-free language reachability (CFL-reachability) is arguably the best-known graph reachability framework in program analysis [15,19,22,23,26,30]. Typically, the framework consists of a frontend and a backend, where the frontend constructs a graph from the source code, and the backend runs CFL-reachability on the graph to obtain properties of the source code [25]. The graphs and grammars depend on specific analyses, but CFL-reachability has a dynamic programming style (sub)cubic-time algorithm [2,20,25,35] for arbitrary graphs and grammars. Faster algorithms exist on special cases [1,17,36].

M. V. Hermenegildo and J. F. Morales (Eds.): SAS 2023, LNCS 14284, pp. 231–258, 2023.
https://doi.org/10.1007/978-3-031-44245-2_12

However, due to the inherent hardness of program analysis, CFL-reachability may not be able to model the exact formulation of the problem [24,37]. A typical example is the interleaved-Dyck-reachability formulation [18,24], which is widely used to simultaneously model function calls/returns [24,26], field reads/writes [29,34], locks/unlocks [11], etc. The interleaved-Dyck language is not context-free [9], and the corresponding graph reachability problem is undecidable [24]. In practice, CFL-reachability can over-approximate computationally hard language reachability problems [24]: the idea is to design a context-free language C that over-approximates the non-context-free language L (meaning that C contains more strings than L).

For a computationally hard L-reachability problem, different CFL-reachability-based approaches over-approximate the solution from different angles. We can straightforwardly intersect the results to achieve better precision. Synchronized pushdown systems [27] essentially employ this idea. The linear conjunctive language reachability work [37] also shows this straightforward intersection can improve precision. However, in this case, different CFL-reachability instances are executed independently. On the other hand, CFLs are not closed under intersection [8,9], so in general, we cannot intersect different CFLs to obtain a new CFL for CFL-reachability. For example, the interleaved-Dyck language [18,37], which is not a CFL, is the intersection of two or more CFLs.

This paper proposes a more synergistic way to "intersect" multiple CFL-reachability-based over-approximations. Specifically, typical CFL-reachability algorithms are of dynamic programming style, which generate "summary edges" from existing graph edges. Our key insight is that when those algorithms generate a summary edge, the existing edges directly contributing to the generation can be recorded. This augmented algorithm can eventually trace a set of original graph edges that contribute to the final reachability results. Therefore, when combining CFL-reachability-based over-approximations based on CFLs $C_1, C_2, \ldots, C_n$, we can run C_2-reachability on the contributing edges of C_1-reachability, as opposed to all edges in the original graph. This process can happen between different C_i's multiple times, which is called *mutual refinement*.

Is the execution order of different CFL-reachability over-approximations important for mutual refinement? We prove in Sect. 4 that given a set of CFL-reachability over-approximations, there exists a unique fix-point, and any order of executing different CFL-reachabilities will reach the fix-point. This is similar to the fix-point theorem [14] and chaotic-iteration algorithms [4,12] in dataflow analysis. The soundness of the fix-point and the fact that it is at least as precise as the straightforward intersection are also proved in Sect. 4. As for the complexity, suppose the CFL is fixed and the number of vertices in the graph is n, then the time complexities of the standard CFL-reachability algorithm [20,25,35] and our augmented algorithm are both $\tilde{O}(n^3)$, and the space complexity is $\tilde{O}(n^2)$ for the standard algorithm and is $\tilde{O}(n^3)$ for our augmented algorithm.

We conduct experiments on two applications: a taint analysis for Java programs obtained from Android apps [10], and a value-flow analysis for LLVM

IR programs obtained from the SPEC CPU 2017 benchmark [28]. On average, compared with the straightforward intersection, mutual refinement achieves a 50.95% precision improvement (measured by the number of reachable pairs) with a 2.65× time increase and a 3.23× space increase on the taint analysis benchmarks, and achieves a 9.37% precision improvement with a 2.55× time increase and a 2.22× space increase on the value-flow analysis benchmarks.

The fast graph simplification algorithm [18] proposed by Li, Zhang, and Reps (abbreviated as the LZR algorithm) also simplify graphs, but the LZR algorithm only works for interleaved-Dyck-reachability while mutual refinement works for any L-reachability preserving CFL-reachability-based over-approximations, and the LZR algorithm is a pre-processing algorithm while mutual refinement is a complete solver. Our taint analysis experiment is interleaved-Dyck reachability, and thus we also evaluate mutual refinement on those graphs simplified by the LZR algorithm: LZR preprocessing can, on average, bring a further precision improvement of 3.27% and reduces the time/space consumption in certain cases. The value-flow analysis experiment is not interleaved-Dyck reachability, so the LZR algorithm is not applicable.

In summary, this paper makes the following main contributions.

- We propose mutual refinement for combining different CFL-reachability over-approximations for hard formal language reachability problems, which can achieve better precision than the straightforward intersection.
- We prove the existence and uniqueness of the fix-point, the soundness, the precision guarantee (being at least as precise as the straightforward intersection), and time/space complexities for mutual refinement.
- We evaluate mutual refinement on two program analysis applications. Experimental results show that mutual refinement can achieve better precision than the straightforward intersection with reasonable extra cost.

This paper is organized as follows. Section 2 gives a motivating example. Section 3 reviews backgrounds and definitions. Section 4 presents mutual refinement and its properties. Section 5 gives experimental results. Section 6 presents discussions. Section 7 surveys related work, and Sect. 8 concludes.

2 Motivating Example

This section motivates mutual refinement using an example of context-sensitive and field-sensitive taint analysis for C++. The analysis first generates a graph from the source code being analyzed, then the source-sink relation from the source code is reduced to the reachability of two vertices in the graph. This is an extended version of the taint analysis mentioned in the work of Huang *et al* [10]. The original analysis is based on interleaved-Dyck reachability, but our motivating example is not. We compare mutual refinement with the straightforward intersection of two different CFL-reachability-based over-approximations.

Example Code. Figure 1 shows a C++ code snippet. The analysis goal is to decide whether the value of the variable s could flow into the variable t. Because

```
#include ...

class Pair {
    int first, second;
    Pair(int fi, int se) : first(fi), second(se) {}
}

int getFirst(Pair p1) {
    return p1.first; // represented by ret1
}

int getSecond(Pair p2) {
    return p2.second; // represented by ret2
}

int main() {
    int s = getSecret();
    Pair a(0, s);
    Pair b(0, 0);
    Pair t(0, 0);
    if (getInput() == "first") {
        int x = getFirst(a);
        t.first = x;
    } else {
        send(getSecond(a));
        int y = getSecond(b);
        t.second = y;
    }
    ...
}
```

Fig. 1. A taint analysis example for C++. The goal is to decide whether the value s can flow into t. The fact is that the value of s cannot flow into t.

t can only contain the first field of a or the second field of b, the answer is that the value of s cannot flow into t.

Graph Reachability Formulation. We use vertices to represent variables and use edges to represent values flowing among variables (Fig. 2). To achieve context-sensitivity and field-sensitivity, we use parenthesis-labeled edges for function calls/returns, and use bracket-labeled edges for field writes/reads.

The taint analysis decides whether the value of s can flow into t (including t's fields). The answer is "yes" if and only if there is a path whose edge labels can be concatenated to a string that represents the interleaving of matched parentheses, matched brackets, and unmatched open brackets. Formally, given an alphabet Σ, we define the interleaving operator [18] $\odot : \Sigma^* \times \Sigma^* \to \mathcal{P}(\Sigma^*)$ as follows, where s, s_1, s_2 are strings and c_1, c_2 are single characters.

$$\begin{aligned}
\epsilon \odot s &= \{s\} \\
s \odot \epsilon &= \{s\} \\
c_1 s_1 \odot c_2 s_2 &= \{c_1 w \mid w \in (s_1 \odot c_2 s_2)\} \cup \{c_2 w \mid w \in (c_1 s_1 \odot s_2)\}.
\end{aligned}$$

For the taint analysis, we are interested in L_T-reachability problem, where $L_T = \bigcup\{s_1 \odot s_2 \mid s_1 \in P, s_2 \in B\}$ and CFLs P and B are defined as follows. Note that we use P or B to denote both the languages and the starting symbols in the

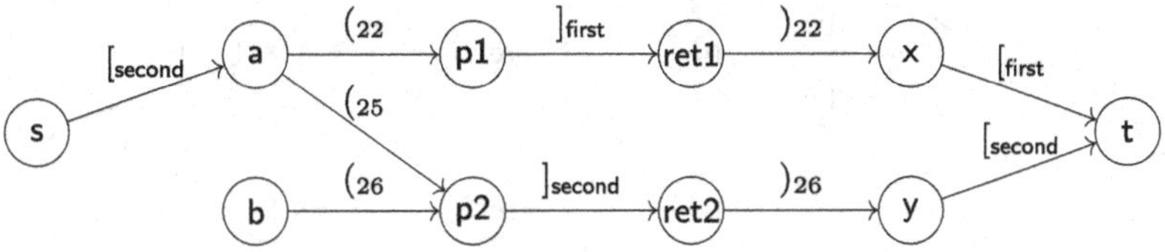

Fig. 2. The taint analysis graph for Fig. 1. Vertices are variables and edges model values flowing among variables: $i \xrightarrow{(_c} j$ represents that i flows into j via the function call at line c; $i \xrightarrow{)_c} j$ represents that i flows into j via the function return at line c; $i \xrightarrow{[_f} j$ represents that i flows into the f field of j; $i \xrightarrow{]_f} j$ represents that the f field of i flows into j.

grammars. L_T is not context-free (which is proved in Sect. 6). We also extend the definition of the interleaving operator $\odot$ to languages, and thus we write $L_T = P \odot B$.

$$P \rightarrow P\,P \mid (_1\,P\,)_1 \mid \ldots \mid (_m\,P\,)_m \mid \epsilon$$

$$B \rightarrow D\,B \mid [_1\,B \mid \ldots \mid [_n\,B \mid \epsilon.$$
$$D \rightarrow D\,D \mid [_1\,D\,]_1 \mid \ldots \mid [_n\,D\,]_n \mid \epsilon.$$

In Fig. 2, there are only two possible paths from s to t. None of these paths satisfy our requirement, so the value of s cannot flow into t.

CFL-Reachability-Based Over-Approximations. We devise two CFLs C_P and C_B to over-approximate L_T. C_P considers only parentheses and treats brackets as empty symbols. C_B considers only brackets and treats parentheses as empty symbols. Both algorithms can be implemented using the well-known CFL-reachability algorithm [20,25,35]. In Fig. 2, both C_P-reachability and C_B-reachability conclude that t is reachable from s. For example, for C_P, t is reachable from s via the path $\mathsf{s} \xrightarrow{[_{\mathsf{second}}} \mathsf{a} \xrightarrow{(_{22}} \mathsf{p1} \xrightarrow{]_{\mathsf{first}}} \mathsf{ret1} \xrightarrow{)_{22}} \mathsf{x} \xrightarrow{[_{\mathsf{first}}} \mathsf{t}$, and for C_B, t is reachable from s via the path $\mathsf{s} \xrightarrow{[_{\mathsf{second}}} \mathsf{a} \xrightarrow{(_{25}} \mathsf{p2} \xrightarrow{]_{\mathsf{second}}} \mathsf{ret2} \xrightarrow{)_{26}} \mathsf{y} \xrightarrow{[_{\mathsf{second}}} \mathsf{t}$. These two conclusions are both false positives.

Straightforward Intersection. One possible method to combine the above two over-approximations is to directly intersect their results, as synchronized pushdown system [27] and linear conjunctive language reachability [37] did. In Fig. 2, however, this method still concludes that t is reachable from s, because the two algorithms both conclude that they are reachable.

Mutual Refinement. To further improve the precision, we first run C_B-reachability, which concludes that t is reachable from s, and the edges contributing to all reachable pairs can be shown in Fig. 3 (parentheses are treated as empty symbols so edges labeled with parentheses are preserved). Now the graph has been simplified. Running C_P-reachability on the graph in Fig. 3 concludes that t is not reachable from s. Thus C_B-reachability "refines" the subsequent

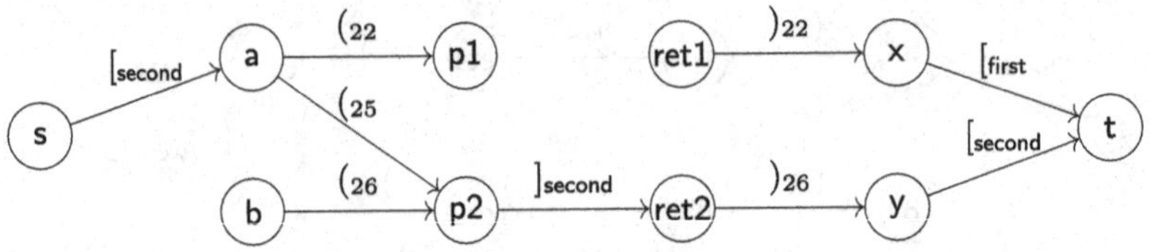

Fig. 3. After running C_B-reachability and tracing only the edges contributing to its results, the graph is simplified. Subsequent execution of C_P-reachability can then conclude that t is not reachable from s.

execution of C_P-reachability. This example shows that mutual refinement can achieve better precision compared with the straightforward intersection.

3 Preliminary

We define L-reachability in Sect. 3.1 and review the standard dynamic programming style algorithm for CFL-reachability in Sect. 3.2. CFL-reachability is used to over-approximate other L-reachability problems in practice.

3.1 L-Reachability

The L-reachability problem is to find pairs (s, t) of vertices such that there exists a path from s to t, and the edge labels along that path form a string in L.

Definition 1 (L-Reachability). *Given a formal language L with a finite alphabet Σ and a finite graph $G = (V, E)$, where each edge $e \in E$ is labeled with a character in Σ, vertex $t \in V$ is L-reachable from vertex $s \in V$ if and only if there exists a finite path (with possibly duplicate vertices and edges) $p = s \xrightarrow{l_1} v_1 \xrightarrow{l_2} \ldots \xrightarrow{l_{n-1}} v_{n-1} \xrightarrow{l_n} t$ in the graph such that the string $l_1 l_2 \ldots l_n$ is in the given formal language. $R(p) = l_1 l_2 \ldots l_n$ is the path string of p. The zero-length path from a vertex to itself forms the empty string. (s, t) is an L-reachable pair. The L-reachability problem is to find the set of all L-reachable pairs.*

Fix a formal language L. Any graph $G = (V, E)$ whose edges are labeled with characters in the alphabet of L essentially gives an instance of the L-reachability problem. We denote this instance as $\langle L, (V, E) \rangle$. There also exist other variants of L-reachability, such as the single-pair reachability, which only cares about the reachability between a specific pair of vertices. In this paper, we focus on all-pairs reachability unless otherwise noted.

3.2 CFL-Reachability

In L-reachability, when the formal language L is a context-free language, the problem is a CFL-reachability problem. CFL-reachability exhibits a popular dynamic programming style cubic-time algorithm [20,25,35], which is shown in

Algorithm 1. The CFL-Reachability Algorithm

```
1: function CFL-REACHABILITY(⟨C, (V, E)⟩)
2:     W ← emptyWorkList()
3:     W.addAll(E)
4:     for X → ϵ ∈ C do
5:         for v ∈ V do
6:             if X⟨v, v⟩ ∉ E then
7:                 add X⟨v, v⟩ to E and W
8:     while W.nonEmpty() do
9:         Y⟨i, j⟩ ← W.pop()
10:        for X → Y ∈ C do
11:            if X⟨i, j⟩ ∉ E then
12:                add X⟨i, j⟩ to E and W
13:        for X → YZ ∈ C do
14:            for Z⟨j, k⟩ ∈ E do
15:                if X⟨i, k⟩ ∉ E then
16:                    add X⟨i, k⟩ to E and W
17:        for X → ZY ∈ C do
18:            for Z⟨k, i⟩ ∈ E do
19:                if X⟨k, j⟩ ∉ E then
20:                    add X⟨k, j⟩ to E and W
21:    return (V, E)
```

Algorithm 1. Given an instance $\langle C, (V, E)\rangle$ of (all-pairs) CFL-reachability problem, we call CFL-REACHABILITY($\langle C, (V, E)\rangle$) in Algorithm 1 to compute the results. The CFL $C = (\Sigma, N, P, S)$ contains the set of terminal symbols Σ, the set of non-terminal symbols N, the set of productions P, and the start symbol S. All productions are in the forms $X \rightarrow YZ$, $X \rightarrow Y$, and $X \rightarrow \epsilon$, where X, Y, and Z are terminal symbols or non-terminal symbols. Any context-free grammar can be transformed into this form [9]. Algorithm 1 works as follows.

1. Initially, all edges in the original graph are added to the worklist (line 3).
2. Then the productions with empty right-hand sides are applied where new edges are added to both the graph and the worklist (lines 4-7).
3. After that, the algorithm removes an edge $Y\langle i, j\rangle$ (connecting vertices i, j with label Y) from the worklist, trying all productions with Y on the right-hand side, adding newly generated edges to both the graph and the worklist, and repeating this process until the worklist becomes empty (lines 8-20).
4. Finally, the updated graph is returned as the result (line 21).

Algorithm 1 shows the process of generating new edges in the graph according to productions, which we call *production applications*. For example, if there is a production $X \rightarrow YZ$ and there are edges $Y\langle i, j\rangle$ and $Z\langle j, k\rangle$ already in the graph, we add a new edge $X\langle i, k\rangle$ to the graph via a production application. Note that when we pop an edge e out from the worklist and process it (lines 8-20), depending on the previously processed edges, some of e's adjacent edges might not be available in the graph yet, thus the current iteration of lines 8–20 may not add all edges that can be generated from e via production applications. However, it is well-known that eventually, all possible edges will be added, and the order of popping out edges from the worklist does not matter.

Theorem 1 (Algorithm 1's Correctness). *When Algorithm 1 terminates, all edges that can be generated by production applications will be in the graph.*

Proof. We prove it by contradiction. Suppose there is an edge e_n, which could be generated by a finite number of production applications, and which is not in the graph produced by Algorithm 1. It is obvious that e_n cannot be in the original edge set. So e_n could be obtained by finitely and positively many production applications. We can denote this process by a sequence $e_1, e_2, \ldots, e_n$, where for all $i \in \{1, 2, \ldots, n\}$, e_i is either in the original graph's edge set or is obtained by applying a production on a set of edges $\{e_{i_1}, e_{i_2}, \ldots, e_{i_{n_i}}\} \subseteq \{e_1, e_2, \ldots, e_{i-1}\}$. Suppose e_j is the first edge in $e_1, e_2, \ldots, e_n$ that is not in the graph produced by Algorithm 1. There must exist such an e_j because according to our assumption, at least e_n is not in the graph produced by Algorithm 1. Again, e_j cannot be in the original edge set. Suppose e_j can be obtained by applying a production on a set of edges $\{e_{j_1}, e_{j_2}, \ldots, e_{j_{n_j}}\} \subseteq \{e_1, e_2, \ldots, e_{j-1}\}$. Since all edges in $\{e_{j_1}, e_{j_2}, \ldots, e_{j_{n_j}}\}$ are in the graph produced by Algorithm 1, when the last edge was popped out, since all productions were tried, Algorithm 1 must add e_j to the graph since all edges in $\{e_{j_1}, e_{j_2}, \ldots, e_{j_{n_j}}\}$ were available in the graph at that time. This is a contradiction.

We briefly explain our notations for time/space complexity. To make the analysis rigorous, we should also consider the time/space complexity of handling numbers. For example, if there are n vertices in the graph and we use $0, 1, \ldots, n-1$ to represent the vertices, then the number $n-1$ itself requires memory of $O(\log n)$, and arithmetic operations on those numbers are not of constant complexity. To focus on dominating factors, instead of using the big-O notation, we use the $\tilde{O}$ notation [3] to hide logarithm factors: $\tilde{O}(f(n))$ represents $O(f(n)(\log n)^k)$ for some constant natural number k.

Complexity Analysis for Algorithm 1. Suppose the grammar of the CFL is fixed, adding one edge to the graph takes constant time, accessing each graph vertex's adjacent vertices takes linear time, and pushing/popping elements to/from the worklist takes constant time. There could be at most $\tilde{O}(|V|^2)$ edges popped out from the worklist at line 9, and for each edge popped out, there could be at most $\tilde{O}(|V|)$ adjacent edges to try in the main **while** loop. Thus the time complexity is $\tilde{O}(|V|^3)$. The space complexity is $\tilde{O}(|V|^2)$ since there could be at most $\tilde{O}(|V|^2)$ edges in the graph and in the worklist.

4 Mutual Refinement

This section formalizes mutual refinement. Specifically, Sect. 4.1 gives an overview; Sect. 4.2 presents the important definition of *contributing edges*;

C-Contributing Edges: $\mathsf{Ctri}(C, (V, E))$

↓ over-approximates

L-Contributing Edges: $\mathsf{Ctri}(L, (V, E))$

Fig. 4. Two important concepts in mutual refinement. L is a formal language whose reachability problem is computationally hard, and C is a context-free language over-approximating L. The set of C-contributing edges $\mathsf{Ctri}(C, (V, E))$ over-approximates the set of L-contributing edges $\mathsf{Ctri}(L, (V, E))$.

Sect. 4.3 presents the algorithm used as individual steps in mutual refinements; Sect. 4.4 presents the complete mutual refinement algorithm.

4.1 Overview

Suppose we have a set of CFL-reachability-based over-approximations using CFLs $C_1, C_2, \ldots, C_m$ for a computationally hard L-reachability problem. For an instance $\langle L, (V, E)\rangle$ of the problem, we first run C_1-reachability. Then we only keep edges that directly or indirectly participated in the construction of S_1 (the start symbol of C_1's grammar) edges. Then we run C_2-reachability and only keep edges participated in the construction of S_2 edges. This process continues until we reach the fix-point: no more edges can be removed. The final reachability result is obtained by executing C_1, C_2, ..., C_m-reachability on the minimum graph and taking the intersection.

4.2 Contributing Edges

The key step of mutual refinement is to over-approximate the set of "useful" edges, *i.e.*, the edges contributing to reachable pairs. This is achieved via formal language over-approximations.

Definition 2 (Formal Language Over-Approximation). *Given two formal languages L_1 and L_2, L_1 over-approximates L_2 if and only if $L_1 \supseteq L_2$.*

Definition 3 (L-Contributing Edges). *For a specific formal language L, given an instance $\langle L, (V, E)\rangle$ of the L-reachability problem, an edge $e \in E$ is an L-contributing edge for this instance if and only if there exists a pair of vertices $u, v \in V$, such that e is part of a finite path p connecting u and v and $R(p) \in L$. The set of such L-contributing edges is denoted as* $\mathsf{Ctri}(L, (V, E))$.

In certain undecidable L-reachability problems (*e.g.*, the interleaved-Dyck-reachability), it can be shown that computing the set $\mathsf{Ctri}(L, (V, E))$ is also undecidable in general [18]. So we need to approximate this set. Suppose we have a context-free language C over-approximating L, then it is straightforward to see that $\mathsf{Ctri}(L, (V, E)) \subseteq \mathsf{Ctri}(C, (V, E))$, because every L-path is also a C-path. Figure 4 summarizes the situation.

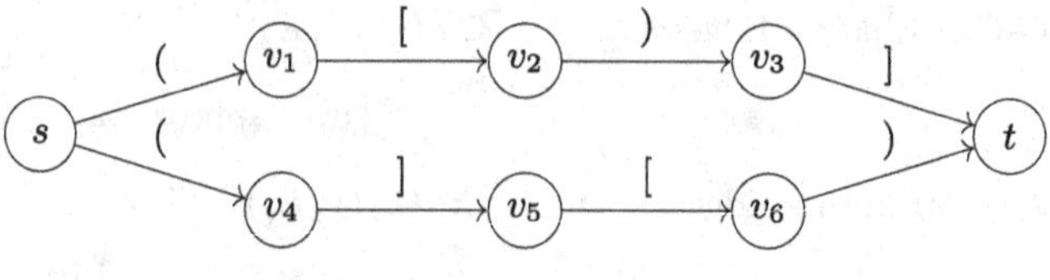

Fig. 5. A Graph illustrating contributing edges.

Example 1 (Contributing Edges). Consider the following example of interleaved-Dyck-reachability, where each string in the interleaved-Dyck language L is an interleaving of two strings from the following two CFLs, respectively.

$$P \rightarrow P\,P \mid (\,P\,) \mid \epsilon$$
$$B \rightarrow B\,B \mid [\,B\,] \mid \epsilon.$$

We use the following context-free language C, which only considers matched parentheses and treats brackets as empty symbols, to over-approximate the interleaved-Dyck language L.

$$C \rightarrow C\,C \mid (\,C\,) \mid [\mid] \mid \epsilon.$$

In the instance of interleaved-Dyck-reachability shown in Fig. 5, the set of L-contributing edges is $\{s \xrightarrow{(} v_1, v_1 \xrightarrow{[} v_2, v_2 \xrightarrow{)} v_3, v_3 \xrightarrow{]} t\}$, while the set of C-contributing edges includes all edges in the original graph.

4.3 Tracing Algorithm

The set of CFL-contributing edges is computable via augmenting the standard CFL-reachability algorithm to trace the edges, which results in Algorithm 2. Given an instance $\langle C, (V, E)\rangle$ of a CFL-reachability problem, we first make the function call RECORD($\langle C, (V, E)\rangle$) to run the CFL-reachability algorithm and record the meta-information "metaInfo", where "metaInfo[e]" contains all edges that directly contributed to the construction of e. Notice that RECORD is almost the same as the standard CFL-reachability algorithm (Algorithm 1), except that we add the highlighted lines to record the meta-information. Then the original graph's C-contributing edges could be obtained by calling COLLECT(metaInfo, E), which recursively collects the contributing edges.[1]

The following theorem demonstrates the correctness of Algorithm 2.

Theorem 2 (Tracing Algorithm's Correctness). *For any instance of CFL-reachability $\langle C, (V, E)\rangle$, we have*

$$\text{COLLECT}(\text{RECORD}(\langle C, (V, E)\rangle)) = \mathsf{Ctri}(C, (V, E)).$$

[1] COLLECT can be implemented using either breadth-first-search or depth-first-search.

Algorithm 2. The Tracing Algorithm

1: **function** RECORD($\langle C, (V, E) \rangle$)
2:     metaInfo $\leftarrow$ emptyMap()
3:     $W \leftarrow$ emptyWorkList()
4:     W.addAll(E)
5:     **for** $X \to \epsilon \in$ CFG **do**
6:         **for** $v \in V$ **do**
7:             **if** $X\langle v, v \rangle \notin E$ **then**
8:                 add $X\langle v, v \rangle$ to E and W
9:     **while** W.nonEmpty() **do**
10:        $Y\langle i, j \rangle \leftarrow W$.pop()
11:        **for** $X \to Y \in$ CFG **do**
12:            metaInfo[$X\langle i, j \rangle$].add($Y\langle i, j \rangle$)
13:            **if** $X\langle i, j \rangle \notin E$ **then**
14:                add $X\langle i, j \rangle$ to E and W
15:        **for** $X \to YZ \in$ CFG **do**
16:            **for** $Z\langle j, k \rangle \in E$ **do**
17:                metaInfo[$X\langle i, k \rangle$].add($Y\langle i, j \rangle, Z\langle j, k \rangle$)
18:                **if** $X\langle i, k \rangle \notin E$ **then**
19:                    add $X\langle i, k \rangle$ to E and W
20:        **for** $X \to ZY \in$ CFG **do**
21:            **for** $Z\langle k, i \rangle \in E$ **do**
22:                metaInfo[$X\langle k, j \rangle$].add($Z\langle k, i \rangle, Y\langle i, j \rangle$)
23:                **if** $X\langle k, j \rangle \notin E$ **then**
24:                    add $X\langle k, j \rangle$ to E and W
25:    **return** $((V, E), \text{metaInfo})$

26:
27: **function** COLLECT$(((V, E), \text{metaInfo}))$
28:    visited $\leftarrow \emptyset$
29:    con $\leftarrow \emptyset$
30:    **function** COLLECTDFS(e)
31:        **if** $e \notin$ visited **then**
32:            visited.add(e)
33:            **if** e's label is a terminal symbol **then**
34:                con.add(e)
35:            **for** $e' \in$ metaInfo[e] **do**
36:                COLLECTDFS(e')
37:    **for** $e \in E$ **do**
38:        **if** e's label is the start symbol **then**
39:            COLLECTDFS(e)
40:    **return** con

Proof. Suppose $e \in$ COLLECT(RECORD($\langle C, (V, E) \rangle$)). According to Algorithm 2, we have $e \in E$, and there exists a finite sequence of edges $e_1 = e, e_2, \ldots, e_n$ (we can move e to the beginning), where each edge is either from the original edge set or obtained from applying one production in C to some preceding edges, e directly or indirectly contributes to e_n, and e_n's label is C's start symbol. So $e \in \mathsf{Ctri}(C, (V, E))$. Conversely, suppose $e \in \mathsf{Ctri}(C, (V, E))$, then $e \in E$ and there exists a finite sequence of edges $e_1 = e, e_2, \ldots, e_n$, where each edge is either from the original edge set or obtained by applying one production in C to some preceding edges, e directly or indirectly contributes to e_n, and e_n's label is C's start symbol. According to Theorem 1, every edge in this sequence must be added to the edge set by Algorithm 1 (and thus also by Algorithm 2). Now let us consider e_n. It is not in the original edge set because its symbol is a non-terminal symbol. Thus e_n can only be obtained by applying one production on some previous edges $\{e_{i_1}, e_{i_2}, \ldots, e_{i_{n_i}}\}$ (which are called the dependency edges of e_n). Since all dependency edges of e_n were added by the algorithm, one edge must be the last one added, and when that one was added, all of e_n's dependency edges were added to the meta-information of e_n (*i.e.*, $\mathsf{metaInfo}(e_n)$). Thus the COLLECTDFS procedure can visit all dependency edges of e_n. Such dependency edges can be reasoned similarly in a depth-first-search manner, and because e_1 directly or indirectly contributes to e_n, eventually COLLECTDFS visits the edge $e_1 = e$. So $e \in \text{COLLECT}(\text{RECORD}(\langle C, (V, E)\rangle))$.

Complexity Analysis for Algorithm 2. For RECORD, suppose the grammar of the CFL is fixed, the graph supports constant time edge addition and linear time adjacent vertices traversal, the worklist supports constant time pushing/popping, and the operations on metaInfo and the edge set corresponding to each key have logarithmic time complexity and linear space complexity with respect to the number of elements. There could be at most $\tilde{O}(|V|^2)$ edges popped out from the worklist at line 10, and for each edge popped out, there could be at most $\tilde{O}(|V|)$ adjacent edges to try in the main **while** loop. The size of metaInfo is bounded by $\tilde{O}(|V|^2)$ and the size of the edge set corresponding to each key is bounded by $\tilde{O}(|V|)$, so each addition operation to metaInfo has a complexity of $\tilde{O}(\log(|V|^2) + \log|V|) = \tilde{O}(\log|V|)$, which can be hidden by our $\tilde{O}$ notation. Thus the time complexity of RECORD is $\tilde{O}(|V|^3)$. The space complexity of RECORD is $\tilde{O}(|V|^3)$ since metaInfo dominates the space complexity and there could be at most $\tilde{O}(|V|^3)$ edge additions to metaInfo. For COLLECT, suppose visited and con also supports logarithm time operations. Consider a new graph where vertices are edges in E, and if $e_2 \in \mathsf{metaInfo}[e_1]$ then we have a "super edge" from e_1 to e_2. It is easy to see that in this new graph, there are at most $\tilde{O}(|V|^2)$ vertices, and the in-degree and out-degree of each vertex are both bounded by $\tilde{O}(|V|)$. Then COLLECT essentially did a depth-first search on this new graph, whose time complexity is determined by the maximum number of "super edges" in this new graph: $\tilde{O}(|V|^2 \times |V| \times c \cdot \log|V|) = \tilde{O}(|V|^3)$. The logarithm factor is due to operations on visited, metaInfo, and con, but is hidden by our notation $\tilde{O}$. The space complexity is bounded by the sizes of the graph ($\tilde{O}(|V|^2)$), visited ($\tilde{O}(|V|^2)$), con ($\tilde{O}(|V|^2)$), metaInfo ($\tilde{O}(|V|^3)$), and the maximum depth of recursive calls ($\tilde{O}(|V|^2)$). Therefore, the space complexity of COLLECT is $\tilde{O}(|V|^3)$.

Table 1. Time/space complexities of Algorithm 1 and Algorithm 2. The CFL size is assumed to be a constant, and the input graph is $G = (V, E)$.

Algorithm	Time Complexity	Space Complexity
Algorithm 1 (The Standard Algorithm)	$\tilde{O}(\|V\|^3)$	$\tilde{O}(\|V\|^2)$
Algorithm 2 (Our Tracing Algorithm)	$\tilde{O}(\|V\|^3)$	$\tilde{O}(\|V\|^3)$

Table 1 compares the time/space complexities of the standard CFL-reachability algorithm (Algorithm 1) and our tracing version (Algorithm 2). In practice, however, the running time and space also depend on the constant and logarithm factors, the computer architecture, etc.

4.4 Mutual Refinement Algorithm

This section precisely defines the mutual refinement algorithm for a computationally hard L-reachability problem with multiple CFL approximations.

Definition 4 (Refinement Sequence). *Given an instance $\langle L, (V, E)\rangle$ of L-reachability problem and m different CFLs $C_1, \ldots, C_m$ ($m \geq 2$), each of which over-approximates L, a refinement sequence is a finite sequence of sets of edges $E_1, \ldots, E_n$, such that $E_1 = E$ and for all $i \geq 2$, E_i is either $\mathsf{Ctri}(C_j, (V, E_k))$ where $j \in \{1, 2, \ldots, m\}$ and $k \in \{1, 2, \ldots, i-1\}$, or $E_j \cap E_k$ where $j, k \in \{1, 2, \ldots, i-1\}$.*

There exists a global minimum edge set (with respect to the set inclusion relation) that can be computed via a fix-point algorithm. This is due to the following monotonicity property of contributing edges.

Lemma 1 (Monotonicity of Contributing Edges). *Given a formal language L, the following formula holds for all problem instances.*

$$E_1 \subseteq E_2 \implies \mathsf{Ctri}(L, (V, E_1)) \subseteq \mathsf{Ctri}(L, (V, E_2))$$

Proof. This is because any L-path in E_1 is also an L-path in E_2.

Theorem 3 (Minimum Edge Set). *Given an instance $\langle L, (V, E)\rangle$ of the L-reachability problem and m different CFLs $C_1, C_2, \ldots, C_m$ ($m \geq 2$), each of which over-approximates L, there exists an edge set $E_{\min}$, which could be obtained by a specific refinement sequence, and which is a subset of all edge sets in all refinement sequences.*

Proof. Consider the process of applying m algorithms successively in an arbitrary order to refine the edge sets: apply C_{i_1}-reachability on E to get E_1, apply C_{i_2}-reachability on E_1 to get E_2, ..., apply C_{i_m}-reachability on E_{m-1} to get E_m, where $C_{i_1}, C_{i_2}, \ldots, C_{i_m}$ is an arbitrary permutation of $C_1, C_2, \ldots, C_m$. For simplicity, we still denote this order as $C_1, C_2, \ldots, C_m$. This is called one round.

Algorithm 3. The Mutual Refinement (MR) Algorithm

```
1: function MR((V, E), {C_1, ..., C_m})
2:     G ← (V, E)
3:     while true do
4:         s ← G.E.size()
5:         for C_i ∈ {C_1, ..., C_m} do
6:             G.E ← COLLECT(RECORD(⟨C_i, G⟩))
7:         if G.E.size() == s then
8:             return G
```

By doing such rounds multiple times until a state where applying another round does not change the edge set, we get the set E_{min}.

First, we prove its termination: after each round, the size of E either decreases or remains the same, but the size of E cannot decrease indefinitely.

Second, we show that E_{min} is indeed the globally minimal set with respect to the subset relation: given any refinement sequence $E_1, \ldots, E_n$, since it is non-increasing with respect to the set inclusion relation, we just need to prove $E_{\text{min}} \subseteq E_n$. We prove this by induction on the lengths of refinement sequences. First, there is only one possible refinement sequence of length 1, which is E itself, and it is obvious that $E_{\text{min}} \subseteq E$. Now suppose that for all refinement sequences of length at most n, E_{min} is a subset of the last edge set in the sequence. Consider an arbitrary refinement sequence of length $n+1$: $E_1, \ldots, E_{n+1}$. Here E_{n+1} is either the intersection of two previous edge sets or obtained by applying C_j-reachability ($j \in \{1, \ldots, m\}$) to one of the previous edge sets. In the first case, by the induction hypothesis, the two previous edge sets all contain E_{min}, so E_{n+1} also contains E_{min}. In the second case, suppose C_j-reachability is applied to E_i ($1 \leq i \leq n$). By the induction hypothesis, we have $E_{\text{min}} \subseteq E_i$, and because the set of contributing edges is monotonic in the sense described in Lemma 1, we further have $E_{\text{min}} = \mathsf{Ctri}(C_j, (V, E_{\text{min}})) \subseteq \mathsf{Ctri}(C_j, (V, E_i)) = E_{n+1}$, where the first equality holds according to the definition of E_{min}.

Algorithm 3 (mutual refinement) gives the complete procedure for finding the minimum edge set described in Theorem 3. It keeps iterating over the given set of algorithms (line 5) until the edge set's size does not change (line 7). Due to Theorem 3, this algorithm is guaranteed to terminate and produce the optimal result among all possible refinement sequences.

Theorem 4 (Mutual Refinement Soundness). *If every CFL in $\{C_1, \ldots, C_m\}$ over-approximates L, then Algorithm 3 does not miss any L-contributing edges.*

Proof. This is immediate from Theorem 2 and Theorem 3.

The final reachability result can be obtained by executing C_1, C_2, ..., C_m-reachability on the minimum graph produced by Algorithm 3, and reporting the pairs that all those CFL-reachability executions report as reachable. In fact, the last iteration of the while loop in Algorithm 3 already does this.

Theorem 5 (Precision Guarantee). *Suppose we have an instance* $\langle L, (V, E)\rangle$ *of L-reachability problem and m different CFLs* $C_1, \ldots, C_m$*, each of which over-approximates L. Let* E_{min} *be the set of edges obtained by executing Algorithm 3 on* (V, E) *and* $C_1, \ldots, C_m$*. Suppose* $P_1, \ldots, P_m$ *are the sets of reachable pairs obtained by executing* $C_1, \ldots, C_m$ *reachabilities on* (V, E)*, and* $Q_1, \ldots, Q_m$ *are the sets of reachable pairs obtained by executing* $C_1, \ldots, C_m$ *reachabilities on* (V, E_{min})*. Then* $\bigcap_{i=1}^{m} Q_i \subseteq \bigcap_{i=1}^{m} P_i$*.*

Proof. Since $E_{\mathsf{min}} \subseteq E$, it is immediate that $\forall i \in \{1, \ldots, m\}, Q_i \subseteq P_i$, because any C_i-path connecting two vertices in (V, E_{min}) is also present in (V, E).

The time and space complexities of Algorithm 3 depend on the number of iterations, which highly depends on the graph structure and the CFLs. $O(|E|)$ is a very loose upper bound of the number of iterations because in each iteration before the last one, we remove at least one edge. Our evaluation (Sect. 5) shows that for specific program analysis problems and graphs with edge sizes up to 184k, the number of iterations can still be within five.

Example 2 (Mutual Refinement Example). If we apply mutual refinement to the motivating example discussed in Sect. 2, where in each round we apply C_B-reachability and C_P-reachability in sequence, then after two rounds, the graph stabilizes. Figure 6 shows this process.

5 Experiments

We evaluate mutual refinement on two applications: a taint analysis for Java programs obtained from Android apps [10], and a value-flow analysis for LLVM IR programs obtained from the SPEC CPU 2017 benchmark [28].

When processing experimental data, we use arithmetic means ($\frac{1}{n}\sum_{i=1}^{n} x_i$) for the average of absolute numbers, and use geometric means ($\sqrt[n]{\prod_{i=1}^{n} x_i}$) for the average of ratios [7]. Also, for the measurement of precision (the number of reachable pairs), we exclude trivial pairs (u, u) and only consider pairs (u, v) where $u \neq v$.

5.1 Experimental Setup

Taint Analysis. We apply our approach to a context-sensitive field-sensitive taint analysis for Java programs obtained from Android apps [10]. The analysis goal is to determine all pairs of variables (s, t) where sensitive information from variable s can flow into variable t. Parentheses model context-sensitivity and brackets model field-sensitivity. A valid path string is an arbitrary interleaving of two strings derived from the two CFLs P and B shown in Fig. 7a. This is the interleaved-Dyck reachability problem, which is undecidable [24].

Unlike the example in Sect. 2, which considers sources/sinks within one function (matched parentheses) and counts flowing into fields as leaks (unmatched brackets), in our experiments, we only count leaks from variables to variables,

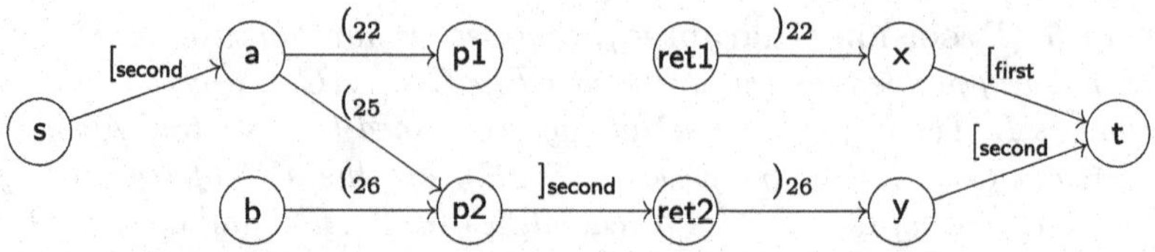

(a) After running C_B-reachability in the first round

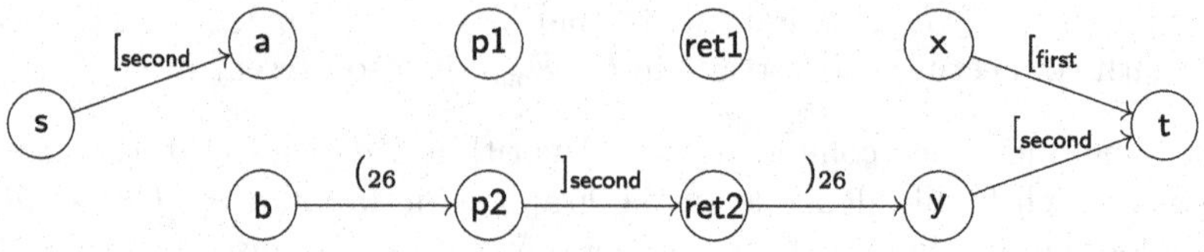

(b) After running C_P-reachability in the first round

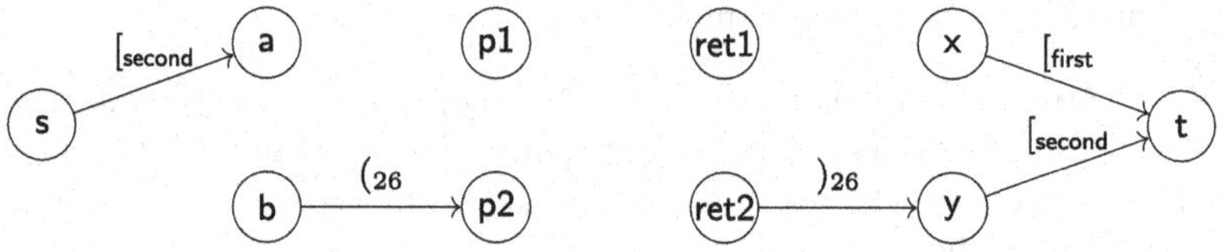

(c) After running C_B-reachability in the second round

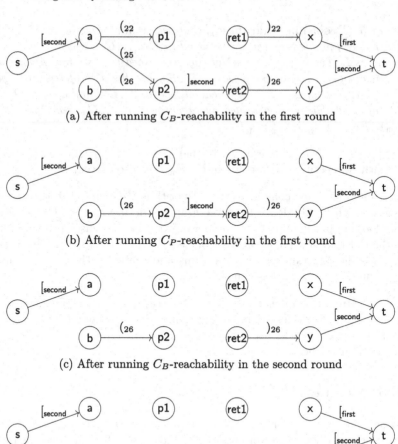

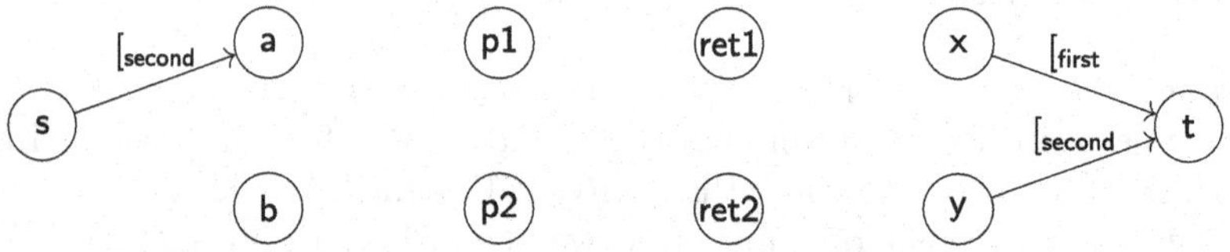

(d) After running C_P-reachability in the second round

Fig. 6. Mutual refinement's iteration process on the motivating example discussed in Sect. 2. It takes two rounds to converge. If we only consider (s,t)-reachability, then the iteration can stop after the second iteration.

thus disallowing unmatched brackets. One reason is that this is the formulation in the original work [10], and the other reason is that we also evaluate the LZR algorithm [18] on these benchmarks, which only supports matched brackets. In general, the grammar can be adjusted according to needs.

To use mutual refinement, we choose two CFLs (C_P, C_B) over-approximating the interleaved-Dyck language L, where C_P models parentheses matching and C_B models brackets matching. Their grammars are shown in Fig. 7b. The execution order is C_P, C_B in each round of mutual refinement.

The benchmarks are selected from the original paper [10]. Specifically, we chose the Contagio malware apps and used the implementation of the client

$$P \to P\,P \mid (_1\,P\,)_1 \mid \ldots \mid (_k\,P\,)_k \mid \epsilon$$

$$B \to B\,B \mid [_1\,B\,]_1 \mid \ldots \mid [_l\,B\,]_l \mid \epsilon$$

$$L = P \odot B$$

(a) The taint analysis is formulated as the well-known interleaved-Dyck-reachability problem.

$$\begin{aligned} C_P &\to C_P\,C_P \mid (_1\,C_P\,)_1 \mid \ldots \mid (_k\,C_P\,)_k \mid I \mid \epsilon \\ I &\to [_1 \mid\,]_1 \mid \ldots \mid [_l \mid\,]_l \end{aligned}$$

$$\begin{aligned} C_B &\to C_B\,C_B \mid [_1\,C_B\,]_1 \mid \ldots \mid [_l\,C_B\,]_l \mid J \mid \epsilon \\ J &\to (_1 \mid\,)_1 \mid \ldots \mid (_k \mid\,)_k \mid \epsilon \end{aligned}$$

(b) We use the above two CFLs C_P and C_B to over-approximate the interleaved-Dyck language.

Fig. 7. The taint analysis formulation and approximation.

analysis to obtain the graphs.[2] We excluded benchmarks that our tool or the original reference's tool failed to handle. Finally, we got 15 benchmarks, and the size information of the APK files and the graphs is shown in Table 2a.

Value-Flow Analysis. We also apply our approach to a context-sensitive value-flow analysis for LLVM IR programs obtained from the SPEC CPU 2017 benchmark [28]. The analysis goal is to determine all pairs of store/load instructions (store v_1 to p_1, load v_2 from p_2) where the value of v_1 can flow into v_2 via intermediate assignments and loads/stores. In this case, context-sensitivity is modeled using matched parentheses; memory stores and loads are modeled using matched brackets (in this case, there is only one type of brackets); normal copies of values are modeled using edges with a special label n. Furthermore, since we are interested in store/load pairs, the first edge in the path string must be a memory store, and the last edge must be a memory load. A valid path string is an interleaving of three strings derived from the three CFLs P, B, and N shown in Fig. 8a where the first symbol must be [and the last symbol must be]. We denote this formal language as L_V. Section 6 shows the existing $D_1 \odot D_k$-reachability problem, whose decidability is currently open [13], is reducible to the L_V-reachability problem.

In order to use mutual refinement, we choose three CFLs (C_P, C_B, and C_E) over-approximating the underlying problem, where C_P models parentheses matching, C_B models brackets matching, and C_E enforces that the first and last edges of the path must be an open bracket and a closed bracket, respectively. Specifically, they have the three grammars shown in Fig. 8b. The execution order is C_P, C_B, C_E in each round of mutual refinement.

The benchmarks are compiled using Clang version 12 [16] to bitcode files. The graphs are generated by the open-source static value-flow analysis framework SVF [31]. We did not include small programs (with bitcode file sizes < 1 MB) or programs that failed to be compiled or linked. Finally, we got 10 benchmarks, and the size information of the bitcode files and the graphs is shown in Table 2a.

[2] https://github.com/proganalysis/type-inference.

$$P \rightarrow P\,P \mid (_1\,P\,)_1 \mid \ldots \mid (_k\,P\,)_k \mid \epsilon$$

$$B \rightarrow B\,B \mid [\,B\,] \mid \epsilon$$

$$N \rightarrow n\,N \mid \epsilon$$

$$L_V = ((P \odot B) \odot N) \cap \{s \mid s = [*]\}$$

(a) The value-flow analysis is formulated as an L_V-reachability problem.

$$C_P \rightarrow C_P\,C_P \mid (_1\,C_P\,)_1 \mid \ldots \mid (_k\,C_P\,)_k \mid I \mid \epsilon$$
$$I \rightarrow [|\,] \mid n$$

$$C_B \rightarrow C_B\,C_B \mid [\,C_B\,] \mid J \mid \epsilon$$
$$J \rightarrow (_1|\,)_1 \mid \ldots \mid (_k|\,)_k \mid n$$

$$C_E \rightarrow [\,K\,]$$
$$K \rightarrow K\,K \mid [|\,] \mid (_1|\,)_1 \mid \ldots \mid (_k|\,)_k \mid n$$

(b) We use the above three CFLs C_P, C_B, and C_E to over-approximate L_V.

Fig. 8. The value-flow analysis formulation and approximation.

Table 2. Benchmark statistics.

Benchmark	APK Size (M)	Graph Size $(\|V\|, \|E\|)$
backflash	0.75	(544, 2048)
batterydoc	0.51	(1674, 4790)
droidkongfu	0.08	(734, 1983)
fakebanker	5.17	(434, 1103)
fakedaum	0.14	(1144, 2603)
faketaobao	0.44	(222, 450)
jollyserv	0.42	(488, 998)
loozfon	0.04	(152, 323)
phospy	0.18	(4402, 15660)
roidsec	0.03	(553, 2026)
scipiex	0.31	(1809, 5820)
simhosy	1.43	(4253, 13768)
skullkey	6.63	(18862, 69599)
uranai	0.07	(568, 1246)
zertsecurity	0.10	(281, 710)

(a) Taint Analysis Graphs.

Benchmark	Bitcode Size (M)	Graph Size $(\|V\|, \|E\|)$
cactus	5.61	(101325, 114805)
imagick	13.68	(103594, 131707)
leela	2.93	(16134, 19110)
nab	1.41	(12727, 13605)
omnetpp	20.80	(171502, 184601)
parest	16.20	(84355, 93493)
perlbench	11.88	(125345, 160958)
povray	7.38	(61802, 71892)
x264	4.68	(49806, 56376)
xz	1.24	(9918, 10767)

(b) Value-flow Analysis Graphs.

Research Questions. Our experiments aim to answer the following questions.

- *RQ1:* Can mutual refinement achieve better precision compared with the straightforward intersection (baseline) on the two applications?
- *RQ2:* What is the time/space overhead that mutual refinement incurs compared with the straightforward intersection (baseline), and how many rounds does mutual refinement take to converge?
- *RQ3:* Can the LZR graph simplification algorithm improve the precision/performance of mutual refinement on the taint analysis application?

Implementation and Experiment Execution. We implemented mutual refinement in C++17.[3] All experiments were performed on a machine running Ubuntu 20.04.2 LTS. We set a timeout of 4 h and a space limit of 128 GB for each algorithm's execution on each benchmark item. For *RQ3*, we used the original implementation of the LZR algorithm available online.[4] Since the LZR algorithm is fast enough, we did not set time/space limits on its executions.

5.2 RQ1: Precision Improvement

According to Theorem 5, mutual refinement's precision is at least as good as the straightforward intersection. We define the precision improvement as $(P_{\mathsf{Baseline}}/P_{\mathsf{MR}}) - 1$, where P_{Baseline} and P_{MR} represent the number of reachable pairs computed by the straightforward intersection (baseline) and mutual refinement, respectively. Table 3 shows that, on average, mutual refinement achieves 50.95% precision improvement on the taint analysis benchmarks and 9.37% precision improvement on the value-flow analysis benchmarks. Note that the improvement greatly depends on specific applications and benchmarks.

Summary: On the two program analysis applications, mutual refinement can achieve visibly better precision compared with the straightforward intersection.

5.3 RQ2: Performance Overhead

Mutual refinement traces the sets of contributing edges, which can cost more time and space. Also, mutual refinement might need several rounds to converge. As shown in Table 3 and Fig. 9, on average, on the taint analysis benchmarks, mutual refinement takes 2.93 rounds to converge and consumes 2.65× time and 3.23× memory compared with the baseline; on the value-flow analysis benchmarks, mutual refinement takes 3.13 rounds to converge and consumes 2.55× time and 2.22× memory compared with the baseline. In some cases, mutual refinement's space consumption can be much higher. For example, mutual refinement incurs a 80.58× space increase on the phospy benchmark in Table 3a. And there is a trend that larger graphs result in larger differences in memory consumption, which reflects the space complexity difference ($\tilde{O}(|V|^2)$ and $\tilde{O}(|V|^3)$). Section 6.4 discusses mutual refinement's memory cost in detail.

However, mutual refinement can also simplify the graph during the execution of each CFL-reachability, while the straightforward intersection cannot. This could lead mutual refinement to consume less resources in certain cases. For example, on the cactus benchmark in Table 3b, mutual refinement consumes less time than the straightforward intersection.

Summary: Mutual refinement typically needs more time and space, but the average time/space increase on the two program analysis applications is within 5×, and the number of iterations needed to converge is within five.

---

[3] The implementation is available on GitHub (https://github.com/sdingcn/mutual-refinement) and Zenodo (https://doi.org/10.5281/zenodo.8191389). Certain low-level data structure optimizations were used.

[4] https://github.com/yuanboli233/interdyck_graph_reduce.

Table 3. Precision and performance results. We present the number of rounds that mutual refinement takes to converge, as well as the comparison of precision/time/space between the straightforward intersection (baseline) and mutual refinement. "-" means time/space limits are exceeded.

Benchmark	Iterations	Precision (Pairs)		Time (Seconds)		Space (MB)	
		Baseline	MR	Baseline	MR	Baseline	MR
backflash	2	6080	2870	0.42	0.67	16.06	36.70
batterydoc	3	8386	5484	0.93	6.06	31.43	133.76
droidkongfu	3	6471	5442	0.32	4.55	16.93	90.06
fakebanker	3	1407	1172	0.04	0.12	9.17	11.96
fakedaum	3	3507	3243	0.28	1.07	18.16	37.40
faketaobao	3	398	328	0.01	0.02	6.98	7.23
jollyserv	3	562	303	0.10	0.14	10.61	15.62
loozfon	2	441	424	0.01	0.04	6.74	9.62
phospy	3	103961	81925	1309.64	9436.26	1202.29	96882.00
roidsec	2	17301	16425	1.79	5.94	28.85	168.93
scipiex	4	20542	10210	69.96	266.33	209.97	3471.78
simhosy	3	100552	41992	102.10	110.78	363.91	1669.46
skullkey	-	-	-	-	-	-	-
uranai	4	353	148	0.11	0.08	10.54	10.56
zertsecurity	3	1969	1110	0.26	0.16	11.24	13.93

(a) Taint Analysis Results.

Benchmark	Iterations	Precision (Pairs)		Time (Seconds)		Space (MB)	
		Baseline	MR	Baseline	MR	Baseline	MR
cactus	4	46502	46421	621.36	419.39	2888.79	9373.77
imagick	-	22091	-	14088.50	-	12211.74	-
leela	3	392	392	0.81	1.94	78.01	122.45
nab	3	1958	1788	0.30	0.87	51.83	70.76
omnetpp	4	90412	50568	76.70	221.21	1769.57	4396.33
parest	3	4571	4571	2.89	8.70	243.79	364.86
perlbench	-	-	-	-	-	-	-
povray	3	7453	7230	18.18	6.43	455.19	260.73
x264	3	61577	60792	47.01	821.81	571.96	10650.62
xz	2	211	211	0.32	2.29	41.10	87.94

(b) Value-flow Analysis Results.

5.4 RQ3: Combination with the LZR Algorithm

The LZR graph simplification algorithm [18] works for interleaved-Dyck-reachability, and is thus applicable to our taint analysis benchmarks as a pre-processing step. One important detail is that the LZR algorithm does graph edge contractions before calculating the contributing edges, while mutual refine-

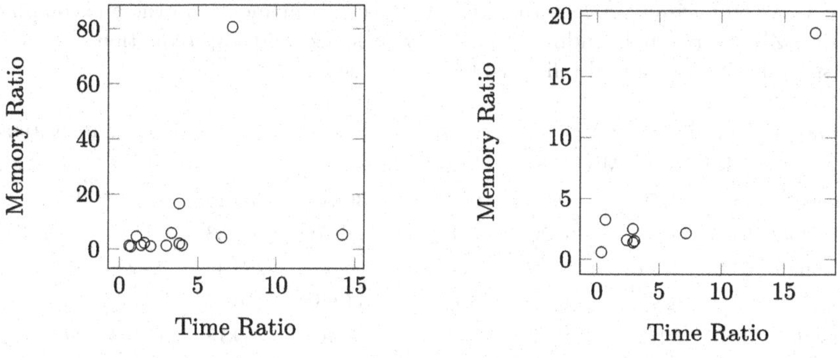

(a) Overhead on taint analysis.

(b) Overhead on value-flow analysis.

Fig. 9. Mutual refinement's performance overhead scatter plots (ratios). Time ratios are mutual refinement's time consumption numbers divided by the baseline's time consumption numbers. Memory ratios are similar.

ment doesn't. This can lead to edges counted as contributing edges in mutual refinement but not counted as contributing edges in the LZR algorithm, because contracting edges can make LZR ignore the contracted edges. As a result, the LZR algorithm can potentially remove certain edges that mutual refinement cannot.

Table 4 compares (1) executing mutual refinement on the original graphs and (2) executing mutual refinement on the graphs simplified by the LZR algorithm. In the (2) case, the time/space consumption includes both algorithms (LZR and MR). On average, LZR can improve the precision of mutual refinement by 3.27%, and this relatively small number shows that mutual refinement itself can already achieve very high precision. Indeed, LZR+MR can reduce 81.38% more edges on average compared with LZR alone. LZR can also boost mutual refinement in terms of time/space consumption, such as the phospy benchmark in Table 4. Notably, the space consumption of LZR+MR is always lower-bounded by 269 MB, and that is because LZR has a minimal memory consumption of roughly 269 MB. This might be due to implementation details.

Summary: LZR can improve mutual refinement's precision, but only to a small extent (3.27% on average). Since LZR is fast, it can boost mutual refinement's performance in certain cases.

6 Discussion

6.1 Generality of Mutual Refinement

Mutual refinement can approximate any language-reachability problem as long as there exist CFL-reachability-based over-approximations. In particular, it is not restricted to the interleaved-Dyck reachability or any particular problem.

Table 4. A comparison between the original mutual refinement and the one combined with the LZR algorithm, including precision, time, space, and edge reduction. "-" means time/space limits for mutual refinement are exceeded.

Benchmark	Precision (Pairs)		Time (Seconds)		Space (MB)		Edge Reduction	
	MR	LZR+MR	MR	LZR+MR	MR	LZR+MR	LZR	LZR+MR
backflash	2870	2870	0.67	0.60	36.70	269.18	677	1434
batterydoc	5484	5438	6.06	1.54	133.76	269.33	1826	3327
droidkongfu	5442	5422	4.55	2.66	90.06	269.40	589	1070
fakebanker	1172	928	0.12	0.17	11.96	269.17	414	745
fakedaum	3243	3243	1.07	0.87	37.40	269.18	1103	1747
faketaobao	328	325	0.02	0.10	7.23	269.13	191	309
jollyserv	303	303	0.14	0.25	15.62	269.01	361	634
loozfon	424	424	0.04	0.08	9.62	269.08	105	189
phospy	81925	80200	9436.26	8849.91	96882.00	69532.63	3838	6659
roidsec	16425	16425	5.94	5.86	168.93	269.12	605	1077
scipiex	10210	10173	266.33	260.05	3471.78	3426.72	1219	2683
simhosy	41992	35419	110.78	78.66	1669.46	1217.93	4801	8866
skullkey	-	-	-	-	-	-	19408	-
uranai	148	148	0.08	0.21	10.56	269.10	566	1063
zertsecurity	1110	1110	0.16	0.22	13.93	269.11	253	438

We have shown two examples L_T and L_V in our motivating example and experiments, and here we show (1) L_T is not a CFL, and (2) $D_1 \odot D_k$-reachability, whose decidability is currently open [13], is reducible to L_V-reachability.

L_T is not a CFL. Suppose L_T is a CFL. We construct a formal language M, each string m of which is an arbitrary interleaving of $p \in P$ and $d \in D$ in Sect. 2, interspersed with an arbitrary number of special symbols $a_1, \ldots, a_l$. Obviously, the language homomorphism

$$f(x) = \begin{cases} [_i \; , x = a_i \\ x \; , \text{otherwise} \end{cases}$$

maps M to L_T. By the assumption L_T is context-free, so M is also context-free since CFL is closed under inverse homomorphisms. Consider the regular language $R = \{s \mid s \text{ does not contain } a_1, \ldots, a_l\}$. Since the intersection of a context-free language and a regular language is also context-free, we have $M \cap R$ is context-free, but this is the interleaved-Dyck language, which is known to be non-context-free [24]. This is a contradiction.

$D_1 \odot D_k$-Reachability is Reducible to L_V-Reachability. $D_1 \odot D_k$ is arbitrary interleaving of two Dyck languages D_1 and D_k, where D_1 is a Dyck language with one kind of parenthesis and D_k is a Dyck language with k kinds of parenthesis. Given any labeled graph consisting of only labels from D_1 and D_k, a pair of vertices (s, t) is $D_1 \odot D_k$-reachable if and only if (s_0, t_0) is L_T-reachable where we just add two vertices s_0 and t_0, and two edges $s_0 \xrightarrow{[} s$ and $t \xrightarrow{]} t_0$, where [and] are the open and close brackets in D_1.

6.2 Different Grammars for the Same CFL

A context-free language can be represented by many different context-free grammars. Ambiguous grammars introduce redundancies, so it can affect mutual refinement's performance because there are more derivations to traverse. However, the choice of grammars does not affect the precision, because we only track L-contributing edges and different grammars refer to the same formal language L. This is also reflected in Algorithm 2: $\mathsf{metaInfo}[e]$ is a set eliminating duplicate tracked edges, and con is also a set eliminating duplicate collected edges.

6.3 Order of Mutual Refinement

In mutual refinement, as Theorem 3 shows, any possible orders of executing the CFL-reachability-based over-approximations $C_1, C_2, \cdots, C_m$ result in the same global minimum. However, different orders might affect the convergence speed. In practice, we can run the available CFL-reachability-based over-approximations on sampled programs to find out a "good" order to use, and then execute the "good" order on all programs. There are other heuristics for order choosing, such as executing the one that can result in the best precision first.

6.4 Cost of Mutual Refinement

As shown in Sect. 5, mutual refinement, in general, needs more time and space than the straightforward intersection. This is because mutual refinement traces the contributing edges and might need more than one iteration to converge. However, after running one CFL-reachability over-approximation, the remaining ones only need to be executed on the simplified graph. Also, in practice, we do not have to wait for the convergence, but can run it for a fixed number of rounds (e.g. two rounds). Other possible optimizations include changing the order of mutual refinement, simplifying the graphs/grammars, etc. Mutual refinement reflects a trade-off between performance and precision.

Memory Overhead of Mutual Refinement. Our experiment shows that in some cases, mutual refinement can take about 80× memory compared with the straightforward intersection. We intuitively explain the reason. Consider the difference between the standard CFL-reachability algorithm (Algorithm 1) and our tracing version (Algorithm 2): in our tracing version, when a new edge is generated, the meta-information about edge dependencies is updated no matter whether the new edge is already in the graph or not. If there are multiple ways to generate the same edge, all of those ways need to be recorded. For example, in the following graph, where we perform the matched-parenthesis reachability with respect to the grammar $S \to S\,S \mid (\,S\,) \mid \epsilon$, there are three ways to generate the summary edge $s \xrightarrow{S} t$, and all edges will be added to the meta information of $s \xrightarrow{S} t$, despite there is only one such summary edge in the final graph. So the memory cost of mutual refinement can be high. Whether this graph pattern occurs in reality depends on the specific analysis details.

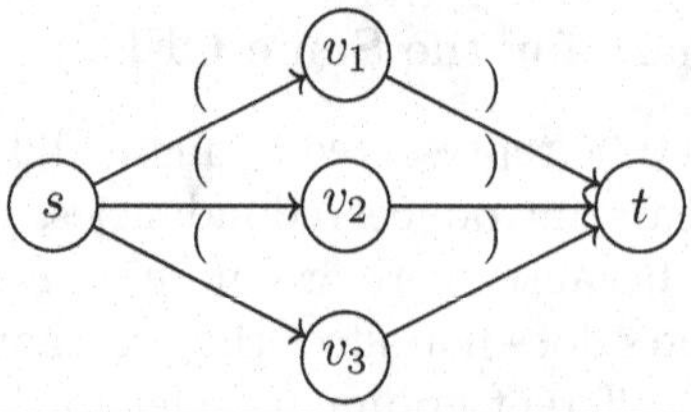

Exploring whether we can reduce the memory cost is an interesting future direction. There exists work compressing information used during static analysis [33].

6.5 Generalization to the Single-Pair Case

In this paper, mutual refinement is formalized to retain the edges contributing to reachable pairs in the CFL-reachability-based over-approximations. Notice that in the single-source-single-target reachability case, we can retain only the edges contributing to the pair that we are interested in, and this can potentially remove even more edges from the graph and thus can also potentially increase the precision as well. We leave this for future work.

6.6 Generalization to Other Algorithms

The idea of tracing in mutual refinement can be potentially generalized to all algorithms using similar "dynamic programming style" approaches. Specifically, as long as the algorithm traverses all edges contributing to the ground truth solution, we can use tracing to extract those edges and use this as a refinement between different such algorithms. It is an interesting future direction to explore the generalization of mutual refinement to broader classes of algorithms.

7 Related Work

CFL-reachability is widely-used in program analysis [15,19,22,23,26,30]. It has a (sub)cubic-time dynamic programming style algorithm [2,20,25,35], and faster algorithms exist in special cases [1,17,36]. CFL-reachability can model function calls/returns [24,26], field reads/writes [29,34], locks/unlocks [11], etc.

In static analysis, many techniques have been proposed to reduce the size of graphs involved in the analysis [5,18,21]. Our mutual refinement process simplifies the graphs, but our main focus is leveraging the information of each CFL-reachability-based over-approximation to refine the results. In particular, the LZR fast graph simplification work [18] also defines similar concepts such as contributing edges, but their algorithm is specific for the interleaved-Dyck-reachability problem, while our mutual refinement works for any L-reachability problems preserving CFL-reachability-based over-approximations. Also, LZR is a pre-processor while mutual refinement is a complete solver.

Interleaved-Dyck-reachability is widely used in program analysis [18,27,37], but it is undecidable [24], so there exist many approximation algorithms. We can use one Dyck language to approximate it and employ the standard cubic-time context-free language reachability algorithm [20,25,35]. The refinement-based context-sensitive points-to analysis work [29] used the method of modeling one Dyck language precisely while approximating the other Dyck language using a regular language [29]. The linear conjunctive language reachability [37] is another formulation of interleaved-Dyck-reachability which is precise, but the corresponding algorithm is approximate. Synchronized pushdown systems [27] model the idea of considering two context-free languages at the same time. Mutual refinement is not restricted to interleaved-Dyck-reachability.

In static analysis and verification, similar strategies of running different approaches in a staged way such that later stages benefit from earlier stages have been studied, such as the Unity – Relay approach [32] to accumulate the precision of different selective context-sensitivity approaches, and the staged verification [6] where faster verifiers run first to reduce the load of later verifiers. Mutual refinement concerns graph-reachability-based program analysis, and we have theorems showing the existence and uniqueness of fix-points.

8 Conclusion

This paper proposed mutual refinement to combine different CFL-reachability over-approximations for computationally hard graph reachability problems. We proved theorems showing the existence and uniqueness of the optimal refinement result, the correctness of mutual refinement, and the precision guarantees. To realize mutual refinement, the modifications to the standard CFL-reachability algorithm are minimal, and the modified version's time/space complexities were carefully analyzed. We also conducted experiments showing that mutual refinement achieved better precision than the straightforward intersection of the sets of reachable vertex pairs, with reasonable extra time and space cost.

Acknowledgement. We thank the anonymous reviewers for their feedback on earlier drafts of this paper. This work was supported, in part, by the United States National Science Foundation (NSF) under grants No. 1917924, No. 2114627, and No. 2237440; and by the Defense Advanced Research Projects Agency (DARPA) under grant N66001-21-C-4024. Any opinions, findings, conclusions, or recommendations expressed in this publication are those of the authors and do not necessarily reflect the views of the above sponsoring entities.

References

1. Chatterjee, K., Choudhary, B., Pavlogiannis, A.: Optimal dyck reachability for data-dependence and alias analysis. Proc. ACM Program. Lang. **2**(POPL), 30:1–30:30 (2018)

2. Chaudhuri, S.: Subcubic algorithms for recursive state machines. In: Proceedings of the 35th ACM SIGPLAN-SIGACT Symposium on Principles of Programming Languages, POPL 2008, San Francisco, California, USA, 7–12 January 2008, pp. 159–169. ACM (2008)
3. Cormen, T.H., Leiserson, C.E., Rivest, R.L., Stein, C.: Introduction to Algorithms. MIT Press, Cambridge (2022)
4. Cousot, P.: Asychronous iterative methods for solving a fixed point system of monotone equations in a complete lattice (1977)
5. Fähndrich, M., Foster, J.S., Su, Z., Aiken, A.: Partial online cycle elimination in inclusion constraint graphs. In: Proceedings of the ACM SIGPLAN 1998 Conference on Programming Language Design and Implementation (PLDI), Montreal, Canada, 17–19 June 1998, pp. 85–96. ACM (1998)
6. Fink, S.J., Yahav, E., Dor, N., Ramalingam, G., Geay, E.: Effective typestate verification in the presence of aliasing. ACM Trans. Softw. Eng. Methodol. **17**(2), 9:1–9:34 (2008)
7. Fleming, P.J., Wallace, J.J.: How not to lie with statistics: the correct way to summarize benchmark results. Commun. ACM **29**(3), 218–221 (1986)
8. Harrison, M.A.: Introduction to Formal Language Theory. Addison-Wesley Longman Publishing Co., Inc. (1978)
9. Hopcroft, J.E., Motwani, R., Ullman, J.D.: Introduction to automata theory, languages, and computation. ACM SIGACT News **32**(1), 60–65 (2001)
10. Huang, W., Dong, Y., Milanova, A., Dolby, J.: Scalable and precise taint analysis for android. In: Proceedings of the 2015 International Symposium on Software Testing and Analysis, ISSTA 2015, pp. 106–117. ACM (2015)
11. Kahlon, V.: Boundedness vs. unboundedness of lock chains: characterizing decidability of pairwise CFL-reachability for threads communicating via locks. In: Proceedings of the 24th Annual IEEE Symposium on Logic in Computer Science, LICS 2009, 11–14 August 2009, Los Angeles, CA, USA, pp. 27–36. IEEE Computer Society (2009)
12. Kildall, G.A.: A unified approach to global program optimization. In: Conference Record of the ACM Symposium on Principles of Programming Languages, Boston, Massachusetts, USA, October 1973, pp. 194–206. ACM Press (1973)
13. Kjelstrøm, A.H., Pavlogiannis, A.: The decidability and complexity of interleaved bidirected dyck reachability. Proc. ACM Program. Lang. **6**(POPL), 1–26 (2022)
14. Kleene, S.C.: Introduction to metamathematics (1952)
15. Kodumal, J., Aiken, A.: The set constraint/CFL reachability connection in practice. In: Proceedings of the ACM SIGPLAN 2004 Conference on Programming Language Design and Implementation 2004, Washington, DC, USA, 9–11 June 2004, pp. 207–218. ACM (2004)
16. Lattner, C., Adve, V.S.: LLVM: a compilation framework for lifelong program analysis & transformation. In: 2nd IEEE/ACM International Symposium on Code Generation and Optimization (CGO 2004), 20–24 March 2004, San Jose, CA, USA, pp. 75–88. IEEE Computer Society (2004)
17. Lei, Y., Sui, Y., Ding, S., Zhang, Q.: Taming transitive redundancy for context-free language reachability. Proc. ACM Program. Lang. **6**(OOPSLA2), 1556–1582 (2022)
18. Li, Y., Zhang, Q., Reps, T.W.: Fast graph simplification for interleaved dyck-reachability. In: Proceedings of the 41st ACM SIGPLAN International Conference on Programming Language Design and Implementation, PLDI 2020, pp. 780–793. ACM (2020)

19. Lu, Y., Shang, L., Xie, X., Xue, J.: An incremental points-to analysis with CFL-reachability. In: Jhala, R., De Bosschere, K. (eds.) CC 2013. LNCS, vol. 7791, pp. 61–81. Springer, Heidelberg (2013). https://doi.org/10.1007/978-3-642-37051-9_4
20. Melski, D., Reps, T.W.: Interconvertibility of a class of set constraints and context-free-language reachability. Theor. Comput. Sci. **248**(1–2), 29–98 (2000)
21. Milanova, A.: Flowcfl: generalized type-based reachability analysis: graph reduction and equivalence of CFL-based and type-based reachability. Proc. ACM Program. Lang. **4**(OOPSLA), 178:1–178:29 (2020)
22. Pratikakis, P., Foster, J.S., Hicks, M.: Existential label flow inference via CFL reachability. In: Yi, K. (ed.) SAS 2006. LNCS, vol. 4134, pp. 88–106. Springer, Heidelberg (2006). https://doi.org/10.1007/11823230_7
23. Rehof, J., Fähndrich, M.: Type-base flow analysis: from polymorphic subtyping to CFL-reachability. In: Conference Record of POPL 2001: The 28th ACM SIGPLAN-SIGACT Symposium on Principles of Programming Languages, London, UK, 17–19 January 2001, pp. 54–66. ACM (2001)
24. Reps, T.: Undecidability of context-sensitive data-dependence analysis. ACM Trans. Program. Lang. Syst. (TOPLAS) **22**(1), 162–186 (2000)
25. Reps, T.W.: Program analysis via graph reachability. Inf. Softw. Technol. **40**(11–12), 701–726 (1998)
26. Reps, T.W., Horwitz, S., Sagiv, S.: Precise interprocedural dataflow analysis via graph reachability. In: Conference Record of POPL 1995: 22nd ACM SIGPLAN-SIGACT Symposium on Principles of Programming Languages, San Francisco, California, USA, 23–25 January 1995, pp. 49–61. ACM Press (1995)
27. Späth, J., Ali, K., Bodden, E.: Context-, flow-, and field-sensitive data-flow analysis using synchronized pushdown systems. Proc. ACM Program. Lang. **3**(POPL), 48:1–48:29 (2019)
28. SPEC: SPEC CPU 2017 (2017). https://www.spec.org/cpu2017/. Accessed 6 Nov 2022
29. Sridharan, M., Bodík, R.: Refinement-based context-sensitive points-to analysis for java. In: Proceedings of the ACM SIGPLAN 2006 Conference on Programming Language Design and Implementation, Ottawa, Ontario, Canada, 11–14 June 2006, pp. 387–400. ACM (2006)
30. Su, Y., Ye, D., Xue, J.: Parallel pointer analysis with CFL-reachability. In: 43rd International Conference on Parallel Processing, ICPP 2014, Minneapolis, MN, USA, 9–12 September 2014, pp. 451–460. IEEE Computer Society (2014)
31. Sui, Y., Xue, J.: SVF: interprocedural static value-flow analysis in LLVM. In: Proceedings of the 25th International Conference on Compiler Construction, pp. 265–266. ACM (2016)
32. Tan, T., Li, Y., Ma, X., Xu, C., Smaragdakis, Y.: Making pointer analysis more precise by unleashing the power of selective context sensitivity. Proc. ACM Program. Lang. **5**(OOPSLA), 1–27 (2021)
33. Xiao, X., Zhang, Q., Zhou, J., Zhang, C.: Persistent pointer information. In: ACM SIGPLAN Conference on Programming Language Design and Implementation, PLDI 2014, Edinburgh, United Kingdom - 09–11 June 2014, pp. 463–474. ACM (2014)
34. Yan, D., Xu, G., Rountev, A.: Demand-driven context-sensitive alias analysis for java. In: Proceedings of the 20th International Symposium on Software Testing and Analysis, ISSTA 2011, Toronto, ON, Canada, 17–21 July 2011, pp. 155–165. ACM (2011)

35. Yannakakis, M.: Graph-theoretic methods in database theory. In: Proceedings of the Ninth ACM SIGACT-SIGMOD-SIGART Symposium on Principles of Database Systems, PODS 1990, pp. 230–242. ACM Press (1990)
36. Zhang, Q., Lyu, M.R., Yuan, H., Su, Z.: Fast algorithms for Dyck-CFL-reachability with applications to alias analysis. In: ACM SIGPLAN Conference on Programming Language Design and Implementation, PLDI 2013, Seattle, WA, USA, 16–19 June 2013, pp. 435–446. ACM (2013)
37. Zhang, Q., Su, Z.: Context-sensitive data-dependence analysis via linear conjunctive language reachability. In: Proceedings of the 44th ACM SIGPLAN Symposium on Principles of Programming Languages, POPL 2017, pp. 344–358. ACM (2017)

ADCL: Acceleration Driven Clause Learning for Constrained Horn Clauses

Florian Frohn(✉) and Jürgen Giesl(✉)

LuFG Informatik 2, RWTH Aachen University, Aachen, Germany
florian.frohn@cs.rwth-aachen.de, giesl@informatik.rwth-aachen.de

Abstract. *Constrained Horn Clauses* (CHCs) are often used in automated program verification. Thus, techniques for (dis-)proving satisfiability of CHCs are a very active field of research. On the other hand, *acceleration techniques* for computing formulas that characterize the N-fold closure of loops have successfully been used for static program analysis. We show how to use acceleration to avoid repeated derivations with recursive CHCs in resolution proofs, which reduces the length of the proofs drastically. This idea gives rise to a novel calculus for (dis)proving satisfiability of CHCs, called *Acceleration Driven Clause Learning (ADCL)*. We implemented this new calculus in our tool LoAT and evaluate it empirically in comparison to other state-of-the-art tools.

1 Introduction

Constrained Horn Clauses (CHCs) are often used for expressing verification conditions in automated program verification. Examples for tools based on CHCs include Korn [19] and SeaHorn [30] for verifying C and C++ programs, JayHorn for Java programs [36], HornDroid for Android apps [12], RustHorn for Rust programs [43], and SmartACE [50] and SolCMC [3] for Solidity. Consequently, techniques for (dis-)proving satisfiability of CHCs (CHC-SAT) are a very active field of research, resulting in powerful tools like Spacer [37], Eldarica [35], FreqHorn [20], Golem [7], Ultimate [17], and RInGEN [38].

On the other hand, *loop acceleration techniques* have been used successfully for static program analyses during the last years, resulting in tools like Flata [9,27] and LoAT [24]. Essentially, such techniques compute quantifier-free first-order formulas that characterize the N-fold closure of the transition relation of

Funded by the Deutsche Forschungsgemeinschaft (DFG, German Research Foundation) - 235950644 (Project GI 274/6-2).

M. V. Hermenegildo and J. F. Morales (Eds.): SAS 2023, LNCS 14284, pp. 259–285, 2023.
https://doi.org/10.1007/978-3-031-44245-2_13

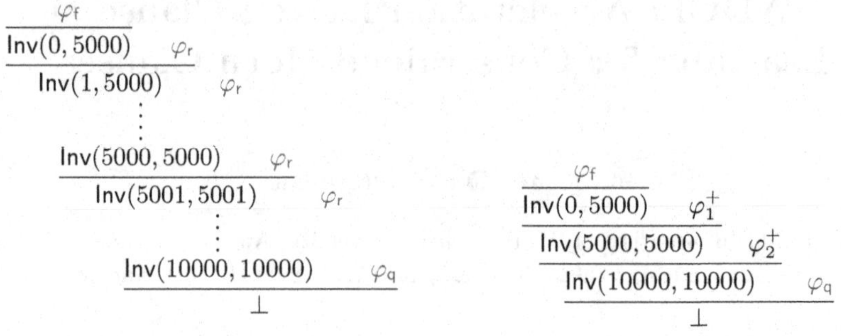

(a) Original Resolution Proof (b) Accelerated Resolution Proof

Fig. 1. Original and Accelerated Resolution Proof

loops without branching in their body. Thus, acceleration techniques can be used when generating verification conditions in order to replace such loops with the closure of their transition relation.

In this paper, we apply acceleration techniques to CHC-SAT, where we restrict ourselves to linear CHCs, i.e., clauses that contain at most one positive and one negative literal with uninterpreted predicates. As our main interest lies in proving *un*satisfiability of CHCs, our approach does not rely on abstractions, in contrast to most other techniques. Instead, we use acceleration to cut off repeated derivations with recursive CHCs while exploring the state space via resolution. In this way, the number of resolution steps that are required to reach a counterexample can be reduced drastically, as new CHCs that are "learned" via acceleration can simulate arbitrarily many "ordinary" resolution steps at once.

Example 1. Consider the following set of CHCs Φ over the theory of linear integer arithmetic (LIA) with a *fact* φ_f, a *rule* φ_r, and a *query* φ_q, where $\top$ and $\bot$ stand for *true* and *false*:[1]

$$\top \implies \mathsf{Inv}(0, 5000) \qquad (\varphi_f)$$

$$\begin{array}{l}\mathsf{Inv}(X_1, X_2) \wedge \\ \quad ((X_1 < 5000 \wedge Y_2 = X_2) \vee (X_1 \geq 5000 \wedge Y_2 = X_2 + 1))\end{array} \implies \mathsf{Inv}(X_1 + 1, Y_2) \quad (\varphi_r)$$

$$\mathsf{Inv}(10000, 10000) \implies \bot \qquad (\varphi_q)$$

Its unsatisfiability can be proven via resolution and arithmetic simplification as shown in Fig. 1a. The proof requires 10001 resolution steps. Using acceleration techniques, we can derive the following two new CHCs from Φ:

$$\mathsf{Inv}(X_1, X_2) \wedge N > 0 \wedge X_1 + N < 5001 \implies \mathsf{Inv}(X_1 + N, X_2) \qquad (\varphi_1^+)$$

$$\mathsf{Inv}(X_1, X_2) \wedge N > 0 \wedge X_1 \geq 5000 \implies \mathsf{Inv}(X_1 + N, X_2 + N) \qquad (\varphi_2^+)$$

[1] `chc-LIA-Lin_052.smt2` from the benchmarks of the CHC Competition '22 [14].

The first CHC φ_1^+ covers arbitrarily many subsequent resolution steps with φ_r where $X_1 < 5000$. Similarly, the second CHC φ_2^+ covers arbitrarily many steps where $X_1 \geq 5000$. Now we can prove unsatisfiability of Φ with just 3 resolution steps, as shown in Fig. 1b.

This idea gives rise to a novel calculus for CHC-SAT, called *Acceleration Driven Clause Learning (ADCL).* ADCL is refutationally complete and can also prove satisfiability, but it does not necessarily terminate.

So far, our implementation in our tool LoAT is restricted to proving unsatisfiability. In program verification (which is one of the most important applications of CHC-SAT), satisfiability usually corresponds to safety, i.e., if an error state is reachable in the original program, then the CHCs derived from the program are unsatisfiable. Hence, LoAT can be used to show reachability of error states in program verification. The "witness" of reachability is a resolution proof ending in a conditional empty clause $\psi \implies \bot$ (where the condition ψ is a formula over the signature of some background theory like LIA), together with a model for ψ. Instantiating the variables in the proof according to the model yields a proof on ground instances. Then this instantiated proof corresponds to a program run that ends in an error state, i.e., a counterexample.

After introducing preliminaries in Sect. 2, we formalize ADCL in Sect. 3. Next, we discuss how to implement ADCL efficiently in Sect. 4. In Sect. 5, we discuss related work, and we show that our approach is highly competitive with state-of-the-art CHC-SAT solvers by means of an empirical evaluation. All proofs can be found in the extended version [26].

2 Preliminaries

We assume that the reader is familiar with basic concepts from many-sorted first-order logic. Throughout this paper, Σ denotes a many-sorted first-order signature that just contains predicates, i.e., we do not consider uninterpreted functions. Moreover, $\mathcal{V}$ denotes a countably infinite set of variables and for each entity e, $\mathcal{V}(e)$ denotes the variables occurring in e. We write $\vec{x}$ for sequences and x_i is the ith element of $\vec{x}$. In the following, we introduce preliminaries regarding *Constrained Horn Clauses* and *acceleration techniques.*

Constrained Horn Clauses are first-order formulas of the form

$$\forall \vec{X}_1, \ldots, \vec{X}_d, \vec{Y}, \vec{Z}.\ \mathsf{F}_1(\vec{X}_1) \wedge \ldots \wedge \mathsf{F}_d(\vec{X}_d) \wedge \psi \implies \mathsf{G}(\vec{Y}) \qquad \text{or}$$
$$\forall \vec{X}_1, \ldots, \vec{X}_d, \vec{Z}.\ \mathsf{F}_1(\vec{X}_1) \wedge \ldots \wedge \mathsf{F}_d(\vec{X}_d) \wedge \psi \implies \bot$$

where $\vec{X}_1, \ldots, \vec{X}_d, \vec{Y}, \vec{Z}$ are pairwise disjoint vectors of pairwise different variables, $\mathsf{F}_1, \ldots, \mathsf{F}_d, \mathsf{G} \in \Sigma$, $\psi \in \mathsf{QF}(\mathcal{A})$ is a quantifier-free first-order formula over the many-sorted signature $\Sigma_{\mathcal{A}}$ of some theory $\mathcal{A}$, and $\mathcal{V}(\psi) \subseteq \vec{X}_1 \cup \ldots \cup \vec{X}_d \cup \vec{Y} \cup \vec{Z}$. We assume that $\mathcal{A}$ is a complete theory with equality and that Σ and $\Sigma_{\mathcal{A}}$ are disjoint, and we usually omit the leading universal quantifier, i.e., all variables in

CHCs are implicitly universally quantified.[2] Moreover, w.l.o.g., we assume that ψ is in negation normal form. In this paper, we restrict ourselves to *linear* CHCs. Thus, we consider CHCs of the following form:

$$\psi \implies \mathsf{G}(\vec{Y}) \quad \text{(fact)} \qquad \mathsf{F}(\vec{X}) \land \psi \implies \bot \quad \text{(query)}$$
$$\mathsf{F}(\vec{X}) \land \psi \implies \mathsf{G}(\vec{Y}) \quad \text{(rule)} \qquad \psi \implies \bot \quad \text{(conditional empty clause)}$$

The premise and conclusion of a CHC is also called *body* and *head*, a CHC is *recursive* if it is a rule where $\mathsf{F} = \mathsf{G}$, and it is *conjunctive* if ψ is a conjunction of literals. Throughout this paper, φ and π always denote CHCs. The *condition* of a CHC φ is $\mathsf{cond}(\varphi) := \psi$. We write $\varphi|_{\psi'}$ for the CHC that results from φ by replacing $\mathsf{cond}(\varphi)$ with ψ'. Typically, the original set of CHCs does not contain conditional empty clauses, but in our setting, such clauses result from resolution proofs that start with a fact and end with a query. A conditional empty clause is called a *refutation* if its condition is satisfiable. We also refer to sets of CHCs as *CHC problems*, denoted Φ or Π.

We call σ an $\mathcal{A}$-*interpretation* if it is a model of $\mathcal{A}$ whose carrier only contains ground terms over $\Sigma_{\mathcal{A}}$, extended with interpretations for Σ and $\mathcal{V}$. Given a first-order formula η over $\Sigma \cup \Sigma_{\mathcal{A}}$, an $\mathcal{A}$-interpretation σ is a *model* of η (written $\sigma \models_{\mathcal{A}} \eta$) if it satisfies η. If such a model exists, then η is *satisfiable*. As usual, $\models_{\mathcal{A}} \eta$ means that η is valid (i.e., we have $\sigma \models_{\mathcal{A}} \eta$ for all $\mathcal{A}$-interpretations σ) and $\eta \equiv_{\mathcal{A}} \eta'$ means $\models_{\mathcal{A}} \eta \iff \eta'$. For sets of formulas H, we define $\sigma \models_{\mathcal{A}} H$ if $\sigma \models_{\mathcal{A}} \bigwedge_{\eta \in H} \eta$. The *ground instances* of a CHC $\eta \land \psi \implies \eta'$ are:

$$\mathsf{grnd}(\eta \land \psi \implies \eta') := \{\eta\sigma \implies \eta'\sigma \mid \sigma \models_{\mathcal{A}} \psi\},$$

where $\eta\sigma$ abbreviates $\sigma(\eta)$, i.e., it results from η by instantiating all variables according to σ. Since $\mathcal{A}$ is complete (i.e., either $\models_{\mathcal{A}} \psi$ or $\models_{\mathcal{A}} \neg\psi$ holds for every closed formula ψ over $\Sigma_{\mathcal{A}}$), $\mathcal{A}$-interpretations σ only differ on Σ and $\mathcal{V}$, and thus we have $\sigma \models_{\mathcal{A}} \varphi$ iff $\sigma \models_{\mathcal{A}} \mathsf{grnd}(\varphi)$.

In the following, we use "::" for the concatenation of sequences, where we identify sequences of length 1 with their elements, i.e., we sometimes write $x :: xs$ instead of $[x] :: xs$ or $x :: y$ instead of $[x, y]$. As usual, $\mathsf{mgu}(s, t)$ is the most general unifier of s and t. The following definition formalizes resolution (where we disregard the underlying theory and just use ordinary syntactic unification). If the corresponding literals of two clauses φ, φ' do not unify, then we define their resolvent to be $\bot \implies \bot$, so that resolution is defined for pairs of arbitrary CHCs. Note that in our setting, the mgu θ is always a variable renaming.

[2] We assume that all arguments of predicates are variables. This is not a restriction, as one can add equations to ψ to identify $\Sigma_{\mathcal{A}}$-terms with fresh variables. To ease the presentation, we also use $\Sigma_{\mathcal{A}}$-terms as arguments of predicates in examples (e.g., in Example 1 we wrote $\top \implies \mathsf{Inv}(0, 5000)$ instead of $Y_1 = 0 \land Y_2 = 5000 \implies \mathsf{Inv}(Y_1, Y_2)$).

Definition 2 (Resolution). *Let φ and φ' be CHCs, where we rename the variables in φ and φ' such that they are disjoint. If*

$$\varphi = (\eta \wedge \psi \implies \mathsf{F}(\vec{x})), \quad \varphi' = (\mathsf{F}(\vec{y}) \wedge \psi' \implies \eta'), \quad \textit{and} \quad \theta = \mathsf{mgu}(\mathsf{F}(\vec{x}), \mathsf{F}(\vec{y})),$$

$$\textit{then} \qquad \mathsf{res}(\varphi, \varphi') := (\eta \wedge \psi \wedge \psi' \implies \eta')\theta.$$

$$\textit{Otherwise,} \qquad \mathsf{res}(\varphi, \varphi') := (\bot \implies \bot).$$

Here, η can also be $\top$ and η' can also be $\bot$. We lift res *to non-empty sequences of CHCs by defining*

$$\mathsf{res}([\varphi_1, \varphi_2] :: \vec{\varphi}) := \mathsf{res}(\mathsf{res}(\varphi_1, \varphi_2) :: \vec{\varphi}) \qquad \textit{and} \qquad \mathsf{res}(\varphi_1) := \varphi_1.$$

We implicitly lift notations and terminology for CHCs to sequences of CHCs via resolution. So for example, we have $\mathsf{cond}(\vec{\varphi}) := \mathsf{cond}(\mathsf{res}(\vec{\varphi}))$ and $\mathsf{grnd}(\vec{\varphi}) := \mathsf{grnd}(\mathsf{res}(\vec{\varphi}))$.

Example 3. Consider a variation $\varPhi'$ of the CHC problem $\varPhi$ from Example 1 where φ_f is replaced by

$$X_1 \leq 0 \wedge X_2 \geq 5000 \implies \mathsf{Inv}(X_1, X_2) \qquad (\varphi'_\mathsf{f})$$

To prove its unsatisfiability, one can consider the resolvent of the sequence $\vec{\varphi} := [\varphi'_\mathsf{f}, \varphi_1^+, \varphi_2^+, \varphi_\mathsf{q}]$:

$$\begin{aligned}
& \mathsf{res}([\varphi'_\mathsf{f}, \varphi_1^+, \varphi_2^+, \varphi_\mathsf{q}]) \\
= \; & \mathsf{res}([\psi \implies \mathsf{Inv}(X_1 + N, X_2), \varphi_2^+, \varphi_\mathsf{q}]) \\
= \; & \mathsf{res}([\psi \wedge N' > 0 \wedge X_1{+}N \geq 5000 \implies \mathsf{Inv}(X_1{+}N{+}N', X_2{+}N'), \varphi_\mathsf{q}]) \quad (\dagger) \\
\equiv_\mathcal{A} \; & \mathsf{res}([X_1 \leq 0 \wedge X_2 \geq 5000 \wedge N' > 0 \implies \mathsf{Inv}(5000 + N', X_2 + N'), \varphi_\mathsf{q}]) \quad (\ddagger) \\
= \; & (X_1 \leq 0 \wedge X_2 \geq 5000 \wedge N' > 0 \wedge 5000 + N' = X_2 + N' = 10000 \implies \bot)
\end{aligned}$$

Here, we have

$$\psi := \mathsf{cond}([\varphi'_\mathsf{f}, \varphi_1^+]) = X_1 \leq 0 \wedge X_2 \geq 5000 \wedge N > 0 \wedge X_1 + N < 5001.$$

In the step marked with ($\dagger$), the variable N' results from renaming N in φ_2^+. In the step marked with ($\ddagger$), we simplified $X_1 + N$ to 5000 for readability, as $\psi \wedge X_1 + N \geq 5000$ implies $X_1 + N = 5000$. If $\sigma(X_1) = 0$ and $\sigma(X_2) = \sigma(N') = 5000$, then $\sigma \models_\mathcal{A} \mathsf{res}(\vec{\varphi})$ and thus $\mathsf{res}(\vec{\varphi})$ is a refutation, so $\varPhi$ is unsatisfiable. By instantiating the variables in the proof according to σ (and setting N to 5000, as we had $X_1 + N = 5000$), we obtain an accelerated resolution proof on ground instances that is analogous to Fig. 1b and serves as a "witness" of unsatisfiability, i.e., a "counterexample" to $\varPhi'$.

Acceleration Techniques are used to compute the N-fold closure of the transition relation of a loop in program analysis. In the context of CHCs, applying an acceleration technique to a recursive CHC φ yields another CHC φ' which, for any instantiation of a dedicated fresh variable $N \in \mathcal{V}(\varphi')$ with a positive integer, has the same ground instances as $\mathsf{res}(\varphi^N)$. Here, φ^N denotes the sequence consisting of N repetitions of φ. In the following definition, we restrict ourselves to conjunctive CHCs, since many existing acceleration techniques do not support disjunctions [8], or have to resort to approximations in the presence of disjunctions [23].

Definition 4 (Acceleration). *An* acceleration technique *is a function* accel *that maps a recursive conjunctive CHC* φ *to a recursive conjunctive CHC such that* $\mathsf{grnd}(\mathsf{accel}(\varphi)) = \bigcup_{n \in \mathbb{N}_{\geq 1}} \mathsf{grnd}(\varphi^n)$.

Example 5. In the CHC problem from Example 1, φ_{r} entails

$$\mathsf{Inv}(X_1, X_2) \wedge X_1 < 5000 \implies \mathsf{Inv}(X_1 + 1, X_2).$$

From this CHC, an acceleration technique would compute φ_1^+.

Note that most theories are not "closed under acceleration". For example, consider the left clause below, which only uses linear arithmetic.

$$\mathsf{F}(X, Y) \implies \mathsf{F}(X + Y, Y) \qquad\qquad \mathsf{F}(X, Y) \wedge N > 0 \implies \mathsf{F}(X + N \cdot Y, Y)$$

Accelerating it yields the clause on the right, which is not expressible with linear arithmetic due to the sub-expression $N \cdot Y$. Moreover, if there is no sort for integers in the background theory $\mathcal{A}$, then an additional sort for the range of N is required in the formula that results from applying accel. For that reason, we consider *many-sorted* first-order logic and theories.

3 Acceleration Driven Clause Learning

In this section, we introduce our novel calculus ADCL for (dis)proving satisfiability of CHC problems. In Sect. 3.1, we start with important concepts that ADCL is based on. Then the ADCL calculus itself is presented in Sect. 3.2. Finally, in Sect. 3.3 we investigate the main properties of ADCL.

3.1 Syntactic Implicants and Redundancy

Since ADCL relies on acceleration techniques, an important property of ADCL is that it only applies resolution to conjunctive CHCs, even if the analyzed CHC problem is not conjunctive. To obtain conjunctive CHCs from non-conjunctive CHCs, we use *syntactic implicants*.

Definition 6 (Syntactic Implicant Projection). *Let $\psi \in \mathsf{QF}(\mathcal{A})$ be in negation normal form. We define:*

$$\begin{aligned}
\mathsf{sip}(\psi,\sigma) &:= \bigwedge\{\ell \text{ is a literal of } \psi \mid \sigma \models_{\mathcal{A}} \ell\} && \text{if } \sigma \models_{\mathcal{A}} \psi \\
\mathsf{sip}(\psi) &:= \{\mathsf{sip}(\psi,\sigma) \mid \sigma \models_{\mathcal{A}} \psi\} \\
\mathsf{sip}(\varphi) &:= \{\varphi|_{\psi} \mid \psi \in \mathsf{sip}(\mathsf{cond}(\varphi))\} && \text{for CHCs } \varphi \\
\mathsf{sip}(\Phi) &:= \bigcup_{\varphi \in \Phi} \mathsf{sip}(\varphi) && \text{for sets of CHCs } \Phi
\end{aligned}$$

Here, sip *abbreviates* syntactic implicant projection.

In contrast to the usual notion of implicants (which just requires that the implicants entail ψ), syntactic implicants are restricted to literals from ψ to ensure that $\mathsf{sip}(\psi)$ is finite. We call such implicants *syntactic* since Definition 6 does not take the semantics of literals into account. For example, the formula $\psi := (X > 0 \wedge X > 1)$ contains the literals $X > 0$ and $X > 1$, and $\models_{\mathcal{A}} X > 1 \implies \psi$, but $(X > 1) \notin \mathsf{sip}(\psi) = \{\psi\}$, because every model of $X > 1$ also satisfies $X > 0$. It is easy to show that $\psi \equiv_{\mathcal{A}} \bigvee \mathsf{sip}(\psi)$, and thus we also have $\Phi \equiv_{\mathcal{A}} \mathsf{sip}(\Phi)$.

Example 7. In the CHC problem of Ex. 1, we have

$$\mathsf{sip}(\mathsf{cond}(\varphi_{\mathsf{r}})) = \{(X_1 < 5000 \wedge Y_2 = X_2), (X_1 \geq 5000 \wedge Y_2 = X_2 + 1)\}.$$

Since $\mathsf{sip}(\varphi)$ is worst-case exponential in the size of $\mathsf{cond}(\varphi)$, we do not compute it explicitly: When resolving with φ, we conjoin $\mathsf{cond}(\varphi)$ to the condition of the resulting resolvent and search for a model σ. This ensures that we do not continue with resolvents that have unsatisfiable conditions. Then we replace $\mathsf{cond}(\varphi)$ by $\mathsf{sip}(\mathsf{cond}(\varphi),\sigma)$ in the resolvent. This corresponds to a resolution step with a conjunctive variant of φ whose condition is satisfied by σ. In other words, our calculus constructs $\mathsf{sip}(\mathsf{cond}(\varphi),\sigma)$ "on the fly" when resolving $\vec{\varphi}$ with φ, where $\sigma \models_{\mathcal{A}} \mathsf{cond}(\vec{\varphi} :: \varphi)$, see Sect. 4 for details. In this way, the exponential blowup that results from constructing $\mathsf{sip}(\varphi)$ explicitly can often be avoided.

As ADCL learns new clauses via acceleration, it is important to prefer more general (learned) clauses over more specific clauses in resolution proofs. To this end, we use the following *redundancy relation* for CHCs.

Definition 8 (Redundancy Relation). *For two CHCs φ and π, we say that φ is* (strictly) redundant *w.r.t. π, denoted $\varphi \sqsubseteq \pi$ ($\varphi \sqsubset \pi$), if $\mathsf{grnd}(\varphi) \subseteq \mathsf{grnd}(\pi)$ ($\mathsf{grnd}(\varphi) \subset \mathsf{grnd}(\pi)$). For a set of CHCs Π, we define $\varphi \sqsubseteq \Pi$ ($\varphi \sqsubset \Pi$) if $\varphi \sqsubseteq \pi$ ($\varphi \sqsubset \pi$) for some $\pi \in \Pi$.*

In the following, we assume that we have oracles for checking redundancy, for satisfiability of $\mathsf{QF}(\mathcal{A})$-formulas, and for acceleration. In practice, we have to resort to incomplete techniques instead. In Sect. 4, we will explain how our implementation takes that into account.

3.2 The ADCL Calculus

A *state* of ADCL consists of a CHC problem Π, containing the original CHCs and all *learned* clauses that were constructed by acceleration, the *trace* $[\varphi_i]_{i=1}^k$, representing a resolution proof, and a sequence $[B_i]_{i=0}^k$ of sets of *blocking clauses*. Clauses $\varphi \sqsubseteq B_i$ must not be used for the $(i+1)^{th}$ resolution step. In this way, blocking clauses prevent ADCL from visiting the same part of the search space more than once. ADCL blocks a clause φ after proving that $\bot$ (and thus unsat) cannot be derived after adding φ to the current trace, or if the current trace $\vec{\varphi} :: \vec{\varphi}'$ ends with φ and there is another "more general" trace $\vec{\varphi} :: \vec{\pi}$ such that $\vec{\varphi}' \sqsubseteq \vec{\pi}$ and $|\vec{\varphi}'| \geq |\vec{\pi}|$, where one of the two relations is strict. In the following, Φ denotes the original CHC problem whose satisfiability is analyzed with ADCL.

Definition 9 (State). *A* state *is a triple*

$$(\Pi, [\varphi_i]_{i=1}^k, [B_i]_{i=0}^k)$$

where $\Pi \supseteq \Phi$ is a CHC problem, $B_i \subseteq \mathsf{sip}(\Pi)$ for each $0 \leq i \leq k$, and $[\varphi_i]_{i=1}^k \in \mathsf{sip}(\Pi)^*$. The clauses in $\mathsf{sip}(\Phi)$ are called original clauses *and all clauses in $\mathsf{sip}(\Pi) \setminus \mathsf{sip}(\Phi)$ are called* learned clauses. *A clause $\varphi \sqsubseteq B_k$ is* blocked, *and φ is* active *if it is not blocked and $\mathsf{cond}([\varphi_i]_{i=1}^k :: \varphi)$ is satisfiable.*

Now we are ready to introduce our novel calculus.

Definition 10 (ADCL). *Let the "backtrack function"* bt *be defined as*

$$\mathsf{bt}(\Pi, [\varphi_i]_{i=1}^k, [B_0, \ldots, B_k]) := (\Pi, [\varphi_i]_{i=1}^{k-1}, [B_0, \ldots, B_{k-1} \cup \{\varphi_k\}]).$$

Our calculus is defined by the following rules.

$$\frac{}{\Phi \rightsquigarrow (\Phi, [], [\varnothing])} \quad \text{(INIT)}$$

$$\frac{\varphi \in \mathsf{sip}(\Pi) \textit{ is active}}{(\Pi, \vec{\varphi}, \vec{B}) \rightsquigarrow (\Pi, \vec{\varphi}{::}\varphi, \vec{B}{::}\varnothing)} \quad \text{(STEP)}$$

$$\frac{\vec{\varphi}^{\circlearrowleft} \textit{ is recursive} \quad |\vec{\varphi}^{\circlearrowleft}| = |\vec{B}^{\circlearrowleft}| \quad \mathsf{accel}(\vec{\varphi}^{\circlearrowleft}) = \varphi}{(\Pi, \vec{\varphi}{::}\vec{\varphi}^{\circlearrowleft}, \vec{B}{::}\vec{B}^{\circlearrowleft}) \rightsquigarrow (\Pi \cup \{\varphi\}, \vec{\varphi}{::}\varphi, \vec{B}{::}\{\varphi\})} \quad \text{(ACCELERATE)}$$

$$\frac{\vec{\varphi}' \sqsubset \mathsf{sip}(\Pi) \quad \textit{or} \quad \vec{\varphi}' \sqsubseteq \mathsf{sip}(\Pi) \wedge |\vec{\varphi}'| > 1}{s = (\Pi, \vec{\varphi}{::}\vec{\varphi}', \vec{B}) \rightsquigarrow \mathsf{bt}(s)} \quad \text{(COVERED)}$$

$$\frac{\textit{all rules and queries from } \mathsf{sip}(\Pi) \textit{ are inactive} \quad \varphi \textit{ is not a query}}{s = (\Pi, \vec{\varphi}{::}\varphi, \vec{B}) \rightsquigarrow \mathsf{bt}(s)} \quad \text{(BACKTRACK)}$$

$$\frac{\vec{\varphi} \textit{ is a refutation}}{(\Pi, \vec{\varphi}, \vec{B}) \rightsquigarrow \mathsf{unsat}} \quad \text{(REFUTE)}$$

$$\frac{\textit{all facts and conditional empty clauses from } \mathsf{sip}(\Pi) \textit{ are inactive}}{(\Pi, [], [B]) \rightsquigarrow \mathsf{sat}} \quad \text{(PROVE)}$$

We write $\overset{\text{I}}{\rightsquigarrow}, \overset{\text{S}}{\rightsquigarrow}, \ldots$ to indicate that INIT, STEP, ... was used for a $\rightsquigarrow$-step. All derivations start with INIT. STEP adds an active CHC φ to the trace. Due to the linearity of CHCs, we can restrict ourselves to proofs that start with a fact or a conditional empty clause, but such a restriction is not needed for the correctness of our calculus and thus not enforced.

As soon as $\vec{\varphi}$ has a recursive suffix $\vec{\varphi}^{\circlearrowleft}$ (i.e., a suffix $\vec{\varphi}^{\circlearrowleft}$ such that $\mathsf{res}(\vec{\varphi}^{\circlearrowleft})$ is recursive), ACCELERATE can be used. Then the suffix $\vec{\varphi}^{\circlearrowleft}$ is replaced by the accelerated clause φ and the suffix $\vec{B}^{\circlearrowleft}$ of sets of blocked clauses that corresponds to $\vec{\varphi}^{\circlearrowleft}$ is replaced by $\{\varphi\}$. The reason is that for learned clauses, we always have $\mathsf{res}(\varphi, \varphi) \sqsubseteq \varphi$, and thus applying φ twice in a row is superfluous. So in this way, clauses that were just learned are not used for resolution several times in a row. As mentioned in Sect. 2, the condition of the learned clause may not be expressible in the theory $\mathcal{A}$. Thus, when ACCELERATE is applied, we may implicitly switch to a richer theory $\mathcal{A}'$ (e.g., from linear to non-linear arithmetic).

If a suffix $\vec{\varphi}'$ of the trace is redundant w.r.t. $\mathsf{sip}(\Pi)$, we can backtrack via COVERED, which removes the last element from $\vec{\varphi}'$ (but not the rest of $\vec{\varphi}'$, since this sequence could now be continued in a different way) and blocks it, such that we do not revisit the corresponding part of the search space. So here the redundancy check allows us to use more general (learned) clauses, if available. Here, it is important that we do not backtrack if $\vec{\varphi}'$ is a single, *weakly* redundant clause. Otherwise, COVERED could always be applied after STEP or ACCELERATE and block the last clause from the trace. Thus, we might falsely "prove" satisfiability.

If no further STEP is possible since all CHCs are inactive, then we BACKTRACK as well and block the last clause from $\vec{\varphi}$ to avoid performing the same STEP again.

If we started with a fact and the last CHC in $\vec{\varphi}$ is a query, then $\mathsf{res}(\vec{\varphi})$ is a refutation and REFUTE can be used to prove unsat.

Finally, if we arrive in a state where $\vec{\varphi}$ is empty and all facts and conditional empty clauses are inactive, then PROVE is applicable as we have exhausted the entire search space without proving unsatisfiability, i.e., Φ is satisfiable. Note that we always have $|\vec{B}| = |\vec{\varphi}| + 1$, since we need one additional set of blocking clauses to block facts. While B_0 is initially empty (see INIT), it can be populated via BACKTRACK or COVERED. So eventually, all facts may become blocked, such that sat can be proven via PROVE.

Example 11. Using our calculus, unsatisfiability of the CHC problem Φ in Example 1 can be proven as follows:

$$\Phi \overset{\text{I}}{\rightsquigarrow} (\Phi, [], [\varnothing])$$

$$\overset{\text{S}}{\rightsquigarrow} (\Phi, [\varphi_{\mathsf{f}}], [\varnothing, \varnothing]) \qquad \top \implies \mathsf{Inv}(0, 5000)$$

$$\overset{\text{S}}{\rightsquigarrow} (\Phi, [\varphi_{\mathsf{f}}, \varphi_{\mathsf{r}}|_{\psi_1}], [\varnothing, \varnothing, \varnothing]) \qquad \mathsf{Inv}(0,5000) \implies \mathsf{Inv}(1,5000)$$
$$\overset{\text{A}}{\rightsquigarrow} (\Pi_1, [\varphi_{\mathsf{f}}, \varphi_1^+], [\varnothing, \varnothing, \{\varphi_1^+\}]) \qquad \mathsf{Inv}(0,5000) \implies \mathsf{Inv}(1,5000)$$
$$\overset{\text{S}}{\rightsquigarrow} (\Pi_1, [\varphi_{\mathsf{f}}, \varphi_1^+, \varphi_{\mathsf{r}}|_{\psi_2}], [\varnothing, \varnothing, \{\varphi_1^+,\}, \varnothing]) \qquad \mathsf{Inv}(5000,5000) \implies \mathsf{Inv}(5001,5001)$$
$$\overset{\text{A}}{\rightsquigarrow} (\Pi_2, [\varphi_{\mathsf{f}}, \varphi_1^+, \varphi_2^+], [\varnothing, \varnothing, \{\varphi_1^+\}, \{\varphi_2^+\}]) \qquad \mathsf{Inv}(5000,5000) \implies \mathsf{Inv}(5001,5001)$$
$$\overset{\text{S}}{\rightsquigarrow} (\Pi_2, [\varphi_{\mathsf{f}}, \varphi_1^+, \varphi_2^+, \varphi_{\mathsf{q}}], [\varnothing, \varnothing, \{\varphi_1^+\}, \{\varphi_2^+\}, \varnothing]) \qquad \mathsf{Inv}(10000,10000) \implies \bot$$
$$\overset{\text{R}}{\rightsquigarrow} \mathsf{unsat}$$

Here, we have:

$$\Pi_1 := \Phi \cup \{\varphi_1^+\} \qquad \psi_1 := X_1 < 5000 \land Y_2 = X_2$$
$$\Pi_2 := \Pi_1 \cup \{\varphi_2^+\} \qquad \psi_2 := X_1 \geq 5000 \land Y_2 = X_2 + 1$$

Beside the state of our calculus, we show a ground instance of the last element φ of $\vec{\varphi}$ which results from applying a model for $\mathsf{cond}(\vec{\varphi})$ to φ. In our implementation, we always maintain such a model. In general, these models are not unique: For example, after the first acceleration step, we might use $\mathsf{Inv}(0,5000) \implies \mathsf{Inv}(X_1,5000)$ for any $X_1 \in [1,5000]$. The reason is that φ_1^+ can simulate arbitrarily many resolution steps with $\varphi_{\mathsf{r}}|_{\psi_1}$, depending on the choice of N.

After starting the derivation with Init, we apply the only fact φ_{f} via Step. Next, we apply φ_{r}, projected to the case $X_1 < 5000$. Since φ_{r} is recursive, we may apply Accelerate afterwards, resulting in the new clause φ_1^+.

Then we apply φ_{r}, projected to the case $X_1 \geq 5000$. Note that the current model (resulting in the ground head-literal $\mathsf{Inv}(1,5000)$) cannot be extended to a model for $\varphi_{\mathsf{r}}|_{\psi_2}$ (which requires $X_1 \geq 5000$). However, as the model is not part of the state, we may choose a different one at any point, which is important for implementing ADCL via *incremental* SMT, see Sect. 4. Hence, we can apply $\varphi_{\mathsf{r}}|_{\psi_2}$ nevertheless.

Now we apply Accelerate again, resulting in the new clause φ_2^+. Finally, we apply the only query φ_{q} via Step, resulting in a conditional empty clause with a satisfiable condition, such that we can finish the proof via Refute.

Later (in Definition 14), we will define *reasonable strategies* for applying the rules of our calculus, which ensure that we use Accelerate instead of applying Step 10001 times in our example.

To see how our calculus proves satisfiability, assume that we replace φ_{q} with

$$\mathsf{Inv}(10000, X_2) \land X_2 \neq 10000 \implies \bot.$$

Then resolution with φ_{q} via the rule Step is no longer applicable and our derivation continues as follows after the second application of Accelerate:

$$(\Pi_2, [\varphi_{\mathsf{f}}, \varphi_1^+, \varphi_2^+], [\varnothing, \varnothing, \{\varphi_1^+\}, \{\varphi_2^+\}])$$
$$\overset{\text{B}}{\rightsquigarrow} (\Pi_2, [\varphi_{\mathsf{f}}, \varphi_1^+], [\varnothing, \varnothing, \{\varphi_1^+, \varphi_2^+\}])$$

$$\overset{\mathrm{B}}{\rightsquigarrow} (\Pi_2, [\varphi_{\mathsf{f}}], [\varnothing, \{\varphi_1^+\}])$$
$$\overset{\mathrm{B}}{\rightsquigarrow} (\Pi_2, [], [\{\varphi_{\mathsf{f}}\}])$$
$$\overset{\mathrm{P}}{\rightsquigarrow} \mathsf{sat}$$

For all three BACKTRACK-steps, φ_{q} is clearly inactive, as adding it to $\vec{\varphi}$ results in a resolvent with an unsatisfiable condition. The first BACKTRACK-step is possible since $\varphi_{\mathsf{r}}|_{\psi_1}$ and φ_1^+ are inactive, as they require $X_1 < 5000$ for the first argument X_1 of their body-literal, but φ_2^+ ensures $Y_1 > 5000$ for the first argument Y_1 of its head-literal. Moreover, $\varphi_{\mathsf{r}}|_{\psi_2}$ and φ_2^+ are blocked, as $\varphi_{\mathsf{r}}|_{\psi_2} \sqsubseteq \varphi_2^+$. The second BACKTRACK-step is performed since $\varphi_{\mathsf{r}}|_{\psi_1}$, $\varphi_{\mathsf{r}}|_{\psi_2}$, φ_1^+, and φ_2^+ are blocked (as $\varphi_{\mathsf{r}}|_{\psi_1} \sqsubseteq \varphi_1^+$ and $\varphi_{\mathsf{r}}|_{\psi_2} \sqsubseteq \varphi_2^+$). The third BACKTRACK-step is possible since $\varphi_{\mathsf{r}}|_{\psi_1}$ and φ_1^+ are blocked, and $\varphi_{\mathsf{r}}|_{\psi_2}$ and φ_2^+ cannot be applied without applying φ_1^+ first, so they are inactive. Thus, we reach a state where the only fact φ_{f} is blocked and hence PROVE applies.

To see an example for COVERED, assume that we apply $\varphi_{\mathsf{r}}|_{\psi_1}$ *twice* before using ACCELERATE. Then the following derivation yields the trace that we obtained after the first acceleration step above:

$$(\Phi, [\varphi_{\mathsf{f}}, \varphi_{\mathsf{r}}|_{\psi_1}], [\varnothing, \varnothing, \varnothing])$$
$$\overset{\mathrm{S}}{\rightsquigarrow} (\Phi, [\varphi_{\mathsf{f}}, \varphi_{\mathsf{r}}|_{\psi_1}, \varphi_{\mathsf{r}}|_{\psi_1}], [\varnothing, \varnothing, \varnothing, \varnothing])$$
$$\overset{\mathrm{A}}{\rightsquigarrow} (\Pi_1, [\varphi_{\mathsf{f}}, \varphi_{\mathsf{r}}|_{\psi_1}, \varphi_1^+], [\varnothing, \varnothing, \varnothing, \{\varphi_1^+\}])$$
$$\overset{\mathrm{C}}{\rightsquigarrow} (\Pi_1, [\varphi_{\mathsf{f}}, \varphi_{\mathsf{r}}|_{\psi_1}], [\varnothing, \varnothing, \{\varphi_1^+\}]) \qquad (\text{as } [\varphi_{\mathsf{r}}|_{\psi_1}, \varphi_1^+] \sqsubset \varphi_1^+)$$
$$\overset{\mathrm{C}}{\rightsquigarrow} (\Pi_1, [\varphi_{\mathsf{f}}], [\varnothing, \{\varphi_{\mathsf{r}}|_{\psi_1}\}]) \qquad (\text{as } \varphi_{\mathsf{r}}|_{\psi_1} \sqsubset \varphi_1^+)$$
$$\overset{\mathrm{S}}{\rightsquigarrow} (\Pi_1, [\varphi_{\mathsf{f}}, \varphi_1^+], [\varnothing, \{\varphi_{\mathsf{r}}|_{\psi_1}\}, \varnothing]) \qquad (\dagger)$$

As one can see in the example above, our calculus uses *forward reasoning*, i.e., it starts with a fact and resolves it with rules until a query applies. Alternatively, one could use *backward reasoning* by starting with a query and resolving it with rules until a fact applies, as in logic programming.

Our calculus could easily be adapted for backward reasoning. Then it would start resolving with a query and aim for resolving with a fact, while all other aspects of the calculus would remain unchanged. Such an adaption would be motivated by examples like

$$\begin{aligned} \mathsf{F}(\ldots) \wedge \ldots &\implies \mathsf{G}(\ldots) \\ \mathsf{G}(\ldots) \wedge \ldots &\implies \mathsf{H}(\ldots) \\ \mathsf{G}(\ldots) \wedge \ldots &\implies \bot \end{aligned}$$

where H is the entry-point of a satisfiable sub-problem. With forward reasoning, ADCL might spend lots of time on that sub-problem, whereas unsatisfiability would be proven after just two steps with backward reasoning. However, in our tests, backward reasoning did not help on any example. Presumably, the reason is that the benchmark set from our evaluation does not contain examples with such a structure. Thus, we did not pursue this approach any further.

3.3 Properties of ADCL

In this section, we investigate the main properties of ADCL. Most importantly, ADCL is sound.

Theorem 12 (Soundness). *If $\Phi \rightsquigarrow^* \mathsf{sat}$, then Φ is satisfiable. If $\Phi \rightsquigarrow^* \mathsf{unsat}$, then Φ is unsatisfiable.*

Proof (Sketch).[3] For unsat, we have $\Phi \rightsquigarrow^* (\Pi, \vec{\varphi}, \vec{B}) \rightsquigarrow \mathsf{unsat}$ where $\Pi \equiv_{\mathcal{A}} \Phi$ and $\vec{\varphi} \in \mathsf{sip}(\Pi)^*$ is a refutation. For sat, assume that Φ is unsatisfiable, but $\Phi \rightsquigarrow s = (\Phi, [], [\varnothing]) \rightsquigarrow^* (\Pi, [], [B]) = s' \rightsquigarrow \mathsf{sat}$. Then there is a refutation $\vec{\varphi} \in \mathsf{sip}(\Pi)^*$ that is minimal in the sense that $\varphi_i \not\sqsubseteq \mathsf{sip}(\Pi)$ for all $1 \le i \le |\vec{\varphi}|$ and $\vec{\varphi}' \not\sqsubseteq \mathsf{sip}(\Pi)$ for all infixes $\vec{\varphi}'$ of $\vec{\varphi}$ whose length is at least 2. We say that $\vec{\varphi}$ is *disabled* by a state $(\Pi', \vec{\varphi}', \vec{B}')$ if $\vec{\varphi}'$ has a prefix $[\varphi'_i]_{i=1}^k$ such that $\varphi_i \equiv_{\mathcal{A}} \varphi'_i$ for all $1 \le i \le k$ and $\varphi_{k+1} \equiv_{\mathcal{A}} \varphi$ for some $\varphi \in B'_k$. Then $\vec{\varphi}$ is disabled by s', but not by s. Let $s^{(i)}$ be the last state in the derivation $\Phi \rightsquigarrow^* \mathsf{sat}$ where $\vec{\varphi}$ is enabled. Then $s^{(i)} \overset{\mathrm{S}}{\rightsquigarrow} s^{(i+1)}$ would imply that $\vec{\varphi}$ is enabled in $s^{(i+1)}$; $s^{(i)} \overset{\mathrm{A}}{\rightsquigarrow} s^{(i+1)}$ would imply that two consecutive clauses in $\vec{\varphi}$ are both equivalent to the newly learned clause, contradicting minimality of $\vec{\varphi}$; $s^{(i)} \overset{\mathrm{C}}{\rightsquigarrow} s^{(i+1)}$ would imply that the trace of $s^{(i)}$ is not minimal, which also contradicts minimality of $\vec{\varphi}$; and $s^{(i)} \overset{\mathrm{B}}{\rightsquigarrow} s^{(i+1)}$ would imply that an element of $\vec{\varphi}$ is strictly redundant w.r.t. the last set of blocking clauses in $s^{(i)}$, which again contradicts minimality of $\vec{\varphi}$. Hence, we derived a contradiction. □

Another important property of our calculus is that it cannot get "stuck" in states other than sat or unsat.

Theorem 13. (Normal Forms). *If $\Phi \rightsquigarrow^+ s$ where s is in normal form w.r.t. $\rightsquigarrow$, then $s \in \{\mathsf{sat}, \mathsf{unsat}\}$.*

Clearly, our calculus admits many unintended derivations, e.g., by applying Step over and over again with recursive CHCs instead of accelerating them. To prevent such derivations, a *reasonable strategy* is required.

Definition 14. (Reasonable Strategy). *We call a strategy for $\rightsquigarrow$* reasonable *if the following holds:*

(1) If $(\Pi, \vec{\varphi}, \vec{B}) \rightsquigarrow^+ (\Pi, \vec{\varphi} :: \vec{\varphi}', \vec{B}')$ for some $\vec{\varphi}'$ as in the definition of Covered, *then* Covered *is used.*
(2) Accelerate *is used with higher preference than* Step.

[3] All full proofs can be found in the extended version [26].

(3) ACCELERATE *is only applied to the shortest recursive suffix* $\vec{\varphi}^{\circlearrowleft}$ *such that* $\mathsf{accel}(\vec{\varphi}^{\circlearrowleft})$ *is not redundant w.r.t.* $\mathsf{sip}(\Pi)$.
(4) If $\vec{\varphi} = []$, *then* STEP *is only applied with facts or conditional empty clauses.*

We write $\rightsquigarrow_{rs}$ *for the relation that results from* $\rightsquigarrow$ *by imposing a reasonable strategy.*

Definition 14 (1) ensures that we backtrack if we added a redundant sequence $\vec{\varphi}'$ of CHCs to the trace. However, for refutational completeness (Theorem 15), it is important that the application of COVERED is only enforced if no new clauses have been learned while constructing $\vec{\varphi}'$ (i.e., Π remains unchanged in the derivation $(\Pi, \vec{\varphi}, \vec{B}) \rightsquigarrow^{+} (\Pi, \vec{\varphi} :: \vec{\varphi}', \vec{B}'))$. The reason is that after applying ACCELERATE, the trace might have the form $\vec{\varphi} = \vec{\varphi}_1 :: \vec{\varphi}_2 :: \mathsf{accel}(\varphi^{\circlearrowleft})$ where $\vec{\varphi}_2 :: \mathsf{accel}(\varphi^{\circlearrowleft}) \sqsubset \mathsf{accel}(\varphi^{\circlearrowleft})$ even if $\vec{\varphi}_2 :: \varphi^{\circlearrowleft}$ was non-redundant before learning $\mathsf{accel}(\varphi^{\circlearrowleft})$. If we enforced backtracking via COVERED in such situations (which would yield the trace $\vec{\varphi}_1 :: \vec{\varphi}_2$), then to maintain refutational completeness, we would have to ensure that we eventually reach a state with the trace $\vec{\varphi}_1 :: \mathsf{accel}(\varphi^{\circlearrowleft}) \sqsubseteq \vec{\varphi}$. However, this cannot be guaranteed, since our calculus does not terminate in general (see Theorem 18).

Definition 14 (2) ensures that we do not "unroll" recursive derivations more than once via STEP, but learn new clauses that cover arbitrarily many unrollings via ACCELERATE instead.

Definition 14 (3) has two purposes: First, it prevents us from learning redundant clauses, as we must not apply ACCELERATE if $\mathsf{accel}(\vec{\varphi}^{\circlearrowleft})$ is redundant. Second, it ensures that we accelerate "short" recursive suffixes first. The reason is that if $\vec{\varphi} = \vec{\varphi}_1 :: \vec{\varphi}_2 :: \vec{\varphi}_3$ where $\vec{\varphi}_2 :: \vec{\varphi}_3$ and $\vec{\varphi}_3$ are recursive, then

$$\mathsf{grnd}(\mathsf{accel}(\vec{\varphi}_2 :: \vec{\varphi}_3)) \stackrel{\text{Def. 4}}{=} \bigcup_{n \in \mathbb{N}_{\geq 1}} \mathsf{grnd}((\vec{\varphi}_2 :: \vec{\varphi}_3)^n)$$
$$\subseteq \bigcup_{n \in \mathbb{N}_{\geq 1}} \bigcup_{m \in \mathbb{N}_{\geq 1}} \mathsf{grnd}((\vec{\varphi}_2 :: \vec{\varphi}_3^m)^n) \stackrel{\text{Def. 4}}{=} \mathsf{grnd}(\mathsf{accel}(\vec{\varphi}_2 :: \mathsf{accel}(\vec{\varphi}_3))),$$

but the other direction ("$\supseteq$") does not hold in general. So in this way, we learn more general clauses.

Definition 14 (4) ensures that the first element of $\vec{\varphi}$ is always a fact or a conditional empty clause. For unsatisfiable CHC problems, the reason is that REFUTE will never apply if $\vec{\varphi}$ starts with a rule or a query. For satisfiable CHC problems, PROVE only applies if all facts and conditional empty clauses are blocked. But in order to block them eventually, we have to add them to the trace via STEP, which is only possible if $\vec{\varphi}$ is empty.

Despite the restrictions in Definition 14, our calculus is still refutationally complete.

Theorem 15. (Refutational Completeness). *If* Φ *is unsatisfiable, then*

$$\Phi \rightsquigarrow_{rs}^{*} \mathsf{unsat}.$$

Proof (Sketch). Given a refutation $\vec{\varphi}$, one can inductively define a derivation $\Phi \rightsquigarrow_{rs}^{*} \mathsf{unsat}$ where each step applies ACCELERATE or STEP. For the latter, it is crucial to choose the next clause in such a way that it corresponds to as many steps from $\vec{\varphi}$ as possible, and that it is maximal w.r.t. $\sqsubset$, to avoid the necessity to backtrack via COVERED. □

However, in general our calculus does not terminate, even with a reasonable strategy. Note that even though CHC-SAT is undecidable for, e.g., CHCs over the theory LIA, non-termination of $\leadsto_{rs}$ is not implied by soundness of ADCL. The reason is that we assume oracles for undecidable sub-problems like SMT, checking redundancy, and acceleration. As acceleration may introduce non-linear integer arithmetic, both SMT and checking redundancy may even become undecidable when analyzing CHCs over a decidable theory like LIA.

To prove non-termination, we extend our calculus by one additional component: A mapping $\mathcal{L} : \mathsf{sip}(\Pi) \to \mathcal{P}(\mathsf{sip}(\Phi)^*)$ from $\mathsf{sip}(\Pi)$ to regular languages over $\mathsf{sip}(\Phi)$, where $\mathcal{P}(\mathsf{sip}(\Phi)^*)$ denotes the power set of $\mathsf{sip}(\Phi)^*$. We will show that this mapping gives rise to an alternative characterization of the ground instances of $\mathsf{sip}(\Pi)$, which will be exploited in our non-termination proof (Theorem 18). Moreover, this mapping is also used in our implementation to check redundancy, see Sect. 4. To extend our calculus, we lift $\mathcal{L}$ from $\mathsf{sip}(\Pi)$ to $\mathsf{sip}(\Pi)^*$ as follows:

$$\mathcal{L}(\varepsilon) := \varepsilon \qquad\qquad \mathcal{L}(\vec{\pi} :: \pi) := \mathcal{L}(\vec{\pi}) :: \mathcal{L}(\pi)$$

Here, "::" is also used to denote language concatenation, i.e., we have

$$\mathcal{L}_1 :: \mathcal{L}_2 := \{\vec{\pi}_1 :: \vec{\pi}_2 \mid \vec{\pi}_1 \in \mathcal{L}_1, \vec{\pi}_2 \in \mathcal{L}_2\}.$$

So while we lift other notations to sequences of transitions via resolution, $\mathcal{L}(\vec{\tau})$ does *not* stand for $\mathcal{L}(\mathsf{res}(\vec{\tau}))$.

Definition 16 (ADCL with Regular Languages). *We extend states (see Definition 9) by a fourth component* $\mathcal{L} : \mathsf{sip}(\Pi) \to \mathcal{P}(\mathsf{sip}(\Phi)^*)$. *The rules* INIT *and* ACCELERATE *of the ADCL calculus (see Definition 10) are adapted as follows:*

$$\frac{\mathcal{L}(\varphi) = \{\varphi\} \text{ for all } \varphi \in \mathsf{sip}(\Phi)}{\Phi \leadsto_{rs} (\Phi, [], [\varnothing], \mathcal{L})} \qquad (\text{INIT})$$

$$\frac{\vec{\varphi}^{\circlearrowleft} \text{ is recursive} \quad |\vec{\varphi}^{\circlearrowleft}| = |\vec{B}^{\circlearrowleft}| \quad \mathsf{accel}(\vec{\varphi}^{\circlearrowleft}) = \varphi \quad \mathcal{L}' = \mathcal{L} \uplus (\varphi \mapsto \mathcal{L}(\vec{\varphi}^{\circlearrowleft})^+)}{(\Pi, \vec{\varphi}::\vec{\varphi}^{\circlearrowleft}, \vec{B}::\vec{B}^{\circlearrowleft}, \mathcal{L}) \leadsto_{rs} (\Pi \cup \{\varphi\}, \vec{\varphi}::\varphi, \vec{B}::\{\varphi\}, \mathcal{L}')} \qquad (\text{ACCELERATE})$$

All other rules from Definition 10 leave the last component of the state unchanged.

Here, $\mathcal{L}(\pi)^+$ denotes the "Kleene plus" of $\mathcal{L}(\pi)$, i.e., we have

$$\mathcal{L}(\pi)^+ := \bigcup_{n \in \mathbb{N}_{\geq 1}} \mathcal{L}(\pi)^n.$$

Note that Definition 16 assumes a reasonable strategy (indicated by the notation $\leadsto_{rs}$). Hence, when ACCELERATE is applied, we may assume $\varphi \notin \mathsf{sip}(\Pi) =$

$\mathrm{dom}(\mathcal{L})$. Otherwise, φ would be redundant and hence a reasonable strategy would not allow the application of ACCELERATE. For this reason, we may write "$\uplus$" in the definition of $\mathcal{L}'$.

The following lemma allows us to characterize the ground instances of elements of $\mathsf{sip}(\Pi)$ via $\mathcal{L}$. Here, we lift grnd to sets by defining $\mathsf{grnd}(X) := \bigcup_{x \in X} \mathsf{grnd}(x)$, where X may be a set of CHCs or a language over CHCs. Thus, $\mathsf{grnd}(\mathcal{L}(\pi))$ is the set of all ground instances of the final resolvents of the sequences in $\mathcal{L}(\pi)$.

Lemma 17. *If $\Phi \leadsto_{rs}^{*} (\Pi, \vec{\varphi}, \vec{B}, \mathcal{L})$ and $\pi \in \mathsf{sip}(\Pi)$, then $\mathsf{grnd}(\pi) = \mathsf{grnd}(\mathcal{L}(\pi))$.*

Now we are ready to prove that, even with a reasonable strategy, ADCL does not terminate.

Theorem 18 (Non-Termination). *There exists a satisfiable CHC problem Φ such that $\Phi \not\leadsto_{rs}^{*} \mathsf{sat}$. Thus, $\leadsto_{rs}$ does not terminate.*

Proof (Sketch). One can construct a satisfiable CHC problem Φ such that all (infinitely many) resolution sequences with Φ are *square-free*, i.e., they do not contain a non-empty subsequence of the form $\vec{\varphi} :: \vec{\varphi}$. For example, this can be achieved by encoding the differences between subsequent numbers of the Thue-Morse sequence [45,46]. As an invariant of our calculus, $\mathcal{L}(\Pi)$ just contains finitely many square-free words for any reachable state $(\Pi, \vec{\varphi}, \vec{B}, \mathcal{L})$. As $\mathsf{grnd}(\Pi) = \mathsf{grnd}(\mathcal{L}(\Pi))$, this means that Π cannot cover all resolution sequences with Φ. Thus, the assumption $\Phi \leadsto_{rs}^{*} \mathsf{sat}$ results in a contradiction. □

The construction from the proof of Theorem 18 can also be used to show that there are non-terminating derivations $\Phi \leadsto_{rs} s_1 \leadsto_{rs} s_2 \leadsto_{rs} \ldots$ where Φ is unsatisfiable. However, in this case there is also another derivation $\Phi \leadsto_{rs}^{*} \mathsf{unsat}$ due to refutational completeness (see Theorem 15).

4 Implementing ADCL

We now explain how we implemented ADCL efficiently in our tool LoAT. Here we focus on proving unsatisfiability. The reason is that our implementation cannot prove sat at the moment, since it uses certain approximations that are incorrect for sat, as detailed below. Thus, when applying PROVE, our implementation returns unknown instead of sat. Our implementation uses Yices [18] and Z3 [44] for SMT solving. Moreover, it is based on the acceleration technique from [23], whose implementation solves recurrence relations with PURRS [4].

Checking Redundancy. To check redundancy in ACCELERATE (as required for reasonable strategies in Definition 14), we use the fourth component $\mathcal{L}$ of states introduced in Definition 16. More precisely, for ACCELERATE, we check if $\mathcal{L}(\vec{\varphi}^{\circlearrowleft})^{+} \subseteq \mathcal{L}(\varphi)$ holds for some learned clause φ. In that case, $\mathsf{accel}(\vec{\varphi}^{\circlearrowleft})$ is redundant due to Lemma 17. Since $\mathcal{L}(\vec{\varphi}^{\circlearrowleft})^{+} \subseteq \mathcal{L}(\varphi)$ is simply an inclusion check for regular languages, it can be implemented efficiently using finite automata. Our implementation uses the automata library libFAUDES [41].

However, this is just a sufficient criterion for redundancy. For example, a learned clause might be redundant w.r.t. an original clause, but such redundancies cannot be detected using $\mathcal{L}$. To see this, note that we have $|\mathcal{L}(\varphi)| = 1$ if φ is an original clause, but $|\mathcal{L}(\varphi)| = \infty$ if φ is a learned clause.

For COVERED, we also check redundancy via $\mathcal{L}$, but if $\vec{\varphi}' = \varphi'$, i.e., if $|\vec{\varphi}'| = 1$, then we only apply COVERED if φ' is an original clause. Then $\mathcal{L}(\varphi') \subseteq \mathcal{L}(\varphi)$ for some $\varphi \neq \varphi'$ implies that φ is a learned clause. Hence, we have $\mathcal{L}(\varphi') \subset \mathcal{L}(\varphi)$, as $|\mathcal{L}(\varphi')| = 1 < |\mathcal{L}(\varphi)| = \infty$. This is just a heuristic, as even $\mathcal{L}(\varphi') \subset \mathcal{L}(\varphi)$ just implies $\varphi' \sqsubseteq \varphi$, but not $\varphi' \sqsubset \varphi$. To see this, consider an original clause $\varphi = (\mathsf{F}(X) \implies \mathsf{F}(0))$. Then $\mathcal{L}(\varphi) = \{\varphi\}$, $\mathsf{accel}(\varphi) \equiv_{\mathcal{A}} \varphi$ (but not necessarily $\mathsf{accel}(\varphi) = \varphi$, as $\mathsf{accel}(\varphi)$ and φ might differ syntactically), and $\mathcal{L}(\mathsf{accel}(\varphi)) = \mathcal{L}(\varphi)^+$. So we have $\mathcal{L}(\varphi) \subset \mathcal{L}(\mathsf{accel}(\varphi))$ and $\varphi \sqsubseteq \mathsf{accel}(\varphi)$, but $\varphi \not\sqsubset \mathsf{accel}(\varphi)$. This is uncritical for proving unsat, but a potential soundness issue for proving sat, which is one reason why our current implementation cannot prove sat.

Implementing STEP and Blocked Clauses. To find an active clause in STEP, we proceed as described before Definition 8, i.e., we search for a suitable element of $\mathsf{sip}(\Pi)$ "on the fly". So we search for a clause $\varphi \in \Pi$ whose body-literal unifies with the head-literal of $\mathsf{res}(\vec{\varphi})$ using an mgu θ. Then we use an SMT solver to check whether

$$\theta(\mathsf{cond}(\mathsf{res}(\vec{\varphi}))) \wedge \theta(\mathsf{cond}(\varphi)) \wedge \bigwedge_{\pi \in B \cap \mathsf{sip}(\varphi)} \neg\theta(\mathsf{cond}(\pi)) \qquad \text{(STEP–SMT)}$$

is satisfiable, where B is the last element of $\vec{B}$. Here, we assume that $\mathsf{res}(\vec{\varphi})$ and φ are variable disjoint (and thus the mgu θ exists). If we find a model σ for STEP–SMT, then we apply STEP with $\varphi|_{\mathsf{sip}(\mathsf{cond}(\varphi),\sigma)}$. So to exclude blocked clauses, we do not use the redundancy check based on $\mathcal{L}$ explained above, but we conjoin the negated conditions of certain blocked clauses to STEP–SMT. To see why we only consider blocked clauses from $\mathsf{sip}(\varphi)$, consider the case that $B = \{\pi\}$ is a singleton. Note that both $\theta(\mathsf{cond}(\varphi))$ and $\theta(\mathsf{cond}(\pi))$ might contain variables that do not occur as arguments of predicates in the (unified) head- or body-literals. So if

$$\begin{aligned}
\varphi &\equiv_{\mathcal{A}} \forall \vec{X}, \vec{Y}_{\varphi}, \vec{X}'.\ \mathsf{F}(\vec{X}) \wedge \psi_{\varphi}(\vec{X}, \vec{Y}_{\varphi}, \vec{X}') \implies \mathsf{G}(\vec{X}'), \\
\varphi' &\equiv_{\mathcal{A}} \forall \vec{X}, \vec{Y}_{\varphi'}, \vec{X}'.\ \mathsf{F}(\vec{X}) \wedge \psi_{\varphi'}(\vec{X}, \vec{Y}_{\varphi'}, \vec{X}') \implies \mathsf{G}(\vec{X}'), \qquad \text{and} \\
\pi &\equiv_{\mathcal{A}} \forall \vec{X}, \vec{Y}_{\pi}, \vec{X}'.\ \mathsf{F}(\vec{X}) \wedge \psi_{\pi}(\vec{X}, \vec{Y}_{\pi}, \vec{X}') \implies \mathsf{G}(\vec{X}'),
\end{aligned}$$

for some $\varphi' \in \mathsf{sip}(\varphi)$, then $\varphi' \sqsubseteq \pi$ iff

$$\models_{\mathcal{A}} \psi_{\varphi'} \implies \exists \vec{Y}_{\pi}.\ \psi_{\pi}. \qquad (\sqsubseteq\text{–EQUIV})$$

Thus, to ensure that we only find models σ such that $\mathsf{sip}(\mathsf{cond}(\varphi), \sigma)$ is not blocked by π, we would have to conjoin

$$\neg(\psi_{\varphi} \implies \exists \vec{Y}_{\pi}.\ \psi_{\pi}) \quad \equiv_{\mathcal{A}} \quad \psi_{\varphi} \wedge \forall \vec{Y}_{\pi}.\ \neg\psi_{\pi}$$

to the SMT problem. Unfortunately, as SMT solvers have limited support for quantifiers, such an encoding is impractical. Hence, we again use a sufficient criterion for redundancy: If

$$\models_{\mathcal{A}} \psi_{\varphi'} \implies \psi_{\pi}, \qquad (\sqsubseteq\text{–SUFFICIENT})$$

then $\sqsubseteq$–EQUIV trivially holds as well. So to exclude conjunctive variants φ' of φ where $\sqsubseteq$–SUFFICIENT is valid, we add

$$\neg(\psi_{\varphi} \implies \psi_{\pi}) \quad \equiv_{\mathcal{A}} \quad \psi_{\varphi} \land \neg\psi_{\pi} \qquad (\not\sqsubseteq\text{–SUFFICIENT})$$

to the SMT problem. If $\vec{Y}_{\pi} \not\subseteq \vec{Y}_{\varphi}$, then satisfiability of $\not\sqsubseteq$–SUFFICIENT is usually trivial. Thus, to avoid increasing the size of the SMT problem unnecessarily, we only add $\not\sqsubseteq$–SUFFICIENT to the SMT problem if $\pi \in \mathsf{sip}(\varphi)$. Instead, we could try to rename variables from $\vec{Y}_{\pi}$ to enforce $\vec{Y}_{\pi} \subseteq \vec{Y}_{\varphi}$. However, it is difficult to predict which renaming is the "right" one, i.e., which renaming would allow us to prove redundancy.

If $B \cap \mathsf{sip}(\varphi)$ contains several clauses $\pi_1, \ldots, \pi_\ell$, then $\sqsubseteq$–SUFFICIENT becomes

$$\models_{\mathcal{A}} \psi_{\varphi'} \implies \mathsf{cond}(\pi_1) \text{ or } \ldots \text{ or } \models_{\mathcal{A}} \psi_{\varphi'} \implies \mathsf{cond}(\pi_\ell) \quad (\sqsubseteq\text{–SUFFICIENT}^+)$$

Instead, our encoding excludes syntactic implicants φ' of φ where

$$\models_{\mathcal{A}} \psi_{\varphi'} \implies \mathsf{cond}(\pi_1) \lor \ldots \lor \mathsf{cond}(\pi_\ell) \qquad (\sqsubseteq\text{–INSUFFICIENT}^+)$$

which is a necessary, but not a sufficient condition for $\sqsubseteq$–SUFFICIENT$^+$. To see why this is not a problem, first note that $\sqsubseteq$–SUFFICIENT$^+$ trivially holds if $\psi_{\varphi'} \in \{\mathsf{cond}(\pi_i) \mid 1 \leq i \leq \ell\}$. Otherwise, we have

$$\models_{\mathcal{A}} (\mathsf{cond}(\pi_1) \lor \ldots \lor \mathsf{cond}(\pi_\ell)) \implies \bigvee \mathsf{sip}(\psi_{\varphi}) \setminus \{\psi_{\varphi'}\}$$

because we assumed $\psi_{\varphi'} \notin \{\mathsf{cond}(\pi_i) \mid 1 \leq i \leq \ell\}$, which implies $\{\mathsf{cond}(\pi_i) \mid 1 \leq i \leq \ell\} \subseteq \mathsf{sip}(\psi_{\varphi}) \setminus \{\psi_{\varphi'}\}$. Together with $\sqsubseteq$–INSUFFICIENT$^+$, this implies

$$\models_{\mathcal{A}} \psi_{\varphi'} \implies \bigvee \mathsf{sip}(\psi_{\varphi}) \setminus \{\psi_{\varphi'}\}.$$

Therefore, we have $\psi_{\varphi} \equiv_{\mathcal{A}} \bigvee \mathsf{sip}(\psi_{\varphi}) \setminus \{\psi_{\varphi'}\}$. Thus, we may assume that $\sqsubseteq$–INSUFFICIENT$^+$ implies redundancy without loss of generality. The reason is that we could analyze the following equivalent CHC problem instead of Π, otherwise:

$$(\Pi \setminus \{\varphi\}) \cup (\mathsf{sip}(\varphi) \setminus \{\varphi'\})$$

Hence, in STEP–SMT, we add (a variable-renamed variant of)

$$\begin{aligned} \neg(\psi_{\varphi} \implies \mathsf{cond}(\pi_1) \lor \ldots \lor \mathsf{cond}(\pi_\ell)) \quad &\equiv_{\mathcal{A}} \quad \psi_{\varphi} \land \neg\mathsf{cond}(\pi_1) \land \ldots \land \neg\mathsf{cond}(\pi_\ell) \\ &\equiv_{\mathcal{A}} \quad \mathsf{cond}(\varphi) \land \bigwedge_{\pi \in B \cap \mathsf{sip}(\varphi)} \neg\mathsf{cond}(\pi) \end{aligned}$$

to the SMT problem.

Example 19. Consider the state (†) from Example 11. First applying STEP with $\varphi_r|_{\psi_1}$ and then applying COVERED yields

$$(\Pi_1, \vec{\varphi}, [\varnothing, \{\varphi_r|_{\psi_1}\}, \{\varphi_r|_{\psi_1}\}])$$

where $\vec{\varphi} = [\varphi_f, \varphi_1^+]$. When attempting a STEP with an element of $\mathsf{sip}(\varphi_r)$, we get:

$$\theta(\mathsf{cond}(\vec{\varphi})) \equiv_{\mathcal{A}} X_1 = 0 \wedge X_2 = 5k \wedge N > 0 \wedge X_1' < 5001 \wedge X_1' = X_1 + N \wedge X_2' = X_2$$
$$\theta(\mathsf{cond}(\varphi_r)) \equiv_{\mathcal{A}} ((X_1' < 5k \wedge Y_2 = X_2') \vee (X_1' \geq 5k \wedge Y_2 = X_2' + 1))$$
$$\bigwedge_{\pi \in B \cap \mathsf{sip}(\varphi_r)} \neg\theta(\mathsf{cond}(\pi)) = \neg\theta(\mathsf{cond}(\varphi_r|_{\psi_1})) \equiv_{\mathcal{A}} X_1' \geq 5k \vee Y_2 \neq X_2'$$

Here, $5k$ abbreviates 5000. Then STEP–SMT is equivalent to

$$X_1 = 0 \wedge X_2 = N = X_1' = X_2' = 5k \wedge Y_2 = 5001.$$

Hence, we have $\sigma \models_{\mathcal{A}} X_1' \geq 5k \wedge Y_2 = X_2' + 1$ for the unique model σ of STEP–SMT, i.e., σ satisfies the second disjunct of $\mathsf{cond}(\varphi_r)$. Thus, we add $\varphi_r|_{\mathsf{sip}(\mathsf{cond}(\varphi_r),\sigma)} = \varphi_r|_{\psi_2}$ to the trace.

Leveraging Incremental SMT. The search for suitable models can naturally be implemented via incremental SMT solving: When trying to apply STEP, we construct θ in such a way that $\theta(\mathsf{cond}(\mathsf{res}(\vec{\varphi}))) = \mathsf{cond}(\mathsf{res}(\vec{\varphi}))$. This is easily possible, as θ just needs to unify predicates whose arguments are duplicate free and pairwise disjoint vectors of variables. Then we push

$$\theta(\mathsf{cond}(\varphi)) \wedge \bigwedge_{\pi \in B \cap \mathsf{sip}(\varphi)} \neg\theta(\mathsf{cond}(\pi)) \qquad \text{(INCREMENTAL)}$$

to the SMT solver. If the model from the previous resolution step can be extended to satisfy INCREMENTAL, then the SMT solver can do so, otherwise it searches for another model. If it fails to find a model, we pop INCREMENTAL, i.e., we remove it from the current SMT problem. ACCELERATE can be implemented similarly by popping $\theta(\mathsf{cond}(\vec{\varphi}^{\circlearrowleft}))$ and pushing $\theta(\mathsf{cond}(\varphi))$ instead.

Note that satisfiability of $\vec{\varphi}$ is an invariant of ADCL. Hence, as soon as the last element of $\vec{\varphi}$ is a query, REFUTE can be applied without further SMT checks. Otherwise, if STEP cannot be applied with any clause, then BACKTRACK or PROVE can be applied without further SMT queries.

Dealing with Incompleteness. As mentioned in Sect. 3, we assumed that we have oracles for checking redundancy, satisfiability of $\mathsf{QF}(\mathcal{A})$-formulas, and acceleration when we formalized ADCL. As this is not the case in practice, we now explain how to proceed if those techniques fail or approximate.

As explained above, SMT is needed for checking activity in STEP. If the SMT solver fails, we assume inactivity. Thus, we do not exhaust the entire search space if we falsely classify active clauses as inactive. Hence, we may miss refutations, which is another reason why our current implementation cannot prove sat.

Regarding acceleration, our implementation of accel may return under-approximations, i.e., we just have $\mathsf{grnd}(\mathsf{accel}(\varphi)) \subseteq \bigcup_{n \in \mathbb{N}_{\geq 1}} \mathsf{grnd}(\varphi^n)$. While this is uncritical for correctness by itself (as learned clauses are still entailed by Φ), it weakens our heuristic for redundancy via $\mathcal{L}$, as we no longer have $\mathsf{grnd}(\varphi) = \mathsf{grnd}(\mathcal{L}(\varphi))$, but just $\mathsf{grnd}(\varphi) \subseteq \mathsf{grnd}(\mathcal{L}(\varphi))$ for learned clauses φ.

Another pitfall when using under-approximating acceleration techniques is that we may have $\vec{\varphi}^{\circlearrowleft} \not\sqsubseteq \mathsf{accel}(\vec{\varphi}^{\circlearrowleft})$. In this case, applying Accelerate can result in an inconsistent trace where $\mathsf{cond}(\vec{\varphi})$ is unsatisfiable. To circumvent this problem, we only add $\mathsf{accel}(\vec{\varphi}^{\circlearrowleft})$ to the trace after removing $\vec{\varphi}^{\circlearrowleft}$ if doing so results in a consistent trace. Here, we could do better by taking the current model σ into account when accelerating $\vec{\varphi}^{\circlearrowleft}$ in order to ensure $\sigma \models_{\mathcal{A}} \mathsf{cond}(\mathsf{accel}(\vec{\varphi}^{\circlearrowleft}))$. We leave that to future work.

Restarts. When testing our implementation, we noticed that several instances "jiggled", i.e., they were solved in some test runs, but failed in others. The reason is a phenomenon that is well-known in SAT solving, called "heavy-tail behavior". Here, the problem is that the solver sometimes gets "stuck" in a part of the state space whose exploration is very expensive, even though finding a solution in another part of the search space is well within the solver's capabilities. This problem also occurs in our implementation, due to the depth-first strategy of our solver (where derivations may even be non-terminating, see Theorem 18). To counter this problem, SAT solvers use restarts [28], where one of the most popular approaches has been proposed by Luby et al. [42]. For SAT solving, the idea is to restart the search after a certain number of conflicts, where the number of conflicts for the next restart is determined by the *Luby sequence*, scaled by a parameter u. When restarting, randomization is used to avoid revisiting the same part of the search space again. We use the same strategy with $u = 10$, where we count the number of learned clauses instead of the number of conflicts. To restart the search, we clear the trace, change the seed of the SMT solver (which may result in different models such that we may use different syntactic implicants), and shuffle the vectors of clauses (to change the order in which clauses are used for resolution).

5 Related Work and Experiments

We presented the novel ADCL calculus for (dis)proving satisfiability of CHCs. Its distinguishing feature is its use of acceleration for learning new clauses. For unsatisfiability, these learned clauses often enable very short resolution proofs for CHC problems whose original clauses do not admit short resolution proofs. For satisfiability, learned clauses often allow for covering the entire (usually infinite) search space by just considering finitely many resolution sequences.

Related Work. The most closely related work is [34], where acceleration is used in two ways: (1) as preprocessing and (2) to generalize interpolants in a CEGAR loop. In contrast to (1), we use acceleration "on the fly" to accelerate resolvents. In contrast to (2), we do not use abstractions, so our learned clauses can directly be used in resolution proofs. Moreover, [34] only applies acceleration to conjunctive clauses, whereas we accelerate conjunctive variants of arbitrary clauses. So in our approach, acceleration techniques are applicable more often, which is particularly useful for finding long counterexamples. However, our approach *solely* relies on acceleration to handle recursive CHCs, whereas [34] incorporates acceleration techniques into a CEGAR loop, which can also analyze recursive CHCs without accelerating them. Thus, the approach from [34] is orthogonal to ADCL. Both (1) and (2) are implemented in Eldarica, but according to its authors, (2) is just supported for transition systems, but not yet for CHCs. Hence, we only considered (1) in our evaluation (named Eld. Acc. below). Earlier, an approach similar to (2) has been proposed in [13], but to the best of our knowledge, it has never been implemented.

Transition power abstraction (TPA) [7] computes a sequence of over-approximations for transition systems where the nth element captures 2^n instead of just n steps of the transition relation. So like ADCL, TPA can help to find long refutations quickly, but in contrast to ADCL, TPA relies on over-approximations.

Some leading techniques for CHC-SAT like GPDR [33] and, in particular, the Spacer algorithm [37], are adaptions of the IC3 algorithm [11] from transition systems to CHCs. IC3 computes a sequence of abstractions of reachable states, aiming to find an abstraction that is inductive w.r.t. the transition relation and implies safety.

Other approaches for CHC-SAT are based on interpolation [17,35], CEGAR and predicate abstraction [29,35], automata [17], machine learning [20,51], bounded model checking (BMC) [6], or combinations thereof.

Related approaches for transition systems include [5] and [10]. The approach of [5] uses acceleration to analyze a sequence of *flattenings* of a given transition system, i.e., under-approximations without nested loops, until a counterexample is found or a fixpoint is reached. Like ADCL, this approach does not terminate in general. However, it does terminate for so-called *flattable* systems. Whether ADCL terminates for flattable systems as well is an interesting question for future work. In contrast to ADCL, [5] has no notion of learning or redundancy, so that the same computations may have to be carried our several times for different flattenings.

The technique of [10] also lifts acceleration techniques to transition systems, but circumvents non-termination by using approximative acceleration techniques in the presence of disjunctions. In contrast, ADCL handles disjunctions via syntactic implicants. Like ADCL, [10, Alg. 2] learns new transitions (Line 9), but only if they are non-redundant (Line 8). However, it applies acceleration to all syntactic self-loops, whereas ADCL explores the state space starting from facts, such that only reachable loops are accelerated. Note that the approach from [10] is very similar to the approach that has been used by earlier versions of LoAT for proving non-termination [24]. We recently showed in [25] that for the purpose of proving non-termination, ADCL is superior to LoAT's earlier approach.

Finally, [40] uses under-approximating acceleration techniques to enrich the control-flow graph of C programs in order to find "deep counterexamples", i.e., long refutations. In contrast to ADCL, [40] relies on external model checkers for finding counterexamples, and it has no notion of redundancy so that the model checker may explore "superfluous" paths that use original instead of accelerated edges of the control-flow graph.

Regarding acceleration, there are many results regarding classes of loops over integer variables where linear arithmetic suffices to express their transitive closure, i.e., they can be accelerated within a decidable theory. The most important such classes are Difference Bounds [16], Octagons [8], Finite Monoid Affine Relations [21], and Vector Addition Systems with States [31]. In an orthogonal line of research, monotonicity-based acceleration techniques have been developed [22,23,40]. While the latter provide fewer theoretical guarantees in terms of completeness and whether the result can be expressed in a decidable logic or not, they are not restricted to loops whose transitive closure is definable in linear arithmetic.

Regarding other theories, the technique from [31] for Vector Addition Systems with States has also been applied to systems over rationals [48]. Similarly, monotonicity-based approaches immediately carry over to rationals or reals. The only approach for acceleration in the presence of Boolean variables that we are aware of is [47]. However, this technique yields over-approximations.

Finally, some acceleration techniques for arrays have been proposed, e.g., [15,32]. The approach of [15] improves the framework of [39] to reason about programs with arrays using a first-order theorem prover by integrating specialized techniques for dealing with array accesses where the indices are monotonically increasing or decreasing. The technique of [32] uses quantifier elimination techniques to accelerate loops where arrays can be separated into *read*- and *write-only* arrays.

Experiments. So far, our implementation of ADCL in LoAT is restricted to integer arithmetic. Thus, to evaluate our approach, we used the examples from the category LIA-Lin (linear CHCs with linear integer arithmetic) from the CHC competition '22 [14], which contains numerous CHC problems resulting from actual program verification tasks. Somewhat surprisingly, these examples contain additional features like variables of type `Bool` and the operators `div` and `mod`. Since variables of type `Bool` are used in most of the examples, we extended our implementation with rudimentary support for `Bool`s. In particular, we implemented a simplistic acceleration technique for `Bool`s (note that we cannot use the approach of [47], as it yields over-approximations). We excluded the 72 examples that use `div` or `mod`, as those operators are not supported by our implementation.

To accelerate CHCs where some variables are of type `Bool`, we use an adaption of the acceleration calculus from [23]. To apply it to $\varphi := (\mathsf{F}(\vec{X}) \wedge \psi \implies \mathsf{F}(\vec{Y}))$, φ needs to be *deterministic*, i.e., there must be a substitution θ such that $\psi \models_{\mathcal{A}} \vec{Y} = \theta(\vec{X})$ and $\mathcal{V}(\theta(\vec{X})) \subseteq \vec{X}$. Then LoAT has to compute a *closed form*, i.e., a vector $\vec{C}$ such that $\vec{C} \equiv_{\mathcal{A}} \theta^N(\vec{X})$. For integer variables, closed forms are computed via recurrence solving. For Boolean variables B, LoAT can only construct a closed form if there is a $k \in \mathbb{N}$ such that $\theta^k(B)$ does not contain Boolean variables, or $\theta^k(B) = \theta^{k+1}(B)$. Once a closed form has been computed, the calculus from [23] can be applied. However, in the presence of Booleans, it has to be restricted to theory-agnostic acceleration techniques. So more precisely, in the presence of Booleans, only the acceleration techniques *monotonic increase* and *monotonic decrease* from [23] can be used.

Using the remaining 427 examples, we compared our implementation with the leading CHC-SAT solvers Spacer [37] (which is part of Z3 [44]), Eldarica [35], and Golem [7]. Additionally, we compared with Z3's implementation of BMC. As mentioned above, Eldarica supports acceleration as preprocessing. Thus, besides Eldarica's default configuration (which does not use acceleration), we also compared with a configuration Eld. Acc. where we enabled this feature. By default, Golem uses the Spacer algorithm, but the Spacer implementation in Z3 performed better in our tests. Thus, we used Golem's implementation of TPA instead, which targets similar classes of examples like ADCL, as explained above. We used Z3 4.11.2, Eldarica 2.0.8, and Golem 0.3.0 and ran our experiments on StarExec [49] with a wallclock timeout of 300s, a cpu timeout of 1200s, and a memory limit of 128GB per example.

The results can be seen in Fig. 2. We evaluated all tools on the 209 examples that do not use `Bools` (Int only) and on the entire benchmark set (Int & Bool). The table on the left shows that LoAT is very competitive w.r.t. proving unsat in terms of solved instances. The entries in the column "unique" show the number of examples where the respective tool succeeds and all others fail. Here we disregard Eld. Acc., as it would be pointless to consider several variants of the same algorithm in such a comparison. If we consider Eld. Acc. instead of Eldarica, then the numbers change according to the values given in parentheses.

The numbers indicate that LoAT is particularly powerful on examples that operate on `Ints` only, but it is also competitive for proving unsatisfiability of examples that may operate on `Bools`, where it is only slightly weaker than Spacer and Z3 BMC. This is not surprising, as the core of LoAT's approach are its acceleration techniques, which have been designed for integers. In contrast, Spacer's algorithm is similar to GPDR [33], which generalizes the IC3 algorithm [11] from transition systems over Booleans to transition systems over theories (like integers), and BMC is theory agnostic.

The figure on the right shows how many proofs of unsatisfiability were found within a given runtime, by each tool. Here, all examples (Int & Bool) are taken into account. LoAT finds many proofs of unsatisfiability quickly (73 proofs within 8 s). Z3 BMC catches up after 12 s (73 proofs for both LoAT and Z3 BMC) and takes over the lead after 14 s (LoAT 73, Z3 BMC 74). Spacer catches up with LoAT after 260 s.

To illustrate LoAT's ability to find short refutations, Table 1 compares the number of resolution steps in LoAT's "accelerated" refutations (that also use learned clauses) with the corresponding refutations that only use original clauses.

		unsat		sat
		solved	unique	solved
Int only	LoAT	30	5 (5)	0
	Z3 BMC	24	1 (1)	23
	Spacer	24	0 (0)	93
	Eldarica	23	0 (–)	122
	Golem TPA	15	0 (0)	45
	Eld. Acc.	21	– (0)	105
Int & Bool	LoAT	78	11 (5)	0
	Z3 BMC	84	5 (5)	28
	Spacer	79	2 (2)	183
	Eldarica	53	0 (–)	165
	Golem TPA	56	0 (0)	73
	Eld. Acc.	56	– (4)	142

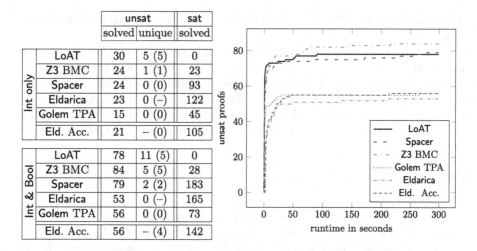

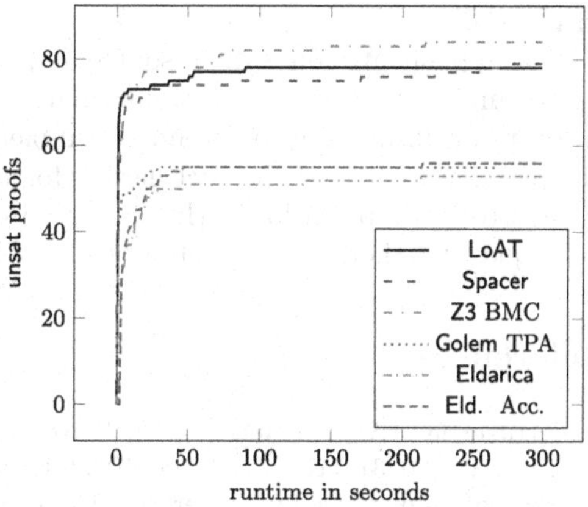

Fig. 2. Comparing LoAT with other CHC solvers

Table 1. Comparing lengths of refutation

example	LoAT's refutation	original refutation
`chc-LIA-Lin_043.smt2`	6	965553
`chc-LIA-Lin_045.smt2`	2	684682683
`chc-LIA-Lin_047.smt2`	3	72536
`chc-LIA-Lin_059.smt2`	3	100000001
`chc-LIA-Lin_154.smt2`	2	134217729
`chc-LIA-Lin_358.smt2`	12	400005
`chc-LIA-Lin_362.smt2`	12	400005
`chc-LIA-Lin_386.smt2`	15	600003
`chc-LIA-Lin_401.smt2`	8	200005
`chc-LIA-Lin_402.smt2`	4	134217723
`chc-LIA-Lin_405.smt2`	9	100012

Here, we restrict ourselves to those instances that can only be solved by LoAT, as the unsatisfiable CHC problems that can also be solved by other tools usually already admit quite short refutations without learned clauses. To compute the length of the original refutations, we instrumented each predicate with an additional argument c. Moreover, we extended the condition of each fact $\psi \implies \mathsf{G}(..., c)$ with $c = 1$ and the condition of each rule $\mathsf{F}(..., c) \wedge \psi \implies \mathsf{G}(..., c')$ with $c' = c + 1$. Then the value of c before applying a query corresponds to the number of resolution steps that one would need if one only used original clauses, and it can be extracted from the model found by the SMT solver. The numbers clearly show that learning clauses via acceleration allows to reduce the length of refutations dramatically. In 76 cases, LoAT learned clauses with non-linear arithmetic.

Our implementation is open-source and available on Github. For the sources, a pre-compiled binary, and more information on our evaluation, we refer to [1,2]. In future work, we plan to extend our implementation to also prove sat, and we will investigate how to construct models for satisfiable CHC problems. Moreover, we want to add support for further theories by developing specialized acceleration techniques. Furthermore, we intend to lift ADCL to non-linear CHCs.

References

1. Artifact for "ADCL: Acceleration Driven Clause Learning for Constrained Horn Clauses" (2023). https://doi.org/10.5281/zenodo.8146788
2. Evaluation of "ADCL: Acceleration Driven Clause Learning for Constrained Horn Clauses" (2023). https://loat-developers.github.io/adcl-evaluation. Source code of LoAT Source code of LoAT available at https://github.com/loat-developers/LoAT/tree/v0.4.0
3. Alt, L., Blicha, M., Hyvärinen, A.E.J., Sharygina, N.: SolCMC: Solidity compiler's model checker. In: Shoham, S., Vizel, Y. (eds.) CAV 2022. LNCS, vol. 13371, pp. 325–338. Springer, Cham (2022). https://doi.org/10.1007/978-3-031-13185-1_16
4. Bagnara, R., Pescetti, A., Zaccagnini, A., Zaffanella, E.: PURRS: towards computer algebra support for fully automatic worst-case complexity analysis. CoRR abs/cs/0512056 (2005). https://doi.org/10.48550/arXiv.cs/0512056
5. Bardin, S., Finkel, A., Leroux, J., Schnoebelen, P.: Flat acceleration in symbolic model checking. In: Peled, D.A., Tsay, Y.-K. (eds.) ATVA 2005. LNCS, vol. 3707, pp. 474–488. Springer, Heidelberg (2005). https://doi.org/10.1007/11562948_35
6. Biere, A.: Bounded model checking. In: Handbook of Satisfiability - Second Edition. Frontiers in Artificial Intelligence and Applications, vol. 336, pp. 739–764. IOS Press (2021). https://doi.org/10.3233/FAIA201002
7. Blicha, M., Fedyukovich, G., Hyvärinen, A.E.J., Sharygina, N.: Transition power abstractions for deep counterexample detection. In: Fisman, D., Rosu, G. (eds.) TACAS 2022. LNCS, vol. 13243, pp. 524–542. Springer, Cham (2022). https://doi.org/10.1007/978-3-030-99524-9_29
8. Bozga, M., Gîrlea, C., Iosif, R.: Iterating octagons. In: Kowalewski, S., Philippou, A. (eds.) TACAS 2009. LNCS, vol. 5505, pp. 337–351. Springer, Heidelberg (2009). https://doi.org/10.1007/978-3-642-00768-2_29
9. Bozga, M., Iosif, R., Konečný, F.: Fast acceleration of ultimately periodic relations. In: Touili, T., Cook, B., Jackson, P. (eds.) CAV 2010. LNCS, vol. 6174, pp. 227–242. Springer, Heidelberg (2010). https://doi.org/10.1007/978-3-642-14295-6_23
10. Bozga, M., Iosif, R., Konečný, F.: Relational analysis of integer programs. Technical report TR-2012-10, VERIMAG (2012). https://www-verimag.imag.fr/TR/TR-2012-10.pdf
11. Bradley, A.R.: SAT-based model checking without unrolling. In: Jhala, R., Schmidt, D. (eds.) VMCAI 2011. LNCS, vol. 6538, pp. 70–87. Springer, Heidelberg (2011). https://doi.org/10.1007/978-3-642-18275-4_7
12. Calzavara, S., Grishchenko, I., Maffei, M.: HornDroid: practical and sound static analysis of Android applications by SMT solving. In: EuroS&P 2016, pp. 47–62. IEEE (2016). https://doi.org/10.1109/EuroSP.2016.16

13. Caniart, N., Fleury, E., Leroux, J., Zeitoun, M.: Accelerating interpolation-based model-checking. In: Ramakrishnan, C.R., Rehof, J. (eds.) TACAS 2008. LNCS, vol. 4963, pp. 428–442. Springer, Heidelberg (2008). https://doi.org/10.1007/978-3-540-78800-3_32
14. CHC Competition. https://chc-comp.github.io
15. Chen, Y., Kovács, L., Robillard, S.: Theory-specific reasoning about loops with arrays using Vampire. In: Kovács, L., Voronkov, A. (eds.) Vampire@IJCAR 2016, pp. 16–32. EPiC 44 (2016). https://doi.org/10.29007/qk21
16. Comon, H., Jurski, Y.: Multiple counters automata, safety analysis and Presburger arithmetic. In: Hu, A.J., Vardi, M.Y. (eds.) CAV 1998. LNCS, vol. 1427, pp. 268–279. Springer, Heidelberg (1998). https://doi.org/10.1007/BFb0028751
17. Dietsch, D., Heizmann, M., Hoenicke, J., Nutz, A., Podelski, A.: Ultimate TreeAutomizer (CHC-COMP tool description). In: De Angelis, E., Fedyukovich, G., Tzevelekos, N., Ulbrich, M. (eds.) HCVS/PERR@ETAPS 2019, pp. 42–47. EPTCS 296 (2019). https://doi.org/10.4204/EPTCS.296.7
18. Dutertre, B.: Yices 2.2. In: Biere, A., Bloem, R. (eds.) CAV 2014. LNCS, vol. 8559, pp. 737–744. Springer, Cham (2014). https://doi.org/10.1007/978-3-319-08867-9_49
19. Ernst, G.: Loop verification with invariants and contracts. In: Finkbeiner, B., Wies, T. (eds.) VMCAI 2022. LNCS, vol. 13182, pp. 69–92. Springer, Cham (2022). https://doi.org/10.1007/978-3-030-94583-1_4
20. Fedyukovich, G., Prabhu, S., Madhukar, K., Gupta, A.: Solving constrained Horn clauses using syntax and data. In: Bjørner, N.S., Gurfinkel, A. (eds.) FMCAD 2018, pp. 1–9 (2018). https://doi.org/10.23919/FMCAD.2018.8603011
21. Finkel, A., Leroux, J.: How to compose Presburger-accelerations: applications to broadcast protocols. In: Agrawal, M., Seth, A. (eds.) FSTTCS 2002. LNCS, vol. 2556, pp. 145–156. Springer, Heidelberg (2002). https://doi.org/10.1007/3-540-36206-1_14
22. Frohn, F., Giesl, J.: Proving non-termination via loop acceleration. In: Barrett, C.W., Yang, J. (eds.) FMCAD 2019, pp. 221–230 (2019). https://doi.org/10.23919/FMCAD.2019.8894271
23. Frohn, F.: A calculus for modular loop acceleration. In: Biere, A., Parker, D. (eds.) TACAS 2020. LNCS, vol. 12078, pp. 58–76. Springer, Cham (2020). https://doi.org/10.1007/978-3-030-45190-5_4
24. Frohn, F., Giesl, J.: Proving non-termination and lower runtime bounds with LoAT (system description). In: Blanchette, J., Kovács, L., Pattinson, D. (eds.) IJCAR 2022. LNCS, vol. 13385, pp. 712–722. Springer, Cham (2022). https://doi.org/10.1007/978-3-031-10769-6_41
25. Frohn, F., Giesl, J.: Proving non-termination by acceleration driven clause learning (short paper). In: Pientka, B., Tinelli, C. (eds.) CADE 2023. LNCS, vol 14132, pp. 220–233. Springer, Cham (2023). Full version appeared in CoRR abs/2304.10166. https://doi.org/10.48550/arXiv.2304.10166
26. Frohn, F., Giesl, J.: ADCL: acceleration driven clause learning for constrained Horn clauses. CoRR abs/2303.01827 (2023). https://doi.org/10.48550/arXiv.2303.01827
27. Ganty, P., Iosif, R., Konečný, F.: Underapproximation of procedure summaries for integer programs. Int. J. Softw. Tools Technol. Transfer **19**(5), 565–584 (2016). https://doi.org/10.1007/s10009-016-0420-7
28. Gomes, C.P., Selman, B., Kautz, H.A.: Boosting combinatorial search through randomization. In: Mostow, J., Rich, C. (eds.) AAAI 1998, pp. 431–437 (1998). https://www.cs.cornell.edu/gomes/pdf/1998_gomes_aaai_iaai_boosting.pdf

29. Grebenshchikov, S., Lopes, N.P., Popeea, C., Rybalchenko, A.: Synthesizing software verifiers from proof rules. In: Vitek, J., Lin, H., Tip, F. (eds.) PLDI 2012, pp. 405–416 (2012). https://doi.org/10.1145/2254064.2254112
30. Gurfinkel, A., Kahsai, T., Komuravelli, A., Navas, J.A.: The SeaHorn verification framework. In: Kroening, D., Păsăreanu, C.S. (eds.) CAV 2015. LNCS, vol. 9206, pp. 343–361. Springer, Cham (2015). https://doi.org/10.1007/978-3-319-21690-4_20
31. Haase, C., Halfon, S.: Integer vector addition systems with states. In: Ouaknine, J., Potapov, I., Worrell, J. (eds.) RP 2014. LNCS, vol. 8762, pp. 112–124. Springer, Cham (2014). https://doi.org/10.1007/978-3-319-11439-2_9
32. Henzinger, T.A., Hottelier, T., Kovács, L., Rybalchenko, A.: Aligators for arrays (tool paper). In: Fermüller, C.G., Voronkov, A. (eds.) LPAR 2010. LNCS, vol. 6397, pp. 348–356. Springer, Heidelberg (2010). https://doi.org/10.1007/978-3-642-16242-8_25
33. Hoder, K., Bjørner, N.: Generalized property directed reachability. In: Cimatti, A., Sebastiani, R. (eds.) SAT 2012. LNCS, vol. 7317, pp. 157–171. Springer, Heidelberg (2012). https://doi.org/10.1007/978-3-642-31612-8_13
34. Hojjat, H., Iosif, R., Konečný, F., Kuncak, V., Rümmer, P.: Accelerating interpolants. In: Chakraborty, S., Mukund, M. (eds.) ATVA 2012. LNCS, pp. 187–202. Springer, Heidelberg (2012). https://doi.org/10.1007/978-3-642-33386-6_16
35. Hojjat, H., Rümmer, P.: The Eldarica Horn solver. In: Bjørner, N.S., Gurfinkel, A. (eds.) FMCAD 2018, pp. 1–7 (2018). https://doi.org/10.23919/FMCAD.2018.8603013
36. Kahsai, T., Rümmer, P., Sanchez, H., Schäf, M.: JayHorn: a framework for verifying Java programs. In: Chaudhuri, S., Farzan, A. (eds.) CAV 2016. LNCS, vol. 9779, pp. 352–358. Springer, Cham (2016). https://doi.org/10.1007/978-3-319-41528-4_19
37. Komuravelli, A., Gurfinkel, A., Chaki, S.: SMT-based model checking for recursive programs. Formal Methods Syst. Design **48**(3), 175–205 (2016). https://doi.org/10.1007/s10703-016-0249-4
38. Kostyukov, Y., Mordvinov, D., Fedyukovich, G.: Beyond the elementary representations of program invariants over algebraic data types. In: Freund, S.N., Yahav, E. (eds.) PLDI 2021, pp. 451–465 (2021). https://doi.org/10.1145/3453483.3454055
39. Kovács, L., Voronkov, A.: Finding loop invariants for programs over arrays using a theorem prover. In: Chechik, M., Wirsing, M. (eds.) FASE 2009. LNCS, vol. 5503, pp. 470–485. Springer, Heidelberg (2009). https://doi.org/10.1007/978-3-642-00593-0_33
40. Kroening, D., Lewis, M., Weissenbacher, G.: Under-approximating loops in C programs for fast counterexample detection. Formal Methods Syst. Design **47**(1), 75–92 (2015). https://doi.org/10.1007/s10703-015-0228-1
41. libFAUDES Library. https://fgdes.tf.fau.de/faudes/index.html
42. Luby, M., Sinclair, A., Zuckerman, D.: Optimal speedup of Las Vegas algorithms. Inf. Process. Lett. **47**(4), 173–180 (1993). https://doi.org/10.1016/0020-0190(93)90029-9
43. Matsushita, Y., Tsukada, T., Kobayashi, N.: RustHorn: CHC-based verification for Rust programs. ACM Trans. Program. Lang. Syst. **43**(4), 15:1–15:54 (2021). https://doi.org/10.1145/3462205
44. de Moura, L., Bjørner, N.: Z3: an efficient SMT solver. In: Ramakrishnan, C.R., Rehof, J. (eds.) TACAS 2008. LNCS, vol. 4963, pp. 337–340. Springer, Heidelberg (2008). https://doi.org/10.1007/978-3-540-78800-3_24
45. OEIS Foundation Inc.: Thue-Morse sequence. The On-Line Encyclopedia of Integer Sequences. https://oeis.org/A010060

46. OEIS Foundation Inc.: First differences of Thue-Morse sequence. The On-Line Encyclopedia of Integer Sequences (1999). https://oeis.org/A029883
47. Schrammel, P., Jeannet, B.: Logico-numerical abstract acceleration and application to the verification of data-flow programs. In: Yahav, E. (ed.) SAS 2011. LNCS, vol. 6887, pp. 233–248. Springer, Heidelberg (2011). https://doi.org/10.1007/978-3-642-23702-7_19
48. Silverman, J., Kincaid, Z.: Loop summarization with rational vector addition systems. In: Dillig, I., Tasiran, S. (eds.) CAV 2019. LNCS, vol. 11562, pp. 97–115. Springer, Cham (2019). https://doi.org/10.1007/978-3-030-25543-5_7
49. Stump, A., Sutcliffe, G., Tinelli, C.: StarExec: a cross-community infrastructure for logic solving. In: Demri, S., Kapur, D., Weidenbach, C. (eds.) IJCAR 2014. LNCS (LNAI), vol. 8562, pp. 367–373. Springer, Cham (2014). https://doi.org/10.1007/978-3-319-08587-6_28
50. Wesley, S., Christakis, M., Navas, J.A., Trefler, R., Wüstholz, V., Gurfinkel, A.: Verifying Solidity smart contracts via communication abstraction in SmartACE. In: Finkbeiner, B., Wies, T. (eds.) VMCAI 2022. LNCS, vol. 13182, pp. 425–449. Springer, Cham (2022). https://doi.org/10.1007/978-3-030-94583-1_21
51. Zhu, H., Magill, S., Jagannathan, S.: A data-driven CHC solver. In: Foster, J.S., Grossman, D. (eds.) PLDI 2018, pp. 707–721 (2018). https://doi.org/10.1145/3192366.3192416

How Fitting is Your Abstract Domain?

Roberto Giacobazzi[1], Isabella Mastroeni[2(✉)], and Elia Perantoni[2]

[1] Department of Computer Science, University of Arizona Tucson, Tucson, USA
rgiacobazzi@gmail.com
[2] Computer Science Department, University of Verona, Verona, Italy
isabella.mastroeni@univr.it, elia.perantoni@studenti.univr.it

Abstract. Abstract interpretation offers sound and decidable approximations for undecidable queries related to program behavior. The effectiveness of an abstract domain is entirely reliant on the abstract domain itself, and the worst-case scenario is when the abstract interpreter provides a response of "don't know", indicating that anything could happen during runtime. Conversely, a desirable outcome is when the abstract interpreter provides information that exceeds a specified level of precision, resulting in a more precise answer. The concept of completeness relates to the level of precision that is forfeited when performing computations within the abstract domain. Our focus is on the domain's ability to express program behaviour, which we refer to as adequacy. In this paper, we present a domain refinement strategy towards adequacy and a simple sound proof system for adequacy, designed to determine whether an abstract domain is capable of providing satisfactory responses to specified program queries. Notably, this proof system is both language and domain agnostic, and can be readily incorporated to support static program analysis.

Keywords: Abstract interpretation · Abstract domain precision · Static analysis

1 Introduction

The accuracy of an abstract interpretation depends upon many factors [13]. (1) The quality of the abstract domain: In this case the abstract domain has to represent in the most precise way all the intermediate invariants that hold at each program point along a computation trace [5,6,10,11,19]. (2) The precision of the fixpoint strategy: In this case an appropriate fixpoint strategy can improve the precision of the analysis either by delaying widening/narrowing or dynamic trace partition [2,8,12,27]. (3) The way the code is written: In this case, the non-compositional nature of the precision of abstract interpretation can be influenced by the way the code is assembled [3,20]. All these factors imply that the design of an optimal (aka, sound and complete) abstract interpretation for static program analysis is a very complex task.

M. V. Hermenegildo and J. F. Morales (Eds.): SAS 2023, LNCS 14284, pp. 286–309, 2023.
https://doi.org/10.1007/978-3-031-44245-2_14

In this paper, we address the first of the above mentioned factors: The quality of the abstract domain. The standard approach is based on the notion of abstract domain refinement [14]. The goal of domain refinement is to remove false alarms by enhancing the expressive power of the abstract domain. In particular, in the last two decades, the notion of completeness, with their global and local refinements [5,17]—the latter called Abstract Interpretation Repair (AIR), perfectly captures the structure of an abstract domain that will produce no false alarm for a given program. This notion has also been weakened towards what is known as *partial completeness* [7] where the precision is evaluated in a metric space built over the abstract domain.

Rather than focusing on eliminating false alarms to achieve completeness, or on weaker forms of completeness that tolerate some level of false alarms, our study is concerned with evaluating the expressiveness of an abstract domain with respect to its ability to represent intermediate invariants in the computation. In particular, when dealing with abstract analysis, it is widely recognized that an abstract domain must allow for the possibility of making no statements regarding the behavior of a computation. This characteristic is critical for enabling the analysis to provide decidable answers to otherwise undecidable questions. The primary objective of adequacy is to prevent excessively imprecise statements with respect to a given concrete assertion. When the level of imprecision exceeds a certain threshold, it is deemed unacceptable, namely not *fitting*, for the purposes of abstract computation. This domain property will be referred to as *adequacy* of the abstract domain.

Like completeness, an abstract domain may be deemed not *adequate* because it is overly abstract. In this scenario, we may question whether it is feasible to *adjust* the abstract domain to ensure adequacy, just as it is possible to eliminate false alarms for achieving completeness by refinement [5,17]. This proposed approach to achieving adequacy involves a refinement strategy that ensures the refined abstract domain approximates computed invariants more accurately than a specified bound τ. However, precisely as it happens for completeness, while the refinement approach is crucial for gaining a deep understanding of adequacy by identifying the elements necessary for enforcing it, it needs the computation of the function/semantics, which may render it an undecidable characterization.

To address this issue, in the context of program analysis, we also introduce a simple proof system, based on structural induction, to verify whether the approximate invariants generated by the abstract interpreter within an abstract domain A are kept below a the given (abstract) bound τ. This is achieved by proving the validity of triples holding on a program $\mathtt{r}$ w.r.t. an input concrete assertions c and an output one d. If $[\![\mathtt{r}]\!]^\sharp_{\mathsf{A}}$ is the abstract semantics of $\mathtt{r}$ given by an abstract interpreter defined on the abstract domain A, namely $[\![\mathtt{r}]\!]^\sharp_{\mathsf{A}} : \mathsf{A} \rightarrow \mathsf{A}$, then if the triple, denoted $\tau \vdash_{\mathsf{A}} \langle \mathsf{c} \rangle\ \mathtt{r}\ \langle \mathsf{d} \rangle$, is derived in the proof system then we can say that A is adequate for $\mathtt{r}$, namely the computation of $\mathtt{r}$ semantics on A is kept under the bound τ. The proof system we introduce, which we refer to as the *abstract domain adequacy logic*, is very simple and can be efficiently checked online using program analysis tools.

Paper Roadmap. Section 2 provides an overview of abstract interpretation and programming language semantics. We chose to treat regular commands as the general programming language to establish a language-agnostic framework. In Sect. 3, we recall abstract domain completeness and introduce the novel concept of abstract domain adequacy. Section 4 outlines the procedure for *adjusting* an abstract domain towards adequacy by refining it. Finally, in Sect. 5, we present a sound proof system for adequacy, and Sect. 6 concludes the paper with closing remarks and potential future directions.

Related Works. Adequacy is a novel approach here proposed for dealing with abstract domain precision. Completeness in abstract interpretation [17] is the closest notion to adequacy, at least in its origin. As we will demonstrate in Sect. 3, the two concepts are incomparable, meaning that neither one is stronger than the other. Nonetheless, the proof system and domain refinement procedures for both concepts employ similar strategies. Specifically, the proof system inherits the locality of the notion of *local completeness* introduced in [4] and [6], which also forms the basis for the refinement strategy in *abstract interpretation repair* (AIR) [5]. As a consequence, the proof systems for global completeness in [19] and local completeness in [6] are logically incomparable with ours. However, the idea of setting a bound on the approximation, which may be weaker than the abstract observation, is a novel aspect of our work.

In the context of local adequacy, as it happens AIR, in general, no optimal (most abstract) refinement exists. Therefore, the process of achieving adequacy can only provide sub-optimal solutions. It should be noted that completeness and adequacy are distinct problems, and as such, the computed refinements produced by the two methods may lead to different domains. An adequate domain may still be incomplete, and thus not a solution in terms of AIR, and vice versa, a solution in terms of AIR may not ensure a bounded abstract computation, and therefore may not be adequate. The technical differences are discussed in Sect. 3.

In [7], the concept of partial completeness is introduced as a means of evaluating the accuracy of an abstract interpretation. This is accomplished by incorporating the abstract domain into a (quasi) metric space, which relaxes the requirement for local completeness to hold up to a metric neighbor of the exact (complete) solution. Along with completeness, partial completeness is also not comparable to adequacy. The latter is not intended to provide any quantitative estimate of the quality of an abstraction but rather an answer of whether the resulting invariant is below (is approximated by) a given bound τ in the abstract domain. This guarantees that at least the information in τ will be included in the computed approximate invariant.

2 Background

If $\mathtt{S}$, $\wp(\mathtt{S})$ denotes the powerset of $\mathtt{S}$. If $f : \mathtt{S} \to \mathtt{T}$, then we often abuse notation by calling f also its additive lifting $f : \wp(\mathtt{S}) \to \wp(\mathtt{T})$ to sets of values: $f(X) \stackrel{\text{def}}{=} \{\, f(x) \,|\, x \in X \subseteq \mathtt{S} \,\}$. If $f : \mathtt{S} \longrightarrow \mathtt{T}$ and $g : \mathtt{T} \to \mathtt{U}$, we denote by $g \circ f$

(or simply gf) their composition. If $f : \mathsf{S} \rightarrow \mathsf{S}$, and $n \in \mathbb{N}$ we define $f^n : \mathsf{S} \rightarrow \mathsf{S}$ inductively as $f^0 \stackrel{\text{def}}{=} id_{\mathsf{S}}$ (the identity on S), $f^{n+1} \stackrel{\text{def}}{=} f \circ f^n$. In a partial ordered structure C, we use $\leq_{\mathsf{C}}$ to denote the partial order relation, $\vee_{\mathsf{C}}$ for lub, $\wedge_{\mathsf{C}}$ for glb, $\top_{\mathsf{C}}$ and $\bot_{\mathsf{C}}$ for respectively the greatest and the least elements (we avoid the pedex C when clear from the context). A function f between ordered structures is monotone if it preserve the order, i.e., $\mathsf{c} \leq_{\mathsf{C}} \mathsf{d} \Rightarrow f(\mathsf{c}) \leq_{\mathsf{C}} f(\mathsf{d})$. It is additive if it preserves arbitrary lubs (co-additivity is dually defined).

2.1 Abstract Interpretation

Abstract interpretation [10,11], is a formal framework for approximating programs semantics defined on a concrete domain C, by means of some abstraction A of C. Given complete lattices C and A, a pair of functions $\alpha : \mathsf{C} \rightarrow \mathsf{A}$ and $\gamma : \mathsf{A} \rightarrow \mathsf{C}$ forms a Galois connection (GC for shorts) if for any $\mathsf{c} \in \mathsf{C}$ and $\mathsf{a} \in \mathsf{A}$ we have $\alpha(\mathsf{c}) \leq_{\mathsf{A}} \mathsf{a} \Leftrightarrow \mathsf{c} \leq_{\mathsf{C}} \gamma(\mathsf{a})$. In this case, α (resp. γ) is the abstraction/left adjoint (resp. concretization/right adjoint), and it is additive (resp. co-additive). Co-additive functions $g : \mathsf{A} \rightarrow \mathsf{C}$ admits left adjoint $g^{-} \stackrel{\text{def}}{=} \lambda \mathsf{c}.\ \bigwedge_{\mathsf{A}} \{\, \mathsf{a} \mid \mathsf{c} \leq_{\mathsf{C}} f(\mathsf{a}) \,\}$. An *upper closure operator* (uco for shorts) $\rho : \mathsf{C} \rightarrow \mathsf{C}$ on a poset C is monotone, idempotent, and extensive, i.e., $\forall x \in \mathsf{C}.\ \mathsf{c} \leq_{\mathsf{C}} \rho(\mathsf{c})$. If in a GC $\alpha \circ \gamma = id_{\mathsf{A}}$ then it is a Galois insertion (GI) and $\gamma \circ \alpha$, simply written $\gamma\alpha$, is an uco. Let us denote by $Abs(\mathsf{C})$ the class of abstract domains (GI or uco) of C. It is well known that $Abs(\mathsf{C})$ is isomorphic to the lattice of all ucos on C, therefore when dealing with GI and clear from the context, we abuse notation by denoting as A both the domain of abstract objects ($\mathsf{A} = \gamma\alpha(\mathsf{C})$) and the closure operator ($\mathsf{A} = \gamma\alpha$). Given an abstract domain $\mathsf{A} \in Abs(\mathsf{C})$ ($\mathsf{A} = \gamma\alpha$) and a concrete function $f : \mathsf{C} \rightarrow \mathsf{C}$, an abstract function $f^{\sharp}_{\mathsf{A}} : \mathsf{A} \rightarrow \mathsf{A}$ is a *sound* approximation of f when $\alpha \circ f \leq_{\mathsf{A}} f^{\sharp}_{\mathsf{A}} \circ \alpha$[1]. The best correct approximation (bca) of f in A is the function $f^{\mathsf{A}} \stackrel{\text{def}}{=} \alpha \circ f \circ \gamma$, any other abstraction is less precise. In this case soundness as domain property is defined as $\mathsf{A} \circ f \leq_{\mathsf{C}} \mathsf{A} \circ f \circ \mathsf{A}$.

2.2 Regular Commands

Following [4,28] (see also [29]) we consider the language Reg_{Exp} of regular commands in the top of Fig. 1 (where $\oplus$ denotes non-deterministic choice and $*$ is the Kleene closure), parametric on a grammar of expressions Exp. This language is general enough to represent control-flow graphs of basic expressions and therefore it covers simple deterministic imperative languages.

The Concrete Semantics. Let Reg_{Exp} be a regular language. We assume the basic transfer expressions have a semantics $(\!| \cdot |\!) : \text{Exp} \rightarrow \mathsf{C} \rightarrow \mathsf{C}$ on a complete lattice C such that $(\!|\mathsf{e}|\!)$ is an additive function. The concrete semantics [28] $[\![\cdot]\!] : \text{Reg}_{\text{Exp}} \rightarrow \mathsf{C} \rightarrow \mathsf{C}$ of regular commands is inductively defined as follows: Let $\mathsf{c} \in \mathsf{C}$

[1] By $\leq_{\mathsf{A}}$ we denote the partial order relation on A.

$$\mathrm{Reg}_{\mathrm{Exp}} \ni \mathtt{r} ::= \mathsf{e} \mid \mathtt{r};\mathtt{r} \mid \mathtt{r} \oplus \mathtt{r} \mid \mathtt{r}^* \qquad \mathsf{e} \in \mathrm{Exp}$$

$$\begin{aligned} \mathfrak{L} &= \mathrm{Reg}_{\mathfrak{L}\,\mathrm{Exp}} \\ \mathfrak{L}\,\mathrm{Exp} \ni \mathsf{e} &::= \mathbf{skip} \mid x := \mathsf{a} \mid \mathsf{b}? \\ \mathrm{AExp} \ni \mathsf{a} &::= x \mid n \mid \mathsf{a} + \mathsf{a} \mid \mathsf{a} - \mathsf{a} \mid \mathsf{a} * \mathsf{a} \\ \mathrm{BExp} \ni \mathsf{b} &::= \mathbf{tt} \mid \mathbf{ff} \mid \mathsf{a} = \mathsf{a} \mid \mathsf{a} \leq \mathsf{a} \mid \mathsf{a} < \mathsf{a} \mid \mathsf{b} \wedge \mathsf{b} \mid \neg \mathsf{b} \\ \mathit{Var} \ni x &\text{ (variables)}, \qquad n \in \mathbb{Z} \text{ (values)} \end{aligned}$$

Fig. 1. The syntax of $\mathrm{Reg}_{\mathrm{Exp}}$, parametric on Exp, and of $\mathfrak{L}$.

$$[\![\mathsf{e}]\!]c \stackrel{\text{def}}{=} (\!|\mathsf{e}|\!)c \qquad [\![\mathtt{r}_1 \oplus \mathtt{r}_2]\!]c \stackrel{\text{def}}{=} [\![\mathtt{r}_1]\!]c \vee_{\mathsf{C}} [\![\mathtt{r}_2]\!]c$$
$$[\![\mathtt{r}_1;\mathtt{r}_2]\!]c \stackrel{\text{def}}{=} [\![\mathtt{r}_2]\!]([\![\mathtt{r}_1]\!]c) \qquad [\![\mathtt{r}^*]\!]c \stackrel{\text{def}}{=} \bigvee_{\mathsf{C}} \{\, [\![\mathtt{r}]\!]^n c \mid n \in \mathbb{N} \,\}$$

The Abstract Semantics. Let $\mathsf{A} \in \mathit{Abs}(\mathsf{C})$, the abstract semantics of regular commands $[\![\cdot]\!]^\sharp_{\mathsf{A}} : \mathrm{Reg}_{\mathrm{Exp}} \to \mathsf{A} \to \mathsf{A}$ on the abstract domain A is defined by structural induction as follows:

$$\begin{aligned} [\![\mathsf{e}]\!]^\sharp_{\mathsf{A}}\mathsf{a} &\stackrel{\text{def}}{=} [\![\mathsf{e}]\!]^{\mathsf{A}}\mathsf{a} \\ [\![\mathtt{r}_1;\mathtt{r}_2]\!]^\sharp_{\mathsf{A}}\mathsf{a} &\stackrel{\text{def}}{=} [\![\mathtt{r}_2]\!]^\sharp_{\mathsf{A}}([\![\mathtt{r}_1]\!]^\sharp_{\mathsf{A}}\mathsf{a}) \\ [\![\mathtt{r}_1 \oplus \mathtt{r}_2]\!]^\sharp_{\mathsf{A}}\mathsf{a} &\stackrel{\text{def}}{=} [\![\mathtt{r}_1]\!]^\sharp_{\mathsf{A}}\mathsf{a} \vee_{\mathsf{A}} [\![\mathtt{r}_2]\!]^\sharp_{\mathsf{A}}\mathsf{a} \\ [\![\mathtt{r}^*]\!]^\sharp_{\mathsf{A}}\mathsf{a} &\stackrel{\text{def}}{=} \bigvee_{\mathsf{A}} \left\{\, ([\![\mathtt{r}]\!]^\sharp_{\mathsf{A}})^n\mathsf{a} \mid n \in \mathbb{N} \,\right\} \end{aligned}$$

where we recall that $[\![\mathsf{e}]\!]^{\mathsf{A}}$ is the bca in A of $[\![\mathsf{e}]\!]$.
By structural induction we can prove that this abstract semantics is monotonic and correct, i.e., $\alpha \circ [\![\mathtt{r}]\!] \leq_{\mathsf{A}} [\![\mathtt{r}]\!]^\sharp_{\mathsf{A}} \circ \alpha$ (or equivalently $\alpha \circ [\![\mathtt{r}]\!] \circ \gamma \leq_{\mathsf{A}} [\![\mathtt{r}]\!]^\sharp_{\mathsf{A}}$).

Programs. We consider standard basic transfer functions for expressions used in deterministic while programs: no-op instruction, assignments and Boolean guards, i.e., we consider the regular language $\mathfrak{L}$ defined in Fig. 1. Hence, we have to deal with integer variables and with stores. Let us denote $\mathit{Var}(\mathtt{r})$ the set of all the variables in $\mathtt{r} \in \mathrm{Reg}_{\mathrm{Exp}}$, and let $\mathsf{C} \stackrel{\text{def}}{=} \wp(\mathbb{M})$ the concrete domain of sets of stores, where the store $\mathbb{m} \in \mathbb{M}$ is a function associating values to a set of variables, i.e., $\mathbb{m} : V \to \mathbb{Z}$, $V \subseteq_f \mathit{Var}$ (finite subset).
In particular, the basic transfer function semantics $(\!|\mathsf{e}|\!) : \mathsf{C} \to \mathsf{C}$ for the expressions of $\mathfrak{L}$, is defined as: $\mathtt{M} \in \mathsf{C}$ (i.e., $\mathtt{M} \subseteq \mathbb{M}$)

$$\begin{aligned} (\!|\mathbf{skip}|\!)\mathtt{M} &\stackrel{\text{def}}{=} \mathtt{M} \\ (\!|x := \mathsf{a}|\!)\mathtt{M} &\stackrel{\text{def}}{=} \{\, \mathbb{m}[x \mapsto (\!|\mathsf{a}|\!)\,\mathbb{m}] \mid \mathbb{m} \in \mathtt{M} \,\} \\ (\!|\mathsf{b}?|\!)\mathtt{M} &\stackrel{\text{def}}{=} \{\, \mathbb{m} \in \mathtt{M} \mid (\!|\mathsf{b}|\!)\,\mathbb{m} = \mathbf{tt} \,\} = \mathtt{M} \cap (\!|\mathsf{b}|\!) \end{aligned}$$

where $(\!|\mathsf{a}|\!) : \mathbb{M} \to \mathbb{Z}$ and $(\!|\mathsf{b}|\!) : \mathbb{M} \to \{\mathbf{tt}, \mathbf{ff}\}$ are the standard evaluation semantics for arithmetic and boolean expressions, respectively, and where we denote $(\!|\mathsf{b}|\!) \stackrel{\text{def}}{=} \{\, \mathbb{m} \in \mathbb{M} \mid (\!|\mathsf{b}|\!)\,\mathbb{m} = \mathbf{tt} \,\}$ the truth semantics of b.

Note that, the concrete semantics of regular language defined above instantiated to $\mathfrak{L}$ corresponds precisely to the denotational semantics defined [9] starting from standard operational semantics of non deterministic choice and iteration [29].

3 From Completeness to Adequacy

Abstract domain completeness is the standard approach used for the characterization of abstract domain precision w.r.t. the computation of the semantics [17]. Let us recall its formal definition.

3.1 Abstract Domain Completeness and its Limits

Let $\mathsf{A} \in Abs(\mathsf{C})$ be an abstraction of C and $f : \mathsf{C} \to \mathsf{C}$ a concrete computation on C, e.g., the program semantics, then the abstract function $f^\sharp_{\mathsf{A}}$ is said to be a *complete/precise* [11,17] approximation of f on A if $\alpha \circ f = f^\sharp_{\mathsf{A}} \circ \alpha$. Intuitively, it means that if we abstract $\mathsf{c} \in \mathsf{C}$ (the input of f), we apply the f approximation $f^\sharp_{\mathsf{A}}$, we obtain the same abstract element that we would have been obtained by abstracting the result of f applied directly on c (without an initial abstraction). Note that, if there exists a complete approximation $f^\sharp_{\mathsf{A}}$ of f, then f^{A} is itself complete. Completeness of f^{A} intuitively means that f^{A} is the most precise approximation of f and, in therefore, completeness can be characterized as a domain property. $\mathsf{A} \in Abs(\mathsf{C})$ is said to be a complete abstraction for f if $\mathsf{A} \circ f \circ \mathsf{A} = \mathsf{A} \circ f$.

In a more general setting, let $f : \mathsf{C}_1 \to \mathsf{C}_2$ be a function on complete lattices C_i (potentially different), and let $\mathsf{A}_i \in Abs(\mathsf{C}_i)$ (for $i \in \{1, 2\}$) be abstractions, respectively, of input and output domains. In this case, we say that $\langle \mathsf{A}_1, \mathsf{A}_2 \rangle$ is a pair of complete abstract domains for f if $\mathsf{A}_2 \circ f = \mathsf{A}_2 \circ f \circ \mathsf{A}_1$.

Note that, this is a global property, since it requires the equality of two functions on all inputs, i.e., $\forall \mathsf{c} \in \mathsf{C}.\ \mathsf{A} \circ f(\mathsf{c}) = \mathsf{A} \circ f \circ \mathsf{A}(\mathsf{c})$. This makes completeness an extremely strong property and indeed, as proved in [4], it holds for all programs in a Turing complete programming language only for trivial abstract domains. This means that the only abstract domains that are complete for all programs are the straightforward ones: the identical abstraction, making abstract and concrete semantics the same, and the top abstraction, making all programs equivalent by abstract semantics. In particular, the authors show that while global completeness can be hard/impossible to achieve, it could well happen that completeness holds locally, i.e. just for some store properties, proving so far what is called local completeness [4], namely $\mathsf{A} \circ f(\mathsf{c}) = \mathsf{A} \circ f \circ \mathsf{A}(\mathsf{c})$ for a fixed point $\mathsf{c} \in \mathsf{C}$. This weakening makes precision strongly dependent on the point c, implying that among points with the same abstraction we may have both complete and incomplete points.

However, both completeness characterizations do not really deal with the loss of precision due to the *choice* of the abstract observation, since it characterizes only whether there is an *extra* loss of precision due to the *computation* on observed/abstracted data (compared with the observation of the concretely computed result). For instance, the $\top$ abstraction, which cannot distinguish any information, is trivially complete, even if it represents the total loss of precision in the observation of data. Therefore, completeness is unable to account for this type of information loss caused by abstraction, which is why we strive to introduce a new concept of precision for abstract domains that can designate $\top$ as entirely imprecise. Graphically, the idea is depicted in Fig. 2 for program semantics. Namely, (local) completeness can only avoid the error depicted as blue area, namely the error due to computation on abstract data compared with the abstraction of the concrete computation, while we aim at bounding the total error depicted, namely the error due to the choice of the abstract domain, independently from its potential completeness.

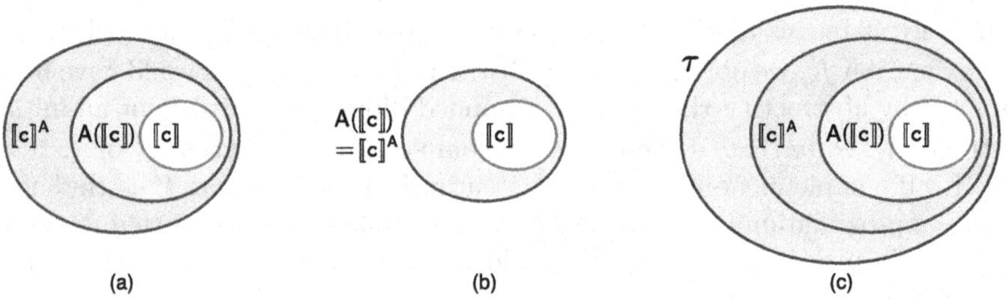

Fig. 2. Program semantics abstraction (a). Complete semantic abstraction (b). Adequacy (c).

3.2 Abstract Domain Adequacy

In order to move the attention to the whole (abstract) image of all the elements with the same abstraction, loosing the dependency on the chosen point imposed by local completeness while keeping a locality of the property, we propose a novel approach referred to as abstract domain adequacy. We can say that abstract domain adequacy allows us to bound (strictly below a fixed threshold) the total amount of approximation due to data abstraction and abstract computation[2]. The idea is to fix a generic bound τ (at the limit $\top$) that we want to confine the loss of precision, namely such that any abstract computation is strictly over-approximated by τ.

[2] Similarly to what happens with completeness, adequacy of any sound abstract operator implies the adequacy of the best correct approximation.

Definition 1 (Abstract domain adequacy w.r.t. τ).
Let C *be a concrete domain,* $f : \mathsf{C} \to \mathsf{C}$, $\mathsf{A} \in Abs(\mathsf{C})$ *one of its abstractions,* $\tau \in \mathsf{A}$ *(i.e.,* $\mathsf{A} = \gamma\alpha$ *and* $\gamma\alpha(\tau) = \tau \in \mathsf{C}$*). Then* A *is adequate w.r.t.* τ *for* f *if*

(Global) $\widetilde{\mathbb{C}}^{\mathsf{A}}(f)_\tau \;\Leftrightarrow\; \forall \mathsf{c} \in \mathsf{C}.\, \mathsf{A} \circ f \circ \mathsf{A}(\mathsf{c}) \lneq_{\mathsf{C}} \tau$ *and*
(Local) $\widetilde{\mathbb{C}}^{\mathsf{A}}_{\mathsf{c}}(f)_\tau \;\Leftrightarrow\; \mathsf{A} \circ f \circ \mathsf{A}(\mathsf{c}) \lneq_{\mathsf{C}} \tau$

when $\tau = \top$ *we simply call* A *adequate for* f*, denoted* $\widetilde{\mathbb{C}}^{\mathsf{A}}(f)$ *and* $\widetilde{\mathbb{C}}^{\mathsf{A}}_{\mathsf{c}}(f)$.

Example 1. Consider $\mathsf{C} = \wp(\mathbb{Z})$ and $\mathsf{A} = Sign$, whose abstract counterpart is depicted on the left of Fig. 3.

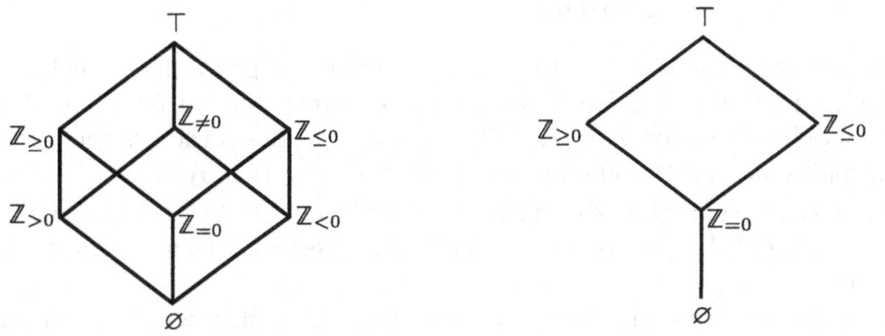

Fig. 3. Abstract domains for signs: *Sign* (left) and $Sign_1$ (right).

Let $f \stackrel{\text{def}}{=} \lambda \mathsf{c}.\, \{\, 2 * n \,|\, n \in \mathsf{c} \,\}$ and let $\mathsf{c} \stackrel{\text{def}}{=} \{0, 2, 4, 6, 8\}$, then we have $\widetilde{\mathbb{C}}^{\mathsf{A}}_{\mathsf{c}}(f)$ since $Sign \circ f \circ Sign(\mathsf{c}) = Sign \circ f(\{\, n \in \mathbb{Z} \,|\, n \geq 0 \,\}) = Sign(\{\, 2n \,|\, n \geq 0, n \in \mathbb{Z} \,\}) = \{\, n \in \mathbb{Z} \,|\, n \geq 0 \,\} \subsetneq \mathbb{Z}$, but $\neg\widetilde{\mathbb{C}}^{\mathsf{A}}_{\mathsf{c}'}(f)$ with $\mathsf{c}' \stackrel{\text{def}}{=} \{-1, 0, 1\}$, since $Sign \circ f \circ Sign(\mathsf{c}') = Sign \circ f(\mathbb{Z}) = Sign(2\mathbb{Z}) = \mathbb{Z}$, which is the top, hence it does not hold globally, i.e., $\neg\widetilde{\mathbb{C}}^{\mathsf{A}}(f)$.
If we consider $g = \lambda \mathsf{c}.\, \{\, n^2 + 2 \,|\, n \in \mathsf{c} \,\}$, and we consider $\tau = \mathbb{Z}_{\geq 0}$, then we have that $\forall \mathsf{c}.\, Sign \circ g \circ Sign(\mathsf{c}) \subseteq \{\, n \in \mathbb{Z} \,|\, n > 0 \,\} \subsetneq \tau$. Hence, $\widetilde{\mathbb{C}}^{\mathsf{A}}(g)_\tau$.

In general, completeness and adequacy are not comparable when $\exists \mathsf{c}.\, \mathsf{A}f(\mathsf{c}) = \top$, since in this case we could have completeness, i.e., $\mathsf{A} \circ f(\mathsf{c}) = \mathsf{A} \circ f \circ \mathsf{A}(\mathsf{c})$ but we cannot satisfy adequacy, i.e., $\mathsf{A} \circ f \circ \mathsf{A}(\mathsf{c}) = \mathsf{A} \circ f(\mathsf{c}) = \top$. Following the other direction, it is clear that adequacy cannot imply completeness. A similar reasoning can be done when we consider adequacy w.r.t. $\tau \neq \top$. In general, we can prove the following relation.

Proposition 1. *Let* C *be a concrete domain,* $f : \mathsf{C} \to \mathsf{C}$ *and* $\mathsf{A} \in Abs(\mathsf{C})$*. Then for any* $\tau \in \mathsf{A}$*, if* $\forall \mathsf{c} \in \mathsf{C}.\, \mathsf{A} \circ f(\mathsf{c}) \lneq_{\mathsf{C}} \tau$ *then* A *complete imply* A *globally adequate w.r.t.* τ *for* f.

Example 2. Let us consider C and f in Example 1, we have shown above that $\neg\widetilde{\mathbb{C}}^{\mathsf{A}}(f)$, but it is trivial to show, and well known, that *Sign* is complete for f, since $\forall \mathsf{c} \in \mathsf{C}.\ Sign \circ f \circ Sign(\mathsf{c}) = Sign \circ f(\mathsf{c})$, since f leaves in the resulting set precisely the same signs that are in the input set, but $\top = \mathbb{Z} = Sign \circ f(\{-1,0,1\}) = Sign(\{-2,0,2\})$. Hence, in this case, completeness does not imply adequacy. On the other side, let $h \stackrel{\text{def}}{=} \lambda \mathsf{c}.\left\{\, (n+2)^2 \,\middle|\, n \in \mathsf{c} \,\right\}$ of the same example, which satisfies adequacy (w.r.t. $\top = \mathbb{Z}$) since $\forall \mathsf{c} \in \mathsf{C}.\ Sign \circ h \circ Sign(\mathsf{c}) \subseteq \left\{\, n \in \mathbb{Z} \,\middle|\, n \geq 0 \,\right\}$, but it is not complete, e.g., $Sign \circ h \circ Sign(\{-1,0,1\}) = Sign \circ h(\mathbb{Z}) = Sign\left\{\, (n+2)^2 \,\middle|\, n \in \mathbb{Z} \,\right\} = \left\{\, n \in \mathbb{Z} \,\middle|\, n \geq 0 \,\right\}$, while $Sign \circ h(\{-1,0,1\}) = Sign(\{1,2,3\}) = \left\{\, n \in \mathbb{Z} \,\middle|\, n > 0 \,\right\}$. Hence, in general, adequacy does not imply completeness.

3.3 Adequacy for $\mathfrak{L}$ Programs

Let us consider now abstract domain adequacy for $\mathfrak{L}$ programs, namely where $f = [\![\mathtt{r}]\!]$, for some $\mathtt{r} \in \mathfrak{L}$. In this case, the concrete domain is $\mathsf{C} = \wp(\mathbb{M})$ and $\mathsf{A} \in Abs(\wp(\mathbb{M}))$ (namely $\leq_{\mathsf{C}}$ is $\subseteq$, while $\leq_{\mathsf{A}}$ still depends on the abstract domain, and in particular on the abstraction α) and we say that A is adequate for $\mathtt{r}$. For the sake of readability, we will write $\widetilde{\mathbb{C}}^{\mathsf{A}}_{\mathsf{c}}(\mathtt{r})$ instead of $\widetilde{\mathbb{C}}^{\mathsf{A}}_{\mathsf{c}}([\![\mathtt{r}]\!])$ (analogous for global adequacy). In this context, we look as properties of elements in $\mathfrak{L}$ related with adequacy.

In [4] the authors introduce a notion of expressability which has a strong relation with completeness. Formally, b is expressible in A if its truth semantics is an element of A, i.e., $(\!|\mathsf{b}|\!) \in \mathsf{A}$. In particular, the authors show that if the semantics of $\mathsf{b}?$ is local complete then b and $\neg\mathsf{b}$ are expressible, while the other implication does not always holds (Lemma III.2 [4]).
As far as adequacy is concerned, the situation is slightly different: while adequacy seems too weak to imply b to be expressible, it is instead implied by the expressability of b.

Definition 2 (b quasi-expressible w.r.t. τ). *Let* $\mathsf{C} = \wp(\mathbb{M})$ *be the concrete domain,* $\mathsf{A} \in Abs(\mathsf{C})$, $\tau \in \mathsf{A}$. *A boolean expression* b, *such that* $(\!|\mathsf{b}|\!) \leq \tau$, *is quasi-expressible w.r.t.* τ *in* A *if there exists* b' *expressible in* A, *i.e.,* $(\!|\mathsf{b}'|\!) \in \mathsf{A}$, *such that* $(\!|\mathsf{b}|\!) \subseteq (\!|\mathsf{b}'|\!)$, $\mathsf{A}((\!|\mathsf{b}|\!)) = \mathsf{A}((\!|\mathsf{b}'|\!)) = (\!|\mathsf{b}'|\!) \subsetneq \tau$.

In other words, a quasi-expressible, w.r.t. τ, boolean expression b has an abstract semantics approximated in A strictly under τ. It is trivial to observe that, if b is not quasi-expressible, w.r.t. τ then $\mathsf{A}((\!|\mathsf{b}|\!)) = \tau$. For instance, consider again the sign domains in Fig. 3. Then the boolean expressions $x \leq 0$ and $0 < x$ are expressible (and therefore quasi-expressible) in *Sign*, since $x \leq 0$ is expressed by $\left\{\, n \,\middle|\, n \leq 0 \,\right\}$ and $0 < x$ by $\left\{\, n \,\middle|\, n < 0 \,\right\}$. Note that $0 < x$ is only quasi-expressible, instead, in $Sign_1$. If we consider the interval domain *Int* and $\tau = [0, +\infty]$, then $10 < x$ is still expressible also w.r.t. τ since its semantics, i.e., $[11, +\infty]$ is strictly contained in τ, $x > 0 \wedge x \ mod\ 2 = 0$, i.e., the set of even numbers greater or equal to 2, is only quasi-expressible w.r.t. τ, since its semantics is contained in the semantics of $x \geq 2$, which is $[2, +\infty] \subsetneq \tau$, while

$x < 100$ is not expressible w.r.t. τ since its semantics is $[-\infty, 99]$, and there is no semantics strictly contained in τ which contains $[-\infty, 99]$.

Theorem 1. *Given* $\mathsf{b} \in \mathrm{BExp}$, *in the hypotheses of Definition 2*

1. *If* b *is quasi-expressible w.r.t* $\tau \in \mathsf{A}$ *then* $\widetilde{\mathbb{C}}^{\mathsf{A}}(\mathsf{b}?)_\tau$;
2. *If* b *is not quasi-expressible w.r.t.* τ *then* $\forall \mathsf{c} \in \mathsf{C}.\, \mathsf{A}(\mathsf{c}) \supseteq \tau$ *we have* $\neg\widetilde{\mathbb{C}}^{\mathsf{A}}_{\mathsf{c}}(\mathsf{b}?)_\tau$.

Proof.

1. Let b be quasi-expressible w.r.t. τ, hence there exists $\mathsf{b}' \in \mathrm{BExp}$ such that $\mathsf{A}(\llparenthesis \mathsf{b} \rrparenthesis) = \mathsf{A}(\llparenthesis \mathsf{b}' \rrparenthesis) = \llparenthesis \mathsf{b}' \rrparenthesis \subsetneq \tau$ and let $\mathsf{c} \in \mathsf{C}$. Then
$$\begin{aligned} \mathsf{A}[\![\mathsf{b}?]\!]\mathsf{A}(\mathsf{c}) = \mathsf{A}\llparenthesis \mathsf{b}? \rrparenthesis \mathsf{A}(\mathsf{c}) &= \mathsf{A}(\mathsf{A}(\mathsf{c}) \cap \llparenthesis \mathsf{b} \rrparenthesis) \subseteq \mathsf{A}(\mathsf{A}(\mathsf{c}) \cap \mathsf{A}(\llparenthesis \mathsf{b} \rrparenthesis)) \\ &= \mathsf{A}(\mathsf{A}(\mathsf{c}) \cap \mathsf{A}(\llparenthesis \mathsf{b}' \rrparenthesis)) = \mathsf{A}(\mathsf{c}) \cap \mathsf{A}(\llparenthesis \mathsf{b}' \rrparenthesis) \\ &\subseteq \mathsf{A}(\llparenthesis \mathsf{b}' \rrparenthesis) = \llparenthesis \mathsf{b}' \rrparenthesis \subsetneq \tau \end{aligned}$$
2. Suppose b is not quasi-expressible w.r.t. τ, i.e., $\mathsf{A}(\llparenthesis \mathsf{b} \rrparenthesis) = \tau$, and $\llparenthesis \mathsf{b} \rrparenthesis \subseteq \tau$, and suppose $\mathsf{A}(\mathsf{c}) \supseteq \tau$, then $\llparenthesis \mathsf{b} \rrparenthesis \subseteq \tau \subseteq \mathsf{A}(\mathsf{c})$ and therefore we trivially have $\mathsf{A}[\![\mathsf{b}?]\!]\mathsf{A}(\mathsf{c}) = \mathsf{A}(\mathsf{A}(\mathsf{c}) \cap \llparenthesis \mathsf{b} \rrparenthesis) = \mathsf{A}(\llparenthesis \mathsf{b} \rrparenthesis) = \tau$.

In other words, when b is quasi-expressible we have the adequacy of the abstract domain w.r.t. its semantics, when we have adequacy of the abstract domain w.r.t. its semantics, we cannot say anything about the possibility to express b, in particular if $\mathsf{A}(\mathsf{c}) \subsetneq \tau$ we always have adequacy w.r.t. τ.

Corollary 1. *Given* $\mathsf{b} \in \mathrm{BExp}$ *and* $\mathsf{A} \in Abs(\mathsf{C})$

1. *If* b *is quasi-expressible then* $\widetilde{\mathbb{C}}^{\mathsf{A}}(\mathsf{b})$;
2. *If* b *is not quasi-expressible (w.r.t.* $\top$*), then* $\forall \mathsf{c} \in \mathsf{C}.\, \mathsf{A}(\mathsf{c}) = \top$ *we have* $\neg\widetilde{\mathbb{C}}^{\mathsf{A}}_{\mathsf{c}}(\mathsf{b}?)$.

4 Adjusting Abstract Domains

In this section, we wonder whether it is possible to *adjust* abstract domains in order to make them locally adequate. First, we realize that, differently from completeness, even when we deal with different input and output abstract domains, i.e., $\mathsf{A}_1 \circ f \circ \mathsf{A}_2$, we have only one possible direction for adjusting the domains, we can only refine them.

A second observation is that it is not always possible to adjust an abstract domain towards adequacy.

Finally, even when possible there may not exist a shell [17], namely a *most abstract* refinement guaranteeing adequacy, but anyway we can adjust the domain towards an optimal refinement guaranteeing adequacy.

For the sake of simplicity, in the following we consider the same domain of input and output, but similar results hold in the most general case.

Proposition 2. *Let* C *be concrete the domain,* $f : \mathsf{C} \to \mathsf{C}$*, and* $\mathsf{A} \in Abs(\mathsf{C})$*. Let* $\mathsf{c} \in \mathsf{C}$ *and* $\tau \in \mathsf{A}$*, if* $f(\mathsf{c}) \not\lneq_{\mathsf{C}} \tau$ *then the abstract domain* A *cannot be adequate.*

For a generic τ, $f(\mathsf{c}) \not\lneq_{\mathsf{C}} \tau$ means that $\tau \leq_{\mathsf{C}} f(\mathsf{c})$ or not comparable, when $\tau = \top$, it means $f(\mathsf{c}) = \top$. The result is trivial, since if A is such that $\mathsf{A} \circ f \circ \mathsf{A}(\mathsf{c}) \lneq_{\mathsf{C}} \tau$ then also $f(\mathsf{c}) \lneq_{\mathsf{C}} \tau$ by extensivity, contradicting the hypothesis. Hence surely adequacy is violated for any possible abstraction A. For instance, if we consider f of Example 1, $\mathsf{c} = \{\, n \in \mathbb{Z} \,|\, n \geq 0 \,\}$ and $\tau = \{\, n \in \mathbb{Z} \,|\, n > 0 \,\}$, then $f(\mathsf{c}) = \{\, 2n \in \mathbb{Z} \,|\, n \geq 0 \,\} \not\lneq_{\mathsf{C}} \tau$ meaning that there not exist abstract domains A adequate for f on c..

Suppose now $f(\mathsf{c}) \lneq_{\mathsf{C}} \tau$, then we may adjust the abstract domain. The following step consists in fixing a first necessary (not sufficient) condition, namely $f \circ \mathsf{A}(\mathsf{c}) \lneq_{\mathsf{C}} \tau$. Indeed it is necessary since, if $\mathsf{A} \circ f \circ \mathsf{A}(\mathsf{c}) \lneq_{\mathsf{C}} \tau$ then, by extensivity, $f \circ \mathsf{A}(\mathsf{c}) \leq_{\mathsf{C}} \mathsf{A} \circ f \circ \mathsf{A}(\mathsf{c}) \lneq_{\mathsf{C}} \tau$. Let us define the following set of elements and domain refinement[3]

$$\mathsf{Ri}^{\tau}_{\mathsf{A}(\mathsf{c})}(\mathsf{A}) \stackrel{\text{def}}{=} \mathsf{A} \boxplus \{\mathsf{d}'\} \text{ with } \mathsf{d}' \in \max\{\, \mathsf{d} \in \mathsf{C} \,|\, \mathsf{d} \geq \mathsf{c},\ f(\mathsf{d}) \lneq_{\mathsf{C}} \tau \ \wedge\ \mathsf{A}(\mathsf{c}) = \mathsf{A}(\mathsf{d}) \,\}$$

where the domain operation $\boxplus$ [5] is defined as follows. Let $\mathsf{A} \in Abs(\mathsf{C})$ and $R \subseteq \mathsf{C}$[4]

$$\mathsf{A} \boxplus R \stackrel{\text{def}}{=} \mathcal{M}(\mathsf{A} \cup R)$$

Proposition 3. *Let* C *be the concrete domain,* $f : \mathsf{C} \to \mathsf{C}$ *monotone, and* $\mathsf{A} \in Abs(\mathsf{C})$*. Suppose* $f(\mathsf{c}) \lneq_{\mathsf{C}} \tau$ *and* $f \circ \mathsf{A}(\mathsf{c}) \not\lneq_{\mathsf{C}} \tau$ *Then* $\mathsf{A}_i \stackrel{\text{def}}{=} \mathsf{Ri}^{\tau}_{\mathsf{A}(\mathsf{c})}(\mathsf{A})$ *is such that* $f \circ \mathsf{A}_i(\mathsf{c}) \lneq_{\mathsf{C}} \tau$.

Proof. Let us denote $\mathsf{R} \stackrel{\text{def}}{=} \max\{\, \mathsf{d} \,|\, \mathsf{d} \in \mathsf{C},\ f(\mathsf{d}) \lneq_{\mathsf{C}} \tau \ \wedge\ \mathsf{A}(\mathsf{c}) = \mathsf{A}(\mathsf{d}) \,\}$ for the sake of readability. Suppose, in particular $\mathsf{A}_i = \mathsf{A} \boxplus \{\mathsf{d}\}$, with $\mathsf{d} \in \mathsf{R}$. Note that $\mathsf{A}_i \in Abs(\mathsf{C})$ by construction, and $\mathsf{A}_i \sqsubseteq \mathsf{A}$. Now, let us observe that $\mathsf{c} \in \mathsf{R}$ since $f(\mathsf{c}) \lneq_{\mathsf{C}} \tau$ by hypothesis, hence $\mathsf{c} \leq_{\mathsf{C}} \mathsf{d}$. Then, by monotonicity of A_i, this means that $\mathsf{A}_i(\mathsf{c}) \leq_{\mathsf{C}} \mathsf{A}_i(\mathsf{d}) = \mathsf{d}$, where the last equality holds by construction. But then, by definition of R, we have $f(\mathsf{d}) \lneq_{\mathsf{C}} \tau$, and therefore $f \circ \mathsf{A}_i(\mathsf{c}) \leq_{\mathsf{C}} f(\mathsf{d}) \lneq_{\mathsf{C}} \tau$.

The following step consists in fixing another necessary (not sufficient) condition, namely $\mathsf{A} \circ f(\mathsf{c}) \lneq_{\mathsf{C}} \tau$, which still may not hold. First of all, let us observe that if $f(\mathsf{c}) \lneq_{\mathsf{C}} \tau$, being $\tau \in \mathsf{A}$, by monotonicity we have $\mathsf{A} \circ f(\mathsf{c}) \leq_{\mathsf{C}} \mathsf{A}(\tau) = \tau$, hence $\mathsf{A} \circ f(\mathsf{c}) \not\lneq_{\mathsf{C}} \tau$ means $\mathsf{A} \circ f(\mathsf{c}) = \tau$. In this case we can refine the output abstract domain to force $\mathsf{A} \circ f(\mathsf{c}) \lneq_{\mathsf{C}} \tau$.
Let us define the following refinement

$$\mathsf{Ro}^{\tau}_{\mathsf{A}(\mathsf{c})}(\mathsf{A}) \stackrel{\text{def}}{=} \mathsf{A} \boxplus \{\mathsf{d}'\} \text{ with } \mathsf{d}' \in \max\{\, f(\mathsf{d}) \,|\, \mathsf{c} \leq \mathsf{d} \in \mathsf{C},\ f(\mathsf{d}) \lneq_{\mathsf{C}} \tau \ \wedge\ \mathsf{A}(\mathsf{c}) = \mathsf{A}(\mathsf{d}) \,\}$$

---

[3] Where max extracts the upper bounds from a set.

[4] Let us recall that $\mathcal{M}$ is the Moore closure, namely the operator closing a set by concrete greatest lower bound, hence making a set a Moore family.

Proposition 4. *Let* C *be the concrete domain,* $f : \mathsf{C} \to \mathsf{C}$ *monotone, and* $\mathsf{A} \in Abs(\mathsf{C})$. *Suppose* $f(\mathsf{c}) \lneq_{\mathsf{C}} \tau$ *and* $\mathsf{A} \circ f(\mathsf{c}) = \tau$. *Then* $\mathsf{A}_o \stackrel{\text{def}}{=} \mathsf{Ro}^{\tau}_{\mathsf{A}(\mathsf{c})}(\mathsf{A})$ *is such that* $\mathsf{A}_o \circ f(\mathsf{c}) \lneq_{\mathsf{C}} \tau$.

Proof. Let us denote the set $\mathsf{R} \stackrel{\text{def}}{=} \max\{f(\mathsf{d}) \,|\, \mathsf{d} \in \mathsf{C},\ f(\mathsf{d}) \lneq_{\mathsf{C}} \tau \wedge \mathsf{A}(\mathsf{c}) = \mathsf{A}(\mathsf{d})\}$ for the sake of readability. Suppose, in particular $\mathsf{A}_o = \mathsf{A} \boxplus \{\mathsf{d}'\}$, with $\mathsf{d}' \in \mathsf{R}$. Note that $\mathsf{A}_o \in Abs(\mathsf{C})$ by construction, and $\mathsf{A}_o \sqsubseteq \mathsf{A}$, namely it is more concrete than A, which means that $\mathsf{A}_o \circ f(\mathsf{c}) \leq_{\mathsf{C}} \mathsf{A} \circ f(\mathsf{c}) = \tau$. Now, let us observe that $f(\mathsf{c}) \in \mathsf{R}$ since $f(\mathsf{c}) \lneq_{\mathsf{C}} \tau$ by hypothesis, hence $f(\mathsf{c}) \leq_{\mathsf{C}} \mathsf{d}'$. Then, by monotonicity of A_o, this means that $\mathsf{A}_o \circ f(\mathsf{c}) \leq_{\mathsf{C}} \mathsf{A}_o(\mathsf{d}') = \mathsf{d}'$, where the last equation holds by construction. But then, by definition of R, we have $\mathsf{d}' \lneq_{\mathsf{C}} \tau$, and therefore $\mathsf{A}_o \circ f(\mathsf{c}) \leq_{\mathsf{C}} \mathsf{d}' \lneq_{\mathsf{C}} \tau$.

Now we can make the final step, combining the two transformations.

Theorem 2. *Let* C *be the concrete domain,* $f : \mathsf{C} \to \mathsf{C}$ *monotone, and* $\mathsf{A} \in Abs(\mathsf{C})$. *Suppose* $f(\mathsf{c}) \lneq_{\mathsf{C}} \tau$, *then let* $\mathsf{A}_i \stackrel{\text{def}}{=} \mathsf{Ri}^{\tau}_{\mathsf{A}(\mathsf{c})}(\mathsf{A})$ *and* $\mathsf{R}^{\tau}_{\mathsf{A}(\mathsf{c})}(\mathsf{A}) \stackrel{\text{def}}{=} \mathsf{Ro}^{\tau}_{\mathsf{A}_i(\mathsf{c})}(\mathsf{A}_i)$, *then* $\mathsf{R}^{\tau}_{\mathsf{A}(\mathsf{c})} \circ f \circ \mathsf{R}^{\tau}_{\mathsf{A}(\mathsf{c})} \lneq_{\mathsf{C}} \tau$.

Proof. By the hypotheses and by Proposition 3 we have that $f \circ \mathsf{A}_i(\mathsf{c}) \lneq_{\mathsf{C}} \tau$. Let us denote $\mathsf{c}' \stackrel{\text{def}}{=} \mathsf{A}_i(\mathsf{c})$, then $f(\mathsf{c}') \lneq \tau$, hence we can build $\mathsf{A}_o \stackrel{\text{def}}{=} \mathsf{Ro}^{\tau}_{\mathsf{A}_i(\mathsf{c}')}(\mathsf{A}_i)$. At this point, by definition and indempotence of A_i we have that

$$\begin{aligned} \mathsf{Ro}^{\tau}_{\mathsf{A}_i(\mathsf{c}')}(\mathsf{A}_i) &= \max\left\{ f(\mathsf{d}) \,\middle|\, \mathsf{d} \in \mathsf{C},\ f(\mathsf{d}) \lneq_{\mathsf{C}} \tau \wedge \mathsf{A}_i(\mathsf{c}') = \mathsf{A}_i(\mathsf{d}) \right\} \\ &= \max\left\{ f(\mathsf{d}) \,\middle|\, \mathsf{d} \in \mathsf{C},\ f(\mathsf{d}) \lneq_{\mathsf{C}} \tau \wedge \mathsf{A}_i(\mathsf{A}_i(\mathsf{c})) = \mathsf{A}_i(\mathsf{d}) \right\} \\ &= \max\left\{ f(\mathsf{d}) \,\middle|\, \mathsf{d} \in \mathsf{C},\ f(\mathsf{d}) \lneq_{\mathsf{C}} \tau \wedge \mathsf{A}_i(\mathsf{c}) = \mathsf{A}_i(\mathsf{d}) \right\} = \mathsf{Ro}^{\tau}_{\mathsf{A}_i(\mathsf{c})}(\mathsf{A}_i) \end{aligned}$$

Hence $\mathsf{A}_o = \mathsf{Ro}^{\tau}_{\mathsf{A}_i(\mathsf{c})}(\mathsf{A}_i) = \mathsf{R}^{\tau}_{\mathsf{A}(\mathsf{c})}(\mathsf{A})$ and $\mathsf{A}_o \sqsubseteq \mathsf{A}_i$. Then by Proposition 4 we have that $\mathsf{A}_o \circ f(\mathsf{c}') \lneq_{\mathsf{C}} \tau$, namely $\mathsf{A}_o \circ f \circ \mathsf{A}_i(\mathsf{c}) \lneq_{\mathsf{C}} \tau$. But then, by $\mathsf{A}_o \sqsubseteq \mathsf{A}_i$ and by monotonicity of the functions involved, we have $\mathsf{A}_o \circ f \circ \mathsf{A}_o(\mathsf{c}) \leq_{\mathsf{C}} \mathsf{A}_o \circ f \circ \mathsf{A}_i(\mathsf{c}) \lneq_{\mathsf{C}} \tau$.

Let us consider a very simple example just to show the process.

Example 3. Consider the sign abstraction $\mathsf{A} = Sign$ on the concrete domain $\mathsf{C} = \wp(\mathbb{Z})$ and $g \stackrel{\text{def}}{=} \lambda \mathsf{c}. \{ n+2 \,|\, n \in \mathsf{c} \}$. Then, if $\mathsf{c} \stackrel{\text{def}}{=} \top = \mathbb{Z}$ we have $g(\mathsf{c}) = \top$, meaning that for the $\top$ element the sign domain cannot be make adequate.
Let us consider now the f function in Example 1, on the same domains and suppose $\tau \stackrel{\text{def}}{=} \mathbb{Z}_{\geq 0}$. Let $\mathsf{c} = \{0, 2, 4\}$, then $f(\mathsf{c}) = \{0, 4, 8\} \subsetneq \tau$, but $f \circ Sign(\mathsf{c}) = f(\mathbb{Z}_{\geq 0}) = \mathbb{Z}_{\geq 0} = \tau$ hence we can try to make the abstract domain adequate for c. Let us observe that for any $n > 0$

$$\mathbb{Z}_{\geq 0} \smallsetminus \{n\} \in \max\left\{ \mathsf{d} \,\middle|\, f(\mathsf{d}) \subsetneq \mathbb{Z}_{\geq 0} \wedge Sign(\mathsf{d}) = \mathbb{Z}_{\geq 0} \right\}$$

since $f(\mathbb{Z}_{\geq 0} \smallsetminus \{n\}) = \mathbb{Z}_{\geq 0} \smallsetminus \{2n\} \subsetneq \tau$, but $Sign(\mathbb{Z}_{\geq 0} \smallsetminus \{n\}) = \mathbb{Z}_{\geq 0}$ since 0 is still in the result. Let us define $Sign' \stackrel{\text{def}}{=} Sign \boxplus (\mathbb{Z}_{\geq 0} \smallsetminus \{8\})$. Now $f \circ Sign'(\mathsf{c}) = f(\mathbb{Z}_{\geq 0} \smallsetminus \{8\}) = \mathbb{Z}_{\geq 0} \smallsetminus \{16\} \subsetneq \tau$, but unfortunately $Sign' \circ f(\mathsf{c}) = Sign'(\{0, 4, 8\}) = \mathbb{Z}_{\geq 0} = \tau$, hence we have to further refine. Then, we have that

$$\mathbb{Z}_{\geq 0} \smallsetminus \{16\} \in \max\left\{ f(\mathsf{d}) \,\middle|\, f(\mathsf{d}) \subsetneq \mathbb{Z}_{\geq 0} \wedge Sign'(\mathsf{d}) = \mathbb{Z}_{\geq 0} \smallsetminus \{8\} \right\}$$

Let $Sign'' \stackrel{\text{def}}{=} Sign' \boxplus \mathbb{Z}_{\geq 0} \smallsetminus \{16\}$, and in this case $Sign'' \circ f(\mathsf{c}) = Sign''(\{0,4,8\}) = \mathbb{Z}_{\geq 0} \smallsetminus \{16\} \subsetneq \tau$ and $Sign'' \circ f \circ Sign''(\mathsf{c}) = Sign'' \circ f(\mathbb{Z}_{\geq 0} \smallsetminus \{8,16\})^5 = Sign''(\mathbb{Z}_{\geq 0} \smallsetminus \{16,32\}) = \mathbb{Z}_{\geq 0} \smallsetminus \{16\} \subsetneq \tau$. In this example, we can also observe that, in general, the refinements do not induce local completeness [5] but only adequacy.

5 Abstract Domain Adequacy Logic

In this section we define a proof system for program analysis of regular commands, parameterized by an abstraction $\mathsf{A} = \gamma\alpha(\mathsf{C})$ on the concrete domain of sets of stores $\mathsf{C} = \wp(\mathbb{M})$. The provable triples of our logic are judgements of the form $\tau \vdash_{\mathsf{A}} \langle \mathsf{c} \rangle\, \mathtt{r}\, \langle \mathsf{d} \rangle$, with $\mathsf{c}, \mathsf{d} \in \mathsf{C}$, $\tau \in \mathsf{A}$ and $\mathtt{r} \in \mathfrak{L}$. $\tau \vdash_{\mathsf{A}} \langle \mathsf{c} \rangle\, \mathtt{r}\, \langle \mathsf{d} \rangle$ guarantees that:

1. $\widetilde{\mathbb{C}}^{\mathsf{A}}_{\mathsf{c}}(\mathtt{r})_\tau$;
2. $[\![\mathtt{r}]\!]^\sharp_{\mathsf{A}} \alpha(\mathsf{c}) \leq_{\mathsf{A}} \alpha(\mathsf{d}) \lneq_{\mathsf{A}} \tau_\alpha \stackrel{\text{def}}{=} \alpha(\tau)$.

The rules are provided in Fig. 4. It is worth noting that, the rule `relax` is added, even if less common, since the rules work with the concrete elements c, and the rule `seq` could be not directly applicable also in cases where the first statement has an output assertion greater than the input assertion of the following statement. In this case the rule $\mathtt{relax}_2$ may not be used or may increase imprecision getting closer to τ.
For instance, consider $\mathtt{r} = \mathtt{r}_1; \mathtt{r}_2$, and consider as output property of $\mathtt{r}_1$ the property $\mathsf{c} = \{0, 10, 20, 30\}$, while the input property for $\mathtt{r}_2$ is $\mathsf{c}' = \{0, 10, 30\}$, then we would have to reduce c or enlarge c' in order to apply rule `seq`. It should be clear that the first direction is surely preferable for not losing precision and only the rule `relax` allows to follow such direction.

Lemma 1. *Let* $\mathsf{C} = \wp(\mathbb{M})$, $\mathsf{A} \in Abs(\mathsf{C})$ *(*$\mathsf{A} = \gamma\alpha$*)*, $\tau \in \mathsf{A}$ *and* $\tau_\alpha \stackrel{\text{def}}{=} \alpha(\tau)$. *Then* $\forall \mathsf{c} \in \mathsf{C}$ *we have that* $\widetilde{\mathbb{C}}^{\mathsf{A}}_{\mathsf{c}}(\mathtt{r})_\tau$ *iff* $\alpha([\![\mathtt{r}]\!]\gamma\alpha(\mathsf{c})) \lneq_{\mathsf{A}} \tau_\alpha$.

Proof. Suppose $\widetilde{\mathbb{C}}^{\mathsf{A}}_{\mathsf{c}}(\mathtt{r})_\tau$, namely such that $\mathsf{A}[\![\mathtt{r}]\!]\mathsf{A}(\mathsf{c}) \subsetneq \tau$, written in terms of the GI it is $\gamma\alpha[\![\mathtt{r}]\!]\gamma\alpha(\mathsf{c}) \subsetneq \tau$, then by monotonicity of α and by properties of GI, we have that

$$\alpha[\![\mathtt{r}]\!]\gamma\alpha(\mathsf{c}) = \alpha\gamma\alpha[\![\mathtt{r}]\!]\gamma\alpha(\mathsf{c}) \leq_{\mathsf{A}} \tau_\alpha$$

Suppose, towards contradiction, that $\alpha[\![\mathtt{r}]\!]\gamma\alpha(\mathsf{c}) = \tau_\alpha$, then since $\gamma(\tau_\alpha) = \gamma\alpha(\tau) = \tau$ being $\tau \in \mathsf{A}$, we would have also

$$\mathsf{A}[\![\mathtt{r}]\!]\mathsf{A}(\mathsf{c}) = \gamma\alpha[\![\mathtt{r}]\!]\gamma\alpha(\mathsf{c}) = \gamma(\tau_\alpha) = \tau$$

contradicting the hypothesis, hence $\alpha[\![\mathtt{r}]\!]\gamma\alpha(\mathsf{c}) \lneq_{\mathsf{A}} \tau_\alpha$.
Suppose now $\alpha[\![\mathtt{r}]\!]\gamma\alpha(\mathsf{c}) \lneq_{\mathsf{A}} \tau_\alpha$, then by monotonicity of γ, we have

$$\mathsf{A}[\![\mathtt{r}]\!]\mathsf{A}(\mathsf{c}) = \gamma\alpha[\![\mathtt{r}]\!]\gamma\alpha(\mathsf{c}) \subseteq \gamma(\tau_\alpha) = \tau$$

Suppose, towards contradiction, that $\gamma\alpha[\![\mathtt{r}]\!]\gamma\alpha(\mathsf{c}) = \gamma(\tau_\alpha)$ then being γ one-to-one, this would imply $\alpha[\![\mathtt{r}]\!]\gamma\alpha(\mathsf{c}) = \tau_\alpha$ contradicting the hypothesis. Hence $\mathsf{A}[\![\mathtt{r}]\!]\mathsf{A}(\mathsf{c}) \subsetneq \tau$.

$$\texttt{transfer:}\ \frac{\widetilde{\mathbb{C}}^{\mathsf{A}}_{\mathsf{c}}(\mathsf{e})_\tau}{\tau \vdash_{\mathsf{A}} \langle \mathsf{c}\rangle\, \mathsf{e}\, \langle [\![\mathsf{e}]\!]\gamma\alpha(\mathsf{c})\rangle}$$

$$\texttt{relax:}\ \frac{\mathsf{c}' \subseteq \mathsf{c} \subseteq \gamma\alpha(\mathsf{c}') \quad \tau \vdash_{\mathsf{A}} \langle \mathsf{c}'\rangle\, \mathtt{r}\, \langle \mathsf{d}'\rangle \quad \mathsf{d} \subseteq \mathsf{d}' \subseteq \gamma\alpha(\mathsf{d})}{\tau \vdash_{\mathsf{A}} \langle \mathsf{c}\rangle\, \mathtt{r}\, \langle \mathsf{d}\rangle}$$

$$\texttt{relax}_2\texttt{:}\ \frac{\mathsf{c} \subseteq \mathsf{c}' \quad \tau \vdash_{\mathsf{A}} \langle \mathsf{c}'\rangle\, \mathtt{r}\, \langle \mathsf{d}'\rangle \quad \alpha(\mathsf{d}') \leq_{\mathsf{A}} \alpha(\mathsf{d}) \lneq_{\mathsf{A}} \tau_\alpha}{\tau \vdash_{\mathsf{A}} \langle \mathsf{c}\rangle\, \mathtt{r}\, \langle \mathsf{d}\rangle}$$

$$\texttt{seq:}\ \frac{\tau \vdash_{\mathsf{A}} \langle \mathsf{c}\rangle\, \mathtt{r}_1\, \langle \mathsf{d}'\rangle \quad \tau \vdash_{\mathsf{A}} \langle \mathsf{d}'\rangle\, \mathtt{r}_2\, \langle \mathsf{d}\rangle}{\tau \vdash_{\mathsf{A}} \langle \mathsf{c}\rangle\, \mathtt{r}_1; \mathtt{r}_2\, \langle \mathsf{d}\rangle} \qquad \texttt{iterate:}\ \frac{\tau \vdash_{\mathsf{A}} \langle \mathsf{c}\rangle\, \mathtt{r}\, \langle \mathsf{d}\rangle \quad \alpha(\mathsf{d}) \leq_{\mathsf{A}} \alpha(\mathsf{c}) \lneq_{\mathsf{A}} \tau_\alpha}{\tau \vdash_{\mathsf{A}} \langle \mathsf{c}\rangle\, \mathtt{r}^*\, \langle \mathsf{c}\rangle}$$

$$\texttt{join:}\ \frac{\tau \vdash_{\mathsf{A}} \langle \mathsf{c}\rangle\, \mathtt{r}_1\, \langle \mathsf{d}_1\rangle \quad \tau \vdash_{\mathsf{A}} \langle \mathsf{c}\rangle\, \mathtt{r}_2\, \langle \mathsf{d}_2\rangle \quad \alpha(\mathsf{d}_1 \cup \mathsf{d}_2) \lneq_{\mathsf{A}} \tau_\alpha}{\tau \vdash_{\mathsf{A}} \langle \mathsf{c}\rangle\, \mathtt{r}_1 \oplus \mathtt{r}_2\, \langle \mathsf{d}_1 \cup \mathsf{d}_2\rangle}$$

Fig. 4. A logic for adequacy w.r.t. τ ($\tau_\alpha \stackrel{\text{def}}{=} \alpha(\tau)$).

Theorem 3. *Let* $\mathsf{c}, \mathsf{d} \in \mathsf{C} = \wp(\mathbb{M})$, $\mathsf{A} \in Abs(\mathsf{C})$ *(*$\mathsf{A} = \gamma\alpha$*)*, $\tau \in \mathsf{A}$ *and* $\tau_\alpha \stackrel{\text{def}}{=} \alpha(\tau)$. *If* $\tau \vdash_{\mathsf{A}} \langle \mathsf{c}\rangle\, \mathtt{r}\, \langle \mathsf{d}\rangle$ *then* (1) $\widetilde{\mathbb{C}}^{\mathsf{A}}_{\mathsf{c}}(\mathtt{r})_\tau$ *and* (2) $[\![\mathtt{r}]\!]^\sharp_{\mathsf{A}}\alpha(\mathsf{c}) \leq_{\mathsf{A}} \alpha(\mathsf{d}) \lneq_{\mathsf{A}} \tau_\alpha$.

Proof. We prove the soundness of the rule system in Fig. 4 by structural induction on the derivation tree of $\tau \vdash_{\mathsf{A}} \langle \mathsf{c}\rangle\, \mathtt{r}\, \langle \mathsf{d}\rangle$, by distinguishing the cases depending on the last rule applied.

`(transfer)`: In this case (1) holds by hypothesis, being the premix of the rule. Then, by Lemma 1 we have $\alpha([\![\mathsf{e}]\!]\gamma\alpha(\mathsf{c})) \lneq_{\mathsf{A}} \tau_\alpha$, and by definition of $[\![\mathsf{e}]\!]^\sharp_{\mathsf{A}}$ we have

$$[\![\mathsf{e}]\!]^\sharp_{\mathsf{A}}\alpha(\mathsf{c}) = (\alpha[\![\mathsf{e}]\!]\gamma)\alpha(\mathsf{c}) = \alpha([\![\mathsf{e}]\!]\gamma\alpha(\mathsf{c})) \lneq_{\mathsf{A}} \tau_\alpha$$

`(relax)`: First of all, let us observe that the hypotheses, by monotonicity and idempotence of $\gamma\alpha$, imply $\gamma\alpha(\mathsf{c}) = \gamma\alpha(\mathsf{c}')$, and therefore, being γ one-to-one, this means that $\alpha(\mathsf{c}) = \alpha(\mathsf{c}')$. Analogously, $\alpha(\mathsf{d}) = \alpha(\mathsf{d}')$. This means that $\alpha([\![\mathtt{r}]\!]\gamma\alpha(\mathsf{c})) = (\alpha[\![\mathtt{r}]\!]\gamma)\alpha(\mathsf{c}) \leq_{\mathsf{A}} [\![\mathtt{r}]\!]^\sharp_{\mathsf{A}}\alpha(\mathsf{c})$ by definition of bca, but then $[\![\mathtt{r}]\!]^\sharp_{\mathsf{A}}\alpha(\mathsf{c}) = [\![\mathtt{r}]\!]^\sharp_{\mathsf{A}}\alpha(\mathsf{c}') \lneq_{\mathsf{A}} \tau_\alpha$ since by hypothesis $\tau \vdash_{\mathsf{A}} \langle \mathsf{c}'\rangle\, \mathtt{r}\, \langle \mathsf{d}'\rangle$, and therefore by inductive hypothesis $[\![\mathtt{r}]\!]^\sharp_{\mathsf{A}}\alpha(\mathsf{c}') \leq_{\mathsf{A}} \alpha(\mathsf{d}') \lneq_{\mathsf{A}} \tau_\alpha$. But then, by definition of bca and by transitivity of $\leq_{\mathsf{A}}$ we have $\alpha([\![\mathtt{r}]\!]\gamma\alpha(\mathsf{c})) \lneq_{\mathsf{A}} \tau_\alpha$. Hence, by Lemma 1 we have (1). As far as (2) is concerned, by we have proved above we have

$$[\![\mathtt{r}]\!]^\sharp_{\mathsf{A}}\alpha(\mathsf{c}) = [\![\mathtt{r}]\!]^\sharp_{\mathsf{A}}\alpha(\mathsf{c}') \leq_{\mathsf{A}} \alpha(\mathsf{d}') = \alpha(\mathsf{d}) \qquad \text{and} \qquad \alpha(\mathsf{d}) = \alpha(\mathsf{d}') \lneq_{\mathsf{A}} \tau_\alpha$$

[5] $\mathbb{Z}_{\geq 0} \smallsetminus \{8, 16\}$ is introduced by $\boxplus$ in *Sign*″.

$\texttt{(relax}_2\texttt{)}$: Note that, by hypothesis $\tau \vdash_{\mathsf{A}} \langle \mathtt{c}' \rangle \mathtt{r} \langle \mathtt{d}' \rangle$, hence by inductive hypothesis, as before, we have $[\![\mathtt{r}]\!]^{\sharp}_{\mathsf{A}} \alpha(\mathtt{c}') \leq_{\mathsf{A}} \alpha(\mathtt{d}') \lneq_{\mathsf{A}} \tau_\alpha$, and therefore

$$\alpha[\![\mathtt{r}]\!]\gamma\alpha(\mathtt{c}) \leq_{\mathsf{A}} [\![\mathtt{r}]\!]^{\sharp}_{\mathsf{A}} \alpha(\mathtt{c}) \leq_{\mathsf{A}} [\![\mathtt{r}]\!]^{\sharp}_{\mathsf{A}} \alpha(\mathtt{c}') \lneq_{\mathsf{A}} \tau_\alpha$$

Then by Lemma 1 this implies $\mathsf{A}[\![\mathtt{r}]\!]\mathsf{A}(\mathtt{c}) \subsetneq \tau$ (condition (1)), and moreover, again by the rule hypotheses and by inductive hypothesis, we have

$$[\![\mathtt{r}]\!]^{\sharp}_{\mathsf{A}} \alpha(\mathtt{c}) \leq_{\mathsf{A}} [\![\mathtt{r}]\!]^{\sharp}_{\mathsf{A}} \alpha(\mathtt{c}') \leq_{\mathsf{A}} \alpha(\mathtt{d}') \leq_{\mathsf{A}} \alpha(\mathtt{d}) \lneq_{\mathsf{A}} \tau_\alpha$$

proving condition (2).

$\texttt{(seq)}$: Let us prove (1). By inductive hypotheses, we have that $[\![\mathtt{r}_1]\!]^{\sharp}_{\mathsf{A}} \alpha(\mathtt{c}) \leq_{\mathsf{A}} \alpha(\mathtt{d}') \lneq_{\mathsf{A}} \tau_\alpha$ and $[\![\mathtt{r}_2]\!]^{\sharp}_{\mathsf{A}} \alpha(\mathtt{d}') \leq_{\mathsf{A}} \alpha(\mathtt{d}) \lneq_{\mathsf{A}} \tau_\alpha$, then by definition of bca and of abstract semantics, and by the monotonicity of the abstract semantics we have that

$$\alpha[\![\mathtt{r}_1;\mathtt{r}_2]\!]\gamma\alpha(\mathtt{c}) \leq_{\mathsf{A}} [\![\mathtt{r}_1;\mathtt{r}_2]\!]^{\sharp}_{\mathsf{A}} \alpha(\mathtt{c}) = [\![\mathtt{r}_2]\!]^{\sharp}_{\mathsf{A}}([\![\mathtt{r}_1]\!]^{\sharp}_{\mathsf{A}} \alpha(\mathtt{c})) \leq_{\mathsf{A}} [\![\mathtt{r}_2]\!]^{\sharp}_{\mathsf{A}} \alpha(\mathtt{d}') \lneq_{\mathsf{A}} \tau_\alpha$$

Hence, by Lemma 1, we have $\mathsf{A}[\![\mathtt{r}]\!]\mathsf{A}(\mathtt{c}) \subsetneq \tau$. As far as (2) is concerned, we have already proved that $[\![\mathtt{r}_1;\mathtt{r}_2]\!]^{\sharp}_{\mathsf{A}} \alpha(\mathtt{c}) \leq_{\mathsf{A}} [\![\mathtt{r}_2]\!]^{\sharp}_{\mathsf{A}} \alpha(\mathtt{d}')$, and $[\![\mathtt{r}_2]\!]^{\sharp}_{\mathsf{A}} \alpha(\mathtt{d}') \leq_{\mathsf{A}} \alpha(\mathtt{d}) \lneq_{\mathsf{A}} \tau_\alpha$ by hypothesis (2) on $\mathtt{r}_2$, and therefore by transitivity we have the thesis.

$\texttt{(iterate)}$: Let us prove that if we have $\tau \vdash_{\mathsf{A}} \langle \mathtt{c} \rangle\ \mathtt{r}\ \langle \mathtt{d} \rangle$ with $\alpha(\mathtt{d}) \leq_{\mathsf{A}} \alpha(\mathtt{c})$, then we have $\tau \vdash_{\mathsf{A}} \langle \mathtt{c} \rangle\ \mathtt{r}^*\ \langle \mathtt{c} \rangle$. We first prove by induction on $n \geq 1$ that $([\![\mathtt{r}]\!]^{\sharp}_{\mathsf{A}})^n \alpha(\mathtt{c}) \leq_{\mathsf{A}} \alpha(\mathtt{d})$. The base ($n = 1$) is the hypothesis of the rule, suppose it holds for $([\![\mathtt{r}]\!]^{\sharp}_{\mathsf{A}})^n$, let us prove for $n+1$, recalling that by structural inductive hypothesis we have that $[\![\mathtt{r}]\!]^{\sharp}_{\mathsf{A}} \alpha(\mathtt{c}) \leq_{\mathsf{A}} \alpha(\mathtt{d}) \subsetneq \tau_\alpha$, and by the rule hypothesis we have $\alpha(\mathtt{d}) \leq_{\mathsf{A}} \alpha(\mathtt{c})$

$$\begin{aligned}([\![\mathtt{r}]\!]^{\sharp}_{\mathsf{A}})^{n+1} \alpha(\mathtt{c}) &= (([\![\mathtt{r}]\!]^{\sharp}_{\mathsf{A}})^n \circ [\![\mathtt{r}]\!]^{\sharp}_{\mathsf{A}}) \alpha(\mathtt{c}) \\ &= ([\![\mathtt{r}]\!]^{\sharp}_{\mathsf{A}})^n ([\![\mathtt{r}]\!]^{\sharp}_{\mathsf{A}} \alpha(\mathtt{c})) \leq_{\mathsf{A}} ([\![\mathtt{r}]\!]^{\sharp}_{\mathsf{A}})^n \alpha(\mathtt{d}) \\ &\leq_{\mathsf{A}} ([\![\mathtt{r}]\!]^{\sharp}_{\mathsf{A}})^n \alpha(\mathtt{c}) \leq_{\mathsf{A}} \alpha(\mathtt{d}) \lneq_{\mathsf{A}} \tau_\alpha\end{aligned}$$

where the last relations hold by inductive hypothesis on n. Hence, for all $n \geq 1$ we have $([\![\mathtt{r}]\!]^{\sharp}_{\mathsf{A}})^n \alpha(\mathtt{c}) \leq_{\mathsf{A}} \alpha(\mathtt{d}) \lneq_{\mathsf{A}} \tau_\alpha$. At this point we have condition (2)

$$\begin{aligned}\alpha([\![\mathtt{r}^*]\!]\gamma\alpha(\mathtt{c})) \leq_{\mathsf{A}} [\![\mathtt{r}^*]\!]^{\sharp}_{\mathsf{A}} \alpha(\mathtt{c}) &= \textstyle\bigvee_{\mathsf{A}\{n\geq 0\}} ([\![\mathtt{r}]\!]^{\sharp}_{\mathsf{A}})^n \alpha(\mathtt{c}) \\ &= ([\![\mathtt{r}]\!]^{\sharp}_{\mathsf{A}})^0 \alpha(\mathtt{c}) \vee_{\mathsf{A}} \textstyle\bigvee_{\mathsf{A}\{n\geq 1\}} ([\![\mathtt{r}]\!]^{\sharp}_{\mathsf{A}})^n \alpha(\mathtt{c}) \\ &\leq_{\mathsf{A}} \alpha(\mathtt{c}) \vee_{\mathsf{A}} \alpha(\mathtt{d}) \leq_{\mathsf{A}} \alpha(\mathtt{c}) \lneq_{\mathsf{A}} \tau_\alpha\end{aligned}$$

by additivity of α and by the rule hypothesis $\alpha(\mathtt{c}) \lneq_{\mathsf{A}} \tau_\alpha$. Finally, condition (1) comes by Lemma 1.

$\texttt{(join)}$: Let us prove (2). By inductive hypotheses we have that $[\![\mathtt{r}_1]\!]^{\sharp}_{\mathsf{A}} \alpha(\mathtt{c}) \leq_{\mathsf{A}} \alpha(\mathtt{d}_1) \lneq_{\mathsf{A}} \tau_\alpha$ and that $[\![\mathtt{r}_2]\!]^{\sharp}_{\mathsf{A}} \alpha(\mathtt{c}) \leq_{\mathsf{A}} \alpha(\mathtt{d}_2) \lneq_{\mathsf{A}} \tau_\alpha$. Hence, by additivity of α we have

$$\begin{aligned}\alpha(\llbracket \mathtt{r}_1 \oplus \mathtt{r}_2 \rrbracket \gamma\alpha(\mathtt{c})) &= (\alpha\llbracket \mathtt{r}_1 \oplus \mathtt{r}_2 \rrbracket \gamma)\alpha(\mathtt{c}) \leq_{\mathsf{A}} \llbracket \mathtt{r}_1 \oplus \mathtt{r}_2 \rrbracket^\sharp_{\mathsf{A}} \alpha(\mathtt{c}) \\ &= \llbracket \mathtt{r}_1 \rrbracket^\sharp_{\mathsf{A}} \alpha(\mathtt{c}) \vee_{\mathsf{A}} \llbracket \mathtt{r}_2 \rrbracket^\sharp_{\mathsf{A}} \alpha(\mathtt{c}) \leq_{\mathsf{A}} \alpha(\mathtt{d}_1) \vee_{\mathsf{A}} \alpha(\mathtt{d}_2) \\ &= \alpha(\mathtt{d}_1 \cup \mathtt{d}_2) \lneq_{\mathsf{A}} \tau_\alpha\end{aligned}$$

By Lemma 1 what we have proved implies also (1), proving the thesis.

Corollary 2. *Let* $\mathsf{C} = \wp(\mathbb{M})$, $\mathsf{A} \in Abs(\mathsf{C})$ *(*$\mathsf{A} = \gamma\alpha$*). If* $\vdash_{\mathsf{A}} \langle \mathtt{c} \rangle\ \mathtt{r}\ \langle \mathtt{d} \rangle$ *then* (1) $\widetilde{\mathbb{C}}^{\mathsf{A}}_{\mathtt{c}}(\mathtt{r})$ *and* (2) $\llbracket \mathtt{r} \rrbracket^\sharp_{\mathsf{A}} \alpha(\mathtt{c}) \leq_{\mathsf{A}} \alpha(\mathtt{d}) \lneq_{\mathsf{A}} \top_{\mathsf{A}}$.

Let us investigate about completeness of this rule system.

Theorem 4. *Let* $\mathtt{c}, \mathtt{d} \in \mathsf{C} = \wp(\mathbb{M})$, $\mathsf{A} \in Abs(\mathsf{C})$ *(*$\mathsf{A} = \gamma\alpha$*),* $\mathtt{r} \in \mathfrak{L}$, $\tau \in \mathsf{A}$ *and* $\tau_\alpha \stackrel{\text{def}}{=} \alpha(\tau)$. (1) $\widetilde{\mathbb{C}}^{\mathsf{A}}_{\mathtt{c}}(\mathtt{r})_\tau$ *and* (2) $\llbracket \mathtt{r} \rrbracket^\sharp_{\mathsf{A}} \alpha(\mathtt{c}) \leq_{\mathsf{A}} \alpha(\mathtt{d}) \lneq_{\mathsf{A}} \tau_\alpha$ *do not imply* $\tau \vdash_{\mathsf{A}} \langle \mathtt{c} \rangle \mathtt{r} \langle \mathtt{d} \rangle$.

Proof (Sketch). We provide an example that cannot be deduced by using the rule system. Consider $\mathtt{r} \stackrel{\text{def}}{=} (x := x * 2; x < 0?)$, let us denote by $\mathtt{r}_1 \stackrel{\text{def}}{=} x := x * 2$ and by $\mathtt{r}_2 \stackrel{\text{def}}{=} x \leq 0?$. Consider the sign domain $\mathsf{A} \stackrel{\text{def}}{=} Sign = \gamma_{\mathsf{S}}\alpha_{\mathsf{S}}$ in Fig. 3 and let us denote by $\alpha_{\mathsf{S}} : \wp(\mathbb{Z}) \to Sign$, and γ_{S} the function associating with each abstract element the represented set, e.g., $\gamma_{\mathsf{S}}(\mathbb{Z}_{\leq 0}) = \{\, n \in \mathbb{Z} \mid n \leq 0 \,\}$, and let $\tau \stackrel{\text{def}}{=} \gamma(\mathbb{Z}_{\leq 0})$. Let $\mathtt{c} \stackrel{\text{def}}{=} \{-10, 0, 10\}$ and $\mathtt{d} \stackrel{\text{def}}{=} \{-10\}$ Then we have that

(1) $\widetilde{\mathbb{C}}^{\mathsf{A}}_{\mathtt{c}}(\mathtt{r})_\tau$, since $Sign\llbracket \mathtt{r} \rrbracket Sign(\{-10, 0, 10\}) = Sign\llbracket \mathtt{r} \rrbracket \mathbb{Z} = Sign(\{\, n \mid n < 0 \,\}) = \{\, n \mid n < 0 \,\} \subsetneq \tau$;
(2) $\llbracket \mathtt{r} \rrbracket^\sharp_{\mathsf{A}} Sign(\mathtt{c}) = \llbracket \mathtt{r} \rrbracket^\sharp_{\mathsf{A}} Sign(\{-10, 0, 10\}) = \llbracket \mathtt{r} \rrbracket^\sharp_{\mathsf{A}} \mathbb{Z} = \mathbb{Z}_{<0} = \alpha_{\mathsf{S}}(\mathtt{d}) \lneq_{Sign} \mathbb{Z}_{\leq 0}$, where trivially $\mathbb{Z}_{\leq 0} = \alpha_{\mathsf{S}}(\tau)$

But, $\widetilde{\mathbb{C}}^{\mathsf{A}}_{\mathtt{c}}(\mathtt{r}_1)_\tau$ does not hold, since $Sign\llbracket \mathtt{r}_1 \rrbracket Sign(\{-10, 0, 10\}) = Sign\llbracket \mathtt{r}_1 \rrbracket \mathbb{Z} = Sign(\mathbb{Z}) = \mathbb{Z} \not\subseteq \tau$, and therefore we cannot find $\mathtt{d}' \in \wp(\mathbb{Z})$ such that $\tau \vdash_{\mathsf{A}} \langle \mathtt{c} \rangle \mathtt{r}_1 \langle \mathtt{d}' \rangle$, making not possible to apply rule `seq`.

The logic above becomes complete if we add/substitute rule (`seq`) with the following rule computing code semantics

$$\mathtt{seq}_1 : \frac{\tau \vdash_{\mathsf{A}} \langle \llbracket \mathtt{r}_1 \rrbracket \gamma\alpha(\mathtt{c}) \rangle\ \mathtt{r}_2\ \langle \mathtt{d} \rangle}{\tau \vdash_{\mathsf{A}} \langle \mathtt{c} \rangle\ \mathtt{r}_1; \mathtt{r}_2\ \langle \mathtt{d} \rangle}$$

and the rule, with infinite premixes

$$\mathtt{iterate}_1 : \frac{\forall n \in \mathbb{N}.\ \tau \vdash_{\mathsf{A}} \langle \mathtt{c} \rangle\ \mathtt{r}^n\ \langle \mathtt{d} \rangle}{\tau \vdash_{\mathsf{A}} \langle \mathtt{c} \rangle\ \mathtt{r}^*\ \langle \mathtt{d} \rangle}$$

where $\mathtt{r}^n$ is a syntactic sugar defined as: $\mathtt{r}^0 \stackrel{\text{def}}{=}$ **skip** and $\mathtt{r}^{n+1} \stackrel{\text{def}}{=} \mathtt{r}^n; \mathtt{r}$. But it is worth noting that in this way the logic itself becomes undecidable requiring to compute a code semantics and to prove infinite conditions for being applied. Let us denote as $\tau \Vdash_{\mathsf{A}} \langle \mathtt{c} \rangle\ \mathtt{r}\ \langle \mathtt{d} \rangle$ the derivation in the rule system in Fig. 4 extended with rules $\mathtt{seq}_1$ and $\mathtt{iterate}_1$.

Theorem 5. *Let* $\mathtt{c}, \mathtt{d} \in \mathsf{C} = \wp(\mathsf{M})$, $\mathsf{A} \in Abs(\mathsf{C})$ *(*$\mathsf{A} = \gamma\alpha$*),* $\mathtt{r} \in \mathfrak{L}$, $\tau \in \mathsf{A}$ *and* $\tau_\alpha \stackrel{\text{def}}{=} \alpha(\tau)$*. If* (1) $\widetilde{\mathbb{C}}^{\mathsf{A}}_{\mathtt{c}}(\mathtt{r})_\tau$ *and* (2) $[\![\mathtt{r}]\!]^\sharp_{\mathsf{A}}\alpha(\mathtt{c}) \leq \alpha(\mathtt{d}) < \tau$ *then we have* $\tau \models_{\mathsf{A}} \langle \mathtt{c} \rangle\, \mathtt{r}\, \langle \mathtt{d} \rangle$.

Proof. Let us prove by structural induction on the language $\mathfrak{L}$.

$\mathtt{r} = \mathtt{e}$: If (1) and (2) hold, then trivially by rule `(transfer)` we have $\tau \models_{\mathsf{A}} \langle \mathtt{c} \rangle \mathtt{e} \langle \mathtt{d} \rangle$.

$\mathtt{r} = \mathtt{r}_1 \oplus \mathtt{r}_2$: Let us consider condition (2), if $[\![\mathtt{r}_1 \oplus \mathtt{r}_2]\!]^\sharp_{\mathsf{A}}\alpha(\mathtt{c}) \leq_{\mathsf{A}} \alpha(\mathtt{d}) \lneq_{\mathsf{A}} \tau_\alpha$ then we have that $[\![\mathtt{r}_1]\!]^\sharp_{\mathsf{A}}\alpha(\mathtt{c}) \vee_{\mathsf{A}} [\![\mathtt{r}_2]\!]^\sharp_{\mathsf{A}}\alpha(\mathtt{c}) \leq_{\mathsf{A}} \alpha(\mathtt{d}) \lneq_{\mathsf{A}} \tau_\alpha$, implying that we have both the relations $[\![\mathtt{r}_1]\!]^\sharp_{\mathsf{A}}\alpha(\mathtt{c}) \leq_{\mathsf{A}} \alpha(\mathtt{Q}) \lneq_{\mathsf{A}} \tau_\alpha$ and $[\![\mathtt{r}_2]\!]^\sharp_{\mathsf{A}}\alpha(\mathtt{c}) \leq_{\mathsf{A}} \alpha(\mathtt{Q}) \lneq_{\mathsf{A}} \tau_\alpha$. By properties of bca, this means that $(\alpha[\![\mathtt{r}_1]\!]\gamma)\alpha(\mathtt{c}) \leq_{\mathsf{A}} [\![\mathtt{r}_1]\!]^\sharp_{\mathsf{A}}\alpha(\mathtt{c}) \lneq_{\mathsf{A}} \tau_\alpha$, but then by Lemma 1 we have $\widetilde{\mathbb{C}}^{\mathsf{A}}_{\mathtt{c}}(\mathtt{r}_1)_\tau$. Analogously we also have $\widetilde{\mathbb{C}}^{\mathsf{A}}_{\mathtt{c}}(\mathtt{r}_2)_\tau$. Hence, by inductive hypothesis implies that $\tau \models_{\mathsf{A}} \langle \mathtt{c} \rangle\, \mathtt{r}_1\, \langle \mathtt{d} \rangle$ and $\tau \models_{\mathsf{A}} \langle \mathtt{c} \rangle\, \mathtt{r}_2\, \langle \mathtt{d} \rangle$, and therefore, by rule `(join)` we have that $\tau \models_{\mathsf{A}} \langle \mathtt{c} \rangle\, \mathtt{r}\, \langle \mathtt{d} \rangle$, being $\alpha(\mathtt{d} \vee \mathtt{d}) = \alpha(\mathtt{d}) \lneq_{\mathsf{A}} \tau_\alpha$.

$\mathtt{r} = \mathtt{r}_1; \mathtt{r}_2$: Suppose $\widetilde{\mathbb{C}}^{\mathsf{A}}_{\mathtt{c}}(\mathtt{r})_\tau$ together with $[\![\mathtt{r}]\!]^\sharp_{\mathsf{A}}(\alpha(\mathtt{c})) \leq_{\mathsf{A}} \alpha(\mathtt{d}) \lneq_{\mathsf{A}} \tau_\alpha$. First of all let us observe that, by definition $[\![\mathtt{r}]\!]^\sharp_{\mathsf{A}}(\alpha(\mathtt{c})) = [\![\mathtt{r}_2]\!]^\sharp_{\mathsf{A}}([\![\mathtt{r}_1]\!]^\sharp_{\mathsf{A}}(\alpha(\mathtt{c})))$. Then, by monotonicity and by construction of abstract semantics we have

$$[\![\mathtt{r}_2]\!]^\sharp_{\mathsf{A}}(\alpha[\![\mathtt{r}_1]\!]\gamma\alpha(\mathtt{c})) \leq_{\mathsf{A}} [\![\mathtt{r}_2]\!]^\sharp_{\mathsf{A}}([\![\mathtt{r}_1]\!]^\sharp_{\mathsf{A}}(\alpha(\mathtt{c}))) \leq_{\mathsf{A}} \alpha(\mathtt{d}) \lneq_{\mathsf{A}} \tau_\alpha$$

which is condition (2) for the hypothesis of rule $(\mathtt{seq}_1)$. As far as (1) is concerned let us observe that

$$\mathsf{A}[\![\mathtt{r}_2]\!]\mathsf{A}([\![\mathtt{r}_1]\!]\gamma\alpha(\mathtt{c})) = \gamma\alpha[\![\mathtt{r}_2]\!]\gamma\alpha[\![\mathtt{r}_1]\!]\gamma\alpha(\mathtt{c}) \subseteq \gamma([\![\mathtt{r}_2]\!]^\sharp_{\mathsf{A}}(\alpha[\![\mathtt{r}_1]\!]\gamma\alpha(\mathtt{c})))$$

where the last holds by definition of $[\![\mathtt{r}_2]\!]^\sharp_{\mathsf{A}}$, and for what we have proved above we have

$$\gamma([\![\mathtt{r}_2]\!]^\sharp_{\mathsf{A}}(\alpha[\![\mathtt{r}_1]\!]\gamma\alpha(\mathtt{c}))) \subseteq \gamma(\tau_\alpha) = \tau$$

Finally, by Lemma 1 it must be $\gamma([\![\mathtt{r}_2]\!]^\sharp_{\mathsf{A}}(\alpha[\![\mathtt{r}_1]\!]\gamma\alpha(\mathtt{c}))) \subsetneq \tau$, since we proved above that $[\![\mathtt{r}_2]\!]^\sharp_{\mathsf{A}}(\alpha[\![\mathtt{r}_1]\!]\gamma\alpha(\mathtt{c})) \lneq_{\mathsf{A}} \tau_\alpha$. Therefore we have (1), i.e., $\mathsf{A}[\![\mathtt{r}_2]\!]\mathsf{A}([\![\mathtt{r}_1]\!]\gamma\alpha(\mathtt{c})) \subsetneq \tau$. At this point, by inductive hypothesis we conclude that $\tau \models_{\mathsf{A}} \langle [\![\mathtt{r}_1]\!]\gamma\alpha(\mathtt{c}) \rangle\, \mathtt{r}_2\, \langle \mathtt{d} \rangle$, and by rule $(\mathtt{seq}_1)$ we derive $\tau \models_{\mathsf{A}} \langle \mathtt{c} \rangle\, \mathtt{r}_1; \mathtt{r}_2\, \langle \mathtt{d} \rangle$.

$\mathtt{r} = \mathtt{r}_1^*$: Suppose $\widetilde{\mathbb{C}}^{\mathsf{A}}_{\mathtt{c}}(\mathtt{r})_\tau$ together with $[\![\mathtt{r}]\!]^\sharp_{\mathsf{A}}(\alpha(\mathtt{c})) \leq_{\mathsf{A}} \alpha(\mathtt{d}) \lneq_{\mathsf{A}} \tau_\alpha$. By definition of abstract semantics, we have $\bigvee_{\mathsf{A}}([\![\mathtt{r}_1]\!]^\sharp_{\mathsf{A}})^n\alpha(\mathtt{c}) = [\![\mathtt{r}_1^*]\!]^\sharp_{\mathsf{A}}\alpha(\mathtt{c}) \leq_{\mathsf{A}} \alpha(\mathtt{d}) \lneq_{\mathsf{A}} \tau_\alpha$, which implies, by definition of least upper bound, that for all n, we have $([\![\mathtt{r}_1]\!]^\sharp_{\mathsf{A}})^n\alpha(\mathtt{c}) \leq_{\mathsf{A}} \alpha(\mathtt{d}) \lneq_{\mathsf{A}} \tau_\alpha$. As before, we can also show that

$$\alpha[\![\mathtt{r}_1^n]\!]\gamma\alpha(\mathtt{c}) \leq_{\mathsf{A}} [\![\mathtt{r}_1^n]\!]^\sharp_{\mathsf{A}}\alpha(\mathtt{c}) = ([\![\mathtt{r}_1]\!]^\sharp_{\mathsf{A}})^n\alpha(\mathtt{c}) \leq_{\mathsf{A}} \alpha(\mathtt{d}) \lneq_{\mathsf{A}} \tau_\alpha$$

since, by induction and by definition, we can observe that $[\![\mathtt{r}_1^n]\!]^\sharp_{\mathsf{A}} = ([\![\mathtt{r}_1]\!]^\sharp_{\mathsf{A}})^n$. Now, by Lemma 1 we also have $\widetilde{\mathbb{C}}^{\mathsf{A}}_{\mathtt{c}}(\mathtt{r}_1^n)_\tau$ for each $n \in \mathbb{N}$, hence by inductive hypothesis we have that $\forall n \in \mathbb{N}.\, \tau \models_{\mathsf{A}} \langle \mathtt{c} \rangle\, \mathtt{r}_1^n\, \langle \mathtt{d} \rangle$. Finally, by rule $(\mathtt{iterate}_1)$ we have that $\tau \models_{\mathsf{A}} \langle \mathtt{c} \rangle\, \mathtt{r}_1^*\, \langle \mathtt{d} \rangle$.

Let us consider some simple examples of derivation. For the sake of simplicity, since the following programs have only one variable x, we abuse notation identifying the domain of stores $\mathbb{M}$ with the domain of values $\mathbb{Z}$. Hence, in the following examples, we will define A directly on $\wp(\mathbb{Z})$.

Example 4. Let us consider the regular command in Reg

$$\mathtt{r} \overset{\text{def}}{=} (x \leq 0?; x := x * 2)^*; 0 \leq x?$$

and $\tau = \top$. Let us consider the abstract domain $\mathsf{A} = Sign$ (let $\mathsf{A} = \gamma_S\alpha_S$) on the left of Fig. 3. For the sake of readability, in the following we identify each abstract element with its meaning, e.g., $\mathbb{Z}_{\leq 0}$ with $\{n \mid n \leq 0\}$. As observe previously, both the boolean expressions in $\mathtt{r}$ are expressible (and therefore quasi-expressible) in *Sign*, since $x \leq 0$ is expressed by $\mathbb{Z}_{\leq 0}$ and $0 \leq x$ by $\mathbb{Z}_{\geq 0}$. By Theorem 1 we have that both $\widetilde{\mathbb{C}}^{\mathsf{A}}_{\mathsf{d}}(x \leq 0?)$ and $\widetilde{\mathbb{C}}^{\mathsf{A}}_{\mathsf{d}}(0 < x?)$ hold for any d. Let us consider an input property $\mathsf{c} \overset{\text{def}}{=} \{-100, -10, 0\}$ ($Sign(\mathsf{c}) = \mathbb{Z}_{\leq 0}$), then $\widetilde{\mathbb{C}}^{\mathsf{A}}_{\mathsf{c}}(x \leq 0?)$ and therefore by rule (transfer):

$$\frac{\widetilde{\mathbb{C}}^{\mathsf{A}}_{\mathsf{c}}(x \leq 0?)}{\vdash_{\mathsf{A}} \langle \mathsf{c} \rangle\; x \leq 0?\; \langle \mathbb{Z}_{\leq 0} \rangle}$$

being $[\![x \leq 0?]\!]Sign(\mathsf{c}) = [\![x \leq 0?]\!]\mathbb{Z}_{\leq 0} = \mathbb{Z}_{\leq 0}$.
Now, note that $Sign\,[\![x := x * 2]\!]\,Sign(\mathbb{Z}_{\leq 0}) = Sign\,[\![x := x * 2]\!]\,\mathbb{Z}_{\leq 0} = \mathbb{Z}_{\leq 0} \subsetneq \top$, hence $\widetilde{\mathbb{C}}^{\mathsf{A}}_{\mathbb{Z}_{\leq 0}}(x := x * 2)$, and therefore we can apply again rule (transfer)

$$\frac{\widetilde{\mathbb{C}}^{\mathsf{A}}_{\mathbb{Z}_{\leq 0}}(x := x * 2)}{\vdash_{\mathsf{A}} \langle \mathbb{Z}_{\leq 0} \rangle\; x := x * 2\; \langle \mathbb{Z}_{\leq 0} \rangle}$$

since $[\![x := x * 2]\!]Sign(\mathbb{Z}_{\leq 0}) = \mathbb{Z}_{\leq 0}$. Finally by rule (seq)

$$\frac{\vdash_{\mathsf{A}} \langle \mathsf{c} \rangle\; x \leq 0?\; \langle \mathbb{Z}_{\leq 0} \rangle \quad \vdash_{\mathsf{A}} \langle \mathbb{Z}_{\leq 0} \rangle\; x := x * 2\; \langle \mathbb{Z}_{\leq 0} \rangle}{\vdash_{\mathsf{A}} \langle \mathsf{c} \rangle\; x \leq 0?; x := x * 2\; \langle \mathbb{Z}_{\leq 0} \rangle}$$

Now, we can apply rule (iterate) obtaining

$$\frac{\vdash_{\mathsf{A}} \langle \mathsf{c} \rangle\; x \leq 0?; x := x * 2\; \langle \mathbb{Z}_{\leq 0} \rangle \quad Sign(\mathbb{Z}_{\leq 0}) = \mathbb{Z}_{\leq 0} = Sign(\mathsf{c}) \subsetneq \top}{\vdash_{\mathsf{A}} \langle \mathsf{c} \rangle\; (x \leq 0?; x := x * 2)^*\; \langle \mathsf{c} \rangle}$$

Finally, by Theorem 1 we have $\widetilde{\mathbb{C}}^{\mathsf{A}}_{\mathsf{c}}(0 \leq x?)$, implying again by rule (transfer)

$$\frac{\widetilde{\mathbb{C}}^{\mathsf{A}}_{\mathsf{c}}(0 \leq x?)}{\vdash_{\mathsf{A}} \langle \mathsf{c} \rangle\; 0 \leq x?\; \langle \mathbb{Z}_{=0} \rangle}$$

since $[\![0 \leq x]\!]Sign(\mathsf{c}) = [\![0 \leq x]\!]\mathbb{Z}_{\leq 0} = \mathbb{Z}_{=0}$ In this way we can conclude, by rule (seq), that $\vdash_{\mathsf{A}} \langle \mathsf{c} \rangle\; (x \leq 0?; x := x * 2)^*; 0 \leq x?\; \langle \mathbb{Z}_{=0} \rangle$, meaning that $\widetilde{\mathbb{C}}^{\mathsf{A}}_{\mathsf{c}}(\mathtt{r})$.

Example 5. Let us consider the regular program $\mathtt{r} \stackrel{\text{def}}{=} \mathtt{r}_1 \oplus \mathtt{r}_2$, where

$$\mathtt{r}_1 \stackrel{\text{def}}{=} (0 < x?; x := x - 1)^*$$
$$\mathtt{r}_2 \stackrel{\text{def}}{=} (x < 100?; x := x + 1)^*$$

Let us consider as abstract domain $\mathsf{A} = \mathit{Int}$ (let $\mathsf{A} = \gamma_{\mathrm{I}}\alpha_{\mathrm{I}}$), $\tau = \gamma_{\mathrm{I}}([0, +\infty])$ and $\mathtt{c} \stackrel{\text{def}}{=} \{0, 10, 20, 30\}$ ($\alpha_{\mathrm{I}}(\mathtt{c}) = [0, 30]$). In the following, for the sake of readability, we identify $[n, m]$ with its meaning $\{i \mid n \leq i \leq m\}$. As already observed, in the considered abstract domain $0 < x$ is expressible w.r.t. τ, while $x < 100$ is not. By Theorem 1, we have $\forall \mathtt{d} \in \mathsf{C}$ that $\widetilde{\mathbb{C}}^{\mathsf{A}}_{\mathtt{d}}(0 < x?)_\tau$ while we have that $\forall \mathtt{d} \subsetneq \tau$ $\widetilde{\mathbb{C}}^{\mathsf{A}}_{\mathtt{d}}(x < 100?)_\tau$, since $\mathit{Int}([\![x < 100?]\!]\mathtt{d}) \subseteq [0, 100] \subsetneq \tau$.
Let us consider $\mathtt{r}_1$ first. By rule `(transfer)`

$$\frac{\widetilde{\mathbb{C}}^{\mathsf{A}}_{\mathtt{c}}(0 < x?)_\tau}{\tau \vdash_{\mathsf{A}} \langle \mathtt{c} \rangle \; 0 < x? \; \langle [1, 30] \rangle}$$

Now we have that $[\![x := x - 1]\!]\mathit{Int}([1, 30]) = [0, 29]$, hence again by rule `(transfer)` we derive

$$\frac{\widetilde{\mathbb{C}}^{\mathsf{A}}_{[1,30]}(x := x - 1)_\tau}{\tau \vdash_{\mathsf{A}} \langle [1, 30] \rangle \; x := x - 1 \; \langle [0, 29] \rangle}$$

being $\mathit{Int}([\![x := x - 1]\!]\mathit{Int}([1, 30])[0, 29] \subsetneq \tau$, and therefore by rule `(seq)` we have $\vdash_{\mathsf{A}} \langle \mathtt{c} \rangle \; 0 < x?; x := x - 1 \; \langle [0, 29] \rangle$. Now, by rule `(iterate)`, we prove

$$\frac{\tau \vdash_{\mathsf{A}} \langle \mathtt{c} \rangle \; 0 < x?; x := x - 1 \; \langle [0, 29] \rangle \quad \mathit{Int}([0, 29]) = [0, 29] \subseteq \mathit{Int}(\mathtt{c}) = [0, 30] \subsetneq \tau}{\tau \vdash_{\mathsf{A}} \langle \mathtt{c} \rangle \; (0 < x?; x := x - 1)^* \; \langle \mathtt{c} \rangle}$$

Let us consider $\mathtt{r}_2$. By rule `(transfer)`

$$\frac{\widetilde{\mathbb{C}}^{\mathsf{A}}_{\mathtt{c}}(x < 100?)_\tau}{\tau \vdash_{\mathsf{A}} \langle \mathtt{c} \rangle \; x < 100? \; \langle [0, 30] \rangle}$$

Now we have that $[\![x := x + 1]\!][0, 30]) = [1, 31]$, hence again by rule `(transfer)` we derive $\vdash_{\mathsf{A}} \langle \mathtt{c} \rangle \; x := x + 1 \; \langle [1, 31] \rangle$, and therefore $\vdash_{\mathsf{A}} \langle \mathtt{c} \rangle \; x < 100?; x := x + 1 \; \langle [1, 31] \rangle$ by rule `(seq)`. In this case, unfortunately $\mathit{Int}([1, 31]) = [1, 31] \not\subseteq \mathit{Int}(\mathtt{c}) = [1, 30]$, hence we cannot apply rule `(iterate)`. Let us consider, instead $\mathtt{c}' \stackrel{\text{def}}{=} \{0, 10, 20, 30, 100\}$ ($\mathit{Int}(\mathtt{c}') = [0, 100]$). Then by rule `(transfer)`

$$\frac{\widetilde{\mathbb{C}}^{\mathsf{A}}_{\mathtt{c}'}(x < 100?)_\tau}{\tau \vdash_{\mathsf{A}} \langle \mathtt{c}' \rangle \; x < 100? \; \langle [0, 99] \rangle}$$

then being $[\![x := x + 1]\!][0, 99]) = [1, 100]$, we have by rule `(transfer)`

$$\frac{\widetilde{\mathbb{C}}^{\mathsf{A}}_{[0,99]}(x := x + 1)_\tau}{\tau \vdash_{\mathsf{A}} \langle [0, 99] \rangle \; x := x + 1 \; \langle [1, 100] \rangle}$$

and therefore $\vdash_{\mathsf{A}} \langle \mathsf{c}' \rangle\, x < 100?; x := x + 1\, \langle [1, 100] \rangle$ by rule (seq). Now by rule (iterate)

$$\frac{\tau \vdash_{\mathsf{A}} \langle \mathsf{c}' \rangle\, x < 100?; x := x + 1\, \langle [1, 100] \rangle \quad Int([1, 100]) = [1, 100] \subseteq Int(\mathsf{c}') = [0, 100] \subsetneq \tau}{\tau \vdash_{\mathsf{A}} \langle \mathsf{c}' \rangle\, (x < 100?; x := x + 1)^*\, \langle \mathsf{c}' \rangle}$$

At this point, by rule (relax$_2$)

$$\frac{\mathsf{c} \subseteq \mathsf{c}' \quad \tau \vdash_{\mathsf{A}} \langle \mathsf{c}' \rangle\, (x < 100?; x := x + 1)^*\, \langle \mathsf{c}' \rangle}{\tau \vdash_{\mathsf{A}} \langle \mathsf{c} \rangle\, (x < 100?; x := x + 1)^*\, \langle \mathsf{c}' \rangle}$$

and therefore we can apply rule (join)

$$\frac{\tau \vdash_{\mathsf{A}} \langle \mathsf{c} \rangle\, (0 < x?; x := x - 1)^*\, \langle \mathsf{c} \rangle \quad \tau \vdash_{\mathsf{A}} \langle \mathsf{c} \rangle\, (x < 100?; x := x + 1)^*\, \langle \mathsf{c}' \rangle \quad \alpha(\mathsf{c}') \lneq_{\mathsf{A}} \tau_\alpha}{\tau \vdash_{\mathsf{A}} \langle \mathsf{c} \rangle\, \mathtt{r}\, \langle \mathsf{c}' \rangle}$$

since $\mathsf{c} \cup \mathsf{c}' = \mathsf{c}'$, meaning that $\widetilde{\mathbb{C}}^{\mathsf{A}}_{\mathsf{c}}(\mathtt{r})_\tau$.

Example 6. In this example, we show that we can derive limits also for diverging loops. Consider $\mathtt{r} = (x \leq 0?; x := 2{*}x)^*$, $\mathsf{A} = Int$ (let $\mathsf{A} = \gamma_{\mathrm{I}}\alpha_{\mathrm{I}}$) and $\tau \stackrel{\text{def}}{=} [-\infty, 0]$. In this case we can observe that if we start from a finite c then it is not possible to apply rule iterate since we enlarge at least one bound of the interval, while if we compute adequacy on a point including the limit we can prove adequacy. Let c be such that $\alpha_{\mathrm{I}}(\mathsf{c}) = [n, 0] \subsetneq [-\infty, 0]$, then $\tau \vdash_{\mathsf{A}} \langle \mathsf{c} \rangle\, x \leq 0?\, \langle \mathsf{c} \rangle$, while $\tau \vdash_{\mathsf{A}} \langle \mathsf{c} \rangle\, x := 2 * x\, \langle \mathsf{d} \rangle$ with $-2n \in \mathsf{d}$, hence $\alpha_{\mathrm{I}}(\mathsf{d}) \not\subseteq \alpha_{\mathrm{I}}(\mathsf{c})$. It is trivial to observe that the only case in which we obtain a result contained in the starting point c is when $\mathsf{c} = [-\infty, n]$ $(n \leq 0)$, since in this case we can derive, in the proof system, that $\tau \vdash_{\mathsf{A}} \langle \mathsf{c} \rangle\, x := 2 * x\, \langle \mathsf{d} \rangle$ with $\mathsf{d} \subseteq [-\infty, 2n] \subseteq [-\infty, n]$.
Let, for instance $n = -10$, then trivially $\tau \vdash_{\mathsf{A}} \langle [-\infty, -10] \rangle\, x \leq 0?\, \langle [-\infty, -10] \rangle$, $\tau \vdash_{\mathsf{A}} \langle [-\infty, -10] \rangle\, x := 2 * x\, \langle [-\infty, -20] \rangle$, hence, by using the composition rule, we prove $\tau \vdash_{\mathsf{A}} \langle [-\infty, -10] \rangle\, x \leq 0?; x := 2 * x\, \langle [-\infty, -20] \rangle$ and being $[-\infty, -20] \subseteq [-\infty, -10]$, we can derive $\tau \vdash_{\mathsf{A}} \langle [-\infty, -10] \rangle\, x \leq 0?; x := 2 * x\, \langle [-\infty, -10] \rangle$. Hence, $\forall \mathsf{c} \in \{\, [-\infty, n] \mid n < 0 \,\}$ we have that $\widetilde{\mathbb{C}}^{\mathsf{A}}_{\mathsf{c}}(\mathtt{r})_{[-\infty,0]}$.

Example 7. Let us consider the regular command in Reg

$$\mathtt{r} \stackrel{\text{def}}{=} (even(x)?; x := x + 1)^*; \oplus(\neg even(x)?; x := x * 2)$$

supposing to add to the language the operator $even(x)$ returning true if x is even, false otherwise, with $\mathsf{A} = Int$ (let $\mathsf{A} = \gamma_{\mathrm{I}}\alpha_{\mathrm{I}}$) and $\tau = \top$. It should be clear that $even(x)$ is not quasi-expressible in A, however we can prove adequacy on some points c. Let $\mathsf{c} = [n, +\infty]$, with $n > 0$, then we have that $\tau \vdash_{\mathsf{A}} \langle \mathsf{c} \rangle even(x)? \langle \mathsf{c} \cap 2\mathbb{Z} \rangle$, since we can trivially prove that $\widetilde{\mathbb{C}}^{\mathsf{A}}_{\mathsf{c}}(even(x))_\tau$. At this point, it holds that $\tau \vdash_{\mathsf{A}} \langle \mathsf{c} \cap 2\mathbb{Z} \rangle x := x{+}1 \langle [n{+}1, +\infty] \cap 2\mathbb{Z}{+}1 \rangle$ by rule (transfer). Hence, by rule (seq) we have $\tau \vdash_{\mathsf{A}} \langle \mathsf{c} \rangle even(x); x := x{+}1 \langle [n{+}1, +\infty] \cap 2\mathbb{Z}{+}1 \rangle$, and being $n > 0$ we have $\mathsf{d} = [n + 1, +\infty] \subseteq [n, +\infty]$ meaning that $\alpha_{\mathrm{I}}(\mathsf{d} \cap 2\mathbb{Z} + 1) = \mathsf{d} \subseteq \alpha_{\mathrm{I}}(\mathsf{c}) = \mathsf{c}$, and therefore $\tau \vdash_{\mathsf{A}} \langle \mathsf{c} \rangle\, (even(x)?; x := x + 1)^*\, \langle \mathsf{c} \rangle$, rule (seq) and by rule (iterate).

On the other hand, $\tau \vdash_{\mathsf{A}} \langle \mathsf{c} \rangle\ \neg even(x)?\ \langle \mathsf{c} \cap 2\mathbb{Z}+1 \rangle$, while $\tau \vdash_{\mathsf{A}} \langle \mathsf{c} \cap 2\mathbb{Z}+1 \rangle\ x := 2x\ \langle [2n, +\infty] \cap 2\mathbb{Z} \rangle$, both by rule (transfer), with $[n, +\infty] \supseteq [2n, +\infty]$. Finally, we have that $\mathsf{c} \cup ([2n, +\infty] \cap 2\mathbb{Z}) = [n, +\infty] \cup ([2n, +\infty] \cap 2\mathbb{Z}) = \mathsf{c}$, which means that $\alpha_{\mathrm{I}}(\mathsf{c}) = [n, +\infty] \subsetneq \tau$. Then we conclude, by rule (join), that $\tau \vdash_{\mathsf{A}} \langle \mathsf{c} \rangle\ \mathtt{r}\ \langle \mathsf{c} \rangle$, i.e., adequacy w.r.t. τ is satisfied.

Example 8. Let us consider a final example with a relational domain such that Octagons [25,26] for the regular command in Reg

$$\mathtt{r} \overset{\text{def}}{=} (y - x \leq 0?; y := y - 1)^*; x - y \leq 0;$$

with $\mathsf{A} = Oct$ (let $\mathsf{A} = \gamma_0\alpha_0$) and $\tau = \{x \leq 5, y \leq 7\}$. In this case, the guard is quasi-expressible. Let us consider $\mathsf{c} \overset{\text{def}}{=} \{y \leq 2, x \leq 1, y - x \leq 2\}$. By Theorem 1, we have $\forall \mathsf{d} \in \mathsf{C}$ that $\widetilde{\mathbb{C}}^{\mathsf{A}}_{\mathsf{d}}(y - x \leq 0?)_\tau$, hence, by rule (transfer), $\tau \vdash_{\mathsf{A}} \langle \mathsf{c} \rangle\, y - x \leq 0?\, \langle \{y \leq 2, x \leq 1, y - x \leq 0\} \rangle$. Then, by rule (transfer) we have also that $\tau \vdash_{\mathsf{A}} \langle \{y \leq 2, x \leq 1, y - x \leq 0\} \rangle y := y - 1 \langle \{y \leq 1, x \leq 1, y - x \leq -1\} \rangle$ and by rule (seq) we have $\tau \vdash_{\mathsf{A}} \langle \mathsf{c} \rangle\, y - x \leq 0?; y := y - 1\, \langle \{y \leq 1, x \leq 1, y - x \leq -1\} \rangle$ (Fig. 5). Then, since $\{y \leq 2, x \leq 1, y - x \leq -1\} \leq_{\mathsf{A}} \mathsf{c}$, we can apply rule (iterate) obtaining $\tau \vdash_{\mathsf{A}} \langle \mathsf{c} \rangle\, (y - x \leq 0?; y := y - 1)^*\, \langle \mathsf{c} \rangle$.
Now, also $x - y \leq 0$ is expressible, hence we have that, by rule (transfer), $\tau \vdash_{\mathsf{A}} \langle \mathsf{c} \rangle x - y \leq 0? \langle \{y \leq 2, x \leq 1, x - y \leq 0, y - x \leq 2\} \rangle$, Hence, we can prove that $\tau \vdash_{\mathsf{A}} \langle \mathsf{c} \rangle\, (y - x \leq 0?; y := y - 1)^*; x - y \leq 0?\, \langle \{y \leq 2, x \leq 1, x - y \leq 0, y - x \leq 2\} \rangle$, again by rule (seq), and therefore we prove adequacy on c.

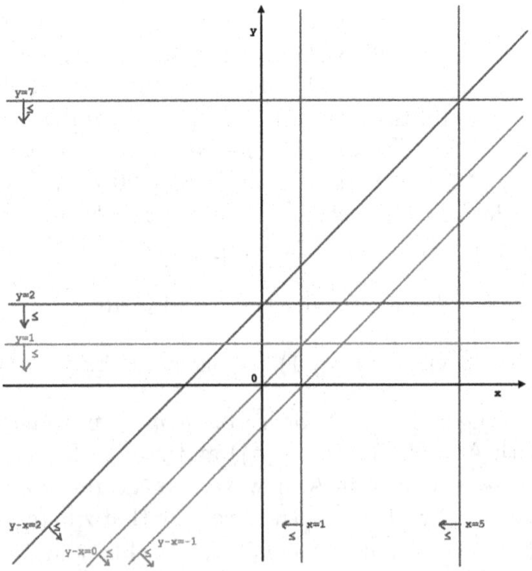

Fig. 5. Graphical representation of octagons in Example 8

6 Conclusions

We introduced the novel notion of adequate abstract domain together with a refinement strategy to adjust abstract domains to make them adequate and a program logic to check whether the abstract interpretation designed on a given abstract domain is adequate. Our program logic is simple and can be checked online during program analysis.

Adequacy is particularly interesting when we are interested to prove whether our abstract interpreter incorporates enough information (here encoded by the bound τ) in the computed invariant. This can have applications beyond program analysis, for instance in language-based security and code protection. In language-based security, as specified by abstract non-interference [15,21,23], adequacy could guarantee that certain amount of information is kept secret or dually it is released in the case of declassification, and this could be analyzed also for dynamic code [1,24]. In code protection the notion of adequacy become stronger than completeness. The standard approach to protect code against program analysis is to make the abstract interpreter maximally imprecise with respect to the given program, which means incomplete [16,18,22]. In this case we may replace completeness with adequacy, and imagine code protecting transformations making an abstract interpreter inadequate for the transformed code. When the chosen bound is $\top$ this corresponds to have a code transformation for which the abstract interpreter is totally blind and cannot extract any meaningful information. Finally, for program verification, it could be interesting to exploit the idea introduced for partial completeness [7], i.e., the use of a metric for weakening completeness, for strengthening adequacy by fixing a maximal distance that we want to guarantee from the fixed bound τ.

References

1. Arceri, V., Mastroeni, I.: Analyzing dynamic code: a sound abstract interpreter for evil eval. ACM Trans. Priv. Secur. **24**(2), 10:1–10:38 (2020)
2. Bourdoncle, F.: Abstract interpretation by dynamic partitioning. J. Funct. Program. **2**(4), 407–435 (1992)
3. Bruni, R., Giacobazzi, R., Gori, R., Garcia-Contreras, I., Pavlovic, D.: Abstract extensionality: on the properties of incomplete abstract interpretations. Proc. ACM Program. Lang. **4**(POPL), 28:1–28:28 (2020). https://doi.org/10.1145/3371096
4. Bruni, R., Giacobazzi, R., Gori, R., Ranzato, F.: A logic for locally complete abstract interpretations. In: Symposium on Logic in Computer Science, LICS, pp. 1–13. IEEE (2021)
5. Bruni, R., Giacobazzi, R., Gori, R., Ranzato, F.: Abstract interpretation repair. In: Jhala, R., Dillig, I. (eds.) PLDI 2022: 43rd ACM SIGPLAN International Conference on Programming Language Design and Implementation, San Diego, CA, USA, 13–17 June 2022, pp. 426–441. ACM (2022)
6. Bruni, R., Giacobazzi, R., Gori, R., Ranzato, F.: A correctness and incorrectness program logic. J. ACM **70**(2), 1–45 (2023)
7. Campion, M., Preda, M.D., Giacobazzi, R.: Partial (in)completeness in abstract interpretation: limiting the imprecision in program analysis. Proc. ACM Program. Lang. **6**(POPL), 1–31 (2022). https://doi.org/10.1145/3498721

8. Cousot, P.: Asynchronous iterative methods for solving a fixed point system of monotone equations in a complete lattice. Res. rep. R.R. 88, Laboratoire IMAG, Université scientifique et médicale de Grenoble, p. 15 Grenoble, France (1977)
9. Cousot, P.: Constructive design of a hierarchy of semantics of a transition system by abstract interpretation. Theor. Comput. Sci. **277**(1–2), 47–103 (2002)
10. Cousot, P., Cousot, R.: Abstract interpretation: a unified lattice model for static analysis of programs by construction or approximation of fixpoints. In: Conference Record of the 4th ACM Symposium on Principles of Programming Languages (POPL 1977), pp. 238–252. ACM Press (1977)
11. Cousot, P., Cousot, R.: Systematic design of program analysis frameworks. In: Conference Record of the 6th ACM Symposium on Principles of Programming Languages (POPL 1979), pp. 269–282. ACM Press (1979)
12. Cousot, P., Cousot, R.: Comparing the Galois connection and widening/narrowing approaches to abstract interpretation. In: Bruynooghe, M., Wirsing, M. (eds.) PLILP 1992. LNCS, vol. 631, pp. 269–295. Springer, Heidelberg (1992). https://doi.org/10.1007/3-540-55844-6_142
13. Cousot, P.: Principles of Abstract Interpretation. MIT Press, Cambridge (2021)
14. Filé, G., Giacobazzi, R., Ranzato, F.: A unifying view of abstract domain design. ACM Comput. Surv. **28**(2), 333–336 (1996)
15. Giacobazzi, R., Mastroeni, I.: Adjoining classified and unclassified information by abstract interpretation. J. Comput. Secur. **18**(5), 751–797 (2010)
16. Giacobazzi, R., Mastroeni, I.: Making abstract interpretation incomplete: modeling the potency of obfuscation. In: Miné, A., Schmidt, D. (eds.) SAS 2012. LNCS, vol. 7460, pp. 129–145. Springer, Heidelberg (2012). https://doi.org/10.1007/978-3-642-33125-1_11
17. Giacobazzi, R., Ranzato, F., Scozzari, F.: Making abstract interpretation complete. J. ACM **47**(2), 361–416 (2000)
18. Giacobazzi, R., Jones, N.D., Mastroeni, I.: Obfuscation by partial evaluation of distorted interpreters. In: Kiselyov, O., Thompson, S.J. (eds.) Proceedings of the ACM SIGPLAN 2012 Workshop on Partial Evaluation and Program Manipulation, PEPM 2012, Philadelphia, Pennsylvania, USA, 23–24 January 23–24 2012, pp. 63–72. ACM (2012)
19. Giacobazzi, R., Logozzo, F., Ranzato, F.: Analyzing program analyses. In: Rajamani, S.K., Walker, D. (eds.) Proceedings of the 42nd Annual ACM SIGPLAN-SIGACT Symposium on Principles of Programming Languages, POPL 2015, Mumbai, India, 15–17 January 2015, pp. 261–273. ACM (2015)
20. Giacobazzi, R., Mastroeni, I.: Making abstract models complete. Math. Struct. Comput. Sci. **26**(4), 658–701 (2016)
21. Giacobazzi, R., Mastroeni, I.: Abstract non-interference: a unifying framework for weakening information-flow. ACM Trans. Priv. Secur. **21**(2), 1–31 (2018)
22. Giacobazzi, R., Mastroeni, I., Preda, M.D.: Maximal incompleteness as obfuscation potency. Formal Aspects Comput. **29**(1), 3–31 (2017)
23. Mastroeni, I.: Abstract interpretation-based approaches to security - A survey on abstract non-interference and its challenging applications. In: Banerjee, A., Danvy, O., Doh, K., Hatcliff, J. (eds.) Semantics, Abstract Interpretation, and Reasoning about Programs: Essays Dedicated to David A. Schmidt on the Occasion of his Sixtieth Birthday, Manhattan, Kansas, USA, 19–20th September 2013. EPTCS, vol. 129, pp. 41–65 (2013)
24. Mastroeni, I., Arceri, V.: Improving dynamic code analysis by code abstraction. In: Lisitsa, A., Nemytykh, A.P. (eds.) Proceedings of the 9th International Workshop

on Verification and Program Transformation, VPT@ETAPS 2021, Luxembourg, Luxembourg, 27th and 28th of March 2021. EPTCS, vol. 341, pp. 17–32 (2021)
25. Minè, A.: The octagon abstract domain. In: AST 2001 in WCRE 2001. pp. 310–319. IEEE, IEEE CS Press (2001)
26. Miné, A.: The octagon abstract domain. Higher Order Symbol. Comput. **19**(1), 31–100 (2006). https://doi.org/10.1007/s10990-006-8609-1
27. Müller, M.N., Fischer, M., Staab, R., Vechev, M.: Abstract interpretation of fixpoint iterators with applications to neural networks. Proc. ACM Program. Lang. **7**(PLDI), 786–810 (2023)
28. O'Hearn, P.W.: Incorrectness logic. Proc. ACM Program. Lang. (POPL) **4**(10), 1–32 (2020)
29. Winskel, G.: The Formal Semantics of Programming Languages: An Introduction. MIT press, Cambridge (1993)

A Product of Shape and Sequence Abstractions

Josselin Giet[1](✉), Félix Ridoux[2,3], and Xavier Rival[1]

[1] INRIA Paris/CNRS/École Normale Supérieure/PSL Research University, Paris, France
{josselin.giet,xavier.rival}@ens.fr

[2] IMDEA Software Institute, Madrid, Spain
felix.ridoux@ens-rennes.fr

[3] Univ Rennes, 35000 Rennes, France

Abstract. Traditional separation logic-based shape analyses utilize inductive summarizing predicates so as to capture general properties of the layout of data-structures, to verify accurate manipulations of, e.g., various forms of lists or trees. However, they also usually abstract away contents properties, so that they may only verify memory safety and invariance of data-structure shapes. In this paper, we introduce a novel abstract domain to describe sequences of values of unbounded size, and track constraints on their length and on extremal values contained in them. We define a reduced product of such a sequence abstraction together with an existing shape abstraction so as to infer both shape and contents properties of data-structures. We report on the implementation of the sequence domain, its integration into a static analyzer for C code, and we evaluate its ability to verify partial functional correctness properties for list and tree algorithms.

Keywords: Shape analysis · Content abstraction · Sorting algorithms

1 Introduction

Dynamically allocated data-structures based on lists, trees or graphs are common due to their flexibility as containers. However, programs using them are notoriously difficult to get right, especially in presence of destructive updates. Indeed, the correctness of such programs relies on a wide spectrum of properties that comprise memory safety (the absence of illegal pointer operations such as the dereference of a null pointer), the preservation of structural invariants like

M. V. Hermenegildo and J. F. Morales (Eds.): SAS 2023, LNCS 14284, pp. 310–342, 2023.
https://doi.org/10.1007/978-3-031-44245-2_15

acyclicity, and subtle functional properties and relationships between the structure layout and its contents such as sortedness. For instance, let us consider a program that inserts an element in a binary search tree. First, it should not cause any runtime error or memory leak. Second, it should not create a cycle or break the tree structure. Third, it should preserve the binary search tree property and be functionally correct, namely ensure that the elements in the tree after insertion are the same as before plus the new element, inserted at the correct position, with respect to the order.

```
struct tree { struct tree *l, *r; int d; };
```

$\mathbf{tree}(\alpha) :=$
$\quad | \ \mathbf{emp} \wedge \alpha = \mathbf{0x0}$
$\quad | \ \exists \alpha_l, \alpha_r, \delta, \alpha.\mathtt{l} \mapsto \alpha_l * \alpha.\mathtt{r} \mapsto \alpha_r * \alpha.\mathtt{d} \mapsto \delta * \mathbf{tree}(\alpha_l) * \mathbf{tree}(\alpha_r) \wedge \alpha \neq \mathbf{0x0}$
$\mathbf{tree_s}(\alpha, S) :=$
$\quad | \ \mathbf{emp} \wedge \alpha = \mathbf{0x0}$
$\quad | \ \exists \alpha_l, \alpha_r, \delta, S_l, S_r, \alpha.\mathtt{l} \mapsto \alpha_l * \alpha.\mathtt{r} \mapsto \alpha_r * \alpha.\mathtt{d} \mapsto \delta * \mathbf{tree_s}(\alpha_l, S_l) * \mathbf{tree_s}(\alpha_r, S_r)$
$\qquad \wedge \alpha \neq \mathbf{0x0} \wedge S = S_l.[\delta].S_r$

Fig. 1. A C tree data-type and associated inductive summarizing predicates

Abstract interpretation [17] provides a general framework to build a sound static analysis from a basic semantics and an abstraction relation, and to verify semantic properties. Notably, it has been applied to verify numerical properties [20,35], the absence of runtime errors [7], string properties [4,25], array properties [19,28–30], liveness properties [55], and security properties [5,24,26]. Several families of shape analyses have also been designed to infer properties of programs manipulating dynamic data-structures, including TVLA [51] and shape analyses based on separation logic [50]. They can reason over structures like lists [12,13] or more general families of structures with an inductive layout [14,31] such as binary trees.

However, few shape analyses reason not only about the layout of data-structures but also about their contents, so as to verify, e.g., that a container consists of the expected collection of elements with the expected multiplicity. While [21,39] handle set predicates, they do not track properties related to element multiplicities or order. Similarly, [41] handles sorting properties of specific families of composite structures in arrays but does not consider general lists or trees. The analyses presented in [9–11] precisely abstract singly-linked lists storing numerical data. They compute numerical properties over these data such as "variable `x` is the sum of all elements in list `l`", or relation between element values and indexes to express sorting. However, it does not handle trees or doubly linked lists. Therefore, in this paper, we seek for an abstraction of data-structure contents that can verify complex invariants (e.g., involving elements orders or multiplicities) as well as some functional properties (like sorting). To illustrate our approach, we consider the classical tree type definition shown in Fig. 1 and assume that we only consider acyclic instances. The inductive predicate **tree** summarizes valid memory regions storing exactly a complete and acyclic tree. More precisely, the predicate $\mathbf{tree}(\alpha)$ either describes an empty tree (then, α

is the null pointer), or a memory region where α points to a valid `tree` block, the `l` and `r` fields of which point to the roots of disjoint (possibly empty) subtrees, as expressed by predicates $\mathbf{tree}(\alpha_l)$ and $\mathbf{tree}(\alpha_r)$. Note that separating conjunction $*$ [50] combines disjoint memory regions. A basic region is either an atomic cell described by a points-to predicate such as $\alpha.\mathtt{d} \mapsto \delta$ or an instance of some inductive predicate. While predicate **tree** describes the layout of memory cells and pointers, it does not convey any information about their contents. By contrast, $\mathbf{tree}_s$ extends **tree** with an additional symbolic parameter S to expose the sequence of values stored in the tree, read from left to right. When the tree is empty, so is its sequence of elements. The sequence stored in a non-empty tree is obtained by first considering the left subtree, then the contents of the root node and finally the right tree. If we additionally require the elements of S be sorted, then $\mathbf{tree}_s(\alpha, S)$ describes binary search trees with root α.

An advantage of this approach is that it allows to split the abstraction into two rather independent components, namely a separation logic based abstraction of the data-structures and another abstraction for properties of sequences of values stored in them. While [39] extends inductive predicates in a similar manner, it only supports set constraints. Therefore, we introduce a new abstract domain devoted to the representation of constraints over sequences. Existing sequence abstractions typically rely on regular expressions or finite automata [3,45,47]. More recently, [4] extends such an abstraction with sub-string, length, and element position constraints. However, these abstractions lack predicates such as constraints over extremal elements or sortedness. Our sequence abstract domain expresses not only relational constraints (it can express that a symbolic sequence is a fragment of another) but also constraints over length, extremal values, and specific predicates like sortedness. Although we use this sequence abstract domain for shape analysis, it could be used independently for other kinds of analyses.

To take advantage of this abstraction in shape analysis, we define a reduced product with a separation logic-based shape abstract domain. This product ties symbolic parameters of inductive predicates in separation logic together with sequence constraints. Sequence constraints that are inferred during the analysis (for instance when unfolding inductive predicates) are passed to the sequence domain. The reduced product also ensures communication between both domains for the computation of abstract operators such as union.

To summarize, we make the following contributions:

- After we overview our analysis in Sect. 2, we introduce a relational abstract domain dedicated to reasoning over sequences in Sect. 3;
- We define a reduced product between the new sequence domain and a separation logic-based abstract domain so as to extend a shape analysis with sequence reasoning capability. We first introduce the basic elements of the reduced product in Sect. 4 in the context of singly-linked lists. We discuss issues related to general inductive predicates in Sect. 5.
- We report on the implementation of our analysis in the MemCAD static analyzer [38] and on its evaluation in Sect. 6. We show that it can cope with the verification of sorting programs and operations over binary search trees.

2 Overview

In this section, we give an overview of the main principles of our static analysis by demonstrating it on the insertion program shown in Fig. 2. When applied to a binary search tree, this function inserts an element at the expected position to preserve sortedness. We study the verification of functional correctness expressed as partial correctness with respect to a pre-condition and a post-condition (Fig. 2). To formalize these, we let **sort** be a symbolic function over sequences of values that maps any sequence to its sorted permutation. Then, the pre-condition assumption assumes that `t` is a well-formed tree described with predicate $\mathbf{tree}_s(\mathtt{t}, S)$ and such that $S = \mathbf{sort}(S)$ (i.e., such that the elements S in `t` are sorted). Likewise, the post-condition asserts that `t` is still a well-formed tree, the contents of which is sorted and comprises exactly the elements in S plus the added value `i`.

```
1  void insert(struct tree* t, int i){
2    // assume tree_s(t, S) ∧ S = sort(S)
3    if(t == null){
4      // ...
5    }else{
6      struct tree* c = t;
7      while(c->d <= i && c->l != null ||
8            c->d > i && c->r != null)
9        c = (c->d <= i) ? c->l : c->r;
10     // ...
11   }
12 } // assert tree_s(t, sort(S.[i]))
```

Fig. 2. Function for insertion in a binary search tree

$$\big(\&\mathtt{t} \mapsto \alpha_0 * \&\mathtt{c} \mapsto \alpha_0 * \mathbf{tree}_s(\alpha_0, S)\big) \quad \wedge \quad (S = \mathbf{sort}(S) \wedge \alpha_0 \neq \mathbf{0x0})$$

(a) Abstract state at the end of line 6

$$\left(\begin{array}{c} \&\mathtt{t} \mapsto \alpha_0 * \&\mathtt{c} \mapsto \alpha_1 \\ * \, \alpha_0.\mathtt{l} \mapsto \alpha_1 * \mathbf{tree}_s(\alpha_1, S_l) \\ * \, \alpha_0.\mathtt{d} \mapsto \delta \\ * \, \alpha_0.\mathtt{r} \mapsto \alpha_2 * \mathbf{tree}_s(\alpha_2, S_r) \end{array}\right) \wedge \left(\begin{array}{c} S = S_l.[\delta].S_r \wedge S = \mathbf{sort}(S) \\ \wedge\, S_l = \mathbf{sort}(S_l) \wedge S_r = \mathbf{sort}(S_r) \\ \wedge\, \mathbf{max}_{S_l} \leq \delta \leq \mathbf{max}_{S_r} \\ \wedge\, \delta \leq \mathtt{i} \wedge \alpha_0, \alpha_1 \neq \mathbf{0x0} \end{array}\right)$$

(b) Abstract state at the end of line 9, first case of the condition

$$\left(\begin{array}{c} \&\mathtt{t} \mapsto \alpha_0 * \&\mathtt{c} \mapsto \alpha' \\ * \, \mathbf{treeseg}_s(\alpha_0, \alpha', S_1 \boxdot S_2) \\ * \, \mathbf{tree}_s(\alpha', S_0) \end{array}\right) \wedge \left(\begin{array}{c} S = S_1.S_0.S_2 \wedge S = \mathbf{sort}(S) \\ \wedge\, S_i = \mathbf{sort}(S_i) \;\; i \in \{0,1,2\} \\ \wedge\, \mathbf{max}_{S_1} \leq \mathtt{i} \leq \mathbf{max}_{S_2} \wedge \mathbf{max}_{S_1} \leq \mathbf{max}_{S_0} \\ \wedge\, \mathbf{min}_{S_0} \leq \mathbf{max}_{S_2} \wedge \alpha_0, \alpha' \neq \mathbf{0x0} \end{array}\right)$$

(c) Abstract state after the first widening

Fig. 3. Selected abstract states

We now discuss the abstraction used by our static analysis. We combine an existing memory abstraction, inspired by separation logic-based shape analyses such as [12,14], a relational numerical abstraction such as convex polyhedra [20], and a novel abstract domain for sequences. Intuitively, the latter describes conjunctions of constraints over both symbolic sequences of values (such as S) and values manipulated by the program. These constraints consist of equalities of pairs of symbolic sequence expressions such as $S' = \mathbf{sort}(S.[\mathtt{i}])$. Moreover, the inductive predicates used in the memory abstraction are instances of the $\mathbf{tree}_s$ predicate of Fig. 1. For instance, the abstract pre-condition simply consists of the memory predicate $\mathbf{tree}_s(\mathtt{t}, S)$ and the sequence predicate $S = \mathbf{sort}(S)$, for some existentially quantified symbolic sequence variable S.

The analysis proceeds by forward abstract interpretation [17]: it computes over-approximate abstract post-conditions for basic statements, and uses widening to enforce the convergence of abstract iterations for loops. Since the analysis uses a reduced product [18], an abstract state consists of a pair of components, namely the shape abstraction that describes the layout of data-structures and the contents' abstraction made of constraints over values and sequences of values. For each analysis step, information stored in either component may be used in order to refine the other, which we discuss next.

We focus on the analysis of the loop that searches for the insertion point in the **else** branch. First, the analysis of the condition test enriches the pre-condition with the constraint $\mathtt{t} \neq \mathtt{null}$ as shown in the abstract state in Fig. 3(a). Then, the analysis continues with the loop. The condition is a disjunction thus the analysis considers each case separately. For the first case, it refines the abstract state to reflect that the condition $\mathtt{c}{-}{>}\mathtt{d} <= \mathtt{i}$ && $\mathtt{c}{-}{>}\mathtt{l}$!= $\mathtt{null}$ evaluates to **true**. Since both memory cells $\mathtt{c}{-}{>}\mathtt{d}$ and $\mathtt{c}{-}{>}\mathtt{l}$ are abstracted by the predicate $\mathbf{tree}_s(\alpha_0, S)$, this predicate needs to be unfolded to enable the analysis of the condition. The first disjunct of inductive predicate $\mathbf{tree}_s$ (Fig. 1), which corresponds to the null pointer, is ruled out by constraint $\mathtt{t} \neq \mathtt{null}$. Therefore, only the second disjunct (non-empty tree) needs be considered. This shows how one component of the abstract state can refine the other. Thus, the analysis generates a new abstract state that exposes the root of the tree and lets α_1, α_2, and δ denote the contents of its `l`, `r`, and `d` fields. We remark that the inductive predicate unfolding also splits the symbolic sequence into $S = S_l.[\delta].S_r$. Then the sequence domain derives that S_l and S_r are sorted since they are subsequences of a sorted sequence. It also infers that all values in S_l are less than δ that is itself less than all values in S_r by definition of **sort**, which writes down $\mathtt{max}_{S_l} \leq \delta \leq \mathtt{min}_{S_r}$. Last, it also retains the numerical constraint $\mathtt{i} \leq \delta$. Figure 3(b) shows the resulting abstract state after the assignment line 9. In the case of the other disjunct, the tree is also unfolded but `c` points to α_2 instead of α_1 and the constraint over `i` and δ is $\delta < \mathtt{i}$.

The widening operator over-approximates abstract union of successive abstract iterates at loop head. In this case, it generalizes abstract states such as the ones shown in Fig. 3(a) and Fig. 3(b) by weakening them locally. Indeed, in all three states, `c` points to a well-formed tree containing a sequence S_0. More-

$$
\begin{aligned}
&\mathbf{treeseg}_s(\alpha, \alpha', S \boxdot S') := \\
&\quad | \ \mathbf{emp} \wedge \alpha = \alpha' \wedge S = S' = [] \\
&\quad | \ \exists \alpha_l, \alpha_r, \mathtt{v}, S_l, S_l', S_r, \alpha.\mathtt{l} \mapsto \alpha_l * \alpha.\mathtt{r} \mapsto \alpha_r * \alpha.\mathtt{d} \mapsto \mathtt{v} * \mathbf{treeseg}_s(\alpha_l, \alpha', S_l \boxdot S_l') \\
&\qquad * \mathbf{tree}_s(\alpha_r, S_r) \wedge \alpha \neq \mathbf{0x0} \wedge S = S_l \wedge S' = S_l'.[\mathtt{v}].S_r \\
&\quad | \ \exists \alpha_l, \alpha_r, \mathtt{v}, S_l, S_r, S_r', \alpha.\mathtt{l} \mapsto \alpha_l * \alpha.\mathtt{r} \mapsto \alpha_r * \alpha.\mathtt{d} \mapsto \mathtt{v} * \mathbf{tree}_s(\alpha_l, S_l) \\
&\qquad * \mathbf{treeseg}_s(\alpha_r, \alpha', S_r \boxdot S_r') \wedge \alpha \neq \mathbf{0x0} \wedge S = S_l.[v].S_r \wedge S = S_r'
\end{aligned}
$$

Fig. 4. Inductive summarizing predicate describing tree segment

over, the remaining of the memory region corresponds to a (possibly empty) partial tree: if it was completed by a tree with root pointed by c, the whole region would form a complete tree with root pointed by t. We call such a partial tree a *tree segment predicate* (the name *segments* comes from the analogy with list segments) and observe that it is can be automatically derived from $\mathbf{tree}_s$ and defined by induction in Fig. 4. When widening synthesizes an instance of $\mathbf{treeseg}_s$ in Fig. 3(c), it needs to infer its sequence argument. The sequence S of elements stored into the whole tree can be split into three parts, S_0, S_1, and S_2 where S_0 is the sequence of elements stored in the subtree pointed to by c and S_1 (resp., S_2) denote the sequence of elements stored in the "left" (resp., "right") part of the tree segment. This implies that the sequence argument of $\mathbf{treeseg}_s$ is not a contiguous sequence. Therefore, it is represented as $S_1 \boxdot S_2$ in the loop invariant Fig. 3(c) where the *placeholder* notation $\boxdot$ stands for the sequence of elements in the "missing subtree" of the segment. When composing $\mathbf{treeseg}_s$ and $\mathbf{tree}_s$ the analysis operations resolve sequences using such $\boxdot$ symbol. Based on this loop invariant, the analysis of the final few assignments of the insertion function produces an abstract state that implies the desired post-condition.

3 Abstract Domain for Sequences

In this section, we define the sequence abstract domain, including its elements and the constraints they denote, its concretization, and its main abstract operators.

3.1 Sequences Abstraction

An element of the abstract domain of sequences is a conjunction of constraints over a finite set of symbolic variables that stand either for sequences of base values, for base values, or for sets of values. Beside sequence equalities and predicates like sortedness, we also consider numerical upper/lower bounds over the values in sequences and multi-set constraints over the collections of values in sequences.

Concrete States. Let $\mathbb{V}$ denote a set of values. Although $\mathbb{V}$ usually denotes a set of scalar values (including addresses), our only assumptions on $\mathbb{V}$ is that it has a total ordering $\preceq$ with extremal values $+\infty, -\infty$. Since our domain constrains both variables that range over $\mathbb{V}$ and variables that range over sequences of values in $\mathbb{V}$, we need several kinds of *symbolic variables.* In the following, we let symbols $\alpha, \alpha_0, \alpha'_0, \beta, \ldots \in \mathbb{X}_n$ denote *value symbolic variables*, namely, variables that stand for a value in $\mathbb{V}$. To express constraints on the set $\mathbb{V}^*$ of all the finite words on alphabet $\mathbb{V}$, we let a separate set $\mathbb{X}_s$, represent *sequence symbolic variables.* We note $S, S_1, S', P, \ldots \in \mathbb{X}_s$ such sequence variables. Finally, we write $\mathcal{M}(\mathbb{V})$ for the set of multisets of values in $\mathbb{V}$ and let $\mathbb{X}_m$ be the set of *multi-set valued symbolic variables.* Moreover, if $S \in \mathbb{X}_s$ is a sequence variable, we attach to it three numerical variables $\texttt{len}_S, \texttt{min}_S, \texttt{max}_S$ in $\mathbb{X}_n$ that respectively denote the length, minimum and maximum value of S, and that there exists a multi-set variable $\texttt{multi}_S \in \mathbb{X}_m$ that denotes the multi-set of its elements.

$$E ::= \texttt{[]} \mid \texttt{[}\alpha\texttt{]} \mid S \mid E.E \mid \textbf{sort}(E) \qquad C\,(\in \mathbb{C}) \;::=\; S = E$$

(a) Syntax of expressions (E) and constraints (C)

$$\llbracket \texttt{[]} \rrbracket_s(\sigma) = \varepsilon \qquad \llbracket \texttt{[}\alpha\texttt{]} \rrbracket_s(\sigma) = \sigma_n(\alpha)$$

$$\llbracket S \rrbracket_s(\sigma) = \sigma_s(S) \qquad \llbracket E_1.E_2 \rrbracket_s(\sigma) = \llbracket E_1 \rrbracket_s(\sigma).\llbracket E_2 \rrbracket_s(\sigma)$$

$$\llbracket \textbf{sort}(E) \rrbracket_s(\sigma) = a_{\pi(1)} \ldots a_{\pi(n)} \text{ where } \begin{cases} \llbracket E \rrbracket(\sigma) = a_1 \ldots a_n \\ \forall i \in [1, n-1], a_{\pi(i)} \preceq a_{\pi(i+1)} \\ \pi \text{ is a permutation of } [1, n] \end{cases}$$

$$(\sigma_n, \sigma_s) \models_s S = E \text{ iff } \sigma_s(S) = \llbracket E \rrbracket_s(\sigma_n, \sigma_s)$$

(b) Semantics

Fig. 5. Sequence expressions and constraints: syntax and semantics

A *concrete state* comprises three functions that map each kind of symbolic variables to elements of the corresponding type. Due to the relationship between a sequence symbolic variable S and $\texttt{len}_S, \texttt{min}_S, \texttt{max}_S$, and $\texttt{multi}_S$, a concrete state is valid if and only if it maps these five variables into consistent objects. Formally:

Definition 1. *A* concrete state *is a tuple* $\sigma = (\sigma_n, \sigma_m, \sigma_s)$ *where the functions* $\sigma_n : \mathbb{X}_n \to \mathbb{V}$, $\sigma_m : \mathbb{X}_m \to \mathcal{M}(\mathbb{V})$, $\sigma_s : \mathbb{X}_s \to \mathbb{V}^*$ *are such that, for all* S *in* $\mathbb{X}_s$,

$$\sigma_s(S) = a_1 \ldots a_n \Rightarrow \begin{cases} \sigma_n(\texttt{min}_S) = \min_i a_i \land \sigma_n(\texttt{max}_S) = \max_i a_i \\ \land\, \sigma_n(\texttt{len}_S) = n \land \sigma_m(\texttt{multi}_S) = \{a_1, \ldots, a_n\} \end{cases}$$

$$\sigma_s(S) = \varepsilon \Rightarrow \begin{cases} \sigma_n(\texttt{min}_S) = +\infty \land \sigma_n(\texttt{max}_S) = -\infty \\ \land\, \sigma_n(\texttt{len}_S) = 0 \land \sigma_m(\texttt{multi}_S) = \emptyset \end{cases}$$

For short, given a state σ, *we note its components* σ_n, σ_m, *and* σ_s. *We write* Σ *for the set of all such concrete states.*

Abstract Sequence Constraints. The sequence abstract domain relies on expressions and constraints over symbolic variables. Their syntax is shown in Fig. 5(a). An expression is either the empty sequence, or a sequence of length one that consists of a value symbolic variable, or a sequence symbolic variable, or a concatenation of expressions, or the sorting of a sequence expression returned by the function **sort** : $E \rightarrow E$, (introduced in Sect. 2). Given a state σ, a sequence expression E evaluates into a sequence of values $[\![E]\!]_s(\sigma)$, as shown in Fig. 5(b). Sequence constraints are *definition constraints* of the form $S = E$, as shown in Fig. 5(a). Allowing only symbolic sequence variables in the left-hand side of equalities somewhat limits expressiveness but simplifies the machine representation of abstract elements. The semantics of constraints is defined based on a satisfaction relation $\models_s$ that is spelled out in Fig. 5(b): we write $(\sigma_n, \sigma_s) \models_s C$ when constraint C holds in concrete state (σ_n, σ_s). We note $\mathbb{C}$ for the set of sequence constraints.

Parameter Abstract Domains. In the following, we assume two abstract domains are fixed, taken as parameters by the sequence abstraction. First, $\mathbb{D}_n^\sharp$ represents numerical constraints and provides a concretization function $\gamma_n : \mathbb{D}_n^\sharp \rightarrow \mathcal{P}(\mathbb{X}_n \rightarrow \mathbb{V})$. Possible choices for $\mathbb{D}_n^\sharp$ include intervals [17], octagons [46], or convex polyhedra [20] abstract domains. Second, $\mathbb{D}_m^\sharp$ represents multi-set constraints and provides a concretization function $\gamma_m : \mathbb{D}_m^\sharp \rightarrow \mathcal{P}(\mathbb{X}_m \rightarrow \mathcal{M}(\mathbb{V}))$. Our implementation uses a variation of the set domain of [39] that describes multi-set constraints.

Sequence Abstraction. An abstract state consists either of a special element $\bot$ that denotes the empty set of concrete states or of a finite conjunction of sequence constraints together with numerical and multi-set constraints:

Definition 2 (Sequence abstraction). *The abstract sequence domain $\Sigma^\sharp$ is defined as $\{\bot\} \uplus \{(\sigma_n^\sharp, \sigma_m^\sharp, C_0 \wedge \ldots \wedge C_n) \mid \sigma_n^\sharp \in \mathbb{D}_n^\sharp, \sigma_m^\sharp \in \mathbb{D}_m^\sharp, C_0, \ldots, C_n \in \mathbb{C}\}$. Furthermore, its concretization $\gamma_\Sigma : \Sigma^\sharp \longrightarrow \mathcal{P}(\Sigma)$ is defined by $\gamma_\Sigma(\bot) = \emptyset$ and:*

$$\begin{aligned}&\gamma_\Sigma(\sigma_n^\sharp, \sigma_m^\sharp, C_0 \wedge \ldots \wedge C_n) = \\ &\quad \big\{(\sigma_n, \sigma_m, \sigma_s) \,\big|\, \sigma_n \in \gamma_n(\sigma_n^\sharp) \wedge \sigma_m \in \gamma_m(\sigma_m^\sharp) \wedge \forall i,\ \sigma_n, \sigma_s \models_s C_i \,\big\}\end{aligned}$$

For consistency, we use $\sigma_s^\sharp$ as a generic notation for a finite conjunction of constraints $C_0 \wedge \ldots \wedge C_n$ and $\sigma^\sharp$ for a generic triple $(\sigma_n^\sharp, \sigma_m^\sharp, \sigma_s^\sharp)$. We remark that the empty conjunction of constraints concretizes into Σ thus we note it $\top$.

Machine Representation. For the sake of algorithmic efficiency, we rely on an optimized machine representation for sequence constraints in non-bottom abstract states. First, we let equality constraints between variables be described by union-find data-structures, which enables the incremental computation of equality classes representatives. Emptiness constraints ($S = [\,]$) and sortedness constraints ($S = \mathbf{sort}(S)$) are marked by tags over sequence variables. Finally, other equality constraints are represented with a map data type, the keys of which are the left hand side variables. For instance, $S = [\alpha]$ boils down to a map entry $S \mapsto [\alpha]$.

3.2 Abstract Operations

We now discuss abstract operations on sequence abstract states. In this subsection, we discuss two operations: $\mathfrak{guard}_{\Sigma}$ refines an abstract sequence element into its conjunction with an additional constraint and $\mathfrak{verify}_{\Sigma}$ attempts to discharge a sequence constraint (so as to, e.g., verify an assertion). We assume that the underlying domains also implement similar operators. For instance, we require the numerical domain to provide an operator $\mathfrak{guard}_n$ that inputs a numerical constraint and a $\sigma_n^\sharp \in \mathbb{D}_n^\sharp$ and refines the latter with that constraint.

Abstract Sequence Condition. First, we consider the *abstract sequence condition* operator $\mathfrak{guard}_{\Sigma} : \mathbb{C} \times \Sigma^\sharp \to \Sigma^\sharp$ which refines an abstract state with an additional sequence constraint. While a naive implementation of $\mathfrak{guard}_{\Sigma}(C, \sigma^\sharp)$ would simply add the constraint C to the conjunction $\sigma_s^\sharp$ component, this would be imprecise in general. Indeed, the conjunction $C \wedge \sigma_s^\sharp$ may be equivalent to $\perp$. Moreover, $C \wedge \sigma_s^\sharp$ may entail constraints that are strictly more precise than those in $\sigma_s^\sharp$.

At a high level, $\mathfrak{guard}_{\Sigma}$ performs three kinds of operations:

1. *Compaction* simplifies constraints by rewriting the right hand side of definition constraints into the left hand side, wherever possible. For example, $S = S'.\texttt{[}\alpha\texttt{]}.S'' \wedge S_1 = S'.\texttt{[}\alpha\texttt{]}$ simplifies into $S = S_1.S'' \wedge S_1 = S'.\texttt{[}\alpha\texttt{]}$.
2. *Saturation* synthesizes additional numerical and multi-set constraints that can be derived from a newly added constraint. For instance, $S = S'.\texttt{[}\alpha\texttt{]}$ entails that $\texttt{len}_S = 1 + \texttt{len}_{S'}$. Likewise, some constraints may entail that a sequence is empty. Another special kind of saturation occurs when the whole state can be reduced to $\perp$ as incompatible constraints are detected. As saturation is the most complex part of $\mathfrak{guard}_{\Sigma}$, we detail it below.
3. *Detection of cyclic constraints* prevents compaction and saturation from adding too many, redundant constraints, and it ensures the termination of algorithms iterating on definitions. We discuss this in Example 2.

We now discuss constraint saturation more in detail:

- The *length constraints saturation* derives numerical constraints from the equality of the length of both sides of a new definition constraint $S = E$. Indeed, such a constraint implies $\texttt{len}_S = \tau_{\texttt{len}}(E)$, which can be added to the $\sigma_n^\sharp$ component using $\mathfrak{guard}_n$, where $\tau_{\texttt{len}}$ is defined by:

$$\tau_{\texttt{len}}(\texttt{[]}) = 0 \qquad \tau_{\texttt{len}}(E.E') = \tau_{\texttt{len}}(E) + \tau_{\texttt{len}}(E') \quad \tau_{\texttt{len}}(S) = \texttt{len}_S$$
$$\tau_{\texttt{len}}(\texttt{[}\alpha\texttt{]}) = 1 \quad \tau_{\texttt{len}}(\textbf{sort}(E)) = \tau_{\texttt{len}}(E)$$

- The *multi-set contents constraints saturation* operates similarly, and derives multi-set equalities from definition constraints. Surely, $S = E$ entails $\texttt{multi}_S = \tau_{\texttt{mul}}(E)$, which can refine the $\sigma_m^\sharp$ part using $\mathfrak{guard}_m$ where $\tau_{\texttt{mul}}$ is defined by:

$$\tau_{\texttt{mul}}(\texttt{[]}) = \emptyset \qquad \tau_{\texttt{mul}}(E.E') = \tau_{\texttt{mul}}(E) \uplus \tau_{\texttt{mul}}(E') \quad \tau_{\texttt{mul}}(S) = \texttt{multi}_S$$
$$\tau_{\texttt{mul}}(\texttt{[}\alpha\texttt{]}) = \{\alpha\} \quad \tau_{\texttt{mul}}(\textbf{sort}(E)) = \tau_{\texttt{mul}}(E)$$

- The *detection of empty sequence variables* derives new definition constraints of the form $S = \texttt{[]}$ when either sequence constraints or numerical constraints entail the emptiness of S. For instance:
  - when $\sigma_s^\sharp$ contains constraints $S' = \texttt{[]}$ and $S'' = \texttt{[]}$, the constraint $S = S'.S''$ simplifies into $S = \texttt{[]}$;
  - when $\sigma_n^\sharp$ contains the constraint $\texttt{len}_S = 0$, then it follows that $S = \texttt{[]}$.
- The *detection of sorted sequence variables* do the same for constraints of the form $S = \textbf{sort}(S)$ thanks to definitions of S and to numerical inequalities:

$$\frac{S = S_1.\ldots.S_n \qquad \forall i, S_i = \textbf{sort}(S_i) \quad \forall i < j, \texttt{max}_{S_i} \leq \texttt{max}_{S_j}}{S = \textbf{sort}(S)}$$

  Such rule is very costly as it checks a quadratic amount of numerical inequalities. Nevertheless, relaxing the rule by only considering the case $j = i + 1$ is not sound, since sequence variables may be empty. Therefore, two consecutive elements in $\sigma_s(S)$ can come from non-consecutive sequence variables.
- The *extremal values inequalities saturation* derives numerical inequalities from a definition constraint $S = E$ by case analysis over the right hand side E, and can be summarized by a set of derivation rules. The rules below describe such reasoning steps:

$$\frac{S = E \qquad \alpha \in \textbf{fv}(E)}{\texttt{min}_S \leq \alpha \leq \texttt{max}_S} \qquad \frac{S = E \qquad S' \in \textbf{fv}(E)}{\texttt{min}_S \leq \texttt{min}_{S'} \qquad \texttt{max}_{S'} \leq \texttt{max}_S}$$

$$\frac{S = \texttt{[]} \qquad \alpha \in \mathcal{X}_n}{\texttt{max}_S < \alpha < \texttt{min}_S} \qquad \frac{S' = \textbf{sort}(S') \qquad S' = \ldots.\texttt{[}\alpha\texttt{]}.S.\ldots}{\alpha \leq \texttt{min}_S}$$

  As an example, the first rule states that numerical constraints can be derived from the knowledge that S is a concatenation of several components including a numerical variable α; in this case novel numeric constraints expressing that α is bounded by the extremal values of S can be added to $\sigma_n^\sharp$ using operator $\mathfrak{guard}_n$. Similarly, the second rule states that the extremal values of a sequence are bounded by the extremal values of any sequence containing it. The third rule states that an empty sequence supports arbitrary bounds. Finally, the fourth rule allows to reason over bounds when a sequence is known to be sorted.
- The *decomposition of equality constraints* synthesizes additional equality constraints that can be derived when two definition constraints $S = E_0$ and $S = E_1$ over the same name can be found in $\sigma_s^\sharp$. Indeed, when both E_0 and E_1 can be decomposed simultaneously, new equalities can be immediately derived:

$$\frac{\texttt{[}\alpha_0\texttt{]}.E_0 = \texttt{[}\alpha_1\texttt{]}.E_1}{\alpha_0 = \alpha_1 \qquad E_0 = E_1} \qquad \frac{S.E_0 = E_1 \qquad S = \texttt{[]}}{E_0 = E_1}$$

  In less obvious decomposition cases, further constraints can still be derived with the help of the numerical constraints. Indeed:

$$\frac{S_0.E_0 = S_1.E_1 \qquad \texttt{len}_{S_0} = \texttt{len}_{S_1}}{S_0 = S_1 \qquad E_0 = E_1}$$

Obviously, this inference may take place only when $\mathtt{lens}_{S_0} = \mathtt{lens}_{S_1}$ can be proved in the numerical domain.

A special case of saturation occurs when incompatible constraints are detected. Then, the whole abstract state is reduced to $\bot$, following the principles of reduced product [18]. As an example, when the abstract state contains the constraints $S = [\alpha]$ and $\mathtt{lens}_S = 0$, such a reduction is performed.

To summarize, the computation of $\mathfrak{guard}_{\Sigma}(C, \sigma^\sharp)$ involves the addition to $\sigma^\sharp$ of a set of constraints that are derived from C. It is conservative in general. The termination of this computation follows from the fact that the added constraints only involve syntactic subcomponents of the elements of C and $\sigma^\sharp_s$.

Example 1. We consider the abstract state of Fig. 3(b) and the constraint $S_1 = S_l.[\delta]$ where S_1 is a new symbolic sequence variable. First, the constraint is added to the abstract state. Second, compaction replaces the pattern $S_l.[\delta]$ with S_1 in all other constraints. Third, the numerical inequality $\alpha \geq \mathtt{max}_{S_1}$ and the sortedness of S_1 entails that S_1 is sorted. Then, $S_1 = \mathbf{sort}(S_1)$ implies that δ is the maximum value of S_1. Moreover, the fact that S_l is a subsequence of S_1 entails that $\mathtt{min}_{S_1} \leq \mathtt{min}_{S_l}$ and $\mathtt{max}_{S_l} \leq \mathtt{max}_{S_1}$. Finally, since $\delta \leq \mathtt{i}$, $\mathfrak{guard}_{\Sigma}$ also derives $\mathtt{max}_{S_1} \leq \mathtt{i}$. Finally, $\mathfrak{guard}_{\Sigma}$ produces:

$$\begin{aligned} S = S_1.S_r \wedge S_1 = S_l.[\delta] \wedge S = \mathbf{sort}(S) \wedge S_i = \mathbf{sort}(S_i),\ i \in \{l, r, 1\} \\ \wedge\, \mathtt{max}_{S_l} \leq \mathtt{max}_{S_1} = \delta \leq \mathtt{max}_{S_r} \wedge \mathtt{min}_{S_1} \leq \mathtt{max}_{S_l} \wedge \delta \leq \mathtt{i} \wedge \alpha_0, \alpha_1 \neq \mathbf{0x0} \end{aligned}$$

Example 2. In this example, we show the detection of mutually cyclic constraints. We consider the abstract state $S_1 = S_2.S' \wedge S_2 = S''.S_3$, and the addition of $S_3 = S_1.S'''$. Inlining definition constraints for S_2 and S_3 would produce the cyclic constraint $S_1 = S''.S_1.S'''.S'$. Thus, this also implies that S', S'', S''' are empty and that S_1, S_2 and S_3 are equal. After removal of the cycle, $\mathfrak{guard}_{\Sigma}$ produces:

$$S' = S'' = S''' = [] \wedge S_1 = S_2 = S_3 \wedge S_1 = S_2.S' \wedge S_2 = S''.S_3$$

Theorem 1 (Soundness of $\mathfrak{guard}_{\Sigma}$). *For all abstract state $\sigma^\sharp$ and constraint C, we have $\{\sigma \in \gamma_{\Sigma}(\sigma^\sharp) \mid \sigma \models_s C\} \subseteq \gamma_{\Sigma}(\mathfrak{guard}_{\Sigma}(C, \sigma^\sharp))$.*

Verification of a Sequence Constraint. Second, we define the *constraint verification operator* $\mathfrak{verify}_{\Sigma} : \Sigma^\sharp \times \mathbb{C} \rightarrow \{\mathbf{false}, \mathbf{true}\}$ which inputs a constraint C and an abstract state $\sigma^\sharp$ and returns **true** when it can prove that $\sigma^\sharp$ entails C. It is conservative in the sense that it may return **false** even when the constraint is satisfied. The computation of $\mathfrak{verify}_{\Sigma}(C, (\sigma^\sharp_n, \sigma^\sharp_m, \sigma^\sharp_s))$ proceeds as follows:

1. If $\sigma^\sharp_s$ is $\bot$, it returns **true**.
2. For definition constraints $S = E$, $\mathfrak{verify}_{\Sigma}$ inlines the definitions of variables, and returns **true** when both sides rewrite into syntactically equal expressions. The absence of cyclic constraints ensures this exploration terminates.
3. Otherwise, it returns **false**.

For constraints of the form $S = \mathbf{sort}(E)$, the operator uses a specific rule (shown below) since variables inside the **sort** function may be arbitrarily reordered. Instead, we take advantage of the multi-set abstract domain to establish that S and E have the same contents.

$$\frac{S = \mathbf{sort}(S) \qquad \mathtt{multi}_S = \tau_{\mathtt{mul}}(E)}{S = \mathbf{sort}(E)}$$

Theorem 2 (Soundness of $\mathfrak{verify}_\Sigma$). *For all abstract state $\sigma^\sharp$ and constraint C, if $\mathfrak{verify}_\Sigma(\sigma^\sharp, C) = \mathbf{true}$ then, we have $\gamma_\Sigma(\sigma^\sharp) \subseteq \{\sigma \in \Sigma \mid \sigma \models_s C\}$.*

3.3 Lattice Operations

We now discuss join, widening and inclusion checking operations for loop analysis. We assume that $\mathbb{D}^\sharp_n$ provides a conservative inclusion test operator $\mathfrak{is\_le}_n$ (it inputs two elements of $\sigma^\sharp_n$ and returns **true** only when it succeeds proving the first is included in the second), an over-approximate join operator $\mathfrak{join}_n$ and a widening $\mathfrak{widen}_n$, and that $\mathbb{D}^\sharp_m$ provides similar operators $\mathfrak{is\_le}_m$, $\mathfrak{join}_m$, and $\mathfrak{widen}_m$, and we build similar operators for $\Sigma^\sharp$.

Inclusion Checking. The inclusion test operator inputs two abstract states and returns a boolean. When it returns **true**, the concretization of the first abstract state is included into that of the second one. The inclusion checking algorithm is based on the constraint representation of abstract states and boils down to a repeated application of $\mathfrak{verify}_\Sigma$.

Definition 3 (Inclusion checking operator). *The operator $\mathfrak{is\_le}_\Sigma : \Sigma^\sharp \times \Sigma^\sharp \to \{\mathbf{true}, \mathbf{false}\}$ is defined by:*

$$\begin{aligned}
&\mathfrak{is_le}_\Sigma((\sigma^\sharp_{n,0}, \sigma^\sharp_{m,0}, \sigma^\sharp_{s,0}), (\sigma^\sharp_{n,1}, \sigma^\sharp_{m,1}, \wedge_i C_i)) \\
&\quad := \mathfrak{is_le}_n(\sigma^\sharp_{n,0}, \sigma^\sharp_{n,1}) \wedge \mathfrak{is_le}_m(\sigma^\sharp_{m,0}, \sigma^\sharp_{m,1}) \wedge (\wedge_i \mathfrak{verify}_\Sigma(C_i, \sigma^\sharp_{s,0}))
\end{aligned}$$

Theorem 3. *The operator $\mathfrak{is\_le}_\Sigma$ is sound in the sense that, for all $\sigma^\sharp_0, \sigma^\sharp_1 \in \Sigma^\sharp$, if $\mathfrak{is\_le}_\Sigma(\sigma^\sharp_0, \sigma^\sharp_1) = \mathbf{true}$, then $\gamma_\Sigma(\sigma^\sharp_0) \subseteq \gamma_\Sigma(\sigma^\sharp_1)$.*

Upper Bounds. As usual, we define two over-approximate upper-bound operators, namely, a classical join operator $\mathfrak{join}_\Sigma : \Sigma^\sharp \times \Sigma^\sharp \to \Sigma^\sharp$ and a widening $\mathfrak{widen}_\Sigma : \Sigma^\sharp \times \Sigma^\sharp \to \Sigma^\sharp$ that ensures termination.

Essentially, the $\mathfrak{join}_\Sigma$ operator proceeds component-wise (like $\mathfrak{is\_le}_\Sigma$ as defined in Definition 3) and essentially preserves sequence constraints that appear in both arguments. In the case of definition constraint, it first saturates the conjunctions of constraints, so as to maximize the possible sets of common constraints. The algorithm of $\mathfrak{widen}_\Sigma$ is similar, except that it does not saturate its left argument for the sake of termination. This implies that $\mathfrak{widen}_\Sigma$ always returns a conjunction of constraints that forms a subset of the constraints of its left argument.

Both operators are sound and furthermore, $\mathfrak{widen}_\Sigma$ guarantees termination.

Theorem 4 (Soundness of join_Σ and $\mathfrak{widen}_\Sigma$, termination of $\mathfrak{widen}_\Sigma$). *For all abstract states $\sigma_0^\sharp$, $\sigma_1^\sharp$, we have: $\gamma_\Sigma(\sigma_0^\sharp) \cup \gamma_\Sigma(\sigma_1^\sharp) \subseteq \gamma_\Sigma(\mathsf{join}_\Sigma(\sigma_0^\sharp, \sigma_1^\sharp))$ and $\gamma_\Sigma(\sigma_0^\sharp) \cup \gamma_\Sigma(\sigma_1^\sharp) \subseteq \gamma_\Sigma(\mathfrak{widen}_\Sigma(\sigma_0^\sharp, \sigma_1^\sharp))$. Moreover, the operator $\mathfrak{widen}_\Sigma$ ensures termination: for all sequence $(\sigma_n^\sharp)_{n\in\mathbb{N}}$ of abstract states the sequence $((\sigma^\sharp)'_n)_{n\in\mathbb{N}}$ defined by $(\sigma^\sharp)'_0 = \sigma_0^\sharp$ and $(\sigma^\sharp)'_{n+1} = \mathfrak{widen}_\Sigma((\sigma^\sharp)'_n, \sigma_{n+1}^\sharp)$ is ultimately stationary.*

Example 3 (Join). In this example, we consider the computation of the join of two abstract states taken from the analysis of the program of Fig. 2. The analysis of the loop at line 7 involves the computation of the join of the three abstract states below. For concision, we omit inequality constraints involving extremal values of empty sequences.

$$\sigma_0^\sharp ::= \begin{cases} S = S_0 \wedge S_1 = S_2 = [] \\ \wedge\, S = \mathbf{sort}(S) \wedge S_i = \mathbf{sort}(S_i), i \in \{0,1,2\} \end{cases}$$
$$\sigma_1^\sharp ::= \begin{cases} S = S_0.S_2 \wedge S_1 = [] \wedge \mathtt{max}_{S_0} \leq \mathtt{min}_{S_2} \wedge \mathtt{i} \leq \mathtt{min}_{S_2} \\ \wedge\, S = \mathbf{sort}(S) \wedge S_i = \mathbf{sort}(S_i), i \in \{0,1,2\} \end{cases}$$
$$\sigma_2^\sharp ::= \begin{cases} S = S_1.S_0 \wedge S_2 = [] \wedge \mathtt{max}_{S_1} \leq \mathtt{min}_{S_0} \wedge \mathtt{max}_{S_1} \leq \mathtt{i} \\ \wedge\, S = \mathbf{sort}(S) \wedge S_i = \mathbf{sort}(S_i), i \in \{0,1,2\} \end{cases}$$

The most notable step is the saturation of the first argument, that injects constraint $S = S_1.S_0.S_2$, as a consequence of $S = S_0$ and $S_1 = S_2 = []$ in $\sigma_0^\sharp$, $S = S_0.S_2$ and $S_1 = []$ in $\sigma_1^\sharp$ and $S = S_1.S_0$ and $S_2 = []$ in $\sigma_2^\sharp$. After this, constraints that hold in only either argument are dropped, as, e.g., constraint $S_1 = []$ in $\sigma_1^\sharp$. The result of the union corresponds to the abstract state in Fig. 3(c).

4 Combination of Sequence Abstraction and Shape Analysis

In this section, we define a shape analysis with inductive predicates that infers invariants about both the layout of data-structures and the sequences of values they store. For the sake of simplicity, we consider only a singly-linked list predicate (Fig. 6) throughout this section, although our analysis and its implementation are parameterized by user-defined inductive predicates [14,15]. The generalization to other structures will be discussed in Sect. 5.

```
struct list { struct list* n; int d; };
```

$\mathbf{lseg}_s(\alpha_0, \alpha_1, S \,\boxdot\,) :=$
$\mid \mathbf{emp} \wedge \alpha_0 = \alpha_1 \wedge S = []$
$\mid \exists \alpha', \delta, S', \alpha_0.\mathtt{n} \mapsto \alpha' * \alpha_0.\mathtt{d} \mapsto \delta * \mathbf{lseg}_s(\alpha', \alpha_1, S' \,\boxdot\,) \wedge \alpha_0 \neq \mathbf{0x0} \wedge S = [\delta].S'$

Fig. 6. A C list data-type and the inductive summarizing predicate describing list segments

4.1 Language and Semantics

Although our implementation is based on the MemCAD analyzer [38] and targets the C language, our formalization only considers a restricted fragment. We let $\mathbb{X}$ denote a finite set of program variables. We consider a basic imperative language, where commands are assignments, conditional statements, loops, and sequences of commands. Expressions are either l-values that evaluate to addresses, or r-values, that evaluate to scalars. An l-value l is either a program variable $\mathtt{v} \in \mathbb{X}$, the access to an l-value field $l.\mathtt{f}$ (for concision, we let $\mathtt{f}$ denote both the field name and the corresponding memory offset), or the dereference $*e$ of an expression e. An r-value e is either a constant $n \in \mathbb{V}$, or the reading of the memory cell defined by an l-value l, or the address $\&l$ or an l-value l, or the application $e_0 \oplus e_1$ of a binary operator to two sub-expressions. For simplicity, we assume here that operators are deterministic and cause no errors. The grammar is shown below:

$$l ::= \mathtt{v} \mid l.\mathtt{f} \mid *e \quad e ::= n \mid l \mid \&l \mid e \oplus e \quad c ::= l = e \mid \mathbf{if}(e)\{c\} \mid \mathbf{while}(e)\{c\} \mid c; c$$

We note $\mathbb{A}$ for the set of addresses, which is a subset of the set of values $\mathbb{V}$. A memory state m is a partial function from addresses to values. We note $\mathbb{M}$ for the set of memory states and let $\emptyset$ denote the empty memory. Furthermore, we assume that each program variable $\mathtt{x}$ has a fixed address denoted by $\underline{\mathtt{x}} \in \mathbb{A}$. Based on these definitions, we set up the program semantics as follows. First, we define the semantics of expressions by induction over their syntax. The semantics of an l-value l is a function $[\![l]\!]_l : \mathbb{M} \to \mathbb{A}$ that maps a memory state m to the address l evaluates to in m. Similarly, the semantics $[\![e]\!]_e : \mathbb{M} \to \mathbb{V}$ of an expression e maps a memory state to a value. Finally, the semantics $[\![c]\!] : \mathcal{P}(\mathbb{M}) \to \mathcal{P}(\mathbb{M})$ of a command c maps any set of input memory states M to the set of all possible output memory states when starting from any $m \in M$. The definition of all three semantics is classical and shown in Fig. 7, where $f_\oplus : \mathbb{V}^2 \to \mathbb{V}$ denotes the semantics of operator $\oplus$.

$$
\begin{array}{rlrl}
[\![\mathtt{x}]\!]_l(m) & := \underline{\mathtt{x}} & [\![n]\!]_e(m) & := n \\
[\![l.\mathtt{f}]\!]_l(m) & := [\![l]\!]_l(m) + \mathtt{f} & [\![l]\!]_e(m) & := m([\![l]\!]_l(m)) \\
[\![*e]\!]_l(m) & := [\![e]\!]_e(m) & [\![\&l]\!]_e(m) & := [\![l]\!]_l(m) \\
 & & [\![e_0 \oplus e_1]\!]_e(m) & := f_\oplus([\![e_0]\!]_e(m), [\![e_1]\!]_e(m))
\end{array}
$$

$$
\begin{array}{rl}
[\![l = e]\!](M) & := \{m[[\![l]\!]_l(m) \mapsto [\![e]\!]_e(m)] \mid m \in M\} \\
[\![\mathbf{if}(e)\{c_0\}]\!](M) & := [\![c_0]\!]\left(\{m \in M \mid [\![e]\!]_e(m) \neq 0\}\right) \cup \{m \in M \mid [\![e]\!]_e(m) = 0\} \\
[\![\mathbf{while}(e)\{c\}]\!](M) & := \{m \in \mathbf{lfp} F \mid [\![e]\!]_e(m) = 0\} \\
 & \quad \text{where } F(M') = M \cup [\![c]\!](m \in M' \mid [\![e]\!]_e(m) \neq 0\}) \\
[\![c_0; c_1]\!](M) & := [\![c_1]\!] \circ [\![c_0]\!](M)
\end{array}
$$

Fig. 7. Semantics of programs

4.2 Combined Memory and Sequence Abstraction

Sequence Aware Shape Abstraction. We start with the definition of abstract memory predicates, following an approach similar to that of separation logic based shape analyses with inductive definitions [12,14], extended with sequence information. As explained early in the section, our formalization considers a single inductive predicate describing list segments, and parameterized with a symbolic sequence variable that stands for the sequence of the values contained in them (Fig. 6). Considering only list segments has two advantages. First, complete lists can be expressed as list segments the last element of which has a "next" field equal to **0x0**. Second, it simplifies reasoning over sequences as it avoids branching structures (considered in Sect. 5). Abstract states rely on scalar symbolic variables in $\mathbb{X}_n$ to denote values and addresses and consist of separating conjunctions [50] of points-to predicates and of list segment predicates:

Definition 4 (Abstract memory states). *The set of* abstract memory states $\mathbb{M}^\sharp$ *is described by the grammar below, where* $\alpha_0, \alpha_1 \in \mathbb{X}_n$ *and* $S \in \mathbb{X}_s$*:*

$$m^\sharp ::= \mathbf{emp} \mid m^\sharp * m^\sharp \mid \alpha_0.\mathtt{f} \mapsto \alpha_1 \mid \mathbf{lseg}_s(\alpha_0, \alpha_1, S \boxdot)$$

We note $\mathbb{M}^\sharp$ *for the set of abstract memory states.*

As usual, **emp** denotes the empty memory region and $m_0^\sharp * m_1^\sharp$ denotes the disjoint union of memory regions described by $m_0^\sharp$ (resp., $m_1^\sharp$). The abstract predicate $\alpha_0.\mathtt{f} \mapsto \alpha_1$ denotes a single memory cell, the address of which is described by α_0 plus the offset of `f` and the contents of which is described by α_1. Finally, $\mathbf{lseg}_s(\alpha_0, \alpha_1, S)$ stands for a (possibly empty) list segment that starts at an address described by α_0, ending with a pointer to address α_1, where each list element consists of two fields, namely, a pointer to the next element and a data field, and such that the sequence of the values of the data fields is described by sequence variable S. In logical terms, the predicate $\mathbf{lseg}_s(\alpha_0, \alpha_1, S)$ is defined inductively as shown in Fig. 6.

As the definition of $\mathbf{lseg}_s$ in Fig. 6 shows, the concretization of abstract memory states indirectly involves sequence variables (and also multi-set variables). Indeed, given an abstract memory state $m^\sharp$ and a sequence variable S that appears in $m^\sharp$, the concretization of $m^\sharp$ also constrains S, $\mathtt{len}_S$, and $\mathtt{multi}_S$. To reflect this, we let the concretization of an abstract memory $m^\sharp$ return a set of tuples that comprise not only a memory state m, but also a valuation that maps each symbolic variable in $m^\sharp$ to a value of the corresponding type (scalar, multi-set, or sequence). Such a valuation boils down to a triple $(\sigma_n, \sigma_m, \sigma_s)$ (Definition 2). The definition of the concretization is based on a set of inductive derivation rules that follow the syntax of abstract memories and unfold the list segment predicates (Fig. 8).

Definition 5 (Concretization of abstract memory states). *The concretization of abstract memory states* $\gamma_{\mathbb{M}}$ *maps an abstract memory* $m^\sharp$ *to a set of pairs* $(m, \sigma) \in \mathbb{M} \times \Sigma$ *and is defined by:*

$$\gamma_{\mathbb{M}}(m^\sharp) = \{(m, \sigma) \mid (m, \sigma) \models_{\mathbb{M}} m^\sharp\}$$

$$\frac{}{\emptyset, \sigma \models_{\mathbb{M}} \mathbf{emp}} \qquad \frac{m = [\sigma_n(\alpha_0) + \mathtt{f} \mapsto \sigma_n(\alpha_1)]}{m, (\sigma_n, \sigma_m, \sigma_s) \models_{\mathbb{M}} \alpha_0.\mathtt{f} \mapsto \alpha_1} \qquad \frac{\forall i, m_i, \sigma \models_{\mathbb{M}} m_i^\sharp}{m_0 \uplus m_1, \sigma \models_{\mathbb{M}} m_0^\sharp * m_1^\sharp}$$

$$\frac{\sigma_n(\alpha_0) = \sigma_n(\alpha_1) \qquad \sigma_n, \sigma_s \models_s S = [\,]}{\emptyset, (\sigma_n, \sigma_m, \sigma_s) \models_{\mathbb{M}} \mathbf{lseg}_s(\alpha_0, \alpha_1, S)}$$

$$\frac{\begin{array}{c} m, (\sigma_n, \sigma_m, \sigma_s) \models_{\mathbb{M}} \alpha_0.\mathtt{n} \mapsto \alpha_2 * \alpha_0.\mathtt{d} \mapsto \alpha_3 * \mathbf{lseg}_s(\alpha_2, \alpha_1, S_1 \boxdot) \\ \sigma_n(\alpha_0) \neq 0 \qquad \sigma_n, \sigma_s \models_s S = [\alpha_3].S_1 \qquad S_1 \text{ fresh} \end{array}}{m, (\sigma_n, \sigma_m, \sigma_s) \models_{\mathbb{M}} \mathbf{lseg}_s(\alpha_0, \alpha_1, S \boxdot)}$$

Fig. 8. Concretization of abstract memory states

As examples of abstract memory states, we refer the reader to the left conjuncts of the three abstract states shown in Fig. 3.

Combined Abstract Domain. The analysis needs to reason accurately over sequence variables not only when they are bound in an inductive predicate, but also when these predicates are unfolded. Thus, it requires a product abstract domain based on the memory abstract domain fixed in Definition 4 and Definition 5 and on the sequence abstract domain introduced in Sect. 3. Moreover, like most shape analyses, it sometimes needs to make case splits due to the disjunctive nature of the inductive predicate $\mathbf{lseg}_s$. Thus, the combined abstraction is defined as follows:

Definition 6 (Combined abstraction). *The elements of the* combined state abstract domain $\mathbb{S}^\sharp$ *are finite disjunctions of pairs of the form* $(m^\sharp, \sigma^\sharp) \in \mathbb{M}^\sharp \times \Sigma^\sharp$. *Furthermore, the concretization* $\gamma_{\mathbb{S}}$ *maps an element* $s^\sharp$ *of* $\mathbb{S}^\sharp$ *into a set of memories* m *and is defined by:*

$$\gamma_{\mathbb{S}}((m^\sharp, \sigma^\sharp)) := \{m \mid \exists \sigma \in \gamma_{\Sigma}(\sigma^\sharp), (m, \sigma) \in \gamma_{\mathbb{M}}(m^\sharp)\} \; \gamma_{\mathbb{S}}(\textstyle\bigvee_i s_i^\sharp) := \bigcup_i \gamma_{\mathbb{S}}(s_i^\sharp)$$

Concatenating Segments. Before we move to the analysis algorithms, we discuss a principle for logical reasoning over segments that many analysis operations rely on. Intuitively, a pair of consecutive segments may be merged into a single segment, that stores a sequence of elements that is the concatenation of the elements in the two initial segments. Reciprocally, it is possible to split a segment based on a partition of the sequence of its elements. The lemma below formalizes this.

Lemma 1 (Concatenation (list predicates)). *We assume* $\alpha_0, \alpha_1, \alpha_2$ *distinct symbolic variables and let* $m_0^\sharp := \mathbf{lseg}_s(\alpha_0, \alpha_1, S_1 \boxdot) * \mathbf{lseg}_s(\alpha_1, \alpha_2, S_2 \boxdot)$, $m_1^\sharp := \mathbf{lseg}_s(\alpha_0, \alpha_2, S \boxdot)$, *and* $\sigma^\sharp := S = S_1.S_2$. *Then, we have (i)* $\gamma_{\mathbb{S}}(m_0^\sharp, \sigma^\sharp) \subseteq \gamma_{\mathbb{S}}(m_1^\sharp, \sigma^\sharp)$, *and (ii) if* $(m, \sigma_1) \in \gamma_{\mathbb{S}}(m_1^\sharp, \sigma^\sharp)$, *then there exists* σ_0 *such that* $(m, \sigma_0) \in \gamma_{\mathbb{S}}(m_0^\sharp, \sigma^\sharp)$ *and, for all* $\beta \in \mathbb{V}$ *such that* $\beta \neq \alpha_1$, $\sigma_0(\beta) = \sigma_1(\beta)$.

4.3 Computation of Abstract Post-conditions

Abstract post-conditions are computed by a pair of families of functions:

- given l-value l and expression e, $\mathfrak{assign}_{\mathbb{S},l=e} : \mathbb{S}^\sharp \to \mathbb{S}^\sharp$ computes an over-approximation for the assignment command $l = e$;
- given expression e, $\mathfrak{guard}_{\mathbb{S},e} : \mathbb{S}^\sharp \to \mathbb{S}^\sharp$ computes an over-approximation for the effect of the condition expression e.

In the following paragraphs, we give the main steps of the algorithms to compute them. They both ensure the soundness conditions that state that, for all l-value l, expression e, and abstract state $s^\sharp \in \mathbb{S}^\sharp$, we have $[\![l = e]\!](\gamma_{\mathbb{S}}(s^\sharp)) \subseteq \gamma_{\mathbb{S}}(\mathfrak{assign}_{\mathbb{S},l=e}(s^\sharp))$ and $\{m \in \gamma_{\mathbb{S}}(s^\sharp) \mid [\![e]\!]_e(m) \neq 0\} \subseteq \gamma_{\mathbb{S}}(\mathfrak{guard}_{\mathbb{S},e}(s^\sharp))$.

Simple Cases. The computation of post-conditions for assignments and tests that involve only fully exposed cells is straightforward and follows classical shape analysis techniques [15]. For instance:

$$\begin{aligned}
&\mathfrak{assign}_{\mathbb{S},\mathtt{x.f=y}}(\underline{\mathtt{x}}.\mathtt{f} \mapsto \alpha_0 * \underline{\mathtt{y}} \mapsto \alpha_1 * m^\sharp, (\sigma_n, \sigma_m, \sigma_s)) \\
&\quad = (\underline{\mathtt{x}}.\mathtt{f} \mapsto \alpha_1 * \underline{\mathtt{y}} \mapsto \alpha_1 * m^\sharp, (\sigma_n, \sigma_m, \sigma_s)) \\
&\mathfrak{guard}_{\mathbb{S},\mathtt{x.f \neq 0x0}}(\underline{\mathtt{x}}.\mathtt{f} \mapsto \alpha_0 * m^\sharp, (\sigma_n, \sigma_m, \sigma_s)) \\
&\quad = (\underline{\mathtt{x}}.\mathtt{f} \mapsto \alpha_0 * m^\sharp, (\mathfrak{guard}_n(\alpha_0 \neq 0, \sigma_n), \sigma_m, \sigma_s))
\end{aligned}$$

where $\mathfrak{guard}_n$ denotes a sound condition test for the numerical domain [20].

Unfolding Inductive Predicates. The more difficult cases in post-conditions arise when some of the memory cells that are affected by the statement are summarized as part of an inductive predicate as, e.g., in $\mathfrak{assign}_{\mathbb{S},\mathtt{x=x.n}}(\underline{\mathtt{x}} \mapsto \alpha_0 * \mathbf{lseg}_s(\alpha_0, \alpha_1, S\boxdot))$. In such cases, some inductive predicates need to be *unfolded*, before falling back to the simpler situation shown in the two aforementioned cases.

The unfolding operation is based on rewriting rules that follow directly from the inductive nature of $\mathbf{lseg}_s$. We note $\rightsquigarrow$ the unfolding relation that rewrites an abstract state into another. Basic cases of $\rightsquigarrow$ proceed as follows:

$$\begin{aligned}
&(\mathbf{lseg}_s(\alpha_0, \alpha_1, S\boxdot) * m^\sharp, (\sigma_n^\sharp, \sigma_m^\sharp, \sigma_s^\sharp)) \\
&\rightsquigarrow \begin{cases} (m^\sharp, \mathfrak{guard}_\Sigma(S = [\,], \mathfrak{guard}_n(\alpha_0 = \alpha_1, \sigma_n^\sharp), \sigma_m^\sharp, \sigma_s^\sharp)) \\ \vee \begin{pmatrix} \alpha_0.\mathtt{n} \mapsto \alpha_2 * \alpha_0.\mathtt{d} \mapsto \alpha_3 * \mathbf{lseg}_s(\alpha_2, \alpha_1, S_1\boxdot) * m^\sharp, \\ \mathfrak{guard}_\Sigma(S = [\alpha_3].S_1, \mathfrak{guard}_n(\alpha_0 \neq 0, \sigma_n^\sharp), \sigma_m^\sharp, \sigma_s^\sharp) \end{pmatrix} \end{cases}
\end{aligned}$$

where α_2, α_3, S_1 are fresh. Unfolding is proved sound by the rules of Fig. 8 in the sense that, for all $s_0^\sharp, s_1^\sharp \in \mathbb{S}^\sharp$, if $s_0^\sharp \rightsquigarrow s_1^\sharp$, then $\gamma_{\mathbb{S}}(s_0^\sharp) \subseteq \gamma_{\mathbb{S}}(s_1^\sharp)$.

The soundness of $\mathfrak{assign}_{\mathbb{S},.}$ and $\mathfrak{guard}_{\mathbb{S},.}$ follows from that of the unfolding relation, from that of the assignment and condition test of the underlying abstract domains, and from the (straightforward) handling of the unfolded cases.

We remark that the main difference compared to baseline shape analyses is that unfolding produces additional predicates about the sequence variables, which are added into the sequence domain. In turn, the addition of these constraints may yield increased precision due to internal reduction.

4.4 Computation of Lattice Operations

The lattice operations required for the analysis of loops comprise the conservative inclusion test and the over-approximation of concrete upper bounds. Moreover, the former is used in the definition of the latter. Again, the algorithms to compute them are based on those of classical shape analyses. Thus, we emphasize the extensions that are required to infer sequence information and refer the reader to [15] for a full description of shape abstraction inclusion and widening algorithms.

Inclusion Checking. The inclusion test function performs a proof search to try to establish inclusion. Although the rule system actually used is more complex, the inclusion proof system can be summarized down to three basic principles. First, when two abstract states have the same abstract memory component, proving inclusion boils down to checking the inclusion in $\Sigma^\sharp$. Second, when the left-hand side contains several inductive predicate instances that can be summarized into one in the right-hand side, the analysis tries to concatenate them using Lemma 1. Third, when the right-hand side can be unfolded and the left-hand side is included into one of the unfolded disjuncts, then the inclusion holds for the initial pair. The rules below formalize these three principles.

$$\frac{\mathfrak{is\_le}_\Sigma(\sigma_l^\sharp, \sigma_r^\sharp) = \textbf{true}}{(m^\sharp, \sigma_l^\sharp) \sqsubseteq (m^\sharp, \sigma_r^\sharp)}$$

$$\frac{\mathfrak{verify}_\Sigma(\sigma_l^\sharp, S = S_1.S_2) = \textbf{true}}{(\mathbf{lseg}_s(\alpha, \beta, S_1 \boxdot) * \mathbf{lseg}_s(\beta, \delta, S_2 \boxdot) * m_l^\sharp, \sigma_l^\sharp) \sqsubseteq (\mathbf{lseg}_s(\alpha, \delta, S \boxdot), \sigma_r^\sharp)}$$

$$\frac{s_r^\sharp \rightsquigarrow \vee_i \overbrace{(m_i^\sharp, \mathfrak{guard}_\Sigma(\sigma_i^\sharp, C_i))}^{s_i^\sharp} \qquad \exists j, \mathfrak{verify}_\Sigma(C_j, \sigma_l^\sharp) = \textbf{true} \wedge (m_l^\sharp, \sigma_l^\sharp) \sqsubseteq s_j^\sharp}{(m_l^\sharp, \sigma_l^\sharp) \sqsubseteq s_r^\sharp}$$

The $\mathfrak{is\_le}_\mathbb{S}$ function takes two abstract states and attempts to construct a proof tree that establishes inclusion based on these principles. The main specificities of the product with a sequence abstract domain are the requirement for $\mathfrak{is\_le}_\mathbb{S}$ to track sequence concatenation constraints and the use of the inclusion checking function of the sequence abstract domain. The soundness of $\mathfrak{is\_le}_\mathbb{S}$ follows from the soundness of the shape inclusion algorithm and of the underlying domains operations:

Theorem 5 (Soundness of $\mathfrak{is\_le}_\mathbb{S}$). *For all $s_0^\sharp, s_1^\sharp \in \mathbb{S}^\sharp$, if $\mathfrak{is\_le}_\mathbb{S}(s_0^\sharp, s_1^\sharp) =$ **true** then $\gamma_\mathbb{S}(s_0^\sharp) \subseteq \gamma_\mathbb{S}(s_1^\sharp)$.*

Join and Widening. The cases of join and widening are more subtle, since these operators may need to introduce $\mathbf{lseg}_s$ predicates together with fresh symbolic sequence variables, and to infer accurate relations over these new variables. Indeed, these algorithms are based on the following two principles:

- when the memory components of the two arguments are equal, we use it for the shape specific part of the result;

- when the memory components of the two arguments differ, they need to be *weakened* by replacing memory fragments with novel instances of $\mathbf{lseg}_s$, with fresh symbolic sequence variables, and by checking inclusion holds using $\mathfrak{is\_le}_{\mathbb{S}}$.

To illustrate the second case, we consider the over-approximation of the two abstract states defined by $s_0^\sharp := (\alpha_0.\mathtt{n} \mapsto \alpha_1 * \alpha_0.\mathtt{d} \mapsto \alpha_3 * \mathbf{lseg}_s(\alpha_1, \alpha_2, S \boxdot), \sigma_0^\sharp)$ and $s_1^\sharp := (\mathbf{lseg}_s(\alpha_0, \alpha_1, S \boxdot) * \alpha_1.\mathtt{n} \mapsto \alpha_2 * \alpha_1.\mathtt{d} \mapsto \alpha_3, \sigma_1^\sharp)$. Clearly, the memory part of both states may be weakened to the same abstract memory $\mathbf{lseg}_s(\alpha_0, \alpha_2, S'' \boxdot)$ where S'' is fresh. This gives the shape specific part of the result. However, in the case of $s_0^\sharp$, this weakening holds under the constraint $S'' = [\alpha_3].S$, whereas it holds under the constraint $S'' = S'.[\alpha_3]$ in the case of $s_1^\sharp$. Therefore, the sequence abstract states should be updated according to these two constraints before calling the corresponding operator in the sequence domain, which produces $\mathfrak{join}_\Sigma(\mathfrak{guard}_\Sigma(S'' = [\alpha_3].S, \sigma_0^\sharp), \mathfrak{guard}_\Sigma(S'' = S'.[\alpha_3], \sigma_1^\sharp))$. Note that this weakening also generates numerical and multi-set constraints. This constraint synthesis issue is carried out by an extension of the inclusion checking algorithm that keeps track of the fresh variables introduced by the widening and accumulates constraints over these.

Theorem 6 (Soundness of $\mathfrak{join}_{\mathbb{S}}, \mathfrak{widen}_{\mathbb{S}}$ and its termination). *The upper bound operator* $\mathfrak{join}_{\mathbb{S}}, \mathfrak{widen}_{\mathbb{S}} : \mathbb{S}^\sharp \times \mathbb{S}^\sharp \to \mathbb{S}^\sharp$ *are sound in the sense that, for all* $s_0^\sharp, s_1^\sharp \in \mathbb{S}^\sharp$, *then* $\gamma_{\mathbb{S}}(s_0^\sharp) \cup \gamma_{\mathbb{S}}(s_1^\sharp) \subseteq \gamma_{\mathbb{S}}(\mathfrak{join}_{\mathbb{S}}(s_0^\sharp, s_1^\sharp))$ *and* $\gamma_{\mathbb{S}}(s_0^\sharp) \cup \gamma_{\mathbb{S}}(s_1^\sharp) \subseteq \gamma_{\mathbb{S}}(\mathfrak{widen}_{\mathbb{S}}(s_0^\sharp, s_1^\sharp))$. *Moreover,* $\mathfrak{widen}_{\mathbb{S}}$ *also ensures the termination property [17].*

4.5 Static Analysis of a Simple Language

The analysis of a command c is a function $[\![c]\!]^\sharp : \mathbb{S}^\sharp \to \mathbb{S}^\sharp$ that over-approximates $[\![c]\!]$. It is defined by induction over the syntax in Fig. 9. Note that the convergence of the sequence of abstract iterates follows from the termination property of $\mathfrak{widen}_{\mathbb{S}}$, and the analysis uses $\mathfrak{is\_le}_{\mathbb{S}}$ to detect stabilization. For conditional statements, we analyze the two branches separately after assuming the corresponding constraint, and we merge the two resulting states using $\mathfrak{join}_{\mathbb{S}}$. It is sound (the proof of soundness is classical [15] and proceeds by induction over the syntax):

Theorem 7 (Soundness). *For all command c,* $[\![c]\!] \circ \gamma_{\mathbb{S}} \dot{\subseteq} \gamma_{\mathbb{S}} \circ [\![c]\!]^\sharp$.

5 Shape and Sequence Predicates for Non-linear Structures

This section discusses the general inductive predicates used by our analysis. While Sect. 4 only considered basic list predicates so as to introduce the analysis in a simpler setup, we now show our analysis handles m-ary trees (thus including lists when $m = 1$), possibly with parent pointers. We require that the

$$\llbracket l = e \rrbracket^\sharp(s^\sharp) := \mathfrak{assign}_{\mathsf{S},l=e}(s^\sharp) \qquad \llbracket c_0; c_1 \rrbracket^\sharp(s^\sharp) := \llbracket c_1 \rrbracket^\sharp \circ \llbracket c_0 \rrbracket^\sharp(s^\sharp)$$
$$\llbracket \mathbf{if}(e)\{c_0\} \rrbracket^\sharp(s^\sharp) := \mathfrak{join}_{\mathsf{S}}\left(\llbracket c_0 \rrbracket^\sharp(\mathfrak{guard}_{\mathsf{S},e\neq 0}(s^\sharp)), \mathfrak{guard}_{\mathsf{S},e=0}(s^\sharp)\right)$$
$$\llbracket \mathbf{while}(e)\{c\} \rrbracket^\sharp(s^\sharp) := \mathfrak{guard}_{\mathsf{S},e=0}(\lim_n s_n^\sharp)$$
$$\text{where } s_0^\sharp := s^\sharp \text{ and } s_{n+1}^\sharp := \mathfrak{widen}_{\mathsf{S}}(s_n^\sharp, \llbracket c \rrbracket^\sharp(\mathfrak{guard}_{\mathsf{S},e\neq 0}(s_n^\sharp)))$$

Fig. 9. Abstract interpretation of a command

sequence arguments of inductive definitions denote (sub-)sets of elements stored in structure (we comment on this restriction in Remark 1). The following paragraphs show the specificities of sequence predicates for such data-structures, the derivation of segment predicates and how it affects analysis operations.

Segment Predicates and Sequence Information. Segment predicates such as **lseg** play a very important role in the analysis, e.g., to analyze data-structure traversals, as in Sect. 2. Basic analysis operations split or merge inductive predicates that describe full structures and segments. As we remarked in Sect. 4, sequence information needs to be maintained when such steps are performed and Lemma 1 provides the method to do so for **lseg**. As observed in Sect. 2, the method derived from Lemma 1 will not work for non linear structures.

Indeed, let us consider the tree segment predicate $\mathbf{treeseg}_s$ shown in Fig. 4, which describes all the possible ways to decompose memory states that store a full tree at node α_0 and where α_1 is the address of one of its subtrees. Equivalently, the memory can be decomposed into a tree segment between α_0 and α_1 and a full tree at root α_1. We note S_0 (resp., S_1) the sequence of elements in the whole structure (resp., the subtree). Figure 10 depicts all possible configurations. In the first case, the subtree and the tree are equal, so the segment is empty and $S_0 = S_1$. In the second case, the subtree at α_1 is a leftmost subtree and $S_0 = S_1.S_r$ for some S_r. The third case is symmetric. The fourth case is the most general and $S_0 = S_l.S_1.S_r$ for some S_l, S_r. Therefore, the most general definition of the sequence(s) of elements in the segment (when the subtree in shown blue is excluded) is $S_0 = S_l \boxdot S_r$, where $\boxdot$ is a placeholder that abstracts the sequence of the elements in the "missing" subtree, and where S_l, S_r may denote the empty sequence.

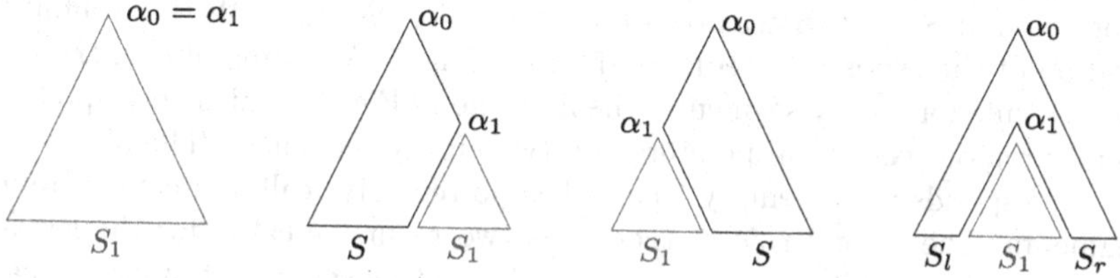

Fig. 10. Concatenation cases for tree segments and full tree predicates

Following this discussion, we now study concatenation of tree segment predicates. Let us assume two disjoint regions respectively abstracted by $\mathbf{treeseg}_s(\alpha, \alpha', S'_l \boxdot S'_r)$ and by $\mathbf{treeseg}_s(\alpha', \alpha'', S''_l \boxdot S''_r)$. Then, the union of these two regions may be abstracted by $\mathbf{treeseg}_s(\alpha, \alpha'', S_l \boxdot S_r)$ where $S_l = S'_l.S''_l$ and $S_r = S''_r.S'_r$. Note that the sequence expression attached to the latter segment is calculated as $S_l.S'_l \boxdot S'_r.S_r = (S_l \boxdot S_r)[\boxdot \leftarrow S'_l \boxdot S'_r]$. Similar reasoning may be carried out to concatenate a segment and a full tree predicate. Based on these observations, we propose a concatenation lemma for $\mathbf{treeseg}_s$:

Lemma 2 (Concatenation (tree case)). *We assume symbolic variables $\alpha, \alpha', \alpha''$ and sequence variables $S, S', S_l, S_r, S'_l, S'_r, S''_l, S''_r$.*

- *Let $m_0^\sharp := \mathbf{treeseg}_s(\alpha, \alpha', S'_l \boxdot S'_r) * \mathbf{tree}_s(\alpha', S')$, $m_1^\sharp := \mathbf{tree}_s(\alpha, S)$ $\sigma^\sharp := S = S'_l.S'.S'_r$. Then, $\gamma_{\mathbb{S}}(m_0^\sharp, \sigma^\sharp) \subseteq \gamma_{\mathbb{S}}(m_1^\sharp, \sigma^\sharp)$.*
- *Let $m_0^\sharp := \mathbf{treeseg}_s(\alpha, \alpha', S'_l \boxdot S'_r) * \mathbf{treeseg}_s(\alpha', \alpha'', S''_l \boxdot S''_r)$, $m_1^\sharp := \mathbf{treeseg}_s(\alpha, \alpha'', S_l \boxdot S_r)$ $\sigma^\sharp := S_l = S'_l.S''_l \wedge S_r = S''_r.S'_r$. Then, $\gamma_{\mathbb{S}}(m_0^\sharp, \sigma^\sharp) \subseteq \gamma_{\mathbb{S}}(m_1^\sharp, \sigma^\sharp)$.*

Derivation of Segment Predicates from Full Predicates. While inductive predicates (e.g., the definition of lists or trees) are user-supplied, our analysis automatically derives the corresponding segment predicates. Indeed, given a full predicate (like $\mathbf{tree}_s$) for an m-ary form of tree (including lists), the segment predicate is obtained by the sequence of steps below:

- each sequence argument S_i is replaced by a marked sequence $S_i \boxdot S'_i$,
- a rule describes empty segments; it abstracts an empty memory region, constrains its extremal points to be equal and its sequence contents to be empty;
- for each inductive rule that contains recursive calls to the inductive predicate, and for each such call c, the segment predicate should include a rule replacing c with a segment instance; moreover, in each such segment rule, the linearity of the sequence concatenations should be reflected by sequence constraints.

As an example, we illustrate this in the case of $\mathbf{tree}_s$:

Example 4 (Tree segments). The definition of $\mathbf{tree}_s$ is shown in Fig. 1. As it has one sequence parameter, the corresponding segment predicate has two, that we note S_0 and S_1 and writes down $\mathbf{treeseg}_s(\alpha, \alpha', S_0 \boxdot S_1)$. We now detail the derivation of the $\mathbf{treeseg}_s$ predicate shown in Fig. 4. As stated above, $\mathbf{treeseg}_s$ includes a rule for empty segments (the first one in Fig. 4), which corresponds to an empty region, two equal pointers and two empty sequences. The first rule of $\mathbf{tree}_s$ corresponds to the empty tree; it has no recursive call and cannot appear in segments. The second rule of $\mathbf{tree}_s$ has two recursive calls (for the left and right subtrees), thus, it gives rise to two rules in $\mathbf{treeseg}_s$, that stand for cases where the segment is in the left (resp., right) subtree. Finally, we consider the constraints over sequences in the last rule (right subtree). Given the notation in Fig. 4, the sequence of values in the whole tree is the argument $S \boxdot S'$ of

$\mathbf{treeseg}_s$ which is equal to $S_l.\mathtt{[}v\mathtt{]}.S_r \boxdot S'_r$ in the last rule. This equality entails the constraints $S = S_l.\mathtt{[}v\mathtt{]}.S_r$ and $S' = S'_r$ which thus appear in the last rule of $\mathbf{treeseg}_s$.

Remark 1 (Limitation of sequence arguments). We observe that the inference of the sequence constraints by linearity as shown in Example 4 can only be achieved since the sequence constraints in $\mathbf{tree}_s$ specify that its segment argument collects a set of elements found at some fields in the structure. As an example, the analysis would not support an alternative definition of $\mathbf{tree}_s$ where the inductive rule would have the sequence constraint $S = \mathbf{sort}(S_l.\mathtt{[v]}.S_r)$, as it does not allow the derivation of precise constraints over sub-sequences for segments. We note that this limitation does not prevent capturing precisely binary search trees in the product abstract domain of Definition 5 with element $\mathbf{tree}_s(\alpha, S) \wedge S = \mathbf{sort}(S)$; instead, it only requires the shape predicate be written in a certain way.

Analysis. The analysis requires users to supply inductive predicates for full structures as well as target pre- and post-conditions. Segment predicates are inferred automatically as shown in the previous paragraph, as well as the appropriate concatenation lemma. Finally, the analysis operators are similar to those shown in Sect. 4, except that they use the concatenation property inferred from the definition of the full structure inductive predicate. For instance, when using the tree inductive predicate of Fig. 1, the analysis infers the segment of Fig. 4 and the concatenation Lemma 2. The analysis satisfies the soundness property of Theorem 7. To conclude the section, we discuss a couple of steps of the computation of widening in the analysis of the program in Fig. 2.

Example 5 (Inclusion checking). We consider the following abstract states:

- $s_0^\sharp = (\alpha.\mathbf{l} \mapsto \alpha_0 * \alpha.\mathbf{d} \mapsto \alpha_1 * \alpha.\mathbf{r} \mapsto \alpha_2 * \mathbf{tree}_s(\alpha_2, S_r), \sigma_0^\sharp)$;
- $s_1^\sharp = (\mathbf{treeseg}_s(\alpha, \alpha_0, S \boxdot S'), \sigma_1^\sharp)$.

Both $s_0^\sharp$ and $s_1^\sharp$ appear during the widening at the first iteration. We study the evaluation of the inclusion test $\mathfrak{is\_le}_{\mathbb{S}}(s_0^\sharp, s_1^\sharp)$. We first remark the following unfoldings (where $\alpha_3, \alpha_4, \alpha_5, S_l$, and S'_l are fresh) yield a similar abstract memory, up to existentially quantified symbolic variable names:

$$\begin{aligned} s_1^\sharp \rightsquigarrow\ & (\alpha.\mathbf{l} \mapsto \alpha_3 * \alpha.\mathbf{d} \mapsto \alpha_4 * \alpha.\mathbf{r} \mapsto \alpha_5 * \mathbf{treeseg}_s(\alpha_3, \alpha_0, S_l \boxdot S'_l) \\ & * \mathbf{tree}_s(\alpha_5, S_r), \sigma_0^\sharp) \wedge S = S_l \wedge S' = S'_l.[\alpha_4].S_r \\ \rightsquigarrow\ & (\alpha.\mathbf{l} \mapsto \alpha_3 * \alpha.\mathbf{d} \mapsto \alpha_4 * \alpha.\mathbf{r} \mapsto \alpha_5 * \mathbf{emp} * \mathbf{tree}_s(\alpha_5, S_r), \\ & \sigma_0^\sharp) \wedge S = S_l \wedge S' = S'_l.[\alpha_4].S_r \wedge S_l = [] \wedge S'_l = [] \wedge \alpha_0 = \alpha_3 \end{aligned}$$

By the definition of $\mathfrak{is\_le}_{\mathbb{S}}$ in Sect. 4.4, $\mathfrak{is\_le}_{\mathbb{S}}(s_0^\sharp, s_1^\sharp)$ returns true if and only if $\mathfrak{is\_le}_{\Sigma}(\sigma_0^\sharp, \sigma_1^\sharp)$, $\mathfrak{verify}_{\Sigma}(\sigma_0^\sharp, S = [])$ and $\mathfrak{verify}_{\Sigma}(\sigma_0^\sharp, S' = [\alpha_1].S_r)$ all return true.

Example 6 (Widening). We now study the computation of the first widening in the analysis of the program shown in Sect. 2. For brevity, we only consider the second disjunct after the condition. The arguments of widening of abstract memory states and the result are shown in Fig. 11. As mentioned in Sect. 4.4, the widening operator seeks for regions that can be described in a similar manner in the both of its arguments, possibly after weakening them. Matching colors in Fig. 11 highlight pairings of similar regions. Recall that all symbolic variables $(\alpha, \alpha_0, \ldots)$ are existentially quantified within a same state. We observe the terms in blue, green and purple are pairwise equal and require no weakening. The areas in red though are not equal. For clarity, we add an **emp** term in $m_0^\sharp$. As observed in Example 5, the matching terms in $m_1^\sharp$ can be weakened into $\mathbf{treeseg}_s(\alpha_0, \alpha_1, S_1 \boxdot S_2)$, provided $S_1 = \texttt{[]}$ and $S_2 = \texttt{[}\delta\texttt{]}.S_r$. The same holds for **emp** in $m_0^\sharp$. The table in the bottom of Fig. 11 summarizes the correspondence between existentially quantified symbolic variables that realizes the association of regions.

The above paragraph describes the computation of the abstract memory state shown in Fig. 3(c). The computation of the sequence abstract state of Fig. 3(c) proceeds by application of $\mathfrak{widen}_\Sigma$.

$$\underbrace{\begin{pmatrix} \&\texttt{t} \mapsto \alpha_0 \\ * \ \&\texttt{c} \mapsto \alpha_0 \\ * \ \mathbf{emp} \\ * \ \mathbf{tree}_s(\alpha_0, S) \end{pmatrix}}_{m_0^\sharp} \quad \underbrace{\begin{pmatrix} \&\texttt{t} \mapsto \alpha_0 * \&\texttt{c} \mapsto \alpha_1 \\ * \ \alpha_0.\texttt{l} \mapsto \alpha_1 * \mathbf{tree}_s(\alpha_1, S_l) \\ * \ \alpha_0.\texttt{d} \mapsto \alpha_2 \\ * \ \alpha_0.\texttt{r} \mapsto \alpha_3 * \mathbf{tree}_s(\alpha_3, S_r) \end{pmatrix}}_{m_1^\sharp} \quad \underbrace{\begin{pmatrix} \&\texttt{t} \mapsto \alpha \\ * \ \&\texttt{c} \mapsto \alpha' \\ * \ \mathbf{treeseg}_s(\alpha, \alpha', S_1 \boxdot S_2) \\ * \ \mathbf{tree}_s(\alpha', S_0) \end{pmatrix}}_{m_f^\sharp}$$

$m_f^\sharp$	α	α'	S_0	S_1	S_2
$m_0^\sharp$	α_0	α_0	S	[]	[]
$m_1^\sharp$	α_0	α_1	S_l	[]	$\texttt{[}\alpha_2\texttt{]}.S_r$

Fig. 11. Shape union between states from Figs. 3(a) and 3(b) (Greek letters denote existentially quantified symbolic variables; identical colors denote similar regions).

6 Implementation and Evaluation

In this section, we report on the implementation and evaluation of the product shape and sequence analysis. We consider the following research questions:

- **(RQ1)** Is the combined analysis of Sect. 4 and Sect. 5 precise enough to prove functional properties on programs implementing classical algorithms over dynamic data-structures (like lists, sorted lists, and binary search trees), and does it help a baseline analysis verify structural invariants are preserved?
- **(RQ2)** Can this analysis successfully verify real-world C libraries?
- **(RQ3)** How significant is the overhead of the combined analysis compared to the baseline?

Table 1. Experimental results on custom examples (Time in milliseconds averaged over 100 runs. For loop iterations, disjoint loops are separated by a semicolon, nested loops by a comma, and the first number corresponds to the outer loop. For inner loops, we take the maximum number of iterations needed to stabilize it.)

Example	without seq			with seq parameters					
	time	#iter	**PrSafe**	time				#iter	**PrSafe**
	all		verified	all	num	seq	shape		+ **Fc** verified
			Singly linked list						
Push	4.0		✓	4.8	0.5	0.5	0.9		✓
Pop	5.1		✓	5.4	0.9	1.4	0.8		✓
Pop (empty)	4.9		✓	4.7	0.8	0.5	1.4		✓
concat	6.5	2	✓	15.7	3.4	3.3	2.7	2	✓
deep copy	12.1	2	✓	20.4	3.7	2.9	5.5	2	✓
length	9.5	3	✓	45.0	22.5	5.0	8.1	3	✓
insert at position	19.0	3	✓	101.9	61.3	7.9	12.2	3	✓
remove at position	17.2	3	✓	92.5	55.5	6.5	12.5	3	✓
inserting in a sorted list	13.5	3	✓	82.5	39.0	10.0	9.2	3	✓
minimum	11.8	3	✓	92.3	42.4	11.1	16.8	3	✓
maximum	11.8	3	✓	93.2	42.9	11.2	17.0	3	✓
insertion sort	24.6	2, 2	✓	714.6	328.6	90.0	126.3	4, 3	✓
bubble sort	40.6	2;2,3	✓ (†)	776.3	399.5	89.2	141.5	3;3,3	✓ (†)
merge	36.8	4	✓	352.2	180.9	41.0	54.9	4	✓
			Binary trees						
Delete leftmost	11.2	3	✓	80.5	38.2	9.4	12.0	3	✓
Delete rightmost	11.5	2	✓	58.1	27.5	6.8	7.6	2	✓
			Binary search trees						
Insertion	25.2	2	✓	150.4	58.0	17.2	15.5	2	✓
Delete max	22.9	2	✗	141.2	68.6	15.2	17.2	2	✓
Delete min	22.0	3	✗	177.9	87.9	19.2	22.8	3	✓
Search (present)	26.6	2	✓	107.2	48.6	15.7	14.4	2	✓
Search (absent)	24.0	3	✓	76.7	29.4	11.4	11.7	3	✓
BST to list (heap sort)	23.8	3	✓	76.5	29.2	11.4	11.7	3	✓
list to BST (heap sort)	34.2	2,2	✓	408.0	188.0	56.5	68.4	3,2	✓

Implementation. We have implemented the sequence abstract domain and the product with the shape abstraction of the MemCAD static analyzer [1,38]. The analysis inputs C programs and user-supplied inductive predicates describing data-structures together with pre- and post-conditions and attempts to verify them, as well as absence of runtime errors. We set convex polyhedra [20] implemented in the Apron library [35] as numerical abstraction and an extension of [39] as multi-set abstraction.

Experiments. We consider two sets of experiments. The first one (Table 1) consists of custom implementations of classical algorithms over lists, sorted lists, and binary search trees and includes sorting, insertion and deletion algorithms. The second (Table 2) collects list data-structure implementations taken from the

Table 2. Experimental results on libraries programs (Time in milliseconds averaged over 100 runs. For loop iterations, disjoint loops are separated by a semicolon, nested loops by a comma, and the first number corresponds to the outer loop. For inner loops, we take the maximum number of iterations needed to stabilize it.)

Example	without seq			with seq parameters					
	time	#iter	**PrSafe**	time				#iter	**PrSafe**
	all		verified	all	num	seq	shape		+ **Fc** verified
			Linux lists						
Init	1.1		✓	2.6	0.2	0.3	1.1		✓
Input	13.6		✓	21.4	2.7	2.4	8.2		✓
Output	22.7		✓	31.5	4.8	4.8	10.5		✓
Output (empty)	33.8		✓	9.3	1.4	1.0	2.5		✓
			FreeRTOS lists						
vListInit	4.3		✓	6.1	1.3	0.4	0.6		✓
vListInsertEnd	23.8		✓	40.3	10.8	1.8	5.3		✓
vListInsert	87.4	4	✓	370.5	202.4	27.2	37.9	4	✓
vListRemove	47.5		✓	163.4	82.6	9.2	20.0		✓
			GDSL (lists)						
Flush	24.3	2	✓	59.4	18.4	5.4	16.1	2	✓
Free	35.3	2	✓ (†)	79.9	25.1	7.4	24.0	2	✓ (†)
Remove head (empty)	34.1		✓	111.9	50.9	6.5	25.4		✓
Remove head (non-empty)	34.0		✓	16.3	5.7	1.1	3.7		✓
Remove tail (empty)	49.5		✓	284.8	165.0	13.6	39.3		✓
Remove tail (non-empty)	49.5		✓	16.2	5.7	1.1	3.6		✓
Search max	69.7	5	✓	708.4	429.7	43.1	145.7	5	PrSafe **Fc**
Search min	69.4	5	✓	634.0	380.3	35.4	131.2	5	PrSafe **Fc**
Search by position	104.5	3;2	✗(†)	1182.8	796.3	40.7	108.2	3;3	✓ (†)

Linux [54] and FreeRTOS [33] operating systems as well as the Generic data-structure library (GDSL) [23], which all involve specificities like back pointers or sentinel nodes. For each data-structure, we provide an inductive definition written in the DSL of MemCAD. This amounts to a single definition a few lines long for each series of tests. For each test, we also specify the pre- and post-condition of procedures. When a procedure may behave differently depending on the shape of their input, we provide two pre-/post-condition pairs. This occurs for the "Pop" function, which does nothing when applied to the empty list. Two target properties are studied:

- **PrSafe**: absence of memory errors and structural preservation (with respect to list or tree invariants but without checking anything about their contents);
- **Fc**: partial functional correctness (including sortedness and the preservation of the elements stored in data-structures).

We ran the experiments on a machine with an i7-8700 processor with 32 Gb of RAM running Ubuntu 18.04. For each test case, we run the analysis *without* and then *with* sequence abstraction to compare runtimes and check if the analyses prove the expected property. When using the analysis without sequence abstraction, only **PrSafe** is considered (this abstraction cannot express **Fc**), whereas the analysis of sequences attempts to discharge both **PrSafe** *and* **Fc**. Table 1 displays raw results for the first series of tests. Table 2 shows the results of the main tests in the second series of tests.

Verification of Complex Properties. As shown in Table 1, the analysis with sequences fully verifies both memory safety and functional correctness (**PrSafe** and **Fc**) for all target codes including three different list sorting programs, operations on binary search trees as well as heap sort (elements of a list are all inserted in an empty binary search tree and collected in a left to right order back into a list). These examples all require the inference of fairly involved invariants. The analysis without sequences can only verify **PrSafe**, yet it fails to do so in several examples, where the use of sequences actually also lets the analysis verify **PrSafe** (in addition to **Fc**). This result is somewhat surprising, as we would not expect sequence information be required to establish basic safety. One caveat is that one example (bubble sort) required the manual insertion of a directive to MemCAD to delay folding. We conjecture the shape folding operator could be improved to avoid this. All other analyses are fully automatic. We conclude the product with sequences not only allows to prove **Fc** even in challenging cases, but may also help with **PrSafe**.

Verification of Real-World Libraries. We now consider Table 2. These examples involve lists with invariants that are considerably more sophisticated than $\mathbf{lseg}_s$, as they are all doubly-linked lists with headers. While GDSL lists contain a pointer to stored value blocks, both Linux and FreeRTOS lists are intrusive lists in the sense of the Linux kernel terminology: the `C` struct containing the `n` and `prev` fields is a substructure of the list node, which implies structure accesses require more complex pointer operations. FreeRTOS lists explicitly store a pointer from substructures to owners, whereas Linux lists rely on pointer arithmetic to access containing blocks. Finally, both FreeRTOS and GDSL lists have a header that stores the number of elements in the lists. FreeRTOS list nodes store a pointer to this header. The analysis with sequences proves both **PrSafe** and **Fc** for all Linux and FreeRTOS primitives. It was also able to fully verify almost all the GDSL list library, although two cases required a manual directive to prevent aggressive folding both with and without sequences (as for bubblesort in Table 1) (they are marked with (†) in the tables). Only two functions for the extraction of minimal/maximal values could not be fully verified with respect to **Fc** (note that **PrSafe** still gets proved): in these codes, the memory widening is too aggressive and folds the node storing the function results, which prevents proving that the returned value is indeed the extremal value in the sequence. All other examples not included in Table 2 are verified. We conclude the analysis handles real-world programs.

Overhead. We now compare performance between the analyses with/without sequences in Tables 1 and 2. While the overhead is modest for the smaller programs, it becomes higher for the more challenging cases, up to roughly 10x-20x. While significant, this cost should be considered in comparison to the much stronger properties proved (i.e., not only **PrSafe** but also partial correctness **Fc** in addition to **PrSafe**). We found two reasons for this increase. First, as shown in the tables, most of the increase is accounted for by the numerical abstract domain partly due to the larger number of symbolic variables that stand for sequence bounds. We believe this overhead could be much reduced with a finer-grained numerical domain packing [7,52]. By contrast, the time spent in memory and sequence domains remains reasonable. Second, the analysis with sequences requires greater numbers of abstract iterates to stabilize loop iterates, as shown in the tables, which explains an important slowdown. This is to be expected due to the more complex value constraints (including polyhedra) used in the analysis with sequences.

7 Related Works

In this section, we discuss previous works on the abstractions of sequences stored in data-structures.

Linear and Contiguous Structures (Arrays and Strings). Several previous works have tried to tie properties of container data-structures with properties of their contents. In particular, [28,29] have extended array abstractions with basic contents properties. More recently [30] introduced array segmentations and [19] made the computation of the array segmentations dynamic during the analysis. The latter two can express that an array is sorted and verify that a function produces sorted arrays. However, they do so with specific predicates rather than an abstraction for sequences. Thus, they cannot express that the set of elements in an array is preserved, which is required to prove a sorting function correct. By contrast, our sequence abstraction handles both sortedness and contents preservation.

Strings and buffers also motivated many research works, as operations on them may incur a security risk. In particular, improper handling of zero terminated strings make opens the door to buffer overrun attacks. Therefore, works such as CSSV [25] abstract the presence or absence of zeroes in strings and their positions in order to verify buffer operations. Besides zeroes, these works do not keep any contents' information.

As noted earlier, several recent works applied concepts such as regular expressions and automata in order to build string abstract domains, that convey precise contents information [3,45,47]. These works are typically aimed at inferring precise information on strings that denote pieces of programs meant to be computed and evaluated at runtime as in the case of JavaScript's `eval` construction. Automata and regular expressions are most adequate for such target properties. More recently, [4] extended these works with length and element position constraints. These abstractions are not aimed at numerical sequences, and fail to express sortedness. By contrast, our sequence abstraction relies on length, extremal elements and sortedness constraints and fails to express regular expressions-based properties as these would not be useful for our intended application. An interesting area of future work would be to build a reduced product of sequence abstractions to combine the expressiveness of these works and of ours.

Shape Analyses for Dynamic Data-Structures. Many abstractions for dynamic data-structures have been proposed. Sagiv *et al.* introduced a shape analysis based on three value logic in [51], that was later extended to handle more complex data-structures such as tree [42]. The seminal work by Reynolds [50], introduced separation logic, that many analyses including ours rely upon. Separation logic has been used in order to reason over not only sequential programs [12] but also concurrent programs [48,57] and to prove properties like linearizability of concurrent data structures [56]. It serves as a basis for structure abstraction in several static analyzers like Smallfoot [12], Facebook Infer [13] (which also performs bi-abduction to synthesize pre- and post-condition pairs), Forester [31] (which uses automata to represent abstract states), and MemCAD [38] (which features a modularized abstract domain). Bi-abduction methods have also been extended to infer inductive predicates on a per-function basis [37] or to infer pre- and post-conditions for programs manipulating lists and using bit-level memory accesses and pointer arithmetic [32]. All the shape abstractions mentioned so far can only keep track of very limited contents properties.

Indeed, inferring precise information about the contents of dynamic data-structures is notoriously difficult, since the memory abstraction layout changes depending on the program point which makes abstraction complex. A first approach to this issue consists in splitting the analysis in two phases, where the first analysis infers only structural invariants and translates the initial program into a purely numerical program, that is taken as input by the second analysis, that discovers numerical invariants. This technique has been applied by [27,43] in order to infer complexity bounds and verify termination of programs based on information on the size of the data-structures. A second approach [14] consists of a reduced product between a memory abstract domain and a numerical abstract domain. While harder to implement, it ensures information can be communicated in both directions between the memory and the value abstract domains, whereas the staged analysis approach only lets the value abstract domain benefit from memory layout information. More recently, [39] combines shape and set abstractions with a reduced product which allows verifying programs on graphs. As it only considers set constraints, it does not capture any order information.

The tools CINV [8] and CELIA [9] (extended with interprocedural analysis support in [11]) are the most closely related to our approach. These static analyzers handle list manipulating programs and are parameterized by an abstract domain called a *data-word domain* to reason on the structure and contents of lists by attaching size or set constraints to them, or constraints quantified over the position of elements, which allows expressing sortedness. Although the heap abstraction does not make explicit use of separation logic the list abstraction follows a similar structure. A first important difference with our work is that CINV and CELIA only handle singly-linked lists, whereas our analysis supports a large range of inductive definitions included doubly linked-lists, trees, binary search trees with and without parent pointers. Indeed, our approach integrates sequence reasoning into a shape analysis that can be parameterized by a wide variety of inductive predicates. This more general scope requires extensions to the analysis algorithms, such as the automatical inference of concatenation lemmas (Lemma 1 and 2) and the use of abstract operators based on them. A second difference comes from the sequence domain and the interaction with it. The data-word domain to handle sortedness relies on a decidable fragment of first order array theory based on constraints of the form $\forall \mathbf{y}, P(\mathbf{y}) \Rightarrow U(\mathbf{y}, Q_1, \ldots)$, where the guard constraint $P(\mathbf{y})$ belongs to a pre-defined, user-provided set of *guard-patterns* constraining the index variables y_j, and U is a conjunction of linear constraints on y_j and $Q_i[y_j]$. This domain does not manipulate symbolic sequence expressions but rather follows a structural approach. For example, the concatenation constraint $S = S_1.S_2$ is expressed as $\forall y_1, y_2, y_1 < \mathtt{len}_{S_1} \wedge y_2 < \mathtt{len}_{S_2} \Rightarrow S_1[y_1] = S[y_1] \wedge S_2[y_2] = S[y_2 + \mathtt{len}_{S_2}]$. Therefore, it requires the user to specify prior to the analysis the appropriate guard pattern. Our sequence abstraction requires no such parameterization.

Provers for Memory and Contents Properties. Separation logic has also been used as foundation for verification tools based on entailment checking procedures, some of which also consider contents properties. Songbird [53] uses a sequent-based approach to attempt deciding implication in a fragment of separation logic enriched with pure predicates. The procedure presented in [34] relies on tree automata to decide implications that involve inductive predicates. SLAD [10] decides entailment on a logic for singly-linked lists and the data stored in them. It handles order constraints on linear structures like lists and arrays. More recently, [22] used bi-abduction to reason about ordered data by explicitly storing bounds on elements in the inductive predicate. This work only considers full structure predicates and does not handle segment predicates. All these tools can be used to discharge implication proof obligations and can be used in verification tools where invariants are either manually written or inferred by some other means.

Additionally, separation logic is also heavily used in approaches based on proof assistants [16]. In that case, contents properties are naturally expressed in the proof assistant language.

Solvers for Sequence Properties. Finally, we remark that our language of sequence constraints based on concatenation of atoms has some similarity with the string logic that can be found in some decision procedures. Though the logic of word equations with at least two atoms is known to be undecidable [49], its quantifier free fragment has a PSPACE complete decision procedure [44]. Following the work of [2] that classifies the field of string constraints solving in three main branches, the automata based approach, using finite state automata to represent the set of constraints [40], the word based approach, that decomposes constraints using algebraic results such as Levi's lemma [6], and the unfolding based approach, which expresses each string variable as a bounded sequence of variables such as bit vectors [36], our abstraction can be categorized as mostly word-based. To the best of our knowledge, no SMT solver is able to reason on the sortedness of word expressions. We refer the reader to [2] for a comprehensive survey on string constraint solving. By comparison with these works, we provide an abstract domain interface on top of the sequence operation, which allows its use in a static analysis tool, following an instance of reduced product [18].

8 Conclusion and Future Works

In this paper, we presented a novel sequence abstract domain that relies on existing numerical and set abstractions, and extended a shape analysis with sequence reasoning. We demonstrated that the resulting analysis can be used in order to verify not only memory safety or structural preservation but also far more advanced correctness properties on a wide variety of inductive structures including various kinds of lists and trees. In particular, it could prove the functional correctness of several list sorting programs and of operations over binary search trees.

A combination of our analysis with a termination analysis [27,55] could verify not only partial correctness but also full correctness, which would be a first interesting direction for future works. Defining a reduced product over abstract domains for sequences would be also a useful research direction, as it would allow to strengthen the expressiveness of the analysis. Last, the evaluation also shows that performance of the combined analysis could be improved with the use of a more efficient dynamic packing [52] for relational constraints.

Acknowledgment. The authors want to thank Thierry Martinez for his work on libraries used by the MemCAD analyzer. This work was supported by the VeriAMOS ANR-18-CE25-0010 French ANR project.

References

1. Artifact for "A Product of Shape and Sequence Abstractions". Zenodo (2023). https://doi.org/10.5281/zenodo.8186871
2. Amadini, R.: A survey on string constraint solving. ACM Comput. Surv. **55**, 1–38 (2021)
3. Arceri, V., Mastroeni, I.: An automata-based abstract semantics for string manipulation languages. In: VPT@Programming (2019)
4. Arceri, V., Olliaro, M., Cortesi, A., Ferrara, P.: Relational string abstract domains. In: Finkbeiner, B., Wies, T. (eds.) VMCAI 2022. LNCS, vol. 13182, pp. 20–42. Springer, Cham (2022). https://doi.org/10.1007/978-3-030-94583-1_2
5. Assaf, M., Naumann, D.A., Signoles, J., Totel, E., Tronel, F.: Hypercollecting semantics and its application to static analysis of information flow. In: POPL (2017)

6. Berzish, M., Ganesh, V., Zheng, Y.: Z3str3: a string solver with theory-aware heuristics. In: FMCAD (2017)
7. Blanchet, B., et al.: A static analyzer for large safety-critical software. In: PLDI (2003)
8. Bouajjani, A., Drăgoi, C., Enea, C., Rezine, A., Sighireanu, M.: Invariant synthesis for programs manipulating lists with unbounded data. In: Touili, T., Cook, B., Jackson, P. (eds.) CAV 2010. LNCS, vol. 6174, pp. 72–88. Springer, Heidelberg (2010). https://doi.org/10.1007/978-3-642-14295-6_8
9. Bouajjani, A., Drăgoi, C., Enea, C., Sighireanu, M.: Abstract domains for automated reasoning about list-manipulating programs with infinite data. In: Kuncak, V., Rybalchenko, A. (eds.) VMCAI 2012. LNCS, vol. 7148, pp. 1–22. Springer, Heidelberg (2012). https://doi.org/10.1007/978-3-642-27940-9_1
10. Bouajjani, A., Drăgoi, C., Enea, C., Sighireanu, M.: Accurate invariant checking for programs manipulating lists and arrays with infinite data. In: Chakraborty, S., Mukund, M. (eds.) ATVA 2012. LNCS, pp. 167–182. Springer, Heidelberg (2012). https://doi.org/10.1007/978-3-642-33386-6_14
11. Bouajjani, A., Drăgoi, C., Enea, C., Sighireanu, M.: On inter-procedural analysis of programs with lists and data. In: PLDI (2011)
12. Calcagno, C., Distefano, D., O'Hearn, P.W., Yang, H.: Footprint analysis: a shape analysis that discovers preconditions. In: Nielson, H.R., Filé, G. (eds.) SAS 2007. LNCS, vol. 4634, pp. 402–418. Springer, Heidelberg (2007). https://doi.org/10.1007/978-3-540-74061-2_25
13. Calcagno, C., Distefano, D., O'Hearn, P., Yang, H.: Compositional shape analysis by means of bi-abduction. In: POPL (2009)
14. Chang, B.Y.E., Rival, X.: Relational inductive shape analysis. In: POPL. ACM (2008)
15. Chang, B.E., Dragoi, C., Manevich, R., Rinetzky, N., Rival, X.: Shape analysis. FNT (1–2) (2020)
16. Charguéraud, A.: Characteristic formulae for the verification of imperative programs. In: ICFP (2011)
17. Cousot, P., Cousot, R.: Abstract interpretation: a unified lattice model for static analysis of programs by construction or approximation of fixpoints. In: POPL. ACM (1977)
18. Cousot, P., Cousot, R.: Systematic design of program analysis frameworks. In: POPL (1979)
19. Cousot, P., Cousot, R., Logozzo, F.: A parametric segmentation functor for fully automatic and scalable array content analysis. In: POPL (2011)
20. Cousot, P., Halbwachs, N.: Automatic discovery of linear restraints among variables of a program. In: POPL (1978)
21. Cox, A., Chang, B.-Y.E., Rival, X.: Automatic analysis of open objects in dynamic language programs. In: Müller-Olm, M., Seidl, H. (eds.) SAS 2014. LNCS, vol. 8723, pp. 134–150. Springer, Cham (2014). https://doi.org/10.1007/978-3-319-10936-7_9
22. Curry, C., Le, Q.L.: Bi-abduction for shapes with ordered data (2020). arXiv https://arxiv.org/abs/2006.10439
23. Darnis, N.: The generic data-structure library (2004). https://directory.fsf.org/wiki/GDSL
24. Distefano, D., Fähndrich, M., Logozzo, F., O'Hearn, P.: Scaling static analyses at Facebook. CACM **62**, 62–70 (2019)
25. Dor, N., Rodeh, M., Sagiv, S.: CSSV: towards a realistic tool for statically detecting all buffer overflows in C. In: PLDI (2003)

26. Ferrara, P., Burato, E., Spoto, F.: Security analysis of the OWASP benchmark with Julia. In: ITASEC (2017)
27. Fiedor, T., Holík, L., Rogalewicz, A., Sinn, M., Vojnar, T., Zuleger, F.: From shapes to amortized complexity. In: Dillig, I., Palsberg, J. (eds.) VMCAI 2018. LNCS, vol. 10747, pp. 205–225. Springer, Cham (2018). https://doi.org/10.1007/978-3-319-73721-8_10
28. Gopan, D., Reps, T.W., Sagiv, S.: A framework for numeric analysis of array operations. In: POPL (2005)
29. Gulwani, S., McCloskey, B., Tiwari, A.: Lifting abstract interpreters to quantified logical domains. In: POPL (2008)
30. Halbwachs, N., Péron, M.: Discovering properties about arrays in simple programs. In: PLDI (2008)
31. Holík, L., Lengál, O., Rogalewicz, A., Šimáček, J., Vojnar, T.: Fully automated shape analysis based on forest automata. In: Sharygina, N., Veith, H. (eds.) CAV 2013. LNCS, vol. 8044, pp. 740–755. Springer, Heidelberg (2013). https://doi.org/10.1007/978-3-642-39799-8_52
32. Holík, L., Peringer, P., Rogalewicz, A., Šoková, V., Vojnar, T., Zuleger, F.: Low-level bi-abduction. In: ECOOP (2022)
33. A. Inc.: The freertos kernel (2022). https://github.com/FreeRTOS
34. Iosif, R., Rogalewicz, A., Vojnar, T.: Deciding entailments in inductive separation logic with tree automata. In: Cassez, F., Raskin, J.-F. (eds.) ATVA 2014. LNCS, vol. 8837, pp. 201–218. Springer, Cham (2014). https://doi.org/10.1007/978-3-319-11936-6_15
35. Jeannet, B., Miné, A.: APRON: a library of numerical abstract domains for static analysis. In: Bouajjani, A., Maler, O. (eds.) CAV 2009. LNCS, vol. 5643, pp. 661–667. Springer, Heidelberg (2009). https://doi.org/10.1007/978-3-642-02658-4_52
36. Kiezun, A., Ganesh, V., Artzi, S., Guo, P.J., Hooimeijer, P., Ernst, M.D.: HAMPI: a solver for word equations over strings, regular expressions, and context-free grammars. ACM Trans. Softw. Eng. Methodol. **21**, 1–28 (2013)
37. Le, Q.L., Gherghina, C., Qin, S., Chin, W.-N.: Shape analysis via second-order bi-abduction. In: Biere, A., Bloem, R. (eds.) CAV 2014. LNCS, vol. 8559, pp. 52–68. Springer, Cham (2014). https://doi.org/10.1007/978-3-319-08867-9_4
38. Li, H., Berenger, F., Chang, B.Y.E., Rival, X.: Semantic-directed clumping of disjunctive abstract states. In: POPL (2017)
39. Li, H., Rival, X., Chang, B.-Y.E.: Shape analysis for unstructured sharing. In: Blazy, S., Jensen, T. (eds.) SAS 2015. LNCS, vol. 9291, pp. 90–108. Springer, Heidelberg (2015). https://doi.org/10.1007/978-3-662-48288-9_6
40. Liang, T., Reynolds, A., Tinelli, C., Barrett, C., Deters, M.: A DPLL(T) theory solver for a theory of strings and regular expressions. In: Biere, A., Bloem, R. (eds.) CAV 2014. LNCS, vol. 8559, pp. 646–662. Springer, Cham (2014). https://doi.org/10.1007/978-3-319-08867-9_43
41. Liu, J., Chen, L., Rival, X.: Automatic verification of embedded system code manipulating dynamic structures stored in contiguous regions. IEEE Trans. Comput. Aided Des. Integr. Circuits Syst. **37**, 2311–2322 (2018)
42. Loginov, A., Reps, T., Sagiv, M.: Automated verification of the Deutsch-Schorr-Waite tree-traversal algorithm. In: Yi, K. (ed.) SAS 2006. LNCS, vol. 4134, pp. 261–279. Springer, Heidelberg (2006). https://doi.org/10.1007/11823230_17
43. Magill, S., Tsai, M.H., Lee, P., Tsay, Y.K.: Automatic numeric abstractions for heap-manipulating programs. In: POPL (2010)
44. Makanin, G.S.: The problem of solvability of equations in a free semigroup. Math. USSR-Sbornik **32**(4) (1977)

45. Midtgaard, J., Nielson, F., Nielson, H.R.: A parametric abstract domain for lattice-valued regular expressions. In: Rival, X. (ed.) SAS 2016. LNCS, vol. 9837, pp. 338–360. Springer, Heidelberg (2016). https://doi.org/10.1007/978-3-662-53413-7_17
46. Miné, A.: The octagon abstract domain. HOSC **19**, 31–100 (2006). https://doi.org/10.1007/s10990-006-8609-1
47. Negrini, L., Arceri, V., Ferrara, P., Cortesi, A.: Twinning automata and regular expressions for string static analysis. In: Henglein, F., Shoham, S., Vizel, Y. (eds.) VMCAI 2021. LNCS, vol. 12597, pp. 267–290. Springer, Cham (2021). https://doi.org/10.1007/978-3-030-67067-2_13
48. O'Hearn, P.W.: Resources, concurrency and local reasoning. In: Gardner, P., Yoshida, N. (eds.) CONCUR 2004. LNCS, vol. 3170, pp. 49–67. Springer, Heidelberg (2004). https://doi.org/10.1007/978-3-540-28644-8_4
49. Quine, W.V.: Concatenation as a basis for arithmetic. J. Symb. Logic **11**(4) (1946). https://doi.org/10.2307/2268308
50. Reynolds, J.: Separation logic: a logic for shared mutable data structures. In: LICS (2002)
51. Sagiv, M., Reps, T., Whilhelm, R.: Solving shape-analysis problems in languages with destructive updating. TOPLAS **20**, 1–50 (1998)
52. Singh, G., Püschel, M., Vechev, M.T.: Fast polyhedra abstract domain. In: POPL (2017)
53. Ta, Q.-T., Le, T.C., Khoo, S.-C., Chin, W.-N.: Automated mutual explicit induction proof in separation logic. In: Fitzgerald, J., Heitmeyer, C., Gnesi, S., Philippou, A. (eds.) FM 2016. LNCS, vol. 9995, pp. 659–676. Springer, Cham (2016). https://doi.org/10.1007/978-3-319-48989-6_40
54. Torvalds, L.: The Linux kernel (2022). https://git.kernel.org
55. Urban, C.: The abstract domain of segmented ranking functions. In: Logozzo, F., Fähndrich, M. (eds.) SAS 2013. LNCS, vol. 7935, pp. 43–62. Springer, Heidelberg (2013). https://doi.org/10.1007/978-3-642-38856-9_5
56. Vafeiadis, V.: Shape-value abstraction for verifying linearizability. In: Jones, N.D., Müller-Olm, M. (eds.) VMCAI 2009. LNCS, vol. 5403, pp. 335–348. Springer, Heidelberg (2008). https://doi.org/10.1007/978-3-540-93900-9_27
57. Vafeiadis, V., Parkinson, M.: A marriage of rely/guarantee and separation logic. In: Caires, L., Vasconcelos, V.T. (eds.) CONCUR 2007. LNCS, vol. 4703, pp. 256–271. Springer, Heidelberg (2007). https://doi.org/10.1007/978-3-540-74407-8_18

Error Localization for Sequential Effect Systems

Colin S. Gordon(✉) and Chaewon Yun

Drexel University, Philadelphia, PA 19104, USA
{csgordon,cy422}@drexel.edu

Abstract. We describe a new concrete approach to giving predictable error locations for sequential (flow-sensitive) effect systems. Prior implementations of sequential effect systems rely on either computing a bottom-up effect and comparing it to a declaration (e.g., method annotation) or leaning on constraint-based type inference. These approaches do not necessarily report program locations that precisely indicate where a program may "go wrong" at runtime.

Instead of relying on constraint solving, we draw on the notion of a residual from literature on ordered algebraic structures. Applying these to effect quantales (a large class of sequential effect systems) yields an implementation approach which accepts exactly the same program as an original effect quantale, but for effect-incorrect programs is guaranteed to fail type-checking with predictable error locations tied to evaluation order. We have implemented this idea in a generic effect system implementation framework for Java, and report on experiences applying effect systems from the literature and novel effect systems to Java programs. We find that the reported error locations with our technique are significantly closer to the program points that lead to failed effect checks.

1 Introduction

Effect systems are a well-established technique for extending a base type system that reasons about input and output shapes and available operations, to also statically reason about behaviors of code. However, error reporting for effect systems has not been systematically studied. Existing implementations of effect systems report errors in one of two ways.

The classic approach is checking that each individual operation's effect is less than some bound [6,28,32,58,68] and reporting errors for any individual operation whose check fails. For example, this is how Java's checked exceptions are handled: every possibly-throwing expression's `throws` clause is checked against that of the enclosing method. This yields highly precise error locations (e.g., reporting specific problematic method invocations or `throw` statements), but applies only for the (common) case of flow-insensitive effect systems.

The more general approach is to raise an error for whatever program point gave rise to a failing constraint during type inference [2,8,34–36,49,52,65], which works for a wide variety of effect systems. However this leads to the well-known

M. V. Hermenegildo and J. F. Morales (Eds.): SAS 2023, LNCS 14284, pp. 343–370, 2023.
https://doi.org/10.1007/978-3-031-44245-2_16

difficulty with localizing mistakes from type inference errors: the constraint which failed may be far away from an actual programmer mistake.

Technically a third possibility is to compare the computed effect of a method body against an annotated or assumed bound. This can work for any effect system, but we know of no implementations taking this approach, which would yield highly imprecise error messages (basically, "this method has an effect error").[1]

This is an unforunate state of affairs: less powerful effect systems have localized error reporting (the first approach), while more powerful flow-sensitive effect systems—arguably in more dire need of precise error reporting—are stuck with error reports that are unpredictable (approach 2) or maximally imprecise (approach 3). This paper shows how to derive precise, predictable error reporting for flow-sensitive effect systems as well, by noticing that the first approach is in fact an error reporting optimization of the third: applied to the same effect system, they accept exactly the same programs, but while the third directly implements typical formalizations, the first in fact cleverly exploits algebraic properties of the third for more precise error reporting. By articulating and generalizing these properties, we obtain a new more precise error reporting mechanism for sequential [66] effect systems.

In the common case of an effect system where effects are partially ordered (or pre-ordered), while type-and-effect checking code with a known upper bound (such as a Java method with a throws clause), it is sufficient to check for each operation (e.g., method invocation or throw statement) whether the effect (e.g., the possibly-thrown checked exceptions) is less than the upper bound (e.g., `throws` clause). If not, an error is reported for that operation. This is a deviation from how such effect systems are typically formalized, which is as a join semilattice, where formally the error would not occur until the least upper bound over *all* subexpressions' effects was compared against the declared bound for the code. Directly implementing this typical formalization is sound, but for a large method provides no direct clue as to where the problematic code may be in the method.

This paper explores in detail why this optimization is valid, and uses that insight to generalize this precise error reporting to *sequential* effect systems. While the validity of this switch from joins in metatheory to local ordering checks in implementations is intuitively clear given basic properties of joins (namely, $\forall X, b. ((\bigsqcup X) \sqsubseteq b) \Leftrightarrow (\forall a \in X. a \sqsubseteq b))$, it is not obvious that a corresponding transformation exists that can be applied to *sequential* effect systems to move from global error checking to incremental error checking. Our contributions include:

- We explicitly identify and explain the common pattern of formalizing an effect system using operators that compute effects, while implementing the systems differently. We explain why this is valid.

[1] Some implementations are designed for effect inference to always succeed, with a secondary analysis rejecting some effects outside the effect system [62,63], and others with unavailable source do not provide enough detail to ascertain their effect checking algorithm [7,18–20,59].

- We generalize this to arbitrary sequential effect systems characterized as effect quantales.
- We describe an implementation of this approach for Java programs in the first implementation framework for sequential effect systems for Java.
- We describe experiments implementing sequential effect systems in this framework and applying them to real Java programs, arguing that this theoretically grounded approach yields precise errors.

2 Background

Effect systems extend traditional type systems with information about side effects of program evaluation, which can be tailored to program behaviors of interest. Applications have included analyzing what regions of memory are accessed [24,46,67]; ensuring data race freedom [1,6,15,17], deadlock freedom [16,29,35,64], or other more targeted concurrency safety properties like safe use of GUI primitives [28,45,68]; checking atomicity in concurrent programs [20,21]; checking safety of dynamic software updates [48]; checking communication properties [2,49]; dataflow properties [4,36] or general safety properties of execution traces [38,61,63].

Effect systems extend the typing judgement to include an additional component, the *effect*, which is a syntactic description of an upper bound on an expression's behavior. The typical judgment form $\Gamma \vdash e : \tau \mid \chi$ is interpreted as meaning the under variable typing assumptions Γ, evaluating expression e will produce a result of type τ (if execution terminates), exhibiting at most behaviors described by χ. Function types are also extended in effect systems to carry a *latent* effect χ, typically written superscript above a function arrow, as in $\tau \xrightarrow{\chi} \tau'$, indicating that χ is a bound on the function body's behavior, which the type rule for function application incorporates into the effect of function invocation.

Most often the (representations of) behaviors an effect system reasons about are assumed to form a join semilattice, and intuitively the effect of an expression is then the least upper bound (join) of the effects of all (executed) subexpressions. But this model of effect systems, while broad and including many useful and powerful effect systems, is incomplete. Many of the effect systems of interest [2, 4,20,21,29,35,36,38,48,49,63,64] have additional structure because they track behaviors sensitive to evaluation order, and therefore have not only a partial ordering on effects to model a notion which behaviors subsume others, but also a notion of sequencing effects to track ordering of behaviour.

Consider using effects to determine where other threads might observe intermediate results of a method in a concurrent program [20,21,72]. There `lock(x);...unlock(x);` is clearly different from `unlock(x);...lock(x);`—in the former case, no other thread in a data-race-free program can observe intermediate states of the ellided section, while in the latter case, another thread could acquire lock `x` and observe changes to the state it protects. *Sequential* effect systems like Flanagan and Qadeer's [20,21] add an additional operator to effect systems, $\triangleright$ in this paper, to model effects occurring in a specific order. $\sqcup$ is retained as the least-upper-bound of effects (e.g., for conditionals). So if `lock(x);` has effect R and `unlock(x)` has effect L (for reasons elaborated in Sect. 3.3), this permits the two code fragments to have different effects due to their different orders: $R \triangleright L = A$ (atomic), while $L \triangleright R = \top$ (non-atomic). This follows the standard type rules for sequential effect systems (the black portions of Fig. 3), where some uses of $\sqcup$ in classic effect systems are replaced by $\triangleright$ where program evaluation order is known.

There is still some active debate as to what the appropriate common model of these *sequential* effect systems should be. They are captured most generally by Tate's effectoids [66] (or equivalently, by polymonads [34]), but these are typically acknowledged to be more general than most systems require. More pragmatic proposals include graded monads [37] and effect quantales [25,27], which differ primarily in what kinds of distributive laws are assumed (or not assumed) for how least-upper-bound and sequencing interact. Gordon [27] gives a detailed survey of general models of sequential effect systems, and their relationships.

We work with sequential effect systems characterized by effect quantales, because their application to mainstream programming languages seems furthest-developed, including general approaches to deriving from a basic effect quantale treatments of loops [27] and constructs derivable from tagged delimited continuations [26] (e.g., exceptions, generators); for related frameworks only single examples exist. Gordon [27] also gives a survey of how a wide range of specific sequential effect systems from the literature are modeled by effect quantales.

Definition 1 (Effect Quantale [27]). *An* effect quantale *is a structure* $Q = \langle E, \sqcup, \triangleright, I \rangle$ *composed of:*

- *A set of effects (behaviors)* E
- *A* partial *join (least-upper-bound)* $\sqcup : E \times E \rightharpoonup E$
- *A* partial *sequencing operator* $\triangleright : E \times E \rightharpoonup E$
- *A unit element* I

such that

- $\langle E, \triangleright, I \rangle$ *is a partial monoid with unit* I *(i.e.,* $\triangleright$ *is an associative operator with left and right unit* I*)*
- $\langle E, \sqcup \rangle$ *is a partial join semilattice (i.e.,* $\sqcup$ *is commutative, associative, and idempotent)*
- $\triangleright$ *distributes over* $\sqcup$ *on both sides*
  - $x \triangleright (y \sqcup z) = (x \triangleright y) \sqcup (x \triangleright z)$
  - $(x \sqcup y) \triangleright z = (x \triangleright z) \sqcup (y \triangleright z)$

Note that when writing relations involving possibly-undefined expressions (e.g., since $x \sqcup y$ may be undefined), we consider two expressions equal if they both evaluate to the same element of E, or are both undefined.[2]

[2] Readers who tire of thinking about partiality can approximate this by imagining there is an additional distinguished error element, greater than all others, and preserved by all operators, representing undefined results, and which is invalid in later type rules (as in the original axiomatization [25]).

From the partial join we can derive a partial order on effects: $x \sqsubseteq y \Leftrightarrow x \sqcup y = y$. Again we must specify the meaning of $\sqsubseteq$ on possibly-undefined expressions: $x \sqsubseteq y$ is defined only if the join of x and y is defined.

Both $\rhd$ and $\sqcup$ are monotone in both arguments, in the sense that if $a \sqsubseteq b$ and $x \sqsubseteq y$, then $a \rhd x \sqsubseteq b \rhd y$ (when the right side is defined) and similarly for $\sqcup$.

Note that any join-semilattice-based effect system can be modeled in this system, using $\bot$ for identity, and reusing join for sequencing as well.

Gordon [27] also describes properties of a partial unary iteration operation $-^*$ used to characterize loop effects, guaranteed to be:

$$\begin{aligned} \text{Extensive } & \forall x.\, x \sqsubseteq x^* \\ \text{Idempotent } & \forall x.\, (x^*)^* = x^* \\ \text{Monotone } & \forall x, y.\, x \sqsubseteq y \Rightarrow x^* \sqsubseteq y^* \\ \text{Foldable } & \forall x.\, (x^*) \rhd (x^*) \sqsubseteq x^* \\ \text{Possibly-Empty } & \forall x.\, I \sqsubseteq x^* \end{aligned}$$

An optimally precise iteration operator can be derived for most effect quantales of interest [27]: all finite effect quantales, and all effect quantales which have finite meets of elements greater than the unit element. This includes all prior specific effect systems considered in the survey section of that paper.

2.1 Implementing Effect Systems

We concern ourselves with implementing effect system checking in a setting where the expected effect of every method in the program is given, rather than inferred. This models a reasonable integration of effects into languages that require explicit method signatures, consistent with a number of prior implementations of effect systems [20,28,32,68]. Experience has shown that while full inference has value, for many effect systems, a reasonable default (or local customization of defaults) is often sufficient to achieve modest annotation overhead. This also models scenarios where full inference has been employed, but manual annotations are required to refine undesirable inferences and force type checking to produce errors in a method that is intended to have a certain effect, but was inferred to have an incompatible effect. We speak of methods because our prototype (Sect. 5) targets Java, but the same principles would apply to procedural or functional languages.

Global Reporting. Many formalizations of effect systems use a join-semilattice or effect-quantale-like formulation of the system, so an implementation can generally compute the effect of an expression bottom-up. The result is that for code with a fixed bound χ (say, the declared effect of a method), the implementation uses the $\sqcup$ and/or $\rhd$ operators to compute the body effect χ', and then once for each method checks that $\chi' \sqsubseteq \chi$. This is a direct implementation of common metatheory for effect systems, but as the only effect *check* occurs at the granularity of entire method or function bodies, there is only one possible error location for such a technique to report: the entire method or function body. For

```
1  @Atomic
2  @ThrownEffect(exception = StringIndexOutOfBoundsException.class,
3                behavior = Atomic.class)
4  public synchronized StringBuffer append(StringBuffer sb) {
5    if (sb == null) {
6        sb = NULL;
7    }
8    int len = sb.length(); // Already atomic
9    int newcount = count + len;
10   if (newcount > value.length)
11     expandCapacity(newcount);
12   sb.getChars(0, len, value, count); // <-- Error: also atomic
13   count = newcount;
14   return this;
15 }
```

Fig. 1. Excerpt from JDK1.4 `StringBuffer` implementation.

example, consider locating the error in Fig. 1, as studied in prior work [20]. This approach would use type rules like those of Fig. 3 to compute the method body's effect, which would be $\top$ (non-atomic). Only then would this be checked against the method annotation that this method should be atomic, and type-checking would fail. At that point, all information that line 12 has critically contributed to the error (because it attempts a second atomic action without synchronization) has been lost, leading to lack of precision in error reporting. We are unaware of any concrete systems that explicitly acknowledge implementing this approach, though language in some papers is suggestive of such an approach (e.g., mentioning that "inspection of a method" with an error revealed a problem, as opposed to indicating an error was flagged on a specific line of code).

Precise Reporting for Commutative Effect Systems. Most effect system implementations are limited to join-semilattice or partial order structures, which ignore program order. Of those with available implementations, all we know of give precise error locations for code expressions which would lead to failing effect system checks by exploiting the trick mentioned in the introduction, that this class of system permits checking effects incrementally by checking if each subexpression's effect is less than the bound, since this is equivalent to computing the join of subexpression effects and comparing to the bound. This is true of all available implementations we are aware of, including Java's checked exceptions [32], the modern implementation of Gordon et al.'s UI effects [28] in the Checker Framework [13,53], Toro and Tanter's framework [68] for gradual effects [60], Rytz et al.'s work for Scala [58], Deterministic Parallel Java [6], and others. As mentioned earlier, this trick does not work for general sequential effect systems.

Constraint-Based Reporting. Most prior implementations of sequential effect systems—and *all* prior implementations *frameworks* for sequential effect systems [8–10,34,52]—use type inference to infer effects. This results in the standard trade-offs for global constraint-based type inference: types (and effects) are inferred with low developer effort when possible, but errors can be cryptic, and implicate program locations unrelated to the error. In particular, these implementations tend to generate subtyping (and subeffecting) constraints from the program structure, which are then solved incrementally by a fixpoint solver. Errors are reported at the location corresponding to the first constraint which is found to be inconsistent. However, that constraint may be totally unrelated to any problematic statement. Consider the brief JavaScript program

```
var x = 3; var y = x; requiresString(y)
```

It is possible for a constraint solver to flag any of the three statements as a type error, assuming the invoked method is typed as requiring a string input. Flagging the first or third lines is reasonable, as they are the sources of the contradiction. However, solvers are permitted to report the middle line as erroneous as well (for storing a number into a string-containing variable), which is not terrible in this case, but becomes problematic with larger blocks of code. This has inspired a wealth of work on various techniques to reduce or partially compensate for (but not eliminate) this unpredictability [11,33,42,44,54,55]. In principle such work is applicable to existing approaches to inferring effects in sequential effect systems [19,50,52], but unpredictability would remain. While details vary between systems, in general this approach could flag any line of code in Fig. 1 as erroneous.

3 Local Errors for Sequential Effect Systems

We would like to obtain precise error reporting for sequential effect systems in general. Because effect quantales subsume the join semilattice model of effect systems [27], we can hope to draw some inspiration from the corresponding optimization on traditional commutative effect systems: that optimization should be a special case of a general solution.

Let us fix an expression e whose effect we would like to ensure is less than χ. Let us assume a set $\{\chi_i \mid i \in \mathsf{Subterms}(e)\}$ where χ_i is the static effect of subterm i from a bottom-up effect synthesis. For now, we will assume all such effects are defined (i.e., that the bottom-up synthesis of effects never results in undefined effects). For the case where effects form a join-semilattice, and all bottom-up computation is joins (no other operators play a role), we can formally relate the global and precise implementations of join-semilattice effect systems by observing

$$\bigsqcup\{\chi_i \mid i \in \mathsf{Subterms}(e)\} \sqsubseteq \chi \Leftrightarrow \forall i \in \mathsf{Subterms}(e).\, \chi_i \sqsubseteq \chi$$

as suggested in the introduction. The left side of the iff expresses the global view that the join of all subexpression effects must be bounded by χ. The right side expresses the local view that each individual subexpression's effect must be less than the bound χ. (This formulation suggests some redundant checks; we return to this later.) One way to express the intuition behind this formula is that performing all of the local checks corresponds to ensuring that each individual χ_i can be further combined with some other effects (here, by join), and the result will still be bounded by χ. Conversely, if there exists some $j \in \mathsf{Subterms}(e)$ such that $\chi_j \not\sqsubseteq \chi$, then no combination with other effects can yield something satisfying the bound χ.

We dub this informal characterization as the notion of *completing* an effect. An effect χ_i *can be completed to* χ if there exists some effect χ' such that the combination of χ_i and χ' is $\sqsubseteq \chi$. The general intuition is that if χ_i can be completed to χ, it is possible to "add more behaviors" to χ_i and obtain an effect less than χ, in the sense that it is possible to extend a program with effect χ_i with additional behaviors such that the overall effect is less than χ. We formalize this later in this section, such that the result will allow precise reporting of error locations, such as line 12 in Fig. 1. But first we must recall and customize a bit of relevant math.

3.1 Residuals

The literature on ordered semigroups [5] and non-commutative substructural logics [23,41] contains many applications of the notion of a *residual* [14,71]:

Definition 2 ((Right) Residual). *A (right)* residual *operation on an ordered monoid M is a binary operation $- \setminus - : M \times M \to M$ such that for any x, y, and z, $x \leq y \setminus z \Leftrightarrow y \cdot x \leq z$*

That is, the right residual $y \setminus z$ of z by y (also read as y under z) is an element of M such that, when sequenced *to the right* of y, yields an element no greater than z (but definitely ordered $\leq z$).

We can adapt this for effect quantales as well:

Definition 3 ((Right) Quantale Residual). *A (right) residual operation on an effect quantale Q is a partial binary operation $- \setminus - : Q \times Q \rightharpoonup Q$ such that for any x, y, and z, $x \sqsubseteq y \setminus z \Leftrightarrow y \rhd x \sqsubseteq z$. A* (right) residuated effect quantale *is an effect quantale with a specified choice of (right) residual operation.*

Consider the case of type-checking $e_1; e_2$, where $\Gamma \vdash e_1 : \chi_1$ and $\Gamma \vdash e_2 : \chi_2$, and ensuring that the effect of the sequential composition of these expressions - $\chi_1 \rhd \chi_2$ - is bounded by χ. A residual on effects can tell us if this is *possible* based on analyzing *only* e_1, in some cases rejecting programs before even analyzing e_2.

If $\chi_1 \setminus \chi$ is undefined, then there *does not exist* χ' such that $\chi_1 \rhd \chi' \sqsubseteq \chi$. If there were some such χ', then by the definition of the residual operation, $\chi' \sqsubseteq \chi_1 \setminus \chi$, which would imply the residual was defined. Thus an implementation could eagerly return an error after synthesizing the effect χ_1 for e_1, and determining the residual was undefined. This is a subtle point about the definition above: it states not only properties of the residual when it is defined, but also requires it to be defined in certain cases.

Many effect quantales have a right residual in the sense of Definition 2, but not all do, and since effect systems are primarily concerned with sound bounds on behavior rather than exact characterizations of behavior, we actually require only a slightly weaker variant of residual:

Definition 4 (Weak (Right) Quantale Residual). *A weak (right) residual operation on an effect quantale Q is a partial binary operation $-\setminus- : Q \times Q \rightharpoonup Q$ such that for any x, y, and z:*

- *Residual bounding: $x \sqsubseteq y \setminus z \Rightarrow y \rhd x \sqsubseteq z$*
- *Residual existence: $y \rhd x \sqsubseteq z \Rightarrow \exists r.\, r = y \setminus z$*
- *Self-residuation: $\exists r.\, z \setminus z = r$*
- *Unit residuation: $I \setminus z = z$*

A (right) residuated effect quantale *is an effect quantale with a specified choice of weak (right) residual operation.*

This is the notion of residual we work with, and this weakening is necessary to capture aspects of non-local control flow [26]. Every residual operation in the remainder of this paper is a weak residual, though for brevity we simply refer to them as residuals. The *total* residual (Definition 3) implies the axioms of the weak residual, so in some cases we present a total residual as a weak residual.

We take this weak right residual to be our formal notion of completion: an effect χ can be completed to χ' if the weak residual $\chi \setminus \chi'$ is defined.

It is worth noting that the literature also contains a definition of left residual, which we could use to similarly issue an eager warning given only χ and χ_2. However, notice that the right residual corresponds to type-checking traversals proceeding in the standard left-to-right evaluation order standard in (most) languages using call-by-value reduction. Because most other analysis tools, and in practice most developer investigation of program-order dependent behaviors proceeds in tandem with evaluation order, we focus solely on the right residual. However, all results in the rest of the paper can be dualized to the left residual. Because we focus exclusively on the right residual, for the rest of the paper we will drop the qualifier "right" and simply refer to unqualified residuals.

This seems a promising approach, but detailing it fully requires also connecting our notion of completion to the way effects are actually combined during type-checking (e.g., most programs are not basic blocks of primitive actions). Before doing so, we build further intuition by describing the residual operations for a few existing effect quantales in the literature, based on Gordon's formalization [27].

3.2 Residual Examples

This section gives several examples of residuated effect quantales, to show that many existing effect systems already naturally satisfy the requirements of our weak residual, so while it is not mathematically the case that all effect quantales have a weak residual, it appears known effect systems typically do. Our extended technical report [31] contains additional examples.

Traditional Commutative Effects. In the case where the effect quantale is simply a (partial) join semilattice (so $\rhd = \sqcup$), the residual is simply:

$$X \setminus Y = Y \text{ when } X \sqsubseteq Y$$

Thus the residual is exactly the local subeffect comparison performed by local implementations of effect checking.

Formal Languages and Quotients Thereof. As formal languages can model sets of acceptable behaviors (and are often used for this purpose, most frequently in automata-theoretic model checking), it is worth considering formal languages as effects. Indeed, languages of finite words over a finite alphabet form an effect quantale: Here we recall a distillation of a number of general behavioral trace effect systems [38,61,63] given by Gordon [27]:

Definition 5 (Finite Trace Effects). *Effects tracking sets of finite event traces, for events in an alphabet Σ, form an effect quantale:*

$$E = \mathcal{P}(\Sigma^*) \setminus \emptyset \qquad X \rhd Y = X \cdot Y \qquad X \sqcup Y = X \cup Y \qquad I = \{\epsilon\}$$

Where sequencing is pairwise concatenation of sets, $X \cdot Y = \{xy \mid x \in X \wedge y \in Y\}$.

We write this effect quantale for a particular alphabet Σ as $\mathsf{FinTrace}(\Sigma)$.

Intuitively, the residual should be defined whenever the dividend is some kind of prefix of all behaviors in the numerator. The formalization is more subtle, but captures this intuition:

$$X \setminus Y = \{w \in \Sigma^* \mid \forall x \in X.\, x \cdot w \in Y\} \text{ when non-empty}$$

That is, the residual $X \setminus Y$ is the set of words which, when sequenced after X, will produce a subset of Y.

Note that this is *not* the quotient of formal languages, which uses the same notation with a different meaning. The (right) *quotient* of X under Y $X \setminus_q Y$ (using the subscript q to distinguish the quotient from the residual) is $\{w \in \Sigma^* \mid \exists x \in X.\, x \cdot w \in Y\}$. Sequencing this after the set X yields $\{xw \mid x \in X \wedge \exists x' \in X.\, x' \cdot w \in Y\}$, which may be larger than Y.

The above (full) residual is in fact an operation that exists in Action Logic, a cousin of Kleene Algebra. Pratt [57] notes that the two are related; in our notation, $X \setminus Y = (X \setminus_q (Y^{-1}))^{-1}$. Since regular languages are closed under complement and quotient, this means they are also closed under residuation, and therefore there is a sub-effect-quantale $\mathsf{Reg}(\Sigma) \subseteq \mathsf{FinTrace}(\Sigma)$ which *also* has weak residuals, which can be computed using operations on finite automata (and mapped back to regular expressions for error reporting).

The induced iteration operator on this effect quantale corresponds to the Kleene star. Note, however, that while these effect quantale operations correspond conveniently to regular expressions, the effect quantale itself is not limited to regular languages: concatenation, union, and Kleene iteration are well-defined operations on *any* formal languages, including context-free, context-sensitive, or recursively enumerable languages.

3.3 Atomicity

Flanagan and Qadeer [20,21] proposed well-known approaches to capturing atomicity as effects. Their original proposal turns out to be a particular finite effect quantale [25,27], whose join semilattice and sequential composition are

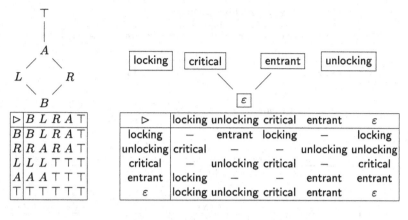

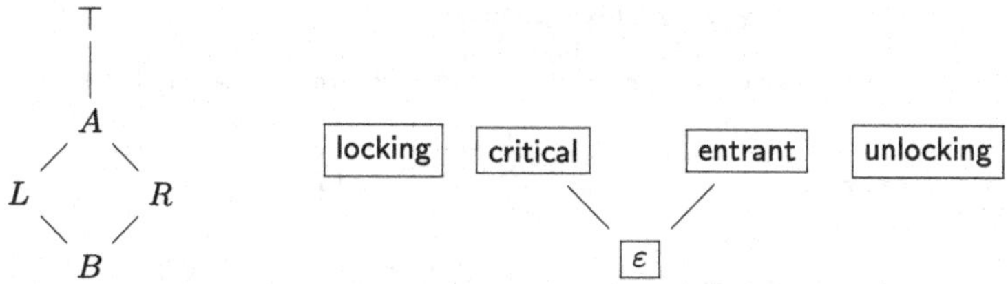

$\rhd$	B	L	R	A	$\top$
B	B	L	R	A	$\top$
R	R	A	R	A	$\top$
L	L	L	$\top$	$\top$	$\top$
A	A	A	$\top$	$\top$	$\top$
$\top$	$\top$	$\top$	$\top$	$\top$	$\top$

(a) Atomicity effects [21]

$\rhd$	locking	unlocking	critical	entrant	ε
locking	–	entrant	locking	–	locking
unlocking	critical	–	–	unlocking	unlocking
critical	–	unlocking	critical	–	critical
entrant	locking	–	–	entrant	entrant
ε	locking	unlocking	critical	entrant	ε

(b) Critical section effects [66].

Fig. 2. Lattices and sequencing for atomicity and critical section (reentrancy) effects. – represents an undefined result for sequential composition.

shown in Fig. 2a[3]] (in the bottom table, the effect in row i sequenced via $\rhd$ with the effect in column j is equal to the effect in cell i, j of the table). The key idea is to adopt Lipton's theory of reduction [43] to label each expression with an effect capturing how it commutes with shared-memory operations in other threads: B for both directions (e.g., thread-local actions), L for left (i.e., earlier, such as lock releases), right (R, later, such as lock acquisitions), atomic A (does not commute, including atomic hardware operations and already-proven-atomic critical sections), or compound $\top$ (interleaves in non-trivial ways with other threads).

Sequential composition captures Lipton's idea that any sequence of R or B actions, followed by at most one atomic A action, then any sequence of L or B actions, can be grouped together as if the whole sequence occurred atomically from the perspective of another thread. We omit iteration for brevity, but the original definition of $(-)^*$ coincides with the results of a general construction on finite effect quantales as well [27].

We can define a (total) residual $\chi \setminus \chi'$ according to the classic mathematical definition: $\chi \setminus \chi' = \bigsqcup\{\chi'' \mid \chi \rhd \chi'' \sqsubseteq \chi'\}$, which is well-defined because the join semilattice is complete. So for example, $L \setminus A$ is the greatest effect which, when sequenced *after* L, yields a result less than A—which in this case works out to be L itself.

3.4 Reentrancy

Tate [66] developed a maximally-general framework for sequential effect systems, and his running example was the system given in Fig. 2b, which has

[3] They subsequently proposed an extension to conditional atomicity [20], which is also an effect quantale when combined with a data race freedom quantale.

$$
\begin{array}{lll}
\textsc{Effects} & \chi \in Q & \text{(effect quantale)} \\
\textsc{Types} & \tau ::= & \mathsf{bool} \mid \mathsf{unit} \mid \tau \xrightarrow{\chi} \tau \\
\textsc{Expressions} & e ::= & x \mid c \mid \lambda^{\chi} x : \tau.\, e \mid e @ e \mid \mathsf{if}\ e\ \mathsf{then}\ e\ \mathsf{else}\ e \mid \mathsf{while}\ e\ e
\end{array}
$$

$$
\boxed{\chi \mapsto \chi \parallel \Gamma \vdash e : \tau \mid \chi}
\qquad
\text{T-Var}\ \frac{\Gamma(x) = \tau}{\chi_0 \mapsto \chi_m \parallel \Gamma \vdash x : \tau \mid I}
\qquad
\text{T-Const}\ \frac{}{\chi_0 \mapsto \chi_m \parallel \Gamma \vdash c : \tau_c \mid I}
$$

$$
\text{T-Lambda}\ \frac{I \mapsto \chi \parallel \Gamma, x : \tau \vdash e : \tau' \mid \chi' \qquad \chi' \sqsubseteq \chi}{\chi_0 \mapsto \chi_m \parallel \Gamma \vdash \lambda^{\chi} x : \tau.\, e : \tau \xrightarrow{\chi} \tau' \mid I}
$$

$$
\text{T-App}\ \frac{\begin{array}{c}\chi_0 \mapsto \chi_m \parallel \Gamma \vdash e_1 : \tau' \xrightarrow{\chi_l} \tau \mid \chi_1 \\ \chi_0 \rhd \chi_1 \mapsto \chi_m \parallel \Gamma \vdash e_2 : \tau \mid \chi_2 \qquad \chi_l \setminus (\chi_2 \setminus (\chi_1 \setminus (\chi_0 \setminus \chi_m)))\ \text{defined}\end{array}}{\chi_0 \mapsto \chi_m \parallel \Gamma \vdash e_1 @ e_2 : \tau \mid \chi_1 \rhd \chi_2 \rhd \chi_l}
$$

$$
\text{T-If}\ \frac{\begin{array}{cc}\chi_0 \mapsto \chi_m \parallel \Gamma \vdash e_c : \mathsf{bool} \mid \chi_c & \chi_0 \rhd \chi_c \mapsto \chi_m \parallel \Gamma \vdash e_t : \tau \mid \chi_t \\ \chi_0 \rhd \chi_c \mapsto \chi_m \parallel \Gamma \vdash e_f : \tau \mid \chi_f & (\chi_t \sqcup \chi_f) \setminus (\chi_c \setminus (\chi_0 \setminus \chi_m))\ \text{defined}\end{array}}{\chi_0 \rhd \chi_m \parallel \Gamma \vdash \mathsf{if}\ e_c\ \mathsf{then}\ e_t\ \mathsf{else}\ e_f : \tau \mid \chi_c \rhd (\chi_t \sqcup \chi_f)}
$$

$$
\text{T-While}\ \frac{\begin{array}{c}\chi_0 \mapsto \chi_m \parallel \Gamma \vdash e_c : \mathsf{bool} \mid \chi_c \\ \chi_0 \rhd \chi_c \mapsto \chi_m \parallel \Gamma \vdash e_b : \tau \mid \chi_b \qquad (\chi_b \rhd \chi_c)^* \setminus (\chi_c \setminus (\chi_0 \setminus \chi_m))\ \text{defined}\end{array}}{\chi_0 \mapsto \chi_m \parallel \Gamma \vdash \mathsf{while}\ e_c\ e_b : \mathsf{unit} \mid \chi_c \rhd (\chi_b \rhd \chi_c)^*}
$$

Fig. 3. Type rules with and without residual checks.

partial joins and sequencing. (He did not describe an iteration operator, but one can be derived from the general construction of iteration operations on finite effect quantals [27].) This is an effect system motivated by tracking critical sections for a single global resource lock which does *not* permit recursive acquisition. This turns out to *also* be a natural effect system for tracking non-reentrant code: the start of a non-reentrant operation can be given the effect locking. Notice that locking $\rhd$ locking is undefined, so attempting to reenter an operation that is non-reentrant will not type-check. This covers non-reentrant locks (as in the original example, and in implementations such as Java's `StampedLock`), but also database APIs that do not support nested transactions (starting and finishing transactions), or the evaluation API for Java's `XPath` expressions (`XPathExpression.evaluate(...)`).

3.5 Connecting Residuals to Type Checking

Figure 3 defines two typing judgments. $\Gamma \vdash e : \tau \mid \chi$ is a standard judgment form for effect systems, interpreted as "under variable typing assumptions Γ, expression e has type τ with effect χ." This judgment is readable in Fig. 3 by ignoring the extensions in blue, and corresponds to a subset of the type rules Gordon [25,27] proved sound for a wide array of possible primitives and state models. In short, the judgment types expressions, using the effect quantale operators to synthesize the effect of the expression, capturing evaluation ordering with $\rhd$ and alternative paths (e.g., in T-If) with $\sqcup$. We call this judgment the *standard judgment*.

Including the text in blue, Fig. 3 defines an additional judgment $\chi_0 \mapsto \chi_m \parallel \Gamma \vdash e : \tau \mid \chi$, interpreted as "under typing assumptions Γ expression e has type τ and effect χ, and moreover if e is executed after effect χ_0, it is still possible for the result to have effect less than χ_m." Later we formalize this interpretation. This extended judgment form performs additional checks (also in blue). These additional checks do not reject (or accept) any additional programs, but restrict how, when, and why programs are rejected.

Lemma 1 (Conservative Extension ✿). *If* $\chi_0 \mapsto \chi_m \parallel \Gamma \vdash e : \tau \mid \chi$, *then* $\Gamma \vdash e : \tau \mid \chi$.

This lemma, and others marked with a ✿ icon, have been mechanically checked in the Coq proof assistant; the proofs are packaged with our artifact [30].

Critically, this result implies than any soundness results holding for the standard judgment are inherited by the extended judgment. Gordon [27] gives generic type safety results for a configurable framework of sequential effect systems, parameterized by primitives and choices of states. Since our standard judgment is an instantiation of that framework (for a specific choice of constants), our extended judgment is also type-safe for appropriate choices of state and primitive semantics. We do not give further consideration to type-safety in this paper, as Gordon's framework can be instantiated to yield type-safety results for all of our examples effect systems (in some cases, demonstrated in that work [27]).

Proving the other direction of the correspondence relies on weakened versions of standard residual properties:

Lemma 2 (Residual Sequencing ✿). *For any effects* $x, y \in Q$ *for a residuated effect quantale* Q, *if* $x \setminus y$ *is defined, then* $x \rhd (x \setminus y) \sqsubseteq y$.

Lemma 3 (Residual Shifting ✿). *For any effects* $x, y, z \in Q$ *for a residuated effect quantale* Q, $(x \rhd y) \setminus z$ *is defined if and only if* $y \setminus (x \setminus z)$ *is defined.*

Lemma 4 (Antitone Residuation ✿). *If* $x \sqsubseteq y$ *and* $y \setminus z$ *is defined, then* $x \setminus z$ *is defined.*

These are enough to prove that the standard typing judgment implies the extended judgment holds, for reasonable choices of χ_0 and χ_m. By reasonable, we mean that it is possible to "reach" χ_m by running code with effect χ_0, then code with the effect the standard judgment assigns, followed by some additional effect, without exceeding a total upper bound of χ_m.

Lemma 5 (Liberal Extension ✿). *If* $\Gamma \vdash e : \tau \mid \chi$, *then for any* χ_0 *and* χ_m *such that* $\chi \setminus (\chi_0 \setminus \chi_m)$ *is defined,* $\chi_0 \mapsto \chi_m \parallel \Gamma \vdash e : \tau \mid \chi$.

Loop Unrolling. While not required for the proof above, readers may wonder if the desired residual is provable for finite loop unrollings, i.e., if $(\chi_b \rhd \chi_c)^n \setminus (\chi_c \setminus (\chi_0 \setminus \chi_m))$ is defined for all naturals n. Indeed it is: the properties of iteration imply $(\chi_b \rhd \chi_c)^n \sqsubseteq (\chi_b \rhd \chi_c)^*$, so this follows from Lemma 4.

Completability. These results highlight that the extended judgment accepts exactly the same programs as the standard judgment, but ensures our informally-stated requirement that the extended judgment checks that given a prefix effect and target bound, the program has a valid effect in that usage context:

Theorem 1 (Completability ✿). *When $\chi_0 \setminus \chi_m$ is defined and $\chi_0 \mapsto \chi_m \parallel \Gamma \vdash e : \tau \mid \chi$, then $\chi \setminus (\chi_0 \setminus \chi_m)$ is defined.*

This result highlights a subtlety of the nested residual checks in several rules. While at a glance it may appear to lump many checks into one since the residuals checked for existence are larger nested residuals, these checks actually verify only one residual definition beyond what is guaranteed by the subexpressions' typing results. Consider as an example T-App. If the antecedent subexpression typings hold, then by Completability $(\chi_1 \setminus (\chi_0 \setminus \chi_m))$ is defined and $\chi_2 \setminus (\chi_1 \setminus (\chi_0 \setminus \chi_m))$ is defined. So T-App is truly checking only the residual with respect to the latent effect of the invoked function. Likewise, T-If and T-While are checking only the residual with respect to the respective constructs, with residuals for the subexpression effects already guaranteed by the antecedents. Later this allows us to ensure that algorithmically, only one residual check is required per source construct, and that if it would fail due to a subexpression rather than the construct being checked, that error would have already been reported when checking the subexpressions individually.

The combination of Theorem 1 and Lemma 5 guarantees that if an expression is well-typed under standard typing, but not under extended typing for a given χ_0 and χ_m with $\chi_0 \setminus \chi_m$ defined, it is because the subexpressions are arranged in a way that is incompatible with the effect context $\chi_0 \mapsto \chi_m$. And because the residual checks in each rule fail (the residual becomes undefined) as soon as any execution prefix's residual is undefined, if the extended judgment rejects a term accepted by the standard judgment, the specific (nested) residual check pinpoints the inadmissible execution prefix for that context.

3.6 Limitations

For the residual to localize errors effectively, it must be the case that some residuals are undefined, since if all residuals exist, then there is no basis for issuing the early errors we seek. A trivial example is the effect quantale given by a group with only the reflexive ordering. In such an effect quantale, it is always possible to start with a prefix effect X and reach a final effect Y by sequencing $X^{-1}Y$ after X, so no residual check will fail—only the final subeffect check in T-Lam. While such effect quantales exist mathematically, we are unaware of any such quantales actually being used as effect systems, as conceptually, they are at odds with the typical goal of an effect system, which is to build a sound summary of (selected) program behavior and reject certain subsets.

Kleene Algebras [40] are iterable effect quantales [27] which are typically used in program analysis, and typically include a least element in lattice order which corresponds to "no behavior" (e.g., an empty set or empty relation). Since most programs are expected to have some kind of behavior, one could modify a

Kleene Algebra to be partial (i.e., removing the least element from its domain) and obtain an effect quantale with meaningful notions of residuals. However, even then there may be "too many" residuals to be useful. For example, in a Kleene Algebra of binary relations (pre- and post-conditions) or of transition functions (e.g., modeling abstract interpretation as a Kleene Algebra [39]), the domain is large enough to admit arbitrary transitions: for any prefix behavior with precondition P as a set of states and ultimate goal postcondition Q as a set of states, the relation $P \times Q$ is non-empty as long as both P and Q are non-empty. So applying our technique to domains like these notions of extensional correctness would require refining the set of transition functions or relations considered, in order to make the residual undefined when no action contained in the actual program could lead to a desired execution. This is less problematic for intensional specifications such as the language-theoretic approaches, because as soon as some execution path commits to a behavior prefix not in the target specification, the residual is undefined.

4 Algorithms

To turn our insights into a tool, we require a type-checking algorithm. Figure 4 shows the core pieces of a type-checking algorithm that accepts exactly the programs well-typed under the extended typing judgment of Fig. 3.[4] We assume that `earlycheck` accepts the contextual and goal effects, type environment, and expression as inputs, and returns a result (a supertype of successful typing results, unbound variable errors, type errors, and effect errors).

The key insight of the residual checking is apparent in the case for applications. This case first type-checks the function position. If that subterm is already problematic then the underlying error is returned. Otherwise, the algorithm continues to ensure the function subterm has a function type, then type-checks the argument position *with a modified progress effect* reflecting that it reduces after the function position (following T-App). If both subterms typecheck (in appropriate contexts), and the argument position is of an appropriate type for the function, then the algorithm checks that the residual corresponding to the final check in T-App is defined, returning success in that case. Note that while there is only one residual check in the application case here, errors are still reported as early as possible in program order. In particular:

- If the function subterm's effect could not be sequenced after χ_0, or the result would not leave the appropriate residual defined, then type-checking of that *subterm* would fail.
- Similarly, if the argument subterm's effect could not be sequenced after χ_0 and the function subterm's effect, type-checking of the argument would fail (note that the function's effect is passed into type-checking for the argument).

[4] The figure uses Java 17's extended switch statements, plus a few notational liberties for operations on effect quantale elements.

```
Result earlycheck(Q χ0, Q χm, env Γ, expr e) {
  switch (e) {
    case Var x:
      Type t = lookup(Γ, x);
      return (t != null) ? new Result(t, I) : new Unbound(x);
    case Const c: return new Success(constType(c), I);
    case Lambda lam:
      Result r =
        earlycheck(I, lam.declEffect(), Γ.with(lam.var(), lam.argty()), lam.body());
      if (!r.isSuccess()) return r;
      Success s = (Success) r;
      return new Success(new FunType(lam.argty(), lam.declEffect(), s.type), I);
    case App app:
      Result resa = earlycheck(χ0, χm, Γ, app.fun);
      if (!resa.isSuccess()) return resa;
      Success sa = (Success) resa;
      /* We know sa.effect\(χ0\χm) is defined */
      if (!sa.type.isFun()) return new BadType(app.fun);
      Result resb =  earlycheck(χ0▷sa.effect, χm, Γ, app.arg);
      if (!resb.isSuccess()) return resb;
      Success sb = (Success) resb;
      /* sb.effect\(sa.effect\(χ0\χm)) defined */
      if (!sa.type.arg.equals(sb.type)) return new BadType(app.arg);
      boolean goodEffect = hasResidual(sa.type.asFunc().latentEffect(),
                                       (sb.effect ⧅ (sa.effect ⧅ (χ0 ⧅ χm)));
      if (goodEffect) {
        return new Success(sa.type.result,
                     sa.effect ▷ sb.effect ▷ sa.type.asFunc().latentEffect());
      } else {
        return new BadEffect(app);
      }
     case If i: ...
     case While w: ...
  }
}
```

Fig. 4. Algorithm for early effect errors.

- The only residual not guaranteed to be defined is the final step of the residual checking, involving the function's *latent* effect, whose interaction with the evaluation context is not implied by the function and argument subterm effects.

The cases for conditionals and loops are similar, checking subexpressions in program order, with only one new explicit residual check in each case.

5 Implementation

We have implemented this approach in a prototype extension of the Checker Framework [13,53] to support sequential effect systems. Currently we support the fragment of Java corresponding to a core object-oriented language: classes, methods (including checking a method override's effect is less than the original's), conditionals, while loops, calls, and switch statements. Exceptions are

```
public abstract class EffectQuantale<Q> {
  public abstract Q LUB(Q l, Q r);
  public abstract Q seq(Q l, Q r);
  public abstract Q unit();
  public abstract Q iter(Q x);
  public abstract Q residual(Q sofar, Q target);
  public boolean LE(Q l, Q r) { return LUB(l, r).equals(r); }
  public boolean isCommutative() { return false; }
  public abstract ArrayList<Class<? extends Annotation>> getValidEffects();
}
```

Fig. 5. Framework interface to effect quantales with effects represented by type Q.

supported through a variant of Gordon's work on tagged delimited continuations [26], described in more detail in our full technical report [31].

The framework extension is parameterized by a choice of effect quantale, represented by the abstract class in Fig. 5, which is parameterized by the representation type `Q` for a given system's effects. It contains operations for $\sqcup$ (`LUB`), $\rhd$ (`seq`), unit, $-^*$ (`iter`), and residual checks (`residual`). Partiality is modeled by returning `null`. A default implementation of $\sqsubseteq$ (`LE`) is provided but can be overridden with more efficient implementations. `getValidEffects()` produces a list of Java annotation types the framework should recognize as being part of this effect quantale.

`isCommutative` indicates whether the effect quantale is commutative, which the framework uses to recover exhaustive error checking for such systems. In general, when the effect of an expression is $\alpha \rhd \beta \rhd \gamma$ and the residual $(\alpha \rhd \beta) \setminus \delta$ is undefined, the framework stops issuing errors about the rest of execution on the same path through the current method, because all residuals with more complete body effects (e.g., $(\alpha \rhd \beta \rhd \gamma) \setminus \delta$) will also be undefined, but not necessarily because of problems with the extensions (i.e., γ may be fine if the problem is β, in which case further errors would be redundant). However, in the case of a commutative $\rhd$, the framework can exploit commutativity to give additional error messages. For example, if $(\alpha \rhd \beta) \setminus \delta$ is undefined as before, then $(\alpha \rhd \beta \rhd \gamma) \setminus \delta$ will also be undefined, but $\alpha \rhd \beta \rhd \gamma = \alpha \rhd \gamma \rhd \beta$, and it is possible that $(\alpha \rhd \gamma) \setminus \delta$ may be defined or undefined, independent of the residual involving β. This is precisely why the standard approach for join-semilattice effect systems of checking individual subexpressions' effects against a bound works and gives all appropriate errors: in our setting, the residual is defined as the bound itself as long as the effect so far is less than the bound, which via commutativity extends to the join of any non-empty subset of body effects being less than the bound. Note however that our approach is general to any commutative effect quantale, including systems like must-effect analysis [47], not just join semilattices.

General checking logic in the Checker Framework (as in the rest of the Java compiler) uses a visitor to traverse ASTs, rather than recursive traversals in Fig. 4. The Java compiler provides the type environment as ambient state in this setting, and the implementation also maintains the current χ_m and χ_0 as visitor state—χ_0 is maintained as a stack of subexpression effects which can be rewound to consider alternate paths (e.g., different branches of a conditional). But the core algorithm is as demonstrated in the application case of Fig. 4, with a single explicit residual check in each case.

We do make two kinds of extensions to the logic. First, in addition to other varieties of loops (which are straightforward adaptations of T-WHILE), we handle additional language constructs present in Java: our handling of exceptions, breaks, and early returns follows an extension of Gordon's work on effect systems for tagged delimited continuations [26]. Gordon defines a transformation of an arbitrary effect quantale that is ignorant of non-local control flow to one that works with tagged delimited continuations. From this, typing rules for checked exceptions, break statements, and early returns can be derived, which we implement. We also extend this construction with residuals, and it is this extension which requires our shift to weak residuals: intuitively, Gordon's construction tracks sets of possible effects for each execution path (normal execution, for each thrown exception, etc.). In general, the *greatest* possible residual for this construction may require modeling an infinite set, while our implementation relies on finite sets. Further details of our handling and residual are given in our extended technical report [31].

Second, when a type error is encountered, the algorithm does not immediately stop. It will immediately report the error, but then sets a flag indicating an error has been found on the current path, suppressing further error reporting. Then traversal continues in order to visit subexpressions that correspond to checking different method bodies (i.e., lambda expressions and anonymous inner classes) and report errors there, which are independent of errors in the surrounding code. When checking conditionals, if an error is encountered in one branch the algorithm resets the flag for an error on the current path and checks the other branch as if it were the only branch (including visiting code later in program order than the whole conditional construct). This permits the implementation to report additional independent errors, rather than allowing errors in one branch to shadow errors in the other.

Our extension inherits the Checker Framework's existing robust support for subtyping, and type generics. While not used in any of our evaluations, the base implementation of the effect visitor extends the base implementation used for the Checker Framework's focus on type qualifiers [22], so effect systems can in principle make use of type qualifiers to determine effects.

Effects are declared as Java annotations targeting method nodes. This unfortunately requires a bit of boilerplate: each effect requires 10 lines of code, but 8 are identical across all declarations (import statements and meta-annotations for the Java compiler to allow them on method declarations and persist them in bytecode), with the remaining lines being the package declaration and one line for naming the actual annotation.

Performance. The execution time of these checkers is dependent primarily on two factors. The first is the underlying effect quantale: if computing sequencing, joins, iteration, and residuals for the underlying effect quantale is particularly slow, this will slow the whole framework. The atomicity and reentrancy effect systems we have implemented (Sect. 6) both have very fast basic effect quantale operations. The second is the cost of working with the control effect transformation of the underlying effect system to handle exceptions, breaks, and non-local returns without individual effect systems needing to address them (see [31]). In the common case (no non-local control flow) an effect represented as an object with an underlying effect representation, and two null pointers, so the operations have very little additional cost over ignoring non-local control entirely. In code that contains non-local control flow or calls methods with checked exceptions, a prefix effect characterizing behavior up to each break, non-local return, throw, and checked exception mentioned in the signatures of called methods. Composing such effects may trigger at most n additional calls to the underlying effect quantale when each effect is tracking at most n non-local behaviors, so the costs do not grow significantly with code complexity.

Critically, since we analyze a single method at a time, even when those sets become large their performance impact is confined to the current method being checked. The only way for complexity of one method to influence the cost of checking another is via method annotations that expose latent effects for a variety of different thrown exceptions in addition to the non-exceptional method body effect. In general the number of such annotations that must appear is dependent not only on the program being analyzed, but also on the specific effect system in use.

In practice, the performance of our implementation, for the inexpensive effect quantales described in the next section, is on par with other existing pluggable type systems in the Checker Framework.

6 Evaluation

The hypothesis underlying this work is that residuals offer a way to localize sequential effect system errors to the earliest program location in program order where a mistake can be recognized, and that this useful precision for developers.

We have implemented two sequential effect systems in this framework to evaluate whether the error locations reported are accurate, which we approach from two angles. First, we reproduce part of Flanagan and Qadeer's evaluation of their atomicity effect system [20], where they found atomicity errors in the then-current JDK (which have since been fixed). The original evaluation simply described the errors as being found as a result of their analysis, with the implication that their tool used global reporting and thus all location of the error was manually driven. Second, we evaluate the accuracy of error reporting for the reentrancy effect system applied to non-reentrant database transactions. This is a common situation across Spring Hibernate, JDBC, and other database systems, and is a situation with non-trivial interactions with exceptions. We find that the residual-based error locations are both predictable and accurate. We evaluate these two systems because they cover both total and partial effect quantales, and because they are simple enough (both are finite with 5 effects each) that we believe we can evaluate the residual-based locations of errors without becoming entangled in deeper questions of how complex error messages are presented, which we believe is important future work for systems with more complex

```
@Atomic
public boolean contentEquals(StringBuffer sb) {
    if (count != sb.length()) // length() is atomic
        return false;
    char v1[] = value;
    char v2[] = sb.getValue(); // <-- Error: second atomic operation
    int i = offset;
    int j = 0;
    int n = count;
    while (n-- != 0) {
        if (v1[i++] != v2[j++])
            return false;
    }
    return true;
}
```

Fig. 6. Excerpt from JDK1.4 `String` implementation.

effects, e.g. Sect. 3.2) where the relationship between the residual's existence and the effects a programmer specifies, are more complex.

A snapshot of our implementation and these case studies is available [30].

6.1 Reproducing Atomicity Errors

We have implemented the earlier of Flanagan and Qadeer's systems for static checking of atomicity via effects [21] (introduced in Sect. 3.3), in 201LOC, 50 of which were for the 5 effect declarations. A full reimplementation would require integration with a data race freedom system [27] (since data races are non-atomic, while well-synchronized memory accesses are both-movers); this version assumes data race freedom. We have run our atomicity checker with residual-based error reporting on some of the JDK1.4 Java classes reported in Flanagan and Qadeer's evaluation to have errors, to check error location accuracy.

The most prominent example in their evaluation was an atomicity violation in the `StringBuffer` code in Fig. 1. The bug in the code is that while the code synchronizes on (locks) the receiver `this`, it performs *two* atomic actions in the body (calls two atomic methods on the argument, which is not locked), even though it is supposed to be atomic. Our prototype reports the second atomic operation, which is the first subexpression in the body that makes it impossible for the remainder of the method to have an overall atomic effect.

Flanagan and Qadeer report a similar bug in `java.lang.String` (of JDK 1.4), shown in Fig. 6. There the same `StringBuffer` methods are involved. Again our technique indicates the exact point in the method beyond which an overall method body effect consistent with the annotation is impossible. In this case, it saves the developer the trouble of looking at most of the method code.

Flanagan and Qadeer also analyzed other parts of the JDK 1.4, but we have had difficulty getting other classes from their evaluation to be accepted with only minor modifications by the modern Java compiler the Checker Framework extends.

```
@Entrant
@ThrownEffect(exception = TxException.class, behavior=Entrant.class)
public void docExample(SessionFactory factory) throws TxException {
  Session sess = factory.openSession();
  Transaction tx = null;
  try {
    tx = sess.beginTransaction();
  } catch (TxException e) {
    sess.close();
    throw e;
  }
  try {
    doWork(tx);
    tx.commit();
  } catch (TxException e) {
    tx.rollback();
    throw e;
  } finally {
    sess.close();
  }
}
```

Fig. 7. Slight refactoring of example from Hibernate documentation.

6.2 Reentrancy

We have also implemented Tate's system for reentrancy checking [66] (introduced in Sect. 3.4). In this system, the critical effect describes code which is safe to use inside a critical section, but which may not begin another (nested) critical section or end the current (presumed) critical section. For our evaluation, rather than focusing on non-reentrant locks (which are little-used in Java), we have focused instead on database transactions, as some database systems (notably Hibernate) do not support nested transactions at all, while general-purpose database interfaces like JDBC leave the behavior of nested transactions up to the particular backend chosen (making the use of nested transactions clearly wrong for some backends, and more generally undefined behavior).

For our case study we focus on a variant of JBoss Hibernate's transaction API.[5] Consider the code in Fig. 7 from Hibernate's documentation.[6] Despite its small size, the main method `docExample` (correctly) handles several significant subtleties. The main transaction itself is in a `try-catch` block, as the session and

[5] This is a variant of the current API with checked exceptions. We must currently use a variant because the Checker Framework's support for stub files (a means to externally annotate compiled JAR files) does not work with multiple checkers "owning" the `@ThrownEffect` annotation. While this certainly affects the real-world applicability of our checker as a tool, it does not impact our evaluation of error reporting accuracy against an extracted copy of the API, and our focus is evaluation of the residual-based error reporting.

[6] https://docs.jboss.org/hibernate/orm/3.2/api/org/hibernate/Session.html#beginTransaction().

transaction methods may throw an exception. The `doWork()` method, a factored out transaction body, is marked `@Critical`. The commit method is annotated as

```
@Unlocking
@ThrownEffect(exception=TxException.class, behavior=Basic.class)
public void commit();
```

indicating that if it succeeds it behaves as if unlocking (i.e., finishing the transaction), while if it throws a `SQLException` the transaction remains open. This ensures that if the body throws an exception, the catch block is checked assuming the code has not yet finished the transaction, requiring the rollback attempt. Because rollback is typically a last-resort fallback, it is annotated as

```
@Unlocking
@ThrownEffect(exception=TxException.class, behavior=Unlocking.class)
public void rollback();
```

since if it fails, the connection is almost certainly broken, and the database will automatically rollback the transaction after a timeout.

Unlike the atomicity system, some sequential compositions in the reentrancy effect system are already undefined (recall Fig. 2b), and would be immediately and locally rejected even without residual-based error detection, which is focused on cases where composition is defined but has already committed the program being analyzed to a course already known to be incompatible with its top-level effect specification. So, for example, attempting to start an additional nested transaction would have effect `@Locking`$\rhd$`@Locking`, which is undefined and would be rejected without our extensions. The additional cases which are rejected earlier due to residual-based error checking are related to the rows of Fig. 2b's $\rhd$ table lacking certain operations: notice that each non-unit row of the table has either $\mathsf{locking}$ and $\mathsf{entrant}$ results, or $\mathsf{unlocking}$ and $\mathsf{critical}$ results. The former rows (for $\mathsf{locking} \rhd -$ and $\mathsf{entrant} \rhd -$) correspond to cases where the code has already committed to being code that must start running *not* inside a transaction, so have no residual with respect to a method-level annotation that the method's code should be able to start inside a transaction (i.e., have the $\mathsf{critical}$ or $\mathsf{unlocking}$) effect.

The additional errors thus manifest in refactoring of the example code's actual work into `doWork`. In large projects, it is easy to lose track of the intended execution context of a method [28], sometimes resulting in developers incorrectly assuming they may need to construct some of that context themselves. While directly starting a nested transaction in the same syntactic scope as another transaction start would be undefined and therefore reported precisely even without our extension (one of the original, informal arguments in favor of effect quantales being partial [27]), factoring the body of the transaction out into this helper method requires annotating the transaction body method with an effect. If it were annotated with `@Entrant`, the call site (specifically) would be rejected as undefined (since `@Locking`$\rhd$`@Entrant` is undefined). Annotating it as `@Critical` (as we do) the call site is accepted, but the factored-out method would be rejected, raising the question of where the error would be reported. Our technique reports the start of the nested transaction as the error location even if it is the first line of code:

```
@Critical
@ThrownEffect(exception=TxException.class, behavior=Critical.class)
public void doWork(Transaction tx) throws TxException {
  ...
  tx.begin(); // <-- error reported
  ...
}
```

Thus also with an effect quantale with partially-defined compositions, residual-based error checking yields additional precise error locations.

7 Related Work

The most closely-related work to ours is that on implementations of sequential effect systems. The implementations we know of for concrete sequential effect systems [20,63] do not have error handling described in the corresponding publications, but are formalized in the standard way which corresponds to the all-at-once method behavior check. It is possible that these systems implemented some kind of eager error reporting in the tools themselves, but the sources are no longer available and in any case these would be optimizations for specific effect systems. Our results establish a profitable eager error reporting strategy for *many* sequential effect systems expressible as effect quantales (it is not necessarily the case that all effect quantales have a residual operator as we propose, but all those described as effect quantales in the literature [27] have residual operators).

There have also been a number of generalized implementations of sequential effect system frameworks. Hicks et al. [34] implement a general elaboration to polymonadic effects, which are equivalent to Tate's productors [66]. They use a constraint-based approach to determine which specific monad each expression should be in (and therefore the effect of each expression). Orchard and Petricek [52] and Bracker and Nilsson [8] implement an embedding of graded monads into Haskell, using typeclass constraints to define the composition and lifting operations. Because this is constraint-based, effect errors will be issued at an arbitrary program point corresponding to a failed constraint, which as in general type inference may be not directly related to the actual mistake in the program. Bracker and Nilsson [9,10] later defined *supermonads*, which generalize many monadic computation types by generalizing to an arbitrary number of parameters to a monadic type (vs. 1 for indexed monads [70], 2 for parameterized monads [3]), and can be used to express polymonads. They also added specialized support for supermonad constraints to Haskell's type inference. Ultimately, because the constraints are still solved in an arbitrary solver-selected order, this suffers from the same problems with unpredictable error locations that exist in the normal Haskell implementations, where errors may be issued in unproblematic program locations, and program changes unrelated to the error may change where an error is reported by affecting constraint solving order. Our approach yields predictable error locations with some guaranteed relevance to actual program errors.

More broadly, there is a wealth of work on better localizing type errors in constraint-based type inference. Many techniques have been applied with a wide variety of trade-offs. Most of this involves searching for a minimal program or type repair that results in inference succeeding [12,44,54,55,73], and reports the location whose term or type was assumed to change or whose type constraint was removed as the most likely error location (in general a program with a general type error may have many incompatible constraints, so the smallest number of changes or removals that fixes the most incompatibilities is likely a source). These approaches are all quite sensible, though both their approaches and setting differs significantly from ours. None of this work on localizing type inference errors treats effects (notably, none of it targets a language in which monads are used to encode effects, though in principle these techniques could be applied to Haskell and thus the Haskell embeddings of effects above). The assumptions available to us for our work are also much stronger in some ways than what is available to the general type inference localization problem. Because sequential effects are so closely coupled with evaluation order, there is a semantically-meaningful notion of best error location, while in general type inference the earliest inconsistency in program order may not be meaningfully related to the actual error location (hence the common practice there of exploring formalizations of the intuitive notions of "minimum changes to fix"). In addition, our effects have far more structure than typical type inference problems, because compared to general bags of constraints as in HM(X) [51] or extensions thereof for object-orientation [56,69], effect quantales afford a convenient algebraic characterization of an operation useful for error location: the residual. As a result, our work is the first which takes an *algebraic* approach to localizing effect errors.

8 Conclusions

We have proposed the first algebraic approach to localizing errors in sequential (flow-sensitive) effect systems, by exploiting the notion of a partial residual. This approach is guaranteed to give more precise error locations than the method-global (and therefore highly imprecise) or constraint-based (and therefore unpredictable) techniques used in all prior sequential effect system implementations, locations which are moreover guaranteed to have relevance to the actual program mistake. We have implemented our technique for Java in a fork of the open source Checker Framework, and shown that our technique gives specific meaningful error messages for previously studied bugs.

Acknowledgements. This work was supported in part by US National Science Foundation Grant #CCF-2007582.

References

1. Abadi, M., Flanagan, C., Freund, S.N.: Types for safe locking: static race detection for Java. ACM Trans. Program. Lang. Syst. **28**(2) (2006)
2. Amtoft, T., Nielson, F., Nielson, H.R.: Type and Effect Systems: Behaviours for Concurrency. Imperial College Press, London (1999)
3. Atkey, R.: Parameterised notions of computation. J. Funct. Program. **19**, 335–376 (2009)
4. Bao, Y., Wei, G., Bračevac, O., Juan, Y., He, Q., Rompf, T.: Reachability types: tracking aliasing and separation in higher-order functional programs. Proc. ACM Program. Lang. **5**(OOPSLA) (2021)
5. Birkhoff, G.: Lattice Theory, Colloquium Publications, vol. 25. American Mathematical Society (1940). Third edition, eighth printing with corrections, 1995
6. Bocchino, R.L., Jr., et al.: A type and effect system for deterministic parallel Java. In: OOPSLA (2009). https://doi.org/10.1145/1640089.1640097
7. Boyapati, C., Lee, R., Rinard, M.: Ownership types for safe programming: preventing data races and deadlocks. In: OOPSLA (2002)
8. Bracker, J., Nilsson, H.: Polymonad programming in Haskell. In: Proceedings of the 27th Symposium on the Implementation and Application of Functional Programming Languages, IFL 2015. Association for Computing Machinery, New York (2015). https://doi.org/10.1145/2897336.2897340
9. Bracker, J., Nilsson, H.: Supermonads: one notion to bind them all. In: Proceedings of the 9th International Symposium on Haskell, pp. 158–169 (2016)
10. Bracker, J., Nilsson, H.: Supermonads and superapplicatives. J. Funct. Program. 103 (2018)
11. Chen, S., Erwig, M.: Counter-factual typing for debugging type errors. In: Proceedings of the 41st ACM SIGPLAN-SIGACT Symposium on Principles of Programming Languages, pp. 583–594 (2014)
12. Chen, S., Erwig, M.: Systematic identification and communication of type errors. J. Funct. Program. **28** (2018)
13. Dietl, W., Dietzel, S., Ernst, M.D., Muşlu, K., Schiller, T.: Building and using pluggable type-checkers. In: ICSE (2011)
14. Dilworth, R.P.: Non-commutative residuated lattices. Trans. Am. Math. Soc. **46**(3), 426–444 (1939)
15. Flanagan, C., Abadi, M.: Object types against races. In: Baeten, J.C.M., Mauw, S. (eds.) CONCUR 1999. LNCS, vol. 1664, pp. 288–303. Springer, Heidelberg (1999). https://doi.org/10.1007/3-540-48320-9_21
16. Flanagan, C., Abadi, M.: Types for safe locking. In: Swierstra, S.D. (ed.) ESOP 1999. LNCS, vol. 1576, pp. 91–108. Springer, Heidelberg (1999). https://doi.org/10.1007/3-540-49099-X_7
17. Flanagan, C., Freund, S.N.: Type-based race detection for Java. In: PLDI (2000). https://doi.org/10.1145/349299.349328
18. Flanagan, C., Freund, S.N., Lifshin, M.: Type inference for atomicity. In: Proceedings of the 2005 ACM SIGPLAN International Workshop on Types in Languages Design and Implementation, pp. 47–58 (2005)
19. Flanagan, C., Freund, S.N., Lifshin, M., Qadeer, S.: Types for atomicity: static checking and inference for Java. ACM Trans. Program. Lang. Syst. (TOPLAS) **30**(4), 1–53 (2008)
20. Flanagan, C., Qadeer, S.: A type and effect system for atomicity. In: PLDI (2003)
21. Flanagan, C., Qadeer, S.: Types for atomicity. In: TLDI (2003)

22. Foster, J.S., Fähndrich, M., Aiken, A.: A theory of type qualifiers. In: Proceedings of the ACM SIGPLAN 1999 Conference on Programming Language Design and Implementation, PLDI 1999, pp. 192–203. ACM (1999). https://doi.org/10.1145/301618.301665
23. Galatos, N., Jipsen, P., Kowalski, T., Ono, H.: Residuated Lattices: An Algebraic Glimpse at Substructural Logics. Studies in Logic and the Foundations of Mathematics, vol. 151. Elsevier (2007)
24. Gifford, D.K., Lucassen, J.M.: Integrating functional and imperative programming. In: Proceedings of the 1986 ACM Conference on LISP and Functional Programming, LFP 1986 (1986)
25. Gordon, C.S.: A generic approach to flow-sensitive polymorphic effects. In: Proceedings of the 31st European Conference on Object-Oriented Programming (ECOOP 2017), Barcelona, Spain (2017). https://doi.org/10.4230/LIPIcs.ECOOP.2017.13
26. Gordon, C.S.: Lifting sequential effects to control operators. In: Proceedings of the 34th European Conference on Object-Oriented Programming (ECOOP 2020), Berlin, Germany (2020). https://doi.org/10.4230/LIPIcs.ECOOP.2020.23
27. Gordon, C.S.: Polymorphic iterable sequential effect systems. ACM Trans. Program. Lang. Syst. (TOPLAS) **43**(1) (2021). https://doi.org/10.1145/3450272
28. Gordon, C.S., Dietl, W., Ernst, M.D., Grossman, D.: $\mathsf{Java}_{\mathsf{UI}}$: effects for controlling UI object access. In: Castagna, G. (ed.) ECOOP 2013. LNCS, vol. 7920, pp. 179–204. Springer, Heidelberg (2013). https://doi.org/10.1007/978-3-642-39038-8_8
29. Gordon, C.S., Ernst, M.D., Grossman, D.: Static lock capabilities for deadlock freedom. In: Proceedings of the 8th ACM SIGPLAN Workshop on Types in Language Design and Implementation (TLDI 2012), Philadelphia, PA, USA (2012). https://doi.org/10.1145/2103786.2103796
30. Gordon, C.S., Yun, C.: Artifact for error localization for sequential effect systems (2023). https://doi.org/10.6084/m9.figshare.23822877
31. Gordon, C.S., Yun, C.: Error localization for sequential effect systems (extended version). No. arXiv cs.PL 2307.15777 (2023). https://doi.org/10.48550/arXiv.2307.15777
32. Gosling, J., Joy, B., Steele, G.L., Bracha, G., Buckley, A.: The Java Language Specification: Java SE 8 Edition. Pearson Education (2014)
33. Hassan, M., Urban, C., Eilers, M., Müller, P.: MaxSMT-based type inference for Python 3. In: Chockler, H., Weissenbacher, G. (eds.) CAV 2018. LNCS, vol. 10982, pp. 12–19. Springer, Cham (2018). https://doi.org/10.1007/978-3-319-96142-2_2
34. Hicks, M., Bierman, G., Guts, N., Leijen, D., Swamy, N.: Polymonadic programming. Electron. Proc. Theor. Comput. Sci. **153**, 79–99 (2014). https://doi.org/10.4204/eptcs.153.7
35. Ivašković, A., Mycroft, A.: A graded monad for deadlock-free concurrency (functional pearl). In: Proceedings of the 13th ACM SIGPLAN International Symposium on Haskell, pp. 17–30 (2020)
36. Ivašković, A., Mycroft, A., Orchard, D.: Data-flow analyses as effects and graded monads. In: 5th International Conference on Formal Structures for Computation and Deduction (FSCD 2020), vol. 167. Dagstuhl (2020)
37. Katsumata, S.: Parametric effect monads and semantics of effect systems. In: POPL (2014)
38. Koskinen, E., Terauchi, T.: Local temporal reasoning. In: CSL/LICS (2014)
39. Kot, L., Kozen, D.: Second-order abstract interpretation via Kleene algebra. Technical report, Cornell University Ithaca (2004)

40. Kozen, D.: Kleene algebra with tests. ACM Trans. Program. Lang. Syst. (TOPLAS) **19**(3), 427–443 (1997). https://doi.org/10.1145/256167.256195
41. Lambek, J.: The mathematics of sentence structure. Am. Math. Mon. **65**(3), 154–170 (1958)
42. Lerner, B.S., Flower, M., Grossman, D., Chambers, C.: Searching for type-error messages. In: Proceedings of the 28th ACM SIGPLAN Conference on Programming Language Design and Implementation, pp. 425–434 (2007)
43. Lipton, R.J.: Reduction: a method of proving properties of parallel programs. Commun. ACM **18**(12), 717–721 (1975). https://doi.org/10.1145/361227.361234
44. Loncaric, C., Chandra, S., Schlesinger, C., Sridharan, M.: A practical framework for type inference error explanation. In: Proceedings of the 2016 ACM SIGPLAN International Conference on Object-Oriented Programming, Systems, Languages, and Applications, pp. 781–799 (2016)
45. Long, Y., Liu, Y.D., Rajan, H.: Intensional effect polymorphism. In: Boyland, J.T. (ed.) 29th European Conference on Object-Oriented Programming (ECOOP 2015). Leibniz International Proceedings in Informatics (LIPIcs), vol. 37, pp. 346–370. Schloss Dagstuhl-Leibniz-Zentrum fuer Informatik (2015). https://doi.org/10.4230/LIPIcs.ECOOP.2015.346. http://drops.dagstuhl.de/opus/volltexte/2015/5221
46. Lucassen, J.M., Gifford, D.K.: Polymorphic effect systems. In: POPL (1988)
47. Mycroft, A., Orchard, D., Petricek, T.: Effect systems revisited—control-flow algebra and semantics. In: Probst, C.W., Hankin, C., Hansen, R.R. (eds.) Semantics, Logics, and Calculi. LNCS, vol. 9560, pp. 1–32. Springer, Cham (2016). https://doi.org/10.1007/978-3-319-27810-0_1
48. Neamtiu, I., Hicks, M., Foster, J.S., Pratikakis, P.: Contextual effects for version-consistent dynamic software updating and safe concurrent programming. In: POPL, pp. 37–49 (2008)
49. Nielson, F., Nielson, H.R.: From CML to process algebras. In: Best, E. (ed.) CONCUR 1993. LNCS, vol. 715, pp. 493–508. Springer, Heidelberg (1993). https://doi.org/10.1007/3-540-57208-2_34
50. Nielson, H.R., Nielson, F.: Communication analysis for concurrent ML. In: Nielson, F. (ed.) ML with Concurrency: Design, Analysis, Implementation, and Application. MCS, pp. 185–235. Springer, Cham (1997). https://doi.org/10.1007/978-1-4612-2274-3_7
51. Odersky, M., Sulzmann, M., Wehr, M.: Type inference with constrained types. Theory Pract. Object Syst. **5**(1), 35 (1999)
52. Orchard, D., Petricek, T.: Embedding effect systems in Haskell. In: Proceedings of the 2014 ACM SIGPLAN Symposium on Haskell, pp. 13–24 (2014)
53. Papi, M.M., Ali, M., Correa, T.L., Jr., Perkins, J.H., Ernst, M.D.: Practical pluggable types for Java. In: ISSTA (2008)
54. Pavlinovic, Z., King, T., Wies, T.: Finding minimum type error sources. In: Proceedings of the 2014 ACM International Conference on Object Oriented Programming Systems Languages & Applications, pp. 525–542 (2014)
55. Pavlinovic, Z., King, T., Wies, T.: Practical SMT-based type error localization. In: Proceedings of the 20th ACM SIGPLAN International Conference on Functional Programming, pp. 412–423 (2015)
56. Pottier, F.: A framework for type inference with subtyping. In: Proceedings of the third ACM SIGPLAN International Conference on Functional Programming (ICFP 1998), pp. 228–238 (1998). https://doi.org/10.1145/291251.289448

57. Pratt, V.: Action logic and pure induction. In: van Eijck, J. (ed.) JELIA 1990. LNCS, vol. 478, pp. 97–120. Springer, Heidelberg (1991). https://doi.org/10.1007/BFb0018436
58. Rytz, L., Odersky, M., Haller, P.: Lightweight polymorphic effects. In: Noble, J. (ed.) ECOOP 2012. LNCS, vol. 7313, pp. 258–282. Springer, Heidelberg (2012). https://doi.org/10.1007/978-3-642-31057-7_13
59. Sasturkar, A., Agarwal, R., Wang, L., Stoller, S.D.: Automated type-based analysis of data races and atomicity. In: Proceedings of the Tenth ACM SIGPLAN Symposium on Principles and Practice of Parallel Programming, pp. 83–94 (2005)
60. Bañados Schwerter, F., Garcia, R., Tanter, E.: A theory of gradual effect systems. In: Proceedings of the 19th ACM SIGPLAN International Conference on Functional Programming, ICFP 2014, pp. 283–295. ACM (2014). https://doi.org/10.1145/2628136.2628149
61. Skalka, C.: Types and trace effects for object orientation. High.-Order Symb. Comput. **21**(3) (2008)
62. Skalka, C., Darais, D., Jaeger, T., Capobianco, F.: Types and abstract interpretation for authorization hook advice. In: 2020 IEEE 33rd Computer Security Foundations Symposium (CSF), pp. 139–152. IEEE (2020)
63. Skalka, C., Smith, S., Van Horn, D.: Types and trace effects of higher order programs. J. Funct. Program. **18**(2) (2008)
64. Suenaga, K.: Type-based deadlock-freedom verification for non-block-structured lock primitives and mutable references. In: Ramalingam, G. (ed.) APLAS 2008. LNCS, vol. 5356, pp. 155–170. Springer, Heidelberg (2008). https://doi.org/10.1007/978-3-540-89330-1_12
65. Talpin, J.P., Jouvelot, P.: Polymorphic type, region and effect inference. J. Funct. Program. **2**(03), 245–271 (1992). https://doi.org/10.1017/S0956796800000393
66. Tate, R.: The sequential semantics of producer effect systems. In: POPL (2013)
67. Tofte, M., Talpin, J.P.: Region-based memory management. Inf. Comput. **132**(2), 109–176 (1997)
68. Toro, M., Tanter, E.: Customizable gradual polymorphic effects for Scala. In: Proceedings of the 2015 ACM SIGPLAN International Conference on Object-Oriented Programming, Systems, Languages, and Applications, OOPSLA 2015, pp. 935–953. ACM (2015). https://doi.org/10.1145/2814270.2814315
69. Trifonov, V., Smith, S.: Subtyping constrained types. In: Cousot, R., Schmidt, D.A. (eds.) SAS 1996. LNCS, vol. 1145, pp. 349–365. Springer, Heidelberg (1996). https://doi.org/10.1007/3-540-61739-6_52
70. Wadler, P., Thiemann, P.: The marriage of effects and monads. Trans. Comput. Logic (TOCL) **4**, 1–32 (2003)
71. Ward, M., Dilworth, R.P.: Residuated lattices. Trans. Am. Math. Soc. **45**(3), 335–354 (1939)
72. Yi, J., Disney, T., Freund, S.N., Flanagan, C.: Cooperative types for controlling thread interference in Java. In: Proceedings of the 2012 International Symposium on Software Testing and Analysis, pp. 232–242 (2012)
73. Zhang, D., Myers, A.C.: Toward general diagnosis of static errors. In: Proceedings of the 41st ACM SIGPLAN-SIGACT Symposium on Principles of Programming Languages, pp. 569–581 (2014)

Scaling up Roundoff Analysis of Functional Data Structure Programs

Anastasia Isychev[1](✉) and Eva Darulova[2]

[1] TU Munich, Munich, Germany
izycheva@in.tum.de
[2] Uppsala University, Uppsala, Sweden
eva.darulova@it.uu.se

Abstract. Floating-point arithmetic is counter-intuitive due to inherent rounding errors that potentially occur at every arithmetic operation. A selection of automated tools now exists to ensure correctness of floating-point programs by computing guaranteed bounds on rounding errors at the end of a computation, but these tools effectively consider only straight-line programs over scalar variables. Much of numerical codes, however, use data structures such as lists, arrays or matrices and loops over these. To analyze such programs today, all data structure operations need to be unrolled, manually or by the analyzer, reducing the analysis to straight-line code, ultimately limiting the analyzers' scalability.

We present the first rounding error analysis for numerical programs written over vectors and matrices that leverages the data structure information to speed up the analysis. We facilitate this with our *functional* domain-specific input language that we design based on a new set of numerical benchmarks that we collect from a variety of domains. Our DSL explicitly carries semantic information that is useful for avoiding duplicate and thus unnecessary analysis steps, as well as enabling abstractions for further speed-ups. Compared to unrolling-based approaches in state-of-the-art tools, our analysis retains adequate accuracy and is able to analyze more benchmarks or is significantly faster, and particularly scales better for larger programs.

Keywords: floating-point arithmetic · rounding error · data structures

1 Introduction

Floating-point arithmetic is notorious for being unintuitive due to its special values as well as rounding operations, the latter inevitably introducing errors at

M. V. Hermenegildo and J. F. Morales (Eds.): SAS 2023, LNCS 14284, pp. 371–402, 2023.
https://doi.org/10.1007/978-3-031-44245-2_17

most arithmetic operations. While special values (Not-a-Number and Infinity) can be explicitly and relatively easily detected during a computation, rounding errors are more tricky as, in general, one does not have results of an exact, infinite-precision computation available for comparison. Static analysis techniques that *soundly* bound rounding errors for all possible inputs, i.e. that compute a guaranteed upper bound on the errors, are thus essential especially for safety-critical systems.

Providing a reasonably accurate sound rounding analysis that tightly bounds rounding errors without extensive over-approximation is intricate already for non-linear *straight-line* code, as the number of recent efforts and tools demonstrates [7–9,13,30,31]. Effectively analyzing finite precision beyond straight-line code, and scaling to larger programs is an open challenge [8,9].

Much of numerical code operates over data structures such as arrays and matrices using some form of loop, for instance when computing statistics during data analyses, performing signal processing or Fourier and stencil transforms in embedded systems, calculating dot products in neural networks, etc. In principle, it is possible to 'unroll' such operations into straight-line code, by assigning individual array elements to scalar variables and unrolling all loops. Existing tools either expect this transformation to be done manually by the user in a tedious and error-prone process [9], or allow the user to specify programs imperatively as loops over arrays and unroll automatically when instructed to do so [13]. One way or another, the rounding error analysis itself is reduced to one over a potentially huge straight-line program, limiting the analyses' scalability.

The alternative standard approach for verifying programs with arrays that abstracts all data structure elements by a single representative are, in general, unsuitable for finite-precision rounding error analysis. The reason for this is that the magnitude of rounding errors directly and significantly depends on the magnitudes of the program inputs. Abstracting data structure elements of different sizes by a single value, resp. interval, leads to over-approximations of the rounding errors, and thus to inaccurate and possibly unusable error bounds.

This paper presents the first rounding error analysis with *explicit* support for operations and bounded loops over array-like data structures (i.e. vectors or lists and matrices). To facilitate this analysis we design a *functional* domain-specific input language (DSL) with operations over lists and matrices that allows to express many commonly used patterns in numerical computing and that serves as the input to our tool.

The benefit of a functional input language is two-fold. First, it allows users to succinctly express their computations and reduces the possibility of common (off-by-one) indexing errors. More importantly, however, a functional language carries *semantic information* that can be *leveraged* by the analysis, removing the need to unroll many operations. For example, loops applying a function to each value in a list (functional `map(`$\lambda x.f(x)$`)`) do not propagate errors between iterations, and a rounding error analysis only has to analyze the loop body once. An unrolling of the loop would lose that high-level information and effectively re-compute the analysis for each loop iteration. For operations that do require unrolling, we show how to use the semantic information to avoid recomputing analysis information that can be effectively over-approximated, further reducing the burden on the analysis. Our abstraction is designed for rounding errors and accounts for different variables' ranges and thus provides a viable tradeoff between analysis accuracy and performance.

We design our input DSL based on a new set of numerical benchmarks that we collected from a variety of domains. We implement our rounding error analysis for this DSL in a tool called DS2L and show that compared to a baseline analysis that unrolls all operations, it can substantially reduce analysis time with little impact on analysis accuracy.

Note that all loops in our DSL are bounded: they are loops over the elements in a data structure (e.g. via higher-order functions). We specifically do not attempt to solve the general problem of rounding errors in unbounded loops [8], but focus on providing an efficient analysis for commonly used operations over data structures.

Our focus is on *scalability* and we thus compare DS2L against the two most scalable (available) rounding error analysis tools Fluctuat [13] and Satire [9]. Our evaluation shows that for benchmarks with large data structure sizes, DS2L scales significantly better: it can analyze many more benchmarks (has fewer timeouts, overflows and infinite error bounds) and is several times faster.

While we evaluate DS2L only on floating-point code to permit a comparison with existing tools, our analysis extends to fixed-point arithmetic as well and DS2L only requires a simple implementation change.

Contributions. In summary, this paper makes the following contributions:

- a new open-source finite-precision benchmark set;
- a fully automated, sound rounding error analysis for programs written in a functional DSL (Sect. 4);
- an open-source implementation of this analysis (Sect. 5);
- an evaluation against state-of-the-art analysis tools (Sect. 6).

The artifact with the benchmark set, DS2L's source code and scripts to run the experiments is available under https://zenodo.org/record/8179028, the source code is also available at https://github.com/malyzajko/daisy.

2 State-of-the-Art in Rounding Error Analysis

Before we explain our own approach, we first provide background on existing rounding error analysis tools that work for straight-line code with arithmetic operations on *scalar* values. Our own analysis (explained in Sect. 4) re-uses this baseline for straight-line arithmetic expressions, and we use it also for comparison in the evaluation (Sect. 6). The vast majority of existing sound rounding error analyses abstract the IEEE-754 [17] floating-point operations with the following equation:

$$x \circ_F y = (x \circ y)(1 + e) + d, |e| \leq \epsilon_M, |d| \leq \delta_M \tag{1}$$

where $\circ \in \{+,-,*,/\}$, $\circ_F$ is the respective floating-point operation, ϵ_M is the machine epsilon and δ_M captures the error due to subnormal numbers. $\epsilon_M = 2^{-53}$ and $\delta_M = 2^{-1075}$ for double-precision floating-point arithmetic that we assume in this paper. $e(x \circ y) + d$ then bounds the worst-case absolute rounding error of an operation $x \circ y$.[1] Errors on individual operations thus depend on the magnitude of the intermediate expressions (such as $x \circ y$), and furthermore propagate through subsequent operations where they may get magnified or diminished, depending on the operation and the ranges.

State-of-the-art rounding error analyses use one of two approaches: dataflow based as implemented in the tools Fluctuat [13] and Daisy [7], or global optimization-based as implemented in FPTaylor [30], Precisa [31] or Satire [9].

The baseline analysis that we choose for straight-line arithmetic operations is of the dataflow type. To compute the overall error, a forward dataflow analysis tracks two abstract domains: one for the (real-valued) ranges at each intermediate operation, and one for the accumulated errors. These are typically computed using interval arithmetic [27] and affine arithmetic [11], respectively. Affine arithmetic can track linear correlations between variables and often (but not always) computes more accurate error bounds than interval arithmetic.

The alternative analysis phrases the computation of the rounding error as a global nonlinear real-valued optimization problem [9,30,31]. We specifically choose a dataflow approach as our base analysis for several reasons. First, it is unclear how to *effectively* use semantic information from the iterators in the global error constraint. Additionally, we identified optimization opportunities when the range information is available separately from the errors. Finally, even though in this paper we focus on floating-point arithmetic for simplicity, dataflow analysis is immediately applicable to fixed-point arithmetic as well, making our analysis more widely applicable. A global symbolic error constraint optimization works well for floats whose dynamic range allows them to represent many values. However, an *efficient usage* of fixed-points requires the integer and fractional bits to be assigned individually for *each subexpression*. To do that, one needs to know the full range of values taken by a (sub-)expression. While it is technically possible to obtain this information also for the symbolic error constraint (for instance, with some other analysis), this incurs significant overhead. Therefore, the global optimization-based approach is only applied to floating-points.

3 DSL for List-Like Data Structures

Before designing our functional domain-specific language for numerical computations (Sect. 3.2), we collected a new set of benchmarks that informed the design of our DSL, and specifically the set of supported operations (Sect. 3.3).

[1] We compute *absolute* errors. While relative errors may seem a more appropriate error measure and some analyses exist [18,29], in practice their computation is limited to applications where 0 does not occur as a possible value (otherwise leading to undefined errors), severely limiting their applicability.

3.1 Benchmark Set

Rounding error analysis on programs that contain operations on data structures such as arrays and loops over them is an open challenge, and correspondingly there is no standard benchmark set yet. The existing FPBench benchmarks [6] cover only straight-line code and a few while-loops but no data structures. We therefore create a new benchmark set that covers different domains where numerical computations are frequent:

- statistical computations: *avg, stdDeviation, variance*
- linear and nonlinear digital filters: *roux1, goubault, harmonic* and *nonlin{1–3}* [25]
- differential equations: *lorenz, pendulum* [8,9]
- signal processing: *alphaBlending* (image mask), *fftvector, fftmatrix* (two versions of forward Fourier transform)
- stencil computations: *convolve2d_size3, sobel3, heat1d* [8,9]
- neural networks: *lyapunov, controllerTora* [20]

Some of the benchmarks from FPBench contain loop bodies of control loops, which we rephrase as loops over arrays of sensor data. Other benchmarks have been collected from scientific publications [8,9,20,25] as well as open-source implementations in different programming languages.

3.2 A Functional DSL

Many verification techniques face the dilemma of either adapting the techniques to work on legacy code and (possibly) giving up some precision, or requiring to rewrite the code with verification in mind and being able to reason about a program in more detail. In this work, we choose the second option, and note that our domain-specific language uses Scala syntax and is similar to other existing functional languages and we thus expect it to be largely familiar to developers.

The goal of our DSL is to allow a convenient way to 1) write programs that perform operations on array-like data structures and 2) to analyze them. Our main insight is that a functional style of programming covers both aspects: it allows for a more succinct representation of programs and it retains high-level semantic information of the operations that can be leveraged by the analysis.

heat1d Example. We illustrate the succinctness of our DSL on one of the benchmarks that we collected from related work [9]. Figure 1 shows the function *heat1d* in the input formats of two different tools. The *heat1d* function takes as input a temperature distribution and computes the temperature at a coordinate `x0` after 32 units of time. The computation requires temperature values for neighboring coordinates which must be repeatedly recomputed, which is essentially a stencil.

The original straight-line version of the *heat1d* benchmark comes from Satire analyzer [9] and includes *1094 lines of code*, 67 of which specify input ranges of (individual) variables, the rest are unrolled loops. Unrolled computations are not only lengthy, but also error-prone and unnatural for a user to write. A more

```c
#include <fluctuat_math.h>
#define N 33
// stencil computations
double heat1d(double (*xm)[N], double (*xp)[N], double* x0) {
int i,j;
for(j=1;j<N; j++) {
  for(i=2; i<(N-j); i++) {
    xm[j][i]=0.25*xm[j-1][i+1]+0.5*xm[j-1][i]+0.25*xm[j-1][i-1];
    xp[j][i]=0.25*xp[j-1][i-1]+0.5*xp[j-1][i]+0.25*xp[j-1][i+1];
  }
  xm[j][0] = 0.25*xm[j-1][1] + 0.5*xm[j-1][0] + 0.25*x0[j-1];
  xp[j][0] = 0.25*xp[j-1][1] + 0.5*xp[j-1][0] + 0.25*x0[j-1];
  x0[j] = 0.25*xm[0][j-1] + 0.5*x0[j-1] + 0.25*xp[0][j-1];
}
return x0[N-1];
}
int main() {
  int i,j;
  double x0[N];
  double xm[N][N];
  double xp[N][N];
  // specify input ranges
  for(i=0; i<N; i++){
    x0[i] = DBETWEEN(1.0, 2.0);
    for(j=0; j<N; j++){
      xm[i][j] = DBETWEEN(1.0, 2.0);
      xp[i][j] = DBETWEEN(1.0, 2.0);
  }}
  heat1d(xm, xp, x0);
  return 0;
}
```

(a) Imperative loop (Fluctuat's input)

```scala
def heat1d(ax: Vector): Real = {
 require(1.0<=ax && ax<=2.0 && ax.size(33))
 if (ax.length() <= 1) {
   ax.head
 } else {
   val coef = Vector(List(0.25, 0.5, 0.25))
   val updCoefs: Vector =
    ax.slideReduce(3,1)(v => (coef*v).sum())
   heat1d(updCoefs)
 }
}
```

(b) Functional style (our DSL)

Fig. 1. heat1d benchmark in input formats for different tools

natural choice when implementing the same algorithm in an imperative style is to use two nested loops. Figure 1a shows the same algorithm written in C formatted for the tool Fluctuat [13]. A loop representation is more succinct—14 lines of code with computations, however it requires loop bounds to be set manually and may lead to index-out-of-bounds errors.

We show the same function *heat1d* written in our functional DSL in Fig. 1b. It uses a sliding window over a list (`slideReduce` operation, explained in more detail in Sect. 3.3) and passes the new values into a recursive call. In contrast to alternative implementations, a functional style program is much shorter—6 lines of code—and eliminates index-out-of-bounds errors as it does not require users to explicitly write elements' indices.

DSL Design. Our DSL is designed for writing numerical algorithms on array-like data structures and was inspired by the popular libraries Lift [15] and TensorFlow [23]. It includes commonly occurring operations on vectors and matrices from the collected benchmarks. When naming DSL functions, we have re-used the names used by Lift and TensorFlow whenever possible and attempted to make other functions' names self-explanatory. We do not expect our current DSL to exhaustively cover all possible numerical programs; rather it serves as a starting point already covering a variety of operations that can and should be extended in the future.

Data Types. Following previous work in rounding error analysis, all values and operations in our DSL are real-valued (as opposed to finite precision), i.e. they have a `Real` type[2]. Real-valued algorithms are more intuitive for a user to write, and easier to analyze as they provide a clear reference semantics. Our DSL provides two data types: a `Vector` is an indexed sequence of `Real` scalar values, and a `Matrix` corresponds to a sequence of vectors of the same length. In the following, we refer to lists (`Vectors`) as vectors, and vectors and matrices as data structures (DSs), for simplicity. Our DSL is purely functional, and as such all data structures are immutable.

To analyze a real-valued program, a user should specify the finite precision, for which the rounding error will be computed. By default our analysis computes the error for a uniform double floating-point precision. Alternative precision assignments can be passed as an additional parameter to our tool and are not a part of the DSL itself.

Input Ranges. Any rounding error analysis requires information on ranges of input variables. Both scalar and DS input ranges can be specified using the `require` clause. The specification should ideally be as precise as possible and provide tight ranges that can be different for some DS elements. We therefore allow two ways to specify input ranges for DSs. If all elements have the same input range, it is enough to specify the range once for the whole DS (`1.0 <= ax && ax <= 2.0`). Additionally, it is possible to specify individual input ranges for subsets of DS elements. For vector elements these ranges are specified as a tuple $((loInd, hiInd), range)$, where $loInd$ and $hiInd$ are the smallest and the largest index of consecutive elements with the input range $range$. For example, to specify that the first and the second element of `ax` in *heat1d* have the input range $[0.0, 0.5]$, we would write `ax.range(0, 1)(0.0, 0.5)`. We also allow individual range specifications on matrices, however, specifying a lower and upper bound of an index range is ambiguous for a matrix. Therefore, we choose a more natural way for specifying special input ranges on matrices: a user has to list the indices of elements for that range. For example, to convey that the first element in the first and second row of a matrix `m` should have the range $[-0.5, 0.5]$, we write `m.specM(Set(Set((0,0),(1,0)),(-0.5,0.5)))`.[3]

DS Size. To analyze operations that traverse a DS, the analysis also needs to know the number of elements in the DS. Our DSL allows to specify the expected *maximum size* of an input data structure—length of a vector, number of rows and columns for a matrix. Having the upper bound on the number of elements in the DS allows us to compute sound results: reported ranges and rounding errors subsume the ranges and errors of programs with input DSs smaller than the specified size.

[2] Precisely, all *fractional* numbers have the type `Real`, while DS sizes and indices have the integer type `Int`.

[3] Admittedly, the `Set()` notation is not the most user-friendly way of input for small specifications. We use it for simplicity of implementation; the notation can be improved with extensions to our parser.

3.3 DSL Functions

Our DSL uses Scala syntax (a representative subset is available in the appendix in Fig. 5); semantically we can roughly split its functions into four groups:

1. *element-wise functions*, such as arithmetic operations and transcendental functions applied to individual elements of a DS;
2. *standard functions*, such as `map`, `fold` and `filter`;
3. *domain-specific* functions, e.g., stencil-like filters, matrix multiplication;
4. *non-numerical* operations, e.g., appending or flipping elements in DS.

Additionally, our DSL supports recursive calls with specific conditional statements. To avoid rounding errors in conditional expressions, we currently limit them to (integer) DS size comparisons `dssize` $\leq c$. Since we only handle *bounded* loops, the DS size must be finite and decreasing in each recursive iteration. Next, we explain the concrete semantics of the DSL functions using pseudocode that makes indices explicit (while they are typically implicit in our DSL). We choose to present the semantics with pseudocode (and not sets of rules), because it is more concise and because it expresses how the operators are ultimately evaluated, which is important for the rounding error analysis.

The semantics of most of our DSL operators is standard. Additionally, our analysis does *not* depend on exactly this DSL's syntax and semantics. We therefore expect our analysis to be *applicable to other (intermediate) representations or languages* with similar semantics. Such representation must (only) be purely functional (immutable variables and DS, no side-effects) and provide a syntactic distinction between different iterators, precisely, the functionality of an iterator must be unambiguous without an additional analysis of the iterator's body.

Element-Wise Functions. They cover arithmetic operations applied to a single DS or a pair of DS, for instance $v1+v2$, where $v1, v2$ are vectors. Semantically these operations are the same as arithmetic operations on scalar numbers. The only difference is that for binary operations on two DS, the operands must have the same dimension. Element-wise operations are defined for both vectors and matrices: the operation is applied to the elements in the operand DSs with the same indices. We also define element-wise operations with constants.

For all unary (`uop`) and binary (`bop`) arithmetic operations the semantics is:

```
a bop b = [a[i] bop b[i] | ∀i∈Indices(a), #Indices(a) == #Indices(b)]
uop(a) = [uop(a[i]) | ∀i∈Indices(a)]
```

In our example function *heat1d* in Fig. 1b (line 8) the expression `coef*v` is an element-wise multiplication of vectors `coef` and `v`: the i-th element of the output vector contains the result of multiplying the i-th element of `coef` with the i-th element of `v`.

Standard Functions. Classic functional-style functions `map`, `fold`, `filter` preserve their semantics. `map` and `fold` are defined on vector elements, and for a matrix on both rows and elements. We add a function `ds.sum()` as syntactic sugar for `fold` with an addition operator to compute a sum of DS elements.

We also extend the map on matrix rows to support indexed iterations with `enumRowsMap(λi,x.f(i,x))`. The function maps over rows of the matrix and applies f to both row's index and elements:

```
m.enumRowsMap(f) = [f(i, m[i,j]) | ∀i∈Rows(m), (i,j)∈Indices(m)]
```

`filter` is defined to apply the conditional to vector elements, and to matrix rows. We do not allow a `filter` on individual matrix elements, as it may result in modified and uneven matrix dimensions.

Domain-Specific Functions. Our DSL defines operations required for implementing neural networks (i.e. matrix multiplication), stencils and image processing filters. We describe the most interesting operations below.

Stencil operations usually require a more complex transformation than `map` or `fold` can provide. The transformations involve an outlook of several elements before and after the current element of a DS, as opposed to accessing a single element in one iteration of `map` and `fold`. Such an outlook is commonly called a sliding window. Our DSL defines it on vectors and matrices with `ds.slideReduce(size, step)(λx.f(x))`, where a window of size `size` shifts by `step` indices at every iteration. For vectors a window is a subset of consecutive elements of length `size`, for matrices a window is a matrix with dimensions `size×size`. A user-supplied function $f(x)$ is then applied to the created window, it returns a scalar value that is saved at the corresponding index of the newly created DS. Intuitively, it is similar to applying a `fold` to a sliding window.

Our example benchmark *heat1d* in Fig. 1b creates a sliding window of 3 vector elements and shifts the window by 1 index at every iteration; the resulting vector `updCoefs` contains results of the `sum()` operation. The pseudocode below explains `ax.slideReduce(3,1)(f)` using explicit indices of the vector `ax`:

```
k=0
∀ i∈ {1..size(ax)-2}:
    v = [ ax[i-1], ax[i], ax[i+1] ]
    updCoefs[k] = coef[0]*v[0] + coef[1]*v[1] + coef[2]*v[2] // f(v) = (coef*v).sum()
    k++
```

The pseudocode contains two indices: i is the index of elements in the original DS `ax`, and k is the index of a sliding window over `ax` and the output vector `updCoefs`.

Our DSL also allows a combination of a sliding window and a `map`, which is useful for implementing signal filters such as the fast Fourier transform. The function `enumSlideFlatMap(n)(λi,x.f(i,x))`, defined on vectors, creates a sliding window of size n that shifts by n indices every iteration. The resulting windows are enumerated and a function $f(i,x)$ transforms every element in the window and saves the results into a new vector. In the FFT implementation in Fig. 2, the sliding window includes 2 elements of the vector `evens` and computes vectors `resleft` and `resright` of the same size as `evens`. The window index `k` is used for accessing elements of the vector `odds` and for computing the filtered values (lines 16 and 22). The pseudocode below explains with explicit indices how `evens.enumSlideFlatMap(2)(f(k,xv))` iterates over the vector `evens`:

```
1  def fftvector(vr: Vector, vi: Vector): Vector = {
     // v: (real part of signal / Fourier coeff.,
3    // imaginary part of signal / Fourier coeff.)
     require(vr >= 68.9 && vr <= 160.43 && vr.size(128) &&
5          vi >= -133.21 && vi <= 723.11 && vi.size(128))
      if (vr.length() == 1)
7       Vector(List(vr.head, vi.head))
      else {
9       val scalar: Real = 1; val Pi: Real = 3.1415926
        val n:Int = vr.length(); val direction:Vector = Vector(List(0.0, -2.0))
11      val evens: Vector = fftvector(vr.everyNth(2, 0), vi.everyNth(2, 0))
        val odds:  Vector = fftvector(vr.everyNth(2, 1), vi.everyNth(2, 1))
13      val resleft: Vector = evens.enumSlideFlatMap(2)((k, xv) => {
          val base: Vector = xv / scalar
15        val oddV: Vector = odds.slice(2 * k, 2 * k + 1)
          val expV: Vector = (direction.*(Pi * k / n)).exp()
17        val offset: Vector = (oddV x expV) / scalar
          base + offset })
19      val resright: Vector = evens.enumSlideFlatMap(2)((k, xv) => {
          val base: Vector = xv / scalar
21        val oddV: Vector = odds.slice(2 * k, 2 * k + 1)
          val expV: Vector = (direction.*(Pi * k / n)).exp()
23        val offset: Vector = (oddV x expV) / scalar
          base - offset })
25      resleft ++ resright  })
```

Fig. 2. Fast Fourier transform filter implemented in our DSL

```
k=0
∀ i∈ {0,2,4,...,size(evens)-2}:
   xv = [ evens[i], evens[i+1] ]
   tmp = f(k, xv) // where tmp is a vector
   res[i] = tmp[0]; res[i+1] = tmp[1]
   k++
```

Non-numerical. Such operations include obtaining a subset of elements (`v.slice(i,j)`), reordering (`m.flipud()`, `m.fliplr()`), appending and prepending elements and rows (`v.+:(elt)`, `m :+ v`). Additionally, our DSL allows to add a zero-padding around a vector or a matrix, and obtain smallest and largest elements of a DS. A special variant of a subset operation `ds.everyNth(n, fromInd)` creates a new DS by taking every n-th element of a vector (or row of a matrix) starting from the index *fromInd*. Our FFT benchmark in Fig. 2 uses the `everyNth` function to obtain subsets of signal values at even and odd indices (lines 11 and 12).

4 Data-Structure Guided Analysis

While a baseline range and error analysis for straight-line code can handle unrolled iterators, it does not make use of implicit additional information that is present in a high-level specification. In an unrolled program each iteration makes up independent expressions to be evaluated, regardless of whether values in consecutive iterations depend on one another. This may result in redundant computations; for instance, a `map` performs the same computation over all elements in a vector and when all those elements have the same specified input range, we only need to analyze the rounding error of the computation once. The same holds for matrix multiplication: each element of the resulting matrix is computed with the same arithmetic expression, but it would appear as a new independent computation if unrolled. When sets of involved elements have the same ranges, it is sufficient to analyze the rounding error of the resulting matrix element once.

We observe that while concrete DS inputs will in general not be the same, a specification of a function to be analyzed will typically provide ranges that in practice often tend to be identical for many inputs. We leverage this in our analysis and compute the ranges and error bounds as rarely as possible. Even though it is not possible to directly apply this approach to iterators where iteration values have dependencies, like `fold`, the analysis can be optimized based on groups of elements with the same specification by introducing suitable over-approximations (see Sect. 4.4).

We first introduce our DS-based concrete and abstract domains before explaining how expressions are analyzed and their analysis is optimized.

4.1 DS-Based Concrete Domain

The goal of our analysis is to collect information about ranges and rounding error bounds for groups of elements. To do so, our concrete domain tracks a tuple (r, f) for each value in a program, where r is the ideal value if a program would be executed with a real numbers semantics, and f is the same value if the program is executed with the finite-precision semantics.

We denote all valid indices of data structures as $Inds^{(n)} = \mathbb{N}^n$, where $n \geq 0$ is the dimension of the DS: $n = 1$ for vectors and $n = 2$ for matrices. For scalar values the set of indices is empty, $n = 0$. Using the indices we define elements of a DS as $\mathbb{V}^{(n)} = Inds^{(n)} \mapsto (\mathbb{R}, \mathbb{F})$. Given a set of elements' values $\mathbb{V}^{(n)}$ we define our concrete domain as $\mathbb{C}^{(n)} = 2^{\mathbb{V}^{(n)}}$, for each dimension of data structures n.

4.2 DS-Based Abstract Domain

We then abstract each tuple (r, f) using a pair of real-valued intervals: $\alpha((r, f)) = (I_R \times I_R)$, where the first interval denotes a range of real values that contains r, and the second tightly bounds the difference between r and f. Here the difference between a real number r and a finite-precision number f represents the rounding error.

Lifted to the DS with dimension n we obtain abstract element's values: $\mathbb{D}^{(n)} = Inds^{(n)} \hookrightarrow (\mathbb{I}_R \times \mathbb{I}_R)$. Note that we are only interested in abstract values of elements with valid indices (as opposed to all possible indices), and use a partial mapping $\hookrightarrow$ to express it in our domain. For invalid indices the mapping is undefined. The abstract domain for our analysis combines all $\mathbb{D}^{(n)}$ with for scalar values, vectors and matrices: $\mathbb{D} = (\mathbb{D}^{(n)})_{n \geq 0}$. Join and meet operators use standard definitions of join and meet on intervals, and are lifted to all valid indices point-wise.

An abstract state $D^{(n)}$ soundly describes a concrete state $C^{(n)}$, that is: $C^{(n)} \subseteq \gamma(D^{(n)})$, where concretization function is defined as follows. Given a set of indices S and a set of mappings from these indices $D^{(n)} = \{i \mapsto (I_i, E_i) | i \in S\}$:

$$\gamma(D^{(n)}) = \{\{i \mapsto (r_j, f_j) | i \in S\} | \forall j. r_j \in I_i, |r_j - f_j| \in E_i\} \tag{2}$$

The abstraction function α is defined as an adjoint of γ: $\alpha(c) = \bigsqcap\{a \mid c \in \gamma(a)\}$, so they form a Galois connection. Each transformation of the abstract state is parametrized with an expression to be evaluated, a mapping of variables' values and computes a new abstract state:

$$[\![\cdot]\!]^\sharp = Expr^{(n)} \rightarrow (Vars \overset{\text{n}}{\mapsto} \mathbb{D}^*) \rightarrow \mathbb{D}^{(n)}, \tag{3}$$

where $\overset{\text{n}}{\mapsto} \mathbb{D}^*$ is a type-preserving mapping that assigns $D^{(0)}$ values to scalar variables, and $D^{(1)}$, $D^{(2)}$ values to vector and matrix literals respectively.

Theorem 1 ***Soundness.*** *Given an abstract state $D \in \mathbb{D}^{(n)}, \{i \mapsto (R, E)\} \in D$ there exists no concrete state $C \in \mathbb{C}^{(n)}$ such that $C \subseteq \gamma(D)$, $\{i \mapsto (r, f)\} \in C$ and $r \notin R \vee |r - f| \notin E$. Moreover, if $D \in \alpha(C)$, $[\![e]\!]C = C'$, and $[\![e]\!]^\sharp D = D'$, then $D' \in \alpha(C')$.*

Proof. (sketch) The theorem states that there is no unsound abstract state in our analysis, and given a sound starting state, our abstract transformations result in a sound end state. The first part follows directly from the definition of interval abstraction and concretization.

The transformations $[\![\cdot]\!]^\sharp$ on data structures are defined for each individual element, which reduces them to transformations on basic blocks. The conditional expressions allowed in the language do not introduce instabilities or discontinuity errors [8,31] and thus do not require special treatment. Precisely, our DSL allows only two types of conditionals: 1) an *integer* comparison of the DS size with a constant in the recursive call, and 2) a comparison with a constant $x \leq c$ inside the `filter` function. As explained later in more detail, our analysis over-approximates the results of `filter` by keeping all DS elements that *may satisfy* the condition. Hence, the result of $[\![\texttt{filter}]\!]^\sharp$ is at least as large as the resulting DS size in concrete semantics, while the DS elements themselves remain unchanged. The result is consistent with the semantics of the input DS size specification and can be used by further iterators over the "filtered" DS. As the conditionals do not introduce instability and all iterators can be unrolled, soundness of our analysis follows from the soundness of the underlying baseline analysis for straight-line code. □

Our functional DSL defines all DS to be immutable, therefore each element of a DS is only assigned once. Our abstract domain does not require updates to individual element's ranges, and all recursive calls are unrolled. Since our analysis handles *only bounded loops* by design, we can unroll all operations, if needed, which is why we do not provide an additional widening operator. While widening in general allows the analysis to terminate quickly, for rounding error analysis the performance/accuracy trade-off is too costly. As our experiments with Fluctuat show (Sect. 6.1), for rounding error bounds, precision lost with widening cannot be recovered, hence an analyser that uses widening in the vast majority of cases reports infinite error bounds, which is sound but not especially meaningful.

4.3 DS Analysis

Both concrete and abstract domains partition DS elements in groups based on their real value and value range respectively. Our implementation describes a group of elements using a *set of indices*. The indices in one group need not be consecutive, the only condition is that they correspond to unique and valid indices of DS elements. Thus when analyzing an operator such as `map`, adding or multiplying by a constant, we only need to run the analysis once per group.

The initial grouping of elements is defined by user range specifications on the input DS. For intermediate variables in the computations, numerical indices for an abstraction of DS elements are inferred during the analysis. Note that the grouping does not change the semantics of functions and operators. As our DSL operates on real numbers, for commutative operations on DS elements their order does not matter. Whenever the analysis encounters an operation where the order of elements does matter, e.g. when computing an accumulator value in `fold`, we sort and split the groups to only contain consecutive elements' indices.

Whenever the expression under analysis contains only scalar values and operations, our analysis re-uses the baseline dataflow rounding error analysis, described in Sect. 2. We next describe how our analysis handles different kinds of DS operations.

Example. We illustrate our abstraction using the running example program in Fig. 3. This contrived example is not part of our benchmark set, we use it here purely for demonstrating the relevant DSL details in a succinct way. Function `fun` takes two input vectors `x` and `y`, both of size 5. An abstraction for vector `x` keeps track of separate ranges for the first two elements and the remaining ones (with indices 2,3,4), i.e. $D_x^{(1)} = \{\{0,1\} \mapsto [0.5, 1.5], \{2,3,4\} \mapsto [0,10]\}$. For the input vector `y` the abstraction also has two groups, but indices in the first group are not consecutive: $D_y^{(1)} = \{\{0,4\} \mapsto [-1,2], \{1,2,3\} \mapsto [0,1.5]\}$.

Map and Element-Wise Operations. Our domains group elements that have the same real range by their indices, such that we can perform range evaluation once for each group. The most prominent example where such evaluation makes a difference for performance is the `map` function, such as on line 4 in Fig. 3. The program multiplies all the elements of the list resulting from `x + y` by 2.0 and adds 1.5. The individual multiplications and additions are independent of each other, i.e. they do not propagate through iterations. For DS elements in one group we thus evaluate the range and error of `i*2.0 + 1.5` only once.

We use a similar approach for element-wise arithmetic operations between two vectors (or two matrices), such as `x + y` in Fig. 3. In contrast to `map`, element-wise operations are binary and we need to take into account *pairs* of ranges. For each unique pair of ranges of operands we compute the range (and error) once.

Matrix Multiplication. Evaluation of matrix multiplication is similar to the element-wise operations, where we compute pairs of ranges. Except, for matrix multiplication the elements, for which we need to know the ranges are located at the left-hand-side matrix row and the right-hand-side matrix column. We

```
def fun(x: Vector, y: Vector): Real = {
  require(x>=0.0 && x<=10.0 && x.size(5) && x.range(0,1)(0.5,1.5) &&
        y>= -1.0 && y<=2.0 && y.size(5) && y.range(1,3)(0.0,1.5))
    val z = (x + y).map(i => i*2.0 + 1.5)
    val r = z.fold(1.0)((acc: Real, i: Real) => acc * sqrt(i))
    r / (x.length()) }
```

Fig. 3. Example program in our DSL

construct an expression for computing the resulting matrix elements internally. For each unique pair of ranges we only evaluate this expression once.

Filter. Filter also takes advantage of the element grouping; our analysis evaluates the condition on each group of DS elements only once. However, `filter` is different from the rest of the functions in our DSL, because its abstract semantics do not exactly mirror the concrete. In the concrete semantics, `ds.filter(`$\lambda x.f(x)$`)` partitions the DS `ds` into two disjoint sets: elements that satisfy `f(x)`, and that satisfy its negation. In the abstract semantics these sets are not necessarily disjoint. Our evaluation `eval` returns an over-approximation of a set of elements from `ds`: the elements that *may* satisfy the condition `f(x)`. Currently we limit expressions in `f(x)` to simple comparisons $x \leq c$ and $x \geq c$, where `x` is the DS element and `c` is a scalar variable or a constant. More complex arithmetic operations are likely to introduce rounding error inside the condition itself, which may lead to a discontinuity error—elements that would have satisfied `f(x)` in a real-valued expression, do not satisfy it under floating-point semantics (or vice versa). We note that complementary techniques for bounding this discontinuity error [8,31] exist that may be integrated into our analysis.

Unrolled Operations. Naturally, not all operations can benefit from a grouping of DS elements alone. The "once-per-range" evaluation cannot be applied on operations that propagate values through multiple iterations (`fold, slideReduce`) or use fresh values at each iteration (for example, loop counters in `enumSlideFlatMap`, `enumRowsMap`). For these functions, the abstraction-guided analysis falls back to the baseline version. It unrolls the iterators and performs range and error evaluation once for each iteration, we then join the ranges (for values and, separately, for errors) to ensure that our results subsume all evaluated iterations. Our analysis handles recursive calls in the same way and unrolls each call as one iteration. Note that for our analysis to terminate, a recursive function must contain an exit condition that uses the (decreasing) length of a DS.
In our running example the analysis unrolls `z.fold` and evaluates ranges and errors of the unrolled expression:

```
1.0 * sqrt(z.at(0)) * sqrt(z.at(1)) * sqrt(z.at(2)) * sqrt(z.at(3)) * sqrt(z.at(4)).
```

Non-numerical Operations. Operations that do not involve arithmetic computations do not introduce new errors, however, they do affect our abstraction. For example, a prepend operation `x.+:(8.0)` will add an element with index 0 and range [8, 8] to the abstraction and shift all indices of `x` by one. If we apply `x.+:(8.0)` to the `x` in the running example, the resulting abstraction will become $D_x^{(1)} = \{\{0\} \mapsto [8,8], \{1,2\} \mapsto [0.5,1.5], \{3,4,5\} \mapsto [0,10]\}$.

Similarly, the `pad` operation adds elements with range $[0, 0]$ around a vector or matrix and re-scales the original elements' indices. Another interesting case of the non-numerical operations is the `x.everyNth(n,k)` function that constructs a new DS by appending every n-th vector element (or every n-th matrix row) starting from the index k and assigning new indices to them. Evaluating `x.everyNth(2,0)` on the $D_x^{(1)}$ from our running example will result in $D_{nth}^{(1)} = \{\{0\} \mapsto [0.5, 1.5], \{1, 2\} \mapsto [0, 10]\}$.

4.4 Optimized Evaluation of `fold`

The `fold` function cannot be evaluated only once per range group, since the accumulator's value changes at every iteration. For analysis, it would thus have to be unrolled. We observed, however, that in many applications the function passed to `fold` has a rather simple structure, such as summing up all elements of the DS. For such simple iterator bodies, the explicit unrolling can be replaced with an optimized evaluation that benefits from grouping of elements.

Our optimization over-approximates the accumulator, thereby effectively eliminating the change in input values from iteration to iteration. The analysis then computes one range per group of elements using a closed-form formula. In general, it is also possible to use approximation of an accumulator and a DS element for the whole loop, not only per group of elements with the same range. However, such a computation will introduce an even larger over-approximation in the result. To keep the bounds reasonably tight, we choose to apply over-approximations rarely. We have implemented this optimization for the most common special cases of lambda functions `f()` that follow next.

Linear Loop. In a linear loop, i.e. $f(ac, el) = a \cdot el + b \cdot ac + c$, if f is executed on a group of elements with the same range $range(el)$, then we can compute the resulting range after n iterations with:

$$range_n = a \cdot range(el) \cdot \sum_{i=0}^{n-1}(b^i) + b^n \cdot init + c \cdot \sum_{i=0}^{n-1}(b^i), \tag{4}$$

where $init$ is the initial value of the accumulator for the current group of elements. The initial accumulator value changes from group to group: it starts with the input parameter of `fold` and for each consecutive group it is replaced with the result of the previous computation. To account for all combinations of signs of linear coefficients a,b,c, we take their ranges to be symmetrical around zero. For generic linear loops, the order of computations matters, therefore we sort and split the groups in the abstraction $D^{(n)}$, such that each group only contains elements with consecutive indices, and the computation is applied to each group in the natural order: starting with the group containing index 0.

There is no simple closed-form equation to compute the rounding errors for linear loops. We therefore unroll the loop for error computations, but we use the over-approximated range of `acc`, pre-computed using Eq. 4. Note that such an evaluation is faster than the full unrolling, since we pre-compute the ranges necessary for error computations.

Sum. A sum of all elements in a vector or matrix is a special case of a linear loop, but in the absence of linear coefficients the range computations are much simpler. For a function $f(acc, el) = acc + el$, we compute one range per group of elements in $D^{(n)}$ abstraction using the formula: $n \cdot range(el) + init$, where n is the number of elements in the group, and $init$ is the initial value of the accumulator for the current group. Note that here the order of groups does not matter, as our DSL specifies a program over real numbers and real-valued sum is associative. The error computation is performed similar to linear loops: we over-approximate the value of `acc` and use the range to compute the error on the unrolled `fold`.

5 Implementation

We implement our analysis in a tool called DS2L in the Scala programming language. For performance reasons, we implement all internal computations using intervals with arbitrary-precision bounds (with outwards rounding for soundness), using the MPFR library [12] with 128 bits of precision. We use the intervals for both range and error computation, and sacrifice some of the error accuracy compared to affine arithmetic that is used by most state-of-the-art analyzers.

We choose to implement the partitioning using sets of indices, among other alternative representations: linear inequalities [3,16], difference-bound matrices [3], and sets of other simple symbolic expressions [5]. We choose a set representation because it does not depend on patterns to group the elements. We have empirically confirmed that on our benchmarks the set representation of index groups performs better than symbolic ranges of consecutive indices. This is because our range evaluation often needs to obtain the range of a DS element with a given index[4], which is a simple inclusion check for sets, but requires additional computation of numerical bounds from symbolic expressions in other representations.

In this paper, we consider only the natural order of evaluation (left-to-right with call-by-value), exactly as it syntactically appears in the program under analysis. For this natural order, DS2L generates executable Scala code and for that code the analysis is sound. Our analysis can also be adapted to other, more efficient, evaluation orders, but determining that order is an orthogonal issue.

6 Experimental Evaluation

We evaluate our DS-based analysis in DS2L in terms of performance and accuracy, focusing on the following research questions:

RQ1 How does DS2L compare to state-of-the-art tools (on large programs)?
RQ2 How does DS-based abstraction affect the accuracy/performance tradeoff?

Benchmarks. We evaluate DS2L on the new benchmark set we collected (Sect. 3.1). The original codes were written in different programming languages.

[4] For instance, taking a single element's range or a range of a group of elements when unrolling an iterator.

Table 1. Benchmarks description: usage of DSL functions and unrolled program sizes for different DS size configurations (in lines of code)

Benchmark	DSL usage						max #ops	Benchmark sizes		
	map	fold	slideRed.	enum*	rec	matMul	in line	small	medium	large
vector benchmarks										
avg		✓					1	101	1001	10001
variance		✓					3	202	2002	20002
stdDev		✓					3	202	2002	20002
roux		✓					3	100	1k	10k
goubalt		✓					3	100	1k	10k
harmonic		✓					3	200	2k	20k
nonlin1		✓					7	200	2k	20k
nonlin2		✓					8	200	2k	20k
nonlin3		✓					6	200	2k	20k
heat1d	✓		✓		✓		5	257	1025	65537
fftvector	✓	✓		✓	✓	✓	4	96	9596	48636
matrix benchmarks										
pendulum		✓					4	404	4004	40004
alphaBlend	✓						4	100	1k	250k
fftmatrix	✓	✓		✓	✓		8	64	6012	30204
conv.2d_sz3			✓				1	162	1458	118098
sobel3			✓				3	972	8748	708588
lorentz		✓					6	141	211	281
lyapunov	✓					✓	(20,200,1000)†	11	101	501
control.Tora	✓					✓	(20,200,1000)†	31	301	1501

† The benchmark contains matrix multiplication, the maximum number of arithmetic operations in one line of code depends on the size of multiplied matrices. Reported values are for (small, medium, large) input DSs.

We have translated them into our functional-style DSL for the purpose of our evaluation and validated our translation with testing. Table 1 displays in more detail which elements of our DSL were used in which benchmarks. Many of the benchmarks operating on vectors have been repurposed from controller loops used in previous work [6] and therefore have similar structure. As an artifact of this translation, our vector-based benchmarks use `fold` frequently.

For each benchmark, we create 12 variants by varying the following:

Size of the Input DS. Input vectors are assigned 100(small), 1k (medium), or 10k (large) elements. Input matrix sizes are 10×10 (small), 100×100 (medium) and 500×500 (large). For benchmarks where the size of a DS is predefined by the algorithm, we take the sizes closest to 10, 100 and 500 (for example, the input matrix for *fftmatrix* has 8×2, 128×2 and 512×2 elements for the small, medium and large setting, respectively). The benchmark input DS size influences the number of operations to be evaluated by the analysis. To give an unambiguous measure of complexity of the programs under analysis, we report the sizes of unrolled programs in Table 1. The reported numbers are lines of code if all operations on DSs would be unrolled to scalar operations, i.e. the number of iterations times number of lines of code computing a scalar value inside each iterator. Since in the absence of DSs there would be no need for non-numerical functions as concatenation of vectors or changing the order of elements in a matrix, we only count lines of code with numerical operations and let-statements. Such unrolled programs could, for example, be used by state-of-the-art rounding error analyzers that operate on straight-line code. Additionally we report the maximum number of arithmetic operations in one line of unrolled code.

Our goal is to efficiently analyze *large* benchmarks. We include small and medium sizes for completeness and to demonstrate scalability, but do not consider DS2L to be necessarily the analysis tool of choice for these.

Range Specification Granularity. We vary the amount of individually specified ranges per DS. The input ranges are specified with either one, i.e. the same, interval for all elements (*AllSame*), different intervals for all elements (*AllDiff*), or for some. When specifying individual ranges for subsets of elements we vary the amount of new range specifications to be 10% and 30% of the input DS size (*Diff10P* and *Diff30P*). For instance, if an input vector has 100 elements *Diff10P* configuration will have 10 additional range specifications, each with an arbitrary amount of elements in it, and the *Diff30P* will have 30 additional range specifications. To avoid any bias by using input ranges that are easier for the analyzer to compute with, we generate all input ranges randomly. Similarly, the amount of elements in one group with special ranges is determined randomly. The smaller ranges of more refined specifications are subsumed by the ranges in AllSame specification.

Experimental Setup. To answer our research questions we evaluate differences in accuracy and performance between a baseline analysis, our new DS abstraction-guided analysis and state-of-the-art tools. To do so, we normalize the reported worst-case rounding error and the running time of the analysis (separately) with respect to a baseline (different for each comparison). Such a normalization is necessary since the running times and error magnitudes vary widely between different benchmarks due to their diverse complexity. We then evaluate the normalized worst-case errors and analysis times.

As running time, we use the reported analysis time of each tool. This is a subset of the total wall-clock running time and excludes, for instance, parsing of the input programs. Since the formats of the input programs differ widely, we consider the analysis time a more meaningful measure for a comparison. We report analysis time averaged over 3 runs. We consider that a tool failed on a benchmark if it either timed out with 30 min, reported an infinite error bound, or encountered some other error. Timeouts were always consistent across all runs on each configuration. Note that the timeout applies to the total running time, including parsing, pre- and post-processing of the results.

As accuracy measure, we use reported absolute worst-case rounding error bounds of each tool for double floating-point precision. For the 13 benchmarks where the return type is a vector or a matrix we take the maximum error of all output DS elements.

All experiments were run on an Intel Xeon machine with 8 CPUs @ 3.50 GHz, 32G of RAM under the OS Ubuntu 22.04. We run both DS2L and a baseline straight-line code analysis in a JVM with 2G memory and 1G stack space.

6.1 State-of-the-Art Tools

We compare DS2L against the state-of-the-art rounding error analyzers Fluctuat [13] and Satire [9]. We choose these two tools, because they are the only tools that natively support data structures and loops over them (Fluctuat), or that analyze straight-line code, but whose abstractions were designed specifically for large program sizes (Satire). In these two dimensions that are relevant for our comparison, Fluctuat and Satire are the state-of-the-art. Satire does include approximations such as not considering higher-order terms that technically affect its soundness, but we ignore this here. DS2L and Fluctuat are 'fully sound'.

We note that an entirely fair comparison is not possible due to the different input formats, as well as different implementation choices such as programming language in which the tools themselves are implemented. Each of our high-level benchmarks written in our functional DSL can be translated to Fluctuat's and Satire's imperative formats in different ways that each may or may not affect the results (no guidelines exist). We manually translate our benchmarks into the tool's input formats by choosing the way that we consider to be natural for a programmer, and so a regular user of the tools would choose, and validate the translation with testing.

In our comparison, we use relative performance and accuracy as a measure of success. DS2L and Fluctuat are deterministic and always report the same error bounds. On some benchmarks Satire reported slightly different errors, we take the largest reported error across the runs. Note that the differences were on the order of 10^{-12}, and taking the average or the smallest error across the runs does not affect the qualitative results.

Fluctuat. Fluctuat can both unroll loops internally and abstract the loop behavior by applying widening. We use the latest available version of Fluctuat provided to us in October 2022.

Fluctuat takes C-programs as input and is itself implemented in C. When translating our benchmarks, we tried to preserve as much functional-style semantics as possible, but had to give up the DS immutability and replace all recursive calls by loops. Furthermore, Fluctuat's library did not support a `max()` function required for implementing the ReLU function in the neural network benchmarks *lyapunov* and *contr.Tora*. We replaced the call to `max()` with an explicit if-then-else statement. Fluctuat does not have a dedicated way of specifying input ranges for data structures, only for scalar values. We therefore assign a range to each element separately, and use loops to assign repeating ranges for the *AllSame* specification. Each benchmark is implemented in a separate function that is called from `main`. We compare DS2L with Fluctuat on all 19 benchmarks.

We run Fluctuat with several different settings:

1. loop iterations are evaluated separately, results joined (merge over all paths—MOP—solution)
2. loops are unrolled until 50k iterations. The largest number of iterations in our benchmarks is 62.5k, however, Fluctuat's setting did not allow us to set the unroll limit higher than 50k.
3. loops are abstracted by widening, nothing is unrolled
4. automatic setting, where Fluctuat finds a suitable number of loop unrollings before applying joins and widening.

Out of all configurations the overall best results were achieved with MOP (which is effectively unrolling) and the explicit unrolling configuration. Fluctuat with MOP and unrolling has timed out less often than other configurations and whenever Flucutat computed non-trivial error bounds, they were exactly the same for all settings. Surprisingly, the automatic configuration of Fluctuat had the highest timeout rate: it failed to produce results within 30 min on 33% of specifications. The pure widening configuration performed better with only 16% rate of timeouts. Since all other settings provided worse or the same results, we compare DS2L's results only to the MOP setting of Fluctuat.

Satire. We use the latest version of Satire available in the open-source GitHub repository[5]. Satire's open-source benchmark set contains pre-processed large unrolled loops, but no original programs that were unrolled. Unfortunately, the original programs with loops were not available (upon request). We have therefore reverse-engineered the loops over data structures from their unrolled versions for two benchmarks *lorenz*, and *heat1d*. Additionally, we translated some of our benchmarks into Satire's input format, which is an imperative DSL that specifies floating-point precision for each variable assignment. We only compare the results on a subset of benchmarks, since we are required to manually unroll the loops, and translate functional operators into imperative code. This translation process is non-trivial, tedious and error prone, especially for complex functions.

Overall, we translated 9 benchmarks that contain a `fold` over an input vector. For these 9 benchmarks we used the same variations in configurations, described above: small, medium, large input DS sizes, and *AllSame, Diff10P, Diff30P, AllDiff* specification granularities. We took Satire's original benchmarks as is: *heat1d* had only one version, that corresponds to our input specification with small input DS and one input range for all elements. The *lorentz* benchmark was available in three different sizes of input DS (20, 30 and 40), and all of them had the same input range for all elements of DS (*AllSame*). In total, we have compared our results on 112 benchmark variations.

We ran Satire with its default parameters and both with and without abstraction. The version with abstraction predictably produced results faster and had fewer timeouts. We therefore compare to the version of Satire with abstraction enabled.

[5] We use the version with the commit hash 8a4816aac6fad4fb86c2af8dc8e634bf0291 2b90.

Table 2. Relative accuracy/performance of state-of-the-art tools compared to DS2L with DS abstraction.

Benchmark size	Accuracy			Performance			# fails	# fails DS2L	total # of bench.
	min	median	max	min	median	max			
Fluctuat									
Small	2.11e−07	0.557	3.55	0.07	0.36	7.22	**2**	10	76
Medium	2.83e−04	0.639	2.91	0.23	**1.98**	4636.52	22	**12**	76
Large	3.60e−02	0.555	2.91	0.66	**24.41**	339.55	60	**25**	76
Satire									
Small	2.98e−07	0.737	3.54	6.33	**24.68**	449.33	6	6	38
Medium	2.07e−10	0.153	3.54	6.32	**39.90**	507.45	12	**8**	37
Large	3.94e−02	0.953	1.34	8.95	**259.64**	767.13	32	**10**	37

6.2 RQ1: Comparison to State-of-the-Art Tools

We compare relative performance and accuracy of state-of-the-art tools normalized against DS2L's results and provide cumulative values in Table 2. The values greater than 1 denote individual benchmarks where DS2L was faster (respectively, more accurate) than the state-of-the-art tool. For instance, value 24.41 means that DS2L is median 24.41 faster than Fluctuat. As it is ambiguous to compute the relative value if one of the tools did not report results, we do not include these cases into the minimum, median and maximum values. Instead we report the number of failures per tool (timeouts, infinite error bounds, overflows). We mark in bold the smaller number of fails per comparison, and median values where DS2L did better than competitors. Note that we provide comparison on small and medium benchmarks for completeness, while our focus lays on large benchmarks.

In addition to normalized values, we present absolute values of our experiments on large benchmarks in Table 3. 'TO' denotes timeouts, other times are reported in seconds. We additionally mark the benchmarks, for which a tool reported overflow or an infinite error bound. For the original Satire benchmark *lorentz*, the missing configurations *Diff10P, Diff30P, AllDiff* with individual ranges for input DS elements are marked with 'na' (non-applicable). Another original benchmark *heat1d* is only defined for a small size of input DS. We provide absolute experimental values for small and medium benchmarks in the appendix.

Accuracy. As expected, state-of-the-art tools often computed tighter error bounds on small and medium benchmarks. However, DS2L was consistently more accurate on the *stdDeviation* benchmark, and the larger (among the two in our set) neural network *controllerTora*. Additionally, Fluctuat reports infinite errors on all medium and large-sized variations of the FFT filter (*fftvector*, *fftmatrix*), while DS2L successfully computes rounding error bounds. Both Fluctuat and DS2L implement—in principle—the same analysis *on the unrolled programs*, and the DS abstractions do not affect accuracy (see Sect. 6.3). The differences in accuracy come from 1) the optimized evaluation of `folds`; 2) DS2L's use of

Table 3. Experimental results on large benchmarks. Reported error bounds are rounded to two digits after decimal point, time is in seconds. "TO" denotes a time-out, "na" stands for non-applicable. **Bold** marks 'winning' values.

	AllSame		*Diff10P*		*Diff30P*		*AllDiff*	
Benchmark	error	time	error	time	error	time	error	time
				DS2L				
avg	5.82e−11	**1.90**	2.86e−11	**5.48**	1.87e−11	**19.73**	**1.51e−11**	**157.63**
variance	7.39e−05	**119.28**	1.92e−05	**248.64**	9.68e−06	**412.39**	6.37e−06	**1144.74**
stdDev	9.01e+03	**118.98**	9.35e−06	**244.51**	4.86e−07	**410.50**	2.70e−07	**1141.30**
roux1	**7.21e−14**	**3.86**	2.46e−13	**10.78**	2.64e−13	**29.88**	2.32e−13	**184.44**
goubault	7.46e−14	**3.93**	8.39e−14	**9.92**	8.39e−14	**27.98**	8.39e−14	**172.90**
harmonic	3.64e−08	**6.55**	1.42e−08	**28.40**	1.13e−08	**100.32**	1.12e−08	**713.85**
nonlin1	*overflow*	–	*overflow*	–	*overflow*	–	*overflow*	–
nonlin2	*overflow*	–	*overflow*	–	*overflow*	–	*overflow*	–
nonlin3	1.08e+74	**766.73**	2.66e+73	**1446.47**	–	TO	–	TO
pendulum	4.69e+81	**1583.05**	–	TO	–	TO	–	TO
heat1d	1.14e−13	**222.82**	7.26e−14	**830.00**	7.14e−14	**874.28**	7.13e−14	**857.08**
conv.2d_size3	3.15e−10	**63.29**	2.88e−10	**111.15**	2.62e−10	**158.94**	–	TO
sobel3	*DivByZero*	–	*DivByZero*	–	*DivByZero*	–	*DivByZero*	–
fftmatrix	**4.39e−08**	325.93	**4.24e−08**	387.76	**3.95e−08**	386.29	**2.97e−08**	399.04
fftvector	**2.02e−08**	262.99	**1.62e−08**	266.15	**1.13e−08**	269.89	**9.84e−09**	278.46
lorentz	3.42e−12	2.33	3.27e−12	2.32	3.27e−12	2.21	1.25e−12	2.27
alphaBlend	3.14e−13	**1.83**	3.14e−13	**47.81**	3.14e−13	**225.50**	–	TO
contr.Tora	2.61e−04	**386.38**	–	TO	–	TO	–	TO
lyapunov	7.02e−08	**104.21**	–	TO	–	TO	–	TO
				Fluctuat				
avg	**2.57e−11**	516.00	**1.83e−11**	475.50	**1.63e−11**	462.00	**1.51e−11**	490.50
variance	–	TO	–	TO	–	TO	–	TO
stdDev	–	TO	–	TO	–	TO	–	TO
roux1	2.10e−13	1310.00	**2.10e−13**	1302.00	**7.52e−14**	1212.50	**1.09e−13**	1295.50
goubault	**6.50e−14**	695.50	**6.45e−14**	726.50	**6.45e−14**	711.00	**1.87e−14**	716.50
harmonic	–	TO	–	TO	–	TO	–	TO
nonlin1	–	TO	–	TO	–	TO	–	TO
nonlin2	–	TO	–	TO	–	TO	–	TO
nonlin3	–	TO	–	TO	–	TO	–	TO
pendulum	–	TO	–	TO	–	TO	–	TO
heat1d	–	TO	–	TO	–	TO	–	TO
conv.2d_size3	–	TO	–	TO	–	TO	–	TO
sobel3	–	TO	–	TO	–	TO	–	TO
fftmatrix	∞	71.33	∞	71.33	∞	71.67	∞	71.00
fftvector	∞	35.67	∞	37.67	∞	116.00	∞	107.33
lorentz	**1.23e−13**	**2.00**	**1.21e−13**	**2.00**	**1.21e−13**	**2.00**	**1.02e−13**	**1.50**
alphaBlend	–	TO	–	TO	–	TO	–	TO
contr.Tora	–	TO	–	TO	–	TO	–	TO
lyapunov	–	TO	–	TO	–	TO	–	TO
				Satire				
avg	3.47e−11	1456.27	2.72e−11	1421.63	2.22e−11	1419.89	2.02e−11	1410.32
variance	–	TO	–	TO	–	TO	–	TO
stdDev	–	TO	–	TO	–	TO	–	TO
roux1	–	TO	–	TO	–	TO	–	TO
goubault	–	TO	–	TO	–	TO	–	TO
harmonic	–	TO	–	TO	–	TO	–	TO
nonlin1	–	TO	–	TO	–	TO	–	TO
nonlin2	–	TO	–	TO	–	TO	–	TO
nonlin3	–	TO	–	TO	–	TO	–	TO
lorentz	1.35e−13	1327.65	*na*	*na*	*na*	*na*	*na*	*na*

intervals instead of affine arithmetic; and 3) internal implementation differences that for the closed-source Fluctuat are not evident. We note that both Fluctuat's and DS2L's reported errors are itself small, and thus practically useful.

Satire reported more accurate results for non-linear benchmarks. On two configurations where DS2L reported overflow for the small input DS size (*AllSame, Diff10P* for *nonlin1* and *Diff10P, Diff30P* for *nonlin2*), Satire successfully reported rounding errors. Predictably, on benchmarks where DS2L used over-approximation of `folds` Satire's reported errors were also smaller. However, on all linear benchmarks except *harmonic* DS2L's accuracy could be recovered by using a non-optimized evaluation of `fold` (while still being faster than Satire, but by a smaller factor). Despite the over-approximation, DS2L was consistently more accurate on the linear *goubault*. Interestingly, DS2L was 3x more accurate than Satire on its original benchmark *heat1d*. Note that the *original* benchmark *heat1d* corresponds to the *AllSame* specification granularity and the small DS size. Experimental data for this setting is available in the appendix in Table 4.

Performance. The performance comparison shows that DS2L scales better to larger programs: it reports results on 50% more *large* benchmarks than Fluctuat and on 59% more than Satire. Additionally, DS2L is faster than Fluctuat on most large and medium-sized benchmarks with a median speedup factor of 25x and 2x respectively. A notable outlier is *alphaBlending*, where DS2L is **4636x** faster than Fluctuat. This is due to the benchmark's internal structure: it contains element-wise operations on matrices, where DS2L's abstraction is particularly efficient.

Satire timed out more often than DS2L on all sizes of benchmarks, and particularly on large benchmarks where it failed to report results on all benchmarks except *avg* and *lorentz* (see Table 3). Moreover, Satire was slower than DS2L by at least **6x** and median **36x** across different sizes of benchmarks including its original benchmarks *heat1d* and *lorentz*.

RQ1 Conclusion: Based on our experimental data, we conclude that DS2L is *significantly faster* than Satire and specifically *scales better* than Fluctuat and Satire to larger programs and is consequently able to report an error for more and larger benchmarks. While DS2L is often less accurate than Fluctuat and Satire, it still produces meaningful accuracy bounds.

6.3 RQ2: DS-Based Abstraction Accuracy/Performance Tradeoff

Our analysis differs from the analysis of the unrolled programs in two main points: it leverages the DS abstraction, and optimizes the evaluation of `folds` (Sect. 4.4). We evaluate the effect of these differences on both accuracy and performance. We split this evaluation into two parts: first, we check the effect of the DS abstraction alone, then we examine the benefits of the optimized `folds`.

DS Abstraction. First, we compare the DS abstraction-based analysis of DS2L to a baseline analysis that works on unrolled code. To avoid confounding factors

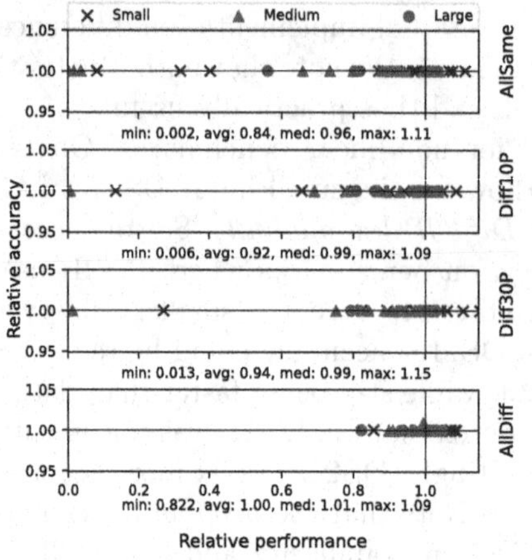

(a) DS2L with abstraction vs. the baseline analysis

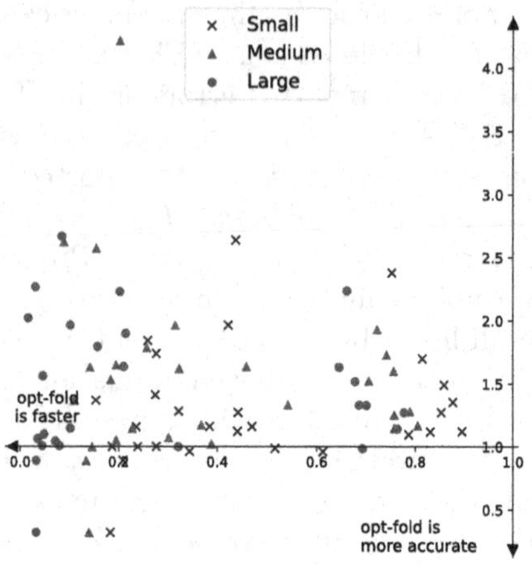

(b) DS2L: Optimized fold vs. unrolled

Fig. 4. Relative performance/accuracy of DS2L in various configurations

such as programming language choice, analysis type etc., we do this comparison on a baseline analysis that we implement within DS2L itself and that shares exactly its analysis for straight-line code. We denote this baseline analysis by BASE. BASE internally unrolls all operations, and thus just like DS2L does not explicitly construct an AST for the entire program, as this may be unnecessarily costly and bias the results. Thus, when comparing DS2L and BASE, the only difference consists in using the corresponding DS abstractions during the analysis. For the purpose of DS abstraction evaluation we use the version of DS2L without over-approximation on `folds`.

Specifically, we compare normalized analysis time and normalized computed worst-case absolute rounding errors per benchmark for each of its 12 variants. Figure 4a summarizes the results, smaller values on both axes are better. The x-axis shows relative analysis time of the DS abstraction analysis to the baseline, values with $x < 1$ denote benchmarks, on which DS2L was faster than BASE. The y-axis represents relative accuracy, values with $y = 1$ show that the worst-case rounding errors reported by DS2L were exactly the same as for BASE. We provide average, median, minimum and maximum relative analysis times for each specification.

For most benchmarks applying the DS abstraction has improved the analysis performance. Predictably, the performance boost was stronger for coarser specifications and close to none on the *AllDiff* specification that assigns each DS element an individual input range. We manually checked the cases where DS2L was slower than BASE. For these cases the absolute time difference is under 0.3 s on small and medium configurations (up to 15% of analysis time), and under 72 s on large configurations (at most 5% of the analysis time). We attribute this to the normal variation in running times and do not see it as a systematic problem.

The computed errors were the same for DS2L and BASE on all benchmarks. This result confirms our expectation that the DS abstractions (without `fold` optimizations) do not change the semantics and therefore do not affect computed rounding errors.

Optimized Folds. We evaluate the effect of our `fold` optimization on top of DS abstraction improvements in Fig. 4b. We compare the relative accuracy and performance on benchmarks with `fold` with and without the optimization. As expected, the optimized `fold` evaluation is faster and less accurate on most benchmarks, these are the points above the x-axis and to the left of the y-axis. The effect is more pronounced on the large benchmarks. Interestingly, in some cases the optimized evaluation reported smaller error bounds despite introducing an over-approximation of ranges. Upon closer inspection we note that some of the randomly generated input range bounds cannot be exactly represented in floating points, hence performing an unrolled error computation on such ranges will include the bounds' rounding error and magnify it (artificially) in subsequent iterations. The accuracy can thus improve in cases where the over-approximated ranges were exactly representable in floats, while corresponding element's input ranges were not.

RQ2 Conclusion: The DS abstraction alone improves the analysis' performance while having no effect on the accuracy. A user may further improve the performance by providing a coarser specification or enabling the optimized evaluation of `folds`, which trades off accuracy for performance.

7 Related Work

Besides Fluctuat [13] and Satire [9], several other tools exist for computing guaranteed upper bounds on rounding errors; Gappa [10], Daisy [7], FPTaylor [30], Real2Float [24], Rosa [8] and PRECiSA [31]. These either implement a dataflow analysis based approach very similar to Fluctuat's or an optimization-based approach similar to Satire. Most of the research has focused on analyzing straight-line numerical expressions as accurately as possible, i.e. computing error bounds as close to the actual errors as possible. Of these, Satire has been shown to be most scalable [9].

A few of these tools can also handle limited programs beyond straight-line expressions. As already discussed, Fluctuat [13] can handle loops via unrolling or with widening, but as we observed widening has limited success with a complex analysis such as the one used to analyze floating-point rounding errors. Rosa [8] provides a more efficient way to bound rounding errors in bounded loops than complete unrolling for a specific type of while loops, but requires invariants about the variable's ranges to be given. Rosa [8] and PRECiSA [31] also support (simple) conditional branches where they also compute the error due to diverging executions between then- and else-branches, in addition to rounding errors of each individual branch. Such techniques are complementary to DS2L's handling of data structures.

In contrast to sound analysis tools, dynamic analysis tools for floating-point programs have less restrictions on the input programs and generally handle whole programs, including loops, conditional branches and data structures. Typically, they execute a program on particular floating-point inputs side-by-side with a shadow execution in a higher precision [2,4,32], for instance implemented using arbitrary-precision arithmetic, that serves as an approximation of the ideal real-valued execution. By their nature, dynamic analyses cannot compute guaranteed bounds on errors, only an estimate of the errors for inputs tried. Several tools use a dynamic analysis to identify inputs that result in particularly large rounding errors [4,32]. Symbolic execution has also been used to find inputs that cause overflow or large precision loss in floating-point programs [1,14,21]. Recent work also combines dynamic and static analysis for identifying, or showing conditional absence of large rounding errors in larger floating-point programs [22].

Abstract interpretation based analyzers such as the industrial-strength Astrée [26], or implementations of different numerical domains such as Apron [19] and ELINA [28] can prove safety of floating-point programs, i.e. the absence of overflows, division-by-zero or out-of-bounds errors by bounding the ranges of variables. They do not, however, quantify rounding errors.

8 Conclusion

We have shown that computing rounding errors over a functional representation of floating-point list programs can be beneficial for analysis performance, by leveraging implicit semantic information present in the high-level representation. Conceptually, our idea appears simple - "just" use a functional input language - and yet, it has not been pursued before. We view this simplicity as a strength, but also note that a effective realization of this idea required a careful design of the DSL and the analysis, as well as substantial implementation effort. Our analysis can generally handle more, and especially larger benchmarks, though some of this performance benefit comes at a trade-off with analysis accuracy. Future work should determine whether it is possible to recover some of this accuracy with minimum performance loss.

A Appendix

Domain Specific Language Syntax. We provide a representative subset of our domain-specific language in Fig. 5. The syntax of all binary arithmetic operations is the same, we therefore omit repeating occurrences.

Experimental Data. We provide the experimental results used to evaluate DS2L in Sect. 6. Table 4 shows results for the small input DSs, Table 5 for medium. Whenever a tool has failed to report the error bound we use "–" to denote it, we also indicate reported *overflow* explicitly, we write ∞ if the reported error bounds were $[-\infty, \infty]$. *'DivByZero'* denotes the case when the analysis detected that the denominator range may include zero. We use "TO" to denote 30-min

```
object Vector {
  def zeroVector(i:Int): Vector
  def zip(v1: Vector, v2: Vector): Matrix
}
case class Vector(data: List[Real]) {
  // uncertainty on the vector
  def +/-(x: Real): Boolean
  // specify one range for the whole vector
  def <=(x: Real): Boolean // also >=
  // specify range for a subset of elements
  def specV(ranges: Set[((Int, Int), (Real, Real))]):
    Boolean
  def size(i: Int): Boolean
  // element-wise operations
  def +(v: Vector): Vector // also -,*,/
  // element-wise elementary functions
  def log(): Vector // sin(), cos(), tan(), ctan(), etc.
  // cross-product
  def x(v: Vector): Vector
  // operations with constants
  def *(c: Real): Vector // also +, /
  // non-arithmetic operations
  def length(): Int
  def at(i: Int): Real
  def slice(i: Int, j: Int): Vector
  def everyNth(i: Int, from: Int): Vector
  // standard functions
  def map(fnc: (Real) => Real): Vector
  def fold(init: Real)(fnc: (Real,Real) => Real): Real
  def filter(fnc: (Real) => Boolean): Vector
  // sliding window
  def slideReduce(size:Int, step: Int)(
    fnc:(Vector) => Real): Vector
  def enumSlideFlatMap(n: Int)(
    fnc: (Int, Vector) => Vector): Vector
  // add zeros padding around the vector
  def pad(i: Int): Vector
  def max(): Real // also min()
  def sum(): Real // syntactic sugar for fold(0.0)(λa,x.a+x)
  // concatenate and add elements
  def ++(v: Vector): Vector // also append :+(_), prepend +:(_)
}
object Matrix {
  def zeroMatrix(i:Int, j:Int): Matrix
}
case class Matrix(data: List[List[Real]]) {
  // < same as in Vector >
  // element-wise operations and elem. functions
  // operations with constants
  // non-arithmetic operations
  // basic functional ops
  // < different from Vector >
  // input spec for range and size
  def specM(ranges: Set[(Set[(Int, Int)], (Real, Real))]):
    Boolean
  def size(i: Int, j: Int): Boolean
  // +non-arithmetic operations
  def row(i: Int): Vector
  def slice(fromI: Int, fromJ: Int)(toI: Int, toJ: Int): Matrix
  def at(i:Int, j: Int): Real
  def numRows(): Int
  def numCols(): Int
  // flip elements upside down
  def flipud(): Matrix // also fliplr() left to right
  def enumRowsMap(fnc: (Int, Vector) => Vector): Matrix
  // operations on individual elements
  def mapElements(fnc: (Real) => Real): Matrix
  def foldElements(init: Real)(fnc: (Real,Real) => Real): Real
}
```

Fig. 5. DSL for numerical programs on data structures

Table 4. Experimental results on small benchmarks. Reported error bounds are rounded to two digits after decimal point, time is in seconds. "TO" denotes a time-out, "na" stands for non-applicable.

Benchmark	*AllSame*		*Diff10P*		*Diff30P*		*AllDiff*	
	error	time	error	time	error	time	error	time
DS2L								
avg	4.62e−13	0.14	2.60e−13	0.17	1.59e−13	0.20	1.42e−13	0.26
variance	5.98e−07	1.06	2.62e−07	1.16	8.82e−08	1.17	6.17e−08	1.32
stdDev	145	0.92	2.81e−08	1.16	3.00e−09	1.09	3.96e−09	1.23
roux1	7.21e−14	0.22	2.26e−13	0.29	2.27e−13	0.34	2.07e−13	0.55
goubault	7.46e−14	0.22	8.38e−14	0.29	7.97e−14	0.33	8.34e−14	0.57
harmonic	1.15e−11	0.31	5.84e−12	0.39	5.81e−12	0.59	5.82e−12	1.09
nonlin1	*overflow*	–	*overflow*	–	1.17e−07	4.07	1.06e−09	4.43
nonlin2	*overflow*	–	*overflow*	–	*overflow*	–	*overflow*	–
nonlin3	7.82e−14	3.85	3.72e−14	4.13	3.18e−14	4.12	2.78e−14	4.55
pendulum	2.27e−13	2.68	2.27e−13	2.74	7.51e−14	3.26	1.73e−13	3.50
heat1d	7.33e−15	1.65	4.79e−15	2.24	4.64e−15	2.22	4.94e−15	2.48
conv.2d_size3	3.15e−10	0.28	1.51e−10	0.30	1.51e−10	0.33	4.07e−11	0.50
sobel3	*DivByZero*	–	*DivByZero*	–	*DivByZero*	–	*DivByZero*	–
fftmatrix	4.29e−12	1.00	4.29e−12	0.95	4.29e−12	1.08	1.88e−12	1.06
fftvector	2.85e−12	0.96	2.40e−12	0.83	1.32e−12	0.89	1.86e−12	0.86
lorentz	4.33e−14	1.29	4.33e−14	1.19	2.55e−14	1.30	3.77e−14	1.28
alphaBlend	3.14e−13	0.07	3.14e−13	0.09	3.14e−13	0.17	3.13e−13	0.74
contr.Tora	1.42e−12	0.43	1.42e−12	1.01	1.20e−12	1.52	1.74e−13	1.38
lyapunov	9.90e−13	0.28	8.87e−13	0.49	6.64e−13	0.67	1.68e−13	0.59
Fluctuat								
avg	2.62e−13	0.11	1.99e−13	0.07	1.62e−13	0.07	1.41e−13	0.07
variance	1.15e−09	6.33	6.17e−10	6.00	3.25e−10	6.00	2.16e−10	6.00
stdDev	516	6.67	1.35e−11	6.00	5.38e−12	6.00	7.13e−12	6.00
roux1	2.10e−13	0.16	1.83e−13	0.12	1.46e−13	0.12	6.80e−14	0.12
goubault	6.50e−14	0.13	6.50e−14	0.09	2.43e−14	0.09	4.67e−14	0.09
harmonic	2.92e−12	0.34	2.47e−12	0.21	2.25e−12	0.21	2.11e−12	0.21
nonlin1	3.07e−14	16.33	2.78e−14	13.00	2.48e−14	13.00	2.73e−14	13.67
nonlin2	∞	16.67	2.83e−12	16.33	1.86e−13	16.67	∞	14.33
nonlin3	7.84e−15	0.55	4.29e−15	0.36	3.53e−15	0.38	3.44e−15	0.48
pendulum	2.15e−13	0.36	2.15e−13	0.20	6.67e−14	0.23	1.63e−13	0.24
heat1d	6.66e−16	12.67	4.44e−16	12.33	4.44e−16	12.67	4.44e−16	12.67
conv.2d_size3	1.24e−10	0.08	6.23e−11	0.08	6.23e−11	0.08	1.56e−11	0.08
sobel3	91.9	0.24	61.6	0.24	61.6	0.24	31.0	0.24
fftmatrix	1.09e−12	0.01	1.09e−12	0.01	1.09e−12	0.01	6.92e−13	0.01
fftvector	6.93e−13	0.01	6.93e−13	0.01	3.46e−13	0.01	6.90e−13	0.00
lorentz	2.16e−14	0.23	2.16e−14	0.23	1.55e−14	0.22	1.90e−14	0.23
alphaBlend	1.56e−13	0.11	1.56e−13	0.12	1.56e−13	0.12	1.55e−13	0.12
contr.Tora	2.28e−12	0.57	1.80e−12	0.58	1.25e−12	0.56	1.17e−13	0.49
lyapunov	8.07e−13	0.09	7.08e−13	0.09	4.58e−13	0.10	9.34e−14	0.10
Satire								
avg	3.65e−13	1.74	2.93e−13	2.22	2.47e−13	2.07	1.93e−13	1.83
variance	1.92e−09	12.22	1.19e−09	16.23	7.57e−10	16.04	4.97e−10	16.54
stdDev	–	TO	–	TO	–	TO	–	TO
roux1	2.55e−13	11.61	2.26e−13	13.39	1.88e−13	13.27	8.58e−14	13.18
goubault	1.14e−13	13.44	1.14e−13	15.37	4.97e−14	14.77	9.74e−14	14.55
harmonic	7.90e−12	19.48	5.01e−12	21.31	4.66e−12	20.48	4.90e−12	20.74
nonlin1	4.28e−14	655.23	3.99e−14	678.74	3.49e−14	687.85	3.87e−14	700.75
nonlin2	-	TO	1.94e−15	100.92	1.94e−15	89.29	–	TO
nonlin3	8.43e−15	32.45	5.62e−15	27.50	4.90e−15	26.09	3.86e−15	28.80
lorentz	9.68e−15	577.99	*na*	*na*	*na*	*na*	*na*	*na*
heat1d	1.98e−14	92.76	*na*	*na*	*na*	*na*	*na*	*na*

Table 5. Experimental results on medium benchmarks. Reported error bounds are rounded to two digits after decimal point, time is in seconds. "TO" denotes a timeout, "na" stands for non-applicable.

	AllSame		*Diff10P*		*Diff30P*		*AllDiff*	
Benchmark	error	time	error	time	error	time	error	time
				DS2L				
avg	3.65e−12	0.47	3.41e−12	0.60	2.01e−12	0.84	1.52e−12	2.25
variance	4.64e−06	4.95	2.42e−06	7.05	7.82e−07	8.66	6.16e−07	14.04
stdDev	1.13e+03	4.96	2.49e−07	6.96	3.11e−08	8.47	3.00e−08	14.27
roux1	7.21e−14	0.84	2.29e−13	1.21	2.41e−13	1.80	2.30e−13	4.04
goubault	7.46e−14	0.83	8.38e−14	1.09	8.39e−14	1.69	8.36e−14	3.77
harmonic	4.56e−10	1.29	1.94e−10	2.03	1.71e−10	3.21	1.59e−10	9.66
nonlin1	*overflow*	–	*overflow*	–	*overflow*	–	*overflow*	–
nonlin2	*overflow*	–	*overflow*	–	*overflow*	–	*overflow*	–
nonlin3	4.32e−05	32.17	2.91e−05	40.75	1.63e−05	49.87	1.16e−05	76.33
pendulum	1.16e−04	28.02	5.50e−05	37.76	5.50e−05	48.87	6.65e−05	85.65
heat1d	1.44e−14	4.20	9.23e−15	6.61	9.09e−15	6.81	9.10e−15	6.82
conv.2d_size3	3.15e−10	0.90	1.68e−10	1.11	2.62e−10	1.43	6.76e−11	2.27
sobel3	*DivByZero*	–	*DivByZero*	–	*DivByZero*	–	*DivByZero*	–
fftmatrix	3.71e−09	55.34	3.66e−09	57.13	3.58e−09	57.89	2.56e−09	59.44
fftvector	1.84e−09	39.84	1.48e−09	39.56	1.12e−09	39.56	1.05e−09	41.12
lorentz	2.28e−13	1.73	2.17e−13	1.69	1.53e−13	1.79	1.84e−13	1.75
alphaBlend	3.14e−13	0.19	3.14e−13	1.00	3.14e−13	1.95	3.14e−13	773.52
contr.Tora	8.75e−08	6.65	6.14e−08	468.52	4.06e−08	485.40	7.33e−09	962.96
lyapunov	5.88e−10	2.90	4.16e−10	96.85	3.37e−10	97.68	1.04e−10	198.28
				Fluctuat				
avg	2.37e−12	3.75	2.06e−12	4.00	1.75e−12	3.00	1.49e−12	3.50
variance	–	TO	–	TO	–	TO	–	TO
stdDev	–	TO	–	TO	–	TO	–	TO
roux1	2.10e−13	8.67	8.16e−14	8.00	5.15e−14	8.00	9.86e−14	8.00
goubault	6.50e−14	5.00	6.50e−14	4.67	6.09e−14	5.00	5.91e−14	5.00
harmonic	1.68e−10	16.00	1.34e−10	14.67	1.16e−10	15.00	1.09e−10	16.00
nonlin1	–	TO	–	TO	–	TO	–	TO
nonlin2	–	TO	–	TO	–	TO	–	TO
nonlin3	2.21e−08	29.67	8.24e−09	30.00	6.02e−09	32.33	6.92e−09	35.50
pendulum	1.12e−04	13.00	5.22e−05	13.67	5.22e−05	16.33	6.33e−05	20.00
heat1d	6.66e−16	236.33	4.44e−16	249.33	4.44e−16	248.33	4.44e−16	247.33
conv.2d_size3	1.24e−10	1.00	1.07e−10	1.33	1.24e−10	1.00	4.09e−11	1.33
sobel3	91.9	6.67	90.3	6.33	86.3	6.67	54.4	6.33
fftmatrix	∞	2.67	∞	2.67	∞	2.67	∞	2.67
fftvector	∞	0.99	∞	2.67	∞	2.67	∞	2.33
lorentz	5.41e−14	0.73	5.28e−14	0.73	4.73e−14	0.73	4.84e−14	0.83
alphaBlend	1.56e−13	744.67	1.56e−13	843.67	1.56e−13	820.33	1.55e−13	743.67
contr.Tora	–	TO	–	TO	–	TO	–	TO
lyapunov	5.69e−10	264.00	4.01e−10	270.50	3.03e−10	269.00	7.89e−11	258.00
				Satire				
avg	3.49e−12	18.70	2.84e−12	15.66	2.34e−12	14.45	2.05e−12	15.99
variance	1.83e−08	476.62	1.09e−08	457.62	6.11e−09	455.67	4.61e−09	458.18
stdDev	–	TO	–	TO	–	TO	–	TO
roux1	2.55e−13	126.46	1.19e−13	118.79	7.00e−14	122.02	1.64e−13	120.40
goubault	1.14e−13	90.19	1.14e−13	83.96	1.10e−13	82.39	9.79e−14	82.82
harmonic	1.62e−11	93.69	1.29e−11	90.72	1.07e−11	89.45	1.03e−11	90.97
nonlin1	–	TO	–	TO	–	TO	–	TO
nonlin2	–	TO	–	TO	–	TO	–	TO
nonlin3	9.17e−15	491.27	6.04e−15	496.15	4.13e−15	468.28	4.94e−15	482.47
lorentz	3.50e−14	875.69	*na*	*na*	*na*	*na*	*na*	*na*
heat1d	*na*	92.76	*na*	*na*	*na*	*na*	*na*	*na*

timeouts and any other tool failures. The reported time is the analysis time in seconds. "*na*" in Satire's results denotes that we did not run Satire on these variations of *heat1d* or *lorentz*, as we only took the original benchmarks that had the same ranges for all input DS elements.

References

1. Barr, E.T., Vo, T., Le, V., Su, Z.: Automatic detection of floating-point exceptions. In: Principles of Programming Languages (POPL) (2013)
2. Benz, F., Hildebrandt, A., Hack, S.: A dynamic program analysis to find floating-point accuracy problems. In: Programming Language Design and Implementation (PLDI) (2012)
3. Cheng, T., Rival, X.: An abstract domain to infer types over zones in spreadsheets. In: Miné, A., Schmidt, D. (eds.) SAS 2012. LNCS, vol. 7460, pp. 94–110. Springer, Heidelberg (2012). https://doi.org/10.1007/978-3-642-33125-1_9
4. Chiang, W., Gopalakrishnan, G., Rakamaric, Z., Solovyev, A.: Efficient search for inputs causing high floating-point errors. In: Symposium on Principles and Practice of Parallel Programming (PPoPP) (2014)
5. Cousot, P., Cousot, R., Logozzo, F.: A parametric segmentation functor for fully automatic and scalable array content analysis. In: Principles of Programming Languages (POPL) (2011)
6. Damouche, N., Martel, M., Panchekha, P., Qiu, C., Sanchez-Stern, A., Tatlock, Z.: Toward a standard benchmark format and suite for floating-point analysis. In: Numerical Software Verification Workshop (NSV) (2016)
7. Darulova, E., Izycheva, A., Nasir, F., Ritter, F., Becker, H., Bastian, R.: Daisy - framework for analysis and optimization of numerical programs. In: Tools and Algorithms for the Construction and Analysis of Systems (TACAS) (2018)
8. Darulova, E., Kuncak, V.: Towards a compiler for reals. ACM Trans. Program. Lang. Syst. **39**(2), 1–28 (2017)
9. Das, A., Briggs, I., Gopalakrishnan, G., Krishnamoorthy, S., Panchekha, P.: Scalable yet rigorous floating-point error analysis. In: International Conference for High Performance Computing, Networking, Storage and Analysis (SC) (2020)
10. De, D., Lauter, C., Melquiond, G.: Assisted verification of elementary functions using Gappa. In: ACM Symposium on Applied Computing (2006)
11. de Figueiredo, L.H., Stolfi, J.: Affine arithmetic: concepts and applications. Numer. Algorithms **37**(1–4), 147–158 (2004)
12. Fousse, L., Hanrot, G., Lefèvre, V., Pélissier, P., Zimmermann, P.: MPFR: a multiple-precision binary floating-point library with correct rounding. ACM Trans. Math. Softw. **33**(2), 13-es (2007)
13. Goubault, E., Putot, S.: Static analysis of finite precision computations. In: Jhala, R., Schmidt, D. (eds.) VMCAI 2011. LNCS, vol. 6538, pp. 232–247. Springer, Heidelberg (2011). https://doi.org/10.1007/978-3-642-18275-4_17
14. Guo, H., Rubio-González, C.: Efficient generation of error-inducing floating-point inputs via symbolic execution. In: International Conference on Supercomputing (ICS) (2020)
15. Hagedorn, B., Stoltzfus, L., Steuwer, M., Gorlatch, S., Dubach, C.: High performance stencil code generation with lift. In: Proceedings of the 2018 International Symposium on Code Generation and Optimization (2018)

16. Halbwachs, N., Péron, M.: Discovering properties about arrays in simple programs. In: Programming Language Design and Implementation (PLDI) (2008)
17. IEEE, C.: IEEE Standard for Floating-Point Arithmetic. IEEE Std 754–2008 (2008)
18. Izycheva, A., Darulova, E.: On sound relative error bounds for floating-point arithmetic. In: Formal Methods in Computer Aided Design (FMCAD) (2017)
19. Jeannet, B., Miné, A.: Apron: A library of numerical abstract domains for static analysis. In: Computer Aided Verification (CAV) (2009)
20. Johnson, T.T., et al.: Arch-comp20 category report: artificial intelligence and neural network control systems (AINNCS) for continuous and hybrid systems plants. In: International Workshop on Applied Verification of Continuous and Hybrid Systems (ARCH20) (2020)
21. Liew, D., Schemmel, D., Cadar, C., Donaldson, A., Zähl, R., Wehrle, K.: Floating-point symbolic execution: a case study in N-version programming. In: ASE (2017)
22. Lohar, D., Jeangoudoux, C., Sobel, J., Darulova, E., Christakis, M.: A two-phase approach for conditional floating-point verification. In: Tools and Algorithms for the Construction and Analysis of Systems (TACAS) (2021)
23. Abadi, M., et al.: TensorFlow: Large-scale machine learning on heterogeneous systems (2015). https://www.tensorflow.org/. Software available from tensorflow.org
24. Magron, V., Constantinides, G., Donaldson, A.: Certified roundoff error bounds using semidefinite programming. ACM Trans. Math. Softw. **43**(4), 1–31 (2017)
25. Miné, A., Breck, J., Reps, T.: An algorithm inspired by constraint solvers to infer inductive invariants in numeric programs. In: Programming Languages and Systems (ESOP) (2016)
26. Miné, A., et al.: Taking static analysis to the next level: proving the absence of run-time errors and data races with astrée. In: ERTS (2016)
27. Moore, R.E., Kearfott, R.B., Cloud, M.J.: Introduction to Interval Analysis. Society for Industrial and Applied Mathematics (2009)
28. Singh, G., Püschel, M., Vechev, M.T.: Fast polyhedra abstract domain. In: Principles of Programming Languages (POPL) (2017)
29. Solovyev, A., Baranowski, M.S., Briggs, I., Jacobsen, C., Rakamaric, Z., Gopalakrishnan, G.: Rigorous estimation of floating-point round-off errors with symbolic Taylor expansions. ACM Trans. Program. Lang. Syst. **41**(1), 1–39 (2019)
30. Solovyev, A., Jacobsen, C., Rakamarić, Z., Gopalakrishnan, G.: Rigorous estimation of floating-point round-off errors with symbolic Taylor expansions. In: Bjørner, N., de Boer, F. (eds.) FM 2015. LNCS, vol. 9109, pp. 532–550. Springer, Cham (2015). https://doi.org/10.1007/978-3-319-19249-9_33
31. Titolo, L., Feliú, M., Moscato, M., Muñoz, C.: An abstract interpretation framework for the round-off error analysis of floating-point programs. In: Verification, Model Checking, and Abstract Interpretation (VMCAI) (2018)
32. Zou, D., Wang, R., Xiong, Y., Zhang, L., Su, Z., Mei, H.: A genetic algorithm for detecting significant floating-point inaccuracies. In: International Conference on Supercomputing (ICS) (2015)

Reverse Template Processing Using Abstract Interpretation

Matthieu Lemerre(✉)

Université Paris-Saclay, CEA, List, 91120 Palaiseau, France
matthieu.lemerre@cea.fr

Abstract. Template languages transform tree-structured data into text. We study the reverse problem, transforming the template into a parser that returns all the tree-structured data that can produce a given text. Programs written in template languages are generally not injective (they have multiple preimages), not affine (some input variables can appear at several locations in the output), and erasing (they provide only a partial view of the source), which makes the problem challenging. We propose to solve this problem using concepts from abstract interpretation, like the denotational style of abstract semantics, soundness, exactness, or reduction, to reason about the precision and the recovery of all the preimages. This work shows that Abstract Interpretation is a very useful theory when reasoning about the reversal of non-injective programs.

1 Introduction

One of the most ubiquitous ways to format data into text is through the use of a *template engine,* or *template processor*. They interpret a program in a *template language*, which consists in a fixed text intertwined with specific *instructions* that produces an *output text*, given tree-structured data as an *input*. The input data often comes from XML, JSON, relational databases, or records from a language providing the data. Examples of such template engines include Apache Freemarker, Mustache, ERB, Jinja, Liquid, XSLT, or StringTemplate [38].

We study the reverse transformation, i.e. the problem of retrieving the input data from the output text. In general, the problem of finding if a program p admits an input that produces a given output w is undecidable. This is the case for the template language that we want to address, as e.g. inversing a template can be used to find the solutions of Diophantine equations, an undecidable problem [28]. Thus, we cannot have an algorithm which is simultaneously *sound* (i.e. does not forget about an input), *complete*, (i.e. does not return incorrect inputs), *terminating*, and working on an *expressive* template language. Another problem is that of *finite representation* of these inputs: if the transformation is not injective (which is rarely the case, as the output is often only a partial view of the input), the set of corresponding inputs can be large or even infinite; we thus want a *finite* representation of this infinite set.

Our solution uses abstract interpretation [8] to solve the reverse transformation of template processing of tree-structured data. Using abstract domains to

M. V. Hermenegildo and J. F. Morales (Eds.): SAS 2023, LNCS 14284, pp. 403–433, 2023.
https://doi.org/10.1007/978-3-031-44245-2_18

finitely represent an infinite set of JSON-like databases, our template reversing algorithm is terminating (Sect. 4), sound (Sect. 5), and works on an expressive template language (which can be easily extended, as shown in Sects. 7 and 8). What we have to give up is completeness; however, most of our operations are complete, and our algorithm can detect if the set of values that it returns is exact or is an over-approximation (Sect. 6). Our experiments (Sect. 8) show that, on practical examples, it is effectively able to retrieve the part of the database that was used to produce a given output.

Specifically, our main contribution is a technique to invert a function by

1. deriving a backward denotational semantics from the forward big-step semantics of the language, with modifications such that the reverse algorithm will need to explore only a finite number of evaluation trees (Sect. 4);
2. using abstract interpretation [8] on this denotational semantics to derive a sound algorithm (Sect. 5), but also to reason about the precision (Sect. 6), simplification by constraint propagation (Sect. 7), and extensions (Sect. 8) of the algorithm.

While we show that template languages are a good fit for applying these techniques, they are quite general and could be reused in other areas of reverse computation[1].

2 Motivation and Example

Our original motivation comes from the following practical problem. In embedded systems, automated generation of code and data in source code is very common, as this minimizes the storage and execution costs in the runtime. Template languages are used to simplify the formatting of this source code.

If it is part of a safety-critical application, this generated source code must be certified. One strategy for this is to certify the code generator. Because an error in this generator can lead to an error when the system runs, such a generator is considered to be critical component which must be qualified at the highest assurance level, which is very costly.

An alternative certification strategy [33] is to develop an *independent checker* that verifies that the generated source code corresponds to safety requirements, independently of how the source was generated (this is similar to the translation validation [40] approach found e.g. in CompCert [26]).

Because an error in such a checker cannot introduce new errors (it can only omit to see existing errors), such a checker is less critical than a code generator and needs only to be qualified at a low assurance level, which is much less costly. The code generator may not even have to be qualified at all, as the certification works on the generated code, independently of its provenance.

Figure 1 represents all the steps of this use-case: on the left, a team of developpers create (manually or automatically) a JSON database containing system

[1] In particular, reverse computation normally focus on injective function, while our technique does require this limitation.

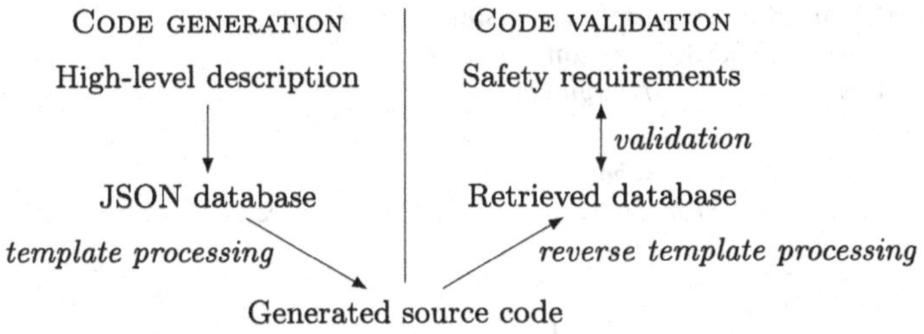

Fig. 1. Verifying generated source code, featuring reverse template processing.

parameters from a high-level description of the system. Template processing is then used to generate source code using these parameters. On the right, the verification team uses the checker first to retrieve a database by parsing the generated source code; this retrieved database can be used to check that the parameters comply with safety requirements. One may wonder why we cannot just reuse the generated JSON database directly: the reason is that this would be considered a common cause of failure by certification authorities, as the verification process must be independent and cannot rely on intermediate artefacts produced by the code generation. On the other hand, the templates can be reused, because they can be viewed as a specification on how the source code has to be generated.

Since such a checker must work from the source code of the safety-critical application, writing a parser extracting the data to validate from the source code is a cumbersome task. When the source code has been produced using templates, our idea is that the parsing can be done by *reversing the template processing* – i.e. evaluating the template backwards, to retrieve the input data from the output text. We can then validate that this retrieved data matches the safety requirements of the system. Figure 1 represents all the steps of this use-case.

Let us examine a concrete example inspired by the actual industrial problem that motivated this work. Consider this example of drones monitoring a sea area from a location in Bermuda. Each drone is assigned a flight plan, which is a sequence of coordinates. Each drone has limited memory, thus the flight plan is generated as a static linked list in source code which is compiled and put inside each drone. To make the flight plan more maintainable, the generation is split in two phases: first, *parameters* are computed and stored in a JSON database; second, source code is generated using a template processor. Figure 2 represents the template generating this linked list, the input parameters, and the resulting code, which can be compiled and linked to the drone autopilot.

Now imagine that the drone must be certified according to safety-critical aeronautics standards. The computation of the flight plan parameters, having to satisfy many antagonistic constraints, is a hard problem (encompassing the traveling salesman), and certifying the code generator producing this flight plan would be hard. Luckily, certifying the code generator is not mandatory, as only the generated code must be certified (independently of how it was generated). The safety requirements on the flight plan code are actually quite simple: (1) the

```
struct coord { float lat; float lon; struct coord *next;};
⟨for c in seq⟩struct coord ⟨= c.name:symbol⟩; ⟨end⟩
struct coord *start = &⟨= first:symbol⟩};
⟨for c in seq⟩
  struct coord ⟨= c.name:symbol⟩ =
  { ⟨= c.lat:float⟩, ⟨= c.lon:float⟩, ⟨if c.last⟩ 0 ⟨else⟩ &⟨= c.next:symbol⟩ ⟨end⟩ };
⟨end⟩
```

$$\begin{bmatrix} \mathit{first} \mapsto \mathit{hamilton} \\ \mathit{seq} \mapsto \begin{bmatrix} \mathit{name} \mapsto \mathit{hamilton} \\ \mathit{lat} \mapsto 32.36 \\ \mathit{lon} \mapsto -64.67 \\ \mathit{last} \mapsto \mathit{false} \\ \mathit{next} \mapsto \mathit{san\_juan} \end{bmatrix} :: \begin{bmatrix} \mathit{name} \mapsto \mathit{san\_juan} \\ \mathit{lat} \mapsto 18.46 \\ \mathit{lon} \mapsto -66.10 \\ \mathit{last} \mapsto \mathit{false} \\ \mathit{next} \mapsto \mathit{miami} \end{bmatrix} :: \begin{bmatrix} \mathit{name} \mapsto \mathit{miami} \\ \mathit{lat} \mapsto 25.76 \\ \mathit{lon} \mapsto -80.19 \\ \mathit{last} \mapsto \mathit{true} \\ \end{bmatrix} \end{bmatrix}$$

```
struct coord { float lat; float lon; struct coord *next;};
struct coord hamilton; struct coord san_juan; struct coord miami;
struct coord *start = &hamilton;
struct coord hamilton = { 32.31, −64.76, &san_juan };
struct coord san_juan = { 18.46, −66.10, &miami };
struct coord miami = { 25.76, −80.19, 0; };
```

Fig. 2. Forward evaluation of the template (top) on the input environment (middle) yields the output text (bottom).

code must provide this data in a format that is suitable for the drone runtime, something which can be specified using the template; (2) the length of the route must be small enough so that the drone does not run out of battery and fall.

To validate the parameters, we cannot just reuse the generated JSON database directly, as this would be considered a common cause of failure by certification authorities. The templates can be reused, as they can be considered as a specification on how the source code has to be formatted. Thus, a suitable strategy to certify compliance of the flight plan source code is to start from the code, and to: 1. Verify that this source code complies with the specified template (this checks safety requirement (1)), and retrieve all the possible input parameters (the JSON databases) that can produce the source code using the template; 2. Verify that each possible input parameters satisfies the safety requirement (2).

Step 2. is application-dependent (Methni et al. [33] provides several examples, such as verifying that communication buffers have sufficient size, that a static schedule plan allows meeting every deadline, etc.), but we propose to automatize step 1. using *reverse template processing.*

3 Background: The RTL Template Language

We study the problem of reversing templates on a simple functional template language, whose syntax and semantics is given here. While simple, this language is quite representative of how typical templates are developed; moreover, we propose extensions to this language in Sect. 8.

$\mathbb{P} \ni p, q$	$\triangleq x \mid p.f$	path
$\mathbb{X} \ni x$		variable names
$\mathbb{F} \ni f$		field names
$\mathbb{W} \ni u, v, w$		word (string)
$\mathbb{T} \ni t$		scalar types

$\mathbb{I} \ni i, j \triangleq w$	fixed word
$\mid \langle = p{:}t \rangle$	replacement
$\mid i\ i$	template concatenation
$\mid \langle \mathtt{if}\ p \rangle\ i\ \langle \mathtt{else} \rangle\ i\ \langle \mathtt{end} \rangle$	conditionals
$\mid \langle \mathtt{for}\ x\ \mathtt{in}\ p \rangle\ i\ \langle \mathtt{end} \rangle$	iterations
$\mid \langle \mathtt{apply}\ \phi\ \mathtt{with}\ x = p \rangle$	function call

Fig. 3. Syntax for the RTL template language

Notations. We write equality by definition as $\triangleq$, word concatenation as $\cdot$, and the empty word as ε. The power set of a set $\mathbb{S}$ is written as $\mathcal{P}(\mathbb{S})$, and the empty set is represented by $\{\}$. The domain of a function φ is represented by $\mathrm{dom}(\varphi)$. We represent by $Seq(\mathbb{S})$ the set of finite sequences of elements in $\mathbb{S}$, and represent a sequence of n elements by $e_0{::}\ldots{::}e_{n-1}$. A sequence of n elements in $\mathbb{S}$ can also be considered as a function $\in [0..n-1] \to \mathbb{S}$.

We use $\mathbb{Y} \rightharpoonup \mathbb{Z}$ to represent the set of partial functions from $\mathbb{Y}$ to $\mathbb{Z}$. If $\Gamma \in \mathbb{Y} \rightharpoonup \mathbb{Z}$, $y \in \mathrm{dom}(\Gamma)$, and $z \in \mathbb{Z}$, we note by $\Gamma[x] \in \mathbb{Z}$ the value bound to x in Γ, and by $\Gamma[y \mapsto z] \in \mathbb{Y} \rightharpoonup \mathbb{Z}$ the replacement of the binding from y to z in Γ. We note by $[]$ a partial function with an empty domain, and by $[y \mapsto z]$ the partial function which binds only y to z (i.e. $[y \mapsto z] = [][y \mapsto z]$). Finally, we note by $\mathit{unbind}(y, \Gamma)$ the restriction of Γ where y is removed from $\mathrm{dom}(\Gamma)$. We represent anonymous functions and partial functions using λ-calculus notation.

Syntax. The template language, whose syntax is given in Fig. 3, manipulates a tree-structured data as its input, and values are referred by paths in that tree. A *path* $p \in \mathbb{P}$ is either a *variable* $x \in \mathbb{X}$, or access to a *field* $f \in \mathbb{F}$ of a record. A template is decomposed into *instructions* $i \in \mathbb{I}$. An instruction is either a fixed word (reproduced as is), a replacement (replaced by the printed representation of a value in a database), a concatenation of two instructions, a conditional, a loop, or a function call. For the sake of simplicity the functions here only take one argument, and we omit the syntax for the definition of functions, which is standard; in particular, recursive calls are allowed.

Databases. A *database* $d \in \mathbb{D}$ is a *tree* defined inductively as either a *scalar* of type t, a *record* from field names to databases, or a *finite sequence* of databases.

$$\mathbb{D} \triangleq \mathbb{D}_s \cup \mathbb{D}_r \cup \mathbb{D}_* \qquad \mathbb{D}_s \triangleq \bigcup_{t \in \mathbb{T}} \mathbb{D}_t \qquad \mathbb{D}_r \triangleq \mathbb{F} \rightharpoonup \mathbb{D} \qquad \mathbb{D}_* \triangleq Seq(\mathbb{D})$$

Scalar types must include integer and boolean types. As we focus on source-code generation, our practical examples also use floating point numbers, symbols (sequence of alphanumeric letters), and quoted strings (delimited by " ").

Environments. An *environment* $\Gamma \in \mathbb{E} = \mathbb{X} \rightharpoonup \mathbb{D}$ is a mapping from variables to databases. For instance, the mapping in the middle of Fig. 2 is an environment, mapping the variables *first* and *seq* to databases; *first* is a scalar (a *symbol*), and *seq* is a sequence of 3 records, each containing only scalar values.

$$\text{FIXED}\quad \frac{}{(\!|w|\!)(\Gamma) = w} \qquad \text{REPLACE}\quad \frac{show_t(\Gamma[p]) = w}{(\!|\langle = p{:}t\rangle|\!)(\Gamma) = w} \qquad \text{CONCAT}\quad \frac{(\!|i|\!)(\Gamma) = u \qquad (\!|j|\!)(\Gamma) = v}{(\!|i\ j|\!)(\Gamma) = u \cdot v}$$

$$\text{IF-TRUE}\quad \frac{\Gamma[p] = true \qquad (\!|i|\!)(\Gamma) = w}{(\!|\langle \texttt{if}\ p\rangle\, i\, \langle \texttt{else}\rangle\, j\, \langle \texttt{end}\rangle|\!)(\Gamma) = w} \qquad \text{IF-FALSE}\quad \frac{\Gamma[p] = false \qquad (\!|j|\!)(\Gamma) = w}{(\!|\langle \texttt{if}\ p\rangle\, i\, \langle \texttt{else}\rangle\, j\, \langle \texttt{end}\rangle|\!)(\Gamma) = w}$$

$$\text{APPLY}\quad \frac{i = \Delta(\phi) \qquad (\!|i|\!)(\Gamma[x \mapsto \Gamma[p]]) = w}{(\!|\langle \texttt{apply}\ \phi\ \texttt{with}\ x = p\rangle|\!)(\Gamma) = w} \qquad \text{FOR}\quad \frac{\Gamma[p] = d_1{::}\ldots{::}d_n \qquad \forall k \in 1..n : (\!|i|\!)(\Gamma[x \mapsto d_k]) = w_k}{(\!|\langle \texttt{for}\ x\ \texttt{in}\ p\rangle\, i\, \langle \texttt{end}\rangle|\!)(\Gamma) = w_1 \cdot\ \ldots\ \cdot w_n}$$

Fig. 4. Big-step operational semantics for RTL.

We extend our notation for variable access in environment, and field access in databases, to handle paths:

$$\Gamma[p.f] \triangleq \Gamma[p][f] \qquad \Gamma[p.f \mapsto v] \triangleq \Gamma[p \mapsto \Gamma[p][f \mapsto v]] \qquad [p.f \mapsto v] \triangleq [p \mapsto [f \mapsto v]]$$

Functions on Scalars. For every scalar type $t \in \mathbb{T}$, we suppose that there exists an injective function $show_t \in \mathbb{D}_t \to \mathbb{W}$ to convert the value into a string, and a partial function $read_t \in \mathbb{W} \rightharpoonup \mathbb{D}_t$ that does the reverse, i.e. their composition is the identity: $\forall s \in \mathbb{D}_t : read_t(show_t(s)) = s$. Note that $read_t$ may fail (e.g. when attemptying to parse "foo" as a number).

Forward Semantics. We now give the normal (forward) semantics for our template language (Fig. 4), in the big-step structural operational style of [22].

$(\!|\cdot|\!)$ is a partial function that takes a template instruction $i \in \mathbb{I}$ and an environment $\Gamma \in \mathbb{E}$, and either produces a word, or fails (when the template tries to access a path not bound in the environment Γ). The evaluation is deterministic.

The evaluation goes as follows: fixed words are copied as is (FIXED). Replacements are done using the value taken from the corresponding field in the database (REPLACE). Concatenated instructions produce a concatenated word (CONCAT). Conditionals depend on the boolean value of a path in the database (IF-TRUE and IF-FALSE); templates which use as a condition a value which is not a boolean fail with an error. The `for` instruction iterates over a sequence, binds each element of the sequence to a variable, evaluates the child instruction with this new environment, and concatenates the results (FOR). The `apply` instruction (APPLY) introduces a new binding which is used in the called function; we assume the existence of a global mapping of definitions Δ from function names to instructions created by parsing the function definitions (the "main" template is attached to the name `main`).

In general the evaluation will start with one or several variables bound, which are the "roots" of the database.

4 Semantics for Reversing Template

We define the *reverse template problem* for i and w as finding the set of all the environments that can produce a word w given a template i. Formally:

Definition 1 (Backward interpretation function). *Given a template i, the* backward interpretation function $[\![i]\!](\cdot)$ *is defined as follows:*

$$[\![i]\!](\cdot) : \mathbb{W} \to \mathcal{P}(\mathbb{E}) \qquad [\![i]\!](w) \triangleq \{\Gamma \in \mathbb{E} : (\!|i|\!)(\Gamma) = w\}$$

We derive a sound algorithm for the reverse template problem in 3 steps:

1. we observe that we can reverse the forward evaluation as a parsing algorithm, but this requires fixing an issue on some `for` template instructions;
2. we define a denotational (i.e. compositional) semantics for the backward interpretation function, that we modify to work around the parsing issue;
3. we define abstract domains that provide finite, computer-manipulable representations of infinite sets of environments, and we use them to derive an algorithm that computes a representation of a superset of $[\![i]\!](w)$.

This section describes the steps 1. and 2., while Sect. 5 presents step 3.

4.1 Parsing as Natural Deduction

To compute $[\![i]\!](\cdot)$, a key observation is that the operational semantics given in Fig. 4 can be read backwards, as a proof search that parses the text according to the template, and use this to retrieve a Γ (this makes use of the correspondance between parse trees and deduction trees observed by Shieber et al. [46]).

This suggests an algorithm that would first use a parser to enumerate all the suitable deduction/parse trees, and solve the associated constraints for each tree (it suffices to translate the template into a context-free grammar that over-approximates the set of words that a template can generate, see Appendix A.1 for details).

Unfortunately, this algorithm fails when the number of parse trees is infinite, which can happen in our language. In Appendix A.1 we show that this happens when the context-free grammar corresponding to the template is cyclic, i.e. a non-terminal can derive into itself without outputing anything else. This can happen notably when a function ϕ may recursively call itself without outputing anything after and before the recursive call, e.g. when ϕ is defined as follows: "⟨`if` *p.cond*⟩ ⟨= *p.data*:*int* ⟩ ⟨`else`⟩ ⟨`apply` ϕ `with` $p = $ *p.next*⟩ ⟨`end`⟩". Note that non-cyclic recursive calls to template functions (e.g. if ϕ is defined as "⟨`if` *p.cond*⟩ ⟨= *p.data*:*int* ⟩ ⟨`else`⟩ (⟨`apply` ϕ `with` $p = $ *p.next*⟩) ⟨`end`⟩") can be handled as in this case, there would still be a finite number of parse trees; further, we explain how to extend our technique to handle cyclic recursive calls to templates in Sect. 8.4). We never encountered such cyclic recursive calls in our real examples (and it is easy to add text in the output to make the recursive call non-cyclic), so in the following we assume that the template has no cyclic recursive calls.

On the contrary, the following pattern is very common. Consider, in Fig. 4, the FOR rule: if the i instruction can produce the empty word ε, then this rule may have an arbitrary large number of antecedents. For instance, in the template:

⟨`for` n `in` *nums*⟩ ⟨`if` *n.odd*⟩ ⟨= *n.id*:*int* ⟩ ⟨`else`⟩ ⟨`end`⟩; ⟨`end`⟩

FOR-ALT

$$\frac{\forall k \in 1..n : w_k \neq \varepsilon \qquad \begin{array}{c} d_1{::}\ldots{::}d_n \text{ subsequence of } \Gamma[p] \\ \forall d : d \in \Gamma[p] \wedge d \notin d_1{::}\ldots{::}d_n \Rightarrow (\!|i|\!)(\Gamma[x \mapsto d]) = \varepsilon \\ \forall k \in 1..n : (\!|i|\!)(\Gamma[x \mapsto d_k]) = w_k \end{array}}{(\!|\langle \texttt{for}\ x\ \texttt{in}\ p\rangle\, i\, \langle \texttt{end}\rangle|\!)(\Gamma) = w_1 \cdot \ \ldots\ \cdot w_n}$$

Fig. 5. Alternative rule for the `for` instruction

applied to the string "11;17;", there can be arbitrarily many n in *nums* which are not *odd*, each of them corresponding to a different parse tree. As in this case the number of parse trees is infinite, the proof search cannot terminate.

To work around this problem, we provide an alternative FOR-ALT rule (Fig. 5, where *subsequences* are not necessarily consecutive). This alternative rule just separates the elements in the sequence that produce an empty string from those that do not, and it is thus easy to prove that both rules are equivalent.

Theorem 1. *The* FOR *and* FOR-ALT *rules are equivalent.*

Using this new rule, the children of a `for` node in a parse tree is now a finite sequence of subtrees each corresponding to a non-empty word, instead of an arbitrary long sequence of subtrees corresponding to either empty or non-empty words (which could thus not be enumerated). The combination of the FOR-ALT rule and restriction on non-cyclic recursive calls makes sure that the number of possible parse trees for any given word is finite, and can thus be enumerated (see Appendix A.1 for a proof).

4.2 A Backward Denotational Semantics

Using Definition 1, we can easily prove that the backward interpretation function $[\![]\!]()$ has the properties given in Fig. 6. But these equations can also act as a denotational semantics for $[\![]\!]()$, i.e. they define the behaviour of $[\![]\!]()$ constructively. To summarize, outputing a fixed word is possible only when the word matches its output; outputing a path constrains this path in the environment; when two templates are concatenated, the environment must fullfill the constraints of both templates; in conditionals the environments must fulfill one of the two cases; as applying a template creates a binding from the formal to actual argument, the reverse evaluation has to perform the opposite operation of unbinding the constraints; finally, handling `for` loops is a combination between concatenation of a finite sequence and unbinding of the loop iterator.

As we explained in Sect. 4.1, this semantics cannot be used "as-is" as the basis for an algorithm, because the `for` rule can perform an infinite number of decompositions. To solve this problem, we have to ignore the elements in sequences that produce an empty string. To do this, we first define *unseq*:

$$\begin{aligned} &\mathit{unseq} : \mathbb{X} \times \mathbb{P} \times \mathit{Seq}(\mathbb{E}) \rightarrow \mathcal{P}(\mathbb{E}) \\ &\mathit{unseq}(x, p, \Gamma_1{::}\ldots{::}\Gamma_n) \triangleq \{\, \Gamma : \quad \Gamma = \mathit{unbind}(x, \Gamma_1) = \ldots = \mathit{unbind}(x, \Gamma_n) \\ &\qquad\qquad\qquad\qquad\qquad\qquad \wedge\ \Gamma_1[x]{::}\ldots{::}\Gamma_n[x] \text{ subsequence of } \Gamma[p] \quad \} \end{aligned}$$

$$
\begin{aligned}
[\![v]\!](w) &= \begin{cases} \mathbb{E} & \text{if } v = w \\ \emptyset & \text{otherwise} \end{cases} \\
[\![\langle = p{:}t\,\rangle]\!](w) &= \{\Gamma \in \mathbb{E} : \Gamma[p] = \mathit{read}_t(u)\} \\
[\![i\ j]\!](w) &= \bigcup_{u \cdot v = w} [\![i]\!](u) \cap [\![j]\!](v) \\
[\![\langle \texttt{if}\ p\rangle\, i\, \langle \texttt{else}\rangle\, j\, \langle \texttt{end}\rangle]\!](w) &= \quad \{\Gamma \in [\![i]\!](w) : \Gamma[p]\} \\
&\quad \cup \{\Gamma \in [\![j]\!](w) : \neg\,\Gamma[p]\} \\
[\![\langle \texttt{apply}\ f\ \texttt{with}\ x = p\rangle]\!](w) &= \{\mathit{unbind}(x, \Gamma) :\ \Gamma \in [\![\Delta(f)]\!](w) \\
&\qquad \wedge \Gamma[p] = \Gamma[x]\} \\
[\![\langle \texttt{for}\ x\ \texttt{in}\ p\rangle\, i\, \langle \texttt{end}\rangle]\!](w) &= \\
\bigcup_{\substack{n \in \mathbb{N} \\ w_1 \cdot w_2 \cdots w_n = u}} \quad \{\ \Gamma : \exists(\Gamma_1, \ldots, \Gamma_n) &\in [\![i]\!](w_1) \times \ldots \times [\![i]\!](w_n), \\
\Gamma[p] &= \Gamma_1[x] :: \ldots :: \Gamma_n[x] \\
\wedge\, \mathit{unbind}(x, \Gamma_1) &= \ldots = \mathit{unbind}(x, \Gamma_n) \quad \}
\end{aligned}
$$

Fig. 6. A denotational semantics for reversing templates.

The idea is that *unseq* takes a variable x, a path p, and a sequence of environments $\Gamma_1{::}\ldots{::}\Gamma_n$ where x is bound, and it retrieves all the Γ where $\Gamma_1{::}\ldots{::}\Gamma_n$ can correspond to a subsequence of the environments that are created in the forward evaluation of a `for` x `in` p instruction applied to an environment Γ.

We also define *emptyseq* as follows:

$$
\begin{aligned}
&\mathit{emptyseq} : \mathbb{I} \times \mathbb{X} \times \mathbb{P} \times \mathit{Seq}(\mathbb{E}) \rightarrow \mathcal{P}(\mathbb{E}) \\
&\mathit{emptyseq}(i, x, p, \Gamma_1{::}\ldots{::}\Gamma_n) \triangleq \{\, \Gamma :\ \forall d \in \Gamma[p] :\ d \neq \Gamma_1[x] \wedge \ldots \wedge d \neq \Gamma_n[x] \\
&\qquad\qquad\qquad\qquad\qquad\qquad \Leftrightarrow \Gamma[x \mapsto d] \in [\![i]\!](\varepsilon) \quad \}
\end{aligned}
$$

Intuitively, the function *emptyseq* constrains the databases d in $\Gamma[p]$, that produce an empty string, to be distinct from those that are in the subsequence $\Gamma_1{::}\ldots{::}\Gamma_n$. Finally, we can modify the rule for `for` templates using these definitions:

$$
[\![\langle \texttt{for}\ x\ \texttt{in}\ p\rangle\, i\, \langle \texttt{end}\rangle]\!](w) \quad = \quad \bigcup_{\substack{n \in \mathbb{N} \\ w_1 \cdot w_2 \cdots w_n = u \\ \forall w_i : w_i \neq \varepsilon}} \quad \bigcup_{\substack{\Gamma_1 \in [\![i]\!](w_1) \\ \vdots \\ \Gamma_n \in [\![i]\!](w_n)}} \begin{array}{l} \mathit{emptyseq}(i, x, p, \Gamma_1{::}\ldots{::}\Gamma_n) \\ \cap\ \ \mathit{unseq}(x, p, \Gamma_1{::}\ldots{::}\Gamma_n) \end{array}
$$

This denotational semantics for reverse template, with the above modified rule for `for` templates, is the basis for our algorithm for sound reversal of templates, provided in the next section.

5 Sound Reversal of Templates

In Sect. 4 we developed a denotational semantics for reversing templates that is compositional and requires only a finite number of parse trees (for a given text). This semantics is not computable because it manipulates infinite sets of databases and environments: for instance, every environment in $\mathbb{E}$ can render the text `"foo"` from the template `"foo"`, and we cannot enumerate $\mathbb{E}$.

A similar problem exists in the setting of sound static analysis of programs, that relies on a program semantics which is not computable due to the handling of infinite (or very large) sets of states $\mathbb{S}$. The solution to this problem is abstract interpretation [8] : the program semantics is approximated by a computation over an *abstract domain* $\mathbb{S}^\sharp$, which is a computer-representable lattice, such that $\mathbb{S}$ and $\mathbb{S}^\sharp$ are (typically) related by a Galois connection. Abstract interpretation is a *sound* method, i.e. it is guaranteed to compute a sound over-approximation of the set of all reachable states of the program; here we propose to use this method to soundly over-approximate the set of all the environments that can produce a given text with a given template.

We first present our *abstract databases* and *abstract environments*, respectively used to represent sets of concrete databases and environments; then our *abstract backward semantics*, which allows computing a sound overapproximation of the backward denotational semantics $[\![]\!]()$. We give the concretisation function γ that provides the formal meaning of the abstract domain by relating abstract elements to the set of concrete elements that it represents, and soundness theorems of all the main operations (we generally omit the proof, as the proof method is standard).

5.1 Abstract Databases

Intuitively, we can see our abstract domains as representing databases as a collection of *constraints*, such that they describe the set of databases that obey these constraints. As there are three different kinds of databases (scalars, records, and sequences), we need three different kinds of constraints to represent them. The domains are presented formally in Fig. 7. We define an *abstract database* $d^\sharp \in \mathbb{D}^\sharp$ to be either a *scalar value* $s \in \mathbb{D}_s$, an *abstract record* $d^\sharp_r \in \mathbb{D}^\sharp_r$ mapping fields to *abstract databases*, an *abstract sequence* $d^\sharp_* \in \mathbb{D}^\sharp_*$, or $\bot$, which represents an unsatisfiable constraint. Its concretisation is defined recursively as representing either a single scalar, the empty set, or a set of abstract databases or abstract sequences.

Remark 1. Our abstract elements cannot represent a set of databases that would contain both a scalar and a record. Thus, the abstraction function α cannot be defined on our domains, and we use a γ-only style of abstract interpretation [10]. Representing such a heterogeneous set is not needed, as abstract databases do not feature a join operator (instead, we perform a *disjunctive completion* [9] by *powerset completion* [2,14] on abstract environments, see Sect. 5.2).

An *abstract record* $d^\sharp_r \in \mathbb{D}^\sharp_r$ is a partial function from fields to abstract databases. Intuitively, each field in the abstract record constrains the corresponding field in the concrete records (fields that are not in the abstract record are unconstrained).

Example 1. Let $d^\sharp_r = [\text{“}a\text{”} \mapsto [\text{“}b\text{”} \mapsto 1]]$. Then:

$$[\text{“}a\text{”} \mapsto 3] \notin \gamma_{\mathbb{D}^\sharp_r}(d^\sharp_r) \qquad [\text{“}d\text{”} \mapsto 8; \text{“}a\text{”} \mapsto [\text{“}b\text{”} \mapsto 1; \text{“}c\text{”} \mapsto 3]] \in \gamma_{\mathbb{D}^\sharp_r}(d^\sharp_r)$$

$$
\begin{array}{rl}
\text{Abstract database} & \mathbb{D}^\sharp = \mathbb{D}_s \cup \mathbb{D}^\sharp_r \cup \mathbb{D}^\sharp_* \cup \{\bot\} \\
\text{Abstract record} & \mathbb{D}^\sharp_r = \mathbb{F} \rightharpoonup \mathbb{D}^\sharp \\
\text{Abstract sequence} & \mathbb{D}^\sharp_* = \mathcal{P}(\mathit{Seq}(\mathbb{D}^\sharp))
\end{array}
$$

$$
\gamma_{\mathbb{D}^\sharp} : \mathbb{D}^\sharp \to \mathcal{P}(\mathbb{D}) \qquad \gamma_{\mathbb{D}^\sharp}(d^\sharp) = \begin{cases} \{d^\sharp\} & \text{if } d^\sharp \in \mathbb{D}_s \\ \gamma_{\mathbb{D}^\sharp_r}(d^\sharp) & \text{if } d^\sharp \in \mathbb{D}^\sharp_r \\ \gamma_{\mathbb{D}^\sharp_*}(d^\sharp) & \text{if } d^\sharp \in \mathbb{D}^\sharp_* \\ \emptyset & \text{if } d^\sharp = \bot \end{cases}
$$

$$
\gamma_{\mathbb{D}^\sharp_r} : \mathbb{D}^\sharp_r \to \mathcal{P}(\mathbb{D}_r) \qquad \gamma_{\mathbb{D}^\sharp_r}(d^\sharp_r) = \{ r \in \mathbb{F} \rightharpoonup \mathbb{D} : \forall f \in \mathrm{dom}(d^\sharp_r), r[f] \in \gamma_{\mathbb{D}^\sharp}(d^\sharp_r[f]) \}
$$

$$
\gamma_{\mathbb{D}^\sharp_*} : \mathbb{D}^\sharp_* \to \mathcal{P}(\mathit{Seq}(\mathbb{D})) \qquad \gamma_{\mathbb{D}^\sharp_*}(d^\sharp_*) = \{ s \in \mathit{Seq}(\mathbb{D}) : \forall d^\sharp_1{::}\ldots{::}d^\sharp_n \in d^\sharp_* : d_1{::}\ldots{::}d_n \text{ subsequence of } s \text{ and } d_1 \in d^\sharp_1 \wedge \ldots \wedge d_n \in d^\sharp_n \}
$$

$$
a^\sharp \sqcap_{\mathbb{D}^\sharp} b^\sharp = \begin{cases} a^\sharp & \text{if } a^\sharp = b^\sharp \\ a^\sharp \sqcap_{\mathbb{D}^\sharp_r} b^\sharp & \text{if } a^\sharp \in \mathbb{D}^\sharp_r \wedge b^\sharp \in \mathbb{D}^\sharp_r \\ a^\sharp \sqcap_{\mathbb{D}^\sharp_*} b^\sharp & \text{if } a^\sharp \in \mathbb{D}^\sharp_* \wedge b^\sharp \in \mathbb{D}^\sharp_* \\ \bot & \text{otherwise} \end{cases}
$$

$$
a^\sharp_r \sqcap_{\mathbb{D}^\sharp_r} b^\sharp_r = \lambda f. \begin{cases} a^\sharp_r[f] & \text{if } f \in \mathrm{dom}(a^\sharp_r) \wedge f \notin \mathrm{dom}(b^\sharp_r) \\ b^\sharp_r[f] & \text{if } f \notin \mathrm{dom}(a^\sharp_r) \wedge f \in \mathrm{dom}(b^\sharp_r) \\ a^\sharp_r[f] \sqcap_{\mathbb{D}^\sharp} b^\sharp_r[f] & \text{if } f \in \mathrm{dom}(a^\sharp_r) \wedge f \in \mathrm{dom}(b^\sharp_r) \end{cases}
$$

$$
a^\sharp_* \sqcap_{\mathbb{D}^\sharp_*} b^\sharp_* = a^\sharp_* \cup b^\sharp_*
$$

Fig. 7. Abstract databases: definitions, concretisations, and abstract intersections.

An *abstract sequence* is defined as a set of sequences of abstract databases. Its intuitive meaning is that the sequences in the set constrains the possible subsequences of the concrete elements.

Intuitively, this set of constraints appears because we do not have another mean to merge constraints over different subsequences of the same sequence. This problem, which is similar to the alignment problem in bidirectional languages [4,24] is studied more in depth in Sect. 7.

Example 2. Let $d^\sharp_* = \{1{::}2, 1{::}3\}$. Then:

$$
\{1{::}2{::}4{::}3, 1{::}5{::}3{::}2, 2{::}1{::}2{::}3\} \subseteq \gamma_{\mathbb{D}^\sharp_*}(d^\sharp_*) \qquad \{2{::}1{::}3, 1{::}3\} \cap \gamma_{\mathbb{D}^\sharp_*}(d^\sharp_*) = \{\}
$$

As shown by this example, some intuitively important relations on the sequences (like the fact that the length of the sequence is known), are not captured by our abstraction; this is explored in Sect. 6.3.

The only operator that we need over abstract databases is *abstract intersection*, defined in Fig. 7, and whose meaning is given by the following theorem:

Theorem 2 (Soundness and exactness of abstract intersection). *Abstract intersection operators* $\sqcap_{\mathbb{D}^\sharp}$, $\sqcap_{\mathbb{D}^\sharp_r}$, *and* $\sqcap_{\mathbb{D}^\sharp_*}$ *are sound and exact:*

$$\begin{aligned}
\forall(a^\sharp, b^\sharp) \in \mathbb{D}^\sharp : &\quad \gamma_{\mathbb{D}^\sharp}(a^\sharp \sqcap_{\mathbb{D}^\sharp} b^\sharp) = \gamma_{\mathbb{D}^\sharp}(a^\sharp) \cap \gamma_{\mathbb{D}^\sharp}(b^\sharp) \\
\forall(a^\sharp_r, b^\sharp_r) \in \mathbb{D}^\sharp_r : &\quad \gamma_{\mathbb{D}^\sharp_r}(a^\sharp_r \sqcap_{\mathbb{D}^\sharp_r} b^\sharp_r) = \gamma_{\mathbb{D}^\sharp_r}(a^\sharp_r) \cap \gamma_{\mathbb{D}^\sharp_r}(b^\sharp_r) \\
\forall(a^\sharp_*, b^\sharp_*) \in \mathbb{D}^\sharp_* : &\quad \gamma_{\mathbb{D}^\sharp_*}(a^\sharp_* \sqcap_{\mathbb{D}^\sharp_*} b^\sharp_*) = \gamma_{\mathbb{D}^\sharp_*}(a^\sharp_*) \cap \gamma_{\mathbb{D}^\sharp_*}(b^\sharp_*)
\end{aligned}$$

5.2 Abstract Environments

Abstract environment $\qquad \mathbb{E}^\sharp = \mathbb{X} \rightharpoonup \mathbb{D}^\sharp$

$$\gamma_{\mathbb{E}^\sharp} : \mathbb{E}^\sharp \to \mathcal{P}(\mathbb{E}) \quad \gamma_{\mathbb{E}^\sharp}(\Gamma^\sharp) = \{\Gamma \in \mathbb{X} \rightharpoonup \mathbb{D} : \forall x \in \mathrm{dom}(\Gamma^\sharp), \Gamma[x] \in \gamma_{\mathbb{D}^\sharp}(\Gamma^\sharp[x])\}$$

$$\mathit{unseq}^\sharp(x, p, \Gamma^\sharp_1 :: \ldots :: \Gamma^\sharp_n) = \left(\bigsqcap_{k\in 1..n}^{\mathbb{E}^\sharp} \mathit{unbind}(x, \Gamma^\sharp_k)\right) \sqcap_{\mathbb{E}^\sharp} [p \mapsto \{\Gamma^\sharp_1[x] :: \ldots :: \Gamma^\sharp_n[x]\}]$$

$$\Gamma^\sharp_1 \sqcap_{\mathbb{E}^\sharp} \Gamma^\sharp_2 = \lambda x. \begin{cases} \Gamma^\sharp_1[x] & \text{if } x \in \mathrm{dom}(\Gamma^\sharp_1) \wedge x \notin \mathrm{dom}(\Gamma^\sharp_2) \\ \Gamma^\sharp_2[x] & \text{if } x \notin \mathrm{dom}(\Gamma^\sharp_1) \wedge x \in \mathrm{dom}(\Gamma^\sharp_2) \\ \Gamma^\sharp_1[x] \sqcap_{\mathbb{D}^\sharp} \Gamma^\sharp_2[x] & \text{if } x \in \mathrm{dom}(\Gamma^\sharp_1) \wedge x \in \mathrm{dom}(\Gamma^\sharp_2) \end{cases}$$

Fig. 8. The *abstract environment* $\mathbb{E}^\sharp$ abstract domain.

Abstract environments $\qquad \mathbb{E}^\sharp_\vee = \mathcal{P}(\mathbb{E}^\sharp)$

$$\gamma_{\mathbb{E}^\sharp_\vee} : \mathbb{E}^\sharp_\vee \to \mathcal{P}(\mathbb{E}) \qquad \gamma_{\mathbb{E}^\sharp_\vee}(e^\sharp) = \bigcup_{\Gamma^\sharp \in e^\sharp} \gamma_{\mathbb{E}^\sharp}(\Gamma^\sharp)$$

$$\top_{\mathbb{E}^\sharp_\vee} = \{[]\} \qquad \bot_{\mathbb{E}^\sharp_\vee} = \{\} \qquad e^\sharp_1 \sqcup_{\mathbb{E}^\sharp_\vee} e^\sharp_2 = e^\sharp_1 \cup e^\sharp_2$$
$$e^\sharp_1 \sqcap_{\mathbb{E}^\sharp_\vee} e^\sharp_2 = \{\Gamma^\sharp_1 \sqcap^\sharp_{\mathbb{E}^\sharp} \Gamma^\sharp_2 : \Gamma^\sharp_1 \in \gamma_{\mathbb{E}^\sharp_\vee}(e^\sharp_1) \wedge \Gamma^\sharp_2 \in \gamma_{\mathbb{E}^\sharp_\vee}(e^\sharp_2)\}$$

Fig. 9. The domain of *abstract environments* $\mathbb{E}^\sharp_\vee$ is the powerset completion of $\mathbb{E}^\sharp$.

Similarly to abstract databases, we define *abstract environments* to represent a set of environments. An *abstract environment* $\Gamma^\sharp \in \mathbb{E}^\sharp$ (Fig. 8) is a mapping from variables to abstract databases. It is very similar to abstract records (except that it is indexed by variables instead of fields); in particular, the concretisation $\gamma_{\mathbb{E}^\sharp}$ and abstract intersection $\sqcap_{\mathbb{E}^\sharp}$ are very similar to the concretisation $\gamma_{\mathbb{D}^\sharp_r}$ and intersection $\sqcap_{\mathbb{D}^\sharp_r}$ of abstract databases.

Theorem 3. $\sqcap_{\mathbb{E}^\sharp}$ *is sound and exact:*

$$\forall(\Gamma_a^\sharp, \Gamma_b^\sharp) \in \mathbb{E}^\sharp : \quad \gamma_{\mathbb{E}^\sharp}(\Gamma_a^\sharp \sqcap_{\mathbb{E}^\sharp} \Gamma_b^\sharp) = \gamma_{\mathbb{E}^\sharp}(\Gamma_a^\sharp) \cap \gamma_{\mathbb{E}^\sharp}(\Gamma_b^\sharp)$$

We define another transfer function on abstract environments, $\mathit{unseq}^\sharp$, that is used to revert a $\langle$`for` x `in` $p\rangle$ $\langle$`end`$\rangle$ instruction: it receives a variable $x \in \mathbb{X}$, a path $p \in \mathbb{P}$, and a sequence of abstract environments in which x is bound; and use this to constrain the path p. Specifically:

Theorem 4 (Soundness and exactness of $\mathit{unseq}^\sharp$). *Let $x \in \mathbb{X}$, $p \in \mathbb{P}$, and $\Gamma_1^\sharp{::}\ldots{::}\Gamma_n^\sharp \in \mathit{Seq}(\mathbb{E}^\sharp)$. Then:*

$$\gamma_{\mathbb{E}^\sharp}(\mathit{unseq}^\sharp(x, p, \Gamma_1^\sharp{::}\ldots{::}\Gamma_n^\sharp)) = \bigcup_{\Gamma_1 \in \Gamma_1^\sharp,\ \ldots,\ \Gamma_n \in \Gamma_n^\sharp} \mathit{unseq}(x, p, \Gamma_1{::}\ldots{::}\Gamma_n)$$

We define the lattice of *abstract environments* $\mathbb{E}_\vee^\sharp$ (Fig. 9) to be the standard *powerset completion* [2,9,14] of $\mathbb{E}^\sharp$.

5.3 Abstract Semantics

Equipped with these abstract domains, we can now propose an algorithm for reversing templates (Fig. 10). This algorithm derives from the backward denotational semantics of Sect. 4.2, using the denotational style of abstract interpretations [44]. This allows, using the soundness theorems on the abstract domains, to prove the soundness of our main algorithm:

Theorem 5 (Soundness of abstract semantics). *Given any template i and word w:*

$$\gamma_{\mathbb{E}_\vee^\sharp}(\llbracket i \rrbracket^\sharp(w)) \supseteq \llbracket i \rrbracket(w)$$

Thanks to the compositional nature of both the abstract and backward denotational semantics, the proof is easily done by induction. It is worth noting that the part where we lose exactness (replacing equality by $\subseteq$) is the abstraction of `for` instructions, as we do not retain the information expressed by *emptyseq* in the backward semantics.

6 Precision and Exactness

We now have a sound algorithm that retrieves a superset of the input environments that can produce a template for a given text.

As shown in Sect. 2, retrieving too many inputs can later lead to false alarms when trying to validate the inputs against requirements. Thus, we want to study whether this set can be sufficiently precise to be of practical use, and when would the algorithm have optimal precision.

$$[\![i]\!]^\sharp(\cdot) : \mathbb{W} \to \mathbb{E}^\sharp_\vee \qquad [\![v]\!]^\sharp(w) = \begin{cases} \top_{\mathbb{E}^\sharp_\vee} & \text{if } v = w \\ \bot_{\mathbb{E}^\sharp_\vee} & \text{otherwise} \end{cases}$$

$$[\![\langle = p{:}t\,\rangle]\!]^\sharp(w) = \{[p \mapsto \mathit{read}_t(u)]\} \qquad [\![i\ j]\!]^\sharp(w) = \bigsqcup_{\substack{\mathbb{E}^\sharp_\vee \\ u \cdot v = w}} [\![i]\!]^\sharp(u) \sqcap_{\mathbb{E}^\sharp_\vee} [\![j]\!]^\sharp(w)$$

$$[\![\langle \texttt{if } p\rangle\, i\, \langle \texttt{else}\rangle\, j\, \langle \texttt{end}\rangle]\!]^\sharp(w) = [\![i]\!]^\sharp(w) \sqcap_{\mathbb{E}^\sharp_\vee} \{[p \mapsto \mathit{true}]\} \sqcup_{\mathbb{E}^\sharp_\vee} [\![j]\!]^\sharp(w) \sqcap_{\mathbb{E}^\sharp_\vee} \{[p \mapsto \mathit{false}]\}$$

$$[\![\langle \texttt{apply } f \texttt{ with } x = p\rangle]\!]^\sharp(w) = \{\, \mathit{unbind}(x, \Gamma^\sharp[p \mapsto \Gamma^\sharp[p] \sqcap_{\mathbb{D}^\sharp} \Gamma^\sharp[x]]) : \Gamma^\sharp \in [\![\Delta(f)]\!]^\sharp(w)\,\}$$

$$[\![\langle \texttt{for } x \texttt{ in } p\rangle\, i\, \langle \texttt{end}\rangle]\!]^\sharp(w) = \bigsqcup_{\substack{\mathbb{E}^\sharp_\vee \\ n \in \mathbb{N} \\ w_1 \cdot w_2 \cdots w_n = u \\ \forall w_i : w_i \neq \varepsilon}} \{\, \mathit{unseq}^\sharp(x, p, \Gamma_1^\sharp :: \ldots :: \Gamma_n^\sharp) : \Gamma_1^\sharp \in [\![i]\!]^\sharp(w_1) \wedge \ldots \wedge \Gamma_n^\sharp \in [\![i]\!]^\sharp(w_n)\,\}$$

Fig. 10. A sound algorithm for reversing templates.

6.1 Optimal Precision

Intuitively, the result of an algorithm for reversing templates would be optimally precise if it returned a single environment, which would be the one used to generate the text. Unfortunately, this is impossible:

Theorem 6. *If some environment Γ exists that generates an output w from a template instruction i, then $[\![i]\!](w)$ is an infinite set.*

Proof. We can create arbitrarily many suitable inputs by adding arbitrary bindings to Γ.

Intuitively, all the bindings that are not used during the evaluation of the template cannot be recovered by the reverse processing, and can have arbitrary values. We thus adopt a more restricted definition of optimal precision by considering only the values bound to paths that are used in the forward evaluation. We first define an order relation $\preccurlyeq$ on databases such that $d_a \preccurlyeq d_b$ means that d_a has fewer bindings than d_b:

Definition 2. *We define a relation $\preccurlyeq \in \mathbb{D} \times \mathbb{D}$ on databases as the smallest relation satisfying:*

- *If $d \in \mathbb{D}_s$ is a scalar, then $d \preccurlyeq d$.*
- *If $d_a, d_b \in \mathbb{D}_r$ are records, $\mathrm{dom}(d_a) \subseteq \mathrm{dom}(d_b)$, and $\forall f \in \mathrm{dom}(d_a) : d_a(f) \preccurlyeq d_b(f)$, then $d_a \preccurlyeq d_b$.*
- *If $d_a, d_b \in \mathbb{D}_*$ are sequences and there exists a subsequence d'_b of d_b such that d_a and d'_b have the same length n, and $\forall k : 0 \leq k \leq (n-1) \Rightarrow d_a(k) \preccurlyeq d'_b(k)$, then $d_a \preccurlyeq d_b$.*

The definition is naturally extended to environments by considering that environments are similar to records (and are the same if field names and variable names are the same set).

Theorem 7. *$\preccurlyeq$ is a partial order.*

Example 3. $[\text{"}a\text{"} \mapsto [\text{"}b\text{"} \mapsto 1{::}3]] \preccurlyeq [\text{"}d\text{"} \mapsto 8; \text{"}a\text{"} \mapsto [\text{"}b\text{"} \mapsto 1{::}2{::}3{::}4; \text{"}c\text{"} \mapsto 3]]$

This relation allows to "minimize" a database to consider only the parts that are relevant for a given template:

Theorem 8. *Let $i \in \mathbb{I}$ be a template instruction, $w \in \mathbb{W}$ be a word, $\Gamma \in \mathbb{E}$ be an environment, such that $(\!|i|\!)(\Gamma) = w$. The set $\{\Gamma' \mid \Gamma' \preccurlyeq \Gamma \wedge (\!|i|\!)(\Gamma') = w\}$ has a minimum, i.e. a unique minimal element. If this minimum is Γ, we say that Γ is* minimal for i.

Proof Sketch. One can collect all the paths that are used during the evaluation of Γ by i, which we call the *footprint* (see Appendix for a formal definition) All the elements corresponding to a path in the footprint must be preserved, otherwise the forward evaluation fails. On the contrary, all the elements that are not in the footprint can be removed without affecting the evaluation. The minimal database is the one that only contains the elements in the footprint.

Thanks to this theorem, we can now partition $[\![i]\!](w)$ into equivalent classes, where Γ and Γ' are equivalent if they can be minimized to the same Γ''; these minimal elements are the representative of the equivalence class. In other word, we can now consider only minimal elements. This allows to define precision as follows:

Definition 3. *Template reversal for a template instruction i and word w is precise if $[\![i]\!](w)$ has only one equivalence class; or equivalently, if only one environment Γ exists such that Γ is minimal for i and $(\!|i|\!)(\Gamma) = w$.*

This definition thus means that there is a unique preimage Γ of w through i, up to minimality. This notion is important for our motivating example: if we can recover this Γ, it means that we have retrieved all the relevant parts of the database that have produced the output.

Remark 2. Another immediate application of program inversion is bidirectional programming [29]: if we first evaluate $(\!|i|\!)(\Gamma) = w$, that w is manually modified, and $[\![i]\!](w')$ returns a single minimal Γ'. Then, using the principle of constant complementation [3,17,29], i.e. adding to Γ' the values of Γ that are not bound to any path in Γ', we can update the database to soundly reflect the edits of w. If the template reversal for i and w' is not precise, then we would have to disambiguate the solution, either asking the user for help, or using hints in the template language.

6.2 Inherent Imprecisions

There are only two reasons why the backward evaluation of a template instruction i for an output w is imprecise (i.e. the computed abstract environments do not form a single equivalence class):

- Either $[\![i]\!](w)$ is imprecise, and the imprecision comes from the template or particular output: there are several minimal preimages of w for the template i.

- Or $[\![i]\!](w)$ is precise, but the imprecision comes from the fact that $[\![i]\!]^\sharp(w)$ is not *exact* [41], meaning that the abstraction introduces further imprecisions.

In this section we study the first source of imprecision, that we call *inherent* imprecisions. An interesting result if template reversal is imprecise for a template i and output w, this means that w is syntactically ambiguous for the grammar corresponding to the template i. More precisely:

Theorem 9. *If $[\![i]\!](w)$ is imprecise, there exists two environments Γ_1 and Γ_2 in $[\![i]\!](w)$ such that the forward evaluation of Γ_1 and Γ_2 (with the original* FOR *rule) produce deduction/parse trees with different shapes.*

Proof Sketch. Suppose that we have Γ_1 and Γ_2 that belong to $[\![i]\!](w)$, are minimal and distinct, and that their evaluation corresponds to deduction trees with the same shape (i.e. the evaluation takes the same branch on conditional tests, and sequences have the same number of elements). The sequence of leaves in a deduction tree is equivalent to a sequence of either fixed strings or calls to $show_t(\Gamma[p])$ for some p, and both sequence must be equal to w. If Γ_1 and Γ_2 have the same parse tree, then this sequence is the same, which means that every $\Gamma[p]$ in the sequence must have the same printed representation. This means that Γ_1 and Γ_2 have equal values for every p in their footprint—which contradicts the fact that Γ_1 and Γ_2 are minimal and distinct.

This theorem is useful, because detecting parsing ambiguity at runtime is relatively easy – for instance the algorithm of $[\![i]\!]^\sharp(w)$, the number of parse trees is the cardinal of the element in $\mathbb{E}^\sharp_\vee$ which is returned (without counting $\bot_{\mathbb{E}^\sharp}$ elements).

Another application of this theorem is that we can enumerate the causes of imprecision in the semantics; it can help the template developer to change the template to fix any ambiguity (e.g. by adding fixed text, e.g. in comments when the output is source code). Imprecisions are due to:

- Ambiguities in concatenation, e.g.
  $[\![\langle = x{:}int\,\rangle\ \langle = y{:}int\,\rangle]\!](123) = \{\,[x \mapsto 1, y \mapsto 23], [x \mapsto 12, y \mapsto 3]\}$
- Ambiguities in loops, e.g.
  $[\![\langle \texttt{for}\ x\ \texttt{in}\ s\rangle\ \langle = x{:}int\,\rangle\ \langle \texttt{end}\rangle]\!](12) = \{[s \mapsto 1{::}2], [s \mapsto 12]\}$
- Ambiguities in conditionals, e.g.
  $[\![\langle \texttt{if}\ c\rangle\, 0\, \langle \texttt{else}\rangle\ \langle = x{:}int\,\rangle\ \langle \texttt{end}\rangle]\!](0) = \{\,[c \mapsto \mathit{true}], [c \mapsto \mathit{false}, x \mapsto 0]\}$
- Loops containing an empty production, e.g.
  $[\![\langle \texttt{for}\ x\ \texttt{in}\ s\rangle\ \langle \texttt{if}\ x.c\rangle\ \langle = x.id{:}int\,\rangle\ \langle \texttt{else}\rangle\ \langle \texttt{end}\rangle\ \langle \texttt{end}\rangle]\!](7) =$
  $$\begin{aligned}\{\,&[s \mapsto [c \mapsto \mathit{false}, id \mapsto 7]],\\ &[s \mapsto [c \mapsto \mathit{true}]{::}[c \mapsto \mathit{false}, id \mapsto 7]],\\ &[s \mapsto [c \mapsto \mathit{true}]{::}[c \mapsto \mathit{true}]{::}[c \mapsto \mathit{false}, id \mapsto 7]], \ldots\}\end{aligned}$$

In concatenation and loops, the ambiguity can often be fixed by inserting fixed string that acts as a separator between two replacements. Note that removal of ambiguity is the reason why, in the language, our replacements take a type argument. Indeed, if, like in many template languages, the replacement could be arbitrary, then the parsing of loop sequences would become highly ambiguous—as it would be possible for separators to be part of the replacement text. For instance, the ambiguity of the following backward evaluation is probably not expected:

$$[\![\langle \texttt{for}\ x\ \texttt{in}\ s\rangle\ \langle = x{:}any\,\rangle;\ \langle \texttt{end}\rangle]\!](\text{``})\texttt{11};22;\text{''} = \{\,[s \mapsto \text{``}\texttt{11}\text{''}{::}\text{``}22\text{''}],[s \mapsto \text{``}\texttt{11};22\text{''}]\}$$

For conditionals, the template should be written such that the languages corresponding to each branch of a conditional do not overlap. One easy way to do it, if the template produces text for a language that allows comments, is to add different comments in the different branches of the condition:

$$[\![\langle \texttt{if}\ c\rangle / * c * /0\,\langle \texttt{else}\rangle\,/*!c * /\langle = x{:}int\,\rangle\,\langle \texttt{end}\rangle]\!](\text{''}/*!c * /0\text{''}) \;=\; \{[c \;\mapsto\; \mathit{false}; x \;\mapsto\; 0]\}$$

6.3 Imprecision Coming from the Abstraction

We now study the second source of imprecision, i.e. imprecisions coming from the abstraction. As we have seen, many of our transfer functions, like abstract intersection, are *exact*. A transfer function $f^\sharp$ is an *exact* [41] (also called forward-complete [19]) approximation of a function f if $f \circ \gamma = \gamma \circ f^\sharp$ (this extends to binary functions).

If S is a set, and $S^\sharp$ is such that $\gamma(S^\sharp) = S$, then $\gamma(f^\sharp(S^\sharp)) = f(S)$. This means that if you only use exact transfer functions in the algorithm for reversing templates (Fig. 10), then the result of the algorithm exactly represents the set of all the inputs of the templates: the algorithm introduces no imprecision.

An important source of inexactness is the join operator. For instance, a join operator on our abstract environment abstract domain $\mathbb{E}^\sharp$, would introduce a catastrophic loss of precision, as when joining two environments $\Gamma_1^\sharp$ and $\Gamma_2^\sharp$, any information known about a variable x bound in only one of the Γ would be lost in the result. This is the reason why we introduced a top-level powerset abstract domain $\mathbb{E}_\vee^\sharp$, which allows performing unions without introducing imprecisions.

There is still one operation in our algorithm which is inexact, which is the handling of sequences. In Sect. 4.2, we introduced the *emptyseq* function to characterize elements in the sequence that produce an empty word. But this information is completely lost in the abstract semantics of Fig. 10.

A simple way to fully recover part of this information, which is very useful in practice, is to use a two-element lattice $\{\mathit{complete}, \mathit{incomplete}\}$ with $\mathit{complete} \sqsubseteq \mathit{incomplete}$, where *complete* means that the abstract element corresponds to the whole sequence, and not to only a subsequence, of the concrete sequence.

We thus change our definition of abstract sequences such that

$$\mathbb{D}_*^\sharp \triangleq \{\mathit{complete}, \mathit{incomplete}\} \times \mathcal{P}(Seq(\mathbb{D}^\sharp))$$

and change the definition of $\gamma_{\mathbb{D}_*^\sharp}$ in Fig. 7 such that "subsequence of" is replaced by "is equal to" when the abstract sequence is *complete*. Finally, in the algorithm computing $[\![\langle \texttt{for}\ x\ \texttt{in}\ p\rangle\, i\, \langle \texttt{end}\rangle]\!]^\sharp(w)$ (Fig. 10), we should set the sequence type to *complete* if the interpretation of the template i cannot produce the empty word, i.e. if $[\![i]\!]^\sharp(\varepsilon) = \bot$.

$$\rho_{\mathbb{D}^\sharp} : \mathbb{D}^\sharp \to \mathbb{D}^\sharp \quad \rho_{\mathbb{D}^\sharp}(d^\sharp) = \begin{cases} d^\sharp & \text{if } d^\sharp \in \mathbb{D}_s \\ \rho_{\mathbb{D}^\sharp_r}(d^\sharp) & \text{if } d^\sharp \in \mathbb{D}^\sharp_r \\ \rho_{\mathbb{D}^\sharp_*}(d^\sharp) & \text{if } d^\sharp \in \mathbb{D}^\sharp_* \end{cases}$$

$$\rho_{\mathbb{D}^\sharp_r} : \mathbb{D}^\sharp_r \to \mathbb{D}^\sharp_r \quad \rho_{\mathbb{D}^\sharp_r}(d^\sharp_r) = \begin{cases} \bot & \text{if } \exists f \in \text{dom}(d^\sharp_r) : \rho[d^\sharp_r[f]] = \bot \\ \lambda f.\rho_{\mathbb{D}^\sharp_r}[d^\sharp_r[f]] & \text{otherwise} \end{cases}$$

$$\rho_{\mathbb{E}^\sharp} : \mathbb{E}^\sharp \to \mathbb{E}^\sharp \quad \rho_{\mathbb{E}^\sharp}(\Gamma^\sharp) = \begin{cases} \bot & \text{if } \exists x \in \text{dom}(\Gamma^\sharp) : \rho_{\mathbb{D}^\sharp_r}[\Gamma^\sharp[x]] = \bot \\ \lambda x.\rho[\Gamma^\sharp[x]] & \text{otherwise} \end{cases}$$

$$\rho_{\mathbb{E}^\sharp_\vee} : \mathbb{E}^\sharp_\vee \to \mathbb{E}^\sharp_\vee \quad \rho_{\mathbb{E}^\sharp_\vee}(e^\sharp) = \{\rho_{\mathbb{E}^\sharp}(\Gamma^\sharp) : \Gamma^\sharp \in e^\sharp \wedge \rho_{\mathbb{E}^\sharp}(\Gamma^\sharp) \neq \bot\}$$

Fig. 11. Some reduction operators for our abstract domains.

With these additions, our abstract algorithm is now exact on the example of Fig. 2, where every `for` instruction cannot produce empty words for any element. We can actually prove this theorem:

Theorem 10. *Let $e^\sharp = [\![i]\!]^\sharp(w)$. If $e^\sharp$ does not contain any incomplete abstract sequences, then the algorithm is exact: $\gamma_{\mathbb{E}^\sharp_\vee}(e^\sharp) = [\![i]\!](w)$*

Combining this theorem with our analysis on inherent imprecisions yields:

Corollary 1. *Let $e^\sharp = [\![i]\!]^\sharp(w)$. If $e^\sharp$ is a singleton and does not contain an incomplete abstract sequence, then $[\![i]\!]^\sharp(w)$ is precise.*

These theorems allow testing if the result of algorithm of Fig. 10 is precise, based only the structure of abstract elements.

Remark 3. If the representation of *complete* abstract sequences is maximally precise, this is not the case for *incomplete* ones. More information could be retained in this case on the elements in the sequence that produce the empty word. This also requires updating operators like the intersection operator, as forgetting about this new information would introduce imprecision.

7 Reduction for Constraint Propagation

Abstract interpretation provides a mean to propagate constraints using an operator called reduction.

Definition 4. *Given an abstract domain $\mathbb{D}^\sharp$, a partial reduction operator $\rho \in \mathbb{D}^\sharp \to \mathbb{D}^\sharp$ is a function such that:*

1. *$\forall d^\sharp \in \mathbb{D}^\sharp : \gamma(\rho(d^\sharp)) = \gamma(d^\sharp)$ (reduction does not change the concretisation)*
2. *$\forall d^\sharp \in \mathbb{D}^\sharp : \rho(d^\sharp) \sqsubseteq^\sharp d^\sharp$ (reduction produces a smaller, simpler abstraction)*

Note that we did not need to define an ordering $\sqsubseteq^\sharp$ on our abstract values up to now so the second condition is less important; a suitable ordering can be defined as $d^\sharp \sqsubseteq^\sharp d'^\sharp \Leftrightarrow \rho(d^\sharp) = \rho(d^\sharp \sqcap d'^\sharp)$.

Removal of $\bot$. There are several places where this operator is useful in our analysis. Figure 11 presents operators for all domains except abstract sequences, that we detail shortly after. The main goal here is to propagate the reductions across all the domains, to remove $\bot$ elements. Indeed, the abstract intersection ($\sqcap$) operators creates $\bot$ elements when the constraints are irreconcilable; this is used in particular, to disambiguate some cases of ambiguous parsing.

Removing these $\bot$ elements is important mainly for performance reasons. Indeed, the $\sqcap_{\mathbb{E}^\sharp_\vee}$ operator has quadratic complexity due to the powerset completion, so removing useless elements early allows to perform fewer computations. Thus, reductions should be performed just after intersections (in practice, it is sometimes easier to interleave the reduction step directly in the definition of the abstract intersection operations).

Reduction of Complete Sequences. Consider the following example, where a sequence appears twice in the template:

$$\left[\!\!\left[\begin{array}{l} A{:}\langle \texttt{for } c \texttt{ in } seq\rangle\ \langle = c.a.:int\,\rangle;\ \langle \texttt{end}\rangle \\ B{:}\langle \texttt{for } c \texttt{ in } seq\rangle\ \langle = c.b.:int\,\rangle;\ \langle \texttt{end}\rangle \end{array}\right]\!\!\right]^\sharp (\texttt{A:1;2;B:3;4;}) =$$
$$[seq \mapsto \{(complete, [a \mapsto 1]{::}[a \mapsto 2]), (complete, [b \mapsto 3]{::}[b \mapsto 4])\}]$$

Following our addition from Sect. 6.3, we can now find out that we retrieved the complete sequence. But the result is not quite the one we would like: what the domain says here is that it saw two complete sequences, but it is unable to merge the elements of the sequence together. The problem here is not a problem of precision, as the concretisation of this domain is optimally precise; the problem comes from the lack of reduction, that the following operator solves. By simplicity this operator is defined $\rho_{\mathbb{D}^\sharp_*}$ on pairs of two elements; the actual operator recursively applies it to every pair until the resulting set can no longer be reduced.

$$\rho_{\mathbb{D}^\sharp_*} : \mathbb{D}^\sharp_* \to \mathbb{D}^\sharp_*$$
$$\rho_{\mathbb{D}^\sharp_*}(\{(complete, d_1{::}\ldots{::}d_n), (\_, d'_1{::}\ldots{::}d'_n)\}) = \{(complete, d_1 \sqcap_{\mathbb{D}^\sharp} d'_1{::}\ldots{::}d_n \sqcap_{\mathbb{D}^\sharp} d'_n)\}$$
$$\rho_{\mathbb{D}^\sharp_*}(\{(\_, d_1{::}\ldots{::}d_n), (complete, d'_1{::}\ldots{::}d'_n)\}) = \{(complete, d_1 \sqcap_{\mathbb{D}^\sharp} d'_1{::}\ldots{::}d_n \sqcap_{\mathbb{D}^\sharp} d'_n)\}$$
$$\rho_{\mathbb{D}^\sharp_*}(\{d_*, d'*\}) = \{d_*, d'_*\} \qquad \text{otherwise}$$

This operator merges together complete sequences when feasible, merging elements based on their positions. Note that it can also merge a complete sequence with a maybe-incomplete one if they have the same number of elements (meaning that the maybe-incomplete sequence is actually complete). Applying this reduction operator on the example above yields the expected result:

$$\rho_{\mathbb{D}^\sharp_*}([seq \mapsto \{(complete, [a \mapsto 1]{::}[a \mapsto 2]), (complete, [b \mapsto 3]{::}[b \mapsto 4])\}]) =$$
$$\left[seq \mapsto \left\{\left(complete, \begin{bmatrix} a \mapsto 1 \\ b \mapsto 3 \end{bmatrix} :: \begin{bmatrix} a \mapsto 2 \\ b \mapsto 4 \end{bmatrix}\right)\right\}\right]$$

Reduction of Partial Sequences. Without any additional information, we cannot learn anything about two partial sequences, because we don't know how to combine different elements together. However, provided that we could uniquely identify elements in the sequence (e.g. using a unique field, or position in the sequence), we could also reduce partial sequences by merging them into a DAG representing the partial order in which elements have been seen.

Such an extension has similarities with the key-based list alignment strategy in bidirectional programming languages [4,24] that allows to match elements between the source and the view when the list was modified using some key. In general, the strategies used in bidirectional programming to reconcile elements in sequences between the source and the updated view, can also be useful to merge information about sequences in our template inversion problem.

8 Implementations and Evaluation

We have implemented this technique on a custom template language called KIT. KIT is a project developed by a small business that develops tools and kernels for safety-critical real-time systems, used in automotive, aerospace & defense, and industrial automation industries. They have developed a custom source-to-source compiler that produces C files based on high-level descriptions of the timing behaviour of their systems. The compiler proceeds in two passes; first it generates an XML database that contains all the low-level parameters, such as the size of the communication buffers of the applications, the authorized inter-process communication between the tasks, or the configuration options used to compile the kernel and the applications. The KIT template engine then process template files using this database to generate C source code containing the application parameters, that will be compiled and linked with the application and kernel code to create an executable describing the whole system.

We proposed template inversion as a possible solution to their problem of independent validation of their generated source code (note that the templates are shared between the generator and validator, but this is not a problem because the templates can be viewed as specifications of the format of the source code). To test our solution, we were given KIT templates and the corresponding output for a sample application. We redeveloped a parser for the KIT language, and a KIT reverse evaluator, in OCaml.

8.1 Extensions for a Full-Featured Template Language

The KIT template language gradually evolved and includes numerous features besides those described in our core language. These features are important for practical usage of the template language. Most of these extensions could be handled by transforming the full KIT language into a "core kit" one:

- `include` directives were handled by inlining (transitively) the included file into the main file;

- Comments are widely used in the KIT files; we just remove them during the lexical analysis of KIT templates;
- There are lexical variations around the instructions which allows adjusting newlines between the source code and the KIT code, also handled during the lexical analysis of KIT templates;
- There are assertions in the code, that are handled using constraints as described below;
- There is a `select` instruction which allows querying for a single element in a sequence. This was handled by updating the definition of path;
- The scalars were untyped, but we created a "catch-all" type consisting in int + symbol + strings + floats, that works in practice for this use-case.
- The template functions are defined in the kit language, and can have more than one argument.

8.2 Arbitrary Expressions

An interesting feature (commonly found in other template languages) is that replacement instructions, and conditionals, can contain *expressions* instead of simple paths. This is beneficial for code generation, as code generators can handle more situations without having to change the database. Consider reversing this HTML-producing template:

<**tr**>⟨**for** *c* **in** *seq*⟩
<**td** **style**="color:⟨**if** *c.temp* < 0⟩ *blue* ⟨**else**⟩ *red* ⟨**end**⟩;">⟨= *c.temp*:*float*⟩</**td**>
⟨**end**⟩</**tr**>

applied to the text:

<**tr**><**td** **style**="color:blue";>−40</**td**><**td** **style**="color:red";>451</**td**></**tr**>

The need for such an expression could be replaced by a change in the input database and a *c.is_temp_negative* test instead, but expressions remove this need. To handle expressions, we simply add our abstract environments $\mathbb{E}^\sharp$ a set of constraints that are bindings of the form *expression* $\mapsto$ *value*. Applied to the above example, this results in:

$$\left\{\begin{array}{l} seq[0].temp < 0 \mapsto true, \\ seq[1].temp < 0 \mapsto false \end{array}\right\}, [seq \mapsto (\mathit{complete}, [temp \mapsto -40]::[temp \mapsto 451])]$$

Updating the transfer functions to modify the constraints when bindings change in `apply` and `for` instructions is fairly easy. Finally, we can change the reduction operator to take constraints into account. One simple way to do that is to substitute paths for their variable if their value is available; for instance, on the above example, the values of $seq[0].temp$ and $seq[1].temp$ are known. This allows to check if the constraint holds; if so, the constraint can be removed, otherwise we can reduce the environment to $\perp$. Thus, after reduction, our example becomes just $[seq \mapsto (\mathit{complete}, [temp \mapsto -40]::[temp \mapsto 451])]$. More complex strategies could be used, e.g. we could try to see if there is a unique solution to the set of constraints using an SMT solver. This strategy suffices for our use case, as we can always add text in the template (as comments in the output text) to add the values of all paths, so that all the constraints can be eliminated by the reduction operator.

8.3 Parsing

We have implemented two versions of our template reversing algorithm. In the first one, we relied on DYPGEN [37], a GLR parser generator for OCaml. The idea of this implementation was that a context-free grammar can be used as an overapproximation of the language that can be produced by a template instruction; semantic actions in the parser can then be used to drop the parse trees that cannot be produced by the template (which corresponds to the case where the backward evaluation of the template returns $\{\}$).

DYPGEN also implements a lexing pass, but it follows the longest match rule, so using it can lead to missing parse trees. Thus, we used single characters as tokens. The generated parser works well on simple examples, but unfortunately, generating the parser for some simple constant texts take several minutes, for instance in header texts like this one:

```
/*********** thread_runtime.c.kit: runtime generation ***********/
```

We measured that building the parsing tables for this bottom-up parser requires a time complexity which is exponential in the number of same characters put side by side. We then opted for direct top-down backtracking [5] implementation of the parsing algorithm, with two optimizations:

- When evaluating $[\![i\ j]\!]^\sharp(w)$, we do not attempt every decomposition of w. Instead, we try to parse i on w, and we ask it to return the set of all the decompositions of w for which it may return an environment, together with the abstract environment. This is much more efficient in particular when analyzing fixed strings, which is the most common template instructions.
- Abstract backward evaluation of a template i is thus a function of type $\mathbb{N} \rightarrow \mathcal{P}(\mathbb{N} \times \mathbb{E}^\sharp_{\mathbb{V}})$, where the integer represents a position in the string. To avoid reanalyzing the same position several times, we use memoization tables, like top-down chart parser [23] or packrat parsers [15].

8.4 Handling Cyclic Recursive Calls

The most important limitation of our implementation is that we do not handle templates that correspond to left-recursive grammars (i.e. that recursively call a template in left position). We implemented this limitation because it is easy to detect if the non-terminal corresponding to a template function is called twice on the same position, which allows returning an error (instead of entering an infinite loop); because cyclic recursive calls did not appear in our industrial examples or case study (it seems difficult to obtain a singleton abstract environment when

Table 1. Evaluation on real-world templates.

KIT template	LoC	Output file	Lines	Chars	Parse time (s)	Equivalent classes
app.psy.runtime.tak.kit	251	app.psy.runtime.tak	345	10158	0.00	1
hal_error_runtime.c.kit	20	hal_error_runtime.c.kit	46	894	0.00	1
hal_runtime.c.kit	39	hal_runtime.c	34	1292	0.00	1
hal_sources.c.kit	63	hal_sources.c	31	838	0.00	1
runtime.c.kit	31	runtime.c	30	737	0.00	1
thread_runtime.c.kit	14	thread_runtime.c	10	164	0.00	1

there are cyclic recursive calls); and because in many cases, it is easy to make the recursive calls non-cyclic (e.g. by systematically inserting parentheses when needed). Still, it is interesting to see if we could lift these limitations.

First, using grammar analysis, it would be theoretically easy to detect left-recursive calls that are not cyclic (i.e. for which the recursive cycle is followed by a terminal or a non-terminal that cannot produce the empty string), and allow the recursion to continue in this case.

Proper handling of truly cyclic recursive calls would require more substantial change, but these changes can be dealt with existing abstract interpretation tools. We can draw ideas from shape analysis to precisely represent the traversal of environments in recursive cycles, such as regular expression on access paths [12] or the inductive predicates of separation logic [6]. We can introduce widening [8] points when analyzing cycling recursive templates to compute an over-approximation of the environments for every possible depth of recursive calls to templates. Thus, abstract interpretation again provides the required tools to implement this extension.

8.5 Evaluation

Research Questions. Our main goal is to evaluate whether reversing template is feasible on real templates. We evaluated the following research questions:

- **RQ0: Soundness check:** does our algorithm return the expected result?
- **RQ1: Efficiency:** how fast is the algorithm?
- **RQ2: Precision:** is the algorithm precise on usual templates and outputs?

Protocol. We focused on 6 representative `.kit` template files given by the industrial company developping its in-house KIT language, together with sample outputs, to evaluate the feasibility of the technique.

The results are given in Table 1, which provides the name of the KIT file, the number of lines (including comments), the name of the output file, its number of lines and character, the time required to parse the file as reported by `time`, and the number of equivalent classes (i.e., number of minimal databases) retrieved by our tool. In all the cases, running the parser on the sample application took

Table 2. Measuring parsing time on large views.

Sequence length	10000	20000	30000	40000
Parsing time (s)	18.8	71.65	148.95	344.22

less than 0.01 s. The computed abstract environment was precise, and a single equivalence class was returned.

To check soundness, we created 7 KIT files corresponding to different ambiguous grammars. In each, our tool could retrieve all the expected abstract environments.

Finally, to evaluate scalability, we created a template with a single `for` template printing numbers separated by ';', and we evaluated it on sequences of different length. The results are reported in Table 2. This table shows that if the execution parsing time is supra-linear in some cases, it is able to handle outputs of fairly large size, sufficient for the generation of code in embedded systems. We could not try larger size has they created a stack overflow within our tool.

Conclusions. The technique had no problem handling existing templates. We feared that reversing the templates on some outputs might be ambiguous and that we would have to perform disambiguation using comments, but it actually never happened. We thus conclude that the technique is viable for reversing templates used to produce embedded systems code.

9 Related Work

Inversion of Injective Programs. Many of the work on program inversion is in the setting of injective functions, that only have a single preimage. In this setting, an early technique for inversion of string-to-string programs is the grammar-based approach of Yellin and Mueckstein [48]. Matsuda et al. [31] extends their idea to first-order functional programs transforming abstract datatypes and, like we do, makes use of the correspondance between evaluation trees and parse trees, and use constraints to recover the input. Finally, Matsuda and Wang [32] extends the technique to programs transforming abstract data types into strings, i.e. transforms a pretty-printer in a parser, which is quite similar to our problem.

We build on this work by using set-based compositional reasoning to handle non-injective functions, which may have multiple pre-images, and by proposing abstract interpretation as a framework to finitely represent these sets. This remove important limitations, such as the need for the function that we want to invert to be injective or to obey other sufficient conditions, such as being affine (variables cannot be duplicated, unlike in Fig. 2) or nonerasing (the view must tell about every variable in the source).

Other techniques for inversing programs that also focus on injective programs include the use of invertible combinators [35], transformation of term rewriting systems [36], or (non-terminating) universal algorithms [1].

A generic technique for writing invertible programs, which do not need to be injective, is logic programming [25]. But logic programming, or, more generally, generation of constraints to be solved by an external solver, cannot finitely represent the set of all solutions, and can only enumerate solutions.

Finally, a related topic is that of bidirectional transformations [11,21], that aim at running programs in reverse, but do so to solve the view-update problem [3]. This problem is formalized using the concept of lenses [16]. A lens is a pair containing a function *get* from a *source* to a *view*, and a function *put* that takes the original source, an updated view, and modifies the source based on the modifications on the view. This problem is distinct from our problem of finding all the preimages of a given function, but is related, and there are interesting convergence point between these problems. In particular, using the *constant complement* approach [3], one can derive a *put* function from inversion of the *get* one, that preserves the part of input not used by the program, an approach called *syntactic bidirectionalization* [17,29].

Approaches Based on Tree Transducers. An important line of work (e.g. [13,18,27,30,34,39,47]) is concerned with the problem of static type checking of XML transformations. In those, the template language is represented by a model which is generally a tree transducer, which takes and produces a tree. Then, given a transducer and a type R_{out} describing the set of outputs, the inverse type checking problem consists in finding the exact set R_{in} of inputs that may produce an output in R_{out}. Such an approach could be used for template inversion of a word w, using the singleton $\{w\}$ as R_{out}.

An important issue here is that the output in our problem is a string, and not a tree; thus the model of program that we would have to use is that of a tree-to-string transducer. Because strings are less structured than trees (which leads to parsing ambiguities when performing the inversion), this problem is more difficult. As said in Seidl et al. [45], "Amazingly little has been known so far for tree-to-string transducers": although their paper provides an algorithm for deciding the equivalence between tree-to-string transducers (using abstract interpretation), to our knowledge no algorithm exists for inverting the execution of such transducers.

Another issue is that if tree transducers represent a model of a template language, this model can differ from practical languages. Tree transducer replace conditions by non-deterministic choice, cannot compute expressions on the input data, and do not incorporate a notion of sequence. Such extensions could be handled by inventing extensions of existing transducers; for instance macro forest transducers [39] can deal with sequences and can be type-checked, albeit with an algorithm of high complexity. We chose abstract interpretation because it provides a framework to efficiently extend and combine different abstractions [9], some of which could be transducers or regular tree languages; and that it allows to explicitly choose the trade-off between precision and efficiency of inverse computation.

Abstract Interpretation. Abstract interpretation [8] is a sound method to derive sound static analysis of programs by the systematic construction of abstract domains [9]. In the canonical abstract interpretation framework, the abstract domain is a lattice which is in Galois-connection with a set, which is often the set of reachable states (or the set of traces) in the program. However, a backward analysis [7] computes an over-approximation of a set of states that can reach some condition, which is related to computing the set of preimages to a function. In program analyzes, backward analyses are usually too imprecise if they are not combined with a forward analysis Rival [43]. In our work, the fact that templates can be approximated using a contex-free grammar that generate a finite number of parse trees for a given output word, where parse trees can be viewed as a kind of evaluation trace, allows a very precise backward analysis (with no need for widening or approximation of joins), but abstract interpretation is still needed to handle the remaining imprecision.

The powerset domain that we use was introduced by Cousot and Cousot [9], and studied by Filé and Ranzato [14]. Bagnara et al. [2] noted that computing a widening operation on this domain is difficult; fortunately we do not need to compute a least fixpoint and thus do not need to introduce a widening operator (even with the introduction of functions in the template, the parse tree for a given output text is always finite).

Ranzato [41] defines two notions of completeness in abstract interpretation, which are completeness and exactness (also called forward-completeness). We use the exactness notion in our paper, to characterize the cases when the abstraction exactly represents the set of possible input environments. Exactness is less commonly used than completeness in abstract interpretation because having exact transfer functions yields an exact representation of the greatest fixpoint, and not of the usual least fixpoint. In our case, exactness can be used because the semantics that we analyze do not need to compute a fixpoint. Ranzato and Zanella [42] also uses exactness to verify properties over Support Vector Machines, which also are loop-free programs.

10 Conclusion

We studied the problem of reversing programs written in template languages, that transform tree-structured data into text. The template language that we use is expressive, and programs in this language are generally not injective (they have multiple preimages), not affine (some input variables can appear at several locations in the output), and erasing (they provide only a partial view of the source); they can use arbitrary expressions, which makes the problem undecidable and challenging. We propose a technique based on deriving a "backward" set-based denotational semantics from the forward big-step semantics, with suitable modifications to avoid the need to perform any fixpoint computation; and to use abstract interpretation to over-approximate this set. Using concepts from abstract interpretation, we can then study useful topics like precision or simplification of the abstract representation of the set of preimages. We believe that these concepts are generally useful when reasoning about reversing non-injective programs, and could find good use in other areas of program inversion, such as bidirectional transformations.

A Appendix

A.1 Template Viewed as a Context-Free Grammar

This appendix explains how templates in the RTL template language may be approximated using a context-free grammar. Figure 12 describes this translation (where | denotes alternative choices, · concatenation, $*$ repetition). G_t is a grammar rule that corresponds to the printed representations of objects of type t.

This translation is not exact but approximate, in that the language

Theorem 11. *Given a template instruction* i *and a word* w*, if there exists* Γ *such that* $(\!|i|\!)(\Gamma)$*, then* w *belongs to the language generated by the context-free grammar* $\mathcal{T}(i)$*.*

$$
\begin{aligned}
\mathcal{T}(w) &\triangleq w\\
\mathcal{T}(\langle= p{:}t\,\rangle) &\triangleq G_t\\
\mathcal{T}(i_1\ i_2) &\triangleq \mathcal{T}(i_1)\cdot\mathcal{T}(i_2)\\
\mathcal{T}(\langle\texttt{if}\ p\rangle\, i_1\,\langle\texttt{else}\rangle\, i_2\,\langle\texttt{end}\rangle) &\triangleq \mathcal{T}(i_1)\mid\mathcal{T}(i_2)\\
\mathcal{T}(\langle\texttt{for}\ x\ \texttt{in}\ p\rangle\, i\,\langle\texttt{end}\rangle) &\triangleq (\mathcal{T}(i))*\\
\mathcal{T}(\langle\texttt{apply}\ \phi\ \texttt{with}\ x=p\rangle) &\triangleq \phi\\
\text{productions} &\triangleq \{\phi\to\mathcal{T}(\Delta(\phi))\mid\phi\in\mathrm{dom}(\Delta)\}
\end{aligned}
$$

Fig. 12. Translation of the RTL template language to a context-free grammar.

Proof. By induction on the instructions of the language.

Given a context-free grammar, we note by $\alpha\Rightarrow\beta$, where α and β are both words over terminals and non-terminals, the fact that β derives from α, meaning that β is obtained from α by substituting a non-terminal by its production [20]. We note by $\Rightarrow^+$ the transitive closure of $\Rightarrow$. We say that a grammar is cyclic if there is a nonterminal ϕ such that $\phi\Rightarrow^+\phi$.

Theorem 12. *Given a context-free grammar, there exists a word* w *for which there is an infinite number of parse trees only if the grammar is cyclic.*

Proof. We suppose that the grammar is not cyclic. We consider a non-terminal ϕ in the grammar. If there is a string such that $\phi\Rightarrow^+\alpha\phi\beta$, then either α or β must derive into a non-empty string (they cannot both derive in the empty string, otherwise the grammar would be cyclic).

This means that given a word w, in any derivation from ϕ to w, ϕ can be replaced only a finite number of time.

As this is true for every non-terminal ϕ and there is a finite number of non-terminals, the derivation from any non-terminal symbol to w must be finite. Because of the correspondence between derivations and parse trees [20], this means that there is a finite number of parse trees.

Thus, if w is a word produced by a template whose translation is a grammar that is not cyclic, then only a finite number of parse trees can parse w. The For-Alt rule is a relaxation of this constraint, allowing a finite number of parse tree even in some cyclic grammars (by considering a variation of context-free grammars where the * of repetition is a native construct).

A.2 Definition of Footprint

Formally, we first extend the set of paths so that they can represent a specific element in a sequence, by adding the $p[k]$ construct:

$$\mathbb{P} \ni p, q \triangleq x \mid p.f \mid p[k]$$

Then, we define the footprint $\mathcal{F}$ of a template instruction i and environment Γ as the set of paths that is used during the evaluation of $(\!|i|\!)(\Gamma)$. The footprint is computable, and is defined recursively in Fig. 13. This function makes use of a substitution function *subst*.

$$\begin{aligned}
\mathit{subst} &: \mathbb{P} \times \mathbb{X} \times \mathbb{P} \to \mathbb{P} \\
\mathit{subst}(x, x, p) &= p \\
\mathit{subst}(y, x, p) &= p \text{ when } y \neq x \\
\mathit{subst}(q.f, x, p) &= \mathit{subst}(q, x, p).f \\
\mathit{subst}(q[k], x, p) &= \mathit{subst}(q, x, p)[k] \\
\mathcal{F} &: \mathbb{I} \times \mathbb{E} \rightharpoonup \mathcal{P}(\mathbb{P}) \\
\mathcal{F}(w, \Gamma) &= \{\} \\
\mathcal{F}(\langle = p{:}t \rangle, \Gamma) &= \{p\} \\
\mathcal{F}(i\ j, \Gamma) &= \mathcal{F}(i, \Gamma) \cup \mathcal{F}(j, \Gamma) \\
\mathcal{F}(\langle \texttt{if } p \rangle\, i\, \langle \texttt{else} \rangle\, j\, \langle \texttt{end} \rangle, \Gamma) &= \begin{cases} \mathcal{F}(i, \Gamma) \cup \{p\} \text{ if } \Gamma[p] = \mathit{true} \\ \mathcal{F}(j, \Gamma) \cup \{p\} \text{ if } \Gamma[p] = \mathit{false} \end{cases} \\
\mathcal{F}(\langle \texttt{apply } f \texttt{ with } x = p \rangle, \Gamma) &= \\
&\{\, \mathit{subst}(q, x, p) : q \in \mathcal{F}(\Delta(f), \Gamma[x \mapsto \Gamma[p]]) \,\} \\
\mathcal{F}(\langle \texttt{for } x \texttt{ in } p \rangle\, i\, \langle \texttt{end} \rangle, \Gamma) &= \\
&\bigcup_{k \in 1..n} \{\mathit{subst}(q, x, p[k]) : q \in \mathcal{F}(i, \Gamma[x \mapsto \Gamma[p][k]])\}
\end{aligned}$$

Fig. 13. Definition of the footprint of a template evaluation

Definition 5. *Given a set of paths $P \in \mathcal{P}(\mathbb{P})$, we define the restriction of an environment $\Gamma \in \mathbb{E}$ to P as follows:*

$$\begin{aligned} \mathit{restrict} &: \mathbb{E} \times \mathcal{P}(\mathbb{P}) \rightarrow \mathbb{E} \\ \mathit{restrict}(\Gamma, P)[p] &= \Gamma[p] \text{ if } p \in P \\ \mathit{restrict}(\Gamma, P)[p] & \text{ is unbound otherwise.} \end{aligned}$$

The fact that the footprint indeed corresponds to the paths that are necessary for the evaluation of the template is given by the following theorems:

Theorem 13. *Let $\mathit{paths}(\Gamma)$ represent all the paths bound in Γ. Then*

1. $(\!|i|\!)(\Gamma) = (\!|i|\!)(\mathit{restrict}(\Gamma, \mathcal{F}(i, \Gamma)))$
2. *If $p \in \mathcal{F}(i, \Gamma)$, then $(\!|i|\!)(\mathit{restrict}(\Gamma, \mathit{paths}(\Gamma) \backslash \{p\})) = \bot$.*

References

1. Abramov, S., Glück, R.: Principles of inverse computation and the universal resolving algorithm. In: Mogensen, T.Æ., Schmidt, D.A., Sudborough, I.H. (eds.) The Essence of Computation. LNCS, vol. 2566, pp. 269–295. Springer, Heidelberg (2002). https://doi.org/10.1007/3-540-36377-7_13
2. Bagnara, R., Hill, P.M., Zaffanella, E.: Widening operators for powerset domains. In: Steffen, B., Levi, G. (eds.) VMCAI 2004. LNCS, vol. 2937, pp. 135–148. Springer, Heidelberg (2004). https://doi.org/10.1007/978-3-540-24622-0_13
3. Bancilhon, F., Spyratos, N.: Update semantics of relational views. ACM Trans. Database Syst. **6**(4), 557–575 (1981)
4. Barbosa, D.M.J., Cretin, J., Foster, N., Greenberg, M., Pierce, B.C.: Matching lenses: alignment and view update. In: 15th ACM SIGPLAN International Conference on Functional programming (ICFP), pp. 193–204. ACM (2010)
5. Birman, A., Ullman, J.D.: Parsing algorithms with backtrack. Inf. Control **23**(1), 1–34 (1973). https://doi.org/10.1016/S0019-9958(73)90851-6
6. Chang, B.Y.E., Rival, X.: Relational inductive shape analysis. In: 35th Symposium on Principles of Programming Languages, POPL 2008, pp. 247–260. ACM, New York (2008)
7. Cousot, P.: Semantic foundations of program analysis. In: Program Flow Analysis: Theory and Applications, chap. 10, pp. 303–342. Prentice-Hall (1981)
8. Cousot, P., Cousot, R.: Abstract interpretation: a unified lattice model for static analysis of programs by construction or approximation of fixpoints. In: 4th Symposium on Principles of Programming Languages (POPL), pp. 238–252 (1977)
9. Cousot, P., Cousot, R.: Systematic design of program analysis frameworks. In: Sixth Symposium on Principles of Programming Languages (POPL), pp. 269–282. ACM Press, New York (1979)
10. Cousot, P., Cousot, R.: Abstract interpretation frameworks. J. Log. Comput. **2**(4), 511–547 (1992)
11. Czarnecki, K., Foster, J.N., Hu, Z., Lämmel, R., Schürr, A., Terwilliger, J.F.: Bidirectional transformations: a cross-discipline perspective. In: Paige, R.F. (ed.) ICMT 2009. LNCS, vol. 5563, pp. 260–283. Springer, Heidelberg (2009). https://doi.org/10.1007/978-3-642-02408-5_19

12. Deutsch, A.: A storeless model of aliasing and its abstractions using finite representations of right-regular equivalence relations. In: International Conference on Computer Languages (ICCL), pp. 2–13. IEEE Computer Society (1992). https://doi.org/10.1109/ICCL.1992.185463
13. Engelfriet, J., Maneth, S.: A comparison of pebble tree transducers with macro tree transducers. Acta Inform. **39**(9), 613–698 (2003)
14. Filé, G., Ranzato, F.: The powerset operator on abstract interpretations. Theor. Comput. Sci. **222**(1–2), 77–111 (1999)
15. Ford, B.: Packrat parsing: simple, powerful, lazy, linear time, functional pearl. In: Seventh International Conference on Functional Programming (ICFP), pp. 36–47. ACM (2002)
16. Foster, J.N., Greenwald, M.B., Moore, J.T., Pierce, B.C., Schmitt, A.: Combinators for bi-directional tree transformations: a linguistic approach to the view update problem. In: 32nd Symposium on Principles of Programming Languages (POPL), pp. 233–246. ACM (2005)
17. Foster, N., Matsuda, K., Voigtländer, J.: Three complementary approaches to bidirectional programming. In: Gibbons, J. (ed.) Generic and Indexed Programming. LNCS, vol. 7470, pp. 1–46. Springer, Heidelberg (2012). https://doi.org/10.1007/978-3-642-32202-0_1
18. Frisch, A., Hosoya, H.: Towards practical typechecking for macro tree transducers. In: Arenas, M., Schwartzbach, M.I. (eds.) DBPL 2007. LNCS, vol. 4797, pp. 246–260. Springer, Heidelberg (2007). https://doi.org/10.1007/978-3-540-75987-4_17
19. Giacobazzi, R., Quintarelli, E.: Incompleteness, counterexamples, and refinements in abstract model-checking. In: Cousot, P. (ed.) SAS 2001. LNCS, vol. 2126, pp. 356–373. Springer, Heidelberg (2001). https://doi.org/10.1007/3-540-47764-0_20
20. Hopcroft, J.E., Motwani, R., Ullman, J.D.: Introduction to Automata Theory, Languages, and Computation, 3rd edn. Pearson (2007)
21. Hu, Z., Schürr, A., Stevens, P., Terwilliger, J.F.: Dagstuhl seminar on bidirectional transformations (BX). SIGMOD Rec. **40**(1), 35–39 (2011)
22. Kahn, G.: Natural semantics. In: Brandenburg, F.J., Vidal-Naquet, G., Wirsing, M. (eds.) STACS 1987. LNCS, vol. 247, pp. 22–39. Springer, Heidelberg (1987). https://doi.org/10.1007/BFb0039592
23. Kay, M.: Algorithm schemata and data structures in syntactic processing. In: Readings in Natural Language Processing, pp. 35–70 (1986)
24. Ko, H., Hu, Z.: An axiomatic basis for bidirectional programming. Principles Program. Lang. **2**(POPL), 41:1–41:29 (2018)
25. Kowalski, R.A.: Predicate logic as programming language. In: Rosenfeld, J.L. (ed.) 6th IFIP Congress on Information Processing, pp. 569–574. North-Holland (1974)
26. Leroy, X.: Formal certification of a compiler back-end or: programming a compiler with a proof assistant. In: 33rd Symposium on Principles of Programming Languages (POPL), pp. 42–54. ACM (2006)
27. Maneth, S., Berlea, A., Perst, T., Seidl, H.: XML type checking with macro tree transducers. In: 24th Symposium on Principles of Database Systems, pp. 283–294. ACM (2005)
28. Matiyasevich, Y.: Диофантовость перечислимых множеств [Enumerable sets are Diophantine]. Dokl. Akad. Nauk SSSR **191**(2), 279–282 (1970). English translation in Soviet Mathematics 11(2), pp. 354–357
29. Matsuda, K., Hu, Z., Nakano, K., Hamana, M., Takeichi, M.: Bidirectionalization transformation based on automatic derivation of view complement functions. In: 12th International Conference on Functional Programming (ICFP), pp. 47–58. ACM (2007)

30. Matsuda, K., Inaba, K., Nakano, K.: Polynomial-time inverse computation for accumulative functions with multiple data traversals. High. Order Symb. Comput. **25**(1), 3–38 (2012)
31. Matsuda, K., Mu, S.-C., Hu, Z., Takeichi, M.: A grammar-based approach to invertible programs. In: Gordon, A.D. (ed.) ESOP 2010. LNCS, vol. 6012, pp. 448–467. Springer, Heidelberg (2010). https://doi.org/10.1007/978-3-642-11957-6_24
32. Matsuda, K., Wang, M.: FliPpr: a system for deriving parsers from pretty-printers. New Gener. Comput. **36**(3), 173–202 (2018)
33. Methni, A., Ohayon, E., Thurieau, F.: ASTERIOS checker: a verification tool for certifying airborne software. In: 10th European Congress on Embedded Real Time Systems (ERTS 2020), Toulouse, France (2020)
34. Milo, T., Suciu, D., Vianu, V.: Typechecking for XML transformers. J. Comput. Syst. Sci. **66**(1), 66–97 (2003)
35. Mu, S.-C., Hu, Z., Takeichi, M.: An injective language for reversible computation. In: Kozen, D. (ed.) MPC 2004. LNCS, vol. 3125, pp. 289–313. Springer, Heidelberg (2004). https://doi.org/10.1007/978-3-540-27764-4_16
36. Nishida, N., Sakai, M.: Completion after program inversion of injective functions. Electron. Notes Theor. Comput. Sci. **237**, 39–56 (2009)
37. Onzon, E.: dypgen: self-extensible parsers and lexers for OCaml (2012). http://dypgen.free.fr
38. Parr, T.J.: Enforcing strict model-view separation in template engines. In: 13th International Conference on World Wide Web (WWW), pp. 224–233. ACM (2004)
39. Perst, T., Seidl, H.: Macro forest transducers. Inf. Process. Lett. **89**(3), 141–149 (2004)
40. Pnueli, A., Siegel, M., Singerman, E.: Translation validation. In: Steffen, B. (ed.) TACAS 1998. LNCS, vol. 1384, pp. 151–166. Springer, Heidelberg (1998). https://doi.org/10.1007/BFb0054170
41. Ranzato, F.: Complete abstractions everywhere. In: Giacobazzi, R., Berdine, J., Mastroeni, I. (eds.) VMCAI 2013. LNCS, vol. 7737, pp. 15–26. Springer, Heidelberg (2013). https://doi.org/10.1007/978-3-642-35873-9_3
42. Ranzato, F., Zanella, M.: Robustness verification of support vector machines. In: Chang, B.-Y.E. (ed.) SAS 2019. LNCS, vol. 11822, pp. 271–295. Springer, Cham (2019). https://doi.org/10.1007/978-3-030-32304-2_14
43. Rival, X.: Understanding the origin of alarms in Astrée. In: Hankin, C., Siveroni, I. (eds.) SAS 2005. LNCS, vol. 3672, pp. 303–319. Springer, Heidelberg (2005). https://doi.org/10.1007/11547662_21
44. Schmidt, D.A.: Abstract interpretation from a denotational-semantics perspective. In: 25th Conference on Mathematical Foundations of Programming Semantics (MFPS). Electronic Notes in Theoretical Computer Science, vol. 249, pp. 19–37. Elsevier (2009)
45. Seidl, H., Maneth, S., Kemper, G.: Equivalence of deterministic top-down tree-to-string transducers is decidable. J. ACM **65**(4), 21:1–21:30 (2018)
46. Shieber, S.M., Schabes, Y., Pereira, F.C.N.: Principles and implementation of deductive parsing. J. Log. Program. **24**(1&2), 3–36 (1995)
47. Tozawa, A.: Towards static type checking for XSLT. In: Symposium on Document Engineering, pp. 18–27. ACM (2001)
48. Yellin, D.M., Mueckstein, E.M.: The automatic inversion of attribute grammars. IEEE Trans. Softw. Eng. **12**(5), 590–599 (1986)

Domain Precision in Galois Connection-Less Abstract Interpretation

Isabella Mastroeni(✉) and Michele Pasqua

University of Verona - Computer Science Department, Verona, Italy
{isabella.mastroeni,michele.pasqua}@univr.it

Abstract. The ever growing pervasiveness of software systems in modern days technology results in an increasing need of *software/program correctness proofs.* The latter, allow developers to spot software failures before production, hence preventing potentially catastrophic repercussions on our society, as in the case of safety-critical infrastructures.

Unfortunately, correctness proofs may fail (even when software is actually correct) due to program analysis imprecision: program analysis sacrifices precision in order to gain decidability. In standard abstract interpretation-based static analyses, such imprecision is "measured" in terms of *completeness* of the chosen observation (i.e., of the chosen abstract domain) w.r.t. the programming language semantics. In this setting, fixed the language language, it is crucial to have decidable techniques to determine whether the chosen abstraction is sufficiently precise to analyze the program under consideration.

In this paper, we characterize abstract domain precision from a novel point of view, providing a formal framework for *characterizing* and (statically) *verifying* abstract domain precision, that can be adopted also in the case of "weakened", i.e., Galois Connection-less, static analysis frameworks. Distinctive examples adopting such frameworks are the Convex Polyhedra and Automata domains, for which standard approaches to reason about analysis precision (i.e., completeness) cannot be applied.

Keywords: Abstract interpretation · Abstract Non-Interference · Completeness · Hyperproperties · (Hyper) Static analysis

1 Introduction

Software-driven technology is becoming more and more pervasive in our everyday life. For this reason, software failures deeply impact our society (think of safety-critical infrastructures, in which software failures may have serious consequences on public safety). This implies that it is extremely important to be confident in what programs do. Dijkstra [15] remarked that *"the only effective way to raise the confidence level of a program significantly is to give a convincing proof of its correctness"*. Program analysis is a prominent method supporting programmers and software engineers in producing reliable software, and abstract interpretation [10,11] is a general framework enabling to design correct-by-construction

M. V. Hermenegildo and J. F. Morales (Eds.): SAS 2023, LNCS 14284, pp. 434–459, 2023.
https://doi.org/10.1007/978-3-031-44245-2_19

program analysis tools. An abstract interpreter provides an approximate sound semantics of a programming language, by computing programs on an (approximate) *abstract domain.* In this context, soundness here means that all true alarms are captured and reported by the analysis. Of course, false alarms may be reported as well, and their presence is in general due to the need of program analysis to make *decidable* the computation of a semantic program property of interest (e.g., variable overflows, formal specifications verification, etc.). When false alarms are not generated, we say the analysis is precise, or *complete.* There is a wide literature about completeness, that spans from the systematic refinement of abstract domains for achieving completeness [25] to the definition of weakened forms of completeness (for instance, verifying completeness locally, on single input properties [5], or by accepting a bounded error in the abstract computation [6]). However, all these works build up on the archetypal abstract interpretation framework adopting Galois connections between concrete and abstract semantics [10,11]. Nevertheless, there are several static analyses developed in weaker frameworks of abstract interpretation [12], where some hypotheses are relaxed. This led, for instance, to the development of powerful numerical static analyzers implementing Convex Polyhedra [13], or abstract domains exploited in machine learning for neural networks verification [1], such as Zonotope [26]. In these relaxed abstract interpretation frameworks, completeness has not been formally studied, even if the absence of false alarms remains surely a crucial point to investigate.

The whole literature concerning abstract domain completeness characterization and enforcing, also its weakened forms, is strongly based on the standard, previous called archetypal, framework of abstract interpretation, that is based on Galois connections (or, equivalently, on upper closure operators). In particular, this framework assumes the existence of the best correct approximation (bca for short) of each concrete element. In the present paper, we reason about completeness in a *weakened framework*, where the bca existence assumption (and the need of Galois connections) is relaxed [12]. In this new, more general, framework we provide a characterization of completeness, together with effective verification techniques. This allows to characterize and verify completeness even in the case of Galois connection-less abstract interpretation.

Paper Contribution. We first propose a possible *formalization* for a weakened abstract interpretation framework (Sect. 3), generalizing the standard one to abstract domains not modeled by means of Galois connections. Then, we exploit its strong correlation with *Abstract Non-Interference* in order to characterize *abstract domain completeness.* Abstract Non-Interference (ANI for short) has been introduced in the context of language-based security as a non-interference policy between observable properties [18,31], but it is a much more general property of computations [23]. In literature, it has been observed that ANI (in all its different variants) can be modeled as a completeness problem [20,21], allowing to exploit completeness transformers, defined in the standard abstract interpretation framework, for deeper understanding ANI in the context of language-based security. However, in [20,21], the authors consider a security-driven notion of

ANI, let us call it *secANI*, where data is partitioned into private and public, and variations of the private input must not affect a property of the public output. Then, they prove that any secANI policy π for a program P can be formulated as a completeness problem for P w.r.t. specific abstractions derived from those defining π. In this paper, we follow the opposite direction: we prove that any completeness problem $\mathcal{C}$ for a program P can be formulated as an ANI (not just secANI) property for P, defined in terms of the abstractions considered in $\mathcal{C}$ (Sect. 4). This becomes particularly useful when we move towards the weaker abstract interpretation framework [12]. Indeed, the completeness results of [25] are built on top of the standard abstract interpretation framework, based on Galois connections, while here we relax such assumption, making our contribution a strict generalization of [25]. Moreover, this relation allows us to adapt the deductive approach defined for ANI [19,22] in order to cope with completeness, providing a logic system for deducing completeness properties (Subsect. 5). Here, the contribution consists in generalizing the proof system provided in [19,22] to deal with generic non-interference properties, not necessarily splitting data in public and private.

Finally, we provide an effective method to verify completeness, by exploiting a hyper static analysis [29], or *hyperanalysis* (Sect. 6). The latter, has been developed to verify *hyperproperties* and, in particular, to verify ANI (that is an hyperproperty). In this way, we can prove that the completeness property of the abstract domains is a hyperproperty of program semantics, and therefore it can be analyzed and verified (even if in restricted versions) by means of an hyperanalysis. Indeed, [32] provides a general methodology for verifying hyperproperties by means of Abstract Interpretation. Here, we show how to define an effective (hyper) static analysis, based on abstract interpretation, making completeness verification decidable.

2 Background

If S is a set, $\wp(S)$ denotes the powerset of S. If $f : S \to T$ is a function, we often abuse notation by calling f also its additive lifting $f : \wp(S) \to \wp(T)$ to sets of values: $f(X) \triangleq \{\, f(x) \,|\, x \in X \subseteq S \,\}$. If $f : S \to T$ and $g : T \to U$, we denote by $g \circ f$ (or simply gf) their composition. If $f : S \to S$, and $n \in \mathbb{N}$ we define $f^n : S \to S$ inductively as: $f^0 \triangleq id_S$ (the identity on S); and $f^{n+1} \triangleq f \circ f^n$.

In ordered structures (e.g., lattices) L we use $\leq_L$ to denote its partial order relation, $\vee_L$ to denote its least upper bound (lub), $\wedge_L$ to denote its greatest lower bound (glb), $\top_L$ to denote its top element and $\bot_L$ to denote its bottom element[1]. A function f on complete lattices is additive if it preserves arbitrary lubs (co-additivity is dually defined). The least fixpoint of $f : C \to C$ on a poset C, when it exists, is denoted *lfp* f. If f is (Scott)continuous on a complete lattice, then *lfp* $f = \bigvee_{n \in \mathbb{N}} f^n(\bot)$.

If $S \subseteq P$ then $\downarrow S \triangleq \{x \in P \mid \exists y \in S \,.\, x \leq y\}$. We will often denote $f(\{x\})$ as $f(x)$ and $\downarrow\{x\}$ as $\downarrow x$.

[1] We avoid the pedex when the structure is clear form the context or it is not relevant.

2.1 Abstract Interpretation

Abstract interpretation [10,11] is a formal framework for approximating programs semantics, defined in terms of a concrete domain C and an abstract domain A of C. Given complete lattices C and A, a pair of functions $\alpha : C \to A$ and $\gamma : A \to C$ forms a Galois connection (GC for short) if for any $x \in C$ and $y \in A$ we have $\alpha(x) \leq_A y \Leftrightarrow x \leq_C \gamma(y)$. In this case, α (resp. γ) is the abstraction/left adjoint (resp. concretization/right adjoint), and it is additive (resp. co-additive). Co-additive functions f admits left adjoint $f^- \triangleq \lambda x.\ \bigwedge\{\ y \,|\, x \leq f(y)\ \}$. An *upper closure operator* (uco for short) $\rho : P \to P$ on a poset P is monotone, idempotent, and extensive (i.e., $\forall x \in P.\ x \leq_P \rho(x)$). If $\alpha \circ \gamma = id_A$ then the GC forms a Galois insertion (GI for short) and $\gamma \circ \alpha$ is an uco. Let us denote by $Abs(C)$ the class of abstract domains (GI or uco) of C. In particular, we denote it by $A_{\alpha,\gamma}$ or by A_ρ depending on what we want to make explicit. The *disjunctive completion* of a domain is defined as: $\curlyvee(\rho) \triangleq \bigsqcup\{\eta \in Abs(C) \mid \eta \sqsubseteq \rho \wedge \eta \text{ is additive}\}$. A closure η is called *partitioning* [35] if $\eta = \mathcal{P}(\eta)$, where $\mathcal{P}(\eta) \triangleq \curlyvee(\{[x]_\eta \mid x \in S\})$, with $[x]_\eta \triangleq \{y \mid \eta(x) = \eta(y)\}$, is the most concrete closure inducing the same partition of η.

Soundness and Completeness. Given an abstract domain $A_{\alpha,\gamma} \in Abs(C)$ and a concrete function $f : C \to C$, an abstract function $f^A : A \to A$ is a *sound* approximation of f when $\alpha \circ f \leq_A f^A \circ \alpha$. The best correct approximation (bca for short) of f in A is the function $\overline{f}^A \triangleq \alpha \circ f \circ \gamma$. Any possible approximation of f is less precise or as precise as the bca of f.

The abstract function f^A is a *complete* [11,25] approximation of f on A if $\alpha \circ f = f^A \circ \alpha$. An abstract domain A is called complete for f if there exists a complete approximation f^A of f. Completeness of f^A intuitively means that f^A is the most precise approximation of f. Completeness can be characterized also in terms of uco. Let $A_\rho \in Abs(C)$, then A is a complete abstraction for f if $\rho \circ f \circ \rho = \rho \circ f$. This implies that completeness is a property of the abstract domain, since if there exists a complete approximation of f, then the bca is itself complete. Abstract domains can be made complete [25]. In a more general setting, let $f : D \to C$ be a function on complete lattices D and C (potentially different), and $A_\rho \in Abs(C)$, $A_\eta \in Abs(D)$ be abstractions, respectively, of input and output domains. In this case, we say that $\langle \rho, \eta \rangle$ is a pair of complete abstract domains for f if $\rho \circ f \circ \eta = \rho \circ f$. A pair of domain transformers can be associated with such completeness problem. We follow [16,24] by defining *domain refinement* τ_r and *simplification* τ_s as any monotone function $\tau_r, \tau_s : Abs(C) \to Abs(C)$ such that $X \subseteq \tau_r(X)$ and $\tau_s(X) \subseteq X$, respectively. In [25], a constructive characterization of the most abstract refinement, called *complete shell*, and of the most concrete simplification, called *complete core*, of any domain, making it complete, for a given continuous function f, is given as a solution of a simple domain equation. Consider the following operators on closures:

$$R_f \triangleq \lambda X.\ \mathcal{M}(\textstyle\bigcup_{y \in X} \mathsf{max}(f^{-1}(\downarrow y))) \qquad C_f \triangleq \lambda X.\ \{y \in L \mid \mathsf{max}(f^{-1}(\downarrow y)) \subseteq X\}$$

where $\mathcal{M}$ denotes the *Moore closure* (i.e., a function that closes all sets by glb) and max retrieves the maximal elements from a set (for the formal details of these constructions see [25]). In [25], the authors proved that the only interesting cases, as far as the refinement and simplification towards completeness are concerned, are respectively the most concrete $\beta \sqsupseteq \rho$ such that $\langle \beta, \eta \rangle$ is complete and the most abstract $\beta \sqsubseteq \eta$ such that $\langle \rho, \beta \rangle$ is complete. In particular, given $A_\rho \in Abs(C)$, the complete shell of $A_\eta \in Abs(D)$ is $\mathcal{R}_f^\rho(\eta) \triangleq \eta \sqcap R_f(\rho)$; and, given $\eta \in uco(D)$, the complete core of $\rho \in uco(C)$ is $\mathcal{C}_f^\eta(\rho) \triangleq \rho \sqcup C_f(\eta)$. When we consider $f : C \to C$ and the constraint $\eta = \rho$, the above construction requires a fixpoint iteration on abstract domains [25].

2.2 The Reference Language

Following the approach of [5] (see also [34,37]) we consider the language $\mathfrak{L}$ of regular commands[2] (RComm in Fig. 1, where $\oplus$ denotes non-deterministic choice and $*$ is the Kleene closure), which is general enough to cover deterministic imperative languages as well as other programming paradigms [5]. The language is parametric on the syntax of basic transfer functions $\mathsf{c} \in$ btFun, that can be instantiated with different kinds of instructions such as, for instance, assignments and boolean guards.

The Concrete Semantics. We consider as concrete semantics a standard denotational semantics. We assume that btFun is provided with a semantics function $(\!| \cdot |\!) :$ btFun $\to (C \to C)$ on a complete lattice C such that $(\!|\mathsf{c}|\!)$ is additive. This assumption is not restrictive since basic transfer functions are always defined by additive lifting [5]. The concrete semantics $[\![\cdot]\!]$: RComm $\to (C \to C)$ of regular commands is then inductively defined as follows:

$$[\![\mathsf{c}]\!]c \triangleq (\!|\mathsf{c}|\!)c \qquad [\![\mathsf{C}_1 \oplus \mathsf{C}_2]\!]c \triangleq [\![\mathsf{C}_1]\!]c \vee [\![\mathsf{C}_2]\!]c$$
$$[\![\mathsf{C}^*]\!]c \triangleq \bigvee\{[\![\mathsf{C}]\!]^n c \mid n \in \mathbb{N}\} \quad [\![\mathsf{C}_1; \mathsf{C}_2]\!]c \triangleq [\![\mathsf{C}_2]\!]([\![\mathsf{C}_1]\!]c)$$

The semantics of regular commands corresponds to the denotational semantics defined in [9] starting from the operational semantics for non deterministic choice and iteration [37].

To complete the language, we consider standard basic transfer functions used in deterministic while languages: skip instruction, assignments and boolean guards, as defined in Fig. 1. In $\mathfrak{L}$ we consider just integers values in $\mathbb{Z}$ and integer variables, where Var is an enumerable set of variable names. Standard imperative language commands can be easily defined by using guarded branching and loop commands as syntactic sugar [5]:

$$\textbf{if } \mathsf{b} \textbf{ then } \mathsf{c}_1 \textbf{ else } \mathsf{c}_2 \textbf{ fi} \triangleq (\mathsf{b}?; \mathsf{c}_1) \oplus (\neg\mathsf{b}?; \mathsf{c}_2) \quad \textbf{while } \mathsf{b} \textbf{ do } \mathsf{c} \textbf{ ew} \triangleq (\mathsf{b}?; \mathsf{c})^*; \neg\mathsf{b}?$$

[2] We choose to keep the language as simple as possible, avoiding non necessary language features, in order to keep the focus on the analysis from a purely semantic point of view.

$$\begin{aligned}
\text{Exp} \ni \mathsf{e} &::= \mathsf{a} \mid \mathsf{b} \\
\text{AExp} \ni \mathsf{a} &::= x \mid n \mid \mathsf{a}+\mathsf{a} \mid \mathsf{a}-\mathsf{a} \mid \mathsf{a}*\mathsf{a} \\
\text{BExp} \ni \mathsf{b} &::= \mathit{true} \mid \mathit{false} \mid \mathsf{e}=\mathsf{e} \mid \mathsf{e}<\mathsf{e} \mid \mathsf{b}\wedge\mathsf{b} \mid \neg\mathsf{b} \\
\mathsf{btFun} \ni \mathsf{c} &::= \mathbf{skip} \mid x := \mathsf{a} \mid \mathsf{b}? \\
\mathsf{RComm} \ni \mathsf{C} &::= \mathsf{c} \mid \mathsf{C};\mathsf{C} \mid \mathsf{C}\oplus\mathsf{C} \mid (\mathsf{C})^* \qquad \mathit{Var} \ni x \text{ (variables)} \qquad \mathbb{Z} \ni n \text{ (values)}
\end{aligned}$$

Fig. 1. Syntax of the language $\mathfrak{L}$ of regular commands.

A program *memory* $\mathsf{m} : V \to \mathbb{Z}$ is a total function from a finite set of variables $V \subseteq Var$ to values. Memory update $[x \mapsto v]$ is defined as usual: $\mathsf{m}[x \mapsto v](x) \triangleq v$, when $x = y$; and $\mathsf{m}[x \mapsto v](y) = \mathsf{m}(y)$ otherwise. Let us call $\mathbb{M} \triangleq V \to \mathbb{Z}$ the set of program memories, the concrete domain of $\mathfrak{L}$ semantics is $C \triangleq \wp(\mathbb{M})$, denoting sets of memories on variables in V. The basic transfer function semantics $(\!|\mathsf{c}|\!) : \wp(\mathbb{M}) \to \wp(\mathbb{M})$ is defined, for a set of memories $\mathsf{M} \subseteq \mathbb{M}$, as:

$$(\!|\mathbf{skip}|\!)\mathsf{M} \triangleq \mathsf{M} \quad (\!|x := \mathsf{a}|\!)\mathsf{M} \triangleq \{\mathsf{m}[x \mapsto \{\!|\mathsf{a}|\!\}\mathsf{m}] \mid \mathsf{m} \in \mathsf{M}\}$$
$$(\!|\mathsf{b}?|\!)\mathsf{M} \triangleq \{\mathsf{m} \in \mathsf{M} \mid \{\!|\mathsf{b}|\!\}\mathsf{m} = \mathit{true}\}$$

where $\{\!|\mathsf{a}|\!\} : \mathbb{M} \to \mathbb{Z}$ and $\{\!|\mathsf{b}|\!\} : \mathbb{M} \to \{\mathit{true}, \mathit{false}\}$ are the standard evaluation semantics for arithmetic and boolean expressions, respectively. For arithmetical expressions, we abuse notation by denoting with $\{\!|\mathsf{a}|\!\}$ also their additive lift to sets of memories.

3 Weak Abstract Interpretation Framework

In the standard abstract interpretation framework [10,11], based on Galois connections, even when only the concretization function is given, a monotone abstraction function always exists and it can be mathematically derived from the concretization (this is guaranteed by the properties of a GC). Whenever such abstraction cannot be defined, as it happens in the case of Convex polyedra [13] or Automata [3] domains, then it means that the concretization does not yields a GC, i.e., it is not co-additive. Indeed, the requirement of having a GC between a concrete domain C and an abstract one A may be in practice too restrictive (e.g., when developing a static analyzer). In [12] the authors provide a more general framework for abstract interpretation, describing *necessary* and *releasable* (i.e., that can be relaxed) assumptions. In particular, it is strictly required that *any concrete element must have an approximation* (to garantee soundness). For instance, this is violated by concretization functions γ mapping the abstract top to a concrete element strictly smaller than the concrete top, i.e., when $\gamma(\top_A) <_C \top_C$. In this case, some concrete elements (those greater that $\gamma(\top_A)$) do not have a sound approximation. Indeed, even if we map all these elements (including $\top_C$) to $\top_A$, then soundness would be violated since the approximation of $\top_C$ would be an object with a strictly smaller concretization[3]. Instead, the existence of the *best approximation* for each concrete element

[3] In GC-based abstract interpretation, this condition is implied by γ being co-additive.

is releasable assumption. The best abstraction does not exist, for instance, when the set of sound approximations is an infinite strictly descending chain or a set of finite/infinite non-comparable strictly decreasing chains [12].

In this section, we provide a *closure*-based characterization of such abstract domains, by formalizing a weakened abstract interpretation framework where the *abstraction* function may be missing and, therefore, where the adoption of the best abstraction assumption is not viable.

Definition 1 (Weak Adjoint). *Let $\gamma : A \to C$ be a monotone and one-to-one*[4] *function such that $\gamma(\top_A) = \top_C$, a* weak adjoint *$\gamma^{\sim} : C \to A$ of γ is any function in $\widetilde{\Gamma}(\gamma)$, where:*

$$\widetilde{\Gamma}(\gamma) \triangleq \{\dot{\alpha} : C \to A \mid \forall c \in C, a \in A.\, c \leq_C \gamma \circ \dot{\alpha}(c) \wedge \dot{\alpha} \circ \gamma(a) = a\}$$

The pair $(\gamma, \gamma^{\sim})$, with $\gamma^{\sim}$ weak adjoint of γ, form a *weak Galois connection.* Hence, a weak adjoint simply fixes the approximations for the meanings of abstract elements given by γ (unique by the on-to-one property of γ), and allows a range of possibilities for the other concrete elements, only forcing soundness, as required in [12]. Hence, Definition 1 gives rise to a *family* of abstraction functions, each depending on the strategy adopted to select the elements in $\{a \in A \mid c \leq_C \gamma(a)\}$ when it does not exist an abstract element a such that $c = \gamma(a)$. For instance, when possible, we could take the minimal elements of such set. Furthermore, when considering a not co-additive γ, then $\gamma^{\sim}$ is in general not monotone. However, when γ is co-additive, taking $\gamma^{\sim}(c) = \mathsf{min}\{a \in A \mid c \leq_C \gamma(a)\}$, we have that $\gamma^{\sim}$ is precisely the left adjoint γ^{-} of γ, since a minimal element always exists and it is unique (the glb).

Theorem 1. *Let $\gamma : A \to C$ be a monotone and one-to-one function such that $\gamma(\top_A) = \top_C$, and $\gamma^{\sim} \in \widetilde{\Gamma}(\gamma)$, then $\gamma^{\sim} \circ \gamma = id$, and $\rho \triangleq \gamma \circ \gamma^{\sim}$ is idempotent, i.e., $\forall c \in C \,.\, \rho \circ \rho(c) = \rho(c)$, and extensive, i.e., $\forall c \in C \,.\, c \leq_C \rho(c)$.*

Proof. For the sake of readability, we denote $\gamma^{\sim}$ more concisely with $\dot{\alpha}$, and we omit the function composition operator.

- $\dot{\alpha}\gamma = id$ holds by construction.
- $\gamma\dot{\alpha}$ is idempotent, indeed: $\gamma\dot{\alpha}\gamma\dot{\alpha} = \gamma(\dot{\alpha}\gamma)\dot{\alpha} = \gamma\dot{\alpha}$.
- $\gamma\dot{\alpha}$ is extensive, indeed: if $c = \gamma(a)$, for some $a \in A$, then $\gamma\dot{\alpha}(c) = \gamma(a) = c$, hence trivially we have $c \leq \gamma\dot{\alpha}(c)$; otherwise, $\gamma\dot{\alpha}(c) \in \gamma(\{a' \in A \mid c \leq_C \gamma(a')\})$, if $\{a' \in A \mid c \leq_C \gamma(a')\} \neq \varnothing$, then its γ image is greater than c, otherwise it is $\top$, again greater than c.

In other words, by losing the abstraction we lose closure monotonicity, while keeping the other properties. We call such operators *weak closures.*

Definition 2 (Weak closure). *Let $\langle C, \leq_C\rangle$ be a poset. Then, $\rho : C \to C$ is a* weak upper closure operator, *or* weak closure, *if it is idempotent and extensive.*

[4] The one-to-one hypothesis is not restrictive, being implicit in the GI-based framework. Indeed, γ can always be made one-to-one by collapsing the elements of A with the same concrete meaning w.r.t. γ.

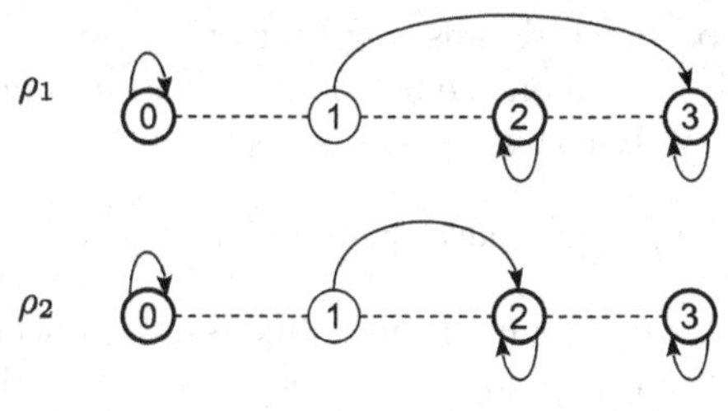

Fig. 2. Different weak closures with the same set of fixpoints.

We denote with $wAbs(C)$ the set of all weak abstract interpretations of C, characterized by a weak GC or, equivalently, by a weak closure.

The set $wAbs(C)$, equipped with the standard point-wise ordering between functions $\sqsubseteq$, forms a partial order. Note that, differently from upper closure operators, weak closures cannot be uniquely identified by the set of their fixpoints. Indeed, it is easy to find different weak closures having the same set of fix points, as depicted in Fig. 2. Here, we have two weak closures ρ_1 and ρ_2[5] on the poset $\langle\{0,1,2,3\},\leq\rangle$, that have the same set of fixpoints $\{0,2,3\}$, even if $\rho_2 \sqsubset \rho_1$.

Example 1. Consider the abstract domain REG [2,3] of automata/regular languages on a finite alphabet Σ. It is well known that automata/regular languages are not closed by infinite intersection, and therefore they do not form an abstract domain in the standard framework. In particular, if we consider as concrete domain the powerset of all strings on the alphabet Σ, i.e., $C = \wp(\Sigma^*)$, we define the abstract domain $\text{REG} \triangleq \{L \subseteq \Sigma^* \mid \exists D \in \text{DFA}.\ L = \mathcal{L}(D)\}$, where DFA is the set of deterministic finite state automata, and $\mathcal{L}(D)$ is the language of strings on Σ accepted by D. Also non-deterministic finite state automata NFA precisely characterize regular languages. The fact that REG is not closed by infinite intersection means that it does not exists an abstraction function associating with any $L \in \wp(\Sigma^*)$ the least regular language containing L. However, a monotone and one-to-one concretization function is the identity (any regular language is a language), hence we can build a weak Galois connection by fixing the regular overapproximation to associate with any L. In order to be a bit more precise, we could provide a way to associate a regular language overapproximating a context-free language. A context-free language L is such that there exists a pushdown automata P, i.e., $P \in PDA$, such that $L = \mathcal{L}(P)$. Then, let $\gamma_{\text{REG}} \triangleq id$ on $\wp(\Sigma^*)$, we define $\gamma^{\sim}_{\text{REG}}$ for each $L \in \wp(\Sigma^*)$ as:

$$\gamma^{\sim}_{\text{REG}}(L) \triangleq \begin{cases} L & \text{if } \exists D \in \text{DFA}.\ L = \mathcal{L}(D) \\ \mathcal{L}(N) & \text{if } \exists P \in \text{PDA}.\ L = \mathcal{L}(P) \ \wedge\ N \triangleq \mathsf{reg}(P) \\ \top & \text{otherwise} \end{cases}$$

[5] The function ρ_2 is also an upper closure operator.

Without entering in too much details, **reg** takes the transition relation δ_P of P (depending also on the symbol on the top of the stack) and defines the transition relation δ_N of a NFA N, ignoring the stack, as:

$$\delta_N(q,a) \triangleq \{q' \mid \exists A \text{ stack symbol in } P.\, \delta(q,a,A) = q'\}$$

Note that, we do not care about decidability issues concerning the existence of DFA and/or PDA, since we do not necessarily need a minimality condition, namely we could map to $\top$ regular or CF languages for which we are not able to provide an automaton.

Completeness (Subsect. 2.1) can be defined in this weakened framework, simply by considering $A_\eta \in wAbs(D)$ and $A_\rho \in wAbs(C)$. In the following, we will call such extended notion *weak completeness*. As we will see in the next sections, some known results holding in the standard abstract interpretation framework hold also in the weak framework, making them applicable even to Galois connection-less abstract domains (like Convex Polyhedra and Automata).

4 Characterizing Weak Completeness

In this section, we characterize domain completeness transformers in the proposed *weakened* framework of abstract interpretation. The existing completeness transformers [25] are strongly based on the monotonicity assumption, relaxed in weak abstract interpretation, hence, they cannot be naively generalized. The idea we propose here consists in exploring the connection between domain completeness and Abstract Non-Interference [18,23], where similar domain transformers have been characterized without using monotonicity.

It is worth noting that, this is not the first attempt to explore such kind of connection. In [20,21], the authors provide a completeness model for ANI in the context of language-based security, where input and output values are only partially observable (i.e., split in public and secret data). In particular, in such previous works we can observe that:

1. abstractions are modeled in the *standard* GC-based abstract interpretation framework (requiring even more restrictive conditions on closures);
2. domain completeness is instantiated (by using *specific* abstractions, e.g., abstracting secret data to the top) to model ANI in language-based security.

In this paper, we will investigate such connection by taking the opposite direction, applicable to a wider context: we will provide an ANI model of domain completeness in the weak framework of abstract interpretation. In particular:

1. abstractions are modeled as *weak* upper closure operators (Definition 2), making the results strictly more general;
2. ANI is instantiated to model abstract domain completeness in the (weak) abstract interpretation framework.

In this way, we can exploit the ANI domain transformers [18,23] for *making abstract domains (weak) complete*, namely complete also in the weak framework of abstract interpretation (i.e., when monotonicity constraint on the closures is relaxed), and to extend the static verification approaches existing for ANI [19, 30,32] to cope with (weak) completeness.

Abstract Non-interference. Non-interference has been introduced in [8,27,36] as a confidentiality policy determining whether the variation of sensible input information has effect on the observable part of the computation. This notion has been weakened by considering the variation of properties affecting a, potentially, abstract computation of functions [23]. Moreover, also the split of data in secret/relevant and public/observable can be seen as an abstraction of the data. Formally, Non-Interference has been generalized and weakened by means of abstract interpretation, as follows.

Definition 3 (Abstract Non-Interference [23]). *Let* $f : D \to C$, $A_\eta \in Abs(D)$ *and* $A_\rho \in Abs(C)$. *We say that* f *satisfies* Abstract Non-Interference[6] *w.r.t.* $\langle \eta, \rho \rangle$, *written* $[\eta]f(\rho)$, *if:*

$$\forall x_1, x_2 \in D.\, \eta(x_1) = \eta(x_2) \;\Rightarrow\; \rho \circ f(x_1) = \rho \circ f(x_2) \tag{1}$$

We recall that, for ANI we have two domain transformers, parametric on the set of observable and relevant input and output data, allowing to characterize: the most concrete harmless (i.e., unable to observe variations) output abstraction ρ (fixed the other observations) [23]; and the most abstract observable input property η, called *revealed information*, (fixed the other observations) [23].

Also Eq. 1 can be defined in the weak abstract interpretation framework, by considering $A_\eta \in wAbs(D)$ and $A_\rho \in wAbs(C)$. In this case we say that f satisfies *weak ANI*.

4.1 Completeness is Abstract Non-Interference

We now show how to require completeness of abstract domains w.r.t. a function means to prove that the function inputs sharing the same property are mapped into outputs that also share the same property (that is precisely ANI). This highlights the strong connection between Completeness and ANI, allowing us to export the domain transformers defined for ANI in the context of static analysis, and precisely in the weak abstract interpretation framework. In addition, there is another important side effect. Completeness has been always characterized as a domain property, even if local completeness [5] showed how much completeness depends on the way the analyzed program is written. Indeed, rewriting completeness as ANI, allows us to see completeness as a program *hyperproperty* [4,29] instead of as a domain property [11,25]. The deep gain in this change

[6] Note that what we call here Abstract Non-Interference is a specific version of the notion in [23], there called narrow.

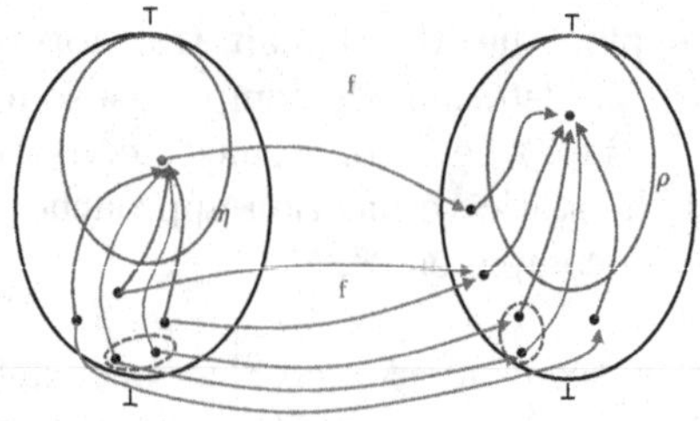

Fig. 3. Completeness is Abstract Non-Interference.

of perspective consists in making it possible to provide a framework for verifying completeness on programs by static analysis. Let us start by proving the connection between completeness and ANI.

Theorem 2. *Let $f : D \to C$, $A_\eta \in wAbs(D)$ and $A_\rho \in wAbs(C)$. We have that $\langle\rho,\eta\rangle$ is weak complete w.r.t f iff f satisfies weak ANI w.r.t. $\langle\eta,\rho\rangle$, namely: $\rho \circ f \circ \eta = \rho \circ f \;\Leftrightarrow\; [\eta]f(\rho)$.*

Proof. ($\Rightarrow$) Suppose $\langle\rho,\eta\rangle$ completeness holds, namely $\forall x \in D \,.\, \rho \circ f \circ \eta(x) = \rho \circ f(x)$. We have to prove that ANI holds, namely $\forall x_1, x_2 \in D \,.\, \eta(x_1) = \eta(x_2) \Rightarrow \rho \circ f(x_1) = \rho \circ f(x_2)$. Suppose $\eta(x_1) = \eta(x_2)$, otherwise the implication vacuously holds. Then we have $\rho \circ f(x_1) = \rho \circ f \circ \eta(x_1) = \rho \circ f \circ \eta(x_2) = \rho \circ f(x_2)$. Hence, ANI $[\eta]f(\rho)$ holds. ($\Leftarrow$) Suppose ANI holds, namely $\forall x_1, x_2 \in D \,.\, \eta(x_1) = \eta(x_2) \Rightarrow \rho \circ f(x_1) = \rho \circ f(x_2)$. We have to prove that $\langle\rho,\eta\rangle$ completeness holds, namely that $\forall x \in D \,.\, \rho \circ f \circ \eta(x) = \rho \circ f(x)$. Let assume that $\eta(x) \neq x$, otherwise completeness trivially holds. Let $x_1 = \eta(x) \in D$ and $x_2 = x \in D$. Then we have $\eta(x_1) = \eta \circ \eta(x) = \eta \circ \eta(x_2) = \eta(x_2)$. Since we suppose that ANI holds, we have that $\eta(x_1) = \eta(x_2)$ implies $\rho \circ f(x_1) = \rho \circ f(x_2)$. By definition, we have that $x_1 = \eta(x)$ and $x_2 = x$, resulting in $\rho \circ f \circ \eta(x) = \rho \circ f(x)$. Since x has been chosen arbitrarily, we can conclude that $\langle\rho,\eta\rangle$ completeness holds.

It is trivial to observe that, since closures are particular (i.e., monotone) weak-closures, by Theorem 2, we have that the equivalence between completeness and ANI holds also in the standard, GC-based, abstract interpretation framework.

Corollary 1. *Let $f : D \to C$, $A_\eta \in Abs(D)$ and $A_\rho \in Abs(C)$. We have that $\langle\rho,\eta\rangle$ is complete w.r.t f iff f satisfies ANI w.r.t. $\langle\eta,\rho\rangle$.*

In other words, completeness requires that all the inputs sharing the same property η are led by f to outputs sharing the same property ρ, while ANI checks the same relation on pairs of computations (as depicted in Fig. 3).

4.2 Making Abstract Domains Weak Complete

Most Concrete Weak Complete Output Observation. Here, we aim at characterizing the (weak) completeness core [25], by exploiting the new formalization of (weak) completeness in terms of (weak) Abstract Non-Interference.

First, let us define the set of all the images by $f : D \to C$ resulting from elements having the same abstraction $A_\eta \in wAbs(D)$, that is, $\forall x \in D$ we define the set $\kappa_f^\eta(x) \triangleq \{f(y) \mid \eta(y) = \eta(x)\}$.

In particular, this means that if $\eta(x_1) = \eta(x_2)$, then also $\kappa_f^\eta(x_1) = \kappa_f^\eta(x_2)$. At this point, we aim at abstracting in the same way all the concrete elements in $\{f(y) \mid \eta(y) = \eta(x)\}$. Following the construction proposed for ANI [18], let us define the following predicate determining which concrete elements do not cause different abstractions for elements in $\{f(y) \mid \eta(y) = \eta(x)\}$. Let $y \in C$:

$$Nint_f^\eta(y) \Leftrightarrow (\exists x \in D\, \exists z \in \kappa_f^\eta(x)\,.\,(y \geq z \Rightarrow y \geq \bigvee \kappa_f^\eta(x)))$$

This predicate holds for y if whenever y is above the image (by f) of an element x, then it is above the images of all the elements sharing the same η property with x.

Finally, let us define $\eta_f^\wedge \triangleq \{y \in C \mid Nint_f^\eta(y)\}$, which is the abstract domain for the output elements of f unable to distinguish the execution of f starting from inputs with the same property η. It is worth noting that, since we characterize $\eta_f^\wedge$ by identifying its fix points, we necessarily obtain an uco. In other words, this simplification provides the most concrete *uco* satisfying completeness, not excluding the potential existence of more concrete weak complete weak closures.

Lemma 1. *Let $f : D \to C$, $A_\eta \in wAbs(D)$ and $A_\rho \in wAbs(C)$, then $\eta_f^\wedge$ is an upper closure operator of C.*

Theorem 3. *Let $f : D \to C$ and $A_\eta \in wAbs(D)$. $\eta_f^\wedge \in uco(C)$ is the* most concrete (not weak) output observation *such that f satisfies ANI w.r.t. $\langle \eta_f^\wedge, \eta \rangle$.*

The previous result provides a characterization of the completeness domain core that is applicable even in the weak abstract interpretation framework. However, as already observed, the construction will always result in a standard upper closure operator, which guarantees the uniqueness of the construction but not necessarily its optimality. Therefore, the development of techniques for constructing optimal solutions in the weak abstract interpretation framework remains an interesting avenue for further study. As expected, whenever we project the construction in the standard framework, this transformer collapses to the well known one presented in [25].

Corollary 2. *If $\rho \in Abs(C)$ and $\eta \in Abs(D)$, then $\rho \sqcup \eta_f^\wedge$ is the most concrete abstraction more abstract than ρ making f to satisfy ANI w.r.t. $\langle \rho \sqcup \eta_f^\wedge, \eta \rangle$ and, hence, it is exactly the* completeness core *[25] of ρ w.r.t. f.*

This corresponds to take only the elements of ρ satisfying the predicate $Nint_f^\eta$. If we aim at computing the most concrete output observation with a fixed input observation we have just to compute precisely $\eta_f^\wedge$.

Example 2. Let us consider a very simple example, the semantics of $0 < x?$, which, for $\mathsf{M} \in \wp(\mathbb{M})$ is $(\!|0 < x?|\!)\mathsf{M} = \mathsf{M} \cap \{\, \mathtt{m} \in \mathbb{M} \mid \mathtt{m}(x) > 0 \,\}$. Let us consider the input observation $\widetilde{Sign} \in wAbs(\wp(\mathbb{M}))$ defined on memories as $\widetilde{Sign}(\mathsf{M}) \triangleq \lambda x \in Var.\ \widetilde{Sign}(\{\mathtt{m}(x) \mid \mathtt{m} \in \mathsf{M}\})$[7] and where, abusing notation, we define

$$\widetilde{Sign} \triangleq \lambda X \in \wp(\mathbb{Z}). \begin{cases} \mathbb{Z}_{\leq 0} \text{ if } X \subseteq \{\, n \in \mathbb{Z} \,|\, n \leq 0 \,\} \triangleq \mathbb{Z}_{\leq 0} \\ \mathbb{Z}_{\geq 0} \text{ if } X \subseteq \{\, n \in \mathbb{Z} \,|\, n \geq 0 \,\} \triangleq \mathbb{Z}_{\geq 0},\ X \neq \{0\} \\ \varnothing \quad \text{if } X = \varnothing \\ \mathbb{Z} \quad \text{otherwise} \end{cases}$$

This is a weak closure since, for instance, $\{0\} \subseteq \{0,1\}$ but $\widetilde{Sign}(\{0\}) = \mathbb{Z}_{\leq 0} \not\leq_{\widetilde{Sign}} \widetilde{Sign}(\{0,1\}) = \mathbb{Z}_{\geq 0}$.
Now, for each M, and therefore for any $\widetilde{Sign}(\mathsf{M})$, we have to build $\kappa^{\widetilde{Sign}}_{(\!|0 < x?|\!)}(\mathsf{M})$, which is the set of all the elements that should have the same output abstraction. Since $\widetilde{Sign}$ has only four fix points, we have only for of such sets:

$$\left\{ (\!|0 < x?|\!)\mathsf{M}' \,\middle|\, \widetilde{Sign}(\mathsf{M}') = [x \mapsto \mathbb{Z}_{\leq 0}] \right\} = \varnothing = \left\{ (\!|0 < x?|\!)\mathsf{M}' \,\middle|\, \widetilde{Sign}(\mathsf{M}') = [x \mapsto \varnothing] \right\}$$
$$\left\{ (\!|0 < x?|\!)\mathsf{M}' \,\middle|\, \widetilde{Sign}(\mathsf{M}') = [x \mapsto \mathbb{Z}_{\geq 0}] \right\} = \mathbb{Z}_{>0} = \left\{ (\!|0 < x?|\!)\mathsf{M}' \,\middle|\, \widetilde{Sign}(\mathsf{M}') = [x \mapsto \mathbb{Z}] \right\}$$

Hence, $\widetilde{Sign}^{\wedge}_{(\!|0 < x?|\!)} = \{\mathbb{Z}, \varnothing, \mathbb{Z}_{>0}\} \cup \{X \mid X \subseteq \mathbb{Z}_{\leq 0}\}$, meaning that any set of positive numbers should be abstracted in the same way in output, while we can observe precisely any set of negative numbers.

Most Abstract Weak Complete Input Perturbation. Now we aim at characterizing the (weak) completeness shell [25], by exploiting the new formalization of (weak) completeness in terms of (weak) Abstract Non-Interference. Note that, in this case we may not have a most abstract complete input perturbation, but a family of optimal input perturbations.

Hence, we are going to identify the set of elements that should share the same input property. Let us characterize the sets of elements that an optimal input perturbation can associate with $x \in D$, depending on $f : D \to C$, $A_\rho \in wAbs(C)$ abstraction on C, where $\mathsf{max}(X)$ extracts the maximal elements from X. Let

$$\rho_f^{\vee} \in \left\{\, \mu : D \to D \,\middle|\, \forall x.\ \mu(x) \in \mathsf{max}\{y \in D \mid \rho f(y) = \rho f(x)\} \,\right\}$$

This function associates with each element the most abstract one (in the worst case it is the identity on the element) sharing the same output observation ρ of its image by f.

Lemma 2. *Let $f : D \to C$, $A_\rho \in wAbs(C)$, then we have $A_{\rho_f^{\vee}} \in wAbs(D)$.*

Theorem 4. *Let $f : D \to C$ and $A_\rho \in wAbs(C)$. We have that $\rho_f^{\vee}$ is maximal, w.r.t. $\sqsubseteq$, among the input observations such that f satisfies ANI w.r.t. $\langle \rho, \rho_f^{\vee} \rangle$.*

The above result characterizes the completeness domain shell even in the weak abstract interpretation framework, and unlike the core, the construction of the

[7] In the following, $\lambda x \in Var.X$ (or $[x \mapsto X]$) denotes the set $\{\mathtt{m} \in \mathbb{M} \mid \mathtt{m}(x) \in X\}$.

shell can result in an optimal solution within the entire weak framework. As expected, whenever we make the construction in the standard framework, this transformer collapses to the well known one designed in [25].

Corollary 3. *If $A_\eta \in Abs(D)$ and $A_\rho \in Abs(C)$, then $\eta \sqcap \rho_f^{\vee}$ is the ANI shell of η w.r.t. f, and therefore it is the* completeness shell [25] *of η w.r.t. f.*

Example 3. Let us consider the simple semantics $(\!|2 * x|\!)\mathsf{M}$ for all $\mathsf{M} \in \wp(\mathbb{M})$. Let Par be the standard parity domain $\{\mathbb{Z}, \mathbb{Z}^{\text{even}}, \mathbb{Z}^{\text{odd}}, \varnothing\}$ returning the parity of sets of integer numbers, let us define

$$\widetilde{ParSign} \triangleq \lambda X \in \wp(\mathbb{Z}).\begin{cases} \mathbb{Z}^{Par(X)}_{\leq 0} & \text{if } X \subseteq \{\, n \in \mathbb{Z} \mid n \leq 0 \,\}, Par(X) \neq \mathbb{Z} \\ \mathbb{Z}^{Par(X)}_{\geq 0} & \text{if } X \subseteq \{\, n \in \mathbb{Z} \mid n \geq 0 \,\},\ X \neq \{0\}, Par(X) \neq \mathbb{Z} \\ Par(X) & \text{otherwise} \end{cases}$$

with fix points denoted $\{\mathbb{Z}, \mathbb{Z}^{\text{even}}, \mathbb{Z}^{\text{odd}}, \mathbb{Z}^{\text{even}}_{\leq 0}, \mathbb{Z}^{\text{odd}}_{\leq 0}, \mathbb{Z}^{\text{even}}_{\geq 0}, \mathbb{Z}^{\text{odd}}_{\geq 0}, \varnothing\}$, where, for instance, $\mathbb{Z}^{\text{even}}_{\leq 0} \triangleq \{\, n \mid n \leq 0, n \text{ even} \,\}$ (analogous for the other cases). As $\widetilde{Sign}$ of the previous example, also $\widetilde{ParSign}$ is a weak closure. In this case, we have to characterize the sets of maximal elements with the same output abstraction, hence we have to find out how many of such sets we have w.r.t. $\widetilde{ParSign}$: First of all we observe that the results may only be of even numbers, hence the only output fix points to consider are those involving even numbers. In the following, we abuse notation by using $\widetilde{ParSign}$ on integers and on memories

$$\begin{aligned} &\max\{\mathsf{M}' \mid \widetilde{ParSign}((\!|2 * x|\!)\mathsf{M}') = [x \mapsto \mathbb{Z}^{\text{even}}_{\leq 0}]\} = [x \mapsto \mathbb{Z}_{\leq 0}] \\ &\max\{\mathsf{M}' \mid \widetilde{ParSign}((\!|2 * x|\!)\mathsf{M}') = [x \mapsto \mathbb{Z}^{\text{even}}_{\geq 0}]\} = [x \mapsto \mathbb{Z}_{\geq 0}] \\ &\max\{\mathsf{M}' \mid \widetilde{ParSign}((\!|2 * x|\!)\mathsf{M}') = [x \mapsto \mathbb{Z}^{\text{even}}]\} = [x \mapsto \mathbb{Z}] \\ &\max\{\mathsf{M}' \mid \widetilde{ParSign}((\!|2 * x|\!)\mathsf{M}') = [x \mapsto \varnothing]\} = [x \mapsto \varnothing] \end{aligned}$$

Hence, $\widetilde{ParSign}^{\vee}_{(\!|2 * x|\!)} = \widetilde{Sign}$, meaning that any more abstract closure would abstract in the same way sets with different output observations, violating ANI.

5 A Deductive System for Completeness

The proposed domain transformers are surely important for deeper understanding how completeness can be characterized, but they do not provide effective methods for retrieving complete abstract domains given a program. In order to make such task effective, we may derive complete domains inductively on the language structure, similarly to what has been done for ANI [19,22]. The idea is to exploit the given transformers on the language expressions, and then to propagate abstractions inductively on regular commands structure.

Indeed, we show how the deductive system for ANI [19,22] can be rewritten for the language $\mathfrak{L}$, in the weak abstract interpretation framework. The inference rules of the deductive system for completeness are given in Fig. 4, where for the sake of readability we write $[\eta]\mathsf{C}(\rho)$ instead of $[\eta][\![\mathsf{C}]\!](\rho)$.

The two axioms of rule **R0** just assert trivial facts, namely that it always holds completeness when the input distinguishes everything or when the output

$$\textbf{R0: } [\eta]\mathsf{C}(\mathbb{T}) \quad [id]\mathsf{C}(\rho) \qquad \textbf{R1: } [\eta]\mathsf{e}(\eta^{\wedge}_{\{\!|\mathsf{e}|\!\}}) \quad [\rho^{\vee}_{\{\!|\mathsf{e}|\!\}}]\mathsf{e}(\rho) \qquad \textbf{R2: } \frac{\eta \sqsubseteq \rho}{[\eta]\mathbf{skip}(\rho)}$$

$$\textbf{R3: } \frac{[\eta]\mathsf{a}(\rho) \quad \eta \sqsubseteq \rho \text{ if } Var \supsetneq \{x\}}{[\eta]\, x := \mathsf{a}(\rho)} \qquad \textbf{R4: } \frac{[\eta]\mathsf{b}(\rho)}{[\eta]\, \mathsf{b}?(\rho)} \qquad \textbf{R5: } \frac{[\eta]\mathsf{C}(\rho) \quad \rho \sqsubseteq \eta}{[\eta]\mathsf{C}^*(\eta)}$$

$$\textbf{R6: } \frac{[\eta]\mathsf{C}_1(\rho) \quad [\eta_1]\mathsf{C}_2(\rho_1) \quad \rho \sqsubseteq \eta_1}{[\eta]\mathsf{C}_1;\ \mathsf{C}_2(\rho_1)} \qquad \textbf{R7: } \frac{[\eta_1]\mathsf{C}_1(\rho_1) \quad [\eta_2]\mathsf{C}_2(\rho_2)}{[\eta_1 \sqcap \eta_2]\mathsf{C}_1 \oplus \mathsf{C}_2(\rho_1 \sqcup \rho_2)}$$

$$\textbf{R8: } \frac{[\eta_1]\mathsf{C}(\rho_1) \quad \eta \sqsubseteq \eta_1 \quad \rho_1 \sqsubseteq \rho}{[\eta]\mathsf{C}(\rho)} \qquad \textbf{R9: } \frac{\forall i \in I\,.\,[\eta_i]\mathsf{C}(\rho) \quad \eta_i \text{ partitioning}}{[\bigsqcup_{i\in I} \eta_i]\mathsf{C}(\rho)}$$

$$\textbf{R10: } \frac{\forall i \in I\,.\,[\eta]\mathsf{C}(\rho_i)}{[\eta]\mathsf{C}(\bigsqcup_{i\in I} \rho_i)} \qquad \textbf{R11: } \frac{\forall i \in I\,.\,[\eta]\mathsf{C}(\rho_i)}{[\eta]\mathsf{C}(\bigsqcap_{i\in I} \rho_i)}$$

Fig. 4. Deriving complete abstractions for the language $\mathfrak{L}$ of regular commands.

does not distinguish anything. Rule **R1** provides the two axioms deriving from the theorems determining complete shell and core of the abstractions involved (Subsect. 4.2), w.r.t. the semantics of the expression. As far as **skip** is concerned **R2**, then still we need the input abstraction η to be more concrete than the output one. **R3**, when dealing with more than one variable, has to ensure (for all the unchanged variables) that η implies ρ. **R4** is quite immediate. Rule **R5** inductively handle iterations. **R6** and **R7** are as expected. Rule **R8** tells us that we can always concretize the input observation and abstract the output observation. Finally, the last rules change input and output abstractions exploiting operations on abstract domains. Note that rule **R9** is applicable only if η_i are all partitioning, namely they necessarily need to be closures, and not just pseudo-closures. This is not a limit of the deductive systems, since all these rule are useful for improving the precision of the deduction but are not necessary for its soundness.

When $[\eta]\mathsf{C}(\rho)$ can be proved in the deductive system in Fig. 4 we write $\vdash [\eta]\mathsf{C}(\rho)$. The pseudo-closures deduced by the derivation $\vdash$ are the most abstract domains for which completeness holds, w.r.t a given program in $\mathfrak{L}$.

Theorem 5 (Soundness). *Let* $\mathsf{C} \in \mathfrak{L}$ *and* $A_\eta, A_\rho \in wAbs(\wp(\mathbb{M}))$. *If* $\vdash [\eta]\mathsf{C}(\rho)$ *then* $\langle \rho, \eta \rangle$ *is (weak) complete for* C.

Example 4. Let $\mathsf{C} \triangleq (0 < x?; x := 2 * x)^*; \neg(0 < x)?$. In this case the concrete domain is $\wp(\mathbb{M})$. Let us consider $\widetilde{Sign}$ defined in Example 2 and $Par\widetilde{Sign}$ in Example 3.

In Example 2 we proved that $[\widetilde{Sign}]0 < x(\widetilde{Sign}^{\wedge}_{(0 < x?)})$. By rule **R4** we have that $[\widetilde{Sign}]0 < x?(\widetilde{Sign}^{\wedge}_{(0 < x?)})$ hence, by rule **R8**, we have $[\widetilde{Sign}]0 < x?(\widetilde{Sign})$, being $\widetilde{Sign}^{\wedge}_{(0 < x?)} \sqsubseteq \widetilde{Sign}$.

Moreover, in Example 3 we proved that $[\widetilde{Sign}]2 * x(\widetilde{ParSign})$. Then, by rule **R3**, having C only one variable, we have that $[\widetilde{Sign}]x := 2 * x(\widetilde{ParSign})$. Hence, we can apply **R6** obtaining $[\widetilde{Sign}]0 < x?; x := 2 * x(\widetilde{ParSign})$, and then, being $\widetilde{ParSign} \sqsubseteq \widetilde{Sign}$, by **R5**, we derive $[\widetilde{Sign}](0 < x?; x := 2 * x)^*(\widetilde{Sign})$.

Finally, we can prove that $[\widetilde{Sign}]\neg(0 < x)(\widetilde{ParSign})$ with a reasoning similar to $0 < x$. Hence, we can apply again **R4** to derive $[\widetilde{Sign}]\neg(0 < x)?(\widetilde{ParSign})$ and **R6** to obtain $[\widetilde{Sign}](0 < x?; x := 2 * x)^*; \neg(0 < x)?(\widetilde{ParSign})$.

6 Statically Verifying (Weak) Completeness

Program verification aims at checking weather a program complies with a specification, i.e. a formal description of what programs are allowed and are not allowed to do. Recently, *hyperproperties* [7] have been introduced in order to formalize those specifications that cannot be checked observing *single* program executions. The behavior (semantics) $\mathcal{S}[\![\mathsf{C}]\!]$ of a program C is usually modeled as *a set* of *denotations* (e.g., execution traces), one for every possible input. In this setting, properties are sets of execution denotations and hyperproperties are collections of sets of executions. This tantamount to say that a program C satisfies a property P iff $\mathcal{S}[\![\mathsf{C}]\!] \subseteq P$, while it satisfies a hyperproperty HP iff $\{\mathcal{S}[\![\mathsf{C}]\!]\} \subseteq HP$. It turns out that a lot of interesting specifications, like (Abstract) Non-Interference, are hyperproperties [4,29] and, hence, they require specific verification mechanisms that go beyond the classic one adopted for program properties. An interesting side effect of our work goes towards the direction advocated in [14] exploring the idea of analyzing static analyses. Indeed, by proving that abstract domain completeness is a program hyperproperty we show how a property of the abstract domain (used for analyzing a program), can be seen as a hyperproperty of the program to analyze, and, hence, that can be statically verified on the program.

In this section, we firstly investigate the correlation between completeness and hyperproperties. In particular, we will shows that abstract domain completeness w.r.t. a program can be restated as a hyperproperty verification problem for such program. Then, by exploiting previous results on hyperproperties verification, we will show how completeness can be statically verified.

6.1 Hypercompleteness: Completeness as a Hyperproperty

Hyperproperties allow to specify complex program specifications (e.g., in the context of concurrent systems or security [7]) and, of course, they are crucial in making precise practical verification mechanisms. But, we believe that hyperproperties play also a more fundamental role in program analysis. Indeed, thanks to the equivalence between completeness and ANI (a hyperproperty), in this section we can prove that *checking completeness of an analysis w.r.t. a program boils down to check a hyperproperty of that program.* Of course such result is just a first step in the field of analyzing program analyses: whether this correlation is limited to completeness or can be generalized to any analysis property deserves further investigation.

A Program Semantics Suited for Hyperproperty Verification. As outlined in [4, 30], in order to verify hyperproperties, it is necessary to lift the concrete semantics to sets of sets, namely we need a *hypersemantics*. In [30], the authors show how to define a *correct* hypersemantics, starting from the concrete language semantics. Correct here means that the hypersemantics contains the concrete one. For instance, in the case of $\mathfrak{L}$, a hypersemantics[8] $[\![\mathsf{C}]\!]_{\mathcal{H}} : \wp(\wp(\mathbb{M})) \rightarrow \wp(\wp(\mathbb{M}))$ of the program C is correct when $[\![\mathsf{C}]\!]\mathsf{M} \in [\![\mathsf{C}]\!]_{\mathcal{H}}\{\mathsf{M}\}$, for any $\{\mathsf{M}\} \subseteq \wp(\mathbb{M})$. With an over-approximation of a (correct) hypersemantics we can soundly verify hyperproperties. The over-approximation is given by an *abstract hypersemantics*, computing on a suitable abstract (hyper)domain.

We can define the hypersemantics of programs in $\mathfrak{L}$ (denoted by the subscript $\mathcal{H}$) following the construction presented in [30,32]. The (hyper) transfer function for basic commands in btFun is $(\!| \cdot |\!)_{\mathcal{H}} : \mathsf{btFun} \rightarrow (\wp(\wp(\mathbb{M})) \rightarrow \wp(\wp(\mathbb{M})))$, where $\wp(\wp(\mathbb{M}))$ is a complete lattice by definition and $(\!|\mathsf{c}|\!)_{\mathcal{H}}$ is the additive lift to sets of the concrete semantics $[\![\mathsf{c}]\!] : \wp(\mathbb{M}) \rightarrow \wp(\mathbb{M})$ of the language. In particular, for any set of sets of memories $\mathfrak{M} \subseteq \wp(\mathbb{M})$ we define:

$$(\!|\mathbf{skip}|\!)_{\mathcal{H}}\mathfrak{M} \triangleq \mathfrak{M} \quad (\!|x := \mathsf{a}|\!)_{\mathcal{H}}\mathfrak{M} \triangleq \{[\![x := \mathsf{a}]\!]\mathsf{M} \mid \mathsf{M} \in \mathfrak{M}\}$$
$$(\!|\mathsf{b}?|\!)_{\mathcal{H}}\mathfrak{M} \triangleq \{(\!|\mathsf{b}|\!)\mathsf{M} \mid \mathsf{M} \in \mathfrak{M}\}$$

The hypersemantics $[\![\cdot]\!]_{\mathcal{H}} : \mathsf{RComm} \rightarrow (\wp(\wp(\mathbb{M})) \rightarrow \wp(\wp(\mathbb{M})))$ of regular commands is inductively defined as follows, for any set of sets of memories $\mathfrak{M} \subseteq \wp(\mathbb{M})$:

$$[\![\mathsf{c}]\!]_{\mathcal{H}}\mathfrak{M} \triangleq (\!|\mathsf{c}|\!)_{\mathcal{H}}\mathfrak{M} \qquad [\![\mathsf{C}_1 \oplus \mathsf{C}_2]\!]_{\mathcal{H}}\mathfrak{M} \triangleq \{[\![\mathsf{C}_1]\!]\mathsf{M} \cup [\![\mathsf{C}_2]\!]\mathsf{M} \mid \mathsf{M} \in \mathfrak{M}\}$$
$$[\![\mathsf{C}^*]\!]_{\mathcal{H}}\mathfrak{M} \triangleq \{\textstyle\bigcup_{n\in\mathbb{N}}\{[\![\mathsf{C}]\!]^n\mathsf{M}\} \mid \mathsf{M} \in \mathfrak{M}\} \quad [\![\mathsf{C}_1;\mathsf{C}_2]\!]_{\mathcal{H}}\mathfrak{M} \triangleq [\![\mathsf{C}_2]\!]_{\mathcal{H}}([\![\mathsf{C}_1]\!]_{\mathcal{H}}\mathfrak{M})$$

Note that, $[\![\mathsf{C}]\!]_{\mathcal{H}}$ is not exactly the lift to sets of $[\![\mathsf{C}]\!]$, but it is a correct approximation [30,32], namely $\{[\![\mathsf{C}]\!]\mathsf{M}\} \subseteq [\![\mathsf{C}]\!]_{\mathcal{H}}\{\mathsf{M}\}$ for any set of memories $\mathsf{M} \subseteq \mathbb{M}$.

Verifying Completeness by Using Program Hypersemantics. Now that we have defined the hypersemantics, we will show how it can be used to verify completeness. To do so, we exploit the equivalence between completeness and ANI and the fact that the latter is a hyperproperty.

The definition of ANI presented in Sect. 4 is given in terms of a generic function f. Hence, ANI for programs in $\mathfrak{L}$ is defined as follows, where we basically instantiate Definition 3 with f being the concrete semantics $[\![\mathsf{C}]\!] : \wp(\mathbb{M}) \rightarrow \wp(\mathbb{M})$ of a program $\mathsf{C} \in \mathfrak{L}$. Let $\eta, \rho \in wAbs(\wp(\mathbb{M}))$, we say that the program C in $\mathfrak{L}$ satisfies (weak) ANI w.r.t. $\langle \eta, \rho \rangle$, written $[\eta]\mathsf{C}(\rho)$, when:

$$\forall \mathsf{M}_1, \mathsf{M}_2 \in \wp(\mathbb{M}) \,.\, \eta(\mathsf{M}_1) = \eta(\mathsf{M}_2) \;\Rightarrow\; \rho([\![\mathsf{C}]\!]\mathsf{M}_1) = \rho([\![\mathsf{C}]\!]\mathsf{M}_2)$$

[8] Note that, an hypersemantics can be given in an abstract way on $\wp(C)$, in the same way we defined the concrete semantics on C in Sect. 2.

Now consider the set $\mathfrak{M}_2^\eta \triangleq \{\{\mathsf{M}_1, \mathsf{M}_2\} \mid \eta(\mathsf{M}_1) = \eta(\mathsf{M}_2)\}$, consisting in the set of memories pairs indistinguishable by the input observation η, and the set $\mathfrak{M}_2^\rho \triangleq \{\{\mathsf{M}_1, \mathsf{M}_2\} \mid \rho(\mathsf{M}_1) = \rho(\mathsf{M}_2)\}$, consisting in the set of memories pairs indistinguishable by the output observation ρ. We can use the hypersemantics $[\![\cdot]\!]_{\mathcal{H}}$ of $\mathfrak{L}$ to perform ANI verification:

$$[\![\mathsf{C}]\!]_{\mathcal{H}} \mathfrak{M}_2^\eta \subseteq \mathfrak{M}_2^\rho \;\Rightarrow\; [\eta]\mathsf{C}(\rho) \tag{2}$$

Indeed, Eq. 2 says that the program C executed from η-equivalent set of memories yields always ρ-equivalent set of memories, that is exactly the definition of ANI w.r.t. $\langle \eta, \rho \rangle$. Note that, this works since ANI is 2-bounded, hence *pairs* of executions are sufficient for verification [30,32]. This, in turn, results into a verification method also for completeness of $[\![\mathsf{C}]\!]$ w.r.t. $\langle \eta, \rho \rangle$, due to its equivalence with ANI.

Theorem 6. *The abstract interpretation $\langle \rho, \eta \rangle$ is (weak) complete for* C *if:*

$$[\![\mathsf{C}]\!]_{\mathcal{H}} \mathfrak{M}_2^\eta \subseteq \mathfrak{M}_2^\rho$$

Proof. The proof is straightforward. Indeed, $[\![\mathsf{C}]\!]_{\mathcal{H}} \mathfrak{M}_2^\eta \subseteq \mathfrak{M}_2^\rho$ implies C satisfies ANI w.r.t. $\langle \eta, \rho \rangle$ (by Eq. 2) and, by Theorem 2, we have C is complete for $\langle \rho, \eta \rangle$.

Note that this is a simple implication since $[\![\mathsf{C}]\!]_{\mathcal{H}}$ is a sound approximation of $[\![\mathsf{C}]\!]$, but it is not the precise additive lift to sets of the concrete semantics [30]. Furthermore, the theorem is given in terms of pseudo-closures, hence we can trivially extend the result to upper closure operators and completeness, in the standard GC-based abstract interpretation framework.

Example 5. Consider the usual non-relational abstraction for memories, approximating a set of memories $\mathsf{M} \in \wp(\mathbb{M}) = \wp(V \to \mathbb{Z})$ by means of a non-relational memory $\mathsf{m}^{nr} \in V \to \wp(\mathbb{Z})$ and a value abstraction $\mathcal{I} \in wAbs(\wp(\mathbb{Z}))$ approximating set of integers to intervals. Consider the program $\mathsf{C} \triangleq x := |x|; ((x > 0)?; x := x-2)^*$ where $|\mathsf{e}|$ is the absolute value operator applied to e that we suppose to add to $\mathfrak{L}$. Then C is not complete for the intervals domain $\mathcal{I}$. Intuitively, the approximation of the concrete semantics on input $\{-1, 1\}$ would yield the interval $\{-1\}$, while the (bca) abstract interpretation on the same input would yield the interval $\{-1, 0\}$. In this setting, $\mathfrak{M}_2^{\mathcal{I}}$ contains all pairs of non-relational memories $\{\mathsf{m}_1^{nr}, \mathsf{m}_2^{nr}\}$ such that $\mathcal{I}(\mathsf{m}_1^{nr}(x)) = \mathcal{I}(\mathsf{m}_2^{nr}(x))$ (for instance $\mathsf{m}_1^{nr}(x) = \{-1, 0, 1\}$ and $\mathsf{m}_2^{nr}(x) = \{-1, 1\}$, that are both approximated in the interval $\{-1, 0, 1\}$). If we execute the hypersemantics on $\mathfrak{M}_2^{\mathcal{I}}$ we will obtain, among others, the set $\{\mathsf{m}_1^{nr'}, \mathsf{m}_2^{nr'}\}$ such that $\mathsf{m}_1^{nr'}(x) = \{-1\}$ and $\mathsf{m}_2^{nr'}(x) = \{-1, 0\}$. But for such non-relational memories we have that $\mathcal{I}(\mathsf{m}_1^{nr'}(x)) = \{-1\} \neq \{-1, 0\} = \mathcal{I}(\mathsf{m}_2^{nr'}(x))$. This means that $[\![\mathsf{C}]\!]_{\mathcal{H}} \mathfrak{M}_2^{\mathcal{I}} \not\subseteq \mathfrak{M}_2^{\mathcal{I}}$, thus violating ANI and, in turn, proving that C is not complete for the interval abstraction.

6.2 Static Analysis for Completeness

As happens for the concrete semantics, also the hypersemantics is in general not computable. To effectively perform a static analysis we indeed need approximation: we need to abstract the computation of the concrete hypersemantics.

The abstract hypersemantics is a correct (and usually computable) approximation of the concrete hypersemantics. In particular, the *abstract hypersemantics* of programs in $\mathfrak{L}$ is a function $[\![\cdot]\!]^A_{\mathcal{H}} : \mathsf{RComm} \to (A \to A)$ on a hyper abstract domain $A_{\alpha,\gamma} \in wAbs(\wp(\wp(\mathbb{M})))$, defined inductively on the structure of regular commands as (here $\sqcup$ is the join of A):

$$[\![\mathsf{c}]\!]^A_{\mathcal{H}} a \triangleq (\alpha \circ [\![\mathsf{c}]\!] \circ \gamma) a \qquad [\![\mathsf{C}_1 \oplus \mathsf{C}_2]\!]^A_{\mathcal{H}} a \triangleq [\![\mathsf{C}_1]\!]^A_{\mathcal{H}} a \sqcup [\![\mathsf{C}_2]\!]^A_{\mathcal{H}} a$$

$$[\![\mathsf{C}^*]\!]^A_{\mathcal{H}} a \triangleq \bigsqcup\{([\![\mathsf{C}]\!]^A_{\mathcal{H}})^n a \mid n \in \mathbb{N}\} \qquad [\![\mathsf{C}_1; \mathsf{C}_2]\!]^A_{\mathcal{H}} a \triangleq [\![\mathsf{C}_2]\!]^A_{\mathcal{H}}([\![\mathsf{C}_1]\!]^A_{\mathcal{H}} a)$$

Note that, even if using the bca for the semantics of basic transfer functions in btFun is quite standard in abstract interpretation [5], effectively computable abstract hypersemantics (i.e. static analyses) may resort to an approximation of the bca.

The Abstract Interpretation for Completeness. To verify ANI and, hence, completeness we can instantiate the *hyperlevel constants* domain of [30] on $\wp(\mathbb{M})$. Note that, nothing changes in the definition of the hyperdomain when we consider a weak closure $\rho \in wAbs(\wp(\mathbb{M}))$, instead of an upper closure operator. In particular, following the construction of [30], we have that $\rho^\bullet = \wp(Atom(\rho)) \cup \{\rho\}$, where $Atom(\rho)$ denotes the sets of atoms of the fixpoints of ρ, namely the elements of ρ just above the bottom. Applying the lifting transformer of [30] we obtain $\mathcal{L}(\rho) \triangleq \lambda\mathfrak{M}.\{\rho(\mathsf{M}) \mid \mathsf{M} \in \mathfrak{M}\}$, for any set of sets of memories $\mathfrak{M} \subseteq \wp(\mathbb{M})$. Composing the two, we obtain $\alpha_\bullet \triangleq \lambda\mathfrak{M}.\rho^\bullet(\mathcal{L}(\rho)(\mathfrak{M}))$, that forms, together with its left adjoint $\gamma_\bullet = \alpha_\bullet^-$, the Galois connection [30]:

$$\langle \wp(\wp(\mathbb{M})), \subseteq \rangle \xrightleftharpoons[\alpha_\bullet]{\gamma_\bullet} \langle \rho^\bullet, \subseteq \rangle$$

By using such abstraction, we have that $\alpha_\bullet(\mathfrak{M}_2^\rho) = Atom(\rho)$, since the set contains only fix points of ρ, which can be seen as constants w.r.t. ρ. Hence, we can approximate the verification of ANI by using an abstract interpretation of the hypersemantics in the hyperdomain $\rho^\bullet$.

Lemma 3. *Let* $[\![\mathsf{C}]\!]^{\rho^\bullet}_{\mathcal{H}}$ *be the abstract interpretation of* C *in* $\rho^\bullet$ *and consider the case where* $\rho \sqsubseteq \eta$. *Then, we have that* $[\![\mathsf{C}]\!]^{\rho^\bullet}_{\mathcal{H}}(\alpha_\bullet(\mathfrak{M}_2^\eta)) \subseteq Atom(\rho) \Rightarrow [\eta]\mathsf{C}(\rho)$.

Proof. Since $[\![\mathsf{C}]\!]^{\rho^\bullet}_{\mathcal{H}}$ is, by design, a correct approximation of $[\![\mathsf{C}]\!]_{\mathcal{H}}$, we have that $[\![\mathsf{C}]\!]_{\mathcal{H}}\mathfrak{M}_2^\eta \subseteq [\![\mathsf{C}]\!]^{\rho^\bullet}_{\mathcal{H}}(\alpha_\bullet(\mathfrak{M}_2^\eta))$. Then, if $[\![\mathsf{C}]\!]^{\rho^\bullet}_{\mathcal{H}}(\alpha_\bullet(\mathfrak{M}_2^\eta)) \subseteq Atom(\rho)$ we obtain that $[\![\mathsf{C}]\!]_{\mathcal{H}}\mathfrak{M}_2^\eta \subseteq Atom(\rho)$. This implies that for each pair of (output) memory sets $\{\mathsf{M}_1, \mathsf{M}_2\} \in [\![\mathsf{C}]\!]_{\mathcal{H}}\mathfrak{M}_2^\eta$, namely sets of memories resulting from the computation of C on η-equivalent (input) memory sets, we have that $\rho^\bullet(\{\mathsf{M}_1, \mathsf{M}_2\}) = \{\mathsf{M}_1, \mathsf{M}_2\}$, since $\{\mathsf{M}_1, \mathsf{M}_2\} \in Atom(\rho)$. But this implies $\rho(\mathsf{M}_1) = \rho(\mathsf{M}_2)$, that is the requirement stated by Abstract Non-Interference.

Note that the requirement of having $\rho \sqsubseteq \eta$ is not too restrictive. Indeed, in static analysis an effectively implementable analyzer is a fixpoint computation that necessarily apply the same abstraction in input and output. Hence, only if we consider η more abstract than ρ we obtain a meaningful analysis. Again, Lemma 3 results into a static analysis method also for completeness, due to its equivalence with ANI.

Theorem 7. *Let* $[\![\mathtt{C}]\!]_{\mathcal{H}}^{\rho^\bullet}$ *be the abstract interpretation of* C *in* $\rho^\bullet$ *and* $\rho \sqsubseteq \eta$. *Then,* $\langle \rho, \eta \rangle$ *is (weak) complete for* C *if* $[\![\mathtt{C}]\!]_{\mathcal{H}}^{\rho^\bullet}(\alpha_\bullet(\mathfrak{M}_2^\eta)) \subseteq Atom(\rho)$.

Proof. The proof is straightforward. Indeed, $[\![\mathtt{C}]\!]_{\mathcal{H}}^{\rho^\bullet}(\alpha_\bullet(\mathfrak{M}_2^\eta)) \subseteq Atom(\rho)$ implies that C satisfies ANI w.r.t. $\langle \eta, \rho \rangle$ (by Lemma 3) and, therefore, by Theorem 2 we have that C is complete for $\langle \rho, \eta \rangle$.

Note that, the inclusion in Lemma 3 and, hence, in Theorem 7 is decidable when we bound the height of $\rho^\bullet$, as explained in [33].

7 Conclusions

Abstract domain completeness is a central issue in the theory of abstract interpretation, that has important practical implications (e.g., precision of abstract interpretation-based static analyses). In this paper, we investigated the connection between domain completeness and Abstract Non-Interference, tackling completeness from a different perspective. This allowed us to adapt the verification mechanisms developed for ANI in order to verify completeness, and to characterize new completeness domain transformers. All such completeness-related machinery has been developed in a weakened closure-based abstract interpretation framework, where we consider abstract domains that do not provide a best correct abstraction (i.e., that do not yield a Galois connection), such as the Convex Polyhedra and the Automata domains.

Such weak abstract interpretation framework has been already introduced in [12], but no formalization was provided in terms of closure-like functions. Indeed, having a general setting for comparing abstractions independently of their representation is quite useful to reason about domains properties, like completeness. In the standard abstract interpretation framework this role is played by upper closure operators but, to the best of our knowledge, there is not an analogous notion for Galois connection-less abstract interpretations. Hence, in the present paper, we introduced *weak-closures*, namely upper closure operators relaxing monotonicity, in order to precisely fill this gap.

A preliminary study on the link between ANI and completeness has been already provided in [20,21], where ANI has been restated as a completeness problem for specific upper closure operators, in the context of language-based security. In the present paper, we followed the opposite direction, by restating completeness as an ANI problem, in the more general setting of weak-closures and not restricted to the specific context of language-based security. As a result, we proved an *equivalence* between completeness and ANI, that holds for abstract domains defined in terms of weak-closures (and, as a trivial consequence, for domains defined on upper closure operators).

As a consequence of the proved equivalence between domain completeness and ANI, in the present paper we highlighted how known domain transformers developed for ANI can be extended to cope with completeness. In particular, we provided transformers making weak-closures complete for a given function and we generalized the deductive system of [19,22], in order to effectively compute the most concrete (weak-)closures that are complete for a given program. Finally, we exploited the static verification mechanisms, based on *hypersemantics* [30], developed for Non-Interference [32] in order to effectively verify ANI and, in turn, completeness (which is, indeed, a hyperproperty of program semantics).

It should be clear that, this paper can be considered only a first step in the direction of abstract interpretation-based static verification of completeness [14], since the connection we considered here is between ANI and the completeness of the best correct approximation (bca) of the semantics. This means that we can only imply completeness for an abstract semantics less precise than the bca. It will indeed deserve further investigation to design static analysis techniques, based on hyper analysis, verifying completeness directly on sound approximations of the bca. It will also worth extending the results to the verification of weaker forms of completeness (e.g., local [5] or partial [6] completeness).

Moreover, the design of static analysis techniques for ANI may become useful also in other fields of application. For instance, *robustness for neural networks* consists in checking whether by performing a perturbation of the input we can observe a variation in the network output classification, where the network can be abstractly interpreted [17]. In this context the idea of statically verifying ANI could be adapted to verify robustness w.r.t. an input perturbation. Clearly, this field of application needs and deserves further work.

A Selected Proofs

Proof (Proof of Lemma 1). We prove that the set $\eta_f^\wedge$ is a Moore family, namely that is closed under greatest lower bound. Let us consider $Y \subseteq \eta_f^\wedge$ and suppose $\exists x \in D \,.\, z \in \kappa_f^\eta(x)$ and such that $\bigwedge Y \geq z$, then $\forall y \in Y$ we have $Y \geq \bigwedge Y \geq z$. But, by definition of Y, this means that $\forall y \in Y$ we have $y \geq \vee\kappa_f^\eta$, hence by definition of glb we have $\bigwedge Y \geq \vee\kappa_f^\eta$, meaning that $\bigwedge Y \in \eta_f^\wedge$.
Suppose now that $\forall x \in D. \forall z \in \kappa_f^\eta(x)$ we have $\bigwedge Y \not\geq z$, hence the implication defining $Nint_f^\eta$ is trivially true and again $\bigwedge Y \in \eta_f^\wedge$.

Proof (Proof of Theorem 3). First of all we have to show that:

$$\forall x_1, x_2 \in D.\, \eta(x_1) = \eta(x_2) \;\Rightarrow\; \eta_f^\wedge \circ f(x_1) = \eta_f^\wedge \circ f(x_2)$$

By construction, $\eta_f^\wedge \circ f(x_1) = \bigwedge\{y \mid y \geq f(x_1) \wedge Nint_f^\eta(y)\}$ and $\eta_f^\wedge \circ f(x_2) = \bigwedge\{y \mid y \geq f(x_2) \wedge Nint_f^\eta(y)\}$. By Lemma 1, we know that also the glb of $Nint_f^\eta$ elements satisfies $Nint_f^\eta$, namely is in the set. Let us prove that if y is such that $Nint_f^\eta(y)$ then it is greater than any image of f. Suppose $y \in \{y \mid y \geq f(x_1) \wedge Nint_f^\eta(y)\}$, then $y \geq f(x_1)$, but $f(x_1) \in \kappa_f^\eta(x_2) = \{f(y) \mid \eta(y) = \eta(x_2)\}$

by hypothesis, but then by $Nint_f^\eta$ hypothesis, $y \geq \bigvee \kappa_f^\eta(x_2) \geq f(x_2)$. Namely $y \in \{y \mid y \geq f(x_2) \wedge Nint_f^\eta(y)\}$. Since we do not have hypotheses on x_1 and x_2, this proves that the two sets are the same, and therefore $\eta_f^\wedge \circ f(x_1) = \eta_f^\wedge \circ f(x_2)$. We now have to prove that it is the most concrete. This come trivially by construction, since $\eta_f^\wedge$ takes all the elements y such that $Nint_f^\eta(y)$, any more concrete domain ρ' must contain w such that $\neg Nint_f^\eta(w)$. But this means that $\exists x \in D\, \exists z \in \kappa_f^\eta(x)$ such that $w \geq z = f(y)$ (for some $y \in D$) but $w \not\geq \bigvee \kappa_f^\eta(x)$, meaning that there must exists $z' \in \kappa_f^\eta(x)$ such that $w \not\geq z' = f(y')$ (for some $y' \in D$). Hence we have $\eta(y) = \eta(y')$ and $\rho' \circ f(y) = z \leq w$ while $\rho' \circ f(y') = z' \not\leq w$ meaning that $\rho' \circ f(y) \neq \rho' \circ f(y')$.

Proof (Proof of Lemma 2). Extensivity holds trivially by definition. Let us prove idempotence. Suppose $\rho_f^\vee(x) = y \in \max\{y \in D \mid \rho \circ f(y) = \rho \circ f(x)\}$. Let us compute $\rho_f^\vee(y) = w \in \max\{w \in D \mid \rho \circ f(w) = \rho \circ f(y)\}$. But the we trivially have that $\rho \circ f(x) = \rho \circ f(y) = \rho \circ f(w)$, hence $w \leq y$ being y maximal, and $y \leq w$ by extensivity of $\rho_f^\vee$, hence $\rho_f^\vee(x) = y = w = \rho_f^\vee(y) = \rho_f^\vee \circ \rho_f^\vee(x)$.

Proof (Proof of Theorem 4). We have to prove that:

$$\forall x_1, x_2.\ \rho_f^\vee(x_1) = \rho_f^\vee(x_2) \ \Rightarrow\ \rho \circ f(x_1) = \rho \circ f(x_2)$$

Suppose that $\rho_f^\vee(x_1) = \rho_f^\vee(x_2)$. Then, $\rho_f^\vee(x_1) = y_1 \in \max\{y \in D \mid \rho \circ f(y) = \rho \circ f(x_1)\}$ and $\rho_f^\vee(x_2) = y_2 \in \max\{y \in D \mid \rho \circ f(y) = \rho \circ f(x_2)\}$, with $y_1 = y_2$, hence $\rho \circ f(x_1) = \rho \circ f(y_1)$ and $\rho \circ f(y_2) = \rho \circ f(x_2)$.

We have now to prove that it is maximal w.r.t. the relative precision order, namely any more abstract abstraction does not satisfy the ANI property. Suppose there exists $\eta' \in wAbs(D)$ more abstract than $\rho_f^\vee$, then it means that there exists $x \in D$ such that $y \triangleq \rho_f^\vee(x) \lneq \eta'(x)$, namely $\eta'(x) \gneq y \in \max\{z \in D \mid \rho \circ f(z) = \rho \circ f(x)\}$. Hence $\eta' \circ \eta'(x) = \eta'(x)$, by idempotence, but $\rho \circ f(\eta'(x)) \neq \rho \circ f(x)$ being y maximal.

Proof (Proof of Theorem 5). Exploiting the correspondence between completeness and Abstract Non-Interference (Theorem 2), we just have to prove that ANI holds. Indeed, we have to prove that if $\vdash [\eta]\mathsf{C}(\rho)$ then $[\eta]\mathsf{C}(\rho)$ holds. Let us prove that all rules in Fig. 4 are sound, namely that the deduced abstraction ensure ANI for P.

Rule **R0:** $\forall x_1, x_2$, independently from the input observation η, we trivially have $\mathbb{T}[\![\mathsf{C}]\!](x_1) = \mathbb{T}[\![\mathsf{C}]\!](x_2)$. On the other hand, $id(x_1) = id(x_2)$ means that $x_1 = x_2$, and therefore trivially, for any ρ, $\rho[\![\mathsf{C}]\!](x_1) = \rho[\![\mathsf{C}]\!](x_2)$.
Rule **R1:** We consider here expressions as base case of the induction. By Corollary 2 we have that $\eta^\wedge_{\{\!|\mathsf{e}|\!\}}$ is such that $\forall x_1, x_2.\ \eta(x_1) = \eta(x_2) \Rightarrow \eta^\wedge_{\{\!|\mathsf{e}|\!\}}\{\!|\mathsf{e}|\!\}(x_1) = \eta^\wedge_{\{\!|\mathsf{e}|\!\}}\{\!|\mathsf{e}|\!\}(x_2)$. Analogous for the other rule by Corollary 3. Note that, in order to be precise we should have to write other two axioms for b; but they are almost the same by considering $\{\!|\mathsf{b}|\!\}$ when computing, respectively, the input and the output observations.

Rule **R2:** In this case we can observe that, $[\eta]\mathbf{skip}(\rho)$ holds iff $\forall x_1, x_2$ we have that $\eta(x_1) = \eta(x_2)$ implies $\rho[\![\mathbf{skip}]\!](x_1) = \rho(x_1) = \rho(x_2) = \rho[\![\mathbf{skip}]\!](x_2)$, and this trivially holds if $\eta \sqsubseteq \rho$.
Rule **R3:** In this case we need the precondition $[\eta]\mathsf{e}(\rho)$, which means that the expression semantics does not change the property, i.e., $\eta(x_1) = \eta(x_2) \Rightarrow \rho(\{\!|\mathsf{e}|\!\}(x_1)) = \rho(\{\!|\mathsf{e}|\!\}(x_2))$. Hence, the assignment is complete if the expression is complete, but if there is more than one variable we need $\eta \sqsubseteq \rho$ for guaranteeing the implication (the assignment behaves like **skip**; on the other potential program viariables). Indeed, $[\![x := \mathsf{e}]\!](x_1) = x_1[x \mapsto \{\!|\mathsf{e}|\!\}(x_1)]$ and $[\![x := \mathsf{e}]\!](x_2) = x_2[x \mapsto \{\!|\mathsf{e}|\!\}(x_2)]$, provides results with the same ρ property since all the variables $y \neq x$, due to the hypotheses $\eta(x_1) = \eta(x_2)$ and $\eta \sqsubseteq \rho$, have values sharing the same ρ property, while for x returns the evaluations of the expression on the two different input memories. These evaluations share precisely the same ρ property by the rule precondition.
Rule **R4:** It is trivial since the semantics of the basic transfer function $\mathsf{b}?$ is precisely the semantics of the boolean expression b.
Rule **R5:** In this case, the proof is obtained by using rule **R2**, **R6** and **R8**. Indeed, when we do not execute $\mathtt{C}$ ($n = 0$) we need in output to observe η (**R2**). When we execute $\mathtt{C}$ one or more times, by induction on $n \geq 1$, by hypotheses and by **R6**, we prove ANI with ρ in output, and therefore by **R8** we prove ANI observing $\eta \sqcup \rho = \eta$.
Rule **R6:** If $\forall x_1, x_2.\ \eta(x_1) = \eta(x_2) \Rightarrow \rho[\![\mathtt{C}_1]\!](x_1) = \rho[\![\mathtt{C}_1]\!](x_2)$ and $\forall y_1, y_2.\ \eta_1(y_1) = \eta_1(y_2) \Rightarrow \rho_1[\![\mathtt{C}_2]\!](y_1) = \rho_1[\![\mathtt{C}_2]\!](y_2)$, then we have that $\forall x_1, x_2. \eta(x_1) = \eta(x_2) \Rightarrow \rho_1[\![\mathtt{C}_2]\!]([\![\mathtt{C}_1]\!](x_1)) = \rho_1[\![\mathtt{C}_2]\!]([\![\mathtt{C}_1]\!](x_2))$. At this point, since $\rho[\![\mathtt{C}_1]\!](x_1) = \rho[\![\mathtt{C}_1]\!](x_2)$ implies $\eta_1[\![\mathtt{C}_1]\!](x_1) = \eta_1[\![\mathtt{C}_1]\!](x_2)$, then we have the thesis.
Rule **R7:** If $\forall x_1, x_2$ we have $\eta_1(x_1) = \eta_1(x_2) \Rightarrow \rho_1[\![\mathtt{C}_1]\!](x_1) = \rho_1[\![\mathtt{C}_1]\!](x_2)$ and $\forall y_1, y_2$ we have $\eta_2(y_1) = \eta_2(y_2) \Rightarrow \rho_2[\![\mathtt{C}_2]\!](y_1) = \rho_2[\![\mathtt{C}_2]\!](y_2)$, then $\forall x_1, x_2$ we have that . $(\eta_1 \sqcap \eta_2)(x_1) = (\eta_1 \sqcap \eta_2)(x_2)$ implies both the equalities $\eta_1(x_1) = \eta_1(x_2)$ and $\eta_2(x_1) = \eta_2(x_2)$, hence we have both $\rho_1[\![\mathtt{C}_1]\!](x_1) = \rho_1[\![\mathtt{C}_1]\!](x_2)$ and $\rho_2[\![\mathtt{C}_2]\!](x_1) = \rho_2[\![\mathtt{C}_2]\!](x_2)$. This implies that, being $[\![\mathtt{C}_1 \oplus \mathtt{C}_2]\!] = [\![\mathtt{C}_1]\!] \cup [\![\mathtt{C}_2]\!]$, $(\rho_1 \sqcup \rho_2)[\![\mathtt{C}_1 \oplus \mathtt{C}_2]\!](x_1) = (\rho_1 \sqcup \rho_2)[\![\mathtt{C}_1 \oplus \mathtt{C}_2]\!](x_2)$.
Rule **R8:** Trivial. Indeed, η implies η_1 and ρ_1 implies ρ.
Rule **R9:** By definition of $\sqcup$ of partitioning closures [28], we have that $\eta_1 \sqcup \eta_2(x_1) = \eta_1 \sqcup \eta_2(x_2)$ implies that either $\eta_1(x_1) = \eta_1(x_2)$ or $\eta_2(x_1) = \eta_2(x_2)$. then by hypothesis, in both cases we have that $\rho[\![\mathtt{C}]\!](x_1) = \rho[\![\mathtt{C}]\!](x_2)$, namely we have the thesis. We can trivially extend the proof to any set I.
Rule **R10:** Trivial by rule **R7**.
Rule **R11:** By definition of $\sqcap$ we have that $\sqcap_i \rho_i[\![\mathtt{C}]\!](x_1) = \bigwedge_i \rho_i[\![\mathtt{C}]\!](x_1)$. By hypothesis if $\eta(x_)) = \eta(x_2)$ then for each $i \in I$ we have $\rho_i[\![\mathtt{C}]\!](x_1) = \rho_i[\![\mathtt{C}]\!](x_2)$, but then $\bigwedge_i \rho_i[\![\mathtt{C}]\!](x_1) = \bigwedge_i \rho_i[\![\mathtt{C}]\!](x_2) = \sqcap_i \rho_i[\![\mathtt{C}]\!](x_2)$, namely we have the thesis.

References

1. Albarghouthi, A.: Introduction to Neural Network Verification (2021). https://doi.org/10.48550/ARXIV.2109.10317, https://arxiv.org/abs/2109.10317
2. Arceri, V., Mastroeni, I.: Analyzing dynamic code: a sound abstract interpreter for evil eval. ACM Trans. Priv. Secur. **24**(2), 10:1–10:38 (2021)
3. Arceri, V., Mastroeni, I., Xu, S.: Static analysis for ECMAScript string manipulation programs. Appl. Sci. **10**, 3525 (2020). https://doi.org/10.3390/app10103525
4. Assaf, M., Naumann, D.A., Signoles, J., Totel, E., Tronel, F.: Hypercollecting semantics and its application to static analysis of information flow. In: Proceedings of POPL, pp. 874–887 (2017)
5. Bruni, R., Giacobazzi, R., Gori, R., Ranzato, F.: A logic for locally complete abstract interpretations. In: Symposium on Logic in Computer Science, LICS, pp. 1–13. IEEE (2021)
6. Campion, M., Dalla Preda, M., Giacobazzi, R.: Partial (in)completeness in abstract interpretation: limiting the imprecision in program analysis. Proc. ACM Program. Lang. **6**(POPL), 1–31 (2022). https://doi.org/10.1145/3498721
7. Clarkson, M.R., Schneider, F.B.: Hyperproperties. J. Comput. Secur. **18**(6), 1157–1210 (2010)
8. Cohen, E.S.: Information transmission in sequential programs. In: et al., D. (ed.) Foundations of Secure Computation, pp. 297–335. Academic Press, New York (1978)
9. Cousot, P.: Constructive design of a hierarchy of semantics of a transition system by abstract interpretation. Theor. Comput. Sci. **277**(1–2), 47–103 (2002)
10. Cousot, P., Cousot, R.: Abstract interpretation: a unified lattice model for static analysis of programs by construction or approximation of fixpoints. In: Conference Record of the 4th ACM Symposium on Principles of Programming Languages (POPL 1977), pp. 238–252. ACM Press (1977)
11. Cousot, P., Cousot, R.: Systematic design of program analysis frameworks. In: Conference Record of the 6th ACM Symposium on Principles of Programming Languages (POPL 1979), pp. 269–282. ACM Press (1979)
12. Cousot, P., Cousot, R.: Abstract interpretation frameworks. J. Logic and Comput. **2**(4), 511–547 (1992)
13. Cousot, P., Halbwachs, N.: Automatic discovery of linear restraints among variables of a program. In: POPL 1978: Proceedings of the 5th ACM SIGACT-SIGPLAN Symposium on Principles of Programming Languages, pp. 84–96. ACM Press (1978). http://doi.acm.org/10.1145/512760.512770
14. Cousot, P., Giacobazzi, R., Ranzato, F.: A^2i: abstract^2 interpretation. Proc. ACM Program. Lang. **3**(POPL), 42:1–42:31 (2019)
15. Dijkstra, E.W.: The humble programmer. Commun. ACM **15**(10), 859–866 (1972). https://doi.org/10.1145/355604.361591
16. Filé, G., Giacobazzi, R., Ranzato, F.: A unifying view of abstract domain design. ACM Comput. Surv. **28**(2), 333–336 (1996)
17. Gehr, T., Mirman, M., Drachsler-Cohen, D., Tsankov, P., Chaudhuri, S., Vechev, M.: Ai2: safety and robustness certification of neural networks with abstract interpretation. In: 2018 IEEE Symposium on Security and Privacy (SP), pp. 3–18 (2018). https://doi.org/10.1109/SP.2018.00058
18. Giacobazzi, R., Mastroeni, I.: Abstract non-interference: parameterizing non-interference by abstract interpretation. In: Proceedings of the 31st Annual ACM SIGPLAN-SIGACT Symposium on Principles of Programming Languages (POPL 2004), pp. 186–197. ACM-Press (2004)

19. Giacobazzi, R., Mastroeni, I.: Proving abstract non-interference. In: Marcinkowski, J., Tarlecki, A. (eds.) CSL 2004. LNCS, vol. 3210, pp. 280–294. Springer, Heidelberg (2004). https://doi.org/10.1007/978-3-540-30124-0_23
20. Giacobazzi, R., Mastroeni, I.: Adjoining declassification and attack models by abstract interpretation. In: Sagiv, M. (ed.) ESOP 2005. LNCS, vol. 3444, pp. 295–310. Springer, Heidelberg (2005). https://doi.org/10.1007/978-3-540-31987-0_21
21. Giacobazzi, R., Mastroeni, I.: Adjoining classified and unclassified information by abstract interpretation. J. Comput. Secur. **18**(5), 751–797 (2010)
22. Giacobazzi, R., Mastroeni, I.: A proof system for abstract non-interference. J. Log. Comput. **20**, 449–479 (2010)
23. Giacobazzi, R., Mastroeni, I.: Abstract non-interference: a unifying framework for weakening information-flow. ACM Trans. Priv. Secur. **21**(2), 1–31 (2018)
24. Giacobazzi, R., Ranzato, F.: Refining and compressing abstract domains. In: Degano, P., Gorrieri, R., Marchetti-Spaccamela, A. (eds.) ICALP 1997. LNCS, vol. 1256, pp. 771–781. Springer, Heidelberg (1997). https://doi.org/10.1007/3-540-63165-8_230
25. Giacobazzi, R., Ranzato, F., Scozzari, F.: Making abstract interpretation complete. J. ACM **47**(2), 361–416 (2000)
26. Girard, A.: Reachability of uncertain linear systems using zonotopes. In: Morari, M., Thiele, L. (eds.) HSCC 2005. LNCS, vol. 3414, pp. 291–305. Springer, Heidelberg (2005). https://doi.org/10.1007/978-3-540-31954-2_19
27. Goguen, J.A., Meseguer, J.: Security policies and security models. In: Proceedings of the IEEE Symposium on Security and Privacy, pp. 11–20. IEEE Computer Society Press (1982)
28. Hunt, S., Mastroeni, I.: The PER model of abstract non-interference. In: Hankin, C., Siveroni, I. (eds.) SAS 2005. LNCS, vol. 3672, pp. 171–185. Springer, Heidelberg (2005). https://doi.org/10.1007/11547662_13
29. Mastroeni, I., Pasqua, M.: Hyperhierarchy of semantics - a formal framework for hyperproperties verification. In: Ranzato, F. (ed.) SAS 2017. LNCS, vol. 10422, pp. 232–252. Springer, Cham (2017). https://doi.org/10.1007/978-3-319-66706-5_12
30. Mastroeni, I., Pasqua, M.: Verifying bounded subset-closed hyperproperties. In: Podelski, A. (ed.) SAS 2018. LNCS, vol. 11002, pp. 263–283. Springer, Cham (2018). https://doi.org/10.1007/978-3-319-99725-4_17
31. Mastroeni, I.: Abstract interpretation-based approaches to security - a survey on abstract non-interference and its challenging applications. In: Banerjee, A., Danvy, O., Doh, K., Hatcliff, J. (eds.) Semantics, Abstract Interpretation, and Reasoning about Programs: Essays Dedicated to David A. Schmidt on the Occasion of his Sixtieth Birthday, Manhattan, Kansas, USA, 19–20th September 2013. EPTCS, vol. 129, pp. 41–65 (2013)
32. Mastroeni, I., Pasqua, M.: Statically analyzing information flows: an abstract interpretation-based hyperanalysis for non-interference. In: Proceedings of the 34th ACM/SIGAPP Symposium on Applied Computing, pp. 2215–2223. Association for Computing Machinery (2019). https://doi.org/10.1145/3297280.3297498
33. Mastroeni, I., Pasqua, M.: Verifying opacity by abstract interpretation. In: Hong, J., Bures, M., Park, J.W., Cerný, T. (eds.) SAC 2022: The 37th ACM/SIGAPP Symposium on Applied Computing, Virtual Event, 25–29 April 2022, pp. 1817–1826. ACM (2022). https://doi.org/10.1145/3477314.3507119
34. O'Hearn, P.W.: Incorrectness logic. Proc. ACM Program. Lang. (POPL) **4**(10), 1-32 (2020)

35. Ranzato, F., Tapparo, F.: Strong preservation as completeness in abstract interpretation. In: Schmidt, D. (ed.) ESOP 2004. LNCS, vol. 2986, pp. 18–32. Springer, Heidelberg (2004). https://doi.org/10.1007/978-3-540-24725-8_3
36. Sabelfeld, A., Myers, A.: Language-based information-flow security. IEEE J. Sel. Areas Commun. **21**(1), 5–19 (2003)
37. Winskel, G.: The Formal Semantics of Programming Languages: An Introduction. MIT Press, Cambridge (1993)

Lifting On-Demand Analysis to Higher-Order Languages

Daniel Schoepe[1(✉)], David Seekatz[2], Ilina Stoilkovska[1], Sandro Stucki[5], Daniel Tattersall[6], Pauline Bolignano[1], Franco Raimondi[1,3], and Bor-Yuh Evan Chang[4,7]

[1] Amazon, London, UK
{schoeped,ilinas,pln,frai}@amazon.com
[2] Calgary, Canada
[3] Middlesex University, London, UK
[4] University of Colorado Boulder, Boulder, USA
[5] Amazon, Gothenburg, Sweden
satucki@amazon.com
[6] Amazon, Seattle, USA
dtatters@amazon.com
[7] Amazon, Boulder, USA
byec@amazon.com

Abstract. In this paper, we present an approach to lift on-demand analysis to higher-order languages. Specifically, our approach bootstraps an *on-demand call graph* construction by leveraging a pair of on-demand data flow analyses. Static analysis is increasingly applied to find subtle bugs or prove deep properties in large, industrial code bases. To effectively do this at scale, analyzers need to both resolve function calls in a precise manner (i.e., construct a precise call graph) and examine only the relevant portion of the program (i.e., be on-demand). A strawman strategy to this problem is to use fast, approximate, whole-program call graph construction algorithms. However, this strategy is generally not adequate for modern languages like JavaScript that rely heavily on higher-order features, such as callbacks and closures, where scalable approximations often introduce unacceptable imprecision. This strategy also limits increasingly sophisticated *on-demand analyses*, which scale by analyzing only parts of a program as needed: the scalability advantages of an on-demand analysis may be thwarted by the need to construct a whole-program call graph. The key insight of this paper is that existing on-demand data flow analyses can themselves be applied in a black-box manner to construct call graphs on demand. We propose a soundness condition for the existing on-demand analyses with respect to partial call graphs, formalize our algorithm as an abstract domain combinator, and prove it sound in Isabelle/HOL. Furthermore, we evaluate a prototype implementation of the resulting on-demand call graph construction algorithm for a subset of JavaScript (using the Synchronized Push-Down Systems framework as the underlying data flow analysis) on benchmarks making heavy use of higher-order functions.

M. V. Hermenegildo and J. F. Morales (Eds.): SAS 2023, LNCS 14284, pp. 460–484, 2023.
https://doi.org/10.1007/978-3-031-44245-2_20

1 Introduction

We consider the problem of lifting on-demand static analyses to higher-order languages—that is, transforming, in a sound manner, an on-demand static analysis relying on an upfront call graph into a fully on-demand analysis constructing its own call graph, even in the presence of first-class functions.

Program analysis approaches are becoming more and more sophisticated, increasingly able to find subtle bugs or prove deep program properties of interest in large code bases [9,26]. There are two key enablers for such advances, especially needed to scale to large industrial applications. One is the ability to reason interprocedurally about the behavior across different functions and modules of a program in a precise manner (rather than, e.g., relying solely on local, intraprocedural information or coarse-grained global information such as types). The other is the capabilty to be on-demand (i.e., to examine only the relevant portion of a program to derive a desired fact on demand).

Reasoning interprocedurally requires access to a *call graph* linking call sites in the program to functions that they may invoke at run time. To apply a static analysis interprocedurally, many tools assume that a call graph is provided upfront, and is consulted by the analysis to determine which parts of the program should be explored. This creates two limitations. First, for higher-order, imperative languages such as JavaScript, the combination of first-class functions with a dynamic heap and object-oriented features may require a deep interleaving between call graph construction and data flow analysis. This arises due to the need to precisely track functions as they flow from the points where they are referenced through higher-order functions, heap cells, inheritance hierarchies, and closure bindings. Without this back-and-forth between call graph construction and data flow analysis, precision might be limited or come at the price of soundness or performance trade-offs. Second, this reliance on an upfront call graph limits the benefit of on-demand techniques—a precise data flow analysis to compute a call graph upfront may significantly negate the benefits of a subsequent on-demand analysis. For example, Stein et al. [32] lift an arbitrary abstract interpretation to be on-demand (and incremental) but still assume an upfront call graph.

The key insight of this work is that existing on-demand intraprocedural data flow analyses can *themselves* be leveraged in a black-box manner to bootstrap an on-demand construction of the call graph. The approach starts from an empty call graph and proceeds by interleaving *backward* data flow queries, resolving which values may flow to a given expression, and *forward* data flow queries, resolving which expressions a given value may flow to. Appropriately interleaving such queries allows us to bootstrap a sound overapproximation of a relevant part of the call graph. This technique allows us to automatically lift the results of on-demand analysis for first-order languages to higher-order ones, thereby further reducing the need for whole-program analysis. As a result, we can parametrically leverage progress on analysis of other challenging language features, allowing the on-demand call graph construction to benefit from the large body of work that already exists on analyzing various combinations of language features, including mutability. Concretely, we make the following contributions:

- We propose a language-agnostic construction for bootstrapping an on-demand call graph, parameterized by a pair of underlying backward and forward on-demand data flow analyses. The two analyses are treated as black boxes, except for the assumption that they can resolve backward and forward queries about data flows between values and expressions with respect to a partial call graph (Sect. 2).
- We present a formalization of our approach as an abstract domain combinator and determine sufficient assumptions on the input analysis and target language to guarantee soundness and termination (Sect. 3). To express soundness, we also introduce a notion of soundness up to a given call graph. This demonstrates a broader approach to formulating and proving soundness of on-demand analyses. Our theoretical results are mechanized in Isabelle/HOL [23]. The theory files are available online [27].
- We evaluate our technique on a prototype implementation that instantiates the approach for a subset of JavaScript, leveraging the intermediate representation of the JavaScript program analyzer TAJS [17], and using Synchronized Push-Down Systems (SPDS) [30] as the underlying data flow analyses. For our evaluation, we use a benchmark set of programs generated via property-based testing techniques, implemented using QuickCheck [5] (Sect. 4). Our results provide some evidence that on-demand call graph construction introduces time savings and explores a smaller portion of the program, when compared with whole-program call graph construction.

2 Overview of Our Approach

In this section, we give an informal overview of our approach to on-demand call graph construction, illustrating the main ideas on a small JavaScript example program (Fig. 1). The presentation in this section is intentionally kept high-level: we assume we are given a forward and a backward data flow analysis that can resolve queries with the help of an existing call graph, but we gloss over the details of how such queries are issued and the formal requirements to make our construction sound. These details are formalized in Sect. 3.

JavaScript programs frequently use callbacks, e.g., to handle user events or interactions between different components in UI frameworks, such as React [21]. Consider the JavaScript snippet in Fig. 1. The function `process` takes two callback arguments: it retrieves data by calling the callback `getData` and passes the result to the callback `handle`. Unfortunately, callbacks complicate the control-flow of programs, which makes them harder to reason about and increases the

```
1  function writeToLog(arg) {
2    log(arg);
3  }
4  function readUserData() {
5    // placeholder for a private
         source
6    return "private userData";
7  }
8  function process(getData, handler) {
9    var data = getData();
10   handler(data);
11 }
12 var handler = writeToLog;
13 process(readUserData, handler);
```

Fig. 1. A JavaScript program logging user data through callbacks

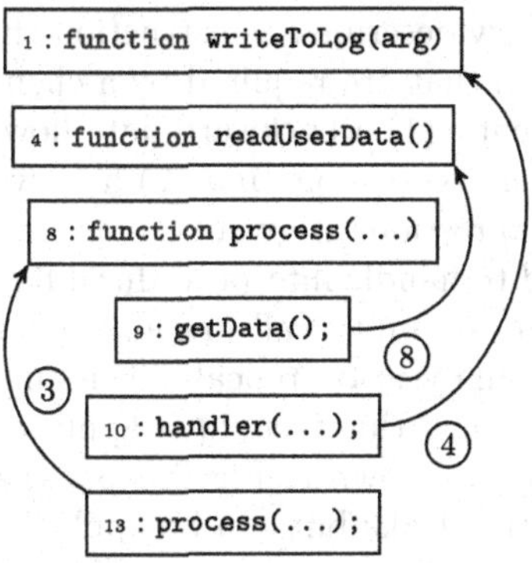

Fig. 2. The call graph constructed for the example program

Query	Step 0	1	2	3	4	5
⟨2, arg, ←⟩	∅	∅	∅	∅	∅	∅
↳⟨1, writeToLog, →⟩		∅	∅	∅	{handler@10}	{handler@10}
↳⟨13, process, ←⟩			∅	{process@8}	{process@8}	{process@8}
↳⟨9, getData, ←⟩						∅
↳⟨8, process, →⟩						

Query	Step 6	7	8	9
⟨2, arg, ←⟩	∅	∅	∅	{private@6}
↳⟨1, writeToLog, →⟩	{handler@10}	{handler@10}	{handler@10}	{handler@10}
↳⟨13, process, ←⟩	{process@8}	{process@8}	{process@8}	{process@8}
↳⟨9, getData, ←⟩	∅	∅	{readUserData@4}	{readUserData@4}
↳⟨8, process, →⟩	∅	{process@13}	{process@13}	{process@13}

Fig. 3. Step-by-step on-demand call graph construction

risk of introducing unintended and undesired behavior. Returning to our example program in Fig. 1, which logs sensitive user data. The leak is not immediately visible since it happens indirectly: `process` is invoked with the arguments `readUserData`, a function returning sensitive data (line 6), and `writeToLog`, a function writing its argument to a public sink (`log` on line 2). Thus, through a sequence of callbacks, the program leaks sensitive user data into a log.

Many existing analyses (e.g., [30]) can detect such leaks, but they typically require a call graph to track interprocedural flows. For example, in order to determine whether `arg` on line 2 might contain sensitive information, an analysis needs to identify all possible calls to `writeToLog`, including indirect ones, such as the call to `handler` on line 10. Constructing a call graph for programs involving callbacks is challenging, particularly for large code bases.

We now describe a construction that lazily computes only those parts of the call graph that are required by a client analysis. This construction relies on two components: (1) a backward data flow analysis that can track which values flow to a given expression, and (2) a forward data flow analysis that determines to which expressions a given value may flow to. Each data flow analysis is only assumed to handle interprocedural flows soundly up to a given call graph. Starting from an empty call graph, we can lazily compute call edges requested by a client analysis by repeatedly issuing queries to the two data flow analyses. We show how this technique applies to the example from Fig. 1; the resulting call graph is shown in Fig. 2. Note that the approach is not limited to tracking information leaks but can be applied to any client analysis requiring call graph information. Furthermore, two different analyses can be used for forward and backward queries as they only communicate through the call graph.

The table in Fig. 3 details the individual steps (1–9) needed to construct the call graph in Fig. 2: each edge in the call graph is labeled by the step number at which it is introduced. The table also tracks the queries issued to the underlying analysis during the process: *backward queries* of the form $\langle \ell, c, \leftarrow \rangle$ to determine which functions can flow to expression c on line ℓ, and *forward queries* of the form $\langle \ell, f, \rightarrow \rangle$ to determine which expressions a function f may flow to. An empty cell in the table indicates that a query has not been issued yet, while $\emptyset$ indicates that a query has been issued but has not yet produced any results. For each step, the table shows how the data flow analyses can make progress given the call graph computed up to this point. This call graph is derived in each step from the answers to queries found so far.

In addition, the table in Fig. 3 also shows the dependency between queries: the "↳" symbol before a query indicates that its result is required to solve an earlier query (i.e., one higher up in the dependency tree). For readability, the table is split into two segments, and should be read following the **Step** number.

Starting from the call to `log` inside function `writeToLog` (on line 2), the client annalysis wants to determine whether `arg` may contain sensitive data. Hence, it issues a backward query $\langle 2, \texttt{arg}, \leftarrow \rangle$ to determine which values flow to `arg` (step 0). Because `arg` is an argument to `writeToLog`, this in turn requires identifying call sites of `writeToLog`, for which a forward query $\langle 1, \texttt{writeToLog}, \rightarrow \rangle$ to identify call sites of `writeToLog` (step 1) is issued.

To answer forward queries about calls to a function f, the algorithm starts by finding syntactic references to f in the code and following the flow of f forwards from those points; such references can be found cheaply by analyzing the scope of variables in the program. In this case, the only such reference occurs in the top-level code, where `writeToLog` is assigned to `handler`, which is passed to `process`. To proceed in identifying call sites of `writeToLog`, the analysis needs to find out how the `handler` argument is used inside call targets. To do so, a query $\langle 13, \texttt{process}, \leftarrow \rangle$ is issued to resolve call targets of the call to `process` on line 13 (step 2). Since this is a direct call, the underlying backward data flow analysis resolves the possible call targets to the function `process` defined on line 8 (step 3); this also adds a call edge to our call graph and allows $\langle 1, \texttt{writeToLog}, \rightarrow \rangle$

to make progress by analyzing the body of `process` to find invocations of its `handler` argument. The data flow analysis then finds a call to `handler` in the body of `process` intraprocedurally, so a call edge is added from that expression to `writeToLog` (step 4). This in turn enables further progress on $\langle 2, \texttt{arg}, \leftarrow\rangle$ which can proceed backwards from this call to resolve what values flow to variable `data`, in this case discovering that the value of `getData` is assigned to `data`. Since `getData` is invoked as a function, another query $\langle 9, \texttt{getData}, \leftarrow\rangle$ needs to be issued to resolve callees of `getData` (step 5).

Because `getData` is passed as a parameter to `process`, further interprocedural analysis is needed to make progress and issue a forward query $\langle 8, \texttt{process}, \rightarrow\rangle$ to find call sites of `process` (step 6). The partial call graph already contains a call edge for `process`, but since this is the first forward query for `process`, there might be additional calls not yet discovered; in this case, however, `process` is only referenced by that call and no additional edges are found (step 7).

This call edge allows the query $\langle 9, \texttt{getData}, \leftarrow\rangle$ to make progress by determining that `getData` points to `readUserData` resulting in a new call edge from `getData()` to `readUserData` (step 8). This in turn triggers further progress of $\langle 2, \texttt{arg}, \leftarrow\rangle$ through the newly added call edge into the body of `readUserData` allowing the data flow analysis to discover that `arg` may contain data from a private source (shown as `private@6` in step 9). This completes the analysis.

The above process is fully on-demand without requiring an analysis of the entire program, aside from identifying syntactic references to functions (which can be determined cheaply through scoping). Additionally, the underlying data flow analyses are reused in a black-box fashion, as long as they allow resolving forward and backward queries up to a given call graph. Rerunning queries when new call edges are added can be avoided when the data flow analyses are incremental and can take newly discovered call edges into account without starting from scratch. Also note that queries make progress independently based on newly discovered call graph edges, rather than requiring to fully resolve each subquery before continuing with a parent query.

2.1 Precision

Different data flow analyses choose different trade-offs in terms of precision and scalability along various dimensions such as context-sensitivity [19], path-sensitivity [8], and how aliasing is handled [10]. For example consider the program in Fig. 4 making use of the JavaScript heap.

A client analysis may need to resolve the calls on lines 15 and 18. Following the algorithm outlined above, this would eventually result in trying to resolve what parameter `f` points to on line 2. A simple data flow analysis that does not track calling contexts may not distinguish between the objects whose `'func'` property is being assigned to in the body of `storeFunc` and therefore report both `function f()` and `function g()` as potential allocation sites of `retrieveFunc(objN)`, resulting in an over-approximate call graph. However, if a calling-context-sensitive analysis is used to resolve call expressions to call tar-

```
1 function storeFunc(obj, f) {
2     obj['func'] = f;
3 }
4 function retrieveFunc(obj) {
5     return obj['func'];
6 }
7 function f() {
8     // ...
9 }
10 function g() {
11     // ...
12 }
13 var obj1 = {};
14 storeFunc(obj1, f);
15 retrieveFunc(obj1)();
16 var obj2 = {};
17 storeFunc(obj2, g);
18 retrieveFunc(obj2)();
```

Fig. 4. JavaScript program with heap use

gets, the query $\langle 15, \texttt{retrieveFunc(obj1)}, \leftarrow \rangle$ returns `function f()` as the only callee, and $\langle 18, \texttt{retrieveFunc(obj2)}, \leftarrow \rangle$ is resolved to `function g()` only.

To see why this is the case, consider the subqueries created during analysis: The initial query $\langle 15, \texttt{retrieveFunc(obj1)}, \leftarrow \rangle$ starts with an empty calling context, the body of `retrieveFunc(obj1)` needs to be analyzed, leading to query $\langle 15, \texttt{retrieveFunc}, \leftarrow \rangle$ to identify the callee, which immediately yields `function retrieveFunc()`. Its analysis in turn yields the fact that the query result is the functions that may flow to `obj1['func']`. In order to analyze how `obj1` is modified by `storeFunc`, another query to resolve the call target on line 14 is needed, returning `function storeFunc()` immediately, adding a call edge to the call graph. This allows the initial query $\langle 15, \texttt{retrieveFunc(obj1)}, \leftarrow \rangle$ to proceed analyzing the body of `storeFunc`. Since we assumed the backward data flow analysis analysis to be calling-context-sensitive, this analysis will use the call on line 14 as the calling context, allowing it to determine that `f` was stored in `obj1['func']`. The calling context of the underlying analysis is preserved in the analysis of an individual query in the same manner as when the underlying analysis is invoked with a precomputed call graph instead.

The same argument applies regardless of the precision of the context sensitivity or how exactly the analysis represents calling contexts and generalizes to other forms of sensitivity, such as field sensitivity.

In more complex cases involving multiple queries, the constructed call graph may contain spurious edges. For example, consider a version of Fig. 1 where the top-level code makes two calls: `process(readUserData, dontWriteToLog)` and `process(readPublicData, writeToLog)`, such that `readPublicData` returns public information and `dontWriteToLog` does not log its argument. In this case, the call on line 10 is (correctly) resolved to call targets `dontWriteToLog` and `writeToLog`, and the call 9 is (correctly) resolved to call targets `readPublicData` and `readUserData`. A standard data flow analysis, when given this call graph, will report a warning when the flow is terminated in the body of `readUserData`. This problem can be addressed by augmenting queries with a context parameter specific to the underlying data flow analyses. In this case, when resolving backward query $\langle 2, \texttt{arg}, \leftarrow \rangle$, additional calling context could be passed to query $\langle 9, \texttt{getData}, \leftarrow \rangle$, eliminating the false positive, while making the analysis more costly as queries now may have to be resolved multiple times with different contexts. We leave such an extension as future work.

2.2 Termination and Soundness

Given that issuing a query may in return issue subqueries, cyclical query dependencies may arise during analysis. The algorithm avoids non-termination due to query cycles by not blocking on a subquery to complete before proceeding. Instead, the algorithm allows each query to make progress whenever any other query finds additional call edges relevant to another query. More precisely, if a query q_1 is processed, which triggers another query q_2 to be issued, and if q_2 in turn again issues q_1, the algorithm discovers that q_1 has already been issued and proceeds with other analysis paths of q_2 that do not depend on q_1 (if there are any). Whenever q_2 finds a call edge, this may allow q_1 to make further progress, in turn possibly allowing further progress of q_2. This process is guaranteed to terminate since, at each step, either the number of query results or the size of the call graph increases, yet both are ultimately bounded by the size of the program. The process is reminiscent of a Datalog-based analysis such as Doop [29] where new tuples being discovered for one relation, may trigger additional rules to apply for another relation, possibly in a mutually recursive fashion. More generally, it is an instance of a fixpoint computation on a finite domain.

Soundness is less straightforward to establish, as it requires issuing all necessary subqueries to eventually discover all the ways in which a given function may be invoked or to find all values flowing to a given expression. To show soundness, we make the assumption that the program under analysis is *closed*, that is, it neither uses reflection nor has entry points that take function arguments. Informally, to see why the on-demand call graph construction algorithm is sound in the absence of reflection, consider how a given function f might be invoked during execution of a closed program. In order for f to be invoked, at least one of the following must hold: (i) f is an entry point to the program, or (ii) a reference to f flows from f's definition to a call site. In other words, references to a function cannot be "guessed" and can be obtained either through a syntactic occurrence of the function's name or through the use of reflection. By starting from such syntactic references, the analysis can track where this function may flow. Similarly, by starting backwards from a call site and using forward analysis to find calls to the surrounding function, the analysis can discover all function definitions flowing to the call site.

Soundness in the presence of reflection requires a way to soundly identify locations where references to a given function may be obtained, for example using an existing reflection analysis [18,20,28]. In practice this may result in significant overapproximation, since analyzing many reflection facilities, for example in Java or JavaScript, requires reasoning about e.g., string computations. We discuss this topic in more detail in Sect. 3.6.

Further, handling programs that are incomplete, that is, programs with missing code such as libraries, is orthogonal to this work. Analyzing incomplete programs with this technique would require incorporating an existing approach for handling to missing code, such as models of missing library functions.

3 On-Demand Call Graph Soundness

In this section, we formally prove the soundness of our approach. We start by introducing a formal, semantic model of programs, call graphs and queries. We define the desired property, *on-demand call graph soundness*, that the call graphs produced by our analysis should satisfy with respect to the given program semantics. We then introduce our algorithm, in the form of a transition system defined by a set of inference rules. Finally, we state our soundness result—that call graphs generated by our rules for a given input program and set of input queries are on-demand sound—and sketch a proof. The full proof has been formalized using Isabelle/HOL and is available online [27].

We choose to depart from the usual abstract interpretation or data flow style presentation in two important ways. First, rather than starting from a concrete program syntax and semantics, we choose to model programs directly as the *collection of (concrete) call-traces* they may produce. We do so because our approach is fundamentally language-agnostic. The call-trace semantics serves as a generic starting point that abstracts over language-specific details while still fitting the abstract interpretation framework. Second, we do not introduce an abstract representation of sets of program traces as it would be used by a realistic analyzer. Instead, we model analyses directly in terms of the (semi-concrete) call-trace semantics. In practice, one does need an abstract domain, and the underlying analysis would typically provide one (e.g., we use SPDS in our prototype implementation). For the purpose of our soundness proof, however, we are primarily interested in the concretization of abstract states back into the concrete call-trace semantics. In our formalization, we therefore skip the indirection through an abstract domain and directly express the analyses as producing sets of concrete traces, while implementations—such as our prototype—use abstract representations that can be queried for various properties that we extract from traces directly in the formal model.

3.1 Program Semantics

Figure 5 defines the language of events in terms of a given set of expressions and functions. In addition, we assume a set of unique *syntactic reference points* where an initial reference to a function is obtained in the program.

$$
\begin{array}{rcl}
\text{call sites } c & \in & \mathbf{CallSite} \\
\text{functions } f & \in & \mathbf{Func} \\
\text{reference points } r & \in & \mathbf{RefPoint} \\
\text{events } e & \in & \mathbf{Event} \\
& ::= & \mathbf{call}(c, f, r) \\
& \mid & \mathbf{enter}(c, f) \\
& \mid & \mathbf{exit}(c, f) \\
& \mid & \mathbf{return}(c, f) \\
& \mid & \mathbf{ref}(f, r) \\
\text{traces } \tau & \in & \mathbf{Event}^* = \mathbf{Trace}
\end{array}
$$

Fig. 5. Syntax of traces and events

Events. Let **CallSite** be the finite set of *call sites* and **Func** the finite set of *function definitions* appearing in some program. Let **RefPoint** be a finite set of *reference points* containing unique identifiers r used to link function calls

```
function f() {           // enter(x(), f)
  return;                // exit(x(), f)
}
var x = f;               // ref(f, r)
x();                     // call(x(), f, r), return(x(), f)
```

Fig. 6. An example program annotated with the events it creates.

to locations where functions are referenced in the source code. To make our approach applicable to a wide range of languages, regardless of their memory model and other features, we model only the language semantics relevant to defining a call graph. To do so, we fix a set **Event** of *events*, where each event $e \in \textbf{Event}$ is one of the following:

- $\textbf{call}(c, f, r)$: A call to function f from call site c, where the reference to f was obtained by the reference point r.
- $\textbf{enter}(c, f)$: Entering the body of callee f, whose call originated from call site c.
- $\textbf{exit}(c, f)$: Exiting the body of callee f, whose call originated from call site c.
- $\textbf{return}(c, f)$: Returning to a call site of function f, whose call originated from call site c.
- $\textbf{ref}(f, r)$: Obtaining a reference to function f with reference point r. This can be either a syntactic reference to f or a use of reflection evaluating to f.

When a function is called, a **call** event is first emitted on the caller side, then an **enter** event is emitted on the callee side. Similarly, when the called function returns, an **exit** event is first created on the callee side, and then a **return** event is created on the caller side. Observe that both the **ref** event and the **call** event contain the reference point r. As we will see in Sect. 3.4, this allows linking the call to a specific reference to the callee that triggered the call. An example program and the created events can be seen in Fig. 6.

Traces and Programs. A *(call) trace* $\tau \in \textbf{Trace}$ is a finite sequence of events. We denote by $|\tau| \in \mathbb{N}$ the length of τ and by τ_i its i-th element, where $0 < i \leq |\tau|$. Given a pair of traces τ, τ', we denote their concatenation by $\tau \cdot \tau'$. We denote by $e_1 \cdots e_n$ the trace consisting of the events $e_1, \ldots, e_n$.

In the following, we fix a program and model its semantics as the (potentially infinite) set of call traces its executions may result in, written $\mathcal{S} \in \mathcal{P}(\textbf{Trace})$. We impose a few restrictions on $\mathcal{S}$ to exclude ill-formed traces that could not be generated by a real program: we assume that events on the caller side are followed by corresponding events on the callee side and vice versa, and that each call to a function f is preceded by obtaining a reference to f. Formally:

- $\mathcal{S}$ is prefix-closed, that is, for every trace $\tau \cdot \tau' \in \mathcal{S}$, the prefix τ is also in $\mathcal{S}$.
- For each trace $\tau \in \mathcal{S}$:
  - If $\tau_i = \textbf{enter}(c, f)$, then $i > 1$ and $\tau_{i-1} = \textbf{call}(c, f, r)$ for $r \in \textbf{RefPoint}$.
  - If $\tau_i = \textbf{call}(c, f, r)$ and $i + 1 \leq |\tau|$, then $\tau_{i+1} = \textbf{enter}(c, f)$.
  - If $\tau = \tau' \cdot \textbf{call}(c, f, r)$, then $\tau \cdot \textbf{enter}(c, f) \in \mathcal{S}$.
  - If $\tau_i = \textbf{exit}(c, f)$, then $\exists j \in \mathbb{N}$, with $0 < j < i$ where $\tau_j = \textbf{enter}(c, f)$

- If $\tau_i = \mathbf{return}(c, f)$, then $i > 1$ and $\tau_{i-1} = \mathbf{exit}(c, f)$.
- If $\tau_i = \mathbf{exit}(c, f)$ and $i + 1 \leq |\tau|$, then $\tau_{i+1} = \mathbf{return}(c, f)$.
- If $\tau_i = \mathbf{call}(c, f, r)$, then $\exists j \in \mathbb{N}$, with $0 < j < i$, such that $\tau_j = \mathbf{ref}(f, r)$.

3.2 Queries

A *client analysis* is an analysis that uses a call graph in order to reason about interprocedural control flow in a program. We distinguish two kinds of *call graph queries* that a client analysis can issue:

1. *callee query*, i.e., a call site $c \in \mathbf{CallSite}$, whose purpose is to find all functions $f \in \mathbf{Func}$ that may have be called at c.
2. *caller query*, i.e., a function $f \in \mathbf{Func}$, whose purpose is to find all call sites $c \in \mathbf{CallSite}$ from which the function f may be called.

Intuitively, callee queries are *backward* data flow queries: given a call site c, we want to find all the reference points in the program before c from which function values can flow to c. Conversely, caller queries are *forward* data flow queries: given a function f, we want to find all the reference points in the program from which f can flow to call sites later on in the program.

In each case, the query implicitly defines a subset of program subtraces containing the reference points of interest. Intuitively, these are the parts of program runs relevant to answering a query. Formally, we first define complete backward subtraces with both start and end points and then close the resulting set of subtraces under suffix: $\textit{complete-bwd-traces}(c) = \{\tau \mid \exists \tau_0 . \tau_0 \cdot \tau \in \mathcal{S} \wedge \tau = \mathbf{ref}(f, r) \cdot \_ \cdot \mathbf{call}(c, f, r)\}$ and $\textit{bwd-traces}(c) = \{\tau_2 \mid \exists \tau_1 . \tau_1 \cdot \tau_2 \in \textit{complete-bwd-traces}(c)\}$. Note that the reference point r is only used to delimit the backward traces relevant to a given call site c. Similarly, we define the set of *forward subtraces* $\textit{fwd-traces}(f)$ for a forward query f, as the subtraces starting with a reference to f, that is, $\textit{fwd-traces}(f) = \{\tau \mid \exists \tau_0 . \tau_0 \cdot \tau \in \mathcal{S} \wedge \tau = \mathbf{ref}(f, \_) \cdot \_\}$.

3.3 Call Graphs

To define an on-demand call graph, we first need the notions of a call graph and a whole-program call graph.

A *call graph* $G \subseteq \mathbf{CallSite} \times \mathbf{Func}$ is a directed graph whose vertices are call sites and functions and whose edges connect a call site $c \in \mathbf{CallSite}$ to a function $f \in \mathbf{Func}$. We write $\mathbf{CG} = \mathbf{CallSite} \times \mathbf{Func}$ for the set of all call graphs. We define the *whole-program call graph* of a program, written *whole-cg*, as the set of all pairs (c, f) that occur on a **call** event in some trace of the program semantics. Formally, $\textit{whole-cg} = \{(c, f) \mid \exists \tau \in \mathcal{S}, 0 < i \leq |\tau| . \tau_i = \mathbf{call}(c, f, \_)\}$.

Let $C \subseteq \mathbf{CallSite}$ and $F \subseteq \mathbf{Func}$ be the sets of callee and caller queries, respectively, that a client analysis issues while analyzing the program. Observe that the whole-program call graph *whole-cg* may be large and include many call edges (c, f) that are never used to answer a call graph query, i.e., such that $c \notin C$ or $f \notin F$. The goal of our on-demand approach is to compute a subgraph G of *whole-cg* containing all the edges needed to answer the queries in C and F.

To characterize such on-demand call graphs G, we introduce the notion of (C, F)-*soundness*. Intuitively, a (C, F)-sound on-demand approximation of a whole-program call graph contains at least the call graph edges necessary to answer all client queries. Formally:

Definition 1 (On-demand call graph soundness). *Let* $C \subseteq$ **CallSite** *and* $F \subseteq$ **Func** *be finite sets of callee and caller queries, respectively. A call graph* $G \subseteq$ **CallSite** $\times$ **Func** *is* on-demand call graph sound *w.r.t.* C *and* F *(or simply* (C, F)-sound*) iff every edge* $(c, f) \in$ *whole-cg is in* G *if either* $c \in C$ *or* $f \in F$*.*

3.4 Answering Call Graph Queries

To construct an on-demand call graph, our algorithm starts from an empty call graph, and gradually adds edges based on answers to the callee queries C and caller queries F issued by the client analysis. To find the answers of these queries, our approach is parameterized by two data flow analyses, defined as follows:

- a forward analysis $\mathscr{F}$: **CG** $\times$ **Func** $\rightarrow \mathcal{P}($**Trace**$)$, used to detect the call sites where a caller query $f \in F$ may have been called; and
- a backward analysis $\mathscr{B}$: **CG** $\times$ **CallSite** $\rightarrow \mathcal{P}($**Trace**$)$, used to detect the functions that a callee query $c \in C$ may call.

For example, to detect the functions that the callee query $x()$ on line 5 in Fig. 6 may call, our algorithm uses a backward data flow analysis to issue a backward query, whose answer contains the function f, defined on line 1. Once f is obtained as an answer, an edge $(x(), f)$ is added to the on-demand call graph.

To guarantee on-demand soundness of the call graph obtained by applying our algorithm, we assume the following about the underlying data flow analyses $\mathscr{F}$ and $\mathscr{B}$. Both data flow analyses are on-demand analyses, that is, intuitively they need only discover interprocedural data flows between a call site c and function f if the given partial call graph contains the edge (c, f). Their answers are an overapproximation of the set of subtraces relevant to a given call graph query. Note that $\mathscr{F}$ and $\mathscr{B}$ are modeled as functions returning sets of traces in order to reason about the soundness of the approach. In practice they would return abstract representations that concretize to sets of traces, which would provide interfaces to determine when data flows to function boundaries.

Next, we define the notions of backward and forward compatibility of a given trace with a partial call graph. These notions are used to restrict the traces that need to be overapproximated by the on-demand analyses $\mathscr{F}$ and $\mathscr{B}$, since they are allowed to only reason about parts of traces relevant to the given query. A trace τ is *forward-compatible* with a call graph G, written $compat^{\rightarrow}(G, \tau)$, if for any event **enter**(c, f) or **return**(c, f) in τ, it holds that $(c, f) \in G$. Similarly, a trace is *backward-compatible* with a call graph G, written $compat^{\leftarrow}(G, \tau)$, if for any event **call**(c, f, r) or **exit**(c, f) in τ, it holds that $(c, f) \in G$. Note that the compatibility definitions are slightly different depending on the direction of the analysis. In the forward case, encountering a call site is easy to identify, but determining the callee-side **enter** event requires resolving which function flows to the call site. In the backward case, reaching the entry point of a function is easy to identify, but not where this function was called. Also, when proceeding backwards, a call site is indicated first by a caller-side **return** event, but its callee needs to be found through additional analysis to identify the corresponding **exit** event. The precise definitions of $\mathit{compat}^{\rightarrow}(G, \tau)$ and $\mathit{compat}^{\leftarrow}(G, \tau)$ can be found in the Isabelle/HOL formalization [27].

Finally, we define the soundness requirements on $\mathscr{F}$ and $\mathscr{B}$. Given a relevant subtrace that is compatible with a given partial call graph, $\mathscr{F}$ should discover next possible event relevant to a query, whereas $\mathscr{B}$ should discover previous possible events. Intuitively, this captures that analyses can make progress on the part of the program that a partial call graph provides enough information about.

Formally, $\mathscr{F}$ is *forward-sound* iff $\{\tau \in \mathit{fwd\text{-}traces}(f) \mid \mathit{compat}^{\rightarrow}(G, \tau)\} \subseteq \mathscr{F}(G, f)$ and if $\tau \cdot \mathbf{enter}(c, f) \in \mathit{fwd\text{-}traces}(f)$ and $\mathit{compat}^{\rightarrow}(G, \tau)$, then $\tau \cdot \mathbf{enter}(c, f) \in \mathscr{F}(G, f)$. Note that this definition entails that $\mathscr{F}(G, f)$ over-approximates all references $\mathbf{ref}(f, r)$ to f as singleton traces $\mathbf{ref}(f, r)$ are compatible with any call graph. Similarly, $\mathscr{B}$ is *backward-sound* iff for any $\tau \in \mathit{bwd\text{-}traces}(c)$ such that $\tau = \tau' \cdot \mathbf{call}(c, f, r)$ and $\mathit{compat}^{\leftarrow}(G, \tau')$, then $\tau \in \mathscr{B}(G, c)$ and if $\mathbf{call}(c, f, r) \in \mathit{bwd\text{-}traces}(c)$, then $\mathbf{call}(c, f, r) \in \mathscr{B}(G, c)$.

If all the assumptions on $\mathscr{F}$ and $\mathscr{B}$ outlined in this section are satisfied, our call graph construction is sound. We make this precise next.

3.5 On-Demand Call Graph Construction as a Transition System

Our on-demand call graph construction algorithm maintains a state consisting of a triple (G, C, F), where G is the currently known call graph, C contains the set of relevant backward queries for callees of call sites $c \in C$ and F contains a set of relevant forward queries for callers of functions $f \in F$.

Figure 7 describes how call graph construction, starting from some call graph construction state can make progress. If the underlying data flow analyses discover a call for a query, either in the forward or backward direction, then we can add the corresponding call edge to the call graph (rules AddFwdCallEdge and AddBwdCallEdge). Note that discovering a call in the forward direction is indicated by an $\mathbf{enter}(\cdot, \cdot)$ event, whereas in the backward direction, this is indicated by a $\mathbf{call}(\cdot, \cdot, \cdot)$ event instead. This difference results from the fact that when proceeding forwards through a function, the caller-side **call** event is always compatible with any partial call graph, whereas discovering the corresponding callee-side **enter** event must have been resolved by the forward analysis. Similarly, in the backward direction, the **enter** event is backward-compatible with any call graph, while the corresponding **call** event is not. The remaining rules describe which additional queries to issue: When reaching a call in either forward or backward direction, the call target needs to be resolved through an additional query (rules ReachedCallBwds and ReachedCallFwds); these rules again exhibit the same difference regarding **enter** and **call** events as for adding call edges to the call graph. Lastly, when reaching the beginning of a function going backwards or the end of a function going forwards, call sites of the containing function need to be resolved through another query to make progress.

$$\frac{\textsc{AddFwdCallEdge}\quad f \in F \qquad \tau \cdot \mathbf{enter}(c,f) \in \mathscr{F}(G,f) \qquad (c,f) \notin G}{(G,C,F) \rightsquigarrow (\{(c,f)\} \cup G, C, F)}$$

$$\frac{\textsc{AddBwdCallEdge}\quad c \in C \qquad \mathbf{ref}(f,r) \cdot \tau \cdot \mathbf{call}(c,f,r) \in \mathscr{B}(G,c) \qquad (c,f) \notin G}{(G,C,F) \rightsquigarrow (\{(c,f)\} \cup G, C, F)}$$

$$\frac{\textsc{ReachedCallFwds}\quad f \in F \tau \cdot \mathbf{call}(c',f',r') \in \mathscr{F}(G,f) \qquad c' \notin C}{(G,C,F) \rightsquigarrow (G, C \cup \{c'\}, F)}$$

$$\frac{\textsc{ReachedCallBwds}\quad c \in C \qquad \mathbf{return}(c',f') \cdot \tau \in \mathscr{B}(G,c) \qquad c' \notin C}{(G,C,F) \rightsquigarrow (G, C \cup \{c'\}, F)}$$

$$\frac{\textsc{ReachedEnterBwds}\quad c \in C \qquad \mathbf{enter}(c',f') \cdot \tau' \in \mathscr{B}(G,c) \qquad f' \notin F}{(G,C,F) \rightsquigarrow (G, C, F \cup \{f'\})}$$

$$\frac{\textsc{ReachedExitFwds}\quad f \in F \qquad \tau \cdot \mathbf{exit}(c,f') \in \mathscr{F}(G,f) \qquad f' \notin F}{(G,C,F) \rightsquigarrow (G, C, F \cup \{f'\})}$$

Fig. 7. On-Demand Call Graph Construction as a transition system

The transition system is intentionally non-deterministic: At each point, multiple rules may be applicable to make progress. The rules can be applied in any order to reach an overapproximation of the relevant parts of the real call graph. We prove soundness of the approach by stating that once the algorithm reaches a fixed point, the call graph is on-demand sound w.r.t. the answered queries.

Theorem 1 (On-Demand Soundness). *For any call graph construction state (G, C, F), if $(G, C, F) \rightsquigarrow^* (G', C', F') \not\rightsquigarrow$, then G' is (C', F')-sound.*

The analysis starts with an empty call graph and non-empty query sets, relying on the special case of the theorem where $G = \emptyset$. As $\rightsquigarrow$ is monotone (discussed below), any queries issued as part of C or F are still present in C' or F'. Based on the intuitions presented in Sect. 2.2, we present a proof sketch summarizing the key techniques. Some definitions and lemma statements are simplified. The full details can be found in the Isabelle/HOL formalization [27].

Proof (sketch). The proof proceeds in four main steps:

1. We first define an intermediate collecting semantics $\rightarrowtail$ that adds subtraces and new queries in the same order as $\rightsquigarrow$ adds call edges and queries. The intermediate collecting semantics maintains the state of forward queries (resp. backward queries) as partial maps $\mathcal{F}$ (resp. $\mathcal{B}$) from functions $f \in \mathbf{Func}$ (resp.

$c \in$ **CallSite**) to subsets of *fwd-traces*(f) (resp. *bwd-traces*(c)). Each step $(\mathcal{F}, \mathcal{B}) \rightarrowtail (\mathcal{F}', \mathcal{B}')$ either adds an event to the end (resp. beginning) of a set in the co-domain of either map. If the event requires no other queries (such as an $\mathbf{ref}(f, r)$ event), then it is added directly. If the new event requires resolving another query (such as function call events), then it is only added if the query it depends on has made enough progress. Alternatively, a step may issue an additional query under similar conditions as $\rightsquigarrow$. Note that this intermediate semantics is more precise as only real events are added to traces. This also renders it not computable.

2. We proceed by proving that $\rightsquigarrow$ overapproximates $\rightarrowtail$. Concretely, we show that if $(\mathcal{F}, \mathcal{B}) \rightarrowtail (\mathcal{F}', \mathcal{B}')$, and $\gamma((G, C, F)) = (\mathcal{F}, \mathcal{B})$, then there exists a new call graph construction state (G', C', F') such that $(G, C, F) \rightsquigarrow (G', C', F')$ and $(\mathcal{F}', \mathcal{B}') \sqsubseteq \gamma((G', C', F'))$, where we write γ for the concretization of a call graph construction state (G, C, F) into subsets of traces for each forward and backward query $(\mathcal{F}, \mathcal{B})$ and $\sqsubseteq$ for a lifting of subset inclusion of traces for each forward and backward query. This is proven using a straightforward induction on $(\mathcal{F}, \mathcal{B}) \rightarrowtail (\mathcal{F}', \mathcal{B}')$.
3. Next, we show that a fixed point of $\rightarrowtail$ approximates all subtraces for the queries that were generated. For this, we need an intermediate definition of well-formedness on the events in the subtraces being discovered. Formally, if $(\mathcal{F}, \mathcal{B}) \not\rightarrowtail$, and $(\mathcal{F}, \mathcal{B})$ is *well-formed*, then for each f such that $\mathcal{F}(f) = T_f$, we have *fwd-traces*$(f) \subseteq T_f$. Similarly, if $\mathcal{B}(c) = T_b$, then it holds that *bwd-traces*$(c) \subseteq T_b$. Well-formedness for forward queries requires that all singleton traces $[\mathbf{ref}(f, \cdot)]$ are included in T_f and that T_f is prefix-closed. Similarly, well-formed backward sets T_b need to include the singleton suffixes of *bwd-traces*(c) in addition to being suffix-closed. To show that a fixed point of $\rightarrowtail$ approximates all subtraces, we proceed by contradiction. Suppose that after reaching a fixed point $(\mathcal{F}, \mathcal{B})$ there is a missing event for a query; hence there must be an earlier missing event. This means there must either be another possible transition $\rightarrowtail$ or an earlier missing event, yielding a contradiction in either case.
4. Combining 2 and 3, we obtain that a fixed point of $\rightsquigarrow$ overapproximates the relevant subset of the whole-program call graph of a given program.

Note that termination follows from the assumption that a fixed program has a finite number of functions and call sites, combined with the monotonicity of $\rightsquigarrow$:

Lemma 1 (Monotonicity). *If* $(G, C, F) \rightsquigarrow (G', C', F')$, *then* $(G, C, F) \sqsubset (G', C', F')$, *where* $\sqsubset$ *denotes lexicographic tuple ordering.*

3.6 Discussion

Reflection. The above algorithm relies on correctly identifying all references to a function f for which call sites need to be determined. In languages without reflection, this can be done easily by identifying where f is referenced syntactically, taking into account scoping rules. However, many languages including Java and JavaScript allow obtaining a reference to a function through the use of reflection. The above definitions assume that an $\mathscr{F}$ correctly overapproximates where a function might be referenced, which entails a reflection analysis in order to soundly analyze programs in the presence of reflection.

Implementation Considerations. We model $\mathscr{F}$ and $\mathscr{B}$ as returning sets of traces that on-demand call graph constructions inspects for certain events. In a real-world implementation, data flow analyses would provide an interface signaling discovered data flows between reference points and call sites as well to a function boundary. Our prototype, described in Sect. 4, interfaces with the automata-based abstraction of SPDS to detect when to issue additional queries or add call graph edges through the listener functionality provided by SPDS.

Non-termination. In the formal model, non-terminating programs are represented as infinite sets of finite traces. In order for an underlying data flow analysis to be considered sound, such infinite sets need to be over-approximated to satisfy the conditions of forward or backward soundness. In practice, this requires a suitable finite representation of an infinite set of traces. For example, consider the program |while(true) f(); |, producing an infinite sequence of call events $\mathbf{call}(f(), f, r)$ for some reference point r along with associated **enter**, **exit**, and **return** events. Assume further that the call target of `f()` produces no additional events. Its denotation is the infinite set $\{S, S \cdot S, S \cdot S \cdot S, \dots\}$ where $S = \mathbf{call}(f, f, r) \cdot \mathbf{enter}(f(), f) \cdot \mathbf{exit}(f(), f) \cdot \mathbf{return}(f(), f)$.

To satisfy the conditions of backward soundness, a backward data flow analysis $\mathscr{B}$ has to include any trace S^n in the set $\mathscr{B}(G, f())$. As discussed, a practical implementation will therefore have to finitely represent an infinite set. For example, a backward analysis may map program locations to potential call targets—in this case mapping `f()` to the function f. In SPDS, this example can be represented using a loop in the call push-down system, adding an edge from `f()` to itself. Similar considerations apply to sound forward data flow analyses.

4 Evaluation

The main research question we explore with our experimental evaluation concerns scalability: A key promise of on-demand call graph construction is the application of more expensive analyses to only relevant parts of a code base, rather than the entire program. This unlocks the possibility to apply analyses that are too expensive to use with a whole-program approach.

In addition to a set of initial queries, issued for the call sites of interest in a given program, our on-demand call graph construction issues queries on which the initial queries depend. As a result, how much of a program is explored during analysis depends on the structure of the program and cannot be bounded upfront—in the worst case, the algorithm may still produce the whole-program call graph. Our experiments evaluate how many queries are resolved in total, for initial sets of various sizes, and report on the potential time savings from on-demand analysis on a set of synthetic benchmarks. The prototype can be found online [27].

Implementation. We implemented the on-demand call graph construction algorithm in a prototype, called MERLIN, for a limited subset of JavaScript. The implementation uses the TAJS [17] intermediate representation and Synchronized Push-Down Systems (SPDS) [30] as the underlying data flow analysis for both forward and backward queries. To support (a subset of) JavaScript in SPDS, the implementation adds backward and forward flow functions on top of an existing language-agnostic SPDS implementation [6]. The implementation supports basic JavaScript features, such as assignments, object allocation and function calls, including closures and accounting for mutability of captured variables. Instantiating SPDS to a sufficiently large subset of JavaScript to analyze real-world code is out of scope for this paper.

To compute a fixed point, MERLIN maintains a set of queries, in addition to the current call graph. A query in this context is represented as a synchronized pushdown system starting from a reference to a function or an call site, depending on the query. Individual queries subscribe to updates about (i) callees of a particular call site, or (ii) call sites of a particular function discovered by other queries. An update may result in adding further transitions in a query's SPDS in the current call graph. Objects are also tracked using SPDS.

When a function entry point is reached by a backward query, or a return statement of a function is reached by a forward query, a new forward query is issued to find call sites of that function. Similarly, when a function call is reached by either a forward or a backward query, a new backward query is issued to resolve possible callees. Based on the results of these new queries, the analysis continues at the function's call sites or a call site's callees.

The asynchronous saturation process described in Sect. 2 is implemented using a reactive programming [12] approach implemented using the Java Virtual Machine's `ForkJoinPool` to resolve queries concurrently. This also enables parallel execution of multiple queries on multi-core machines.

Synthetic Benchmarks. We evaluate MERLIN against a set of synthetic benchmarks generated using the property-based testing library QuickCheck [5]. To capture non-trivial dependencies between the call graph queries, the generated programs heavily use higher-order functions, and treat functions as first class values, reflecting the dynamic nature of JavaScript programs. That is, functions are passed along a chain of functions, both as arguments and return values, before they are eventually called.

Each generated program has between 6000 and 10000 lines of code, including whitespace and braces. Figure 8 shows a (simplified) excerpt from an example in the benchmark set, where function `chainTarget106` is returned from a function via `returnAFunc100`, the return value of which is invoked in `fun57`. The benchmarks contain between 600 and 900 functions, with higher-order call chains of up to length 4. We leave an investigation of typical usage patterns of higher-order functions in JavaScript for future work.

```
function fun57(arg57) {
    ((chainTarget106)((fun57)((retAFunc100)(someIdentifier))))(someIdentifier
        );
}
function retAFunc100(arg615) {
    return chainTarget106;
}
function chainTarget106(arg614) {}
```

Fig. 8. Example output by QuickCheck-based benchmark generator

Results. We ran the experiments on an AWS EC2 instance of type `c5.4xlarge` with Intel Xeon Platinum 8124M CPU with 16 cores and 32 GiB memory. We use Correto version 17.0.6.10.1 with a stack size limit of 512 MiB and heap size limit of 16 GiB. For each program, MERLIN's analysis is run multiple times, with increasing the number of initial call graph queries in each iteration. The set of initial call graph queries is constructed by randomly selecting call sites occurring in the benchmark programs. This simulates a client analysis that issues queries for a subset of all call sites in the program. In the limit, issuing a query for every function call approximates a whole-program analysis. Our experiments also simulate a whole-program analysis by querying all call sites in the program.

The results of running MERLIN on the synthetic benchmarks are shown in Fig. 9. Overall, the wall clock time (Fig. 9a) grows super-linearly with the number of resolved queries. The number of queries that need to be resolved (Fig. 9d) increases with the number of initial queries, matching the intuitive expectation that on-demand call graph construction explores only a part of the program on our benchmark set. Similarly, the wall clock time increases with the number of resolved queries, albeit to a lesser extent due to the use of parallelism. Memory consumption (Fig. 9b) remains relatively constant, indicating a significant fixed memory cost in our implementation.

As shown in Fig. 9a, whole-program analysis results (indicated by black boxes) often require less wall clock time to resolve than smaller initial sets of queries. This effect is due to the use of parallelism in the prototype: As demonstrated by Fig. 9c, whole-program analysis runs require as much or more CPU time to be resolved. However, but due to starting the analysis for all queries in parallel, they make better use of available CPU cores in the same span of wall clock time. This effect is somewhat in line with intuitive expectations: If a smaller set of queries is requested, there are less unrelated data flows to analyze, lowering the opportunities for parallelism. On the contrary, a whole-program analysis benefits from parallelism because many paths through a program can be analyzed independently. We double-check this explanation by reporting single-threaded results on the same benchmark set in Appendix A. This observation allows client analyses to fine-tune the strategy for call graph construction depending on the

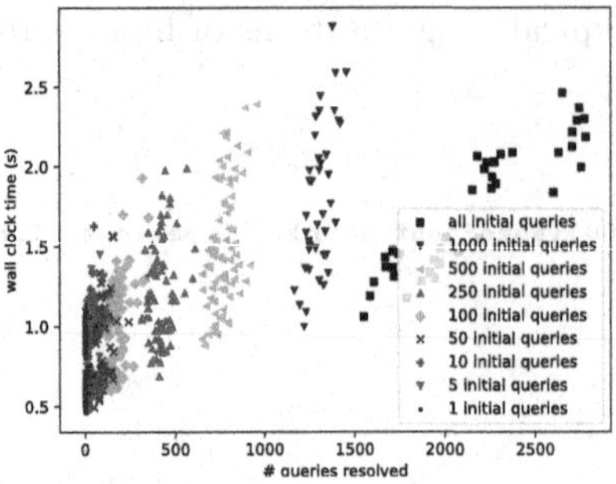

(a) Wall clock time

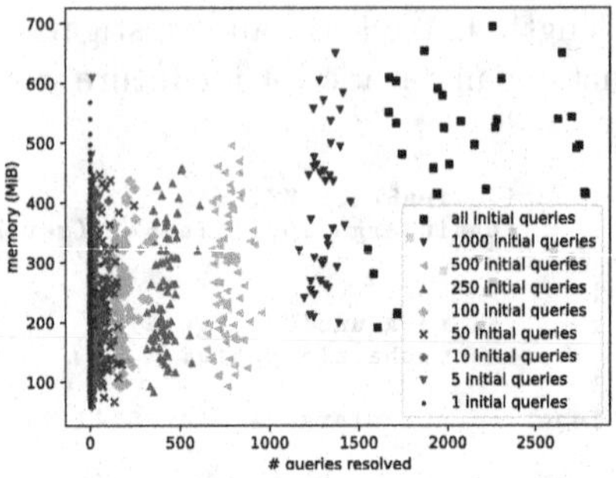

(b) Memory usage per set of initial queries

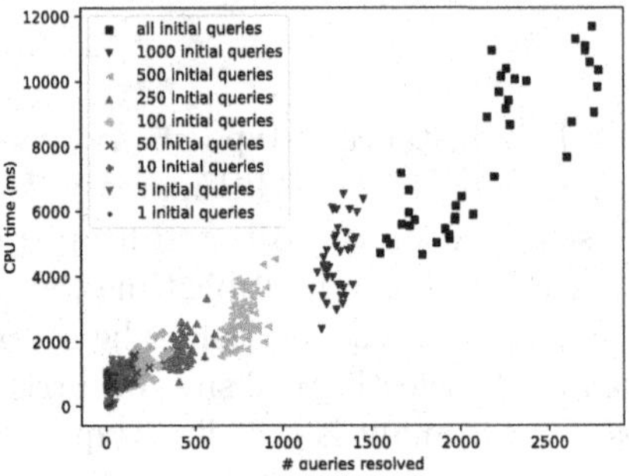

(c) CPU time

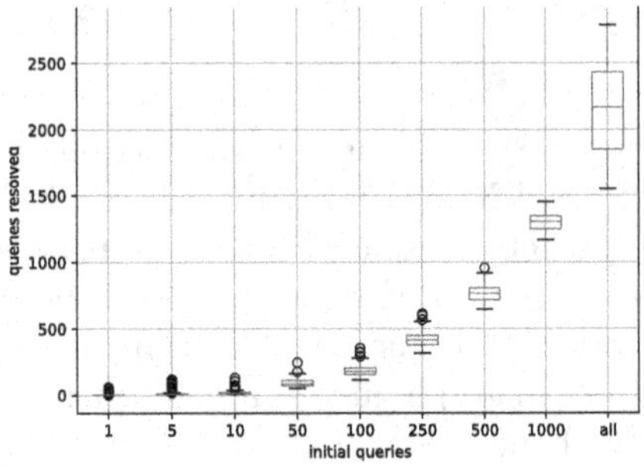

(d) Average number of queries resolved

Fig. 9. Running MERLIN on synthetic benchmarks. The x-axis shows the size of each initial query set. The data points depict executions on different benchmark files. For each initial query set size, the same file is randomly sampled multiple times. Each initial query set is run independently without keeping intermediate results between runs.

scenario. On an end-user machine, using all available CPU cores may degrade the overall system performance too much to be viable, making on-demand analysis preferable. Electricity usage, environmental concerns, and battery life are other factors that make reducing CPU time relevant.

While the reduction in wall clock time based on the number queries to be resolved is often not significant compared to a whole-program analysis with the same technique, this data provides evidence that only a part of the program needs to be explored in order to answer a limited set of call graph queries. This effect may become more relevant in very large code bases or when using highly precise, expensive data flow analyses.

Threats to Validity. The memory usage reported in Fig. 9 is subject to measurement inaccuracies. CPU time and memory usage were measured using JVM internals with varying levels of guarantees. For example, memory usage is measured by first asking the JVM to perform garbage collection via `System.gc()`, but this is not guaranteed to garbage-collect all unreachable objects in the JVM heap. As a result, memory usage may include state produced by previous analysis batches. Additionally, while all the internal state of all SPDS solvers is retained when measuring the memory consumption, there may be temporary data that is garbage-collected before the memory measurement is taken.

Limitations. As supporting the whole JavaScript langauge in SPDS is out of scope for this paper, MERLIN currently does not support all JavaScript language features, motivating evaluation on synthetic benchmarks that may not be representative of real-world JavaScript code. Instead, MERLIN presents an initial evaluation of whether this approach can be implemented using a realistic state-of-the-art data flow analysis. As a result, the above experiments do not show how much time is saved on real-world code, given the fact that many common JavaScript features are deliberately not used in the synthetic benchmark code, and the generated programs may use patterns that may not translate to patterns found in real-world code. Nevertheless, the subset of JavaScript that MERLIN supports and the set of synthetic benchmarks is sufficient to show the usefulness of on-demand call graph construction. We list the current limitations of MERLIN below, and consider addressing them as part of future work.

In the current implementation, MERLIN does not support dynamic property access, prototype inheritance, reflection, and JavaScript builtins. This may produce unsound results in practice. Moreover, context sharing between different queries is limited, even though this is in principle supported by the SPDS approach; this results in lower precision of our results than necessary. Since MERLIN reuses the TAJS [17] intermediate interpretation, it can only directly analyze EcmaScript 5 [11] programs, which in practice can be mitigated by transpiling code written in newer EcmaScript dialects using tools such as Babel [1].

Finally, MERLIN produces a large number of conceptually unnecessary queries, SPDS represents possible call stacks abstractly using a push-down system, where the system's stack contains program locations. To avoid querying for call sites when reaching a function boundary, the pushdown system could be consulted to approximate the possible elements at the top of the stack at this location. While SPDS constructs another automaton encoding the reachable configurations of the pushdown system using an existing approach [3,13], it is unclear whether this automaton allows extracting the required information. We leave leveraging call stack abstraction of SPDS to support this as future work.

5 Related Work

Demand Control-Flow Analysis [15] (Demand-CFA) tackles the problem of performing the functional equivalent of on-demand call graph construction for a purely functional lambda calculus, and similarly divides its approach into interdependent forward and backward queries. The key distinguishing feature of our work is providing a parameterized construction leveraging data flow analyses to support impure languages with non-functional features. In contrast, Demand-CFA fixes the specific analyses used for resolving expressions and finding call sites. This approach is sufficient in the context of a purely functional language, but translation to a language with imperative features introduces a large design space of how to trade-off precision and scalability. By providing a parameterized approach, we sidestep such trade-offs and provide a modular building block.

Another line of work aims to make whole-program call graph construction scalable enough to apply to large code bases. A prominent example is Class-Hierarchy Analysis [7] (CHA) and subsequent work [2] in the context of object-oriented languages. CHA achieves scalability by making use of nominal typing to resolve higher-order behavior resulting from dynamic dispatch. Since all subtyping relationships are explicit in the syntax (for example, in the form of `extends` and `implements` clauses in Java), this is straightforward to compute efficiently. However, this approach is harder to apply to languages that use functions as first-class values without potentially introducing a large amount of imprecision. For example, given a higher-order function accepting a function of type `int -> int` as input, considering each function with this type (out of potentially many) as a potential callee in the body of the higher-order function might lead to many spurious call edges in practice. Using functions as first-class values is common practice in JavaScript, and is becoming common in more languages, for example through Java's introduction of lambda expressions [25] and streams [24]. Similarly, fast and scalable approaches exist for whole-program JavaScript call graph construction. Feldthaus et al. [14] present an underapproximate call graph construction algorithm for JavaScript that scales to usage inside an integrated development environment (IDE), which places strict requirements on how fast the analysis can be performed. However, in order to achieve this level of performance, the approach is intentionally unsound and misses call edges. Nielsen et. al [22] also present a highly scalable approach to call graph construction sacrificing soundness in some cases. While our implementation is also unsound in the presence of the same features that cause unsoundness in their work, our theoretical approach provides strong soundness guarantees.

Another well-known approach is variable-type analysis (VTA) [33], which produces reasonably scalable whole-program call graphs in the presence of higher-order functions and heap objects without requiring deep interleavings between the call graph construction and the data flow analysis. However, VTA's performance may render it too slow in certain contexts, e.g. for in-IDE use on large applications. To achieve this level of scalability, VTA's precision is constrained by its heap abstraction, while our approach allows for the use of more precise heap abstractions while hopefully remaining scalable for large code bases.

A key motivation for our work is the common theme of other analysis approaches assuming a precomputed call graph. Such examples include practical bug detection tools such as Infer [4], as well as theoretical results on Demanded Abstract Interpretation [32] that allow turning whole-program analyses into demand-driven analyses transparently. The latter example in particular may allow turning a whole-program data flow analysis into a fully demand-driven analysis by (i) obtaining an on-demand, but still call-graph-dependent, data flow analysis by applying Demanded Abstract Interpretation, and (ii) lifting the call graph requirement using the approach presented in this paper.

Our work relies on the existence of sufficiently precise on-demand data flow analyses, an area that has seen improvements recently. Notably, Synchronized Push-Down Systems [30] reconcile the conflict between precise tracking of field accesses and calling contexts. Boomerang [31] provides another on-demand data flow analysis supporting exactly the same forward and backward queries required to instantiate our approach.

Our approach of issuing additional queries that allow each other to make progress in a mutually recursive fashion is inspired by Datalog-based analyses such as Doop [29] and CodeQL [16]. Datalog analyses, however, directly build a call graph together with a specific points-to analysis and do not typically allow plugging in another points-to analysis instead. Further, we are not aware of on-demand analyses implemented in Datalog. The formalization of our approach may also provide a starting point to reason about soundness of Datalog-based analyses, which has not been extensively studied formally.

6 Conclusions

We present an approach for bootstrapping an on-demand call graph, leveraging underlying forward and backward data flow analyses. Our approach is parametric in the underlying analyses assuming only a notion of soundness up to a partial call graph. Based on this notion of soundness, we formalize our call graph construction and prove it sound (mechanized in Isabelle/HOL). Our prototype MERLIN implements this approach for a subset of JavaScript using Synchronized Push-Down Systems [30] for both forward and backward data flow analysis. We evaluate MERLIN on a synthetic benchmark set. The results indicate that on-demand call graph construction indeed has the potential to improve scalability by only exploring the relevant part of programs in the benchmark.

Acknowledgments. This paper describes work performed in part while David Seekatz was an Applied Scientist Intern at Amazon. Franco Raimondi holds concurrent appointments at Middlesex University and as an Amazon Scholar. Bor-Yuh Evan Chang holds concurrent appointments at the University of Colorado Boulder and as an Amazon Scholar. This paper describes work performed at Amazon and is not associated with Middlesex University nor the University of Colorado Boulder.

We are particularly grateful to Fangyi Zhou and Martin Schaef for their discussions and feedback on several drafts of this paper. We thank the anonymous reviewers for their helpful comments and feedback. This research was conducted in the Prime Video Automated Reasoning team and we are grateful to the entire team for their support.

A Single-Threaded Performance Results

Figure 10 shows the benchmark results when run on a single core, demonstrating that the faster whole-program results are caused by better CPU utilization.

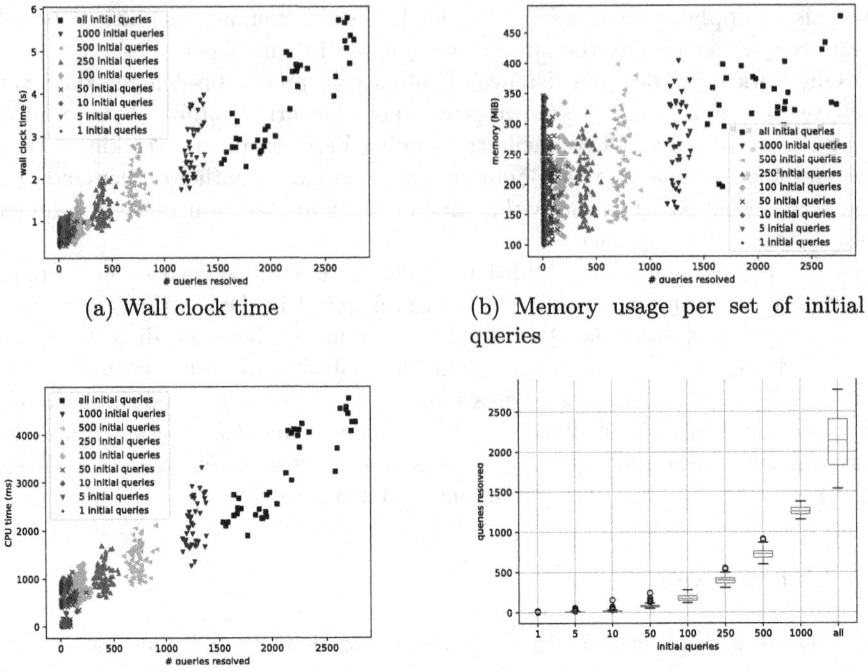

(a) Wall clock time

(b) Memory usage per set of initial queries

(c) CPU time

(d) Average number of queries resolved

Fig. 10. Single-threaded performance results

References

1. Babel: Babel. https://babeljs.io/. Accessed 01 Apr 2023
2. Bacon, D.F., Sweeney, P.F.: Fast static analysis of C++ virtual function calls. In: Anderson, L., Coplien, J. (eds.) Proceedings of the 1996 ACM SIGPLAN Conference on Object-Oriented Programming Systems, Languages & Applications (OOPSLA 1996), San Jose, California, USA, 6–10 October 1996, pp. 324–341. ACM (1996)
3. Bouajjani, A., Esparza, J., Maler, O.: Reachability analysis of pushdown automata: application to model-checking. In: Mazurkiewicz, A., Winkowski, J. (eds.) CONCUR 1997. LNCS, vol. 1243, pp. 135–150. Springer, Heidelberg (1997). https://doi.org/10.1007/3-540-63141-0_10
4. Calcagno, C., Distefano, D.: Infer: an automatic program verifier for memory safety of C programs. In: Bobaru, M., Havelund, K., Holzmann, G.J., Joshi, R. (eds.) NFM 2011. LNCS, vol. 6617, pp. 459–465. Springer, Heidelberg (2011). https://doi.org/10.1007/978-3-642-20398-5_33
5. Claessen, K., Hughes, J.: Quickcheck: a lightweight tool for random testing of Haskell programs. In: Odersky, M., Wadler, P. (eds.) Proceedings of the Fifth ACM SIGPLAN International Conference on Functional Programming (ICFP 2000), Montreal, Canada, 18–21 September 2000, pp. 268–279. ACM (2000)

6. CodeShield: de.fraunhofer.iem.SPDS. https://github.com/codeshield-security/spds. Accessed 30 Jan 2022
7. Dean, J., Grove, D., Chambers, C.: Optimization of object-oriented programs using static class hierarchy analysis. In: Tokoro, M., Pareschi, R. (eds.) ECOOP 1995. LNCS, vol. 952, pp. 77–101. Springer, Heidelberg (1995). https://doi.org/10.1007/3-540-49538-X_5
8. Dillig, I., Dillig, T., Aiken, A.: Sound, complete and scalable path-sensitive analysis. In: Gupta, R., Amarasinghe, S.P. (eds.) Proceedings of the ACM SIGPLAN 2008 Conference on Programming Language Design and Implementation, Tucson, AZ, USA, 7–13 June 2008, pp. 270–280. ACM (2008)
9. Distefano, D., Fähndrich, M., Logozzo, F., O'Hearn, P.W.: Scaling static analyses at Facebook. Commun. ACM **62**(8), 62–70 (2019). https://doi.org/10.1145/3338112
10. Diwan, A., McKinley, K.S., Moss, J.E.B.: Type-based alias analysis. In: Davidson, J.W., Cooper, K.D., Berman, A.M. (eds.) Proceedings of the ACM SIGPLAN 1998 Conference on Programming Language Design and Implementation (PLDI), Montreal, Canada, 17–19 June 1998, pp. 106–117. ACM (1998)
11. ECMA International: ECMAScript language specification, 5th edition (2011). https://www.ecma-international.org/ecma-262/5.1/
12. Elliott, C., Hudak, P.: Functional reactive animation. In: Jones, S.L.P., Tofte, M., Berman, A.M. (eds.) Proceedings of the 1997 ACM SIGPLAN International Conference on Functional Programming (ICFP 1997), Amsterdam, The Netherlands, 9–11 June 1997, pp. 263–273. ACM (1997)
13. Esparza, J., Hansel, D., Rossmanith, P., Schwoon, S.: Efficient algorithms for model checking pushdown systems. In: Emerson, E.A., Sistla, A.P. (eds.) CAV 2000. LNCS, vol. 1855, pp. 232–247. Springer, Heidelberg (2000). https://doi.org/10.1007/10722167_20
14. Feldthaus, A., Schäfer, M., Sridharan, M., Dolby, J., Tip, F.: Efficient construction of approximate call graphs for JavaScript IDE services. In: Notkin, D., Cheng, B.H.C., Pohl, K. (eds.) 35th International Conference on Software Engineering, ICSE 2013, San Francisco, CA, USA, 18–26 May 2013, pp. 752–761. IEEE Computer Society (2013)
15. Germane, K., McCarthy, J., Adams, M.D., Might, M.: Demand control-flow analysis. In: Enea, C., Piskac, R. (eds.) VMCAI 2019. LNCS, vol. 11388, pp. 226–246. Springer, Cham (2019). https://doi.org/10.1007/978-3-030-11245-5_11
16. GitHub: CodeQL. https://codeql.github.com/. Accessed 29 Jan 2022
17. Jensen, S.H., Møller, A., Thiemann, P.: Type analysis for Javascript. In: Palsberg, J., Su, Z. (eds.) SAS 2009. LNCS, vol. 5673, pp. 238–255. Springer, Heidelberg (2009). https://doi.org/10.1007/978-3-642-03237-0_17
18. Landman, D., Serebrenik, A., Vinju, J.J.: Challenges for static analysis of Java reflection: literature review and empirical study. In: Uchitel, S., Orso, A., Robillard, M.P. (eds.) Proceedings of the 39th International Conference on Software Engineering, ICSE 2017, Buenos Aires, Argentina, 20–28 May 2017, pp. 507–518. IEEE/ACM (2017)
19. Lhoták, O., Hendren, L.: Context-sensitive points-to analysis: is it worth it? In: Mycroft, A., Zeller, A. (eds.) CC 2006. LNCS, vol. 3923, pp. 47–64. Springer, Heidelberg (2006). https://doi.org/10.1007/11688839_5
20. Li, Y., Tan, T., Xue, J.: Understanding and analyzing Java reflection. ACM Trans. Softw. Eng. Methodol. **28**(2), 7:1-7:50 (2019)
21. Meta: React. https://reactjs.org/. Accessed 06 Feb 2022

22. Nielsen, B.B., Torp, M.T., Møller, A.: Modular call graph construction for security scanning of Node.js applications. In: Cadar, C., Zhang, X. (eds.) 30th ACM SIGSOFT International Symposium on Software Testing and Analysis, ISSTA 2021, Virtual Event, Denmark, 11–17 July 2021, pp. 29–41. ACM (2021)
23. Nipkow, T., Wenzel, M., Paulson, L.C.: 5. the rules of the game. In: Nipkow, T., Wenzel, M., Paulson, L.C. (eds.) Isabelle/HOL. LNCS, vol. 2283, pp. 67–104. Springer, Heidelberg (2002). https://doi.org/10.1007/3-540-45949-9_5
24. Oracle: Java streams. https://docs.oracle.com/javase/8/docs/api/java/util/stream/package-summary.html. Accessed 02 Feb 2022
25. Oracle: Lambda expressions for the Java programming language (2014). https://jcp.org/aboutJava/communityprocess/final/jsr335/index.html
26. Sadowski, C., Aftandilian, E., Eagle, A., Miller-Cushon, L., Jaspan, C.: Lessons from building static analysis tools at google. Commun. ACM **61**(4), 58–66 (2018). https://doi.org/10.1145/3188720
27. Schoepe, D.: Lifting on-demand analysis to higher-order languages (artifact). Static Anal. Symp. (2023). https://doi.org/10.5281/zenodo.8189312
28. Smaragdakis, Y., Balatsouras, G., Kastrinis, G., Bravenboer, M.: More sound static handling of Java reflection. In: Feng, X., Park, S. (eds.) APLAS 2015. LNCS, vol. 9458, pp. 485–503. Springer, Cham (2015). https://doi.org/10.1007/978-3-319-26529-2_26
29. Smaragdakis, Y., Bravenboer, M.: Using datalog for fast and easy program analysis. In: de Moor, O., Gottlob, G., Furche, T., Sellers, A. (eds.) Datalog 2.0 2010. LNCS, vol. 6702, pp. 245–251. Springer, Heidelberg (2011). https://doi.org/10.1007/978-3-642-24206-9_14
30. Späth, J., Ali, K., Bodden, E.: Context-, flow-, and field-sensitive data-flow analysis using synchronized pushdown systems. Proc. ACM Program. Lang. **3**(POPL), 48:1–48:29 (2019)
31. Späth, J., Do, L.N.Q., Ali, K., Bodden, E.: Boomerang: demand-driven flow- and context-sensitive pointer analysis for Java. In: Krishnamurthi, S., Lerner, B.S. (eds.) 30th European Conference on Object-Oriented Programming, ECOOP 2016, 18–22 July 2016, Rome, Italy. LIPIcs, vol. 56, pp. 22:1–22:26. Schloss Dagstuhl - Leibniz-Zentrum für Informatik (2016)
32. Stein, B., Chang, B.E., Sridharan, M.: Demanded abstract interpretation. In: Freund, S.N., Yahav, E. (eds.) 42nd ACM SIGPLAN International Conference on Programming Language Design and Implementation, PLDI 2021, Virtual Event, Canada, 20–25 June 2021, pp. 282–295. ACM (2021)
33. Sundaresan, V., et al.: Practical virtual method call resolution for Java. In: Rosson, M.B., Lea, D. (eds.) Proceedings of the 2000 ACM SIGPLAN Conference on Object-Oriented Programming Systems, Languages & Applications, OOPSLA 2000, Minneapolis, Minnesota, USA, 15–19 October 2000, pp. 264–280. ACM (2000)

Octagons Revisited
Elegant Proofs and Simplified Algorithms

Michael Schwarz(✉) and Helmut Seidl

Technische Universität München, Garching, Germany
{m.schwarz, helmut.seidl}@tum.de

Abstract. Weakly relational domains have enjoyed tremendous success in the area of program analysis, since they offer a decent compromise between precision and efficiency. *Octagons*, in particular, have widely been studied to obtain efficient algorithms which, however, come with intricate correctness arguments. Here, we provide simplified cubic time algorithms for computing the closure of *Octagon* abstract relations both over the rationals and the integers which avoid introducing auxiliary variables. They are based on a more general formulation by means of 2-*projective* domains which allows for an elegant short correctness proof. The notion of 2-projectivity also lends itself to efficient algorithms for incremental normalization. For the *Octagon* domain, we also provide an improved construction for linear programming based best abstract transformers for affine assignments.

Keywords: weakly relational domains · octagons · 2-decomposable relational domains · Floyd-Warshall algorithm

1 Introduction

While for intricate verification tasks, monolithic relational domains such as the polyhedra abstract domain [8] are indispensable, they are considered prohibitively expensive. Therefore, *weakly relational* domains have been proposed which can only express simple relational properties, but scale better to larger programs. Examples of such domains to capture numerical properties are the *Two Variables Per Inequality* domain [27], or domains given by a finite set of *linear templates* [25]. The most prominent example of a template numerical domain is the *Octagon* domain [20,21] which allows tracking upper and lower bounds not only of program variables but also of sums and differences of *two* program variables. One such octagon abstract relation could, e.g., be given by the conjunction

$$(-x \leq -5) \wedge (x \leq 10) \wedge (x + y \leq 0) \wedge (x - z \leq 1)$$

Octagons thus can be considered as a mild extension of the non-relational domain of *Intervals* for program variables. An efficient comparison of octagon abstract

The original version of this chapter was previously published non-open access. A Correction to this chapter is available at https://doi.org/10.1007/978-3-031-44245-2_24

M. V. Hermenegildo and J. F. Morales (Eds.): SAS 2023, LNCS 14284, pp. 485–507, 2023.
https://doi.org/10.1007/978-3-031-44245-2_21

relations for inclusion, is enabled by canonical representations where all implied bounds are made explicit. Such representations are called *closed*. In the given example, the upper bounds

$$(y \leq -5) \wedge (-z \leq -4)$$

are implied and therefore are included into the closed representation.

Procedures for computing closures of octagons over rationals or integers have been given by Miné [20] where an improved closure algorithm for integers later has been provided by Bagnara et al. [1,2]. Further practical improvements are discussed in [4]. All these algorithms have in common that they introduce auxiliary variables for negated program variables $-z$ in order to represent each octagon as a difference bound matrix (DBM), and then apply dedicated techniques for these [19], namely, the *Floyd-Warshall* algorithm [6]. The auxiliary variables, however, must additionally be taken care of by the algorithm which blurs the simplicity of the idea, and also complicates the correctness argument.

Here, we take another approach. To provide efficient procedures for the *Octagon* domain with simple proofs, we identify two generic properties of relational domains which are sufficient for an abstract version of the *Floyd-Warshall* algorithm to provide *normal forms*. Normalization takes calculations on abstract relations between 1, 2, and 3 variables as black boxes and uses these to infer abstract 1 or 2-variable relations mediated by other variables. Our normalization algorithm can be instantiated for rational octagons as well as integer octagons or other instances of the class of weakly relational domains satisfying our criteria.

The first criterion is 2-*decomposability* as introduced in [26] which requires that each abstract relation can be uniquely reconstructed from its projections onto sub-clusters of variables of size at most 2. The second criterion is called *2-projectivity*. This property means that each variable x can be eliminated from an abstract relation by considering projections onto at most 2-variable clusters. If both criteria are satisfied, our algorithm returns the normal form. The key correctness argument can be provided on two pages. Our abstract setting also provides an elegant algorithm for *incremental* normalization, i.e., for re-establishing the normal form after improving the relationship between two variables. In practice, such improvements may occur as the abstract effect of guards in the program which are expressible as abstract relations. For the *Octagon* domain over rationals or integers, we provide improved abstract transformers for affine assignments based on linear programming.

2 Relational Domains

Let us recall basic definitions for relational domains. We mostly follow the notation used in [26] where the notion of 2-decomposability has been introduced. Let $\mathcal{X}$ be some finite set of variables. A *relational domain* $\mathcal{R}$ is a lattice with least element $\bot$ and greatest element $\top$ which provides the monotonic operations

$$\begin{aligned} [\![x \leftarrow e]\!]^\sharp &: \mathcal{R} \rightarrow \mathcal{R} \text{ (assignment to variable } x \text{ with right-hand } e) \\ r|_Y &: \mathcal{R} \rightarrow \mathcal{R} \text{ (restriction to } Y \subseteq \mathcal{X}) \\ [\![?c]\!]^\sharp &: \mathcal{R} \rightarrow \mathcal{R} \text{ (guard for condition } c) \end{aligned}$$

for some languages e of expressions and c of conditions, respectively.

The given operations are meant to provide the abstract transformers for the basic operations of programs. Restricting a relation r to a subset Y of variables amounts to *forgetting* all information about variables in $\mathcal{X}\backslash Y$. Thus, we require that

$$\begin{array}{lll} r|_{\mathcal{X}} & = r & \\ r|_{\emptyset} & = \top & \\ r|_{Y_1} & \sqsupseteq r|_{Y_2} & \text{when } Y_1 \subseteq Y_2 \\ (r|_{Y_1})|_{Y_2} & = r|_{Y_1 \cap Y_2} & \end{array} \tag{1}$$

Restriction therefore is *idempotent*. For guards with condition c, we require that

$$[\![?c]\!]^\sharp r = r \sqcap [\![?c]\!]^\sharp (r|_V) \tag{2}$$

where V is the set of variables occurring inside c.

For a *numerical* relational domain, we additionally require for $Y \subseteq \mathcal{X}$ that

$$([\![x \leftarrow e]\!]^\sharp r)\big|_Y = r|_Y \qquad (x \notin Y) \tag{3}$$

$$([\![x \leftarrow e]\!]^\sharp r)\big|_Y = ([\![x \leftarrow e]\!]^\sharp (r|_{Y \cup V}))\big|_Y \qquad (x \in Y) \tag{4}$$

where V is the set of variables occurring in e. Intuitively, this means that an assignment to the variable x does not affect relational information for any set Y of variables with $x \notin Y$. To determine the effect for a set Y of variables containing x, it suffices to additionally take the variables into account which occur in the right-hand side e. This property may, e.g., be violated if the relational domain also represents points-to information so that updates to x may also affect relational information for sets of variables not containing x.

Example 1. For numerical variables, a variety of such relational domains have been proposed, e.g., (conjunctions of) *affine equalities* [16,22,23] or *affine inequalities* [8]. For affine equalities or inequalities, projection onto a subset of Y of variables corresponds to the geometric projection onto the sub-space defined by Y, combined with arbitrary values for variables $z \notin Y$. The abstract effect of a guard c onto a given conjunction r can be realized as $r \wedge c = r \wedge (c \wedge r|_V)$ if c is a linear equality or inequality, respectively, using variables from V. The abstract effect of an assignment $x \leftarrow e$ with affine right-hand side e, finally, can be reduced to the addition of new constraints and projection onto sub-spaces. Relational domains may also be constructed for non-numerical values, e.g., by maintaining *finite* subsets of value maps. □

3 Weakly Relational Domains

One way to tackle the high cost of relational domains is to track relationships not between all variables, but only between *subclusters* of variables. We call such domains *Weakly Relational Domains.*

For a subset $Y \subseteq \mathcal{X}$, let $\mathcal{R}^Y = \{r \mid r \in \mathcal{R}, r|_Y = r\}$ the set of all abstract values from $\mathcal{R}$ that contain only information on those variables in Y. For any collection $\mathcal{S} \subseteq 2^{\mathcal{X}}$ of *clusters* of variables, a relation $r \in \mathcal{R}$ can be *approximated* by a meet of relations from $\mathcal{R}^Y, Y \in \mathcal{S}$ since for every $r \in \mathcal{R}$,

$$r \sqsubseteq \bigsqcap\{r|_Y \mid Y \in \mathcal{S}\} \tag{5}$$

holds. Schwarz et al. [26] introduce the notion of 2-*decomposable* relational domains. These are domains where the full value can be recovered from the restriction to all clusters $[\mathcal{X}]_2$ of variables of size at most 2, and all finite least upper bounds can be recovered by computing within these clusters only, i.e., where

$$r = \bigsqcap\left\{r|_p \mid p \in [\mathcal{X}]_2\right\} \tag{6}$$

$$(\bigsqcup R)|_p = \bigsqcup\left\{r|_p \mid r \in R\right\} \quad (p \in [\mathcal{X}]_2) \tag{7}$$

holds for each abstract relation $r \in \mathcal{R}$ and each finite set of abstract relations $R \subseteq \mathcal{R}$. The most prominent example of a 2-decomposable domain is the *Octagon* domain [20] – either over rationals or integers, while *affine equalities* or *affine inequalities* are examples of domains that are not 2-decomposable.

Each value r from a 2-decomposable relational domain $\mathcal{R}$ can be represented as the meet of its restrictions to 2-clusters, i.e., by the collection $\left\langle r|_p\right\rangle_{p\in[\mathcal{X}]_2}$. This representation is called 2-*normal*, and an algorithm to compute it, *normalization*. Consider an *arbitrary* collection $\langle s_p\rangle_{p\in[\mathcal{X}]_2}$ with $s_p \in \mathcal{R}^p$ with $r = \bigsqcap\{s_p \mid p \in [\mathcal{X}]_2\}$. Then $r|_p \sqsubseteq s_p$ always holds, while equality need not hold. In the *Octagon* domain over the rationals or the integers, the 2-normal representation of an octagon value corresponds to its *strong closure* and *tight closure*, respectively, as described in [1,20]. Here, we do not distinguish between different types of closure for rational and integer octagons. Instead, we call a non-$\perp$ octagon O over a numerical set of values $\mathbb{I} \in \{\mathbb{Q}, \mathbb{Z}\}$ *closed* if for each octagon combination ℓ, the upper bound b_ℓ equals the minimal value $b \in \mathbb{I}$ such that $\ell \leq b$ is implied by O, or ∞ if no such bound exists.

While for rational octagons, closure in cubic time was already proposed by Miné [20], it is much more recent that a corresponding algorithm was provided for integer octagons [1,2]. Here, we re-consider these results. By referring to 2-decomposable domains instead of to octagons, we succeed in providing a conceptually simple normalization algorithm with a simple correctness proof, from which cubic closure algorithms for the *Octagon* domains can be derived.

4 2-Projectivity

Subsequently, we assume that $\mathcal{R}$ is an arbitrary 2-decomposable domain over some set $\mathcal{X}$ of variables. Assume that $r \in \mathcal{R}$ is given by $r = \bigsqcap\{s_p \mid p \in [\mathcal{X}]_2, s_p \in \mathcal{R}^p\}$. Then, we consider the following constraint system in the unknowns $r_p, p \in [\mathcal{X}]_2$, over $\mathcal{R}$,

$$r_{\{x,y\}} \sqsubseteq s_{\{x,y\}} \sqcap \left(r_{\{x,z\}} \sqcap r_{\{z,y\}}\right)\big|_{\{x,y\}} \tag{8}$$

for $x, y, z \in \mathcal{X}$. All right-hand sides of the constraint system (8) are monotonic.

Proposition 1. *The collection* $\langle r|_p \rangle_{p \in [\mathcal{X}]_2}$ *is a solution of constraint system* (8).

Proof. Let $x, y, z \in \mathcal{X}$. Then

$$r|_{\{x,y\}} = r|_{\{x,y\}} \sqcap r|_{\{x,y\}} \sqsubseteq s_{\{x,y\}} \sqcap r|_{\{x,y\}} \sqsubseteq s_{\{x,y\}} \sqcap \left(r|_{\{x,z\}} \sqcap r|_{\{z,y\}} \right)\Big|_{\{x,y\}} \square$$

From Proposition 1, we conclude that the *greatest* solution of (8) – if it exists – is an overapproximation of the normal representation of r. In general, the Kleene fixpoint iteration for computing greatest solutions of constraint systems (8) may not terminate. Let us call a 2-decomposable relational domain $\mathcal{R}$ *2-projective* when from each abstract relation r, each single variable can be eliminated by using projections onto clusters from $[\mathcal{X}]_2$ only, i.e., when for every $Y \subseteq \mathcal{X}$, $z \in \mathcal{X} \backslash Y$, $y_j \in Y \cup \{z\}$, $r' \in \mathcal{R}^Y$, and $r_{\{z,y_j\}} \in \mathcal{R}^{\{z,y_j\}}$,

$$\left(r_{\{z,y_1\}} \sqcap \ldots \sqcap r_{\{z,y_k\}} \sqcap r'\right)\big|_Y = r' \sqcap \textstyle\bigsqcap_{i,j=1}^{k} \left(r_{\{z,y_i\}} \sqcap r_{\{z,y_j\}}\right)\big|_{Y \cap \{y_i,y_j\}} \quad (9)$$

Proposition 2. *The following 2-decomposable domains are 2-projective:*

1. *rational octagons;*
2. *integer octagons;*
3. *2-variable rational affine inequalities;*
4. *2-variable rational affine equalities.*

Proof. Let us consider the claims (1) and (2) for octagons. Intuitively, their correctness follows from the correctness of *Fourier-Motzkin* elimination of a single variable z from a system of inequalities. In general, this holds only for rational inequalities as considered for claim (1). However, it also holds for systems of integer inequalities – given that all coefficients are integer and all non-zero coefficients of z are either 1 or -1.

Let us call a linear combination $\sum_{x \in \mathcal{X}} a_x \cdot x$ an *octagon* combination if at most two of the coefficients a_x are non-zero and these are then from $\{-1, 1\}$. For a subset Y of variables, let L_Y denote the set of all octagon combinations with variables from Y. An integer octagon constraint is of the form $\ell \leq b$ where ℓ is a linear octagon combination and the bound b is integer or ∞.

Subsequently, we represent an abstract octagon relation over Y by a *closed* conjunction

$$\textstyle\bigwedge_{\ell \in L_Y} \ell \leq b_\ell \quad (10)$$

of octagon constraints with variables from Y if the octagon is satisfiable, or $\perp$ if it is not. Here, the conjunction (10) is satisfiable and closed iff

$$\begin{array}{ll} 0 \leq b_\ell + b_{-\ell} & \text{if } \ell \in L_Y \\ b_\ell \leq (b_{\ell_1} + b_{\ell_2})/c & \text{if } \ell_1 \neq \ell_2 \text{ and } c \cdot \ell = \ell_1 + \ell_2 \end{array}$$

holds for some $c \in \{1, 2\}$. Here, factor 2 occurs if one variable x occurs both in ℓ_1 and ℓ_2 with the same sign, while another variable y occurs with different signs, i.e.,

$$c \cdot \ell = (x + y) + (x - y) = 2 \cdot x$$

In case of octagons over rationals, the operator "/" denotes division, whereas in case of octagons over integers, it denotes *integer* division, i.e., may include rounding downwards. By definition, the closed representation of an abstract octagon relation is also 2-normal.

For computing the closure for an arbitrary conjunction r of octagon constraints with one or two variables only, we may first determine the least given upper bound b_ℓ for each occurring octagon linear combination ℓ. As a result, we obtain at most 8 octagon constraints for which satifiability (over rationals or integers) can be decided in constant time. Provided the conjunction is satisfiable, all implied tighter upper bounds (over rationals or integers) can be inferred.

Example 2. Consider the integer octagon given by conjunction of the constraints

$$x + y \leq -2 \qquad x - y \leq 5 \qquad -x + y \leq 0$$

By adding up constraints with positive and negative occurrences of the same variable, we derive that

$$y \leq -1 \qquad x \leq 1$$

must also hold, while no further bounds can be inferred. If the conjunction of octagon constraints additionally has the inequality

$$-x - y \leq 0$$

then, by adding this to the first inequality, we derive

$$0 \leq -2$$

– which is false – implying that the octagon equals $\bot$. □

Assume that each non-$\bot$ value $r_{\{y_j,z\}}$, $y_j \in Y \cup \{z\}$, is represented as a *closed* conjunction of octagon constraints with variables from $\{y_j, z\}$. Assume likewise, that $r' \neq \bot$ is represented by a conjunction of octagon constraints with variables from Y only.

For each pair y_i, y_j of variables from $Y \cup \{z\}$, the abstract value

$$(r_{\{y_i,z\}} \wedge r_{\{y_j,z\}})\big|_{Y \cap \{y_i,y_j\}} \tag{11}$$

can be obtained by means of Fourier-Motzkin elimination of z, applied to the closed conjunctions of octagon constraints representing $r_{\{y_i,z\}}$, and $r_{\{y_j,z\}}$, respectively. In order to see this, we note that all occurring non-zero coefficients of z in the constraints of $r_{\{y_i,z\}}$ as well as $r_{\{y_j,z\}}$ are from $\{-1, 1\}$. Consider a constraint $\ell \leq b$ of the resulting conjunction. Three cases may occur.

- ℓ may contain occurrences of both variables y_i and y_j – each with coefficients in $\{-1, 1\}$.
- ℓ may contain a single occurrence of one variable, w.l.o.g., y_i, whose coefficient now is in $\{-2, -1, 1, 2\}$. In case the coefficient of y_i is in $\{-2, 2\}$, ℓ is still equivalent to an octagon constraint for y_i only. If the constraint, e.g., is $2 \cdot y_i \leq 7$, then it is equivalent to $y_i \leq 3.5$ over rationals, and to $y_i \leq 3$ over the integers.

- ℓ does not contain any occurrences of variables. In this case, it is either equivalent to true and can be abandoned, or equivalent to false – implying that (11) equals $\bot$.

We conclude that the expression (11), when satisfiable, can be represented by a conjunction of octagon constraints using variables y_i and y_j. Thus, the right-hand side of Eq. (9) for rational as well as integer octagons is equivalent to the result of Fourier-Motzkin elimination of z. This implies claim (2).

Example 3. Assume an integer octagon $r = r' \wedge r_{\{y_1,z\}} \wedge r_{\{y_2,z\}}$ where

$$\begin{aligned} r' &= y_1 + y_2 \leq 7 \\ r_{\{y_1,z\}} &= (y_1 + z \leq -1) \wedge (y_1 \leq 3) \wedge (-z \leq 4) \\ r_{\{y_2,z\}} &= (y_2 - z \leq 5) \wedge (-y_2 \leq 1) \end{aligned}$$

Fourier-Motzkin elimination of z adds the additional constraint

$$y_1 + y_2 \leq 4$$

Projection onto the subset $Y = \{y_1, y_2\}$ according to (9) therefore results in the conjunction of constraints

$$(y_1 + y_2 \leq 7) \wedge (y_1 \leq 3) \wedge (y_1 + y_2 \leq 4) \wedge (-y_2 \leq 1)$$

which can be further simplified to $(y_1 \leq 3) \wedge (y_1 + y_2 \leq 4) \wedge (-y_2 \leq 1)$. □

Example 4. The following 2-decomposable domains are not 2-projective:

1. Finite sets of 2-variable maps;
2. Implications between interval constraints. □

Proof. For (1), let $\mathcal{X} = \{a, x, y, z\}$ where variables range over values from the set $\{1, 2, 3\}$ and maps from variables to such sets are used as the abstraction. Consider now:

$$r_{\{a,x\}} = \{a \mapsto \{1,2\}\} \qquad r_{\{a,y\}} = \{a \mapsto \{2,3\}\} \qquad r_{\{a,z\}} = \{a \mapsto \{3,1\}\}$$

where all other r_p, $p \in [\mathcal{X}]_2$ have the value $\top$. Then,

$$\left(r_{\{a,x\}} \sqcap r_{\{a,y\}} \sqcap r_{\{a,z\}} \sqcap \top\right)\Big|_{\{x,y,z\}} = \bot$$

but, in violation of property (9),

$$\begin{aligned} &\top \sqcap (r_{\{a,x\}} \sqcap r_{\{a,x\}})\big|_{\{x\}} \sqcap (r_{\{a,y\}} \sqcap r_{\{a,y\}})\big|_{\{y\}} \sqcap (r_{\{a,z\}} \sqcap r_{\{a,z\}})\big|_{\{z\}} \\ &\sqcap (r_{\{a,x\}} \sqcap r_{\{a,y\}})\big|_{\{x,y\}} \sqcap (r_{\{a,x\}} \sqcap r_{\{a,z\}})\big|_{\{x,z\}} \sqcap (r_{\{a,y\}} \sqcap r_{\{a,z\}})\big|_{\{y,z\}} \\ =\ &\top \sqcap \top \sqcap \top \sqcap \top \sqcap (\{a \mapsto \{1,2\}\} \sqcap \{a \mapsto \{2,3\}\})|_{\{x,y\}} \sqcap \\ &(\{a \mapsto \{1,2\}\} \sqcap \{a \mapsto \{3,1\}\})|_{\{x,z\}} \sqcap (\{a \mapsto \{2,3\}\} \sqcap \{a \mapsto \{3,1\}\})|_{\{y,z\}} \\ =\ &(\{a \mapsto \{2\}\})|_{\{x,y\}} \sqcap (\{a \mapsto \{1\}\})|_{\{x,z\}} \sqcap (\{a \mapsto \{3\}\})|_{\{x,z\}} \sqcap \\ =\ &\top \sqcap \top \sqcap \top = \top \end{aligned}$$

The domain of implications between interval constraints consists of finite conjunctions of the form

$$x \in I \implies y \in I'$$

for variables x and y and I, I' either intervals or the empty set, ordered by implication. In particular, $x \in \emptyset$ may be written as False, while $x \in [-\infty, \infty]$ is denoted by True.

Now, consider the same set $\mathcal{X} = \{a, x, y, z\}$ of variables as for claim (1) and let

$$\begin{aligned} r_{\{a,x\}} &= \{\mathsf{True} \implies a \in [1,2]\} \\ r_{\{a,y\}} &= \{\mathsf{True} \implies a \in [2,3]\} \\ r_{\{a,z\}} &= \{a \in [2,2] \implies \mathsf{False}\} \end{aligned}$$

where all other r_p, $p \in [\mathcal{X}]_2$ have the value $\top$. Then,

$$\left(r_{\{a,x\}} \sqcap r_{\{a,y\}} \sqcap r_{\{a,z\}} \sqcap \top\right)\Big|_{\{x,y,z\}} = \mathsf{False} = \bot$$

but

$$\begin{aligned} &\top \wedge (r_{\{a,x\}} \wedge r_{\{a,x\}})\big|_{\{x\}} \wedge (r_{\{a,y\}} \wedge r_{\{a,y\}})\big|_{\{y\}} \wedge (r_{\{a,z\}} \wedge r_{\{a,z\}})\big|_{\{z\}} \\ &\wedge (r_{\{a,x\}} \wedge r_{\{a,y\}})\big|_{\{x,y\}} \wedge (r_{\{a,x\}} \wedge r_{\{a,z\}})\big|_{\{x,z\}} \wedge (r_{\{a,y\}} \wedge r_{\{a,z\}})\big|_{\{y,z\}} \\ = &\top \wedge \top \wedge \top \wedge \top \wedge (\{\mathsf{True} \implies a \in [1,2]\} \wedge \{\mathsf{True} \implies a \in [2,3]\})|_{\{x,y\}} \wedge \\ &(\{\mathsf{True} \implies a \in [1,2]\} \wedge \{a \in [2,2] \implies \mathsf{False}\})|_{\{x,z\}} \wedge \\ &(\{\mathsf{True} \implies a \in [2,3]\} \wedge \{a \in [2,2] \implies \mathsf{False}\})|_{\{y,z\}} \\ = &(\mathsf{True} \implies a \in [2,2])|_{\{x,y\}} \wedge (\mathsf{True} \implies a \in [1,1])|_{\{x,z\}} \wedge \\ &(\mathsf{True} \implies a \in [3,3])|_{\{x,z\}} \\ = &\top \wedge \top \wedge \top = \top \end{aligned}$$

which means property (9) is violated. □

Subsequently, assume that the 2-decomposable domain $\mathcal{R}$ is 2-projective. We show that under this assumption, the greatest solution of the constraint system (8) exists and *coincides* with the normal representation. Moreover, we provide an efficient algorithm for performing the normalization.

Assume that $\mathcal{X} = \{x_1 \ldots x_n\}$, and let $X_r = \{x_1, \ldots, x_r\}$, and $\bar{X}_r = \mathcal{X} \backslash X_r$ for $r = 0, \ldots, n$. Assume that we are given $s_p \in \mathcal{R}^p$, $(p \in [\mathcal{X}]_2)$. For $x, y \in \mathcal{X}$, we define the sequence

$$\begin{aligned} s^{(0)}_{\{x,y\}} &= s_{\{x\}} \sqcap s_{\{y\}} \sqcap s_{\{x,y\}} \\ s^{(r)}_{\{x,y\}} &= s^{(r-1)}_{\{x,y\}} \sqcap \left(s^{(r-1)}_{\{x,x_r\}} \sqcap s^{(r-1)}_{\{x_r,y\}}\right)\Big|_{\{x,y\}} \qquad \text{for } r > 0: \end{aligned}$$

Proposition 3. *Let $\bar{s} = \bigsqcap\{s_p \mid p \in [\mathcal{X}]_2\}$ be the abstract relation represented by $\langle s_p \rangle_{p \in [\mathcal{X}]_2}$. Let $p \in [\mathcal{X}]_2$. For $r = 0, \ldots, n$,*

1. *$s^{(r)}_p \sqsubseteq s^{(r)}_{\{x\}}$ for each $x \in p$;*
2. $$\bar{s}|_{\bar{X}_r \cup \{x,y\}} = \bigsqcap \left\{ s^{(r)}_p \mid p \subseteq \bar{X}_r \cup \{x,y\}, 1 \leq |p| \leq 2 \right\} \qquad (12)$$

Proof. For $r = 0$, the proposition holds by definition. Now assume that $r > 0$ and the assertion already holds for $r-1$. For $p = \{x, y\}$, we calculate

$$\begin{aligned} s^{(r)}_{\{x,y\}} &= s^{(r-1)}_{\{x,y\}} \sqcap \left(s^{(r-1)}_{\{x,x_r\}} \sqcap s^{(r-1)}_{\{x_r,y\}}\right)\Big|_{\{x,y\}} \sqsubseteq s^{(r-1)}_{\{x\}} \sqcap s^{(r-1)}_{\{x,x_r\}}\Big|_{\{x,y\}} \\ &\sqsubseteq s^{(r-1)}_{\{x\}} \sqcap s^{(r-1)}_{\{x,x_r\}}\Big|_{\{x\}} = s^{(r)}_{\{x\}} \end{aligned}$$

and the first claim follows. For the second claim Eq. (12), consider the case $x_r \notin \{x, y\}$. Then

$$\begin{aligned} \bar{s}|_{\bar{X}_r\cup\{x,y\}} &= \left(\bar{s}|_{\bar{X}_{r-1}\cup\{x,y\}}\right)\Big|_{\bar{X}_r\cup\{x,y\}} \\ &= \left(\bigsqcap\left\{s^{(r-1)}_p \mid p \subseteq \bar{X}_{r-1}\cup\{x,y\}, 1\leq|p|\leq 2\right\}\right)\Big|_{\bar{X}_r\cup\{x,y\}} && \text{(by induction hypothesis)} \\ &= \left(\bigsqcap\left\{s^{(r-1)}_p \mid p \subseteq \bar{X}_r\cup\{x,y\}, 1\leq|p|\leq 2\right\} \sqcap \bigsqcap\left\{s^{(r-1)}_{\{z,x_r\}} \mid z \in \bar{X}_{r-1}\cup\{x,y\}\right\}\right)\Big|_{\bar{X}_r\cup\{x,y\}} \\ &= \bigsqcap\left\{s^{(r-1)}_p \mid p \subseteq \bar{X}_r\cup\{x,y\}, 1\leq|p|\leq 2\right\} \sqcap \\ &\quad \bigsqcap\left\{\left(s^{(r-1)}_{\{z_1,x_r\}} \sqcap s^{(r-1)}_{\{x_r,z_2\}}\right)\Big|_{(\bar{X}_r\cup\{x,y\})\cap\{z_1,z_2\}} \mid z_1, z_2 \in \bar{X}_r\cup\{x,y\}\right\} \sqcap \\ &\quad \bigsqcap\left\{\left(s^{(r-1)}_{\{z_1,x_r\}} \sqcap s^{(r-1)}_{\{x_r\}}\right)\Big|_{(\bar{X}_r\cup\{x,y\})\cap\{z_1\}} \mid z_1 \in \bar{X}_r\cup\{x,y\}\right\} \\ &\quad \sqcap s^{(r-1)}_{\{x_r\}}\Big|_{(\bar{X}_r\cup\{x,y\})\cap\{x_r\}} && \text{(by Eq. (9))} \\ &= \bigsqcap\left\{s^{(r-1)}_p \mid p \subseteq \bar{X}_r\cup\{x,y\}, 1\leq|p|\leq 2\right\} \sqcap \\ &\quad \bigsqcap\left\{\left(s^{(r-1)}_{\{z_1,x_r\}} \sqcap s^{(r-1)}_{\{x_r,z_2\}}\right)\Big|_{\{z_1,z_2\}} \mid z_1, z_2 \in \bar{X}_r\cup\{x,y\}\right\} \sqcap \\ &\quad \bigsqcap\left\{\left(s^{(r-1)}_{\{z_1,x_r\}} \sqcap s^{(r-1)}_{\{x_r\}}\right)\Big|_{\{z_1\}} \mid z_1 \in \bar{X}_r\cup\{x,y\}\right\} \sqcap s^{(r-1)}_{\{x_r\}}\Big|_{\emptyset} \\ &= \bigsqcap\left\{s^{(r-1)}_p \mid p \subseteq \bar{X}_r\cup\{x,y\}, 1\leq|p|\leq 2\right\} \sqcap \\ &\quad \bigsqcap\left\{\left(s^{(r-1)}_{\{z_1,x_r\}} \sqcap s^{(r-1)}_{\{x_r,z_2\}}\right)\Big|_{\{z_1,z_2\}} \mid z_1, z_2 \in \bar{X}_r\cup\{x,y\}\right\} && \text{(by claim (1))} \\ &= \bigsqcap\left\{s^{(r)}_p \mid p \subseteq \bar{X}_r\cup\{x,y\}, 1\leq|p|\leq 2\right\} \end{aligned}$$

and the assertion holds. For the second but last equality, we used that the meet in the second but last row is non-empty, since

$$s^{(r-1)}_{\{x_r\}}\Big|_{\emptyset} \sqsupseteq s^{(r-1)}_{\{x_r\}}\Big|_{\{z_1\}} \sqsupseteq s^{(r-1)}_{\{z_1,x_r\}}\Big|_{\{z_1\}} \sqsupseteq s^{(r-1)}_{\{z_1,x_r\}}\Big|_{\{z_1,z_2\}} \sqsupseteq s^{(r-1)}_{\{z_1,x_r\}} \sqcap s^{(r-1)}_{\{z_1,x_r\}}\Big|_{\{z_1,z_2\}}$$

holds for each $z_1, z_2 \in \bar{X}_r \cup \{x, y\}$. Now let $x_r \in \{x, y\}$. Then $\bar{X}_r \cup \{x, y\} = \bar{X}_{r-1} \cup \{x, y\}$. W.l.o.g., let $x = x_r$. Then $s^{(r-1)}_{\{x,x_r\}} = s^{(r-1)}_{\{x\}}$ and $s^{(r-1)}_{\{x_r,y\}} = s^{(r-1)}_{\{x,y\}}$. Hence by claim (1), $s^{(r)}_{\{x,y\}} = s^{(r-1)}_{\{x,y\}}$. Accordingly,

$$\begin{aligned} \bar{s}|_{\bar{X}_r\cup\{x,y\}} &= \bar{s}|_{\bar{X}_{r-1}\cup\{x,y\}} \\ &= \bigsqcap\left\{s^{(r-1)}_p \mid p \subseteq \bar{X}_{r-1}\cup\{x,y\}, 1\leq|p|\leq 2\right\} && \text{(by induction hypothesis)} \\ &= \bigsqcap\left\{s^{(r-1)}_{\{z_1,z_2\}} \sqcap s^{(r-1)}_{\{z_1,x\}} \sqcap s^{(r-1)}_{\{x,z_2\}} \mid z_1, z_2 \in \bar{X}_{r-1}\cup\{x,y\}\right\} \\ &= \bigsqcap\left\{s^{(r)}_p \mid p \subseteq \bar{X}_r\cup\{x,y\}, 1\leq|p|\leq 2\right\} \end{aligned}$$

□

Thus, provided $\mathcal{R}$ fulfills Eq. 9, we obtain for $k = n$:

$$\bar{s}|_{\{x,y\}} = s^{(n)}_{\{x,y\}} \sqcap s^{(n)}_{\{x\}} \sqcap s^{(n)}_{\{y\}} = s^{(n)}_{\{x,y\}}$$

Subsequently, we consider Algorithm 1. It consists of one application of the *Floyd-Warshall* algorithm, as is. For that to be sufficient, an initialization round is performed upfront to ensure that each value $t_{\{x,y\}}$ not only subsumes $s_{\{x,y\}}$, but also $s_{\{x\}}$ and $s_{\{y\}}$. The complexity of the proposed algorithm is $\mathcal{O}(n^3)$ if calculations with abstract relations over at most three variables, i.e., from $\mathcal{R}^Y$ for every $Y \subseteq \mathcal{X}$ with $|Y| \leq 3$, can be performed in constant time. For Algorithm 1, we find:

Theorem 1. *Assume that $\langle t_p \rangle_{p \in [\mathcal{X}]_2}$ is the collection of values returned by Algorithm 1 for the collection $\langle s_p \rangle_{p \in [\mathcal{X}]_2}$. Let $\bar{s} = \bigsqcap\{s_p \mid p \in [\mathcal{X}]_2\}$ the abstract relation represented by $\langle s_p \rangle_{p \in [\mathcal{X}]_2}$. Then for each $p \in [\mathcal{X}]_2$,*

1. *$\bar{s}|_p \sqsubseteq t_p$;*
2. *If the 2-decomposable domain $\mathcal{R}$ is 2-projective, then $\bar{s}|_p = t_p$ holds. In that case, $\langle t_p \rangle_{p \in [\mathcal{X}]_2}$ is the greatest solution of the constraint system* (8)*.*

Thus, Algorithm 1 provides a cubic time normalization procedure – whenever $\mathcal{R}$ is 2-decomposable and 2-projective. We remark that the initializing first loop cannot be abandoned. When $\mathcal{R}$ is not 2-projective, but 2-decomposable, the algorithm still computes *overapproximations* of normal representations.

Proof. Let $p \in [\mathcal{X}]_2$. By Proposition 1, $\bar{s}|_p \sqsubseteq t_p$ holds, since the right-hand sides of the constraint system (8) are all monotonic, and starting from the initial values provided in the first loop, each update to some $t_{\{x,y\}}$ in the second loop, corresponds to one update performed by the evaluation of some right-hand side of (8). Therefore, the first assertion follows.

Now assume that the 2-decomposable relational domain $\mathcal{R}$ additionally is 2-projective. Let $t_p^{(r)}$ denote the value of t_p attained after the iteration of the second loop for the variable x_r. By induction on r, we verify by means of Proposition 3 that for all $p \in [\mathcal{X}]_2$, $t_p^{(r)} \sqsubseteq s_p^{(r)}$ holds for all $r = 0, \ldots, n$. In particular, $t_p = t_p^{(n)} \sqsubseteq \bar{s}|_p$, and the second assertion of the theorem follows. □

Algorithm 1: The variant of the *Floyd-Warshall* algorithm to compute (an overapproximation of) normalization.

```
for x, y ∈ 𝒳 do
    t_{x,y} := s_{x,y} ⊓ s_{x} ⊓ s_{y}                    // initialization
for z ∈ 𝒳 do
    for x, y ∈ 𝒳 do
        t_{x,y} := t_{x,y} ⊓ (t_{x,z} ⊓ t_{z,y})|_{x,y}
return ⟨t_p⟩_{p∈[𝒳]_2}
```

Example 5. Given a (finite) set of constants, the *Pairs* domain consists of false or conjunctions $\bigwedge\{\phi_p \mid p \in [\mathcal{X}]_2\}$ where for $p \in [\mathcal{X}]_2$, ϕ_p is true or a disjunction of conjunctions of atomic propositions $x = c$, $x \in p$. It is ordered by logical implication. Consider, e.g., $r = \phi_{\{x,y\}} \wedge \phi_{\{y,z\}}$ with $\phi_{\{x,y\}} \equiv (x = a) \vee (x = b \wedge y = c)$ and $\phi_{\{y,z\}} \equiv (y = d \wedge z = b)$. Then $r|_{\{x,y\}} = (x = a \wedge y = d)$. Likewise, $r|_{\{y,z\}} = (y = d \wedge z = b)$ and $r|_{\{x,z\}} = (x = a \wedge z = b)$.

Assume each $r \in R$ is represented by $r = \bigwedge\{r|_p \mid p \in [\mathcal{X}]_2\}$, and define for $p \in [\mathcal{X}]_2$, ϕ_p as the least upper bound of formulas $r|_p, r \in R$. Then $\bar{r} = \bigwedge\{\phi_p \mid p \in [\mathcal{X}]_2\}$ is an upper bound of R and, in fact, the least upper bound. For some $p \in [\mathcal{X}]_2$, then by definition, $\bar{r}|_p \Rightarrow \phi_p$. By monotonicity of the restriction, on the other hand, $r|_p \Rightarrow \bar{r}|_p$ for all $r \in R$. Therefore, $\phi_p \Rightarrow \bar{r}|_p$ as well, and the claim follows. While being 2-decomposable, the *Pairs* domain is not 2-projective. Let, e.g.,

$$\begin{aligned} s_{\{w,x\}} &= (w = \texttt{"fun1"} \wedge x = \texttt{\&f1}) \vee (w = \texttt{"fun3"} \wedge x = \texttt{\&f2}) \\ s_{\{w,y\}} &= (w = \texttt{"fun2"}) \vee (w = \texttt{"fun3"}) \\ s_{\{w,z\}} &= (w = \texttt{"fun1"} \wedge z = \texttt{\&f1}) \vee (w = \texttt{"fun2"} \wedge z = \texttt{\&f1}) \end{aligned}$$

and all other $s_p =$ true. Then, Algorithm 1 computes

$$\begin{aligned} t_{\{w\}} &= t_{\{w,x\}} = t_{\{w,y\}} = t_{\{w,z\}} = \mathsf{false} & t_{\{y\}} &= \mathsf{true} \\ t_{\{x\}} &= t_{\{x,y\}} = (x = \texttt{\&f1}) \vee (x = \texttt{\&f2}) & t_{\{y,z\}} &= t_{\{z\}} = (z = \texttt{\&f1}) \\ t_{\{x,z\}} &= (x = \texttt{\&f1} \wedge z = \texttt{\&f1}) \vee (x = \texttt{\&f2} \wedge z = \texttt{\&f1}) \end{aligned}$$

which is an overapproximation of the normalization given by $\bar{s}|_p =$ false for $p \in [\mathcal{X}]_2$. Here, the normalization happens to coincide with the greatest solution of constraint system (8). □

Example 6. According to Proposition 2, the domains of rational as well as integer octagons are 2-decomposable and 2-projective. Therefore, Algorithm 1 computes the exact 2-normal form, and thus provides us with cubic time closure algorithms for these. □

5 Incremental Normalization

If the condition c of a guard can be abstracted by some abstract relation $r_c \in \mathcal{R}$, then the transfer function $[\![?c]\!]^\sharp$ can be chosen as $[\![?c]\!]^\sharp r = r \sqcap r_c$. Assume that the relational domain $\mathcal{R}$ is 2-decomposable as well as 2-projective, and that r_c is represented as the meet $r_{p_1} \sqcap \ldots \sqcap r_{p_k}$ for $p_j \in [\mathcal{X}]_2$. Then, the normalization of $r \sqcap r_c$ can be computed *incrementally*. For the octagon domain over integers, Chawdhary et al. [4] give quadratic incremental closure algorithms. Just like theirs, our algorithm for incremental normalization is based on the Floyd-Warshall algorithm, i.e., Algorithm 1.

Algorithm 2: Incremental version of the FLOYD-WARSHALL algorithm to incrementally compute (an overapproximation of) 2-normal forms when clusters t_p, $p \subseteq V$, with $|p| = 2$ have potentially received new values.

```
for z ∈ V do
    for x, y ∈ 𝒳 do
        t_{x,y} := t_{x,y} ⊓ (t_{x,z} ⊓ t_{z,y})|_{x,y}
return ⟨t_p⟩_{p∈[𝒳]_2}
```

In our setting, adding new constraints amounts to improving some clusters $r_{\{a,b\}}$ where a and b are from some set $V \subseteq \mathcal{X}$. For simplicity, we require that only clusters $r_{\{a,b\}}$ with $a \neq b$ are improved. This allows us in the adaption of Algorithm 1 to avoid the initialization loop. Whenever $\mathcal{X}$ contains more than one variable, this extra requirement is no limitation, though, as a constraint involving only the variable z may just be added to any 2-variable cluster p with $z \in p$. (When $\mathcal{X}$ contains only one variable, no normalization is required.) Normalization then is computed by the modified version of Algorithm 1 given in Algorithm 2.

Theorem 2. *Assume a 2-normal collection of values of some 2-decomposable relational domain* $S = \langle s_p \rangle_{p \in [\mathcal{X}]_2}$*, and a collection* $S_1 = \langle s'_{p'} \rangle_{p' \subseteq V, |p'|=2}$ *with* $s'_{p'} \sqsubseteq s_{p'}$ *for all* p'*. Assume that* $\langle t_p \rangle_{p \in [\mathcal{X}]_2}$ *is the collection of values returned by Algorithm 2 for the collection* $S' = \langle s_p \rangle_{p \in [\mathcal{X}]_2, (p \not\subseteq V \vee |p| \neq 2)} \cup S_1$ *Let* $\bar{s} = \bigsqcap S'$ *the abstract relation represented by* S'*. Then for each* $p \in [\mathcal{X}]_2$*,*

1. $\bar{s}|_p \sqsubseteq t_p$*;*
2. *If the 2-decomposable domain* $\mathcal{R}$ *is 2-projective, then* $\bar{s}|_p = t_p$ *holds. In that case,* $\langle t_p \rangle_{p \in [\mathcal{X}]_2}$ *is the greatest solution of constraint system* (8)*.*

Proof. Let $p \in [\mathcal{X}]_2$. $\bar{s}|_p \sqsubseteq t_p$ holds since, as observed before, all right-hand sides of the constraint system (8) are monotonic and the individual update steps of Algorithm 2 each correspond to updates performed by the evaluations of the right-hand sides of (8). Thus, the first statement follows.

Now consider the case where the relational domain is additionally 2-projective. The invariant which the non-incremental Algorithm 1 attains after the initialization holds by construction here. Let $t_p^{(r)}$ denote the value of t_p attained after the iteration of the second loop for the r-th variable in the non-incremental Algorithm 1. We choose the order of the iteration of variables in the second loop such that the variables in V are considered last. Then, for the first $|\mathcal{X} \setminus V|$ iterations $t_p^{(r-1)} = t_p^{(r)}$, as the original collection $\langle s_p \rangle_{p \in [\mathcal{X}]_2}$ was normalized. Therefore, it suffices to execute the last $|V|$ iterations of the second loop of Algorithm 1 which is identical to Algorithm 2. Thus, by Theorem 1, the claim follows. □

We have thus shown that re-establishing normalization (and thus closure) after adding octagon constraints for m variables is in $\mathcal{O}(m \cdot n^2)$.

6 Abstract Transformers for Linear Assignments

Assume we are given a normalized value r over the set $\mathcal{X}$ of program variables from some 2-decomposable relational domain. Assume further that we are given an assignment a of the form $x \leftarrow e$ where e is an expression over some subset $V \subseteq \mathcal{X}$, and assume that the relational domain satisfies properties (3) and (4). Let $r \in \mathcal{R}$ denote the relational value before the assignment and assume r is already normalized where $r_p = r|_p$ has already been computed for all $p \in [\mathcal{X}]_2$. Let $r' = [\![\mathsf{a}]\!]^\sharp\, r$ denote the relational value after the assignment. Then, for every $p \in [\mathcal{X}]_2$ with $x \notin p$, $r'|_p = r|_p = r_p$. In order to compute the normalization of r', it therefore suffices to compute the values $r'_p = r'|_p$ for $x \in p$, i.e., a *linear* number of clusters p. Now consider some variable $y \in \mathcal{X}$. Because of property (4), we have that

$$\begin{aligned} r'_p &= [\![\mathsf{a}]\!]^\sharp r\big|_{\{x,y\}} \\ &= \left([\![\mathsf{a}]\!]^\sharp r|_{V\cup\{x,y\}}\right)\Big|_{\{x,y\}} \\ &= \left([\![\mathsf{a}]\!]^\sharp(\textstyle\bigsqcap\{r_p \mid p \subseteq V \cup \{x,y\}\})\right)\big|_{\{x,y\}} \end{aligned}$$

i.e., the abstract value $r'_{\{x,y\}}$ requires taking into account only clusters $p \in [\mathcal{X}]_2$ with variables from $V \cup \{x, y\}$. We conclude:

Proposition 4. *Assume that computations on abstract relations from $\mathcal{R}$ over a bounded set of variables is constant time, and assume that the assignment a refers only to a bounded number of variables. Assume further that the abstract relation $r \in \mathcal{R}$ is normalized. Then a normalization of the relation $[\![\mathsf{a}]\!]^\sharp r$ can be computed in linear time.* □

7 Linear Programming with Octagon Constraints

Let us turn to the implementation of best abstract transformers for assignments for the octagon domain (over rationals as well as over integers). For the octagon domain, an abstract transformer for assignments can be constructed by adding octagon constraints. This works well for right-hand sides of the form $y + c$ or $-y + c$ for variables y and constants c. For more general right-hand sides such as, e.g., $3 \cdot y - 2 \cdot z$, the best transformer can instead be expressed by means of *optimization* problems [25].

Assume that the octagon is provided by bounds $b_\ell, \ell \in L_V$ for some subset $V \subseteq \mathcal{X}$ of variables. Depending on the sign of a variable occurring in a linear combination ℓ, we say it occurs *positively* or *negatively*. Consider the optimization problem of maximizing a linear objective function taking variables from V subject to the given set of octagon constraints

$$\begin{array}{ll} \textbf{maximize } \sum_{z\in V} a_z \cdot z & \\ \textbf{subject to } \ell \le b_\ell & (\ell \in L_V) \end{array} \tag{13}$$

When interpreted over the rationals, optimal solutions can be computed in time *polynomial* in the *size* of the linear program (i.e., the number of bits to spell it out) [15] or exponential time in the number of variables if simplex type algorithms are used [17]. To this general approach, we here add one more observation, namely, that over the rationals, the set of octagon constraints to be satisfied in optimization problems can be restricted to constraints where each occurring variable $z \in V$ occurs with the same sign as the coefficient a_z of z in the objective function: this considerably reduces the number of constraints to be considered.

Proposition 5. *Assume that we are given the rational octagon linear program (13) where $a_z > 0$ for all $z \in V$. If the octagon corresponding to the constraints is closed, then the same result is obtained when the constraints are restricted to octagon linear combinations z and $z + y$ for $z, y \in V$ and $z \neq y$.*

Proof. The proof of the proposition is obtained by means of the *dual* linear program:

$$\begin{array}{ll} \textbf{minimize} & \sum_{\ell \in L_V} y_\ell \cdot b_\ell \\ \textbf{subject to} & (\sum_{z \text{ in } \ell} y_\ell) - (\sum_{-z \text{ in } \ell} y_\ell) = a_z \quad (z \in V) \\ & \qquad\qquad\qquad\qquad\qquad\quad y_\ell \geq 0 \quad (\ell \in L_V) \end{array} \tag{14}$$

If the original program is unbounded, then so is the program with the restricted set of constraints. Therefore, assume that the original linear program is bounded. Then the dual optimization problem has a feasible solution $y_\ell, \ell \in L_V$, where the minimal gain b is attained, i.e., $\sum_{\ell \in L_V} y_\ell \cdot b_\ell = b$. It remains to prove that b can be attained by a feasible solution $y_\ell, \ell \in L$, where $y_\ell = 0$ for all octagon combinations ℓ which contain negations. We proceed by induction on the number of octagon combinations ℓ with negative occurrences of variables from V. Assume that there are octagon combinations ℓ with negated occurrences of z and $y_\ell > 0$. Consider the linear constraint in (13) for z

$$\left(\sum_{j=1}^{r} y_\ell\right) - \left(\sum_{j'=1}^{r'} y_{\ell'_{j'}}\right) = a_z$$

where ℓ_j enumerates all octagon combinations with positive and $\ell'_{j'}$ enumerates all octagon combinations with negative occurrences of z. Since $r' > 0$ and $a_z > 0$, also $r > 0$. If $y_{\ell_r} \geq y_{\ell'_{r'}}$, we proceed to eliminate the octagon combination $\ell'_{r'}$ with a negative occurrence of z and proceed to eliminate also all other negative occurrences of z by constructing a solution y'_ℓ with the same gain b where $y'_{\ell'_{r'}} = 0$. If $\ell_r + \ell'_{r'} = 0$, then either no further variable is contained in $\ell_r, \ell'_{r'}$ or the same variable z' occurs with opposite signs. Then we set $y'_{\ell_r} = y'_{\ell'_{r'}} = 0$ and $y'_p = y_p$ otherwise.

Now assume that $\ell_r + \ell'_{r'}$ is a linear combination different from 0. Then it either is equivalent to an octagon combination not involving variable z, or $2z'$ or $2 \cdot (-z')$ for some variable z' different from z. In order to deal with all these cases consistently, we introduce a correction factor c as 1 if the sum is an octagon linear combination, and 2 otherwise. Let q denote the octagon combination with

$c \cdot q = \ell_r + \ell'_{r'}$. Since the octagon r is closed, $c \cdot b_q \le b_{\ell_r} + b_{\ell'_{r'}}$ holds. Let $y'_\ell, \ell \in L_V$, be defined by

$$y'_\ell = \begin{cases} y_{\ell_r} - y_{\ell'_{r'}} \text{ if } \ell = \ell_r \\ 0 \text{ if } \ell = \ell'_{r'} \\ y_\ell + c \cdot y_{\ell'_{r'}} \text{ if } c \cdot \ell = q \\ y_\ell \text{ otherwise} \end{cases}$$

We claim that $y'_\ell, \ell \in L$, is again a feasible solution, i.e., satisfies all constraints, where the same gain b is attained. Concerning the gain, we have

$$\begin{aligned} y_{\ell_r} \cdot b_{\ell_r} + y_{\ell'_{r'}} \cdot b_{\ell'_{r'}} + y_q \cdot b_q &= (y_{\ell_r} - y_{\ell'_{r'}}) \cdot b_{\ell_r} + y_{\ell'_{r'}} \cdot (b_{\ell_r} + b_{\ell'_{r'}}) + y_q \cdot b_q \\ &\ge y'_{\ell_r} \cdot b_{\ell_r} + y'_q \cdot b_q \end{aligned}$$

As the gain b was already minimal, we conclude that the gain for the y'_ℓ has not changed. It remains to show that the y'_ℓ form a feasible solution of the constraints in (13). By construction, the equation for z is satisfied (we reduce y_{ℓ_r} with a positive occurrence of z by the same amount as $y_{\ell'_{r'}}$ with a negative occurrence). If q contains a variable z' which is then different from z, then this variable must occur in $\ell_r, \ell'_{r'}$ or both and if so, with the same sign. If it is contained only in $\ell'_{r'}$, then $y_{\ell'_{r'}}$ in the left-hand side of the constraint for z' is replaced with 0, while at the same time y_q is increased with y_{ℓ_r}. If it is contained only in ℓ_r, then y_{ℓ_r} in the left-hand side of the constraint for z' is decreased with $y_{\ell'_{r'}}$, while at the same time y_q is increased with y_{ℓ_r}. If it is contained both in ℓ_r and $\ell'_{r'}$, then y_{ℓ_r} in the left-hand side of the constraint for z' is decreased with $y_{\ell'_{r'}}$, $y_{\ell'_{r'}}$ is set to 0, y_q is increased with $2 \cdot y_{\ell'_{r'}}$.

Thus, in all cases, the equation is satisfied for the y'_p.

We conclude that the combination ℓ_r can equivalently be removed by means of the octagon combination q not involving the variable z.

Therefore, now assume that $y_{\ell'_{r'}} > y_{\ell_r}$ where, w.l.o.g., the maximal value of the non-zero y_{ℓ_j} equals y_{ℓ_r}. If $\ell_r + \ell'_{r'} = 0$, then $b_{\ell_r} + b_{\ell'_{r'}} = 0$ (otherwise the gain were not minimal). Therefore, we set $y'_{\ell_r} = 0$, $y'_{\ell'_{r'}} = y_{\ell'_{r'}} - y_{\ell_r}$, and $y'_\ell = \ell_p$ otherwise to obtain a feasible solution where the minimal gain is attained. At the same time, the number of octagon combinations ℓ with $y'_\ell > 0$ where z occurs positively has decreased. Therefore, assume that $\ell_r + \ell'_{r'}$ is different from 0. Then there is a coefficient $c \in \{1, 2\}$ and an octagon constraint q such that $c \cdot q = \ell_r + \ell'_{r'}$ and $c \cdot b_q \le b_{\ell_r} + b_{\ell'_{r'}}$. Then we set

$$y'_\ell = \begin{cases} 0 \text{ if } \ell = \ell_r \\ y_{\ell'_{r'}} - y_{\ell_r} \text{ if } \ell = \ell'_{r'} \\ y_q + c \cdot y_{\ell_r} \text{ if } \ell = q \\ y_\ell \text{ otherwise} \end{cases}$$

Again, we obtain a feasible solution where the gain has not increased, but the number of octagon combinations ℓ with $y'_\ell > 0$ where z occurs positively has decreased. Altogether, we conclude that, without increasing the gain, the feasible solution y_ℓ can be adjusted such that $y_\ell = 0$ for ℓ whenever ℓ contains negative occurrences of variables in V.

As a result, we obtain as the dual of the simplified LP problem

$$\begin{array}{lll} \textbf{minimize} & \sum_{z_1 \in V} y_{z_1} \cdot b_{z_1} + \sum_{z_2 \in V \setminus \{z_1\}} y_{z_1+z_2} \cdot b_{z_1+z_2} & \\ \textbf{subject to} & y_{z_1} + \sum_{z_2 \in V \setminus \{z_1\}} y_{z_1+z_2} = a_{z_1} & (z_1 \in V) \\ & y_{z_1} \geq 0 & (z_1 \in V) \\ & y_{z_1+z_2} \geq 0 & (z_1, z_2 \in V, z_1 \neq z_2) \end{array} \tag{15}$$

Example 7. Assume that the set of program variables consists of x, z_1, z_2, z_3, that our goal is to maximize the linear objective function $2z_1 + 3z_2 + z_3$ subject to the octagon constraints

$$z_1 + z_2 \leq 10 \qquad z_1 + z_3 \leq 1 \qquad z_2 + z_3 \leq 1$$

The dual linear program then is given by

$$\begin{array}{ll} \textbf{minimize} & y_1 \cdot 10 + y_2 + y_3 \\ \textbf{subject to} & y_1 + y_2 = 2 \quad y_1 + y_3 = 3 \quad y_2 + y_3 = 1 \\ & y_1, y_2, y_3 \geq 0 \end{array}$$

In this case, there is just one possible solution for the y_i, namely,

$$y_1 = 2.5 \quad y_2 = 0.5 \quad y_3 = 0.5$$

—implying that the optimal value is given by $25 + 0.5 + 0.5 = 26$. □

For an optimization problem with integer octagon constraints, we may, in principle, proceed as for rationals. Solving integer linear programs with octagon constraints precisely, however, is NP-hard. This can be seen, e.g., by reduction from the NP-complete *maximum clique problem*, i.e., the problem of deciding whether the maximal size of a clique in an undirected graph exceeds some bound. Let $G = (V, E)$ denote a finite undirected graph, and choose V as the set of variables. Then we construct the integer optimization problem

$$\begin{array}{lll} \textbf{maximize} & \sum_{x \in V} x & \\ \textbf{subject to} & x + y \leq 1 & (\{x, y\} \notin E) \\ & -x \leq 0 & (x \in V) \\ & x \leq 1 & (x \in V) \end{array}$$

The constraints are all integer octagon constraints, while the solution to the optimization problem equals the maximal size of a clique. Since the construction of the integer optimization problem from the instance of the clique problem can be done in polynomial time, it follows that to decide whether the optimal value for an integer linear program with octagon constraints exceeds some value, is NP-hard.

8 Abstract Assignments for Octagons

Assume that we are given an affine assignment of the form

$$x \leftarrow b + \sum_{z \in V} a_z \cdot z$$

and that the octagon before the assignment is a closed octagon r with coefficients $b_\ell, \ell \in L_{\mathcal{X}}$. W.l.o.g., assume that x does not occur in the right-hand side, i.e., $x \notin V$. Over the rationals, the best upper bound b'_ℓ for the octagon combination ℓ with x occurring in ℓ is obtained by a linear program of the form (13). Depending on ℓ, the objective functions are

ℓ	objective function
x	$\sum_{z \in V} a_z \cdot z$
$-x$	$\sum_{z \in V} -a_z \cdot z$
$x + y$	$y + \sum_{z \in V} a_z \cdot z$
$x - y$	$-y + \sum_{z \in V} a_z \cdot z$
$-x + y$	$y + \sum_{z \in V} -a_z \cdot z$
$-x - y$	$-y + \sum_{z \in V} -a_z \cdot z$

The best abstract transformer $[\![\mathsf{a}]\!]^\sharp$ then is given by

$$[\![\mathsf{a}]\!]^\sharp(r) = r|_{\mathcal{X} \setminus \{x\}} \wedge r_x \tag{16}$$

where r_x denotes the conjunction

$$(x \leq b + b'_x) \wedge \bigwedge_{z \neq x} (x + z \leq b + b'_{x+z}) \wedge (x - z \leq b + b'_{x-z}) \wedge \\ (-x + z \leq b'_{-x+z} - b) \wedge (-x - z \leq b'_{-x-z} - b)$$

Over the integers, we can proceed analogously to the rational case by solving the corresponding integer optimization problems. Since these, in general, are NP-hard, we prefer for integer octagons, to rely on rational *relaxations* of the corresponding ILP problems. This means that for each octagon combination ℓ, we determine the best rational upper bound b_ℓ after the assignment (as determined by the corresponding LP problem) which is tightened to $\lfloor b_\ell \rfloor$ to obtain a sound upper bound for ℓ over the integers. We remark that for integer octagons, an alternative formulation of abstract transformers for affine assignments has been provided in [21]. The transformer there is based on the optimal abstract transformer for rational polyhedra in [9] whose bounds are tightened and subsequently over-approximated by octagon constraints. The latter step also requires solving appropriate (relaxed) LP problems, which are essentially the same as we solve – only that we benefit from a reduced number of octagon constraints to be taken into account by each LP problem. We obtain:

Theorem 3. *For the octagon domain over the rationals, the best transformer* (16) *for a linear assignment can be computed in polynomial time. For n program variables and a constant number of variables occurring in the assignment, the best transformer can be computed in time $\mathcal{O}(n)$.*

□

Proof. Assume that the octagon before the assignment is closed. Due to Proposition 5, the octagon transformer for linear assignments satisfies properties (4) and (3). Therefore by Proposition 4, only a linear number of optimization problems must be solved. Over the rationals, the optimal upper bound to an octagon combination can be determined by solving an LP problem – which is known to be possible in polynomial time. Note that due to Proposition 5, the set of octagon constraints to be taken into account can be reduced to constraints with octagon combinations where the signs of variables match the corresponding signs occurring in the objective function.

If the right-hand side contains only a bounded number of variables, each of the LP problems will refer to a bounded number of variables only, and thus can be solved in constant time (e.g., by using the Simplex algorithm). Since only $\mathcal{O}(n)$ many of these problems must be solved, the overall runtime is linear. □

Over the integers, on the other hand, the solution of the relaxed integer LP problem for a sound bound to an octagon combination can be obtained as the solution to the corresponding relaxed rational LP problem, and the argument proceeds as in the rational case. As a corollary, we therefore obtain:

Corollary 1. *For the octagon domain over the integers, the integer relaxation of* (16) *for a linear assignment can be computed in polynomial time. For n program variables and a constant number of variables occurring in the assignment, the relaxed best transformer can be computed in time $\mathcal{O}(n)$.* □

9 Related Work

Since being introduced by Miné [20,21], the weakly relational numerical domain of *Octagons* has found widespread application in the analysis and verification of programs and is part, e.g., of the highly successful static analyzer ASTRÉE [3,7]. While normalization has been known to be cubic time for rational octagons right from the beginning [20], it was open whether this also holds true for integer octagons. This question has been settled affirmatively by Bagnara et al. [1]. Sankaranarayanan et al. [25] proposed using techniques from linear programming to compute best transformers for linear assignments. Chawdhary et al. [4] investigated the problem of improved quadratic algorithms for incremental closure, i.e., adding one further octagon constraint. Implementations of *Octagons* are provided, e.g., by the APRON library [14] and ELINA [10]. Various *Octagon* algorithms are practically evaluated by Gange et al. [12].

Extensions of octagons have been considered by Péron and Halbwachs [24] and Chen et al. [5]. For these extensions, however, known normalization algorithms turn out to be rather expensive so that more practical *approximate* normalizations have been proposed. Figure 1 gives an overview over some weakly relational domains, whether they are 2-decomposable and whether they are also 2-projective as well as the best time complexities for (approximate) normalization in the number of variables.

Domain	2-decomposable	2-projective	Normalization
Integer Octagons [20]	✓	✓	$\mathcal{O}(n^3)$
Rational Octagons [20]	✓	✓	$\mathcal{O}(n^3)$
TVPI [27][a]	✓	✓	$\mathcal{O}(n^3 \log^2 n)$
Pentagons [18]	✓	✓	$\mathcal{O}(n^3)$
Weighted Hexagons [11]	✓	✓	$\mathcal{O}(n^3)$
Logahedra [13]	✓	✓	$\mathcal{O}(n^3)$
dDBM [24][b]	✓	✗ (Appendix A)	$O(n^3)$ rat.; $O(n^5)$ ints
AVO [5]	✓	✗ (Appendix A)	$O(2^n \cdot n^3)$ rat.; ? ints
Pairs (Example 5)	✓	✗	?

Fig. 1. Various weakly relational domains, whether they are 2-projective and 2-decomposable, and the complexity of their normalization operation. [a](For TVPI: As operations on values for 3 variables are in $\mathcal{O}(\log^2 n)$.) [b](For int dDBM: Approximate normalization up-to emptiness. Checking emptiness is exponential.)

10 Conclusion and Future Work

We have provided an algorithm for normalizing octagon abstract relations over rationals as well as over integers. For that, we introduced the notion of 2-decomposability for relational domains and provided a cubic-time algorithm based on *Floyd-Warshall* which overapproximates normalization. For the subclass of 2-projective domains comprising, e.g., integer or rational *Octagons*, it computes the *exact* 2-normal form. The major benefit of the resulting algorithm is its simplicity. For the instance of the *Octagon* domain, e.g., the closure is obtained without duplication of variables. The general setup also provides us with a quadratic algorithm for *incremental* normalization. For octagons, we also reconsidered the construction of best abstract transformers for affine assignments by means of linear programming. Over the rationals, we observe that only those octagon constraints need to be taken into account where the sign of each occurring variable z agrees with the sign of the occurrence of z in the respective objective functions. This, again, may result in a significant speedup when it comes to practical implementations.

In future work, we would like to provide a new implementation of *Octagon* domains based on our algorithms and evaluate its practical performance on realistic examples. Combining our algorithms with orthogonal techniques such as online decomposition [28] in particular seems like a promising line of inquiry. We also would like to explore in greater detail the potential of further, perhaps non-numerical 2-decomposable domains.

Acknowledgements. This work was supported in part by Deutsche Forschungsgemeinschaft (DFG) - 378803395/2428 ConVeY.

A 2-Projectivity for Extensions of Octagons

Here, we investigate extensions to the *Octagon* domain and the domain of difference bounds, respectively, that have been proposed in the literature, and investigate whether they are 2-decomposable and 2-projective.

Example 8. Consider the domain of difference-bound matrices enhanced with disequalities [24] where $\mathcal{X} = \{a, b, c\}$. This domain is 2-decomposable. Now, for 2-projectivity, let, e.g.,

$$\begin{aligned} r_{\{a,b\}} &= (a - b \leq -1 \wedge b \neq 98 \wedge b \neq 97) \\ r_{\{a,c\}} &= (c \leq 99) \\ r_{\{b,c\}} &= (b - c \leq -1) \end{aligned}$$

and all other $r_p = \top$. We remark that, by abuse of notation, we write $b \neq 98$ instead of introducing a dedicated variable c_{98} and constraints $b \neq c_{98} \wedge c_{98} \leq 98 \wedge 0 - c_{98} \leq -98$, and analogously for $b \neq 97$. Now, consider (9) with $Y = \{a, c\}$, $z = b$, $r' = \{c \leq 99\}$ Then,

$$\begin{aligned} &\left(r_{\{b\}} \wedge r_{\{b,a\}} \wedge r_{\{b,c\}} \wedge r'\right)\Big|_{Y} \\ &= \left(r_{\{b\}} \wedge r_{\{b,a\}} \wedge r_{\{b,c\}} \wedge r'\right)\Big|_{\{a,c\}} \\ &= (c \leq 99 \wedge a - c \leq -2 \wedge c \leq 95) \\ &\neq (c \leq 99 \wedge a - c \leq -2 \wedge c \leq 97) \\ &= (c \leq 99) \wedge \top \wedge \top \wedge \top \wedge (a - c \leq -2) \wedge \top \wedge \top \\ &= (c \leq 99) \wedge \left(r_{\{b\}} \wedge r_{\{b\}}\right)\Big|_{\emptyset} \wedge \left(r_{\{a,b\}} \wedge r_{\{a,b\}}\right)\Big|_{\{a\}} \wedge \left(r_{\{b,c\}} \wedge r_{\{b,c\}}\right)\Big|_{\{c\}} \\ &\quad \wedge \left(r_{\{a,b\}} \wedge r_{\{b,c\}}\right)\Big|_{\{a,c\}} \wedge \left(r_{\{b\}} \wedge r_{\{b,a\}}\right)\Big|_{\{a\}} \wedge \left(r_{\{b\}} \wedge r_{\{b,c\}}\right)\Big|_{\{c\}} \\ &= r' \wedge \bigwedge_{i,j=1}^{k} \left(r_{\{b,y_i\}} \wedge r_{\{b,y_j\}}\right)\Big|_{Y \cap \{y_i,y_j\}} \end{aligned}$$

and the domain thus is not 2-projective. □

Example 9. Consider the domain of octagons enhanced with additional constraints for the absolute values of variables [5], i.e., with additional constraints of the form $\pm|x| \pm |y| \leq c$ and $\pm|x| \pm y \leq c$. This domain is 2-decomposable. Now, for 2-projectivity, let, e.g.,

$$\begin{aligned} r_{\{a,d\}} &= a - |d| \leq 2 \\ r_{\{b,c\}} &= b + c \leq 5 \\ r_{\{b,d\}} &= b - d \leq 5 \\ r_{\{c,d\}} &= -c + d \leq 2 \wedge -|d| \leq 0 \end{aligned}$$

with all other $r_p = \top$ for $p \in [\mathcal{X}]_2$. Now, consider (9) with $Y = \{a, b, c\}$, $z = d$, $r' = (b + c \leq 5)$.

$$
\begin{aligned}
&(r_{\{d\}} \wedge r_{\{d,a\}} \wedge r_{\{d,b\}} \wedge r_{\{d,c\}} \wedge r')\big|_Y \\
&= (r_{\{d\}} \wedge r_{\{d,a\}} \wedge r_{\{d,b\}} \wedge r_{\{d,c\}} \wedge r')\big|_{\{a,b,c\}} \\
&= b + c \leq 5 \wedge b - c \leq 7 \wedge b \leq 6 \wedge a + b \leq 9 \\
&\neq b + c \leq 5 \wedge b - c \leq 7 \wedge b \leq 6 \\
&= b + c \leq 5 \wedge \top \wedge \top \wedge \{b - c \leq 7\} \\
&= b + c \leq 5 \wedge (a - |d| \leq 2 \wedge b - d \leq 5)|_{\{a,b\}} \\
&\quad \wedge (a - |d| \leq 2 \wedge (-c + d \leq 2 \wedge -|d| \leq 0))|_{\{a,c\}} \wedge \\
&\quad (b - d \leq 5 \wedge (-c + d \leq 2 \wedge -|d| \leq 0))|_{\{b,c\}} \\
&= b + c \leq 5 \wedge (r_{\{d,a\}} \wedge r_{\{d,b\}})\big|_{\{a,b\}} \wedge (r_{\{d,a\}} \wedge r_{\{d,c\}})\big|_{\{a,c\}} \wedge (r_{\{d,b\}} \wedge r_{\{d,c\}})\big|_{\{b,c\}} \\
&= \{b + c \leq 5\} \wedge \\
&\quad (r_{\{d,a\}})\big|_{\{a\}} \wedge (r_{\{d,a\}} \wedge r_{\{d,b\}})\big|_{\{a,b\}} \wedge (r_{\{d,a\}} \wedge r_{\{d,c\}})\big|_{\{a,c\}} \wedge \\
&\quad (r_{\{d,b\}})\big|_{\{b\}} \wedge (r_{\{d,b\}} \wedge r_{\{d,c\}})\big|_{\{b,c\}} \wedge \\
&\quad (r_{\{d,c\}})\big|_{\{c\}} \\
&= \{b + c \leq 5\} \wedge \\
&\quad (r_{\{d,a\}} \wedge r_{\{d,a\}})\big|_{\{a\}} \wedge (r_{\{d,a\}} \wedge r_{\{d,b\}})\big|_{\{a,b\}} \wedge (r_{\{d,a\}} \wedge r_{\{d,c\}})\big|_{\{a,c\}} \\
&\quad \wedge (r_{\{d,a\}} \wedge r_{\{d,d\}})\big|_{\{a\}} \wedge \\
&\quad (r_{\{d,b\}} \wedge r_{\{d,b\}})\big|_{\{b\}} \wedge (r_{\{d,b\}} \wedge r_{\{d,c\}})\big|_{\{b,c\}} \wedge (r_{\{d,b\}} \wedge r_{\{d,d\}})\big|_{\{b\}} \wedge \\
&\quad (r_{\{d,c\}} \wedge r_{\{d,c\}})\big|_{\{c\}} \wedge (r_{\{d,c\}} \wedge r_{\{d,d\}})\big|_{\{c\}} \wedge \\
&\quad (r_{\{d,d\}} \wedge r_{\{d,d\}})\big|_{\{\emptyset\}} \\
&= r' \wedge \textstyle\bigwedge_{i,j=1}^{k} (r_{\{d,y_i\}} \wedge r_{\{d,y_j\}})\big|_{Y \cap \{y_i,y_j\}}
\end{aligned}
$$

and the domain thus is not 2-projective. □

References

1. Bagnara, R., Hill, P.M., Zaffanella, E.: An improved tight closure algorithm for integer octagonal constraints. In: Logozzo, F., Peled, D.A., Zuck, L.D. (eds.) VMCAI 2008. LNCS, vol. 4905, pp. 8–21. Springer, Heidelberg (2008). https://doi.org/10.1007/978-3-540-78163-9_6 ISBN: 978-3-540-78163-9
2. Bagnara, R., Hill, P.M., Zaffanella, E.: Weakly-relational shapes for numeric abstractions: improved algorithms and proofs of correctness. Formal Methods Syst. Des. **35**(3), 279–323 (2009). https://doi.org/10.1007/s10703-009-0073-1
3. Blanchet, B., et al.: A static analyzer for large safety-critical software. In: Proceedings of the ACM SIGPLAN 2003 Conference on Programming Language Design and Implementation, PLDI 2003, pp. 196–207. Association for Computing Machinery, New York (2003). https://doi.org/10.1145/781131.781153. ISBN: 1581136625
4. Chawdhary, A., Robbins, E., King, A.: Incrementally closing octagons. Formal Methods Syst. Des. **54**(2), 232–277 (2019). https://doi.org/10.1007/s10703-017-0314-7
5. Chen, L., Liu, J., Miné, A., Kapur, D., Wang, J.: An abstract domain to infer octagonal constraints with absolute value. In: Müller-Olm, M., Seidl, H. (eds.) SAS 2014. LNCS, vol. 8723, pp. 101–117. Springer, Cham (2014). https://doi.org/10.1007/978-3-319-10936-7_7

6. Cormen, T.H., Leiserson, C.E., Rivest, R.L., Stein, C.: Introduction to Algorithms. MIT Press, Cambridge (2009)
7. Cousot, P., Cousot, R., Feret, J., Mauborgne, L., Miné, A., Rival, X.: Why does astrée scale up? Form. Methods Syst. Des. **35**(3), 229–264 (2009). https://doi.org/10.1007/s10703-009-0089-6. ISSN: 0925-9856
8. Cousot, P., Halbwachs, N.: Automatic discovery of linear restraints among variables of a program. In: Aho, A.V., Zilles, S.N., Szymanski, T.G. (eds.) Conference Record of the Fifth Annual ACM Symposium on Principles of Programming Languages, Tucson, Arizona, USA, January 1978, pp. 84–96, ACM Press (1978). https://doi.org/10.1145/512760.512770
9. Cousot, P., Halbwachs, N.: Automatic discovery of linear restraints among variables of a program. In: Proceedings of the 5th ACM SIGACT-SIGPLAN Symposium on Principles of Programming Languages, POPL 1978, pp. 84–96. Association for Computing Machinery, New York (1978). https://doi.org/10.1145/512760.512770. ISBN: 9781450373487
10. ELINA: ELINA: ETH library for numerical analysis (2018). https://elina.ethz.ch/
11. Fulara, J., Durnoga, K., Jakubczyk, K., Schubert, A.: Relational abstract domain of weighted hexagons. Electron. Notes Theor. Comput. Sci. **267**(1), 59–72 (2010). https://doi.org/10.1016/j.entcs.2010.09.006
12. Gange, G., Ma, Z., Navas, J.A., Schachte, P., Søndergaard, H., Stuckey, P.J.: A fresh look at zones and octagons. ACM Trans. Program. Lang. Syst. **43**(3), 1–51 (2021). https://doi.org/10.1145/3457885. ISSN: 0164-0925
13. Howe, J.M., King, A.: Logahedra: a new weakly relational domain. In: Liu, Z., Ravn, A.P. (eds.) ATVA 2009. LNCS, vol. 5799, pp. 306–320. Springer, Heidelberg (2009). https://doi.org/10.1007/978-3-642-04761-9_23
14. Jeannet, B., Miné, A.: APRON: a library of numerical abstract domains for static analysis. In: Bouajjani, A., Maler, O. (eds.) CAV 2009. LNCS, vol. 5643, pp. 661–667. Springer, Heidelberg (2009). https://doi.org/10.1007/978-3-642-02658-4_52
15. Karmarkar, N.: A new polynomial-time algorithm for linear programming. In: Proceedings of the Sixteenth Annual ACM Symposium on Theory of Computing, pp. 302–311 (1984)
16. Karr, M.: Affine relationships among variables of a program. Acta Informatica **6**, 133–151 (1976). https://doi.org/10.1007/BF00268497
17. Klee, V., Minty, G.J.: How good is the simplex algorithm. Inequalities **3**(3), 159–175 (1972)
18. Logozzo, F., Fähndrich, M.: Pentagons: a weakly relational abstract domain for the efficient validation of array accesses. In: Proceedings of the 2008 ACM Symposium on Applied Computing, SAC 2008, pp. 184–188. Association for Computing Machinery, New York (2008). https://doi.org/10.1145/1363686.1363736. ISBN: 9781595937537
19. Miné, A.: A new numerical abstract domain based on difference-bound matrices. In: Danvy, O., Filinski, A. (eds.) PADO 2001. LNCS, vol. 2053, pp. 155–172. Springer, Heidelberg (2001). https://doi.org/10.1007/3-540-44978-7_10
20. Miné, A.: The octagon abstract domain. In: WCRE 2001, p. 310. IEEE Computer Society (2001). https://doi.org/10.1109/WCRE.2001.957836
21. Miné, A.: The octagon abstract domain. High. Order Symbol. Comput. **19**(1), 31–100 (2006). https://doi.org/10.1007/s10990-006-8609-1. ISSN: 1388-3690
22. Müller-Olm, M., Seidl, H.: Precise interprocedural analysis through linear algebra. In: Jones, N.D., Leroy, X. (eds.) Proceedings of the 31st ACM SIGPLAN-SIGACT Symposium on Principles of Programming Languages, POPL 2004, Venice, Italy,

14–16 January 2004, pp. 330–341. ACM (2004). https://doi.org/10.1145/964001.964029
23. Müller-Olm, M., Seidl, H.: Analysis of modular arithmetic. ACM Trans. Program. Lang. Syst. **29**(5), 29 (2007). https://doi.org/10.1145/1275497.1275504
24. Péron, M., Halbwachs, N.: An abstract domain extending difference-bound matrices with disequality constraints. In: Cook, B., Podelski, A. (eds.) VMCAI 2007. LNCS, vol. 4349, pp. 268–282. Springer, Heidelberg (2007). https://doi.org/10.1007/978-3-540-69738-1_20
25. Sankaranarayanan, S., Sipma, H.B., Manna, Z.: Scalable analysis of linear systems using mathematical programming. In: Cousot, R. (ed.) VMCAI 2005. LNCS, vol. 3385, pp. 25–41. Springer, Heidelberg (2005). https://doi.org/10.1007/978-3-540-30579-8_2 ISBN: 978-3-540-30579-8
26. Schwarz, M., Saan, S., Seidl, H., Erhard, J., Vojdani, V.: Clustered relational thread-modular abstract interpretation with local traces. In: Wies, T. (ed.) ESOP 2023. LNCS, vol. 13990, pp. 28–58. Springer, Cham (2023). https://doi.org/10.1007/978-3-031-30044-8_2
27. Simon, A., King, A., Howe, J.M.: Two variables per linear inequality as an abstract domain. In: Leuschel, M. (ed.) LOPSTR 2002. LNCS, vol. 2664, pp. 71–89. Springer, Heidelberg (2003). https://doi.org/10.1007/3-540-45013-0_7
28. Singh, G., Püschel, M., Vechev, M.: A practical construction for decomposing numerical abstract domains. Proc. ACM Program. Lang. **2**(POPL), 1–28 (2018). https://doi.org/10.1145/3158143

Polynomial Analysis of Modular Arithmetic

Thomas Seed[1], Chris Coppins[1], Andy King[1(✉)], and Neil Evans[2]

[1] University of Kent, Canterbury CT2 7NZ, UK
a.m.king@kent.ac.uk

[2] AWE Aldermaston, Reading RG7 4PR, UK

Abstract. The modular polynomial abstract domain, MPAD, is proposed, whose invariants are systems of polynomial equations that hold modulo a power of 2. Its domain operations are founded on a closure operation, but unlike conventional polynomial abstractions, MPAD satisfies the ascending chain condition, can model both positive and negative polynomial guards, and can infer invariants previously out of reach.

Keywords: abstract interpretation · modular arithmetic · polynomial invariants

1 Introduction

One step in the evolution of a numeric abstract domain is when the domain, originally conceived for idealised, arbitrary-precision arithmetic, is adapted to machine arithmetic to better suit its working environment. This adaption is more often a leap than a step because the domain operations typically need to be fundamentally reimagined to model modular arithmetic. It has taken more than two decades for each of the classical abstract domains of ranges [7,15], difference constraints [9] and linear equalities [20], to be adjusted to a modular setting, as realised in, respectively, sign agnostic range analysis [11], modular differences [12] and linear equalities modulo a power of two [27]. The tenor of these works is that operating over modular integers is not a restriction, but rather the natural domain for deriving invariants over fixed-width integers, which are the norm in mainstream programming languages.

Modular Polynomial Abstract Domain. For inferring polynomial invariants, one might be forgiven for considering the additional complexity of modular arithmetic to be an irritation, justified only by the desire to faithfully model machine integers and avoid missing invariants. In this paper we challenge this view by demonstrating how Modular Polynomial Abstract Domain (MPAD) can simplify the discovery of polynomial equalities. Contrary to non-modular approaches [4,8,17,22,23,25,29–31], MPAD is a finite lattice. The finiteness of modular polynomials has been observed before [33], and exploited in a backwards analysis [33] over programs equipped with polynomial assignment, non-deterministic assignment and negative guards (discussed in Sect. 7). Our work takes modular polynomials in a new direction, literally forwards, enabling MPAD to be combined [5]

M. V. Hermenegildo and J. F. Morales (Eds.): SAS 2023, LNCS 14284, pp. 508–539, 2023.
https://doi.org/10.1007/978-3-031-44245-2_22

with classic numeric domains [24]. Like [33], MPAD obviates the need to specify the shape of an invariant up-front (in a template) [29,31], or limit the syntactic form of the program [17,18,23], or drop high-degree polynomials [30].

Closure of Modular Systems. Fundamental to MPAD is the concept of a closed polynomial system. A system of polynomials is closed if it cannot be further augmented with polynomials without restricting its solution set. Ensuring a closed representation is essential to ensure that entailment of a given constraint can always be checked. Morever, mirroring a construction used for the Octagon domain [24], we demonstrate that join and projection can be calculated, without omitting polynomials that actually hold, when they are applied to closed systems. It follows that MPAD can infer all modular polynomial invariants for programs with polynomial and non-deterministic assignments, and non-deterministic branching. Though preserved by join and projection, closedness is lost when intersecting two polynomial systems to compute their meet. To resolve this, we present a divide-and-conquer algorithm for computing closure, thus ensuring a closed representation throughout the analysis.

Expressiveness. MPAD can model positive and negative polynomial guards, that is, assume $(p = 0)$ and assume $(p \neq 0)$ statements where p is a polynomial. Support for negative guards is a direct consequence of working with fixed-width integers: an integer assumes a non-zero value if and only if one of its bits is set, a property that can be expressed in MPAD. The finiteness of MPAD also allows a best transformer [28] to be mechanically calculated. For instance, the best transformer for the 3-bit bitvector operation $x \,\&\, y = z$ is the system S:

$$\begin{array}{ll}
xy^3 + xy^2 + 5yz^2 + 2xy + 5z^2 + 2z, & xyz + 7xz^2 + 7yz^2 + z^3, \\
xz^3 + xz^2 + 5z^3 + 6xz + 5z^2 + 6z, & y^2z + 7yz^2 + yz + 7z^2, \\
yz^3 + 5yz^2 + z^3 + 2yz + 5z^2 + 2z, & 4xy + 4z, \\
x^2y + 5xy^2 + 6xz^2 + 6yz^2 + 6z^3 + 5xy + 3z^2, & 4xz + 4z, \\
x^2z + 7xz^2 + 5xz + 3z^2, & 4yz + 4z
\end{array}$$

where each polynomial $p \in S$ is satisfied by every assignment of the form $x, y \in \{0, \ldots, 7\}$ and $z = (x \& y) \mod 8$. This, and other best abstractions, can only be calculated [28] because MPAD satisfies the ascending chain condition.

Contributions. To summarise, this paper makes the following contributions:

- We introduce closure for MPAD, showing that it is preserved by join and projection but must be re-established after meet to retain all invariants;
- We present a divide-and-conquer algorithm for computing closure, introducing reductions and shortcuts that simplify its calculation;
- We show how redundant calculation can be removed from the algorithm (of Buchberger for modular polynomials [2]) which sits behind closure;
- We show that using MPAD in forwards analysis can derive invariants that cannot be derived with existing domains (because of its support for guards).

Roadmap. Section 2 introduces MPAD, providing the minimum of detail for following the example of Sect. 6.5. The domain operations of MPAD are built atop of Gröbner bases, which are introduced in Sect. 3. (The detail of Sect. 3.5 can be skipped on first reading since it is only necessary for Sect. 6.6.) Sect. 4 explains how join can be calculated in terms of variable elimination and Gröbner bases. Section 5 introduces covers of polynomial systems, providing an algorithm for computing them. It also shows how meet can be reduced to closure. Section 6 presents correctness and precision results for MPAD over polynomial programs, and concludes with an illustrative example. Section 7 reviews related work and Sect. 8 concludes.

2 Modular Polynomial Abstract Domain

This section abstractly specifies MPAD, and its domain operations, with minimal mathematical machinery. The problems of how to finitely represent the elements of MPAD and compute meet, join and projection are deferred to later sections.

2.1 Modular Arithmetic

Let $\omega \geq 1$, $m = 2^\omega$ and $\mathbb{Z}_m = \{0, \ldots, m-1\}$ be an abstraction of machine arithmetic over ω-bit integers [26,27]. The relation $\equiv_m \subseteq \mathbb{Z} \times \mathbb{Z}$ is defined by $x \equiv_m y$ if there exists $k \in \mathbb{Z}$ such that $x - y = km$. Atop, the operation $\cdot \pmod{m} : \mathbb{Z} \to \mathbb{Z}_m$ is defined $x \pmod{m} = y$ where $y \in \mathbb{Z}_m$ uniquely satisfies $x \equiv_m y$. The unary operation $- : \mathbb{Z}_m \to \mathbb{Z}_m$ and the dyadic operations $+, \cdot : \mathbb{Z}_m \times \mathbb{Z}_m \to \mathbb{Z}_m$ are then defined: $-x = (\hat{-}x) \pmod{m}$, $x + y = (x \hat{+} y) \pmod{m}$ and $x \cdot y = (x \hat{\cdot} y) \pmod{m}$ where $\hat{-}, \hat{+}, \hat{\cdot}$ denote the classical operations over $\mathbb{Z}$. If $x \in \mathbb{Z}_m$ then $y \in \mathbb{Z}_m$ is a multiplicative inverse of x if $x \cdot y = 1$. Note that $x \in \mathbb{Z}_m$ has a multiplicative inverse iff it is odd, in which case the inverse is unique. In particular, if $\omega > 1$ then $\mathbb{Z}_m$ is not a field, since 2 has no multiplicative inverse.

2.2 Polynomials

Let $\boldsymbol{x} = \langle x_1, \ldots, x_d \rangle$ be a vector of variables. A monomial over $\boldsymbol{x}$ is an expression $\boldsymbol{x}^{\boldsymbol{\alpha}} = x_1^{\alpha_1} \cdots x_d^{\alpha_d}$ where $\boldsymbol{\alpha} = \langle \alpha_1, \ldots, \alpha_d \rangle \in \mathbb{N}^d$. A term over $\boldsymbol{x}$ is an expression $t = c\boldsymbol{x}^{\boldsymbol{\alpha}}$ where $c \in \mathbb{Z}_m$ and $\boldsymbol{x}^{\boldsymbol{\alpha}}$ is a monomial. A polynomial over $\boldsymbol{x}$ is an expression $t_1 + \cdots + t_s$ where each t_i is a term over $\boldsymbol{x}$, the case $s = 0$ corresponding to the 0 polynomial. The set of polynomials over $\boldsymbol{x}$ is denoted $\mathbb{Z}_m[\boldsymbol{x}]$.

A polynomial $p = t_1 + \cdots + t_s$ is normalised if either $s = 0$ or else for all $t_i = c_i \boldsymbol{x}^{\boldsymbol{\alpha}_i}$ and $t_j = c_j \boldsymbol{x}^{\boldsymbol{\alpha}_j}$ it holds that $c_i \neq 0$ and if $i \neq j$ then $\boldsymbol{\alpha}_i \neq \boldsymbol{\alpha}_j$. By repeatedly combining the coefficients of terms with equal monomials, and deleting terms with coefficient 0, a polynomial can be transformed into a normalised form. Two polynomials are considered equal if they have equal normal forms, up to the ordering of terms. If $c\boldsymbol{x}^{\boldsymbol{\alpha}}$ is a term then $\mathsf{vars}(c\boldsymbol{x}^{\boldsymbol{\alpha}}) = \{x_i \mid \alpha_i > 0\}$, which is extended to polynomials by $\mathsf{vars}(p) = \bigcup_{t \in p} \mathsf{vars}(t)$.

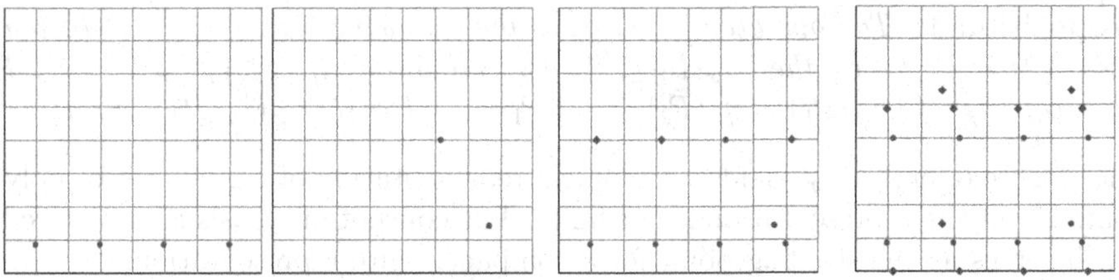

(a) $\gamma_{\boldsymbol{x}}(Q_1)$ (b) $\gamma_{\boldsymbol{x}}(Q_2)$ (c) $\gamma_{\boldsymbol{x}}(\langle Q_1' \rangle_{\boldsymbol{x}} \cap \langle Q_2 \rangle_{\boldsymbol{x}})$ (d) $\gamma_{\boldsymbol{x}}(\langle Q_1 \rangle_{\boldsymbol{x}} \cap \langle Q_2 \rangle_{\boldsymbol{x}})$

Fig. 1. Dyadic join with and without closure

For $p \in \mathbb{Z}_m[\boldsymbol{x}]$, $d = |\boldsymbol{x}|$ and $\boldsymbol{a} \in \mathbb{Z}_m^d$ let $[\![p]\!]_{\boldsymbol{x}}(\boldsymbol{a})$ denote evaluating p at $\boldsymbol{a}$ by substituting each a_i for x_i in p, and calculating the resulting arithmetical expression. Through this definition, a set of polynomials in $\mathbb{Z}_m[\boldsymbol{x}]$ is a symbolic description of a set of points, interpreted by $\gamma_{\boldsymbol{x}}$ as follows:

Definition 1. *The concretisation map* $\gamma_{\boldsymbol{x}} : \wp(\mathbb{Z}_m[\boldsymbol{x}]) \to \wp(\mathbb{Z}_m^d)$ *where* $d = |\boldsymbol{x}|$ *is defined:* $\gamma_{\boldsymbol{x}}(P) = \{\boldsymbol{a} \in \mathbb{Z}_m^d \mid [\![p]\!]_{\boldsymbol{x}}(\boldsymbol{a}) = 0 \text{ for all } p \in P\}$

The set of points $\gamma_{\boldsymbol{x}}(P)$ is the solution (or zero) set of the set P of polynomials over $\boldsymbol{x}$. For a single $p \in \mathbb{Z}_m[\boldsymbol{x}]$, let $\gamma_{\boldsymbol{x}}(p) = \gamma_{\boldsymbol{x}}(\{p\})$.

Example 1. Let $\boldsymbol{x} = \langle x, y \rangle$ and $Q_1, Q_2 \subseteq \mathbb{Z}_{256}[\boldsymbol{x}]$ where

$$Q_1 = \{\, 4x + 132, y + 228 \,\} \quad Q_2 = \left\{ \begin{array}{lll} x^2 + x + 123y + 130, & xy + 108y + 128, \\ 2x + 23y + 54, & y^2 + 82y, & 128y \end{array} \right\}$$

The solutions sets $\gamma_{\boldsymbol{x}}(Q_1)$ and $\gamma_{\boldsymbol{x}}(Q_2)$ are plotted as points in $[0, 255]^2$ in Fig. 1(a) and Fig. 1(b) respectively. Here, the grid lines represent increments of 32. Although Q_1 is linear it has 4 solutions, namely (31, 28), (95, 28), (159, 28) and (223, 28), because $31 \cdot 4 \equiv_{256} 95 \cdot 4 \equiv_{256} 159 \cdot 4 \equiv_{256} 223 \cdot 4 \equiv_{256} 124 \equiv_{256} -132$.

2.3 Closure

Suppose $P \subseteq \mathbb{Z}_m[\boldsymbol{x}]$, $p \in \mathbb{Z}_m[\boldsymbol{x}]$ and $\gamma_{\boldsymbol{x}}(P) \subseteq \gamma_{\boldsymbol{x}}(p)$. Then $\gamma_{\boldsymbol{x}}(P \cup \{p\}) = \gamma_{\boldsymbol{x}}(P)$, thus P can be augmented with p without restricting its solution set. This is the intuition behind the following definition:

Definition 2. *The operator* $\uparrow_{\boldsymbol{x}}$: $\wp(\mathbb{Z}_m[\boldsymbol{x}]) \to \wp(\mathbb{Z}_m[\boldsymbol{x}])$ *is defined by:* $\uparrow_{\boldsymbol{x}} P = \{p \in \mathbb{Z}_m[\boldsymbol{x}] \mid \gamma_{\boldsymbol{x}}(P) \subseteq \gamma_{\boldsymbol{x}}(p)\}$

The following result collects fundamental properties of $\uparrow_{\boldsymbol{x}}$. The first three together imply that $\uparrow_{\boldsymbol{x}}$ is a closure operator on $\langle \wp(\mathbb{Z}_m[\boldsymbol{x}]), \subseteq \rangle$. The fourth implies that $\uparrow_{\boldsymbol{x}}$ constructs a canonical representation of a system of polynomials. The fifth shows that the canonical representation preserves the solution set.

Proposition 1. *The operator $\uparrow_{x}$ satisfies the following: (1) $P \subseteq \uparrow_{x} P$ (extensive); (2) if $P_1 \subseteq P_2$ then $\uparrow_{x} P_1 \subseteq \uparrow_{x} P_2$ (monotonic); (3) $\uparrow_{x} \uparrow_{x} P = \uparrow_{x} P$ (idempotent); (4) $\gamma_{x}(P_1) = \gamma_{x}(P_2)$ iff $\uparrow_{x} P_1 = \uparrow_{x} P_2$; (5) $\gamma_{x}(\uparrow_{x} P) = \gamma_{x}(P)$.*

The closure operator $\uparrow_{x}$ yields a canonical representation of a given set of polynomials, yet the representation is not finite. The concept of a basis is introduced, which serves as the starting point for a compact, finite representation:

Definition 3. *If $B \subseteq \mathbb{Z}_m[\boldsymbol{x}]$ then $\langle B \rangle_{x} = \{\sum_{i=1}^{s} u_i p_i | \, s \in \mathbb{N}, p_i \in B, u_i \in \mathbb{Z}_m[\boldsymbol{x}]\}$*

The set of polynomials $\langle B \rangle_{x}$ is an ideal in that it is closed under addition with a polynomial from B and multiplication with an arbitrary polynomial (not necessarily drawn from B). The ideal $\langle B \rangle_{x}$ is said to be generated by B, which is called the basis. In particular the solutions of $\langle B \rangle_{x}$ are those of B itself and the sets found by applying closure are ideals themselves:

Lemma 1. *(1) $\gamma_{x}(\langle B \rangle_{x}) = \gamma_{x}(B)$ and (2) If $P = \uparrow_{x} P$ then $P = \langle P \rangle_{x}$.*

Generating P from itself is enough to show that P is an ideal, but does not provide the necessary finite representation. However, it has long been known that ideals of polynomials admit a finite basis [16], at least for polynomials whose coefficients are drawn from a field. This classical result, which can be interpreted as a statement on representation, adapts naturally to the setting of polynomials over modular integers, as will be explained in Sect. 3.

Example 2. Returning to Example 1, $\uparrow_{x} Q_1$ and $\uparrow_{x} Q_2$ admit the finite representations $\uparrow_{x} Q_1 = \langle Q_1' \rangle_{x}$ and $\uparrow_{x} Q_2 = \langle Q_2 \rangle_{x}$ where $Q_1' = \{x^2+2x+1, 4x+132, y+228\}$. Observe $31^2 + 2 \cdot 31 + 1 = 1024 \equiv_{256} 0$. Similarly it follows $\gamma_{x}(x^2+2x+1) \supseteq \{(31,y),(95,y),(159,y),(233,y) \mid y \in \mathbb{Z}_{256}\}$. Thus $x^2+2x+1 \in \uparrow_{x} Q_1$. However, $x^2+2x+1 \notin \langle Q_1 \rangle_{x}$. To see this, consider the expansion of the polynomial $p(4x+132)+q(y+228) = 4(xp+33p+57q)+yq$. Observe that any term t occurring in this polynomial that is independent of y must be a term of $4(xp+33p+57q)$. But then, the coefficient of t must be a multiple of 4. In particular, there cannot exist p, q for which $x^2+2x+1 = p(4x+132)+q(y+228)$, since x^2 (and in fact $2x$ and 1 as well) is independent of y but has coefficient 1. Hence Q_1 must be enlarged to obtain a basis for $\uparrow_{x} Q_1$.

2.4 MPAD

The closure operator characterises the elements of our abstract domain:

Definition 4. $\mathsf{MPAD}_m[\boldsymbol{x}] = \{P \subseteq \mathbb{Z}_m[\boldsymbol{x}] \mid \uparrow_{x} P = P\}$

Elements of $\mathsf{MPAD}_m[\boldsymbol{x}]$ are said to be closed. If $P_1 \subseteq P_2$ then $\gamma_{x}(P_1) \supseteq \gamma_{x}(P_2)$ thus to align with $\langle \wp(\mathbb{Z}_m^d), \subseteq \rangle$ the domain $\mathsf{MPAD}_m[\boldsymbol{x}]$ adopts superset ordering:

Proposition 2. *$\langle \mathsf{MPAD}_m[\boldsymbol{x}], \sqsubseteq, \bot, \top, \sqcap, \sqcup \rangle$ is a finite lattice, where*

$$\sqsubseteq = \supseteq \quad \bot = \mathbb{Z}_m[\boldsymbol{x}] \quad \top = \uparrow_{x} \emptyset \quad P_1 \sqcap P_2 = \uparrow_{x} (P_1 \cup P_2) \quad P_1 \sqcup P_2 = P_1 \cap P_2$$

Join and meet are specified set theoretically rather than algorithmically. Observe too that MPAD is finite even though there are no bounds, a priori, put on the degree of any polynomial. This follows from the finiteness of $\mathbb{Z}_m$ and the closure construction that underlies MPAD. To observe this, consider the function space $F = \{[\![p]\!]_{\boldsymbol{x}} \mid p \in \mathbb{Z}_m[\boldsymbol{x}]\} \subseteq \mathbb{Z}_m^d \to \mathbb{Z}_m$. Since the space $\mathbb{Z}_m^d \to \mathbb{Z}_m$ is finite there exists $p_1, \ldots, p_\ell \in \mathbb{Z}_m[\boldsymbol{x}]$ such that $F = \{[\![p_i]\!]_{\boldsymbol{x}} \mid i \in [1, \ell]\}$. To see how F determines the structure of $\mathsf{MPAD}_m[\boldsymbol{x}]$, define $p \equiv q$ iff $[\![q]\!]_{\boldsymbol{x}}(\boldsymbol{a}) = [\![p]\!]_{\boldsymbol{x}}(\boldsymbol{a})$ for all $\boldsymbol{a} \in \mathbb{Z}_m^d$. Let $P \in \mathsf{MPAD}_m[\boldsymbol{x}]$ and $p \in P$. Observe $p \equiv p_i$ for some $i \in [1, \ell]$ and $\gamma_{\boldsymbol{x}}(P) \subseteq \gamma_{\boldsymbol{x}}(p) = \gamma_{\boldsymbol{x}}(p_i)$ hence $p_i \in P$. Conversely, if $p_j \in P$ and $p_j \equiv q$ then $q \in P$. Therefore there exists $I \subseteq [1, \ell]$ such that $P = \{q \in \mathbb{Z}_m[\boldsymbol{x}] \mid q \equiv p_i, i \in I\}$. Thus $\mathsf{MPAD}_m[\boldsymbol{x}]$ only has a finite number of elements.

Example 3. Continuing from Example 2, let

$$Q' = \left\{ \begin{array}{l} x^3 + x + 13y^2 + 11y + 126, \\ x^2y + xy + 14y^2 + 24y, \\ 2x^2 + xy + 19y^2 + 97y + 78, \\ xy^2 + 22y^2 + 116y, \quad y^3 + 22y^2 + 72y \\ 2xy + 19y^2 + 110y, \quad 128y, \\ 4x + 2y^2 + 82y + 108, \quad 32y^2 + 64y \end{array} \right\} \quad Q = \left\{ \begin{array}{l} x^2y + xy + 14y^2 + 24y, \\ xy^2 + 22y^2 + 116y, \\ 2xy + 19y^2 + 110y, \\ 4x + 2y^2 + 82y + 108, \\ y^3 + 22y^2 + 72y, \\ 32y^2 + 64y, \quad 128y \end{array} \right\}$$

Then, $\langle Q_1' \rangle_{\boldsymbol{x}} \sqcap \langle Q_2 \rangle_{\boldsymbol{x}} = \langle Q' \rangle_{\boldsymbol{x}}$ and $\langle Q_1 \rangle_{\boldsymbol{x}} \sqcap \langle Q_2 \rangle_{\boldsymbol{x}} = \langle Q \rangle_{\boldsymbol{x}}$. Again, we defer the discussion of how Q and Q' are calculated. Observe from Figs. 1(a), 1(b) and 1(c) that $\gamma_{\boldsymbol{x}}(\langle Q_1' \rangle_{\boldsymbol{x}}) \cup \gamma_{\boldsymbol{x}}(\langle Q_2 \rangle_{\boldsymbol{x}}) \subseteq \gamma_{\boldsymbol{x}}(\langle Q' \rangle_{\boldsymbol{x}})$ as required, the diamond points indicating those introduced by join itself. The diamonds in Fig. 1(d) are extraneous points introduced by calculating $\langle Q_1 \rangle_{\boldsymbol{x}} \sqcap \langle Q_2 \rangle_{\boldsymbol{x}}$ rather than $\langle Q_1' \rangle_{\boldsymbol{x}} \sqcap \langle Q_2 \rangle_{\boldsymbol{x}}$. This illustrates that operating on arbitrary bases is not generally sufficient to maintain precision, thus motivating the need for closure.

Finally, the following result asserts that MPAD enjoys mathematical properties that simplify the application of abstract interpretation:

Proposition 3. $\langle \wp(\mathbb{Z}_m^d), \subseteq \rangle \underset{\gamma_{\boldsymbol{x}}}{\overset{\alpha_{\boldsymbol{x}}}{\rightleftarrows}} \langle \mathsf{MPAD}_m[\boldsymbol{x}], \sqsubseteq \rangle$ *is a Galois insertion, where* $\alpha_{\boldsymbol{x}}(A) = \{p \in \mathbb{Z}_m[\boldsymbol{x}] \mid A \subseteq \gamma_{\boldsymbol{x}}(p)\}$

2.5 Null Polynomials

Recall $\top = \uparrow_{\boldsymbol{x}} \emptyset = \{p \in \mathbb{Z}_m[\boldsymbol{x}] \mid \gamma_{\boldsymbol{x}}(\emptyset) \subseteq \gamma_{\boldsymbol{x}}(p)\}$. It follows $\top = \{p \in \mathbb{Z}_m[\boldsymbol{x}] \mid \forall \boldsymbol{a} \in \mathbb{Z}_m^d . [\![p]\!]_{\boldsymbol{x}}(\boldsymbol{a}) = 0\}$ because $\gamma_{\boldsymbol{x}}(\emptyset) = \mathbb{Z}_m^d$. Such polynomials are referred to as vanishing or null polynomials [14] and represent universally valid constraints.

Example 4. Let $\boldsymbol{x} = \langle x, y \rangle$. Then in $\mathbb{Z}_{16}[\boldsymbol{x}]$, $\top = \langle N \rangle_{\boldsymbol{x}}$ where

$$N = \left\{ \begin{array}{c} x^6 + x^5 + x^4 + 7x^3 + 6x^2 \ (p_1), \qquad 2x^4 + 4x^3 + 6x^2 + 4x \ (p_2), \\ x^4y^2 + x^4y + 2x^3y^2 + 2x^3y + 3x^2y^2 + 3x^2y + 2xy^2 + 2xy \ (p_3), \\ x^2y^4 + 2x^2y^3 + 3x^2y^2 + 2x^2y + xy^4 + 2xy^3 + 3xy^2 + 2xy \ (p_4), \\ y^6 + y^5 + y^4 + 7y^3 + 6y^2 \ (p_5) \qquad 2y^4 + 4y^3 + 6y^2 + 4y \ (p_6), \\ 4x^2y^2 + 4x^2y + 4xy^2 + 4xy, \quad 8x^2 + 8x, \qquad 8y^2 + 8y \end{array} \right\}$$

The p_i annotations are for future reference (Example 22).

Somewhat surprisingly an algorithm exists for finitely enumerating the set of null polynomials, hence computing $\top$, for any given number of variables and bit-width [14, Theorem 3.3]. It is tempting to remove null polynomials from bases, since they are vacuous as constraints. Unfortunately, this is not generally possible without sacrificing the canonical representation property of closure.

3 Gröbner Bases

This section provides a primer on Gröbner bases over modulo integers.

3.1 Rank and Divisibility in $\mathbb{Z}_m$

Let $\mid \subseteq \mathbb{Z}^2$ denote the divisibility relation over integers: $a \mid b$ iff b is divisible by a. The rank [26] of $a \in \mathbb{Z}_m$ is defined: $\mathsf{rank}_\omega(a) = \max\{j \in \mathbb{N} \mid 2^j \mid a\}$ if $a > 0$ otherwise ω, and can be computed by counting the number of trailing zeros in the binary representation of a [34].

Example 5. In $\mathbb{Z}_{256}$ where $\omega = 8$, $\mathsf{rank}_8(0) = 8$, $\mathsf{rank}_8(15) = 0$ and $\mathsf{rank}_8(56) = 3$.

If $a \in \mathbb{Z}_m$ then $a = 2^{\mathsf{rank}_\omega(a)}d$ for some odd d. If $a \neq 0$ then $d = a/2^{\mathsf{rank}_\omega(a)}$ is unique and the expression $2^{\mathsf{rank}_\omega(a)}d$ is referred to as the rank decomposition of a. For completeness, we declare $0 = 2^\omega \cdot 1$ be the rank decomposition of 0.

Example 6. In $\mathbb{Z}_{256}$, $0 = 2^8 \cdot 1$, $15 = 2^0 \cdot 15$ and $56 = 2^3 \cdot 7$ are rank decompositions.

For $a_1 \in \mathbb{Z}_m$ and $a_2 \in \mathbb{Z}_m \setminus \{0\}$, a_1 is divisible by a_2 if $a_1 = ba_2$ for some divisor $b \in \mathbb{Z}_m$. This occurs iff $\mathsf{rank}_\omega(a_1) \geq \mathsf{rank}_\omega(a_2)$, in which case, if $a_i = 2^{k_i}d_i$ is the rank decomposition of each a_i, then $b = 2^{k_1-k_2}d_1{d_2}^{-1}$ where ${d_2}^{-1}$ is the multiplicative inverse of d_2 (which exists since d_2 is odd).

3.2 Monomial Orderings

Gröbner bases are founded on the concept of reduction, which simplifies a polynomial with respect to a set of polynomials. To define reduction it is necessary to order the terms in a polynomial, leading to the concept of monomial ordering:

Definition 5. *A total order $\prec$ over monomials $\boldsymbol{x}^{\boldsymbol{\alpha}}$ is a monomial ordering if: (1) $1 \prec \boldsymbol{x}^{\boldsymbol{\alpha}}$ for all $\boldsymbol{\alpha} > \boldsymbol{0}$ and (2) if $\boldsymbol{x}^{\boldsymbol{\alpha}_1} \prec \boldsymbol{x}^{\boldsymbol{\alpha}_2}$ then $\boldsymbol{x}^{\boldsymbol{\alpha}_1}\boldsymbol{x}^{\boldsymbol{\beta}} \prec \boldsymbol{x}^{\boldsymbol{\alpha}_2}\boldsymbol{x}^{\boldsymbol{\beta}}$ for all $\boldsymbol{x}^{\boldsymbol{\alpha}_1}$, $\boldsymbol{x}^{\boldsymbol{\alpha}_2}$ and $\boldsymbol{x}^{\boldsymbol{\beta}}$.*

If $\prec$ is a monomial ordering then $\preceq$ will denote its non-strict version. Note that monomial orderings are well-orderings, hence there is no infinite decreasing chain $\boldsymbol{x}^{\boldsymbol{\alpha}_1} \succ \boldsymbol{x}^{\boldsymbol{\alpha}_2} \succ \cdots$ of monomials.

Example 7. Let $\boldsymbol{y} = \langle x_{j_1}, \ldots, x_{j_d} \rangle$ be a permutation of $\boldsymbol{x}$ and $<$ denote lexicographical ordering over $\mathbb{N}^d$. Then, the lexicographical ordering $\prec_{\boldsymbol{y}}$, defined by $\boldsymbol{x}^{\boldsymbol{\alpha}} \prec_{\boldsymbol{y}} \boldsymbol{x}^{\boldsymbol{\beta}}$ iff $\langle \alpha_{j_1}, \ldots, \alpha_{j_d} \rangle < \langle \beta_{j_1}, \ldots, \beta_{j_d} \rangle$, is a monomial ordering.

Monomial orderings add structure to polynomials: specifically, if $p \neq 0$ then p can be uniquely expressed as $p = c\boldsymbol{x}^{\alpha} + q$ where $c \neq 0$ and all monomials $\boldsymbol{x}^{\beta}$ in q satisfy $\boldsymbol{x}^{\beta} \prec \boldsymbol{x}^{\alpha}$. Making use of this additional structure we define:

Definition 6. *Let $\prec$ be a monomial ordering over $\boldsymbol{x}$ and $p = c\boldsymbol{x}^{\alpha} + q$ where $c \neq 0$ and all monomials $\boldsymbol{x}^{\beta}$ in q satisfy $\boldsymbol{x}^{\beta} \prec \boldsymbol{x}^{\alpha}$. Then, (1) $\mathsf{lt}_{\prec}(p) = c\boldsymbol{x}^{\alpha}$, (2) $\mathsf{lm}_{\prec}(p) = \boldsymbol{x}^{\alpha}$ and (3) $\mathsf{lc}_{\prec}(p) = c$ are respectively the leading term, monomial and coefficient of p with respect to $\prec$.*

3.3 Reduction

Reduction is analogous to integer division with remainder:

Definition 7. *Let $p, q, r \in \mathbb{Z}_m[\boldsymbol{x}]$, $p \neq 0$, $q \neq 0$ and $\prec$ a monomial ordering. Then, p is $\prec$-reducible by q to r, denoted $p \rightarrow_{\prec,q} r$, if $\mathsf{lt}_{\prec}(p) = t\,\mathsf{lt}_{\prec}(q)$ and $p = tq + r$ for some term t.*

Reducibility lifts to sets $B \subseteq \mathbb{Z}_m[\boldsymbol{x}]$ by $\rightarrow_{\prec,B} = \bigcup_{p \in B} \rightarrow_{\prec,p}$. Furthermore, let $\rightarrow^{+}_{\prec,B}$ (resp. $\rightarrow^{*}_{\prec,B}$) denote the transitive (resp. transitive, reflexive) closure of $\rightarrow_{\prec,B}$. If $p \rightarrow^{+}_{\prec,B} r$ for some r then p is said to be $\prec$-reducible by B, otherwise $\prec$-irreducible by B, denoted $p \not\rightarrow_{\prec,B}$.

Example 8. Let $\boldsymbol{x} = \langle x, y, a \rangle$ and $B \subseteq \mathbb{Z}_{16}[\boldsymbol{x}]$ where

$$B = \left\{ \begin{matrix} x + a^2 + 7a + 7 \;\; (p_1),\; y + a^2 + 7a + 7 \; (p_2), \\ a^3 + a^2 + 7a + 7 \; (p_3),\; 2a^2 + 14 \qquad\qquad (p_4),\; 8a + 8 \; (p_5) \end{matrix} \right\}$$

Now, let $p = xa + 15 \in \mathbb{Z}_{16}[\boldsymbol{x}]$ and $\prec = \prec_{\boldsymbol{x}}$. Then, $\mathsf{lt}_{\prec}(p) = xa = a\,\mathsf{lt}_{\prec}(p_1)$ and $p = ap_1 + r_1$ where $r_1 = 15a^3 + 9a^2 + 9a + 15$, hence $p \rightarrow_{\prec,p_1} r_1$. Similarly, $\mathsf{lt}_{\prec}(r_1) = 15a^3 = 15\,\mathsf{lt}_{\prec}(p_3)$ and $r_1 = 15p_3 + r_2$ where $r_2 = 10a^2 + 6$, hence $r_1 \rightarrow_{\prec,p_3} r_2$. Finally, $\mathsf{lt}_{\prec}(r_2) = 10a^2 = 5\,\mathsf{lt}_{\prec}(p_4)$ and $r_2 = 5p_4 + r_3$ where $r_3 = 0$, hence $r_2 \rightarrow_{\prec,p_4} r_3$. Thus, $p \rightarrow_{\prec,p_1} r_1 \rightarrow_{\prec,p_3} r_2 \rightarrow_{\prec,p_4} r_3$, hence $p \rightarrow^{+}_{\prec,B} 0$.

Note p is $\prec$-reducible by B iff $\mathsf{lt}_{\prec}(p)$ is divisible by $\mathsf{lt}_{\prec}(q)$ for some $q \in B$, where a term t_1 is divisible by a term t_2 if $t_1 = t_2 t_3$ for some term t_3. Moreover, reduction eliminates the leading term of a polynomial, leaving a residue polynomial comprised of strictly smaller terms with respect to $\prec$:

Lemma 2. *If $p \rightarrow^{+}_{\prec,B} r \neq 0$ then $\mathsf{lm}_{\prec}(r) \prec \mathsf{lm}_{\prec}(p)$.*

Since monomial orderings are well-orderings, the previous result implies that a sequence of reductions cannot continue ad infinitum and must eventually terminate with the 0 polynomial. In this case, it follows that $p \in \langle B \rangle_{\boldsymbol{x}}$, hence reduction provides a test for membership in an ideal:

Proposition 4. *If $p \rightarrow^{*}_{\prec,B} 0$ then $p \in \langle B \rangle_{\boldsymbol{x}}$.*

But reduction against an arbitrary basis B does not lead to a complete test for membership in $\langle B \rangle_{\boldsymbol{x}}$, hence motivating Gröbner bases.

3.4 Gröbner Bases

With reduction in place, the concept of Gröbner basis can be introduced:

Definition 8. *Let $B \subseteq \mathbb{Z}_m[\boldsymbol{x}]$ and $\prec$ a monomial ordering over $\boldsymbol{x}$. Then, $G \subseteq \langle B \rangle_{\boldsymbol{x}}$ is a Gröbner basis for $\langle B \rangle_{\boldsymbol{x}}$ with respect to $\prec$ if for all $p \in \langle B \rangle_{\boldsymbol{x}}$, if $p \neq 0$ then p is $\prec$-reducible by G.*

Gröbner bases provide a complete test for membership in $\langle B \rangle_{\boldsymbol{x}}$, as asserted by:

Lemma 3. *If G is a Gröbner basis for $\langle B \rangle_{\boldsymbol{x}}$ with respect to $\prec$ then for all $p \in \langle B \rangle_{\boldsymbol{x}}$, $p \rightarrow^*_{\prec,G} 0$.*

Example 9. Let $\boldsymbol{x} = \langle x, y \rangle$, $\prec = \prec_{\boldsymbol{x}}$ and $p \in \mathbb{Z}_{16}[\boldsymbol{x}]$ where $p = 4x$. Moreover, let $B = \{p_1, p_2\} \subseteq \mathbb{Z}_{16}[\boldsymbol{x}]$ where $p_1 = 2x^2y + 2x^2 + 6xy + x$ and $p_2 = 4y + 4$. Then, $p = 12p_1 + (10x^2 + 10x)p_2 \in \langle B \rangle_{\boldsymbol{x}}$, yet $p \not\rightarrow_{\prec,B}$, thus B is not a Gröbner basis with respect to $\prec$. However, it can be shown if $p_3 = 6x$ and $p_4 = 3x$ then $G = \{p_1, p_2, p_3, p_4\}$ is a Gröbner basis for $\langle B \rangle_{\boldsymbol{x}}$ with respect to $\prec$. Note that p is $\prec$-reducible by $p_4 \in G$. Indeed, $p \rightarrow_{\prec,p_4} 0$, hence $p \rightarrow^*_{\prec,G} 0$, as predicted by the previous result.

3.5 Buchberger's Algorithm

Classically [3], Gröbner bases are computed by evaluating S-polynomials:

Definition 9. *Let $\prec$ be a monomial ordering over $\boldsymbol{x}$. The S-polynomial of $p_1, p_2 \in \mathbb{Z}_m[\boldsymbol{x}]$ with respect to $\prec$ is defined:*

$$S_{\prec}(p_1, p_2) = d_2 2^{k-k_1} \boldsymbol{x}^{\boldsymbol{\alpha}-\boldsymbol{\alpha}_1} p_1 - d_1 2^{k-k_2} \boldsymbol{x}^{\boldsymbol{\alpha}-\boldsymbol{\alpha}_2} p_2$$

where, if $p_i = 0$ then $k_i = \omega$, $d_i = 1$ and $\boldsymbol{\alpha}_i = \boldsymbol{0}$, else $2^{k_i} d_i$ is the rank decomposition of $\mathsf{lc}_{\prec}(p_i)$ and $\boldsymbol{x}^{\boldsymbol{\alpha}_i} = \mathsf{lm}_{\prec}(p_i)$, $k = \max(k_1, k_2)$ and $\boldsymbol{\alpha} = \max(\boldsymbol{\alpha}_1, \boldsymbol{\alpha}_2)$.

Example 10. If $p_1 = 2x^2y + 2x^2 + 6xy + x$ and $p_2 = 4y + 4$ then it follows $\mathsf{S}_{\prec}(p_1, p_2) = 2(2xy^2 + 6xy + 2y^2 + y) - y^2(4x + 4) = 12xy + 2y$ and $\mathsf{S}_{\prec}(p_1, 0) = 8(2xy^2 + 6xy + 2y^2 + y) - xy^2(0) = 8y$.

Note that $\mathsf{lt}_{\prec}(d_2 2^{k-k_1} \boldsymbol{x}^{\boldsymbol{\alpha}-\boldsymbol{\alpha}_1} p_1) = \mathsf{lt}_{\prec}(d_1 2^{k-k_2} \boldsymbol{x}^{\boldsymbol{\alpha}-\boldsymbol{\alpha}_2} p_2)$, hence the S-polynomial $\mathsf{S}_{\prec}(p_1, p_2)$ leads to a cancellation of leading terms. In particular, the S-polynomial $\mathsf{S}_{\prec}(p_1, 0)$ eliminates the leading term of p_1, and possible other terms as well. This deviates from the classical case of fields, where only multiplying by 0 can eliminate a leading term. S-polynomials then yield an effective criterion [2, Theorem 30] to determine if a given basis is a Gröbner basis.

Theorem 1 (Buchberger's criterion). *Let $\prec$ be a monomial ordering and $B = \{p_1, \ldots, p_s\} \subseteq \mathbb{Z}_m[\boldsymbol{x}]$. If $S_{\prec}(p_i, p_j) \rightarrow^*_{\prec,B} 0$ and $S_{\prec}(p_i, 0) \rightarrow^*_{\prec,B} 0$ for all $1 \leq i < j \leq s$ then B is a Gröbner basis for $\langle B \rangle_{\boldsymbol{x}}$ with respect to $\prec$.*

```
function gb_≺(B = {p_1, ..., p_s} ⊆ Z_m[x])
begin
  G := B
  S := {(p_i, p_j) | 1 ≤ i < j ≤ s} ∪ {(p_i, 0) | 1 ≤ i ≤ s}
  while (S ≠ ∅)
    let s = (f_1, f_2) ∈ S
    S := S \ {s}
    p := S_≺(f_1, f_2)
    let p →*_{≺,G} r where r ↛_{≺,G}
    if (r ≠ 0)
      S := S ∪ {(g, r) | g ∈ G} ∪ {(r, 0)}
      G := G ∪ {r}
    end if
  end while
  return G
end
```

Fig. 2. Gröbner basis algorithm over integers modulo 2^{ω}

Buchberger's criterion justifies Buchberger's algorithm for constructing Gröbner bases. Figure 2 presents a version of Buchberger's algorithm [2] that takes $B \subseteq \mathbb{Z}_m[\boldsymbol{x}]$ and a monomial ordering $\prec$ over $\boldsymbol{x}$ and returns a Gröbner basis for $\langle B \rangle_{\boldsymbol{x}}$ with respect to $\prec$. The algorithm maintains a basis G, initialised to B, and a set of unverified S-polynomials S. The algorithm attempts to verify that G is a Gröbner basis by reducing each S-polynomial pair in S against it. If some S-polynomial does not reduce, it yields a new element which is added to G, and generates further S-polynomials. The algorithm terminates when all S-polynomials for the current basis reduce to 0, at which point Buchberger's criterion applies to show the result, henceforth denoted $\mathsf{gb}_{\prec}(B)$, is a Gröbner basis. Observe that $B \subseteq G$ on each iteration of the while loop hence $B \subseteq \mathsf{gb}_{\prec}(B)$.

4 Calculating Variable Elimination and Join

This section explains how variable elimination can be computed using Gröbner bases, and how variable elimination can be combined with a relaxation to compute the join of two ideals finitely represented as bases.

4.1 Variable Elimination

A generic projection function $\pi_i(\langle a_1, \ldots, a_\ell \rangle) = \langle a_1, \ldots, a_{i-1}, a_{i+1}, \ldots, a_\ell \rangle$ is used to formulate elimination. The presentation of elimination commences with a syntactic version which removes polynomials that contains a given variable:

Definition 10. *(Syntactic) variable elimination is an operation* $\mathsf{elim}[x_j]$ *where* $\mathsf{elim}[x_j] : \wp(\mathbb{Z}_m[\boldsymbol{x}]) \to \wp(\mathbb{Z}_m[\pi_j(\boldsymbol{x})])$ *defined by* $\mathsf{elim}[x_j](P) = P \cap \mathbb{Z}_m[\pi_j(\boldsymbol{x})]$

The following result demonstrates that abstraction and elimination commute. The result is formulated in terms of the natural lifting of π_j from the function space $\mathbb{Z}_m^d \to \mathbb{Z}_m^{d-1}$ to $\wp(\mathbb{Z}_m^d) \to \wp(\mathbb{Z}_m^{d-1})$.

Proposition 5. *If $A \subseteq \mathbb{Z}_m^d$ then $\mathsf{elim}[x_j](\alpha_{\boldsymbol{x}}(A)) = \alpha_{\pi_j(\boldsymbol{x})}(\pi_j(A))$.*

It follows from this result that elimination preserves closure:

Corollary 1. *If $P \in \mathsf{MPAD}_m[\boldsymbol{x}]$ then $\mathsf{elim}[x_j](P) \in \mathsf{MPAD}_m[\pi_j(\boldsymbol{x})]$.*

Example 11. Consider $B = \{wx + 10w, 15wx^2 + wx + x^2 + 15x\} \subseteq \mathbb{Z}_{16}[w, x]$ and observe $\mathsf{elim}[w](B) = \emptyset$. However $(x^2 + 7x + 8)(wx + 10w) + (x + 2)(15wx^2 + wx + x^2 + 15x) = x^3 + x^2 + 14x$ hence $x^3 + x^2 + 14x \in \langle B\rangle_{\langle w,x\rangle}$. Since $w \notin \mathsf{vars}(x^3 + x^2 + 14x)$ it follows $x^3 + x^2 + 14x \in \mathsf{elim}[w](\langle B\rangle_{\langle w,x\rangle})$. In particular, $\mathsf{elim}[w](\langle B\rangle_{\langle w,x\rangle}) \neq \{0\} = \langle\emptyset\rangle_{\langle x\rangle} = \langle \mathsf{elim}[w](B)\rangle_{\langle x\rangle}$.

The previous example shows that syntactic variable elimination is not well-behaved with respect to ideal generation, thus motivating the following:

Definition 11. *(Semantic) variable elimination is a relation $\rightarrow_{\mathsf{elim}[x_j]}$ where $\rightarrow_{\mathsf{elim}[x_j]} \subseteq \wp(\mathbb{Z}_m[\boldsymbol{x}]) \times \wp(\mathbb{Z}_m[\pi_j(\boldsymbol{x})])$ defined by $B \rightarrow_{\mathsf{elim}[x_j]} B'$ iff $\mathsf{elim}[x_j](\langle B\rangle_{\boldsymbol{x}}) = \langle B'\rangle_{\pi_j(\boldsymbol{x})}$*

Proposition 6. *Let $B \subseteq \mathbb{Z}_m[\boldsymbol{x}]$ and B' be a Gröbner basis for $\langle B\rangle_{\boldsymbol{x}}$ with respect to $\prec_{\boldsymbol{y}}$ where $\boldsymbol{y}$ is a permutation of $\boldsymbol{x}$ and $y_1 = x_j$. Then $B \rightarrow_{\mathsf{elim}[x_j]} \mathsf{elim}[x_j](B')$.*

The previous result can be stated more generally in terms of elimination orderings [1]; the restriction to lexicographical ordering is adopted merely to simplify the presentation. Consistent with this choice, $\mathsf{gb}_{\prec_{\boldsymbol{y}}}$ is henceforth abbreviated to $\mathsf{gb}_{\boldsymbol{y}}$, again purely to streamline the exposition.

Example 12. Let $B = \{wx + 10w, 15wx^2 + wx + x^2 + 15x\} \subseteq \mathbb{Z}_{16}[w, x, y]$. Then, $\mathsf{gb}_{\langle w,x,y\rangle}(B) = B \cup \{wx + 3x^2 + 13x, 2w + x^2 + 15x, x^3 + x^2 + 14x\}$. It therefore follows $B \rightarrow_{\mathsf{elim}[w]} \{x^3 + x^2 + 14x\}$.

Example 13. Let $B = \{w(x+3), w(y+9), (1-w)(x+6), (1-w)(y+2)\}$. Then,

$$\begin{aligned}
\mathsf{gb}_{\langle w,x,y\rangle}(B) &= B \cup \{w + 7y + 14, \quad x + 5y, \quad y^2 + 11y + 2\}\\
\mathsf{gb}_{\langle w,y,x\rangle}(B) &= B \cup \{w + 5x + 14, \quad y + 13x, \quad x^2 + 9x + 2\}
\end{aligned}$$

Thus $B \rightarrow_{\mathsf{elim}[w]} B'$ and $B \rightarrow_{\mathsf{elim}[w]} B''$ where $B' = \{x + 5y, y^2 + 11y + 2\}$ and $B'' = \{y + 13x, x^2 + 9x + 2\}$ illustrating why $\rightarrow_{\mathsf{elim}[w]}$ is defined as a relation. To see $\langle B'\rangle_{\langle x,y\rangle} = \langle B''\rangle_{\langle x,y\rangle}$ observe $x + 5y \rightarrow_{y+13x} 0$ and

$$\begin{aligned}
y^2 + 11y + 2 &\rightarrow_{y+13x} 3xy + 11y + 2\\
&\rightarrow_{y+13x} 9x^2 + 11y + 2 \rightarrow_{x^2+9x+2} 15x + 11y \rightarrow_{y+13x} 0
\end{aligned}$$

Similarly, $p \rightarrow_{B'} 0$ for all $p \in B''$.

4.2 Join

Once variable elimination is in place, join can be calculated by adapting a standard relaxation [1] to the current setting. The result, which provides a way of intersecting ideals, hence calculating join, is stated in terms of a lifted product $qP = \{qp \mid p \in P\}$ where $P \subseteq \mathbb{Z}_m[\boldsymbol{x}]$ and $q \in \mathbb{Z}_m[\boldsymbol{x}]$:

Proposition 7. *Let* $\langle B_1 \rangle_{\boldsymbol{x}}, \langle B_2 \rangle_{\boldsymbol{x}} \in \mathit{MPAD}_m[\boldsymbol{x}]$. *If* $w \notin \mathsf{vars}(B_1 \cup B_2)$ *then* $\langle B_1 \rangle_{\boldsymbol{x}} \cap \langle B_2 \rangle_{\boldsymbol{x}} = \langle B \rangle_{\boldsymbol{x}}$ *whenever* $wB_1 \cup (1-w)B_2 \rightarrow_{\mathit{elim}[w]} B$

Example 14. Let $\boldsymbol{x} = \langle x, y \rangle$ and $B_1, B_2 \subseteq \mathbb{Z}_{16}[\boldsymbol{x}]$ where $B_1 = \{x + 10\}$, $B_2 = \{x^2 + 15x\}$ and $I_i = \langle B_i \rangle_{\boldsymbol{x}}$. Both I_i are closed, that is, $I_i = \uparrow I_i$. Let

$$B = wB_1 \cup (1-w)B_2 = \{wx + 10w, 15wx^2 + wx + x^2 + 15x\}$$

By Example 11, $B \rightarrow_{\mathsf{elim}[w]} \{x^3 + x^2 + 14x\}$, hence $\langle B_1 \rangle_{\boldsymbol{x}} \sqcup \langle B_2 \rangle_{\boldsymbol{x}} = \langle x^3 + x^2 + 14x \rangle_{\boldsymbol{x}}$.

Figures 3(a), 3(b) and 3(i) depict $\gamma_{\boldsymbol{x}}(I_1)$, $\gamma_{\boldsymbol{x}}(I_2)$ and $\gamma_{\boldsymbol{x}}(I_1 \sqcup I_2)$ respectively. Observe $(8, y) \in \gamma_{\boldsymbol{x}}(I_1 \sqcup I_2)$ but $(8, y) \notin \gamma_{\boldsymbol{x}}(I_1) \cup \gamma_{\boldsymbol{x}}(I_2)$ for any $y \in \mathbb{Z}_{16}$. These additional points, which are introduced by join itself, stem not from the relaxation $wB_1 \cup (1-w)B_2$ which introduces w, but the elimination of w from $\mathsf{gb}_{\langle w,x,y \rangle}(B)$ which derives a unary polynomial representation over x alone. To see this, observe $B[x \mapsto 8] = \{8w, 8w + 8\}$ and $B[x \mapsto 14] = \{14w + 12, 10w + 6\}$ both have no solutions.

Example 15. Figure 3 presents a series of examples of join on $\mathbb{Z}_{16}[\boldsymbol{x}]$ for $\boldsymbol{x} = \langle x, y \rangle$. Figures 3(a)–(h) depict $\gamma_{\boldsymbol{x}}(I_i)$ for $I_i = \langle B_i \rangle_{\boldsymbol{x}}$ where $I_i = \uparrow I_i$ and B_i are as follows:

$$\begin{array}{ll} B_3 = \{x + 3, \quad y + 9\} & B_6 = \{x^2, \quad xy^4 + xy^2 + 2xy, \quad 2xy^2 + 2xy, \quad 4x\} \\ B_4 = \{x + 6, \quad y + 2\} & B_7 = \{x^4y + x^2y + 2xy, \quad 2x^2y + 2xy, \quad y^2, \quad 4y\} \\ B_5 = \{x^2, \quad 4x, \quad y\} & B_8 = \{x + y\} \end{array}$$

For comparison, the yellow points give the best abstraction of $\gamma_{\boldsymbol{x}}(I_i)$ using systems of linear congruences modulo 16 (linear polynomials).

Figures 3(i)–(p) depict $\gamma_{\boldsymbol{x}}(I_i \sqcup I_j)$ for various combinations of $i, j \in \{1, \ldots, 8\}$, illustrating where a polynomial representation introduces additional points via join. Observe that join induces a loss of information as witnessed by additional points of the form $(8, y)$ and $(14, y)$ in $\gamma_{\boldsymbol{x}}(I_1 \sqcup I_2)$. Again, the yellow points give the join of the best linear abstractions, which can be computed by combining a relaxation with variable elimination [21]. To illustrate the working, consider B_3 and B_4 rewritten as follows:

$$B_3 = \{x \equiv_{16} -3, \quad y \equiv_{16} -9\} \qquad B_4 = \{x \equiv_{16} -6, \quad y \equiv_{16} -2\}.$$

The relaxation introduces fresh variables x', y', x'', y'' and μ:

$$\begin{array}{lll} x \equiv_{16} x' + x'' & x' \equiv_{16} -3\mu & x'' \equiv_{16} -6(1-\mu) \\ y \equiv_{16} y' + y'' & y' \equiv_{16} -9\mu & y'' \equiv_{16} -2(1-\mu) \end{array}$$

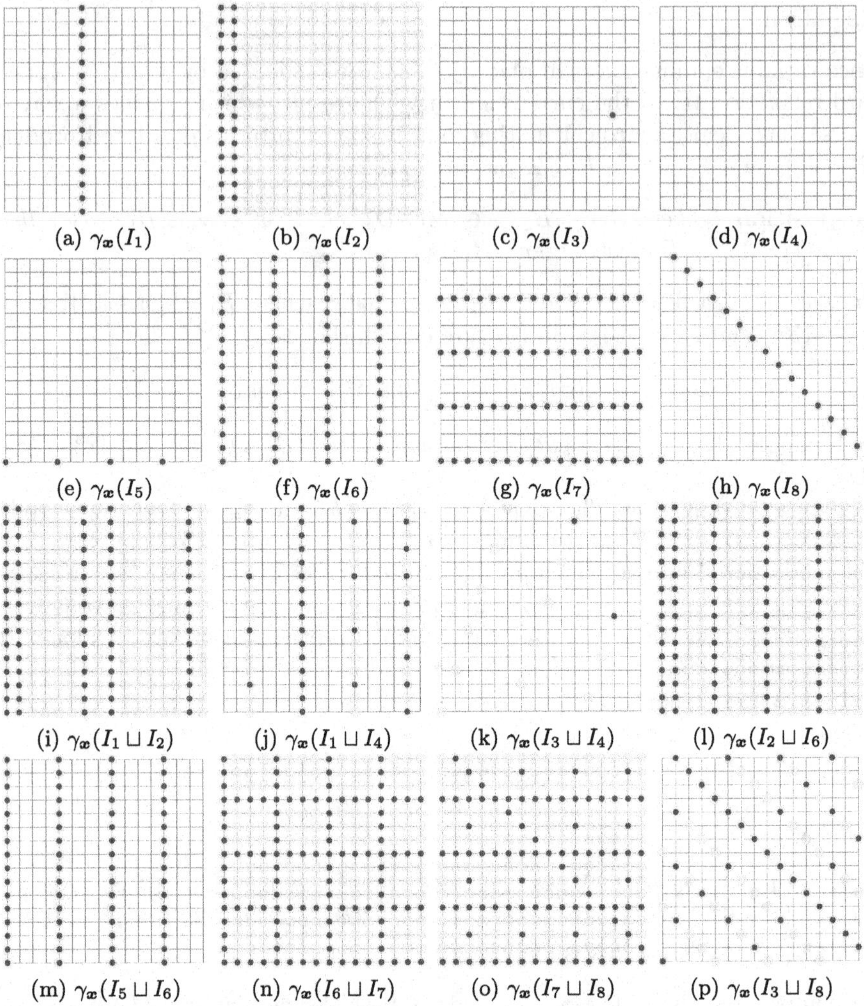

Fig. 3. Examples of join on $\mathbb{Z}_{16}[\boldsymbol{x}]$ for $\boldsymbol{x} = \langle x, y \rangle$

Eliminating x', y', x'' and y'' gives a system of two congruences: $x \equiv_{16} 3\mu - 6$ and $y \equiv_{16} -7\mu - 2$. Rearranging for μ gives $\mu \equiv_{16} 2 - 5x$ hence $y \equiv_{16} 3x$ as illustrated in Fig. 3(k). The other linear joins are computed likewise.

Note the loss of precision in using linear, rather than polynomial, abstractions. For instance, the set $\gamma_{\boldsymbol{x}}(I_2)$ can only be approximated by a trivial (unconstrained) linear system, which loses all information. Moreover, as demonstrated in Figs. 3(j)–(k) and Figs. 3(n)–(p), even if the arguments to a (polynomial) join are representable via linear systems, the result may not be.

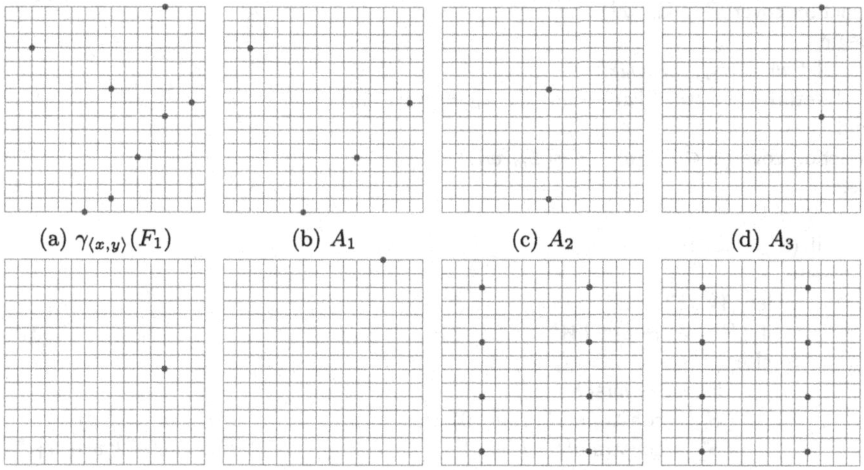

(a) $\gamma_{\langle x,y\rangle}(F_1)$ (b) A_1 (c) A_2 (d) A_3

(e) A_4 (f) A_5 (g) $\gamma_{\langle x,y\rangle}(F_2)$ (h) A_6

Fig. 4. Covers of F_1 over $\langle w_1\rangle$ and F_2 over $\langle w_1, w_2\rangle$

5 Calculating Closure and Meet

This section addresses how to finitely compute closure. The problem is reduced to that of computing a cover of a system of polynomials. A cover provides a way to decompose closure to sub-problems for which closure can be computed directly. A divide-and-conquer algorithm is introduced for computing a cover, which exploits a simplification procedure based on Gröbner bases, to avoid superfluous work. The section concludes by showing how meet can be computed using closure.

5.1 Covering

An algorithm for closure is formulated in terms of the concept of a cover, which is itself defined through a lifting of polynomial evaluation $[\![p]\!]_{\boldsymbol{x}}(\boldsymbol{a})$ to a vector of polynomials $\boldsymbol{p} = \langle p_1, \ldots, p_n\rangle$ by $[\![\boldsymbol{p}]\!]_{\boldsymbol{x}}(\boldsymbol{a}) = \langle [\![p_1]\!]_{\boldsymbol{x}}(\boldsymbol{a}), \ldots, [\![p_n]\!]_{\boldsymbol{x}}(\boldsymbol{a})\rangle$.

Definition 12. *Let* $\mathcal{W} \subseteq \mathbb{Z}_m[\boldsymbol{w}]^d$*,* $A \subseteq \mathbb{Z}_m^d$ *and* $F \subseteq \mathbb{Z}_m[\boldsymbol{x}]$*. Then*

- $\mathcal{W}$ *is a cover of* A *over* $\boldsymbol{w}$ *iff* $A = \{[\![\boldsymbol{W}]\!]_{\boldsymbol{w}}(\boldsymbol{a}) \mid \boldsymbol{W} \in \mathcal{W} \wedge \boldsymbol{a} \in \mathbb{Z}_m^{|\boldsymbol{w}|}\}$
- $\mathcal{W}$ *is a cover of* F *over* $\boldsymbol{w}$ *iff* $\mathcal{W}$ *is a cover of* $\gamma_{\boldsymbol{x}}(F)$ *over* $\boldsymbol{w}$

Example 16. Figures 4(a) and (g) depict $\gamma_{\boldsymbol{x}}(F_1)$ and $\gamma_{\boldsymbol{x}}(F_2)$ for $\boldsymbol{x} = \langle x, y\rangle$ where

$$F_1 = \{x + 3y^3 + 4y^2 + 7y + 10, \quad y^4 + 7y^2 + 8y\} \quad F_2 = \{2x + 10, \quad 4y + 12\}$$

Figures 4(b), (c) and (d) illustrate $A_i = \{[\![\boldsymbol{W}_i]\!]_{\boldsymbol{w}}(\boldsymbol{a}) \mid \boldsymbol{a} \in \mathbb{Z}_m^1\}$ for $\boldsymbol{w} = \langle w_1\rangle$ where $\boldsymbol{W}_1 = \langle 4w_1 + 6, 4w_1\rangle$, $\boldsymbol{W}_2 = \langle 8, 8w_1 + 1\rangle$ and $\boldsymbol{W}_3 = \langle 12, 8w_1 + 7\rangle$. Observe

```
function cover(F ⊆ Z_m[x])
begin
    let w = ⟨w_1, ..., w_d⟩
    return cover(w, F[x_1 ↦ w_1, ..., x_d ↦ w_d])
end
function cover(S ∈ Z_m[w]^d × ℘(Z_m[w]))
begin
    S' = simplify(S)
    if (S' = nil) return ∅
    else
        let ⟨W, F⟩ = S'
        if (F = ∅) return {W}
        else
            let w_i ∈ vars(F)
            S'_0 = constrain(S', 1, w_i, 0)          (* F ∪ {w_i − 2^1 w} *)
            S'_1 = constrain(S', 1, w_i, 1)          (* F ∪ {w_i − 2^1 w + 1} *)
            return cover(S'_0) ∪ cover(S'_1)
        end if
    end if
end
```

Fig. 5. The cover algorithm

$\{\boldsymbol{W}_i\}$ is a cover of A_i and since $\gamma_{\boldsymbol{x}}(F_1) = A_1 \cup A_2 \cup A_3$, $\{\boldsymbol{W}_1, \boldsymbol{W}_2, \boldsymbol{W}_3\}$ is a cover of F_1 over $\boldsymbol{w}$. The set of 4 vectors $\{\boldsymbol{W}_1, \boldsymbol{W}_2, \boldsymbol{W}_4, \boldsymbol{W}_5\}$ where $\boldsymbol{W}_4 = \langle 12, 7\rangle$ and $\boldsymbol{W}_5 = \langle 12, 15\rangle$ is also a cover of F_1, illustrating that covers are not unique. The polynomial vectors $\boldsymbol{W}_4$ and $\boldsymbol{W}_5$ define single points and suggest how a cover can be constructed for an arbitrary $F \subseteq \mathbb{Z}_m[\boldsymbol{w}]$ by putting $\mathcal{W} = \{\boldsymbol{a} \mid \boldsymbol{a} \in \gamma_{\boldsymbol{x}}(F)\}$. The vector $\boldsymbol{w}$ is not necessarily unary as the cover $\{\boldsymbol{W}_6\}$ of F_2 over $\boldsymbol{w} = \langle w_1, w_2\rangle$ illustrates where $\boldsymbol{W}_6 = \langle 8w_1 + 3, 4w_2 + 1\rangle$ and $\gamma_{\boldsymbol{x}}(F_2) = A_6 = \{[\![\boldsymbol{W}_6]\!]_w(\boldsymbol{a}) \mid \boldsymbol{a} \in \mathbb{Z}_m^2\}$, and $\gamma_{\boldsymbol{x}}(F_2)$ and A_6 are illustrated in Figs. 4(g) and (h) respectively.

The challenge is to compute a cover over some $\boldsymbol{w}$ for arbitrary $F \subseteq \mathbb{Z}_m[\boldsymbol{x}]$ without naively enumerating all points of $\gamma_{\boldsymbol{x}}(F)$. To this end, Fig. 5 presents a divide-and-conquer algorithm that recursively decomposes $\gamma_{\boldsymbol{x}}(F)$ into subsets following the structure of F. Ultimately the function computes a cover $\mathcal{W} \subseteq \mathbb{Z}_m[\boldsymbol{w}]^d$ for F over $\boldsymbol{w}$ where $|\boldsymbol{w}| = d = |\boldsymbol{x}|$. The function cover depends on three auxiliary functions, simplify, constrain and safe all of which are listed in Fig. 6. The function cover and its auxiliaries operate on pairs $S = \langle \boldsymbol{W}, F\rangle$ where $\boldsymbol{W} \in \mathbb{Z}_m[\boldsymbol{w}]^d$ is a vector of polynomials and $F \subseteq \mathbb{Z}_m[\boldsymbol{w}]$ is a system. The vector $\boldsymbol{W}$ provides a lens to interpret the solutions of F, as is formalised below:

Definition 13. *The concretisation map* $\gamma_{\boldsymbol{w}} : \mathbb{Z}_m[\boldsymbol{w}]^d \times \wp(\mathbb{Z}_m[\boldsymbol{w}]) \to \wp(\mathbb{Z}_m^d)$ *is defined:* $\gamma_{\boldsymbol{w}}(\langle \boldsymbol{W}, F\rangle) = \{[\![\boldsymbol{W}]\!]_w(\boldsymbol{a}) \mid \boldsymbol{a} \in \gamma_{\boldsymbol{w}}(F)\}$

```
function simplify(⟨W, F⟩ ∈ Z_m[w]^d × ℘(Z_m[w]))
begin
    F' = gb_w(F)
    S' = ⟨W, F'⟩
    if (c ∈ F' where c ∈ Z_m \ {0})
        return nil
    else if (2^(ω−j)(w_i + r) ∈ F' where j > 0 ∧ r ∈ Z_m[w_{i+1}, ..., w_d] ∧ safe(W, w_i, r))
        S'' = constrain(S', j, w_i, r)          (* F ∪ {w_i − 2^j w + r} *)
        return simplify(S'')
    else
        return S'
    end if
end
function constrain(⟨W, F⟩ ∈ Z_m[w]^d × Z_m[w], j ∈ N, w_i ∈ w, r ∈ Z_m[w_{i+1}, ..., w_d])
begin
    F ∪ {w_i − 2^j w + r} →_elim[w_i] F'
    W' = W[w_i ↦ 2^j w − r]
    if (W'_i = 2^ω w + q ∧ q ∈ Z_m[w_{i+1}, ..., w_d]) F'' = F'[w ↦ 0]
    else F'' = F'[w ↦ w_i]
    return ⟨W'[w ↦ w_i], F''⟩
end
function safe(W ∈ Z_m[w]^d, w_i ∈ w, r ∈ Z_m[w_{i+1}, ..., w_d])
begin
    let W = ⟨2^(k_1) w_1 + q_1, ..., 2^(k_d) w_d + q_d⟩
    if (c y^α ∈ r, w_ℓ ∈ vars(y) where k_i + rank(c) < k_ℓ) return false
    else return true
end
```

Fig. 6. The simplify, constrain and safe functions

Example 17. Consider $S_b = \langle \boldsymbol{W}_b, F_b \rangle$ and $S_c = \langle \boldsymbol{W}_c, F_c \rangle$, where $\boldsymbol{W}_b = \langle w_1, 2w_2 \rangle$, $\boldsymbol{W}_c = \langle w_1, 4w_2 \rangle$ and

$$F_b = \left\{ \begin{array}{c} w_1^2 + w_1 + 6w_2 + 12, \\ 2w_1w_2 + 4w_1, \quad 4w_2^2, \quad 8w_2 \end{array} \right\} \qquad F_c = \left\{ \begin{array}{c} w_1^2 + w_1 + 12w_2 + 12, \\ 4w_1w_2 + 4w_1 \end{array} \right\}$$

Figure 8(b) illustrates $\gamma_w(F_b)$ as translucent points and $\gamma_w(S_b)$ as opaque points. Observe $\langle 8, 2 \rangle, \langle 8, 10 \rangle \in \gamma_w(F_b)$ and $[\![\boldsymbol{W}_b]\!]_w(\langle 8, 2 \rangle) = \langle 8, 4 \rangle = [\![\boldsymbol{W}_b]\!]_w(\langle 8, 10 \rangle)$. Hence, in general, there is a many-to-one relationship between $\gamma_w(F_b)$ and $\gamma_w(S_b)$. Figure 8(c) depicts $\gamma_w(F_c)$ and $\gamma_w(S_c)$ using the same convention. Observe too that $\gamma_w(S_b) = \gamma_w(S_c)$ but the cardinality of $\gamma_w(F_c)$ is 4-fold that of $\gamma_w(S_c)$ since $\boldsymbol{W}_c = \langle w_1, 4w_2 \rangle$.

Observe that if $\mathcal{W} \subseteq \mathbb{Z}_m[\boldsymbol{w}]^d$ is a cover for $F \subseteq \mathbb{Z}_m[\boldsymbol{x}]$ over $\boldsymbol{w}$ then $\gamma_x(F) = \cup\{\gamma_w(\langle \boldsymbol{W}, \emptyset \rangle) \mid \boldsymbol{W} \in \mathcal{W}\}$. Thus a cover is formed from pairs $\langle \boldsymbol{W}, F \rangle$ that are degenerate in that $F = \emptyset$. The rationale behind cover is thus to decompose a single pair $\langle \boldsymbol{W}, F \rangle$ where $\boldsymbol{W} = \boldsymbol{w}$ into a collection of degenerate pairs:

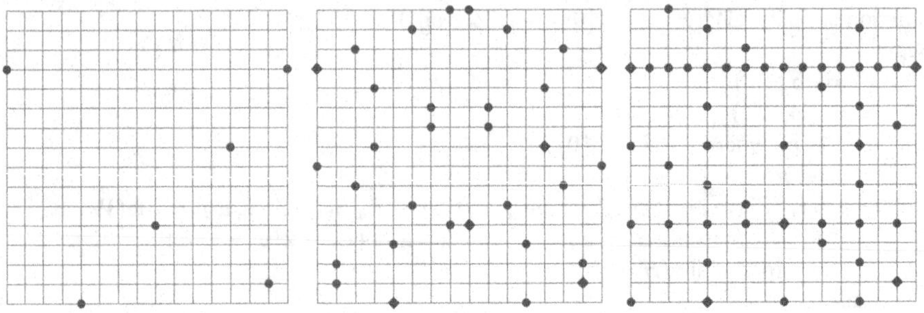

(a) $\gamma_{\boldsymbol{x}}(F)$ (b) $\gamma_{\boldsymbol{x}}(F_3)$ (c) $\gamma_{\boldsymbol{x}}(F_4)$

Fig. 7. Solution sets for F, F_3 and F_4

Example 18. Consider computing a cover for the system

$$F = \{x^2 + x + 7y^2 + 11y + 12, \quad xy + 4x + 10y^2\}$$

over $\boldsymbol{w} = \langle w_1, w_2\rangle$. The set $\gamma_{\boldsymbol{x}}(F)$ is plotted in Fig. 7(a). The top-level cover function expresses F as the pair $S_a = \langle \boldsymbol{W}_a, F_a\rangle$ where

$$\boldsymbol{W}_a = \boldsymbol{w} \qquad F_a = \{w_1^2 + w_1 + 7w_2^2 + 11w_2 + 12, \quad w_1w_2 + 4w_1 + 10w_2^2\}$$

Since $[\![\boldsymbol{W}_a]\!]_{\boldsymbol{w}}(\boldsymbol{b}) = \boldsymbol{b}$ for all $\boldsymbol{b} \in \mathbb{Z}_m^2$, it follows $\gamma_{\boldsymbol{w}}(S_a) = \gamma_{\boldsymbol{x}}(F)$.

The cover function invokes both simplify and constrain. The function simplify performs simplification, either returning nil, indicating $\gamma_{\boldsymbol{w}}(\langle \boldsymbol{W}, F\rangle) = \emptyset$, or $S' = \langle \boldsymbol{W}', F'\rangle$ where $\gamma_{\boldsymbol{w}}(S) = \gamma_{\boldsymbol{w}}(S')$ (possibly with $S = S'$). The first substantive action of simplify is to calculate a Gröbner basis F' for the ideal $\langle F\rangle_{\boldsymbol{w}}$ using the variable ordering $\boldsymbol{w}$. If there exists a constant polynomial $c \in F'$ such that $c \neq 0$ then this reveals $\gamma_{\boldsymbol{w}}(F) = \gamma_{\boldsymbol{w}}(F') = \emptyset$ hence $\gamma_{\boldsymbol{w}}(S) = \emptyset$. Otherwise, constrain is invoked if F' contains a polynomial of the form $2^{\omega-j}(w_i + r)$ where $r \in \mathbb{Z}_m[w_{i+1}, \dots, w_d]$, $0 < j \leq \omega$ and the safety check $\mathsf{safe}(\boldsymbol{W}, w_i, r)$ is satisfied. The added polynomial $w_i - 2^j w + r$ asserts that $w_i + r$ is a multiple of 2^j, which is a direct consequence of $2^{\omega-j}(w_i + r)$. The safety check ensures that the addition of $2^{\omega-j}(w_i + r)$ does not induce a coupling between the variables of $\boldsymbol{w}$, specifically those arising in r, that would compromise the termination argument behind simplify and cover. The safety check is vacuously satisfied if $\mathsf{vars}(r) = \emptyset$.

Simplification is used in tandem with splitting, the latter employed by cover only when the former cannot infer new information. When constrain is invoked from cover, two pairs S'_0 and S'_1 are derived from $S' = \langle \boldsymbol{W}', F'\rangle$ for which $\gamma_{\boldsymbol{w}}(S') = \gamma_{\boldsymbol{w}}(S'_0) \cup \gamma_{\boldsymbol{w}}(S'_1)$. The pairs S'_0 and S'_1 are formed by adding $w_i - 2w + 0$ and $w_i - 2w + 1$ to F', which stipulate, respectively, whether w_i takes an even or an odd value. Note, in this case, $\mathsf{constrain}(S', 1, w_i, r)$ is called with $\mathsf{vars}(r) = \emptyset$, hence $\mathsf{safe}(\boldsymbol{W}, w_i, r)$ holds independently of $\boldsymbol{W}$ and w_i and need not be deployed within the body of cover itself. The cover function is then recursively applied to S'_0 and S'_1 to compute two covers, which are combined by set union. The function returns a singleton set $\{\boldsymbol{W}\}$ when $F = \emptyset$.

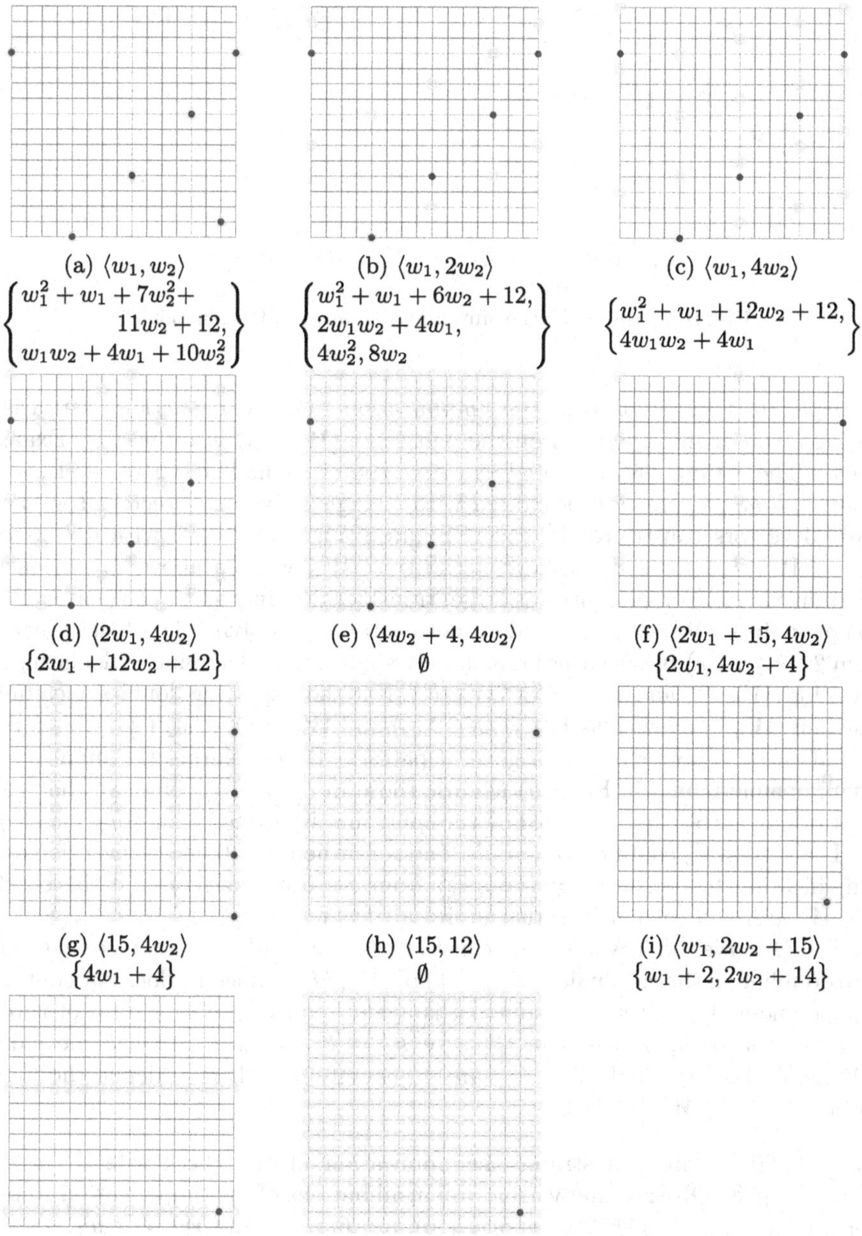

(a) $\langle w_1, w_2 \rangle$
$\left\{\begin{array}{r} w_1^2 + w_1 + 7w_2^2 + \\ 11w_2 + 12, \\ w_1w_2 + 4w_1 + 10w_2^2 \end{array}\right\}$

(b) $\langle w_1, 2w_2 \rangle$
$\left\{\begin{array}{l} w_1^2 + w_1 + 6w_2 + 12, \\ 2w_1w_2 + 4w_1, \\ 4w_2^2, 8w_2 \end{array}\right\}$

(c) $\langle w_1, 4w_2 \rangle$
$\left\{\begin{array}{l} w_1^2 + w_1 + 12w_2 + 12, \\ 4w_1w_2 + 4w_1 \end{array}\right\}$

(d) $\langle 2w_1, 4w_2 \rangle$
$\{2w_1 + 12w_2 + 12\}$

(e) $\langle 4w_2 + 4, 4w_2 \rangle$
$\emptyset$

(f) $\langle 2w_1 + 15, 4w_2 \rangle$
$\{2w_1, 4w_2 + 4\}$

(g) $\langle 15, 4w_2 \rangle$
$\{4w_1 + 4\}$

(h) $\langle 15, 12 \rangle$
$\emptyset$

(i) $\langle w_1, 2w_2 + 15 \rangle$
$\{w_1 + 2, 2w_2 + 14\}$

(j) $\langle 14, 2w_2 + 15 \rangle$
$\{2w_2 + 14\}$

(k) $\langle 14, 1 \rangle$
$\emptyset$

Fig. 8. Covering F: $\gamma_y(F_n)$ (large, translucent points) and $\gamma_y(S_n)$ (small, opaque points) for $S_n = \langle \boldsymbol{W}_n, F_n \rangle$

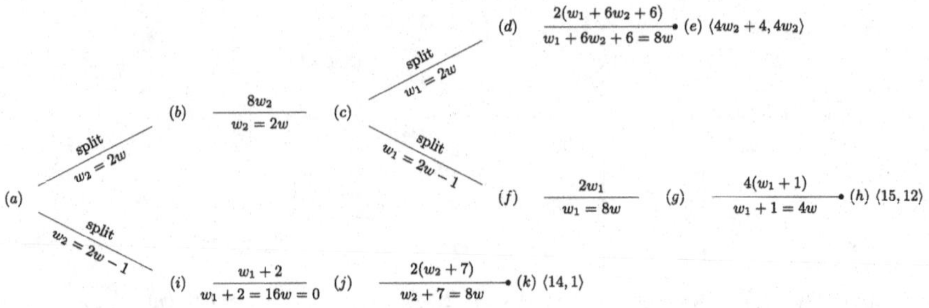

Fig. 9. Covering F: the simplification and splitting actions

Example 19. Figure 9 presents the simplification and splitting actions that arise during a run of the algorithm on the pair $S_a = \langle \boldsymbol{W}_a, F_a \rangle$ introduced in Example 18. The actions are presented as a tree rooted at node a where the leaves, nodes e, h and k, are each decorated with a single polynomial vector. Together these 3 vectors constitute the cover. Figure 8 augments Fig. 9 with details of $S_n = \langle \boldsymbol{W}_n, F_n \rangle$ for each node n of the tree: $\boldsymbol{W}_n$ written above F_n. In each diagram $\gamma_w(F_n)$ is represented as large, translucent points and $\gamma_w(S_n)$ as small, opaque points. Observe that F_a does not contain any polynomial of the general form $2^{\omega-j}(w_i + r)$ hence cover immediately splits the problem into calculating a cover for $\langle \boldsymbol{W}_b, F_b \rangle$ and a cover for $\langle \boldsymbol{W}_i, F_i \rangle$. Note how splitting doubles a leading constant: $\boldsymbol{W}_a = \boldsymbol{w}$ whereas $\boldsymbol{W}_b = \langle w_1, 2w_2 \rangle$ and $\boldsymbol{W}_i = \langle w_1, 2w_2 + 1 \rangle$. This form of scaling by a power of 2 is a general pattern. By comparing the number of small, opaque points in Fig. 8(a) against those in (b) and (i), observe that the solutions of $\gamma_w(S_a)$ are preserved by the split, that is, $\gamma_w(S_a) = \gamma_w(S_b) \cup \gamma_w(S_i)$.

The system F_b contains $8w_2 = 2^{4-1}(w_2 + r)$ where $r = 0$ hence cover deploys simplification to derive $S_c = \langle \boldsymbol{W}_c, F_c \rangle$ from S_b. Since $\mathsf{vars}(r) = \emptyset$ the check $\mathsf{safe}(\boldsymbol{W}, w_i, r)$ is vacuously satisfied. Recall from Example 17 that $\gamma_w(S_b) = \gamma_w(S_c)$. Observe too how a leading constant is again doubled, with a commensurate doubling in the cardinality of $\gamma_w(F_c)$ over $\gamma_w(F_b)$. Since F_c does not contain any polynomial $2^{\omega-j}(w_i + r)$ splitting is again applied to give a total of three branches that emanate from a. Observe $F_e = F_g = F_h = \emptyset$ hence the pairs $\langle \boldsymbol{W}_e, F_e \rangle$, $\langle \boldsymbol{W}_g, F_g \rangle$ and $\langle \boldsymbol{W}_h, F_h \rangle$ are degenerate and thereby define the final cover $\{\boldsymbol{W}_e, \boldsymbol{W}_g, \boldsymbol{W}_h\}$ over $\boldsymbol{w}$.

Example 20. Figure 9 illustrates the application of the check $\mathsf{safe}(\boldsymbol{W}, w_i, r)$ within simplify. Observe that $\mathsf{vars}(r) = \emptyset$ in all but one of the simplification steps. For the step that applies $2(w_1 + 6w_2 + 6)$, $r = 6w_2 + 6$ and $\boldsymbol{W} = \langle 2^1 w_1, 2^2 w_2 \rangle$. The polynomial r contains a single term $6w_2$, which contains the single variable w_2. The test $\mathsf{safe}(\boldsymbol{W}, w_1, r)$ thus reduces to a single inequality $k_1 + \mathsf{rank}(6) < k_2$ which is false since $k_1 = 1$, $\mathsf{rank}(6) = 1$ and $k_2 = 2$. Thus safe returns true.

The cover function, and its auxiliaries, are justified by two independent sets of results, the first establishing termination of simplify and cover and the second proving that cover is indeed a cover. The headline results are stated below:

Theorem 2. *simplify and cover terminate.*

Theorem 3. *Let $F \subseteq \mathbb{Z}_m[\boldsymbol{x}]$ and cover$(F) = \mathcal{W} \subseteq \mathbb{Z}_m^d[\boldsymbol{w}]$. Then $\mathcal{W}$ is a cover of F over $\boldsymbol{w}$.*

Example 21. Returning again to F_1 and F_2 of Example 16, cover computes $\mathcal{W}_1 = \{\langle 4w_2 + 6, 4w_2\rangle, \langle 8, 8w_2 + 1\rangle, \langle 12, 8w_2 + 7\rangle\}$ and $\mathcal{W}_2 = \{\langle 8w_1 + 3, 4w_2 + 1\rangle\}$ over $\boldsymbol{w} = \langle w_1, w_2\rangle$, where the 3 vectors of $\mathcal{W}_1$ corresponds to A_1, A_2 and A_3 respectively and the single vector constituting $\mathcal{W}_2$ corresponds to A_6 of Fig. 4, but with a different parametric variable w_2 from w_1 used in Example 16.

5.2 Closure

This section explains how a cover provides a vehicle for computing closure. A closed set of polynomials can be represented by different bases, and therefore a relation is introduced to express when one basis represents the closure of another:

Definition 14. *The relation $\rightarrow_{cl[\boldsymbol{x}]} \subseteq \wp(\mathbb{Z}_m[\boldsymbol{x}])^2$ is defined $B \rightarrow_{cl[\boldsymbol{x}]} B'$ iff $\uparrow_{\boldsymbol{x}} \langle B\rangle_{\boldsymbol{x}} = \langle B'\rangle_{\boldsymbol{x}}$.*

The following lemma provides a method for computing $\uparrow_{\boldsymbol{x}} \langle F\rangle_{\boldsymbol{x}}$ when $\{\boldsymbol{W}\}$ is a singleton cover for F. The lemma is stated by lifting the elimination relation to vectors of variables defined thus $B \rightarrow_{\mathsf{elim}[\epsilon]} B$ and $B \rightarrow_{\mathsf{elim}[y:\boldsymbol{y}]} B''$ iff $B \rightarrow_{\mathsf{elim}[y]} B'$ and $B' \rightarrow_{\mathsf{elim}[\boldsymbol{y}]} B''$. The computational tactic given in the lemma amounts to augmenting null polynomials with d polynomials which equate each variable x_ℓ with W_ℓ and then applying variable elimination:

Lemma 4. *Suppose $\boldsymbol{W} \in \mathbb{Z}_m[\boldsymbol{w}]^d$, $\top = \langle N\rangle_{\boldsymbol{w}}$ and $\{x_1 - W_1, \ldots, x_d - W_d\} \cup N \rightarrow_{\mathsf{elim}[\boldsymbol{w}]} B \subseteq \mathbb{Z}_m[\boldsymbol{x}]$. Then, $\langle B\rangle_{\boldsymbol{x}} = \alpha_{\boldsymbol{x}}(\{[\![\boldsymbol{W}]\!]_{\boldsymbol{w}}(\boldsymbol{a}) \mid \boldsymbol{a} \in \mathbb{Z}_m^{|\boldsymbol{w}|}\})$.*

Example 22. To illustrate this tactic, recall from Example 21 that $\{\boldsymbol{W}\}$ is a cover of F_2 over $\boldsymbol{w} = \langle w_1, w_2\rangle$ where $\boldsymbol{W} = \langle 8w_1 + 3, 4w_2 + 1\rangle$. Recall too from Example 4 that $\top = \langle N\rangle_{\boldsymbol{x}}$ where $\boldsymbol{x} = \langle x, y\rangle$. Observe $N' = N[x \mapsto w_1, y \mapsto w_2]$ is also a set of nulls, albeit over $\mathbb{Z}_m[\boldsymbol{w}]$. Let $p'_i = p_i[x \mapsto w_1, y \mapsto w_2]$ using the abbreviations of Example 4. Then $\mathsf{gb}_{\boldsymbol{w}:\boldsymbol{x}}(\{x - W_1, y - W_2\} \cup N']) = B$ where

$$B = \left\{\begin{array}{c} p'_1,\quad p'_2,\quad p'_3,\quad p'_4,\quad 2w_1y + 6w_1 + w_2x + w_2 + x + 3y + 10, \\ w_1^4y + w_1^4 + 4w_1^3 + w_1^2y + 5w_1^2 + 4w_1 + w_2x + w_2 + 3y + 13, \\ w_1^2w_2y + 3w_1^2w_2 + w_1w_2y + 3w_1w_2,\quad w_1x + 5w_1,\quad 8w_1 + x + 13, \\ \hline w_2^3y + 3w_2^3 + w_2^2y + 3w_2^2, w_2^2x + w_2^2 + w_2x + w_2y + y + 15, \\ p'_5,\quad p'_6,\quad 2w_2y + 2w_2 + y + 15,\quad 4w_2 + 3y + 13, \\ \hline x^2 + 7,\quad xy + x + y + 9,\quad 2x + 10,\quad y^2 + 2y + 13,\quad 4y + 12 \end{array}\right\}$$

The three regions delineate polynomials depending on both w_1 and w_2 (top), w_2 but not w_1 (middle) and neither w_1 nor w_2 (bottom). It thus follows that $\{x - W_1, y - W_2\} \cup N' \rightarrow_{\mathsf{elim}[w_1]} B'$ where

$$B' = \left\{\begin{array}{c} w_2^3y + 3w_2^3 + w_2^2y + 3w_2^2, w_2^2x + w_2^2 + w_2x + w_2y + y + 15, \\ p'_5,\quad p'_6,\quad 2w_2y + 2w_2 + y + 15,\quad 4w_2 + 3y + 13, \\ \hline x^2 + 7,\quad xy + x + y + 9,\quad 2x + 10,\quad y^2 + 2y + 13,\quad 4y + 12 \end{array}\right\}$$

B' is a Gröbner basis (with respect to $\prec_{\langle w,x,y\rangle}$), hence $B' \rightarrow_{\mathsf{elim}[w_2]} B''$ where

$$B'' = \{x^2 + 7, \quad xy + x + y + 9, \quad 2x + 10, \quad y^2 + 2y + 13, \quad 4y + 12\}$$

Composing the two eliminations yields $\{x - W_1, y - W_2\} \cup N' \rightarrow_{\mathsf{elim}[\boldsymbol{w}]} B''$. Note that it is only necessary to compute a single Gröbner basis to derive B''. Observe that each polynomial of B'' satisfies the points of $\gamma_{\boldsymbol{x}}(F_2)$ illustrated in Fig. 4(g).

The following theorem generalises this tactic to arbitrary covers:

Theorem 4. *Let $B \subseteq \mathbb{Z}_m[\boldsymbol{x}]$, $\top = \langle N\rangle_{\boldsymbol{w}}$ and $\mathcal{W} \subseteq \mathbb{Z}_m[\boldsymbol{w}]^d$ be a cover for B over $\boldsymbol{w}$. Suppose for each $\boldsymbol{W} \in \mathcal{W}$, $\{x_1 - W_1, \ldots, x_d - W_d\} \cup N \rightarrow_{\mathsf{elim}[\boldsymbol{w}]} B_{\boldsymbol{W}}$ and $\langle B'\rangle_{\boldsymbol{x}} = \bigsqcup_{\boldsymbol{W}\in\mathcal{W}} \langle B_{\boldsymbol{W}}\rangle_{\boldsymbol{x}}$. Then, $B \rightarrow_{\mathsf{cl}[\boldsymbol{x}]} B'$.*

Example 23. Now recall from Example 19 that $\{\boldsymbol{W}_e, \boldsymbol{W}_h, \boldsymbol{W}_k\}$ is a cover of

$$F = \{x^2 + x + 7y^2 + 11y + 12, \quad xy + 4x + 10y^2\}$$

over $\boldsymbol{w} = \langle w_1, w_2\rangle$ where $\boldsymbol{W}_e = \langle 4w_2 + 4, 4w_2\rangle$, $\boldsymbol{W}_h = \langle 15, 12\rangle$ and $\boldsymbol{W}_k = \langle 14, 1\rangle$. To apply the theorem, $B_{\boldsymbol{W}_e}$ is derived by $\{x - (4w_2 + 4), y - 4w_2\} \cup N \rightarrow_{\mathsf{elim}[\boldsymbol{w}]} B_{\boldsymbol{W}_e}$. Since $\boldsymbol{W}_e$ depends only on w_2, $B_{\boldsymbol{W}_e}$ can be computed by $\{x - (4w_2 + 4), y - 4w_2\} \cup N' \rightarrow_{\mathsf{elim}[w_2]} B_{\boldsymbol{W}_e}$ where $\top = \langle N'\rangle_{\langle w_2\rangle}$. To that end, note $\mathsf{gb}_{\langle w_2,x,y\rangle}(\{x - (4w_2 - 4), y - 4w_2\} \cup N') = B'_{\boldsymbol{W}_e}$ where

$$B'_{\boldsymbol{W}_e} = \left\{ \begin{array}{c} w_2^6 + w_2^5 + w_2^4 + 3w_2^3 + w_2^2 y + 2w_2^2 + w_2 y, \\ 2w_2^4 + w_2^2 y + 2w_2^2 + w_2 y + y, \quad w_2^3 y + w_2 y + 2y, \\ 2w_2 y + 2y, \quad 4w_2 + 3y, \quad x + 3y + 12, \quad y^2, \quad 4y \end{array} \right\}$$

thus $B_{\boldsymbol{W}_e} = \{x + 3y + 12, y^2, 4y\}$ is computed avoiding nulls containing w_1.

The bases $B_{\boldsymbol{W}_h}$ and $B_{\boldsymbol{W}_k}$ can be derived without recourse to elimination or any nulls since $\boldsymbol{W}_h$ and $\boldsymbol{W}_k$ are independent of w_1 and w_2 hence put

$$B_{\boldsymbol{W}_h} = \{x-15, y-12\} = \{x+1, y+4\} \qquad B_{\boldsymbol{W}_k} = \{x-14, y-1\} = \{x+2, y+15\}$$

By Theorem 4 $\uparrow_{\boldsymbol{x}} \langle F\rangle_{\boldsymbol{x}} = \langle B\rangle_{\boldsymbol{x}}$ where $\langle B\rangle_{\boldsymbol{x}} = \langle B_{\boldsymbol{W}_e}\rangle_{\boldsymbol{x}} \sqcup \langle B_{\boldsymbol{W}_h}\rangle_{\boldsymbol{x}} \sqcup \langle B_{\boldsymbol{W}_k}\rangle_{\boldsymbol{x}}$ giving

$$B = \{x^2 + x + 7y^2 + 11y + 12, \quad xy + 4x + 10y^2, \quad y^3 + 7y^2 + 8y, \quad 4y^2 + 12y\}$$

All the polynomials of B satisfy the points $\gamma_{\boldsymbol{x}}(F)$ plotted in Fig. 7(a). Observe

$$F' = \{x^2 + x + 7y^2 + 11y + 12, \quad xy + 4x + 10y^2, \quad y^3 + 7y^2 + 8y\}$$

is a Gröbner basis for $\langle F\rangle_{\boldsymbol{x}}$ with respect to $\prec_{\boldsymbol{x}}$. Since $4y^2 + 12y$ is irreducible by F' it follows $4y^2 + 12y \notin \langle F\rangle_{\boldsymbol{x}}$ which is why closure augments F with $4y^2 + 12y$.

5.3 Meet

Despite the central importance of meet, this section is relatively short, since the following proposition demonstrates how meet can be reduced to closure:

Proposition 8. *Let* $\langle B_1 \rangle_{\boldsymbol{x}}, \langle B_2 \rangle_{\boldsymbol{x}} \in \mathsf{MPAD}_m[\boldsymbol{x}]$. *If* $B_1 \cup B_2 \rightarrow_{\mathsf{cl}[\boldsymbol{x}]} B$ *then* $\langle B_1 \rangle_{\boldsymbol{x}} \sqcap \langle B_2 \rangle_{\boldsymbol{x}} = \langle B \rangle_{\boldsymbol{x}}$.

Example 24. Consider $F_3, F_4 \subseteq \mathbb{Z}_{16}[x, y]$ where $F_3 = \{x^2+x+7y^2+11y+12\}$ and $F_4 = \{xy+4x+10y^2\}$ and let $F = F_3 \cup F_4$. The solution sets $\gamma_{\boldsymbol{x}}(F)$, $\gamma_{\boldsymbol{x}}(F_3)$ and $\gamma_{\boldsymbol{x}}(F_4)$ are plotted in Figs. 7(a), (b) and (c) respectively. The diamond points in Figs. 7(b) and (c) are those contained in both $\gamma_{\boldsymbol{x}}(F_3)$ and $\gamma_{\boldsymbol{x}}(F_4)$ and show $\gamma_{\boldsymbol{x}}(F) = \gamma_{\boldsymbol{x}}(F_1) \cap \gamma_{\boldsymbol{x}}(F_2)$. Now, Example 23 shows $F \rightarrow_{\mathsf{cl}[\boldsymbol{x}]} B$ where

$$B = \{x^2 + x + 7y^2 + 11y + 12, \quad xy + 4x + 10y^2, \quad y^3 + 7y^2 + 8y, \quad 4y^2 + 12y\}$$

thus $\langle F_3 \rangle_{\boldsymbol{x}} \sqcap \langle F_4 \rangle_{\boldsymbol{x}} = \langle B \rangle_{\boldsymbol{x}}$. As noted in Example 23, $4y^2 + 12y \notin \langle F \rangle_{\boldsymbol{x}}$ hence $\langle F \rangle_{\boldsymbol{x}} \neq \langle B \rangle_{\boldsymbol{x}}$.

6 Forwards Analysis of Polynomial Programs

In this section, the class of polynomial programs is introduced for which a concrete semantics is defined over sets of points drawn from $\mathbb{Z}_m^d$. The corresponding abstract semantics over MPAD defines a forwards analysis. The development builds to show the soundness of the analysis, as well as state a precision result for programs consisting solely of polynomial assignments, non-deterministic assignments and non-deterministic branching. The section concludes with an illustrative example for a program which computes the modular inverse.

6.1 Polynomial Programs

Let $\boldsymbol{x} = \langle x_1, \ldots, x_d \rangle$ denote a vector of program variables. A polynomial program over $\boldsymbol{x}$ is a graph $G = \langle N, E, n^* \rangle$ where N is a finite set of program points, $E \subseteq N \times \mathsf{Stmt} \times N$ is a finite set of annotated edges and $n^* \in N$ is the entry point into G. The set Stmt of program statements is defined:

$$x_j := p \quad | \quad x_j := * \quad | \quad \mathsf{assume}\ (p = 0) \quad | \quad \mathsf{assume}\ (p \neq 0)$$

where $x_j := *$ and $x_j := p$ denote, respectively, non-deterministic assignment to the variable x_j and polynomial assignment to x_j for some $p \in \mathbb{Z}_m[\boldsymbol{x}]$. The assume statements for $p = 0$ and $p \neq 0$ provide a linguistic abstraction for positive and negative guards, respectively expressing that p is satisfied, and conversely p is not satisfied, by an assignment to $\boldsymbol{x}$.

6.2 Concrete Semantics

To define the concrete semantics, let $\boldsymbol{a}[j \mapsto c] = \langle a_1, \ldots, a_{j-1}, c, a_{j+1}, \ldots, a_d \rangle$ for $\boldsymbol{a} \in \mathbb{Z}_m^d$, $c \in \mathbb{Z}_m$ and j a variable index denote a vector update. The concrete semantics is then formulated in terms of a set of (concrete) transfer functions $[\![s]\!] : \wp(\mathbb{Z}_m^d) \to \wp(\mathbb{Z}_m^d)$, one for each program statement s, defined as follows:

$$\begin{aligned}
[\![x_j := p]\!](A) &= \{(\boldsymbol{a})[j \mapsto c] \mid \boldsymbol{a} \in A, c = [\![p]\!]_{\boldsymbol{x}}(\boldsymbol{a})\} \\
[\![x_j := *]\!](A) &= \{(\boldsymbol{a})[j \mapsto c] \mid \boldsymbol{a} \in A, c \in \mathbb{Z}_m\} \\
[\![\mathsf{assume}\ (p = 0)]\!](A) &= \{\boldsymbol{a} \in A \mid [\![p]\!]_{\boldsymbol{x}}(\boldsymbol{a}) = 0\} \\
[\![\mathsf{assume}\ (p \neq 0)]\!](A) &= \{\boldsymbol{a} \in A \mid [\![p]\!]_{\boldsymbol{x}}(\boldsymbol{a}) \neq 0\}
\end{aligned}$$

Observe that the function space $N \to \wp(\mathbb{Z}_m^d)$ is ordered point-wise: $\theta \sqsubseteq \theta'$ iff $\theta(n) \subseteq \theta'(n)$ for all $n \in N$. Thus the concrete semantics can be defined as follows:

Definition 15. *The concrete semantics for* $G = \langle N, E, n^* \rangle$ *is the least map* $\theta : N \to \wp(\mathbb{Z}_m^d)$ *satisfying:*

- $\mathbb{Z}_m^d \subseteq \theta(n^*)$
- $[\![s]\!](\theta(n)) \subseteq \theta(n')$ *for all* $\langle n, s, n' \rangle \in E$

6.3 Abstract Semantics

Analogous to the concrete semantics, the abstract semantics for $G = \langle N, E, n^* \rangle$ is defined in terms of a set of (abstract) transfer functions. For a statement s, $[\![s]\!] : \mathsf{MPAD}_m[\boldsymbol{x}] \to \mathsf{MPAD}_m[\boldsymbol{x}]$ is defined thus:

$$\begin{aligned}
[\![x_j := p]\!](P) &= \{q \in \mathbb{Z}_m[\boldsymbol{x}] \mid q[p/x_j] \in P\} \\
[\![x_j := *]\!](P) &= \uparrow_{\boldsymbol{x}} \mathsf{elim}[x_j](P) \\
[\![\mathsf{assume}\ (p = 0)]\!](P) &= \uparrow_{\boldsymbol{x}} (\{p\} \cup P) \\
[\![\mathsf{assume}\ (p \neq 0)]\!](P) &= \textstyle\bigsqcup_{k=1}^{\omega} [\![\mathsf{assume}\ (2^{\omega-k}p + 2^{\omega-1} = 0)]\!](P)
\end{aligned}$$

Here, the notation $q[p/x_j]$ denotes the polynomial constructed by substituting p for every instance of x_j in q. To comprehend the encoding for $\mathsf{assume}(p \neq 0)$, suppose $\boldsymbol{a} \in \mathbb{Z}_m$ such that $[\![p]\!]_{\boldsymbol{x}}(\boldsymbol{a}) \neq 0$. Observe there exists some $1 \leq k \leq \omega$ such that $[\![p]\!]_{\boldsymbol{x}}(\boldsymbol{a})$ has 1 in its k-th lowest bit position and 0 in all lower bits. Therefore $[\![2^{\omega-k}p + 2^{\omega-1}]\!]_{\boldsymbol{x}}(\boldsymbol{a}) = 0$. Conversely, if $[\![2^{\omega-k}p + 2^{\omega-1}]\!]_{\boldsymbol{x}}(\boldsymbol{a}) = 0$ then $[\![p]\!]_{\boldsymbol{x}}(\boldsymbol{a})$ has 1 in its k-th lowest bit position hence $[\![p]\!]_{\boldsymbol{x}}(\boldsymbol{a}) \neq 0$.

The function space $N \to \mathsf{MPAD}_m[\boldsymbol{x}]$ is likewise ordered point-wise: $\sigma \sqsubseteq \sigma'$ iff $\sigma(n) \sqsubseteq \sigma'(n)$ for all $n \in N$, allowing the abstract semantics to be defined thus:

Definition 16. *The abstract semantics for* $G = \langle N, E, n^* \rangle$ *is the least map* $\sigma : N \to \mathsf{MPAD}_m[\boldsymbol{x}]$ *satisfying:*

- $\top \sqsubseteq \sigma(n^*)$
- $[\![s]\!](\theta(n)) \sqsubseteq \sigma(n')$ *for all* $\langle n, s, n' \rangle \in E$

Since MPAD is finite, the abstract semantics can be concretely computed by fixed-point iteration; an example of such a procedure is illustrated in Sect. 6.5. The relationship between the concrete and abstract semantics is developed in the following section. The following result details how the abstract transfer functions are actually computed:

Proposition 9. *Let* $\langle B\rangle_{\boldsymbol{x}} \in \mathsf{MPAD}_m[\boldsymbol{x}]$ *and* $w \notin \mathsf{vars}(B)$. *Then:*

- *If* $B \cup \{w - p\} \rightarrow_{\mathsf{elim}[x_j]} B'$ *and* $B' \cup \{x_j - w\} \rightarrow_{\mathsf{elim}[w]} B''$ *then it follows* $[\![x_j := p]\!](\langle B\rangle_{\boldsymbol{x}}) = \langle B''\rangle_{\boldsymbol{x}}$.
- *If* $B \rightarrow_{\mathsf{elim}[x_j]} B'$ *and* $B' \rightarrow_{\mathsf{cl}[\boldsymbol{x}]} B''$ *then* $[\![x_j := *]\!](\langle B\rangle_{\boldsymbol{x}}) = \langle B''\rangle_{\boldsymbol{x}}$.
- *If* $\{p\} \cup B \rightarrow_{\mathsf{cl}[\boldsymbol{x}]} B'$ *then* $[\![\mathsf{assume}\ (p = 0)]\!](\langle B\rangle_{\boldsymbol{x}}) = \langle B'\rangle_{\boldsymbol{x}}$.

6.4 Correctness and Precision

Key to establishing correctness and precision of the analysis are the following results. The first elucidates the relationship between concrete and abstract join using the abstraction map $\alpha_{\boldsymbol{x}} : \wp(\mathbb{Z}_m^d) \rightarrow \mathsf{MPAD}_m[\boldsymbol{x}]$ introduced in Proposition 3:

Proposition 10. *Suppose* $P_1, P_2 \in \mathsf{MPAD}_m[\boldsymbol{x}]$ *where* $P_1 = \alpha_{\boldsymbol{x}}(A_1), P_2 = \alpha_{\boldsymbol{x}}(A_2)$ *for some* $A_1, A_2 \subseteq \mathbb{Z}_m^d$. *Then* $P_1 \sqcup P_2 = \alpha_{\boldsymbol{x}}(A_1 \cup A_2)$.

The second result demonstrates soundness of each of the abstract transfer functions, as well as optimality for the two assignment operations:

Proposition 11. *Let* $A \subseteq \mathbb{Z}_m^d$ *and* $P = \alpha_{\boldsymbol{x}}(A)$ *so that* $P \in \mathsf{MPAD}_m[\boldsymbol{x}]$. *Then*

$$\begin{aligned}
\alpha_{\boldsymbol{x}}([\![x_j := p]\!](A)) &= [\![x_j := p]\!](P)\\
\alpha_{\boldsymbol{x}}([\![x_j := *]\!](A)) &= [\![x_j := *]\!](P)\\
\alpha_{\boldsymbol{x}}([\![\mathsf{assume}\ (p = 0)]\!](A)) &\sqsubseteq [\![\mathsf{assume}\ (p = 0)]\!](P)\\
\alpha_{\boldsymbol{x}}([\![\mathsf{assume}\ (p \neq 0)]\!](A)) &\sqsubseteq [\![\mathsf{assume}\ (p \neq 0)]\!](P)
\end{aligned}$$

With these results in the place, the following theorem can be demonstrated:

Theorem 5. *If the concrete and the abstract semantics for* $G = \langle N, E, n^*\rangle$ *are* $\theta : N \rightarrow \wp(\mathbb{Z}_m^d)$ *and* $\sigma : N \rightarrow \mathsf{MPAD}_m[\boldsymbol{x}]$ *respectively then:*

$$\alpha_{\boldsymbol{x}}(\theta(n)) \sqsubseteq \sigma(n) \text{ for all } n \in N$$

If G is free from $\mathsf{assume}\ (p = 0)$ *and* $\mathsf{assume}\ (p \neq 0)$ *statements then:*

$$\alpha_{\boldsymbol{x}}(\theta(n)) = \sigma(n) \text{ for all } n \in N$$

In particular, MPAD provides a sound analysis for polynomial programs, and moreover finds all modular polynomial invariants for programs consisting of polynomial and non-deterministic assignments and non-deterministic branching.

6.5 Illustrative Example

To illustrate how MPAD can be applied, consider the algorithm [34] listed in Fig. 10(a). The algorithm computes the multiplicative inverse of an (odd) modular integer $a \in \mathbb{Z}_m$. The variables x, y and a all store a ω-bit (unsigned) integer. The algorithm is abstracted by the polynomial program represented in Fig. 10(b) where $\boldsymbol{x} = \langle x, y, a\rangle$, the nodes are $N = \{0, \ldots, 7\}$ and the entry node is 0. Each

```
function inverse(a)
assume (a odd)
begin
   y := 1
   do
      x := y
      y := x * (2 − a * x)
   while (x ≠ y)
   assert (a * x = 1)
   return x
end
```

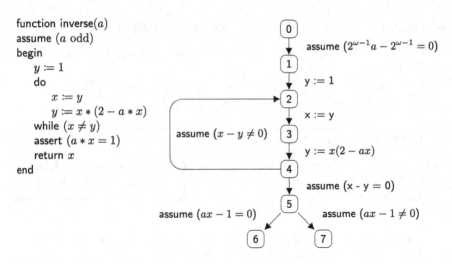

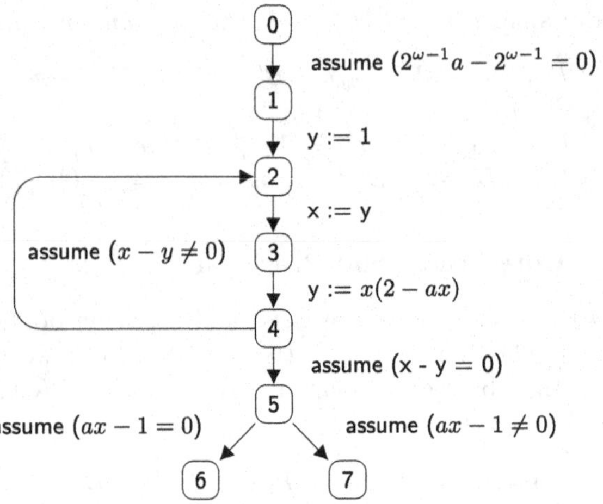

Fig. 10. An algorithm and flow graph for computing the multiplicative inverse

edge is decorated with a polynomial assignment or an assumption involving a polynomial equality or a polynomial disequality.

The statement assume (a odd) is rendered as assume $(2^{\omega-1}a - 2^{\omega-1} = 0)$, where the (linear) polynomial $2^{\omega-1}a - 2^{\omega-1} = 0$ expresses that a is odd. The control-flow for the **do** ... **while** is represented as two edges decorated with assume $(x - y \neq 0)$ and assume $(x - y = 0)$, which, respectively, encode the loop condition $x \neq y$ and its negation. The control flow for the assert statement is expressed through two edges decorated with assume $(ax - 1 = 0)$ and assume $(ax - 1 \neq 0)$, where the node 7 is reached if the assertion fails.

Figure 11 presents each σ_k computed by a work-list algorithm primed with the edges that flow from 0. The second column displays the worklist w_k. The selected edge $\langle n, n' \rangle \in w_k$ is always the first listed in w_k. For instance, at step 4, the edge $\langle 4, 2 \rangle$ is selected, rather than $\langle 4, 5 \rangle$. The third column displays σ_{k+1} as a function of the σ_k: σ_k if no update occurred, else $\sigma_k[n' \mapsto P]$ where $P \in \mathsf{MPAD}_m[\boldsymbol{x}]$. Polynomials that appear multiply are referenced with a label: p_a, p_b, etc. Most significantly, the table demonstrates $\sigma_{14}(7) = \bot$ thus assert $(a * x = 1)$ must succeed (this can be seen from $ax - 1 \rightarrow^*_{\prec, \sigma_{13}(5)} 0$). No other abstract domain can verify this code because the invariants are both polynomial and modular and the analysis requires polynomial guards; indeed the manual proof of correctness of the algorithm [34] relies on both polynomial manipulation and observing $a^2(2^\omega) = 0 \mod 2^\omega$.

Since a positive polynomial guard is modelled by meet, detailed commentaries are only given for a polynomial assignment and a negative guard:

Polynomial Assignment. When $k = 1$, the edge $\langle 1, 2 \rangle$ is selected, corresponding to the statement $y := 1$. From the table it follows $\sigma_1(1) = P_0 = \langle B_0 \rangle_{\boldsymbol{x}}$. To model the assignment, first the basis B_0 is adjoined with the polynomial $w - 1$. Here,

k	w_k	σ_{k+1}
0	$\{\langle 0,1\rangle\}$	$\sigma_0[1 \mapsto \langle x^4a + x^4 + 2x^3a + 2x^3 + 3x^2a + 3x^2 + 2xa + 2x\ (p_a),$ $2x^2y^2a + 2x^2y^2 + 2x^2ya +$ $2x^2y + 2xy^2a + 2xy^2 + 2xya + 2xy,$ $x^2a^2 + 7x^2 + xa^2 + 7x\ (p_b), 4x^2a + 4x^2 + 4xa + 4x\ (p_c),$ $y^4a + y^4 + 2y^3a + 2y^3 + 3y^2a + 3y^2 + 2ya + 2y,$ $y^2a^2 + 7y^2 + ya^2 + 7y, 4y^2a + 4y^2 + 4ya + 4y,$ $a^3 + a^2 + 7a + 7\ (p_d), 2a^2 + 14\ (p_e), 8a + 8\ (p_f)\rangle_{\boldsymbol{x}}]$
1	$\{\langle 1,2\rangle\}$	$\sigma_1[2 \mapsto \langle p_a, p_b, p_c, y + 15\ (p_g), p_d, p_e, p_f\rangle_{\boldsymbol{x}}]$
2	$\{\langle 2,3\rangle\}$	$\sigma_2[3 \mapsto \langle x + 15\ (p_h), p_g, p_d, p_e, p_f\rangle_{\boldsymbol{x}}]$
3	$\{\langle 3,4\rangle\}$	$\sigma_3[4 \mapsto \langle p_h, y + a + 14, p_d, p_e, p_f\rangle_{\boldsymbol{x}}]$
4	$\{\langle 4,2\rangle, \langle 4,5\rangle\}$	$\sigma_4[2 \mapsto \langle p_a, p_b, p_c, xy + 15x + 7y + 9, y^2 + ya + 5y + 7a + 2\ (p_i),$ $ya^2 + 7y + a^2 + 7\ (p_j), 2ya + 2y + 6a + 6\ (p_k),$ $8y + 8\ (p_l), p_d, p_e, p_f\rangle_{\boldsymbol{x}}]$
5	$\{\langle 2,3\rangle, \langle 4,5\rangle\}$	$\sigma_5[3 \mapsto \langle x + 7y + 8\ (p_m), p_i, p_j, p_k, p_l, p_d, p_e, p_f\rangle_{\boldsymbol{x}}]$
6	$\{\langle 3,4\rangle, \langle 4,5\rangle\}$	$\sigma_6[4 \mapsto \langle x^2 + 2x + 3y + 3a + 7\ (p_n),$ $xy + 3x + a + 11, xa + 3x + y + 11,$ $4x + 2y + 2a + 8\ (p_o), y^2 + 2y + a^2 + 6a + 6\ (p_q),$ $ya + y + a^2 + 7a + 6\ (p_r), 4y + 4a + 8\ (p_s), p_d, p_e, p_f\rangle_{\boldsymbol{x}}]$
7	$\{\langle 4,2\rangle, \langle 4,5\rangle\}$	$\sigma_7[2 \mapsto \langle p_a, x^2y + 7x^2 + 8x + 7y + 9, p_b, p_c, xy^2 + 15x + y^2 + 15,$ $xya + xy + 7xa + 7x + ya + y + 7a + 7,$ $2xy + 14x + y^2 + ya + 3y + 7a + 4,$ $y^3 + y^2 + 7y + 7\ (p_t), y^2a + y^2 + 7a + 7\ (p_u),$ $2y^2 + 14\ (p_v), p_j, p_k, p_l, p_d, p_e, p_f\rangle_{\boldsymbol{x}}]$
8	$\{\langle 2,3\rangle, \langle 4,5\rangle\}$	$\sigma_8[3 \mapsto \langle p_m, p_t, p_u, p_v, p_j, p_k, p_l, p_d, p_e, p_f\rangle_{\boldsymbol{x}}]$
9	$\{\langle 3,4\rangle, \langle 4,5\rangle\}$	$\sigma_9[4 \mapsto \langle p_n,$ $xy + xa + 2x + 3y + 3a + 6, xa^2 + 3x + 2y + a^2 + 2a + 7,$ $2xa + 2x + 6a + 6, p_o, p_q, p_r, p_s, p_d, p_e, p_f\rangle_{\boldsymbol{x}}]$
10	$\{\langle 4,2\rangle, \langle 4,5\rangle\}$	σ_{10}
11	$\{\langle 4,5\rangle\}$	$\sigma_{11}[5 \mapsto \langle x + a^2 + 7a + 7\ (p_w), y + a^2 + 7a + 7\ (p_x), p_d, p_e, p_f\rangle_{\boldsymbol{x}}]$
12	$\{\langle 5,6\rangle, \langle 5,7\rangle\}$	$\sigma_{12}[6 \mapsto \langle p_w, p_x, p_d, p_e, p_f\rangle_{\boldsymbol{x}}]$
13	$\{\langle 5,7\rangle\}$	σ_{13}

Fig. 11. Updates to the state map

w is a new variable that represents the value of y after the assignment and the polynomial $w - 1$ expresses that this value must equal 1. Then, y is eliminated from $B_0 \cup \{w - 1\}$, to reflect that y is overwritten during the assignment. This elimination step is achieved in two phases. First, a Gröbner basis is computed for $\langle B_0 \cup \{w - 1\}\rangle_{\boldsymbol{x}}$ with respect to a lexicographical ordering $\langle y, x, w, a\rangle$ over the variables, yielding

$$\left\{\begin{array}{c} y^4a + y^4 + 2y^3a + 2y^3 + 3y^2a + 3y^2 + 2ya + 2y, \\ 2y^2x^2a + 2y^2x^2 + 2y^2xa + 2y^2x + 2yx^2a + 2yx^2 + 2yxa + 2yx, \\ y^2a^2 + 7y^2 + ya^2 + 7y, \quad 4y^2a + 4y^2 + 4ya + 4y, \\ x^4a + x^4 + 2x^3a + 2x^3 + 3x^2a + 3x^2 + 2xa + 2x, \quad x^2a^2 + 7x^2 + xa^2 + 7x, \\ 4x^2a + 4x^2 + 4xa + 4x, \quad w + 15, \quad a^3 + a^2 + 7a + 7, \quad 2a^2 + 14, \quad 8a + 8 \end{array}\right\}$$

Then, all polynomials involving y are deleted:

$$B_0' = \left\{ \begin{array}{l} x^4a + x^4 + 2x^3a + 2x^3 + 3x^2a + 3x^2 + 2xa + 2x, \\ x^2a^2 + 7x^2 + xa^2 + 7x, \quad 4x^2a + 4x^2 + 4xa + 4x, \\ w + 15, \quad a^3 + a^2 + 7a + 7, \quad 2a^2 + 14, \quad 8a + 8 \end{array} \right\}$$

the Gröbner basis ensuring that this deletion does not lose information. To finalise the assignment, a Gröbner basis is computed for $\langle B_0' \cup \{w - y\}\rangle_{\boldsymbol{x}}$ with respect to the lexicographical ordering $\langle w, y, x, a\rangle$, then all constraints containing w are deleted, yielding:

$$B_1 = \left\{ \begin{array}{l} x^4a + x^4 + 2x^3a + 2x^3 + 3x^2a + 3x^2 + 2xa + 2x, \\ x^2a^2 + 7x^2 + xa^2 + 7x, \quad 4x^2a + 4x^2 + 4xa + 4x, \\ y + 15, \quad a^3 + a^2 + 7a + 7, \quad 2a^2 + 14, \quad 8a + 8 \end{array} \right\}$$

Negative Polynomial Guard. When $k = 4$, the edge $\langle 4, 2\rangle$ is selected, the edge corresponding to the statement $\mathsf{assume}\ (x - y \neq 0)$. From the table it follows $\sigma_3(4) = \langle B_3\rangle_{\boldsymbol{x}}$ where

$$B_3 = \{x + 15, \quad y + a + 14, \quad a^3 + a^2 + 7a + 7, \quad 2a^2 + 14, \quad 8a + 8\}$$

To effect the operation, closure is separately applied to four bases:

$$\begin{array}{lll} B_3 \cup \{8(x - y) + 8\} & \rightarrow_{\mathsf{cl}[\boldsymbol{x}]} & B_{4,1} = \{1\} \\ B_3 \cup \{4(x - y) + 8\} & \rightarrow_{\mathsf{cl}[\boldsymbol{x}]} & B_{4,2} = \{x + 15,\ y + a + 14,\ a^2 + 2a + 1,\ 4a + 4\} \\ B_3 \cup \{2(x - y) + 8\} & \rightarrow_{\mathsf{cl}[\boldsymbol{x}]} & B_{4,3} = \{x + 15,\ y + a + 14,\ a^2 + 7,\ 2a + 6\} \\ B_3 \cup \{(x - y) + 8\} & \rightarrow_{\mathsf{cl}[\boldsymbol{x}]} & B_{4,4} = \{x + 15,\ y + 7,\ a + 7\} \end{array}$$

The intuition is that each $\gamma_{\boldsymbol{x}}(B_{4,k})$ is the subset of $\boldsymbol{a} \in \gamma_{\boldsymbol{x}}(B_3)$ for which the k least-significant bits of $[\![x - y]\!]_{\boldsymbol{x}}(\boldsymbol{a})$ store the value 2^{k-1}. Thus $\gamma_{\boldsymbol{x}}(B_{4,1})$ is the subset of $\boldsymbol{a} \in \gamma_{\boldsymbol{x}}(B_3)$ for which the least bit of $[\![x - y]\!]_{\boldsymbol{x}}(\boldsymbol{a})$ is $2^0 = 1$; $\gamma_{\boldsymbol{x}}(B_{4,2})$ is the subset for which the 2 least bits of $[\![x - y]\!]_{\boldsymbol{x}}(\boldsymbol{a})$ store $2^1 = 2$, etc. Since $[\![x - y]\!]_{\boldsymbol{x}}(\boldsymbol{a}) \neq 0$ holds precisely when at least one bit is set, it follows $P_4 = \bigsqcup_{k=1}^{4} \langle B_{4,k}\rangle_{\boldsymbol{x}} \in \mathsf{MPAD}_m[\boldsymbol{x}]$ satisfies the property above. In fact, in this case $P_4 = P_3$, hence the abstract execution of $\mathsf{assume}\ (x - y \neq 0)$ does not strengthen the polynomial constraints even though $B_{4,1} = \{1\}$ reveals that the difference between x and y is never odd.

6.6 Implementation

Buchberger's algorithm, like many in symbolic computation, has poor worst-case complexity [19]. Performance can be dramatically improved, however, by factoring out redundant s-polynomial calculations (and the ensuing reductions) using the so-called Gebauer and Möller rules [13]. To reestablish these rules for modular polynomials, let $B = \{p_1, \ldots, p_s\} \subseteq \mathbb{Z}_m[\boldsymbol{x}] \setminus \{0\}$ and put $\boldsymbol{p} = \langle p_1, \ldots, p_s\rangle$ and $\boldsymbol{t} = \langle \mathsf{lt}_{\prec}(p_1), \ldots, \mathsf{lt}_{\prec}(p_s)\rangle$. A vector $\boldsymbol{q} \in \mathbb{Z}_m[\boldsymbol{x}]^s$ is a syzygy of $\boldsymbol{t}$ iff $\boldsymbol{q} \cdot \boldsymbol{t} = 0$. The set $\mathsf{syz}(\boldsymbol{t})$ of syzygies of $\boldsymbol{t}$ forms a module. It can be shown

[13] that if $\boldsymbol{q} \cdot \boldsymbol{p} \rightarrow_{\prec,B} 0$ for all syzygies $\boldsymbol{q}$ in a module-basis for $\mathsf{syz}(\boldsymbol{t})$, then B is a Gröbner basis. Letting $\{\boldsymbol{e}_1, \ldots, \boldsymbol{e}_s\}$ denote the standard basis for $\mathbb{Z}_m[\boldsymbol{x}]^s$, $k_i = \mathsf{rank}(\mathsf{lc}_\prec(p_i))$ and $t_{i,j} = \mathsf{lcm}(t_i, t_j)/t_i$, the principle syzygies π_i and $\pi_{i,j}$ are defined:

$$\pi_i = 2^{\omega - k_i}\boldsymbol{e}_i \quad \text{and} \quad \pi_{i,j} = t_{i,j}\boldsymbol{e}_i - t_{j,i}\boldsymbol{e}_j \text{ where } 1 \leq i < j \leq s$$

The following result yields a condition for detecting redundant principle syzygies:

Proposition 12. *Given* $\mathbf{t} = \langle t_1, \ldots, t_s \rangle$ *be a vector of non-zero terms. Then*

$$\frac{\mathit{lcm}(t_i, t_j, t_k)}{\mathit{lcm}(t_i, t_j)}\boldsymbol{\pi}_{i,j} + \frac{\mathit{lcm}(t_i, t_j, t_k)}{\mathit{lcm}(t_j, t_k)}\boldsymbol{\pi}_{j,k} + \frac{\mathit{lcm}(t_i, t_j, t_k)}{\mathit{lcm}(t_k, t_i)}\boldsymbol{\pi}_{k,i} = 0$$

and, in particular, if t_k *divides* $\mathit{lcm}(t_i, t_j)$ *then* $\boldsymbol{\pi}_{i,j}$ *is in the submodule generated by* $\boldsymbol{\pi}_{j,k}$ *and* $\boldsymbol{\pi}_{k,i}$

Principle syzygies align with S-polynomials: π_i and $\pi_{i,j}$ correspond to $\mathsf{S}_\prec(p_i, p_i)$ and $\mathsf{S}_\prec(p_i, p_j)$ respectively. Thus, the above result can be reinterpreted for S-polynomials as follows: given polynomials $p_i, p_j, p_k \in \mathbb{Z}_m[\boldsymbol{x}]$ such that $\mathsf{lt}_\prec(p_i)$ divides $\mathsf{lcm}(\mathsf{lt}_\prec(p_j), \mathsf{lt}_\prec(p_k))$ then the S-polynomial $\mathsf{S}_\prec(p_i, p_k)$ can be dropped (from S in Fig. 2) if $\mathsf{S}_\prec(p_i, p_k)$ and $\mathsf{S}_\prec(p_i, p_j)$ are (eventually) computed. Although this rule mirrors the triple criteria of [13], modular polynomials offer additional redundancy rules. Together these rules reduce the running time from hours on the above 4-bit example to 510 ms on a 2.5 GHz 16 GB Macbook.

Our implementation is 9293 LOC of Scala3 and is stratified in 3 layers: the worklist-driven fixpoint engine, the domain operations and the underlying Gröbner basis solver. For bit-widths of 8, 12 and 16, the running times are 1,398 ms 5,894 ms and 54,019 ms respectively (though the actual target for our work is AVR micro-controller code which is merely 8-bit). To scale to these higher bit-widths, it is necessary to reduce the numbers of terms in each polynomial. Rather surprisingly, this can be achieved on-the-fly as a polynomial is generated term-by-term rather than as a post-processing step which is applied to some (huge) polynomial derived from an arithmetic operation. To illustrate, consider summing two polynomials q_1 and q_2 where $q_1 = t_1 + r_1$ and $q_2 = t_2 + r_2$ and t_1 and t_2 are leading terms with the same powers. The term $t = t_1 + t_2$ is computed then reduced (whenever possible) with a null polynomial whose leading term divides t to give a simplified polynomial q. Then we apply the same tactic to sum $q + r_1$ to give a polynomial s and apply the same tactic yet again to sum $s + r_2$. A null polynomial whose leading terms divides t can be found directly, provided one exists, without resorting to search or even a lookup table. In fact, given t, the null can be found simply by multiplying terms together [32, definition 9]. For example, if $\omega = 4$ and $t = 3x^2y^3$ then the null polynomial $3x^2y^3 + 7x^2y^2 + 6x^2y + 13xy^3 + 9xy^2 + 10xy$ is found by expanding $3x(x-1)y(y-1)(y-2)$ so that $q = 9x^2y^2 + 10x^2y + 3xy^3 + 7xy^2 + 6xy$. The degree of the leading term of $q_1 + q_2$ is then reduced from x^2y^3 to x^2y^2. Applying this tactic repeatedly keeps the number of terms small in all arithmetic operations. (The tactic is not mentioned in [2] but appears to be a dynamic version of the technique used in [33] that applies null (vanishing) polynomials to statically bound the representation of polynomials.)

7 Related Work

Momentum for migrating abstract domains from idealised arithmetic to machine arithmetic is growing [10–12,21,26,27], driven by the desire to soundly model program behaviour and low-level code. Some of these domains [10,21,26,27] satisfy the ascending chain condition, which is key to computing best transformers [28] though, to our knowledge, this observation has not been previously made.

Early approaches to deriving (non-modular) polynomial invariants employed forwards [29] and backwards [25] abstract interpretation over domains of polynomial ideals. In the former case, termination of the analysis requires a widening operator to remove polynomials of high degree, since polynomial ideals over $\mathbb{Q}$ do not satisfy the ascending chain condition. In the latter case, the analysis is primed with a template polynomial of bounded degree; linear systems are then solved to find assignments to the (symbolic) coefficients of the templates, which yield the polynomial invariants. An alternative approach [31], also employing template polynomials, directly encodes the conditions for a given template polynomial to be an invariant as a parametric linear system, which can then be solved with suitable methods [6]. None of these analyses is complete and [25] concludes, "It is a challenging open problem whether or not the set of all polynomial relations can be computed not just ones of some given form".

This challenge [25] has motivated subsequent work [17,18,23,30], which restrict the form of programs that can be analysed, either to those containing only simple loops [30], P-solvable loops [23] or affine programs [17] (where a variable is assigned to an affine expression). State-of-the-art in computing all polynomial relations focuses on affine programs [17] where the problem is reduced to that of computing the Zariski closure of the semigroup generated by a finite set of rational square matrices. However, it is not clear how this approach extends to general polynomial assignments, particularly those in a modular setting.

A more promising line of enquiry in this vein [33] seeks to adapt backwards abstract interpretation to inferring non-modular polynomial invariants [25] to a modular setting. The insight is that it is possible to bound the degree of the template polynomial without losing precision, by exploiting the fact that any modular polynomial is semantically equivalent to one with degree at most $1.5(\omega + d)$. Building on this bound, the analysis of [33, pp. 311] seeks to infer all polynomial invariants for programs consisting of polynomial and non-deterministic assignments, non-deterministic branching and polynomial disequality guards. For disequality guards, the weakest precondition transformer is defined as $[\![p \neq 0]\!]^T q = \{ pq \}$ [33, pp. 306]. The subtlety of the modular setting is that the pre-condition pq can vanish, compromising soundness. To illustrate, put $p = 2x$ and $q = 128x$ in $\mathbb{Z}_{256}[x]$. Then $pq = (2x)(128x) = 256x^2 = 0$, which holds vacuously. Now observe that the assignment $x = 1$, which satisfies 0, passes the disequality guard $2x \neq 0$ but violates q. Thus the weakest precondition transformer is actually unsound. This not only illustrates the delicacy of modular reasoning, but suggests that the ability to reason about disequalities, even imprecisely, is a key advantage of the present work.

By design, the analysis [33] does not support equality guards, as these are not readily handled [33, pp. 301] by weakest precondition transformers. However, handling equalities is sometimes necessary, as demonstrated by the worked example, where $x - y = 0$ is required for inferring $ax - 1 = 0$ at program exit. Interestingly, the analysis [33] does not rely on Gröbner basis computations, but rather only exploits reduction and properties of null polynomials to detect fixed points. Although this finesses the need for Gröbner bases, it is not clear how they can be avoided when computing join in forwards analysis.

8 Conclusions

Working over modular integers is not merely more realistic, but reshapes the domain operations which can and need be applied. Widening is unnecessary since modular integers induce a domain of polynomial invariants which satisfies the ascending chain condition. Negative polynomial guards can be supported by partitioning the solution set of a polynomial disequality into sets of integers whose least bits equal a power of two. MPAD extends the scope of invariant discovery as demonstrated on an algorithm for calculating a multiplicative inverse.

Acknowledgements. We thank the anonymous reviewers for their insightful comments and Helmut Seidl for kindly checking the vanishing precondition example. This work was supported, in part, by EPSRC grant EP/T014512/1.

References

1. Adams, W., Loustaunau, P.: An Introduction to Gröbner Bases. American Mathematical Society (1994)
2. Brickenstein, M., Dreyer, A., Greuel, G., Wedler, M., Wienand, O.: New developments in the theory of Gröbner bases and applications to formal verification. J. Pure Appl. Algebra **213**, 1612–1635 (2009)
3. Buchberger, B.: An algorithm for finding the basis elements of the residue class ring of a zero dimensional polynomial ideal. J. Symb. Comput. **41**, 475–511 (2006)
4. Cacher, D., Jensen, T., Jobin, A., Kirchner, F.: Inference of polynomial invariants for imperative programs: a farewell to Gröbner bases. Sci. Comput. Program. **93**, 89–109 (2014)
5. Codish, M., Mulkers, A., Bruynooghe, M., Garcia De La Banda, M., Hermenegildo, M.: Improving abstract interpretations by combining domains. Trans. Program. Lang. Syst. **17**(1), 28–44 (1995)
6. Collins, G., Hong, H.: Partial cylindrical algebraic decomposition for quantifier elimination. J. Symb. Comput. **12**, 299–328 (1991)
7. Cousot, P., Cousot, R.: Abstract interpretation: a unified lattice model for static analysis of programs by construction or approximation of fixpoints. In: Principles of Programming Languages, pp. 238–252. ACM Press (1977)

8. de Oliveira, S., Bensalem, S., Prevosto, V.: Polynomial invariants by linear algebra. In: Artho, C., Legay, A., Peled, D. (eds.) ATVA 2016. LNCS, vol. 9938, pp. 479–494. Springer, Cham (2016). https://doi.org/10.1007/978-3-319-46520-3_30
9. Dill, D.L.: Timing assumptions and verification of finite-state concurrent systems. In: Sifakis, J. (ed.) CAV 1989. LNCS, vol. 407, pp. 197–212. Springer, Heidelberg (1990). https://doi.org/10.1007/3-540-52148-8_17
10. Elder, M., Lim, J., Sharma, T., Andersen, T., Reps, T.: Abstract domains of affine relations. Trans. Program. Lang. Syst. **36**(4), 1–73 (2014)
11. Gange, G., Navas, J., Schachte, P., Søndergaard, H., Stuckey, P.: Interval analysis and machine arithmetic: why signedness ignorance is bliss. Trans. Program. Lang. Syst. **37**(1), 1–35 (2014)
12. Gange, G., Søndergaard, H., Stuckey, P.J., Schachte, P.: Solving difference constraints over modular arithmetic. In: Bonacina, M.P. (ed.) CADE 2013. LNCS (LNAI), vol. 7898, pp. 215–230. Springer, Heidelberg (2013). https://doi.org/10.1007/978-3-642-38574-2_15
13. Gebauer, R., Möller, H.: On an installation of Buchberger's algorithm. J. Symb. Comput. **6**(2/3), 275–286 (1988)
14. Greuel, G.M., Seelisch, F., Wienand, O.: The Gröbner basis of the ideal of vanishing polynomials. J. Symb. Comput. **46**(5), 561–570 (2011)
15. Harrison, W.: Compiler analysis of the value ranges for variables. IEEE Trans. Softw. Eng. **3**(3), 243–250 (1977)
16. Hilbert, D.: Über die Theorie der Algebraischen Formen. Math. Ann. **36**(4), 473–534 (1890)
17. Hrushovski, E., Ouaknine, J., Pouly, A., Worrell, J.: Polynomial invariants for affine programs. In: Logic in Computer Science, pp. 530–539. ACM Press (2018)
18. Humenberger, A., Jaroschek, M., Kovács, L.: Invariant generation for multi-path loops with polynomial assignments. In: Dillig, I., Palsberg, J. (eds.) VMCAI 2018. LNCS, vol. 10747, pp. 226–246. Springer, Cham (2018). https://doi.org/10.1007/978-3-319-73721-8_11
19. Huynh, D.: A super-exponential lower bound for Gröbner bases and Church-Rosser commutative Thue systems. Inf. Control **68**(1–3), 196–206 (1986)
20. Karr, M.: Affine relationships among variables of a program. Acta Informatica **6**(2), 133–151 (1976)
21. King, A., Søndergaard, H.: Inferring congruence equations using SAT. In: Gupta, A., Malik, S. (eds.) CAV 2008. LNCS, vol. 5123, pp. 281–293. Springer, Heidelberg (2008). https://doi.org/10.1007/978-3-540-70545-1_26
22. Kovács, L.: Reasoning algebraically about P-solvable loops. In: Ramakrishnan, C.R., Rehof, J. (eds.) TACAS 2008. LNCS, vol. 4963, pp. 249–264. Springer, Heidelberg (2008). https://doi.org/10.1007/978-3-540-78800-3_18
23. Kovács, L.: A complete invariant generation approach for P-solvable loops. In: Pnueli, A., Virbitskaite, I., Voronkov, A. (eds.) PSI 2009. LNCS, vol. 5947, pp. 242–256. Springer, Heidelberg (2010). https://doi.org/10.1007/978-3-642-11486-1_21
24. Miné, A.: The octagon abstract domain. High. Order Symb. Comput. **19**(1), 31–100 (2006)
25. Müller-Olm, M., Seidl, H.: Computing polynomial program invariants. Inf. Process. Lett. **91**, 233–244 (2004)
26. Müller-Olm, M., Seidl, H.: Analysis of modular arithmetic. In: Sagiv, M. (ed.) ESOP 2005. LNCS, vol. 3444, pp. 46–60. Springer, Heidelberg (2005). https://doi.org/10.1007/978-3-540-31987-0_5

27. Müller-Olm, M., Seidl, H.: Analysis of modular arithmetic. Trans. Program. Lang. Syst. **29**(5), 1–26 (2007)
28. Reps, T., Sagiv, M., Yorsh, G.: Symbolic implementation of the best transformer. In: Steffen, B., Levi, G. (eds.) VMCAI 2004. LNCS, vol. 2937, pp. 252–266. Springer, Heidelberg (2004). https://doi.org/10.1007/978-3-540-24622-0_21
29. Rodríguez-Carbonell, E., Kapur, D.: An abstract interpretation approach for automatic generation of polynomial invariants. In: Giacobazzi, R. (ed.) SAS 2004. LNCS, vol. 3148, pp. 280–295. Springer, Heidelberg (2004). https://doi.org/10.1007/978-3-540-27864-1_21
30. Rodríguez-Carbonell, E., Kapur, D.: Generating all polynomial invariants in simple loops. J. Symb. Comput. **42**, 443–476 (2007)
31. Sankaranarayanan, S., Sipma, H.B., Manna, Z.: Non-linear loop invariant generation using Gröbner bases. In: Principles of Programming Languages, pp. 318–329. ACM Press (2004)
32. Seed, T.: Program verification using polynomials over modular arithmetic. Ph.D. thesis, University of Kent (2021). https://doi.org/10.22024/UniKent/01.02.90261. https://kar.kent.ac.uk/90261/
33. Seidl, H., Flexeder, A., Petter, M.: Analysing all polynomial equations in $\mathbb{Z}_{2^w}$. In: Alpuente, M., Vidal, G. (eds.) SAS 2008. LNCS, vol. 5079, pp. 299–314. Springer, Heidelberg (2008). https://doi.org/10.1007/978-3-540-69166-2_20
34. Warren, H.: Hacker's Delight. Addison-Wesley, Boston (2012)

Boosting Multi-neuron Convex Relaxation for Neural Network Verification

Xuezhou Tang, Ye Zheng, and Jiaxiang Liu(✉)

Shenzhen University, Shenzhen, China
2110276137@email.szu.edu.cn, jiaxiang0924@gmail.com,
zhengyeah@foxmail.com

Abstract. Formal verification of neural networks is essential for their deployment in safety-critical real-world applications, such as autonomous driving and cyber-physical controlling. Multi-neuron convex relaxation is one of the mainstream methods to improve verification precision. However, existing techniques rely on empirically selecting neuron groups before performing multi-neuron convex relaxation, which may yield redundant yet expensive convex hull computations. This paper proposes a volume approximation based approach for selecting neuron groups. We approximate the volumes of convex hulls for all group candidates, without calculating their convex hulls. The group candidates with small volumes are then selected for convex hull computation, aiming at ruling out unnecessary convex hulls with loose relaxation. We implement our approach as the neural network verification tool FaGMR, and evaluate it against state-of-the-art tools including Prima, α,β-CROWN, and ERAN on neural networks trained by MNIST and CIFAR-10. The experimental results demonstrate that FaGMR is more efficient than these tools, yet with the same or sometimes better verification precision.

Keywords: Neural network verification · Multi-neuron relaxation · Volume approximation

1 Introduction

The increasing adoption of neural networks in many safety-critical scenarios has underscored their safety and robustness. However, the existence of adversarial examples is revealed to be a severe threat. That is, there exist perturbed inputs (e.g. images) that are human-imperceptible but give rise to misclassification by a neural network. For example, forged traffic signs can fool certain autonomous driving systems [16]. They look almost the same for humans, yet making auto-driving systems output incorrect predictions, hence leading to unexpected behaviors.

This work is supported by the National Natural Science Foundation of China (61836005), the Natural Science Foundation of Guangdong Province (2022A1515011458, 2022A1515010880), and the Shenzhen Science and Technology Innovation Program (JCYJ20210324094202008).

M. V. Hermenegildo and J. F. Morales (Eds.): SAS 2023, LNCS 14284, pp. 540–563, 2023.
https://doi.org/10.1007/978-3-031-44245-2_23

A large body of research aims to find adversarial examples based on testing (see a survey [30]). They are usually effective in falsifying robustness. Notwithstanding, the fact that these techniques discover no adversarial examples does not guarantee robustness. On the other hand, *formal verification*, which is complementary to testing, mathematically proves the robustness of a given neural network against perturbed inputs, thus providing a formal guarantee for safety-critical applications.

Formal verification of neural networks usually needs to compute the output range of a neural network given a perturbed input range. Computing an output for a single input is trivial, but computing an output region for an input region is significantly more complex. The difficulty arises from the composition of the non-linear activation functions, which leads to a highly non-linear input-output relation of the neural network. So the key challenge is to handle the enormous non-linear functions in a precise and scalable manner.

Convex relaxation methods *over-approximate* the non-linear activation functions with convex polytopes, usually represented as linear constraints. Among them, single-neuron convex relaxation based methods over-approximate each neuron separately (e.g., [20,21,28,29,33]). These methods do not capture the interdependencies between neurons, so they are fundamentally less precise than multi-neuron convex relaxation based methods. The latter takes multiple neurons jointly into account, designing over-approximations for groups of neurons [17,19,24]. An essential problem of multi-neuron relaxation based methods lies in convex hull computations. Typically, in the first step, these methods select groups of neurons of size k ($k \geq 2$) in the same activation layer. For each group, the $\mathbb{R}^k \times \mathbb{R}^k$ input-output relation of its activation functions is then over-approximated jointly. The over-approximation is performed by computing a convex hull of the input-output relation, represented by a set of linear constraints. It is believed that the more groups of neurons are considered and the more overlap between groups is allowed, the more precise verification results can be achieved. However, NP-hardness of convex hull computation problems limits the number of groups to be selected. For instance, adopting an exact convex hull computing algorithm, KPoly [19] partitions the neurons of an activation layer into small sets of size $n_s \leq 5$ and only selects groups of $k \leq 3$ neurons within each partition. PRIMA [17] proposes a polynomial-time method for approximating convex hulls, hence allowing to consider a larger number of groups in a reasonable time limit. Similarly, it partitions all neurons with respect to n_s and selects a subset of all size-k groups within each partition. But the parameter n_s in PRIMA is significantly larger than that in KPoly, yielding significant precision improvement. Nevertheless, these parameters and the selection of groups are decided empirically. They may not perform equally well on different verification problems, even on different activation layers in the same network. On the other hand, we observe that there may exist redundant groups, in the sense that the constraints of their convex hulls are implied by the constraints generated by other groups. Convex hull computations of these redundant groups are unnecessary and should be avoided.

In this paper, we seek to improve the efficiency of multi-neuron convex relaxation based methods by heuristically selecting neuron groups. The main idea is to evaluate the tightness of over-approximation by the volume of the convex hull. The exact calculation of volumes of (high-dimensional) convex hulls is infeasible. More importantly, it does not avoid the unnecessary convex hull computations. We propose to instead under- and over-approximate the volumes of convex hulls without the need for computing the convex hulls. Neuron groups with small estimated volumes will be selected while groups with large volumes are eliminated. In such a way, some unnecessary yet expensive convex hull computations are avoided.

For evaluation, we implement our approach as a neural network verification tool FaGMR (**Fa**st **G**rouping for **M**ulti-neuron **R**elaxation). We compare FaGMR with state-of-the-art tools Prima [17], α,β-CROWN [28] and ERAN [23] on neural networks trained by the widely-used datasets MNIST and CIFAR-10. The experimental results show that FaGMR is faster than Prima, α,β-CROWN, and ERAN, by spending on average 11.2%, 43.1%, and 15.2% less verification time respectively. Meanwhile, FaGMR successfully verifies at least the same number of verification problems as Prima and ERAN, and on average 46.7% more than α,β-CROWN.

Our contributions are summarized as follows:

- We propose a volume approximation based approach to automatically select neuron groups for multi-neuron relaxation methods. It allows to avoid unnecessary yet expensive convex hull computations, hence boosting the efficiency of multi-neuron relaxation methods.
- We implement our approach as a verification tool FaGMR and conduct an extensive evaluation, demonstrating the efficacy of our approach.

Tool Availability. To foster further research, we place FaGMR into the public domain. The source code is available at https://github.com/formes20/FaGMR.

Organization. Section 2 recalls necessary backgrounds on neural network verification and the multi-neuron relaxation method. Our approach is presented in Sect. 3 and evaluated in Sect. 4. Related work is discussed in Sect. 5. We conclude our presentation in Sect. 6.

2 Preliminaries

Notations. We reserve lowercase Latin and Greek letters $a, b, x, \dots, \theta, \dots$ for scalars, bold $\boldsymbol{a}$ for vectors, capitalized bold $\boldsymbol{A}$ for matrices, and capitals A, calligraphic $\mathcal{A}$ or blackboard bold $\mathbb{A}$ for sets. Similarly, scalar functions are denoted as $f : \mathbb{R}^d \to \mathbb{R}$ and vector valued functions as $\boldsymbol{f} : \mathbb{R}^d \to \mathbb{R}^k$. Given n elements, the number of k-combinations is represented by $\binom{n}{k}$.

2.1 Neural Network Verification

A *(feedforward) neural network* $\boldsymbol{h}(\boldsymbol{x}) : \mathcal{X} \to \mathbb{R}^{|\mathcal{Y}|}$ is a $|\mathcal{Y}|$-dimensional vector valued function from the input space $\mathcal{X}$ to the output space $\mathcal{Y}$. Specifically, $\boldsymbol{h}(\boldsymbol{x})$ is the interleaved composition of affine function layers $\boldsymbol{g}_i(\boldsymbol{x}) = \boldsymbol{W}_i\boldsymbol{x} + \boldsymbol{b}_i$, with non-linear activation layers $\boldsymbol{f}_i(\boldsymbol{x})$:

$$\boldsymbol{h}(\boldsymbol{x}) = \boldsymbol{g}_\ell \circ \boldsymbol{f}_\ell \circ \boldsymbol{g}_{\ell-1} \circ \cdots \circ \boldsymbol{f}_1 \circ \boldsymbol{g}_0(\boldsymbol{x})$$

where ℓ is the number of hidden layers. $\boldsymbol{f}_i(\boldsymbol{x})$ applies non-linear activation functions in an element-wise manner. If $\boldsymbol{h}(\boldsymbol{x})$ is a classification neural network, it will output the index c of its maximum output vector component, i.e. $c = \arg\max_j \boldsymbol{h}(\boldsymbol{x})_j$.

A neural network verification problem commonly needs to verify the *robustness* property. A robust neural network must satisfy the smoothness assumption [8], i.e., for any input $\boldsymbol{x}$ and a small perturbation $\boldsymbol{\delta}$, $\boldsymbol{h}(\boldsymbol{x}+\boldsymbol{\delta}) \approx \boldsymbol{h}(\boldsymbol{x})$ should hold. In the case of classification tasks, this assumption conforms to the visual capabilities of human: if $\boldsymbol{x}$ looks similar to $\boldsymbol{x}'$, they should belong to the same class.

Formally, perturbed inputs are defined by an l_p-norm ball neighborhood of $\boldsymbol{x}$:

$$\mathbb{B}^p_\theta(\boldsymbol{x}) = \{\boldsymbol{x}' = \boldsymbol{x} + \boldsymbol{\delta} \mid \|\boldsymbol{\delta}\|_p \le \theta\}$$

where θ is the *perturbation threshold* that bounds $\boldsymbol{\delta}$. We would like to verify that the neural network $\boldsymbol{h}(\boldsymbol{x})$ does not misclassify any perturbed input in this region.

Definition 1. *Given a neural network $\boldsymbol{h}(\boldsymbol{x})$, an input $\boldsymbol{x} \in \mathcal{X}$ and a perturbation threshold θ, a* verification problem *is to give the truth value of the following statement:*

$$\arg\max_j \boldsymbol{h}(\boldsymbol{x})_j = \arg\max_j \boldsymbol{h}(\boldsymbol{x}')_j, \quad \textit{for each } \boldsymbol{x}' \in \mathbb{B}^p_\theta(\boldsymbol{x}).$$

If the statement in Definition 1 is true, we conclude that the neural network $\boldsymbol{h}$ is robust with respect to the input $\boldsymbol{x}$ against the perturbation threshold θ.

2.2 Multi-neuron Convex Relaxation

Multi-neuron convex relaxation based methods like PRIMA [17] solve neural network verification problems (Definition 1) by encoding them as linear optimization problems. Specifically, given a neural network $\boldsymbol{h}$, an input $\boldsymbol{x}$ and a perturbation threshold θ, these methods encode the whole network $\boldsymbol{h}$ w.r.t. the (convex) region $\mathbb{B}^p_\theta(\boldsymbol{x})$ via linear constraints, define a linear optimization objective for the target statement $\arg\max_j \boldsymbol{h}(\boldsymbol{x})_j = \arg\max_j \boldsymbol{h}(\boldsymbol{x}')_j$, and finally invoke an LP solver to obtain a bound determining whether $\boldsymbol{h}$ is robust. Note that all affine function layers $\boldsymbol{g}_i$ in $\boldsymbol{h}$ can be described exactly by linear constraints, while the non-linear activation layers $\boldsymbol{f}_i$ have to be over-approximated using linear constraints in their input-output spaces. Given a non-linear activation layer, conventional single-neuron convex relaxation based methods (e.g. [20,21,28,29,33]) take each single neuron in turn to generate neuron-wise over-approximations, accumulated as the layer-wise over-approximation. Instead, multi-neuron convex relaxation based methods select (possibly overlapping) groups of neurons, generate linear constraints for each group of neurons as group-wise over-approximations, then accumulate them as the layer-wise over-approximation. By capturing interdependencies between different neurons when obtaining group-wise over-approximations, multi-neuron relaxation methods achieve tighter over-approximations.

We now review the multi-neuron constraints leveraged by PRIMA [17] that our approach focuses on.

Let us fix some single activation layer. Assume a layer-wise input polytope $\mathcal{S}$ constraining all the inputs of the layer, and a group $G = \{v_1, v_2, \ldots, v_k\}$ of neurons of size $k \geq 2$. PRIMA starts the multi-neuron relaxation for G by projecting $\mathcal{S}$ onto the input dimensions of the group G, i.e. onto the $(x_1, x_2, \ldots, x_k)$-space, where x_i denotes the input of the neuron v_i. More precisely, PRIMA computes an octahedral over-approximation $\mathcal{P}_G$ of the projection instead of an exact projection, following the idea of KPOLY [19]. Then for the k-dimensional $\mathcal{P}_G$, PRIMA computes a $2k$-dimensional convex over-approximation $\mathcal{K}_G$ of the input-output relation of G through its novel *Split-Bound-Lift Method (SBLM)*. The linear constraints constituting the polytope $\mathcal{K}_G$ are the expected multi-neuron constraints for the group G. SBLM constructs $\mathcal{K}_G$ from $\mathcal{P}_G$ via two phases: splitting and lifting. In the following, we omit the subscript G, using $\mathcal{P}$ and $\mathcal{K}$ for clarity when causing no ambiguity.

Splitting. Assume that the activation function in the neural network is $f : \mathbb{D} \rightarrow \mathbb{R}$. The splitting phase requires a set of intervals $\mathcal{D}^j$ covering the domain $\mathbb{D}$. We will focus on the activation function ReLU : $\mathbb{R} \rightarrow \mathbb{R}$ defined by $\text{ReLU}(x) = \max(x, 0)$ when introducing PRIMA and our approach in the following for simplicity, and generalize our approach to activation functions Sigmoid and Tanh in Sect. 3.4. For the ReLU activation function, the required intervals are $\mathcal{D}^1 = (-\infty, 0]$ and $\mathcal{D}^2 = [0, +\infty)$, whose union covers the domain $\mathbb{D} = \mathbb{R}$. These intervals are instantiated w.r.t. the neuron v_i as $\mathcal{D}_i^1 = \{\boldsymbol{x} \in \mathbb{R}^k \mid x_i \leq 0\}$ and $\mathcal{D}_i^2 = \{\boldsymbol{x} \in \mathbb{R}^k \mid x_i \geq 0\}$. The splitting phase splits $\mathcal{P}$ according to the intervals $\mathcal{D}^j$ w.r.t. input variables x_i iteratively, considering one variable at a step. Without loss of generality, we (randomly) choose the splitting ordering $v_k, v_{k-1}, \ldots, v_1$. That is, the splitting phase splits w.r.t. x_k first, then x_{k-1} and so on, finally x_1. Formally, the splitting phase works as follows.

Definition 2 (Splitting). *Given a size-k group $G = \{v_1, \ldots, v_k\}$ of neurons and a polytope $\mathcal{P}$ in the $(x_1, \ldots, x_k)$-space. The* splitting *phase is performed by*

$$\mathcal{P}_\epsilon^{(0)} = \mathcal{P};$$
$$\mathcal{P}_{\tau,j}^{(i+1)} = \mathcal{P}_\tau^{(i)} \cap \mathcal{D}_{k-i}^j, \quad \textit{for } 0 \leq i < k \textit{ and } j \in \{1, 2\}$$

where ϵ denotes the empty sequence, and τ a sequence of length i containing 1 *and/or* 2*. The polytopes $\mathcal{P}_{\{1,2\}^k}^{(k)}$ are obtained after splitting, called* quadrants.

Intuitively, at the i-th ($0 \leq i < k$) step, the input variable x_{k-i} is considered. Each polytope $\mathcal{P}_\tau^{(i)}$ obtained after the previous step is split by the hyperplane $\{\boldsymbol{x} \in \mathbb{R}^k \mid x_{k-i} = 0\}$, generating two polytopes $\mathcal{P}_{\tau,1}^{(i+1)}$ and $\mathcal{P}_{\tau,2}^{(i+1)}$. Note that for each polytope $\mathcal{P}_\tau^{(i)}$ generated during splitting, the length of τ equals i. The splitting phase can be regarded as constructing a complete binary tree. The initial polytope $\mathcal{P}$ is the root. All the generated polytopes $\mathcal{P}_\tau^{(i)}$ constitute the nodes, with i being the depth and τ the path from the root. The 2^k quadrants $\mathcal{P}_{\{1,2\}^k}^{(k)}$ are the leaves.

Lifting. The lifting phase extends and combines the 2^k k-dimensional quadrants into one $2k$-dimensional polytope, during which convex hulls are computed. Similar to splitting, this phase also progresses step by step, extending polytopes by one dimension corresponding to an output variable at each step. The lifting ordering is the reverse of the splitting one: $v_1, v_2, \ldots, v_k$. That is, the quadrants in the $(x_1, \ldots, x_k)$-space are lifted to the $(x_1, \ldots, x_k, y_1)$-space first, then $(x_1, \ldots, x_k, y_1, y_2)$-space and so on, where y_i denotes the output of neuron v_i. The resulting polytope $\mathcal{K}$ after the lifting phase is in the $(x_1, \ldots, x_k, y_1, \ldots, y_k)$-space.

The lifting phase requires a set of bounds $\mathcal{B}^j$ corresponding to the intervals $\mathcal{D}^j$, bounding the output of the activation function. Each $\mathcal{B}^j$ is a pair of linear functions of the form

$$\mathcal{B}^j = (a_j^{\leq}, a_j^{\geq}),$$

where $a_j^{\leq}$ and $a_j^{\geq}$ are linear functions satisfying

$$a_j^{\leq}(x) \leq f(x) \leq a_j^{\geq}(x), \text{ for each } x \in (\mathcal{D}^j \cap [\underline{x}, \overline{x}]),$$

where $\underline{x}$ and $\overline{x}$ are concrete lower and upper bounds of x, respectively. For the ReLU activation function, the required bounds are $\mathcal{B}^1 = (0, 0)$ and $\mathcal{B}^2 = (x, x)$. They are instantiated w.r.t. the neuron v_i as $\mathcal{B}_i^1 = \{\boldsymbol{x} \in \mathbb{R}^{k+i} \mid 0 \leq y_i \leq 0\} = \{\boldsymbol{x} \in \mathbb{R}^{k+i} \mid y_i = 0\}$ and $\mathcal{B}_i^2 = \{\boldsymbol{x} \in \mathbb{R}^{k+i} \mid x_i \leq y_i \leq x_i\} = \{\boldsymbol{x} \in \mathbb{R}^{k+i} \mid y_i = x_i\}$. Note that $\mathcal{B}_i^j$ is $(k+i)$-dimensional due to the lifting ordering, precisely, being in the $(x_1, \ldots, x_k, y_1, \ldots, y_i)$-space. Formally, the lifting phase progresses as follows.

Definition 3 (Lifting). *Given a size-k group $G = \{v_1, \ldots, v_k\}$ of neurons and 2^k quadrants $\mathcal{P}_{\{1,2\}^k}^{(k)}$ obtained by splitting. The* lifting *phase is performed by*

$$\mathcal{K}_{\{1,2\}^k}^{(0)} = \mathcal{P}_{\{1,2\}^k}^{(k)};$$

$$\mathcal{K}_\tau^{(i+1)} = \operatorname{conv}\Big((\mathrm{e}_{y_{i+1}}(\mathcal{K}_{\tau,1}^{(i)}) \cap \mathcal{B}_{i+1}^1) \cup (\mathrm{e}_{y_{i+1}}(\mathcal{K}_{\tau,2}^{(i)}) \cap \mathcal{B}_{i+1}^2) \Big), \quad \text{for } 0 \leq i < k$$

where $\operatorname{conv}(\cdot)$ *denotes the convex hull, and* $\mathrm{e}_y(\mathcal{A}) = \mathcal{A} \times \mathbb{R}$ *extends* $\mathcal{A}$ *by the dimension* y *for any set* $\mathcal{A}$. *The polytope* $\mathcal{K} = \mathcal{K}_\epsilon^{(k)}$ *is the output of the lifting phase, as well as the SBLM.*

PRIMA computes the convex hull conv(·) via its novel *Partial Double Description Method (PDDM)*, which we do not detail in this paper. Intuitively, the lifting phase progresses as per the binary tree constructed during the splitting phase, from the leaves to the root. At the i-th ($0 \le i < k$) step, any two children $\mathcal{K}_{\tau,1}^{(i)}$ and $\mathcal{K}_{\tau,2}^{(i)}$ of the same parent are extended by a new dimension y_{i+1}, and bounded by $\mathcal{B}^1$ and $\mathcal{B}^2$, respectively. The convex hull $\mathcal{K}_{\tau}^{(i+1)}$ of their union is put at the position of their parent. All quadrants are combined along the tree until only one polytope $\mathcal{K}$ is obtained at the root.

3 Volume Approximation Based Grouping

Before generating multi-neuron constraints for a given group of neurons as presented in Sect. 2.2, a key problem is that which and how many groups we should select to generate constraints. For an activation layer with n neurons, given the group size k, it is certainly ideal to consider all $\binom{n}{k}$ possible size-k groups. Nevertheless, computing multi-neuron constraints for each of them is too expensive due to the high complexity of convex hull computation, even by using SBLM. Empirically selecting groups by pre-defined parameters, like in KPOLY and PRIMA, is an efficient and effective solution in some scenarios. But we observe that sometimes these grouping strategies may lead to *redundant* groups, in the sense that the generated multi-neuron constraints for them are implied by the constraints for other groups.

Example 1. Assume that three neurons v_1, v_2, and v_3 are in the same activation layer, the group size $k = 2$. There are three possible groups $G_1 = \{v_1, v_2\}$, $G_2 = \{v_1, v_3\}$ and $G_3 = \{v_2, v_3\}$. Assume that the octahedral over-approximations for them are respectively

$$\begin{aligned}\mathcal{P}_{G_1} &= \{\boldsymbol{x} \in \mathbb{R}^2 \mid x_1 + x_2 \le 3,\ x_1 - x_2 \le 3,\ -x_1 + x_2 \le 3,\ -x_1 - x_2 \le 3,\\ &\qquad -1 \le x_1 \le 1,\ -2 \le x_2 \le 2\},\\ \mathcal{P}_{G_2} &= \{\boldsymbol{x} \in \mathbb{R}^2 \mid x_1 + x_3 \le 2,\ x_1 - x_3 \le 2,\ -x_1 + x_3 \le 2,\ -x_1 - x_3 \le 2,\\ &\qquad -1 \le x_1 \le 1,\ -1 \le x_3 \le 1\},\\ \mathcal{P}_{G_3} &= \{\boldsymbol{x} \in \mathbb{R}^2 \mid x_2 + x_3 \le 3,\ x_2 - x_3 \le 3,\ -x_2 + x_3 \le 3,\ -x_2 - x_3 \le 3,\\ &\qquad -2 \le x_2 \le 2,\ -1 \le x_3 \le 1\}.\end{aligned}$$

The multi-neuron constraints generated by PRIMA are as follows, where $\mathcal{C}_{G_i}$ denotes the constraints of the output polytope $\mathcal{K}_{G_i}$ by SBLM:

$$\begin{aligned}\mathcal{C}_{G_1} &= \{0.5x_1 - y_1 \le 0.5,\ 0.5x_2 - y_2 \le 1,\ -x_2 + y_2 \le 0.36,\\ &\qquad -x_1 + y_1 \le 0.18,\ y_1 \le 1,\ y_2 \le 1\},\\ \mathcal{C}_{G_2} &= \{0.5x_1 - y_1 \le 0.5,\ 0.5x_3 - y_3 \le 1,\ -x_3 + y_3 \le 0.18,\\ &\qquad -x_1 + y_1 \le 0.18,\ y_1 \le 1,\ y_3 \le 1\},\\ \mathcal{C}_{G_3} &= \{0.5x_3 - y_3 \le 0.5,\ 0.5x_2 - y_2 \le 1,\ -x_2 + y_2 \le 0.36,\\ &\qquad -x_3 + y_3 \le 0.18,\ y_2 \le 1,\ y_3 \le 1\}.\end{aligned}$$

One can verify that $\mathcal{C}_{G_1}$ is implied by $\mathcal{C}_{G_2} \cup \mathcal{C}_{G_3}$. It means that the constraints in $\mathcal{C}_{G_1}$ are useless when accumulated into the layer-wise over-approximation which already includes $\mathcal{C}_{G_2}$ and $\mathcal{C}_{G_3}$. Therefore, $\mathcal{C}_{G_1}$ and thus the corresponding group G_1 are redundant.

The multi-neuron constraint generation, especially the convex hull computation therein, for the redundant groups like G_1 in Example 1 is unnecessary and should be avoided for efficiency. However, convex hull computation in high-dimension is unavoidable if we would like to identify these redundant groups precisely. Adopting the idea in [21], which considers in the single-neuron case an over-approximation with smaller area as a tighter over-approximation, we expect redundant groups to generate looser over-approximations (i.e. the polytopes $\mathcal{K}_G$) with larger (high-dimensional) volumes. Instead of exact volumes, our approach computes the approximations of the volumes in order to avoid expensive calculation in high-dimension for both convex hulls and exact volumes. The groups with larger approximated volumes are then discarded since they are more likely redundant. As a result, our approach produces neuron groups that may include fewer redundant ones, while their multi-neuron constraints preserve precision.

3.1 Overview of Our Approach

Our approach follows the multi-neuron relaxation framework. The key idea in our approach is to fast compute the volume approximations of all possible size-k neuron groups *before* selecting some of them to generate multi-neuron constraints.

Each neuron in the activation layer is processed iteratively. For each neuron, our approach comprises the following three steps: volume approximation, group selection, and convex hull computation. Figure 1 shows the workflow to select neuron groups involving the neuron v_i, when $k = 2$.

1. *Volume approximation.* Computing the precise volume of a $2k$-dimensional convex hull generated for a size-k neuron group is time-consuming. Therefore, we leverage the approximation methods detailed in Sect. 3.2 to under- and over-approximate the volume of the convex hull for each group candidate, in order to decide whether it will be selected for the $2k$-dimensional convex hull generation. Our volume approximation methods are based on Betke and Henk [4]. We improve their method for the over-approximation by utilizing the volume of the octahedron $\mathcal{P}$ to make the approximation tighter. Our over-approximation is hence obtained via k-dimensional calculation of the exact volume of $\mathcal{P}$ that can be done by off-the-shelf volume tools. It may reduce some $2k$-dimensional computations of unnecessary convex hulls. In the case where $k = 2$ and v_i is considered, Fig. 1 demonstrates that the under- and over-approximations of the volumes of all group candidates (of size 2) containing v_i are calculated.
2. *Neuron group selection.* Once under- and over-approximated volumes have been computed for all the group candidates, "better" candidates are selected. Our selecting strategy prefers those groups with smaller volumes. It will select the groups with very small over-approximated volumes, and eliminate the

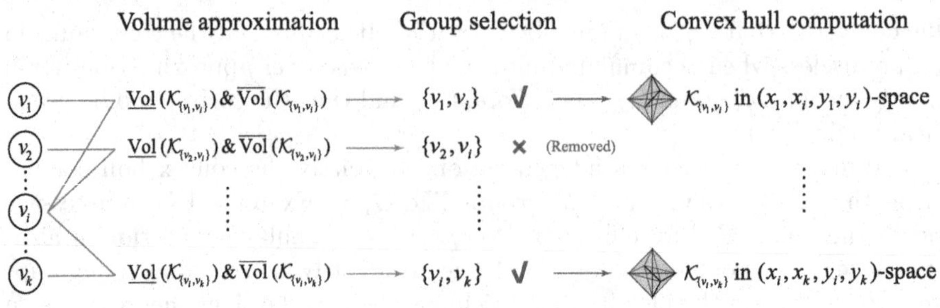

Fig. 1. Workflow of Our Approach to Select Groups for v_i ($k = 2$)

groups with very large under-approximated volumes. The details can be found in Sect. 3.3. In Fig. 1, we can see that some group candidates (e.g. $\{v_2, v_i\}$) are weeded out by our selecting strategy. Only some groups (e.g. $\{v_1, v_i\}$ and $\{v_i, v_k\}$) are passed to the following convex hull solving step.

3. *Convex hull computation.* After the groups are decided, their $2k$-dimensional convex hulls are computed. The computation can be performed by existing techniques. Specifically, our implementation leverages SBLM and PDDM in PRIMA due to their efficiency and exactness. This step obtains the convex hull, thus the multi-neuron constraints, for each selected group. For instance, the convex hull $\mathcal{K}_{\{v_1,v_i\}}$ in the (x_1, x_i, y_1, y_i)-space for the selected group $\{v_1, v_i\}$ in Fig. 1.

3.2 Volume Approximation

Given a group G of neurons, we detail in this section how to approximate the volume of the generated convex hull $\mathcal{K}_G$ (presented in Sect. 2.2) *without* actually computing the convex hull. Following the notations in Sect. 2.2, we denote the neuron group of size k as $G = \{v_1, \ldots, v_k\}$, the octahedral over-approximation input to SBLM as $\mathcal{P}$, and the convex hull output by SBLM as $\mathcal{K}$.

For an arbitrary (convex) d-dimensional polytope $\mathcal{Q} \in \mathbb{R}^d$, we denote its (high-dimensional) volume as $\mathrm{Vol}(\mathcal{Q})$, the under- and over-approximations of the volume as $\underline{\mathrm{Vol}}(\mathcal{Q})$ and $\overline{\mathrm{Vol}}(\mathcal{Q})$, respectively. That is, $\underline{\mathrm{Vol}}(\mathcal{Q}) \leq \mathrm{Vol}(\mathcal{Q}) \leq \overline{\mathrm{Vol}}(\mathcal{Q})$. Betke and Henk gave in [4] an algorithm to calculate the under- and over-approximations as follows.

Lemma 1 ([4]). *Given an arbitrary (convex) polytope $\mathcal{Q} \in \mathbb{R}^d$, the under- and over-approximations of the volume of $\mathcal{Q}$ can be calculated by*

$$\underline{\mathrm{Vol}}(\mathcal{Q}) = \frac{1}{d!} \cdot \prod_{i=1}^{d} (u_i - l_i)$$

$$\overline{\mathrm{Vol}}(\mathcal{Q}) = \prod_{i=1}^{d} (u_i - l_i)$$

where $[l_i, u_i]$ *is the range of the* i*-th dimension of* $\mathcal{Q}$.

We adopt the under-approximation given by Lemma 1 in our approach to calculate the under-approximated volume $\underline{\mathrm{Vol}}(\mathcal{K})$ of the convex hull $\mathcal{K}$.

On the other hand, for the over-approximated volume, the one given by Lemma 1 intuitively over-approximates the polytope via the high-dimensional box represented by the Cartesian product $\prod_{i=1}^{d}[l_i, u_i]$. The result is generic, but not tight enough for our purpose, since the convex hull $\mathcal{K}$ we consider is obtained by specific construction and thus has specific characteristics. Generally speaking, we over-approximate in our approach the convex hull $\mathcal{K}$ with a $2k$-dimensional *prism* [22].

A d-dimensional prism is geometrically formed by parallel segments of the same length drawn from all the points of a $(d-1)$-dimensional polytope called *base*. The volume of a prism $\mathcal{Q}$ with the base $\mathcal{S}$ can be computed by $\mathrm{Vol}(\mathcal{Q}) = \mathrm{Vol}(\mathcal{S}) \cdot h$, where h is the *height* of the prism. We have the following property about the over-approximations and the volumes of the generated convex hulls during the lifting phase (Definition 3).

Lemma 2. *Given a size-*k *group* $G = \{v_1, \ldots, v_k\}$ *of neurons and the polytope* $\mathcal{P}$ *input to SBLM, for any* $0 \le i \le k$*, each polytope* $\mathcal{K}_\mathcal{T}^{(i)}$ *generated during the lifting phase satisfies:*

$$\mathcal{K}_\mathcal{T}^{(i)} \subseteq \mathcal{Q}^{(i)},$$

$$\mathrm{Vol}(\mathcal{Q}^{(i)}) = \mathrm{Vol}(\mathcal{P}) \cdot \prod_{j=1}^{i} (\overline{y_j} - \underline{y_j}), \text{ and}$$

$$\mathrm{Vol}(\mathcal{K}_\mathcal{T}^{(i)}) \le \mathrm{Vol}(\mathcal{P}) \cdot \prod_{j=1}^{i} (\overline{y_j} - \underline{y_j}),$$

where $\mathcal{Q}^{(i)} = \mathcal{P} \times \prod_{j=1}^{i}[\ \underline{y_j}, \overline{y_j}\ ]$, $\underline{y_j}$ *and* $\overline{y_j}$ *denote the lower and upper bounds of the* y_j*-dimension of* $\mathcal{K}_\mathcal{T}^{(i)}$*, respectively.*

Proof. We prove by induction on i.

- For the base case $i = 0$, $\mathcal{K}_\mathcal{T}^{(0)} = \mathcal{P}_\mathcal{T}^{(k)} \subseteq \mathcal{P} = \mathcal{Q}^{(0)}$ by Definitions 2 and 3. It trivially holds that $\mathrm{Vol}(\mathcal{Q}^{(0)}) = \mathrm{Vol}(\mathcal{P})$. The third statement $\mathrm{Vol}(\mathcal{K}_\mathcal{T}^{(0)}) \le \mathrm{Vol}(\mathcal{P})$ follows from the first two.
- For the induction step, assuming the three statements hold when $i = m$, we prove that they hold as well when $i = m+1$. By Definition 3,

$$\mathcal{K}_\mathcal{T}^{(m+1)} = \mathrm{conv}\Big((\mathrm{e}_{y_{m+1}}(\mathcal{K}_{\mathcal{T},1}^{(m)}) \cap \mathcal{B}_{m+1}^1) \cup (\mathrm{e}_{y_{m+1}}(\mathcal{K}_{\mathcal{T},2}^{(m)}) \cap \mathcal{B}_{m+1}^2) \Big).$$

And by induction hypothesis, we have both $\mathcal{K}_{\mathcal{T},1}^{(m)} \subseteq \mathcal{Q}^{(m)}$ and $\mathcal{K}_{\mathcal{T},2}^{(m)} \subseteq \mathcal{Q}^{(m)}$. Hence,

$$\mathcal{K}_\mathcal{T}^{(m+1)} \subseteq \mathrm{conv}\Big((\mathrm{e}_{y_{m+1}}(\mathcal{Q}^{(m)}) \cap \mathcal{B}_{m+1}^1) \cup (\mathrm{e}_{y_{m+1}}(\mathcal{Q}^{(m)}) \cap \mathcal{B}_{m+1}^2) \Big).$$

Recall that for any i, $\mathcal{B}_i^1 = \{\boldsymbol{x} \in \mathbb{R}^{k+i} \mid y_i = 0\}$ and $\mathcal{B}_i^2 = \{\boldsymbol{x} \in \mathbb{R}^{k+i} \mid y_i = x_i\}$, so both $\mathcal{B}_{m+1}^1$ and $\mathcal{B}_{m+1}^2$ can be over-approximated by $\{\boldsymbol{x} \in \mathbb{R}^{k+m+1} \mid \underline{y_{m+1}} \leq y_{m+1} \leq \overline{y_{m+1}}\}$. Therefore, we further get

$$\begin{aligned}\mathcal{K}_{\mathcal{T}}^{(m+1)} \subseteq \operatorname{conv}\Big(&(\mathrm{e}_{y_{m+1}}(\mathcal{Q}^{(m)}) \cap \{\boldsymbol{x} \in \mathbb{R}^{k+m+1} \mid \underline{y_{m+1}} \leq y_{m+1} \leq \overline{y_{m+1}}\})\\ &\cup(\mathrm{e}_{y_{m+1}}(\mathcal{Q}^{(m)}) \cap \{\boldsymbol{x} \in \mathbb{R}^{k+m+1} \mid \underline{y_{m+1}} \leq y_{m+1} \leq \overline{y_{m+1}}\})\Big)\\ = \operatorname{conv}\Big(&(\mathrm{e}_{y_{m+1}}(\mathcal{Q}^{(m)}) \cap \{\boldsymbol{x} \in \mathbb{R}^{k+m+1} \mid \underline{y_{m+1}} \leq y_{m+1} \leq \overline{y_{m+1}}\})\Big)\\ = \operatorname{conv}\Big(&\mathcal{Q}^{(m)} \times [\,\underline{y_{m+1}}, \overline{y_{m+1}}\,]\Big).\end{aligned}$$

Since $\mathcal{Q}^{(m)} = \mathcal{P} \times \prod_{j=1}^{m} [\,\underline{y_j}, \overline{y_j}\,]$ by definition, $\mathcal{Q}^{(m)} \times [\,\underline{y_{m+1}}, \overline{y_{m+1}}\,]$ is convex. So $\operatorname{conv}\Big(\mathcal{Q}^{(m)} \times [\,\underline{y_{m+1}}, \overline{y_{m+1}}\,]\Big) = \mathcal{Q}^{(m)} \times [\,\underline{y_{m+1}}, \overline{y_{m+1}}\,]$. Then,

$$\mathcal{K}_{\mathcal{T}}^{(m+1)} \subseteq \mathcal{Q}^{(m)} \times [\,\underline{y_{m+1}}, \overline{y_{m+1}}\,] = \mathcal{P} \times \prod_{j=1}^{m+1} [\,\underline{y_j}, \overline{y_j}\,] = \mathcal{Q}^{(m+1)}.$$

The first statement is proved.

For the second statement, because $\mathcal{Q}^{(m+1)} = \mathcal{Q}^{(m)} \times [\,\underline{y_{m+1}}, \overline{y_{m+1}}\,]$, it is a prism formed by the base $\mathcal{Q}^{(m)}$ and parallel segments along the y_{m+1}-axis, and the height is $\overline{y_{m+1}} - \underline{y_{m+1}}$. Thus its volume $\mathrm{Vol}(\mathcal{Q}^{(m+1)}) = \mathrm{Vol}(\mathcal{Q}^{(m)}) \cdot (\overline{y_{m+1}} - \underline{y_{m+1}})$. By induction hypothesis, $\mathrm{Vol}(\mathcal{Q}^{(m)}) = \mathrm{Vol}(\mathcal{P}) \cdot \prod_{j=1}^{m} (\overline{y_j} - \underline{y_j})$, it then follows that

$$\mathrm{Vol}(\mathcal{Q}^{(m+1)}) = \mathrm{Vol}(\mathcal{Q}^{(m)}) \cdot (\overline{y_{m+1}} - \underline{y_{m+1}}) = \mathrm{Vol}(\mathcal{P}) \cdot \prod_{j=1}^{m+1} (\overline{y_j} - \underline{y_j}).$$

Finally, the third statement follows from the first two, which concludes our proof. □

Lemma 2 states that each convex hull generated during the lifting phase in SBLM can be over-approximated by a prism. It moreover tells that the volume of the prism can be calculated through the volume of the input polytope $\mathcal{P}$ and the bounds of all y_i-dimensions. Now we have our main theorem for the volume approximation.

Theorem 1 (Volume approximation). *Given a size-k group $G = \{v_1, \ldots, v_k\}$ of neurons and the polytope $\mathcal{P}$ input to SBLM, the volume $\mathrm{Vol}(\mathcal{K})$ of the convex hull $\mathcal{K}$ output by SBLM is bounded by $\underline{\mathrm{Vol}}(\mathcal{K})$ and $\overline{\mathrm{Vol}}(\mathcal{K})$ as follows:*

$$\underline{\mathrm{Vol}}(\mathcal{K}) = \frac{1}{(2k)!} \cdot \prod_{i=1}^{k} \left((\overline{x_i} - \underline{x_i}) \cdot (\overline{y_i} - \underline{y_i})\right),$$

$$\overline{\mathrm{Vol}}(\mathcal{K}) = \mathrm{Vol}(\mathcal{P}) \cdot \prod_{i=1}^{k} (\overline{y_i} - \underline{y_i}),$$

where $\underline{x_i}$ *and* $\overline{x_i}$ *(resp.,* $\underline{y_i}$ *and* $\overline{y_i}$*) denote the lower and upper bounds of the* x_i*-dimension (resp.,* y_i*-dimension) of* $\mathcal{K}$*, respectively.*

Proof. The lower bound is derived by applying Lemma 1, while the upper bound by Definition 3 and Lemma 2. □

In Theorem 1, the bounds of each x_i can be computed by $\underline{x_i} = \min_{\boldsymbol{x}\in\mathcal{P}} x_i$ and $\overline{x_i} = \max_{\boldsymbol{x}\in\mathcal{P}} x_i$. Recall that the bounding linear functions required by the lifting phase for ReLU are $\mathcal{B}^1 = (a_1^{\leq}, a_1^{\geq}) = (0, 0)$ and $\mathcal{B}^2 = (a_2^{\leq}, a_2^{\geq}) = (x, x)$. The bounds of each y_i can be computed by $\underline{y_i} = \min_{\boldsymbol{x}\in\mathcal{P}}(a_1^{\leq}(x_i), a_2^{\leq}(x_i)) = \min_{\boldsymbol{x}\in\mathcal{P}}(0, x_i) = 0$ and $\overline{y_i} = \max_{\boldsymbol{x}\in\mathcal{P}}(a_1^{\geq}(x_i), a_2^{\geq}(x_i)) = \max_{\boldsymbol{x}\in\mathcal{P}}(0, x_i) = \overline{x_i}$. Theorem 1 indicates that the under- and over-approximations of the volume $\mathrm{Vol}(\mathcal{K})$ can be calculated via the volume of the easily generated, low-dimensional $\mathcal{P}$ as well as the bounds of all dimensions, without actually computing the computationally expensive, high-dimensional $\mathcal{K}$.

3.3 Detailed Algorithm

The details of our approach are presented in Algorithm 1. It takes as input the group size k, the set V of all neurons in the considered activation layer, and the pre-computed lower bounds $\mathcal{L}$ and upper bounds $\mathcal{U}$ of all neurons in the neural network. The algorithm outputs the set $\mathcal{G}$ of groups that will be sent for convex hull computation to generate multi-neuron constraints.

The algorithm first filters out all the *fixed* neurons (line 2), whose inputs have lower bounds greater than 0 or upper bounds less than 0. The filtering is performed by the function FILTER(·). All *unfixed* neurons constitute the set V'. Any group with size k consisting of the neurons in V' is a group candidate. All $\binom{|V'|}{k}$ group candidates are generated (line 3). For each neuron v_i in V', our algorithm iteratively selects groups $\mathcal{G}_i$ whose convex hulls are needed (lines 5–14). Each iteration starts with collecting group candidates containing v_i (line 5). Then for each group candidate G, the approximated volumes of its corresponding convex hull $\mathcal{K}_G$ are computed (lines 9–10), during which the octahedral over-approximation $\mathcal{P}_G$ is calculated by the function GETOCTAAPPR(·) provided in PRIMA. With the under- and over-approximations of $\mathrm{Vol}(\mathcal{K}_G)$, the algorithm decides whether the candidate G should be selected (line 12), according to the selecting strategy implemented in SELECT(·) that is detailed in Algorithm 2. Finally, all groups selected iteratively are accumulated together (line 14).

Algorithm 2 shows our selecting strategy given the current set $\mathcal{G}_i$ of selected groups and approximated volumes. When no group is selected (i.e. $\mathcal{G}_i = \emptyset$), the group candidate G is selected (lines 1–2). If the over-approximated volume is small enough, all selected groups can be abandoned and only G will be selected (lines 3–4). Correspondingly, if the under-approximated volume is large enough, G should be dropped (lines 5–6). Otherwise, G is added (lines 7–8). Intuitively, our selecting strategy attempts to select the groups with very small over-approximated volumes, as well as to eliminate the candidates with

Algorithm 1. Volume Approximation based Grouping (for a Single Layer)

Input: the target neural network $\boldsymbol{h}$, group size k, the set V of all neurons in the layer, pre-computed bounds $\mathcal{L}$ and $\mathcal{U}$ of all neurons in $\boldsymbol{h}$
Output: the set $\mathcal{G}$ of groups for convex hull computation

$\mathcal{G} \leftarrow \emptyset$
Select only unfixed neurons: $V' \leftarrow \text{FILTER}(V, \mathcal{L}, \mathcal{U})$
$\mathcal{GC} \leftarrow \text{GENCANDIDATE}(V', k)$
for all $v_i \in V'$ **do**
  Get group candidates involving v_i: $\mathcal{GC}_i \leftarrow \text{COLLECT}(v_i, \mathcal{GC})$
  Initialize selected groups involving v_i: $\mathcal{G}_i \leftarrow \emptyset$
  for all $G \in \mathcal{GC}_i$ **do**
    if $\underline{\text{Vol}}(\mathcal{K}_G)$ and $\overline{\text{Vol}}(\mathcal{K}_G)$ are not available **then**
      Compute octahedral over-approximation: $\mathcal{P}_G \leftarrow \text{GETOCTAAPPR}(G, \mathcal{L}, \mathcal{U}, \boldsymbol{h})$
      Volume approximation: calculate $\underline{\text{Vol}}(\mathcal{K}_G)$ and $\overline{\text{Vol}}(\mathcal{K}_G)$ by Theorem 1
    end if
    Update $\mathcal{G}_i$: $\mathcal{G}_i \leftarrow \text{SELECT}(\mathcal{G}_i, G, \underline{\text{Vol}}(\mathcal{K}_G), \overline{\text{Vol}}(\mathcal{K}_G))$
  end for
  $\mathcal{G} \leftarrow \mathcal{G} \cup \mathcal{G}_i$
end for
return $\mathcal{G}$

Algorithm 2. Selecting Strategy $\text{SELECT}(\cdot)$

Input: the set $\mathcal{G}_i$ of currently selected groups for neuron v_i, group candidate G, approximated volumes $\underline{\text{Vol}}(\mathcal{K}_G)$ and $\overline{\text{Vol}}(\mathcal{K}_G)$
Output: the updated set $\mathcal{G}'_i$ of selected groups for neuron v_i

if $\mathcal{G}_i = \emptyset$ **then**
  $\mathcal{G}'_i \leftarrow \{G\}$
else if $\overline{\text{Vol}}(\mathcal{K}_G) \leq \max_{G' \in \mathcal{G}_i}(\underline{\text{Vol}}(\mathcal{K}_{G'}))$ **then**
  $\mathcal{G}'_i \leftarrow \{G\}$
else if $\underline{\text{Vol}}(\mathcal{K}_G) \geq \min_{G' \in \mathcal{G}_i}(\overline{\text{Vol}}(\mathcal{K}_{G'}))$ **then**
  $\mathcal{G}'_i \leftarrow \mathcal{G}_i$
else
  $\mathcal{G}'_i \leftarrow \mathcal{G}_i \cup \{G\}$
end if
return $\mathcal{G}'_i$

very large under-approximated volumes. It conservatively keeps the candidates otherwise, in order to prevent losing precision.

We give a detailed example to illustrate our algorithms.

Example 2. Assume that there are five neurons in the ReLU activation layer. That is, $V = \{v_1, v_2, v_3, v_4, v_5\}$. Let the group size $k = 2$, and the pre-computed bounds be $x_1 \in [-1, 1]$, $x_2 \in [-2, 2]$, $x_3 \in [-1, 1]$, $x_4 \in [-3, 3]$, and $x_5 \in [-\frac{1}{2}, \frac{1}{2}]$. All neurons are unfixed, so $V' = V = \{v_1, v_2, v_3, v_4, v_5\}$. All $\binom{5}{2} = 10$ group candidates are

$$\mathcal{GC} = \{\{v_1, v_2\}, \{v_1, v_3\}, \{v_1, v_4\}, \{v_1, v_5\}, \\ \{v_2, v_3\}, \{v_2, v_4\}, \{v_2, v_5\}, \{v_3, v_4\}, \{v_3, v_5\}, \{v_4, v_5\}\}.$$

We start with $v_1 \in V'$. Collecting group candidates in $\mathcal{GC}$ that contain v_1, we have $\mathcal{GC}_1 = \{\{v_1, v_2\}, \{v_1, v_3\}, \{v_1, v_4\}, \{v_1, v_5\}\}$. $\mathcal{G}_1$ is then initialized as $\mathcal{G}_1 = \emptyset$. For all $G \in \mathcal{GC}_1$, the under- and over-approximated volumes are calculated:

- By function GETOCTAAPPR($\cdot$) in PRIMA, the octahedral over-approximations are

$$\begin{aligned}
\mathcal{P}_{\{v_1,v_2\}} = \{\boldsymbol{x} \in \mathbb{R}^2 \mid\ & x_1 + x_2 \le 3,\ -x_1 + x_2 \le 1,\ x_1 - x_2 \le 1, \\
& -x_1 - x_2 \le 3,\ -1 \le x_1 \le 1,\ -2 \le x_2 \le 2\}, \\
\mathcal{P}_{\{v_1,v_3\}} = \{\boldsymbol{x} \in \mathbb{R}^2 \mid\ & x_1 + x_3 \le 2,\ -x_1 + x_3 \le \frac{1}{2},\ x_1 - x_3 \le \frac{1}{2}, \\
& -x_1 - x_3 \le 2,\ -1 \le x_1 \le 1,\ -1 \le x_3 \le 1\}, \\
\mathcal{P}_{\{v_1,v_4\}} = \{\boldsymbol{x} \in \mathbb{R}^2 \mid\ & x_1 + x_4 \le 4,\ -x_1 + x_4 \le 2,\ x_1 - x_4 \le 2, \\
& -x_1 - x_4 \le 4,\ -1 \le x_1 \le 1,\ -3 \le x_4 \le 3\}, \\
\mathcal{P}_{\{v_1,v_5\}} = \{\boldsymbol{x} \in \mathbb{R}^2 \mid\ & x_1 + x_5 \le \frac{3}{2},\ -x_1 + x_5 \le \frac{1}{2},\ x_1 - x_5 \le \frac{1}{2}, \\
& -x_1 - x_5 \le \frac{3}{2},\ -1 \le x_1 \le 1,\ -\frac{1}{2} \le x_5 \le \frac{1}{2}\}.
\end{aligned}$$

- By Theorem 1, the approximated volumes are

$$\begin{aligned}
\underline{\mathrm{Vol}}(\mathcal{K}_{\{v_1,v_2\}}) &= \frac{2}{3}, & \overline{\mathrm{Vol}}(\mathcal{K}_{\{v_1,v_2\}}) &= 4, \\
\underline{\mathrm{Vol}}(\mathcal{K}_{\{v_1,v_3\}}) &= \frac{1}{6}, & \overline{\mathrm{Vol}}(\mathcal{K}_{\{v_1,v_3\}}) &= 1, \\
\underline{\mathrm{Vol}}(\mathcal{K}_{\{v_1,v_4\}}) &= \frac{3}{2}, & \overline{\mathrm{Vol}}(\mathcal{K}_{\{v_1,v_4\}}) &= 9, \\
\underline{\mathrm{Vol}}(\mathcal{K}_{\{v_1,v_5\}}) &= \frac{1}{24}, & \overline{\mathrm{Vol}}(\mathcal{K}_{\{v_1,v_5\}}) &= \frac{1}{2}.
\end{aligned}$$

  Note that we invoke QHULL [3] to compute $\mathrm{Vol}(\mathcal{P})$ in Theorem 1.

From $\mathcal{G}_1 = \emptyset$, Algorithm 2 updates $\mathcal{G}_1$ for each $G \in \mathcal{GC}_1$ (line 12 in Algorithm 1):

- When $G = \{v_1, v_2\}$, since $\mathcal{G}_1 = \emptyset$, it is updated to $\mathcal{G}_1 = \{G\} = \{\{v_1, v_2\}\}$.
- When $G = \{v_1, v_3\}$, since $\overline{\mathrm{Vol}}(\mathcal{K}_G) = 1 \not\le \frac{2}{3} = \underline{\mathrm{Vol}}(\mathcal{K}_{\{v_1,v_2\}}) = \max_{G' \in \mathcal{G}_1}(\underline{\mathrm{Vol}}(\mathcal{K}_{G'}))$, and $\underline{\mathrm{Vol}}(\mathcal{K}_G) = \frac{1}{6} \not\ge 4 = \overline{\mathrm{Vol}}(\mathcal{K}_{\{v_1,v_2\}}) = \min_{G' \in \mathcal{G}_1}(\overline{\mathrm{Vol}}(\mathcal{K}_{G'}))$, $\mathcal{G}_1$ is updated to $\{\{v_1, v_2\}\} \cup \{G\} = \{\{v_1, v_2\}, \{v_1, v_3\}\}$.
- When $G = \{v_1, v_4\}$, since $\overline{\mathrm{Vol}}(\mathcal{K}_G) = 9 \not\le \frac{2}{3} = \underline{\mathrm{Vol}}(\mathcal{K}_{\{v_1,v_2\}}) = \max_{G' \in \mathcal{G}_1}(\underline{\mathrm{Vol}}(\mathcal{K}_{G'}))$, and $\underline{\mathrm{Vol}}(\mathcal{K}_G) = \frac{3}{2} \ge 1 = \overline{\mathrm{Vol}}(\mathcal{K}_{\{v_1,v_3\}}) = \min_{G' \in \mathcal{G}_1}(\overline{\mathrm{Vol}}(\mathcal{K}_{G'}))$, then G is dropped and $\mathcal{G}_1$ remains $\{\{v_1, v_2\}, \{v_1, v_3\}\}$.
- When $G = \{v_1, v_5\}$, since $\overline{\mathrm{Vol}}(\mathcal{K}_G) = \frac{1}{2} \le \frac{2}{3} = \underline{\mathrm{Vol}}(\mathcal{K}_{\{v_1,v_2\}}) = \max_{G' \in \mathcal{G}_1}(\underline{\mathrm{Vol}}(\mathcal{K}_{G'}))$, $\mathcal{G}_1$ is updated to $\{G\} = \{\{v_1, v_5\}\}$.

Finally, $\mathcal{G}_1 = \{\{v_1, v_5\}\}$.

Then $v_2 \in V'$ is considered. $\mathcal{GC}_2 = \{\{v_1, v_2\}, \{v_2, v_3\}, \{v_2, v_4\}, \{v_2, v_5\}\}$. The process is similar. The obtained set of selected groups containing v_2 is $\mathcal{G}_2 = \{\{v_1, v_2\}, \{v_2, v_3\}, \{v_2, v_5\}\}$.

Similarly, we get $\mathcal{G}_3 = \{\{v_3, v_5\}\}$, $\mathcal{G}_4 = \{\{v_4, v_5\}\}$, and $\mathcal{G}_5 = \{\{v_1, v_5\}, \{v_2, v_5\}, \{v_3, v_5\}, \{v_4, v_5\}\}$ for the neurons v_3, v_4 and v_5, respectively.

Lastly, the set of selected groups for the whole activation layer is $\mathcal{G} = \bigcup_{i=1}^{5} \mathcal{G}_i = \{\{v_1, v_2\}, \{v_2, v_3\}, \{v_1, v_5\}, \{v_2, v_5\}, \{v_3, v_5\}, \{v_4, v_5\}\}$. As a result, our approach eliminates $|\mathcal{GC}| - |\mathcal{G}| = 10 - 6 = 4$ group candidates.

3.4 Generalization

Our approach is presented until now for the ReLU activation function. However, note that the ReLU function only plays a role when instantiating the intervals $\mathcal{D}^j$ and the bounds $\mathcal{B}^j$ required by SBLM (Sect. 2.2). The characteristics of the ReLU function are not necessary for our approach. Our approach can be generalized, as SBLM in [17], to the Sigmoid function $\sigma(x) = \frac{e^x}{e^x+1}$ and the Tanh function $\tanh(x) = \frac{e^x - e^{-x}}{e^x + e^{-x}}$ by instantiating $\mathcal{D}^j$ and $\mathcal{B}^j$ differently.

Following [17], assuming $x \in [\underline{x}, \overline{x}]$, the intervals are instantiated as $\mathcal{D}^1 = (-\infty, c]$ and $\mathcal{D}^2 = [c, +\infty)$, where the constant c is chosen to minimize the area of the abstraction of a single neuron in the input-output plane. And the single-neuron abstraction of the activation function f (Sigmoid or Tanh) is defined by the bounds $\mathcal{B}^j = (a_j^{\leq}, a_j^{\geq})$ instantiated using the bounds from [21] as:

$$f(x) \leq a_j^{\geq}(x) = f(u_j) + (x - u_j) \cdot \begin{cases} \frac{f(u_j) - f(l_j)}{u_j - l_j}, & \text{if } u_j \leq 0, \\ \min(f'(u_j), f'(l_j)), & \text{otherwise}, \end{cases}$$

$$f(x) \geq a_j^{\leq}(x) = f(l_j) + (x - l_j) \cdot \begin{cases} \frac{f(u_j) - f(l_j)}{u_j - l_j}, & \text{if } l_j \geq 0, \\ \min(f'(u_j), f'(l_j)), & \text{otherwise}, \end{cases}$$

where l_j and u_j denote the lower and upper bounds of $\mathcal{D}^j \cap [\underline{x}, \overline{x}]$, respectively, and f' for the derivative of f. Using the above instantiation, our approach is applicable to the neural networks with Sigmoid and Tanh activation functions.

4 Experiments

We implement our approach as a neural network verifier FaGMR (**Fast** **G**rouping for **M**ulti-neuron **R**elaxation) based on Prima, by replacing its grouping strategy with our volume approximation based approach. In this section, we evaluate the efficiency and effectiveness of FaGMR on common benchmarks. Specifically, we compare FaGMR against our baseline Prima in Sect. 4.2. It is further compared in Sect. 4.3 with two other state-of-the-art verifiers from the Verification of Neural Networks Competition (VNN-COMP) 2021 [2]: α, β-CROWN [28] and ERAN [23]. They are representatives of mainstream verification techniques. Section 4.4 shows the results of FaGMR on Sigmoid and Tanh neural networks.

Table 1. Neural networks used in the experiments. "Type" is the network structure: fully-connected (FC), convolutional (Conv), or Residual. "Training" is the used robust training technique: non-robust (NOR), PGD [14], or DiffAI [15].

Dataset	Model	Training	Type	Neurons	Layers	Activation
MNIST	5 × 100	NOR	FC	510	5	ReLU
	9 × 100	NOR	FC	810	9	ReLU
	6 × 200	NOR	FC	1010	6	ReLU
	6 × 500	NOR	FC	3000	6	Sigmoid
	6 × 500	NOR	FC	3000	6	Tanh
	ConvMed	PGD	Conv	3604	3	ReLU
	ConvMed	PGD	Conv	3604	3	Sigmoid
	ConvMed	PGD	Conv	3604	3	Tanh
	ConvBig	DiffAI	Conv	48064	6	ReLU
CIFAR-10	ConvSmall	DiffAI	Conv	3604	3	ReLU
	ConvMed	PGD	Conv	5703	3	ReLU
	ResNet2b	DiffAI	Residual	11364	13	ReLU

4.1 Experiment Configurations

Neural Networks. The evaluation is conducted on two widely-used datasets: MNIST and CIFAR-10. In particular, besides fully-connected and convolutional network structures, our evaluation includes a large ResNet network. Table 1 shows the details about all the networks used in our experiments. They are benchmarks from VNN-COMP 2021 [2] and can be downloaded at [23].

Robustness Property. As most works do, we consider the l_∞-norm perturbation on correctly classified inputs from the datasets. All verifiers are asked to answer verification problems as defined by Definition 1. More successfully verified problems mean better precision. In general, the perturbation thresholds θ are chosen as the same as those in [17].

Parameters of FaGMR. FaGMR chooses $k = 3$, which is claimed as the optimal option in Prima. That is, FaGMR considers size-3 neuron groups for convex relaxation.

Machine and Software. All experiments are conducted on a 12-core 2.20 GHz Intel Xeon Sliver 4212 platform with 64GB memory. FaGMR is implemented in Python 3.7 and uses Gurobi 9.5.1 [10] for LP solving. Qhull [3] is employed to compute Vol($\mathcal{P}$) in Theorem 1.

4.2 Comparison of Verification Precision and Runtime

We first compare the verification precision and runtime of FaGMR against Prima, the state-of-the-art multi-neuron relaxation tool as well as the baseline

Table 2. Comparison of FAGMR against PRIMA. "Total" is the number of verification problems, θ for the perturbation threshold, "#group" for average number of selected groups, "time" for average runtime (in seconds), and "#verified" for the number of successfully verified problems. The best data are highlighted.

Network		Total	θ	PRIMA-all			PRIMA-para			FAGMR		
				#group	time	#verified	#group	time	#verified	#group	time	#verified
MNIST	5 × 100	979	0.015	11.0	43.9	974	10.4	38.8	974	**8.7**	**33.5**	**974**
			0.026	45.6	52.8	970	37.4	47.0	970	**25.5**	**40.3**	**970**
	9 × 100	947	0.026	1.5k	96.8	891 (20)*	338.0	61.6	911	**138.8**	**57.6**	**911**
	6 × 200	972	0.015	1.6k	106.7	959	1.5k	68.6	958	**877.0**	**57.6**	**959**
	ConvMed	983	0.026	324.2	99.7	973 (2)	207.5	60.1	975	**108.4**	**54.8**	**975**
	ConvBig	929	0.03	366.4	114.7	922 (4)	259.3	**89.6**	924 (2)	**125.5**	96.9	**926**
CIFAR-10	ConvSmall	471	4/255	3.0k	49.0	452	2.3k	34.6	452	**1.4k**	**24.2**	**452**
	ConvMed	312	2/255	15.4k	649.5	288 (7)	2.4k	251.6	295	**1.8k**	**223.6**	**295**
	ResNet2b	161	1/255	-	-	-	7.0k	407.5	158	**1.1k**	**199.4**	**158**

* in parentheses is the number of out-of-memory cases.
\- results omitted due to lack of availability (over 50% out-of-memory cases).

that FAGMR is built on. For thorough evaluation, the comparison includes the following two variants of PRIMA discussed in [17]:

- PRIMA-all: It selects all possible k-neuron groups in an activation layer.
- PRIMA-para: It defines parameters n_s and s, partitions the neurons of an activation layer into sets of size n_s, and selects for each set a subset of all size-k groups that pairwise overlap by at most s. It is the default in PRIMA.

We use the suggested $k = 3$ for all three verifiers FAGMR, PRIMA-all, and PRIMA-para. For PRIMA-para, the default configuration ($n_s = 70$, $s = 1$) in its implementation is used. The three verifiers are compared on 8 different networks of various sizes. The results are shown in Table 2.

In Table 2, FAGMR successfully verifies the most problems in all cases, and outperforms PRIMA-all and PRIMA-para w.r.t. runtime in most cases. Particularly, observe that for the MNIST 6×200 network with $\theta = 0.015$, FAGMR verifies one more problem than PRIMA-para while being 16.0% ($\approx (68.6-57.6)/68.6$) faster, and it is 46.0% faster than PRIMA-all yet achieving the same verification precision. For the large network CIFAR-10 ResNet2b, FAGMR successfully verifies the same number of problems as PRIMA-para, but is much (51.1%) faster. On some complicated benchmarks, the MNIST ConvBig with $\theta = 0.03$ for instance, both PRIMA-all and PRIMA-para run out of memory in several problems, but FAGMR does not, because it selects a much less number of groups for convex relaxation. All the benchmarks demonstrate that FAGMR effectively reduces the number of neuron groups. As a result, FAGMR reduces the verification time by 11.2% on average compared to PRIMA-para, but with negligible precision loss compared to PRIMA-all. The comparison confirms the effectiveness and efficiency of FAGMR.

Details of Runtime. The efficiency improvement of FAGMR comes from selecting less number of neuron groups, which decreases the time cost for both

Table 3. Detailed runtime of FaGMR and Prima (in seconds). T_{gr} is the time for neuron grouping, T_{cg} the time for multi-neuron constraint generation, T_{lp} the time for LP solving.

Network	θ	Prima-all			Prima-para			FaGMR		
		T_{gr}	T_{cg}	T_{lp}	T_{gr}	T_{cg}	T_{lp}	T_{gr}	T_{cg}	T_{lp}
MNIST 5 × 100	0.015	0.4	7.7k	34.8k	0.4	5.0k	32.6k	132	**2.2k**	**30.0k**
	0.026	0.4	9.0k	41.1k	0.4	6.4k	39.0k	350	**2.8k**	**35.8k**
CIFAR-10 ConvSmall	2/255	1.4	3.0k	2.6k	1.4	3.0k	2.6k	2.7	**2.1k**	**2.3k**
	4/255	2.3	15.0k	6.8k	2.3	9.9k	5.1k	9.8	**4.5k**	**3.2k**

constraint generation and solving. We quantitatively analyze the influence of group reduction by dividing the runtime into three parts:

- T_{gr}: time for grouping;
- T_{cg}: time for constraint generation;
- T_{lp}: time for LP solving.

Table 3 shows the detailed runtime for some benchmarks. All the time is the total time spent on all verification problems. We can see that FaGMR spends more time for neuron grouping (T_{gr}) than both Prima-all and Prima-para, due to the volume approximation and comparison. However, the grouping time is negligible compared to the time for multi-neuron constraint generation (T_{cg}) and LP solving (T_{lp}). The increased grouping time of FaGMR brings significant efficiency improvements in both constraint generation and LP solving. For instance, in the MNIST 5×100 network with $\theta = 0.015$, $T_{gr} + T_{cg}$ for FaGMR is 70.0% ($\approx (7.7 - 2.332)/7.7$) and 53.4% less than Prima-all and Prima-para, respectively. And the total runtime ($T_{gr} + T_{cg} + T_{lp}$) of FaGMR is 24.0% and 14.0% faster than Prima-all and Prima-para, respectively.

Notice that for the CIFAR-10 ConvSmall network with $\theta = 2/255$ in Table 3, Prima-all and Prima-para have the same T_{gr}, T_{cg} and T_{lp}. It is because there are only a few number of unfixed neurons that need to be grouped in such verification problems with the small perturbation threshold, making the statically chosen grouping parameters of Prima-para ineffective. Our dynamic grouping strategy in FaGMR however avoids this to some extent, yielding respectively 30.0% and 11.5% efficiency improvement in T_{cg} and T_{lp}.

4.3 Comparison with Other State-of-the-Art Verifiers

We have shown the effectiveness and efficiency of FaGMR compared to its baseline Prima, the state-of-the-art multi-neuron relaxation verifier. In this section, FaGMR is further compared against α, β-CROWN [28] and ERAN [23], two outstanding verifiers in VNN-COMP 2021 [2]. For α, β-CROWN, we use its default configuration, under which it performs complete verification using Branch and Bound (BaB). For ERAN, we use its multi-neuron relaxation technique with default $n_s = 70$ and $s = 1$. The detailed settings are as follows.

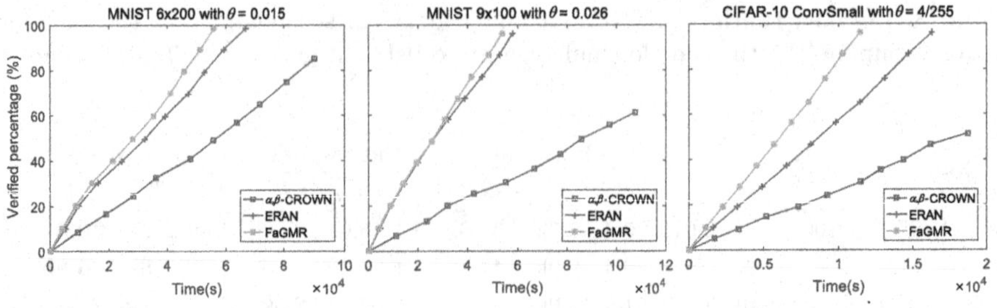

Fig. 2. Verified Percentage of FaGMR, α, β-CROWN and ERAN w.r.t. Runtime. Three benchmarks consist of 972, 947, and 471 verification problems, respectively.

- α, β-CROWN: BaB verifier with 20 β-CROWN iterations; CPU mode; timeout for each task being 300 s; MILP refinement enabled; PGD attack disabled. The configuration files for different networks can be found at its repository[1] with names `network_name.yaml`.
- ERAN: incomplete verifier with `refinepoly` domain; $n_s = 70$ and $s = 1$ for multi-neuron relaxation; CPU mode; MILP disabled. The configuration file is available here.[2]

Figure 2 shows the comparison results on three neural networks. The y-axes stand for the verified percentage and the x-axes for the runtime. The figure illustrates that the verified percentage increases as the time passes. The fact that a trend line is steeper indicates that its corresponding verifier is more efficient.

Figure 2 demonstrates that α, β-CROWN eventually verifies the least verification problems among the three tools on each network. It is mostly because α, β-CROWN utilizes single-neuron relaxation techniques that inherently lead to lower precision than multi-neuron relaxation leveraged by both FaGMR and ERAN. FaGMR achieves similar verification precision to ERAN on these three benchmarks. Precisely, it successfully verifies one more problem than ERAN on the MNIST 6×200 network when $\theta = 0.015$, and exactly the same number of problems on the other two networks. For efficiency, we can easily see that FaGMR outperforms the other two tools on all three networks.

The experimental results show that FaGMR is also competitive among the state-of-the-art verifiers using different techniques.

4.4 Comparison on Sigmoid and Tanh Neural Networks

FaGMR is applicable to the neural networks with activation functions Sigmoid and Tanh as presented in Sect. 3.4. In this section, we compare FaGMR against Prima-para on such networks. Prima-all is excluded due to out-of-memory

[1] https://github.com/Verified-Intelligence/alpha-beta-CROWN/tree/main/complete_verifier/exp_configs/.

[2] https://github.com/formes20/FaGMR/blob/main/code/tf_verify/config.py.

Table 4. Comparison of FAGMR against PRIMA-para on Sigmoid and Tanh networks. "Total" is the number of verification problems, θ for the perturbation threshold, "#group" for average number of selected groups, "time" for average runtime (in seconds), and "#verified" for the number of successfully verified problems. The best data are highlighted.

Network		Total	Activation	θ	PRIMA-para			FAGMR		
					#group	time	#verified	#group	time	#verified
MNIST	6 × 500	95	Sigmoid	0.012	6.2k	640.9	95	**3.8k**	**570.0**	**95**
	ConvMed	99	Sigmoid	0.014	6.3k	255.6	99	**5.9k**	**252.5**	**99**
	6 × 500	99	Tanh	0.005	406.6	211.8	97 (1)*	**184.8**	**194.9**	**98**
	ConvMed	98	Tanh	0.005	1.2k	220.4	98	**446.3**	**191.8**	**98**

* in parentheses is the number of out-of-memory cases.

issues on these activation functions. Specifically, we choose two MNIST networks 6 × 500 and ConvMed with Sigmoid and Tanh activation functions (see Table 1), then conduct the comparison experiments similar to Sect. 4.2.

Similarly, Table 4 shows that FAGMR outperforms PRIMA-para on these networks with activation functions Sigmoid and Tanh. Specifically, by reducing the number of selected groups, FAGMR is on average 8.3% faster than PRIMA-para. In particular, it successfully verifies one more problem than PRIMA-para on the 6 × 500 Tanh network when $\theta = 0.005$ due to the latter's out-of-memory issue, while obtaining the same precision on the other three benchmarks.

5 Related Work

According to the completeness of verification results, neural network verification methods can be categorized into complete methods and incomplete ones.

Complete Verification. Complete verification methods can describe the exact behavior of a neural network w.r.t. an input region. They can be further classified into: (i) SAT/SMT based methods [7,11,12], which encode the verification problem into an SAT/SMT query; (ii) Mixed-integer linear programming (MILP) based methods [1,5,7], which encode the verification problem into an MILP problem and then invoke MILP solvers; (iii) Branch-and-Bound based methods, which split non-linear activation functions into linear pieces [6,25,27,28], or split the input region to be small enough so that the neural network behaves linearly on each input sub-region [26]. Complete methods are usually limited in scalability because of the computational complexity.

Incomplete Verification. Incomplete verification methods often relax non-linear activations such as ReLU to speed up verification. Most incomplete methods attempt to develop efficient and precise over-approximations for a given activation function (e.g. [18,20,21,28,29,33], see a survey in [13]). FAGMR belongs to this category. It applies convex relaxation to over-approximate non-linear activation functions, hence is incomplete but is faster and more scalable than complete methods. Among incomplete verification methods, single-neuron convex relaxation based methods consider each neuron separately and over-approximate its activation function. They are very efficient (e.g., [9,18,20,21,28,29,31–33]), but their verification precision is proved to be limited by a convex relaxation barrier [18]. Instead, multi-neuron convex relaxation methods [17,19,24] suggest over-approximating multiple neurons jointly for higher precision, hence breaking down the barrier faced by single-neuron relaxation. Our work follows this promising direction and improves the efficiency of existing techniques.

6 Conclusion

We have presented a fast and effective neuron grouping strategy for multi-neuron convex relaxation methods. The key idea is to compute the volume approximations of all possible neuron group candidates and then select better groups according to the approximated volumes. The evaluation shows that our approach effectively reduces verification time and achieves competitive verification precision compared to the state-of-the-art tools.

Acknowledgements. We thank all the anonymous reviewers and Gagandeep Singh for their invaluable comments and suggestions.

References

1. Anderson, R., Huchette, J., Ma, W., Tjandraatmadja, C., Vielma, J.P.: Strong mixed-integer programming formulations for trained neural networks. Math. Program. **183**(1), 3–39 (2020). https://doi.org/10.1007/s10107-020-01474-5
2. Bak, S., Liu, C., Johnson, T.T.: The second international verification of neural networks competition (VNN-COMP 2021): summary and results. CoRR abs/2109.00498 (2021). https://arxiv.org/abs/2109.00498
3. Barber, C.B., Dobkin, D.P., Huhdanpaa, H.: Qhull: Quickhull algorithm for computing the convex hull. Astrophysics Source Code Library, pp. ascl-1304 (2013)
4. Betke, U., Henk, M.: Approximating the volume of convex bodies. Discret. Comput. Geom. **10**(1), 15–21 (1993). https://doi.org/10.1007/BF02573960
5. Botoeva, E., Kouvaros, P., Kronqvist, J., Lomuscio, A., Misener, R.: Efficient verification of ReLU-based neural networks via dependency analysis. In: The Thirty-Fourth AAAI Conference on Artificial Intelligence, AAAI 2020, The Thirty-Second Innovative Applications of Artificial Intelligence Conference, IAAI 2020, The Tenth AAAI Symposium on Educational Advances in Artificial Intelligence, EAAI 2020, New York, NY, USA, 7–12 February 2020, pp. 3291–3299. AAAI Press (2020). https://ojs.aaai.org/index.php/AAAI/article/view/5729
6. Bunel, R., Lu, J., Turkaslan, I., Torr, P.H.S., Kohli, P., Kumar, M.P.: Branch and bound for piecewise linear neural network verification. J. Mach. Learn. Res. **21**, 42:1–42:39 (2020). http://jmlr.org/papers/v21/19-468.html
7. Ehlers, R.: Formal verification of piece-wise linear feed-forward neural networks. In: D'Souza, D., Narayan Kumar, K. (eds.) ATVA 2017. LNCS, vol. 10482, pp. 269–286. Springer, Cham (2017). https://doi.org/10.1007/978-3-319-68167-2_19

8. Goodfellow, I.J., Bengio, Y., Courville, A.C.: Deep Learning. Adaptive Computation and Machine Learning. MIT Press (2016). http://www.deeplearningbook.org/
9. Goubault, E., Palumby, S., Putot, S., Rustenholz, L., Sankaranarayanan, S.: Static analysis of ReLU neural networks with tropical polyhedra. In: Drăgoi, C., Mukherjee, S., Namjoshi, K. (eds.) SAS 2021. LNCS, vol. 12913, pp. 166–190. Springer, Cham (2021). https://doi.org/10.1007/978-3-030-88806-0_8
10. Gurobi Optimization: Gurobi Optimizer. http://www.gurobi.com
11. Katz, G., Barrett, C., Dill, D.L., Julian, K., Kochenderfer, M.J.: Reluplex: an efficient SMT solver for verifying deep neural networks. In: Majumdar, R., Kunčak, V. (eds.) CAV 2017. LNCS, vol. 10426, pp. 97–117. Springer, Cham (2017). https://doi.org/10.1007/978-3-319-63387-9_5
12. Katz, G., et al.: The Marabou framework for verification and analysis of deep neural networks. In: Dillig, I., Tasiran, S. (eds.) CAV 2019. LNCS, vol. 11561, pp. 443–452. Springer, Cham (2019). https://doi.org/10.1007/978-3-030-25540-4_26
13. Liu, C., Arnon, T., Lazarus, C., Strong, C.A., Barrett, C.W., Kochenderfer, M.J.: Algorithms for verifying deep neural networks. Found. Trends Optim. **4**(3–4), 244–404 (2021). https://doi.org/10.1561/2400000035
14. Madry, A., Makelov, A., Schmidt, L., Tsipras, D., Vladu, A.: Towards deep learning models resistant to adversarial attacks. CoRR abs/1706.06083 (2017). http://arxiv.org/abs/1706.06083
15. Mirman, M., Gehr, T., Vechev, M.T.: Differentiable abstract interpretation for provably robust neural networks. In: Dy, J.G., Krause, A. (eds.) Proceedings of the 35th International Conference on Machine Learning, ICML 2018, Stockholmsmässan, Stockholm, Sweden, 10–15 July 2018. Proceedings of Machine Learning Research, vol. 80, pp. 3575–3583. PMLR (2018). http://proceedings.mlr.press/v80/mirman18b.html
16. Morgulis, N., Kreines, A., Mendelowitz, S., Weisglass, Y.: Fooling a real car with adversarial traffic signs. CoRR abs/1907.00374 (2019). http://arxiv.org/abs/1907.00374
17. Müller, M.N., Makarchuk, G., Singh, G., Püschel, M., Vechev, M.T.: PRIMA: general and precise neural network certification via scalable convex hull approximations. Proc. ACM Program. Lang. **6**(POPL), 1–33 (2022). https://doi.org/10.1145/3498704
18. Salman, H., Yang, G., Zhang, H., Hsieh, C., Zhang, P.: A convex relaxation barrier to tight robustness verification of neural networks. In: Wallach, H.M., Larochelle, H., Beygelzimer, A., d'Alché-Buc, F., Fox, E.B., Garnett, R. (eds.) Advances in Neural Information Processing Systems 32: Annual Conference on Neural Information Processing Systems 2019, NeurIPS 2019, Vancouver, BC, Canada, 8–14 December 2019, pp. 9832–9842 (2019)
19. Singh, G., Ganvir, R., Püschel, M., Vechev, M.T.: Beyond the single neuron convex barrier for neural network certification. In: Wallach, H.M., Larochelle, H., Beygelzimer, A., d'Alché-Buc, F., Fox, E.B., Garnett, R. (eds.) Advances in Neural Information Processing Systems 32: Annual Conference on Neural Information Processing Systems 2019, NeurIPS 2019, Vancouver, BC, Canada, 8–14 December 2019, pp. 15072–15083 (2019). https://proceedings.neurips.cc/paper/2019/hash/0a9fdbb17feb6ccb7ec405cfb85222c4-Abstract.html
20. Singh, G., Gehr, T., Mirman, M., Püschel, M., Vechev, M.T.: Fast and effective robustness certification. In: Bengio, S., Wallach, H.M., Larochelle, H., Grauman, K., Cesa-Bianchi, N., Garnett, R. (eds.) Advances in Neural

Information Processing Systems 31: Annual Conference on Neural Information Processing Systems 2018, NeurIPS 2018, Montréal, Canada, 3–8 December 2018, pp. 10825–10836 (2018). https://proceedings.neurips.cc/paper/2018/hash/f2f446980d8e971ef3da97af089481c3-Abstract.html

21. Singh, G., Gehr, T., Püschel, M., Vechev, M.T.: An abstract domain for certifying neural networks. Proc. ACM Program. Lang. **3**(POPL), 41:1–41:30 (2019). https://doi.org/10.1145/3290354
22. Sommerville, D.M.: Introduction to the Geometry of N Dimensions. Courier Dover Publications (2020)
23. SRI Lab: ETH robustness analyzer for neural networks (ERAN) (2022). https://github.com/eth-sri/eran
24. Tjandraatmadja, C., Anderson, R., Huchette, J., Ma, W., Patel, K., Vielma, J.P.: The convex relaxation barrier, revisited: tightened single-neuron relaxations for neural network verification. In: Larochelle, H., Ranzato, M., Hadsell, R., Balcan, M., Lin, H. (eds.) Advances in Neural Information Processing Systems 33: Annual Conference on Neural Information Processing Systems 2020, NeurIPS 2020, 6–12 December 2020, Virtual (2020). https://proceedings.neurips.cc/paper/2020/hash/f6c2a0c4b566bc99d596e58638e342b0-Abstract.html
25. Wang, S., Pei, K., Whitehouse, J., Yang, J., Jana, S.: Efficient formal safety analysis of neural networks. In: Bengio, S., Wallach, H.M., Larochelle, H., Grauman, K., Cesa-Bianchi, N., Garnett, R. (eds.) Advances in Neural Information Processing Systems 31: Annual Conference on Neural Information Processing Systems 2018, NeurIPS 2018, Montréal, Canada, 3–8 December 2018, pp. 6369–6379 (2018). https://proceedings.neurips.cc/paper/2018/hash/2ecd2bd94734e5dd392d8678bc64cdab-Abstract.html
26. Wang, S., Pei, K., Whitehouse, J., Yang, J., Jana, S.: Formal security analysis of neural networks using symbolic intervals. In: Enck, W., Felt, A.P. (eds.) 27th USENIX Security Symposium, USENIX Security 2018, Baltimore, MD, USA, 15–17 August 2018, pp. 1599–1614. USENIX Association (2018). https://www.usenix.org/conference/usenixsecurity18/presentation/wang-shiqi
27. Wang, S., et al.: Beta-CROWN: efficient bound propagation with per-neuron split constraints for neural network robustness verification. In: Ranzato, M., Beygelzimer, A., Dauphin, Y.N., Liang, P., Vaughan, J.W. (eds.) Advances in Neural Information Processing Systems 34: Annual Conference on Neural Information Processing Systems 2021, NeurIPS 2021, 6–14 December 2021, Virtual, pp. 29909–29921 (2021). https://proceedings.neurips.cc/paper/2021/hash/fac7fead96dafceaf80c1daffeae82a4-Abstract.html
28. Xu, K., et al.: Fast and complete: enabling complete neural network verification with rapid and massively parallel incomplete verifiers. In: 9th International Conference on Learning Representations, ICLR 2021, Virtual Event, Austria, 3–7 May 2021. OpenReview.net (2021). https://openreview.net/forum?id=nVZtXBI6LNn
29. Zhang, H., Weng, T., Chen, P., Hsieh, C., Daniel, L.: Efficient neural network robustness certification with general activation functions. In: Bengio, S., Wallach, H.M., Larochelle, H., Grauman, K., Cesa-Bianchi, N., Garnett, R. (eds.) Advances in Neural Information Processing Systems 31: Annual Conference on Neural Information Processing Systems 2018, NeurIPS 2018, Montréal, Canada, 3–8 December 2018, pp. 4944–4953 (2018)
30. Zhang, J.M., Harman, M., Ma, L., Liu, Y.: Machine learning testing: survey, landscapes and horizons. IEEE Trans. Softw. Eng. **48**(2), 1–36 (2022)

31. Zhao, Z., Zhang, Y., Chen, G., Song, F., Chen, T., Liu, J.: CLEVEREST: accelerating CEGAR-based neural network verification via adversarial attacks. In: Singh, G., Urban, C. (eds.) SAS 2022. LNCS, vol. 13790, pp. 449–473. Springer, Cham (2022). https://doi.org/10.1007/978-3-031-22308-2_20
32. Zheng, Y., Liu, J., Shi, X.: MpBP: verifying robustness of neural networks with multi-path bound propagation. In: Roychoudhury, A., Cadar, C., Kim, M. (eds.) Proceedings of the 30th ACM Joint European Software Engineering Conference and Symposium on the Foundations of Software Engineering, ESEC/FSE 2022, Singapore, Singapore, 14–18 November 2022, pp. 1692–1696. ACM (2022). https://doi.org/10.1145/3540250.3558924
33. Zheng, Y., Shi, X., Liu, J.: Multi-path back-propagation method for neural network verification. Ruan Jian Xue Bao/J. Softw. **33**(7), 2464–2481 (2022). http://www.jos.org.cn/1000-9825/6585.htm. (in Chinese)

Correction to: Octagons Revisited

Elegant Proofs and Simplified Algorithms

Michael Schwarz and Helmut Seidl

Correction to:
Chapter 21 in: M. V. Hermenegildo and J. F. Morales (Eds.): *Static Analysis*, LNCS 14284, https://doi.org/10.1007/978-3-031-44245-2_21

Chapter 21 was previously published non-open access. It has now been changed to open access under a CC BY 4.0 license and the copyright holder updated to 'The Author(s)'. The book has also been updated with these changes.

The updated version of this chapter can be found at https://doi.org/10.1007/978-3-031-44245-2_21

M. V. Hermenegildo and J. F. Morales (Eds.): SAS 2023, LNCS 14284, p. C1, 2024.
https://doi.org/10.1007/978-3-031-44245-2_24

Author Index

A
Abbasi, Rosa 41
Arceri, Vincenzo 65

B
Boillot, Jérôme 84
Bolignano, Pauline 460

C
Campion, Marco 114
Cao, Shangtong 139
Chang, Bor-Yuh Evan 460
Chen, Yanbin 164
Coppins, Chris 508

D
D'Antoni, Loris 3
Dalla Preda, Mila 114
Darulova, Eva 41, 371
Dimovski, Aleksandar S. 190, 212
Ding, Shuo 231
Dolcetti, Greta 65

E
Evans, Neil 508

F
Ferdinand, Christian 10
Feret, Jérôme 84
Frohn, Florian 259

G
Giacobazzi, Roberto 114, 286
Giesl, Jürgen 259
Giet, Josselin 310
Gordon, Colin S. 343
Guo, Yao 139

H
He, Ningyu 139

I
Isychev, Anastasia 371

K
Kästner, Daniel 10
King, Andy 508

L
Lemerre, Matthieu 403
Liu, Jiaxiang 540

M
Mastroeni, Isabella 286, 434

P
Pasqua, Michele 434
Perantoni, Elia 286

R
Raimondi, Franco 460
Ridoux, Félix 310
Rival, Xavier 310

S
Schoepe, Daniel 460
Schwarz, Michael 485
Seed, Thomas 508
Seekatz, David 460
Seidl, Helmut 485
Singh, Gagandeep 28
Stade, Yannick 164
Stoilkovska, Ilina 460
Stucki, Sandro 460

T
Tang, Xuezhou 540
Tattersall, Daniel 460

M. V. Hermenegildo and J. F. Morales (Eds.): SAS 2023, LNCS 14284, pp. 565–566, 2023.
https://doi.org/10.1007/978-3-031-44245-2

U
Urban, Caterina 114

W
Wang, Haoyu 139
Wilhelm, Reinhard 10

Y
Yun, Chaewon 343

Z
Zaffanella, Enea 65
Zhang, Qirun 231
Zheng, Ye 540

Printed in the United States
by Baker & Taylor Publisher Services